DIRECTORY *of* local authorities 2015

SWEET & MAXWELL THOMSON REUTERS

Published in 2015 by
Thomson Reuters (Professional) UK Limited
trading as Sweet & Maxwell,
Friars House, 160 Blackfriars Road, London, SE1 8EZ
(Registered in England & Wales, Company No 1679046.
Registered Office and address for service:
2nd floor, 1 Mark Square, Leonard Street, London EC2A 4EG)

For further information on our products and services, visit
www.sweetandmaxwell.co.uk

Typeset by Infolaw Ltd, London
Printed and bound in Great Britain by Ashford Colour Press, Gosport, Hants

No natural forests were destroyed to make this product;
only farmed timber was used and re-planted.

A CIP catalogue record for this book
is available from the British Library

ISBN 9780 4140 51027

Contents

Introduction

Local Authorities *1* *Index to Local Authorities 2* *London Authorities 6* *Local Authorities in England 17* *Local Authorities in Wales 87* *Local Authorities in Scotland 93* **1**

Gazetteer *101* **2**

Principal Mortgage Lenders *199* **3**

Courts *205* **4**

Government Departments *221* **5**

Police Forces *223* **6**

Health Authorities *231* **7**

Land Registry *Land Registry Offices 233* *Land Registration Table 235* **8**

HM Revenue and Customs *243* **9**

Probate Registries *247* **10**

Rent Assessment Panels and the Rent Service *249* **11**

High Court Enforcement Officers *By District 251* *Addresses 270* **12**

Utilities *279* **13**

General Addresses *283* **14**

Conveyancing Fees and Charges *295* *Residential Fees 302* *Commercial Fees 316* **15**

Introduction

The Directory of Local Authorities is a database of information about local authorities in England, Wales and Scotland, particularly for those involved in conveyancing searches, together with related information concerning conveyancing fees/charges and land registration.

Part 1 contains information about the London boroughs, metropolitan authorities, county councils, unitary authorities and district councils of England (including those with city, royal borough or borough status) and the county councils and county boroughs of Wales. The Directory contains similar information regarding Scottish councils, although, of course, all searches are made in the Register of Sasines in Edinburgh.

Authorities may be located in a number of ways. If the relevant district is known, it may be accessed directly by name; if not then the appropriate authority can be found using the indexes or the Gazetteer in Part 2. This contains 25,000 place names of parishes, cities, towns, villages and other smaller identifiable places.

The Directory also contains the names and addresses of a number of other types of organisations which practitioners may wish to contact in Parts 3–14.

The publishers would appreciate notification of any changes of contact details for any authority or organisation listed, or any errors which may have come to light.

As in the past we welcome suggestions for the improvement of subsequent editions.

Every effort has been made to ensure that details given were correct at May 1, 2015.

Part 1

Local Authorities

This part of the Directory provides the names and addresses of the metropolitan counties, non-metropolitan county councils and district councils both metropolitan and non-metropolitan in England and Wales, established by the Local Government Acts 1972,1985, 1992 and 1998, and operational since April 2009. City and royal borough status may be conferred on district councils by HM The Queen under the prerogative of Letters Patent, while the 1972 Act makes provision for district councils to petition Her Majesty for a grant of borough status. Many district councils, metropolitan and non-metropolitan, have been granted city, royal borough or borough status, and their chairmen are styled 'mayor', or, in the case of some cities, 'lord mayor'.

Unitary authorities in England are styled 'District Council' (unless having city status). In Wales they are styled 'County Council' or 'County Borough'. All the local authorities in Greater London are designated 'London Borough' except for Kensington & Chelsea and Kingston upon Thames, which have Royal London Borough status, Westminster, which has City status, and the Corporation of London.

In cases where this publication is used by solicitors in conveyancing transactions, it should be noted that the addresses given for local authorities incorporate the local land charge section, and for such searches, application should be made to the local authority concerned, not the county council. They will merely have to forward the request for searches to the local authority as they do not usually hold lists. Local authorities have emphasised the need for the submission of up-to-date plans, of which two copies are usually necessary.

As this Directory is primarily used by solicitors making local searches, the addresses given of the district councils are those to which a solicitor would apply for this purpose. Separate addresses are also given for building control, council tax, planning and highways departments when applicable.

In the event that a commons search is deemed necessary, application should be made to the county authority, for which the addresses given relate to the legal department or secretariat.

This part also provides the names and addresses of the unitary authorities in Scotland, styled 'Council', established by the Local Government Act 1992, and operational since April 1, 1996. It should be remembered by English practitioners that the procedure for making local searches is different in Scotland, where all searches are made in the General Register of Sasines at the Department of the Registers of Scotland, to which enquiry should be made for further details. It is worth noting here, however, that it is usual to employ professional searchers, and that it is the responsibility of the seller, not the buyer, to make the search.

The offices may be applied to for specific matters such as planning and environmental health, roads, drainage water and the council tax.

The Land Registration (Scotland) Act 1979 which came into force early in 1981 laid the foundation for a system of land registration in Scotland and individual areas will gradually be drawn into its ambit. Practitioners should therefore be vigilant as to the progress of this Act.

Also note that National Parks in England and Wales are independent special purpose local authorities, which have operated as separate authorities since April 1996 in Wales and April 1997 in England. In particular, they are the statutory unitary planning authorities for their areas. Contact information is provided under National Park Authorities in the General Addresses section.

Authorities' document exchange (DX) numbers and facsimile numbers are given in addition to addresses and telephone numbers.

Index to Local Authorities

The following lists give the names of the metropolitan counties, county councils, district and unitary authorities for England, Wales and Scotland. The name of each authority is followed by the reference number under which the name and address of the authority is listed in the Directory. English counties are numbered 1 to 49, and districts and unitary authorities 1.1, 1.2 etc, according to the county in which they fall. London authorities are numbered 1 to 33 with the prefix 'L' for clarity, Welsh authorities 1 to 22, prefixed 'W', and Scottish authorities 1 to 32, prefixed 'S'.

England: Metropolitan Counties

Greater Manchester 19
Merseyside 29
South Yorkshire 39
Tyne & Wear 43
West Midlands 45
West Yorkshire 47

England: County Councils, and former County Councils

Avon 1 (abolished)
Bedfordshire 2 (abolished)
Berkshire 3 (abolished)
Buckinghamshire 5
Cambridgeshire 6
Cheshire 7 (abolished)
Cleveland 8 (abolished)
Cornwall 9 (abolished)
Cumbria 10
Derbyshire 11
Devon 12
Dorset 13
Durham 14 (abolished)
East Sussex 16
Essex 17
Gloucestershire 18
Hampshire 20
Hereford & Worcester 21 (abolished)
Hertfordshire 22
Humberside 23 (abolished)
Isle of Wight 24
Kent 25
Lancashire 26
Leicestershire 27
Lincolnshire 28
Norfolk 30
Northamptonshire 31
Northumberland 32 (abolished)
North Yorkshire 33
Nottinghamshire 34
Oxfordshire 35
Shropshire 37 (abolished)
Somerset 38
Staffordshire 40
Suffolk 41
Surrey 42
Warwickshire 44
West Sussex 46
Wiltshire 48 (abolished)
Worcestershire 49

England: London Authorities

Barking & Dagenham L1
Barnet L2
Bexley L3
Brent L4
Bromley L5
Camden L6
Corporation of London L7
Croydon L8
Ealing L9
Enfield L10
Greenwich L11
Hackney L12
Hammersmith & Fulham L13
Haringey L14
Harrow L15
Havering L16
Hillingdon L17
Hounslow L18
Islington L19
Kensington & Chelsea L20
Kingston upon Thames L21
Lambeth L22
Lewisham L23
Merton L24
Newham L25
Redbridge L26
Richmond upon Thames L27
Southwark L28
Sutton L29
Tower Hamlets L30
Waltham Forest L31
Wandsworth L32
Westminster L33

England: District and Unitary Authorities

Unitary authorities are marked (U)

Adur 46.7
Allerdale 10.2
Alnwick *see Northumberland*
Amber Valley 11.6
Arun 46.5
Ashfield 34.4
Ashford 25.12
Aylesbury Vale 5.2
Babergh 41.6
Barnsley 39.1
Barrow-in-Furness 10.6
Basildon 17.10
Basingstoke & Deane 20.1
Bassetlaw 34.1
Bath *see Bath & North East Somerset*
Bath & North East Somerset (U) 38.6
Bedford (U) 2.1
Berwick-upon-Tweed *see Northumberland*
Beverley *see East Riding of Yorkshire*
Birmingham 45.5
Blaby 27.6
Blackburn with Darwen (U) 26.10
Blackpool (U) 26.4
Blyth Valley *see Northumberland*
Bolsover 11.5
Bolton 19.2
Boothferry *see East Riding of Yorkshire and North Lincs*
Boston 28.5
Bosworth *see Hinckley & Bosworth*
Bournemouth (U) 13.7
Bracknell Forest (U) 3.6
Bradford 47.1
Braintree 17.2
Breckland 30.3
Brentwood 17.9
Bridgnorth *see Shropshire*
Brighton & Hove (U) 16.3
Bristol (U) 4.1
Broadland 30.5
Bromsgrove 49.2
Broxbourne 22.7
Broxtowe 34.5
Burnley 26.12
Bury 19.3
Calderdale 47.3
Cambridge 6.6
Cannock Chase 40.7
Canterbury 25.5
Caradon *see Cornwall*
Carlisle 10.1
Carrick *see Cornwall*
Castle Morpeth *see Northumberland*
Castle Point 17.13
Central Bedfordshire (U) 2.2
Charnwood 27.2
Chelmsford 17.7

Cheltenham 18.4
Cherwell 35.2
Cheshire West and Chester (U) 7.3
Cheshire East (U) 7.5
Chester *see Cheshire West and Chester*
Chesterfield 11.2
Chester-le-Street *see Durham*
Chichester 46.2
Chiltern 5.4
Chorley 26.9
Christchurch 13.8
Cleethorpes *see North East Lincolnshire*
Colchester 17.3
Congleton *see Cheshire East*
Copeland 10.4
Corby 31.1
Cornwall (U) 9.1
Cotswold 18.5
Coventry 45.7
Craven 33.5
Crawley 46.1
Crewe & Nantwich *see Cheshire East*
Dacorum 22.4
Darlington (U) 14.8
Dartford 25.1
Daventry 31.4
Derby City (U) 11.7
Derbyshire Dales 11.3
Derwentside *see Durham*
Doncaster 39.2
Dover 25.6
Dudley 45.3
Durham (U) 14.1
Durham City *see Durham*
Easington *see Durham*
Eastbourne 16.5
East Cambridgeshire 6.4
East Devon 12.7
East Dorset 13.3
East Hampshire 20.6
East Hertfordshire 22.3
Eastleigh 20.9
East Lindsey 28.2
East Northamptonshire 31.3
East Riding of Yorkshire (U) 15.2
East Staffordshire 40.5
East Yorkshire *see East Riding of Yorkshire*
Eden 10.3
Ellesmere Port & Neston *see Cheshire West and Chester*
Elmbridge 42.5
Epping Forest 17.6
Epsom & Ewell 42.6
Erewash 11.8
Exeter 12.6
Fareham 20.10
Fenland 6.2
Forest Heath 41.2
Forest of Dean 18.2
Fylde 26.5
Gateshead 43.3
Gedling 34.7
Gillingham *see Medway Towns*
Glanford *see North Lincolnshire*
Gloucester 18.3
Gosport 20.11
Gravesham 25.2
Gt Yarmouth 30.6
Grimsby *see North East Lincolnshire*
Guildford 42.7
Halton (U) 7.2
Hambleton 33.2
Harborough 27.8
Harlow 17.5
Harrogate 33.6
Hart 20.2
Hartlepool (U) 14.9
Hastings 16.6
Havant 20.13
Herefordshire (U) 21.1
Hertsmere 22.10
High Peak 11.1
Hinckley & Bosworth 27.4
Holderness *see East Riding of Yorkshire*
Horsham 46.3
Hove *see Brighton & Hove*
Huntingdon 6.3
Hyndburn 26.11
Ipswich 41.7
Isle of Wight (U) 24.1
Kennet *see Wiltshire*
Kerrier *see Cornwall*
Kettering 31.2
King's Lynn & West Norfolk 30.2
Kingston upon Hull (U) 15.1
Kingswood *see South Gloucestershire*
Kirklees 47.4
Knowsley 29.4
Lancaster 26.1
Langbaurgh *see Redcar & Cleveland*
Leeds 47.2
Leicester City (U) 27.5
Lewes 16.4
Lichfield 40.8
Lincoln 28.3
Liverpool 29.2
Luton (U) 2.4
Macclesfield *see Cheshire East*
Maidstone 25.10
Maldon 17.8
Malvern Hills 49.4
Manchester 19.6
Mansfield 34.2
Medina *see Isle of Wight*
Medway Towns, The (U) 25.3
Melton 27.3
Mendip 38.2
Mid Bedfordshire *see Central Bedfordshire*
Mid Devon 12.4
Middlesbrough (U) 33.9
Mid Suffolk 41.4
Mid Sussex 46.4
Milton Keynes (U) 5.1
Mole Valley 42.8
New Forest 20.7
Newark and Sherwood 34.3
Newbury *see West Berkshire*
Newcastle-under-Lyme 40.2
Newcastle upon Tyne 43.1
Northampton 31.5
Northavon *see South Gloucestershire*
North Cornwall *see Cornwall*
North Devon 12.2
North Dorset 13.2
North East Derbyshire 11.4
North East Lincolnshire (U) 28.9
North Hertfordshire 22.1
North Kesteven 28.4
North Lincolnshire (U) 28.8
North Norfolk 30.1
North Somerset (U) 38.7
North Shropshire *see Shropshire*
North Tyneside 43.2
North Warwickshire 44.1
North West Leicestershire 27.1
North Wiltshire *see Wiltshire*
Northumberland (U) 32.1
Norwich 30.4
Nottingham (U) 34.6
Nuneaton & Bedworth 44.2
Oadby & Wigston 27.7
Oldham 19.7
Oswestry *see Shropshire*
Oxford 35.5
Pendle 26.13
Penwith *see Cornwall*
Peterborough (U) 6.1
Plymouth (U) 12.8
Poole (U) 13.6
Portsmouth (U) 20.12
Preston 26.6
Purbeck 13.5
Reading (U) 3.2
Redcar & Cleveland (U) 33.10
Redditch 49.3
Reigate & Banstead 42.9
Restormel *see Cornwall*
Ribble Valley 26.3
Richmondshire 33.1
Rochdale 19.4
Rochester *see Medway Towns*
Rochford 17.11
Rossendale 26.14
Rother 16.2
Rotherham 39.4
Rugby 44.3
Runnymede 42.1
Rushcliffe 34.8
Rushmoor 20.3
Rutland (U) 36.1
Ryedale 33.3
St Albans 22.5
St Edmundsbury 41.3
St Helens 29.3
Salford 19.5
Salisbury *see Wiltshire*
Sandwell 45.4
Scarborough 33.4
Scunthorpe *see North Lincolnshire*
Sedgefield *see Durham*
Sedgemoor 38.1
Sefton 29.1
Selby 33.8
Sevenoaks 25.8
Sheffield 39.3
Shepway 25.13
Shrewsbury & Atcham *see Shropshire*
Shropshire (U) 37.1
Slough (U) 3.5
Solihull 45.6
Southampton (U) 20.8
South Bedfordshire *see Central Bedfordshire*
South Bucks 5.5
South Cambridgeshire 6.5
South Derbyshire 11.9
Southend (U) 17.14
South Gloucestershire (U) 18.7
South Hams 12.9
South Holland 28.7
South Kesteven 28.6
South Lakeland 10.5
South Norfolk 30.7
South Northamptonshire 31.7
South Oxfordshire 35.3
South Ribble 26.7
South Shropshire *see Shropshire*
South Somerset 38.5
South Staffordshire 40.6
South Tyneside 43.4
South Wight *see Isle of Wight*
Spelthorne 42.2
Stafford 40.4
Staffordshire Moorlands 40.1
Stevenage 22.2
Stockport 19.9
Stockton-on-Tees (U) 14.10
Stoke-on-Trent (U) 40.3
Stratford-upon-Avon 44.5
Stroud 18.6
Suffolk Coastal 41.5
Sunderland 43.5
Surrey Heath 42.3
Swale 25.4
Swindon (U) 48.2
Tameside 19.10
Tamworth 40.9
Tandridge 42.10

1

Taunton Deane 38.4
Teesdale *see Durham*
Teignbridge 12.5
Telford & Wrekin, The (U) 37.4
Tendring 17.4
Test Valley 20.4
Tewkesbury 18.1
Thamesdown *see Swindon*
Thanet 25.7
Three Rivers 22.8
Thurrock (U) 17.12
Tonbridge & Malling 25.9
Torbay (U) 12.10
Torridge 12.1
Trafford 19.8
Tunbridge Wells, Royal 25.11
Tynedale *see Northumberland*
Uttlesford 17.1
Vale Royal *see Cheshire West and Chester*
Vale of White Horse 35.4
Wakefield 47.5
Walsall 45.2
Wansbeck *see Northumberland*
Wansdyke *see Bath & North East Somerset*
Warrington (U) 7.1
Warwick 44.4
Watford 22.9
Waveney 41.1
Waverley 42.11
Wealden 16.1
Wear Valley *see Durham*
Wellingborough 31.6
Welwyn Hatfield 22.6
West Berkshire (U) 3.1
West Devon 12.3
West Dorset 13.1
West Lancashire 26.8
West Lindsey 28.1
West Oxfordshire 35.1
West Somerset 38.3
West Wiltshire *see Wiltshire*
Weymouth & Portland 13.4
Wigan 19.1
Wiltshire (U) 48.1
Winchester 20.5
Windsor & Maidenhead (U) 3.4
Wirral 29.5
Woking 42.4
Wokingham (U) 3.3
Wolverhampton 45.1
Woodspring *see North Somerset*
Worcester 49.5
Worthing 46.6
Wychavon 49.6
Wycombe 5.3
Wyre 26.2
Wyre Forest 49.1
York (U) 33.7

Wales: Unitary Authorities

Anglesey W1
Blaenau Gwent W2
Bridgend W3
Caerphilly W4
Cardiff W5
Carmarthenshire W6
Ceredigion W7
Conwy W8
Denbighshire W9
Flintshire W10
Gwynedd W11
Merthyr Tydfil W12
Monmouthshire W13
Neath Port Talbot W14
Newport W15
Pembrokeshire W16
Powys W17
Rhondda Cynon Taff W18
Swansea W19
Torfaen W20
Vale of Glamorgan W21
Wrexham W22

Scotland: Unitary Authorities

Aberdeenshire S1
Angus S2
Argyll & Bute S3
City of Aberdeen S4
City of Dundee S5
City of Edinburgh S6
City of Glasgow S7
Clackmannanshire S8
Dumfries & Galloway S10
East Ayrshire S11
East Dunbartonshire S12
East Lothian S13
East Renfrewshire S14
Falkirk S15
Fife S16
Highland S17
Inverclyde S18
Midlothian S19
Moray S20
North Ayrshire S21
North Lanarkshire S22
Orkney S23
Perth & Kinross S24
Renfrewshire S25
Scottish Borders S30
Shetland Islands S26
South Ayrshire S27
South Lanarkshire S28
Stirling S29
West Dunbartonshire S9
West Lothian S31
Western Isles S32

Former County Councils: pre–1974

The following list gives the names of county councils existing before the Local Government Act 1972 took effect on April 1, 1974. Each name is followed by the name(s) of the successor county council(s) and/or metropolitan authority by which it was absorbed.

Anglesey *Gwynedd*
Bedfordshire *Bedfordshire*
Berkshire *Berkshire, Oxfordshire*
Brecknockshire *Gwent, Mid Glamorgan, Powys*
Buckinghamshire *Berkshire, Buckinghamshire*
Caernarvonshire *Gwynedd*
Cambridgeshire & Isle of Ely *Cambridgeshire*
Cardiganshire *Dyfed*
Carmarthenshire *Dyfed*
Cheshire *Greater Manchester, Merseyside, Cheshire, Derbyshire*
Cornwall *Cornwall*
Cumberland *Cumbria*
Denbighshire *Clwyd, Gwynedd*
Derbyshire *Derbyshire*
Devon *Devon*
Dorset *Dorset*
Durham *Tyne & Wear, Cleveland, Durham*
Essex *Essex*
Flintshire *Clwyd*
Glamorganshire *Mid Glamorgan, South Glamorgan, West Glamorgan*
Gloucestershire *Avon, Gloucestershire*
Hampshire *Dorset, Hampshire*
Herefordshire *Hereford & Worcester*
Hertfordshire *Hertfordshire*
Huntingdon & Peterborough *Cambridgeshire*
Isle of Wight *Isle of Wight*
Kent *Kent*
Lancashire *Greater Manchester, Merseyside, Cheshire, Cumbria, Lancashire*
Leicestershire *Leicestershire*
Lincolnshire (Holland) *Lincolnshire*
Lincolnshire (Kesteven) *Lincolnshire*
Lincolnshire (Lindsey) *Humberside, Lincolnshire*
Merionethshire *Clwyd, Gwynedd*
Monmouthshire *Gwent, Mid Glamorgan, South Glamorgan*
Montgomeryshire *Powys*
Norfolk *Norfolk*
Northamptonshire *Northamptonshire*
Northumberland *Tyne & Wear, Northumberland*
Nottinghamshire *South Yorkshire, Nottinghamshire*
Oxfordshire *Oxfordshire*
Pembrokeshire *Dyfed*
Radnorshire *Powys*
Rutland *Leicestershire*
Shropshire *Shropshire*
Somerset *Avon, Somerset*

Staffordshire *West Midlands, Staffordshire*
Suffolk (East) *Norfolk, Suffolk*
Suffolk (West) *Suffolk*
Surrey *Surrey, West Sussex*
Sussex (East) *East Sussex, West Sussex*
Sussex (West) *West Sussex*
Warwickshire *West Midlands, Warwickshire*
Westmorland *Cumbria*
Wiltshire *Wiltshire*
Worcestershire *West Midlands, Hereford & Worcester*
Yorkshire (East Riding) *Humberside, North Yorkshire*
Yorkshire (North Riding) *Cleveland, Durham, North Yorkshire*
Yorkshire (West Riding) *Greater Manchester, South Yorkshire, West Yorkshire, Cumbria, Humberside, Lancashire, North Yorkshire*

1

Former County Councils

The following list gives the names of county councils existing before the Local Government Act 1992 took effect on April 1 in 1995, 1996, 1997, 1998 and 2009. Each name is followed by the reference number(s) of the successor council(s) (unitary authority(ies)) by which it was absorbed.

Avon 4.1, 18.7, 38.6 38.7
Bedfordshire 2.1, 2.2
Berkshire 3.1 3.6
Cheshire 7.3, 7.5
Cleveland 14.9 14.10, 33.9 33.10
Clwyd W1, W10, W11, W17, W22
Cornwall 9.1
Durham, Co 14.1
Dyfed W8, W9, W16
Gwent W3, W6, W13, W15, W20
Gwynedd W1, W2, W5
Hereford & Worcester 21.1, 49.1 49.7
Humberside 15.1, 28.8 28.9
Isle of Wight 24.1
Mid-Glamorgan W4, W6, W7, W12, W18, W21
Northumberland 32.1
North Yorkshire (York) only 33.7
Powys W17
Shropshire 37.1
South Glamorgan W7, W21
West Glamorgan W14, W19
Wiltshire 48.1

Former Regional and Islands Councils

The following list gives the names of regional and island councils existing before the Local Government Act 1992 took effect on 1 April 1996. Each name is followed by the reference number(s) of the successor council(s) (unitary authority(ies)) by which it was absorbed.

Borders S30
Central S8, S15, S29
Dumfries & Galloway S10
Fife S16
Grampian S1, S4, S20
Highland S17
Lothian S6, S13, S19, S31
Strathclyde S3, S7, S9, S11, S12, S14, S18, S21, S22, S25, S27, S28
Tayside S2, S5, S24
Orkney S23
Shetland S26
Western Isles S32

Local Authorities in London

L1 Barking & Dagenham London Borough Council

Website: www.lbbd.gov.uk
Main Switchboard: 020 8215 3000
Conveyancing Searches: Local Land Charges, Room 104 Grnd Fl, Town Hall, 1 Town Sq, Barking IG11 7LU
Tel: 020 8227 3426 Fax: 020 8227 3490
e-mail: llcservice@lbbd.gov.uk
Note: Formerly: pt Barking B, pt Dagenham B
Council Tax: Council Tax Section, Elevate Barking & Dagenham Direct, 90 Stour Rd, Dagenham RM10 7JD
Tel: 020 8278 2504
Environmental & Enforcement: Mr D Henaghan, Director, Town Hall, 1 Town Sq, Barking IG11 7LU
Tel: 020 8227 5700
Solicitor to the Council: Paul Feild, Senior Lawyer, The Legal Practice, Civic Centre, Rainham Rd Nth, Dagenham RM10 7BN
Tel: 020 8227 3133
e-mail: paul.feild@BDTLegal.org.uk
Water Services: Thames Water and Essex & Suffolk Water

L2 Barnet London Borough Council

Website: www.barnet.gov.uk
Main Switchboard: 020 8359 2000
Conveyancing Searches: Local Land Charges, Bldg 4 North London Business Pk, Oakleigh Rd Sth, London N11 1NP
Tel: 020 8359 5591 Fax: 0871 594 8117
DX: 37106 Whetstone
e-mail: locallandcharges@barnet.gov.uk
Note: Formerly: Arkley UD, Burnt Oak UD, Cricklewood UD, East Barnet UD, Edgware UD, pt Elstree UD, Finchley UD, Friern Barnet UD, Golders Green UD, Hendon UD, Mill Hill UD, Muswell Hill UD, Southgate UD, Totteridge UD, Whetstone UD
Building Control, Highways & Planning: Environmental Services, North London Business Pk, Oakleigh Rd Sth, London N11 1NP
Tel: 020 8359 3000 Fax: 0870 889 6818
e-mail: first.contact@barnet.gov.uk
Council Tax: Council Tax, Finance Dept, North London Business Pk, Bldg 4, Oakleigh Rd Sth, London N11 1NP
Tel: 020 8359 2608 (N&E)/ 2609 (S&W) Fax: 020 8359 2273
e-mail: local.taxation@barnet.gov.uk
Environmental Services: Environmental Services, Bldg 4, North London Business Pk, Oakleigh Rd Sth, London N11 1NP
Tel: 020 8359 2000 Fax: 020 8359 4887
Social Services & Housing: Community Services, North London Business Pk, Oakleigh Rd Sth, London N11 1NP
Tel: 020 8359 2000 Fax: 020 8359 4887
Solicitor to the Council: Margaret Martinus, Head of Legal, Bldg 4, North London Business Pk, Oakleigh Rd Sth, London N11 1NP
Tel: 020 8359 2545 Fax: 020 8359 2680
DX: 59318 Hendon
e-mail: margaret.martinus@barnet.gov.uk
Note: Based in the London Borough of Brent
Water Services: Thames Water and Three Valleys Water

L3 Bexley London Borough Council

Website: www.bexley.gov.uk
Main Switchboard: 020 8303 7777
Conveyancing Searches: Land Charges, Civic Offices, 2 Watling St, Bexleyheath, Kent DA6 7AT
Tel: 020 3045 4000 Fax: 020 3045 5817
DX: 31807 Bexleyheath (FAO Land Charges)
e-mail: land.charges@bexley.gov.uk
Note: Formerly: Bexley MB, Erith MB, Crayford UD, Sidcup UD, pt Thamesmead, Welling
Building Control: Building Control, Civic Offices, 2 Watling St, Bexleyheath DA6 7AT
Tel: 020 3045 7777 Fax: 020 3045 5817
DX: 31807 Bexleyheath (FAO Building Control)
e-mail: building.control@bexley.gov.uk
Council Tax: Finance Dept – Capita Managed Services Ltd, Town Hall, Erith DA8 1TL
Tel: 0345 302 2317 Fax: 01322 356069
DX: 31807 Bexleyheath
e-mail: bexley.ctax@secure.capita.co.uk
Environmental Health: Environmental Health & Trading Standards, Civic Offices, 2 Watling St, Bexleyheath DA6 7AT
Tel: 020 3045 5602 Fax: 020 8308 1300
DX: 31807 Bexleyheath (FAO Env Health)
Highways & Amenities: Public Realm Management, Footscray Offices, 1st Fl, Maidstone Rd, Sidcup DA14 5HS
Tel: 020 8303 7777 Fax: 020 8309 4429
DX: 31807 Bexleyheath
Planning: Town Planning Dept – Development Control, Civic Offices, 2 Watling St, Bexleyheath DA6 7AT
Tel: 020 8303 7777 Fax: 020 3045 5817
DX: 31807 Bexleyheath (FAO Planning)
e-mail: development.control@bexley.gov.uk
Solicitor to the Council: Akinola Alabi, Legal Dept, Civic Offices, 2 Watling St, Bexleyheath DA6 7AT
Tel: 020 8303 7777 Fax: 020 3045 5449
DX: 31807 Bexleyheath
e-mail: akin.alabi@bexley.gov.uk
Transport & Traffic Services: Transport Planning & Development, Civic Offices, 2 Watling St, Bexleyheath DA6 7AT
Tel: 020 3045 5852 Fax: 020 3045 5899
DX: 38107 Bexleyheath (FAO Highways)
Water Services: Thames Water

L4 Brent London Borough Council

Website: www.brent.gov.uk
Main Switchboard: 020 8937 1234
Conveyancing Searches: Local Land Charges, Brent Civic Centre, Engineers Way, Wembley HA9 0FJ
Tel: 020 8937 5351
e-mail: locallandcharges@brent.gov.uk
Note: Formerly: Wembley MB, Willesden MB
Environmental Health: Environmental Health Dept, Brent Civic Centre, Engineers Way, Wembley HA9 0FJ
Tel: 020 8937 5252 Fax: 020 8937 5150
Other Departments: Brent Civic Centre, Engineers Way, Wembley HA9 0FJ
Solicitor to the Council: Head of Legal Services, Brent Civic Centre, Engineers Way, Wembley HA9 0FJ
Tel: 020 8937 1292 Fax: 020 8937 1313
Water Services: Thames Water and Three Valleys Water

L5 Bromley London Borough Council

Website: www.bromley.gov.uk
Main Switchboard: 020 8464 3333
Conveyancing Searches: Renewal & Recreation Dept, Bromley Civic Centre, Stockwell Cl, Bromley BR1 3UH
Tel: 020 8461 7909 Fax: 020 8461 7769
DX: 5727 Bromley
e-mail: land.charges@bromley.gov.uk
Note: Formerly: Beckenham B, Bromley B, Orpington UD, Penge UD, Chislehurst UD
Building Control: Renewal & Recreation Dept, Civic Centre, Stockwell Cl, Bromley BR1 3UH
Tel: 020 8313 4313 Fax: 020 8313 4604
e-mail: buildingcontrol@bromley.gov.uk
Council Tax: Council Tax, Exchequer Ho, Widmore Rd, Bromley BR1 3XU
Tel: 020 8242 9312
e-mail: council.tax@bromley.gov.uk
Environmental Health & Trading Standards: Environmental Services, Civic Centre, Stockwell Cl, Bromley BR1 3UH
Tel: 020 8313 4830 Fax: 020 8313 4450
e-mail: ehts.customer@bromley.gov.uk
Highways: Environmental Services, Civic Centre, Stockwell Cl, Bromley BR1 3UH
Tel: 020 8464 3333 Fax: 020 8313 4707
e-mail: csc@bromley.gov.uk
Planning: Renewal & Recreation Dept, Civic Centre, Stockwell Cl, Bromley BR1 3UH
Tel: 020 8313 4956 Fax: 020 8461 7769
DX: 5727 Bromley
e-mail: planning@bromley.gov.uk
Solicitor to the Council: Mark Bowen, Legal & Democratic Services, Civic Centre, Stockwell Cl, Bromley BR1 3UH
Tel: 020 8313 4355 Fax: 020 8290 0608
DX: 5727 Bromley
e-mail: mark.bowen@bromley.gov.uk
Water Services: Thames Water

L6 Camden London Borough Council

Website: www.camden.gov.uk
Main Switchboard: 020 7974 4444
Conveyancing Searches: Shirley Jackdeo, Local Land Charges Mgr, 5th Fl, Town Hall Extension, Argyle St, London WC1H 8EQ
Tel: 020 7974 5660 Fax: 020 7974 2546
DX: 2106 Euston
e-mail: local.landcharges@camden.gov.uk
Note: Formerly: Hampstead MB, Holborn MB, St Pancras MB
Building Control: Environment Dept, 6th Fl, Town Hall Extension, Argyle St, London WC1H 8EQ
Tel: 020 7974 6941 Fax: 020 7974 5603
DX: 2106 Euston
e-mail: building.control@camden.gov.uk
Environmental Health & Consumer Protection: Diane Fleming, Team Mgr, Environment Dept, Town Hall Extension, Argyle St, London WC1H 8EQ
Tel: 020 7974 5613 Fax: 020 7974 1680
DX: 2106 Euston
e-mail: env.health@camden.gov.uk
Highways: Helena Kakouratos, Team Mgr, Environment Dept, 4th Fl, Camden Town Hall Extension, Argyle St, London WC1H 8EQ
Tel: 020 7974 6956 Fax: 020 7974 5585
DX: 2106 Euston
e-mail: helena.kakouratos@camden.gov.uk
Planning: Planning Advice & Information Team, 5th Fl, Camden Town Hall Extension, Argyle St, London WC1H 8EQ
Tel: 020 7974 5613 Fax: 020 7974 1930
DX: 2106 Euston
Solicitor to the Council: Andrew Maughan, Head of Legal Services, 2nd Fl, Town Hall, Judd St, London WC1H 9JE
Tel: 020 7974 5656 Fax: 020 7974 5837
DX: 2106 Euston
e-mail: andrew.maughan@camden.gov.uk
Water Services: Thames Water

L7 City of London

Website: www.cityoflondon.gov.uk
Main Switchboard: 020 7606 3030
Conveyancing Searches: Local Land Charges Section, Dept of The Built Environment, PO Box 270, Guildhall, London EC2P 2EJ
Tel: 020 7332 1710 Fax: 020 7332 1806
DX: 121784 Guildhall
e-mail: plans@cityoflondon.gov.uk
Building Control: District Surveyor's Office, Dept of The Built Environment, PO Box 270, Guildhall, London EC2P 2EJ
Tel: 020 7332 1000 Fax: 020 7332 1968
DX: 121781 Guildhall
e-mail: district.surveyor@cityoflondon.gov.uk
Council Tax: Chamberlain, PO Box 270, Guildhall, London EC2P 2EJ
Tel: 020 7606 3030 Fax: 020 7332 1991
DX: 121781 Guildhall
e-mail: chb-secriat@cityoflondon.gov.uk
Planning: Department of The Built Environment, PO Box 270, Guildhall, London EC2P 2EJ
Tel: 020 7332 1710 Fax: 020 7332 1806
DX: 121784 Guildhall
e-mail: plans@cityoflondon.gov.uk
Solicitor to the Council: Comptroller & City Solicitor, PO Box 270, Guildhall, London EC2P 2EJ
Tel: 020 7606 3030 Fax: 020 7600 3389
DX: 121783 Guildhall
e-mail: ccs.contact@cityoflondon.gov.uk
Water Services: Thames Water

L8 Croydon London Borough Council

Website: www.croydon.gov.uk
Main Switchboard: 020 8726 6000
Conveyancing Searches: Chief Executives Dept, Local Land Charges Team, Bernard Weatherill Ho, 8 Mint Walk, Croydon CR0 1EA
Tel: 020 8407 1331
DX: 136018 Croydon 17
e-mail: local.landcharges@croydon.gov.uk
Note: Formerly: Croydon CB, Coulsdon and Purley UD
Council Tax: Chief Executives Dept, Council Tax, Bernard Weatherill Ho, 8 Mint Walk, Croydon CR0 1EA
Tel: 020 8726 7000
e-mail: croytax@croydon.gov.uk
Environmental Health: Adult Services, Health & Housing, Bernard Weatherill Ho, 8 Mint Walk, Croydon CR0 1EA
Tel: 020 8726 6000
Other depts: All other depts, Bernard Weatherill Ho, 8 Mint Walk, Croydon CR0 1EA
Tel: 020 8726 6000
Planning: Planning & Environment, Bernard Weatherill Ho, 8 Mint Walk, Croydon CR0 1EA
Tel: 020 8726 6000 Fax: 020 8760 5408
e-mail: development.management@croydon.gov.uk

Solicitor to the Council: Julie Belvir, Director of Democratic & Legal Services, Bernard Weatherill Ho, 8 Mint Walk, Croydon CR0 1EA
Tel: 020 8726 6000
DX: 136017 Croydon 17
e-mail: julia.belvir@croydon.gov.uk
Water Services: Thames Water

L9 Ealing London Borough Council

Website: www.ealing.gov.uk
Main Switchboard: 020 8825 5000
Conveyancing Searches: Local Land Charges, Perceval Ho, 14–16 Uxbridge Rd, London W5 2HL
Tel: 020 8825 8998
DX: 5106 Ealing
e-mail: landcharges@ealing.gov.uk
Council Tax: Council Tax, Perceval Ho, 14–16 Uxbridge Rd, London W5 2HL
Tel: 020 8825 7050
DX: 5106 Ealing
e-mail: revenues@ealing.gov.uk
Environmental Health: Environmental Health & Consumer Services, Perceval Ho, 14–16 Uxbridge Rd, London W5 2HL
Tel: 020 8825 5000
DX: 5106 Ealing
e-mail: environmentalhealth@ealing.gov.uk
Highways: Transport Services, Perceval Ho, 14–16 Uxbridge Rd, London W5 2HL
Tel: 020 8825 7388
DX: 5106 Ealing
e-mail: transportservices@ealing.gov.uk
Planning & Building Control: Planning & Building Control, Perceval Ho, 14–16 Uxbridge Road, London W5 2HL
Tel: 020 8825 6600
DX: 5106 Ealing
e-mail: planning@ealing.gov.uk
Solicitor to the Council: Helen Harris, Director of Legal Services, Perceval Ho, 14–16 Uxbridge Rd, London W5 2HL
Tel: 020 8825 8615
DX: 5106 Ealing
e-mail: harrish@ealing.gov.uk
Water Services: Thames Water and Three Valleys Water

L10 Enfield London Borough Council

Website: www.enfield.gov.uk
Main Switchboard: 020 8379 1000
Conveyancing Searches: Land Charges, 1st Fl, Civic Centre, PO Box 50, Silver St, Enfield EN1 3XA
Tel: 020 8379 4125
DX: 90615 Enfield
e-mail: landcharges@enfield.gov.uk
Note: Formerly: Edmonton MB, Enfield MB, Southgate MB
Environmental Health: Environmental Health, Civic Centre, Silver St, Enfield EN1 3XA
Solicitor to the Council: Asmat Hussain, Assistant Director of Legal Services, Civic Centre, PO Box 50, Silver St, Enfield EN1 3XA
Tel: 020 8379 6438 Fax: 020 8379 6492
DX: 90615 Enfield
e-mail: asmat.hussain@enfield.gov.uk
Water Services: Thames Water

L11 Greenwich London Borough Council

Website: www.greenwich.gov.uk
Main Switchboard: 020 8854 8888
Conveyancing Searches: Land Charges, The Woolwich Centre, 35 Wellington St, Woolwich, London SE18 6HQ
Tel: 020 8921 5087/8/9 Fax: 020 8921 5370
DX: 400852 Woolwich 5
e-mail: local-land-charges@greenwich.gov.uk
Note: Formerly: pt Blackheath MB, pt Charlton MB, Greenwich MB, pt Sidcup UD, pt Woolwich MB. DX is for Land Charges only
Building Control: Building Control, 2nd Fl, Crown Building, 48 Woolwich New Rd, Woolwich SE18 6HQ
Tel: 020 8921 5413 Fax: 020 8921 5544
e-mail: building.control@greenwich.gov.uk
Council Tax: Treasurer, Council Tax, Valley Ho, PO Box 4794, Charlton SE7 7DJ
Tel: 020 8921 4147 Fax: 020 8293 4192
e-mail: counciltax@greenwich.gov.uk
Environmental Health: Directorate of Public Services, Riverside Ho, Woolwich High St, Woolwich SE18 6DN
Tel: 020 8854 8888
e-mail: [forename.surname]@greenwich.gov.uk
Highways: Highways Central Admin (THE), Peggy Middleton Ho, 50 Woolwich New Rd, Woolwich SE18 6HQ
Tel: 020 8921 5419 Fax: 020 8855 9324
e-mail: [forename.surname]@greenwich.gov.uk
Planning: Planning, Peggy Middleton Ho, 50 Woolwich New Rd, Woolwich SE18 6HQ
Tel: 020 8921 5222/5019 Fax: 020 8921 5442
e-mail: planningapps@greenwich.gov.uk
Solicitor to the Council: Russell Power, Head of Law & Governance, 5th Fl, Riverside Ho West, Woolwich High St, Woolwich SE18 6ON
Tel: 020 8921 5105 Fax: 020 8921 5556
DX: 400851 Woolwich 5
e-mail: russell.power@greenwich.gov.uk
Water Services: Thames Water

L12 Hackney London Borough Council

Website: www.hackney.gov.uk
Main Switchboard: 020 8356 3000
Conveyancing Searches: Land Charges Dept, Planning & Regulatory Services, 2 Hillman St, London E8 1FB
Tel: 020 8356 8295 Fax: 020 8356 8110
DX: 124200 Hackney 3
e-mail: landcharges@hackney.gov.uk
Note: Formerly: Hackney MB, Shoreditch MB, Stoke Newington MB
Council Tax: Council Tax Service, Hackney Service Centre, 1 Hillman St, London E8 1DY
Tel: 020 8356 3154 Fax: 020 8356 3613/3683
e-mail: council.tax@hackney.gov.uk
Environmental Health: Environmental Health Dept (The Private Sector Housing), Stoke Newington Municipal Offices, Stoke Newington Church St, London N16 0JR
Tel: 020 8356 4866 Fax: 020 8356 4758
e-mail: environmental.health@hackney.gov.uk
Highways: Highways & Engineering Team, Kelton Ho, 89–115 Mare St, London E8 4RU
Tel: 020 8356 2897 Fax: 020 8356 8142
Planning & Building Control: Building Control Service, Planning & Regulatory Services, 2 Hillman St, London E8 1FB
Tel: 020 8356 8124 (Building Control); 7715 (Planning)
Fax: 020 8356 8122 (Building Control); 8087 (Planning)
e-mail: buildingcontrol.bpt@hackney.gov.uk

Solicitor to the Council: Yinka Owa, Assistant Director of Legal and Democratic, Legal Services, 1 Hillman St, London E8 1HE
Tel: 020 8356 6234 Fax: 020 8356 6174
DX: 124200 Hackney 3
e-mail: yinka.owa@hackney.gov.uk
Water Services: Thames Water

L13 Hammersmith & Fulham London Borough Council

Website: www.lbhf.gov.uk
Main Switchboard: 020 8748 3020
Conveyancing Searches: Transport & Technical Services, Town Hall Extension, 6th Fl, King St, Hammersmith, London W6 9JU
Tel: 020 8753 2233
DX: 32759 Hammersmith 2
e-mail: land_charges@lbhf.gov.uk
Council Tax: Council Tax Office, Town Hall Extension, 2nd Fl, King St, Hammersmith, London W6 9JU
Tel: 020 8600 7777 Fax: 020 8753 1578
e-mail: localtaxation@lbhf.gov.uk
Highways Dept: Highways Dept, Town Hall Extension, 5th Fl, King St, Hammersmith, London W6 9JU
Tel: 020 8753 1081 Fax: 020 8753 3035
e-mail: environment@lbhf.gov.uk
Planning, Building Control: Transport & Technical Services, Town Hall Extension, 6th Fl, King St, London W6 9JU
Tel: 020 8753 1081
e-mail: environment@lbhf.gov.uk
Solicitor to the Council: Michael Cogher, Assistant Director of Legal & Democratic Services, Town Hall, 1st Fl, Hammersmith, London W6 9JU
Tel: 020 8753 2700 Fax: 020 8753 2711
DX: 32768 Hammersmith 2
e-mail: michael.cogher@lbhf.gov.uk
Water Services: Thames Water

L14 Haringey London Borough Council

Website: www.haringey.gov.uk
Main Switchboard: 020 8489 0000
Conveyancing Searches: Land Charges, Alexandra Ho, 10 Station Rd, Wood Green, London N22 7TR
Tel: 020 8489 3797/8 Fax: 020 8489 3948
DX: 156930 Wood Green 5
e-mail: land.charges@haringey.gov.uk
Note: Formerly: Hornsey B, Tottenham B, Wood Green B
Borough Engineer: Transportation Planning, River Pk Ho, 225 High Rd, Wood Green, London N22 8HQ
Tel: 020 8489 5573 Fax: 020 8489 5577
Building Control: Planning Policy & Development, 639 High Rd, Tottenham, London N17 8BD
Tel: 020 8489 1000 Fax: 020 8489 5229
e-mail: building.control@haringey.gov.uk
Council Tax: Alexandra Ho, 10 Station Rd, London N22 7TR
Tel: 020 8489 1000 Fax: 020 8489 3940
e-mail: council.tax@haringey.gov.uk
Highways: Highways and Traffic Design, River Pk Ho, 225 High Rd, Wood Green, London N17 8BD
Tel: 020 8489 1335 Fax: 020 8489 1399
Planning & Environmental Health: Planning & Environmental Health, 639 High Rd, Tottenham, London N17 8BD
Tel: 020 8489 5538 Fax: 020 8489 5553
Solicitor to the Council: Head of Legal Services, River Pk Ho, 225 High Rd, Wood Green, London N22 8HQ
Tel: 020 8489 3974 Fax: 020 8489 3835
DX: 35651 Wood Green 1
Water Services: Thames Water

L15 Harrow London Borough Council

Website: www.harrow.gov.uk
Main Switchboard: 020 8863 5611
Conveyancing Searches: Land Charges Dept, Registration Services, Civic Centre, Station Rd, Harrow HA1 2UX
Tel: 020 8424 1270 Fax: 020 8424 1414
DX: 30450 Harrow 3
e-mail: landcharges@harrow.gov.uk
Note: Formerly: Harrow B
Council Tax: Access Harrow, PO Box 731, Civic Centre, Station Rd, Harrow, Middlesex HA1 2DT
Tel: 020 8901 2610
Planning: Civic 1, Civic Centre, Station Rd, Harrow, Middlesex HA1 2UY
Tel: 020 8901 2650
e-mail: planning.applications@harrow.gov.uk
Solicitor to the Council: Hugh Peart, Director of Legal Services, Harrow Legal Services, PO Box 2, Civic Centre, Harrow HA1 2UH
Tel: 020 8863 5611 x 2287 Fax: 020 8424 1557
DX: 30450 Harrow 3
e-mail: hugh.peart@harrow.gov.uk
Water Services: Thames Water and Three Valleys Water

L16 Havering London Borough Council

Website: www.havering.gov.uk
Main Switchboard: 01708 434343
Conveyancing Searches: Land Charges, Town Hall, Main Rd, Romford RM1 3BD
Tel: 01708 432425 Fax: 01708 432482
DX: 312102 Romford 16
e-mail: landsearches@havering.gov.uk
Note: Formerly: Romford MB, Hornchurch UD
Building Control: 8th Fl, Mercury Ho, Mercury Grdns, Romford RM1 3SL
Tel: 01708 432 700
e-mail: buildingcontrol@havering.gov.uk
Council Tax: Town Hall, Main Rd, Romford RM1 3BD
Tel: 01708 433 997
e-mail: counciltax@havering.gov.uk
Environmental Health: 10th Fl, Mercury Ho, Mercury Grdns, Romford RM1 3SL
Tel: 01708 432 777
e-mail: environmental.health@havering.gov.uk
Solicitor to the Council: Interim Director, Legal & Governance, Town Hall, Main Rd, Romford RM1 3BD
Tel: 01708 432 484 Fax: 01708 432 482
Water Services: Thames Water and Anglian Water

L17 Hillingdon London Borough Council

Website: www.hillingdon.gov.uk
Main Switchboard: 01895 250111
Conveyancing Searches: Local Land Charges, 3N/03, Civic Centre, High St, Uxbridge UB8 1UW
Tel: 01895 250624
e-mail: locallandcharges@hillingdon.gov.uk
Note: Formerly: Uxbridge B, Hayes and Harlington UD, Ruislip-Northwood UD, Yiewsly & West Drayton UD
Building Control: A Oloyede, Building Control Manager, Civic Centre, 3N/03, Uxbridge UB8 1UW
Tel: 01895 250804
e-mail: buildingcontrol@hillingdon.gov.uk
Council Tax: Council Tax, 1S/02 Civic Centre, High St, Uxbridge UB8 1UW
Tel: 01895 250000 Fax: 01895 250879
e-mail: ctax@hillingdon.gov.uk

Environmental Services: 3 North, Civic Centre, High St, Uxbridge, Middlesex UB8 1UW
Tel: 01895 250 574 Fax: 01895 277 476
e-mail: environmentalhealthdutyofficer@hillingdon.gov.uk
Planning: 3N/01, Civic Centre, High St, Uxbridge, Middlesex UB8 1UW
Tel: 01895 250 230
e-mail: planning@hillingdon.gov.uk
Solicitor to the Council: Rajesh Alagh, Borough Solicitor, Civic Centre, Uxbridge UB8 1UW
Tel: 01895 250617 Fax: 01895 250784
DX: 45101 Uxbridge
e-mail: ralagh@hillingdon.gov.uk
Water Services: Thames Water and Three Valleys Water

L18 Hounslow London Borough Council

Website: www.hounslow.gov.uk
Main Switchboard: 020 8583 2000
Conveyancing Searches: Land Charges, Civic Centre, Lampton Rd, Hounslow TW3 4DN
Tel: 020 8583 2093/4 Fax: 020 8583 2092
DX: 3505 Hounslow
e-mail: landcharges@hounslow.gov.uk
Note: Formerly: Brentford & Chiswick B, Heston & Isleworth B, Feltham UD
Building Control: Borough Planning Dept, Civic Centre, Lampton Rd, Hounslow TW3 4DN
Tel: 020 8583 5403 Fax: 020 8583 5405
e-mail: buildingcontrol@hounslow.gov.uk
Council Tax: Council Tax Office, Civic Centre, Lampton Rd, Hounslow TW3 4DN
Tel: 020 8583 4242 Fax: 020 8583 4788
e-mail: counciltax@hounslow.gov.uk
Planning: Civic Centre, Lampton Rd, Hounslow TW3 4DN
Tel: 020 8583 5555
e-mail: planning@hounslow.gov.uk
Solicitor to the Council: Mr Terry Welsh, Civic Centre, Lampton Rd, Hounslow TW3 4DN
Tel: 020 8583 2022 Fax: 020 8583 2055
DX: 3505 Hounslow
e-mail: terry.welsh@hounslow.gov.uk
Water Services: Thames Water

L19 Islington London Borough Council

Website: www.islington.gov.uk
Main Switchboard: 020 7527 2000
Conveyancing Searches: Local Land Charges Section, 3rd Fl Environment & Regeneration, 222 Upper St, London N1 1XR
Tel: 020 7527 3297/3148 Fax: 020 7527 3370
e-mail: landsearches@islington.gov.uk
Building Control: Building Control, 222 Upper St, London N1 1YA
Tel: 020 7457 5999 Fax: 020 7457 5998
Engineers: Technical & Environmental (Engineers), PO Box 3333, 222 Upper St, London N1 1YA
Tel: 020 7527 2857 Fax: 020 7527 2134
Environmental Services: Technical & Environmental (Environmental Services), 222 Upper St, London N1 1YA
Tel: 020 7527 3420/3033/3217 Fax: 020 7527 3057
Planning: Planning, 222 Upper St, London N1 1YR
Tel: 020 7527 2813 Fax: 020 7527 2731
Solicitor to the Council: Louise Round, Director of Corporate Resources, Town Hall, Upper St, London N1 2UD
Tel: 020 7527 2000 x 3174 Fax: 020 7527 3243
DX: 122230 Upper Islington
Water Services: Thames Water

L20 Kensington & Chelsea Royal London Borough Council

Website: www.rbkc.gov.uk
Main Switchboard: 020 7361 3000
Conveyancing Searches: Land Charges, Town Hall, Hornton St, London W8 7NX
Tel: 020 7361 3554 Fax: 020 7361 3464
DX: 84016 Kensington High Street 2
e-mail: land.charges@rbkc.gov.uk
Note: Formerly: Chelsea MB, Kensington MB
Building Control: Building Control Section, Room 343, KensingtonTown Hall, Hornton St, London W8 7NX
Tel: 020 7361 3838 Fax: 020 7361 3820
e-mail: building.control@rbkc.gov.uk
Council Tax: Council Tax Dept, Town Hall, Hornton St, London W8 7NX
Tel: 020 7361 3005 Fax: 020 7368 0303
e-mail: counciltax@rbkc.gov.uk
Environmental Health: Environmental Health, Council Offices, 37 Pembroke Rd, London W8 6PW
Tel: 020 7361 3002 Fax: 020 7341 5200
e-mail: environmentalhealth@rbkc.gov.uk
Highways: Highway Section, Town Hall, Hornton St, London W8 7NX
Tel: 020 7361 3001 Fax: 020 7361 3156
Planning: Planning Dept, Town Hall, Hornton St, London W8 7NX
Tel: 020 7361 3012 Fax: 020 7361 3463
e-mail: planning@rbkc.gov.uk
Solicitor to the Council: Michael Cogher, Director of Legal Services, Town Hall, Hornton St, London W8 7NX
Tel: 020 7361 2180 Fax: 020 7361 2764
DX: 84015 Kensington High Street 2
e-mail: michael.cogher@rbkc.gov.uk
Water Services: Thames Water

L21 Kingston upon Thames Royal London Borough Council

Website: www.kingston.gov.uk
Main Switchboard: 020 8547 5000
Conveyancing Searches: Local Land Charges, Guildhall, High St, Kingston upon Thames KT1 1EU
Tel: 020 8547 4634
Fax: 020 8547 5127 local land charges only
DX: 31515 Kingston upon Thames
e-mail: local.landcharges@rbk.kingston.gov.uk
Note: Formerly: Kingston upon Thames B, Malden & Coombe MB, Surbiton MB
Building Control, Highways & Planning: Environmental Services, Guildhall 2, High St, Kingston upon Thames KT1 1EU
Tel: 020 8547 5002
Fax: 020 8547 5363 (Pla); 4460 (Bldg Cont); 5926 (Hwys)
Council Tax: Council Tax, Guildhall 2, High St, Kingston upon Thames KT1 1EU
Tel: 020 8547 5007 Fax: 020 8547 5648
Environmental Health: Community Services, Guildhall, High St, Kingston upon Thames KT1 1EU
Tel: 020 8547 5004 Fax: 020 8547 5568
Solicitor to the Council: Mr N A Bishop, Head of Legal Services, Guildhall, High St, Kingston upon Thames KT1 1EU
Tel: 020 8547 5110 Fax: 020 8547 5127
DX: 31515 Kingston upon Thames
Water Services: Thames Water

L22 Lambeth London Borough Council

Website: www.lambeth.gov.uk
Main Switchboard: 020 7926 1000
Conveyancing Searches: Land Charges Section, Town Hall, Brixton Hill, London SW2 1RW
Tel: 020 7926 3145/2188 Fax: 020 7926 2361
DX: 132670 Brixton 2
e-mail: personalsearch@lambeth.gov.uk
Note: Formerly: Lambeth MB, pt Wandsworth MB
Building Control: Building Control Dept, Phoenix Ho, 10 Wandsworth Rd, London SW8 2LL
Tel: 020 7926 9000 Fax: 020 7926 1155
e-mail: buildingcontrol@lambeth.gov.uk
Council Tax: Council Tax Office, Olive Morris Ho, 18 Brixton Hill, London SW2 1RL
Tel: 0345 302 2312 Fax: 020 7926 9483
e-mail: lambethctax@capita.co.uk
Environmental Health: Regulatory Services, 2 Herne Hill Rd, London SE24 0AU
Tel: 020 7926 6111 Fax: 020 7926 6130
e-mail: regulatoryservices@lambeth.gov.uk
Highways: Highways Infrastructure, Blue Star Hse, 234–244 Stockwell Rd, London SW9 9SP
Tel: 020 7926 9000 Fax: 020 7926 6201
e-mail: tandhcallcentre@lambeth.gov.uk
Planning: Planning Dept, Phoenix Ho, 10 Wandsworth Rd, London SW8 2LL
Tel: 020 7926 1180 Fax: 020 7926 1171
e-mail: tpac@lambeth.gov.uk
Solicitor to the Council: Mark Hynes, Director of Legal and Democratic Services, Room 203, 2nd Fl, Town Hall, Brixton, London SW2 1RW
Tel: 020 7926 2209 Fax: 020 7926 2361
e-mail: mhynes@lambeth.gov.uk
Water Services: Thames Water

L23 Lewisham London Borough Council

Website: www.lewisham.gov.uk
Main Switchboard: 020 8314 6000
Conveyancing Searches: Land Charges, Laurence Ho, 3rd Fl, 1 Catford Rd, London SE6 4SW
Tel: 020 8314 6262 Fax: 020 8314 3127
e-mail: landcharges@lewisham.gov.uk
Note: Formerly: Deptford MB, Lewisham MB
Building Control: Building Control, Laurence Ho, 4th Fl, 1 Catford Rd, London SE6 4SW
Tel: 020 8314 8233 Fax: 020 8314 3138
e-mail: building.control@lewisham.gov.uk
Council Tax: Directorate of Finance & Support, Council Tax Unit, Laurence Ho, Ground Fl Access point, 1 Catford Rd, London SE6 4SW
Tel: 020 8690 9666 Fax: 020 8314 3165
e-mail: counciltax@lewisham.gov.uk
Environmental Health: Laurence Ho, 4th Fl, 1 Catford Rd, London SE6 4SW
Tel: 020 8314 6789 Fax: 020 8314 2594
e-mail: environmentalhealth@lewisham.gov.uk
Highways: Highways, Wearside Services Centre, Wearside Rd, Lewisham, London SE13 3EZ
Tel: 020 8314 7171 Fax: 020 8297 9835
e-mail: highways@lewisham.gov.uk
Planning: Planning Services, Laurence Ho, 3rd Fl, 1 Catford Rd, London SE6 4SW
Tel: 020 8314 7400 Fax: 020 8314 3127
e-mail: planning@lewisham.gov.uk
Solicitor to the Council: Kath Nicholson, Head of Law, Legal Services, 3rd Fl, Lewisham Town Hall, Catford Rd, London SE6 4RU
Tel: 020 8314 7648 Fax: 020 8314 3107
DX: 139500 Lewisham 4
e-mail: kath.nicholson@lewisham.gov.uk
Water Services: Thames Water

L24 Merton London Borough Council

Website: www.merton.gov.uk
Main Switchboard: 020 8274 4901
Conveyancing Searches: Local Land Charges, Merton Civic Centre, London Rd, Morden SM4 5DX
Tel: 020 8545 3350
DX: 41650 Morden
e-mail: locallandcharges@merton.gov.uk
Note: Formerly: Mitcham B, Wimbledon B, Merton & Morden UD
Building Control: Civic Centre, 14th Fl, London Rd, Morden, Surrey SM4 5DX
Tel: 020 8545 3145 Fax: 020 8543 6085
DX: 41650 Morden
e-mail: buildingcontrol@merton.gov.uk
Council Tax: Civic Centre, 2nd Fl, London Road, Morden, Surrey SM4 5DX
Tel: 020 8274 4904 Fax: 020 8545 3960
DX: 41650 Merton
e-mail: local.taxation@merton.gov.uk
Environmental Health: Civic Centre, 14th Floor, London Rd, Morden, Surrey SM4 5DX
Tel: 020 8545 3441 Fax: 020 8545 4025
DX: 41650 Morden
e-mail: ehcommercial@merton.gov.uk
Highways: Civic Centre, 13th Floor, London Rd, Morden, Surrey SM4 5DX
Tel: 020 8545 3428 Fax: 020 8545 3199
DX: 41650 Morden
e-mail: trafficandhighways@merton.gov.uk
Planning: Civic Centre, 14th Floor, London Rd, Morden, Surrey SM4 5DX
Tel: 020 8545 3777 Fax: 020 8543 6085
DX: 41650 Morden
e-mail: planning@merton.gov.uk
Solicitor to the Council: Paul Evans, Merton Civic Centre, London Rd, Morden SM4 5DX
Tel: 020 8545 3163 / 3338 Fax: 020 8545 3244
DX: 41650 Morden
e-mail: paul.evans@merton.gov.uk
Water Services: Thames Water

L25 Newham London Borough Council

Website: www.newham.gov.uk
Main Switchboard: 020 8430 2000
Conveyancing Searches: Land Charges, 1st Fl, West Wing, Newham Dockside, 1000 Dockside Rd, London E16 2QU
Tel: 020 3373 0996 Fax: 020 8557 8981
DX: 4706 East Ham
e-mail: land.charges@newham.gov.uk
Note: Formerly: East Ham CB, West Ham CB, pt Woolwich MB
Building Control: Building Control Service, Newham Dockside, 1000 Dockside Rd, London E16 2QU
Tel: 020 3373 8200
Council Tax: Council Tax Offices, PO Box 23504, London E15 4UU
Tel: 020 8430 2000 Fax: 020 8430 1026
e-mail: counciltax@newham.gov.uk

Environmental Health: Newham Dockside, 1000 Dockside Rd, London E16 2QU
Tel: 020 8430 2000 Fax: 020 8430 4434
Highways & Planning (1): Newham Dockside, 1000 Dockside Rd, London E16 2QU
Tel: 020 3373 8300
Highways & Planning (2): Newham Dockside, 1000 Dockside Rd, London E16 2QU
Tel: 020 8430 2000
Solicitor to the Council: Helen Sidwell, Deputy Director & Head of Legal Services, Newham Dockside, 1000 Dockside Rd, London E16 2QU
Tel: 020 8430 2000 Fax: 020 8470 0480
e-mail: helen.sidwell@newham.gov.uk
Water Services: Thames Water

L26 Redbridge London Borough Council

Website: www.redbridge.gov.uk
Main Switchboard: 020 8554 5000
Conveyancing Searches: Land Charges Dept, 3rd Fl, Town Hall, 128–142 High Rd, Ilford, Essex IG1 1DD
Tel: 020 8708 2139 Fax: 020 8708 2981
DX: 134261 Ilford 8
e-mail: landcharges@redbridge.gov.uk
Note: Formerly: Ilford B, Wanstead & Woodford B, pt Dagenham B, pt Chigwell UD
Building Control & Planning: Town Hall, 128–142 High Rd, Ilford, Essex IG1 1DD
Tel: 020 8708 2175 (planning); 020 8708 2530 (bldg)
Fax: 020 8708 2062 (planning); 020 8708 2985 (bldg)
DX: 134620 Ilford 8
e-mail: planning.enquiry@redbridge.gov.uk
Note: buildingcontrol@redbridge.gov.uk
Council Tax: Council Tax Offices, 22–26 Clements Rd, Ilford IG1 1BD
Tel: 020 8708 5670 Fax: 020 8708 4313
e-mail: council.tax@redbridge.gov.uk
Environmental Health: Environmental and Civil Protection, 8 Perth Terrace, Perth Rd, Ilford IG2 6AT
Tel: 020 8708 5473 Fax: 020 8708 5506
e-mail: public.protection@redbridge.gov.uk
Highways: Highways & Cleansing Services, Lynton Ho, 255–259 High Rd, Ilford IG1 1NN
Tel: 020 8708 3632 Fax: 020 8708 3970
Solicitor to the Council: Simon Goodwin, Borough Solicitor and Secretary, PO Box 2, Town Hall, 4th Fl, 128–142 High Rd, Ilford IG1 1DD
Tel: 020 8708 2201 Fax: 020 8708 2981
DX: 134261 Ilford 8
e-mail: simon.goodwin@redbridge.gov.uk
Water Services: Thames Water

L27 Richmond upon Thames London Borough Council

Website: www.richmond.gov.uk
Main Switchboard: 0845 612 2660
Conveyancing Searches: Local Land Charges, Civic Centre, 44 York St, Twickenham TW1 3BZ
Tel: 020 8891 7774
DX: 200027 Twickenham
e-mail: landcharges@richmond.gov.uk
Note: Formerly: Barnes B, Richmond B, Twickenham B
Other depts: Civic Centre, 44 York St, Twickenham TW1 3BZ
Tel: 0845 612 2660
Solicitor to the Council: Mrs Helen White, Interim Head of Legal Services, Civic Centre, 44 York St, Twickenham TW1 3BZ
e-mail: legalservices@richmond.gov.uk
Water Services: Thames Water

L28 Southwark London Borough Council

Website: www.southwark.gov.uk
Main Switchboard: 020 7525 5000
Conveyancing Searches: Local Land Charges, Communities Law & Governance, Southwark Council, PO Box 64529, London SE1P 5LX
Tel: 020 7525 7392 Fax: 020 7525 7675
DX: 136148 London Bridge 7
e-mail: landcharges2@southwark.gov.uk
Note: Formerly: Bermondsey MB, Camberwell MB, Southwark MB
Building Control: Building Control Officer, PO Box 64529, London SE1P 5LX
Tel: 0845 600 1285 Fax: 020 7525 5575/5593
e-mail: building.control@southwark.gov.uk
Council Tax: Council Tax Section, LB Southwark, PO Box 64529, London SE1P 5LX
Tel: 020 7525 1850
e-mail: counciltax@southwark.gov.uk
Environmental Management: Environmental Management, PO Box 64529, London SE1P 5LX
e-mail: environment@southwark.gov.uk
Planning and Economic Development: Regeneration Dept (Planning), PO Box 64529, London SE1P 5LX
Tel: 020 7525 5403 Fax: 020 7525 5575/5593
e-mail: planning.enquiries@southwark.gov.uk
Public Protection: Public Protection Dept, Community Safety & Enforcement, 3rd Fl, PO Box 64529, London SE1P 5LX
Tel: 020 7525 5777
e-mail: environment@southwark.gov.uk
Solicitor to the Council: Deborah Collins, Communities Law & Governance, PO Box 64529, London SE1P 5LX
Tel: 020 7525 7630 Fax: 020 7525 7554
DX: 136146 London Bridge 7
e-mail: deborah.collins@southwark.gov.uk
Water Services: Thames Water

L29 Sutton London Borough Council

Website: www.sutton.gov.uk
Main Switchboard: 020 8770 5070
Conveyancing Searches: Local Land Charges Dept, 24 Denmark Rd, Carshalton SM5 2JG
Tel: 020 8770 5107 Fax: 020 8770 6201
DX: 134341 Sutton 11
e-mail: landcharges@sutton.gov.uk
Note: Formerly: Beddington & Walling B, Sutton & Cheam B, Carshalton UD
Building Control, Planning, Highways & Environmental Health: 24 Denmark Rd, Carshalton SM5 2JG
Tel: 020 8770 5070 Fax: 020 8770 6201
Council Tax: Civic Offices, St Nicholas Way, Sutton SM1 1EA
Solicitor to the Council: Stephen Lawrence, Executive Head of Legal Services, Civic Offices, Gifford Ho, St Helier Ave, Morden SM4 6HY
Water Services: Thames Water

L30 Tower Hamlets London Borough Council

Website: www.towerhamlets.gov.uk
Main Switchboard: 020 7364 5000
Conveyancing Searches: Land Charges Dept, Town Hall, Mulberry Place, PO Box 55739, 5 Clove Cres, London E14 1BY
Tel: 020 7364 5009 Fax: 020 7364 4515
DX: 42679 Isle of Dogs
e-mail: landcharges@towerhamlets.gov.uk
Note: Formerly: Bethnal Green MB, Poplar MB, Stepney MB

Building Control: Building Control Offices, Town Hall, Mulberry Place, PO Box 55739, 5 Clove Cres, London E14 2BG
Tel: 020 7364 5009 Fax: 020 7364 5265
e-mail: buildingcontrol@towerhamlets.gov.uk
Council Tax: Revenue Services, The Town Hall, Mulberry Pl, PO Box 55739, 5 Clove Cres, London E14 2BG
Tel: 020 7364 5002 Fax: 020 7364 4456
e-mail: counciltax@towerhamlets.gov.uk
Environmental Health: Environmental Health & Protection, Mulberry Pl (AH), PO Box 55739, 5 Clove Cres, London E14 2BG
Tel: 020 7364 5008 Fax: 020 7364 6831
e-mail: environmentalhealth@towerhamlets.gov.uk
Highways: Mulberry Pl, PO Box 55739, 5 Clove Cres, London E14 2BG
Tel: 020 7364 6924 Fax: 020 7364 6711
Planning: Mulberry Pl, PO Box 55739, 5 Clove Cres, London E14 2BG
Tel: 020 7364 5009 Fax: 020 7364 4536
e-mail: planning@towerhamlets.gov.uk
Solicitor to the Council: Isabella Freeman, Head of Legal, Mulberry Pl, 5 Clove Cres, London E14 2BG
Tel: 020 7364 4801 Fax: 020 7364 4804
DX: 42679 Isle of Dogs
e-mail: isabella.freeman@towerhamlets.gov.uk
Water Services: Thames Water

L31 Waltham Forest London Borough Council

Main Switchboard: 020 8496 3000
Conveyancing Searches: Land Charges, Sycamore Ho, Town Hall Complex, Forest Rd, London E17 4JA
Tel: 020 8496 4566/4662
DX: 124540 Waltham Forest
e-mail: jackiesteward@walthamforest.gov.uk
Note: Formerly: Chingford B, Leyton B, Walthamstow B
Building Control & Planning: Building Control & Planning Dept, Development Management, Sycamore Ho, Town Hall Complex, Forest Rd, London E17 4JA
Tel: 020 8496 6723 Fax: 020 8496 6902
DX: 124540 Waltham Forest
Council Tax: Council Tax Office, Town Hall, Forest Rd, London E17 4JA
Tel: 020 8527 6600 Fax: 020 8509 0074
Environmental Health: Sycamore Ho, Town Hall, Forest Rd, London E17 4JA
Tel: 020 8496 2219
DX: 124540 Waltham Forest
Highways: Low Hall, Argall Ave, London E10 7AS
Tel: 020 8496 1034 Fax: 020 8496 2664
Solicitor to the Council: Daniel Fenwick, Director of Governance and Law, Waltham Forest Town Hall, Forest Rd, London E17 4JA
Tel: 020 8496 4295 Fax: 020 8523 4967
DX: 124540 Waltham Forest
Water Services: Thames Water

L32 Wandsworth London Borough Council

Website: www.wandsworth.gov.uk
Main Switchboard: 020 8871 6000
Conveyancing Searches: Land Charges, Town Hall, Wandsworth High St, London SW18 2PU
Tel: 020 8871 7664 Fax: 020 8871 7528
DX: 59054 Wandsworth Nth
e-mail: locallandcharges@wandsworth.gov.uk
Note: Formerly: Battersea MB, pt Wandsworth MB
Building Control: Town Hall, Wandsworth High St, London SW18 2PU
Tel: 020 8871 7620
e-mail: buildingcontrol@wandsworth.gov.uk
Council Tax: Town Hall, Wandsworth High St, London SW18 2PU
Tel: 020 8871 8081
e-mail: counciltax@wandsworth.gov.uk
Environmental Services: Environmental Services, Technical Services, 5th Fl, Wandsworth Town Hall, Wandsworth High St, London SW18 2PU
Tel: 020 8871 6127 Fax: 020 8871 6964
e-mail: esd@wandsworth.gov.uk
Planning: Town Hall, Wandsworth High St, London SW18 2PU
Tel: 020 8871 8871
e-mail: boroughplanner@wandsworth.gov.uk
Solicitor to the Council: Mr Martin Walker, Borough Solicitor, Town Hall, Wandsworth High St, London SW18 2PU
Tel: 020 8871 6110 Fax: 020 8871 7506
DX: 59054 Wandsworth North
e-mail: mwalker@wandsworth.gov.uk
Water Services: Thames Water

L33 Westminster City Council

Website: www.westminster.gov.uk
Main Switchboard: 020 7641 6000
Conveyancing Searches: Local Land Charges, Westminster City Council, PO Box 240, Victoria St, London SW1E 6QP
Tel: 020 7641 2413 Fax: 020 7641 6069
DX: 2310 Victoria
e-mail: landcharges@westminster.gov.uk
Note: Formerly: City of Westminster MB, Paddington MB, St Marylebone MB
Building Control: Building Control, 11th Fl, Westminster City Hall, 64 Victoria St, London SW16 6QP
Tel: 020 7641 7230 Fax: 020 7641 7115
e-mail: districtsurveyors@westminster.gov.uk
Council Tax (1): Council Tax street addresses A-K, PO Box 4009, London SW1E 6QZ
Tel: 0845 302 3400 Fax: 020 8315 2194
e-mail: westminstercounciltax1@capita.co.uk (A-K)
Note: Minicom/textphone: 0845 070 0281
Council Tax (2): Council Tax (street addresses L-Z), PO Box 4009, London SW1E 6QZ
Tel: 0845 3023 400 Fax: 020 7641 6044
e-mail: westminstercounciltax2@capita.co.uk
Note: Minicom/textphone 0845 070 0281
Environmental Health: Environmental Health Consultation Team, Westminster City Hall, 64 Victoria St, London SW1E 6QP
Tel: 020 7641 3161 Fax: 020 7641 3436
e-mail: ehcttechnicalsupport@westminster.gov.uk
Highways: Highways, 12th Fl, City Hall, 64 Victoria St, London SW1E 6QP
Tel: 020 7641 2642 Fax: 020 7641 2046
DX: 2310 Victoria
Planning: City Planning and Development, City Hall, 64 Victoria St, London SW1E 6QP
Tel: 020 7641 2513 Fax: 020 7641 3124
e-mail: planninginformation@westminster.gov.uk
Note: www.westminster.gov.uk/planning
Solicitor to the Council: Peter Large, Head of Legal Services, 15th Fl, City Hall, Westminster, London SW1E 6QP
Tel: 020 7641 8078 Fax: 020 7641 3325
DX: 2310 Victoria
e-mail: plarge@westminster.gov.uk
Water Services: Thames Water

London Postal Districts by Code

The following list gives the London Postal Codes, the name of the postal district and the London Boroughs (in parentheses) in which they are situated.

E1 Eastern (Head) District (Tower Hamlets)
E2 Bethnal Green (Hackney, Tower Hamlets)
E3 Bow (Tower Hamlets)
E4 Chingford (Waltham Forest)
E5 Clapton (Hackney)
E6 East Ham (Newham)
E7 Forest Gate (Newham, Waltham Forest)
E8 Hackney (Hackney, Waltham Forest)
E9 Homerton (Hackney, Tower Hamlets)
E10 Leyton (Waltham Forest)
E11 Leytonstone (Waltham Forest)
E12 Manor Park (Newham, Redbridge)
E13 Plaistow (Newham)
E14 Poplar (Tower Hamlets)
E15 Stratford (Hackney, Newham, Waltham Forest)
E16 Victoria Dock (Newham)
E17 Walthamstow (Waltham Forest)
E18 Woodford and South Woodford (Redbridge, Waltham Forest)
EC1 Eastern Central (Head) District (Corporation of London, Islington)
EC2 Eastern Central (Head) District (Corporation of London, Islington)
EC3 Eastern Central (Head) District (Corporation of London, Tower Hamlets)
EC4 Eastern Central (Head) District (Camden, Corporation of London)
N1 Northern (Head) District (Camden, Islington)
N2 East Finchley (Barnet, Haringey)
N3 Finchley (Barnet)
N4 Finsbury Park (Haringey, Islington)
N5 Highbury (Islington)
N6 Highgate (Camden, Haringey)
N7 Holloway (Islington)
N8 Hornsey (Haringey, Islington)
N9 Lower Edmonton (Enfield)
N10 Muswell Hill (Barnet, Haringey)
N11 New Southgate (Barnet, Enfield, Haringey)
N12 North Finchley (Barnet)
N13 Palmers Green (Enfield, Haringey)
N14 Southgate (Barnet, Enfield)
N15 South Tottenham (Hackney, Haringey)
N16 Stoke Newington (Hackney, Haringey)
N17 Tottenham (Haringey)
N18 Upper Edmonton (Enfield)
N19 Upper Holloway (Camden, Haringey, Islington)
N20 Whetstone (Barnet)
N21 Winchmore Hill (Enfield)
N22 Wood Green (Enfield, Haringey)
NW1 North Western (Head) District (Camden, Westminster)
NW2 Cricklewood (Barnet, Brent, Camden)
NW3 Hampstead (Barnet, Camden)
NW4 Hendon (Barnet)
NW5 Kentish Town (Camden)
NW6 Kilburn (Camden, Westminster)
NW7 Mill Hill (Barnet)
NW8 St Johns Wood (Camden, Westminster)
NW9 The Hyde (Barnet, Brent)
NW10 Willesden (Brent, Ealing, Hammersmith & Fulham)
NW11 Golders Green (Barnet, Camden)
SE1 South Eastern (Head) District (Lambeth, Southwark)
SE2 Abbey Wood (Bexley, Greenwich)
SE3 Blackheath (Greenwich, Lewisham)
SE4 Brockley (Lewisham)
SE5 Camberwell (Lambeth, Southwark)
SE6 Catford (Lewisham)
SE7 Charlton (Greenwich)
SE8 Deptford (Greenwich, Lewisham, Southwark)
SE9 Eltham (Greenwich, Lewisham)
SE10 Greenwich (Greenwich, Lewisham)
SE11 Kennington (Lambeth, Southwark)
SE12 Lee (Greenwich, Lewisham)
SE13 Lewisham (Greenwich, Lewisham)
SE14 New Cross (Lewisham, Southwark)
SE15 Peckham (Lewisham, Southwark)
SE16 Rotherhithe (Lewisham, Southwark)
SE17 Walworth (Southwark)
SE18 Woolwich (Bexley, Greenwich)
SE19 Norwood (Croydon, Lambeth, Southwark)
SE20 Anerley (Bromley)
SE21 Dulwich (Lambeth, Southwark)
SE22 East Dulwich (Southwark)
SE23 Forest Hill (Lewisham, Southwark)
SE24 Herne Hill (Lambeth)
SE25 South Norwood (Croydon)
SE26 Sydenham (Bromley, Lewisham, Southwark)
SE27 West Norwood (Croydon, Lambeth)
SE28 Thamesmead (Bexley, Greenwich)
SW1 South Western (Head) District (Kensington & Chelsea, Westminster)
SW2 Brixton (Lambeth)
SW3 Chelsea (Kensington & Chelsea)
SW4 Clapham (Lambeth, Wandsworth)
SW5 Earls Court (Hammersmith & Fulham, Kensington & Chelsea)
SW6 Fulham (Hammersmith & Fulham, Kensington & Chelsea)

SW7 South Kensington (Kensington & Chelsea, Westminster)
SW8 South Lambeth (Lambeth, Wandsworth)
SW9 Stockwell (Lambeth)
SW10 West Brompton (Hammersmith & Fulham, Kensington & Chelsea)
SW11 Battersea (Wandsworth)
SW12 Balham (Lambeth, Wandsworth)
SW13 Barnes (Richmond upon Thames)
SW14 Mortlake (Richmond upon Thames)
SW15 Putney (Richmond upon Thames, Wandsworth)
SW16 Streatham (Croydon, Lambeth, Wandsworth)
SW17 Tooting (Lambeth, Merton, Wandsworth)
SW18 Wandsworth (Wandsworth)
SW19 Wimbledon (Merton, Wandsworth)
SW20 West Wimbledon (Kingston upon Thames, Merton)
W1 Western (Head) District (Camden, Westminster)
W2 Paddington (Westminster)
W3 Acton (Ealing, Hammersmith & Fulham)
W4 Chiswick (Ealing, Hammersmith & Fulham, Hounslow)
W5 Ealing (Ealing)
W6 Hammersmith (Hammersmith & Fulham, Hounslow)
W7 Hanwell (Ealing)
W8 Kensington (Kensington & Chelsea)
W9 Maida Vale (Camden, Westminster)
W10 North Kensington (Hammersmith & Fulham, Kensington & Chelsea, Westminster)
W11 Notting Hill (Kensington & Chelsea)
W12 Shepherds Bush (Ealing, Hammersmith & Fulham)
W13 West Ealing (Ealing)
W14 West Kensington (Hammersmith & Fulham, Kensington & Chelsea)
WC1 Western Central (Head) District (Camden, Islington)
WC2 Western Central (Head) District (Camden, Westminster)

1

London Postal Districts by Name

This section comprises an alphabetical list of London Postal Districts with their respective postal codes. The London Boroughs in which they are situated are shown in parentheses.

Abbey Wood (Bexley, Greenwich) SE2
Acton (Ealing, Hammersmith & Fulham) W3
Anerley (Bromley) SE20
Balham (Lambeth, Wandsworth) SW12
Barnes (Richmond upon Thames) SW13
Battersea (Wandsworth) SW11
Bethnal Green (Hackney, Tower Hamlets) E2
Blackheath (Greenwich, Lewisham) SE3
Bow (Tower Hamlets) E3
Brixton (Lambeth) SW2
Brockley (Lewisham) SE4
Camberwell (Lambeth, Southwark) SE5
Catford (Lewisham) SE6
Charlton (Greenwich) SE7
Chelsea (Kensington & Chelsea) SW3
Chingford (Waltham Forest) E4
Chiswick (Ealing, Hammersmith & Fulham, Hounslow) W4
Clapham (Lambeth, Wandsworth) SW4
Clapton (Hackney) E5
Cricklewood (Barnet, Brent, Camden) NW2
Deptford (Greenwich, Lewisham, Southwark) SE8
Dulwich (Lambeth, Southwark) SE21
Ealing (Ealing) W5
Earls Court (Hammersmith & Fulham, Kensington & Chelsea) SW5
East Dulwich (Southwark) SE22
East Finchley (Barnet, Haringey) N2
East Ham (Newham) E6
Eastern (Head) District (Tower Hamlets) E1
Eastern Central (Head) District (Camden, Corporation of London) EC4
Eastern Central (Head) District (Corporation of London, Islington) EC1
Eastern Central (Head) District (Corporation of London, Islington) EC2
Eastern Central (Head) District (Corporation of London, Tower Hamlets) EC3
Eltham (Greenwich, Lewisham) SE9
Finchley (Barnet) N3
Finsbury Park (Haringey, Islington) N4
Forest Gate (Newham, Waltham Forest) E7
Forest Hill (Lewisham, Southwark) SE23
Fulham (Hammersmith & Fulham, Kensington & Chelsea) SW6
Golders Green (Barnet, Camden) NW11
Greenwich (Greenwich, Lewisham) SE10
Hackney (Hackney, Waltham Forest) E8
Hammersmith (Hammersmith & Fulham, Hounslow) W6
Hampstead (Barnet, Camden) NW3
Hanwell (Ealing) W7
Hendon (Barnet) NW4
Herne Hill (Lambeth) SE24
Highbury (Islington) N5
Highgate (Camden, Haringey) N6
Holloway (Islington) N7
Homerton (Hackney, Tower Hamlets) E9
Hornsey (Haringey, Islington) N8
Kennington (Lambeth, Southwark) SE11
Kensington (Kensington & Chelsea) W8
Kentish Town (Camden) NW5

Kilburn (Camden, Westminster) NW6
Lee (Greenwich, Lewisham) SE12
Lewisham (Greenwich, Lewisham) SE13
Leyton (Waltham Forest) E10
Leytonstone (Waltham Forest) E11
Lower Edmonton (Enfield) N9
Maida Vale (Camden, Westminster) W9
Manor Park (Newham, Redbridge) E12
Mill Hill (Barnet) NW7
Mortlake (Richmond upon Thames) SW14
Muswell Hill (Barnet, Haringey) N10
New Cross (Lewisham, Southwark) SE14
New Southgate (Barnet, Enfield, Haringey) N11
North Finchley (Barnet) N12
North Kensington (Hammersmith & Fulham, Kensington & Chelsea, Westminster) W10
North Western (Head) District (Camden, Westminster) NW1
Northern (Head) District (Camden, Islington) N1
Norwood (Croydon, Lambeth, Southwark) SE19
Notting Hill (Kensington & Chelsea) W11
Paddington (Westminster) W2
Palmers Green (Enfield, Haringey) N13
Peckham (Lewisham, Southwark) SE15
Plaistow (Newham) E13
Poplar (Tower Hamlets) E14
Putney (Richmond upon Thames, Wandsworth) SW15
Rotherhithe (Lewisham, Southwark) SE16
Shepherds Bush (Ealing, Hammersmith & Fulham) W12
South Eastern (Head) District (Lambeth, Southwark) SE1
South Kensington (Kensington & Chelsea, Westminster) SW7
South Lambeth (Lambeth, Wandsworth) SW8
South Norwood (Croydon) SE25
South Tottenham (Hackney, Haringey) N15
South Western (Head) District (Kensington & Chelsea, Westminster) SW1
Southgate (Barnet, Enfield) N14
St Johns Wood (Camden, Westminster) NW8
Stockwell (Lambeth) SW9
Stoke Newington (Hackney, Haringey) N16
Stratford (Hackney, Newham, Waltham Forest) E15
Streatham (Croydon, Lambeth, Wandsworth) SW16
Sydenham (Bromley, Lewisham, Southwark) SE26
Thamesmead (Bexley, Greenwich) SE28
The Hyde (Barnet, Brent) NW9
Tooting (Lambeth, Merton, Wandsworth) SW17
Tottenham (Haringey) N17
Upper Edmonton (Enfield) N18
Upper Holloway (Camden, Haringey, Islington) N19
Victoria Dock (Newham) E16
Walthamstow (Waltham Forest) E17
Walworth (Southwark) SE17
Wandsworth (Wandsworth) SW18
West Brompton (Hammersmith & Fulham, Kensington & Chelsea) SW10
West Ealing (Ealing) W13
West Kensington (Hammersmith & Fulham, Kensington & Chelsea) W14
West Norwood (Croydon, Lambeth) SE27
West Wimbledon (Kingston upon Thames, Merton) SW20
Western (Head) District (Camden, Westminster) W1
Western Central (Head) District (Camden, Islington) WC1
Western Central (Head) District (Camden, Westminster) WC2
Whetstone (Barnet) N20
Willesden (Brent, Ealing, Hammersmith & Fulham) NW10
Wimbledon (Merton, Wandsworth) SW19
Winchmore Hill (Enfield) N21
Wood Green (Enfield, Haringey) N22
Woodford and South Woodford (Redbridge, Waltham Forest) E18
Woolwich (Bexley, Greenwich) SE18

Local Authorities in England

2 Bedfordshire

2.0 Bedfordshire County Council (abolished)

County Council abolished as from 1 April 2009. Bedford BC is Bedford Council (Unitary) and Mid Bedfordshire DC and South Bedfordshire DC have merged to form Central Bedfordshire Council (Unitary).

2.1 Bedford Council (U)

Website: www.bedford.gov.uk
Main Switchboard: 01234 267422
Conveyancing Searches: Local Land Charges, Borough Hall, Cauldwell St, Bedford MK42 9AP
Tel: 01234 276389
DX: 117105 Bedford 4
e-mail: locallandcharges@bedford.gov.uk
Note: Tel/Fax for Land Charges only
Building Control: Building Control, Borough Hall, Cauldwell St, Bedford MK42 5AP
Tel: 01234 718097
DX: 117105 Bedford 4
e-mail: buildingcontrol@bedford.gov.uk
Council Tax: Local Taxation & Revenues, Borough Hall, Cauldwell St, Bedford MK42 9AP
Tel: 01234 718097
DX: 117105 Bedford 4
e-mail: localtax@bedford.gov.uk
Environmental Health: Environmental Health, Rogers Court, Kingsway, Bedford MK42 9BA
Tel: 01234 267422
DX: 117105 Bedford 4
e-mail: ehadmin@bedford.gov.uk
Highways: Bedford Borough Council, Borough Hall, Cauldwell St, Bedford MK42 9AP
Tel: 01234 718003
DX: 117105 Bedford 4
e-mail: highways.helpdesk@bedford.gov.uk
Planning: Planning, Borough Hall, Cauldwell St, Bedford MK42 9AP
Tel: 01234 718068
DX: 117105 Bedford 4
e-mail: planning@bedford.gov.uk
Solicitor to the Council: Mr M Gough, Borough Hall, Cauldwell St, Bedford MK42 9AP
Tel: 01234 718206 Fax: 01234 718266
DX: 117105 Bedford 4
Water Services: Geodesys (Anglian Water Services)

2.2 Central Bedfordshire Council (U)

Website: www.centralbedfordshire.gov.uk
Main Switchboard: 0300 300 8000
Conveyancing Searches: Local Land Charges, Priory Ho, Monks Walk, Chicksands SG17 5TQ
Tel: 0300 300 8052
DX: 153440 Shefford
e-mail: land.charges@centralbedfordshire.gov.uk
Building Control: Planning Services, Priory Ho, Monks Walk, Chicksands SG17 5TQ
Tel: 0300 300 8307
DX: 153440 Shefford
e-mail: building.control@centralbedfordshire.gov.uk
Council Tax: Head of Revenues & Benefits, Watling Ho, High St Nth, Dunstable, Beds LU6 1LF
Tel: 0300 300 8306
Environmental Health: Head of Environmental Health Services, Priory Ho, Monks Walk, Chicksands SG17 5TQ
Tel: 0300 300 8302
DX: 153440 Shefford
Highways: Development Control 2, Priory Ho, Monks Walk, Chicksands SG17 5TQ
Tel: 0300 300 8308
DX: 153440 Shefford
Planning: Head of Planning Services, Priory Ho, Monks Walk, Chicksands SG17 5TQ
Tel: 0300 300 8307
DX: 153440 Shefford
Solicitor to the Council: Head of Democratic & Legal Services, Priory Ho, Monks Walk, Chicksands SG17 5TQ
Tel: 0300 300 8000
DX: 153440 Shefford
Water Services: Anglian Water (Geodesys) and Thames Water Property Insight, (for areas south of Dunstable)

2.4 Luton Council (U)

Website: www.luton.gov.uk
Main Switchboard: 01582 546000
Conveyancing Searches: Local Land Charges Service, Legal Services, Luton Borough Council, Town Hall, Luton LU1 2BQ
Tel: 01582 546042 Fax: 01582 547137 (Land Charges Dept)
DX: 5926 Luton
e-mail: landcharges@luton.gov.uk
Building Control: Town Hall, George St, Luton LU1 2BQ
Tel: 01582 546607 Fax: 01582 546993
e-mail: build.control@luton.gov.uk
Council Tax: Revenues Division, Corporate & Customer Services, Luton Borough Council, Town Hall, George St, Luton LU1 2BQ
Tel: 01582 510350 / Hotline: 0300 7900 340
Fax: 01582 546977
DX: 5926 Luton
e-mail: revenues@luton.gov.uk
Environmental Health: Town Hall, George St, Luton LU1 2BQ
Tel: 01582 510330 Fax: 01582 546676
Planning: Development Control Manager, Town Hall, George St, Luton LU1 2BQ
Tel: 01582 546317
e-mail: developmentcontrol@luton.gov.uk
Solicitor to the Council: Richard Stevens, Head of Legal Services, Apex Ho, 30–34 Upper George St, Luton LU1 2RD
Tel: 01582 546020 Fax: 01582 547140
DX: 5926 Luton
Water Services: Thames Water (except Poynters Rd, Luton: Anglian Water)

3 Berkshire

3.0 Berkshire County Council (abolished)

Royal County Council abolished as from 1 April 1998.

3.1 West Berkshire District Council (U)

Website: www.westberks.gov.uk
Main Switchboard: 01635 42400
Conveyancing Searches: Land Charges, Council Offices, Market St, Newbury RG14 5LD
Tel: 01635 519465
DX: 30825 Newbury
e-mail: smann@westberks.gov.uk
Building Control, Council Tax & Planning: Council Offices, Market St, Newbury RG14 5LD
Environmental Health: Public Protection, Council Offices, Market St, Newbury RG14 5LD
Tel: 01635 42400
DX: 30825 Newbury
Highways: Highways & Engineering, Council Offices, Market St, Newbury RG14 5LD
Tel: 01635 42400
Solicitor to the Council: David Holling, Head of Legal Services, Council Offices, Market St, Newbury RG14 5LD
Tel: 01635 519422 Fax: 01635 519431
DX: 30825 Newbury
e-mail: d.holling@westberks.gov.uk
Water Services: Thames Water (Asset Data Services)

3.2 Reading Borough Council (U)

Website: www.reading.gov.uk
Main Switchboard: 01189 37 37 37
Conveyancing Searches: Land Charges, Civic Centre, Reading RG1 7AE
Tel: 01189 37 2363 Fax: 01189 37 2320
DX: 40124 Reading (Castle Street)
Building Control: Building Control, Level 8, Civic Centre, Reading RG1 7AE
Tel: 0118 937 3787
DX: 40124 Reading (Castle St)
e-mail: building.control@reading.gov.uk
Council Tax: Local Taxation, PO Box 26, Civic Centre, Reading RG1 7TD
Tel: 0118 937 3727
DX: 40124 Reading (Castle St)
Environmental Health: Environmental Health, Civic Centre, Reading RG1 7AE
Tel: 0118 937 3787
DX: 40124 Reading (Castle St)
e-mail: hep@reading.gov.uk
Highways: Highways Team, Civic Centre, Reading RG1 7AE
Tel: 0118 937 3787
e-mail: vaughan.norris@reading.gov.uk
Planning: Planning Team, Level 8, Civic Centre, Reading RG1 7AE
Tel: 0118 937 3787
DX: 40124 Reading (Castle St)
e-mail: plgadmin@reading.gov.uk
Solicitor to the Council: Chris Brooks, Head of Legal & Democratic Services, Civic Centre, Reading RG1 7AE
Tel: 0118 937 2602 Fax: 0118 937 2767
DX: 40124 Reading (Castle Street)
e-mail: chris.brooks@reading.gov.uk
Water Services: Thames Water

3.3 Wokingham Borough Council (U)

Website: www.wokingham.gov.uk
Main Switchboard: 0118 974 6000
Conveyancing Searches: Head of Local Land Charges, PO Box 151, Shute End, Wokingham RG40 1WH
Tel: 0118 974 6532 Fax: 0118 978 9078
DX: 33506 Wokingham
e-mail: landcharges@wokingham.gov.uk
Building Control: Building Control, Council Offices, PO Box 155, Shute End, Wokingham RG40 1WH
Tel: 0118 974 6375
DX: 33506 Wokingham
Council Tax: Finance Dept, Council Offices, PO Box 152, Shute End, Wokingham RG40 1WH
Tel: 0118 974 6602 Fax: 0118 974 6631
DX: 33506 Wokingham
Environmental Health: Public Protection Dept, Council Offices, PO Box 155, Shute End, Wokingham RG40 1WH
Tel: 0118 974 6376 Fax: 0118 974 6385
DX: 33506 Wokingham
e-mail: john.mullaney@wokingham.gov.uk
Highways: Place & Neighbourhood Services, Council Offices, PO Box 153, Shute End, Wokingham RG40 1WL
Tel: 0118 974 6332
DX: 33506 Wokingham
e-mail: highwayops@wokingham.gov.uk
Planning: Planning Services, Council Offices, PO Box 157, Shute End, Wokingham RG40 1WH
Tel: 0118 974 6428 Fax: 0118 974 6484
DX: 33506 Wokingham
e-mail: ian.jordan@wokingham.gov.uk
Solicitor to the Council: Mary Severin, Council Offices, PO Box 151, Shute End, Wokingham RG40 1WH
Tel: 0118 974 6520 Fax: 0118 978 9078
DX: 33506 Wokingham
e-mail: mary.severin@wokingham.gov.uk
Water Services: Thames Water (Asset Data Services)

3.4 Windsor & Maidenhead Royal Borough (U)

Website: www.rbwm.gov.uk
Main Switchboard: 01628 683800
Conveyancing Searches: Local Land Charges & Commons Registrations, Town Hall, St Ives Rd, Maidenhead SL6 1RF
Tel: 01628 796292/3 Fax: 01628 776031
DX: 6422 Maidenhead 1
e-mail: land.charges@rbwm.gov.uk
Note: Tel/fax for Land Charges and Commons Registrations only
Building Control: Building Control Consultancy, Town Hall, St Ives Rd, Maidenhead SL6 1RF
Tel: 01628 796870 / 01628 796885 (24hr Inspection Hotline)
Fax: 01628 796886
DX: 6422 Maidenhead 1
Council Tax: PO Box 3446, Town Hall, St Ives Rd, Maidenhead SL6 1NY
Tel: 01628 683850
e-mail: council.tax@rbwm.gov.uk
Highways: Highways Dept, Town Hall, St Ives Rd, Maidenhead SL6 1RF
Tel: 01628 683806
DX: 6422 Maidenhead 1
Other depts:
Tel: 01628 798888 Fax: 01628 796408
Planning: Development Control, Town Hall, St Ives Rd, Maidenhead SL6 1RF
Tel: 01628 683810
DX: 6422 Maidenhead 1
e-mail: planning.maidenhead@rbwm.gov.uk
Solicitor to the Council: Head of Legal Services, Town Hall, St Ives Rd, Maidenhead SL6 1RF
Tel: 01628 796014 Fax: 01628 796408
DX: 6422 Maidenhead
Water Services: Thames Water

3.5 Slough Borough Council (U)

Website: www.slough.gov.uk
Main Switchboard: 01753 475111
Conveyancing Searches: Local Land Charges Service, St Martin's Place, 51 Bath Rd, Slough SL1 3UF
Tel: 01753 875039
DX: 42270 Slough West
e-mail: landcharges@slough.gov.uk
Building Control, Environmental Health, Highways & Planning: Slough Building Control Services, St Martin's Place, 51 Bath Rd, Slough SL1 3UF
Tel: 01753 875810 (Bldg Ctrl); 477340 (Plng); 875255 (Env Hlth) Fax: 01753 875809
e-mail: buildingcontrol@slough.gov.uk
Note: foodandsafety@slough.gov.uk
Council Tax: Housing & Neighbourhood Services Dept, Council Tax Manager, PO Box 1733, Slough SL1 1FS
Tel: 01753 475111 Fax: 01753 875369
e-mail: counciltax@slough.gov.uk
Solicitor to the Council: Steven Quayle, Law & Corporate Governance, Town Hall, Bath Rd, Slough SL1 3UQ
Tel: 01753 875004 Fax: 01753 875183
DX: 42270 Slough West
Water Services: Thames Water

3.6 Bracknell Forest Borough Council (U)

Website: www.bracknell-forest.gov.uk
Main Switchboard: 01344 352000
Conveyancing Searches: Registrar of Local Land Charges, Time Sq, Market St, Bracknell RG12 1JD
Tel: 01344 352000
DX: 33611 Bracknell
e-mail: lindabell@bracknell-forest.gov.uk
Building Control, Highways & Planning: Environment, Time Sq, Market St, Bracknell RG12 1JD
Tel: 01344 352000
DX: 33611 Bracknell
Council Tax: Revenue Services, PO Box 3559, Bracknell RG12 1WY
Tel: 01344 352011 Fax: 01344 352201
Environmental Health: Time Sq, Market St, Bracknell RG12 1JD
Solicitor to the Council: Alex Jack, Borough Solicitor, Corporate Services – Legal, Easthampstead Ho, Town Sq, Bracknell RG12 1AQ
Tel: 01344 352000 Fax: 01344 352236
Water Services: Thames Water

4 Bristol

4.1 Bristol City Council (U)

Website: www.bristol.gov.uk
Main Switchboard: 0117 922 2000
Conveyancing Searches: Local Land Charges, 3rd Fl, Bazaar Wing, Brunel Ho, PO Box 3176, Bristol BS3 9FS
Tel: 0117 922 3506
DX: 7827 Bristol 1
e-mail: landcharges@bristol.gov.uk
Building Control, Highways & Planning: Planning Searches (PLACE), 1st Fl, Bazaar Wing, Brunel Ho, PO Box 3176, Bristol BS3 9FS
Tel: 0117 922 3861
DX: 7827 Bristol 1
e-mail: planning.searches@bristol.gov.uk
Council Tax: Local Taxation Division, PO Box 968, Bristol BS99 1ZG
Tel: 0117 922 2900
DX: 7827 Bristol
Environmental Health: Environmental Health Services, Brunel Ho, PO Box 3176, Bristol BS3 9FS
Tel: 01179 222500
DX: 7827 Bristol
e-mail: pollution@bristol.gov.uk
Solicitor to the Council: Sanjay Prashar, Service Director, Legal and Democratic Services, Brunel Ho, PO Box 3176, Bristol BS3 9FS
Tel: 0117 922 2839
DX: 7827 Bristol 1
e-mail: sanjay.prashar@bristol.gov.uk
Water Services: Bristol Water and Wessex Water

1

5 Buckinghamshire

5.0 Buckinghamshire County Council

Website: www.buckscc.gov.uk
Main Switchboard: 01296 395000
Search Address: Legal & Democratic Services, County Hall, Walton St, Aylesbury HP20 1UA
Tel: 01296 383689
DX: 97401 Aylesbury 2
e-mail: legal@buckscc.gov.uk
Solicitor to the Council: Mrs Anne Davies, Head of Legal & Democratic Services, County Hall, Walton St, Aylesbury HP20 1UA
Tel: 01296 383689
DX: 97401 Aylesbury 2
e-mail: adavies@buckscc.gov.uk

5.1 Milton Keynes Council

Website: www.miltonkeynes.gov.uk
Main Switchboard: 01908 691691
Conveyancing Searches: Land Charges Dept, Civic Offices, 1 Saxon Gate East, Central Milton Keynes MK9 3EJ
Tel: 01908 252317 Fax: 01908 252211
e-mail: land.charges@milton-keynes.gov.uk
Building Control: Building Control, Civic Offices, 1 Saxon Gate East, Central Milton Keynes MK9 3EJ
Tel: 01908 252403
e-mail: building.control@milton-keynes.gov.uk
Council Tax: Revenue Services, PO Box 5327, Civic Offices, 1 Saxon Gate East, Central Milton Keynes MK9 3EJ
Tel: 01908 253794 Fax: 01908 253707
Other depts: Civic Offices, as before
Solicitor to the Council: Sharon Bridglasingh, Head of Legal Services, Civic Offices, 1 Saxon Gate East, Central Milton Keynes MK9 3HG
Tel: 01908 691691 Fax: 01908 252273
Water Services: Anglian Water (Geodesys)

5.2 Aylesbury Vale District Council

Website: www.aylesburyvaledc.gov.uk
Main Switchboard: 01296 585858
Conveyancing Searches: Land Charges Section, The Gateway, Gatehouse Rd, Aylesbury HP19 8FF
Tel: 01296 585039
DX: 4130 Aylesbury 1
e-mail: landcharges@aylesburyvaledc.gov.uk
Building Control: Building Control, The Gateway, Gatehouse Rd, Aylesbury HP19 8FF
Tel: 01296 585460
e-mail: bcontrol@aylesburyvaledc.gov.uk

Council Tax: Council Tax Dept, The Gateway, Gatehouse Rd, Aylesbury HP19 8FF
Tel: 01296 585299
e-mail: counciltax@aylesburyvaledc.gov.uk
Environmental Health: Environmental Health, The Gateway, Gatehouse Rd, Aylesbury HP19 8FF
Tel: 01296 585605
e-mail: envhealth@aylesburyvaledc.gov.uk
Highways: Bucks County Council
Planning: Planning Dept, The Gateway, Gatehouse Rd, Aylesbury HP19 8FF
Tel: 01296 585679
e-mail: devcon@aylesburyvaledc.gov.uk
Solicitor to the Council: Head of Legal Services, The Gateway, Gatehouse Rd, Aylesbury HP19 8FF
Tel: 01296 585024
DX: 4130 Aylesbury 1
e-mail: legal@aylesburyvaledc.gov.uk
Water Services: Thames Water and Anglian Water

5.3 Wycombe District Council

Website: www.wycombe.gov.uk
Main Switchboard: 01494 461000
Conveyancing Searches: Local Land Charges, Queen Victoria Rd, High Wycombe HP11 1BB
Tel: 01494 421180
DX: 4411 High Wycombe 1
e-mail: elections@wycombe.gov.uk
Building Control: Queen Victoria Rd, High Wycombe HP11 1BB
Tel: 01494 461000
DX: 4411 High Wycombe 1
Council Tax: Queen Victoria Rd, High Wycombe HP11 1BB
Tel: 01494 461000
DX: 4411 High Wycombe 1
Environmental Health: Queen Victoria Rd, High Wycombe HP11 1BB
Tel: 01494 461000
DX: 4411 High Wycombe 1
Highways: Bucks County Council
Planning: Queen Victoria Rd, High Wycombe HP11 1BB
Tel: 01494 461000
DX: 4411 High Wycombe 1
Solicitor to the Council: District Solicitor, Queen Victoria Rd, High Wycombe HP11 1BB
Tel: 01494 421252
DX: 4411 High Wycombe 1
Water Services: Thames Water

5.4 Chiltern District Council

Website: www.chiltern.gov.uk
Main Switchboard: 01494 729000
Conveyancing Searches: Land Charges Section, King George V Ho, King George V Rd, Amersham HP6 5AW
Tel: 01494 732007/8
DX: 50711 Amersham
e-mail: landcharges@chiltern.gov.uk
Building Control: Building Control, Capswood, Oxford Rd, Denham UB9 4LH
Tel: 01895 837296
DX: 40261 Gerrards Cross
e-mail: buildingcontrol@southbucks.gov.uk
Council Tax, Environmental Health & Planning: Council Offices, as before
Highways: Bucks County Council
Solicitor to the Council: Mrs J Swift, King George V Ho, King George V Rd, Amersham HP6 5AW
Tel: 01494 729000
DX: 50711 Amersham
e-mail: legal@chiltern.gov.uk
Water Services: Thames Water

5.5 South Bucks District Council

Website: www.southbucks.gov.uk
Main Switchboard: 01895 837 200
Conveyancing Searches: Local Land Charges, Council Offices, Capswood, Oxford Rd, Denham UB9 4LH
Tel: 01895 837 329/370 Fax: 01895 837 277
DX: 40261 Gerrards Cross
e-mail: locallandcharges@southbucks.gov.uk
Building Control: Building Control, Council Offices, Capswood, Oxford Rd, Denham UB9 2LH
Tel: 01895 837296
DX: 40261 Gerrards Cross
e-mail: buildingcontrol@southbucks.gov.uk
Council Tax: Council Tax, Council Offices, Capswood, Oxford Rd, Denham UB9 4LH
Tel: 01895 837200
DX: 40261 Gerrards Cross
Environmental Health: Environmental Health, Council Offices, Capswood, Oxford Rd, Denham UB9 4LH
Tel: 01895 837200
DX: 40261 Gerrards Cross
e-mail: envhealth@southbucks.gov.uk
Highways: Bucks County Council
Planning: Planning, Council Offices, Capswood, Oxford Rd, Denham UB9 4LH
Tel: 01895 837200
DX: 40261 Gerrards Cross
e-mail: planning@southbucks.gov.uk
Solicitor to the Council: Joanna Swift, Capswood, Oxford Rd, Denham UB9 4LH
Tel: 01895 837232
DX: 40261 Gerrards Cross
e-mail: joanna.swift@southbucks.gov.uk
Water Services: Thames Water

6 Cambridgeshire

6.0 Cambridgeshire County Council

Website: www.cambridgeshire.gov.uk
Main Switchboard: 0345 045 5200
Search Address: Cambridgeshire Archives, Box RES1009, Shire Hall, Castle Hill, Cambridge CB3 0AP
Tel: 01223 699399 (Gen.enqs)
e-mail: cals@cambridgeshire.gov.uk
Head of Legal Services: Christopher Jones, Shire Hall, RES 1001, Castle Hill, Cambridge CB3 0AP
Tel: 01223 699386 Fax: 01223 717074
DX: 137872 Cambridge 9
e-mail: christopher.jones@cambridgeshire.gov.uk

6.1 Peterborough City Council (U)

Website: www.peterborough.gov.uk
Main Switchboard: 01733 747474
Conveyancing Searches: Local Land Charges, Bayard PL, Broadway, Peterborough PE1 1FD
Tel: 01733 452220
DX: 12310 Peterborough 1
e-mail: local.landcharges@peterborough.gov.uk

Building Control: Environmental Services Planning Services, Town Hall, Bridge St, Peterborough PE1 1HF
Tel: 01733 453422
DX: 12310 Peterborough 1
e-mail: buildingcontrol@peterborough.gov.uk
Council Tax: Revenues & Benefits Service, Town Hall, Bridge St, Peterborough PE1 1HF
Tel: 01733 452258 Fax: 01733 452585
DX: 12310 Peterborough 1
e-mail: local.taxation@peterborough.gov.uk
Environmental Health: Environmental Services Environmental & Public Protection, Bayard PL, Broadway, Peterborough PE1 1AY
Tel: 01733 747474 Fax: 01733 863811
DX: 12310 Peterborough 1
e-mail: wmhd@peterborough.gov.uk
Highways: Environmental Services Highways Infrastructure, Stuart Ho, St John's St, Peterborough PE1 5DD
Tel: 01733 747474 Fax: 01733 753459
DX: 12310 Peterborough 1
e-mail: highways@peterborough.gov.uk
Planning: Development Dept, Operations Directorate, Town Hall, Brdge St, Peterborough PE1 1HF
Tel: 01733 453410 Fax: 01733 453410
e-mail: planningcontrol@peterborough.gov.uk
Solicitor to the Council: Helen Edwards, Legal Services, Town Hall, Bridge St, Peterborough PE1 1HG
Tel: 01733 747474 Fax: 01733 452299
DX: 12310 Peterborough 1
e-mail: ask@peterborough.gov.uk
Water Services: Anglian Water

6.2 Fenland District Council

Website: www.fenland.gov.uk
Main Switchboard: 01354 654321
Conveyancing Searches: Local Land Charges Team, Fenland Hall, County Rd, March PE15 8NQ
Tel: 01354 654321 Fax: 01354 606914
e-mail: landcharges@fenland.gov.uk
Building Control: CNC Building Control, King's Lynn & West Norfolk, The Boathouse Business Centre, 1 Harbour Sq, Nene Parade, Wisbech PE13 3BH
Tel: 0808 168 5041
e-mail: enquiries@cncbuildingcontrol.gov.uk
Environmental Health: Director of Environment & Leisure, The Base, Melbourne Ave, March PE15 0EN
Tel: 01354 654321
e-mail: environmentalservices@fenland.gov.uk
Highways: Cambridgeshire County Council
Planning: Development Services, Fenland Hall, County Rd, March PE15 8NQ
Tel: 01354 654321
e-mail: planning@fenland.gov.uk
Solicitor to the Council: Chief Solicitor, Fenland Hall, County Rd, March PE15 8NQ
Tel: 01354 654321 Fax: 01354 606914
Water Services: Geodesys Ltd

6.3 Huntingdon District Council

Website: www.huntingdonshire.gov.uk
Main Switchboard: 01480 388388
Conveyancing Searches: Local Land Charges Section, Pathfinder Ho, St Mary's St, Huntingdon PE29 3TN
Tel: 01480 388043 Fax: 01480 388061
DX: 140316 Huntingdon SC
e-mail: land.charges@huntsdc.gov.uk
Highways: Cambridgeshire County Council
Other depts: as before,
Tel: 01480 388388 Fax: 01480 388099
Solicitor to the Council: Mr Colin Meadowcroft, Head of Legal Estates, as before,
Tel: 01480 388021 Fax: 01480 388061
e-mail: mail@huntsdc.gov.uk
Water Services: Geodesys

6.4 East Cambridgeshire District Council

Website: www.eastcambs.gov.uk
Main Switchboard: 01353 665555
Conveyancing Searches: Legal Services, The Grange, Nutholt Lane, Ely CB7 4EE
Tel: 01353 665555 Fax: 01353 665240
e-mail: landcharges@eastcambs.gov.uk
Building Control: Building Control,
Tel: 01353 665555 Fax: 01353 665240
e-mail: bcservices@eastcambs.gov.uk
Council Tax: Council Tax,
Tel: 0845 072 6000
e-mail: counciltax@angliarevenues.gov.uk
Environmental Health & Planning: The Grange, as before,
Tel: 01353 665555 Fax: 01353 665240
Highways: Cambridgeshire County Council
Solicitor to the Council: Principal Solicitor, Legal Services, The Grange, Nutholt Lane, Ely CB7 4EE
Tel: 01353 665555 Fax: 01353 668803
DX: 41001 Ely
Water Services: Geodesys

6.5 South Cambridgeshire District Council

Website: www.scambs.gov.uk
Main Switchboard: 03450 450 500
Conveyancing Searches: Land Charges, South Cambridgeshire Hall, Cambourne Business Park, Cambourne, Cambridge CB23 6EA
Tel: 01954 713064/713222/713065 Fax: 01954 713150
DX: 729500 Cambridge 15
e-mail: land.charges@scambs.gov.uk
Building Control: Building Control, as before,
Tel: 0345 045 0062 (Inspections) / 01954 713203 (Gen Enqs)
DX: 729500 Cambridge 15
e-mail: building.control@scambs.gov.uk
Council Tax: Council Tax, as before,
Tel: 0345 045 0064 Fax: 01954 713122
DX: 729500 Cambridge 15
e-mail: revenues@scambs.gov.uk
Environmental Health: Health & Environmental Services, as before,
Tel: 0345 045 0063 Fax: 01954 713248
DX: 729500 Cambridge 15
e-mail: env.health@scambs.gov.uk
Highways: Cambridgeshire County Council
Planning: Planning Dept, as before,
Tel: 03450 455215 (Dev'lt Control); 03450 455216 (Dev'lt Servs)
DX: 729500 Cambridge 15
e-mail: planning@scambs.gov.uk
Principal Solicitor: Legal & Democratic Services Mgr, Legal & Land Charges, as before,
Tel: 01954 713027 Fax: 01954 713150
DX: 729500 Cambridge 15
e-mail: legal.office@scambs.gov.uk
Water Services: Geodesys

6.6 Cambridge City Council

Website: www.cambridge.gov.uk
Main Switchboard: 01223 457000
Conveyancing Searches: Land Charges, PO Box 700, Cambridge CB11 0JH
Tel: 01223 457417
DX: 5854 Cambridge
e-mail: land.charges@cambridge.gov.uk
Note: 2 copies of location plan required
Building Control: Building Control, Department of Environment & Planning, PO Box 700, Cambridge CB1 0JH
Tel: 01223 457118 Fax: 01223 457129
DX: 5854 Cambridge
e-mail: buildingcontrol@cambridge.gov.uk
Council Tax: Council Tax Office, PO Box 700, Cambridge CB1 0JH
Tel: 01223 715333
DX: 5854 Cambridge
e-mail: benefits@cambridge.gov.uk
Environmental Health: Environmental Health, PO Box 700, Cambridge CB1 0JH
Tel: 01223 457000
DX: 5854 Cambridge
e-mail: envhealth@cambridge.gov.uk
Highways: Cambridgeshire County Council
Planning: Planning Dept, PO Box 700, Cambridge CB1 0JH
Tel: 01223 457200 Fax: 01223 457109
DX: 5854 Cambridge
e-mail: planning@cambridge.gov.uk
Solicitor to the Council: Simon Pugh, Head of Legal Services, Legal Services, PO Box 700, Cambridge CB1 0JH
Tel: 01223 457401 Fax: 01223 457409
DX: 5854 Cambridge
e-mail: simon.pugh@cambridge.gov.uk
Water Services: Geodesys

7 Cheshire

7.0 Cheshire County Council (abolished)

County Council abolished as from 1 April 2009. Ellesmere Port & Neston BC, Vale Royal BC and Chester City Council merged to create Cheshire West and Chester Borough Council (Unitary). Macclesfield BC, Crewe & Nantwich BC and Congleton BC merged to form Cheshire East Borough Council (Unitary).

7.1 Warrington Borough Council (U)

Website: www.warrington.gov.uk
Main Switchboard: 01925 443322
Conveyancing Searches: Assistant Chief Executives, Quattro, 4th Fl, Buttermarket St, Warrington WA1 2QB
Tel: 01925 442160 Fax: 01925 442044
DX: 17760 Warrington
e-mail: landcharges@warrington.gov.uk
Building Control, Environmental Health and Highways: Environment and Regeneration Dept, New Town Ho, Ground Fl, Warrington WA1 2NH
Tel: 01925 443322
Council Tax: Benefits & Exchequer Services, New Town Ho, Buttermarket St, Warrington WA1 2NH
Tel: 01925 443210 Fax: 01925 443211
e-mail: counciltax@warrington.gov.uk
Housing Services: Housing Advice Centre, Housing Plus, The Gateway, 85–101 Sankey St, Warrington WA1 1SR
Tel: 01925 246868 Fax: 01925 246897
e-mail: housingadvice@warrington.gov.uk
Planning: Environment and Regeneration Dept, New Town Ho, Buttermarket St, Warrington WA1 2NH
Tel: 01925 442819 Fax: 01925 442823
e-mail: devcontrol@warrington.gov.uk
Solicitor to the Council: Tim Date, Solicitor to the Council, Quattro Bldg, Buttermarket St, Warrington WA1 2NH
Tel: 01925 442150 Fax: 01925 413449
DX: 17760 Warrington
e-mail: tdate1@warrington.gov.uk
Water Services: United Utilities

7.2 Halton Borough Council (U)

Website: www.halton.gov.uk
Main Switchboard: 0303 333 4300
Conveyancing Searches: Local Land Charges, Legal Services, Municipal Bldg, Kingsway, Widnes WA8 7QF
Tel: 0151 511 7792 Fax: 0151 471 7527
e-mail: landcharges@halton.gov.uk
Building Control, Environmental Health, Planning & Highways: Environment Dept, Municipal Bldg, Kingsway, Widnes WA8 7QF
Tel: 0151 511 6565 Fax: 0151 471 7304
e-mail: Building.control@halton.gov.uk
Environmental.protection@halton.gov.uk
Forward.planning@halton.gov.uk
Council Tax: Council Tax, Catalyst Ho, Sankey St, Widnes WA8 0GH
Tel: 0151 511 8930 Fax: 0151 471 7308
Other depts: Policy & Corporate, Municipal Bldg, Kingsway, Widnes WA8 7QF
Tel: 0151 511 7839 Fax: 0151 471 7302
Solicitor to the Council: Mr Mark Reaney, Operation Directoral and Monitoring Officer, Municipal Bldg, Kingsway, Widnes WA8 7QF
Tel: 0151 511 6006 Fax: 0151 471 7527
Water Services: United Utilities

7.3 Cheshire West and Chester County Borough Council (U)

Website: www.cheshirewestandchester.gov.uk
Main Switchboard: 0300 1238 123
Conveyancing Searches: Local Land Charges Unit, Nicholas Ho, 1 Blackfriars, Chester CH1 2NU
Tel: 0300 123 7027
DX: 722041 Winsford 2
e-mail: llc@cheshirewestandchester.gov.uk
Building Control: Regulatory Services – Building Control, Wyvern Ho, The Drumber, Winsford CW7 1AH
Tel: 0300 123 7027
DX: 722411 Chester 17
e-mail: building.control@cheshirewestandchester.gov.uk
Council Tax: Revenue and Benefits Dept, PO Box 187, Ellesmere Port CH34 9DB
Tel: 0300 123 7022
e-mail: counciltax@cheshirewestandchester.gov.uk
Environmental Health: Environmental Health, Wyvern Ho, The Drumber, Winsford CW7 1AH
Tel: 0300 123 8123
e-mail: environmentalprotection@cheshirewestandchester.gov.uk
Highways: Chester, Ellesmereport and Neston Area Highways Office, Guilden Sutton Depot, Guilden Sutton, Chester CH3 7EX
Tel: 0300 123 8123
e-mail: engch@cheshirewestandchester.gov.uk

Highways: Winsford and Northwich Area Highways Office, Phoenix Ho, Clough Rd, Winsford CW7 4BD
Tel: 0300 123 8123
e-mail: engvr@cheshirewestandchester.gov.uk
Planning: Development Management, Nicholas Ho, 1 Blackfriars, Chester CH1 2NU
Tel: 0300 123 7027
DX: 722411 Chester 17
e-mail: planning@cheshirewestandchester.gov.uk
Solicitor to the Council: Legal Services, HQ 2nd Fl, 58 Nicholas St, Chester CH1 2NP
Tel: 0300 123 8123
Water Services: Welsh Water/United Utilities

7.5 Cheshire East County Borough Council (U)

Website: www.cheshireeast.gov.uk
Main Switchboard: 0300 1235 500
Conveyancing Searches: Registrar of Local Land Charges, Municipal Buildings, Earle St, Crewe CW1 2BJ
Tel: 0300 123 5014 Fax: 01270 537009
e-mail: landcharges@cheshireeast.gov.uk
Building Control: Building Control Section, Sandbach Enterprise Centre, Wesley Ave, Sandbach CW11 1DG
Tel: 01270 375278/53/56
e-mail: buildingcontrol@cheshireeast.gov.uk
Council Tax: Revenue Serives, PO Box 622, Crewe CW1 9JH
Tel: 0300 123 5013 Fax: 01625 504848
e-mail: ctax@cheshireeast.gov.uk
Environmental Health: Environmental Health, Westfields, Middlewich Rd, Sandbach CW11 1HZ
Tel: 0300 123 5015
e-mail: environmentalprotection@cheshireeast.gov.uk
Highways: Highways Team, Floor 6, Delamere Ho, Delamere St, Crewe CW1 2LL
Tel: 0300 123 5020 Fax: 01270 371158
e-mail: cheshireeasttraffic@cheshireeast.gov.uk
Planning: Planning Dept, PO Box 606, Muncipal Buildings, Crewe CW1 9HP
Tel: 0300 123 5014
e-mail: planning@cheshireeast.gov.uk
Solicitor to the Council: Mr Andrew Leadbetter, Legal Services Manager, Westfields, Middlewich Rd, Sandbach CW11 1HZ
Tel: 01270 529948
e-mail: andrew.leadbetter@cheshireeast.gov.uk
Water Services: United Utilities

9 Cornwall

9.0 Cornwall County Council (abolished)

County Council abolished as from 1 April 2009. North Cornwall DC, Restormel BC, Caradon DC, Penwith DC, Kerrier DC, Carrick DC and Cornwall County Council combined to form Cornwall Council (Unitary).

9.1 Cornwall Council (U)

Website: www.cornwall.gov.uk
Main Switchboard: 0300 1234 100
Conveyancing Searches: see under area offices
Area Central 1 (formerly Carrick): Room F2.04, Circuit Ho, St Clement St, Truro TR1 1DT
Tel: 01872 224401
DX: 81232 Truro
e-mail: landcharges.central1@cornwall.gov.uk
Note: 2 copies of OS extract showing boundaries of property to be searched edged red
Area Central 2 (formerly Restormel): 39 Penwinnick Rd, St Austell PL25 5DR
Tel: 01726 223630 Fax: 01726 223301
DX: 144560 St Austell 3
e-mail: landcharges.central2@cornwall.gov.uk
Note: 2 copies of OS extract showing boundaries of property to be searched edged red
Area East 1 (formerly North Cornwall): 3–5 Barn La, Bodmin PL31 1LZ
Tel: 01208 265612 Fax: 01208 265683
e-mail: landcharges.east1@cornwall.gov.uk
Note: 2 copies of OS extract showing boundaries of property to be searched edged red
Area East 2 (formerly Caradon): Luxstowe Ho, Greenbank Rd, Liskeard PL14 3DZ
Tel: 01579 341421 Fax: 01579 341426
e-mail: landcharges.east2@cornwall.gov.uk
Note: 2 copies of OS extract showing boundaries of property to be searched edged red
Area West 1 (formerly Kerrier & Penwith): Dolcoath Ave, Camborne TR14 8SX
Tel: 0300 123 4151 Fax: 01209 614099
e-mail: landcharges.west2@cornwall.gov.uk
Note: 2 copies of OS extract showing boundaries of property to be searched edged red
Highways: Highways Dept, Room F2.05, Circuit Ho, St Clement St, Truro TR1 1DT
Tel: 0300 123 4222
DX: 81232 Truro
e-mail: roadtransportandparking@cornwall.gov.uk
Solicitor to the Council: Head of Legal & Democratic Services, County Hall, Treyew Rd, Truro TR1 3AY
e-mail: enquiries@cornwall.gov.uk
Water Services: South West Water

10 Cumbria

10.0 Cumbria County Council

Website: www.cumbria.gov.uk
Main Switchboard: 01228 606060
Search Address: Legal Services Unit, The Courts, English St, Carlisle CA3 8LZ
Tel: 01228 606060 Fax: 01228 227380
DX: 63023 Carlisle
e-mail: info@cumbria.gov.uk

10.1 Carlisle City Council

Website: www.carlisle.gov.uk
Main Switchboard: 01228 817000
Conveyancing Searches: Governance Directorate, Civic Centre, Rickergate, Carlisle CA3 8QG
Tel: 01228 817554 Fax: 01228 817072
DX: 63037 Carlisle
e-mail: landcharges@carlisle.gov.uk
Building Control: Economic Development Directorate, Civic Centre, as before,
Tel: 01228 817000 Fax: 01228 817199
e-mail: bc@carlisle.gov.uk
Council Tax: Community Engagement Directorate, Civic Centre, as before,
Tel: 01228 817200 Fax: 01228 817266
e-mail: customerservices@carlisle.gov.uk
Environmental Health: Local Environment Directorate, Civic Centre, as before,
Tel: 01228 817559 Fax: 01228 817346
e-mail: environmentalhealth@carlisle.gov.uk

Highways: Cumbria Highways, Carlisle local practice, Parkhouse Bldg, Baron Way, Kingmoor Business Pk, Carlisle CA6 4SJ
Tel: 01228 673078 Fax: 01228 227662
e-mail: customerservices@cumbriahighways.org.uk
Planning: Director of Economic Development, Civic Centre, as before,
Tel: 01228 817000 Fax: 01228 817199
e-mail: customerservices@carlisle.gov.uk
Solicitor to the Council: Mr M D Lambert, Director of Governance, Civic Centre, Rickergate, Carlisle CA3 8QG
Tel: 01228 817019 Fax: 01228 817072
e-mail: markl@carlisle.gov.uk
Water Services: United Utilities

10.2 Allerdale Borough Council

Website: www.allerdale.gov.uk
Main Switchboard: 01900 702702
Conveyancing Searches: Land Charges Dept, Allerdale Ho, Workington, Cumbria CA14 3YJ
Tel: 01900 702720 Fax: 01900 702698
DX: 62861 Workington
e-mail: land.charges@allerdale.gov.uk
Building Control: Building Control, Allerdale Ho, as before,
Tel: 01900 702520
e-mail: building.control@allerdale.gov.uk
Council Tax: Council Tax, Allerdale Ho, Workington CA14 3YJ
Tel: 01900 702530 Fax: 01900 702507
e-mail: revenues@allerdale.gov.uk
Highways: Cumbria Highways, Highway Depot, Joseph Noble Rd, Lillyhall Ind Est, Workington CA14 4JH
Tel: 0845 609 6609 Fax: 01900 702507
e-mail: betterhighways.allerdale@cumbriahighways.org.uk
Planning: Planning, Allerdale Ho, as before,
Tel: 01900 702702
e-mail: planning@allerdale.gov.uk
Solicitor to the Council: Mr N Fardon, Borough Solicitor, Allerdale Ho, Workington CA14 3YJ
Tel: 01900 702528
DX: 62861 Workington 1
e-mail: nick.fardon@allerdale.gov.uk
Water Services: United Utilities

10.3 Eden District Council

Website: www.eden.gov.uk
Main Switchboard: 01768 817817
Conveyancing Searches: Dept of Corporate & Legal Services, Town Hall, Penrith CA11 7QF
Tel: 01768 817817 Fax: 01768 890732
e-mail: land.charges@eden.gov.uk
Building Control: Planning Services, Mansion Ho, Penrith CA11 7YG
Tel: 01768 212373/212313 (North Team); 01768 212342 (South Team) Fax: 01768 212320
e-mail: building.control@eden.gov.uk
Council Tax: Finance Dept, Town Hall, Penrith CA11 7QF
Tel: 01768 212216/212242 Fax: 01768 890470
e-mail: counciltax@eden.gov.uk
Environmental Health: Environmental Services, Mansion Ho, Penrith CA11 7YG
Tel: 01768 817817 Fax: 01768 890470
e-mail: env.health@eden.gov.uk
Highways: Cumbria County Council
Planning: Planning Services, Mansion Ho, Penrith CA11 7YG
Tel: 01768 817817 Fax: 01768 890732
e-mail: planning.services@eden.gov.uk
Solicitor to the Council: Paul Foote, Director of Corporate & Legal Services, Town Hall, Penrith CA11 7QF
Tel: 01768 817817 Fax: 01768 890470
e-mail: dcls@eden.gov.uk
Water Services: United Utilities and Northumbrian Water

10.4 Copeland Borough Council

Website: www.copeland.gov.uk
Main Switchboard: 0845 054 8600
Conveyancing Searches: Land Charges Section, The Copeland Centre, Catherine St, Whitehaven CA28 7SJ
Tel: 0845 0548 600 Fax: 01946 598311
DX: 62904 Whitehaven
e-mail: personalsearches@copeland.gov.uk
Building Control: Building Control, The Copeland Centre, Catherine St, Whitehaven CA28 7SJ
Tel: 01946 598409/598413 Fax: 01946 598306
e-mail: building.control@copeland.gov.uk
Council Tax: Council Tax, The Copeland Centre, Catherine St, Whitehaven CA28 7SJ
Tel: 0845 054 8600
e-mail: ctax@copeland.gov.uk
Highways: Cumbria Highways, Richmond Ho, Catherine St, Whitehaven CA28 7QY
Tel: 0845 609 6609 Fax: 01228 673111
e-mail: contact@cumbriahighways.gov.uk
Other depts: The Council Offices, as before
Planning: Planning Policy Team, The Copeland Centre, Catherine St, Whitehaven CA28 7SJ
Tel: 0845 054 8600
e-mail: ldf@copeland.gov.uk
Solicitor to the Council: Martin J. Epson, Chief Legal Officer, The Copeland Centre, Catherine St, Whitehaven CA28 7SJ
Tel: 01946 598515 Fax: 01946 598311
DX: 62904 Whitehaven
e-mail: mjepson@copelandbc.gov.uk
Water Services: United Utilities

10.5 South Lakeland District Council

Website: www.southlakeland.gov.uk
Main Switchboard: 01539 733333
Conveyancing Searches: Director (People & Places), South Lakeland Ho, Lowther St, Kendal LA9 4DL
Tel: 01539 793331 Fax: 01539 740300
DX: 63428 Kendal 1
e-mail: landcharges@southlakeland.gov.uk
Note: A clear up-to-date location plan (in duplicate) to a minimum scale of 1:2500 showing correct curtilage of property is required with every search.
Building Control: Director (People & Places), South Lakeland Ho, Lowther St, Kendal LA9 4DL
Tel: 01539 733333 Fax: 01539 740300
DX: 63428 Kendal 1
e-mail: building.control@southlakeland.gov.uk
Council Tax: Revenues & Benefits, South Lakeland Ho, Lowther St, Kendal LA9 4DQ
Tel: 01539 733333 Fax: 01539 740300
DX: 63428 Kendal 1
e-mail: counciltax@southlakeland.gov.uk
Environmental Health: Environmental Protection Group, Neighbourhood Services, South Lakeland Ho, Lowther St, Kendal LA9 4UD
Tel: 01539 733333 Fax: 01539 740300
DX: 63428 Kendal 1
e-mail: publicprotection@southlakeland.gov.uk
Highways: Cumbria Highways

Planning: Director (People & Places), South Lakeland Ho, Lowther St, Kendal LA9 4DL
Tel: 01539 733333 Fax: 01539 740300
DX: 63428 Kendal 1
e-mail: development.management@southlakeland.gov.uk
Property Management: Social Enterprise, South Lakeland Ho, Lowther St, Kendal LA9 4UE
Tel: 01539 797420 Fax: 01539 740300
DX: 63428 Kendal 1
Solicitor to the Council: Matthew Neal, Principal Solicitor, South Lakeland Ho, Lowther St, Kendal LA9 4UQ
Tel: 01539 733333 Fax: 01539 740300
DX: 63428 Kendal 1
e-mail: m.neal@southlakeland.gov.uk
Technical Services: Parking Services, South Lakeland Ho, Lowther St, Kendal LA9 4UQ
Tel: 01539 733333 Fax: 01539 740300
DX: 63428 Kendal 1
e-mail: parking@southlakeland.gov.uk
Water Services: United Utilities

10.6 Barrow-in-Furness Borough Council

Website: www.barrowbc.gov.uk
Main Switchboard: 01229 876543
Conveyancing Searches: Local Land Charges Department, Barrow-in-Furness Borough Council, Town Hall, Duke St, Barrow-in-Furness LA14 2LD
Tel: 01229 876364/876337 Fax: 01229 876515
DX: 63917
e-mail: bbclandcharges@barrowbc.gov.uk
Building Control: Building Control Dept, Town Hall, Duke St, Barrow-in-Furness, Cumbria LA14 2LD
Tel: 01229 876481
e-mail: buildcontrol@barrowbc.gov.uk
Council Tax: Council Tax, Town Hall, Duke St, Barrow-in-Furness LA14 2LD
Tel: 01229 404242 Fax: 01229 404740
e-mail: counciltax@barrowbc.gov.uk
Environmental Health: Environmental Health Dept, Town Hall, Duke St, Barrow-in-Furness, Cumbria LA14 2LD
Tel: 01229 876543
e-mail: envhealth@barrowbc.gov.uk
Highways: Cumbria County Council
Planning: Planning Dept, Town Hall, Duke St, Barrow-in-Furness LA14 2LD
Tel: 01229 876543 Fax: 01229 876508
e-mail: consultplanning@barrowbc.gov.uk
Solicitor to the Council: Legal & Administration Dept, Town Hall, Duke St, Barrow-in-Furness LA14 2LD
Tel: 01229 876346 Fax: 01229 876515
DX: 63917 Barrow-in-Furness
Water Services: United Utilities

11 Derbyshire

11.0 Derbyshire County Council

Website: www.derbyshire.gov.uk
Main Switchboard: 01629 533190
Search Address: Legal & Democratic Services, County Hall, Matlock DE4 3AG
Tel: 01629 580000 Fax: 01629 538326
e-mail: john.mcelvaney@derbyshire.gov.uk
Solicitor to the Council: Mr John Mcelvaney, Director of Legal Services, County Hall, Smedley St, Matlock DE4 3AG
Tel: 01629 538303 Fax: 01629 538326
e-mail: john.mcelvaney@derbyshire.gov.uk

11.1 High Peak Borough Council

Website: www.highpeak.gov.uk
Main Switchboard: 0345 129 7777
Conveyancing Searches: Local Land Charges Section, Buxton Town Hall, Market Pl, Buxton SK17 6EL
Tel: 0345 129 7777 Fax: 01663 752055
e-mail: land-searches@highpeak.gov.uk
Building Control: High Peak Building Control Services, Municipal Bldgs, Glossop SK13 8AF
Tel: 0845 129 7777/01298 28400 x3752 Fax: 01663 751766
e-mail: buildingcontrol@highpeak.gov.uk
Council Tax: High Peak Borough Council, Town Hall, Buxton SK17 6EL
Tel: 0345 129 4858 Fax: 01298 27639
e-mail: counciltax@highpeak.gov.uk
Environmental Health: Environment & Health, Town Hall, Buxton SK17 6EL
Tel: 0345 129 7777 Fax: 01298 28425
e-mail: environmental@highpeak.gov.uk
Highways: Derbyshire County Council
Legal Services: Jeanette Marsh, Legal Services Manager, Council Offices, Hayfield Rd, Chapel-en-le-Frith, High Peak SK23 0QJ
Tel: 0845 129 7777 Fax: 01663 752055
e-mail: jeanettemarsh@highpeak.gov.uk
Planning: Planning, Municipal Bldgs, Glossop SK13 8AF
Tel: 0845 129 7777 Fax: 01457 860290
e-mail: planning@highpeak.gov.uk
Water Services: North West Water and Severn Trent Water

11.2 Chesterfield Borough Council

Website: www.chesterfield.gov.uk
Main Switchboard: 01246 345345
Conveyancing Searches: Governance, Legal Section, Town Hall, Rose Hill, Chesterfield S40 1LP
Tel: 01246 345303 Fax: 01246 345356
DX: 12356 Chesterfield 1
e-mail: local.searches@chesterfield.gov.uk
Building Control: BCN Consultancy, Town Hall, Rose Hill, Chesterfield S40 1LP
Tel. 01246 345817 Fax: 01246 345910
e-mail: building.control@bcnconsultancy.co.uk
Council Tax: Maureen Madin/Carolyn Szadura, Revenues & Benefits Manager, PO Box 100, 85 New Sq, Chesterfield S40 1SN
Tel: 01246 345497/345502 Fax: 01246 345486
e-mail: billing@chesterfield.gov.uk
Environmental Health: Environmental Services, Town Hall, Rose Hill, Chesterfield S40 1LP
Tel: 01246 345741 Fax: 01246 345760
e-mail: env.health@chesterfield.gov.uk
Highways: Derbyshire County Council
Planning: Planning Service, Town Hall, as before,
Tel: 01246 345811 Fax: 01246 345809
DX: 12356 Chesterfield 1
e-mail: planning@chesterfield.gov.uk
Solicitor to the Council: Sara Goodwin, Head of Governance, Town Hall, as before,
Tel: 01246 345309 Fax: 01246 345270
DX: 12356 Chesterfield 1
e-mail: sara.goodwin@chesterfield.gov.uk
Water Services: Severn Trent Water and Yorkshire Water, Note: Drainage enquiries via Yorkshire Water

1

11.3 Derbyshire Dales District Council

Website: www.derbyshiredales.gov.uk
Main Switchboard: 01629 761100
Conveyancing Searches: Land Charges, Corporate Services Dept, Town Hall, Matlock DE4 3NN
Tel: 01629 761270 Fax: 01629 761307
e-mail: landcharges@derbyshiredales.gov.uk
Building Control: Planning & Development Services Dept, as before,
Tel: 01629 761321 Fax: 01629 761163
DX: 27259 Matlock
e-mail: buildingcontrol@derbyshiredales.gov.uk
Council Tax: Benefits Section, Town Hall, Bank Rd, Matlock DE4 3NN
Tel: 01629 761222 Fax: 01629 761295
e-mail: revenues@derbyshiredales.gov.uk
Environmental Health: Community Services Dept, as before,
Tel: 01629 761212 Fax: 01629 761165
DX: envhealth@derbyshiredales.gov.uk
Highways: Derbyshire County Council,
Tel: 0845 605 8058
e-mail: call.centre@derbyshire.gov.uk
Planning – Peak National Park: Peak National Park Authority, Aldern Ho, Baslow Rd, Bakewell DE45 1AE
Tel: 01629 816200 Fax: 01629 816310
e-mail: planning@peakdistrict.gov.uk
Solicitor to the Council: Mr Phillip Horsfield, Corporate Services Dept, Town Hall, Matlock DE4 3NN
Tel: 01629 761200 Fax: 01629 761148
e-mail: phillip.horsfield@derbyshiredales.gov.uk
Water Services: Severn Trent Water

11.4 North East Derbyshire District Council

Website: www.ne-derbyshire.gov.uk
Main Switchboard: 01246 231111
Conveyancing Searches: Local Land Charges Section, Council Ho, Saltergate, Chesterfield S40 1LF
Tel: 01246 217152/7151 Fax: 01246 217447
e-mail: connectne@ne-derbyshire.gov.uk
Building Control: BCN Consultancy, Town Hall, Rose Hill, Chesterfield S40 1LP
Tel: 01246 345905/345345 Fax: 01246 345910
e-mail: building.control@bcnconsultancy.co.uk
Council Tax: Connect NE Council Tax & Benefits, Council Ho, Saltergate, Chesterfield, Derbyshire S40 1LF
Tel: 01246 217600 Fax: 01246 217444
e-mail: connectne@ne-derbyshire.gov.uk
Environmental Health: Environmental Health, Council Ho, Saltergate, Chesterfield S40 1LF
Tel: 01246 231111 Fax: 01246 217447
e-mail: connectne@ne-derbyshire.gov.uk
Highways: Derbyshire County Council
Planning: Planning, Council Ho, as before,
Tel: 01246 231111 Fax: 01246 217447
e-mail: developmentcontrol@ne-derbyshire.gov.uk
Solicitor to the Council: Mrs N Smith, Council Ho, Saltergate, Chesterfield S40 1LF
Tel: 01246 231111 Fax: 01246 217443
e-mail: naomi.smith@ne-derbyshire.gov.uk
Water Services: Severn Trent Water and Yorkshire Water

11.5 Bolsover District Council

Website: www.bolsover.gov.uk
Main Switchboard: 01246 242424
Conveyancing Searches: Legal Services, The Arc, High St, Clowne S43 4JY
Tel: 01246 242424 Fax: 01246 242354
e-mail: land.charges@bolsover.gov.uk
Building Control: BCN Consultancy, Town Hall, Rose Hll, Chesterfield S40 1LP
Tel: 01246 345817/345905
e-mail: building.control@bcnconsultancy.co.uk
Council Tax: Revenue Services, The Arc, High St, Clowne S43 4JY
Tel: 01246 242436
e-mail: benefits@bolsolver.gov.uk
Environmental Health: Environmental Health, The Arc, High St, Clowne S43 4JY
Tel: 01246 242424
e-mail: enquiries@bolsover.gov.uk
Highways: Derbyshire County Council
Planning: Planning Services, The Arc, High St, Clowne S43 4JY
Tel: 01246 242424
e-mail: dev.control@bolsover.gov.uk
Solicitor to the Council: Mrs S Sternberg, Solicitor to the Council, The Arc, High St, Clowne S43 4JY
Tel: 01246 242414
Technical Services: Regeneration, The Arc, High St, Clowne S43 4JY
Water Services: Severn Trent Water

11.6 Amber Valley Borough Council

Website: www.ambervalley.gov.uk
Main Switchboard: 01773 570222
Conveyancing Searches: Local Land Charges, Town Hall, Market Pl, Ripley, Derbyshire DE5 3BT
Tel: 01773 841357 Fax: 01773 841357
e-mail: land.charges@ambervalley.gov.uk
Building Control: Building Control, Town Hall, Market Pl, Ripley DE5 3BT
Tel: 01773 841521 Fax: 01773 841523
e-mail: buildinginspections@ambervalley.gov.uk
Council Tax: Financial Services Dept, Town Hall, Market Pl, Ripley DE5 3BT
Tel: 01773 841440 Fax: 01773 841407
e-mail: council.tax@ambervalley.gov.uk
Environmental Health: Environmental Health & Leisure Division, Town Hall, Market Pl, Ripley DE5 3BT
Tel: 01773 841335 Fax: 01773 841523
e-mail: envhealth@ambervalley.gov.uk
Highways: Derbyshire County Council
Planning: Development Division, Town Hall, Market Pl, Ripley DE5 3BT
Tel: 01773 841571 Fax: 01773 841523
e-mail: development@ambervalley.gov.uk
Solicitor to the Council: Mr Paul Benski, Principal Solicitor, Town Hall, Market Pl, Ripley DE5 3BT
Tel: 01773 570222 Fax: 01773 841616
e-mail: enquiry@ambervalley.gov.uk
Water Services: Severn Trent Water

11.7 Derby City Council (U)

Website: www.derby.gov.uk
Main Switchboard: 01332 293111
Conveyancing Searches: Resources Directorate, The Council Ho, Corporation St, Derby DE1 2FS
Tel: 01332 640805 Fax: 01332 640666
e-mail: landcharges@derby.gov.uk
Building Control: Building Consultancy, The Council Ho, Corporation St, Derby DE1 2FS
Tel: 01332 640796 Fax: 01332 643299
e-mail: buildingcontrol@derby.gov.uk

Council Tax: Customer Service Centre, The Council Ho, Corporation St, Derby DE1 2FS
Tel: 0333 200 6900 Fax: 01332 643299
e-mail: council.tax@derby.gcsx.gov.uk
Environmental Health: Environmental Services, The Council Ho, Corporation St, Derby DE1 2FS
Tel: 01332 642020 Fax: 01332 643299
Highways: Regeneration & Community, The Council Ho, Corporation St, Derby DE1 2FS
Tel: 01332 293111 Fax: 01332 643299
e-mail: highwaysdevelopmentcontrol@derby.gov.uk
Planning: Development Management Neighbourhoods, The Council Ho, Corporation St, Derby DE1 2FS
Tel: 01332 640795 Fax: 01332 643299
e-mail: developmentcontrol@derby.gov.uk
Solicitor to the Council: Stuart Leslie, Director of Legal & Democratic Services, The Council Ho, Corporation St, Derby DE1 2FS
Tel: 01332 293111 Fax: 01332 643299
DX: 723460 Derby 20
Water Services: Severn Trent Water

11.8 Erewash Borough Council

Website: www.erewash.gov.uk
Main Switchboard: 0115 907 2244
Conveyancing Searches: Local Land Charges, Town Hall, Ilkeston DE7 5RP
Tel: 0115 907 1145 Fax: 0115 907 2259
DX: 10318 Ilkeston
e-mail: landcharges@erewash.gov.uk
Building Control: Planning & Regeneration, Town Hall, Long Eaton, Notts NG10 1HU
Tel: 0115 907 2229/2236 Fax: 0115 907 2237
DX: 10318 Ilkeston
e-mail: buildingcontrol@erewash.gov.uk
Council Tax: Council Tax Dept, Wharncliffe Rd, Ilkeston DE7 5SE
Tel: 0115 907 1001/1004 Fax: 0115 907 1069
DX: 10318 Ilkeston
e-mail: counciltax@erewash.gov.uk
Environmental Health: Environmental Health, Merlin Ho, Merlin Way, Ilkeston DE7 4RA
Tel: 0115 907 2244 ext 3820 Fax: 0115 931 6079
DX: 10318 Ilkeston
e-mail: environmentalhealth@erewash.gov.uk
Highways: Derbyshire County Council
Planning: Planning & Regeneration, Town Hall, Long Eaton, Notts NG10 1HU
Tel: 0115 907 2244 ext 3391 Fax: 0115 907 2267
DX: 10318 Ilkeston
e-mail: planning@erewash.gov.uk
Solicitor to the Council: Mr Brandon Morris, Head of Law & Corporate Governance, Town Hall, Ilkeston DE7 5RP
Tel: 0115 907 1132 Fax: 0115 907 1121
DX: 10318 Ilkeston
e-mail: brendan.morris@erewash.gov.uk
Water Services: Severn Trent Water

11.9 South Derbyshire District Council

Website: www.south-derbys.gov.uk
Main Switchboard: 01283 595795
Conveyancing Searches: Land Charges Dept, Civic Offices, Civic Way, Swadlincote DE11 0AH
Tel: 01283 595851
DX: 23912 Swadlincote
e-mail: land.charges@south-derbys.gov.uk
Building Control: Building Control Services, Civic Offices, Civic Way, Swadlincote DE11 0AH
Tel: 01283 228757 Fax: 01283 595850
e-mail: building.control@south-derbys.gov.uk
Council Tax: Revenue Service, Civic Offices, Civic Way, Swadlincote DE11 0AH
Tel: 01283 595971 Fax: 01283 595857
e-mail: ctaxnndr@south-derbys.gov.uk
Environmental Health: Environmental Health Section, Civic Offices, Civic Way, Swadlincote DE11 0AH
Tel: 01283 595724 Fax: 01283 595855
e-mail: environmental.health@south-derbys.gov.uk
Highways: Derbyshire County Council
Other depts: Civic Offices, Civic Way, Swadlincote DE11 0AH
Tel: 01283 221000 Fax: 01283 228734
DX: 23912 Swadlincote
e-mail: land.charges@south-derbys.gov.uk
Planning: Planning Services, Civic Offices, Civic Way, Swadlincote DE11 0AH
Tel: 01283 228706
e-mail: planning@south-derbys.gov.uk
Solicitor to the Council: Miss Ardip Kaur, Civic Offices, Civic Way, Swadlincote DE11 0AH
Water Services: Severn Trent Water

12 Devon

12.0 Devon County Council

Website: www.devon.gov.uk
Main Switchboard: 0845 155 1015
Search Address: County Solicitor, County Hall, Room G26, Topsham Rd, Exeter EX2 4QD
Tel: 0845 155 1015 Fax: 01392 382286
DX: 744970 Exeter 31
e-mail: customerrelations-mailbox@devon.gov.uk

12.1 Torridge District Council

Website: www.torridge.gov.uk
Main Switchboard: 01237 428700
Conveyancing Searches: Local Land Charges Team, Riverbank Ho, Bideford EX39 2QG
Tel: 01237 428765/428766 Fax: 01237 425972
DX: 53606 Bideford
e-mail: land.charges@torridge.gov.uk
Building Control & Planning: Planning Dept, Riverbank Ho, Bideford EX39 2QG
Tel: 01237 428724 (Bldg Control) / 428711 (Planning Support) Fax: 01237 478849
DX: 53606 Bideford
e-mail: bc.admin@torridge.gov.uk / planning.policy@torridge.gov.uk / planning.support@torridge.gov.uk
Council Tax: Council Tax Dept, Bridge Bldgs, Bideford EX39 2HT
Tel: 01237 428900 Fax: 01237 424299
DX: 53606 Bideford
e-mail: council.tax@torridge.gov.uk
Environmental Protection: Environmental Health & Public Protection, Bridge Bldgs, Bridge St, Bideford EX39 2HT
Tel: 01237 428810 Fax: 01237 474407
DX: 53606 Bideford
e-mail: environmental.protection@torridge.gov.uk
Highways: Devon County Council

Solicitor to the Council: Legal Services, Riverbank Ho, Bideford EX39 2QG
Tel: 01237 428700 (main switchboard) Fax: 01237 478849
DX: 53606 Bideford
Water Services: South West Water

12.2 North Devon District Council

Website: www.northdevon.gov.uk
Main Switchboard: 01271 327711
Conveyancing Searches: Local Land Charges Registry, Lynton Ho, Commercial Rd, Barnstaple EX31 1DG
Tel: 01271 388406 Fax: 01271 343968
e-mail: landcharges@northdevon.gov.uk
Building Control: Lynton Ho, as before,
Tel: 01271 388202 Fax: 01271 388201
e-mail: buildingcontrol@northdevon.gov.uk
Council Tax: Lynton Ho, as before,
Tel: 01271 327711 Fax: 01271 326134
e-mail: counciltax@northdevon.gov.uk
Environmental Health: Lynton Ho, as before,
Tel: 01271 388870
e-mail: customerservices@northdevon.gov.uk
Highways: Devon County Council
Planning: Lynton Ho, as before,
Tel: 01271 388288 Fax: 01271 388293
e-mail: planning@northdevon.gov.uk
Solicitor to the Council: Ken Miles, Lynton Ho, as before,
Tel: 01271 388262 Fax: 01271 374312

12.3 West Devon Borough Council

Website: www.westdevon.gov.uk
Main Switchboard: 01822 813600
Conveyancing Searches: Land Charges Office, Kilworthy Pk, Drake Rd, Tavistock PL19 0BZ
Tel: 01822 813667 Fax: 01822 813634
DX: 82405 Tavistock
e-mail: landcharges@westdevon.gov.uk
Note: searches@westdevon.gov.uk; 2 plans required for each search if submitted by post or DX; 1 plan if submitted by email.
Building Control: Building Control: Devon Building Control Partnership, Teignbridge District Council, Forde Ho, Brunel Rd, Newton Abbot TQ12 4XX
Tel: 01626 215793
DX: 121075 Newton Abbot 5
e-mail: mail@devonbuildingcontrol.gov.uk
Council Tax Dept: Council Tax, Kilworthy Pk, Drake Rd, Tavistock PL19 0BZ
Tel: 01822 618800
DX: 82405 Tavistock
e-mail: counciltax@westdevon.gov.uk
Environmental Health: Environmental Health, Kilworthy Pk, Drake Rd, Tavistock PL19 0BZ
Tel: 01822 813600
DX: 82405 Tavistock
e-mail: environmentalhealth@westdevon.gov.uk
Highways: Devon County Council
Other depts: Kilworthy Pk, Drake Rd, Tavistock PL19 0BZ
Tel: 01822 813600 Fax: 01822 813634
DX: 82405 Tavistock
Planning – Dartmoor National Park: Planning Dept, Dartmoor National Park Authority, Parke, Bovey Tracey, Newton Abbot TQ13 9JQ
Tel: 01626 832093 Fax: 01626 834684
Solicitor to the Council: Mrs Catherine Bowen, Borough Solicitor, Kilworthy Park, Drake Rd, Tavistock PL19 0BZ
Tel: 01822 813600 Fax: 01822 813634
DX: 82405 Tavistock
e-mail: cbowen@westdevon.gov.uk
Water Services: South West Water

12.4 Mid Devon District Council

Website: www.middevon.gov.uk
Main Switchboard: 01884 255255
Conveyancing Searches: Registrar of Local Land Charges, Phoenix Ho, Phoenix La, Tiverton EX16 6PP
Tel: 01884 255255 Fax: 01884 234318
DX: 49011 Tiverton
e-mail: customerfirst@middevon.gov.uk
Building Control & Planning: Planning & Regeneration Service, Phoenix Ho, Phoenix La, Tiverton EX16 6PP
Tel: 01884 255255 Fax: 01884 234235
e-mail: customerfirst@middevon.gov.uk
Council Tax: Revenues, Phoenix Ho, Phoenix La, Tiverton EX16 6PP
Tel: 01884 255255 Fax: 01884 234318
e-mail: customerfirst@middevon.gov.uk
Environmental Health: Enviromental Services, Phoenix Ho, Phoenix La, Tiverton EX16 6PP
Tel: 01884 255255 Fax: 01884 234256
e-mail: customerfirst@middevon.gov.uk
Highways: Devon County Council
Solicitor to the Council: Legal Services Manager, Phoenix Ho, Phoenix La, Tiverton EX16 6PP
Tel: 01884 255255 Fax: 01884 234318
DX: 49011 Tiverton
e-mail: customerfirst@middevon.gov.uk
Water Services: South West Water

12.5 Teignbridge District Council

Website: www.teignbridge.gov.uk
Main Switchboard: 01626 361101
Conveyancing Searches: Land Charges Department, Forde Ho, Council Offices, Brunel Rd, Newton Abbot TQ12 4XX
Tel: 01626 215124
DX: 121075 Newton Abbot 5
e-mail: landcharges@teignbridge.gov.uk
Building Control: Dept of Planning and Environmental Services, Forde Ho, Brunel Rd, Newton Abbot TQ12 4XX
Tel: 01626 215793
e-mail: mail@devonbuildingcontrol.gov.uk
Council Tax: Revenues and Benefits, PO Box 2, Forde Ho, Newton Abbot TQ12 4YR
Tel: 01626 215000 Fax: 01626 215538
e-mail: revandbens@teignbridge.gov.uk
Environmental Health: Dept of Planning and Environmental Services, Forde Ho, Brunel Rd, Newton Abbot TQ12 4XX
Tel: 01626 361101
e-mail: ehealth@teignbridge.gov.uk
Highways: Devon County Council
Planning: Dept of Planning and Environmental Services, Forde Ho, Brunel Rd, Newton Abbot TQ12 4XX
Tel: 01626 215743
e-mail: planning@teignbridge.gov.uk
Solicitor to the Council: Duncan Moors, Solicitor to the Council, Legal & Democratic Services, Forde Ho, Newton Abbot TQ12 4XX
Tel: 01626 215163 Fax: 01626 215169
DX: 121075 Newton Abbot 5 (Legal Dept)
e-mail: duncan.moors@teignbridge.gov.uk
Water Services: South West Water

12.6 Exeter City Council

Website: www.exeter.gov.uk
Main Switchboard: 01392 277888
Conveyancing Searches: Land Charges, Civic Centre, Paris St, Exeter EX1 1JJ
Tel: 01392 265128 Fax: 01392 265495
DX: 8323 Exeter
e-mail: land.charges@exeter.gov.uk
Council Tax: Council Tax Registration Officer,
Tel: 01392 277888 Fax: 01392 265265
Highways: Devon County Council, County Hall, Topsham Rd, Exeter
Tel: 01392 382295
DX: 8345
Solicitor to the Council: Ms Baan Al-Khafaji, Principal Solicitor, Corporate Manager of Legal Services, Civic Centre, Paris St, Exeter EX1 1JN
Tel: 01392 277888 Fax: 01392 265265
DX: 8323 Exeter
e-mail: bkhafaji@exeter.gov.uk
Water Services: South West Water

12.7 East Devon District Council

Website: www.eastdevon.gov.uk
Main Switchboard: 01395 516551
Conveyancing Searches: Local Land Charges, Council Offices, Knowle, Sidmouth EX10 8HL
Tel: 01395 571532
DX: 48705 Sidmouth
e-mail: lcharges@eastdevon.gov.uk
Building Control: Building Control, Council Offices, as before
Tel: 01395 517482 Fax: 01395 517551
DX: 48705 Sidmouth
e-mail: buildingcontrol@eastdevon.gov.uk
Council Tax: Finance, Council Offices, as before
Tel: 01395 517446
DX: 48705 Sidmouth
e-mail: counciltax@eastdevon.gov.uk
Environmental Health: Environment, Council Offices, as before
Tel: 01395 517456 Fax: 01395 517407
e-mail: environmentalhealth@eastdevon.gov.uk
Planning: Environment Directorate, Council Offices, as before
Tel: 01395 517475
DX: 48705 Sidmouth
e-mail: planning@eastdevon.gov.uk
Solicitor to the Council: Legal Services, Council Offices, Knowle, Sidmouth EX10 8HL
Tel: 01395 516551 Fax: 01395 517507
DX: 48705 Sidmouth
e-mail: legal@eastdevon.gov.uk
Water Services: South West Water

12.8 Plymouth City Council (U)

Website: www.plymouth.gov.uk
Main Switchboard: 01752 668000
Conveyancing Searches: Local Land Charges, Legal Services, Civic Centre, Armada Way, Plymouth PL1 2AA
Tel: 01752 304478 Fax: 01752 306083
DX: 8278 Plymouth 2
e-mail: llcplymouth@plymouth.gov.uk
Other depts: Civic Centre, Plymouth PL1 2EW
Tel: 01752 668000
Solicitor to the Council: David Shepperd, Head of Legal Services, 1st Fl, Civic Centre, Armada Way, Plymouth PL1 2AA
Tel: 01752 306116 Fax: 01752 306083
DX: 8278 Plymouth 2
e-mail: dave.shepperd@plymouth.gov.uk
Water Services: South West Water

12.9 South Hams District Council

Website: www.southhams.gov.uk
Main Switchboard: 01803 861234
Conveyancing Searches: Planning, Economy & Community, Land Charges Office, Follaton Ho, Plymouth Rd, Totnes TQ9 5NE
Tel: 01803 861127 (Direct); 01803 861234
Fax: 01803 861166
DX: 300050 Totnes 2
e-mail: landcharges@southhams.gov.uk
Highways Dept: Devon County Council
Other depts: Dartmoor National Park Authority, Parke, Bovey Tracey, Newton Abbot TQ13 9JQ
Tel: 01626 832093 Fax: 01626 834684
e-mail: hq@dartmoor-npa.gov.uk
Search Queries: Devon County Council, Land Charges Office, County Hall, Exeter EX2 4QD
Tel: 01392 382295 Fax: 01392 382286
DX: 8345 Exeter
Solicitor to the Council & Monitoring Officer: Delyth Jenkins Evans, Follaton Ho, Plymouth Rd, Totnes TQ9 5NE
Tel: 01803 861234 Fax: 01803 866151
DX: 300050 Totnes 2
e-mail: delyth.jenkins-evans@southhams.gov.uk
Water Services: South West Water

12.10 Torbay Council (U)

Website: www.torbay.gov.uk
Main Switchboard: 01803 201201
Conveyancing Searches: Land Charges Dept, Town Hall, Castle Circus, Torquay TQ1 3DR
Tel: 01803 207107
DX: 59006 Torquay 1
e-mail: landcharges@torbay.gov.uk
Building Control & Planning: Spatial Planning, Town Hall, Castle Circus, Torquay TQ1 3DR
Tel: 01803 208097 Fax: 01803 208858
DX: 59006 Torquay 1
e-mail: building.control@torbay.gov.uk/planning@torbay.gov.uk
Council Tax: Exchequer & Benefits, Town Hall, Castle Circus, Torquay TQ1 3DR
Tel: 01803 207207 Fax: 01803 207234
DX: 59006 Torquay 1
e-mail: council.tax@torbay.gov.uk
Environmental Health: Community Safety, Commerce Ho, Abbey Rd, Torquay TQ2 5PJ
Tel: 01803 208025 Fax: 01803 208854
DX: 59006 Torquay 1
e-mail: community.safetyadmin@torbay.gov.uk
Highways: Highways & Engineering Division, Town Hall, Castle Circus, Torquay TQ1 3DR
Tel: 01803 207740 Fax: 01803 207670
DX: 59006 Torquay 1
e-mail: highways@torbay.gov.uk
Solicitor to the Council: Mrs A Bond, Town Hall, Castle Circus, Torquay TQ1 3DR
Tel: 01803 201201 Fax: 01803 207492
DX: 59006 Torquay 1
Water Services: South West Water

13 Dorset

13.0 Dorset County Council

Website: www.dorsetforyou.com
Main Switchboard: 01305 221000
Search Address: Legal & Democratic Services, County Hall, Colliton Pk, Dorchester DT1 1XJ
Tel: 01305 221000 Fax: 01305 224399
DX: 8716 Dorchester
Solicitor to the Council: Jonathan Mair, Head of Legal & Democratic Services, County Hall, Colliton Pk, Dorchester DT1 1XJ
Tel: 01305 224181 Fax: 01305 224399
DX: 8716 Dorchester
e-mail: j.e.mair@dorsetcc.gov.uk

13.1 West Dorset District Council

Website: www.dorsetforyou.com
Main Switchboard: 01305 251010
Conveyancing Searches: Land Charges, South Walks Ho, South Walks Rd, Dorchester DT1 1UZ
Tel: 01305 252212
e-mail: landcharges@westdorset-dc.gov.uk
Council Tax: Council Tax Office, South Walks Ho, South Walks Rd, Dorchester DT1 1UZ
Tel: 01305 251010
Highways: Dorset County Council
Other depts: South Walks Ho, South Walks Rd, Dorchester DT1 1UZ
Solicitor to the Council: Melanie Earnshaw, Council Offices, North Quay, Weymouth DT4 8TA
Water Services: Wessex Water and South West Water

13.2 North Dorset District Council

Website: www.dorsetforyou.com/northdorset
Main Switchboard: 01258 454111
Conveyancing Searches: Local Land Charges, 'Nordon', Salisbury Rd, Blandford Forum DT11 7LL
Tel: 01258 484023
DX: 142920 Blandford Forum 2
e-mail: landcharges@north-dorset.gov.uk
Building Control: Building Control, Nordon, Salisbury Rd, Blandford Forum DT11 7LL
Tel: 01258 484266
DX: 142920 Blandford Forum 2
e-mail: buildingcontrol_DL@north-dorset.gov.uk
Council Tax: Revenue Services, Nordon, Salisbury Rd, Blandford Forum DT11 7LL
Tel: 01258 454111 Fax: 01258 484185
DX: 142920 Blandford Forum 2
e-mail: customerservicesdl@north-dorset.gov.uk
Environmental Health: Environmental Health, Nordon, Salisbury Rd, Blandford Forum DT11 7LL
Tel: 01258 484381 Fax: 01258 484298
DX: 142920 Blandford Forum 2
e-mail: envlicens@north-dorset.gov.uk
Highways: Dorset County Council
Planning: Planning Service, Nordon, Salisbury Rd, Blandford Forum DT11 7LL
Tel: 01258 484201 Fax: 01258 484230
DX: 142920 Blandford Forum 2
e-mail: d3@north-dorset.gov.uk
Solicitor to the Council: Mr S Caundle, Nordon, Salisbury Rd, Blandford Forum DT11 7LL
Tel: 01258 484016
e-mail: scaundle@north-dorset.gov.uk
Water Services: Wessex Water Development Group

13.3 East Dorset District Council

Website: www.dorsetforyou.com
Main Switchboard: 01202 795096
East Dorset District Council & Christchurch Borough Council are now working in partnership.
Conveyancing Searches: Local Land Charges Section, Council Offices, Furzehill, Wimborne BH21 4HN
Tel: 01202 795163
e-mail: local.landcharges@christchurchandeastdorset.gov.uk
Highways: Dorset County Council
Other depts: Council Offices, Furzehill, Wimborne BH21 4HN
Tel: 01202 795096
Solicitor to the Council: Mr Keith Mallett, Solicitor to the Council, Civic Offices, Bridge St, Christchurch BH23 1AZ
Tel: 01202 495000
e-mail: kmallett@christchurchandeastdorset.gov.uk
Water Services: Wessex Water

13.4 Weymouth & Portland Borough Council

Website: www.weymouth.gov.uk
Main Switchboard: 01305 838000
Conveyancing Searches: Development Management, Council Offices, North Quay, Weymouth DT4 8TA
Tel: 01305 838202 Fax: 01305 838600
e-mail: landcharges@weymouth.gov.uk
Building Control: Local Environment, Council Offices, North Quay, Weymouth DT4 8TA
Tel: 01305 838327 Fax: 01305 838600
e-mail: buildingcontrol@weymouth.gov.uk
Council Tax: Revenues & Benefits Services, Glyde Path Ho, Glyde Path Rd, Dorchester DT1 1JB
Tel: 01305 211900
e-mail: j.monelle@weymouth.gov.uk
Environmental Health: Pollution & Private Sector Housing, Council Offices, North Quay, Weymouth DT4 8TA
Tel: 01305 838432 Fax: 01305 766684
e-mail: envhealth@weymouth.gov.uk
Highways: Dorset County Council
Planning: Development Management, Council Offices, North Quay, Weymouth DT4 8TA
Tel: 01305 838342 Fax: 01305 838600
e-mail: planning@weymouth.gov.uk
Solicitor to the Council: Ms Melanie Earnshaw, Head of Governance, Council Offices, North Quay, Weymouth DT4 8TA
Tel: 01305 838212 Fax: 01305 838438
e-mail: melanieearnshaw@weymouth.gov.uk
Water Services: Wessex Water

13.5 Purbeck District Council

Website: www.dorsetforyou.com/purbeck
Main Switchboard: 01929 556561
Conveyancing Searches: Planning & Community Services, Westport Ho, Worgret Rd, Wareham BH20 4PP
Tel: 01929 557224 Fax: 01929 552688
e-mail: landcharges@purbeck-dc.gov.uk
Building Control: Planning & Community Services, Westport Ho, as above,
Tel: 01929 557307 Fax: 01929 552688
e-mail: buildingcontrol@purbeck-dc.gov.uk
Council Tax: Revenue & Benefits Unit, Westport Ho, as above,
Tel: 01929 557656 Fax: 01929 552688
e-mail: counciltax@purbeck-dc.gov.uk
Environmental Health: Public Health & Housing Services, Westport Ho, as above,
Tel: 01929 557239 Fax: 01929 552688
e-mail: publichealth@purbeck-dc.gov.uk

Highways: Dorset County Council,
Tel: 01305 251000
Planning: Planning & Community Services, Westport Ho, as above,
Tel: 01929 557273 Fax: 01929 552688
e-mail: planning@purbeck-dc.gov.uk
Solicitor to the Councl: Chief Executive's Office, Westport Ho, as above,
Tel: 01929 557223 Fax: 01929 552688
e-mail: davidfairbairn@purbeck-dc.gov.uk
Water Services: Wessex Water

13.6 Poole Borough Council (U)

Website: www.poole.gov.uk
Main Switchboard: 01202 633633
Conveyancing Searches: Legal & Democratic Services, Civic Centre, Poole BH15 2RU
Tel: 01202 262816 Fax: 01202 633527
DX: 123820 Poole 7
e-mail: landcharges@poole.gov.uk
Building Control: Building Consultancy Services, Room 206, Civic Centre, Poole BH15 2RU
Tel: 01202 633250 Fax: 01202 633244
DX: 123820 Poole 7
e-mail: bldg.consult@poole.gov.uk
Council Tax: Revenue & Benefits Financial Services, Civic Centre, Poole BH15 2RU
Tel: 01202 634234 Fax: 01202 633150
DX: 123820 Poole 7
e-mail: financialservices@poole.gov.uk
Environmental Health: Environmental and Consumer Protection Services, Unit 1, Newfields Business Park, 2 Stinsford Rd, Poole BH17 0NF
Tel: 01202 261700 Fax: 01202 261717
DX: 123820 Poole 7
e-mail: environment@poole.gov.uk
Highways: Highways & Transportation Services, St John's Ho, Serpentine Rd, Poole BH15 2DX
Tel: 01202 262000 Fax: 01202 262091
DX: 123820 Poole 7
e-mail: transportation@poole.gov.uk
Planning: Planning & Regeneration, Civic Centre, Poole BH15 2RU
Tel: 01202 633321 Fax: 01202 633345
DX: 123820 Poole 7
e-mail: planning@poole.gov.uk
Solicitor to the Council: Mr Tim Martin, Head of Legal & Democratic Services, Civic Centre, Poole BH15 2RU
Tel: 01202 633478 Fax: 01202 262818
DX: 123820 Poole 7
e-mail: t.martin@poole.gov.uk

13.7 Bournemouth Borough Council (U)

Website: www.bournemouth.gov.uk
Main Switchboard: 01202 451451
Conveyancing Searches: Law & Corporate Governance & Legal & Democratic, Town Hall, Bourne Ave, Bournemouth BH2 6DY
Tel: 01202 451119/451120 Fax: 01202 451003
DX: 156942 Bournemouth 3
e-mail: locallandcharges@bournemouth.gov.uk
Building Control, Highways & Planning: Planning & Transport, Town Hall Annexe, St Stephen's Rd, Bournemouth BH2 6EA
Tel: 01202 451411
Fax: 01202 451005 (Plan); 01202 451010 (Bldg Ctrl)
e-mail: planning@bournemouth.gov.uk
Council Tax: Resources, Revenue & Benefits Services, Town Hall, Stephen's Rd, Bournemouth BH2 6EB
Tel: 01202 451597 Fax: 01202 451004
e-mail: revenue&benefits@bournemouth.gov.uk
Environmental Health: Public Protection, Town Hall, St Stephen's Rd, Bournemouth BH2 6LL
Tel: 01202 451451 Fax: 01202 451000
DX: 7615 Bournemouth
e-mail: foodandhealthandsafety@bournemouth.gov.uk
Highways: Technical Services, Town Hall Annexe, St Stephen's Rd, Bournemouth BH2 6EA
Tel: 01202 451340
e-mail: roger.ball@bournemouth.gov.uk
Solicitor to the Council: Tanya Coulter, Service Director, Legal & Democratic, Town Hall, Bourne Ave, Bournemouth BH2 6DY
Tel: 01202 454944 Fax: 01202 451001
DX: 156942 Bournemouth 3
e-mail: tanya.coulter@bournemouth.gov.uk
Water Services: Wessex Water

13.8 Christchurch Borough Council

Website: www.dorsetforyou.com
Main Switchboard: 01202 795096
Christchurch Borough Council and East Dorset District Council are now working in partnership.
Conveyancing Searches: Local Land Charges Section, Council Offices, Furzehill, Wimborne BH21 4HN
Tel: 01202 795163
e-mail: local.landcharges@christchurchandeastdorset.gov.uk
Highways: Dorset County Council
Solicitor to the Council: Keith Mallett, Head of Legal and Democratic Services, Civic Offices, Bridge St, Christchurch BH23 1AZ
Tel: 01202 795096
e-mail: k.mallett@christchurchandeastdorset.gov.uk
Water Services: Wessex Water

14 Durham, Co

14.0 County Durham County Council (abolished)

County Council abolished as from 1 April 2009. Derwentside DC, Chester-le-Street DC, Wear Valley DC, City of Durham DC, Easington DC, Teesdale DC, Sedgefield BC and Durham County Council combined to form Durham County Council (Unitary).

14.1 Durham County Council (U)

Website: www.durham.gov.uk
Main Switchboard: 0300 123 7070 / 0191 383 4567
Conveyancing Searches: County Hall, Durham DH1 5UL
Tel: 03000 269734
Building Control: Planning Services, County Hall, Durham DH1 5UL
Tel: 03000 261867
Council Tax: Revenues & Benefits, Council Offices, Spennymoor DH16 6JU
Tel: 03000 260410
Environmental Health: County Hall, Durham DH1 5UL
Tel: 03000 260924
Highways: County Hall, Durham DH1 5UL
Tel: 03000 267455
Planning: Planning Services, County Hall, Durham DH1 5UL
Tel: 03000 267334

Solicitor to the Council: Mrs Colette Longbottom, Legal Services, County Hall, Durham DH1 5UL
Tel: 03000 269732
DX: 722100 Durham 16
Water Services: Northumbrian Water

14.8 Darlington Borough Council (U)

Website: www.darlington.gov.uk
Main Switchboard: 01325 380651
Conveyancing Searches: Land Charges, Dept of Resources Services, Town Hall, Darlington DL1 5QT
Tel: 01325 388336 Fax: 01325 388318
DX: 69280 Darlington 6
e-mail: land.charges@darlington.gov.uk
Building Control: Building Control Division, 14 Harewood Hill, Darlington DL3 7HY
Tel: 01325 406214 Fax: 01325 388362
DX: 69280 Darlington 6
e-mail: buildingcontrolenquiries@darlington.gov.uk
Council Tax: Revenue & Collection Services, Town Hall, Darlington DL1 5QT
Tel: 01325 388373 Fax: 01325 388244
DX: 69280 Darlington 6
e-mail: revenue.queries@darlington.gov.uk
Environmental Health: Environmental & Consumer Protection Division, Town Hall, Darlington DL1 5QT
Tel: 01325 388799 Fax: 01325 388555
DX: 69280 Darlington 6
e-mail: customerservices@darlington.gov.uk
Highways: Highways Dept, Town Hall, Darlington DL1 5QT
Tel: 01325 388799 Fax: 01325 388724
DX: 69280 Darlington 6
Planning: Development & Environment Dept, Town Hall, Darlington DL1 5QT
Tel: 01325 388799 Fax: 01325 388900
DX: 69280 Darlington 6
e-mail: planning.enquiries@darlington.gov.uk
Solicitor to the Council: Ms C Whitehead, Borough Solicitor, Town Hall, Darlington DL1 5QT
Tel: 01325 388307 Fax: 01325 388318
DX: 69280 Darlington 6
e-mail: catherine.whitehead@darlington.gov.uk
Water Services: Northumbrian Water

14.9 Hartlepool Borough Council (U)

Website: www.hartlepool.gov.uk
Main Switchboard: 01429 266522
Conveyancing Searches: Local Land Charges Section, Civic Centre, Victoria Rd, Hartlepool TS24 8AY
Tel: 01429 523088 Fax: 01429 523701
DX: 60669 Hartlepool 1
e-mail: landcharges@hartlepool.gov.uk
Building Control, Highways & Planning: Regeneration & Planning Dept, Bryan Hanson Ho, Hanson Sq, Hartlepool TS24 7BT
Tel: 01429 266522 Fax: 01429 523599
DX: 60669 Hartlepool 1
e-mail: customer.service@hartlepool.gov.uk
Council Tax: Finance Division, Civic Centre, Victoria Rd, Hartlepool TS24 8AY
Tel: 01429 266522 Fax: 01429 523112
DX: 60669 Hartlepool 1
e-mail: benefits@hartlepool.gov.uk
Environmental Health: Public Protection Division, Civic Centre, Victoria Rd, Hartlepool TS24 8AY
Tel: 01429 266522 Fax: 01429 523308
DX: 60669 Hartlepool 1
e-mail: environmental.protection@hartlepool.gov.uk
Highways: Highways, 1 Church St, Hartlepool TS24 7DS
Tel: 01429 266522
e-mail: highways@hartlepool.gov.uk
Solicitor to the Council: Chief Solicitor, Legal Division, Civic Centre, Victoria Rd, Hartlepool TS24 8AY
Tel: 01429 266522 Fax: 01429 523005
DX: 60669 Hartlepool 1
Water Services: Northumbrian Water

14.10 Stockton-on-Tees Borough Council (U)

Website: www.stockton.gov.uk
Main Switchboard: 01642 393939
Conveyancing Searches: Law & Democracy, PO Box 11, Municipal Bldgs, Church Rd, Stockton-on-Tees TS18 1LD
Tel: 01642 526319 Fax: 01642 393092
DX: 60611 Stockton
e-mail: land.charges@stockton.gov.uk
Building Control & Planning: Development & Neighbourhood Services, PO Box 11, Municipal Buildings, Stockton-on-Tees TS18 1LD
Tel: 01642 527068 Fax: 01642 526048
DX: 60611 Stockton
e-mail: developmentservices@stockton.gov.uk
Council Tax: Resources, PO Box 410, Kingsway Ho, West Precinct, Billingham TS23 2YD
Tel: 01642 397108 Fax: 01642 526813
e-mail: council.tax@stockton.gov.uk
Environmental Health: Community Protection, PO Box 232, 16 Church Rd, Stockton-on-Tees TS18 1XD
Tel: 01642 526575 Fax: 01642 524743
DX: 60611 Stockton
e-mail: environmental.health@stockton.gov.uk
Highways: Development & Neighbourhood Services, PO Box 229, Kingsway Ho, West Precinct, Billingham TS23 2YL
Tel: 01642 393939 Fax: 01642 526713
DX: 60611 Stockton
e-mail: technicalservices@stockton.gov.uk
Solicitor to the Council: David Bond, Director of Law & Democracy, Municipal Bldgs, Church Rd, Stockton-on-Tees TS18 1LD
Tel: 01642 527061 Fax: 01642 393092
DX: 60611 Stockton
e-mail: david.bond@stockton.gov.uk
Water Services: Northumbrian Water

15 East Riding of Yorkshire

15.1 Kingston upon Hull City Council (U)

Website: www.hullcc.gov.uk
Main Switchboard: 01482 300300
Conveyancing Searches: Local Land Charges, Room 155, The Guildhall, Alfred Gelder St, Hull HU1 2AA
Tel: 01482 613258 Fax: 01482 613310
DX: 11934 Hull 1
e-mail: landcharges@hullcc.gov.uk
Building Control: Building Control, Kingston Ho, Bond St, Kingston upon Hull HU1 3ER
Tel: 01482 612326 Fax: 01482 612310
DX: 11934 Hull 1
e-mail: hull.building.control@hullcc.gov.uk
Chief Executive: The Guildhall, Room 22, Alfred Gelder St, Hull HU1 2AA
Tel: 01482 615000 Fax: 01482 613111
DX: 11934 Hull 1
e-mail: chief.executive@hullcc.gov.uk

Council Tax: Treasury Bldg, PO Box 15, Guildhall Rd, Kingston upon Hull HU1 2AB
Tel: 01482 300300 Fax: 01482 613562
DX: 11934 Hull 1
e-mail: ctaxsr@hullcc.gov.uk
Environmental Health: Public Protection, 33 Witham, Hull HU9 1DB
Tel: 01482 300300
DX: 11934 Hull 1
e-mail: public.protection@hullcc.gov.uk
Highways: Streetscene Services, Kingston Ho, Bond St, Kingston upon Hull HU1 3ER
Tel: 01482 300300
DX: 11934 Hull 1
e-mail: highways.admin.team@hullcc.gov.uk
Planning: Planning Dept, Kingston Ho, Bond St, Kingston upon Hull HU1 3ER
Tel: 01482 612345 Fax: 01482 612350
DX: 11934 Hull 1
e-mail: planning.policy@hullcc.gov.uk
Solicitor to the Council: Paul Thompson, Guildhall, Alfred Gelder St, Kingston upon Hull HU1 2AA
Tel: 01482 300300 Fax: 01482 615112
DX: 11934 Hull 1
e-mail: paul.thompson@hullcc.gov.uk
Water Services: Yorkshire Water

15.2 East Riding of Yorkshire Council (U)

Website: www.east-riding.gov.uk
Main Switchboard: 01482 887700
Conveyancing Searches: Land Charges, County Hall, Beverley HU17 9BA
Tel: 01482 393170/1/2/3/4 Fax: 01482 393175
DX: 28318 Beverley
e-mail: landcharges@eastriding.gov.uk
Building Control & Planning: Planning (Development Services), County Hall, Beverley HU17 9BA
Tel: 01482 887700
DX: 28318 Beverley
e-mail: beverley.bc@eastriding.gov.uk
Council Tax: Finance, County Hall, Beverley HU17 9BA
Tel: 01482 394747 Fax: 01482 394749
DX: 28318 Beverley
e-mail: council.tax@eastriding.gov.uk
Environmental Health: Public Protection, County Hall, Beverley HU17 9BA
Tel: 01482 887700
DX: 28318 Beverley
e-mail: pollution.control@eastriding.gov.uk
Highways: Highways & Engineering Services, County Hall, Beverley HU17 9BA
Tel: 01482 393760 Fax: 01482 393709
DX: 28318 Beverley
e-mail: beverley.bc@eastriding.gov.uk
Solicitor to the Council: Matthew Buckley, Head of Legal, Law Admin Property & Planning, County Hall, Beverley HU17 9BA
Water Services: Yorkshire Water/Safe-move

16 East Sussex

16.0 East Sussex County Council

Website: www.eastsussexcc.gov.uk
Main Switchboard: 01273 481000
Search Address: Governance Services Dept, Legal Services Team, PO Box 2714, County Hall, Lewes BN7 1UE
Tel: 01273 481939 Fax: 01273 481900
DX: 97482 Lewes 3
e-mail: legal.services@eastsussex.gov.uk

16.1 Wealden District Council

Website: www.wealden.gov.uk
Main Switchboard: 01323 443322
Conveyancing Searches: Environmental Services, Local Land Charges Section, Council Offices, Vicarage La, Hailsham BN27 2AX
Tel: 01892 602431 Fax: 01892 602523
DX: 38303 Hailsham
e-mail: landcharges@wealden.gov.uk
Building Control: Planning Dept, Building Control Section, Council Offices, Vicarage La, Hailsham BN27 2AX
Tel: 01892 602010/602005 Fax: 01892 602777
Council Tax: Council Tax Dept, Council Offices, Vicarage La, Hailsham BN27 2AX
Tel: 01323 444385 Fax: 01323 443146
Environmental Health: Environmental Health Dept, Council Offices, Town Hall, Bexhill-on-Sea TN39 3JX
Tel: 01323 443322
Highways: East Sussex County Council, Transport & Environment Section
Planning: Planning Dept (Information), Council Offices, Vicarage La, Hailsham BN27 2AX
Tel: 01892 602510 Fax: 01892 602586
DX: 38303 Hailsham
e-mail: planning.information@wealden.gov.uk
Planning – South Downs National Park: North St, Midhurst GU29 9DH
Tel: 0300 303 1053
Solicitor to the Council: Solicitor & Legal Services Manager, Council Offices, Vicarage La, Hailsham BN27 2AX
Tel: 01892 602438 Fax: 01892 602223
Water Services: Southern Water Services

16.2 Rother District Council

Website: www.rother.gov.uk
Main Switchboard: 01424 787878
Conveyancing Searches: Planning Division, Town Hall, Bexhill-on-Sea TN39 3JX
Tel: 01424 787878
DX: 8103 Bexhill-on-Sea
e-mail: landcharges@rother.gov.uk
Building Control: Planning Division, Town Hall, as before,
Tel: 01424 787670/71 Fax: 01424 787672
DX: 8103 Bexhill-on-Sea
e-mail: buildingcontrol@rother.gov.uk
Council Tax: Finance, PO Box 60, Bexhill-on-Sea TN39 3ZF
Tel: 01424 787730 Fax: 01424 787755
DX: 8103 Bexhill-on-Sea
e-mail: counciltax@rother.gov.uk
Environmental Health: Environmental Health Division Services Directorate, Town Hall, as before,
Tel: 01424 787550 Fax: 01424 787547
DX: 8103 Bexhill-on-Sea
e-mail: envhealth@rother.gov.uk
Highways: East Sussex County Council

Planning: Planning Division, Town Hall, as before,
Tel: 01424 787606/600 Fax: 01424 787657
DX: 8103 Bexhill-on-Sea
e-mail: planning@rother.gov.uk
Solicitor to the Council: Mr D Edwards, Town Hall, Bexhill-on-Sea TN39 3JX
Tel: 01424 787840 Fax: 01424 787879
DX: 8103 Bexhill-on-Sea
e-mail: david.edwards@rother.gov.uk
Water Services: South East Water & Southern Water

16.3 Brighton & Hove Council (U)

Website: www.brighton-hove.gov.uk
Main Switchboard: 01273 290000
Conveyancing Searches: Local Land Charge Unit, Brighton Town Hall, Bartholomew Sq, Brighton BN1 1JA
Tel: 01273 292007 Fax: 01273 291948
DX: 2704 Brighton 1
e-mail: landcharges@brighton-hove.gov.uk
Building Control: Building Control, Hove Town Hall, Norton Rd, Hove BN3 3BQ
Tel: 01273 292030 Fax: 01273 292310
e-mail: building.control@brighton-hove.gov.uk
Council Tax: Brighton & Hove Council, PO Box 2929, Brighton BN1 1PS
Tel: 01273 291291 Fax: 01273 291234
e-mail: council.tax@brighton-hove.gov.uk
Environmental Services: Environmental Protection, Bartholomew Ho, 2nd Fl, Bartholomew Sq, Brighton BN1 1JP
Tel: 01273 2924266
e-mail: ehl.environmentalprotection@brighton-hove.gov.uk
Other depts: Brighton & Hove City Council, Kings Ho, Grand Ave, Hove BN3 2LS
Tel: 01273 290000
Solicitor to the Council: Abraham Ghebre-Ghiorghis, Head of Law, King's Ho, Grand Ave, Hove BN3 2LS
Tel: 01273 291500 Fax: 01273 291545
DX: 59286 Hove
Water Services: Southern Water

16.4 Lewes District Council

Website: www.lewes.gov.uk
Main Switchboard: 01273 471600
Conveyancing Searches: Local Land Charges Dept, Southover Ho, Southover Rd, Lewes BN7 1AB
Tel: 01273 471600
DX: 3118 Lewes 1
e-mail: locallandcharges@lewes.gov.uk
Building Control & Planning: Planning Dept, Southover Ho, Southover Rd, Lewes BN7 1AB
Tel: 01273 471600
DX: 3118 Lewes 1
e-mail: planning@lewes.gov.uk
Council Tax: Council Tax Section, Southover Ho, Southover Rd, Lewes BN7 1AB
Tel: 01273 471600
e-mail: localtax@lewes.gov.uk
Environmental Health: Southover Ho, Southover Rd, Lewes BN7 1AB
Tel: 01273 471600
DX: 3118 Lewes 1
e-mail: ehealth@lewes.gov.uk
Highways: East Sussex County Council
Other depts: Southover Ho, Southover Rd, Lewes BN7 1AB
Solicitor to the Council: C Knight, Head of Legal & Democratic Services, Southover Ho, Southover Rd, Lewes BN7 1AB
Tel: 01273 471600
DX: 3118 Lewes 1
e-mail: legal@lewes.gov.uk
Water Services: Southern Water Services Ltd.

16.5 Eastbourne Borough Council

Website: www.eastbourne.gov.uk
Main Switchboard: 01323 410000
Conveyancing Searches: Corporate Services Division, Local Land Charges Section, 1 Grove Rd, Eastbourne BN21 4TW
Tel: 01323 415015 Fax: 01323 415994
DX: 6921 Eastbourne
e-mail: landcharges@eastbourne.gov.uk
Building Control: Building Control, 1 Grove Rd, Eastbourne BN21 4TW
Tel: 01323 415217 Fax: 01323 415995
DX: 6921 Eastbourne
e-mail: buildingcontrol@eastbourne.gov.uk
Environmental Health: Norman Kinnish, Director of Economy, Tourism & Environment, Environmental Health Section, 1 Grove Rd, Eastbourne BN21 4TW
Tel: 01323 415350 Fax: 01323 415997
DX: 6921 Eastbourne
e-mail: environmentalhealth@eastbourne.gov.uk
Finance Manager: Peter Stabb, Financial Management Services, 1 Grove Rd, Eastbourne BN21 4TW
Tel: 01323 415107 Fax: 01323 415999
DX: 6921 Eastbourne
e-mail: peter.stabb@eastbourne.gov.uk
Highways: Highways Section, 68 Grove Rd, Eastbourne BN21 4UH
Tel: 0345 608 0193
e-mail: highways@eastsussex.gov.uk
Planning & Strategy: Development Planning, 68 Grove Rd, Eastbourne BN21 4UH
Tel: 01323 415219 Fax: 01323 415995
DX: 6921 Eastbourne
e-mail: planning@eastbourne.gov.uk
Solicitor to the Council: Jeremy Chambers, Head of Legal Services, 68 Grove Rd, Eastbourne BN21 4UH
Tel: 01323 410000 Fax: 01323 415994
DX: 6921 Eastbourne
e-mail: legal&property@eastbourne.gov.uk
Water Services: Southern Water

16.6 Hastings Borough Council

Website: www.hastings.gov.uk
Main Switchboard: 01424 781066
Conveyancing Searches: LLPG & Local Land Charges, 85–86 Castleham Rd, St Leonards-on-Sea TN38 9NT
Tel: 01424 451093
e-mail: landchar@hastings.gov.uk
Building Control: Rother & Hastings Building Control Partnership, Town Hall, London Rd, Bexhill, E.Sussex TN39 3JX
Tel: 01424 787680
DX: 8103 Bexhill-on-Sea
e-mail: buildingcontrol@rother.gov.uk
Council Tax: Revenue Services, Aquila Ho, Breeds Pl, Hastings TN34 3UY
Tel: 01424 451081 Fax: 01424 451541
e-mail: counciltax@hastings.gov.uk
Environmental Health: Environmental Protection, Aquila Ho, Breeds Pl, Hastings TN34 3UY
Tel: 01424 451079 Fax: 01424 451133
e-mail: envprotection@hastings.gov.uk

Highways: East Sussex County Council
Planning: Development Control, Aquila Ho, Breeds Pl, Hastings TN34 3UY
Tel: 01424 451090 Fax: 01424 783305
e-mail: dcenquiries@hastings.gov.uk
Solicitor to the Council: Borough Solicitor, Aquila Ho, Breeds Pl, Hastings TN34 3UY
Tel: 01424 781066 Fax: 01424 781743
e-mail: legaldept@hastings.gov.uk
Water Services: Southern Water

17 Essex

17.0 Essex County Council

Website: www.essex.gov.uk
Main Switchboard: 0845 743 0430
Search Address: Chief Executive's Office, County Hall, Market Rd, Chelmsford CM1 1QH
Tel: 01245 431103
e-mail: lisa.white@essex.gov.uk
Solicitor to the Council: Philip Thomson, County Solicitor, Legal Services, County Hall, Market Rd, Chelmsford CM1 1QH
Tel: 01245 506760 Fax: 01245 357335
DX: 123300 Chelmsford 7
e-mail: philip.thomson@essex.gov.uk

17.1 Uttlesford District Council

Website: www.uttlesford.gov.uk
Main Switchboard: 01799 510510
Conveyancing Searches: Local Land Charges, Council Offices, London Rd, Saffron Walden CB11 4ER
Tel: 01799 510418/510419 Fax: 01799 510392
e-mail: vrogacs@uttlesford.gov.uk
Building Control & Environmental Health: Operations Directorate, Council Offices, as before,
Tel: 01799 510539 Fax: 01799 510499
DX: 200307 Saffron Walden
e-mail: buildingcontrol@uttlesford.gov.uk
Council Tax: Resources, Council Offices, as before
Highways: Essex Highways, Springfield Highways Depot, Colchester Rd, Springfield CM2 5PU
Tel: 01245 342955
Planning: Development Directorate, Council Offices, London Rd, Saffron Walden CB11 4ER
Tel: 01799 510675 Fax: 01799 510500
DX: 200307 Saffron Walden
e-mail: lrusling@uttlesford.gov.uk
Solicitor to the Council: Mr M J Perry, Solicitor to the Council, Council Offices, London Rd, Saffron Walden CB11 4ER
Tel: 01799 510416 Fax: 01799 510550
DX: 200307 Saffron Walden
e-mail: mperry@uttlesford.gov.uk

17.2 Braintree District Council

Website: www.braintree.gov.uk
Main Switchboard: 01376 552525
Conveyancing Searches: Local Land Charges Section, Causeway Ho, Bocking End, Braintree CM7 9HB
Tel: 01376 557789
e-mail: maxine.steele@braintree.gov.uk
Note: (Land Charges only)
Environmental Health & Planning: Planning & Environmental Services, Causeway Ho, Bocking End, Braintree CM7 9HB
Tel: 01376 552525
Highways: Essex Highways, County Hall, Market Rd, Chelmsford CM1 1QH
Tel: 01245 342583
e-mail: landcharges@essexhighways.org
Solicitor to the Council: Ian Hunt, Head of Law & Governance, Causeway Ho, Bocking End, Braintree CM7 9HB
Tel: 01376 552525
e-mail: ianhu@braintree.gov.uk
Water Services: Anglian Water (Geodesys)

17.3 Colchester Borough Council

Website: www.colchester.gov.uk
Main Switchboard: 01206 282222
Conveyancing Searches: Land Charges Section, Professional Services, Rowan Ho, 33 Sheepen Rd, Colchester CO3 3WG
Tel: 01206 282248/01206 282425 Fax: 01206 282598
DX: 729040 Colchester 15
e-mail: landcharges@colchester.gov.uk
Building Control: Building Control, Commercial Services, Rowan Ho, 33 Sheepen Rd, Colchester CO3 3WG
Tel: 01206 508646 Fax: 01206 282598
DX: 729040 Colchester 15
e-mail: tony.tarran@colchester.gov.uk
Council Tax: Corporate & Financial Management, Rowan Ho, 33 Sheepen Rd, Colchester CO3 3WG
Tel: 01206 282309 Fax: 01206 282319
DX: 729040 Colchester 15
Environmental Health: Environmental Control, Professional Services, Rowan Ho, 33 Sheepen Rd, Colchester CO3 3WG
Tel: 01206 282596 Fax: 01206 282598
DX: 729040 Colchester 15
Highways: Essex Highways, 910 The Crescent, Colchester CO4 9QQ
Solicitor to the Council: Mr A Weavers, Principal Lawyer, Rowan Ho, 33 Sheepen Rd, Colchester CO3 3WG
Tel: 01206 282213 Fax: 01206 573911
DX: 729040 Colchester 15
e-mail: andrew.weavers@colchester.gov.uk
Water Services: Geodesys

17.4 Tendring District Council

Website: www.tendringdc.gov.uk
Main Switchboard: 01255 686868
Conveyancing Searches: Local Land Charges, Council Offices, Thorpe Rd, Weeley CO16 9AJ
Tel: 01255 686577
DX: 34660 Clacton
e-mail: lcharges@tendringdc.gov.uk
Building Control: Life Opportunities – Private Sector Housing, Town Hall, Station Rd, Clacton-on-Sea, Essex CO15 1SE
Tel: 01255 686744 Fax: 01255 686406
DX: 34660 Clacton
e-mail: pshousing@tendringdc.gov.uk
Council Tax: 88–90 Pier Ave, Clacton-on-Sea CO15 1TN
Tel: 01255 686822 Fax: 01255 686405
DX: 34660 Clacton
e-mail: council.tax@tendringdc.gov.uk
Environmental Services: Public Experience, Council Offices, Thorpe Rd, Weeley, Clacton-on-Sea CO16 9AJ
Tel: 01255 686868 Fax: 01255 686404
DX: 34660 Clacton
e-mail: environmental.services@tendringdc.gov.uk
Highways: Essex County Council

Planning: Planning & Building Control Service, Council Offices, Thorpe Rd, Weeley, Clacton-on-Sea CO16 9AJ
Tel: 01255 686161/111
Fax: 01255 686417; Building Control 01255 686425
DX: 34660 Clacton
e-mail: planning.services@tendringdc.gov.uk
Solicitor to the Council: Lisa Hastings, Legal Services, Town Hall, Station Rd, Clacton-on-Sea CO15 1SE
Tel: 01255 686564
DX: 34660 Clacton
Water Services: Anglian Water (Geodesys)

17.5 Harlow District Council

Website: www.harlow.gov.uk
Main Switchboard: 01279 446611
Conveyancing Searches: Local Land Charges Dept, Legal Section, Civic Centre, The Water Gardens, Harlow CM20 1WG
Tel: 01279 446696 Fax: 01279 446638
DX: 40550 Harlow 1
e-mail: christine.warnes@harlow.gov.uk
Building Control: Building Control, Civic Centre 3rd Fl, The Water Gardens, Harlow CM20 1WG
Tel: 01279 446859 Fax: 01279 446560
DX: 40550 Harlow 1
e-mail: buildingcontrol@harlow.gov.uk
Council Tax: Council Tax Unit, Civic Centre 3rd Fl, The Water Gardens, Harlow CM20 1WG
Tel: 01279 446688 Fax: 01279 446635
DX: 40550 Harlow 1
e-mail: council.tax@harlow.gov.uk
Environmental Health: Environmental Health, Civic Centre 3rd Fl, The Water Gardens, Harlow CM20 1WG
Tel: 01279 446111 Fax: 01279 446638
DX: 40550 Harlow 1
e-mail: env.health@harlow.gov.uk
Highways: Essex County Council,
Tel: 01279 446 655
DX: 40550 Harlow 1
e-mail: highways@harlow.gov.uk
Planning: Planning Services, Civic Centre 3rd Fl, The Water Gardens, Harlow CM20 1WG
Tel: 01279 446598 Fax: 01279 446639
DX: 40550 Harlow 1
Solicitor to the Council: Head of Legal Services, Civic Centre, The Water Gardens, Harlow CM20 1WG
Tel: 01279 446037 Fax: 01279 446638
DX: 40550 Harlow 1
Water Services: Thames Water Utilities

17.6 Epping Forest District Council

Website: www.eppingforestdc.gov.uk
Main Switchboard: 01992 564000
Conveyancing Searches: Corporate Support Services (Local Land Charges), Civic Offices, High St, Epping CM16 4BZ
Tel: 01992 564079 Fax: 01992 564588
DX: 40409 Epping
e-mail: jtautz@eppingforestdc.gov.uk
Highways: Essex County Council
Other depts: Civic Offices, as before
Solicitor to the Council: Miss Colleen O'Boyle, Civic Offices, High St, Epping CM16 4BZ
Tel: 01992 564475 Fax: 01992 578018
DX: 40409 Epping
e-mail: coboyle@eppingforestdc.gov.uk
Water Services: Thames Water

17.7 Chelmsford Council

Website: www.chelmsford.gov.uk
Main Switchboard: 01245 606606
Conveyancing Searches: Sustainable Communities, Land Charges – Development Management, Civic Centre, Duke St, Chelmsford CM1 1JE
Tel: 01245 606858 Fax: 01245 606559
DX: 123305 Chelmsford 7
e-mail: llcmailbox@chelmsford.gov.uk
Building Control: Building Control Services, PO Box 7544, Civic Centre, Chelmsford CM1 1XP
Tel: 01245 606431 Fax: 01245 606288
DX: 123305 Chelmsford 7
e-mail: building.control@chelmsford.gov.uk
Council Tax: Financial Services, PO Box 457, Civic Centre, Duke St, Chelmsford CM1 1JE
Tel: 01245 606780 Fax: 01245 606693
DX: 123305 Chelmsford 7
e-mail: revenues@chelmsford.gov.uk
Environmental Health: Public Health & Protection Services, Civic Centre, Coval La, Chelmsford CM1 1JE
Tel: 01245 606606 Fax: 01245 606681
DX: 123305 Chelmsford 7
e-mail: environmental.services@chelmsford.gov.uk
Highways: Essex Highways, Service Management Office 2, Springfield Highways Depot, Colchester Rd, Chelmsford CM2 5PU
Tel: 0845 603 7631
Planning: Planning Services, Civic Centre, Coval La, Chelmsford CM1 1JE
Tel: 01245 606826 Fax: 01245 606526
DX: 123305 Chelmsford 7
e-mail: town.planning@chelmsford.gov.uk
Solicitor to the Council: Ann Coronel, Legal & Democratic Services Manager, Civic Centre, Duke St, Chelmsford CM1 1JE
Tel: 01245 606416 Fax: 01245 606245
DX: 123305 Chelmsford 7
e-mail: ann.coronel@chelmsford.gov.uk
Water Services: Geodesys

17.8 Maldon District Council

Website: www.maldon.gov.uk
Main Switchboard: 01621 854477
Conveyancing Searches: Land Charges Dept, Council Offices, Princes Rd, Maldon CM9 5DL
Tel: 01621 854477 Fax: 01621 852575
e-mail: local.landcharges@maldon.gov.uk
Building Control: Building Control, Council Offices, Princes Rd, Maldon CM9 5DL
Tel: 01621 854477 Fax: 01621 852575
e-mail: building.control@maldon.gov.uk
Council Tax: Revenues & Benefits, Council Offices, Princes Rd, Maldon CM9 5DL
Tel: 01621 854477 Fax: 01621 852575
e-mail: benefits@maldon.gov.uk
Environmental Health: Environmental Health, Council Offices, Princes Rd, Maldon CM9 5DL
Tel: 01621 854477 Fax: 01621 852575
e-mail: customer.services@maldon.gov.uk
Highways: Essex Highways, PO Box 11, County Hall, Chelmsford CM1 1QH
Tel: 01245 342692
DX: 3322 Chelmsford
e-mail: highwayrecords@essexhighways.org
Solicitor to the Council: see Essex County Council
Water Services: Anglian Water

17.9 Brentwood Borough Council

Website: www.brentwood.gov.uk
Main Switchboard: 01277 312500
Conveyancing Searches: Land Charges Section, Town Hall, Ingrave Rd, Brentwood CM15 8AY
Tel: 01277 312625 Fax: 01277 312625
DX: 5001 Brentwood
e-mail: land.charges@brentwood.gov.uk
Building Control: Building Control Services, Town Hall, Ingrave Rd, Brentwood CM15 8AY
Tel: 01277 312532 Fax: 01277 312747
DX: 5001 Brentwood
e-mail: buildingsurveying@brentwood.gov.uk
Council Tax: Council Tax & Benefits, Town Hall, Ingrave Rd, Brentwood CM15 8AY
Tel: 01277 312500 Fax: 01277 312743
DX: 5001 Brentwood
e-mail: revenue@brentwood.gov.uk
Environmental Health: Environmental Health Services, Town Hall, Ingrave Rd, Brentwood CM15 8AY
Tel: 01277 312504 Fax: 01277 312526
DX: 5001 Brentwood
e-mail: envhealth@brentwood.gov.uk
Highways: Town Hall, Ingrave Rd, Brentwood CM15 8AY
Tel: 01277 312500 Fax: 01277 312684
DX: 5001 Brentwood
e-mail: highways@brentwood.gov.uk
Planning: Planning Services, Town Hall, Ingrave Rd, Brentwood CM15 8AY
Tel: 01277 312620 Fax: 01277 312743
DX: 5001 Brentwood
e-mail: planning@brentwood.gov.uk
Solicitor to the Council: Brian Keane, Executive Law & Policy Officer, Town Hall, Ingrave Rd, Brentwood CM15 8AY
Tel: 01277 312555 Fax: 01277 312744
DX: 5001 Brentwood
e-mail: brian.keane@brentwood.gov.uk
Water Services: Anglian Water (t/a Geodesys) and Thames Water Property Insight

17.10 Basildon District Council

Website: www.basildon.gov.uk
Main Switchboard: 01268 533333
Conveyancing Searches: Local Land Charges Registrar, Basildon Centre, St Martin's Sq, Basildon SS14 1DL
Tel: 01268 294199/294465 Fax: 01268 294162
DX: 53008 Basildon
e-mail: landcharges@basildon.gov.uk
Council Tax: Council Tax, Council Offices, Basildon Centre, St Martin's Sq, Basildon SS14 1DL
Tel: 01268 533333
DX: 53008
Environmental Health: Environmental Health, Basildon Centre, St Martin's Sq, Basildon SS14 1DL
Tel: 01268 294292
DX: 53008 Basildon
e-mail: environmentalhealth@basildon.gov.uk
Highways: Engineers, Childerditch Industrial Pk, Brentwood, Essex CM13 3HD
Tel: 0845 603 7631
Planning: Planning, Basildon Centre, St Martin's Sq, Basildon SS14 1DL
Tel: 01268 533333 Fax: 01268 294162
DX: 53008 Basildon
e-mail: planning@basildon.gov.uk
Solicitor to the Council: Ms Lorraine Brown, Manager of Legal & Estates, Basildon Centre, St Martin's Sq, Basildon SS14 1DL
Tel: 01268 294461
DX: 53008 Basildon
Water Services: Geodesys

17.11 Rochford District Council

Website: www.rochford.gov.uk
Main Switchboard: 01702 546366
Conveyancing Searches: Land Charges, Council Offices, South St, Rochford SS4 1BW
Tel: 01702 318191 Fax: 01702 318154
DX: 39751 Rochford
e-mail: sarah.orchard@rochford.gov.uk
Building Control: Head of Planning Services, Council Offices, South St, Rochford SS4 1BW
Tel: 01702 318081 Fax: 01702 318181
DX: 39751 Rochford
e-mail: shaun.scrutton@rochford.gov.uk
Council Tax: Head of Community Services, Council Offices, South St, Rochford SS4 1BW
Tel: 01702 546366 Fax: 01702 318129
DX: 39751 Rochford
e-mail: jeremy.bourne@rochford.gov.uk
Environmental Health: Head of Environmental Services, Council Offices, South St, Rochford SS4 1BW
Tel: 01702 546366 Fax: 01702 545737
DX: 39751 Rochford
e-mail: richard.evans@rochford.gov.uk
Highways: Mouchel Ltd, Victoria Ho, 101–105 Victoria Rd, Chelmsford CM1 1JR
Tel: 01245 247000 Fax: 01245 247001
DX: 3322 Chelmsford
e-mail: highwayrecords@mouchel.com
Planning: Head of Planning Services, Council Offices, South St, Rochford SS4 1BW
Tel: 01702 318191 Fax: 01702 545737
DX: 39751 Rochford
e-mail: shaun.scrutton@rochford.gov.uk
Solicitor to the Council: Head of Legal Services, Council Offices, South St, Rochford SS4 1BW
Tel: 01702 546366 Fax: 01702 318154
DX: 39751 Rochford
e-mail: albert.bugeja@rochford.gov.uk
Water Services: Geodesys

17.12 Thurrock Council (U)

Website: www.thurrock.gov.uk
Main Switchboard: 01375 652652
Conveyancing Searches: Local Land Charges, Sustainable Communities, Civic Offices, New Rd, Grays RM17 6SL
Tel: 01375 652052/3 Fax: 01375 652780
DX: 141048 Grays 3
e-mail: land.charges@thurrock.gov.uk
Building Control: Civic Offices, New Rd, Grays RM17 6SL
Tel: 01375 652008 Fax: 01375 652359
DX: 141048 Grays 3
e-mail: buildingcontrol@thurrock.gov.uk
Environmental Health: Public Protection, Civic Offices, New Rd, Grays RM17 6SL
Tel: 01375 652955
DX: 141048 Grays 3
e-mail: general.enquiries@thurrock.gov.uk

Highways: Engineering Services, Curzon Depot, Manor Way, Grays RM17 6BQ
Tel: 01375 366100 / 754763
DX: 141048 Grays 3
e-mail: highways@thurrock.gov.uk
Planning: Development Management, Civic Offices, New Rd, Grays RM17 6SL
Tel: 01375 652 291 Fax: 01375 652 787
DX: 141048 Grays 3
e-mail: development.control@thurrock.gov.uk
Solicitor to the Council: Head of Legal Services, Civic Offices, New Rd, Grays RM17 6SL
Tel: 01375 652041 Fax: 01375 652782
DX: 141040 Grays 3
Water Services: Anglian Water

17.13 Castle Point Borough Council

Website: www.castlepoint.gov.uk
Main Switchboard: 01268 882200
Conveyancing Searches: Support Services, Council Offices, Kiln Rd, Thundersley, Benfleet SS7 1TF
Tel: 01268 882437 Fax: 01268 882453
DX: 39603 Hadleigh
e-mail: landcharges@castlepoint.gov.uk
Building Control: Council Offices, Kiln Rd, Thundersley, Benfleet SS7 1TF
Tel: 01268 882200 Fax: 01268 882455
DX: 39603 Hadleigh
e-mail: planning@castlepoint.gov.uk
Environmental Health: Council Offices, Kiln Rd, Thundersley, Benfleet SS7 1TF
Tel: 01268 882200 Fax: 01268 882455
DX: 39603 Hadleigh
e-mail: info@castlepoint.gov.uk
Highways: Essex County Council
Other depts: Council Tax, Freepost CL3636, Chelmsford, Essex CM1 ILX
Tel: 08457 430430
e-mail: counciltax@essexcc.gov.uk
Solicitor to the Council: Andrew Smith, Borough Solicitor & Monitoring Officer, Council Offices, Kiln Rd, Thundersley, Benfleet SS7 1TF
Tel: 01268 882200 Fax: 01268 882453
DX: 39603 Hadleigh
e-mail: asmith@castlepoint.gov.uk
Water Services: Anglian (drainage)/Essex & Suffolk (drinking water)

17.14 Southend-on-Sea Borough Council (U)

Website: www.southend.gov.uk
Main Switchboard: 01702 215000
Conveyancing Searches: Land Charges, PO Box 6, Civic Centre, Victoria Ave, Southend SS2 6ER
Tel: 01702 215124
DX: 2812 Southend
e-mail: landcharges@southend.gov.uk
Building Control, Environmental Health, Planning & Highways: Department of Enterprise, Tourism and the Environment, PO Box 6, Civic Centre, Victoria Ave, Southend-on-Sea SS2 6ER
Tel: 01702 215000
e-mail: buildingcontrol@southend.gov.uk
Council Tax: The Borough Treasurer, PO Box 2, Civic Centre, Victoria Ave, Southend-on-Sea SS2 6ER
Tel: 01702 215000
Solicitor to the Council: Support Services, Civic Centre, Victoria Ave, Southend-on-Sea SS2 6ER
Tel: 01702 215000 Fax: 01702 215110
DX: 2812 Southend
e-mail: legalanddemocraticservices@southend.gov.uk
Water Services: Geodesys

18 Gloucestershire

18.0 Gloucestershire County Council

Website: www.gloucestershire.gov.uk
Main Switchboard: 01452 425000
Search Address: Legal & Democratic Services, Quayside Ho, Quay St, Gloucester GL1 2TZ
Tel: 01452 425203 Fax: 01452 426790
DX: 133275 Gloucester 11 (Legal)
e-mail: stephen.higginbotham@gloucestershire.gov.uk
Solicitor to the Council: N J Roberts, Director of Law & Administration, Quayside Ho, Quay St, Gloucester GL1 2TZ
Tel: 01452 425201 Fax: 01452 426790
DX: 133275 Gloucester 11 (Legal)
e-mail: nigel.roberts@gloucestershire.gov.uk

18.1 Tewkesbury Borough Council

Website: www.tewkesbury.gov.uk
Main Switchboard: 01684 295010
Conveyancing Searches: Borough Development, Development Services, Council Offices, Gloucester Rd, Tewkesbury GL20 5TT
Tel: 01684 272024 Fax: 01684 272227
DX: 11406 Tewkesbury
e-mail: landcharges@tewkesbury.gov.uk
Note: 1 copy of 2500 scale plan required with every search; no expedition facilities
Building Control: Cheltenham Borough Council, Built Environment, Municipal Offices, Cheltenham GL50 9SA
Tel: 01242 264390
e-mail: buildingcontrol@cheltenham.gov.uk
Council Tax: Resources, Council Offices, Gloucester Rd, Tewkesbury GL20 5TT
Tel: 01684 272111 Fax: 01684 272157
DX: 11406 Tewkesbury
e-mail: revenues@tewkesbury.gov.uk
Environmental Health: Borough Development, Environmental & Housing Services, Council Offices, Gloucester Rd, Tewkesbury GL20 5TT
Tel: 01684 272191 Fax: 01684 272146
DX: 11406 Tewkesbury
e-mail: ehenquiries@tewkesbury.gov.uk
Highways: Gloucestershire Highways, Imperial Gate Business Pk, Corinium Ave, Barnwood, Gloucester GL4 3BW
Tel: 08000 514 514
e-mail: highways@gloucester.gov.uk
Planning: Development Services, Developmemnt Management, Council Offices, Gloucester Rd, Tewkesbury GL20 5TT
Tel: 01684 272151 Fax: 01684 272227
DX: 11406 Tewkesbury
e-mail: techadmin@tewkesbury.gov.uk
Solicitor to the Council: Borough Solicitor, Legal Services, Council Offices, Gloucester Rd, Tewkesbury GL20 5TT
Tel: 01684 272011 Fax: 01684 272040
DX: 11406 Tewkesbury
Water Services: Severn Trent Water

18.2 Forest of Dean District Council

Website: www.fdean.gov.uk
Main Switchboard: 01594 810000
Conveyancing Searches: Land Charges Section, Council Offices, High St, Coleford GL16 8HG
Tel: 01594 812509 Fax: 01594 812470
DX: 94102 Coleford
e-mail: land.charges@fdean.gov.uk
Building Control: Council Offices, High St, Coleford GL16 8HG
Tel: 01594 810000
Council Tax: Council Tax Dept, Council Offices, High St, Coleford GL16 8HG
Tel: 01594 810000 Fax: 01594 812590
Environmental Health: Council Offices, High St, Coleford GL16 8HG
Tel: 01594 810000
Highways: Gloucestershire County Council
Planning: Council Offices, High St, Coleford GL16 8HG
Tel: 01594 810000 Fax: 01594 812314
Solicitor to the Council: Mrs C Hughes, Council Offices, High St, Coleford GL16 8HG
Tel: 01594 812510 Fax: 01594 812515
Water Services: Severn Trent Water & Welsh Water

18.3 Gloucester City Council

Website: www.gloucester.gov.uk
Main Switchboard: 01452 396396
Conveyancing Searches: Head of Legal & Policy Development, Herbert Warehouse, The Docks, Gloucester GL1 2EQ
Tel: 01452 396116 Fax: 01452 396398
DX: 7516 Gloucester 1 (Legal)
e-mail: landc@gloucester.gov.uk
Building Control: Building Control, Herbert Warehouse, The Docks, Gloucester GL1 2EQ
Tel: 01452 396771 Fax: 01452 396763
DX: 7516 Gloucester 1 (Plan)
e-mail: buildingcontrol@gloucester.gov.uk
Council Tax: Head of Finance, Herbert Warehouse, The Docks, Gloucester GL1 2EQ
Tel: 01452 396495 Fax: 01452 396404
DX: 7516 Gloucester 1 (Rev)
e-mail: revenues@gloucester.gov.uk
Environmental Health: Head of Public Protection, Herbert Warehouse, The Docks, Gloucester GL1 2EQ
Tel: 01452 396396 Fax: 01452 396340
e-mail: heretohelp@gloucester.gov.uk
Highways: Gloucestershire County Council
Solicitor to the Council: Ms Sue Mullins, Head of Legal & Policy Development, Herbert Warehouse, The Docks, Gloucester GL1 2EQ
Tel: 01452 396110 Fax: 01452 396398
DX: 7516 Gloucester
e-mail: sue.mullins@gloucester.gov.uk
Water Services: Severn Trent Water

18.4 Cheltenham Borough Council

Website: www.cheltenham.gov.uk
Main Switchboard: 01242 264328
Conveyancing Searches: Built Environment, Municipal Offices, Promenade, Cheltenham GL50 9SA
Tel: 01242 264328
e-mail: locallandcharges@cheltenham.gov.uk
Other depts: Municipal Offices, Promenade, Cheltenham GL50 9SA
Tel: 01242 264312
e-mail: builtenvironment@cheltenham.gov.uk
Solicitor to the Council: Assistant Director (Legal & Democratic Services), Council Offices, Gloucester Rd, Tewkesbury GL20 5TT
Tel: 01684 272691
e-mail: legalservices@tewkesbury.gov.uk
Water Services: Severn Trent Water

18.5 Cotswold District Council

Website: www.cotswold.gov.uk
Main Switchboard: 01285 623000
Conveyancing Searches: Land Charges, Trinity Rd, Cirencester GL7 1PX
Tel: 01285 623000 Fax: 01285 623916
DX: 144421 Cirencester 2
e-mail: landcharges@cotswold.gov.uk
Building Control: Trinity Rd, as before,
Tel: 01285 623 000 Fax: 01285 623 905
e-mail: buildingcontrol@cotswold.gov.uk
Council Tax: Trinity Rd, as before,
Tel: 01285 623000
e-mail: revenues@cotswold.gov.uk
Environmental Health: Trinity Rd, as before,
Tel: 01285 623000
Highways: Gloucestershire County Council,
e-mail: highwayrecords@gloucestershire.gov.uk
Planning: Trinity Rd, as before,
Tel: 01285 623 000
e-mail: planning@cotswold.gov.uk
Solicitor to the Council: Ms B Patel, Legal & Property Services, Trinity Rd, as before,
e-mail: bhavna.patel@cotswold.gov.uk
Water Services: Thames Water, Severn Trent and Wessex Water

18.6 Stroud District Council

Website: www.stroud.gov.uk
Main Switchboard: 01453 766321
Conveyancing Searches: The Registration of Local Land Charges, Council Offices, Ebley Mill, Westward Rd, Stroud GL5 4UB
Tel: 01453 754854 Fax: 01453 754937
e-mail: locallandcharges@stroud.gov.uk
Highways: Gloucestershire Highways, Imperial Gate Business Pk, Corinium Ave, Barnwood, Gloucester GL4 3BW
Tel: 08000 514 514
e-mail: highways@gloucester.gov.uk
Solicitor to the Council: Ms Patricia Adley, Council Offices, Ebley Mill, Westward Rd, Stroud GL5 4UB
Tel: 01453 766321 x 4370 Fax: 01453 754937
e-mail: patricia.adley@stroud.gov.uk
Water Services: Severn Trent Water and Wessex Water

18.7 South Gloucestershire District Council (U)

Website: www.southglos.gov.uk
Main Switchboard: 01454 868686
Conveyancing Searches: Land Charges (Thornbury), Castle St, Thornbury BS35 1HF
Tel: 01454 863060 Fax: 01454 862609
DX: 48357 Thornbury
e-mail: locallandcharges@southglos.gov.uk
Building Control: Planning, Transportation & Environmental Services,
Tel: 01454 868004 Fax: 01454 863454
Council Tax: Revenues & Benefits, Nibley Ct, 3 Turner Dr, Yate BS37 5YU
Tel: 01454 868003 Fax: 01454 863005

Highways: Engineering Services Section, Planning, Transportation & Environmental Services, Network Services, Broad La, Engine Common, Yate BS17 5PN
Tel: 01454 864568 Fax: 01454 863630
Other depts: Planning, Transportation & Environmental Services,
Tel: 01454 868686 Fax: 01454 863642
Solicitor to the Council: John McCormack, Head of Legal & Democratic Services, Council Offices, Castle St, Thornbury BS35 1HF
Tel: 01454 863021 Fax: 01454 865979
DX: 48357 Thornbury
Water Services: Wessex Water

19 Greater Manchester

19.1 Wigan Borough Council

Website: www.wigan.gov.uk
Main Switchboard: 01942 244991
Conveyancing Searches: Local Land Charges Section, Town Hall, Library St, Wigan WN1 1YN
Tel: 01942 827125/6/7 Fax: 01942 827154
DX: 702075 Wigan 2
e-mail: landcharges@wigan.gov.uk
Building Control: Places: Economy Waste and Infrastructure, Planning & Transport (Land Searches), Wigan Council, PO Box 100, Wigan WN1 3DS
Tel: 01942 489150 x89150
e-mail: planningsearches@wigan.gov.uk
Council Tax: Resources Directorate, Citizen Support Services (Awards & Taxation), Wigan Council, PO Box 100, Wigan WN1 3DS
Tel: 01942 828644 x3644 Fax: 01942 828613
e-mail: revenues@wigan.gov.uk
Environmental Health: Places Directorate, Business Compliance & Improvement, Wigan Council, PO Box 100, Wigan WN1 3DS
Tel: 01942 489626 x89626 Fax: 01942 404222
e-mail: ep@wigan.gov.uk
Highways: Places Directorate, Infrastructure Asset Management Group, PO Box 100, Wigan WN1 3DS
Tel: 01942 489279 x89279 Fax: 01942 404222
e-mail: lorraine.jackson@wigan.gov.uk
Planning: Places: Economy, Waste & Infrastructure, Planning & Transport (Land Searches), Wigan Council, PO Box 100, Wigan WN1 3DS
Tel: 01942 489150 x89150
e-mail: planningsearches@wigan.gov.uk
Solicitor to the Council: Mr John Mitchell, Assistant Director, Legal Resources Directorate, Wigan Council Town Hall, Library St, Wigan WN1 1YN
Tel: 01942 827026 x2026 Fax: 01942 827093
DX: 702075 Wigan 2
Water Services: United Utilities

19.2 Bolton Borough Council

Website: www.bolton.gov.uk
Main Switchboard: 01204 333333
Conveyancing Searches: Development & Regeneration, Spatial Data, 3rd Fl, Town Hall, Victoria Sq, Bolton BL1 1RU
Tel: 01204 331137 / 331324
e-mail: spatialdatagroup@bolton.gov.uk
Building Control: Building Control Service, Regeneration Dept, Room 309, 3rd Fl, Town Hall, Victoria Sq, Bolton BL1 1RU
Tel: 01204 336033 Fax: 01204 336399
DX: 716633 Bolton 10
e-mail: building.control@bolton.gov.uk
Council Tax: Council Tax Office, Finance Dept, Town Hall, Bolton BL1 1RX
Tel: 01204 331 599
DX: 716633 Bolton 10
e-mail: council.tax@bolton.gov.uk
Environmental Health: Environmental Services, Castle Hill Centre, Castleton St, Bolton BL2 2JW
Tel: 01204 336505
e-mail: environmentalhealth@bolton.gov.uk
Highways & Sewer: Highways & Engineering, 4th Fl, Wellsprings, Victoria Sq, Bolton BL1 1US
Tel: 01204 336458 Fax: 01204 336499
e-mail: highways@bolton.gov.uk
Planning: Developing & Regeneration, Planning Support, 3rd Fl, Town Hall, Bolton BL1 1RU
Tel: 01204 336000 Fax: 01204 336399
e-mail: planning.control@bolton.gov.uk
Solicitor to the Council: Helen Gorman, Borough Solicitor, Chief Executive's Dept, Town Hall, Bolton BL1 1RU
Tel: 01204 333333 Fax: 01204 331040
DX: 716633 Bolton 10
e-mail: helen.gorman@bolton.gov.uk
Water Services: United Utilities

19.3 Bury Metropolitan Borough Council

Website: www.bury.gov.uk
Main Switchboard: 0161 253 5000
Conveyancing Searches: Chief Executive's, Town Hall, Knowsley St, Bury BL9 0SW
Tel: 0161 253 5243 Fax: 0161 253 5248
Building Control: Resources & Regulation Dept, 3 Knowsley Pl, Duke St, Bury BL9 0EJ
Tel: 0161 253 5313 Fax: 0161 253 5290
e-mail: building.control@bury.gov.uk
Council Tax: Financial Services Division, Resources & Regulation Dept, Whittaker St, Radcliffe M26 2DT
Tel: 0161 253 5656 Fax: 0161 253 7039
e-mail: counciltax@bury.gov.uk
Environmental Health: Resources & Regulation Dept, 3 Knowsley Pl, Duke St, Bury BL9 0EJ
Tel: 0161 253 5353 Fax: 0161 253 5578
e-mail: customercontactteam@bury.gov.uk
Highways: Resources & Regulation Dept, 3 Knowsley Pl, Duke St, Bury BL9 0EJ
Tel: 0161 253 5828
e-mail: engcon@bury.gov.uk
Planning: Resources & Regulation Dept, 3 Knowsley Pl, Duke St, Bury BL9 0EJ
Tel: 0161 253 5432 Fax: 0161 253 5290
e-mail: planning@bury.gov.uk
Solicitor to the Council: Jayne Hammond, Director of Legal & Democratic Services, Town Hall, Knowsley St, Bury BL9 0SW
Tel: 0161 253 5237 Fax: 0161 253 5119
e-mail: j.m.hammond@bury.gov.uk
Water Services: United Utilities

19.4 Rochdale Borough Council

Website: www.rochdale.gov.uk
Main Switchboard: 01706 647474
Conveyancing Searches: Legal & Democratic Services, 1st Fl, Brook Ho, Oldham Rd, Middleton, Manchester M24 1AY
Tel: 01706 647474 x 4702
DX: 129053 Middleton
e-mail: legal@rochdale.gov.uk
Building Control, Environmental Health & Planning: Planning & Regulation Services, Number One Riverside, Smith St, Rochdale OL16 1XU
Tel: 01706 924327 Fax: 01706 924628
e-mail: development.control@rochdale.gov.uk
Council Tax: Revenues & Benefit Services, Number One Riverside, Smith St, Rochdale OL16 1XU
Tel: 0845 121 2970 Fax: 01706 926186
e-mail: council.tax@rochdale.gov.uk
Environmental Health: Environmental Health, Number One Riverside, Smith St, Rochdale OL16 1XU
Tel: 0845 121 2971 Fax: 01706 924185
e-mail: environmental.health2@rochdale.gov.uk
Highways: 1st Fl, Brook Ho, Oldham Rd, Middleton, Manchester M24 1AY
Tel: 0845 121 2979
DX: 129053 Middleton
e-mail: engineers@rochdale.gov.uk
Solicitor to the Council: Borough Solicitor (Linda Fisher), Number One Riverside, Smith St, Rochdale OL16 1XU
Tel: 01706 924702
DX: 22831 Rochdale
Water Services: United Utilities

19.5 Salford City Council

Website: www.salford.gov.uk
Main Switchboard: 0161 794 4711
Conveyancing Searches: Land Charges Section, Civic Centre, Chorley Rd, Swinton M27 5DA
Tel: 0161 793 3124 Fax: 0161 794 6480
DX: 712100 Swinton 2
e-mail: land.charges@salford.gov.uk
Building Control: Building Control Section, Urban Vision, Emerson Ho, Albert St, Eccles M30 0TE
Tel: 0161 779 6175 Fax: 0161 779 6002
e-mail: building.control@salford.gov.uk
Council Tax: Finance Division, Civic Centre, Chorley Rd, Swinton M27 5AW
Tel: 0161 909 6502
e-mail: benefitenquiries@salford.gov.uk
Environmental Health: Environment Directorate, Turnpike Ho, 631 Eccles New Rd, Salford M50 1SW
Tel: 0161 7370551
e-mail: environment@salford.gov.uk
Highways: Highways Section, Urban Vision, Emerson Ho, Albert St, Eccles M30 0TE
Tel: 0161 909 6505 Fax: 0161 779 6006
e-mail: highway.services@urbanvision.org.uk
Planning: Planning Section, Urban Vision, Emerson Ho, Albert St, Eccles M30 0TE
Tel: 0161 906 6545 Fax: 0161 779 6002
e-mail: planningcontact@salford.gov.uk
Water Services: United Utilities

19.6 Manchester City Council

Website: www.manchester.gov.uk
Main Switchboard: 0161 234 5000
Conveyancing Searches: Chief Executive's (Planning Division), Land Charges, PO Box 314, Manchester M60 2JR
Tel: 0161 234 3144/4649/4604 Fax: 0161 234 4099
DX: 714441 Manchester 23
e-mail: landcharges@manchester.gov.uk
Council Tax: Council Tax Service, PO Box 147, Manchester MI5 5TU
Tel: 0161 234 5002 Fax: 0161 953 8226
e-mail: ctax.enquiries@manchester.gov.uk
Solicitor to the Council: Susan Orrell, City Solicitor, PO Box 532, Town Hall, Albert Sq, Manchester M60 2LA
Tel: 0161 234 3087 Fax: 0161 234 3207
e-mail: s.orrell@manchester.gov.uk
Water Services: United Utilities

19.7 Oldham Borough Council

Website: www.oldham.gov.uk
Main Switchboard: 0161 770 3000
Conveyancing Searches: Land Charges Office, Room 222, Civic Centre, West St, Oldham OL1 1UL
Tel: 0161 770 4849
DX: 710000 Oldham-Civic Centre
e-mail: land.charges@oldham.gov.uk
Note: Tel is for Local Land Charges
Building Control: Transportation & Planning, Level 3, Civic Centre, West St, Oldham OL1 1UG
Tel: 0161 770 4122 Fax: 0161 770 4103
e-mail: buildingcontrolteam@oldham.gov.uk
Council Tax: Revenues Team, Level 2, Henshaw Ho, Cheapside, Oldham OL1 1NY
Tel: 0161 770 6622 Fax: 0161 770 6944
e-mail: council.tax@oldham.gov.uk
Environmental Health: Environmental Services, Chadderton Town Hall, Middleton Rd, Chadderton OL9 6PP
Tel: 0161 770 2244 Fax: 0161 770 4500
e-mail: environmentalhealth@oldham.gov.uk
Highways: Highways & Engineering, Henshaw Ho, Cheapside, Oldham OL1 1NY
Tel: 0161 770 4333 Fax: 0161 770 3411
e-mail: ts.traffic@oldham.gov.uk
Planning: Transportation & Planning, Level 3, Civic Centre, West St, Oldham OL1 1UG
Tel: 0161 770 4105 Fax: 0161 770 3104
e-mail: planning@oldham.gov.uk
Solicitor to the Council: Mr Paul Entwistle, Borough Solicitor, Civic Centre, Room 442, West St, Oldham OL1 1UH
Tel: 0161 770 4822 Fax: 0161 770 5185
e-mail: paul.entwistle@oldham.gov.uk
Water Services: United Utilities

19.8 Trafford Borough Council

Website: www.trafford.gov.uk
Main Switchboard: 0161 912 2000
Conveyancing Searches: Legal & Democratic Services, Trafford Town Hall, Talbot Rd, Stretford, Greater Manchester M32 0TH
Tel: 0161 912 4258 Fax: 0161 912 4294
e-mail: landcharges@trafford.gov.uk
Building Control & Planning: Chief Planning Officer, Trafford Town Hall, Talbot Rd, Stretford, Greater Manchester M32 0TH
Tel: 0161 912 3149 Fax: 0161 912 3179
e-mail: building.control@trafford.gov.uk

Council Tax: Finance Dept, Council Tax Section, PO Box 65, Sale M33 6BY
Tel: 0161 912 2020 Fax: 0161 912 2369
e-mail: council.tax@trafford.gov.uk
Environmental Health: Public Protection, Trafford Town Hall, Talbot Rd, Stretford M32 0TH
Tel: 0161 912 4916/18 Fax: 0161 912 1133
e-mail: environmental.health@trafford.gov.uk
Highways: Highway Maintenance Services, Carrington Depot, Carrington M31 4WS
Tel: 0161 912 5517 Fax: 0161 912 5555
Solicitor to the Council: Ms Jane Le Fevre, Director of Legal & Democratic Services, Trafford Town Hall, Talbot Rd, Stretford, Trafford, Greater Manchester M32 0TH
Tel: 0161 912 4215 Fax: 0161 912 4294
e-mail: jane.lefevre@trafford.gov.uk
Water Services: United Utilities

19.9 Stockport Borough Council

Website: www.stockport.gov.uk
Main Switchboard: 0161 480 4949
Conveyancing Searches: Stockport Legal Services, Town Hall, Edward St, Stockport SK1 3XE
Tel: 0161 474 3352 Fax: 0161 474 3234
DX: 22605 Stockport 2
e-mail: landcharges@stockport.gov.uk
Building Control: Building Control, Stopford Ho, Piccadilly, Stockport SK1 3XE
Tel: 0161 474 3658/3575/3571
e-mail: building.bc@stockport.gov.uk
Council Solicitor: Mr Barry Khan, Service Director (Legal & Property), 2nd Fl, Stopford Ho, Stockport SK1 3XE
Tel: 0161 474 5873 Fax: 0161 477 9530
DX: 22605 Stockport 2
e-mail: barry.khan@stockport.gov.uk
Council Tax: Council Tax Section, Stopford Ho, Piccadilly, Stockport SK1 3XE
Tel: 0161 217 6014 Fax: 0161 474 5202
Environmental Health: Environmental Health & Trading Standards, Stopford Ho, Piccadilly, Stockport SK1 3XE
Tel: 0161 474 4181 Fax: 0161 474 4369
e-mail: environmental.health@stockport.gov.uk
Highways: Transportation Policy Team, Hygarth Ho, Wellington Rd (103), Stockport SK1 3TT
Tel: 0161 474 4394 Fax: 0161 474 4833
e-mail: transportation@stockport.gov.uk
Planning: Planning Services – Development Management, Stopford Ho, Piccadilly, Stockport SK1 3XE
Tel: 0161 474 3541/3569 Fax: 0161 474 4337
e-mail: planning.dc@stockport.gov.uk

19.10 Tameside Borough Council

Website: www.tameside.gov.uk
Main Switchboard: 0161 342 8355
Conveyancing Searches: Land Charges/Planning & Building Control, Council Offices, Wellington Rd, Ashton-under-Lyne OL6 6DL
Tel: 0161 342 2153 Fax: 0161 342 3111
e-mail: landcharges@tameside.gov.uk
Solicitor to the Council: Sandra Stewart, Borough Solicitor, Council Offices, Wellington Rd, Ashton-under-Lyne OL6 6DL
Tel: 0161 342 3028 Fax: 0161 342 3840
e-mail: sandra.stewart@tameside.gov.uk
Water Services: United Utilities

20 Hampshire

20.0 Hampshire County Council

Website: www.hants.gov.uk
Main Switchboard: 01962 841841
Search Address: Corporate Services, Elizabeth II Ct, The Castle, Winchester SO23 8UJ
Tel: 01962 841841 Fax: 01962 867273
DX: 2510 Winchester
e-mail: info@hants.gov.uk
Solicitor to the Council: Mr Kevin Gardner, Head of Legal Services, Hampshire County Council, Elizabeth II Ct, The Castle, Winchester SO23 8UJ
Tel: 01962 847381 Fax: 01962 867273
DX: 2510 Winchester
e-mail: kevin.gardner@hants.gov.uk

20.1 Basingstoke & Deane Borough Council

Website: www.basingstoke.gov.uk
Main Switchboard: 01256 844844
Conveyancing Searches: Land Charges Section, Planning & Development, Civic Offices, London Rd, Basingstoke RG21 4AH
Tel: 01256 844844 Fax: 01256 841945
DX: 3008 Basingstoke
e-mail: hilary.brummell@basingstoke.gov.uk
Building Control: Civic Offices, as before
Council Tax: Local Tax & Benefits, Parklands, London Rd, Basingstoke RG21 4AH
Tel: 01256 844844 Fax: 01256 844710
DX: 3008 Basingstoke
Environmental Health: Civic Offices, as before
Highways: Hampshire County Council
Planning: Civic Offices, as before
Solicitor to the Council: Melanie O'Sullivan, Civic Offices, London Rd, Basingstoke RG21 4AH
Water Services: Thames Water & Southern Water

20.2 Hart District Council

Website: www.hart.gov.uk
Main Switchboard: 01252 622122
Conveyancing Searches: Local Land Charges, Civic Offices, Harlington Way, Fleet GU51 4AE
Tel: 01252 774419 Fax: 01252 774410 (Land Charges)
DX: 32632 Fleet
e-mail: locallandcharges@hart.gov.uk
Environmental Health: Environmental Health, Council Offices, Harlington Way, Fleet GU51 4AE
Tel: 01252 774421 Fax: 01252 774464
DX: 32632 Fleet
e-mail: eh@hart.gov.uk
Highways: Hampshire County Council
Other depts: Civic Offices, Harlington Way, Fleet GU51 4AE
Tel: 01252 622122 Fax: 01252 626886 (General)
DX: 32632 Fleet
e-mail: enquiries@hart.gov.uk
Solicitor to the Council: Karen Saunders, Shared Legal Services, Basingstoke & Deane Borough Council, Civic Offices, London Rd, Basingstoke RG21 4AH
e-mail: karen.saunders@basingstoke.gov.uk
Water Services: Thames Water

20.3 Rushmoor Borough Council

Website: www.rushmoor.gov.uk
Main Switchboard: 01252 398398
Conveyancing Searches: Local Land Charges & Searches Section, Council Offices, Farnborough Rd, Farnborough GU14 7JU
Tel: 01252 398911 Fax: 01252 524017
DX: 122250 Farnborough 2
e-mail: landcharges@rushmoor.gov.uk
Note: Plan required – location plan required in all cases
Building Control: Building Control Services, Council Offices, as before,
Tel: 01252 398398 Fax: 01252 398726
e-mail: buildingcontrol@rushmoor.gov.uk
Council Tax: Local Taxation, Council Offices, as before,
Tel: 01252 398912 Fax: 01252 524017
e-mail: localtax@rushmoor.gov.uk
Environmental Health: Environmental Health Services, Council Offices, as before,
Tel: 01252 398398 Fax: 01252 398088
e-mail: environmentalhealth@rushmoor.gov.uk
Highways: Highway Searches, Capital Ho, 48–52 Andover Rd, Winchester SO23 7BH
Tel: 01962 832193
e-mail: land.charges@hants.gov.uk
Planning: Planning Services, Council Offices, as before,
Tel: 01252 398398 Fax: 01252 398726
e-mail: plan@rushmoor.gov.uk
Private Sector Housing Services: Private Sector Housing Services, Council Offices, as before,
Tel: 01252 398398 Fax: 01252 398088
e-mail: privatehousing@rushmoor.gov.uk
Solicitor to the Council: Solicitor to the Council, Council Offices, Farnborough Rd, Farnborough GU14 7JU
Tel: 01252 398601 Fax: 01252 524017
DX: 122250 Farnborough 2
e-mail: legal@rushmoor.gov.uk
Water Services: Thames Water

20.4 Test Valley Borough Council

Website: www.testvalley.gov.uk
Main Switchboard: 01264 368000
Conveyancing Searches: Land Charges, Beechhurst, Weyhill Rd, Andover, Hants SP10 3AJ
Tel: 01264 368407 Fax: 01264 368408
DX: 123080 Andover 6
e-mail: land.charges@testvalley.gov.uk
Building Control: Building Control, Council Offices, Duttons Rd, Romsey SO51 8XG
Tel: 01794 527700/01264 368052 Fax: 01794 527888
e-mail: buildingcontrol@testvalley.gov.uk
Council Tax: Revenues Services, Council Offices, Beech Hurst, Weyhill Rd, Andover SP10 3AJ
Tel: 01264 368000 Fax: 01264 368599
e-mail: counciltax@testvalley.gov.uk
Environmental Health: Environment & Health Service, Beech Hurst, Weyhill Rd, Andover, Hants SP10 3AJ
Tel: 01264 368000 / 01794 527700 Fax: 01264 368149
e-mail: envhealth@testvalley.gov.uk
Highways: Hampshire County Council
Planning: Planning Services, Council Offices, Beech Hurst, Weyhill Rd, Andover SP10 3AJ
Tel: 01264 368000 Fax: 01264 368199
e-mail: planning@testvalley.gov.uk
Solicitor to the Council: Mrs S Tovey, Legal Services, Council Offices, Beech Hurst, Weyhill Rd, Andover SP10 3AJ
Tel: 01264 368401 Fax: 01264 368449
e-mail: legal@testvalley.gov.uk
Water Services: Southern Water

20.5 Winchester City Council

Website: www.winchester.gov.uk
Main Switchboard: 01962 840222
Conveyancing Searches: Land Charges Dept, City Offices, Colebrook St, Winchester SO23 9LJ
Tel: 01962 848281 Fax: 01962 843069
DX: 120400 Winchester 5
e-mail: www.landcharges@winchester.gov.uk
Note: Main Reception Fax: 01962 841365
Building Control: Building Control Dept, City Offices, Colebrook St, Winchester SO23 9LJ
Tel: 01962 848322
e-mail: buildingcontrol@winchester.gov.uk
Environmental Health: Environmental Health Dept, City Offices, Colebrook St, Winchester SO23 9LJ
Tel: 01962 848358
e-mail: health@winchester.gov.uk
Highways: Hampshire County Council
Planning: Planning Dept, City Offices, Colebrook St, Winchester SO23 9LJ
Tel: 01962 848548
e-mail: planning@winchester.gov.uk
Solicitor to the Council: Howard Bone, Head of Legal Services, City Offices, Colebrook St, Winchester SO23 9LJ
Tel: 01962 840222 Fax: 01962 841365
Water Services: Southern Water

20.6 East Hampshire District Council

Website: www.easthants.gov.uk
Main Switchboard: 01730 266551
Conveyancing Searches: Land Charges Dept, Penns Pl, Petersfield GU31 4EX
Tel: 01730 234251/234262 Fax: 01730 234263
DX: 100403 Petersfield
e-mail: land.charges@easthants.gov.uk
Building Control: Building Control, Penns Pl, Petersfield GU31 4EX
Tel: 01730 234207 Fax: 01730 234210
DX: 100403 Petersfield
e-mail: julie.hesketh@easthants.gov.uk
Council Tax: Revenues & Benefits, Penns Pl, Petersfield GU31 4EX
Tel: 01730 234400 Fax: 01730 260645
DX: 100403 Petersfield
Environmental Health: Environmental Health, Penns Pl, Petersfield GU31 4EX
Tel: 01730 234323/234304 Fax: 01730 234330
DX: 100403 Petersfield
Highways: Hampshire County Council
Planning: Planning Development, Penns Pl, Petersfield GU31 4EX
Tel: 01730 234248/46 Fax: 01730 234348
DX: 100403 Petersfield
Solicitor to the Council: Mr N Leach, Principal Solicitor, Penns Pl, Petersfield GU31 4EX
Tel: 01730 234088 Fax: 01730 233935
DX: 100403 Petersfield
e-mail: nick.leach@easthants.gov.uk
Water Services: Southern Water and Thames Water

20.7 New Forest District Council

Website: www.nfdc.gov.uk
Main Switchboard: 023 8028 5000
Conveyancing Searches: Land Charges, Appletree Ct, Beaulieu Rd, Lyndhurst SO43 7PA
Tel: 023 8028 5383 Fax: 023 8028 5555
DX: 123010 Lyndhurst 2
e-mail: landcharges@nfdc.gov.uk
Building Control: Planning & Transportation, Appletree Ct, as before,
Tel: 023 8028 5245
e-mail: building.control@nfdc.gov.uk
Council Tax: Council Tax Officer, Customer Services, Town Hall, Avenue Rd, Lymington SO41 9ZG
Tel: 01590 646111 Fax: 023 8028 5733
e-mail: taxandbenefits@nfdc.gov.uk
Environmental Health: Public Health & Community Safety, Appletree Ct, as before,
Tel: 023 8028 5411 Fax: 023 8028 5596
e-mail: envhealth.commadmin@nfdc.gov.uk
Highways: Hampshire County Council, The Castle, Winchester SO23 8UD
Tel: 0845 6035638
Planning: Planning & Transportation, Appletree Ct, as before,
Tel: 023 8028 5345 Fax: 023 8028 5555
DX: 123010 Lyndhurst 2
e-mail: dev.control@nfdc.gov.uk
Planning (Outside NFDC Area): New Forest National Park Authority, Lymington Town Hall, Avenue Rd, Lymington SO41 9ZG
Tel: 01590 646600
e-mail: dev.control@newforestnpa.gov.uk
Solicitor to the Council: Grainne O'Rourke, Chief Solicitor, Appletree Ct, Beaulieu Rd, Lyndhurst SO43 7PA
Tel: 023 8028 5000 Fax: 023 8028 5555
DX: 123010 Lyndhurst 2
e-mail: grainne.o'rourke@nfdc.gov.uk
Water Services: Southern Water & Wessex Water

20.8 Southampton City Council (U)

Website: www.southampton.gov.uk
Main Switchboard: 023 8022 3855
Conveyancing Searches: Local Land Charges Services, Civic Centre, Southampton SO14 7LY
Tel: 023 8083 2980
DX: 115710 Southampton 17 Land Charges Dept
e-mail: land.charges@southampton.gov.uk
Note: 2 copies HM Land Registry filed plan with each search
Building Control: Building Control Services, Civic Centre, Southampton SO14 7LU
Tel: 023 8083 2558
DX: 115710 Southampton 17 Building Control
e-mail: building.control@southampton.gov.uk
Common Land Searches: Local Land Charges Services, Civic Centre, Southampton SO14 7LY
Tel: 023 8083 2980
DX: 115710 Southampton 17 Land Charges Dept
e-mail: land.charges@southampton.gov.uk
Note: 2 copies HM Land Registry filed plan with each search
Council Tax: Local Taxation Services, Fl 2, One Guildhall Sq, Southampton SO14 7LD
Tel: 023 8083 3006
DX: 115710 Southampton 17 Council Tax
e-mail: council.tax@southampton.gov.uk
Environmental Health: Housing Solutions / Private Housing Division, Floor 5, One Guildhall Sq, Southampton SO14 7LD
Tel: 023 8083 2606
DX: 115710 Southampton 17 Housing Solutions
Planning & Development: Planning & Development Services, Civic Centre, Southampton SO14 7LY
Tel: 023 8083 2603
DX: 115710 Southampton 17 Planning Dept
e-mail: planning@southampton.gov.uk
Solicitor to the Council: Mark Heath, Solicitor to the Council, Civic Centre, Southampton SO14 7LT
Tel: 023 8022 3855 x2028 Fax: 023 8083 2308
DX: 115710 Southampton 17
e-mail: mark.heath@southampton.gov.uk
Water Services: Southern Water

20.9 Eastleigh Borough Council

Website: www.eastleigh.gov.uk
Main Switchboard: 023 8068 8000
Conveyancing Searches: Land Charges, Eastleigh Ho, Upper Market St, Eastleigh SO50 9FD
Tel: 023 8068 8115 Fax: 023 8065 2023
DX: 122381 Eastleigh 2
e-mail: landcharges@eastleigh.gov.uk
Other depts: Eastleigh Ho, Upper Market St, Eastleigh SO50 9FD
Tel: 023 8068 8000 Fax: 023 8068 8257
DX: 122381 Eastleigh 2
e-mail: direct@eastleigh.gov.uk
Solicitor to the Council: Richard Ward, Head of Legal Services, Eastleigh Ho, Upper Market St, Eastleigh SO50 9FD
Tel: 023 8068 8000 Fax: 023 8062 9277
DX: 122381 Eastleigh 2
e-mail: richard.ward@eastleigh.gov.uk
Water Services: Southern Water

20.10 Fareham Borough Council

Website: www.fareham.gov.uk
Main Switchboard: 01329 236100
Conveyancing Searches: Land Charges Section, Dept of Community, Civic Offices, Civic Way, Fareham PO16 7AZ
Tel: 01329 236100 Fax: 01329 824505
DX: 40814 Fareham
e-mail: landsearches@fareham.gov.uk
Building Control: Building Control Partnership, Depot Offices, Broadcut, Fareham PO16 8SP
Tel: 01329 824823
DX: 40814 Fareham
e-mail: bcpartnership@fareham.gov.uk
Council Tax: Finance and Resources Dept, Civic Offices, Civic Way, Fareham PO16 7AZ
Tel: 01329 236100 Fax: 01329 822732
DX: 40814 Fareham
e-mail: counciltax@fareham.gov.uk
Environmental Health: Regulatory & Democratic Services, Civic Offices, Civic Way, Fareham PO16 7AZ
Tel: 01329 236100 Fax: 01329 822732
DX: 40814 Fareham
e-mail: health@fareham.gov.uk
Highways: Hampshire County Council
Planning: Planning & Development, Civic Offices, Civic Way, Southampton PO16 7AZ
Tel: 01329 236100
DX: 40814 Fareham
e-mail: planning@fareham.gov.uk

Solicitor to the Council: Richard Ivory, HR & Democratic Services, Southampton & Fareham Legal Services, Southampton City Council, Southbrook Rise, 4–8 Millbrook Rd East, Fareham SO15 1YG
Tel: 023 8083 2974
e-mail: richard.ivory@southampton.gov.uk
Water Services: Southern Water

20.11 Gosport Borough Council

Website: www.gosport.gov.uk
Main Switchboard: 023 9258 4242
Conveyancing Searches: Land Charges Section, Town Hall, High St, Gosport PO12 1EB
Tel: 023 9254 5221 Fax: 023 9254 5587
DX: 136567 Gosport 2
e-mail: land.charges@gosport.gov.uk
Building Control: Building Control Partnership, Civic Offices, Fareham PO16 7TT
Tel: 01329 236100 Fax: 01329 822732
e-mail: bcpartnership@fareham.gov.uk
Highways: Hampshire County Council
Other depts: Town Hall, as before
Solicitor to the Council: Linda Edwards, Borough Solicitor, Town Hall, High St, Gosport PO12 1EB
Tel: 023 9258 4242 Fax: 023 9254 5587
DX: 136567 Gosport 2
e-mail: linda.edwards@gosport.gov.uk
Water Services: Southern Water

20.12 Portsmouth City Council (U)

Website: www.portsmouth.gov.uk
Main Switchboard: 023 9283 4092
Conveyancing Searches: Local Land Charges Dept, Legal Services, Civic Offices, Guildhall Sq, Portsmouth PO1 2PX
Tel: 023 9283 4063/4065 Fax: 023 9283 4076
e-mail: land.charges@portsmouthcc.gov.uk
Building Control: Building Control Services, Civic Offices, Guildhall Sq, Portsmouth PO1 2AU
Tel: 023 9283 4722/4606 Fax: 023 9283 4103
e-mail: buildcontrol@portsmouthcc.gov.uk
City Solicitor: Michael Lawther, Civic Offices, Guildhall Sq, Portsmouth PO1 2PX
Tel: 023 9283 4123 Fax: 023 9283 4076
e-mail: michael.lawther@portsmouthcc.gov.uk
Council Tax: Local Taxation (Council Tax), Civic Offices, Guildhall Sq, Portsmouth PO1 2BE
Tel: 023 9268 8588 / 023 9283 4556 Fax: 023 9283 4500
e-mail: localtaxation@portsmouthcc.gov.uk
Environment and Public Protection: Civic Offices, Guildhall Sq, Portsmouth PO1 2PQ
Tel: 023 9283 4167 Fax: 023 9283 4519
e-mail: public.protection@portsmouthcc.gov.uk
Highways, Transport & Street Management: Civic Offices, Guildhall Sq, Portsmouth PO1 2BG
Tel: 023 9283 4092
e-mail: cityhelpdesk@portsmouthcc.gov.uk
Planning: Planning Services, Civic Offices, Guildhall Sq, Portsmouth PO1 2AU
Tel: 023 9283 4334 Fax: 023 9283 4660
e-mail: planning@portsmouthcc.gov.uk
Private Sector Housing: Private Sector Housing, Civic Offices, Guildhall Sq, Portsmouth PO1 2AZ
Tel: 023 9268 8369
e-mail: housing.privatesector@portsmouthcc.gov.uk
Water Services: Southern Water

20.13 Havant Borough Council

Website: www.havant.gov.uk
Main Switchboard: 023 9247 4174
Conveyancing Searches: Land Charges, Planning & Development Services, Civic Offices, Civic Centre Rd, Havant PO9 2AX
Tel: 023 9244 6236 Fax: 023 9244 6588
DX: 50005 Havant
e-mail: land.charges@havant.gov.uk
Highways: Hampshire County Council
Solicitor to the Council: Paul Griffith, Democratic Services, Civic Offices, Civic Centre Rd, Havant PO9 2AX
Tel: 023 9244 6201 Fax: 023 9248 0263
DX: 50005 Havant
e-mail: paul.griffith@havant.gov.uk
Water Services: Southern Water

21 Herefordshire

21.0 Hereford and Worcester County Council (abolished)

Hereford and Worcester County Council abolished from 1 April 1998. Separate Lieutenancy created for Herefordshire.

21.1 Herefordshire Council (U)

Website: www.herefordshire.gov.uk
Main Switchboard: 01432 260000
Conveyancing Searches: Economy, Communities & Corporate, Local Land Charges Section, Town Hall, Hereford HR1 2PJ
Tel: 01432 260997
DX: 135297 Hereford 3
e-mail: landcharges@herefordshire.gov.uk
Note: 2 plans required.
Building Control & Planning: Planning Directorate, Blueschool Ho, Blueschool St, Hereford HR1 2ZB
Tel: 01432 261938/260386
Council Tax: Revenues, PO Box 224, Hereford HR1 2XW
Tel: 01432 260360
Environmental Health: Environment Services Directorate, Blueschool Ho, Blueschool St, Hereford HR1 2ZB
Tel: 01432 261761 Fax: 01432 261982
Highways: Environment – Highways & Transportation, PO Box 236, Plough La, Hereford HR4 0WZ
Tel: 01432 260969
Solicitor to the Council: Legal & Democratic Services, Shirehall, St Peters Sq, Hereford HR1 2HY
Tel: 01432 260200
DX: 135296 Hereford 3
Water: Welsh Water / Severn Trent

22 Hertfordshire

22.0 Hertfordshire County Council

Website: www.hertsdirect.org
Main Switchboard: 0300 123 4040
Search Address: Legal Services, County Hall, Pegs Lane, Hertford SG13 8DE Fax: 01992 555508
DX: 145781 Hertford 4
e-mail: [firstname.surname]@hertfordshire.gov.uk
Solicitor to the Council: Mrs K Pettitt, Chief Legal Officer, County Hall, Pegs Lane, Hertford SG13 8DE
Tel: 0300 123 4040 Fax: 01992 555508
DX: 145781 Hertford 4
e-mail: kathryn.pettitt@hertfordshire.gov.uk

22.1 North Hertfordshire District Council

Website: www.north-herts.gov.uk
Main Switchboard: 01462 474000
Conveyancing Searches: Local Land Charges Dept, Council Offices, Gernon Rd, Letchworth Garden City SG6 3JF
Tel: 01462 474538 Fax: 01462 474391
DX: 31317 Letchworth Garden City
e-mail: land.charges@north-herts.gov.uk
Building Control: PO Box 480, M33 0DE
Tel: 01462 474355/474000 Fax: 01462 474229
DX: 31317 Letchworth Garden City
e-mail: building.control@north-herts.gov.uk
Council Tax: Finance Dept, Town Lodge, Gernon Rd, Letchworth Garden City SG6 3JF
Tel: 01462 474000 Fax: 01462 474496
DX: 31317 Letchworth Garden City
Environmental Health: Housing & Public Protection, Council Offices, Gernon Rd, Letchworth Garden City SG6 3JF
Tel: 01462 474000 Fax: 01462 474546
DX: 31317 Letchworth Garden City
e-mail: env.health@north-herts.gov.uk
Planning: Planning Control & Conservation, Council Offices, Gernon Rd, Letchworth SG6 3JF
Tel: 01462 474000 Fax: 01462 474558
DX: 31317 Letch
e-mail: planning.control@north-herts.gov.uk
Solicitor to the Council: Legal Services, Council Offices, Gernon Rd, Letchworth SG6 3JF
Tel: 01462 474000 Fax: 01462 474227
DX: 31317 Letchworth Garden City
e-mail: legal.support@north-herts.gov.uk

22.2 Stevenage Borough Council

Website: www.stevenage.gov.uk
Main Switchboard: 01438 242242
Conveyancing Searches: Registrar of Local Land Charges, Daneshill Ho, Danestrete, Stevenage SG1 1HN
Tel: 01438 242964/242302 Fax: 01438 242353
e-mail: land.searches@stevenage.gov.uk
Highways: Hertfordshire County Council
Other depts: Daneshill Ho, Danestrete, Stevenage SG1 1HN
Tel: 01438 242242 Fax: 01438 242566
Solicitor to the Council: Paul Froggatt, Borough Solicitor, Daneshill Ho, Danestrete, Stevenage SG1 1HN
Tel: 01438 242212 Fax: 01438 242197
e-mail: paul.froggatt@stevenage.gov.uk
Water Services: Thames Water (majority); Anglian Water (part)

22.3 East Hertfordshire District Council

Website: www.eastherts.gov.uk
Main Switchboard: 01279 655261
Conveyancing Searches: Land Charges Section, Wallfields, Pegs La, Hertford SG13 8EQ
Tel: 01279 655261 Fax: 01279 502281
DX: 50431 Bishop's Stortford
e-mail: landcharges@eastherts.gov.uk
Building Control & Planning: Planning & Environment Dept, Council Offices, Wallfields, Pegs La, Hertford SG13 8EQ
Tel: 01279 655261
DX: 50431 Bishop's Stortford
e-mail: building.control@eastherts.gov.uk
Council Tax: Council Tax Dept, Wallfields, Pegs Lane, Hertford SG13 8EQ
Tel: 01279 655261
DX: 50431 Bishop's Stortford
e-mail: revenues@eastherts.gov.uk
Environmental Health: Planning & Environment Dept, Council Offices, Wallfields, Pegs La, Hertford SG13 8EQ
Tel: 01279 655261
e-mail: environmental.health@eastherts.gov.uk
Highways: Hertfordshire County Council
Solicitor to the Council: Mr Simon Drinkwater, Director of Neighbourhood Services, Wallfields, Pegs La, Hertford SG13 8EQ
Tel: 01279 655261
e-mail: simon.drinkwater@eastherts.gov.uk
Water Services: Thames Water

22.4 Dacorum Borough Council

Website: www.dacorum.gov.uk
Main Switchboard: 01442 228000
Conveyancing Searches: Land Charges, Civic Centre, Marlowes, Hemel Hempstead HP1 1HH
Tel: 01442 228674 (direct dial for Jeanne Byrne)
Fax: 01442 228161
DX: 8804 Hemel Hempstead
e-mail: land.charges@dacorum.gov.uk
Building Control: Alex Chrusciak, Group Mgr, Development Management & Planning, Civic Centre, Marlowes, Hemel Hempstead HP1 1HH
Tel: 01442 228590
e-mail: building.control@dacorum.gov.uk
Other depts: Mr James Doe, Assistant Director, Planning, Development & Regeneration, Civic Centre, as before, Fax: 01442 228583
e-mail: james.doe@dacorum.gov.uk
Solicitor to the Council: Steven Baker, Solicitor to the Council, Civic Centre, Marlowes, Hemel Hempstead HP1 1HH
Tel: 01442 228229 Fax: 01442 240897
DX: 8804 Hemel Hempstead
e-mail: steven.baker@dacorum.gov.uk
Water Services: Thames Water (Asset Data Services)

22.5 St Albans City and District Council

Website: www.stalbans.gov.uk
Main Switchboard: 01727 866100
Conveyancing Searches: Legal, Democratic and Regulatory Services, District Council Offices, St Peter's St, St Albans AL1 3JE
Tel: 01727 819513/819511 Fax: 01727 819255
DX: 6178 St Albans 1
e-mail: landcharges@stalbans.gov.uk
Solicitor to the Council: Head of Legal, Democratic and Regulatory Services, District Council Offices, St Peter's St, St Albans AL1 3JE
Tel: 01727 819502 Fax: 01727 819255
DX: 6178 St Albans 1
e-mail: legal@stalbans.gov.uk
Water Services: Thames Water

22.6 Welwyn Hatfield Borough Council

Website: www.welhat.gov.uk
Main Switchboard: 01707 357000
Conveyancing Searches: Land Charges Section, Council Offices, The Campus, Welwyn Garden City AL7 6AE
Tel: 01707 357357/8*/357351 Fax: 01707 357475/357373
DX: 30075 Welwyn Garden City 1
e-mail: locallandcharges@welhat.gov.uk
Building Control: Building Control Dept, Council Offices, The Campus, Welwyn Garden City AL8 6AE
Tel: 01707 357000
DX: 30075 Welwyn Garden City 1
e-mail: buildingcontrol@welhat.gov.uk

Council Tax: Council Tax, Council Offices, The Campus, Welwyn Garden City AL7 6AE
Tel: 01707 357000 Fax: 01707 357484
DX: 30075 Welwyn Garden City 1
Environmental Health: Environmental Health Dept, Council Offices, The Campus, Welwyn Garden City AL8 6AE
Tel: 01707 357000
DX: 30075 Welwyn Garden City 1
e-mail: e.health@welhat.gov.uk
Highways: Hertfordshire County Council
Planning: Planning Dept, Council Offices, The Campus, Welwyn Garden City AL8 6AE
Tel: 01707 357000
DX: 30075 Welwyn Garden City 1
e-mail: planning@welhat.gov.uk
Solicitor to the Council: Head of Law & Administration (Solicitor), Council Offices, The Campus, Welwyn Garden City AL7 6AE
Tel: 01707 357000 x 2575 Fax: 01707 357373
DX: 30075 Welwyn Garden City
e-mail: m.martinus@welhat.gov.uk
Water Services: Thames Water (Asset Data Services)

22.7 Broxbourne Borough Council

Website: www.broxbourne.gov.uk
Main Switchboard: 01992 785555
Conveyancing Searches: Land Charges Section, Borough Offices, Bishop's College, Churchgate, Cheshunt EN8 9XQ
Tel: 01992 785552 Fax: 01992 350555
e-mail: landcharges@broxbourne.gov.uk
Building Control: Dept of Environmental Services, Borough Offices, Bishop's College, Churchgate, Cheshunt EN8 9XQ
Tel: 01992 785566 Fax: 01992 350555
e-mail: buildingcontrol@broxbourne.gov.uk
Council Tax: Dept of Resources, Borough Offices,, Bishop's College, Churchgate, Cheshunt EN8 9XQ
Tel: 01992 785555
e-mail: counciltax@broxbourne.gov.uk
Environmental Health: Dept of Environmental Services, Borough Offices, Bishop's College, Churchgate, Cheshunt EN8 9XQ
Tel: 01992 785555 Fax: 01992 350555
e-mail: envhealth@broxbourne.gov.uk
Highways: Hertfordshire County Council
Planning: Dept of Environmental Services, Borough Offices, Bishop's College, Churchgate, Cheshunt EN8 9XQ
Tel: 01992 785510 Fax: 01992 350555
e-mail: planning@broxbourne.gov.uk
Solicitor to the Council: Mr G Miles, Borough Offices, Bishop's College, Cheshunt EN8 9XJ
Tel: 01992 785555 Fax: 01992 350555
e-mail: legal@broxbourne.gov.uk
Water Services: Thames Water

22.8 Three Rivers District Council

Website: www.threerivers.gov.uk
Main Switchboard: 01923 776611
Conveyancing Searches: Land & Property Information Section, Three Rivers Ho, Northway, Rickmansworth WD3 1RL
Tel: 01923 727107 Fax: 01923 727377
DX: 38271 Rickmansworth
e-mail: enquiries@threerivers.gov.uk
Note: Note: Customer Service Centre answers basic enquiries
Building Control: Building Control, Three Rivers Ho, Northway, Rickmansworth WD3 1RL
Tel: 01923 776611
e-mail: enquiries@threerivers.gov.uk
Council Tax: Council Tax (shared service), Town Hall, Watford, WD17 3EX
Tel: 01923 776611
e-mail: revenues@threerivers.gov.uk
Environmental Health: Environmental Health, Three Rivers Ho, Northway, Rickmansworth WD3 1RL
Tel: 01923 776611 Fax: 01923 896119
DX: 38271 Rickmansworth
e-mail: enquiries@threerivers.gov.uk
Highways: Hertfordshire County Council
Planning: Development Management, Three Rivers Ho, Northway, Rickmansworth WD3 1RL
Tel: 01923 776611 Fax: 01923 896119
DX: 38271 Rickmansworth
e-mail: enquiries@threerivers.gov.uk
Solicitor to the Council: Anne Morgan, Solicitor to the Council, Three Rivers Ho, Northway, Rickmansworth WD3 1RL
Tel: 01923 776611 Fax: 01923 896119
DX: 38271 Rickmansworth
e-mail: enquiries@threerivers.gov.uk
Water Services: Thames Water

22.9 Watford Borough Council

Website: www.watford.gov.uk
Main Switchboard: 01923 226400
Conveyancing Searches: Local Land Charges, Town Hall, Watford WD17 3EX
Tel: 01923 278282 Fax: 01923 278562
DX: 51529 Watford 2
e-mail: linda.edwards@watford.gov.uk
Building Control & Planning: Planning & Development, Town Hall, Watford WD17 3EX
Tel: 01923 226400 Fax: 01923 278478
DX: 51529 Watford 2
e-mail: planninganddevelopment@watford.gov.uk
Council Tax: Revenues & Benefits, Town Hall, Watford WD17 3EX
Tel: 01923 226400 Fax: 01923 226133
DX: 51529 Watford 2
e-mail: revenuesandbenefits@watford.gov.uk
Environmental Services: Environmental Services, Town Hall, Watford WD17 3EX
Tel: 01923 278503 Fax: 01923 230765
DX: 51529 Watford 2
e-mail: alan.gough@watford.gov.uk
Highways: Hertfordshire County Council
Legal & Property Services: Carol Chen, Town Hall, Watford WD17 3EX
Tel: 01923 278350 Fax: 01923 278366
DX: 51529 Watford 2
e-mail: carol.chen@watford.gov.uk
Water Services: Thames Water

22.10 Hertsmere Borough Council

Website: www.hertsmere.gov.uk
Main Switchboard: 020 8207 2277
Conveyancing Searches: Local Land Charges, Civic Offices, Elstree Way, Borehamwood WD6 1WA
Tel: 020 8207 7491 Fax: 020 8207 7555
DX: 45602 Borehamwood
e-mail: landcharges@hertsmere.gov.uk
Other depts: Civic Offices, Elstree Way, Borehamwood WD6 1WA
Tel: 020 8207 2277
DX: 45602 Borehamwood
e-mail: customer.services@hertsmere.gov.uk

Solicitor to the Council: Head of Legal Services, Civic Offices, Elstree Way, Borehamwood WD6 1WA Fax: 020 8207 7555
DX: 45602 Borehamwood
e-mail: legal@hertsmere.gov.uk
Water Services: Thames Water

24 Isle of Wight

24.0 Isle of Wight County Council (replaced by unitary)

Isle of Wight County Council replaced by the new unitary authority named Isle of Wight Council as from April 1, 1995.

24.1 Isle of Wight Council (U)

Website: www.iwight.com
Main Switchboard: 01983 821000
Conveyancing Searches: Local Land Charges Section, County Hall, High St, Newport, Isle of Wight PO30 1UD
Tel: 01983 821000 Fax: 01983 823344
DX: 56361 Newport IOW
e-mail: llcgeneralenquiries@iow.gov.uk
Council Tax: Director of Resources, Council Offices, The Broadway, Sandown, Isle of Wight PO36 9EA
Tel: 01983 821000 Fax: 01983 823900
DX: 56361 Newport IOW
e-mail: council.tax@iow.gov.uk
Environmental Health: Environmental Health, Jubilee Stores, The Quay, Newport, Isle of Wight PO30 2EH
Tel: 01983 823000 Fax: 01983 529804
DX: 56361 Newport IOW
e-mail: eh@iow.gov.uk
Highways & Drainage: Island Roads, St Christopher Ho, 42 Daish Way, Newport, Isle of Wight PO30 5XJ
Tel: 01983 822440
e-mail: info@islandroads.com
Planning & Building Control: Planning Services, Council Offices, Seaclose, Fairlee Rd, Newport, Isle of Wight PO30 2QS
Tel: 01983 821000 Fax: 01983 823563
DX: 56361 Newport IOW
e-mail: building.control@iow.gov.uk / development@iow.gov.uk
Solicitor to the Council: Strategic Manager, Legal Services, County Hall, High St, Newport, Isle of Wight PO30 1UD
Tel: 01983 821000 Fax: 01983 823699
DX: 56361 Newport (IOW)
e-mail: legal.services@iow.gov.uk
Water Services: Southern Water

25 Kent

25.0 Kent County Council

Website: www.kent.gov.uk/legal
Main Switchboard: 03000 414141
Search Address: Geoff Wild, Director of Governance & Law, Sessions Ho, County Hall, Maidstone ME14 1XQ
Tel: 01622 694302
DX: 123693 Maidstone 6
e-mail: geoff.wild@kent.gov.uk
Common Land Searches: Countryside Access Service, Commons Registration, 2nd Fl, Invicta Ho, County Hall, Maidstone ME14 1XX
Tel: 01622 221533 Fax: 01622 221636
DX: 123694 Maidstone 6
e-mail: land.searches@kent.gov.uk
Highways: Kent Highway Definition Team, 1st Fl, Invicta Ho, County Hall, Maidstone ME14 1XX
Tel: 0845 824 7800 Fax: 01622 66602
DX: 123690 Maidstone 6
e-mail: kent.highwayservices@kent.gov.uk
Solicitor to the Council: Geoff Wild, Director of Governance & Law, Sessions Ho, County Hall, Maidstone ME14 1XQ
Tel: 03000 416840
DX: 123693 Maidstone 6
e-mail: geoff.wild@kent.gov.uk

25.1 Dartford Borough Council

Website: www.dartford.gov.uk
Main Switchboard: 01322 343434
Conveyancing Searches: Strategic Directorate, Civic Centre, Home Gdns, Dartford DA1 1DR
Tel: 01322 343281 Fax: 01322 343047
DX: 142726 Dartford 7
e-mail: propertyinformation@dartford.gov.uk
Building Control: Building Control, Civic Centre, as before,
Tel: 01322 343238 Fax: 01322 343222
e-mail: building.control@dartford.gov.uk
Council Tax: Council Tax, Civic Centre, as before,
Tel: 01322 343700 Fax: 01322 343968
e-mail: council.tax@dartford.gov.uk
Environmental Health: Environmental Health Services, Civic Centre, as before,
Tel: 01322 343374 Fax: 01322 343963
e-mail: environmental.admin@dartford.gov.uk
Highways: Kent County Council, West Kent Divisional Offices, Joynes Ho, New Rd, Gravesend DA11 0AT
Tel: 01474 544061
Planning: Planning Dept, Civic Centre, as before,
Tel: 01322 343203 Fax: 01322 343047
e-mail: planning.dc@dartford.gov.uk
Solicitor to the Council: Marie Kelly-Stone, Legal Services, Civic Centre, Home Gdns, Dartford DA1 1DR
Tel: 01322 343416 Fax: 01322 343422
DX: 31908 Dartford
e-mail: marie.kelly-stone@dartford.gov.uk
Water Services: Thames Water & Southern Water

25.2 Gravesham Borough Council

Website: www.gravesham.gov.uk
Main Switchboard: 01474 564422
Conveyancing Searches: Land Charges, Civic Centre, Windmill St, Gravesend DA12 1AU
Tel: 01474 337245 Fax: 01474 337299
DX: 6804 Gravesend
e-mail: jayne.pike@gravesham.gov.uk
Building Control: STG Building Control Partnership, Foord Annexe, East Gate Ho, High St, Rochester ME1 1EW
Tel: 01634 331600 Fax: 01634 331299
DX: 6804 Gravesend
e-mail: building@stgbc.co.uk
Council Tax: Financial Services, Civic Centre, Windmill St, Gravesend DA12 1AU
Tel: 01474 337700 Fax: 01474 337453
DX: 6804 Gravesend
e-mail: debtors@gravesham.gov.uk
Environmental Health & Highways: Environmental & Public Health Services, Civic Centre, Windmill St, Gravesend DA12 1AU
Tel: 01474 337334 Fax: 01474 337296
DX: 6804 Gravesend

Solicitor to the Council: Mr Michael J Hayley, Head of Legal Services, Civic Centre, Windmill St, Gravesend DA12 1AU
Tel: 01474 337256 Fax: 01474 337299
DX: 6804 Gravesend
e-mail: mike.hayley@gravesham.gov.uk
Water Services: Southern Water

25.3 Medway Council (U)

Website: www.medway.gov.uk
Main Switchboard: 01634 306000
Conveyancing Searches: Local Land Charges, Medway Council, Gun Wharf, Dock Rd, Chatham, Kent ME4 4TR
Tel: 01634 332733 Fax: 01634 332845
DX: 140142 Chatham 8
e-mail: landcharges@medway.gov.uk
Building Control: STG Building Control Partnership, East Gate Ho, High St, Rochester ME1 1GW
Tel: 01634 331133 Fax: 01634 331299
e-mail: building@stgbc.org.uk
Council Tax: MRBS, Gun Wharf, Dock Rd, Chatham, Kent ME4 4TR
Tel: 01634 332222
e-mail: ctax@medway.gov.uk
Planning, Highways & Environmental Health: Regeneration, Community & Culture, Gun Wharf, Dock Rd, Chatham, Kent ME4 4TR
Tel: 01634 306000
Solicitor to the Council: Assistant Director, Legal and Corporate Services, Gun Wharf, Dock Rd, Chatham, Kent ME4 4TR
Tel: 01634 306000 Fax: 01634 332845
DX: 140142 Chatham 8
Water Services: Southern Water

25.4 Swale Borough Council

Website: www.swale.gov.uk
Main Switchboard: 01795 417850
Conveyancing Searches: Administration & Legal Service Unit, Swale Hse, East St, Sittingbourne ME10 3HT
Tel: 01795 417173/417331 Fax: 01795 417327
DX: 59900 Sittingbourne II
e-mail: landcharges@swale.gov.uk
Council Tax: Swale Borough Council, Swale Ho, as before,
Tel: 01795 417555 Fax: 01795 417488
e-mail: ctax@swale.gov.uk
Solicitor to the Council: Ms Monica Blades-Chase, Borough Solicitor, Legal & Democratic Services, Swale Ho, East St, Sittingbourne ME10 3HT
Tel: 01795 424341 Fax: 01795 417327
DX: 59900 Sittingbourne 11
e-mail: legal@swale.gov.uk
Water Services: Southern Water

25.5 Canterbury City Council

Website: www.canterbury.gov.uk
Main Switchboard: 01227 862000
Conveyancing Searches: Planning and Regeneration, Military Rd, Canterbury CT1 1YW
Tel: 01227 862178 Fax: 01227 862020
DX: 99713 Canterbury 3
e-mail: locallc@canterbury.gov.uk
Building Control: Planning and Regeneration, Military Rd, Canterbury CT1 1YW
Tel: 01227 862513 Fax: 01227 785970
e-mail: building.control@canterbury.gov.uk
Council Tax: Council Tax Section, Military Rd, Canterbury CT1 1YW
Tel: 01227 862000 / 862300 Fax: 01227 862020
e-mail: council.tax@canterbury.gov.uk
Environmental Health: Direct Services, Neighbourhood Services, Military Rd, Canterbury CT1 1YW
Tel: 01227 862202 Fax: 01227 450847
e-mail: envhealth@canterbury.gov.uk
Highways: Kent County Council
Planning – Development Control: Development Management, Military Rd, Canterbury CT1 1YW
Tel: 01227 862178 Fax: 01227 862020
DX: 99713 Canterbury 3
e-mail: development.management@canterbury.gov.uk
Planning – Local Plans: Planning Policy, Military Rd, Canterbury CT1 1YW
Tel: 01227 862178 Fax: 01227 862020
DX: 99713 Canterbury 3
e-mail: planning.policy@canterbury.gov.uk
Solicitor to the Council: Sarah Bowman, Head of Legal Services, Military Rd, Canterbury CT1 1YW
Tel: 01227 862011
DX: 99713 Canterbury 3
e-mail: sarah.bowman@canterbury.gov.uk
Water Services: Southern Water

25.6 Dover District Council

Website: www.dover.gov.uk
Main Switchboard: 01304 821199
Conveyancing Searches: Local Land Charges, Council Offices, White Cliffs Business Park, Dover CT16 3PJ
Tel: 01304 872354
DX: 6312 Dover
e-mail: landcharges@dover.gov.uk
Building Control: Assets & Building Control, Council Offices, White Cliffs Business Park, Dover CT16 3PJ
Tel: 01304 872495
DX: 6312 Dover
e-mail: buildingcontrol@dover.gov.uk
Council Tax: Council Offices, White Cliffs Business Park, Dover CT16 3PF
Tel: 01304 872199
DX: 6312 Dover
e-mail: customerservices@dover.gov.uk
Environmental Health: Regulatory Services, Council Offices, White Cliffs Business Park, Dover CT16 3PQ
Tel: 01304 872428 Fax: 01304 872217
DX: 6312 Dover
e-mail: envhealth@dover.gov.uk
Planning: Regeneration & Development, Council Offices, White Cliffs Business Park, Dover CT16 3PJ
Tel: 01304 872486
DX: 6312 Dover
e-mail: developmentcontrol@dover.gov.uk
Solicitor to the Council: Harvey Rudd, Legal, Council Offices, White Cliffs Business Park, Dover CT16 3PJ
Tel: 01304 872321 Fax: 01304 872325
DX: 6312 Dover
e-mail: legal@dover.gov.uk
Water Services: Southern Water

25.7 Thanet District Council

Website: www.thanet.gov.uk
Main Switchboard: 01843 577000
Conveyancing Searches: Local Land Charges Section, PO Box 9, Cecil St, Margate CT9 1XZ
Tel: 01843 577450 Fax: 01843 290906
DX: 30555 Margate
e-mail: land.charges@thanet.gov.uk
Solicitor to the Council: Corporate & Regulatory Manager, PO Box 9, Cecil St, Margate CT9 1XZ
Tel: 01843 577005 Fax: 01843 290906
DX: 30555 Margate
Water Services: Southern Water

25.8 Sevenoaks District Council

Website: www.sevenoaks.gov.uk
Main Switchboard: 01732 227000
Conveyancing Searches: Local Land Charges, Council Offices, Argyle Rd, Sevenoaks TN13 1HG
Tel: 01732 227000
DX: 30006 Sevenoaks
e-mail: land.charges@sevenoaks.gov.uk
Building Control: Building Control, Council Offices, Argyle Rd, Sevenoaks TN13 1HG
Tel: 01732 227376
e-mail: building.control@sevenoaks.gov.uk
Council Tax: Council Tax & Benefits, Council Offices, Argyle Rd, Sevenoaks TN13 1HG
Tel: 01732 227000 Fax: 01732 743052
DX: 30006 Sevenoaks
e-mail: revenues@sevenoaks.gov.uk
Environmental Health: Environmental Health Partnership – Dartford & Sevenoaks, Dartford Borough Council, Civic Centre, Home Gdns, Dartford DA1 1DR
Tel: 01322 343434 Fax: 01322 343963
DX: 142726 Dartford 7
e-mail: eh.support@dartford.gov.uk
Highways: Kent County Council
Planning: Planning Services, Council Offices, Argyle Rd, Sevenoaks TN13 1HG
Tel: 01732 227000 Fax: 01732 740693
DX: 30006 Sevenoaks
e-mail: planning.information@sevenoaks.gov.uk
Solicitor to the Council: Christine Nuttall, Head of Legal Services, Council Offices, Argyle Rd, Sevenoaks TN13 1HG
Tel: 01732 227245 Fax: 01732 743052
DX: 30006 Sevenoaks
e-mail: christine.nuttall@sevenoaks.gov.uk
Water Services: Southern Water or Thames Water

25.9 Tonbridge & Malling Borough Council

Website: www.tmbc.gov.uk
Main Switchboard: 01732 844522
Conveyancing Searches: Local Land Charges Section, Legal Services, Gibson Bldg, Gibson Dr, Kings Hill, West Malling ME19 4LZ
Tel: 01732 876124
e-mail: land.charges@tmbc.gov.uk
Building Control: Building Control, Council Offices, Argyle Rd, Sevenoaks TN13 1HG
Tel: 01732 227376
e-mail: building.control@sevenoaks.gov.uk
Council Tax: Financial Services, Gibson Bldg, Gibson Dr, Kings Hill, West Malling ME19 4LZ
Tel: 01732 876100 Fax: 01732 873530
e-mail: financial.services@tmbc.gov.uk
Environmental Health: Environmental Health & Housing Services, Gibson Bldg, Gibson Dr, Kings Hill, West Malling ME19 4LZ
Tel: 01732 876186 Fax: 01732 841421
e-mail: environmental.protection@tmbc.gov.uk
Highways: Kent County Council
Planning: Planning Services, Gibson Bldg, Gibson Dr, Kings Hill, West Malling ME19 4LZ
Tel: 01732 876318 Fax: 01732 876363
e-mail: planning.applications@tmbc.gov.uk
Solicitor to the Council: Mr Adrian Stanfield, Central Services Director, Gibson Bldg, Gibson Dr, Kings Hill, West Malling ME19 4LZ
Tel: 01732 876346 Fax: 01732 842170
e-mail: adrian.stanfield@tmbc.gov.uk
Water Services: Southern Water (majority); Thames Water

25.10 Maidstone Borough Council

Website: www.maidstone.co.uk
Main Switchboard: 01622 602000
Conveyancing Searches: Local Land Charges Section, Maidstone Ho, King St, Maidstone, Kent ME15 6JQ
Tel: 01622 602251
DX: 4819 Maidstone
e-mail: landcharges@maidstone.gov.uk
Building Control: Building Control, Maidstone Ho, King St, Maidstone, Kent ME15 6JQ
Tel: 01622 602220 Fax: 01622 602972
e-mail: building@maidstone.gov.uk
Council Tax: Revenues & Benefits, Maidstone Ho, King St, Maidstone, Kent ME15 6JQ
Tel: 01622 602003 (Revenues)/01622 602557 (Benefits)
Fax: 01622 602974 (Revenues)/01622 602974 (Benefits)
e-mail: counciltax@maidstone.gov.uk
Environmental Health: Environmental Health, Maidstone Ho, King St, Maidstone, Kent ME15 6JQ
Tel: 01622 602202 Fax: 01622 602972
Highways: Kent County Council
Planning: Planning, Maidstone Ho, King St, Maidstone ME15 6JQ
Tel: 01622 602736 Fax: 01622 602972
e-mail: developmentcontrol@maidstone.gov.uk
Solicitor to the Council: Paul Fisher, Head of Corporate Law & Monitoring,
Tel: 01622 602006 Fax: 01622 602974
DX: 4819 Maidstone
e-mail: paulfisher@maidstone.gov.uk
Water Services: Southern Water

25.11 Tunbridge Wells Borough Council

Website: www.tunbridgewells.gov.uk
Main Switchboard: 01892 526121
Conveyancing Searches: Land Charges Section, Town Hall, Royal Tunbridge Wells, Kent TN1 1RS
Tel: 01892 526121 Fax: 01892 534227
DX: 3929 Tunbridge Wells 1
e-mail: landcharges@tunbridgewells.gov.uk
Building Control: Building Control Services, Town Hall, as before,
Tel: 01892 526121 Fax: 01892 534227
DX: 3929 Tunbridge Wells 1
e-mail: building.control@tunbridgewells.gov.uk
Council Tax & Environmental Health: Revenues, Town Hall, as before,
Tel: 01892 526121 Fax: 01892 554133
DX: 3929 Tunbridge Wells 1
e-mail: counciltax@tunbridgewells.gov.uk
Highways: Kent County Council

Planning: Planning Dept, Town Hall, as before,
Tel: 01892 526121 Fax: 01892 534227
DX: 3929 Tunbridge Wells 1
Solicitor to the Council: Paul Cummins, Head of Legal Services, Town Hall, Tunbridge Wells TN1 1RS
Tel: 01892 526121 Fax: 01892 554027
DX: 3929 Tunbridge Wells 1
e-mail: info@tunbridgewells.gov.uk
Water Services: Southern Water

25.12 Ashford Borough Council

Website: www.ashford.gov.uk
Main Switchboard: 01233 331111
Conveyancing Searches: Planning & Development Services, Land Charges Section, Civic Centre, Tannery Lane, Ashford TN23 1PL
Tel: 01233 330284 Fax: 01233 330286
DX: 151140 Ashford (Kent) 7
e-mail: land.charges@ashford.gov.uk
Building Control: Civic Centre, as before
Council Tax (Commercial Properties): Canterbury City Council
Council Tax (Residential Properties): Civic Centre, as before
Environmental Health: Civic Centre, as before
Highways: Kent County Council
Planning: Civic Centre, as before
Solicitor to the Council: Mr T W Mortimer, Legal Services Manager, Civic Centre, Tannery Lane, Ashford TN23 1PL
e-mail: terry.mortimer@ashford.gov.uk
Note: Land Charges under jurisdiction of the Property Services Manager
Water Services: Southern Water

25.13 Shepway District Council

Website: www.shepway.gov.uk
Main Switchboard: 01303 853000
Conveyancing Searches: Local Land Charges, Civic Centre, Castle Hill Ave, Folkestone CT20 2QY
Tel: 01303 853206 Fax: 01303 853316
DX: 4912 Folkestone
e-mail: land.charges@shepway.gov.uk
Note: Tel No is Land Charges only.
Other depts: Civic Centre, as before
Solicitor to the Council: Amandeep Khroud, Principal Solicitor, Civic Centre, Castle Hill Ave, Folkestone CT20 2QY
Tel: 01303 853248 Fax: 01303 853548
DX: 4912 Folkestone
Water Services: Southern Water,
Note: (for 2.4.1, 2.4.2, 37 & 38 only)

26 Lancashire

26.0 Lancashire County Council

Website: www.lancashire.gov.uk
Main Switchboard: 0845 053 0000
Search Address: Legal Services Group, Office of the Chief Executive, PO Box 78, County Hall, Preston PR1 8XJ
Tel: 01772 533773 Fax: 01772 533612
DX: 710928 Preston County Hall

26.1 Lancaster City Council

Website: www.lancaster.gov.uk
Main Switchboard: 01524 582000
Conveyancing Searches: Legal Services, Town Hall, Dalton Sq, Lancaster LA1 1PJ
Tel: 01524 582034 Fax: 01524 582030
DX: 63531 Lancaster
e-mail: sbutterworth@lancaster.gov.uk
Building Control: Town Hall, Marine Rd, Morecambe LA4 5AF
Tel: 01524 582369 Fax: 01524 582353
DX: 63531 Lancaster
e-mail: buildingcontrol@lancaster.gov.uk
Council Tax: Town Hall, Lancaster LA1 1PJ
Tel: 01524 582000 Fax: 01524 582160
DX: 63531 Lancaster
Environmental Health: Morecambe Town Hall, Marine Rd, East Morecambe LA4 5AF
Tel: 01524 582676 Fax: 01524 582709
e-mail: environmentalhealth@lancaster.gov.uk
Highways: Lancashire County Council
Planning: Town Hall, Marine Rd, Morecambe LA4 5AF
Tel: 01524 582343 Fax: 01524 582323
DX: 63531 Lancaster
e-mail: developmentcontrol@lancaster.gov.uk
Solicitor to the Council: Sarah Taylor, Chief Officer (Governance), Town Hall, Lancaster LA1 1PJ
Tel: 01524 582025 Fax: 01524 582368
DX: 63531 Lancaster
e-mail: staylor@lancaster.gov.uk
Water: United Utilities

26.2 Wyre Borough Council

Website: www.wyre.gov.uk
Main Switchboard: 01253 891000
Conveyancing Searches: Local Land Charges Section, Wyre Civic Centre, Breck Rd, Poulton-le-Fylde FY6 7PU
Tel: 01253 891000 Fax: 01253 899000
e-mail: landcharges@wyre.gov.uk
Council Tax, Building Control, Environmental Health & Planning: address as before
Highways: Lancashire County Council
Solicitor to the Council: Mary Grimshaw, Senior Solicitor, Wyre Civic Centre, Breck Rd, Poulton-le-Fylde FY6 7PU
Tel: 01253 891000 Fax: 01253 899000
e-mail: mary.grimshaw@wyre.gov.uk
Water Services: United Utilities

26.3 Ribble Valley Borough Council

Website: www.ribblevalley.gov.uk
Main Switchboard: 01200 425111
Conveyancing Searches: Legal Dept, Local Land Charges Officer, Council Offices, Church Walk, Clitheroe BB7 2RA
Tel: 01200 414405 Fax: 01200 414485
Building Control: Geoff Lawson, Council Offices, Church Walk, Clitheroe BB7 2RA
Tel: 01200 414508
e-mail: geoff.lawson@ribblevalley.gov.uk
Council Tax: Mark Edmondson, Council Offices, Church Walk, Clitheroe BB7 2RA
Tel: 01200 414504
e-mail: mark.edmondson@ribblevalley.gov.uk
Environmental Health: James Russell, Council Offices, Church Walk, Clitheroe BB7 2RA
Tel: 01200 414466
e-mail: james.russell@ribblevalley.gov.uk
Highways: Lancashire County Council
Planning: John Macholc, Council Offices, Church Walk, Clitheroe BB7 2RA
Tel: 01200 414502
e-mail: john.macholc@ribblevalley.gov.uk
Solicitor to the Council: Diane Rice, Head of Legal & Democratic Services, Council Offices, Church Walk, Clitheroe BB7 2RA
Tel: 01200 414418 Fax: 01200 414485
e-mail: diane.rice@ribblevalley.gov.uk
Water Services: United Utilities

26.4 Blackpool Borough Council (U)

Website: www.blackpool.gov.uk
Main Switchboard: 01253 477477/477166
Conveyancing Searches: Local Land Charges, PO Box 17, Town Hall, Blackpool FY1 1NF
Tel: 01253 476334 Fax: 01253 476201
e-mail: land.charges@blackpool.gov.uk
Building Control: Building Control, PO Box 17, Town Hall, Blackpool FY1 1LZ
Tel: 01253 476219 Fax: 01253 476201
e-mail: building.control@blackpool.gov.uk
Council Tax: Revenues & Benefits Division, PO Box 50, Town Hall, Blackpool FY1 1AD
Tel: 01253 478741 Fax: 01253 478900
DX: 742010 Blackpool 18
e-mail: revenues@blackpool.gov.uk
Environmental Health: Neighbourhood Services, 125 Albert Rd, Blackpool FY1 4PW
Tel: 01253 477477 Fax: 01253 478010
e-mail: env.protection@blackpool.gov.uk
Highways: Transportation Division, Layton Depot, Plymouth Rd, Blackpool FY3 7HW
Tel: 01253 477477 Fax: 01253 476314
e-mail: customer.first@blackpool.gov.uk
Planning: Planning Division, PO Box 17, Corporation St, Blackpool FY1 1LZ
Tel: 01253 476229 Fax: 01253 476201
e-mail: planning@blackpool.gov.uk
Solicitor to the Council: Head of Legal Services, PO Box 11, Town Hall, Blackpool FY1 1NB
Tel: 01253 477450 Fax: 01253 477149
DX: 742010 Blackpool 18
e-mail: legal.services@blackpool.gov.uk

26.5 Fylde Borough Council

Website: www.fylde.gov.uk
Main Switchboard: 01253 658658
Conveyancing Searches: Land Charges, Strategic Development Services, Town Hall, Lytham St Annes FY8 1LW
Tel: 01253 658507
e-mail: landcharges@fylde.gov.uk
Building Control: Built Environment Unit, Town Hall, Lytham St Annes FY8 1LW
Tel: 01253 658658
e-mail: buildingcontrol@fylde.gov.uk
Council Tax: Town Hall, as before
Environmental Health: Consumer Wellbeing & Protection Business Unit, Town Hall, Lytham St Annes FY8 1LW
Highways: Lancashire County Council
Planning: Built Environment Unit, Town Hall, Lytham St Annes FY8 1LW
Tel: 01253 658658
e-mail: planning@fylde.gov.uk
Solicitor to the Council: Mr I Curtis, Governance & Partnerships, Town Hall, Lytham St Annes FY8 1LW
e-mail: ianc@fylde.gov.uk
Water Services: United Utilities

26.6 Preston City Council

Website: www.preston.gov.uk
Main Switchboard: 01772 906000
Conveyancing Searches: Local Land Charges, Town Hall, Lancaster Rd, Preston PR1 2RL
Tel: 01772 906119 Fax: 01772 906323
e-mail: landcharges@preston.gov.uk
Building Control, Environmental Health, Planning: Director of Environmental Services, Lancastria Ho, Lancaster Rd, Preston PR1 2RH
Tel: 01772 906581 Fax: 01772 906762
e-mail: devcon@preston.gov.uk
Council Tax: Director of Finance & Property Services, Town Hall, Lancaster Rd, Preston PR1 2RL
Tel: 01772 906969 Fax: 01772 906195
e-mail: ctax@preston.gov.uk
Highways: Lancashire County Council
Solicitor to the Council: Angela Harrison, Governance Director, Town Hall, Lancaster Rd, Preston PR1 2RL
Tel: 01772 906105 Fax: 01772 906195
e-mail: corporateservices@preston.gov.uk

26.7 South Ribble Borough Council

Website: www.southribble.gov.uk
Main Switchboard: 01772 421491
Conveyancing Searches: Local Land Charges Department, Civic Centre, West Paddock, Leyland PR25 1DH
Tel: 01772 625283 Fax: 01772 622287
e-mail: landcharges@southribble.gov.uk
Highways: Lancashire County Council
Other depts: Civic Centre, as before
Solicitor to the Council: David Whelan, Legal Services Manager, Civic Centre, West Paddock, Leyland PR25 1DH
Tel: 01772 625279 Fax: 01722 622287
e-mail: d.whelan@southribble.gov.uk
Water Services: United Utilities

26.8 West Lancashire Borough Council

Website: www.westlancs.gov.uk
Main Switchboard: 01695 577177
Conveyancing Searches: Corporate Services, Council Offices, 52 Derby St, Ormskirk L39 2DF
Tel: 01695 585160 Fax: 01695 585082
e-mail: stephen.tinsley@westlancs.gov.uk
Building & Planning: Planning Services, Council Offices, as before,
Tel: 01695 585132 Fax: 01695 585113
e-mail: john.harrison@westlancs.gov.uk
Council Tax: ACE, Council Offices, as before,
Tel: 01695 585005 Fax: 01695 585229
e-mail: shirley.stankowski@westlancs.gov.uk
Environmental Health: Community Services, Stanley Depot, Stanley Way, Skelmersdale WN8 8EE
Tel: 01695 585202 Fax: 01695 585126
e-mail: david.tilleray@westlancs.gov.uk
Highways: Lancashire County Council
Solicitor to the Council: Corporate Services, Council Offices, 52 Derby St, Ormskirk L39 2DF
Tel: 01695 585001 Fax: 01695 585082
e-mail: terry.broderick@westlancs.gov.uk
Water Services: United Utilities

26.9 Chorley Borough Council

Website: www.chorley.gov.uk
Main Switchboard: 01257 515151
Conveyancing Searches: Partnerships, Planning & Policy, Civic Offices, Union St, Chorley PR7 1AL
Tel: 01257 515151 Fax: 01257 515150
DX: 18411 Chorley 1
e-mail: landcharges@chorley.gov.uk
Building Control: Building Control, Civic Offices, Union St, Chorley PR7 1AL
Tel: 01257 515151 Fax: 01257 515150
DX: 18411 Chorley 1
e-mail: dcon@chorley.gov.uk

Council Tax: Council Tax Dept, Civic Offices, Union St, Chorley PR7 1AL
Tel: 01257 515151 Fax: 01257 515150
DX: 18411 Chorley 1
e-mail: contact@chorley.gov.uk
Environmental Health: People & Places, Civic Offices, Union St, Chorley PR7 1AL
Tel: 01257 515151 Fax: 01257 515150
DX: 18411 Chorley 1
e-mail: contact@chorley.gov.uk
Highways: Lancashire County Council Surveyors, Highways Info (Searches), PO Box 9 , Guild Ho, County Hall, Preston PR1 8RD
Tel: 01772 221611 Fax: 01772 533015
e-mail: enquiries@lancashire.gov.uk
Planning: Planning Dept, Civic Offices, Union St, Chorley PR7 1AL
Tel: 01257 515151 Fax: 01257 515150
DX: 18411 Chorley 1
e-mail: dcon@chorley.gov.uk
Solicitor to the Council: Chris Moister, Head of Governance, Town Hall, Market St, Chorley PR7 1DP
Tel: 01257 515151 Fax: 01257 515150
DX: 18411 Chorley 1
e-mail: chris.moister@chorley.gov.uk
Water Services: United Utilities

26.10 Blackburn with Darwen Borough Council (U)

Website: www.blackburn.gov.uk
Main Switchboard: 01254 585585
Conveyancing Searches: Regeneration & Environment Dept, Land Charges Section, Development Control, Lower Gnd Fl, Town Hall, King William St, Blackburn BB1 7DY
Tel: 01254 585242
e-mail: landcharges@blackburn.gov.uk
Building Control: Pennine Lancashire Building Control, Blackburn Enterprise Centre, Suite 11, Furthergate, Blackburn BB1 3HQ
Tel: 01254 505022 Fax: 01254 505023
e-mail: bc@pennine lancsplace.org
Council Tax: Director of Finance, Capita Finance, Council Tax Service, Admail 3860, Blackburn BB1 1WB
Tel: 0845 070 1066 Fax: 01254 273799
e-mail: revenues@blackburn.gov.uk
Environmental Health: Environment, Housing & Neighbourhoods, Whitedove Offices, Roman Rd Industrial Est, Davyfield Rd, Blackburn BB1 2LX
Tel: 01254 267637 Fax: 01254 267672
e-mail: environmental.health@blackburn.gov.uk
Note: public.protection@blackburn.gov.uk
Highways: Capita Property & Infrastructure, Capita Blackburn Business Centre, Castleway Ho, 17 Preston New Rd, Blackburn BB1 1AU
Tel: 01254 273493 Fax: 01254 273333
e-mail: highways@capita.co.uk
Planning: Regeneration & Environment Dept, Development Control, Lower Grnd Fl, Town Hall, King William St, Blackburn BB1 7DY
Tel: 01254 585960
e-mail: planning@blackburn.gov.uk
Solicitor to the Council: HR & Legal, Fl H, Town Hall, King William St, Blackburn BB1 7DY
Tel: 01254 585411
Water Services: United Utilities

26.11 Hyndburn Borough Council

Website: www.hyndburnbc.gov.uk
Main Switchboard: 01254 388111
Conveyancing Searches: Policy & Corporate Governance, Scaitcliffe Ho, Ormerod St, Accrington BB5 0PF
Tel: 01254 388111 Fax: 01254 392597
e-mail: enquiries@hyndburnbc.gov.uk
Council Tax: Council Tax Section, Financial Services Section, Town Hall, Broadway, Accrington BB5 1LA
Tel: 01254 388111 Fax: 01254 235308
e-mail: enquiries@hyndburnbc.gov.uk
Highways: Lancashire County Council
Housing & Environmental Health: Environmental Health Section, 20 Cannon St, Accrington BB5 1NJ
Tel: 01254 388111 Fax: 01254 386711
e-mail: enquiries@hyndburnbc.gov.uk
Planning & Building Control: Planning Section, Scaitcliffe Ho, Ormerod St, Accrington BB5 0PF
Tel: 01254 388111 Fax: 01254 391625
e-mail: planning@hyndburnbc.gov.uk
Solicitor to the Council: Jane Ellis, Head of Legal & Democratic Services, Scaitcliffe Ho, Ormerod St, Accrington BB5 0PF
Tel: 01254 388111 Fax: 01254 392597
e-mail: jane.ellis@hyndburnbc.gov.uk
Water Services: United Utilities

26.12 Burnley Borough Council

Website: www.burnley.gov.uk
Main Switchboard: 01282 425011
Conveyancing Searches: Local Land Charges, Town Hall, Manchester Rd, Burnley BB11 9SA
Tel: 01282 425011 x3262
e-mail: landcharges@burnley.gov.uk
Building Control & Planning: Housing & Development Control, Parker Lane Offices, Burnley BB11 2DT
Tel: 01282 425011 x3297
e-mail: planning@burnley.gov.uk
Council Tax: Revenues & Benefits Service, Contact Centre, Parker La, Burnley BB11 2DT
Tel: 01282 425011
e-mail: benefits@burnley.gov.uk / localtaxation@burnley.gov.uk
Environmental Health: Environmental Health, Parker Lane Offices, Parker La, Burnley BB11 2DT
Tel: 01282 425011 x3304
e-mail: envhealth@burnley.gov.uk
Highways: Lancashire County Council
Solicitor to the Council: Mr David Talbot, Senior Solicitor, Law & Regulation, Town Hall, Manchester Rd, Burnley BB11 9SA
Tel: 01282 425011 ext 7141
e-mail: dtalbot@burnley.gov.uk
Water Services: United Utilities

26.13 Pendle Borough Council

Website: www.pendle.gov.uk
Main Switchboard: 01282 661661
Conveyancing Searches: Land Charges Section, Democratic & Legal Section, Town Hall, Market St, Nelson BB9 7LG
Tel: 01282 661639 Fax: 01282 661630
DX: 14669 Nelson
e-mail: land.charge@pendle.gov.uk
Council Tax: Treasury Services, No.1 Market St, Nelson BB9 7LG
Tel: 01282 878993 Fax: 01282 608448
DX: 14669 Nelson

Environmental Health: Environmental Health & Urban Renewal, Fleet St Depot, Fleet St, Nelson BB9 7YQ
Tel: 01282 661661 Fax: 01282 661750
DX: 14669 Nelson
Highways: Lancashire County Council
Planning & Building Control: Planning & Building Control Services, Town Hall, Market St, Nelson BB9 7LG
Tel: 01282 661661 Fax: 01282 661720
DX: 14669 Nelson
Solicitor to the Council: Richard Townson, Democratic & Legal Services Manager, Town Hall, Market St, Nelson BB9 7LG
Tel: 01282 661650 Fax: 01282 661630
DX: 14669 Nelson
Water: Unitied Utilities & Yorkshire Water

26.14 Rossendale Borough Council

Website: www.rossendale.gov.uk
Main Switchboard: 01706 217777
Conveyancing Searches: Registrar of Local Land Charges, Futures Park, Bacup OL13 0BB
Tel: 01706 238632 Fax: 01706 214112
e-mail: locallandcharges@rossendalebc.gov.uk
Development & Environmental Services: Futures Park, Bacup, Lancs OL13 0BB
Tel: 01706 217777
Highways: Lancashire County Council
Planning: Planning, Futures Park, Bacup OL13 0BB
Tel: 01706 217777
Solicitor to the Council: Legal Services, Futures Park, Bacup, Lancs OL13 0BB
Tel: 01706 217777
Water Services: United Utilities

27 Leicestershire

27.0 Leicestershire County Council

Website: www.leics.gov.uk
Main Switchboard: 0116 232 3232
Search Address: Chief Executive's Dept, County Hall, Leicester Rd, Glenfield, Leicester LE3 8RA
Tel: 0116 232 3232 Fax: 0116 305 6260
DX: 729262 Leicester 30
e-mail: chiefexecs@leics.gov.uk
Solicitor to the Council: David Morgan, County Solicitor, County Hall, Leicester Rd, Glenfield, Leicester LE3 8RA
Tel: 0116 305 6006 Fax: 0116 305 6221
DX: 729262 Leicester 30
e-mail: elizabeth.mccalla@leics.gov.uk

27.1 North West Leicestershire District Council

Website: www.nwleicestershire.gov.uk
Main Switchboard: 01530 454545
Conveyancing Searches: Land Charges, Council Offices, Whitwick Rd, Coalville, Leicester LE67 3FJ
Tel: 01530 454513 Fax: 01530 454690
DX: 23662 Coalville
e-mail: land.charges@nwleicestershire.gov.uk
Building Control: David Darlington, Council Offices, Whitwick Rd, Coalville, Leicester LE67 3FJ
Tel: 01530 454692 Fax: 01530 454690
DX: 23662 Coalville
e-mail: building.control@nwleicestershire.gov.uk
Council Tax: North West Leicestershire Revenues & Benefits, Hinckley & Bosworth BC, Council Offices, Argents Mead, Hinckley LE10 1BZ
Tel: 01455 238141
Highways: Leicestershire County Council
Planning: Mr C Elston, Council Offices, Whitwick Rd, Coalville, Leicester LE67 3FJ
Tel: 01530 454545 Fax: 01530 454506
DX: 23662 Coalville
Solicitor to the Council: Mr D Gill, Council Offices, Whitwick Rd, Coalville, Leicester LE67 3FJ
Tel: 01530 454772 Fax: 01530 454506
DX: 23662 Coalville
e-mail: dave.gill@nwleicestershire.gov.uk
Water Services: Severn Trent Water

27.2 Charnwood Borough Council

Website: www.charnwood.gov.uk
Main Switchboard: 01509 263151
Conveyancing Searches: Land Charges, Strategic Support, Southfields, Southfields Rd, Loughborough LE11 2TN
Tel: 01509 634993/4/5 Fax: 01509 231260
DX: 19628 Loughborough
e-mail: land.charges@charnwood.gov.uk
Building Control: Building Control Services, Southfields Rd, Loughborough LE11 2TN
Tel: 01509 634924 Fax: 01509 260536
DX: 19628 Loughborough
e-mail: building.control@charnwood.gov.uk
Council Tax: Southfields Rd, Loughborough LE11 2TN
Tel: 01509 634884 Fax: 01509 634880
DX: 19628 Loughborough
e-mail: charnwood.counciltax@secure.capita.co.uk
Environmental Health: Housing & Health, Southfields, Southfields Rd, Loughborough LE11 2TN Fax: 01509 211703
DX: 19628 Loughborough
e-mail: env.house@charnwood.gov.uk
Highways: Leicestershire County Council
Planning: Development, Southfields Rd, Loughborough LE11 2TN
Tel: 0116 263151
DX: 19628 Loughborough
e-mail: development.control@charnwood.gov.uk
Solicitor to the Council: Sanjit Sull, Legal Services, Strategic Support, Council Offices, Southfields, Southfields Rd, Loughborough LE11 2TN
Tel: 01509 263151 Fax: 01509 263791
DX: 19628 Loughborough
Water Services: Severn Trent Water

27.3 Melton Borough Council

Website: www.melton.gov.uk
Main Switchboard: 01664 502502
Conveyancing Searches: Regulatory Services, Parkside, Station Approach, Burton St, Melton Mowbray LE13 1GH
Tel: 01664 502502 Fax: 01664 410283
e-mail: reception@melton.gov.uk
Building Control: Regulatory Services, Parkside, Station Approach, Burton St, Melton Mowbray LE13 1GH
Tel: 01664 502502
e-mail: buildingcontrol@melton.gov.uk
Council Tax: Revenues & Benefits, Parkside, Station Approach, Burton St, Melton Mowbray LE13 1GH
Tel: 01664 502502
e-mail: customerservices@melton.gov.uk
Environmental Health: Regulatory Services, Parkside, Station Approach, Burton St, Melton Mowbray LE13 1GH
e-mail: environmentalhealth@melton.gov.uk
Highways: Leicestershire County Council
Planning: Regulatory Services, Parkside, Station Approach, Burton St, Melton Mowbray LE13 1GH
e-mail: developmentcontrol@melton.gov.uk

Solicitor to the Council: Mrs V Wenham, Parkside, Station Approach, Burton St, Melton Mowbray LE13 1GH
Tel: 01664 502502 Fax: 01664 410283
e-mail: vwenham@melton.gov.uk
Water Services: Severn Trent Water and Anglian Water, Note: Anglian Water for Buckminster, Sewston, Cold Overton & Knossington only.

27.4 Hinckley & Bosworth Borough Council

Website: www.hinckley-bosworth.gov.uk
Main Switchboard: 01455 238141
Conveyancing Searches: Local Land Charges, Blaby District Council, Council Offices, Desford Rd, Narborough LE19 2EP
Tel: 0116 272 7578
e-mail: land.charges@blaby.gov.uk
Building Control: Building Control, Council Offices, Hinckley Hub, Rugby Rd, Hinckley LE10 0FR
Tel: 01455 238141 Fax: 01455 619897
e-mail: buildingcontrol@hinckley-bosworth.gov.uk
Council Tax: Head of Finance & ICT, Hinckley Hub, Rugby Rd, Hinckley LE10 0FR
Tel: 01455 238141 Fax: 01455 251519
e-mail: revenues@hinckley-bosworth.gov.uk
Environmental Health: Head of Health & Environment, Hinckley Hub, Rugby Rd, Hinckley LE10 0FR
Tel: 01455 238141 Fax: 01455 234590
e-mail: esadmin@hinckley-bosworth.gov.uk
Highways: Leicestershire County Council
Planning: Head of Culture & Development, Hinckley & Bosworth Borough Council, Hinckley Hub, Rugby Rd, Hinckley LE10 0FR
Tel: 01455 238141 Fax: 01455 619897
e-mail: planning@hinckley-bosworth.gov.uk
Solicitor to the Council: Miss Horton, Principal Solicitor, Hinkley Hub, Rugby Rd, Hinckley LE10 0FR
Tel: 01455 238141
DX: 716429 Hinckley
e-mail: legal.services@hinckley-bosworth.gov.uk
Water Services: Severn Trent Water

27.5 Leicester City Council (U)

Website: www.leicester.gov.uk
Main Switchboard: 0116 252 7000
Conveyancing Searches: Legal Services, New Walk Centre A10, Welford Pl, Leicester LE1 6ZG
Tel: 0116 252 6356 Fax: 0116 223 9102
DX: 10908 Leicester 1
e-mail: land-charges@leicester.gov.uk
Building Control: Regeneration & Culture Dept, as before,
Tel: 0116 252 6652 Fax: 0116 254 6316
e-mail: buildingcontrol@leicester.gov.uk
Council Tax: Housing Dept, Local Taxation, as before,
Tel: 0116 299 3900
e-mail: council.tax@leicester.gov.uk
Environmental Health & Highways: Regeneration & Culture Dept, as before,
Tel: 0116 252 7001 Fax: 0116 255 9289
e-mail: environment.helpline@leicester.gov.uk
Planning: Community Services Dept, Leicester Rd, Glenfield, Leicester LE3 8TD
Tel: 0116 252 7249 Fax: 0116 252 7273
e-mail: planningcontrol@leicester.gov.uk
Solicitor to the Council: Director of Legal Services, New Walk Centre, Welford Pl, Leicester LE1 6ZG
Tel: 0116 252 6302 Fax: 0116 285 8993
DX: 10908 Leicester 1
e-mail: legal-services@leicester.gov.uk
Water: Severn Trent

27.6 Blaby District Council

Website: www.blaby.gov.uk
Main Switchboard: 0116 275 0555
Conveyancing Searches: Local Land Charges, Council Offices, Desford Rd, Narborough, Leicester LE19 2EP
Tel: 0116 272 7579 Fax: 0116 272 7596
e-mail: land.charges@blaby.gov.uk
Building Control: Building Control, Council Offices, Desford Rd, Narborough, Leicester LE19 2EP
Tel: 0116 272 7533 Fax: 0116 272 7599
e-mail: building.control@blaby.gov.uk
Council Tax: Revenues, Council Offices, Desford Rd, Narborough. Leicester LE19 2EP
Tel: 0116 275 0555 Fax: 0116 275 0368
DX: 706890 Narborough
e-mail: revenues@blaby.gov.uk
Environmental Health: Environmental Health, Council Offices, Desford Rd, Narborough, Leicester LE19 2EP
Tel: 0116 275 0555
e-mail: environmental.health@blaby.gov.uk
Highways & Transportation: Leicestershire County Council
Planning: Planning Delivery Team, Council Offices, Desford Rd, Narborough, Leicester LE19 2EP
Tel: 0116 272 7705 Fax: 0116 272 7593
e-mail: planning@blaby.gov.uk
Solicitor to the Council: Corporate Services, Council Offices, Desford Rd, Narborough, Leicester LE19 2EP
Tel: 0116 272 7641 Fax: 0116 272 7596
e-mail: legal.services@blaby.gov.uk
Water Services: Severn Trent Water

27.7 Oadby & Wigston Borough Council

Website: www.oadby-wigston.gov.uk
Main Switchboard: 0116 288 8961
Conveyancing Searches: Land Charges, Council Offices, Bushloe Ho, Station Rd, Wigston LE18 2DR
Tel: 0116 257 2637 Fax: 0116 288 7828
e-mail: landcharges@oadby-wigston.gov.uk
Building Control: Built Environment, Council Offices, as before,
Tel: 0116 257 2657 Fax: 0116 257 2707
e-mail: buildingcontrol@oadby-wigston.gov.uk
Council Tax: Revenues & Benefits, Council Offices, as before
Tel: 0116 257 2625 Fax: 0116 288 7828
e-mail: revenues@oadby-wigston.gov.uk
Environmental Health: Environmental Health, Council Offices, as before,
Tel: 0116 257 2601 / 2669 Fax: 0116 257 2743
e-mail: envhealth@oadby-wigston.gov.uk
Highways: Leicestershire County Council
Planning: Development Control, Council Offices, as before,
Tel: 0116 257 2636 Fax: 0116 288 7828
e-mail: planning@oadby-wigston.gov.uk
Solicitor to the Council: Head of Corporate Resources, Council Offices, Bushloe Ho, Station Rd, Wigston LE18 2DR
Tel: 0116 257 2602 Fax: 0116 288 7828
e-mail: corporateresources@oadby-wigston.gov.uk
Water Services: Severn Trent Water

27.8 Harborough District Council

Website: www.harborough.gov.uk
Main Switchboard: 01858 828282
Conveyancing Searches: Registrar of Local Land Charges, The Symington Bldg, Adam & Eve St, Market Harborough LE16 7AG
Tel: 01858 821333 Fax: 01858 821000
DX: 27317 Market Harborough
e-mail: landcharges@harborough.gov.uk

Building Control: The Symington Bldg, Adam & Eve St, Market Harborough LE16 7AG
Tel: 01858 828282 Fax: 01858 821000
DX: 27317 Market Harborough
e-mail: building.control@harborough.gov.uk
Council Tax:
Tel: 01455 255791
DX: 27317 Market Harborough
e-mail: hdc.council.tax@hinckley-bosworth.gov.uk
Environmental Health: The Symington Bldg, Adam & Eve St, Market Harborough LE16 7AG
Tel: 01858 828282 Fax: 01858 821000
DX: 27317 Market Harborough
Highways: Leicestershire County Council
Planning: The Symington Bldg, Adam & Eve St, Market Harborough LE16 7AG Fax: 01858 821000
DX: 27317 Market Harborough
e-mail: planning@harborough.gov.uk
Solicitor to the Council: Ms Verina Wenham, Head of Legal Dept, The Symington Bldg, Adam & Eve St, Market Harborough LE16 7AG Fax: 01858 821000
DX: 27317 Market Harborough
Water Services: Anglian Water Services & Severn Trent Water

28 Lincolnshire

28.0 Lincolnshire County Council

Website: www.lincolnshire.gov.uk
Main Switchboard: 01522 552222
Search Address: Legal Services Lincolnshire, 45–49 Newland, Lincoln LN1 1XZ
Tel: 01522 552573 Fax: 01522 552138
DX: 701680 Lincoln 5
Solicitor to the Council: Mr D Coleman, Chief Legal Officer, Legal Services, Lincolnshire, 45–49 Newland, Lincoln LN1 1XZ
Tel: 01522 552134 Fax: 01522 552138
DX: 701680 Lincoln 5
e-mail: david.coleman@lincolnshire.gov.uk

28.1 West Lindsey District Council

Website: www.west-lindsey.gov.uk
Main Switchboard: 01427 676676
Conveyancing Searches: Local Land Charges Dept, Guildhall, Marshall's Yard, Gainsborough DN21 2NA
Tel: 01427 676624/5 Fax: 01427 675169
DX: 27214 Gainsborough
e-mail: locallandcharges@west-lindsey.gov.uk
Building Control: Building Control, Guildhall, Marshall's Yard, Gainsborough DN21 2NA
Tel: 01427 676672 Fax: 01427 675159
DX: 27214 Gainsborough
e-mail: building.control@west-lindsey.gov.uk
Council Tax: Revenues Dept, Guildhall, Marshall's Yard, Gainsborough DN21 2NA
Tel: 01427 676676 Fax: 01427 675170
Environmental Health: Public Protection, Guildhall, Marshall's Yard, Gainsborough DN21 2NA
Tel: 01427 676676 Fax: 01427 811579
Highways: Lincolnshire County Council
Planning: Planning Dept, Guildhall, Marshall's Yard, Gainsborough DN21 2NA
Tel: 01427 676676 Fax: 01427 675168
e-mail: planning.customer.care@westlindsey.gov.uk
Solicitor to the Council: West Lindsey District Council, Guildhall, Marshall's Yard, Gainsborough DN21 2NA
Tel: 01427 676676 Fax: 01427 675170
DX: 27214 Gainsborough
Water Services: Severn Trent Water and Anglian Water

28.2 East Lindsey District Council

Website: www.e-lindsey.gov.uk
Main Switchboard: 01507 601111
Conveyancing Searches: Local Land Charges, Tedder Hall, Manby Pk, Louth LN11 8UP
Tel: 01507 613006/613005 Fax: 01507 329047
e-mail: landcharges@e-lindsey.gov.uk
Building Control: Building Control, Tedder Hall, Manby Pk, Louth LN11 8UP
Tel: 01507 601111/613188 Fax: 01507 600206
e-mail: customerservices@e-lindsey.gov.uk
Council Tax: Finance Dept, Tedder Hall, Manby Pk, Louth LN11 8UP
Tel: 01507 601111 Fax: 01507 600206
e-mail: customerservices@e-lindsey.gov.uk
Environmental Health: Environmental Services Dept, Tedder Hall, Manby Pk, Louth LN11 8UP
Tel: 01507 601111 Fax: 01507 600206
e-mail: customerservices@e-lindsey.gov.uk
Highways: Highways Dept, City Hall, Beaumont Fee, Lincoln LN1 1DN
Tel: 01522 552222 Fax: 01522 552811
e-mail: customerservices@e-lindsey.gov.uk
Planning: Planning Dept, Tedder Hall, Manby Pk, Louth LN11 8UP
Tel: 01507 601111 Fax: 01507 600206
e-mail: customerservices@e-lindsey.gov.uk
Solicitor to the Council: Chief Executive's Dept, Tedder Hall, Manby Pk, Louth LN11 8UP
Tel: 01507 329401 Fax: 01507 600206
Water Services: Geodesys

28.3 Lincoln City Council

Website: www.lincoln.gov.uk
Main Switchboard: 01522 881188
Conveyancing Searches: Land Charges, Director of Development & Environmental Services, City Hall, Beaumont Fee, Lincoln LN1 1DF
Tel: 01522 873291 Fax: 01522 567934
e-mail: landcharges@lincoln.gov.uk
Building Control: Building Control, City Hall, Beaumont Fee, Lincoln LN1 1DF
Tel: 01522 873709 Fax: 01522 567934
e-mail: building.control@lincoln.gov.uk
Council Tax: Council Tax, Director of Resources, City Hall, Beaumont Fee, Lincoln LN1 1DB
Tel: 01522 881188 Fax: 01522 542569
Environmental Health: Director of Development & Environmental Services, City Hall, Beaumont Fee, Lincoln LN1 1DH
Tel: 01522 873249 Fax: 01522 567934
e-mail: environmental.health@lincoln.gov.uk
Highways: Lincolnshire County Council
Planning: Director of Development & Environmental Services, City Hall, Beaumont Fee, Lincoln LN1 1DF
Tel: 01522 873484 Fax: 01522 567934
e-mail: developmentteam@lincoln.gov.uk
Solicitor to the Council: Carolyn Wheater, City Hall, Beaumont Fee, Lincoln LN1 1DD
Tel: 01522 881188 Fax: 01522 521736
e-mail: legal@lincoln.gov.uk
Water Services: Geodesys

28.4 North Kesteven District Council

Website: www.n-kesteven.gov.uk
Main Switchboard: 01529 414155
Conveyancing Searches: Democratic Services, Council Offices, Kesteven St, Sleaford NG34 7EF
Tel: 01529 414155 Fax: 01529 413956
DX: 26909 Sleaford
e-mail: land_charges@n-kesteven.gov.uk
Building Control & Environmental Services: Council Offices, Kesteven St, Sleaford NG34 7EF
Tel: 01529 414155 Fax: 01529 413956
e-mail: customer_services@n-kesteven.gov.uk
Highways: Lincolnshire County Council
Highways & Planning: Transportation Group, District Planning Authority, Council Offices, Kesteven St, Sleaford NG34 7EF
Tel: 01529 414155 Fax: 01529 413956
e-mail: planning@n-kesteven.gov.uk
Water Services: Anglian/Geodesys

28.5 Boston Borough Council

Website: www.boston.gov.uk
Main Switchboard: 01205 314200
Conveyancing Searches: Licensing & Local Land Charges, Municipal Bldgs, West St, Boston PE21 8QR
Tel: 01205 314200 Fax: 01205 364604
e-mail: landcharges@boston.gov.uk
Building Control: Building Control, Municipal Bldgs, West St, Boston PE21 8QR
Tel: 01205 314200 Fax: 01205 314297
e-mail: buildingcontrol@boston.gov.uk
Council Tax: Council Tax, Municipal Bldgs, West St, Boston PE21 8QR
Tel: 01205 314200 Fax: 01205 364604
e-mail: revs@boston.gov.uk
Environmental Health: Environmental Health, Municipal Bldgs, West St, Boston PE21 8QR
Tel: 01205 314200 Fax: 01205 364604
e-mail: envserv@boston.gov.uk
Highways: Lincolnshire County Council
Other depts: Municipal Bldgs, West St, Boston PE21 8QR
Tel: 01205 314200 Fax: 01205 364604
e-mail: info@boston.gov.uk
Planning: Development Control, Municipal Bldgs, West St, Boston PE21 8QR
Tel: 01205 314200 Fax: 01205 364604
e-mail: planning@boston.gov.uk
Solicitor to the Council: Legal Services Lincolnshire, Municipal Bldgs, West St, Boston PE21 8QR
Tel: 01205 314200 Fax: 01205 314328
e-mail: legalservices@lincolnshire.gov.uk
Water Services: Anglian Water

28.6 South Kesteven District Council

Website: www.southkesteven.gov.uk
Main Switchboard: 01476 406080
Conveyancing Searches: Land Charges, St Peters Hill, Grantham NG31 6PZ
Tel: 01476 406080 Fax: 01476 406018
DX: 27024 Grantham
e-mail: landcharges@southkesteven.gov.uk
Highways: Lincolnshire County Council
Solicitor to the Council: Service Manager, Legal Services, Council Offices, St Peters Hill, Grantham NG31 6PZ
Tel: 01476 406080 Fax: 01476 406000
DX: 27024 Grantham
e-mail: j.armstrong@southkesteven.gov.uk
Water Services: Geodesys & Severn Trent Water

28.7 South Holland District Council

Website: www.sholland.gov.uk
Main Switchboard: 01775 761161
Conveyancing Searches: Land Charges Section, Planning & Development, Council Offices, Priory Rd, Spalding PE11 2XE
Tel: 01775 764445 Fax: 01775 762937
e-mail: landcharge@sholland.gov.uk
Building Control: Building Control Section, Council Offices, Priory Rd, Spalding PE11 2XE
Tel: 01775 761161 Fax: 01775 762937
e-mail: bcadmin@sholland.gov.uk
Council Tax: Finance, Council Offices, Priory Rd, Spalding PE11 2XE
Tel: 01775 761161 Fax: 01775 711253
e-mail: counciltax@sholland.gov.uk
Environmental Services: Environmental Services Dept, Council Offices, Priory Rd, Spalding PE11 2XE
Tel: 01775 761161 Fax: 01775 711054
e-mail: pollution@sholland.gov.uk
Highways: Lincolnshire County Council
Planning: Planning & Development, Council Offices, Priory Rd, Spalding PE11 2XE
Tel: 01775 761161 Fax: 01775 710772
e-mail: localplan@sholland.gov.uk
Solicitor to the Council: Head of Legal & Member Services, Council Offices, Priory Rd, Spalding PE11 2XE
Tel: 01775 761161 Fax: 01775 711253
e-mail: jscarsbrook@sholland.gov.uk
Water Services: Anglian Water

28.8 North Lincolnshire District Council (U)

Website: www.northlincs.gov.uk
Main Switchboard: 01724 296296
Conveyancing Searches: Land Charges, Civic Centre, Ashby Rd, Scunthorpe DN16 1AB
Tel: 01724 296246 Fax: 01724 281705
DX: 14717 Scunthorpe 1
e-mail: landcharges@northlincs.gov.uk
Building Control: Civic Centre, Ashby Rd, Scunthorpe DN16 1AB
Tel: 01724 296296 Fax: 01724 297872
Council Tax: Hewson Ho, Station Rd, Brigg DN20 8EG
Tel: 01724 296296
Environmental Health: Church Square Ho, PO Box 138, Scunthorpe DN15 6XP
Tel: 01724 296296 Fax: 01724 297897
Highways: 8–9 Billet Lane, Normanby Enterprise Pk, Scunthorpe DN15 9YH
Tel: 01724 296296
Planning: Civic Centre, Ashby Rd, Scunthorpe DN16 1AB
Tel: 01724 296296 Fax: 01724 297871
Solicitor to the Council: Mr Jon Hogg, Head of Legal Services, Civic Centre, Ashby Rd, Scunthorpe DN16 1AB
Tel: 01724 296296 Fax: 01724 296219
DX: 14717 Scunthorpe 1
Water Services: Geodesys & Severn Trent Water

28.9 North East Lincolnshire Borough Council (U)

Website: www.nelincs.gov.uk
Main Switchboard: 01472 313131
Conveyancing Searches: Local Searches, Law & Democratic Services, Municipal Offices, Town Hall Sq, Grimsby DN31 1HU
Tel: 01472 324001 Fax: 01472 324022
DX: 13536 Grimsby 1
e-mail: locallandcharges@nelincs.gov.uk

1

Building Control & Planning: Building Control & Planning, Origin 1, Origin Way, Europarc, Grimsby DN37 9TZ
Tel: 01472 324213 Fax: 01472 324216
e-mail: bc@nelincs.gov.uk
Note: planning@nelincs.gov.uk
Council Tax: Finance – Billing & Collection, Civic Offices, Knoll St, Cleethorpes DN35 8LN
Tel: 01472 326287 Fax: 01472 324322
e-mail: counciltax@nelincs.gov.uk
Environmental Health: Public Protection – Environmental Health, Thrunscoe Centre, Highgate, Cleethorpes DN35 8NX
Tel: 01472 324722 Fax: 01472 324767
e-mail: environmental.health@nelincs.gov.uk
Environmental Services: Neighbourhood Services, Doughty Rd, Grimsby DN32 0LL
Tel: 01472 326756 Fax: 01472 324819
e-mail: customerrequests@nelincs.gov.uk
Highways: Highways & Transport, Origin One, Origin Way, Genesis Europarc, Grimsby DN37 9TZ
Tel: 01472 324528 Fax: 01472 325657
e-mail: customerrequests@nelincs.gov.uk
Solicitor to the Council: Strategic Business Support, Municipal Offices, Town Hall Sq, Grimsby DN31 1HU
Tel: 01472 313131 Fax: 01472 324022
DX: 13536 Grimsby 1
e-mail: tony.maione@nelincs.gov.uk
Water Services: Anglian Water

29 Merseyside

29.1 Sefton Metropolitan Borough Council

Website: www.sefton.gov.uk
Main Switchboard: 0845 140 0845
Conveyancing Searches: Planning Services, Magdalen Ho, 30 Trinity Rd, Bootle L20 3NJ
Tel: 0151 934 2199
e-mail: land.charges@sefton.gov.uk
Building Control – South: Building Control, Ground Fl, Magdalen Ho, 30 Trinity Rd, Bootle L20 3NJ
Tel: 0151 934 4622 Fax: 0151 934 4627
e-mail: building@sefton.gov.uk
Common Land Searches: Land Charges, Planning Services, Magdalen Ho, 30 Trinity Rd, Bootle L20 3NJ
Tel: 0151 934 2199/2019
e-mail: land.charges@sefton.gov.uk
Council Tax: Council Tax Section, Finance Dept, PO Box 21, Bootle L20 3US
Tel: 0845 140 0845 Fax: 0151 934 4334
e-mail: rev-and-bens.web@sefton.gov.uk
Environmental Health – North Sefton: Environment Dept, Crown Bldgs, 9/11 Eastbank St, Southport PR8 1DL
Tel: 0151 934 2095 Fax: 0151 934 2220
e-mail: etscontact@sefton.gov.uk
Environmental Health – South Sefton: Environment Dept, Magdalen Ho, 30 Trinity Rd, Bootle L20 3NJ
Tel: 0845 140 0845 Fax: 0151 934 4276
e-mail: epd@sefton.gov.uk
Highways: Highways Development Council, Magdalen Ho, Bootle L20 3NJ
Tel: 0151 934 4175 Fax: 0151 934 4627
e-mail: hdc.planapps@sefton.gov.uk
Planning – South Sefton: Planning Dept, Ground Fl, Magdalen Ho, 30 Trinity Rd, Bootle L20 3NJ
Tel: 0151 934 3583 Fax: 0151 934 3587
e-mail: planning.department@sefton.gov.uk
Solicitor to the Council: Mrs Jill Coule, Head of Corporate Legal Services, Magdalen Ho, 30 Trinity Rd, Bootle L20 3NJ
Tel: 0151 934 2031
e-mail: jill.coule@sefton.gov.uk
Water Services: United Utilities

29.2 Liverpool City Council

Website: www.liverpool.gov.uk
Main Switchboard: 0151 233 3000
Conveyancing Searches: Local Search Unit, Municipal Bldgs, Dale St, Liverpool L2 2DH
Tel: 0151 233 3021
e-mail: landcharges@liverpool.gov.uk
Building Surveyors: Building Control, Municipal Bldgs, as above,
Tel: 0151 233 3021
e-mail: building.control@liverpool.gov.uk
Council Tax: Post Revenues Services, PO Box 834, Liverpool L69 2UT
Tel: 0151 233 3008/9
e-mail: revenue.service@liverpool.gov.uk
Environmental Health: Municipal Bldgs, as above,
Tel: 0151 233 4579
e-mail: environmental.health@liverpool.gov.uk
Highways: Highways and Transportation, 4th Fl, Cunard Bldgs, Liverpool L1 5JW
Tel: 0151 233 3001/3000
e-mail: highways.management@liverpool.gov.uk
Planning: Planning & Development Service, Municipal Bldgs, as above,
Tel: 0151 233 3021
e-mail: planningandbuildingcontrol@liverpool.gov.uk
Note: development.plans@liverpool.gov.uk
Solicitor to the Council: Mrs Janette McLoughlin, 2nd Fl, Municipal Bldgs, Dale St, Liverpool L69 2DH
Tel: 0151 225 2130
Water Services: United Utilities

29.3 St Helens Borough Council

Website: www.sthelens.gov.uk
Main Switchboard: 01744 676789
Conveyancing Searches: Licensing and Land Charges Officer, Wesley Ho, Corporation St, St Helens WA10 1HP
Tel: 01744 676289 Fax: 01744 676290
DX: 19484 St Helens
e-mail: landcharges@sthelens.gov.uk
Building Control: Chief Building Control Officer, Town Hall, Victoria Sq, St Helens WA10 1HP
Tel: 01744 676242 Fax: 01744 676255
DX: 19484 St Helens
e-mail: buildingcontrol@sthelens.gov.uk
Conveyancing: Assistant Chief Executive – Legal & Admin Services, Town Hall, Victoria Sq, St Helens WA10 1HP
Tel: 01744 673202 Fax: 01744 733337
DX: 19484 St Helens
e-mail: angelasanderson@sthelens.gov.uk
Council Tax: Assistant Chief Executive – Finance, Town Hall, Victoria Sq, St Helens WA10 1HP
Tel: 01744 676789 Fax: 01744 733337
DX: 19484 St Helens
e-mail: counciltax@sthelens.gov.uk
Environmental Health: Environmental Health Officer, Wesley Hse, Victoria Sq, St Helens WA10 1HE
Tel: 01744 676339 Fax: 01744 676365
DX: 19484 St Helens
e-mail: environmentalhealth@sthelens.gov.uk

Highways: Environmental Protection Dept, Wesley Hse, Corporation St, St Helens WA10 1HE
Tel: 01744 676386 Fax: 01744 673363
DX: 19484 St Helens
e-mail: jimdutton@sthelens.gov.uk
Planning: Development Services Mgr, Town Hall, Victoria Sq, St Helens WA10 1HP
Tel: 01744 676157 Fax: 01744 676154
DX: 19484 St Helens
e-mail: planning@sthelens.gov.uk
Solicitor to the Council: Angela Sanderson, Asst Chief Executive, Legal & Administrative Services, Town Hall, Victoria Sq, St Helens WA10 1HP
Tel: 01744 673202 Fax: 01744 733337
DX: 19484 St Helens
e-mail: angelasanderson@sthelens.gov.uk
Water Services: United Utilities

29.4 Knowsley Metropolitan Borough Council

Website: www.knowsley.gov.uk
Main Switchboard: 0151 489 6000
Conveyancing Searches: Corporate Resources, PO Box 24, Municipal Bldgs, Archway Rd, Huyton, Knowsley, Merseyside L36 9YU
Tel: 0151 443 3551 Fax: 0151 449 3650
DX: 713891 Huyton 3
e-mail: propertysearchinformation@knowsley.gov.uk
Building Control, Highways & Planning: Planning & Development, Yorkon Bldg, Archway Rd, Huyton, Knowsley L36 9FB
Tel: 0151 443 2380 Fax: 0151 480 0267
e-mail: planning@knowsley.gov.uk
Council Tax: Finance, Municipal Bldg, Cherryfield Drive, Kirkby, Knowsley L33 1TX
Tel: 0151 443 4476 Fax: 0151 443 3661
e-mail: local.taxation@knowsley.gov.uk
Environmental Health: Public Health & Consumer Protection, Municipal Bldgs, Cherryfield Dr, Kirkby L32 1TX
Tel: 0151 443 4723 Fax: 0151 289 7488
e-mail: environmentalhealth@knowsley.gov.uk
Solicitor to the Council: Mr M Dearing, Head of Legal Services, Municipal Bldg, Archway Rd, Huyton, Knowsley L36 9YU
Tel: 0151 443 3672 Fax: 0151 443 3550
DX: 713891 Huyton 3
e-mail: mike.dearing@knowsley.gov.uk
Water Services: North West Water

29.5 Wirral Metropolitan Borough Council

Website: www.wirral.gov.uk
Main Switchboard: 0151 606 2000
Conveyancing Searches: Local Land Charges Section, Regeneration, Housing & Planning, North Annexe, Wallasey Town Hall, Brighton St, Wallasey, Wirral CH44 8ED
Tel: 0151 691 8256 Fax: 0151 691 8532
e-mail: landcharges@wirral.gov.uk
Building Control: Building Control, North Annexe, Brighton St, Wallasey CH44 8ED
Tel: 0151 691 8454
e-mail: buildingcontrol@wirral.gov.uk
Council Tax: Council Tax Section, PO Box 2, Birkenhead CH41 6BU
Tel: 0151 666 4128 Fax: 0151 666 3334/8
e-mail: counciltax@wirral.gov.uk
Environmental Health: Private Sector Housing, North Annexe, Brighton St, Wallasey CH44 8ED
Tel: 0151 691 8156
Highways: Highway Maintenance Admin Team, Cheshire Lines Bldg, Canning St, Birkenhead CH41 1ND
Tel: 0151 606 2004 Fax: 0151 606 2582
e-mail: shaunbrady@wirral.gov.uk
Planning: Planning & Economic Devlt, Regeneration, North Annexe, Wallasey Town Hall, Brighton St, Wallasey, Wirral CH44 8ED
Tel: 0151 691 8125 Fax: 0151 691 8532
e-mail: planed@wirral.gov.uk
Solicitor to the Council: Dept of Law, HR and Asset Management, Town Hall, Brighton St, Wallasey CH44 8ED
Tel: 0151 691 8498 Fax: 0151 691 8468/0151 691 8482
Water Services: United Utilities & Babtie Group

1

30 Norfolk

30.0 Norfolk County Council

Website: www.norfolk.gov.uk
Main Switchboard: 0344 800 8020
Search Address: Environment, Transport & Development Dept, County Hall, Martineau Lane, Norwich, Norfolk NR1 2SG
Tel: 01603 223224 Fax: 01603 627258
DX: 135927 Norwich 13
e-mail: etd.registry@norfolk.gov.uk
Solicitor to the Council: Chief Executive – Legal Services, County Hall, Martineau Lane, Norwich NR1 2DH
Tel: 0344 800 8020 Fax: 01603 222899
DX: 135926 Norwich 13 (Legal Services)
e-mail: information@norfolk.gov.uk

30.1 North Norfolk District Council

Website: www.northnorfolk.org
Main Switchboard: 01263 513811
Conveyancing Searches: Land Charges Section, Council Offices, Holt Rd, Cromer NR27 9EN
Tel: 01263 516013
DX: 31008 Cromer
e-mail: landcharges@north-norfolk.gov.uk; electronic.search@north-norfolk.gov.uk
Council Tax, Building Control, Environmental Health & Planning: Council Offices, Holt Rd, Cromer NR27 9EN
Tel: 01263 513811 Fax: 01263 515042
DX: 31008 Cromer
e-mail: ctaxreg@north-norfolk.gov.uk
Note: building.control@north-norfolk.gov.uk; ep@north-norfolk.gov.uk; planningpolicy@north-norfolk.gov.uk
Highways: Norfolk County Council
Solicitor to the Council: Ms E Duncan, Legal Services Manager, Council Offices, Holt Rd, Cromer NR27 9EN
Tel: 01263 516045 Fax: 01263 515042
DX: 31008 Cromer
e-mail: emma.duncan@north-norfolk.gov.uk
Water Services: Anglian Water/Geodesys

30.2 King's Lynn & West Norfolk Borough Council

Website: www.west-norfolk.gov.uk
Main Switchboard: 01553 616200
Conveyancing Searches: Central Services, King's Ct, Chapel St, King's Lynn PE30 1EX
Tel: 01553 616268 Fax: 01553 616728
DX: 57825 King's Lynn
e-mail: land.charges@west-norfolk.gov.uk
Highways: Norfolk County Council
Other depts: as before

Solicitor to the Council: Nicola Leader, Legal Services Manager, King's Ct, Chapel St, King's Lynn PE30 1EX
Tel: 01553 616270 Fax: 01533 616728
DX: 57825 King's Lynn
e-mail: nicola.leader@west-norfolk.gov.uk
Water Services: Anglian Water/Geodesys

30.3 Breckland District Council

Website: www.breckland.gov.uk
Main Switchboard: 01362 656870
Conveyancing Searches: Land Charges, Elizabeth Ho, Walpole Loke, Dereham NR19 1EE
Tel: 01362 656384 Fax: 01362 696771
DX: 743950 Dereham 2
e-mail: land.charges@breckland.gov.uk
Council Tax: Revenues, Breckland Ho, St Nicholas St, Thetford IP24 1BT
Tel: 01362 656871 Fax: 01842 756513
e-mail: finance@breckland.gov.uk
Environmental Health: Environmental Health, Elizabeth Ho, Walpole Loke, Dereham NR19 1EE
Tel: 01362 656878
e-mail: healthandsafety@breckland.gov.uk
Highways: Norfolk County Council
Planning & Building Control: Planning & Building Control, Elizabeth Ho, Walpole Loke, Dereham NR19 1EE
Tel: 01362 656228 Fax: 01362 696771
DX: 743950 Dereham 2
e-mail: building.control@breckland.gov.uk
Solicitor to the Council: District Solicitor, Legal Services, Elizabeth Ho, Walpole Loke, Dereham NR19 1EE
Tel: 01362 656870 Fax: 01362 690821
DX: 743950 Dereham 2
Water Services: Geodesys

30.4 Norwich City Council

Website: www.norwich.gov.uk
Main Switchboard: 0844 980 3333
Conveyancing Searches: Land Charges Section, City Hall, St Peter's St, Norwich NR2 1NH
Tel: 01603 212050 Fax: 01603 213000
DX: 5278 Norwich
e-mail: landsearches@norwich.gov.uk
Building Control: CNC Building Control Consultancy, South Norfolk District Council, South Norfolk Ho, Swan La, Long Stratton NR15 2XE
Tel: 01508 535300
e-mail: enquiries@cncbuildingcontrol.gov.uk
Council Tax: Revenue Services, City Hall, Norwich NR2 1WJ
Tel: 0844 980 3333 Fax: 01603 213000
e-mail: revenues@norwich.gov.uk
Environmental Health: Environmental Health, City Hall, St Peter's St, Norwich NR2 1NH
Tel: 0844 980 3333 Fax: 01603 213002
Highways: Transportation Policy, City Hall, St Peter's St, Norwich NR2 1NH
Tel: 0344 980 3333 Fax: 01603 213000
e-mail: info@norwich.gov.uk
Planning: Planning, Directorate of Development, City Hall, St Peter's St, Norwich NR2 1WP
Tel: 0844 980 3333 Fax: 01603 213000
e-mail: info@norwich.gov.uk
Solicitor to the Council: David Johnson, Solicitor to the Council, NPLAN, County Hall, Marineau La, Norwich NR1 2DH
Tel: 01603 222215
e-mail: enquiries@nplan.co.uk
Water Services: Anglian Water

30.5 Broadland District Council

Website: www.broadland.gov.uk
Main Switchboard: 01603 431133
Conveyancing Searches: Local Land Charges, Thorpe Lodge, 1 Yarmouth Rd, Thorpe St Andrew, Norwich NR7 0DU
Tel: 01603 430586
e-mail: land.charges@broadland.gov.uk
Council Tax: Revenue Services, Thorpe Lodge, 1 Yarmouth Rd, Thorpe St Andrew, Norwich NR7 0DU
Tel: 01603 430600/01 Fax: 01603 430531
e-mail: council.tax@broadland.gov.uk
Environmental Health: Environmental Services, Thorpe Lodge, 1 Yarmouth Rd, Thorpe St Andrew, Norwich NR7 0DU
Tel: 01603 430534 Fax: 01603 430616
e-mail: environ.protection@broadland.gov.uk
Highways: Norfolk County Council
Planning: Planning, Thorpe Lodge, 1 Yarmouth Rd, Thorpe St Andrew, Norwich NR7 0DU
Tel: 01603 430509
e-mail: planning.administration@broadland.gov.uk
Water Services: Geodesys

30.6 Great Yarmouth Borough Council

Website: www.great-yarmouth.gov.uk
Main Switchboard: 01493 856100
Conveyancing Searches: Land Charges, Town Hall, Hall Plain, Great Yarmouth NR30 2QF
Tel: 01493 846650/664
DX: 41121 Great Yarmouth 1
e-mail: landcharges@great-yarmouth.gov.uk
Building Control: Building Control, Town Hall, Hall Plain, Great Yarmouth NR30 2QF
Tel: 01493 846396
DX: 41121 Great Yarmouth 1
e-mail: buildingcontrol@great-yarmouth.gov.uk
Council Tax: Council Tax, Greyfriars Ho, Greyfriars Way, Great Yarmouth NR30 2QF
Tel: 01493 846244
DX: 41121 Great Yarmouth 1
e-mail: ctax@great-yarmouth.gov.uk
Environmental Health: Environmental Health Dept, Town Hall, Hall Plain, Great Yarmouth NR30 2QF
Tel: 01493 846478
DX: 41121 Great Yarmouth 1
e-mail: health@great-yarmouth.gov.uk
Highways: Norfolk County Council
Planning: Planning, Town Hall, Hall Plain, Great Yarmouth NR30 2QF
Tel: 01493 846169/695
DX: 41121 Great Yarmouth 1
e-mail: plan@great-yarmouth.gov.uk
Solicitor to the Council: Mr C F Skinner, nplaw, County Hall, Martineau Lane, Norwich NR1 2DH
e-mail: general.nplaw@norfolk.gov.uk
Water Services: Anglian Water and Essex & Suffolk Water

30.7 South Norfolk District Council

Website: www.south-norfolk.gov.uk
Main Switchboard: 01508 533633
Conveyancing Searches: Land Charges Team, South Norfolk Ho, Swan La, Long Stratton NR15 2XE
Tel: 01508 533676 Fax: 01508 533625
e-mail: landcharges@s-norfolk.gov.uk
Building Control: CNC Building Control, South Norfolk Ho, Swan La, Long Stratton NR15 2XE
Tel: 01508 535300
e-mail: enquiries@cncbuildingcontrol.gov.uk

Council Tax: Council Tax, South Norfolk Ho, as before,
Tel: 01508 533775 Fax: 01508 533622
DX: 130080 Long Stratton 2
e-mail: counciltax@s-norfolk.gov.uk
Highways: Norfolk County Council
Planning: Planning, South Norfolk Ho, Swan Ln, Long Stratton NR15 2XE
Tel: 01508 533813
e-mail: planning@cncbuildingcontrol.gov.uk
Solicitor to the Council: NPLAW, Norfolk County Council, County Hall, Martineau La, Norwich NR1 2DH
Tel: 01603 638123
Water Services: Anglian Water/Geodesys

31 Northamptonshire

31.0 Northamptonshire County Council

Website: www.northamptonshire.gov.uk
Main Switchboard: 01604 236236
Search Address: Investigation, Searches & Definitive Map, Northamptonshire Highways, Riverside Ho, Bedford Rd, Northampton NN1 5XN
Tel: 01604 364420
e-mail: landsearches@kierwsp.co.uk
Solicitor to the Council: Ms Penny Osborne, Head of Legal Services, PO Box 104, County Hall, Northampton NN1 1AW
Tel: 01604 237036
e-mail: posborne@northamptonshire.gov.uk

31.1 Corby Borough Council

Website: www.corby.gov.uk
Main Switchboard: 01536 464000
Conveyancing Searches: Registrar of Local Land Charges, Legal & Democratic Service, Deene Ho, New Post Office Sq, Corby NN17 1GD
Tel: 01536 464026 Fax: 01536 464645
DX: 12915 Corby
e-mail: land.charges@corby.gov.uk
Council Tax & Building Control: Building Control, Deene Ho, New Post Office Sq, Corby NN17 1GD
Tel: 01536 464171 Fax: 01536 464634
DX: 12915 Corby
e-mail: building.control@corby.gov.uk
Environmental Health: Environmental Health Dept, Deene Ho, New Post Office Sq, Corby NN17 1GD
Tel: 01536 464052 Fax: 01536 464644
DX: 12915 Corby
Highways: Northamptonshire Highways
Planning: Planning, Deene Ho, New Post Office Sq, Corby NN17 1GD
Tel: Planning 01536 464177 Fax: Planning 01536 464634
DX: 12915 Corby
e-mail: planning.services@corby.gov.uk
Solicitor to the Council: Legal Services, Deene Ho, New Post Office Sq, Corby NN17 1GD
Tel: 01536 464679 Fax: 01536 464109
DX: 12915 Corby
e-mail: nigel.channer@corby.gov.uk
Water Services: Geodesys

31.2 Kettering Borough Council

Website: www.kettering.gov.uk
Main Switchboard: 01536 410333
Conveyancing Searches: Head of Development Services, Municipal Offices, Bowling Green Rd, Kettering NN15 7QX
Tel: 01536 534220 Fax: 01536 410795
e-mail: landcharges@kettering.gov.uk
Building Control: Head of Development Services, as before,
Tel: 01536 534250 Fax: 01536 410795
e-mail: buildingcontrol@kettering.gov.uk
Council Tax: Head of Income & Debt Management, Municipal Offices, Bowling Green Rd, Kettering NN15 7QX
Tel: 01536 534235 Fax: 01536 410795
e-mail: counciltax@kettering.gov.uk
Environmental Health: Head of Environmental Health, as before,
Tel: 01536 534307 Fax: 01536 410795
e-mail: environmentalhealth@kettering.gov.uk
Highways: Northamptonshire County Council
Planning: Head of Development Services, as before,
Tel: 01536 534316 Fax: 01536 410795
e-mail: planning@kettering.gov.uk
Solicitor to the Council: Head of Democratic & Legal Services, Municipal Offices, Bowling Green Rd, Kettering NN15 7QX
Tel: 01536 534209 Fax: 01536 532424
Water Services: Geodesys

31.3 East Northamptonshire District Council

Website: www.east-northamptonshire.gov.uk
Main Switchboard: 01832 742000
Conveyancing Searches: Land Charges Manager, Cedar Dr, Thrapston NN14 4LZ
Tel: 01832 742141 Fax: 01832 734839
DX: 701611 Thrapston
e-mail: lcharges@east-northamptonshire.gov.uk
Building Control: address as before,
Tel: 01832 742139 Fax: 01832 742128
e-mail: building.control@east-northamptonshire.gov.uk
Council Tax: address as before,
Tel: 01832 742000
e-mail: revenues@east-northamptonshire.gov.uk
Environmental Health: Environmental Services, address as before,
Tel: 01832 742000
e-mail: environment@east-northamptonshire.gov.uk
Highways: Northamptonshire County Council
Planning: Planning Services, as before,
Tel: 01832 742225
e-mail: planning@east-northamptonshire.gov.uk
Solicitor to the Council: Mr N Pritchard, Legal Officer, Cedar Dr, Thrapston NN14 4LZ
Tel: 01832 742151 Fax: 01832 734839
DX: 701611 Thrapston
e-mail: ndpritchard@east-northamptonshire.gov.uk
Water Services: Anglian Water/Geodesys

31.4 Daventry District Council

Website: www.daventrydc.gov.uk
Main Switchboard: 01327 871100
Conveyancing Searches: Land Charges Section, Civic Offices, Lodge Rd, Daventry NN11 4FP
Tel: 01327 302314
DX: 21965 Daventry
e-mail: jrussell@daventrydc.gov.uk
Building Control & Planning: Planning & Building Control Sections, Civic Offices, Lodge Rd, Daventry NN11 4FP
Tel: 01327 871100 Fax: 01327 300011
DX: 21965 Daventry
Council Tax: Finance, Civic Offices, Lodge Rd, Daventry NN11 4FP
Tel: 01327 871100
DX: 21965 Daventry

Environmental Health: Environmental Health Section, Civic Offices, Lodge Rd, Daventry NN11 4FP
Tel: 01327 302464 Fax: 01327 300011
DX: 121965 Daventry
Highways: Land Searches,
Tel: 01604 364470 Fax: 01604 654466
DX: 12481 Northampton 1
Solicitor to the Council: District Law, Civic Offices, Lodge Rd, Daventry NN11 4FP
Tel: 01327 302426 Fax: 01327 300011
DX: 21965 Daventry
e-mail: geoffhollands@kettering.gov.uk
Water Services: Anglian Water, Severn Trent Water and Thames Water (Western Division)

31.5 Northampton Borough Council

Website: www.northampton.gov.uk
Main Switchboard: 01604 837837
Conveyancing Searches: Local Land Charges, John Dryden Ho, The Lakes, Bedford Rd, Northampton NN4 7YD
Tel: 01604 363936 Fax: 01604 838503
e-mail: landcharges@northampton.gov.uk; landcharges@northamptonshire.gov.uk
Building Control: Building Control, The Guildhall, St Giles Sq, Northampton NN1 1DE
Tel: 01604 838920 Fax: 01604 838984
Council Tax: Council Tax Dept, The Guildhall, St Giles Sq, Northampton NN1 1DE
Tel: 01604 837500 Fax: 01604 838768
Environmental Health: Environmental Health, Westbridge, St Jamesmill Rd, Northampton NN5 5JW
Tel: 01604 838789 Fax: 01604 838755
Highways: Northamptonshire County Council (MGWSP)
Planning: Planning, Surveying & Highways Depts, The Guildhall, St Giles Sq, Northampton NN1 1DE
Tel: 01604 838910 Fax: 01604 838795
Solicitor to the Council: Borough Secretary, Legal Services, The Guildhall, St Giles Sq, Northampton NN1 1DE
Tel: 01604 837837 Fax: 01604 838554
e-mail: solicitors@northampton.gov.uk
Water Services: Geodesys

31.6 Wellingborough Borough Council

Website: www.wellingborough.gov.uk
Main Switchboard: 01933 229777
Conveyancing Searches: Local Land Charges, Council Offices, Swanspool Ho, Doddington Rd, Wellingborough NN8 1BP
Tel: 01933 231568
e-mail: llcsearches@wellingborough.gov.uk
Building Control & Health: Environmental Protection & Building Control, Swanspool Ho, Doddington Rd, Wellingborough NN8 1BP
Tel: 01933 229777
Council Tax: Revenues & Benefits, Council Offices, 1 Tithe Barn Rd, Wellingborough NN8 1BN
Tel: 01933 229777 Fax: 01933 231629
e-mail: revenueservices@wellingborough.gov.uk
Highways: Northamptonshire County Council
Planning: Planning & Local Development, Council Offices, Swanspool Ho, Doddington Rd, Wellingborough NN8 1PB
Tel: 01933 229777
e-mail: planning@wellingborough.gov.uk
Solicitor to the Council: Head of Legal Services, Council Offices, Swanspool Ho, Doddington Rd, Wellingborough NN8 1BP
Tel: 01933 229777 Fax: 01933 231506
Water Services: Anglian Water

31.7 South Northamptonshire District Council

Website: www.southnorthants.gov.uk
Main Switchboard: 01327 322322
Conveyancing Searches: Law & Governance, The Forum, Moat La, Towcester NN12 6AD
Tel: 01327 322116 Fax: 01327 322114
DX: 16938 Towcester
e-mail: landcharges@southnorthants.gov.uk
Highways: Northamptonshire County Council
Solicitor to the Council: Kevin Lane, Head of Law & Governance, The Forum, as above,
Tel: 0300 0030107 Fax: 01327 322114
DX: 16938 Towcester
e-mail: kevin.lane@cherwellandsouthnorthants.gov.uk
Water Services: Anglian Water and Thames Water

32 Northumberland

32.0 Northumberland County Council (abolished)

County Council abolished as from 1 April 2009. Berwick-upon-Tweed BC, Alnwick DC, Tynedale DC, Castle Morpeth BC, Wansbeck DC, Blyth Valley BC now combined with Northumberland County Council to form Northumberland County Council (Unitary).

32.1 Northumberland Council (U)

Website: www.northumberland.gov.uk
Main Switchboard: 0845 600 6400
Conveyancing Searches: Land Charges Section, County Hall, Morpeth NE61 2EF
Tel: 0845 600 6400 Fax: 01670 533238
e-mail: landchargesoffice@northumberland.gov.uk
Building Control: Building Control, Loansdean, Morpeth NE61 2AP
e-mail: buildingcontrol@northumberland.gov.uk
Council Tax: Council Tax Dept, Wansbeck Sq, Ashington NE63 9XL
Tel: 0845 600 6400 Fax: 01670 534117
e-mail: ask@northumberland.gov.uk
Environmental Health: County Hall, Morpeth NE61 2EF
Tel: 0845 600 6400 Fax: 01670 534117
e-mail: ask@northumberland.gov.uk
Highways: County Hall, Morpeth NE61 2EF
Tel: 0845 600 6400 Fax: 01670 534117
e-mail: ask@northumberland.gov.uk
Planning: Planning, County Hall, Morpeth NE61 2EF
Solicitor to the Council: Head of Legal Services, County Hall, Morpeth NE61 2EF
Tel: 01670 533202 Fax: 01670 533238
Water: Northumbrian Water

33 North Yorkshire

33.0 North Yorkshire County Council

Website: www.northyorks.gov.uk
Main Switchboard: 0845 872 7374
Search Address: Legal & Democratic Services, County Hall, Racecourse La, Northallerton DL7 8AD
Tel: 0845 872 7374 Fax: 01609 780447
e-mail: legal.services@northyorks.gov.uk
Solicitor to the Council: Carole Dunn, Assistant Chief Executive, Legal & Democratic Services, County Hall, Racecourse La, Northallerton DL7 8AD
Tel: 01609 532953 Fax: 01609 780447
e-mail: legal.services@northyorks.gov.uk

33.1 Richmondshire District Council

Website: www.richmondshire.gov.uk
Main Switchboard: 01748 829100
Conveyancing Searches: Local Land Charges, Mercury Ho, Station Rd, Richmond DL10 4JX
Tel: 01748 827138
e-mail: llcsearches@richmondshire.gov.uk
Building Control & Planning: Building Control, Suite 2, Coxwold Ho, Easingwold Business Pk, Stillington Rd, Easingwold YO61 3FB
Tel: 01347 822 703
e-mail: buildingcontrol@richmondshire.gov.uk
Council Tax: Council Tax Office, Financial Unit, Mercury Ho, Station Rd, Richmond DL10 4JX
Tel: 01748 829100 Fax: 01748 822257
e-mail: local.taxation@richmondshire.gov.uk
Environmental Health: Environmental Unit, Friars Wynd, Richmond DL10 4RT
Tel: 01748 829100 Fax: 01748 826186
DX: 65047 Richmond NY
e-mail: environment@richmondshire.gov.uk
Highways: North Yorkshire County Council
Solicitor to the Council: Callum KcKeon, Mercury Ho, Station Rd, Richmond DL10 4JX
Tel: 01748 829100 Fax: 01748 825071
DX: 65047 Richmond NY
Water Services: Yorkshire Water and Northumbrian Water

33.2 Hambleton District Council

Website: www.hambleton.gov.uk
Main Switchboard: 0845 1211555
Conveyancing Searches: Land Charges, Civic Centre, Stone Cross, Northallerton DL6 2UU
Tel: 01609 767009/767008 Fax: 01609 767264
DX: 61650 Northallerton 1
e-mail: landcharges@hambleton.gov.uk
Building Control: North Yorkshire County Council, Suite 2, Coxwold Ho, Easingwold Business Pk, Easingwold, York YO61 3FB
Tel: 01347 822703 Fax: 01609 767248
e-mail: buildingcontrol@hambleton.gov.uk
Council Tax: Resources, Civic Centre, Stone Cross, Northallerton DL6 2UU
Tel: 0845 121 1555 Fax: 01609 767228
DX: 61650 Northallerton 1
e-mail: revenues@hambleton.gov.uk
Environmental Health: Planning & Environmental Services, Civic Centre, Stone Cross, Northallerton DL6 2UU
Tel: 0845 121 1555 Fax: 01609 767228
DX: 61650 Northallerton 1
e-mail: ehealth@hambleton.gov.uk
Highways: North Yorkshire County Council,
Tel: 0845 872 7374
e-mail: highwaysmaintenance@northyorks.gov.uk
Planning: Planning & Environmental Services, Civic Centre, Stone Cross, Northallerton DL6 2UU
Tel: 01609 767167 / 0845 121 1555 Fax: 01609 767228
DX: 61650 Northallerton 1
e-mail: dcenquiries@hambleton.gov.uk
Solicitor to the Council: Martyn Richards, Head of Legal & Democratic Services, Civic Centre, Stone Cross, Northallerton DL6 2UU
Tel: 01609 767010 Fax: 01609 767264
DX: 61650 Northallerton 1
e-mail: martyn.richards@hambleton.gov.uk
Water Services: Northumbrian Water and Yorkshire Water

33.3 Ryedale District Council

Website: www.ryedale.gov.uk
Main Switchboard: 01653 600666
Conveyancing Searches: Local Land Charges Dept, Ryedale Ho, Old Malton Rd, Malton YO17 7HH
Tel: 01653 600666 x271 or 310 Fax: 01653 690834
DX: 723622 Malton 2
e-mail: landcharges@ryedale.gov.uk
Building Control: Suite 2, Coxwold Ho, Easingwold Business Pk, Easingwold, York YO61 3FB
Tel: 01347 822703
e-mail: buildingcontrol@ryedale.gov.uk
Council Tax: Ryedale Ho, Malton YO17 7HH
Tel: 01653 600666 Fax: 01653 699889
e-mail: ctax@ryedale.gov.uk
Environmental Health: Ryedale Ho, Malton YO17 7HH
Tel: 01653 600666 Fax: 01653 600764
e-mail: envhealth@ryedale.gov.uk
Highways: North Yorkshire County Council
Planning: Ryedale Ho, Malton YO17 7HH
Tel: 01653 600666 Fax: 01653 690834
DX: 723620 Malton 2
e-mail: dm@ryedale.gov.uk
Solicitor to the Council: K Anthony Winship, Solicitor to the Council, Ryedale Ho, as before,
DX: 723621 Malton 2
e-mail: anthony.winship@ryedale.gov.uk
Water Services: Yorkshire Water

33.4 Scarborough Borough Council

Website: www.scarborough.gov.uk
Main Switchboard: 01723 232323
Conveyancing Searches: Local Land Charges Unit, Central Administration, Town Hall, St Nicholas St, Scarborough YO11 2HG
Tel: 01723 232488 Fax: 0870 238 4159
e-mail: locallandcharges@scarborough.gov.uk
Building Control: North Yorkshire Building Control Partnership,
e-mail: enquiries@NYBCP.org
Environmental Health: Dept of Environmental Health, St Nicholas St, Town Hall, Scarborough YO11 2HG
Tel: 01223 232323 (Customer First)
Highways (part): North Yorkshire County Council
Planning: Development Control, Town Hall, St Nicholas St, Scarborough YO11 2HG
Tel: 01723 232323 Fax: 0870 191 3997
e-mail: planning.services@scarborough.gov.uk
Planning (Moors): North Yorkshire Moors National Park Authority, The Old Vicarage, Bondgate, Helmsley YO62 5BP
Tel: 01439 770657 Fax: 01439 770691
e-mail: info@northyorkmoors-npa.gov.uk
Solicitor to the Council: Lisa Dixon, Legal Services Manager, Town Hall, St Nicholas St, Scarborough YO11 2HG
Tel: 01723 232348 Fax: 01723 501665
e-mail: lisa.dixon@scarborough.gov.uk
Water Services: Yorkshire Water

33.5 Craven District Council

Website: www.cravendc.gov.uk
Main Switchboard: 01756 700600
Conveyancing Searches: Ms J Bosher-Norcliffe, 1 Belle Vue Sq, Broughton Rd, Skipton BD23 1FJ
Tel: 01756 706239
e-mail: landcharges@cravendc.gov.uk

Building Control: Building Control Surveyors, 1 Belle Vue Sq, Broughton Rd, Skipton BD23 1FJ
Tel: 01756 706469
e-mail: buildingcontrol@cravendc.gov.uk
Council Tax: Finance Dept, Council Tax Section, 1 Belle Vue Sq, Broughton Rd, Skipton BD23 1FJ
Tel: 01756 700600
e-mail: customerservices@cravendc.gov.uk
Environmental Health: Environmental Health, 1 Belle Vue Sq, Broughton Rd, Skipton BD23 1FJ
Tel: 01756 706357/706359
e-mail: environmentalhealth@cravendc.gov.uk
Highways: North Yorkshire County Council
Solicitor to the Council: Legal Services, 1 Belle Vue Sq, Broughton Rd, Skipton BD23 1FJ
Tel: 01756 706234 Fax: 01756 706257
e-mail: legals@cravendc.gov.uk
Water: Yorkshire Water / United Utilities

33.6 Harrogate Borough Council

Website: www.harrogate.gov.uk
Main Switchboard: 01423 500600
Conveyancing Searches: Registrar of Local Land Charges, Development Services, Knapping Mount, West Grove Rd, Harrogate HG1 2AE
Tel: 01423 556066
DX: 11962 Harrogate
e-mail: landchar@harrogate.gov.uk
Building Control: Building Control, Council Offices, Crescent Gdns, Harrogate HG1 2SE
Tel: 01423 556555 Fax: 01423 556550
Council Tax: Council Tax, Council Offices, Crescent Gdns, Harrogate HG1 2SE
Tel: 01423 556677
e-mail: benefitsrevenues@harrogate.gov.uk
Highways: North Yorkshire County Council
Solicitor to the Council: Chief Solicitor, Council Offices, Crescent Gdns, Harrogate HG1 2SE
Tel: 01423 556015 Fax: 01423 556010
DX: 11962 Harrogate
Water Services: Yorkshire Water (Safe-Move)

33.7 City of York Council (U)

Website: www.york.gov.uk
Main Switchboard: 01904 551550
Conveyancing Searches: Local Land Charges, West Offices, Station Rise, York YO1 6GA
Tel: 01904 551363
DX: 720621 York 21
e-mail: landcharges@york.gov.uk
Building Control: West Offices, Station Rise, York YO1 6GA
Tel: 01904 551333
e-mail: building.control@york.gov.uk
Council Tax: Resources Group, West Offices, Station Rise, York YO1 6GA
Tel: 01904 551558 Fax: 01904 551047
Enviromental Health: Environmental Regulation, Eco Dept, Hazel Ct, James St, York YO10 3DS
Tel: 01904 551550
Solicitor to the Council: Head of Legal Services, West Offices, Station Rise, York YO1 6GA
Tel: 01904 551004

33.8 Selby District Council

Website: www.selbydistrictcouncil.gov.uk
Main Switchboard: 01757 705101
Conveyancing Searches: Land Charges, Civic Centre, Doncaster Rd, Selby YO8 9FT
Tel: 01757 705101 Fax: 01757 292229
e-mail: landcharges@selby.gov.uk
Building Control: Building Control, Suite 2, Coxwold Ho, Easingwold Business Park, Easingwold YO61 3FB
Tel: 01347 822703 Fax: 01347 824279
e-mail: maria.podgorski@nybcp.org
Council Tax & NNDR: Local Taxation, Civic Centre, Doncaster Rd, Selby YO8 9FT
Tel: 01757 705101 Fax: 01757 292229
e-mail: localtaxation@selby.gov.uk
Environmental Health: Environmental Health, Civic Centre, Doncaster Rd, Selby YO8 9FT
Tel: 01757 705101 Fax: 01757 292229
e-mail: envhealth@selby.gov.uk
Highways: North Yorkshire County Council
Planning: Planning, Civic Centre, Doncaster Rd, Selby YO8 9FT
Tel: 01757 705101 Fax: 01757 292229
e-mail: planning@selby.gov.uk
Solicitor to the Council: Legal Services, Civic Centre, Doncaster Rd, Selby YO8 9FT
Tel: 01757 705101 Fax: 01757 292229
e-mail: legal@selby.gov.uk
Water Services: Yorkshire Water

33.9 Middlesbrough Borough Council (U)

Website: www.middlesbrough.gov.uk
Main Switchboard: 01642 245432
Conveyancing Searches: Legal & Democratic Services, PO Box 503, Town Hall, Russell St, Middlesbrough TS1 9FX
Tel: 01642 729770 Fax: 01642 729882
DX: 60532 Middlesbrough
e-mail: landcharges@middlesbrough.gov.uk
Building Control & Planning: Community Protection Service, PO Box 504, Civic Centre, Middlesbrough TS1 9FY
Tel: 01642 729375 Fax: 01642 729967
e-mail: buildingcontrol@middlesbrough.gov.uk
Council Tax: Finance Dept, PO Box 2, Middlesbrough Ho, 50 Corporation Rd, Middlesbrough TS1 2YL
Tel: 01642 726007 Fax: 01642 726989
e-mail: ctax@middlesbrough.gov.uk
Environmental Health: Community Protection, 3rd & 5th Fl, Vancouver Ho, Middlesbrough TS1 9FW
Tel: 01642 728158 Fax: 01642 728960
e-mail: enservices@middlesbrough.gov.uk
Highways, Transportation Services, Environment: Transport & Design, Vancouver Ho, PO Box 502, Gurney St, Middlesbrough TS1 9FW
Tel: 01642 728644 Fax: 01642 728969
e-mail: jointsupportservices@mouchel-middlesbrough.com
Solicitor to the Council: Bryn Roberts, Legal Services Manager, PO Box 503, Municipal Bldgs, Russell St, Middlesbrough TS1 9FX
Tel: 01642 729738 Fax: 01642 729882
DX: 60532 Middlesbrough
e-mail: bryn_roberts@middlesbrough.gov.uk
Water Services: Northumbrian Water Sewerage Dept

33.10 Redcar & Cleveland Borough Council (U)

Website: www.redcar-cleveland.gov.uk
Main Switchboard: 01642 774774
Conveyancing Searches: Chief Executive's Dept, Redcar & Cleveland Ho, Kirkleatham St, Redcar TS10 1RT
Tel: 01642 444003 Fax: 01642 444004
DX: 60041 Normanby
Building Control: Building Control, Dept of Regeneration, Redcar & Cleveland Ho, Kirkleatham St, Redcar TS10 1RT
Tel: 01287 612361
e-mail: kevin_johnson@redcar-cleveland.gov.uk
Council Tax: Council Tax Dept., Belmont Ho, Rectory La, Guisborough TS14 7FD
Tel: 01642 774774 Fax: 01642 771102
e-mail: council_tax@redcar-cleveland.gov.uk
Other depts: Department of Area Management, Belmont Ho, Rectory La, Guisborough TS14 7FD
Tel: 01642 774774 Fax: 01287 612468
DX: 60041 Normanby
Solicitor to the Council: Richard Frankland, Director of Corporate Resources, Redcar & Cleveland Ho, Kirkleatham St, Redcar TS10 1RT
Tel: 01642 444405 Fax: 01642 444578
DX: 60041 Normanby
e-mail: richard_frankland@redcar-cleveland.gov.uk
Water Services: Northumbrian Water

34 Nottinghamshire

34.0 Nottinghamshire County Council

Website: www.nottinghamshire.gov.uk
Main Switchboard: 0115 982 3823
Search Address: County Hall, West Bridgford, Nottingham NG2 7QP
Tel: 0300 500 8080 Fax: 0115 977 3815
DX: 723420 West Bridgford 2
Solicitor to the Council: Heather Dickinson, Group Mgr, Legal & Democratic Services, County Hall, West Bridgford, Nottingham NG2 7QP
Tel: 0115 977 4835 Fax: 0115 977 3815
DX: 723420 West Bridgford 2
e-mail: heather.dickinson@nottscc.gov.uk

34.1 Bassetlaw District Council

Website: www.bassetlaw.gov.uk
Main Switchboard: 01909 533533
Conveyancing Searches: Land Charges Unit, Queen's Bldgs, Potter St, Worksop S80 2AH
Tel: 01909 533277 Fax: 01909 535524
DX: 723180 Worksop 3
e-mail: land.charges@bassetlaw.gov.uk
Building Control: Principal Building Control Surveyor, Queen's Bldgs, as before,
Tel: 01909 533130 Fax: 01909 482622
DX: 723180 Worksop 3
e-mail: building.control@bassetlaw.gov.uk
Council Tax: Local Taxation, Queen's Bldgs, as before,
Tel: 01909 533258/34 Fax: 01909 535506
DX: 723180 Worksop 3
e-mail: revenues@bassetlaw.gov.uk
Environmental Health: Queen's Bldgs, Potter St, Worksop S80 2AH
Tel: 01909 533219 / 01777 713764
DX: 723180 Worksop 3
e-mail: customer.services@bassetlaw.gov.uk
Highways: Nottinghamshire County Council
Planning: Planning Services, Queen's Bldgs, Potter St, Worksop S80 2AH
Tel: 01909 533446/72/92 Fax: 01909 482622
DX: 723180 Worksop 3
e-mail: planning@bassetlaw.gov.uk
Solicitor to the Council: Solicitor, Queen's Bldgs, Potter St, Worksop S80 2AH
Tel: 01909 533176
DX: 723180 Worksop 3
e-mail: customer.services@bassetlaw.gov.uk
Water Services: Severn Trent Water

34.2 Mansfield District Council

Website: www.mansfield.gov.uk
Main Switchboard: 01623 463463
Conveyancing Searches: Legal Services, Civic Centre, Chesterfield Rd Sth, Mansfield NG19 7BH
Tel: 01623 463063 Fax: 01623 463900
e-mail: locallandcharges@mansfield.gov.uk
Highways: Nottinghamshire County Council
Other depts: Civic Centre, as before
Solicitor to the Council: Mrs Anita Bradley, Head of Corporate Administration, Civic Centre, Chesterfield Rd South, Mansfield NG19 7BH
Tel: 01623 463463 Fax: 01623 463900
e-mail: abradley@mansfield.gov.uk
Water Services: Severn Trent Water

34.3 Newark & Sherwood District Council

Website: www.newark-sherwooddc.gov.uk
Main Switchboard: 01636 650000
Conveyancing Searches: Technical Support Business Unit, Kelham Hall, Kelham, Newark NG23 5QX
Tel: 01636 650000
e-mail: customerservices@nsdc.info
Building Control: Business Control Business Unit, Kelham Hall, Kelham, Newark NG23 5QX
Tel: 01636 650000
e-mail: bcsupport@nsdc.info
Council Tax: Revenues & Benefits Business Unit, Kelham Hall, Kelham, Newark NG23 5QX
Tel: 01636 650000
e-mail: council.tax@nsdc.info
Environmental Health: Environmental Services Business Unit, Kelham Hall, Kelham, Newark NG23 5QX
Tel: 01636 650000
e-mail: customerservices@nsdc.info
Highways: Nottinghamshire County Council
Planning: Development Business Unit, Kelham Hall, Kelham, Newark NG23 5QX
Tel: 01636 650000
e-mail: customerservices@nsdc.info
Solicitor to the Council: Mrs Kirsty Cole, Deputy Chief Executive, Kelham Hall, Kelham, Newark NG23 5QX
Tel: 01636 650000
e-mail: kirsty.cole@nsdc.info
Water Services: Severn Trent Water and Anglian Water

34.4 Ashfield District Council

Website: www.ashfield-dc.gov.uk
Main Switchboard: 01623 450000
Conveyancing Searches: Land Charges, Council Offices, Urban Rd, Kirkby-in-Ashfield NG17 8DA
Tel: 01623 457313 Fax: 01623 457033
e-mail: landcharges@ashfield-dc.gov.uk

Building Control & Planning: Development Advice & Building Control, Council Offices, as before,
Tel: 01623 457172 Fax: 01623 457033
e-mail: planning.admin@ashfield-dc.gov.uk
Highways: Nottinghamshire County Council
Solicitor to the Council: Legal, Council Offices, Urban Rd, Kirkby-in-Ashfield NG17 8DA
Tel: 01623 457312 Fax: 01623 457585
Water Services: Severn Trent Water

34.5 Broxtowe Borough Council

Website: www.broxtowe.gov.uk
Main Switchboard: 0115 917 7777
Conveyancing Searches: Land Charges, Council Offices, Foster Ave, Beeston, Nottingham NG9 1AB
Tel: 0115 917 3285 Fax: 0115 917 3131
e-mail: landcharges@broxtowe.gov.uk
Building Control and Planning: Directorate of Planning & Community Development, Council Offices, as before,
Tel: 0115 917 3466 Fax: 0115 917 3377
e-mail: pabc@broxtowc.gov.uk
Council Tax: Directorate of Finance, Council Offices, as before,
Tel: 0115 917 7777 Fax: 0115 917 3683
e-mail: billing@broxtowe.gov.uk
Environmental Health: Directorate of Housing, Health & Leisure, Council Offices, as before,
Tel: 0115 917 3446 Fax: 0115 917 3394 (Housing); 0115 917 3377 (H & L)
e-mail: hhl@broxtowe.gov.uk
Highways: Directorate of Technical & Works Services, Council Offices, as before,
Tel: 0115 917 3046 Fax: 0115 917 3038
e-mail: highways@broxtowe.gov.uk
Solicitor to the Council: Simon Smith, Head of Legal Services, Council Offices, Foster Ave, Beeston, Nottingham NG9 1AB
Tel: 0115 917 7777 Fax: 0115 917 3131
e-mail: legal@broxtowe.gov.uk
Water Services: Severn Trent Water

34.6 Nottingham City Council (U)

Website: www.nottinghamcity.gov.uk
Main Switchboard: 0115 876 4939/4389/4388
Conveyancing Searches: Local Land Charges Section, Resources Dept, Loxley Ho, Station St, Nottingham NG2 3NG
Tel: 0115 876 4389
DX: 719182 Nottingham 34
e-mail: locallandcharges@nottinghamcity.gov.uk
Building Control & Planning: Building Control Service, Loxley Ho, Station St, Nottingham NG2 3NG
Tel: 0115 876 4028 Fax: 0115 876 3234
e-mail: building.control@nottinghamcity.gov.uk
Council Tax: Council Tax Enquiries, Contact Centre, Angel Row, Nottingham NG1 6HP
Tel: 0115 841 5550
e-mail: counciltax@nottinghamcity.gov.uk
Environmental Health: Environmental Services Dept, Exchange Bldgs, Smithy Row, Nottingham NG1 2BS
Tel: 0115 876 1166
e-mail: public.health@nottinghamcity.gov.uk
Highways: Highways Section, Loxley Ho, Station St, Nottingham NG2 3NG
Tel: 0115 876 5402 Fax: 0115 915 6150
e-mail: highways@nottinghamcity.gov.uk
Solicitor to the Council: Legal Services Manager, Corporate Services, Loxley Ho, Station St, Nottingham NG2 3NG
Tel: 0115 876 4332 Fax: 0115 915 4004
DX: 719182 Nottingham 34
Water Services: Severn Trent Water

34.7 Gedling Borough Council

Website: www.gedling.gov.uk
Main Switchboard: 0115 901 3901
Conveyancing Searches: Land Charges, Civic Centre, Arnot Hill Pk, Arnold, Nottingham NG5 6LU
Tel: 0115 901 3971 Fax: 0115 901 3758
e-mail: landcharges@gedling.gov.uk
Building Control: Building Control, Civic Centre, Arnot Hill Pk, Arnold, Nottingham NG5 6LU
Tel: 0115 901 3740 Fax: 0115 901 3758
e-mail: buildingcontrol@gedling.gov.uk
Council Tax: Civic Centre, Arnot Hill Pk, Arnold, Nottingham NG5 6LU
Tel: 0115 901 3950 Fax: 0115 901 3978
e-mail: counciltax@gedling.gov.uk
Environmental Health: Public Protection, Civic Centre, Arnot Hill Pk, Arnold, Nottingham NG5 6LU
Tel: 0115 901 3972 Fax: 0115 901 3758
e-mail: environmentalhealth@gedling.gov.uk
Highways: Nottinghamshire County Council,
Tel: 08449 808080
e-mail: enquiries@nottscc.gov.uk
Planning: Planning, Civic Centre, Arnot Hill Pk, Arnold, Nottingham NG5 6LU
Tel: 0115 901 3971 Fax: 0115 901 3758
e-mail: developmentcontrol@gedling.gov.uk
Solicitor to the Council: Legal Services, Civic Centre, Arnot Hill Park, Arnold, Nottingham NG5 6LU
Tel: 0115 901 3896 Fax: 0115 901 3920
Water Services: Severn Trent

34.8 Rushcliffe Borough Council

Website: www.rushcliffe.gov.uk
Main Switchboard: 0115 981 9911
Conveyancing Searches: Land Charges, The Civic Centre, Pavilion Rd, West Bridgford, Nottingham NG2 5FE
Tel: 0115 981 9911; direct line 0115 914 8513/9148575
Fax: 0115 914 8452
e-mail: landcharges@rushcliffe.gov.uk
Building Control: Building Control Dept, The Civic Centre, Pavilion Rd, West Bridgford, Nottingham NG2 5FE
Tel: 0115 981 9911 Fax: 0115 914 8452
e-mail: buildingcontrol@rushcliffe.gov.uk
Environmental Health: Environmental Health, The Civic Centre, Pavilion Rd, West Bridgford, Nottingham NG2 5FE
Tel: 0115 981 9911 Fax: 0115 914 8574
e-mail: environmentalhealth@rushcliffe.gov.uk
Highways: Nottinghamshire County Council
Other depts: The Civic Centre, Pavilion Rd, West Bridgford, Nottingham NG2 5FE
Planning: Development Control, The Civic Centre, Pavilion Rd, West Bridgford, Nottingham NG2 5FE
Tel: 0115 981 9911 Fax: 0115 914 8452
e-mail: developmentcontrol@rushcliffe.gov.uk
Solicitor to the Council: P J Cox, Borough Solicitor, The Civic Centre, Pavilion Rd, West Bridgford, Nottingham NG2 5FE
Tel: 0115 981 9911 Fax: 0115 945 5882
e-mail: pcox@rushcliffe.gov.uk
Water Services: Severn Trent Water

35 Oxfordshire

35.0 Oxfordshire County Council

Website: www.oxfordshire.gov.uk
Main Switchboard: 01865 792422
Search Address: Peter G Clark, County Solicitor, Law & Culture, County Hall, New Rd, Oxford OX1 1ND
Tel: 01865 323907 Fax: 01865 783361
DX: 4310 Oxford
e-mail: peter.clark@oxfordshire.gov.uk
Solicitor to the Council: Mr Peter Clark, County Solicitor, County Hall, New Rd, Oxford OX1 1ND
Tel: 01865 323907 Fax: 01865 783361
DX: 4310 Oxford
e-mail: peter.clark@oxfordshire.gov.uk

35.1 West Oxfordshire District Council

Website: www.westoxon.gov.uk
Main Switchboard: 01993 861000
Conveyancing Searches: Local Land Charges, Elmfield, New Yatt Rd, Witney OX28 1PB
Tel: 01993 861440 Fax: 01993 861451
e-mail: land.charges@westoxon.gov.uk
Building Control: Building Control Section, Elmfield, New Yatt Rd, Witney OX28 1PB
Tel: 01993 861430 Fax: 01993 861451
e-mail: building.control@westoxon.gov.uk
Council Tax: Local Taxation Services, PO Box 303, Witney OX28 1WR
Tel: 01993 861040 Fax: 01993 861051
e-mail: local.taxation@westoxon.gov.uk
Environmental Health: Environmental Services, Elmfield, New Yatt Rd, Witney OX28 1PB
Tel: 01993 861000 Fax: 01993 861053
e-mail: community.services@westoxon.gov.uk
Highways: Oxfordshire County Council
Planning: Planning Services, Elmfield, New Yatt Rd, Witney OX28 1PB
Tel: 01993 861420 Fax: 01993 861451
e-mail: planning@westoxon.gov.uk
Solicitor to the Council: Keith Butler, Head of Legal Services, Council Offices, Woodgreen, Witney OX28 6NB
Tel: 01993 861590 Fax: 01993 861450
e-mail: legal@westoxon.gov.uk
Water Services: Thames Water

35.2 Cherwell District Council

Website: www.cherwell.gov.uk
Main Switchboard: 01295 227001
Conveyancing Searches: Law & Governance, Land Charges, Bodicote Ho, Bodicote, Banbury OX15 4AA
Tel: 01295 221596
DX: 24224 Banbury
e-mail: local.charges@cherwell-dc.gov.uk
Building Control: Planning, Housing & Economy Directorate, Building Control & Engineering Services, Bodicote Ho, Bodicote, Banbury OX15 4AA
Tel: 0300 003 0200
DX: 24224 Banbury
e-mail: building.control@cherwellandsouthnorthants.gov.uk
Council Tax: Customer Service & Resources Directorate, Finance Dept, PO Box 27, Banbury, Oxfordshire OX15 4BH
Tel: 01295 227000
DX: 24224 Banbury
e-mail: council.tax@cherwell-dc.gov.uk
Environmental Services: Environment & Community Directorate, Environmental Services, Bodicote Ho, Bodicote, Banbury OX15 4AA
Tel: 01295 227007
DX: 24224 Banbury
e-mail: customer.services@cherwell-dc.gov.uk
Highways: Oxfordshire County Council
Legal and Democratic Services: Head of Law & Governance, Bodicote Ho, Bodicote, Banbury OX15 4AA
DX: 24224 Banbury
Planning: Planning, Housing & Economy Directorate, Development Control & Major Development, Bodicote Ho, Bodicote, Banbury OX15 4AA
Tel: 01295 227006
DX: 24224 Banbury
e-mail: planning@cherwell-dc.gov.uk
Water Services: Thames Water/Anglian Water/Severn Trent Water

1

35.3 South Oxfordshire District Council

Website: www.southoxon.gov.uk
Main Switchboard: 01491 823000
Conveyancing Searches: Land Charges Dept, Benson La, Crowmarsh Gifford, Wallingford OX10 8AY
Tel: 01491 823621 Fax: 01491 823625
DX: 144122 Wallingford 2
e-mail: land.charges@southoxon.gov.uk
Building Control: Building Control Services, Benson La, Cromarsh Gifford, Wallingford OX10 8AY
e-mail: building.control@southandvale.gov.uk
Council Tax: Council Tax, South Oxfordshire District Council, PO Box 872, Erith DA8 1UN
Tel: 0345 302 2313
Environmental Health: Environmental Services Dept, Benson La, Crowmarsh Gifford, Wallingford OX10 8NL Fax: 01491 823201
DX: 144120 Wallingford 2
e-mail: env.health@southoxon.gov.uk
Highways: Oxfordshire County Council
Planning: Planning Dept, Benson La, Crowmarsh Gifford, Wallingford OX10 8NJ
Tel: 01491 823740/50 Fax: 01491 823746
DX: 144120 Wallingford 2
e-mail: planning@southoxon.gov.uk
Solicitor to the Council: The Solicitor to the Council, Legal & Democratic Services, Benson La, Crowmarsh Gifford, Wallingford OX10 8QS
Tel: 01491 823345 Fax: 01491 823658
DX: 144121 Wallingford 2
e-mail: legal@southoxon.gov.uk
Water Services: Thames Water

35.4 Vale of White Horse District Council

Website: www.whitehorsedc.gov.uk
Main Switchboard: 01235 520202
Conveyancing Searches: Land Charges Section, Benson La, Crowmarsh Gifford, Wallingford OX10 8ED
Tel: 01235 540445
e-mail: land.charges@whitehorsedc.gov.uk
Building Control: Building Control Team, Benson La, Crowmarsh Gifford, Wallingford OX10 8ED
Tel: 01235 540357 Fax: 01235 540397
e-mail: building.control@southandvale.gov.uk
Council Tax: Council Tax, Vale of White Horse DC, PO Box 88, Erith DA8 1UN
Environmental Health: Benson La, Crowmarsh Gifford, Wallingford OX10 8ED
Tel: 01235 520202

Head of Legal Services: Ian Price, Benson La, Crowmarsh Gifford, Wallingford OX10 8ED
Tel: 01235 540302 Fax: 01235 547609
Highways: Oxfordshire County Council
Planning: Planning, Benson La, Crowmarsh Gifford, Wallingford OX10 8ED
Water Services: Thames Water

35.5 Oxford City Council

Website: www.oxford.gov.uk
Main Switchboard: 01865 249811
Conveyancing Searches: Planning Business Unit, St Aldate's Chambers, 109–113 St Aldates, Oxford OX1 1DS
Tel: 01865 249811 Fax: 01865 252144
DX: 4309 Oxford
e-mail: cslc@oxford.gov.uk
Building Control: Building Control, St Aldate's Chambers, 109–113 St Aldate's, Oxford OX1 1DS
Tel: 01865 249811 Fax: 01865 252198
DX: 4309 Oxford
e-mail: buildingcontrol@oxford.gov.uk
Council Tax: Revenues & Benefits Business Unit, St Aldate's Chambers, 8109–113 St Aldate's, Oxford OX1 1DS
Tel: 01865 249811 Fax: 01865 252475
DX: 4309 Oxford
e-mail: counciltax@oxford.gov.uk
Environmental Health: Environmental Health Business Unit, St Aldate's Chambers, 109–113 St Aldate's, Oxford OX1 1DS
Tel: 01865 249811 Fax: 01865 252344
DX: 4309 Oxford
e-mail: environment@oxford.gov.uk
Highways: Oxfordshire County Council
Planning: Planning Business Unit, St Aldate's Chambers, 109–113 St Aldate's, Oxford OX1 1DS
Tel: 01865 249811 Fax: 01865 252144
DX: 4309 Oxford
e-mail: planning@oxford.gov.uk
Solicitor to the Council: Legal & Democratic Services Business Unit, Town Hall, St Aldate's, Oxford OX1 1BX
Tel: 01865 249811 Fax: 01865 252694
DX: 4309 Oxford
Water Services: Thames Water

36 Rutland

36.1 Rutland County Council (U)

Website: www.rutland.gov.uk
Main Switchboard: 01572 722577
Conveyancing Searches: Land Charges Section, Council Offices, Catmose, Oakham LE15 6HP
Tel: 01572 722577 Fax: 01572 758307
DX: 28340 Oakham
e-mail: landcharges@rutland.gov.uk
Building Control: via Land Charges
Council Tax: Revenues, Council Offices, Catmose, Oakham LE15 6HP
Tel: 01572 722577 Fax: 01572 758307
DX: 28340 Oakham
Environmental Health: via Land Charges
Highways & Planning: via Land Charges
Solicitor to the Council: Legal Services, Peterborough City Council, Town Hall, Bridge St, Peterborough PE1 1HG
Tel: 01733 452621 Fax: 01733 452220
DX: 12310 Peterborough 1
Water Services: Severn Trent Water and Anglian Water

37 Shropshire

37.0 Shropshire County Council (abolished)

County Council abolished as from 1 April 2009. Oswestry BC, North Shropshire DC, Shrewsbury & Atcham BC, South Shropshire DC and Bridgnorth DC are now combined with Shropshire County Council to form Shropshire Council (Unitary).

37.1 Shropshire Council (U)

Website: www.shropshire.gov.uk
Main Switchboard: 0345 678 9000
Conveyancing Searches: Development Services, The Shirehall, Abbey Foregate, Shrewsbury SY2 6ND
Tel: 0345 6789004
e-mail: customer.service@shropshire.gov.uk
Building Control: Development Services, The Shirehall, Abbey Foregate, Shrewsbury SY2 6ND
Tel: 0345 678 9004 Fax: 01743 252619
e-mail: buildingcontrol@shropshire.gov.uk
Council Tax: Resources, The Shirehall, Abbey Foregate, Shrewsbury SY2 6ND
Tel: 0345 678 9002
e-mail: council.tax@shropshire.gov.uk
Environmental Health: Public Protection, The Shirehall, Abbey Foregate, Shrewsbury SY2 6ND
Tel: 0345 678 9000
e-mail: public.protection@shropshire.gov.uk
Highways: Development Services, The Shirehall, Abbey Foregate, Shrewsbury SY2 6ND
Tel: 0345 678 9006
e-mail: customer.services@shropshire.gov.uk
Planning: Development Management, The Shirehall, Abbey Foregate, Shrewsbury SY2 6ND
Tel: 0345 678 9004
e-mail: customer.service@shropshire.gov.uk
Solicitor to the Council: Claire Porter, Head of Legal Services, The Shirehall, Abbey Foregate, Shrewsbury SY2 6ND
Tel: 01743 252763 Fax: 01743 252795
DX: 702024 Shrewsbury 2
Water Services: Dwr Cymru (Welsh Water)/Severn Trent Water/North West Water

37.4 Telford & Wrekin Council (U)

Website: www.telford.gov.uk
Main Switchboard: 01952 380000
Conveyancing Searches: Land Charges, Legal Services, Addenbrook Ho, Ironmasters Way, Telford TF3 4NT
Tel: 01952 383247 Fax: 01952 383253
DX: 712120 Telford 5
e-mail: landcharges@telford.gov.uk
Building Control & Planning: Building Control, Development Management, Wellington Civic Offices, PO Box 457, Telford TF2 2FH
Tel: 01952 384555 Fax: 01952 384110
DX: 712121 Telford 5
e-mail: buildingcontrol@telford.gov.uk
Council Tax: Revenues & Benefits Services, Addenbrook Ho, Ironmasters Way, Telford TF3 4NT
Tel: 01952 383838 Fax: 01952 383991
e-mail: council.tax@telford.gov.uk
Environmental Health: Environmental Health, Darby Ho, Lawn Central, Telford TF3 4LE
Tel: 01952 381818 Fax: 01952 381806
DX: 712122 Telford 5
e-mail: environmental.health@telford.gov.uk

Highways: Highways & Transport, Darby Ho, Lawn Central, Telford TF3 4LE
Tel: 01952 380000 Fax: 01952 384835
DX: 712122 Telford 5
e-mail: highways@telford.gov.uk
Planning: Development Management, PO Box 457, Wellington Civic Offices, Telford TF2 2FH
Tel: 01952 380380 Fax: 01952 384110
e-mail: planning.control@telford.gov.uk
Solicitor to the Council: Law Democracy & People Services, Addenbrook Ho, Ironmasters Way, Telford TF3 4NT
DX: 712120 Telford 5
e-mail: jonathon.eatough@telford.gov.uk
Water Services: Severn Trent Water

38 Somerset

38.0 Somerset County Council

Website: www.somerset.gov.uk
Main Switchboard: 0845 345 9166
Search Address: Land Charges, County Hall, Taunton TA1 4DY
Tel: 01823 355515 Fax: 01823 356113/114
DX: 122470 Taunton 7
e-mail: landcharges@somerset.gov.uk
Solicitor to the Council: Ms Catherine Witham, County Hall, Taunton TA1 4DY
Tel: 01823 355022
e-mail: cwitham@somerset.gov.uk

38.1 Sedgemoor District Council

Website: www.sedgemoor.gov.uk
Main Switchboard: 0845 4082540
Conveyancing Searches: Legal Services Dept, Bridgwater Ho, King Sq, Bridgwater TA6 3AR
Tel: 01278 435324 Fax: 01278 435500
DX: 745440 Bridgwater 7
e-mail: land.charges@sedgemoor.gov.uk
Building Control & Planning: Development Services,
Tel: 0845 4082545 Fax: 01278 444076
e-mail: building.control@sedgemoor.gov.uk
Council Tax: Revenues,
Tel: 0845 4082541 Fax: 01278 435772
e-mail: ctax@sedgemoor.gov.uk
Environmental Health: Environmental Health & Strategic Housing, Bridgwater Ho, King Sq, Bridgwater TA6 3AR
Highways: Somerset County Council
Solicitor to the Council: Ms Melanie Wellman, Group Mgr, Legal & Democratic Services, Bridgwater Ho, King Sq, Bridgwater TA6 3AR
Tel: 01278 435734 Fax: 01278 435500
DX: 745440 Bridgwater 7
e-mail: melanie.wellman@sedgemoor.gov.uk
Water Services: Wessex Water

38.2 Mendip District Council

Website: www.mendip.gov.uk
Main Switchboard: 0300 303 8588
Conveyancing Searches: Land Charges Section, Cannards Grave Rd, Shepton Mallet BA4 5BT
Tel: 0300 303 8588 Fax: 01749 346263
DX: 43001 Shepton Mallet
e-mail: landcharges@mendip.gov.uk
Note: One copy of plan required
Building Control: Building Control Services, Cannards Grave Rd, Shepton Mallet BA4 5BT
Tel: 0300 303 8588 Fax: 01749 346263
DX: 43001 Shepton Mallet
e-mail: buildingcontrol@mendip.gov.uk
Council Tax, Environmental Health & Planning: Council Tax, Environmental Health & Planning, Cannards Grave Rd, Shepton Mallet BA4 5BT
Tel: 0300 303 8588 Fax: 01749 346263
DX: 43001 Shepton Mallet
e-mail: customerservices@mendip.gov.uk
Highways: Somerset County Council
Solicitor to the Council: Legal Section, Cannards Grave Rd, Shepton Mallet BA4 5BT
Tel: 0300 303 8588 Fax: 01749 346263
DX: 43001 Shepton Mallet
e-mail: legal@mendip.gov.uk
Water Services: Wessex Water

38.3 West Somerset District Council

Website: www.westsomersetonline.gov.uk
Main Switchboard: 01643 703704
Conveyancing Searches: Local Land Charges, West Somerset Ho, Killick Way, Williton, Taunton TA4 4QA
Tel: 01984 635274 Fax: 01984 635257
DX: 117701 Williton
e-mail: landcharges@westsomerset.gov.uk
Note: 2 plans required with EVERY search request
Building Control & Environmental Health: West Somerset Ho, Killick Way, Williton, Taunton TA4 4QA
Tel: 01643 703704
DX: 117701 Williton
e-mail: builtenvironment@westsomerset.gov.uk
Note: envhealth&licensing@westsomerset.gov.uk
Council Tax: Council Tax, West Somerset Ho, Killick Way, Williton, Taunton TA4 4QA Fax: 01643 703033
DX: 117701 Williton
e-mail: customerservices@westsomerset.gov.uk
Highways: Somerset County Council,
Note: Area split. Contact either Planning Services, Council Offices, as above or Exmoor National Park, Exmoor Hse, Dulverton
Planning: Planning Dept, West Somerset Ho, Killick Way, Williton, Taunton TA4 4QA
Tel: 01984 635314
DX: 117701 Williton
e-mail: planningemail@westsomerset.gov.uk
Water Services: Wessex Water and South West Water

38.4 Taunton Deane Borough Council

Website: www.tauntondeane.gov.uk
Main Switchboard: 01823 356356
Conveyancing Searches: Land Charges Dept, Deane Ho, Belvedere Rd, Taunton TA1 1HE
Tel: 01823 356315 Fax: 01823 356329
Highways: Somerset County Council
Solicitor to the Council: Roy Pinney, Legal & Democratic Services Manager, Deane Ho, Belvedere Rd, Taunton TA1 1HE
e-mail: r.pinney@tauntondeane.gov.uk
Water Services: Wessex Water and South West Water

38.5 South Somerset District Council

Website: www.southsomerset.gov.uk
Main Switchboard: 01935 462462
Conveyancing Searches: Head of Legal & Corporate Services, Local Land Charges Section, Council Offices, Brympton Way, Yeovil BA20 2DS
Tel: 01935 462462 Fax: 01935 462666
e-mail: landcharges@southsomerset.gov.uk
Building Control: Building Control Unit, Council Offices, Brympton Way, Yeovil BA20 2DS
Tel: 01935 462462
e-mail: building.control@southsomerset.gov.uk
Community Resource Centre: Community Resource Centre, Manor Stables, Hendford, Yeovil BA20 1UN
Tel: 01935 462535
e-mail: community.resources@southsomerset.gov.uk
Council Tax: Local Taxation Service, Council Offices, Brympton Way, Yeovil BA20 2HT
Tel: 01935 462462 Fax: 01935 462551
e-mail: council.tax@southsomerset.gov.uk
Environmental Health: Environmental Protection, Council Offices, Brympton Way, Yeovil BA20 2DS
Tel: 01935 462462
e-mail: pollution.control@southsomerset.gov.uk
Highways: Somerset County Council
Housing: Yarlington Housing Group, South Somerset Ho, Alvington, Yeovil BA22 8WN
Tel: 01935 404533 Fax: 01935 404500
Planning: Planning Admin, Council Offices, Brympton Way, Yeovil BA20 2HT
Tel: 01935 462462
e-mail: planning@southsomerset.gov.uk
Solicitor to The Council: South Somerset District Council, Head of Legal & Corporate Services, Council Offices, Brympton Way, Yeovil BA20 2HY
Tel: 01935 462462 Fax: 01935 462666
e-mail: legal@southsomerset.gov.uk
Water Services: Wessex Water and South West Water

38.6 Bath & North East Somerset District Council (U)

Website: www.bathnes.gov.uk
Main Switchboard: 01225 477000
Conveyancing Searches: Land Charges, Lewis Ho, Manvers St, Bath BA1 1JG
Tel: 01225 477092
DX: 8047 Bath
e-mail: land_charges@bathnes.gov.uk
Note: The above address is for Common Registration Searches also
Building Control: Building Control, Lewis Ho, Manvers St, Bath BA1 1JG
Tel: 01225 477517 Fax: 01225 477637
Council Tax: Revenue Services, The Guildhall, Bath BA1 5AW
Tel: 01225 477024 Fax: 01225 477379
Environmental Health: Environmental & Consumer Services, 9–10 Bath St, Bath BA1 1SN
Tel: 01225 477502 Fax: 01225 477674
Highways: Highways & Transportation, Riverside Temple St, Keynsham, Bristol BS31 1LA
Tel: 01225 395239
Planning: Planning & Development Services, Lewis Ho, Manvers St, Bath BA1 1JG
Tel: 01225 477676 Fax: 01225 477592
Solicitor to the Council: Vernon Hitchman, Solicitor to the Council, Riverside, Temple St, Keynsham, Bristol BS31 1LA
Tel: 01225 477000 Fax: 01225 394043
DX: 30109 Keynsham
e-mail: vernon_hitchman@bathnes.gov.uk
Water Services: Wessex Water

38.7 North Somerset District Council (U)

Website: www.n-somerset.gov.uk
Main Switchboard: 01934 888888
Conveyancing Searches: Land Charges Team, Town Hall, Walliscote Grove Rd, Weston-super-Mare BS23 1UJ
Tel: 01934 634942/634943 / 01275 884107
DX: 8411 Weston-super-Mare
e-mail: llcharges@n-somerset.gov.uk
Council Tax: Director of Finance & Resources, Town Hall, Walliscote Grove Rd, Weston-super-Mare BS23 1UJ
Tel: 01934 888144 Fax: 01934 634898
e-mail: n-somersetctax@liberata.com
Environmental Health: Director of Development & Environment, Town Hall, Walliscote Grove Rd, Weston-super-Mare BS23 1UJ
Tel: 01934 888888 Fax: 01934 634634
DX: 8411 Weston-super-Mare
Highways: Director of Development & Environment, Town Hall, Walliscote Grove Rd, Weston-Super-Mare BS23 1UJ
Tel: 01934 888802
Other depts: Planning/Building Control, Director of Development & Environment, Town Hall, Walliscote Grove Rd, Weston-super-Mare BS23 1UJ
Tel: 01275 884550
e-mail: bc.info@n-somerset.gov.uk
Solicitor to the Council: Head of Legal and Democratic Services, Town Hall, Walliscote Grove Rd, Weston-super-Mare BS23 1AE
Tel: 01275 884325 Fax: 01934 418194
DX: 8411 Weston-super-Mare
Water Services: Wessex Water

39 South Yorkshire

39.1 Barnsley Metropolitan Borough Council

Website: www.barnsley.gov.uk
Main Switchboard: 01226 770770
Conveyancing Searches: Borough Secretary's Dept, Local Land Charges Section, PO Box 634, Barnsley S70 9GG
Tel: 01226 773054 Fax: 01226 773097
DX: 12266 Barnsley 1
e-mail: locallandcharges@barnsley.gov.uk
Building Control: Planning & Regulatory Services, PO Box 604, Barnsley S70 9FE
Tel: 01226 770770
Council Tax: Council Tax Dept, Borough Treasurer, PO Box 63, Barnsley S70 2TJ
Tel: 01226 770770
Environmental Health: Planning & Regulatory Services, PO Box 602, Barnsley S70 9FB
Tel: 01226 770770
Highways: Environmental Services, PO Box 601, Barnsley S70 9FA
Housing: Strategic Housing, PO Box 603, Barnsley S70 9FD
Tel: 01226 770770
Planning: Planning & Regulatory Services, PO Box 604, Barnsley S70 9FE
Tel: 01226 770770

Solicitor to the Council: Andrew Frosdick, Borough Secretary and Solicitor to the Council, PO Box 609, Barnsley S70 9FH
Tel: 01226 773006 Fax: 01226 772499
Water Services: Yorkshire Water (Safe Move)

39.2 Doncaster Metropolitan Borough Council

Website: www.doncaster.gov.uk
Main Switchboard: 01302 736000
Conveyancing Searches: Local Land Charges, Floor 2, Civic Office, Waterdale, Doncaster DN1 3BU
Tel: 01302 734638
DX: 12569 Doncaster
e-mail: landcharges.legal@doncaster.gov.uk
Building Control: Building Control, Floor 2, Civic Office, Waterdale, Doncaster DN1 3BU
Tel: 01302 734848
e-mail: building.control@doncaster.gov.uk
Council Tax: Directorate of Financial Services, Colonnades Ho, Duke St, Doncaster DN1 1ER
Tel: 01302 734454 Fax: 01302 734373
e-mail: localtaxation@doncaster.gov.uk
Environmental Health: Public Health, Floor 2, Civic Office, Waterdale, Doncaster DN1 3BU
Tel: 01302 737573 Fax: 01302 737038
e-mail: nuisance.team@doncaster.gov.uk
Highways: Highways Management, Floor 2, Civic Office, Waterdale, Doncaster DN1 3BU
Tel: 01302 735059
e-mail: network.management@doncaster.gov.uk
Solicitor to the Council: Mr Roger Harvey, Assistant Director of Legal & Democratic Services, Floor 2, Civic Office, Waterdale, Doncaster DN1 3BU
Tel: 01302 734646
DX: 12569 Doncaster
e-mail: roger.harvey@doncaster.gov.uk
Water Services: Yorkshire Water, Severn Trent Water and Anglian Water

39.3 Sheffield City Council

Website: www.sheffield.gov.uk
Main Switchboard: 0114 272 6444
Conveyancing Searches: Legal & Governance, Local Land Charges Registry, Town Hall, Sheffield S1 2HH
Tel: 0114 273 4033/38
DX: 10580 Sheffield
e-mail: landcharges@sheffield.gov.uk
Building Control: Building Standards, 2–10 Carbrook Hall Rd, Sheffield S1 2DB
Tel: 0114 273 4168/5543/4170 Fax: 0114 273 5174
e-mail: buildingcontrol@sheffield.gov.uk
Council Tax: Council Tax Office, First Point, Howden Ho, Sheffield S1 2SH
Tel: 0114 273 6633 Fax: 0114 273 6808
e-mail: council.tax@sheffield.gov.uk
Environmental Health: Development, Environment & Leisure, 2–10 Carbrook Hall Rd, Sheffield S9 2DB
Tel: 0114 273 5774/7410/7411/4651 Fax: 0114 274 6464
e-mail: environmentalservicesadmin@sheffield.gov.uk
Highways: Development Services, Transport & Highways Division, Howden Ho, Sheffield S1 2HH
Tel: 01142 736125
e-mail: highwayrecords@sheffield.gov.uk
Planning: Land & Planning, Howden Ho, Sheffield S1 2SH
Tel: 0114 203 9178
e-mail: planningdc@sheffield.gov.uk
Water Services: Yorkshire Water

39.4 Rotherham Metropolitan Borough Council

Website: www.rotherham.gov.uk
Main Switchboard: 01709 382121
Conveyancing Searches: Environment & Development Services (Planning & Regeneration), Land Charges Section, Bailey Ho, Rawmarsh Rd, Rotherham S60 1TD
Tel: 01709 823890 Fax: 01709 823809
e-mail: eds-landcharges@rotherham.gov.uk
Building Control: Planning & Regeneration, Bailey Ho, Rawmarsh Rd, Rotherham S60 1TD
Tel: 01709 823847/823899 Fax: 01709 823845
e-mail: building.control@rotherham.gov.uk
Council Tax: Financial Services, Civic Bldgs, Walker Place, Rotherham S65 1UF
Tel: 01709 336006
e-mail: council.tax@rotherham.gov.uk
Highways: Environment & Development Services (Streetpride), Bailey Ho, Rawmarsh Rd, Rotherham S60 1TD
Tel: 01709 382121/823812 Fax: 01709 370506/366958
e-mail: streetpride@rotherham.gov.uk
Housing & Environmental Health: Housing & Environmental Health Services, Reresby Ho, Bow Bridge Close, Rotherham S60 1BY
Tel: 01709 382121
e-mail: environmental.management@rotherham.gov.uk
Solicitor to the Council: Mr Timothy Mumford, Head of Legal Services, The Council Offices, Doncaster Gate, Rotherham S65 1DJ
Tel: 01709 382121 Fax: 01709 823598
DX: 12606 Rotherham 1
e-mail: tim.mumford@rotherham.gov.uk
Water Services: Yorkshire Water and Severn Trent Water

40 Staffordshire

40.0 Staffordshire County Council

Website: www.staffordshire.gov.uk
Main Switchboard: 0300 111 8000
Search Address: Nick Bell, Chief Executive, Wedgwood Bldg, Tipping St, Stafford ST16 2DH
Tel: 01785 276100 Fax: 01785 277347
DX: 712320 Stafford 5
e-mail: nick.bell@staffordshire.gov.uk
Solicitor to the Council: John Tradewell, Director of Law & Transformation, Wedgwood Bldg, Tipping St, Stafford ST16 2DH
Tel: 01785 276102 Fax: 01785 277347
DX: 712320 Stafford 5
e-mail: john.tradewell@staffordshire.gov.uk

40.1 Staffordshire Moorlands District Council

Website: www.staffsmoorlands.gov.uk
Main Switchboard: 0345 605 3010
Conveyancing Searches: Registrar of Local Land Charges, PO Box 136, Buxton SK17 1AQ
Tel: 01538 395470
e-mail: land.charges@staffsmoorlands.gov.uk
Building Control, Council Tax, Environmental Health: PO Box 136, Buxton SK17 1AQ
Tel: 0345 6053010
Highways: Staffordshire County Council
Planning: Planning, PO Box 136, Buxton SK17 1AQ
Tel: 0345 605 3013
Solicitor to the Council: Mark Trillo, Corporate Director & Monitoring Officer, PO Box 136, Buxton SK17 1AQ
Tel: 0345 605 3010
e-mail: mark.trillo@staffsmoorlands.gov.uk

Water Services: Severn Trent Water and North West Water

40.2 Newcastle-under-Lyme Borough Council

Website: www.newcastle-staffs.gov.uk
Main Switchboard: 01782 717717
Conveyancing Searches: Central Services, Civic Offices, Merrial St, Newcastle-under-Lyme ST5 2AG
Tel: 01782 717717; direct line 01782 742232 Fax: 01782 711032
DX: 20959 Newcastle-under-Lyme
e-mail: land.charges@newcastle-staffs.gov.uk
Building Control: Civic Centre, Glebe St, Stoke-on-Trent, Staffs ST4 1RF
Tel: 01782 232266
Highways: Staffordshire County Council
Other depts: as before
Solicitor to the Council: Principal Solicitor, Civic Offices, Merrial St, Newcastle-under-Lyme ST5 2AG
Tel: 01782 742201
DX: 20959 Newcastle-under-Lyme
e-mail: instructionsforlegal@newcastle-staffs.gov.uk
Water Services: Severn Trent and North West Water

40.3 Stoke-on-Trent City Council (U)

Website: www.stoke.gov.uk
Main Switchboard: 01782 234567
Conveyancing Searches: Local Land Charges, City Renewal, PO Box 630, Civic Centre, Glebe St, Stoke-on-Trent ST4 1HH
Tel: 01782 232775 Fax: 01782 232171
DX: 21058 Stoke-on-Trent
e-mail: land.charges@stoke.gov.uk
Building Control: City Renewal, Civic Centre, Glebe St, Stoke-on-Trent ST4 1HH
Tel: 01782 232459 Fax: 01782 232171
DX: 21058 Stoke-on-Trent
e-mail: bas@stoke.gov.uk
Council Tax: Business Services, PO Box 632, Swann Ho, Boothen Rd, Stoke-on-Trent ST4 4TS
Tel: 01782 233777 Fax: 01782 232312
DX: 21058 Stoke-on-Trent
e-mail: revenues@stoke.gov.uk
Highways: Highways Network Management, Civic Centre, Glebe St, Stoke-on-Trent ST4 1HH
Tel: 01782 231934 Fax: 01782 232171
DX: 21058 Stoke-on-Trent
e-mail: kat.lacy@stoke.gov.uk
Planning: Development Management, Civic Centre, Glebe St, Stoke-on-Trent ST4 1HH
Tel: 01782 232372 Fax: 01782 232171
DX: 21058 Stoke-on-Trent
e-mail: planning.apps@stoke.gov.uk
Regulatory Services: Housing, Environmental & Neighbourhood Services, PO Box 2452, Hanley Town Hall, Albion St, Hanley, Stoke-on-Trent ST1 1XP
Tel: 01782 232065 Fax: 01782 236496
DX: 21058 Stoke-on-Trent
e-mail: public.protection@stoke.gov.uk
Solicitor to the Council: Mr Paul Hackney, Assistant Director, Legal Services, Civic Centre, Glebe St, Stoke-on-Trent ST4 1HH
Tel: 01782 232800 Fax: 01782 232377
DX: 21058 Stoke-on-Trent
e-mail: paul.hackney@stoke.gov.uk
Water Services: Severn Trent Water

40.4 Stafford Borough Council

Website: www.staffordbc.gov.uk
Main Switchboard: 01785 619000
Conveyancing Searches: Planning and Regeneration Service, Land Charges Section, Civic Centre, Riverside, Stafford ST16 3AQ
Tel: 01785 619534
DX: 723321 Stafford 7
e-mail: landcharges@staffordbc.gov.uk
Building Control, Council Tax, Environmental Health & Planning: Civic Centre, Riverside, Stafford ST16 3AQ
Tel: 01543 464507 / 01785 619157
e-mail: buildingcontrol@cannockchasedc.gov.uk
Note: revenues@staffordbc.gov.uk; ehadmin@staffordbc.gov.uk; planning@staffordbc.gov.uk
Highways: Staffordshire County Council
Solicitor to the Council: Mr Alistair Welch, Head of Law & Administration, Civic Centre, Riverside, Stafford ST16 3AQ
Tel: 01785 619204 Fax: 01785 619119
e-mail: awelch@staffordbc.gov.uk
Water: Severn Trent Water

40.5 East Staffordshire Borough Council

Website: www.eaststaffsbc.gov.uk
Main Switchboard: 01283 508000
Conveyancing Searches: Local Land Charges Dept, Legal and Democratic Services, ESBC, PO Box 8045, Burton upon Trent DE14 9JG
Tel: 01283 508000 Fax: 01283 508388
e-mail: locallandcharges@eaststaffsbc.gov.uk
Building Control, Planning, Environmental Health & Engineers: ESBC, PO Box 8045, Burton upon Trent DE14 9JG
Tel: 01283 508000 Fax: 01283 508388
Council Tax: Service Commissioning, ESBC, PO Box 8045, Burton upon Trent DE14 1JG
Tel: 01283 508000
e-mail: council.tax@eaststaffsbc.gov.uk
Highways: Staffordshire County Council
Solicitor to the Council: David Duckitt, Legal Services Manager, ESBC, PO Box 8045, Burton upon Trent DE14 9JG
Tel: 01283 508000 Fax: 01283 508388
e-mail: david.duckitt@eaststaffsbc.gov.uk
Water Services: Severn Trent Water

40.6 South Staffordshire District Council

Website: www.sstaffs.gov.uk
Main Switchboard: 01902 696000
Conveyancing Searches: Local Land Charges, Council Offices, Wolvehampton Rd, Codsall, South Staffordshire WV8 1PX
Tel: 01902 696116/696138 Fax: 01902 696143
DX: 18036 Codsall
e-mail: landcharges@sstaffs.gov.uk
Building Control: Council Offices, Wolverhampton Rd, Codsall, South Staffordshire WV8 1PX
Tel: 01902 696440 Fax: 01902 696434
DX: 18036 Wolverhampton
e-mail: buildingcontrol@sstaffs.gov.uk
Council Tax: Council Tax Dept, PO Box 1644, Wolverhampton WV8 1ZF
Tel: 01902 696664 Fax: 01902 696630
e-mail: taxation@sstaffs.gov.uk
Highways: Staffordshire County Council

Solicitor to the Council: Head of Legal Services, Council Offices, Wolverhampton Rd, Codsall, South Staffordshire WV8 1PX
Tel: 01902 696100 Fax: 01902 696800
DX: 18036 Wolverhampton
Water Services: Severn Trent Water

40.7 Cannock Chase District Council

Website: www.cannockchasedc.gov.uk
Main Switchboard: 01543 462621
Conveyancing Searches: Legal Dept, Civic Centre, PO Box 28, Beecroft Rd, Cannock WS11 1BG
Tel: 01543 464636 Fax: 01543 464321
e-mail: locallandcharges@cannockchasedc.gov.uk
Building Control: Stafford Borough Council, Civic Centre, Riverside, Stafford ST16 3AQ
Tel: 01543 464507
Council Tax, Environmental Health & Planning: Civic Centre, as before
Highways: Staffordshire County Council
Solicitor to the Council: Head of Legal & Democratic Services, Civic Centre, PO Box 28, Beecroft Rd, Cannock WS11 1BG
Tel: 01543 462621
Water Services: Severn Trent Water & South Staffordshire Water

40.8 Lichfield District Council

Website: www.lichfielddc.gov.uk
Main Switchboard: 01543 308000
Conveyancing Searches: Democratic, Development & Legal Services, Land Charges Section, District Council Ho, Frog La, Lichfield WS13 6YZ
Tel: 01543 309650 Fax: 01543 308068
e-mail: landcharges@lichfielddc.gov.uk
Building Control: Democratic, Development & Legal Services, District Council Ho, Frog La, Lichfield WS13 6YZ
Tel: 01543 308157 Fax: 01543 308068
e-mail: bchotline@lichfielddc.gov.uk
Council Tax: Revenues & Benefits, District Council Ho, Frog La, Lichfield WS13 6YX
Tel: 01543 308880 Fax: 01543 309899
e-mail: revenues@lichfielddc.gov.uk / benefits@lichfielddc.gov.uk
Environmental Health: Community Housing & Health, District Council Ho, Frog La, Lichfield WS13 6YX
Tel: 01543 308700 Fax: 01543 309899
e-mail: helen.titterton@lichfielddc.gov.uk
Highways: Staffordshire County Council
Planning: Democratic, Development & Legal Services, District Council Ho, Frog La, Lichfield WS13 6YZ
Tel: 01543 308000 Fax: 01543 308200
e-mail: devcontrol@lichfielddc.gov.uk
Solicitor to the Council: Bal Nahal, Democratic, Development & Legal Services, District Council Ho, Frog La, Lichfield WS13 6YU
Tel: 01543 308002 Fax: 01543 309899
e-mail: bal.nahal@lichfielddc.gov.uk
Water Services: Severn Trent Water

40.9 Tamworth Borough Council

Website: www.tamworth.gov.uk
Main Switchboard: 01827 709709
Conveyancing Searches: Land Charges Dept, Marmion Ho, Lichfield St, Tamworth B79 7BZ
Tel: 01827 709257 Fax: 01827 709271
e-mail: locallandcharges@tamworth.gov.uk
Building Control: Lichfield and Tamworth Building Control, Marmion Ho, Lichfield St, Tamworth B79 7BZ
Tel: 01543 308157 Fax: 01543 308068
e-mail: bchotline@lichfielddc.gov.uk
Council Tax: Council Tax, Marmion Ho, Lichfield St, Tamworth B79 7BZ
Tel: 01827 709530 Fax: 01827 709546
e-mail: counciltax@tamworth.gov.uk
Environmental Health: Environmental Health, Marmion Ho, Lichfield St, Tamworth B79 7BZ
Tel: 01827 709428 Fax: 01827 709434
Highways: Staffordshire County Council
Planning: Planning Dept, Marmion Ho, Lichfield St, Tamworth B79 7BZ
Tel: 01827 709281/709282 Fax: 01827 709277
e-mail: planningadmin@tamworth.gov.uk
Solicitor to the Council: Mrs Jane Hackett, Marmion Ho, Lichfield St, Tamworth B79 7BZ
Tel: 01827 709258 Fax: 01827 709271
e-mail: jane-hackett@tamworth.gov.uk
Water Services: Severn Trent Water

41 Suffolk

41.0 Suffolk County Council

Website: www.suffolk.gov.uk
Main Switchboard: 0345 606 6067
Search Address: Lead Lawyer (Commercial Practice Group), Suffolk Legal (Scrutiny & Monitoring), Constantine Ho, 5 Constantine Rd, Ipswich IP1 2DH
Tel: 01473 264220 Fax: 01473 263010
DX: 87951 Ipswich
e-mail: david.holt@suffolkcc.gov.uk
Solicitor to the Council: Solicitor to the Council and Head of Legal (Scrutiny & Monitoring), Constantine Ho, as above,
Tel: 01473 260860 Fax: 01473 263010
DX: 87951 Ipswich
e-mail: timothy.earl@suffolk.gov.uk

41.1 Waveney District Council

Website: www.waveney.gov.uk
Main Switchboard: 01502 562111
Conveyancing Searches: Regeneration & Environment Portfolio, Local Land Charges Section, Town Hall, High St, Lowestoft NR32 1HS
Tel: 01502 523243 Fax: 01502 514617
DX: 41220 Lowestoft
e-mail: landcharges@waveney.gov.uk
Building Control & Planning: Regeneration & Environment Portfolio, Building Control, Town Hall, High St, Lowestoft NR32 1HS
Tel: 01502 523044 Fax: 01502 514617
DX: 41220 Lowestoft
e-mail: buildingcontrol@waveney.gov.uk
Council Tax: Revenues & Benefits, PO Box 96, Lowestoft NR32 1HW
Tel: 01502 523435 Fax: 01502 523310
e-mail: council.tax@waveney.gov.uk
Environmental Health: Regeneration & Environment Portfolio, Environmental Services, Town Hall, High St, Lowestoft NR32 1HS
Tel: 01502 523117 Fax: 01502 523150
DX: 41220 Lowestoft
e-mail: environment@waveney.gov.uk
Highways: Suffolk County Council

Solicitor to the Council: Mrs Nargif Sultan, Solicitor to the Council, Town Hall, High St, Lowestoft NR32 1HS
Tel: 01502 523233 Fax: 01502 589327
DX: 41220 Lowestoft
Water: Geodesys Ltd

41.2 Forest Heath District Council

Website: www.forest-heath.gov.uk
Main Switchboard: 01638 719000
Conveyancing Searches: The Registrar, Land Charges, Council Offices, College Heath Rd, Mildenhall IP28 7EY
Tel: 01638 719319 Fax: 01638 716493
e-mail: lc@forest-heath.gov.uk
Building Control, Environmental Health & Planning: College Heath Rd, Mildenhall, Suffolk IP28 7EY
Tel: 01638 719000 Fax: 01638 716493
Council Tax: Council Tax, Breckland Ho, St Nicholas St, Thetford IP24 1BT
Tel: 01362 656871
e-mail: contactus@breckland.gov.uk
Highways: Suffolk County Council, Highways Dept., Endeavour Ho, 8 Russell St, Ipswich, Suffolk IP1 2BY
Tel: 01473 264190 Fax: 01473 216825
e-mail: land.charges@suffolk.gov.uk
Solicitor to the Council: Mr P Heard, Solicitor, Council Offices, College Heath Rd, Mildenhall IP28 7EY
Tel: 01638 719309 Fax: 01638 716493
e-mail: peter.heard@forest-heath.gov.uk
Water Services: Geodesys

41.3 St Edmundsbury Borough Council

Website: www.stedmundsbury.gov.uk
Main Switchboard: 01284 763233
Conveyancing Searches: Economy and Environment Directorate, West Suffolk Ho, Western Way, Bury St Edmunds IP33 3YU
Tel: 01284 763233 Fax: 01284 757369
DX: 57223 Bury St Edmunds
e-mail: land.charges@stedsbc.gov.uk
Building Control & Planning: Economy and Environment Directorate, West Suffolk Ho, Western Way, Bury St Edmunds IP33 3YU
Tel: 01284 763233 Fax: 01284 757374/8
DX: 57223 Bury St Edmunds
e-mail: planning.helpdesk@stedsbc.gov.uk
Council Tax: Resources Directorate, West Suffolk Ho, Western Way, Bury St Edmunds IP33 3YU
Tel: 01284 757275 Fax: 01284 757279
DX: 57223 Bury St Edmunds
e-mail: revenues@stedsbc.gov.uk
Environmental Health: Community Directorate, West Suffolk Ho, Western Way, Bury St Edmunds IP33 3YU
Tel: 01284 763233 Fax: 01284 757039
e-mail: env.health@stedsbc.gov.uk
Highways: Suffolk County Council
Solicitor to the Council: Miss Joy Bowes, Legal & Democratic Services, West Suffolk Ho, Western Way, Bury St Edmunds IP33 3YU
Tel: 01284 763233 Fax: 01284 757155
e-mail: legal.services@stedsbc.gov.uk
Water Services: Anglian Water

41.4 Mid Suffolk District Council

Website: www.midsuffolk.gov.uk
Main Switchboard: 01449 724500
Conveyancing Searches: Information Management and ICT, Council Offices, 131 High St, Needham Mkt, Ipswich IP6 8DL
Tel: 01449 724695 / 724686 Fax: 01449 724696
e-mail: land.charges@midsuffolk.gov.uk
Building Control: Building Control, Council Offices, as before,
Tel: 01449 724512
e-mail: buildingcontrol@midsuffolk.gov.uk
Council Tax: Council Tax, Council Offices, as before,
Tel: 01473 825798
e-mail: customer.services@babergh.gov.uk
Environment: Food & Safety and Environmental Protection, Council Offices, as before,
Tel: 0845 606 6170
e-mail: customerservice@midsuffolk.gov.uk
Highways: Endeavour Ho, 8 Russell St, Ipswich, Suffolk IP1 2BX
Tel: 0845 606 6067
e-mail: customerservice@midsuffolk.gov.uk
Planning: Planning, Council Offices, as before,
Tel: 01449 724612
e-mail: planningadmin@midsuffolk.gov.uk
Solicitor to the Council: District Monitoring Officer, Corporate Organisation: Governance & Law, Council Offices, High St, Needham Market, Ipswich IP6 8DL
Tel: 01449 724679 Fax: 01449 724696
e-mail: legalteam@midsuffolk.gov.uk
Water Services: Geodesys & Anglian Water Services

41.5 Suffolk Coastal District Council

Website: www.suffolkcoastal.gov.uk
Main Switchboard: 01394 383789
Conveyancing Searches: Registrar of Local Land Charges, Land Charges Dept, Council Offices, Melton Hill, Woodbridge IP12 1AU
Tel: 01394 444265
DX: 41400 Woodbridge
e-mail: land.charges@suffolkcoastal.gov.uk
Highways: Suffolk County Council
Solicitor to the Council: Mrs Hilary Slater, Solicitor to the Council, Council Offices, Melton Hill, Woodbridge IP12 1AU
Tel: 01394 383789 Fax: 01394 444770
DX: 41400 Woodbridge
e-mail: hilary.slater@suffolkcoastal.gov.uk
Water Services: Geodesys

41.6 Babergh District Council

Website: www.babergh.gov.uk
Main Switchboard: 01473 826622
Conveyancing Searches: Land Charges, Council Offices, Corks La, Hadleigh, Ipswich IP7 6SJ
Tel: 01473 826629 Fax: 08702 206197
DX: 85055 Exchange Babergh
e-mail: land.charges@babergh.gov.uk
Building Control: Council Offices, as before,
Tel: 01473 825853/825749 Fax: 01473 825708
e-mail: building.control@babergh.gov.uk
Council Tax: Council Offices, as before,
Tel: 01473 825798 Fax: 01473 823954
Environmental Health: Council Offices, as before
Highways: Suffolk County Council
Planning: Council Offices, as before,
Tel: 01473 825858

Solicitor to the Council: Head of Corporate Organisation, Council Offices, Corks La, Hadleigh, Ipswich IP7 6SJ
Tel: 01473 825712 Fax: 01473 825742
DX: 85055 Babergh
Water Services: Geodesys

41.7 Ipswich Borough Council

Website: www.ipswich.gov.uk
Main Switchboard: 01473 432000
Conveyancing Searches: Local Land Charges Section, Grafton Ho, 15/17 Russell Rd, Ipswich IP1 2DE
Tel: 01473 432340/432341/432866 Fax: 01473 432974
DX: 3225 Ipswich
e-mail: land.charges@ipswich.gov.uk
Planning: Planning, Grafton Ho, 15/17 Russell Rd, Ipswich IP1 2DE
Tel: 01473 432904 / 432907
DX: 3225 Ipswich
Solicitor to the Council: Ms Claire Barritt, Head of Corporate Services, Grafton Ho, 15/17 Russell Rd, Ipswich IP1 2DE
Tel: 01473 432320 Fax: 01473 433737
DX: 3225 Ipswich
e-mail: claire.barritt@ipswich.gov.uk
Water Services: Geodesys

42 Surrey

42.0 Surrey County Council

Website: www.surreycc.gov.uk
Main Switchboard: 03456 009009
Search Address: Legal Services, County Hall, Penrhyn Rd, Kingston upon Thames KT1 2DN
Tel: 020 8541 9088 Fax: 020 8541 9115
DX: 31509 Kingston upon Thames
e-mail: legal.records@surreycc.gov.uk
Solicitor to the Council: Mrs Ann Charlton, Head of Legal Services, County Hall, Penrhyn Rd, Kingston upon Thames KT1 2DN
Tel: 020 8541 9001 Fax: 020 8541 9005
DX: 31509 Kingston-upon-Thames
e-mail: ann.charlton@surreycc.gov.uk

42.1 Runnymede Borough Council

Website: www.runnymede.gov.uk
Main Switchboard: 01932 838383
Conveyancing Searches: Local Land Charges Section, Civic Centre, Station Rd, Addlestone KT15 2AH
Tel: 01932 425660/425662 Fax: 01932 838384
DX: 46350 Addlestone
e-mail: land.charges@runnymede.gov.uk
Building Control: Building Control, Civic Centre, Station Rd, Addlestone KT15 2AH
Tel: 01932 425135
e-mail: david.jones@runnymede.gov.uk
Council Tax: Council Tax, Civic Centre, Station Rd, Addlestone KT15 2AH
Tel: 01932 838383
e-mail: counciltax@runnymede.gov.uk
Highways: Surrey County Council
Solicitor to the Council: Legal, Civic Centre, Station Rd, Addlestone KT15 2AH
Tel: 01932 425643 Fax: 01932 838384
DX: 46350 Addlestone
e-mail: andrew.atkinson@runnymede.gov.uk
Water Services: Thames Water

42.2 Spelthorne Borough Council

Website: www.spelthorne.gov.uk
Main Switchboard: 01784 451499
Conveyancing Searches: Local Land Charges, Council Offices, Knowle Green, Staines TW18 1XB
Tel: 01784 446483
DX: 98044 Staines 2
e-mail: land.charges@spelthorne.gov.uk
Building Control: Building Control, Council Offices, Knowle Green, Staines TW18 1XB
Tel: 01784 446368
DX: 98044 Staines 2
e-mail: building.control@spelthorne.gov.uk
Council Tax: Council Tax, Council Offices, Knowle Green, Staines TW18 1XB
Tel: 01784 451499
DX: 98044 Staines 2
e-mail: c.tax@spelthorne.gov.uk
Environmental Health: Environmental Health, Council Offices, Knowle Green, Staines TW18 1XB
Tel: 01784 446291
DX: 98044 Staines 2
e-mail: environmental.health.domestic@spelthorne.gov.uk
Highways: Surrey County Council
Planning: Planning, Council Offices, Knowle Green, Staines TW18 1XB
Tel: 01784 444273
DX: 98044 Staines 2
e-mail: planning.development.control@spelthorne.gov.uk
Solicitor to the Council: Mr M Graham, Head of Legal Services, Council Offices, Knowle Green, Staines TW18 1XB
Tel: 01784 446229
DX: 98044 Staines 2
e-mail: m.graham@spelthorne.gov.uk
Water Services: Thames Water (Asset Data Services)

42.3 Surrey Heath Borough Council

Website: www.surreyheath.gov.uk
Main Switchboard: 01276 707100
Conveyancing Searches: Regulatory Services, Surrey Heath Ho, Knoll Rd, Camberley GU15 3HD
Tel: 01276 707305 Fax: 01276 707337
DX: 32722 Camberley
e-mail: landcharges@surreyheath.gov.uk
Building Control: Transformation, Surrey Heath Ho, Knoll Rd, Camberley GU15 3HD
Tel: 01276 707223 Fax: 01276 707266
DX: 32722 Camberley
e-mail: building.control@surreyheath.gov.uk
Council Tax: Council Tax, Surrey Heath Ho, Knoll Rd, Camberley GU15 3HD
Tel: 01276 707176 Fax: 01276 707440
DX: 32722 Camberley
e-mail: revenues@surreyheath.gov.uk
Environmental Health: Community Services, Surrey Heath Ho, Knoll Rd, Camberley GU15 3HD
Tel: 01276 707330 Fax: 01276 707177
DX: 32722 Camberley
e-mail: environmental.health@surreyheath.gov.uk
Highways: Surrey County Council
Planning: Regulatory Services, Surrey Heath Ho, Knoll Rd, Camberley GU15 3HD
Tel: 01276 707222 Fax: 01276 707218
DX: 32722 Camberley
e-mail: development.control@surreyheath.gov.uk

Solicitor to the Council: Head of Legal Services, Surrey Heath Ho, Knoll Rd, Camberley GU15 3HD
Tel: 01276 707304 Fax: 01276 707446
DX: 32722 Camberley
e-mail: legal.services@surreyheath.gov.uk
Water Services: Thames Water Utilities

42.4 Woking Borough Council

Website: www.woking.gov.uk
Main Switchboard: 01483 755855
Conveyancing Searches: Land Charges, Customer Services, Civic Offices, Gloucester Sq, Woking GU21 6YL
Tel: 01483 743035 Fax: 01483 776335
DX: 2931 Woking
e-mail: landcharges@woking.gov.uk
Building Control: Building Control, Civic Offices, as before,
Tel: 01483 756842
e-mail: buildingcontrol@woking.gov.uk
Highways: Surrey County Council
Solicitor to the Council: Peter Bryant, Borough Secretary & Solicitor, Civic Offices, Gloucester Sq, Woking GU21 1YL
Tel: 01483 755855 Fax: 01483 768746
DX: 2831 Woking
e-mail: wokbc@woking.gov.uk
Water Services: Thames Water

42.5 Elmbridge Borough Council

Website: www.elmbridge.gov.uk
Main Switchboard: 01372 474474
Conveyancing Searches: Local Land Charges, Planning Services, Civic Centre, High St, Esher KT10 9SD
Tel: 01372 474195 Fax: 01372 474973
DX: 36302 Esher
e-mail: lcharges@elmbridge.gov.uk
Note: 24 hour information line: 01372 474197.
Highways: Surrey County Council, Highway Information Team
Other depts: Civic Centre, High St, Esher KT10 9SD
Tel: 01372 474474
DX: 36302 Esher
Solicitor to the Council: Mr Alan Harrison, Head of Legal Services, Civic Centre, High St, Esher KT10 9SD
Tel: 01372 474192 Fax: 01372 474973
DX: 36302 Esher
e-mail: legalservices@elmbridge.gov.uk
Water Services: Thames Water

42.6 Epsom & Ewell Borough Council

Website: www.epsom-ewell.gov.uk
Main Switchboard: 01372 732000
Conveyancing Searches: Support Services, Town Hall, The Parade, Epsom KT18 5BY
Tel: 01372 732000 Fax: 01372 732720
DX: 30713 Epsom
e-mail: contactus@epsom-ewell.gov.uk
Building Control, Council Tax, Environmental Health, Planning: Town Hall, The Parade, Epsom KT18 5BY
Tel: 01372 732000
DX: 37013 Epsom
Highways: Surrey County Council
Solicitor to the Council: Mr Simon Young, Chief Solicitor, Town Hall, The Parade, Epsom KT18 5BY
Tel: 01372 732000 Fax: 01372 732111
DX: 30713 Epsom
e-mail: syoung@epsom-ewell.gov.uk
Water Services: Thames Water

42.7 Guildford Borough Council

Website: www.guildford.gov.uk
Main Switchboard: 01483 505050
Conveyancing Searches: Planning Services, Local Land Charges Section, Millmead Ho, Millmead, Guildford GU2 4BB
Tel: 01483 444080 Fax: 01483 444996
DX: 2472 Guildford 1
e-mail: landcharges@guildford.gov.uk
Building Control & Planning: Planning Services, Millmead Ho, Millmead, Guildford GU2 4BB
Tel: 01483 444585
e-mail: buildingcontrol@guildford.gov.uk
Council Tax: Revenue & Payments Services, Council Tax, Millmead Ho, Millmead, Guildford GU2 4BB
Tel: 01483 444864 Fax: 01483 444874
e-mail: ctax@guildford.gov.uk
Environmental Health: Environmental Health & Licensing Services, Millmead Ho, Millmead, Guildford GU2 4BB
Tel: 01483 505050 Fax: 01483 444546
e-mail: environmentalhealth@guildford.gov.uk
Highways: Surrey County Council
Solicitor to the Council: Mr S Gerrard, Interim Head of Legal & Democratic Services, Millmead Ho, Millmead, Guildford GU2 4BB
Tel: 01483 444042
DX: 2472 Guildford 1
e-mail: stephen.gerrard@guildford.gov.uk
Water Services: Thames Water

42.8 Mole Valley District Council

Website: www.molevalley.gov.uk
Main Switchboard: 01306 885001
Conveyancing Searches: Land Charges Section, Pippbrook, Dorking RH4 1SJ
Tel: 01306 879132 Fax: 01306 879190
DX: 57306 Dorking
e-mail: land.charges@molevalley.gov.uk
Highways: Surrey County Council
Solicitor to the Council: Mr Chris Harris, Solicitor, Pippbrook, Dorking RH4 1SJ
Tel: 01306 885001 Fax: 01306 876821
DX: 57306 Dorking
e-mail: chris.harris@molevalley.gov.uk
Water Services: Thames Water/Southern Water

42.9 Reigate & Banstead Borough Council

Website: www.reigate-banstead.gov.uk
Main Switchboard: 01737 276000
Conveyancing Searches: Legal Services Manager, Town Hall, Castlefield Rd, Reigate RH2 0SH
Tel: 01737 276068 Fax: 01737 276070
DX: 54102 Reigate 2
e-mail: maggie.judd@reigate-banstead.gov.uk
Building Control, Environmental Health & Planning: Environmental Services, Town Hall, Castlefield Rd, Reigate RH2 0SH
Tel: 01737 276000 Fax: 01737 276260
DX: 54102 Reigate 2
e-mail: contactus@reigate-banstead.gov.uk
Council Tax: Council Tax Office, Town Hall, Castlefield Rd, Reigate RH2 0SH
Tel: 01737 276000 Fax: 01737 276513
DX: 54102 Reigate 2
e-mail: council.tax@reigate-banstead.gov.uk

Solicitor to the Council: Head of Legal & Property Services, Town Hall, Castlefield Rd, Reigate RH2 0SH
Tel: 01737 276000 Fax: 01737 276070
DX: 54102 Reigate 2
e-mail: michael.graham@reigate-banstead.gov.uk
Water Services: Thames Water

42.10 Tandridge District Council

Website: www.tandridge.gov.uk
Main Switchboard: 01883 722000
Conveyancing Searches: Land Charges, Council Offices, 8 Station Rd East, Oxted RH8 0BT
Tel: 01883 732878/732879 Fax: 01883 722015
DX: 39359 Oxted
e-mail: landcharges@tandridge.gov.uk
Building Control: Building Control, Council Offices, 8 Station Rd East, Oxted RH8 0BT
Tel: 01883 722000 Fax: 01883 722015
DX: 39359 Oxted
e-mail: buildingcontrol@tandridge.gov.uk
Council Tax: Department of Resources, Council Offices, 8 Station Rd East, Oxted RH8 0BT
Tel: 01883 732932/0845 9400470 Fax: 01883 722015
DX: 39359 Oxted
e-mail: ctax@tandridge.gov.uk
Highways: Surrey County Council
Other depts: Department of Environmental Protection, Council Offices, 8 Station Rd East, Oxted RH8 0BT
Tel: 01883 722000 Fax: 01883 722015
DX: 39359 Oxted
Planning: Planning, Council Offices, 8 Station Rd East, Oxted RH8 0BT
Tel: 01883 722000 Fax: 01883 722015
DX: 39359 Oxted
e-mail: planningapplications@tandridge.gov.uk
Solicitor to the Council: Mr C Moore, Assistant Chief Executive (Legal), Council Offices, 8 Station Rd East, Oxted RH8 0BT
Tel: 01883 732740 Fax: 01883 722015
DX: 39359 Oxted
e-mail: cmoore@tandridge.gov.uk
Water Services: Thames Water/Southern Water

42.11 Waverley Borough Council

Website: www.waverley.gov.uk
Main Switchboard: 01483 523333
Conveyancing Searches: Jack Andrew, Land Charges Administrator, Council Offices, The Burys, Godalming GU7 1HR
Tel: 01483 523272
DX: 58303 Godalming 1
e-mail: landcharges@waverley.gov.uk
Building Control: Council Offices, The Burys, Godalming GU7 1HR
Tel: 01483 523323
e-mail: buildingcontrol@waverley.gov.uk
Council Tax: Council Offices, The Burys, Godalming GU7 1HR
Tel: 01483 523500
e-mail: counciltax@waverley.gov.uk
Environmental Health: Community Services, Council Offices, The Burys, Godalming GU7 1HR
Tel: 01483 523393
e-mail: environmentalhealth@waverley.gov.uk
Highways: Surrey County Council
Planning: Corporate Services and Planning, Council Offices, The Burys, Godalming GU7 1HR
Tel: 01483 523583
e-mail: planningenquiries@waverley.gov.uk
Solicitor to the Council: Daniel Bainbridge, Borough Solicitor, Council Offices, The Burys, Godalming GU7 1HR
Tel: 01483 523235
DX: 58303 Godalming 1
e-mail: daniel.bainbridge@waverley.gov.uk
Water Services: Thames Water and Southern Water

43 Tyne & Wear

43.1 Newcastle upon Tyne City Council

Website: www.newcastle.gov.uk
Main Switchboard: 0191 278 7878
Conveyancing Searches: Land Charges, Legal Services, Civic Centre, Barras Bridge, Newcastle upon Tyne NE99 2BN
Tel: 0191 211 5146 Fax: 0191 211 4887
DX: 62552 Jesmond
e-mail: landcharges@newcastle.gov.uk
Building Control, Council Tax, Environmental Health, Highways & Planning: Civic Centre, Barras Bridge, Newcastle upon Tyne NE99 2BN
Tel: 0191 232 8520
Solicitor to the Council: John Softly, Chief Legal Officer, Civic Centre, Barras Bridge, Newcastle upon Tyne NE99 2BN
Tel: 0191 2777122 Fax: 0191 277 7127
DX: 62552 Jesmond
e-mail: john.softly@newcastle.gov.uk
Water Services: Northumbrian Water

43.2 North Tyneside Borough Council

Website: www.northtyneside.gov.uk
Main Switchboard: 0845 200 0101
Conveyancing Searches: North Tyneside Council, Local Land Charges, Legal Governance & Commercial Services, Quadrant 3rd Fl Left, The Silverlink North, Cobalt Business Pk, North Tyneside NE27 0BY
Tel: 0191 643 2200 Fax: 0191 643 2430
e-mail: land.charges@northtyneside.gov.uk
Building Control: Building Control, North Tyneside Council, Quadrant 1st Fl Left, The Silverlink North, Cobalt Business Pk, North Tyneside NE27 0BY
Tel: 0191 643 2200
e-mail: building.control@northtyneside.gov.uk
Council Tax: Council Tax, Quadrant 1st Fl Right, The Silverlink North, Colbalt Business Pk, North Tyneside NE27 0BY
Tel: 0845 200 0104
e-mail: team.revenue@northtyneside.gov.uk
Environmental Health: Environmental Health, North Tyneside Council. Quadrant 1st Fl Left, The Silverlink North, Cobalt Business Pk, North Tyneside NE27 0BY
Tel: 0191 6436635 Fax: 0191 6432391
e-mail: environmental.health@northtyneside.gov.uk
Highways and Environment: Highway Maintenance, Quadrant 1st Fl Left, The Silverlink North, Cobalt Business Pk, North Tyneside NE27 0BY
Tel: 0845 200 0103
e-mail: highways.environment@northtyneside.gov.uk
Planning: Planning, Quadrant 1st Fl Left, The Silverlink North, Cobalt Business Pk, North Tyneside NE27 0BY
Tel: 0191 643 2310 Fax: 0191 643 2426
e-mail: planning.enforcement@northtyneside.gov.uk

Solicitor to the Council: Head of Legal, Governance & Commercial Services, Quadrant 3rd Fl Left, The Silverlink North, Cobalt Business Pk, North Tyneside NE27 0BY
Tel: 0191 643 5339 Fax: 0191 643 2451
Water Services: Northumbrian Water Ltd.

43.3 Gateshead Borough Council

Website: www.gateshead.gov.uk
Main Switchboard: 0191 433 3000
Conveyancing Searches: Legal & Corporate Services, Civic Centre, Regent St, Gateshead NE8 1HH
Tel: 0191 433 2195 Fax: 0191 433 3256
DX: 60308 Gateshead 1
e-mail: landcharges@gateshead.gov.uk
Building Control: Regulatory Services, Civic Centre, Regent St, Gateshead NE8 1HH
Tel: 0191 433 3144 Fax: 0191 478 3491
e-mail: labc@gateshead.gov.uk
Council Tax: Finance & ICT Central Services, Civic Centre, Regent St, Gateshead NE8 1HH
Tel: 0191 433 3729 Fax: 0191 433 2066
e-mail: counciltax@gateshead.gov.uk
Environmental Health: Regulatory Services, Development & Enterprise, Civic Centre, Regent St, Gateshead NE8 1HH
Tel: 0191 433 3926 Fax: 0191 4774827
e-mail: environmentalhealth@gateshead.gov.uk
Highways: Development & Enterprise, Civic Centre, Regent St, Gateshead NE8 1HH
Tel: 0191 433 3132 Fax: 0191 477 8422
e-mail: customerservices@gateshead.gov.uk
Planning: Development Control, Civic Centre, Regent St, Gateshead NE8 1HH
Tel: 0191 433 3416 Fax: 0191 477 8422
e-mail: customerservices@gateshead.gov.uk
Solicitor to the Council: Mr Mike Barker, Civic Centre, Regent St, Gateshead NE8 1HH
Tel: 0191 433 3000 Fax: 0191 478 2755
DX: 60308 Gateshead 1
Water Services: Northumbrian Water

43.4 South Tyneside Borough Council

Website: www.southtyneside.info
Main Switchboard: 0191 427 1717
Conveyancing Searches: Business & Area Management, Head of Legal Services, Town Hall & Civic Offices, Westoe Rd, South Shields NE33 2RL
Tel: 0191 424 7229/7231 Fax: 0191 455 0208
DX: 60850 South Shields 4
e-mail: landcharges@southtyneside.gov.uk
Building Control & Planning: Economic Regeneration, Head of Regulatory Services, Town Hall & Civic Offices, Westoe Rd, South Shields NE33 2RL
Tel: 0191 427 1717 Fax: 0191 427 7171
Council Tax: Council Tax Office, Town Hall & Civic Offices, Westoe Rd, South Shields NE33 2RL
Tel: 0191 424 4330
e-mail: council.tax@southtyneside.gov.uk
Environmental Health: Economic Regeneration, Head of Regulatory Services, Town Hall & Civic Offices, Westoe Rd, South Shields NE33 2RL
Tel: 0191 427 1717 Fax: 0191 427 0469
Highways: Business & Area Management, Head of Sustainable Community, Middlefields, Heddon Way, South Shields NE34 0NT
Tel: 0191 427 2652 Fax: 0191 427 2061
Legal Services: Head of Legal Services, Town Hall & Civic Offices, Westoe Rd, South Shields NE33 2RL
Tel: 0191 427 1717 Fax: 0191 455 0208
DX: 60850 South Shields 4
Water Services: Northumbrian Water

43.5 Sunderland City Council

Website: www.sunderland.gov.uk
Main Switchboard: 0191 520 5555
Conveyancing Searches: Law & Governance, Land Charges, Civic Centre, Burdon Rd, Sunderland SR2 7DN
Tel: 0191 561 1018 Fax: 0191 553 1020
DX: 60729 Sunderland
e-mail: land.charges@sunderland.gov.uk
Building Control: Office of the Chief Executive, Building Control, Sunderland City Library & Arts Centre, Upper Fl, 28–32 Fawcett St, Sunderland SR1 1RE
Tel: 0191 561 1550 Fax: 0191 553 1466
DX: 60729 Sunderland
e-mail: buildingcontrol@sunderland.gov.uk
Council Tax: Commercial & Corporate Services, Civic Centre, Burdon Rd, Sunderland SR2 7DN
Tel: 0191 561 1814 Fax: 0191 553 1854
DX: 60729 Sunderland
e-mail: council.tax@sunderland.gov.uk
Environmental Health: Office of the Chief Executive, Jack Crawford Ho, Commercial Rd, Sunderland SR2 8QR
Tel: 0191 566 1488 Fax: 0191 523 7963
DX: 60729 Sunderland
e-mail: cityandneighbourhood@sunderland.gov.uk
Highways: Office of the Chief Executive, Highjway Asset Management, Jack Crawford Ho, Commercial Rd, Sunderland SR2 8QR
Tel: 0191 561 1615
DX: 60729 Sunderland
e-mail: highway.records@sunderland.gov.uk
Planning: Office of the Chief Executive, Development Control, Sunderland City Library & Arts Centre, Upper Fl, 28–32 Fawcett St, Sunderland SR1 1RE
Tel: 0191 561 1564 Fax: 0191 514 5099
DX: 60729 Sunderland
e-mail: dc@sunderland.gov.uk
Solicitor to the Council: Head of Law & Governance, Civic Centre, Burdon Rd, Sunderland SR2 7DN
Tel: 0191 561 1805 Fax: 0191 553 2020
DX: 60729 Sunderland
e-mail: elaine.waugh@sunderland.gov.uk
Water Services: Northumbrian Water

44 Warwickshire

44.0 Warwickshire County Council

Website: www.warwickshire.gov.uk
Main Switchboard: 01926 410410
Search Address: Law & Governance, PO Box 9, Shire Hall, Warwick CV34 4RR
Tel: 01926 410410 Fax: 01926 412326
DX: 723362 Warwick 5
Solicitor to the Council: Greta Needham, Head of Law & Governance, PO Box 9, Shire Hall, Warwick CV34 4RR
Tel: 01926 410410 Fax: 01926 412326
DX: 723362 Warwick 5
e-mail: gretaneedham@warwickshire.gov.uk

44.1 North Warwickshire Borough Council

Website: www.northwarks.gov.uk
Main Switchboard: 01827 715341
Conveyancing Searches: Central Services, The Council Ho, South St, Atherstone CV9 1DE
Tel: 01827 715341 Fax: 01827 719225
e-mail: llc@northwarks.gov.uk
Building Control: c/o Nuneaton & Bedworth Borough Council,
e-mail: building.control@nuneatonandbedworth.gov.uk
Council Tax: Resources (Revenues and Benefits Division), The Council Ho, South St, Atherstone CV9 1DE
Tel: 01827 715341 Fax: 01827 719225
e-mail: counciltax@northwarks.gov.uk
Environmental Health: Environment Division, Old Bank Ho, 129 Long St, Atherstone CV9 1DE
Tel: 01827 715341
e-mail: environmentalhealth@northwarks.gov.uk
Highways: Warwickshire County Council
Planning: Planning Division, The Council Ho, South St, Atherstone CV9 1DE
Tel: 01827 715341
e-mail: planningcontrol@northwarks.gov.uk
Solicitor to the Council: Mr Steve Maxey, Assistant Chief Executive, The Council Ho, South St, Atherstone CV9 1DE
Tel: 01827 715341 Fax: 01827 719225
e-mail: stevemaxey@northwarks.gov.uk
Water Services: Severn Trent

44.2 Nuneaton & Bedworth Borough Council

Website: www.nuneatonandbedworth.gov.uk
Main Switchboard: 024 76376376
Conveyancing Searches: Planning & Public Protection – Land Charges, Town Hall, Coton Rd, Nuneaton CV11 5AA
Tel: 024 7637 6361 Fax: 024 7637 6214
DX: 16458 Nuneaton 1
e-mail: land.charges@nuneatonandbedworth.gov.uk
Building Control & Planning: Planning & Public Protection, Town Hall, Coton Rd, Nuneaton CV11 5AA
Tel: 024 7637 6328 Fax: 024 7637 6214
DX: 16458 Nuneaton 1
e-mail: building.control@nuneatonandbedworth.gov.uk
Note: planning@nuneatonandbedworth.gov.uk
Council Tax: Finance & Procurement, Council Ho, Coton Rd, Nuneaton CV11 5AA
Tel: 024 7637 6530 Fax: 024 7637 6433
DX: 16458 Nuneaton 1
e-mail: benefits.section@nuneatonandbedworth.gov.uk
Environmental Health: Planning & Public Protection, Town Hall, Coton Rd, Nuneaton CV11 5AA
Tel: 024 7637 6328 Fax: 024 7637 6214
DX: 16458 Nuneaton 1
e-mail: env.health@nuneatonandbedworth.gov.uk
Highways: Warwickshire County Council, Environment & Economy, PO Box 43, Shire Hall, Warwick CV34 4SX
Tel: 01926 412708 Fax: 08702 428149
DX: 723360 Warwick
e-mail: searches@warwickshire.gov.uk
Solicitor to the Council: Legal & Democratic Support Services, Town Hall, Coton Rd, Nuneaton CV11 5AA
Tel: 024 7637 6234 Fax: 024 7637 6238
DX: 16458 Nuneaton 1
e-mail: legal@nuneatonandbedworth.gov.uk
Water Services: Severn Trent Water

44.3 Rugby Borough Council

Website: www.rugby.gov.uk
Main Switchboard: 01788 533533
Conveyancing Searches: Local Land Charges Section, Town Hall, Evreux Way, Rugby CV21 2RR
Tel: 01788 533560 Fax: 01788 533778
DX: 11681 Rugby
e-mail: land.charges@rugby.gov.uk
Note: A current OS plan will be required for all searches.
Building Control: Planning & Recreation Services, Town Hall, Evreux Way, Rugby CV21 2RR
Tel: 01788 533790 Fax: 01788 533778
DX: 11681 Rugby
e-mail: building.control@rugby.gov.uk
Council Tax: Resources, Town Hall, Evreux Way, Rugby CV21 2RR
Tel: 01788 533488 Fax: 01788 533409
DX: 11681 Rugby
e-mail: council.tax@rugby.gov.uk
Highways: Warwickshire County Council
Housing & Environmental Health: Housing Services & Environmental Services, Town Hall, Evreux Way, Rugby CV21 2RR
Tel: 01788 533533 Fax: 01788 533409
DX: 11681 Rugby (HEH)
e-mail: contact.centre@rugby.gov.uk
Planning: Planning & Recreation Services, Town Hall, Evreux Way, Rugby CV21 2RR
Tel: 01788 533759 Fax: 01788 533778
DX: 11681 Rugby
e-mail: rbc.planning@rugby.gov.uk
Solicitor to the Council: Deborah Tyrrell, Principal Solicitor, Town Hall, Evreux Way, Rugby CV21 2RR
Tel: 01788 533533 Fax: 01788 533567
DX: 11681 Rugby
e-mail: deborah.tyrell@rugby.gov.uk
Water Services: Severn Trent Water

44.4 Warwick District Council

Website: www.warwickdc.gov.uk
Main Switchboard: 01926 450000
Conveyancing Searches: Land Charges, Riverside Ho, Milverton Hill, Leamington Spa CV32 5HZ
Tel: 01926 456607 Fax: 01926 456609
DX: 29123 Leamington Spa 1
e-mail: landcharges@warwickdc.gov.uk
Building Control: Head of Planning, Riverside Ho, Milverton Hill, Leamington Spa CV32 5HZ
Tel: 01926 456516 Fax: 01926 456542
DX: 29123 Leamington Spa 1
e-mail: planning_bcontrol@warwickdc.gov.uk
Council Tax: Head of Revenues & Customer Services, PO Box 258, Leamington Spa CV32 5RU
Tel: 01926 456066 Fax: 01926 456059
e-mail: ctaxenquiries@warwickdc.gov.uk
Environmental Health: Head of Environmental Health, PO Box 2176, Riverside Ho, Milverton Hill, Leamington Spa CV32 5QF
Tel: 01926 450000 Fax: 01926 456746
DX: 29123 Leamington Spa 1
Highways: Warwickshire County Council
Planning: Head of Planning, Riverside Ho, Milverton Hill, Leamington Spa CV32 5HZ
Tel: 01926 456536 x3368 Fax: 01926 456542
DX: 29123 Leamington Spa 1
e-mail: planning_west@warwick.gov.uk

Solicitor to the Council: David Carter, Strategic Director, Customers, Workforce & Governance, Warwickshire County Council, PO Box 9, Shire Hall, Warwick CV34 4RR
Tel: 01926 412798 Fax: 01926 413704
DX: 723362 Warwick 5
e-mail: legal@warwickshire.gov.uk
Water Services: Severn Trent Water

44.5 Stratford-upon-Avon District Council

Website: www.stratford.gov.uk
Main Switchboard: 01789 267575
Conveyancing Searches: Local Land Charges, Elizabeth Ho, Church St, Stratford-upon-Avon CV37 6HX
Tel: 01789 267575/260223 Fax: 01789 260630
DX: 700737 Stratford-upon-Avon 2
e-mail: landcharges@stratford-dc.gov.uk
Building Control, Council Tax, Environmental Health & Planning: Elizabeth Ho, as before,
Tel: 01789 260626 Fax: 01789 260630
e-mail: buildingcontrol@stratford-dc.gov.uk
Highways: Warwickshire County Council
Solicitor to the Council: Elizabeth Ho, Church St, Stratford-upon-Avon CV37 6HX
Tel: 01789 267575 Fax: 01789 260789
DX: 700737 Stratford-upon-Avon 2
Water Services: Severn Trent Water/Thames Water

45 West Midlands

45.1 Wolverhampton City Council

Website: www.wolverhampton.gov.uk
Main Switchboard: 01902 556556
Conveyancing Searches: Legal Services, Civic Centre, St Peter's Sq, Wolverhampton WV1 1RG
Tel: 01902 555028 Fax: 01902 554970
Building Control: Building Consultancy, Regeneration & Environment, Civic Centre, St Peter's Sq, Wolverhampton WV1 1RP
Tel: 01902 555595 Fax: 01902 555587
Council Tax: Council Tax Finance Section, PO Box 250, Wolverhampton WV2 1AX
Tel: 01902 555805/6 Fax: 01902 555885
Environmental Health: Regeneration & Environment, Civic Centre, St Peter's Sq, Wolverhampton WV1 1RG
Tel: 01902 554303 Fax: 01902 554329
Highways: Transport Network Management, Regeneration & Environment, Heantun Ho, Salop St, Wolverhampton WV3 0SQ
Tel: 01902 555755 Fax: 01902 555794
Planning: Regeneration & Environment, Civic Centre, St Peter's Sq, Wolverhampton WV1 1RP
Tel: 01902 555604 Fax: 01902 555403
Solicitor to the Council: S Kembrey, Solicitor to the Council & Assistant Director Governance, Civic Centre, St Peter's Sq, Wolverhampton WV1 1RG
Tel: 01902 554910 Fax: 01902 554970
Water Services: Severn Trent Water

45.2 Walsall Metropolitan Borough Council

Website: www.walsall.gov.uk
Main Switchboard: 01922 650000
Conveyancing Searches: Registrar of Local Land Charges, Local Land Charges, Planning & Building Control, Civic Centre, Darwall St, Walsall WS1 1DG
Tel: 01922 652667 Fax: 01922 623234
e-mail: locallandcharges@walsall.gov.uk
Building Control: Planning & Building Control, Civic Centre, Darwall St, Walsall WS1 1DG
Tel: 01922 652677 Fax: 01922 623234
e-mail: buildingcontrol@walsall.gov.uk
Council Tax: The Local Taxation Unit, PO Box 23, Walsall WS1 1TP
Tel: 01922 650000 Fax: 01922 723337
e-mail: counciltax@walsall.gov.uk
Environmental Health: Pollution Control, Engineering & Transportation, Civic Centre, Darwall St, Walsall WS1 1DG
Tel: 01922 658040 Fax: 01922 654800
Solicitor to the Council: Head of Legal Services, Town Hall, Lichfield St, Walsall WS1 1TP
Tel: 01922 654822 Fax: 01922 646142
DX: 12149 Walsall
Water Services: Severn Trent Water

45.3 Dudley Metropolitan Borough Council

Website: www.dudley.gov.uk
Main Switchboard: 0300 555 2345
Conveyancing Searches: Local Land Charges, Law & Governance, Directorate of Corporate Resources, 5 Ednam Rd, Dudley DY1 1HL
Tel: 01384 815336/815340/816815 Fax: 01384 814084
DX: 741443 Dudley 7
e-mail: landcharges@dudley.gov.uk
Building Control & Planning: Directorate of the Urban Environment, 3 St James's Rd, Dudley DY1 1HZ
Tel: 01384 814136 Fax: 01384 814126
e-mail: building.control@dudley.gov.uk
Council Tax: Customer Services, Directorate of Corporate Resources, The Council Ho, Priory Rd, Dudley DY1 1HG
Tel: 01384 814939 / 0300 555 8000 Fax: 01384 815358
e-mail: revenue.finance@dudley.gov.uk
Environmental Health: Directorate of the Urban Environment – Planning & Environmental Health, 3 St James' Rd, Dudley DY1 1HZ
Tel: 01384 814136 Fax: 01384 814627
e-mail: enviroprotect.due@dudley.gov.uk
Highways: Directorate of the Urban Environment, Traffic & Road Safety, The Council Ho, Mary Stevens Pk, Stourbridge DY8 2AA
Tel: 01384 814450/4429 Fax: 01384 814428
Solicitor to the Council: Director, Directorate of Corporate Resources, Council Ho, Priory Rd, Dudley DY1 1HF
Tel: 01384 815300
Water Services: Severn Trent Water

45.4 Sandwell Metropolitan Borough Council

Website: www.sandwell.gov.uk
Main Switchboard: 0121 569 2200 / 0845 358 2200
Conveyancing Searches: Local Land Charges, Sandwell Council Ho, PO Box 2374, Oldbury B69 3DE
Tel: 0121 569 3256/3257
DX: 710072 Sandwell
e-mail: angela_price@sandwell.gov.uk
Council Tax: Council Tax, Sandwell Council Ho, PO Box 237, Sale M33 6GY
Tel: 0845 3510015
e-mail: contact@sandwell.gov.uk
Environmental Health: Environmental Health & Trading Standards, Court Ho, 335–337 High St, West Bromwich B70 8LU
Tel: 0121 569 6600

Planning, Highways & Building Control: Regeneration and Economy, Sandwell Council Ho, PO Box 2374, Oldbury B69 3DE
Tel: 0121 569 4055/4054
DX: 710072 Sandwell
e-mail: planning@sandwell.gov.uk
Solicitor to the Council: Mr Jan Britton, Chief Executive, Sandwell Council Ho, PO Box 2374, Oldbury B69 3DE
Tel: 0121 569 2200 Fax: 0121 569 3210
DX: 710070 Sandwell
Water Services: Severn Trent Water

45.5 Birmingham City Council

Website: www.birmingham.gov.uk/landcharges
Main Switchboard: 0121 303 1111
Conveyancing Searches: Local Land Charges Registry, PO Box 28, Birmingham B1 1TU
Tel: 0121 303 4839
e-mail: land.charges@birmingham.gov.uk
Building Control: Building Consultancy Division, PO Box 28, Birmingham B1 1TU
Tel: 0121 675 7006
e-mail: building.consultancy@birmingham.gov.uk
Council Tax: Central Income Section, Revenues Directorate, PO Box 4092, Birmingham B4 7AD
Tel: 0121 303 5530
e-mail: revenue.cis@birmingham.gov.uk
Environmental Health: Environmental Protection Unit, 581 Tyburn Rd, Erdington B24 9RF
Tel: 0121 303 9900/5440 Fax: 0121 303 9901/5436
e-mail: publichealth@birmingham.gov.uk
Highways: Private Rented Services, Suite 6 Waterlinks Ho, Richard St, Birmingham B7 4AA
Tel: 0121 303 4009 Fax: 0121 303 1475
Planning: Planning Dept, Birmingham B1 1TU
Tel: 0121 303 1115 Fax: 0121 303 4838
e-mail: planning.enquiries@birmingham.gov.uk
Solicitor to the Council: M F N Ahmad, Chief Legal Officer, King Edward Ho, 135a New St, Birmingham B2 4QJ
Tel: 0121 303 2066
DX: 13053 Birmingham 1
Transportation: Transportation Strategy, Birmingham B2 2JE
Tel: 0121 675 3615/3611/3613 Fax: 0121 303 6379
e-mail: highwaysinformation@birmingham.gov.uk
Water Services: Severn Trent Water

45.6 Solihull Metropolitan Borough Council

Website: www.solihull.gov.uk
Main Switchboard: 0121 704 6000
Conveyancing Searches: Land Charges, Council Ho, Solihull B91 9TX
Tel: 0121 704 6013/6014
e-mail: landcharges@solihull.gov.uk
Building Control & Planning: Planning Services, PO Box 11652, Solihull B91 9YA
Tel: 0121 704 8008
e-mail: planning@solihull.gov.uk
Council Tax: Council Tax, PO Box 1761, Council Ho, Solihull B91 9RR
Tel: 0121 704 8100
Environmental Health: Public Protection, PO Box 18, Council Ho, Solihull B91 3QB
Tel: 0121 704 8000
e-mail: publicprotection@solihull.gov.uk
Highways: Places Directorate, Transport, Highways & the Environment, Council Ho, Solihull B91 3QT
Tel: 0121 704 8004
e-mail: highwaysearches@solihull.gov.uk
Solicitor to the Council: Phillip Lloyd Williams, Director of Corporate Governance, Legal Services, Council Ho, Manor Sq, Solihull B91 3QB
Tel: 0121 704 6003
e-mail: legal@solihull.gov.uk
Water Services: Severn Trent Water

45.7 Coventry City Council

Website: www.coventry.gov.uk
Main Switchboard: 024 7683 3333
Conveyancing Searches: Local Land Charges Team, Council Ho, Earl St, Coventry CV1 5RR
Tel: 024 7683 3124/3127 Fax: 024 7683 3204
DX: 18868 Coventry 2
e-mail: landcharges@coventry.gov.uk
Building Control: Building Regulation, Fl 2, Civic Centre 4, Muck Park St, Coventry CV1 2PY
Tel: 01926 456519 Fax: 01926 456542
DX: 18868 Coventry 2
e-mail: buildingcontrol@coventry.gov.uk
Council Tax: Council Tax Team, Council Ho, Earl St, Coventry CV1 5RR
Tel: 024 7683 1111 Fax: 024 7683 3837
e-mail: counciltax@coventry.gov.uk
Environmental Health: Public Protection, Broadgate Ho, Broadgate, Coventry CV1 1NH
Tel: 024 7683 3333
DX: 18868 Coventry 2
e-mail: coventrydirect@coventry.gov.uk
Highways & Planning: City Development Directorate, Tower Block, Much Park St, Coventry CV1 2PY
Tel: 024 7683 3333 (H); 024 7683 1212 (Planning)
DX: 18868 Coventry 2
e-mail: planning@coventry.gov.uk
Solicitor to the Council: Christine Forde, Assistant Director Legal & Democratic Services, Council Ho, Earl St, Coventry CV1 5RR
Tel: 024 7683 1587 Fax: 024 7683 3770
DX: 18868 Coventry 2
Water Services: Severn Trent Water

46 West Sussex

46.0 West Sussex County Council

Website: www.westsussex.gov.uk
Main Switchboard: 01243 777100
Search Address: County Secretary's Group, County Hall, West St, Chichester PO19 1RG
Tel: 01243 777777 Fax: 01243 777952
DX: 30330 Chichester
e-mail: county.secretary@westsussex.gov.uk
Solicitor to the Council: Mr Tony Kershaw, Head of Legal Services, County Secretary's Group, County Hall, West St, Chichester PO19 1RQ
Tel: 01243 777100 Fax: 01243 777952
DX: 30330 Chichester
e-mail: tony.kershaw@westsussex.gov.uk

46.1 Crawley Borough Council

Website: www.crawley.gov.uk
Main Switchboard: 01293 438000
Conveyancing Searches: Registrar of Local Land Charges, Town Hall, The Boulevard, Crawley RH10 1UZ
Tel: 01293 438278/438525 Fax: 01293 511803
DX: 57139 Crawley
e-mail: landcharges@crawley.gov.uk

Building Control: Building Services-Horsham District Council, Park Nth, North St, Horsham RH12 1RL
Tel: 01403 215151 Fax: 01403 215599
DX: 57609 Horsham
e-mail: building.control@horsham.gov.uk
Highways: West Sussex County Council
Other depts: Town Hall, as before
Solicitor to the Council: Mrs Anne-Maria Brown, Town Hall, The Boulevard, Crawley RH10 1UZ
Tel: 01293 438292
Water Services: Thames Water

46.2 Chichester District Council

Website: www.chichester.gov.uk
Main Switchboard: 01243 785166
Conveyancing Searches: Local Land Charges Section, East Pallant Ho, East Pallant, Chichester PO19 1TY
Tel: 01243 534664; 785166 x 4664 Fax: 01243 776766
DX: 30340 Chichester
e-mail: landcharges@chichester.gov.uk
Building Control: Environment and Economic Services, East Pallant Ho, East Pallant, Chichester PO19 1TY
Tel: 01243 534734 Fax: 01243 776766
DX: 30340 Chichester
e-mail: contact@chichester.gov.uk
Council Tax: Revenues Systems, East Pallant Ho, East Pallant, Chichester PO19 1TY
Tel: 01243 534501 Fax: 01243 776766
DX: 30340 Chichester
e-mail: counciltax@chichester.gov.uk
Environmental Health: Environmental Health Services, East Pallant Ho, East Pallant, Chichester PO19 1TY
Tel: 01243 534598 Fax: 01243 776766
e-mail: environmentalhealth@chichester.gov.uk
Highways: West Sussex County Council
Planning: Development Management, East Pallant Ho, East Pallant, Chichester PO19 1TY
Tel: 01243 534734 Fax: 01243 534563
e-mail: dcplanning@chichester.gov.uk
Solicitor to the Council: David Stewart, Legal Practice Manager, East Pallant Ho, East Pallant, Chichester PO19 1TY
Tel: 01243 785166 x 4663 Fax: 01243 776766
DX: 30340 Chichester
e-mail: dstewart@chichester.gov.uk

46.3 Horsham District Council

Website: www.horsham.gov.uk
Main Switchboard: 01403 215100
Conveyancing Searches: Local Land Charges, Development Management, Horsham District Council, Park North, North St, Horsham RH12 1RL
Tel: 01403 215472 Fax: 01403 215396
DX: 57609 Horsham 6
e-mail: landcharges@horsham.gov.uk
Building Control: Council Offices, as before,
Tel: 01403 215151
e-mail: building.control@horsham.gov.uk
Council Tax: Council Offices, as before
Environmental Health: Council Offices, as before
Highways: West Sussex County Council
Planning: Council Offices, as before,
Tel: 01403 215187
e-mail: planning@horsham.gov.uk
Solicitor to the Council: Ms Liz Creswick, Council Solicitor, Council Offices, Park North, North St, Horsham RH12 1RL
Tel: 01403 215100 Fax: 01403 215487
DX: 57609 Horsham 6
e-mail: liz.creswick@horsham.gov.uk
Water Services: Southern Water/Thames Water (Northern part of district only)

46.4 Mid Sussex District Council

Website: www.midsussex.gov.uk
Main Switchboard: 01444 458166
Conveyancing Searches: Local Land Charges, Oaklands Rd, Haywards Heath RH16 1SS
Tel: 01444 477444 Fax: 01444 477461
DX: 300320 Haywards Heath 1
e-mail: landcharges@midsussex.gov.uk
Building Control, Housing & Environmental Health: Housing, Environmental Health & Building Control Division, Oaklands Rd, Haywards Heath RH16 1SS
Tel: 01444 477126 (Bldg Control); 01444 477019 (Env Health)
e-mail: envhealth@midsussex.gov.uk
Council Tax: Revenue Services Division, Oaklands Rd, Haywards Heath RH16 1SS
Tel: 01444 477564 Fax: 01444 255308
e-mail: revenue@centralsussex.gov.uk
Highways: West Sussex County Council
Planning: Economic Promotion & Planning, Development Management Business Unit, Oaklands Rd, Haywards Heath RH16 1SS
Tel: 01444 458166 Fax: 01444 477461
DX: 300320 Haywards Heath 1
e-mail: planningenquiries@midsussex.gov.uk
Solicitor to the Council: Paul Collick, Acting Legal Officer, Oaklands, Oaklands Rd, Haywards Heath RH16 1SS
Tel: 01444 458166 Fax: 01444 450027
DX: 300320 Haywards Heath 1
e-mail: paulc@midsussex.gov.uk
Water Services: Southern Water & Thames Water

46.5 Arun District Council

Website: www.arun.gov.uk
Main Switchboard: 01903 737500
Conveyancing Searches: Local Land Charges, Planning & Economic Regeneration Dept, Civic Centre, Maltravers Rd, Littlehampton BN17 5LF
Tel: 01903 737780 Fax: 01903 730442
DX: 57406 Littlehampton
e-mail: landcharges@arun.gov.uk
Highways: West Sussex County Council
Planning: for those within the South Downs National Park: South Downs National Park, Hatton Ho, Bepton Rd, Midhurst GU29 9LU
Tel: 0300 303 1053
e-mail: planning@southdowns.gov.uk
Solicitor to the Council: Wendy Ashenden-Bax, Solicitor to the Council, Civic Centre, Maltravers Rd, Littlehampton BN17 5LF
Tel: 01903 737500 Fax: 01903 716019
DX: 57046 Littlehampton
e-mail: wendy.ashendenbax@arun.gov.uk
Water Services: Southern Water

46.7 Adur & Worthing District Council

Website: www.worthing.gov.uk / www.adur.gov.uk
Main Switchboard: 01903 239999
Conveyancing Searches: Local Land Charges Dept, Portland Ho, 44 Richmond Rd, Worthing BN11 1HS
Tel: 01903 221490/221038/221116
e-mail: landcharges@adur-worthing.gov.uk
Building Control & Planning: Development Management, Portland Ho, 44 Richmond Rd, Worthing BN11 1HS
Tel: 01903 239999
DX: 142965 Worthing 10
e-mail: planning@adur-worthing.gov.uk
Environmental Health: Environmental Health, Portland Ho, 44 Richmond Rd, Worthing BN11 1HS
Tel: 01903 239999
e-mail: environmental.support@adur-worthing.gov.uk
Highways: West Sussex County Council
Solicitor to the Council: Susan Sale, Corporate and Cultural Services, Portland Ho, 44 Richmond Rd, Worthing BN11 1HS
Tel: 01903 221119
e-mail: legal.admin@adur-worthing.gov.uk
Water Services: Southern Water

47 West Yorkshire

47.1 City of Bradford Metropolitan District Council

Website: www.bradford.gov.uk
Main Switchboard: 01274 432111
Conveyancing Searches: Local Land Charges Team, Jacobs Well, Bradford BD1 5RW
Tel: 01274 432238
e-mail: landcharges.team@bradford.gov.uk
Building Control: Building Control Dept, Jacobs Well, Bradford BD1 5RW
Tel: 01274 433807 Fax: 01274 435081
e-mail: buildingcontrol@bradford.gov.uk
Council Tax: Britannia Ho, Hall Ings, Bradford BD1 1HX
Tel: 01274 437792 Fax: 01274 437888
Environmental Health: Environmental Health Dept, Jacobs Well, Bradford BD1 5RW
Tel: 01274 434366
e-mail: epadmin@bradford.gov.uk
Highways: Highways Dept, Jacobs Well, Bradford BD1 5RW
Tel: 01274 437417 Fax: 01274 431330
Planning: Planning Dept, Jacobs Well, BD1 5RW
Tel: 01274 434605 Fax: 01274 722840
e-mail: councilcontact.planning@bradford.gov.uk
Solicitor to the Council: City Solicitor's Office, City Hall, Bradford BD1 1HY
Tel: 01274 432496 Fax: 01274 730337
Water Services: Safemove

47.2 Leeds City Council

Website: www.leeds.gov.uk
Main Switchboard: 0113 222 4444
Conveyancing Searches: Legal, Licensing & Registration Services, Local Land Charges Section, Civic Hall, Leeds LS1 1UR
Tel: 0113 247 4015/6 Fax: 0113 224 3279
DX: 715295 Leeds 33
e-mail: locallandcharges@leeds.gov.uk
Council Tax: Resources, Revenues & Benefits, PO Box 60, 2 Great George St, Leeds LS2 8JR
Tel: 0113 222 4404 Fax: 0113 247 5874
e-mail: council.tax@leeds.gov.uk
Highways & Transportation: City Services, Selectapost 6, Street Registry Section, Ring Rd, Middleton, Leeds LS10 4AX
Tel: 0113 222 4407 Fax: 0113 247 8428
e-mail: highways@leeds.gov.uk
Other depts: Chief Executive, Civic Hall, Leeds LS1 1UR
Planning: City Development, The Leonardo Bldg, 2 Rossington St, Leeds LS2 8HD
Tel: 0113 2224409
e-mail: dec@leeds.gov.uk
Solicitor to the Council: Chief Legal Services Officer, St Georges Ho, 40 Gt George St, Leeds LS1 3DL
Water Services: Yorkshire Water (Safemove)

1

47.3 Calderdale Borough Council

Website: www.calderdale.gov.uk
Main Switchboard: 0845 245 6000
Conveyancing Searches: Local Land Charges Section, Springhall Mansions, Huddersfield Rd, Halifax HX1 0AQ
Tel: 01422 393053 Fax: 01422 392147
e-mail: locallandcharges@calderdale.gov.uk
Building Control: Planning Services, 2nd Fl Northgate Ho, Northgate, Halifax HX1 1UN
Tel: 01422 392221
e-mail: buildingcontrol@calderdale.gov.uk
Council Tax: Finance Service, Council Tax Section, Princess Bldgs, Princess St, Halifax HX1 1TP
Tel: 0845 2458000 Fax: 01422 393533
e-mail: council.tax@calderdale.gov.uk
Environmental Health: Environmental Health Services, Northgate Ho, Northgate, Halifax HX1 1UN
Tel: 01422 392373 Fax: 01422 392399
e-mail: environmental.health@calderdale.gov.uk
Highways: Engineering Services, Highway Development Control, Northgate Ho, Halifax HX1 1UN
Tel: 01422 392176/125 Fax: 01422 392193
e-mail: highways@engineering.gov.uk
Planning: Planning Services, Planning & Building Control Sections, Northgate Ho, Halifax HX1 1UN
Tel: 01422 392237 Fax: 01422 392238
e-mail: town.planning@calderdale.gov.uk
Solicitor to the Council: Ian Hughes, Head of Democratic Services, Northgate Ho, Halifax HX1 1UN
Tel: 01422 393091
e-mail: ian.hughes@calderdale.gov.uk
Water Services: Yorkshire Water (Bradford)

47.4 Kirklees Council

Website: www.kirklees.gov.uk
Main Switchboard: 01484 221000
Conveyancing Searches: Local Land Charges Services, Flint St Depot, Flint St, Huddersfield HD1 6LG
Tel: 01484 416655
e-mail: land.charges@kirklees.gov.uk
Building Control: Building Control Dept, Flint St Depot, Flint St, Huddersfield HD1 6LG
Tel: 01484 221550
e-mail: building.control@kirklees.gov.uk
Council Tax: Council Tax Dept, Civic Centre 1, PO Box A4, Huddersfield HD1 2NF
Tel: 01484 414900
e-mail: revenues.benefits@kirklees.gov.uk
Environmental Health: Environmental Health, Flint St Depot, Flint St, Huddersfield HD1 6LG
Tel: 01484 414739
e-mail: pollution@kirklees.gov.uk

Highways: Highways Registry, Flint St Depot, Flint St, Huddersfield HD1 6LG
Tel: 01484 221000
e-mail: highways.ross@kirklees.gov.uk
Housing Services (Heavy Woollen Areas): Private Sector Housing, Civic Centre 3, High St, Huddersfield HD1 2PR
Tel: 01484 221000
Housing Services (Huddersfield/Agbrigg Areas): Private Sector Housing, Civic Centre 3, High St, Huddersfield HD1 2PR
Tel: 01484 221000
Planning: Development Control Support Unit, PO Box B93, Civic Centre Phase III, Market St, Huddersfield HD1 2JR
Tel: 01484 414746
e-mail: planning.contactcentre@kirklees.gov.uk
Solicitor to the Council: Vanessa Redfearn, Solicitor to the Council, Civic Centre 3, Market St, Huddersfield HD1 2TG
Tel: 01484 221441
DX: 710090 Huddersfield 8
e-mail: vanessa.redfearn@kirklees.gov.uk
Water Services: Yorkshire Water Services (Safemove)

47.5 Wakefield Metropolitan District Council

Website: www.wakefield.gov.uk
Main Switchboard: 0845 850 6506
Conveyancing Searches: Local Land Charges, County Hall, Bond St, Wakefield WF1 2QW
Tel: 01924 305260 Fax: 01924 305263
e-mail: landcharges@wakefield.gov.uk
Council Tax: Revenues & Benefits Service, Wakefield One, PO Box 700, Wakefield WF1 2EB
Tel: 0844 90 20 205
e-mail: ctaxgeneral@wakefield.gov.uk
Environmental Health: Environmental Health, Wakefield One, PO Box 700, Wakefield WF1 2EB
Tel: 0845 8506 506 Fax: 01924 306419
e-mail: ep@wakefield.gov.uk
Planning & Building: Planning & Regeneration, Wakefield One, PO Box 700, Wakefield WF1 2EB
Tel: 0845 8506 506 Fax: 01924 306690
e-mail: devcontrol@wakefield.gov.uk
Solicitor to the Council: Bernadette Livesey, Service Director Legal & Governance, County Hall, Bond St, Wakefield WF1 1QW
Tel: 01924 305011 Fax: 01924 305243
e-mail: legalservices@wakefield.gov.uk
Transportation & Engineering: Highways & Engineering, Wakefield One, PO Box 700, Wakefield WF1 2EB
Tel: 0845 8506 506 Fax: 01924 306310
e-mail: customerservices@wakefield.gov.uk
Water Services: Yorkshire Water (Safemove)

48 Wiltshire

48.0 Wiltshire County Council (abolished)

County Council abolished as from 1 April 2009. North Wiltshire DC, West Wiltshire DC, Kennet DC, Salisbury DC and Wiltshire County Council are now combined to form Wiltshire Council (Unitary).

48.1 Wiltshire Council (U)

Website: www.wiltshire.gov.uk
Main Switchboard: 0300 456 0100
Conveyancing Searches: Local Land Charges, County Hall, Bythesea Rd, Trowbridge BA14 8JN
Tel: 0300 003 4574
DX: 116892 Trowbridge 3
e-mail: locallandchargesnorth@wiltshire.gov.uk, locallandchargeseast@wiltshire.gov.uk, locallandchargessouth@wiltshire.gov.uk, locallandchargeswest@wiltshire.gov.uk
Building Control: Building Control Dept, County Hall, as above,
e-mail: buildingcontrolcentral@wiltshire.gov.uk, buildingcontrolnorth@wiltshire.gov.uk, buildingcontrolsouth@wiltshire.gov.uk
Council Tax: Revenues and Benefits, County Hall, as above,
Tel: 01225 770342 Fax: 01225 770333
e-mail: revsandbens@wiltshire.gov.uk
Environmental Health: Environmental Health, County Hall, as above,
Tel: 01225 776655
e-mail: publicprotectionwest@wiltshire.gov.uk, publicprotectionnorth@wiltshire.gov.uk, publicprotectioneast@wiltshire.gov.uk, publicprotectionsouth@wiltshire.gov.uk
Highways: Highways, County Hall, as above,
Tel: 01225 777234
e-mail: clarence@wiltshire.gov.uk
Planning: Development Control, County Hall, as above,
Tel: 0300 456 0100
e-mail: developmentmanagementwest@wiltshire.gov.uk, developmentmanagementnorth@wiltshire.gov.uk, developmentmanagementeast@wiltshire.gov.uk, developmentmanagementsouth@wiltshire.gov.uk
Solicitor to the Council: Ian Gibbons, County Hall, Bythesea Rd, Trowbridge BA14 8JN
Tel: 01225 713052 Fax: 01225 713998
DX: 116892 Trowbridge 3
e-mail: iangibbons@wiltshire.gov.uk
Water Services: Wessex Water, Thames Water & Southern Water

48.2 Swindon Borough Council (U)

Website: www.swindon.gov.uk
Main Switchboard: 01793 445500
Conveyancing Searches: Local Land Charges, 4th Fl, Wat Tyler West, Beckhampton St, Swindon SN1 2JH
Tel: 01793 466246/466359 Fax: 01793 466458
DX: 133055 Swindon 16
e-mail: landcharges@swindon.gov.uk
Building Control: Building Control, 4th Fl, Wat Tyler West, Beckhampton St, Swindon SN1 2JH
Tel: 01793 445502 Fax: 01793 466166
DX: 133055 Swindon 16
e-mail: buildingcontrol@swindon.gov.uk
Council Tax: Customer Services, Revenues & Benefits, Wat Tyler Ho, Beckhampton St, Swindon SN1 2JH
Tel: 0345 302 2316 Fax: 01793 464344
DX: 133055 Swindon 16
e-mail: customerservices@swindon.gov.uk
Environmental Health: Environmental Health – Protection, Wat Tyler Ho, Beckhampton St, Swindon SN1 2JH
Tel: 01793 445501
DX: environmentalprotection@swindon.gov.uk

Highways: Highways Management Unit, Wat Tyler West, Beckhampton St, Swindon SN1 2JH
Tel: 01793 445500 Fax: 01793 466446
DX: 133055 Swindon 16
e-mail: highwayrecords@swindon.gov.uk
Planning: Development Control, Wat Tyler West, Beckhampton St, Swindon SN1 2JH
Tel: 01793 445500 Fax: 01793 466459
DX: 133055 Swindon 16
e-mail: sbcdc@swindon.gov.uk
Solicitor to the Council: Mr Stephen Taylor, Director of Law & Corporate Governance, Civic Offices, Euclid St, Swindon SN1 2JH
Tel: 01793 463012 Fax: 01793 490420
DX: 133055 Swindon 16
e-mail: staylor@swindon.gov.uk
Water Services: Thames Water

49 Worcestershire

49.0 Worcestershire County Council

Website: www.worcestershire.gov.uk
Main Switchboard: 01905 763763
Search Address: Head of Legal & Democratic Services, County Hall, Spetchley Rd, Worcester WR5 2NP
Tel: 01905 766335 Fax: 01905 766677
DX: 29941 Worcester 2
e-mail: legalservices@worcestershire.gov.uk
Solicitor to the Council: Simon Mallinson, Head of Legal & Democratic Services, County Hall, Spetchley Rd, Worcester WR5 2NP
Tel: 01905 766652 Fax: 01905 766677
DX: 29441 Worcester 2
e-mail: smallinson@worcestershire.gov.uk

49.1 Wyre Forest District Council

Website: www.wyreforestdc.gov.uk
Main Switchboard: 01562 732928
Conveyancing Searches: Local Land Charges, Wyre Forest Ho, Finepoint Way, Kidderminster DY11 7WF
Tel: 01562 732713/732714
e-mail: land.charges@wyreforestdc.gov.uk
Building Control & Planning: Economic Prosperity and Place, Wyre Forest Ho, Finepoint Way, Kidderminster DY11 7WF
Tel: 01562 732928
e-mail: dev.control@wyreforestdc.gov.uk
Council Tax: Council Tax Dept, Wyre Forest Ho, Finepoint Way, Kidderminster DY11 7WF
Tel: 01562 732928 Fax: 01562 732659
e-mail: counciltaxsection.revenue.wfdcrev@wyreforestdc.gov.uk
Environmental Health: Environmental Health, Worcestershire Regulatory Services, Wyatt Ho, Farrier St, Worcester WR1 3BH
Tel: 01905 822799
Highways: Wyre Forest Highways Partnership Unit, Worcestershire County Council, County Hall, Spetchley Rd, Worcester WR5 2XC
Tel: 01905 766213
Solicitor to the Council: Solicitor to the Council, Wyre Forest Ho, Finepoint Way, Kidderminster DY11 7WF
Tel: 01562 732715
e-mail: caroline.newlands@wyreforestdc.gov.uk
Water Services: Severn Trent

49.2 Bromsgrove District Council

Website: www.bromsgrove.gov.uk
Main Switchboard: 01527 881288
Conveyancing Searches: Planning & Regeneration, Council Ho, Burcot Lane, Bromsgrove B60 1AA
Tel: 01527 881420 Fax: 01527 881313
e-mail: locallandcharges@bromsgroveandredditch.gov.uk
Note: p.baggott@bromsgrove.gov.uk
Building Control: Planning & Regeneration, Council Ho, as before,
Tel: 01527 881402
e-mail: b.control@bromsgroveandreddditch.gov.uk
Council Tax: Financial Services, Council Ho, as before
Environmental Health: Environmental Health, Worcestershire Regulatory Services, PO Box 866, Worcester WR1 9DP
Tel: 01905 822799 Fax: 01905 617132
e-mail: wrsenquiries@worcsregservices.gov.uk
Highways: Worcestershire County Council,
Tel: 0845 607 2005
e-mail: worcestershirehub@worcester.gov.uk
Planning: Planning, Council Ho, as before,
e-mail: pec@bromsgrove.gov.uk
Solicitor to the Council: Claire Felton, Head of Legal, Equalities & Democratic Services, Council Ho, Burcot Lane, Bromsgrove B60 1AA
e-mail: c.felton@bromsgroveandredditch.gov.uk
Water Services: Severn Trent Water

49.3 Redditch Borough Council

Website: www.redditchbc.gov.uk
Main Switchboard: 01527 64252
Conveyancing Searches: Local Land Charges, Town Hall, Walter Stranz Sq, Redditch B98 8AH
Tel: 01527 64252 (direct line) Fax: 01527 534138
e-mail: locallandcharges@bromsgroveandredditch.gov.uk
Building Control, Council Tax, Environmental Health and Planning: Town Hall, Walter Stranz Sq, Redditch B98 8AH
Tel: 01527 64252 (switchboard) Fax: 01527 534138
e-mail: [firstname.surname]@redditchbc.gov.uk
Highways: Worcestershire County Council
Solicitor to the Council: Clare Flanagan, Solicitor, Town Hall, Walter Stranz Sq, Redditch B98 8AH
Tel: 01527 64252 x3173 Fax: 01527 534138
e-mail: clare.flanagan@bromsgroveandredditch.gov.uk
Water Services: Severn Trent Water

49.4 Malvern Hills District Council

Website: www.malvernhills.gov.uk
Main Switchboard: 01684 862151
Conveyancing Searches: Local Land Charges Section, The Council Ho, Avenue Rd, Malvern WB14 3AF
Tel: 01684 862151 Fax: 01684 862369
DX: 17608 Malvern
e-mail: land.charges@malvernhills.gov.uk
Building Control: Building Control, The Council Ho, Avenue Rd, Malvern WR14 3AF
Tel: 01684 862223 Fax: 01684 862499
DX: 17608 Malvern
e-mail: building.control@malvernhills.gov.uk
Council Tax: Financial Services, Portland Ho, Church St, Malvern WR14 2BA
Tel: 01684 822733 Fax: 01684 862474
DX: 17608 Malvern
e-mail: worcestershirehub@malvernhills.gov.uk
Engineering: Technical Services, Portland Ho, Church St, Malvern WR14 2BA
Tel: 01684 862151 Fax: 01684 862498
DX: 17608 Malvern

Environmental Services: Environmental Services, Council Ho, Avenue Rd, Malvern WR14 3AF
Tel: 01684 862151 Fax: 01684 862481
DX: 17608 Malvern
Highways: Worcestershire County Council,
Tel: 0845 607 2005
e-mail: worcestershirehub@worcester.gov.uk
Planning: Planning Services, Malvern Hills District Council, Council Ho, Avenue Rd, Malvern WR14 3AF
e-mail: worcestershirehub@malvernhills.gov.uk
Solicitor to the Council: Nigel Snape, Head of Legal Services, The Council Ho, Avenue Rd, Malvern WR14 3AF
Tel: 01684 892700 Fax: 01684 892552
DX: 17608 Malvern
e-mail: nigelsnape@malvernhills.gov.uk
Water Services: Severn Trent Water

49.5 Worcester City Council

Website: www.worcester.gov.uk
Main Switchboard: 01905 722233
Conveyancing Searches: Local Land Charges, Planning Section, Director of Development Services, Worcester City Council Museum & Art Gallery, Foregate St, Worcester WR1 1DT
Tel: 01905 722023/4 Fax: 01905 722370
e-mail: landcharges@worcester.gov.uk
Building Control: Building Control Section, Director of Development Services, The Council Ho, Avenue Rd, Malvern WR14 3AF
Tel: 01684 862223
e-mail: building.control@malvernhills.gov.uk
Council Tax: Worcester City Council, Revenues & Benefits, PO Box 11, Pershore WR10 1PU
Tel: 01905 722233
e-mail: revenues@swrbss.org
Environmental Health: Worcestershire Regulatory Services, PO Box 866, Worcester WR1 9DP
e-mail: wrsenquiries@worcegservices.gov.uk
Highways: Worcestershire County Council,
Tel: 01905 763763
e-mail: worcestershirehub@worcester.gov.uk
Planning: Planning Section, Director of Development Services, Worcester City Council Museum & Art Gallery, Foregate St, Worcester WR1 1DT
Tel: 01905 722555 Fax: 01905 722370
e-mail: planning@worcester.gov.uk
Solicitor to the Council: Mr T O'Gara, Worcester City Council Museum & Art Gallery, Foregate St, Worcester WR1 1DT
Tel: 01905 722019 Fax: 01905 722370
e-mail: timothy.ogara@worcester.gov.uk
Water: Severn Trent

49.6 Wychavon District Council

Website: www.wychavon.gov.uk
Main Switchboard: 01386 565000
Conveyancing Searches: Corporate Database, Civic Centre, Queen Elizabeth Drive, Pershore WR10 1PT
Tel: 01386 565001
DX: 25934 Pershore
e-mail: locallandcharges@wychavon.gov.uk
Building Control & Planning: South Worcestershire Building Control Partnership, The Council Ho, Avenue Rd, Malvern WR14 3AF
Tel: 01684 862 223
e-mail: mail@southworcestershirebuildingcontrol.gov.uk
Council Tax: South Worcestershire Shared Services, Wychavon Revenues & Benefits, PO Box 11, Pershore WR10 1PU
Tel: 03004 560560
e-mail: revenues@southworcestershirerevenues.gov.uk
Environmental Health: Worcestershire Regulatory Services,
Tel: 01905 822799
e-mail: wrsenquiries@worcsregsservices.gov.uk
Highways: Worcestershire County Council,
Tel: 01905 763763
e-mail: worcestershirehub@worcestershire.gov.uk
Planning: Housing & Planning Dept, Civic Centre, Queen Elizabeth Dr, Pershore WR10 1PT
Tel: 01386 565565
DX: 25934 Pershore
e-mail: planning@wychavon.gov.uk
Solicitor to the Council: Mr Ian Marshall, Head of Legal Support Services, Civic Centre, Queen Elizabeth Drive, Pershore WR10 1PT
Tel: 01386 565000 Fax: 01386 561089
DX: 25934 Pershore
e-mail: ian.marshall@wychavon.gov.uk
Water Services: Severn Trent Water

50 Isles of Scilly

50.1 Isles of Scilly Council (U)

Website: www.scilly.gov.uk
Main Switchboard: 01720 424000
Conveyancing Searches: Planning & Development Dept, Town Hall, St Mary's, Isles of Scilly TR21 0LW
Tel: 01720 424350 Fax: 01720 424017
e-mail: searches@scilly.gov.uk
Building Control & Planning: Planning & Development Dept, Town Hall, as above,
Tel: 01720 424350 Fax: 01720 424017
e-mail: planning@scilly.gov.uk
Council Tax: Council Tax, Town Hall, as above,
Tel: 01720 424000 Fax: 01720 424017
e-mail: apritchard@scilly.gov.uk
Environmental Health & Highways: Environmental Health / Infrastructure, Town Hall, as above,
Tel: 01720 424000 Fax: 01720 424017
e-mail: enquiries@scilly.gov.uk
Solicitor to the Council: Democratic & Corporate Development, Town Hall, as above,
Tel: 01720 4245000 Fax: 01720 424017
e-mail: enquiries@scilly.gov.uk
Water Services: Infrastructure, Town Hall, as above,
Tel: 01720 424000 Fax: 01720 424017
e-mail: enquiries@scilly.gov.uk

Local Authorities in Wales

W1 Anglesey County Council (U)

Website: www.ynysmon.gov.uk
Main Switchboard: 01248 750057
Conveyancing Searches: Legal Services, Local Land Charges Section, Council Offices, Llangefni LL77 7TW
Tel: 01248 752573/752172 Fax: 01248 752132
DX: 701771 Llangefni
e-mail: ijxcs@anglesey.gov.uk
Building Control: Planning & Environment, Council Offices, Llangefni LL77 7TW
Tel: 01248 752428 Fax: 01248 752232
Council Tax: Finance Dept, Council Offices, Llangefni LL77 7TW
Tel: 01248 752602 Fax: 01248 752233
Environmental Health: Planning & Environment, Council Offices, Llangefni LL77 7TW
Tel: 01248 752820 Fax: 01248 752880
Highways: Highway Services, Council Offices, Llangefni LL77 7TW
Tel: 01248 752300 Fax: 01248 724839
Planning: Planning & Environment, Council Offices, Llangefni LL77 7TW
Tel: 01248 752428 Fax: 01248 752430
Solicitor to the Council: Ms Lyn Ball, Director of Legal Services, Council Offices, Llangefni, Anglesey LL77 7TW
Tel: 01248 752568 Fax: 01248 752132
DX: 701771 Llangefni
e-mail: lbxcs@anglesey.gov.uk
Water Services: Welsh Water

W2 Blaenau Gwent County Borough Council (U)

Website: www.blaenau-gwent.gov.uk
Main Switchboard: 01495 311556
Conveyancing Searches: Legal & Corporate Section, Governance Division, Municipal Offices, Civic Centre, Ebbw Vale NP23 6XB
Tel: 01495 355087 Fax: 01495 357789
DX: 43956 Ebbw Vale
e-mail: audra.williams@blaenau-gwent.gov.uk
Building Control & Planning: Planning Dept, Council Offices, High St, Blaina NP13 3XD
Tel: 01495 355518 Fax: 01495 355598
DX: 43956
e-mail: planning@blaenau-gwent.gov.uk
Council Tax: Resources Dept, Municipal Offices, Civic Centre, Ebbw Vale NP23 6XB
Tel: 01495 355212 Fax: 01495 356132
DX: 43956
e-mail: ctax@blaenau-gwent.gov.uk
Environmental Health: Public Protection Services, Anvil Ct, Church St, Abertillery NP13 1DB
Tel: 01495 357813 Fax: 01495 355834
DX: 43956
e-mail: environmental.health@blaenau-gwent.gov.uk
Highways: Technical Services, Baldwin Ho, Festival Pk, Ebbw Vale NP23 8ED
Tel: 01495 355384
DX: 43956
e-mail: clive.rogers@blaenau-gwent.gov.uk
Solicitor to the Council: Miss Andrea Jones, Head of Legal & Corporate Services, Municipal Offices, Civic Centre, Ebbw Vale NP23 6XB
Tel: 01495 355013 Fax: 01495 355291
DX: 43956 Ebbw Vale
e-mail: andrea.jones@blaenau-gwent.gov.uk
Water Services: Dwr Cymru – Welsh Water

W3 Bridgend County Borough Council (U)

Website: www.bridgend.gov.uk
Main Switchboard: 01656 643643
Conveyancing Searches: Land Charges, Civic Offices, Angel St, Bridgend CF31 4WB
Tel: 01656 643124
DX: 151420 Bridgend 6
e-mail: landcharges@bridgend.gov.uk
Building Control: Building Control, Civic Offices, as before,
Tel: 01656 643408
e-mail: meryl.morgan@bridgend.gov.uk
Council Tax: Council Tax, Civic Offices, as before,
Tel: 01656 643391
Environmental Health: Environmental Health, Civic Offices, as before,
Tel: 01656 643260
e-mail: publicprotection@bridgend.gov.uk
Highways: Transport & Engineering, Civic Offices, Angel St, Bridgend CF31 4WB
Tel: 01656 642525/642530/642527 Fax: 01656 642580
e-mail: highwaysearches@bridgend.gov.uk
Planning: Planning, Civic Offices, as before,
Tel: 01656 643177
e-mail: planning@bridgend.gov.uk
Solicitor to the Council: Assistant Chief Executive, Legal & Regulatory Services, Civic Offices, PO Box 4, Angel St, Bridgend CF31 4WB
Water Services: Welsh Water

W4 Caerphilly County Borough Council (U)

Website: www.caerphilly.gov.uk
Main Switchboard: 01443 815588 / 01495 226622
Conveyancing Searches: Land Charges, Planning Division, Pontllanfraith Ho, Blackwood Rd, Pontllanfraith, Blackwood NP12 2YW
Tel: 01495 235012 Fax: 01495 235013
e-mail: landcharges@caerphilly.gov.uk
Building Control: Directorate of Environment, Council Offices, Civic Centre, Blackwood Rd, Pontllanfraith, Blackwood NP12 2YW
Tel: 01495 235053 Fax: 01495 235013
e-mail: buildingcontrol@caerphilly.gov.uk
Council Tax: Directorate of Chief Executives, Council Offices, Caerphilly County B.C., Penallta Ho, Tredomen Pk, Ystrad Mynach CF82 7PG
Tel: 01443 863002 Fax: 01443 864087
e-mail: counciltax@caerphilly.gov.uk
Environmental Health: Directorate of the Environment, Pontllanfraith Ho, Pontllanfraith, Blackwood NP12 2YW
Tel: 01443 866544 Fax: 01495 235016
e-mail: enviroservices@caerphilly.gov.uk
Highways: Highways Customer Care, Pontllanfraith Ho, Blackwood Rd, Pontllanfraith, Blackwood NP12 2YW
Tel: 01443 866551
e-mail: engineering@caerphilly.gov.uk

Planning: Tim Stephens, Development Control Manager, Pontllanfraith Ho, Blackwood Rd, Pontllanfraith, Blackwood NP12 2YW
Tel: 01495 235359 Fax: 01495 235013
e-mail: planning@caerphilly.gov.uk
Solicitor to the Council: Legal & Democratic Services, Council Offices, Caerphilly County B.C., Penallta Ho, Tredomen Pk, Ystrad Mynach CF82 7PG
Tel: 01443 815588 Fax: 01443 863154
e-mail: legalsgo@caerphilly.gov.uk

W5 Cardiff County Council (U)

Website: www.cardiff.gov.uk
Main Switchboard: 029 2087 2000
Conveyancing Searches: Local Land Charges, County Hall, Room 473, Atlantic Wharf, Cardiff CF10 4UW
Tel: 029 2087 2510/2513/2435
DX: 200753 Cardiff Bay
e-mail: locallandcharges@cardiff.gov.uk
Building Control & Environmental Health: Building Control Services, County Hall, Atlantic Wharf, Cardiff CF10 4UW
e-mail: buildingcontrol@cardiff.gov.uk
Council Tax: Financial Services, City Hall, Cathays Park, Cardiff CF10 5ND
Tel: 029 2087 2087 Fax: 029 2087 1115
e-mail: ctax@cardiff.gov.uk
Solicitor to the Council: County Solicitor, Rm 477, County Hall, Cardiff CF10 4UW
Tel: 029 20872421 Fax: 029 20872488
Water Services: Dwr Cymru – Welsh Water

W6 Carmarthenshire County Council (U)

Website: www.carmarthenshire.gov.uk
Main Switchboard: 01267 234567
Conveyancing Searches: Local Land Charges Unit (Chief Executive's Dept), County Hall, Carmarthen SA31 1JP
Tel: 01267 224071/224075 Fax: 01267 224695
DX: 744630 Carmarthen 10
e-mail: landcharges@carmarthenshire.gov.uk
Building Control: Regeneration Dept (Building Control), Building 16, Park Dewi Sant, Jobswell Rd, Carmarthen SA31 3HB
Tel: 01267 246002 Fax: 01267 246017
DX: 51410 Carmarthen
e-mail: building.control@carmarthenshire.gov.uk
Council Tax: Council Tax Dept, Ty Elwyn, Llanelli SA15 3AP
Tel: 01554 742200 Fax: 01554 754188
e-mail: counciltax@carmarthenshire.gov.uk
Environmental Health (Area East): Social Care & Housing Dept, Town Hall, Ammanford SA18 3BE
Tel: 01269 598222
e-mail: schbsuammanford@carmarthenshire.gov.uk
Environmental Health (Area South & West): as before, Ty Elwyn, Llanelli SA15 3AP
Tel: 01554 899311
e-mail: schbsullanelli@carmarthenshire.gov.uk
Highways: Technical Services Dept (Highways), Room 9, Block 2, Parc Myrddin, Richmond Terrace, Carmarthen SA31 228163
Tel: 01267 228163
e-mail: highwaysearches@carmarthenshire.gov.uk
Planning (All Areas): Regeneration Dept (Planning), Civic Offices, Crescent Rd, Llandeilo SA19 6HW
Tel: 01558 825285
e-mail: planningsearches@carmarthenshire.gov.uk
Solicitor to the Council: Ms Linda Rees-Jones, Acting Head of Administration & Law, County Hall, Carmarthen SA31 1JP
Tel: 01267 224012 Fax: 01267 230848
DX: 744630 Carmarthen 10
Water Services: Welsh Water,
Note: Drainage: Sewerage Operating Contractors Mid & West Wales. Freephone: 0800 0855936.

W7 Ceredigion (formerly Cardiganshire) County Council (U)

Website: www.ceredigion.gov.uk
Main Switchboard: 01545 570881
Conveyancing Searches: Land Charges, Neuadd Ceredigion, Penmorfa, Aberaeron SA46 0PA
Tel: 01545 574152 Fax: 01545 572039
DX: 745510 Aberaeron 2
e-mail: locallc@ceredigion.gov.uk
Building Control: Highways, Property & Works, County Hall, Market St, Aberaeron SA46 0AT
Tel: 01545 570881 Fax: 01545 572589
e-mail: hpw@ceredigion.gov.uk
Council Tax: Council Tax, Finance Department, Canolfan Rheidol, Rhodfa Padarn, Llanbadarn Fawr, Aberystwyth SY23 3UE
Tel: 01970 633252
e-mail: revenues@ceredigion.gov.uk
Environmental Health & Planning: Environmental Services & Housing, Neuadd Ceredigion, Penmorfa, Aberaeron SA46 0PA
Tel: 01545 572151
e-mail: envhealth@ceredigion.gov.uk
Highways: Highways, Property & Works, County Hall, Market St, Aberaeron SA46 0AT
Tel: 01545 570881 Fax: 01545 572589
e-mail: hpw@ceredigion.gov.uk
Solicitor to the Council: Claire Jones, Chief Executive's Dept, Penmorfa, Aberaeron SA46 0PA
Tel: 01545 570881 Fax: 01545 572029
DX: 745510 Aberaeron 2
e-mail: clairej@ceredigion.gov.uk
Water Services: Welsh Water

W8 Conwy County Borough Council (U)

Website: www.conwy.gov.uk
Main Switchboard: 01492 574000
Conveyancing Searches: Local Search Section, Civic Offices, Abergale Rd, Colwyn Bay, Conwy LL29 8AR
Tel: 01492 576095 Fax: 01492 596102
DX: 24628 Conwy
e-mail: regulatory.services@conwy.gov.uk
Building Control: Building & Housing Regulation, Civic Offices, Abergele Rd, Colwyn Bay LL29 8AR
Tel: 01492 574186 Fax: 01492 512637
e-mail: building.control@conwy.gov.uk
Council Tax: Finance Dept, Bodlondeb, Conwy LL32 8DU
Tel: 01492 576607 Fax: 01492 576260
DX: 24628 Conwy
e-mail: ctax.enquiries@conwy.gov.uk
Environmental Health: Regulatory Services, Civic Offices, Colwyn Bay LL29 8AR
Tel: 01492 575242 Fax: 01492 575204
DX: 24628 Conwy
e-mail: regulatory.services@conwy.gov.uk
Highways: Highways Dept, The Heath, Penmaenmawr Rd, Llanfairfechan LL33 0PF
Tel: 01492 575491 Fax: 01248 575500
e-mail: highwaymaintenance@conwy.gov.uk

Planning: Planning Dept, Civic Offices, Colwyn Bay LL29 8AR
Tel: 01492 575271 Fax: 01492 512637
DX: 24628 Conwy
e-mail: cynllun.plan@conwy.gov.uk
Solicitor to the Council: Mr Iwan Davies, Head of Legal Services, Bodlondeb, Conwy LL32 8DU
Tel: 01492 576110 Fax: 01492 576116
DX: 24628 Conwy
e-mail: iwan.davies@conwy.gov.uk
Water Services: Welsh Water

W9 Denbighshire County Council (U)

Website: www.denbighshire.gov.uk
Main Switchboard: 01824 706000
Conveyancing Searches: Land Charges, Council Offices, Caledfryn Smithfield Rd, Denbigh LL16 3RJ
Tel: 01824 706918
e-mail: local-land-charges@denbighshire.gov.uk
Building Control: Planning & Building Control, Caledfryn, Smithfield Rd, Denbigh LL16 3RJ
Tel: 01824 706717 Fax: 01824 706953
e-mail: building.control@denbighshire.tov.uk
Council Tax: Director of Resources, Russell Ho, Churton Rd, Rhyl LL18 3DP
Tel: 01824 706468 Fax: 01824 706306
e-mail: revenues@denbighshire.gov.uk
Environmental Health: Public Protection, County Hall, Wynnstay Rd, Ruthin LL15 1YN
Tel: 01824 706080 Fax: 01824 706051
e-mail: envhealth@denbighshire.gov.uk
Highways: Environment, Caledfryn, Smithfield Rd, Denbigh LL16 3RJ
Tel: 01824 706101 Fax: 01824 706180
e-mail: highways@denbighshire.gov.uk
Solicitor to the Council: County Clerk, County Hall, Wynnstay Rd, Ruthin LL15 1YN
Tel: 01824 712562 Fax: 01824 706293
DX: 21839 Ruthin
e-mail: dcc-admin@denbighshire.gov.uk
Water Services: Welsh Water

W10 Flintshire County Council (U)

Website: www.flintshire.gov.uk
Main Switchboard: 01352 752121
Conveyancing Searches: Planning & Environment, County Hall, Mold CH7 6NF
Tel: 01352 702334/5/3 Fax: 01352 702399
DX: 708591 Mold 4
e-mail: land.charges@flintshire.gov.uk
Building Control: Planning & Environment, County Hall, Mold CH7 6NF
Tel: 01352 703417 Fax: 01352 703615
DX: 708590 Mold 4
Council Tax: Corporate Services, County Hall, Mold CH7 6NA
Tel: 01352 704848 Fax: 01352 704850
DX: 708590 Mold 4
e-mail: localtaxation.contactcentre@flintshire.gov.uk
Environmental Health: Public Protection Environment Directorate, County Hall, Mold CH7 6NF
Tel: 01352 703440 Fax: 01352 703441
DX: 708590 Mold 4
Highways: Environment Directorate, County Hall, Mold CH7 6NF
Tel: 01352 704617 Fax: 01352 755024
DX: 708590 Mold 4
Planning: Planning & Environment, County Hall, Mold CH7 6NF
Tel: 01352 703228 Fax: 01352 756444
DX: 708590 Mold 4
e-mail: planningreception@flintshire.gov.uk
Solicitor to the Council: Corporate Services, County Hall, Mold CH7 6NA
Tel: 01352 702344 Fax: 01352 702494
DX: 708590 Mold 4
Water Services: Dwr Cymru – Welsh Water

W11 Gwynedd Council (U)

Website: www.gwynedd.gov.uk
Main Switchboard: 01766 771000
Conveyancing Searches – Arfon and Dwyfor Areas: Democracy & Legal Service, Council Offices, Shirehall St, Caernarfon LL55 1SH
Tel: 01286 679647
DX: 713561 Caernarfon 5
e-mail: enquiries@gwynedd.gov.uk
Conveyancing Searches – Meirionnydd area: Democracy & Legal Service, Council Offices, Penarlag, Dolgellau LL40 2YB
Tel: 01341 422341 Fax: 01341 423984
DX: 711444 Dolgellau
e-mail: enquiries@gwynedd.gov.uk
Building Control: Gwynedd Consultancy, Council Offices, Shirehall St, Caernarfon LL55 1SH
Tel: 01766 771000 Fax: 01286 682771
DX: 713561 Caernarfon 5
e-mail: buildingcontrol@gwynedd.gov.uk
Council Tax: Finance Revenue Unit, Gwynedd Council, Penrallt, Caernarfon LL55 1BN
Tel: 01286 682689 Fax: 01286 677136
DX: 713560 Caernarfon 5
e-mail: counciltax@gwynedd.gov.uk
Environmental Health: Public Protection Service, Council Offices, Swyddfa Arfon, Penrallt LL55 1BN
Tel: 01766 771000
e-mail: gyc@gwynedd.gov.uk
Highways: Transportation Service, County Offices, Shirehall St, Caernarfon LL55 1SH
Tel: 01286 672255 Fax: 01286 675961
DX: 713560 Caernarfon 5
e-mail: enquiries@gwynedd.gov.uk
Planning (Main Office): Planning Service, Ffordd y Cob, Pwllheli LL53 5AA
Tel: 01766 771000
e-mail: planning@gwynedd.gov.uk
Solicitor to the Council: Dilys Phillips, Head of Democratic and Legal, County Offices, Shirehall St, Caernarfon LL55 1SH
Tel: 01286 679015 Fax: 01286 673993
DX: 713561 Caernarfon 5
e-mail: dilysaphillips@gwynedd.gov.uk
Water Services: Welsh Water

W12 Merthyr Tydfil County Borough Council (U)

Website: www.merthyr.gov.uk
Main Switchboard: 01685 725000
Conveyancing Searches: Estates Dept Land Charges Section, Unit 5, Triangle Business Pk, Pentrebach, Merthyr Tydfil CF48 4TQ
Tel: 01685 725294
e-mail: landcharges@merthyr.gov.uk
Note: A plan is required

Building Control & Planning: Planning Dept (Building Control), Unit 5, Triangle Business Pk, Pentrebach, Merthyr Tydfil CF48 4TQ
Tel: 01685 726263
e-mail: building.control@merthyr.gov.uk
Council Tax: Council Tax Office, Civic Centre, Castle St, Merthyr Tydfil CF47 8AN
Tel: 01685 725074 Fax: 01685 722146
e-mail: revenues@merthyr.gov.uk
Environmental Health: Environmental Health, Civic Centre, Castle St, Merthyr Tydfil CF47 8AN
Tel: 01685 725000 Fax: 01685 722146
Highways: Highways Dept, Unit 20, Merthyr Tydfil Industrial Pk, Pentrebach, Merthyr Tydfil CF48 4DR
Tel: 01685 724939 Fax: 01443 693872
e-mail: highways@merthyr.gov.uk
Solicitor to the Council: Legal Division, Civic Centre, Castle St, Merthyr Tydfil CF47 8AN
Tel: 01685 725283 Fax: 01685 725060
Water Services: Welsh Water

W13 Monmouthshire County Council (U)

Website: www.monmouthshire.gov.uk
Main Switchboard: 01633 644644
Conveyancing Searches: Land Charges Section, PO Box 106, Caldicot NP26 9AN
Tel: 01633 644073 / 644075
DX: 131331 Usk 2
e-mail: landcharges@monmouthshire.gov.uk
Note: Not accepted without plans
Building Control & Planning: Planning & Building Control, PO Box 106, Caldicot NP26 9AN
Tel: 01633 644644
DX: 131331 Usk 2
e-mail: buildingcontrol@monmouthshire.gov.uk
Note: planning@monmouthshire.gov.uk
Council Tax: Revenue Section, PO Box 106, Caldicot NP26 9AN
Tel: 01633 644630
e-mail: counciltax@monmouthshire.gov.uk
Environmental Health: Environmental Health, PO Box 106, Caldicot NP26 9AN
Tel: 01633 644644
Highways: Highways Dept, PO Box 106, Caldicot NP26 9AN
Tel: 01633 644644
DX: 131331 Usk 2
Solicitor to the Council: Robert Tranter, Head of Legal Services, PO Box 106, Caldicot NP26 9AN
Tel: 01633 644644
DX: 131331 Usk 2
e-mail: roberttranter@monmouthshire.gov.uk
Water Services: Welsh Water and Hyder

W14 Neath Port Talbot County Borough Council (U)

Website: www.npt.gov.uk
Main Switchboard: 01639 686868
Conveyancing Searches: Finance and Corporate Services, Head of Legal Services, Land Charges Section, Civic Centre, Port Talbot SA13 1PJ
Tel: 01639 763345 Fax: 01639 763417
DX: 135226 Port Talbot 2
e-mail: landcharges@npt.gov.uk
Building Control: Environment Directorate, Head of Planning, Building Control Section, The Quays, Brunel Way, Baglan Energy Pk, Baglan SA11 2GG
Tel: 01639 686820 Fax: 01639 686101
e-mail: building.control@npt.gov.uk
Council Tax (Neath): Finance & Corporate Services, Head of Revenue Services, Council Tax Section, Civic Centre, Neath SA11 3QZ
Tel: 01639 686840
e-mail: council.tax@npt.gov.uk
Council Tax (Port Talbot): Finance & Corporate Services, Head of Revenue Services, Council Tax Section, Civic Centre, Port Talbot SA13 1PJ
Tel: 01639 763152 Fax: 01639 763382
e-mail: council.tax@npt.gov.uk
Environmental Health: Social Services, Health & Housing, Environmental Health & Trading Standards, Civic Centre, Neath SA11 3QZ
Tel: 01639 685678 Fax: 01639 685677
e-mail: ehts@npt.gov.uk
Highways: Environment, Network Management Section, The Quays, Brunel Way, Baglan Pk, Baglan SA11 2GG
Tel: 01639 686764 Fax: 01639 764250
e-mail: environment@npt.gov.uk
Planning: Environment Directorate, Building Control Dept, The Quays, Brunel Way, Baglan Energy Pk, Baglan SA11 2GG
Tel: 01639 686764 Fax: 01639 764250
e-mail: planning@npt.gov.uk
Solicitor to the Council: Head of Legal Services, Finance & Corporate Services, Civic Centre, Port Talbot SA13 1PJ
Tel: 01639 763369 Fax: 01639 763370
DX: 135226 Port Talbot 2
Water Services: Welsh Water

W15 Newport City Council (U)

Website: www.newport.gov.uk
Main Switchboard: 01633 656656
Conveyancing Searches: Local Land Charges Section, Civic Centre, Newport NP20 4UR
Tel: 01633 210776 / 210777 Fax: 01633 244721
DX: 99463 Newport Gwent 3
e-mail: land.charges@newport.gov.uk
Building Control: Building Control, Civic Centre, as before
e-mail: building.control@newport.gov.uk
Council Tax: Council Tax, Civic Centre, as before
e-mail: counciltax@newport.gov.uk
Environmental Health: Environmental Health, Civic Centre, as before
e-mail: environmental.health@newport.gov.uk
Highways: Highways, as before
e-mail: streetscene@newport.gov.uk
Planning: Planning, as before
e-mail: planning@newport.gov.uk
Solicitor to the Council: Gareth Price, Head of Law and Standards, Civic Centre, Newport NP20 4UR
Tel: 01633 656656 Fax: 01633 244721
DX: 99463 Newport Gwent 3
Water Services: Welsh Water

W16 Pembrokeshire County Council (U)

Website: www.pembrokeshire.gov.uk
Main Switchboard: 01437 764551
Conveyancing Searches: Legal & Committee, County Hall, Haverfordwest SA61 1TP
Tel: 01437 775788 Fax: 01437 776493
DX: 98295 Haverfordwest
e-mail: landcharges@pembrokeshire.gov.uk
Building Control: Building Control, County Hall, Haverfordwest SA61 1TP
Tel: 01437 775251/775897
e-mail: richard.lawrence@pembrokeshire.gov.uk

Highways: Highways, County Hall, Haverfordwest SA61 1TP
Tel: 01437 775184
e-mail: stephen.roberts@pembrokeshire.gov.uk
Planning: Planning Dept, County Hall, Haverfordwest SA61 1TP
Tel: 01437 776373
e-mail: charlotte.jenkins@pembrokeshire.gov.uk
Solicitor to the Council: H J Miller, Head of Legal & Committee Services, County Hall, Haverfordwest SA61 1TP
Tel: 01437 775779 Fax: 01437 775303
DX: 98295 Haverfordwest
e-mail: huw.miller@pembrokeshire.gov.uk
Water Services: Welsh Water

W17 Powys County Council (U)

Website: www.powys.gov.uk
Main Switchboard: 01938 552828
Conveyancing Searches: Land Charges Section, Neuadd Maldwyn, Severn Rd, Welshpool SY21 7AS
Tel: 01938 551111
DX: 29213 Welshpool
e-mail: land.charges@powys.gov.uk
Building Control: Building Control, Neuadd Brycheiniog, Cambrian Way, Brecon LD3 7HR
Tel: 01874 612353
Environmental Health: Environmental Health, Neuadd Maldwyn, Severn Rd, Welshpool SY21 7AS
Tel: 01938 551121
Highways: Highways, County Hall, Spa Rd East, Llandrindod Wells LD1 5LG
Tel: 01597 826663
Planning (Montgomeryshire): Planning (Montgomeryshire), Neuadd Maldwyn, Severn Rd, Welshpool SY21 7AS
Tel: 01938 551259
Planning (Brecknockshire & Radnorshire): Planning, The Gwalia, Ithon Rd, Llandrindod Wells LD1 6AA
Tel: 01597 827177
Solicitor to the Council: Mr R C Pinney, County Hall, Spa Rd East, Llandrindod Wells LD1 5LG
Tel: 01597 826630 Fax: 01597 826220
Water Services: Babtie Group & Severn Trent (Montgom') / Hyder & Severn Trent (Breckn'/Radn')

W18 Rhondda Cynon Taf County Borough Council (U)

Website: www.rctcbc.gov.uk
Main Switchboard: 01443 424000
Conveyancing Searches: Land Charges Section, Unit 2, Maritime Business Pk, Maritime Industrial Estate, Pontypridd CF37 1NY
Tel: 01443 490100 Fax: 01443 485776
e-mail: landcharges@rhondda-cynon-taff.gov.uk
Building Control & Planning: Sardis Ho, Pontypridd CF37 1DU
Tel: 01443 494700 Fax: 01443 494888
e-mail: planningservices@rhondda-cynon-taff.gov.uk
Council Tax: Finance Services, Bronwydd Ho, Porth CF39 9DL
Tel: 01443 681081
e-mail: revenues@rhondda-cynon-taff.gov.uk
Environmental Health: Unit B1 Dinas Isaf, Williamstown, Porth
Tel: 01443 442100
Highways: Sardis Ho, Sardis Rd, Pontypridd CF37 1DU
Tel: 01443 494700 Fax: 01443 494705
Solicitor to the Council: Mr Paul Lucas, Director of Legal & Democratic Services, Unit 2 Maritime Business Pk, Pontypridd CF37 1NY
Tel: 01443 424105 Fax: 01443 424114
e-mail: paullucas@rhondda-cynon-taff.gov.uk

Water Services: Welsh Water

W19 Swansea City & County Council (U)

Website: www.swansea.gov.uk
Main Switchboard: 01792 636000
Conveyancing Searches: Legal Services, Civic Centre, Oystermouth Rd, Swansea SA1 3SN
Tel: 01792 636150 Fax: 01792 636763
DX: 743540 Swansea 22
e-mail: locallandcharges@swansea.gov.uk
Building Control & Environmental Health: Environment, Civic Centre, Oystermouth Rd, Swansea SA1 4PE
Tel: 01792 635636 Fax: 01792 635644
Council Tax: Finance Dept, The Guildhall, Swansea SA1 4NR
Tel: 01792 635382 Fax: 01792 635895
e-mail: council.tax@swansea.gov.uk
Highways: Environmental Dept, Clydach Depot, Clydach, Swansea SA6 5BY
Tel: 01792 843330
e-mail: highways@swansea.gov.uk
Planning: Planning Dept, Civic Centre, Oystermouth Rd, Swansea SA1 3SN
Tel: 01792 635701 Fax: 01792 635719
e-mail: planning@swansea.gov.uk
Solicitor to the Council: Mr Patrick Arran, Head of Legal Services, Civic Centre, Oystermouth Rd, Swansea SA1 3SN
Tel: 01792 636699 Fax: 01792 636340
DX: 743540 Swansea 22
e-mail: patrick.arran@swansea.gov.uk
Water Services: Welsh Water

W20 Torfaen County Borough Council (U)

Website: www.torfaen.gov.uk
Main Switchboard: 01495 762200
Conveyancing Searches: Corporate Resources, Civic Centre, Pontypool NP4 6YB
Tel: 01495 742655 Fax: 01495 742670
DX: 44257 Pontypool
e-mail: julie.jenkins@torfaen.gov.uk
Council Tax: Finance Dept, Civic Centre, Pontypool NP4 6YB
Tel: 01495 766129
e-mail: revs&bens@torfaen.gov.uk
Environmental Health, Planning & Building Control: Planning & Public Protection, County Hall, Cwmbran NP44 2WN
Tel: 01633 648095/647640 Fax: 01633 647328
e-mail: planning@torfaen.gov.uk
Highways: Operational Services, County Hall, Cwmbran NP44 2WN
Tel: 01495 762200 Fax: 01633 648017
e-mail: streetscene@torfaen.gov.uk
Solicitor to the Council: Lynda Willis, Chief Legal Officer, Civic Centre, Pontypool NP4 6YB
Tel: 01495 742660
DX: 44257 Pontypool
e-mail: lynda.willis@torfaen.gov.uk
Water Services: Welsh Water

W21 Vale of Glamorgan County Borough Council (U)

Website: www.valeofglamorgan.gov.uk
Main Switchboard: 01446 700111
Conveyancing Searches: Land Charges, Civic Offices, Holton Rd, Barry CF63 4RU
Tel: 01446 709417/8 Fax: 01446 709193
DX: 38553 Barry

1

Building Control: Planning & Transportation, Dock Offices, Barry Docks, Barry CF63 4RT
Tel: 01446 704842 Fax: 01446 704843
DX: 38553 Barry
Council Tax: Council Tax Collection/Registration, Civic Offices, Holton Rd, Barry CF63 4RU
Tel: 01446 709564 Fax: 01446 709275
DX: 38553 Barry
e-mail: counciltax@valeofglamorgan.gov.uk
Environmental Health: Legal & Regulatory Services, Civic Offices, Holton Rd, Barry CF63 4RU
Tel: 01446 709804 Fax: 01446 709828
DX: 38553 Barry
Highways: Building Control, Economic Development, Planning, Transport & Highways, Dock Office, Subway Rd, Barry CF62 4RT
Tel: 02920 673085 Fax: 02920 673198
DX: 38553 Barry
Planning: Building Control, Economic Development, Planning, Transport & Highways, Dock Offices, Barry Docks, Barry CF63 4RT
Tel: 01446 704658 Fax: 01446 704847
DX: 38553 Barry
Solicitor to the Council: Mr P H Evans, Director of Legal & Regulatory Services, Civic Offices, Holton Rd, Barry CF66 4RU
Tel: 01446 709400 Fax: 01446 701189
DX: 38553 Barry
Water Services: Welsh Water

W22 Wrexham County Borough Council (U)

Website: www.wrexham.gov.uk
Main Switchboard: 01978 292000
Conveyancing Searches: Community Wellbeing & Development Dept, Lorol St, Wrexham LL11 1LG
Tel: 01978 292021 Fax: 01978 292502
DX: 721924 Wrexham 4
e-mail: landcharges@wrexham.gov.uk
Building Control & Planning: Community Wellbeing & Development Dept, Lord St, Wrexham LL11 1LG
Tel: 01978 292016 Fax: 01978 292502
DX: 721924 Wrexham 4
e-mail: planning@wrexham.gov.uk
Council Tax: Finance Dept, Lambpit St, Wrexham LL11 1AR
Tel: 01978 292031 Fax: 01978 292702
e-mail: counciltax@wrexham.gov.uk
Environmental Health: Housing & Public Protection Dept, Ruthin Rd, Wrexham LL13 7TU
e-mail: neil.underwood@wrexham.gov.uk
Highways: Environment Dept, Abbey Rd, Wrexham Industrial Estate, Wrexham LL13 8ZE
Solicitor to the Council: Head of Corporate & Customer Services, Guildhall, Wrexham LL11 1AY
Tel: 01978 292202 Fax: 01978 292207
DX: 721924 Wrexham 4
e-mail: trevor.coxon@wrexham.gov.uk
Water: Welsh Water

Local Authorities in Scotland

S1 Aberdeenshire Council (U)

Website: www.aberdeenshire.gov.uk
Main Switchboard: 08456 081207
Conveyancing Searches: Building Standards, Gordon Ho, Blackhall Rd, Inverurie AB51 3WA
Tel: 01467 620981
DX: LP–3 Inverurie
e-mail: building.standards@aberdeenshire.gov.uk
Council Tax: Finance Dept, Gordon Ho, Blackhall Rd, Inverurie AB51 3WA
Tel: 08456 081201
e-mail: council.tax@aberdeenshire.gov.uk
Environmental Health: Environmental Health, Gordon Ho, Blackhall Rd, Inverurie AB51 3WA
Tel: 01467 628159 Fax: 01467 628358
DX: LP–3 Inverurie
e-mail: environmental@aberdeenshire.gov.uk
Highways: Transportation & Infrastructure, Woodhill Ho, Westburn Rd, Aberdeen AB16 5GB
Tel: 01224 665520
e-mail: transportation@aberdeenshire.gov.uk
Planning (Central): Winston Ho, 29 Castle St, Banff AB45 1DQ
Tel: 01261 813210 Fax: 01261 813281
DX: LP–7 Banff
e-mail: bb.planapps@aberdeenshire.gov.uk, ga.planapps@aberdeenshire.gov.uk
Planning (North): Arbuthnot Ho, 62 Board St, Peterhead AB42 1DA
Tel: 01779 483724 Fax: 01779 483727
e-mail: bu.planapps@aberdeenshire.gov.uk, fo.planapps@aberdeenshire.gov.uk
Planning (South): Viewmount, Arduthie Rd, Stonehaven AB39 2DQ
Tel: 01569 768300 Fax: 01569 766549
DX: LP–5Stonehaven
e-mail: ma.planapps@aberdeenshire.gov.uk
Solicitor to the Council: Director of Legal & Governance, Woodhill Ho, Westburn Rd, Aberdeen AB16 5GB
Tel: 01224 665430
Water Services: North of Scotland Water Authority

S2 Angus Council (U)

Website: www.angus.gov.uk
Main Switchboard: 08452 777778
Conveyancing Searches: Resources, Legal & Democratic Services, Angus Ho, Orchardbank Business Park, Forfar DD8 1AN
Tel: 01307 461460 Fax: 01307 476299
DX: LP8
e-mail: legdem@angus.gov.uk
Building Control & Planning: Communities, Planning & Place, County Bldgs, Market St, Forfar DD8 0LG
Tel: 01307 461774 Fax: 01307 461895
e-mail: planning@angus.gov.uk
Council Tax: Resources, Corporate Improvement & Finance, Invertay Ho, Maule St, Monifieth DD5 4JG
Tel: 01382 536570 Fax: 01382 535086
e-mail: revenquiry@angus.gov.uk
Environmental Health: Communities, Regulatory & Protective Services, County Bldgs, Market St, Forfar DD8 3WR
Tel: 01307 461460 Fax: 01307 473388
e-mail: envhealth@angus.gov.uk
Highways: Communities, Technical & Property Services, County Bldgs, Market St, Forfar DD8 3WR
Tel: 01307 473289 Fax: 01307 473388
e-mail: roads@angus.gov.uk
Solicitor to the Council: Sheona Hunter, Head of Legal & Democratic Services, Angus Ho, Orchardbank Business Pk, Forfar DD8 1AN
Tel: 01307 461460 Fax: 01307 476299
DX: LP8 Forfar
e-mail: legdem@angus.gov.uk
Water Services: Scottish Water

1

S3 Argyll & Bute Council (U)

Website: www.argyll-bute.gov.uk
Main Switchboard: 01546 602127
Conveyancing Searches: Governance & Law, Kilmory Castle, Lochgilphead PA31 8RT
Tel: 01546 604377 Fax: 01546 604435
DX: 599700 Lochgilphead
e-mail: eileen.wallace@argyll-bute.gov.uk
Building Control & Planning: Planning & Regulatory Services, Manse Brae, Lochgilphead PA31 8RD
Tel: 01546 604618 Fax: 01546 604237
e-mail: purchasing.dis@argyll-bute.gov.uk
Council Tax: Strategic Finance, Witchburn Rd, Campbeltown PA28 6JU
Tel: 01546 605511 Fax: 01586 553050
e-mail: ctax1@argyll-bute.gov.uk
Environmental Services: Planning & Regulatory Services, Kilmory Castle, Lochgilphead PA31 8RT
Tel: 01546 604292 Fax: 01546 604410
DX: 599700 Lochgilphead
e-mail: alan.morrison@argyll-bute.gov.uk
Highways: Roads and Amenity Services, Manse Brae, Lochgilphead PA31 8RD
Tel: 01546 604687 Fax: 01546 604631
Solicitor to the Council: Charles Reppke, Head of Governance & Law, Kilmory Castle, Lochgilphead PA31 8RT
Tel: 01546 604192 Fax: 01546 604359
DX: 599700 Lochgilphead
e-mail: charles.reppke@argyll-bute.gov.uk
Water Services: Scottish Water

S4 City of Aberdeen Council (U)

Website: www.aberdeencity.gov.uk
Main Switchboard: 08456 080910
Conveyancing Searches: Development Management Team, St Nicholas Ho, Broad St, Aberdeen AB10 1GY
Tel: 01224 523470 Fax: 01224 636181
DX: 529452 Aberdeen 9
e-mail: pi@aberdeencity.gov.uk
Note: Operate a one-stop service: all information (including water). No need to contact Scottish Water.
Building Control: Enterprise, Planning and Infrastructure, 8th Fl, St Nicholas Ho, as before,
Tel: 01224 523470 Fax: 01224 636181
DX: 529452 Aberdeen 9
e-mail: pi@aberdeencity.gov.uk
Council Tax: Council Tax and Benefits Section – Council Tax, Finance, 27–29 Crown Ho, Aberdeen AB11 6HA
Tel. 0845 000 0021 Fax: 01224 632343
e-mail: counciltax@aberdeencity.gov.uk

Environmental Health: Housing & the Environment, 4th Fl, St Nicholas Ho, Broad St, Aberdeen AB10 1BY
Tel: 01224 523440/522945 Fax: 01224 647333
e-mail: poll@aberdeencity.gov.uk
Highways: Environment & Infrastructure (Roads), Neighbourhood Services South, St Nicholas Ho, Broad St, Aberdeen AB10 1WL
Tel: 01224 522700 Fax: 01224 626301
Planning: Development Management Team, 8th Fl, St Nicholas Ho, Broad St, Aberdeen AB10 1GY
Tel: 01224 523470 Fax: 01224 636181
e-mail: pi@aberdeencity.gov.uk
Solicitor to the Council: Robert Loughridge, Asst Director of Legal & Democratic Services, Town Ho, Broad St, Aberdeen AB10 1AQ
Tel: 01224 522524 Fax: 01224 522491
DX: 529450 Aberdeen 9
Water Services: Scottish Water,
Note: All property enquiries are co-ordinated by the Property Enquiries Section of City Development Services.

S5 Dundee City Council (U)

Website: www.dundeecity.gov.uk
Main Switchboard: 01382 434000
Conveyancing Searches: Support Services, 21 City Sq, Dundee DD1 3BY
Tel: 01382 434202 Fax: 01382 434666
DX: LP 38
e-mail: roger.mennie@dundeecity.gov.uk
City Development: City Development, Dundee Ho, North Lindsay St, Dundee DD1 1QE
Tel: 01382 433610
DX: LP 38
e-mail: mike.galloway@dundeecity.gov.uk
Council Tax: Finance, Dundee Ho, North Lindsay St, Dundee DD1 1QE
Tel: 01382 433359 Fax: 01382 433045
e-mail: marjory.stewart@dundeecity.gov.uk
Environment: Environmental Dept, 353 Clepington Rd, Dundee
Tel: 01382 434729 Fax: 01382 436226
e-mail: ken.laing@dundeecity.gov.uk
Solicitor to the Council: Roger Mennie, Head of Democratic & Legal Services, 21 City Sq, Dundee DD1 3BY
Tel: 01382 434577 Fax: 01382 434666
DX: LP 38
e-mail: roger.mennie@dundeecity.gov.uk
Water Services: North of Scotland Water Authority

S6 City of Edinburgh Council (U)

Website: www.edinburgh.gov.uk
Main Switchboard: 0131 200 2000
Conveyancing Searches: City Development Dept, Waverley Ct, 4 East Market St, Edinburgh EH8 8BG
Tel: 0131 529 3550 Fax: 0131 529 6206
e-mail: commercial.property@edinburgh.gov.uk
Building Control, Highways & Planning: City Development Dept, Waverley Ct, 4 East Market St, Edinburgh EH8 8BG
Tel: 0131 529 7826 Fax: 0131 529 6206
e-mail: buildingwarrant.applications@edinburgh.gov.uk
Council Tax: Revenues Division, PO Box 12331, Chesser Ho, Edinburgh EH11 3YR
Tel: 0131 469 5000 Fax: 0131 469 5010
e-mail: revenuesbenefits@edinburgh.gov.uk
Environmental Health: Environment & Consumer Services, Chesser Ho, 500 Gorgie Rd, Edinburgh EH11 3YJ
Tel: 0131 529 3030 Fax: 0131 469 5849
e-mail: environmentalhealth@edinburgh.gov.uk
Solicitor to the Council: Gillian Lindsay, Council Solicitor, City Chambers, High St, Edinburgh EH1 1YJ
Tel: 0131 200 2000 Fax: 0131 529 3603
e-mail: gill.lindsay@edinburgh.gov.uk
Water Services: East of Scotland Water Authority

S7 City of Glasgow Council (U)

Website: www.glasgow.gov.uk
Main Switchboard: 0141 287 2000
Conveyancing Searches: Legal Services, City Chambers, George Sq, Glasgow G2 1DU
Tel: 0141 287 4132 Fax: 0141 287 5662
DX: GW 145
Council Tax: Financial Services, City Chambers, George Sq, Glasgow G1 1JE
Tel: 0845 600 8040 Fax: 0141 287 7674
Environmental Health: Land & Environmental Services, 231 George St, Glasgow G1 1RX
Tel: 0845 270 1558 Fax: 0141 287 5588
e-mail: public.health@eps.glasgow.gov.uk
Highways: Land & Environmental Services, 231 George St, Glasgow G2 7AD
Tel: 0141 287 9000 Fax: 0141 287 9059
e-mail: les@glasgow.gov.uk
Planning: Development & Regeneration Services, 229 George St, Glasgow G1 1QU
Tel: 0141 287 8555 Fax: 0141 287 8444
e-mail: regeneration@drs.glasgow.gov.uk
Solicitor to the Council: Anne-Marie O'Donnell, Executive Director of Corporate Services, City Chambers, George Sq, Glasgow G2 1DU
Tel: 0141 287 4522 Fax: 0141 287 3627
Water Services: Scottish Water

S8 Clackmannanshire Council (U)

Website: www.clacksweb.org.uk
Main Switchboard: 01259 450000
Conveyancing Searches: Administration & Legal Services, Greenfield, Alloa FK10 2AD
Tel: 01259 450000 Fax: 01259 452021
DX: LP 9
Building Control, Highways & Environmental Health: Development & Environmental Services, Kilncraigs, Greenside St, Alloa FK10 1EB
Tel: 01259 450000/452560 Fax: 01259 727301
e-mail: building.standards@clacks.gov.uk
Council Tax: Finance & Corporate Services, Council Tax Team, Kilncraigs, Greenside St, Alloa FK10 1EB
Tel: 01259 450000/226237
e-mail: counciltax@clacks.gov.uk
Planning: Development & Environmental Services, Kilncraigs, Greenside St, Alloa FK10 1EB
Tel: 01259 450000 Fax: 01259 727301
e-mail: devplan@clacks.gov.uk
Solicitor to the Council: David Thomson, Head of Administration & Legal Services, Greenfield, Alloa FK10 2AD
Tel: 01259 450000 Fax: 01259 452021
Water Services: East of Scotland Water Authority

S9 West Dunbartonshire Council (U)

Website: www.west-dunbarton.gov.uk
Main Switchboard: 01389 737000
Conveyancing Searches: Planning Services, Council Offices, Clydebank G81 1TG
Tel: 01389 738209 Fax: 01389 738584
e-mail: buildingandplanning@west-dunbarton.gov.uk

Building Control & Planning: Planning & Building Standards, Housing, Environmental and Economic Development, Council Offices, Roseberry Pl, Clydebank G81 1TG
Tel: 01389 738575 Fax: 01389 738584
e-mail: buildingandplanning@west-dunbarton.gov.uk
Council Tax: Finance Services, Council Offices, Garshake Rd, Dumbarton G82 3PU
Tel: 01389 738282 Fax: 01389 737472
e-mail: council.tax@west-dunbarton.gov.uk
Environmental Health Section: Environmental Health Section, West Dunbartonshire Council, Council Offices, Clydebank G81 1TG
Tel: 01389 738627/738652 Fax: 01389 738674
e-mail: environmental.health@west-dunbarton.gov.uk
Solicitor to the Council: Peter Hessett, Legal & Administrative Services, Council Offices, Garshake Rd, Dumbarton G82 3PU
Tel: 01389 737800 Fax: 01389 737870
e-mail: peter.hessett@west-dunbarton.gov.uk
Water Services: Scottish Water

S10 Dumfries & Galloway Council (U)

Website: www.dumgal.gov.uk
Main Switchboard: 030 33 33 3000
Conveyancing Searches: Dumfries & Galloway Council, Council Offices, English St, Dumfries DG1 2DD
Tel: 030 33 33 3000 Fax: 01387 260034
e-mail: cis@dumgal.gov.uk
Council Tax: Financial Services, Carruthers Ho, English St, Dumfries DG1 2HP
Tel: 01387 260266 Fax: 01387 260326
Environmental Health: Operations Manager, Environmental Standards, Municipal Chambers, Buccleuch St, Dumfries DG1 2AD
Tel: 030 33 33 3000
e-mail: environmental-standards@dumgal.gov.uk
Planning: Operations Manager, Planning & Environment, Kirkbank Ho, English St, Dumfries DG1 2HS
Tel: 01387 260100 Fax: 01387 260188
e-mail: p&e.directorssecretary@dumgal.gov.uk
Solicitor to the Council: Legal Services, Council Offices, English St, Dumfries DG1 2DD
Tel: 01387 260000 Fax: 01387 247803
DX: LP–9
e-mail: head.legal.services@dumgal.gov.uk
Water Services: West of Scotland Water

S11 East Ayrshire Council (U)

Website: www.east-ayrshire.gov.uk
Main Switchboard: 01563 576000
Conveyancing Searches: Property Enquiry Reports, Democratic Services, Council Headquarters, London Rd, Kilmarnock KA3 7BU
Tel: 01563 576571 Fax: 01563 576245
DX: LP18 DXKK23 (Receive only)
e-mail: propertyenquiries@east-ayrshire.gov.uk
Building Control & Planning: Planning and Economic Development, The Johnnie Walker Bond, 15 Strand St, Kilmarnock KA1 1HU
Tel: 01563 576781/576778 Fax: 01563 576774
e-mail: planning.service@east-ayrshire.gov.uk
Council Tax: Finance Service, Opera Ho, 8 John Finnie St, Kilmarnock KA1 1DD
Tel: 01563 554400
e-mail: council.tax@east-ayrshire.gov.uk
Environmental Health: Finance & Corporate Support, Legal Procurement & Regulatory Services, Environmental Health, Civic Centre Sth, John Dickie St, Kilmarnock KA1 1HN
Tel: 01563 576856 Fax: 01563 503125
e-mail: bill.gilchrist@east-ayrshire.gov.uk
Highways: Roads & Transportation, The Johnnie Walker Bond, 15 Strand St, Kilmarnock KA1 1HU
Tel: 01563 503185 Fax: 01563 503178
e-mail: roads@east-ayrshire.gov.uk
Housing: Housing Dept, Housing Asset Services, Holmquarry Rd, Kilmarnock KA1 4EP
Tel: 01563 555715 Fax: 01563 555738
e-mail: gordon.mckenzie@east-ayrshire.gov.uk
Solicitor to the Council: David Mitchell, Head of Legal, Procurement & Regulatory Services, Council Headquarters, London Rd, Kilmarnock KA3 7BU
Tel: 01563 576161 Fax: 01563 576179
DX: LP18 DXKK23 (receive only)
e-mail: david.mitchell@east-ayrshire.gov.uk
Water Services: Scottish Water

S12 East Dunbartonshire Council (U)

Website: www.eastdunbarton.gov.uk
Main Switchboard: 0300 123 4510
Conveyancing Searches: Legal Services, Broomhill Industrial Estate, Kelsyth Rd, Kirkintilloch G66 1TF
Tel: 0300 123 4510
DX: LP7-Kirkintilloch
Building Control: Building Standards, Southbank Business Park, Kirkintilloch G66 1XQ
Tel: 0300 123 4510
e-mail: buildingstandards@eastdunbarton.gov.uk
Council Tax: Council Tax Dept, 2–4 West High St, Kirkintilloch G66 1AD
Tel: 0300 123 4510
e-mail: counciltax@eastdunbarton.gov.uk
Environmental Health: Environmental Health, Southbank Business Pk, Kirkintilloch G66 1XQ
Tel: 0300 123 4510
e-mail: environmental.health@eastdunbarton.gov.uk
Highways: Roads & Neighbourhood Services, Broomhill Industrial Estate, Kilsyth Rd, Kirkintilloch G66 1QF
Tel: 0300 123 4510
e-mail: roadservices@eastdunbarton.gov.uk
Planning: Development & Enterprise, Southbank Business Park, Kirkintilloch G66 1XQ
Tel: 0300 123 4510
e-mail: planning@eastdunbarton.gov.uk
Water: Scottish Water

S13 East Lothian Council (U)

Website: www.eastlothian.gov.uk
Main Switchboard: 01620 827827
Conveyancing Searches: Service Manager – Legal and Procurement, John Muir Ho, Brewery Pk, Haddington EH41 3HA
Tel: 01620 827770 Fax: 01620 827253
e-mail: legal@eastlothian.gov.uk
Building Control: Environment (Building Standards), John Muir Ho, Brewery Pk, Haddington EH41 3HA
Tel: 01620 827216 Fax: 01620 827723
e-mail: buildingstandards@eastlothian.gov.uk
Council Tax: Council Tax Dept, PO Box 13251, Haddington EH41 3YG
Tel: 01875 824314 Fax: 01620 827149
e-mail: counciltax@eastlothian.gov.uk

1

Education & Community Services: Education, John Muir Ho, Brewery Pk, Haddington EH41 3HA
Tel: 01620 827616 Fax: 01620 827291
e-mail: educationenquiries@eastlothian.gov.uk
Environmental Health: Environmental and Consumer Services, John Muir Ho, Brewery Pk, Haddington EH41 3HA
Tel: 01620 827365 Fax: 01620 827918
e-mail: ehts@eastlothian.gov.uk
Highways: Roads, John Muir Ho, Brewery Pk, Haddington EH41 3HA
Tel: 01875 824305 Fax: 01620 827710
e-mail: transportation@eastlothian.gov.uk
Planning: Planning, John Muir Ho, Brewery Pk, Haddington EH41 3HA
Tel: 01620 827216 Fax: 01620 827723
e-mail: planning@eastlothian.gov.uk
Solicitor to the Council: Morag Ferguson, Service Manager – Legal, John Muir Ho, Haddington EH41 3HA
Tel: 01620 827770 Fax: 01620 827253
e-mail: legal@eastlothian.gov.uk
Water Services: East of Scotland Water Authority & Scottish Water

S14 East Renfrewshire Council (U)

Website: www.eastrenfrewshire.gov.uk
Main Switchboard: 0141 577 3000
Conveyancing Searches: Legal Services, Council Headquarters, Eastwood Pk, Rouken Glen Rd, Giffnock G46 6UG
Tel: 0141 577 3021 Fax: 0141 577 3834
DX: 501600 Giffnock
e-mail: gerry.mahon@eastrenfrewshire.gov.uk
Building Control: Building Control, 2 Spiersbridge Way, Spiersbridge Business Pk, Thornliebank G46 8NG
Tel: 0141 577 3895/3878 Fax: 0141 577 3781
e-mail: gillian.mccarney@eastrenfrewshire.gov.uk
Chief Solicitor: Mr Gerry Mahon, Legal Services, Council Headquarters, Eastwood Park, Rouken Glen Rd, Giffnock G46 6UG
Tel: 0141 577 3024 Fax: 0141 577 3834
DX: 501600 Giffnock
e-mail: gerry.mahon@eastrenfrewshire.gov.uk
Council Tax: Revenue Services, Barrhead Council Offices, 211 Main St, Barrhead G78 1SY
Tel: 0141 577 3295 Fax: 0141 577 3255
e-mail: ctax@eastrenfrewshire.gov.uk
Environmental Health: Environment Dept (Cleansing, Parks & Protective Services Division), Thornliebank Depot, Carnwadric Rd, Thornliebank G46 8HR
Tel: 0141 577 3785 Fax: 0141 577 8622
DX: 501601 Giffnock
e-mail: john.davidson@eastrenfrewshire.gov.uk
Highways: Environment Dept (Roads, Planning & Transportation Division), 2 Spiersbridge Way, Spiersbridge Business Pk, Thornliebank G46 8NG
Tel: 0141 577 3417 Fax: 0141 577 3414
e-mail: roads@eastrenfrewshire.gov.uk
Planning: Environment Dept (Roads, Planning & Transportation Division), 2 Spiersbridge Way, Spiersbridge Business Pk, Thornliebank G46 8NG
Tel: 0141 577 3895/3878 Fax: 0141 577 3781
DX: 501601 Giffnock
e-mail: gillian.mccarney@eastrenfrewshire.gov.uk
Water Services: Scottish Water

S15 Falkirk Council (U)

Website: www.falkirk.gov.uk
Main Switchboard: 01324 506070
Conveyancing Searches: Law & Administration Services, Municipal Bldgs, West Bridge St, Falkirk FK1 5RS
Tel: 01324 506070 Fax: 01324 506071
DX: LP1 – Falkirk 2
e-mail: director.la@falkirk.gov.uk
Building Control: Building Standards, Development Services, Abbotsford Ho, David's Loan, Bainsford, Falkirk FK2 7YZ
Tel: 01324 504985 Fax: 01324 504709
DX: LP3-Falkirk 2
e-mail: buildingcontrol@falkirk.gov.uk
Council Tax: Finance Services, Falkirk Council, Municipal Bldgs, West Bridge St, Falkirk FK1 5RS
Tel: 01324 506070 Fax: 01324 506363
e-mail: director.finance@falkirk.gov.uk
Environmental Health: Environmental Protection Unit, Abbotsford Ho, David's Loan, Bainsford, Falkirk FK2 7YZ
Tel: 01324 504982 Fax: 01324 504709
DX: LP3-Falkirk 2
e-mail: envhealth@falkirk.gov.uk
Highways & Planning: Development Services, Abbotsford Ho, David's Loan, Bainsford, Falkirk FK2 7YZ
Tel: 01324 504950 Fax: 01324 504709
DX: LP3-Falkirk 2
e-mail: planenv@falkirk.gov.uk
Solicitor to the Council: Rosemary Glackin, Law & Administration Services, Municipal Bldgs, West Bridge St, Falkirk FK1 5RS
Tel: 01324 506070 Fax: 01324 506288
DX: LP1-Falkirk 2
e-mail: director.la@falkirk.gov.uk
Water Services: Scottish Water

S16 Fife Council (U)

Website: www.fifedirect.org.uk
Main Switchboard: 0845 155 0000
Conveyancing Searches: Legal Services (Conveyancing & Contracts), Corporate Services, Fife Ho, North St, Glenrothes KY7 5LT
Tel: 0845 155 0000 Fax: 01592 583155
DX: 561502 Glenrothes 3
e-mail: jane.donaldson@fife.gov.uk
Council Tax: Benefits & Council Tax Team, PO Box 18015, North St, Glenrothes KY7 5YJ
Tel: 08451 551144
e-mail: benctax@fife.gov.uk
Environmental Health: Enterprise, Planning & Protective Services, Kingdom Ho, Kingdom Ave, Glenrothes KY7 5LY
Tel: 08451 555555 x442284 (direct line)
e-mail: keith.winter@fife.gov.uk
Highways: Transportation & Environmental Services, Bankhead Central, Bankhead Pk, Glenrothes KY7 6GH
Tel: 08451 550000
e-mail: bob.mclellan@fife.gov.uk
Planning & Building Control: Enterprise, Planning & Protective Services, Kingdom Ho, Kingdom Ave, Glenrothes KY7 5LY
Tel: 08451 555555
Solicitor to the Council: Chief Legal Officer, Legal Services, Corporate Services, Fife Ho, North St, Glenrothes KY7 5LT
Tel: 0845 155 0000 Fax: 01592 583155
e-mail: iain.matheson@fife.gov.uk
Water Services: Scottish Water

S17 Highland Council (U)

Website: www.highland.gov.uk
Main Switchboard: 01349 886606
Conveyancing Searches: see under Area Offices
Area Office: Badenoch and Strathspey: Area Office, Ruthven Rd, Kingussie PH21 1EJ
Tel: 01540 664502 Fax: 01540 661004
Area Office: Caithness: Area Office, Girnigoe St, Wick KW1 4HW
Tel: 01955 607719 Fax: 01955 607706
Area Office: Inverness: Area Office, Town Ho, High St, Inverness IV1 1JJ
Tel: 01463 785100 Fax: 01463 724291
Area Office: Lochaber: Area Office, Lochaber Ho, High St, Fort William PH33 6EL
Tel: 01397 707256 Fax: 01397 702178
Area Office: Nairn: Area Office, The Court Ho, High St, Nairn IV12 4AU
Tel: 01667 458500 Fax: 01667 452056
Area Office: Ross and Cromarty: Area Office, High St, Dingwall IV15 9RY
Tel: 01349 868527 Fax: 01349 863510
Area Office: Skye and Lochalsh: Area Office, Tigh na Sgire, Park La, Portree IV51 9GP
Tel: 01478 612341 Fax: 01478 613824
Area Office: Sutherland: Area Office, Drummuig, Golspie KW10 6TA
Tel: 01408 635200
Building Control & Planning: Planning & Development Service, Council Offices, Glenurquhart Rd, Inverness IV3 5NX
Tel: 01463 702250 Fax: 01463 702298
e-mail: planning@highland.gov.uk
Council Tax: Finance Service, Glenurquhart Rd, Inverness IV3 5YX
Tel: 0800 393811 Fax: 01463 702320
e-mail: finance@highland.gov.uk
Note: Freefone: Caithness, Sutherland and Lochaber: 0800 611681; Inverness, Nairn and Badenoch & Strathspey: 0800 393811; Ross & Cromarty and Skye & Lochalsh: 0800 122182
Environmental Health: T.E.C. (Transport, Environmental & Community Works) Services, Glenurquhart Rd, Inverness IV3 5NX
Tel: 01463 702500 Fax: 01463 702606
e-mail: tecs@highland.gov.uk
Highways: T.E.C. Services, Glenurquhart Rd, Inverness IV3 5NX
Tel: 01463 702646 Fax: 01463 702606
e-mail: tecs@highland.gov.uk
Solicitor to the Council: Stewart Fraser, Head of Legal & Democratic Services, Glenurquhart Rd, Inverness IV3 5NX
Tel: 01463 702112 Fax: 01463 702182
e-mail: legal-hq@highland.gov.uk
Water Services: Scottish Water

S18 Inverclyde Council (U)

Website: www.inverclyde.gov.uk
Main Switchboard: 01475 717171
Conveyancing Searches: Legal Services, Municipal Bldgs, Clyde Sq, Greenock PA15 1LX
Tel: 01475 712139 Fax: 01475 712137
e-mail: legal@inverclyde.gov.uk
Building Control & Planning: Planning Services, Municipal Bldgs, Clyde Sq, Greenock PA15 1LY
Tel: 01475 712406 Fax: 01475 712468
e-mail: devcont.planning@inverclyde.gov.uk
Council Tax: Finance Dept, 1st Fl, Municipal Bldgs, Clyde Sq, Greenock PA15 1LX
Tel: 01475 712961 Fax: 01475 712168
e-mail: council.tax@inverclyde.gov.uk
Environmental Health: Safer and Inclusive Communities, 50 West Stewart St, Greenock PA15 1YA
Tel: 01475 714200
e-mail: safer.communities@inverclyde.gov.uk
Highways: Transportation & Roads, 71 East Hamilton St, Greenock PA15 2UA
Tel: 01475 714800 Fax: 01475 714825
e-mail: roads@inverclyde.gov.uk
Legal & Administration: Gerard Malone, Head of Legal & Property Services, Municipal Bldgs, Clyde Sq, Greenock PA15 1LX
Tel: 01475 712139 Fax: 01475 712137
e-mail: gerard.malone@inverclyde.gov.uk
Water Services: West of Scotland Water Authority

S19 Midlothian Council (U)

Website: www.midlothian.gov.uk
Main Switchboard: 0131 270 7500
Conveyancing Searches: Corporate Resources, Fairfield Ho, 8 Lothian Rd, Dalkeith EH22 3AA
Tel: 0131 271 3368 (Planning); 0131 663 1103 (Roads)
Fax: 0131 271 3537 (Planning); 0131 654 2797 (Roads)
DX: 540568 Dalkeith (receipt only)
e-mail: see Planning and Roads
Building Control: Building Standards, Corporate Resources, Fairfield Ho, 8 Lothian Rd, Dalkeith EH22 3AA
Tel: 0131 271 3320 Fax: 0131 271 3537
DX: 540568 Dalkeith (receipt only)
e-mail: building-standards@midlothian.gov.uk
Council Tax: Revenues & Benefits Services, Corporate Resources, Buccleuch Ho, 1 White Hart St, Dalkeith EH22 1AE
Tel: 0131 271 3201 Fax: 0131 271 3599
DX: 540568 Dalkeith (receipt only)
e-mail: revenues.enquiries@midlothian.gov.uk
Environmental Health: Environmental Health & Trading Standards, Communities and Wellbeing, Fairfield Ho, 8 Lothian Rd, Dalkeith EH22 3ZH
Tel: 0131 271 3318 Fax: 0131 271 3537
DX: 540568 Dalkeith (receipt only)
e-mail: environmentalhealth@midlothian.gov.uk
Highways: Roads Services, Corporate Resources, Dundas Bldgs, 62a Polton St, Bonnyrigg EH19 3YD
Tel: 0131 663 1103 Fax: 0131 654 2797
DX: 540568 Dalkeith (receipt only)
e-mail: commercial.services@midlothian.gov.uk
Planning: Development Management, Corporate Resources, Fairfield Ho, 8 Lothian Rd, Dalkeith EH22 3AA
Tel: 0131 271 3302 Fax: 0131 271 3537
DX: 540568 Dalkeith (receipt only)
e-mail: development.management@midlothian.gov.uk
Solicitor to the Council: Legal and Secretariat, Corporate Resources, Midlothian Ho, Buccleuch St, Dalkeith EH22 1DJ
Tel: 0131 270 7500 Fax: 0131 271 3107
DX: 540568 Dalkeith (receipt only)
e-mail: jim.clifford@midlothian.gov.uk
Water Services: Scottish Water

1

S20 Moray Council (U)

Website: www.moray.gov.uk
Main Switchboard: 01343 543451
Conveyancing Searches: Head of Legal & Democratic Services, Council Offices, High St, Elgin IV30 1BX
Tel: 01343 543451 Fax: 01343 563221
DX: 520666
e-mail: ldsadmin@moray.gov.uk
Solicitor to the Council: Head of Legal & Democratic Services, Council Offices, High St, Elgin IV30 1BX
Tel: 01343 543451 Fax: 01343 563221
DX: 520666
e-mail: ldsadmin@moray.gov.uk
Water Services: Scottish Water

S21 North Ayrshire Council (U)

Website: www.north-ayrshire.gov.uk
Main Switchboard: 0845 603 0590
Conveyancing Searches: Corporate Services – Planning, Cunninghame Ho, Irvine KA12 8EE
Tel: 01294 324757 Fax: 01294 324372
e-mail: propertyenquiries@north-ayrshire.gov.uk
Note: Property enquiries only
Council Tax: Financial Services, Cunninghame Ho, Irvine KA12 8EE
Tel: 0845 603 0592 Fax: 01294 324544
e-mail: counciltax@north-ayrshire.gov.uk
Environmental Health: Corporate Services, 1st Fl, Cunninghame Ho, Irvine KA12 8EE
Tel: 01294 324300 Fax: 01294 324360
e-mail: environmentalhealth@north-ayrshire.gov.uk
Highways: Roads, Perceton Ho, Irvine KA11 2AL
Tel: 01294 225200 Fax: 01294 225244
e-mail: headofroads@northayrshire.gov.uk
Planning: Legal & Protective Services (Legal, Development Ctrl, Building Ctrl), Cunninghame Ho, Irvine KA12 8EE
Tel: 01294 324319 Fax: 01294 324372
DX: IR 11
Solicitor to the Council: Ian Mackay, Cunninghame Ho, Irvine KA12 8EE
Tel: 01294 324385 Fax: 01294 324394
DX: IR11
e-mail: imackay@north-ayrshire.gov.uk
Water Services: West of Scotland Water Authority

S22 North Lanarkshire Council (U)

Website: www.northlanarkshire.gov.uk
Main Switchboard: 01698 403200
Conveyancing Searches: Corporate Services, Civic Centre, Windmillhill St, Motherwell ML1 1AB
Tel: 01698 302443 Fax: 01698 302351
Council Tax: Finance and Customer Services, 7 Scott St, Motherwell ML1 1SX
Tel: 01698 302930
DX: 571700
e-mail: revenue@northlan.gov.uk
Highways, Planning, Building Standards & Environmental Health: Environmental Services, Fleming Ho, 2 Tryst Rd, Cumbernauld G67 1JW
Tel: 01236 632500 Fax: 01698 302115
e-mail: esenquiries@northlan.gov.uk
Legal Services: Head of Legal Services, Corporate Services, Civic Centre, Windmillhill St, Motherwell ML1 1AB
Tel: 01698 302554 Fax: 01698 302211
DX: 571701 Motherwell 2
Water Services: Scottish Water

S23 Orkney Islands Council (U)

Website: www.orkney.gov.uk
Main Switchboard: 01856 873535
Conveyancing Searches: Corporate Services, Legal Services, Council Offices, School Pl, Kirkwall KW15 1NY
Tel: 01856 873535 Fax: 01856 876941
e-mail: corporate.services@orkney.gov.uk
Building Control: Development & Infrastructure, Council Offices, as before,
Tel: 01856 873535
e-mail: business.standards@orkney.gov.uk
Council Tax: Corporate Services, Finance, Council Offices, as before,
Tel: 01856 873535 Fax: 01856 876158
e-mail: corporateservices@orkney.gov.uk
Environmental Health: Development & Infrastructure, Council Offices, as before,
Tel: 01856 873535 Fax: 01856 886450
e-mail: env-health@orkney.gov.uk
Highways: Development & Infrastructure, Council Offices, as before,
Tel: 01856 873535 Fax: 01856 876094
e-mail: developmentandinfrastructure@orkney.gov.uk
Planning: Development & Infrastructure, Council Offices, as before,
Tel: 01856 873535
e-mail: planning@orkney.gov.uk
Solicitor to the Council: Head of Legal Services, Council Offices, School Pl, Kirkwall KW15 1NY
Tel: 01856 873535 Fax: 01856 876941
e-mail: corporateservices@orkney.gov.uk
Water Services: Scottish Water

S24 Perth & Kinross Council (U)

Website: www.pkc.gov.uk
Main Switchboard: 01738 475000
Conveyancing Searches: The Environment Service, Pullar Ho, 35 Kinnoull St, Perth PH1 5GD
Tel: 01738 476476 Fax: 01738 476410
e-mail: es@pkc.gov.uk
Building Control: The Environment Service, Pullar Ho, 35 Kinnoull St, Perth PH1 5GD
Tel: 01738 475300 Fax: 01738 476410
e-mail: buildingstandards@pkc.gov.uk
Customer Services: Customer Service Centre, Perth & Kinross Council, 2 High St, Perth PH1 5PH
Tel: 01738 475000 Fax: 01738 475497
e-mail: enquiries@pkc.gov.uk
Environmental Health: The Environment Service, Pullar Ho, 35 Kinnoull St, Perth PH1 5GD
Tel: 01738 476476 Fax: 01738 475210
e-mail: es@pkc.gov.uk
Highways: The Environment Service, Pullar Ho, 35 Kinnoull St, Perth PH1 5GD
Tel: 01738 476476 Fax: 01738 476410
e-mail: rtas@pkc.gov.uk
Planning: The Environment Service, Pullar Ho, 35 Kinnoull St, Perth PH1 5GD
Tel: 01738 475300 Fax: 01738 476410
e-mail: developmentplan@pkc.gov.uk

S25 Renfrewshire Council (U)

Website: www.renfrewshire.gov.uk
Main Switchboard: 0300 300 0330
Conveyancing Searches: Finance & Corporate Services, Renfrewshire Ho, Cotton St, Paisley PA1 1TR
Tel: 0141 618 7163 Fax: 0141 618 6070
DX: 590702
e-mail: cs@renfrewshire.gov.uk
Building Control & Planning: Development & Housing Services, Renfrewshire Ho, Cotton St, Paisley PA1 1JD
Tel: 0141 618 7933 Fax: 0141 618 7935
e-mail: pt@renfrewshire.gov.uk
Council Tax: Finance & Corporate Services, Renfrewshire Ho, Cotton St, Paisley PA1 1HY
Tel: 0300 300 0300 Fax: 0141 618 7052
e-mail: council-tax.finit@renfrewshire.gov.uk
Environmental Health: Environmental Services, Renfrewshire Ho, Cotton St, Paisley PA1 1BR
Tel: 0141 618 7626
e-mail: es@renfrewshire.gov.uk
Head of Legal & Democratic Services: Mr Kenneth Graham, Renfrewshire Ho, Cotton St, Paisley PA1 1TR
Tel: 0141 618 7360 Fax: 0141 618 6070
DX: 590702
e-mail: cs@renfrewshire.gov.uk
Roads: Community Resources, Renfrewshire Ho, Cotton St, Paisley PA1 1LL
Tel: 0141 618 7932
e-mail: pt@renfrewshire.gov.uk
Water Services: Scottish Water

S26 Shetland Islands Council (U)

Website: www.shetland.gov.uk
Main Switchboard: 01595 693535
Conveyancing Searches: Governance & Law – Legal Division, 8 North Ness Business Pk, Lerwick ZE1 0LZ
Tel: 01595 744550 Fax: 01595 744585
e-mail: legal.services@shetland.gov.uk
Building Control & Planning: Planning, 8 North Ness Business Park, Lerwick ZE1 0LZ
Tel: 01595 744800 Fax: 01595 744804
e-mail: development.plans@shetland.gov.uk
Council Tax: Finance, 8 North Ness Business Pk, Lerwick ZE1 0LZ
Tel: 01595 744683 Fax: 01595 744661
e-mail: local.taxation@shetland.gov.uk
Environmental Health: Infrastructure Services, Charlotte Ho, Commercial Rd, Lerwick ZE1 0LX
Tel: 01595 745250 Fax: 01595 744802
e-mail: environmental.health@shetland.gov.uk
Highways: Infrastructure Services, Gremista, Lerwick ZE1 0PX
Tel: 01595 744866 Fax: 01595 744869
e-mail: roads@shetland.gov.uk
Solicitor to the Council: Jan R Riise, Executive Manager, 8 North Ness Business Pk, Lerwick ZE1 0LZ
Tel: 01595 744550 Fax: 01595 744585
e-mail: legal.services@shetland.gov.uk
Water Services: Scottish Water

S27 South Ayrshire Council (U)

Website: www.south-ayrshire.gov.uk
Main Switchboard: 0300 123 0900
Conveyancing Searches: Property Enquiry Services and Estates, Newton Ho, 30 Green St La, Ayr KA8 8BH
Tel: 01292 612970/613095
e-mail: laura.penman@south-ayrshire.gov.uk, david.lewis@south-ayrshire.gov.uk
Council Tax: Revenues & Benefits, Ground Fl, County Bldgs, 10 Wellington Sq, Ayr KA7 1DR
Tel: 01292 612664
e-mail: council.tax@south-ayrshire.gov.uk
Environmental Health: Environmental Health, Burns Ho, Burns Statue Sq, Ayr KA7 1UT
Tel: 01292 618222 Fax: 01292 288755
e-mail: environmental.health@south-ayrshire.gov.uk
Highways: Development, Safety & Regulation, Planning & Transportation, Burns Ho, Burns Statue Sq, Ayr KA7 1UT
Tel: 01292 612000 (main switchboard) Fax: 01292 616260
Planning & Building Control: Development Safety & Regulation (Planning Services), Burns Ho, Burns Statue Sq, Ayr KA7 1UT
Tel: 01292 616107 Fax: 01292 616161
e-mail: planning.development@south-ayrshire.gov.uk
Solicitor to the Council: Ralph Riddiough, Head of Legal & Democratic Services, County Bldgs, Wellington Sq, Ayr KA7 1DR
Tel: 01292 612400 (Personal Assistant) Fax: 01292 612188
DX: LP32 AYR
e-mail: ralph.riddiough@south-ayrshire.gov.uk
Water Services: Scottish Water

S28 South Lanarkshire Council (U)

Website: www.southlanarkshire.gov.uk
Main Switchboard: 0303 123 1015
Conveyancing Searches: Legal Services, Floor 13, Almada St, Hamilton ML3 0AA
Tel: 01698 455935 Fax: 01698 455035
DX: 579641 Hamilton 3
Building Control & Planning: Enterprise Resources, 154 Montrose Cres, Hamilton ML3 6LB
Tel: 0303 123 1015
e-mail: enterprise.hq@southlanarkshire.gov.uk
Council Tax: Housing & Technical Resources, Council Offices, Brandongate, 1 Leechlee Rd, Hamilton ML3 0XB
Tel: 0303 123 1010
e-mail: benefitsandrevenues.hamilton@southlanarkshire.gov.uk
Environmental Health: Environmental Services, Montrose Ho, 154 Montrose Cres, Hamilton ML3 6LB
Tel: 0303 123 1020
Highways: Roads & Transportation Services, Enterprise Resources, Montrose Ho, 154 Montrose Cres, Hamilton ML3 6LB
Tel: 0303 123 1015
e-mail: enterprise.hq@southlanarkshire.gov.uk
Solicitor to the Council: Geraldine McCann, Head of Legal Services, Floor 13, Almada St, Hamilton ML3 0AA
Tel: 01698 454526 Fax: 01698 454523
DX: 579641 Hamilton 3
e-mail: geraldine.mccann@southlanarkshire.gov.uk
Water Services: West of Scotland Water Authority

S29 Stirling Council (U)

Website: www.stirling.gov.uk
Main Switchboard: 0845 277 7000
Conveyancing Searches: Head of Environment Services, Old Viewforth, Stirling FK8 2ET
Tel: 0845 277 7000
e-mail: info@stirling.gov.uk
Building Control: Municipal Bldgs, 2 Corn Exchange Rd, Stirling FK2 2HU
e-mail: info@stirling.gov.uk
Council Tax: Council Tax, Teith Ho, Kerse Rd, Stirling FK7 7QA

Environmental Health: Municipal Bldgs, 2 Corn Exchange Rd, Stirling FK8 2HU
e-mail: info@stirling.gov.uk
Planning: Municipal Bldgs, 2 Corn Exchange Rd, Stirling FK8 2HU
e-mail: planning@stirling.gov.uk
Solicitor to the Council: Liz Duncan, Old Viewforth, Stirling FK8 2ET
Tel: 0845 277 7000 / 01786 233108
e-mail: duncanl@stirling.gov.uk
Water Services: Scottish Water

S30 Scottish Borders Council (U)

Website: www.scotborders.gov.uk
Main Switchboard: 0300 100 1800
Conveyancing Searches: Service Director, Regulatory Services, Council Headquarters, Newtown St Boswells, Melrose TD6 0SA
Tel: 01835 824000
DX: LP 1 Newtown St Boswells
e-mail: bfrater@scotborders.gov.uk
Building Control & Planning: Service Director, Regulatory Services, Council Heqdquarters, Newtown St Boswells, Melrose TD6 0SA
Council Tax: Service Director, Neighbourhood Services, Council Headquarters, Newtown St Boswells, Melrose TD6 0SA
Tel: 01835 825013
e-mail: jcraig@scotborders.gov.uk
Environmental Health: Service Director, Regulatory Services, Council Headquarters, Newtown St Boswells, Melrose TD6 0SA
Highways: Roads, Council Headquarters, Newtown St Boswells, Melrose TD6 0SA
Solicitor to the Council: Chief Legal Officer, Council Headquarters, Newtown St Boswells, Melrose TD6 0SA
Water Services: Scottish Water

S31 West Lothian Council (U)

Website: www.westlothian.gov.uk
Main Switchboard: 01506 280000
Conveyancing Searches: Legal Services, West Lothian Civic Centre, Howden South Rd, Livingston EH54 6FF
Tel: 01506 280000
e-mail: corine.paterson@westlothian.gov.uk
Building Control: Building Standards, West Lothian Civic Centre, as above,
Tel: 01506 280000 Fax: 01506 282489
e-mail: buildingstandards@westlothian.gov.uk
Council Tax: The Revenues Unit, St David Ho, South Bridge St, Bathgate EH48 1TT
Tel: 01506 282020
e-mail: counciltax@westlothian.gov.uk
Environmental Health: Environmental Health & Trading Standards, West Lothian Civic Centre, as above,
Tel: 01506 280000 Fax: 01506 282489
e-mail: environmentalhealth@westlothian.gov.uk
Highways: Roads & Transportation, Whitehill Ho, Whitehill Industrial Estate, Bathgate EH48 2HA
Tel: 01506 280000
e-mail: customer.service@westlothian.gov.uk
Planning: Development Planning, West Lothian Civic Centre, as above,
Tel: 01506 280000 Fax: 01506 282489
e-mail: localplan@westlothian.gov.uk
Solicitor to the Council: Carol Johnson, Chief Solicitor, West Lothian Civic Centre, Howden South Rd, Livingston EH54 6FF
Tel: 01506 280000
e-mail: legal.services@westlothian.gov.uk
Water Services: Scottish Water

S32 Western Isles/Comhairle nan Eilean Siar Council (U)

Website: www.cne-siar.gov.uk
Main Switchboard: 0845 600 7090
Conveyancing Searches: Executive Office, Council Offices, Sandwick Rd, Stornoway, Isle of Lewis HS1 2BW
Tel: 01851 709204 Fax: 01851 705349
e-mail: lmcdonald@cne-siar.gov.uk
Building Control & Planning: Development Dept, Council Offices, as before,
Tel: 01851 822690 Fax: 01851 705349
e-mail: planning@cne-siar.gov.uk
Council Tax: Revenues Section, Council Offices, as before,
Tel: 01851 709293 / 709296 Fax: 01851 705349
e-mail: counciltax@cne-siar.gov.uk
Environmental Health: Development Dept, Council Offices, as before,
Tel: 01851 822694 (Stornoway); 01870 604990 (Balivanich)
e-mail: eh@cne-siar.gov.uk
Highways: Technical Services, Council Offices, as above,
Tel: 01851 709465 Fax: 01851 705349
e-mail: iain.mackinnon@cne-siar.gov.uk
Solicitor to the Council: Lesley-Ann McDonald, Head of Executive Office, Sandwick Rd, Stornoway, Isle of Lewis HS1 2BW
Tel: 01851 709263 Fax: 01851 705349
e-mail: lmcdonald@cne-siar.gov.uk
Water Services: North of Scotland Water

Part 2

Gazetteer

The Gazetteer is a list of the names in alphabetical order of most towns, parishes, villages and other places with their own identities in England, Wales and Scotland and should be used to find the appropriate authority if not known. Each name is followed by the reference number under which the name and address of the authority is listed in the Directory. English districts and unitary authorities are numbered 1.1, 1.2 etc, London authorities L1 etc, Welsh authorities W1 etc, and Scottish authorities S1 etc. Where there is more than one place with the same name, the county or district is also given to assist identification. The word '(part)' after a place name indicates that the place spans the boundary between the two or more authorities given; an asterisk (*) denotes that there are two places of the same name in the same county. If the practitioner is in doubt as to the exact situation of a property, it may be useful to consult a large scale map.

In the case of a place known as, eg, North Turton, look under both 'Turton' and 'North' as the various authorities label places within their jurisdictions differently. This also applies to prefixes such as East, West, Upper, Lower, Greater and Smaller. Practitioners are reminded of the importance of submitting Ordnance Survey extracts with the property curtilages clearly defined to enable officers to answer district council enquiries efficiently and accurately.

Aarons Hill 38.5
Ab Kettleby 27.3
Ab Lench 49.6
Abbas Combe 38.5
Abberley 49.4
Abberton (Essex) 17.3
Abberton (Worcs) 49.6
Abbess Roding 17.6
Abbey 25.4
Abbey Green 44.2
Abbey Green (Shrop) 37.1
Abbey Hulton 40.3
Abbey St Bathans S30
Abbey Village 26.9
Abbey Wood (part) L3, L11
Abbeycwmhir W17
Abbeydale (Gloucs) 18.3
Abbeydale (Worcs) 49.3
Abbeydore 21.1
Abbeymead 18.3
Abbeymeads 48.2
Abbots Barton 20.5
Abbots Bickington 12.1
Abbots Bromley 40.5
Abbots Langley 22.8
Abbots Leigh 38.7
Abbots Morton 49.6
Abbots Ripton 6.3
Abbots Salford 44.5
Abbotsbury 13.1
Abbotsfield 38.4
Abbotsham 12.1
Abbotskerswell 12.5
Abbotsley 6.3
Abbotstone 20.5
Abbotswood 20.4
Abbotts Ann 20.4
Abbotts Barton 20.5
Abbotts Worthy 20.5
Abdon 37.1
Abenbury W22
Aber W11
Aberaeron W7
Aberaman W18
Aberangell W11
Aberarad W6
Aberarder S17
Aberargie S24
Aberavon W14
Aberbanc W7
Aberbargoed W4
Aberbeeg (part) W2, W4
Aberbran W17
Abercanaid W12
Abercarn W4
Abercegir W17
Abercerdin W3
Aberchirder S1
Abercorn S31
Abercrave W17
Abercregan W14
Abercromby 29.2
Abercwmboi W18
Abercynon W18
Aberdalgie S24
Aberdare W18
Aberdaron W11
Aberdeen S4
Aberdesach W11
Aberdour (Fife) S16
Aberdulais W14
Aberdyfi W11
Aberedw W17
Abererch W11
Aberfan W12
Aberfeldy S24
Aberffraw W1
Aberford (see Lotherton)
Aberfoyle S29
Abergarwed W14
Abergavanny 38.5
Abergavenny W13
Abergeirw W11
Abergele W8
Aberglaslyn W11
Abergorlech W6
Abergwesyn W17
Abergwili W6
Abergwynfi W14
Abergynolwyn W11
Aberhafesp W17
Aberhill S16
Aberhosan W17
Aberkenfig W3
Aberlady S13
Aberlemno S2
Aberllefenni W11
Aberlour S20
Abermorddu W10
Abermule W17
Abernant (Carm) W6
Abernant (Rhondda) W18
Abernethy S24
Abernyte S24
Aberporth W7
Abersoch W11
Abersychan W20
Aberthaw W21
Aberthin W21
Abertillery W2
Abertridwr W4
Abertysswg W4
Aberuthven S24
Aberwheeler W9
Aberyscir W17
Aberystwyth W7
Abingdon 35.4
Abinger (part) 42.8
Abinger Bottom 42.8
Abinger Common 42.8
Abinger Hammer (part)
42.7, 42.8
Abington (Lanarks') S28
Abington (N'hants) 31.5
Abington Pigotts 6.5
Abney 11.3
Abney Grange 11.3
Above Derwent 10.2
Aboyne & Glentanar S1
Abram 19.1
Abriachan S17
Abridge 17.6
Abson 18.7
Abthorpe 31.7
Aby with Greenfield 28.2
Acaster Malbis 33.7
Acaster Selby 33.8
Accrington 26.11
Achahoish S3
Achaphubuil S17
Acharacle S17
Acharn S24
Achavanich S17
Achgarve S17
Achiemore S17
Achiltibuie S17
Achilty S17
Achintee S17
Achintraid S17
Achmore (Highland) S17
Achmore (W Isles) S32
Achnahaird S17
Achnamara S3
Achnasheen S17
Achnashellach S17
Achosnich S17
Achscrabster S17
Achtorneed S17
Achurch (Thorpe Achurch)
31.3

Ackenthwaite 10.5
Ackergill S17
Acklam (Malton) (N Yorks) 33.3
Acklam (Middlesbrough) 33.9
Acklington 32.1
Ackton 47.5
Ackworth 47.5
Ackworth Moor Top 47.5
Acle 30.5
Acocks Green 45.5
Acol 25.7
Acomb (N'land) 32.1
Acomb (York) 33.7
Aconbury 21.1
Acre 26.14
Acrefair W22
Acresford (part) 11.9, 27.1
Acrise 25.13
Acthorpe 28.2
Acton & District 7.5
Acton (Staffs) 40.2
Acton (Suffolk) 41.6
Acton (Wrexham) W22
Acton (part) L9, L13
Acton Beauchamp 21.1
Acton Bridge 7.3
Acton Burnell 37.1
Acton Green (part) L9
Acton Lea 37.1
Acton Reynald 37.1
Acton Round 37.1
Acton Scott 37.1
Acton Trussell 40.6
Acton Turville 18.7
Adamsdown W5
Adamton S27
Adbaston 40.4
Adber 13.1
Adbury 20.1
Adcote (part) 37.1
Adderbury, East & West 35.2
Adderley 37.1
Adderley Green 40.3
Adderstone with Lucker 32.1
Addiewell S31
Addingham (Cumbria) 10.3
Addingham (W Yorks) 47.1
Addington (Bucks) 5.2
Addington (Kent) 25.9
Addlestone 42.1
Addlethorpe 28.2
Adeney 37.4
Adfa W17
Adforton 21.1
Adgarley (see Stainton)
Adgestone 24.1
Adisham 25.5
Adlestrop 18.5
Adlingfleet 15.2
Adlington (Cheshire) 7.5
Adlington (Lancs) 26.9
Admaston (Shrop) 37.4
Admaston (Staffs) 40.5
Admington 44.5
Adsborough 38.4
Adsdean 46.2
Adstock 5.2
Adstone 31.7
Advent 9.1
Adversane 46.3
Advie S17
Adwell 35.3
Adwick-le-Street 39.2
Adwick-on-Dearne 39.2
Ae S10
Affetside (part) 19.2, 19.3
Affpuddle 13.5
Afonwen (Flint) W10
Afonwen (Gwynedd) W11
Agden* 7.3, 7.5
Agglethorpe (see Coverham)
Aglionby 10.1
Aigburth 29.2
Aighton 26.3
Aiketgate 10.3
Aikton 10.2
Ailby (see Rigsby)
Ailsa Craig S27
Ailsworth 6.1
Ainderby Miers with Holtby 33.2
Ainderby Quernhow 33.2
Ainderby Steeple 33.2
Ainley Top 47.3
Ainsdale (part) 29.1
Ainstable (part) 10.1, 10.3
Ainsworth 19.3
Ainthorpe 33.4
Aintree (part) 29.1, 29.2
Airdrie S22
Airedale 47.5
Airlie S2
Airmyn 15.2
Airth S15
Airton 33.5
Airyholme 33.3
Aisby* 28.1, 28.6
Aiskew 33.2
Aislaby (N Yorks) 33.4
Aislaby (Pickering) (N Yorks) 33.3
Aislaby (Stockton) 14.10
Aisthorpe 28.1
Akebar 33.1
Akeld 32.1
Akeley 5.2
Akenham 41.4
Albany 43.5
Albaston 9.1
Alberbury with Cardeston 37.1
Albert Village 27.1
Albourne 46.4
Albrighton 37.1
Albrighton, nr Shrewsbury 37.1
Alburgh 30.7
Albury (Herts) 22.3
Albury (Oxon) 35.3
Albury (Surrey) 42.7
Alby with Thwaite 30.1
Alcaig S17
Alcaston 37.1
Alcester 44.5
Alciston 16.1
Alcombe 38.3
Alconbury 6.3
Alconbury Weston 6.3
Alcumlow (see Moreton)
Aldborough 30.1
Aldbourne 48.1
Aldbrough 15.2
Aldbrough-St-John 33.1
Aldbury 22.4
Aldeburgh 41.5
Aldeby 30.7
Aldenham 22.10
Alderbury 48.1
Alderford 30.5
Alderholt 13.3
Alderley 18.6
Alderley Edge 7.5
Aldermaston 3.1
Alderminster 44.5
Aldermoor 20.8
Alderney 13.6
Aldersey 7.3
Aldershaw 40.8
Aldershot 20.3
Alderton (Gloucs) 18.1
Alderton (N'hants) 31.7
Alderton (Shrop) 37.1
Alderton (Suffolk) 41.5
Alderton (Wilts) 48.1
Alderwasley 11.6
Aldfield 33.6
Aldford 7.3
Aldham (Essex) 17.3
Aldham (Suffolk) 41.6
Aldingbourne 46.5
Aldingham 10.5
Aldington (Kent) 25.12
Aldington (Worcs) 49.6
Aldon (Shrop) 37.1
Aldon (Som) 38.5
Aldreth 6.4
Aldridge 45.2
Aldringham-cum-Thorpeness 41.5
Aldrington 16.3
Aldsworth (part) 18.5, 46.2
Aldwark (Derbys) 11.3
Aldwark (N Yorks) 33.2
Aldwick 46.5
Aldwincle 31.3
Aldworth 3.1
Aled W8
Alethorpe 30.1
Alexandria S9
Aley Green 2.2
Alfold (part) 42.11, 46.2
Alford S1
Alford (Lincs) 28.2
Alford (Shrop) 37.1
Alford (Som) 38.5
Alfreton 11.6
Alfrick 49.4
Alfriston 16.1
Algarkirk 28.5
Alhampton 38.2
Alice Holt 20.6
Alkborough 28.8
Alkerton 35.2
Alkham 25.6
Alkington (Gloucs) 18.6
Alkington (Shrop) 37.1
Alkmonton 11.3
Alkrington 19.4
All Cannings 48.1
All Saints (E Devon) 12.7
All Saints South Elmham 41.1
All Stretton (part) 37.1
Allandale S15
Allanton S22
Allbrook 20.9
Allendale 32.1
Allengrove 10.1
Allenheads 32.1
Allens Green 22.3
Allensmore 21.1
Allenton 11.7
Allenwood 10.1
Aller 38.5
Allerby 10.2
Allerford 38.3
Allerston, North & South 33.3
Allerthorpe (E Yorks) 15.2
Allerthorpe (see Swainby)
Allerton (Mersey) 29.2
Allerton (W Yorks) 47.1
Allerton Bywater 47.2
Allerton Mauleverer with Hopperton 33.6
Allerwash 32.1
Allesley 45.7
Allestree (part) 11.6, 11.7
Allet Common 9.1
Allexton 27.8
Allhallows (Cumbria) 10.2
Allhallows (Kent) 25.3
Alligin S17
Allington (Dorset) 13.1
Allington (Kent) 25.10
Allington (Lincs) 28.6
Allington (Wilts) (part) 48.1
Allington (Wrexham) W22
Allithwaite, Upper & Lower 10.5
Alloa S8
Allonby 10.2
Allostock 7.3
Alloway S27
Allowenshay 38.5
Allscott 37.4
Allt Goch W8
Alltami W10
Alltmawr W17
Alltwalis W6
Alltwen W14
Almaveor 9.1
Almeley 21.1
Almer 13.3
Almington 40.2
Almodington 46.2
Almondbank S24
Almondbury 47.4
Almondell S31

Almondsbury 18.7
Alne 33.2
Alness S17
Alnham 32.1
Alnmouth 32.1
Alnwick 32.1
Alperton L4
Alphamstone 17.2
Alpheton 41.6
Alpington 30.7
Alport* 11.3
Alpraham 7.5
Alresford (Essex) 17.4
Alresford (Hants) 20.5
Alrewas 40.8
Alsager (part) 7.5
Alsagers Bank 40.2
Alsop-en-le-Dale 11.3
Alston with Garrigill 10.3
Alstonefield 40.1
Altandhu S17
Altarnun 9.1
Altass S17
Altcar Little 29.1
Altham 26.11
Althorne 17.8
Althorp 31.4
Althorpe (see Keadby)
Altnaharra S17
Altofts 47.5
Alton (Derbys)* 11.4, 11.6
Alton (Hants) 20.6
Alton (Staffs) 40.1
Alton Barnes 48.1
Alton Pancras 13.1
Alton Priors 48.1
Altrincham 19.8
Alum Bay 24.1
Alum Rock 45.5
Alva S8
Alvah S1
Alvanley 7.3
Alvaston (Cheshire) 7.5
Alvaston (Derby) 11.7
Alvechurch 49.2
Alvecote 44.1
Alvediston 48.1
Alveley 37.1
Alverdiscott 12.1
Alverstoke 20.11
Alverstone Garden Village 24.1
Alverton (Corn) 9.1
Alverton (Notts) 34.3
Alves S20
Alvescot 35.1
Alveston (Gloucs) 18.7
Alveston (Warks) 44.5
Alvie S17
Alvingham 28.2
Alvington (Gloucs) 18.2
Alvington (Som) 38.5
Alwalton 6.1, 6.3
Alweston 13.1
Alwington 12.1
Alwinton 32.1
Alwoodley 47.2
Alyth S24
Ambaston 11.9
Amber Hill 28.5
Ambergate 11.6
Amberley (Gloucs) 18.6
Amberley (W Sussex) 46.3
Ambersham 46.2
Amble 32.1
Amblecote 45.3
Ambler Thorn 47.1
Ambleside 10.5
Ambleston W16
Ambrosden 35.2
Amcotts 28.8
Amen Corner 3.6
Amersham (Bucks) 5.4
Amersham (Som) 38.5
Amesbury 48.1
Ameysford 13.3
Amington 40.9
Amisfield S10
Amlwch W1
Amlwch Port W1
Ammanford W6
Amotherby 33.3
Ampfield 20.4
Ampleforth 33.3
Ampney Crucis 18.5
Ampney St Mary 18.5
Ampney St Peter 18.5
Amport 20.4
Ampthill 2.2
Ampton 41.3
Amroth (part) W6, W16
Amulree S24
Ancaster 28.6
Ancells Park 20.2
Anchor (Shrop) W17
Anchorsholme 26.4
Ancoats 19.6
Ancroft 32.1
Ancrum S30
Ancton 46.5
Anderby 28.2
Anderson 13.2
Anderton (Cheshire) 7.3
Anderton (Corn) 9.1
Anderton (Lancs) 26.9
Andover 20.4
Andoversford 18.5
Andwell 20.1
Anelog W11
Anerley L5
Anfield 29.2
Angarrack 9.1
Angersleigh 38.4
Angerton (Cumbria) 10.5
Angerton (N'land) 32.1
Angle W16
Anglezarke 26.9
Angmering 46.5
Angram Grange 33.2
Anick 32.1
Anlaby 15.2
Anlaby Common 15.2
Anmer 30.2
Anmore 20.5
Anna Valley 20.4
Annan S10
Annathill S22
Annbank S27
Annesley 34.4
Annesley Woodhouse 34.4
Annfield Plain 14.1
Annitsford 43.2
Ansdell 26.5
Ansdore (Waltham) 25.5
Ansford 38.5
Ansley 44.1
Anslow 40.5
Anstey (Hants) 20.6
Anstey (Herts) 22.3
Anstey (Leics) 27.2
Anstruther, Easter & Wester S16
Ansty (W Sussex) 46.4
Ansty (Warks) 44.3
Ansty (Wilts) 48.1
Anthill 20.5
Antingham 30.1
Anton's Gowt 28.2
Antony 9.1
Antrobus 7.3
Antron (Mabe) 9.1
Antron (Porthleven) 9.1
Anvil Green (Waltham) 25.5
Anwick 28.4
Apedale 40.2
Apethorpe 31.3
Apley 28.1
Apperknowle 11.4
Apperley Bridge 47.1
Appin S3
Appleby (Cumbria) 10.3
Appleby (Lincs) 28.8
Appleby Magna 27.1
Appleby Parva 27.1
Applecross S17
Appledore (Devon) 12.1
Appledore (Kent) (part) 25.12, 25.13
Appledram 46.2
Appleford 35.4
Appleshaw 20.4
Appleton (Cheshire) 7.1
Appleton (Norfolk) (see Flitcham)
Appleton Roebuck 33.8
Appleton Thorn 7.1
Appleton Wiske 33.2
Appleton with Eaton 35.4
Appleton, East & West 33.1
Appleton-le-Moors 33.3
Appleton-le-Street 33.3
Appletreehall S30
Appletreewick 33.5
Appley 38.4
Appley Bridge (part) 19.1, 26.8
Apse Heath 24.1
Apsley 20.1
Aqueduct 37.4
Arabella S17
Arbirlot S2
Arborfield 3.3
Arbroath S2
Arbury 44.2
Archdeacon Newton 14.8
Archiestown S20
Arclid 7.5
Ardcharnich S17
Ardclach S17
Arddleen W17
Ardeley 22.3
Arden with Ardenside 33.3
Ardencaple S3
Ardens Grafton 44.5
Ardentinny S3
Ardeonaig S29
Ardersier S17
Ardgay S17
Ardgour S17
Ardindrean S17
Ardingly 46.4
Ardington 35.4
Ardleigh 17.4
Ardler S24
Ardley 35.2
Ardlussa S3
Ardmore S17
Ardnave S3
Ardneaskan S17
Ardrishaig S3
Ardroil Sands S32
Ardross S17
Ardrossan S21
Ardsley, East & West 47.2
Ardtalla S3
Ardtalnaig S24
Arduaine S3
Ardubh S17
Ardvasar S17
Ardvourlie S32
Ardwell S10
Ardwick 19.6
Arford 20.6
Argoed W4
Arisaig S17
Arkendale 33.6
Arkengarthdale 33.1
Arkesden 17.1
Arkholme 26.1
Arksey 39.2
Arkwright Town 11.4
Arlecdon & Frizington 10.4
Arlescote 44.5
Arlesey 2.2
Arleston 37.4
Arley 44.1
Arlingham 18.6
Arlington (Devon) 12.2
Arlington (E Sussex) 16.1
Arlington (Gloucs) 18.5
Armadale (Highland) S17
Armadale (Lothian) S31
Armathwaite (part) 10.1, 10.3
Arminghall 30.7
Armitage Bridge 47.4
Armitage with Handsacre 40.8
Armscote 44.5
Armston (Barnwell) 31.3
Armstrong 43.5
Armthorpe 39.2

2

Arncliffe 33.5
Arncott (Upper & Lower) 35.2
Arncroach S16
Arne 13.5
Arnesby 27.8
Arnewood 20.7
Arnisdale S17
Arnish S32
Arniston S19
Arnold (E Yorks) 15.2
Arnold (Notts) 34.7
Arnos Vale 4.1
Arnprior S29
Arnside 10.5
Aros S3
Arpinge 25.13
Arrad Foot 10.5
Arram 15.2
Arrathorne 33.1
Arreton 24.1
Arrina S17
Arrington 6.5
Arrow 44.5
Artafallie S17
Arthington 47.2
Arthingworth 31.4
Arthog W11
Arthuret 10.1
Artington 42.7
Arundel (Mersey) 29.2
Arundel (W Sussex) 46.5
Arwarton 41.6
Asby 10.3
Ascot (part) 3.4, 3.6
Ascott 44.5
Ascott-under-Wychwood 35.1
Asenby 33.6
Asfordby 27.3
Asfordby Hill 27.3
Asgarby* 28.2, 28.4
Ash (Derbys) 11.9
Ash (Kent)* 25.6, 25.8
Ash (Shrop) 37.1
Ash (Som) 38.5
Ash (Surrey) 42.7
Ash Bank 40.1
Ash Green 44.2
Ash Magna 37.1
Ash Parva 37.1
Ash Priors 38.4
Ash Thomas 12.4
Ashampstead 3.1
Ashbocking 41.4
Ashbourne 11.3
Ashbrittle 38.4
Ashbrooke 43.5
Ashburnham & Penhurst 16.2
Ashburton 12.5
Ashbury (Oxon) 35.4
Ashby (N Lincs) 28.8
Ashby (Norfolk) 30.6
Ashby (Suffolk) 41.1
Ashby Folville 27.3
Ashby Magna 27.8
Ashby Parva 27.8
Ashby Puerorum 28.2
Ashby St Ledgers 31.4
Ashby St Mary 30.7
Ashby Woulds 27.1
Ashby de la Launde 28.4
Ashby with Scremby 28.2
Ashby-cum-Fenby 28.9
Ashby-de-la-Zouch 27.1
Ashchurch 18.1
Ashcombe (Devon) 12.5
Ashcott 38.1
Ashdon 17.1
Ashe 20.1
Ashe Park 20.1
Ashe Warren 20.1
Asheldham 17.8
Ashen 17.2
Ashen Cross 38.5
Ashendon 5.2
Asheridge 5.4
Ashey 24.1
Ashfield 9.1
Ashfield-cum-Thorpe 41.4
Ashfields 37.1
Ashford (Devon) 12.2
Ashford (Hants) 20.7
Ashford (Kent) 25.12
Ashford (Shrop) 37.1
Ashford (Surrey) 42.2
Ashford Bowdler 37.1
Ashford Carbonell 37.1
Ashford Common 42.2
Ashford Hill 20.1
Ashford-in-the-Water 11.3
Ashgate (part) 11.2, 11.4
Ashgill S28
Ashill (Devon) 12.4
Ashill (Norfolk) 30.3
Ashill (Som) 38.5
Ashingdon 17.11
Ashington (N'land) 32.1
Ashington (Som) 38.5
Ashington (W Sussex) 46.3
Ashkirk S30
Ashland 5.1
Ashlett 20.7
Ashleworth 18.1
Ashley (Cambs) 6.4
Ashley (Cheshire) 7.5
Ashley (Dorset) 13.3
Ashley (Gloucs) 18.5
Ashley (Hants)* 20.4, 20.7
Ashley (Kent) 25.6
Ashley (N'hants) 31.2
Ashley (Staffs) 40.2
Ashley Down 4.1
Ashley Green 5.4
Ashley Heath 40.2
Ashley Warren 20.1
Ashley-cum-Silverly 6.4
Ashleyhay 11.6
Ashmanhaugh 30.1
Ashmansworth 20.1
Ashmore 13.2
Ashorne 44.5
Ashover 11.4
Ashow 44.4
Ashperton 21.1
Ashprington 12.9
Ashreigney 12.1
Ashridge 22.4
Ashtead 42.8
Ashton (Bristol) 4.1
Ashton (Cambs) 6.1
Ashton (Cheshire) 7.3
Ashton (Corn) 9.1
Ashton (Devon) 12.5
Ashton (Here) (see Eye, Moreton & Ashton)
Ashton (Lancs) 26.6
Ashton (N'hants)* 31.3, 31.7
Ashton Court 38.7
Ashton Gate 4.1
Ashton Keynes 48.1
Ashton Vale 4.1
Ashton with Stodday 26.1
Ashton-in-Makerfield (part) 19.1, 29.3
Ashton-on-Mersey 19.8
Ashton-under-Hill 49.6
Ashton-under-Lyne 19.10
Ashurst (Hants) 20.7
Ashurst (Kent) 25.11
Ashurst (W Sussex) 46.3
Ashurst Wood (part) 16.1, 46.4
Ashwater 12.1
Ashwell (Herts) 22.1
Ashwell (Rutland) 36.1
Ashwellthorpe 30.7
Ashwick 38.2
Ashwicken 30.2
Askam-in-Furness 10.6
Aske 33.1
Askern 39.2
Askerswell 13.1
Askerton 10.1
Askett 5.3
Askham (Cumbria) 10.3
Askham (Notts) 34.1
Askham Bryan 33.7
Askham Richard 33.7
Askrigg 33.1
Askwith 33.6
Aslackby 28.6
Aslacton 30.7
Aslockton 34.8
Aspall 41.4
Aspatria 10.2
Aspenden 22.3
Aspley (Notts) 34.6
Aspley (W Yorks) 47.4
Aspley Guise 2.2
Aspley Heath (Beds) 2.2
Aspley Heath (Warks) 44.5
Aspull 19.1
Asselby 15.2
Asserby 28.2
Asserton 48.1
Assington 41.6
Astcote 31.7
Asterby 28.2
Asterleigh (see Kiddington)
Asterley 37.1
Asterton 37.1
Asthal 35.1
Astley 37.1
Astley (Gtr M'chester) 19.1
Astley (Shrop) 37.1
Astley (Warks) 44.1
Astley (Worcs) 49.4
Astley Abbots 37.1
Astley Village 26.9
Aston (Berks) 3.3
Aston (Cheshire)* 7.3, 7.5
Aston (Flint) W10
Aston (Herts) 22.3
Aston (S Yorks) 39.4
Aston (Shrop)* 37.1, 37.4
Aston (Staffs) 40.2
Aston (W Mids) 45.5
Aston Abbots 5.2
Aston Bampton & Shifford 35.1
Aston Botterell 37.1
Aston Cantlow 44.5
Aston Clinton 5.2
Aston Crews 21.1
Aston Flamville 27.6
Aston Ingham 21.1
Aston Magna 18.5
Aston Munslow 37.1
Aston Pigott 37.1
Aston Rogers 37.1
Aston Rowant 35.3
Aston Sandford 5.2
Aston Somerville 49.6
Aston Subedge 18.5
Aston Tirrold 35.3
Aston Upthorpe 35.3
Aston-Eyre 37.1
Aston-by-Budworth 7.5
Aston-by-Stone 40.4
Aston-juxta-Mondrum 7.5
Aston-le-Walls 31.7
Aston-on-Clun 37.1
Aston-upon-Trent 11.9
Astwell 31.7
Astwick 2.2
Astwith 11.5
Astwood 5.1
Astwood Bank (part) 49.3
Aswarby 28.4
Aswardby 28.2
Atch Lench 49.6
Atcham 37.1
Athelhampton 13.1
Athelington 41.4
Athelney 38.4
Athelstaneford S13
Atherfield 24.1
Atherfield Green 24.1
Atherington (Devon) 12.2
Atherington (W Sussex) 46.5
Atherstone (Som) 38.5
Atherstone (Warks) 44.1
Atherstone-on-Stour 44.5
Atherton (part) 19.1, 19.2
Atley Hill (South Cowton) 33.2
Atlow 11.3
Attenborough 34.5
Atterbury 5.1

Atterby 28.1
Attleborough (Norfolk) 30.3
Attleborough (Warks) 44.2
Attlebridge 30.5
Atwick 15.2
Atworth 48.1
Auberrow 21.1
Aubourn 28.4
Auchenblae S1
Auchencairn S10
Auchencrow S30
Auchendinny S19
Auchendoir & Kearn S1
Auchengate S27
Auchengray S28
Auchenheath S28
Auchenmalg S10
Auchincruive S27
Auchinleck S11
Auchinloch S22
Auchintibber S28
Auchmithie S2
Auchnagatt S1
Auchnarrow S20
Auchterarder S24
Auchtercairn S17
Auchterderran S16
Auchterless S1
Auchtermuchty S16
Auchtertool S16
Auckland Park 14.1
Auckley 39.2
Audenshaw 19.10
Audleby 28.1
Audlem 7.5
Audley 40.2
Audleys Wood 20.1
Aughton (E Yorks) 15.2
Aughton (Lancs)* 26.8
Aughton (S Yorks) 39.4
Aukengill S17
Auldearn S17
Auldgirth S10
Auldhouse S28
Ault Hucknall 11.5
Aultbea S17
Aultgrishan S17
Aultguish S17
Aunby 28.6
Aunsby 28.4
Aust 18.7
Austen Fen 28.2
Austerfield 39.2
Austerlands 19.7
Austerson 7.5
Austhorpe 47.2
Austonley 47.4
Austrey 44.1
Austwick 33.5
Authorpe 28.2
Avebury 48.1
Aveley 17.12
Avening 18.5
Averham 34.3
Avery Hill L11
Aveton Gifford 12.9
Aviemore S17
Avington 20.5
Avishayes 38.5
Avoch S17
Avon Castle 13.3
Avon Dassett 44.5
Avonbridge S15
Avonbury 21.1
Avonmouth 4.1
Avonwick 12.9
Awbridge 20.4
Awliscombe 12.7
Awre 18.2
Awsworth 34.5
Axbridge 38.1
Axford (Hants) 20.1
Axford (Wilts) 48.1
Axmansford 20.1
Axminster 12.7
Axmouth 12.7
Axton W10
Aychley 37.1
Aycliffe (part) 14.1, 14.8
Aycliffe Village (Durham) 14.1
Aylburton 18.2
Aylesbeare 12.7
Aylesbury 5.2
Aylesby 28.9
Aylesford (part) 25.9, 25.10
Aylesham 25.6
Aylmerton 30.1
Aylsham 30.5
Aylton 21.1
Aylworth 18.5
Aymestrey 21.1
Aynho 31.7
Ayot St Lawrence 22.6
Ayot St Peter 22.6
Ayr S27
Aysgarth 33.1
Ayside 10.5
Ayston 36.1
Aythorpe Roding 17.1
Ayton (Scottish Borders) S30
Ayton (T & W) 43.5
Azerley 33.6
Babbacombe 12.10
Babbinswood 37.1
Babcary 38.5
Babel W6
Babell W10
Babington 38.2
Babraham 6.5
Babworth 34.1
Bachau W1
Bache 7.3
Back S32
Backbarrow 10.5
Backe W6
Backford 7.3
Backford Cross (part) 7.3
Backwell 38.7
Backwell Common 38.7
Backwell Green 38.7
Backworth 43.2
Baconsthorpe 30.1
Bacton (Here) 21.1
Bacton (Norfolk) 30.1
Bacton (Suffolk) 41.4
Bacup 26.14
Badachro S17
Badbury 48.2
Badbury Wick 48.2
Badby 31.4
Badcall S17
Badcaul S17
Baddeley Edge 40.3
Baddeley Green 40.3
Baddesley Clinton 44.4
Baddesley Ensor 44.1
Baddiley 7.5
Baddington 7.5
Baden Hill 18.7
Badenscallie S17
Badger 37.1
Badgers Cross 38.5
Badgers Mount 25.8
Badgeworth (Gloucs) 18.1
Badgworth (Som) 38.1
Badingham 41.5
Badingsgill S30
Badland W17
Badlesmere 25.4
Badley 41.4
Badluarach S17
Badminton 18.7, W2
Badralloch S17
Badsey (Worcs) 49.6
Badshot Lea 42.11
Badsworth 47.5
Badwell Ash 41.4
Bag Enderby 28.2
Bagborough 38.4
Bagby 33.2
Bagendon 18.5
Bagillt W10
Baginton 44.4
Baglan W14
Bagley 37.1
Bagley Marsh 37.1
Bagnall 40.1
Bagpath 18.5
Bagshot 42.3
Bagstone 18.7
Bagthorpe 34.4
Bagthorpe with Barmer 30.2
Baguley 19.6
Bagworth 27.4
Baildon 47.1
Baildon Green 47.1
Bailey (Cumbria) 10.1
Bailey (Lancs) 26.3
Bailiff Bridge 47.3
Baillieston S7
Bainbridge 33.1
Bainsford S15
Bainton (Cambs) 6.1
Bainton (E Yorks) 15.2
Bainton (Oxon) 35.2
Bakersfield (part) 34.6
Bakestone Moor 11.5
Bakewell 11.3
Bala W11
Balachraggan S17
Balado S24
Balallan S32
Balbeggie S24
Balblair S17
Balby 39.2
Balchrick S17
Balcombe 46.4
Baldersby 33.6
Baldersdale 14.1
Balderstone (Gtr M'chester) 19.4
Balderstone (Lancs) 26.3
Balderton 34.3
Baldingstone 19.3
Baldock 22.1
Baldwinholme 10.1
Baldwins Gate 40.2
Bale 30.1
Balerno S6
Balfron S29
Balham (part) L22, L32
Balintore S17
Balivanich S32
Balk 33.2
Balkeerie S2
Balkholme 15.2
Balkiellie S2
Ball Common 38.5
Ball Green 40.3
Ball Hill 20.1
Ballachulish, North & South S17
Ballantrae S27
Ballater S1
Balleigh S17
Ballencrieff S13
Ballidon 11.3
Ballinger 5.4
Ballingham 21.1
Ballingry S16
Ballinluig S24
Ballinshoe S2
Ballintuim S24
Balloch (Highland) (part) S17
Balloch (W Dunbarton) (part) S9
Balls Cross 46.2
Balls Green 16.1
Ballygrant S3
Balmacara S17
Balmaclellan S10
Balmaha S29
Balmedie S1
Balmer 37.1
Balmer Lawn 20.7
Balmerino S16
Balmoral S1
Balmore S12
Balmullo S16
Balnacoil S17
Balnacra S17
Balnaguard S24
Balne 33.8
Balquhidder S29
Balsall 45.6
Balsall Common 45.6
Balsall Heath 45.5
Balscote 35.2
Balsham 6.5

Baltasound S26
Balterley (part) 7.5, 40.2
Baltonsborough 38.2
Balvicar S3
Bamber Bridge (part) 26.7, 26.9
Bamburgh 32.1
Bamford (Derbys) 11.1
Bamford (Gtr M'chester) 19.4
Bamfurlong 19.1
Bampton (Cumbria) 10.3
Bampton (Devon) 12.4
Bampton (Oxon) 35.1
Banavie S17
Banbury 35.2
Bancffosfelen W6
Banchory S1
Banchory-Devenick S1
Banchory-Ternan S1
Bancroft 5.1
Bancroft Park 5.1
Bancycapel W6
Bancyfelin W6
Bancyffordd W6
Bandrake Head 10.5
Banff S1
Bangley 40.8
Bangor W11
Bangor-is-y-coed W22
Bangor-on-Dee W22
Bangour S31
Banham 30.3
Bank 20.7
Bank Lane 19.3
Bank Top 47.1
Bankend S10
Bankfoot (Perth & Kinross) S24
Bankfoot (W Yorks) 47.1
Bankhead 10.5
Bankhead (Aberdeen) S4
Banknewton 33.5
Banknock S15
Banks (Cumbria) 10.1
Banks (Lancs) 26.8
Bankshill S10
Banningham 30.1
Bannockburn S29
Banstead 42.9
Bantham 12.9
Banton S22
Banwell 38.7
Banwen W14
Banwy W17
Bapchild 25.4
Baptist Mills 4.1
Bapton 48.1
Bar Hill 6.5
Barbaraville S17
Barber Green 10.5
Barbon 10.5
Barbreck S3
Barbridge 7.5
Barby 31.4
Barcheston 44.5
Barclose 10.1
Barcombe 16.4
Barcombe Cross 16.4
Barcombe Mills 16.4
Barcroft 47.1
Barden (N Yorks)* 33.1, 33.5
Barden (Som) 38.3
Bardfield Saling (see Salings, The)
Bardney 28.1
Bardney Causeway 28.4
Bardon 27.1
Bardon Mill 32.1
Bardowie S12
Bardsea 10.5
Bardsey Island W11
Bardsey-cum-Rigton 47.2
Bardsley 19.7
Bardwell 41.3
Barford (Hants) 20.6
Barford (Norfolk) 30.7
Barford (Warks) 44.4
Barford St John & Barford St Michael 35.2
Barford St Martin 48.1
Barforth 14.1
Barfrestone 25.6
Bargate (Derbys) 11.6
Bargeddie S22
Bargoed W4
Bargrennan S10
Barham (Cambs) 6.3
Barham (Kent) 25.5
Barham (Suffolk) 41.4
Barholm 28.6
Barkby 27.2
Barkby Thorpe 27.2
Barkers Green 37.1
Barkestone-le-Vale 27.3
Barkham (Berks) 3.3
Barkham (Som) 38.3
Barking & Dagenham L1
Barking (Suffolk) 41.4
Barkisland 47.3
Barkla Shop 9.1
Barkston (Lincs) 28.6
Barkston Ash 33.8
Barkway 22.1
Barland W17
Barlaston 40.4
Barlavington 46.2
Barlborough 11.5
Barlby 33.8
Barlestone 27.4
Barley (Herts) 22.1
Barley (Lancs) 26.13
Barley Mow 43.3
Barleythorpe 36.1
Barlinch 38.3
Barling Magna 17.11
Barlings 28.1
Barlow (N Yorks) 33.8
Barlow (T & W) 43.3
Barlow Grange 11.4
Barlow Lees 11.4
Barmby Moor 15.2
Barmby-on-the-Marsh 15.2
Barmer (see Bagthorpe)
Barming 25.10
Barmishaw 47.1
Barmoor 32.1
Barmouth (Abermaw) W11
Barmpton (Durham) 14.8
Barmston (E Yorks) 15.2
Barmston (T & W) 43.5
Barnack 6.1
Barnacle (Shilton) 44.3
Barnacre with Bonds 26.2
Barnard Castle 14.1
Barnardiston 41.3
Barnburgh (Doncaster) (part) 39.1, 39.2
Barnby (N Yorks) 33.4
Barnby (Suffolk) 41.1
Barnby Dun with Kirk Sandall 39.2
Barnby Moor 34.1
Barnby in the Willows (Notts) 34.3
Barnes L27
Barnes (Park Area) 43.5
Barnet L2
Barnetby-le-Wold 28.8
Barney 30.1
Barngates 10.5
Barnham (Suffolk) 41.3
Barnham (W Sussex) 46.5
Barnham Broom 30.7
Barnhead S2
Barnhill S20
Barningham (Durham) 14.1
Barningham (Suffolk) 41.3
Barningham Winter 30.1
Barnoldby-le-Beck 28.9
Barnoldswick 26.13
Barns Green 46.3
Barnsbury L19
Barnsley (Gloucs) 18.5
Barnsley (S Yorks) 39.1
Barnsole 25.6
Barnstaple 12.2
Barnston (Essex) 17.1
Barnston (Mersey) 29.5
Barnstone 34.8
Barnt Green 49.2
Barnton 7.3
Barnwell (N'hants) 31.3
Barnwell (T & W) 43.5
Barnwood 18.3
Barons Court L13
Barony (see Evenwood)
Barr S27
Barr Common 45.2
Barra S32
Barrachan S10
Barraclough 26.3
Barras 10.3
Barrasford 32.1
Barrhead S14
Barrhill S27
Barrington (Cambs) 6.5
Barrington (Gloucs) 18.5
Barrington (N'land) 32.1
Barrington (Som) 38.5
Barrington Hill 38.5
Barripper 9.1
Barrmill S21
Barrock S17
Barrow (Cheshire) 7.3
Barrow (Cumbria) 10.6
Barrow (Lancs) 26.3
Barrow (Rutland) 36.1
Barrow (Shrop) 37.1
Barrow (Som) 38.5
Barrow (Suffolk) (see Denham)
Barrow Common 38.7
Barrow Court 38.7
Barrow Green 25.4
Barrow Gurney 38.7
Barrow Haven 28.8
Barrow Hill 11.2
Barrow Island 10.6
Barrow Moor 40.1
Barrow upon Soar 27.2
Barrow upon Trent 11.9
Barrow-in-Furness 10.6
Barrow-upon-Humber 28.8
Barrowby 28.6
Barrowden 36.1
Barrowford 26.13
Barrows Green 10.5
Barry (Angus) S2
Barry (Vale Glam) W21
Barsby 27.3
Barsham (Norfolk) 30.1
Barsham (Suffolk) 41.1
Barston 45.6
Bartestree 21.1
Barthomley 7.5
Bartle 26.6
Bartley 20.7
Bartley Green 45.5
Bartley Heath 20.2
Bartley Wood Business Park 20.2
Bartlow 6.5
Barton (Beds) 2.2
Barton (Cambs) 6.5
Barton (Cheshire) 7.3
Barton (Cumbria) 10.3
Barton (Gloucs) 18.5
Barton (Lancs) 26.6
Barton (N Yorks) 33.1
Barton (Oxon) 35.5
Barton (Som) 38.7
Barton (Warks) 44.5
Barton Bendish 30.2
Barton Blount 11.9
Barton Hartshorne 5.2
Barton Hill 4.1
Barton Mills 41.2
Barton St David 38.5
Barton Seagrave 31.2
Barton Stacey 20.4
Barton Turf 30.1
Barton in Fabis 34.8
Barton on Sea 20.7
Barton-in-the-Beans 27.4
Barton-le-Clay 2.2
Barton-le-Street 33.3
Barton-le-Willows 33.3
Barton-on-the-Heath 44.5
Barton-under-Needwood 40.5

Barton-upon-Humber 28.8
Barugh (Gt & Little) 33.3
Barugh Green 39.1
Barvas S32
Barway 6.4
Barwell 27.4
Barwick (Herts) 22.3
Barwick (Norfolk) 30.2
Barwick (Som) 38.5
Barwick in Elmet 47.2
Baschurch 37.1
Bascote 44.5
Bascote Heath 44.5
Basford (Cheshire) 7.5
Basford (Notts) 34.6
Basford (Staffs) (part) 40.2, 40.3
Bashall Eaves 26.3
Bashley 20.7
Basildon (Berks) 3.1
Basildon (Essex) 17.10
Basing 20.1
Basing View 20.1
Basingstoke 20.1
Basingstoke Business Park (Chineham) 20.1
Baslow & Bubnell 11.3
Bason Bridge 38.1
Bassenthwaite 10.2
Bassett 20.8
Bassett Down (part) 48.1, 48.2
Bassingbourn-cum-Kneesworth 6.5
Bassingfield 34.8
Bassingham 28.4
Bassingthorpe 28.6
Baston 28.6
Bastwick (see Repps)
Baswich 40.4
Batchley 49.3
Batchmere 46.2
Batcombe (Dorset) 13.1
Batcombe (Som) 38.2
Batesway 40.8
Bath 38.6
Bathampton 38.6
Bathealton 38.4
Batheaston 38.6
Batherton 7.5
Bathford 38.6
Bathgate S31
Bathley 34.3
Bathpool (Corn) 9.1
Bathpool (Som) 38.4
Batley 47.4
Batley Carr 47.4
Batsford 18.5
Batson 12.9
Battersby (Ingleby Greenhow) 33.2
Battersea L32
Battisford 41.4
Battle (E Sussex) 16.2
Battle (Powys) W17
Battlefield 37.1
Battlesbridge (part) 17.7, 17.11
Battlesden 2.2
Battleton 38.3
Battram 27.1
Battramsley 20.7
Battyeford 47.4
Baughurst 20.1
Baughurst Common 20.1
Baulking 35.4
Baumber 28.2
Baunton 18.5
Bausley with Criggion W17
Bavington 32.1
Bawburgh 30.7
Bawdeswell 30.3
Bawdrip 38.1
Bawdsey 41.5
Bawsey 30.2
Bawtry 39.2
Baxenden 26.11
Baxter Howe 33.3
Baxterley 44.1
Bayble S32
Baycliff 10.5
Baydon (part) 48.1, 48.2
Bayfield 30.1
Bayford (Herts) 22.3
Bayford (Som) 38.5
Baylham 41.4
Baylis 3.5
Baynard's Green 35.2
Bayston Hill (Hook-a-Gate) 37.1
Bayswater L33
Bayton 49.4
Bayview S32
Bayvil W16
Bayworth 35.4
Beach 18.7
Beachampton 5.2
Beachamwell 30.3
Beachley 18.2
Beacon 9.1
Beacon Hill (Burghclere, Highclere) 20.1
Beacon Hill (Surrey) 42.11
Beacon's Bottom 5.3
Beaconsfield (part) 5.4, 5.5
Beadlam 33.3
Beadlow 2.2
Beadnell 32.1
Beaford 12.1
Beal (N Yorks) 33.8
Beal (N'land) 32.1
Bealings, Gt & Little 41.5
Beam Bridge (Som) 38.4
Beambridge (Shrop) 37.1
Beamhurst 40.5
Beaminster 13.1
Beamish, East & West (part) 14.1
Beamsley 33.5
Bean 25.1
Beanhill 5.1
Bear Cross 13.7
Bear Wood (Dorset) (part) 13.6, 13.7
Beare Green 42.8
Bearley 44.5
Bearpark 14.1
Bearsden S12
Bearsted 25.10
Bearstone 37.1
Bearwardcote 11.9
Bearwood (Berks) 3.3
Bearwood (W Mids) 45.4
Beattock S10
Beauchamp Roding 17.6
Beaudesert 44.5
Beaufort W2
Beaulieu 20.7
Beauly S17
Beaumaris W1
Beaumont 10.1
Beaumont Chase 36.1
Beaumont-cum-Moze 17.4
Beaurepaire 20.1
Beausale 44.4
Beauworth 20.5
Beaworthy (part) 12.3
Bebington 29.5
Beccles 41.1
Becconsall (see Hesketh)
Beck Foot (Cumbria) 10.5
Beck Hill 47.1
Beck Row 41.2
Beckbury 37.1
Beckenham (part) L5, L8, L23
Beckering (see Holton)
Beckermonds 33.5
Beckfield 33.7
Beckfoot (W Yorks) 47.1
Beckford 49.6
Beckham, East & West 30.1
Beckhampton 48.1
Beckhead 10.5
Beckingham (Lincs) 28.4
Beckingham (Notts) 34.1
Beckington 38.2
Beckley (E Sussex) 16.2
Beckley (Hants) 20.7
Beckley (Oxon) 35.3
Beckside 10.5
Bedale 33.2
Beddau W18
Beddgelert W11
Beddingham 16.4
Bedfield 41.4
Bedford 2.1
Bedham 46.2
Bedhampton 20.13
Bedingfield 41.4
Bedingham 30.7
Bedlam 37.1
Bedlington 32.1
Bedlington Station 32.1
Bedlinog W12
Bedminster 4.1
Bedminster Down 4.1
Bedmond 22.8
Bednall 40.6
Bednall Head 40.6
Bedrule S30
Bedstone 37.1
Bedwas W4
Bedwellty Village W4
Bedwelty Pits W2
Bedworth 44.2
Bedworth Heath 44.2
Bedworth Hill 44.2
Bedworth Woodlands 44.2
Beeby 27.2
Beech 20.6
Beech Hill (Berks) 3.1
Beech Hill (Hants) 20.6
Beech Pike 18.5
Beechcliffe 47.1
Beechdale 34.6
Beechingstoke 48.1
Beechwood 33.9
Beecraigs S31
Beedon 3.1
Beeford 15.2
Beehive 38.5
Beeley 11.3
Beelsby 28.9
Beelsby Top 28.9
Beenham 3.1
Beer (Devon) 12.7
Beer (Som) 38.5
Beer Hackett 13.1
Beer Mill 38.5
Beercrocombe 38.5
Beesands 12.9
Beesby (see Hawerby)
Beesby in the Marsh 28.2
Beeson 12.9
Beeston (Beds) 2.2
Beeston (Cheshire) 7.3
Beeston (Notts) 34.5
Beeston Regis 30.1
Beeston Rylands 34.5
Beeston St Andrew 30.5
Beeston St Lawrence 30.1
Beeston with Bittering 30.3
Beeswing S10
Beetham (Cumbria) 10.5
Beetham (Som) 38.5
Beetley 30.3
Begbroke 35.2
Begelly W16
Beggearnhuish 38.3
Beguildy W17
Begwary 2.1
Beighton (Norfolk) 30.5
Beighton (S Yorks) 39.3
Beith S21
Bekesbourne 25.5
Belaugh 30.5
Belbroughton 49.2
Belchamp Otten 17.2
Belchamp St Paul 17.2
Belchamp Walter 17.2
Belchford 28.2
Belfield 19.4
Belford 32.1
Belgrano W8
Belgrave 40.9
Belgravia L33
Belhelvie S1
Belhus 17.12
Bell Bridge 40.8
Bell Busk 33.5
Bell End 49.2

2

Bell Vale 46.2
Bellamour 40.8
Bellaport 37.1
Belle Vale 29.2
Belleau 28.2
Bellehiglash S20
Bellerby 33.1
Bellingdon 5.4
Bellinge 31.5
Bellingham 32.1
Bells Mains S19
Bells Yew Green 16.1
Bellsbank S11
Bellshill S22
Bellsquarry S31
Belmesthorpe 36.1
Belmont (Durham) 14.1
Belmont (Here) 21.1
Belmont (Lancs) 26.10
Belper 11.6
Belph 11.5
Belsay 32.1
Belsize L6, 22.8
Belstead 41.6
Belstone 12.3
Belthorn (part) 26.10, 26.11
Beltinge (Herne Bay) 25.5
Belton (Leics) 27.1
Belton (Lincs) 28.6
Belton (N Lincs) 28.8
Belton (Norfolk) 30.6
Belton-in-Rutland 36.1
Belvedere L3
Belvoir 27.3
Bembridge 24.1
Bempton 15.2
Ben Rhydding 47.1
Benacre 41.1
Benbecula S32
Benchill 19.6
Bendish 22.1
Benefield 31.3
Benenden 25.11
Benfieldside 14.1
Benfleet 17.13
Bengate 30.1
Bengeo 22.3
Benhall 41.5
Benholm S1
Beningbrough 33.2
Benington (Herts) 22.3
Benington (Lincs) 28.5
Benllech W1
Benningholme 15.2
Benniworth 28.2
Benover, Yalding 25.10
Benridge 32.1
Bensham 43.3
Benson 35.3
Bent Lont 37.1
Benter 38.2
Bentham, High & Low 33.5
Bentilee 40.3
Bentley (Hants) 20.6
Bentley (S Yorks) 39.2
Bentley (Suffolk) 41.6
Bentley (Warks) 44.1
Bentley (Worcs) 49.2
Bentley Heath (Herts) 22.10
Bentley Heath (W Mids) 45.6
Bentley Pauncefoot 49.2
Benton Square 43.2
Benton* 43.1, 43.2
Bentpath S10
Bents S31
Bentworth 20.6
Benwell 43.1
Benwick 6.2
Beoley 49.2
Bepton 46.2
Berden 17.1
Bere Alston 12.3
Bere Ferrers 12.3
Bere Regis 13.5
Berehill 20.1
Bergh Apton 30.7
Berinsfield 35.3
Berkeley 18.6
Berkhamsted 22.4
Berkley 38.2
Berkswell 45.6
Berkswich 40.4
Bermondsey L28
Bermuda 44.2
Bernera S32
Berneray S32
Berners Roding 17.6
Bernisdale S17
Berrick Salome 35.3
Berriedale S17
Berrier 10.3
Berriew W17
Berrington 37.1
Berrow (Som) 38.1
Berrow (Worcs) 49.4
Berrow Hill (part) 49.3
Berry Brow 47.4
Berry Hill (Gloucs) 18.2
Berry Hill (Staffs) 40.3
Berry Pomeroy 12.9
Berrydown 20.1
Berrynarbor 12.2
Bersham W22
Bersted, North, South & Central 46.5
Berth-ddu W10
Berthengam W10
Berthllwyd W12
Bervie S1
Berwick 16.1
Berwick Bassett 48.1
Berwick Hill 32.1
Berwick Hills 33.9
Berwick St James 48.1
Berwick St John 48.1
Berwick St Leonard 48.1
Berwick-upon-Tweed 32.1
Bescaby 27.3
Besford (Shrop) 37.1
Besford (Worcs) 49.6
Bessacarr 39.2
Bessels Green 25.8
Besselsleigh 35.4
Besses O' Th' Barn 19.3
Bessingham 30.1
Besthorpe (Norfolk) 30.3
Besthorpe (Notts) 34.3
Bestwood 34.6
Bestwood Lodge 34.7
Bestwood Park 34.6
Bestwood St Albans 34.7
Bestwood Village 34.7
Beswick (E Yorks) 15.2
Beswick (Gtr M'chester) 19.6
Betchton 7.5
Betchworth 42.8
Bethel (Anglesey) W1
Bethel (Gwynedd) W11
Bethersden 25.12
Bethesda (Gwynedd) W11
Bethesda (Pemb) W16
Bethlehem W6
Bethnal Green (part) L12, L30
Betley 40.2
Betsham 25.1
Betteshanger 25.6
Bettiscombe 13.1
Bettisfield (Shrop) (part) 37.1
Bettisfield (Wrexham) (part) W22
Betton 37.1
Bettws (Bridgend) W3
Bettws (Powys) W17
Bettws Disserth W17
Bettws Gwerfil Goch W9
Bettws Ifan W7
Bettws Newydd W13
Bettws-y-Crwyn 37.1
Bettyhill S17
Betws W6
Betws Garmon W11
Betws Lleucu W7
Betws-y-coed W8
Betws-yn-Rhos W8
Beulah (Card) W7
Beulah (Powys) W17
Beveley 37.4
Bevendean 16.3
Bevercotes 34.1
Bevere 49.6
Beverley (E Yorks) 15.2
Beverstone 18.5
Bevington 44.5
Bevois Valley 20.8
Bewaldeth 10.2
Bewbush 46.1
Bewcastle 10.1
Bewdley 49.1
Bewerley 33.6
Bewholme 15.2
Bewick, Old & New 32.1
Bewsey 7.1
Bewshaugh 32.1
Bexhill 16.2
Bexley L3
Bexley (Maypole) 25.1
Bexley Hill 46.2
Bexleyheath L3
Bexton 7.5
Beyton 41.4
Bibstone 18.7
Bibury 18.5
Bicester 35.2
Bickenhall 38.4
Bickenhill 45.6
Bicker 28.5
Bickershaw 19.1
Bickerstaffe 26.8
Bickerton 7.5
Bickington* 12.2, 12.5
Bickland (part) 9.1
Bickleigh* 12.4, 12.9
Bickley L5
Bickley (Cheshire) 7.3
Bickmarsh 49.6
Bicknacre 17.7
Bicknoller 38.3
Bicknor 25.10
Bickton 20.7
Bicton (Devon) 12.7
Bicton (Shrop)* 37.1
Bidborough 25.11
Bidden 20.1
Biddenden 25.12
Biddenham 2.1
Biddesden Lane 48.1
Biddestone 48.1
Biddick 43.5
Biddisham 38.1
Biddlesden 5.2
Biddlestone 32.1
Biddulph 40.1
Biddulph Park 40.1
Bideford 12.1
Bidford-on-Avon 44.5
Bidston 29.5
Bidwell 2.2
Bielby 15.2
Bieldside S4
Bierley 47.1
Bierton with Broughton 5.2
Bigbury (Devon) 12.9
Bigby (Lincs) 28.1
Biggar S28
Biggar Village 10.6
Biggin (N Yorks) 33.8
Biggin by Hartington 11.3
Biggin by Hulland 11.3
Biggin Hill L5
Biggleswade 2.2
Bighton 20.5
Bignall End 40.2
Bignor 46.2
Bilborough 34.6
Bilbrook (Som) 38.3
Bilbrook (Staffs) 40.6
Bilbrough 33.8
Bilbster S17
Bildeston 41.6
Bill Quay 43.3
Billericay 17.10
Billesdon 27.8
Billesley (W Mids) 45.5
Billesley (Warks) 44.5
Billingbear (part) 3.3, 3.4, 3.6
Billingborough 28.6
Billinge (part) 19.1, 29.3

Billingford* 30.3, 30.7
Billingham 14.10
Billinghay 28.4
Billingley 39.1
Billingshurst 46.3
Billingsley 37.1
Billington 26.3
Billington, Gt & Little (Beds) 2.2
Billockby 30.6
Billy Row 14.1
Bilsborrow 26.2
Bilsby 28.2
Bilsdale Midcable 33.2
Bilsdale West Side 33.3
Bilsington 25.12
Bilsthorpe 34.3
Bilston S19
Bilston (part) 45.1, 45.2
Bilstone 27.4
Bilting (Godmersham) 25.12
Bilton (part) 15.1, 15.2
Bilton in Ainsty 33.6
Bin Weston 37.1
Binbrook 28.2
Binchester 14.1
Bincombe (Dorset) (part) 13.1, 13.4
Bincombe (Som) 38.5
Binderton 46.2
Binegar 38.2
Binfield 3.6
Binfield Heath 35.3
Binfields 20.1
Bingfield 32.1
Bingham 34.8
Binghams Melcombe 13.1
Bingley 47.1
Bings Heath* 37.1
Binham 30.1
Binley (Hants) 20.1
Binley (W Mids) 45.7
Binley Woods 44.3
Binns, The S31
Binsey 35.5
Binstead 24.1
Binsted (Hants) 20.6
Binsted (W Sussex) 46.5
Binton 44.5
Bintree 30.3
Birch (Essex) 17.3
Birch (Gtr M'chester) 19.4
Birch (Shrop) 37.1
Birch Green 22.3
Birch Hill 3.6
Birch Vale 11.1
Bircham 30.2
Birchanger (Essex) 17.1
Birchanger (Som) 38.3
Birchencliffe 47.4
Bircher 21.1
Birches Head 40.3
Birchfields 45.5
Birchgrove W19
Birchington 25.7
Birchley 29.3
Birchley Heath 44.1
Birchmoor 44.1
Birchover 11.3
Birchwood (Cheshire) 7.1
Birchwood (Som) 38.5
Bircotes 34.1
Birdbrook 17.2
Birdbush 48.1
Birdforth 33.2
Birdham 46.2
Birdholme 11.2
Birdingbury 44.3
Birdlip 18.5
Birdsall 33.3
Birdsedge 47.4
Birdsmoorgate 13.1
Birdwell 39.1
Birdwood 18.2
Birgham S30
Birk Brow 33.10
Birkby (N Yorks) 33.2
Birkby (W Yorks) 47.4
Birkdale 29.1
Birkenhead 29.5
Birkenshaw (S Lanarks) S28
Birkenshaw (W Yorks) 47.4
Birkenside S19
Birkholme 28.6
Birkin 33.8
Birkrigg 10.5
Birley 21.1
Birling 25.9
Birlingham 49.6
Birmingham 45.5
Birnam S24
Birnbeck Island 38.7
Birnie S20
Birsay S23
Birse S1
Birstall (Leics) 27.2
Birstall (W Yorks) 47.4
Birstall Smithies 47.4
Birstwith 33.6
Birthorpe 28.6
Birtle (part) 19.3, 19.4
Birtley (N'land) 32.1
Birtley (T & W) 43.3
Birtsmorton 49.4
Bisbrooke 36.1
Biscathorpe 28.2
Biscovey 9.1
Bisham 3.4
Bishampton 49.6
Bishop Auckland 14.1
Bishop Burton 15.2
Bishop Middleham 14.1
Bishop Monkton 33.6
Bishop Norton 28.1
Bishop Sutton 38.6
Bishop Thornton 33.6
Bishop Wilton 15.2
Bishop's Castle 37.1
Bishop's Caundle 13.1
Bishop's Gate 3.4
Bishop's Green 20.1
Bishop's Stortford 22.3
Bishop's Tawton 12.2
Bishop's Waltham 20.5
Bishopbriggs S12
Bishopdale 33.1
Bishops Cannings 48.1
Bishops Cleeve 18.1
Bishops Frome 21.1
Bishops Hull 38.4
Bishops Itchington 44.5
Bishops Lydeard 38.4
Bishops Nympton 12.2
Bishops Offley 40.4
Bishops Sutton 20.5
Bishops Tachbrook 44.4
Bishopsbourne 25.5
Bishopsbridge 28.1
Bishopsgarth 14.10
Bishopside, High & Low 33.6
Bishopsteignton 12.5
Bishopstoke 20.9
Bishopston (Bristol) 4.1
Bishopston (Swansea) W19
Bishopstone (Bucks) 5.2
Bishopstone (E Sussex) 16.4
Bishopstone (Here) 21.1
Bishopstone (Herne Bay) 25.5
Bishopstone (Wilts)* 48.1, 48.2
Bishopstrow 48.1
Bishopswood (Hants) 20.1
Bishopswood (Here) 21.1
Bishopswood (Som) 38.4
Bishopswood (Staffs) 40.6
Bishopsworth 4.1
Bishopthorpe 33.7
Bishopton (Durham) 14.8
Bishopton (Renfrew) S25
Bishopton (Warks) 44.5
Bishopwearmouth 43.5
Bishton W15
Bisley (Surrey) 42.3
Bisley with Lypiatt 18.6
Bispham (part) 26.4, 26.8
Bissoe 9.1
Bisterne 20.7
Bitchet Green 25.8
Bitchfield 28.6
Bittadon 12.2
Bittaford 12.9
Bittering, Magna & Parva (see Beeston)
Bitterley 37.1
Bitterne 20.8
Bitterne Park 20.8
Bitterscote 40.9
Bittesby 27.8
Bittescombe 38.3
Bitteswell 27.8
Bitton 18.7
Bix 35.3
Bixley 30.7
Blaby 27.6
Black Bourton 35.1
Black Callerton 43.1
Black Cross 9.1
Black Dam 20.1
Black Dog 12.4
Black Heddon 32.1
Black Hill 47.1
Black Lake 45.4
Black Lane 19.3
Black Notley 17.2
Black Torrington 12.1
Blackawton 12.9
Blackbank 44.2
Blackbird Leys 35.5
Blackborough 12.4
Blackboys 16.1
Blackbrook (Derbys) 11.6
Blackbrook (Mersey) 29.3
Blackbrook (Staffs) 40.2
Blackbrook (Surrey) 42.8
Blackburn (Aberdeen) S1
Blackburn (Lancs) 26.10
Blackburn (W Lothian) S31
Blackbushe 20.2
Blackcliffe 44.5
Blackcraig S10
Blackdown (Dorset) 13.1
Blackdown (W Sussex) 46.2
Blackdown (Warks) 44.4
Blacker Hill 39.1
Blackfell 43.5
Blackfield 20.7
Blackford S24
Blackford (Cumbria) 10.1
Blackford (Shrop) 37.1
Blackford (Som) 38.5
Blackford Bridge 19.3
Blackfordby 27.1
Blackfords 40.7
Blackfriars 19.5
Blackhall 14.1
Blackhall Mill 43.3
Blackham 16.1
Blackheath L11
Blackheath (Surrey) 42.11
Blackheath (W Mids) 45.4
Blackheath (part) L11, L23
Blackhill 14.1
Blackland 48.1
Blackley (Gtr M'chester) 19.6
Blackley (W Yorks) 47.3
Blacklunans S24
Blackmill W3
Blackmoor (Hants) 20.6
Blackmoor (Som) 38.4, 38.7
Blackmoorfoot 47.4
Blackmore 17.9
Blackmore End (Wethersfield) 17.2
Blackness S15
Blacknest (Berks) 3.4
Blacknest (Hants) 20.6
Blacko 26.13
Blackpool 26.4
Blackridge S31
Blackrod 19.2
Blackshaw 47.3
Blackshaw Moor 40.1
Blackshawhead 47.3
Blackshiels S19
Blackstone 46.3
Blackthorn 31.5
Blackthorn (part) 35.2
Blacktoft 15.2

Blackwall L30
Blackwater (Corn) 9.1
Blackwater (Hants) 20.2
Blackwater (Som) 38.5
Blackwaterfoot S21
Blackwell (Derbys)* 11.5
Blackwell (Warks) 44.5
Blackwell (Worcs) 49.2
Blackwell in the Peak (Derbys)* 11.3
Blackwood W4
Blackwood (S Lanarks) S28
Bladbean 25.13
Bladnoch S10
Bladon 35.1
Blaen Dowlais W12
Blaenau W6
Blaenau Ffestiniog W11
Blaenavon W20
Blaenclydach W18
Blaencwm W18
Blaenffos W16
Blaengarw W3
Blaengwawr W18
Blaengwrach W14
Blaengwynfi W14
Blaenhonddan W14
Blaenllechau W18
Blaenpennal W7
Blaenrheidol W7
Blaenrhondda W18
Blaenwaun W6
Blaenycoed W6
Blagdon (N'land) 32.1
Blagdon (Som) 38.7
Blagdon Hill 38.4
Blagrove 48.2
Blaich S17
Blaina W2
Blainslie S30
Blair Atholl S24
Blairdrummond S29
Blairgowrie S24
Blairhall S16
Blairingone S24
Blairlogie S29
Blairmore S17
Blairninich S17
Blaisdon 18.2
Blaise Hamlet 4.1
Blakedown 49.1
Blakelands 5.1
Blakelaw 43.1
Blakeley 37.1
Blakeley Green 45.1
Blakelow 7.5
Blakemere 21.1
Blakemoor 32.1
Blakenall 45.2
Blakeney (Gloucs) 18.2
Blakeney (Norfolk) 30.1
Blakenhall 7.5
Blakeshall 49.1
Blakesley 31.7
Blanchland 32.1
Blandford Forum 13.2
Blandford St Mary 13.2
Blanefield S29
Blankney 28.4
Blantyre S28
Blasford Hill 17.7
Blashford 20.7
Blaston 27.8
Blatchbridge 38.2
Blatherwycke 31.3
Blawith 10.5
Blaxhall 41.5
Blaxton 39.2
Blaydon 43.3
Bleaberry Rigg 10.1
Bleadney 38.2
Bleadon 38.7
Bleak Street 38.5
Blean 25.5
Bleasby (Lincs) 28.1
Bleasby (Notts) 34.3
Bleasby Moor 28.1
Bleasdale 26.2
Bleatarn 10.3
Bleddfa W17
Bledington 18.5
Bledlow 5.3
Bledlow Ridge 5.3
Blencarn 10.3
Blencowe 10.3
Blendworth 20.6
Blenheim 35.1
Blennerhasset 10.2
Bletchingdon 35.2
Bletchingley 42.10
Bletchley (Bucks) 5.1
Bletchley (Shrop) 37.1
Bletherston W16
Bletsoe 2.1
Blewbury 35.4
Blickling 30.5
Blidworth 34.3
Blindbothel 10.2
Blindcrake 10.2
Blindley Heath 42.10
Blindmore 38.5
Blisland 9.1
Bliss Gate (Rock) 49.1
Blissford 20.7
Blistshill 37.4
Blisworth 31.7
Blithbury 40.8
Blithfield 40.5
Blithford 40.8
Blo' Norton 30.3
Blockley 18.5
Bloemfontein 14.1
Blofield 30.5
Bloomsbury L6
Blore with Swinscoe 40.1
Blowick 29.1
Blowing House 9.1
Bloxham 35.2
Bloxholm 28.4
Bloxwich 45.2
Bloxworth 13.5
Blubberhouses 33.6
Blue Anchor (Corn) 9.1
Blue Anchor (Som) 38.3
Blue Bell Hill 25.9
Blue Bridge 5.1
Blue Town 25.4
Bluebell 37.4
Blundellsands 29.1
Blundeston 41.1
Blunham 2.2
Blunsdon 48.2
Bluntington 49.1
Bluntisham 6.3
Blunts 9.1
Blurton 40.3
Blyborough 28.1
Blyford 41.1
Blymhill 40.6
Blyth (N'land) 32.1
Blyth (Notts) 34.1
Blythburgh 41.5
Blythe Bridge (part) 40.1, 40.4
Blyton 28.1
Blyton Carr 28.1
Bo'ness S15
Boarhills S16
Boarhunt 20.5
Boars Hill 35.4
Boarshaw 19.4
Boarstall 5.2
Boat of Garten S17
Bobbing 25.4
Bobbington 40.6
Bobbingworth 17.6
Bockhampton, North, Middle & South 13.8
Bocking 47.1
Bocking (see Braintree & Bocking)
Bockleton 49.4
Boconnoc 9.1
Bodafon W1
Boddam (Shetland) S26
Bodden 38.2
Boddington (Gloucs) 18.1
Bodedern W1
Bodelwyddan W9
Bodenham (Here) 21.1
Bodenham (Wilts) 48.1
Bodfari W9
Bodffordd W1
Bodham 30.1
Bodiam 16.2
Bodicote 35.2
Bodinnick 9.1
Bodle Street 16.1
Bodmin 9.1
Bodney 30.3
Bodorgan W1
Bodsham 25.13
Boduan W11
Bodwrog W1
Bog Row 43.5
Boghall S19
Bogindollo S2
Bognor Regis 46.5
Bogthorn 47.1
Bogwood S19
Bohortha 9.1
Bojewyan 9.1
Bolahaul W6
Bolam (Durham) 14.1
Bolam (N'land) 32.1
Bolas Heath 37.4
Bolas Magna 37.4
Bolbeck Park 5.1
Bold 29.3
Bold Heath 29.3
Boldmere 45.5
Boldon Colliery 43.4
Boldre 20.7
Boldron 14.1
Bole 34.1
Bolehall 40.9
Bolehill, Wirksworth 11.3
Bolenowe 9.1
Boley Park 40.8
Bolham 12.4
Bolingey 9.1
Bollington 7.5
Bolney 46.4
Bolnhurst 2.1
Bolsover 11.5
Bolster Moor 47.4
Bolsterstone 39.3
Bolstone 21.1
Boltby 33.2
Bolter End 5.3
Bolton S13
Bolton (Cumbria) 10.3
Bolton (E Yorks) 15.2
Bolton (Gtr M'chester) 19.2
Bolton (W Yorks) 47.1
Bolton Abbey 33.5
Bolton by Bowland 26.3
Bolton Percy 33.8
Bolton Woods 47.1
Bolton-le-Sands 26.1
Bolton-on-Swale 33.1
Bolton-upon-Dearne 39.1
Boltons 10.2
Boltons, The L20
Bolventor (part) 9.1
Bomarsund 32.1
Bomere Heath 37.1
Bonaly S6
Bonar Bridge S17
Bonawe S3
Bonby 28.8
Boncath W16
Bonchester Bridge S30
Bonchurch 24.1
Bondleigh 12.3
Bonds (see Barnacre)
Bonehill 40.8
Boney Hay 40.8
Bonham 48.1
Bonhill S9
Boningale 37.1
Bonkyl S30
Bonningate, Crook 10.5
Bonnington 25.12
Bonnybridge S15
Bonnyrigg S19
Bonsall 11.3
Bontddu W11
Bontnewydd W11
Bonvilston W21
Bonwick 15.2
Bonymaen W19

Booker 5.3
Bookham 42.8
Booley 37.1
Boorley Green 20.9
Boosbeck 33.10
Booth 47.3
Bootham 33.7
Boothby Graffoe 28.4
Boothby Pagnell 28.6
Boothen 40.3
Boothorpe 27.1
Booths Hill 7.1
Boothstown (part) 19.1, 19.5
Boothtown 47.3
Boothville 31.5
Bootle (Cumbria) 10.4
Bootle (Mersey) 29.1
Booton 30.5
Boozer Pit 38.5
Boraston 37.1
Borden 25.4
Borden, Milland 46.2
Border 38.5
Bordesley (W Mids) 45.5
Bordesley (Worcs) (part) 49.2, 49.3
Bordesley Green 45.5
Bordley 33.5
Bordon 20.6
Boreatton 37.1
Boreham (part) 17.2, 17.7
Boreham Street 16.1
Borehamwood 22.10
Boreland S10
Borgue (Dumfries & Galloway) S10
Borgue (Highland) S17
Borley 17.2
Borough Fen 6.1
Borough Green 25.9
Borough Post 38.4
Borough, The L28
Boroughbridge 33.6
Borras W22
Borras Park (Wrexham) W22
Borrowash 11.8
Borrowby (Scarborough) 33.4
Borrowby (Thirsk) 33.2
Borrowdale 10.2
Borstal 25.3
Borth W7
Borth-y-Gest W11
Borthwick S19
Borve S32
Borwick 26.1
Bosbury 21.1
Boscarne 9.1
Boscastle 9.1
Boscaswell 9.1
Boscobel 37.1
Boscombe (Wilts) 48.1
Boscombe, East & West 13.7
Bosham 46.2
Bosherston W16
Bosley 7.5

Bossall (see Buttercrambe)
Bossiney 9.1
Bossingham 25.5
Bossington (Hants) 20.4
Bossington (Kent) 25.5
Bossington (Som) 38.3
Bostock 7.3
Boston 28.5
Boston Spa 47.2
Bosullow 9.1
Boswell 28.2
Botallack 9.1
Botany Bay (Staffs) 40.8
Botcheston 27.4
Botesdale 41.4
Bothal 32.1
Bothamsall 34.1
Bothel 10.2
Bothenhampton 13.1
Bothenwood 13.3
Bothwell S28
Botley (Hants) (part) 20.5, 20.9
Botley (Oxon) (part) 35.4, 35.5
Botolph Claydon 5.2
Bottesford (N Lincs) 28.8
Bottesford (Notts) 27.3
Bottisham 6.4
Bottlesford 48.1
Bottomboat 47.5
Botton (see Wray)
Botts Green 44.1
Botusfleming 9.1
Botwnnog W11
Bough Beech 25.8
Boughrood W17
Boughton (N'hants) 31.4
Boughton (Norfolk) 30.2
Boughton (Notts) 34.3
Boughton Aluph 25.12
Boughton Lees 25.12
Boughton Malherbe 25.10
Boughton Monchelsea 25.10
Boughton Street 25.4
Boughton under Blean 25.4
Boulby 33.10
Boulderclough 47.3
Bouldon 37.1
Boulge 41.5
Boulston (see Uzmaston)
Boulton 11.7
Boundary (Staffs) 40.1
Boundary (part) 11.9, 27.1
Bounds Green L14
Boundstone 42.11
Bourn 6.5
Bournbrook 45.5
Bourne (Lincs) 28.6
Bourne (Som) 38.7
Bourne (Surrey) 42.11
Bourne End (Beds) 2.2
Bourne End (Bucks) 5.3
Bourne Valley 13.6
Bournemouth (Central) 13.7
Bournheath 49.2
Bournmoor 14.1

Bournville 45.5
Bourtie S1
Bourton (Bucks) 5.2
Bourton (Dorset) 13.2
Bourton (Oxon) 35.4
Bourton (Som) 38.7
Bourton (Warks) 44.3
Bourton (Wilts) 48.1
Bourton, Great & Little 35.2
Bourton-on-the-Hill 18.5
Bourton-on-the-Water 18.5
Boustead Hill 10.1
Bouth 10.5
Boveridge 13.3
Boverton W21
Bovey Tracey 12.5
Bovingdon 22.4
Bovingdon Green 5.3
Bow (Devon) 12.4
Bow (London) L30
Bow Brickhill 5.1
Bow Street W7
Bowburn 14.1
Bowden S30
Bowden Hill 48.1
Bowdens 38.5
Bowdon 19.8
Bower S17
Bower Ashton 4.1
Bower Chalke 48.1
Bower Hinton 38.5
Bowers Gifford 17.10
Bowes 14.1
Bowes Park L14
Bowhill S16
Bowland S30
Bowland Bridge 10.5
Bowland Forest 26.3
Bowland with Leagram 26.3
Bowlee 19.3
Bowlhead Green 42.11
Bowling (W Dunbar) S9
Bowling (W Yorks) 47.1
Bowlish 38.2
Bowmanstead 10.5
Bowmore S3
Bowness-on-Solway 10.2
Bowness-on-Windermere 10.5
Bowriefauld S2
Bowring Park (part) 29.2, 29.4
Bowscale 10.3
Bowscar 10.3
Bowsden 32.1
Bowston 10.5
Bowthorpe 30.4
Box 48.1
Boxford (Berks) 3.1
Boxford (Suffolk) 41.6
Boxgrove 46.2
Boxhill 42.8
Boxley 25.10
Boxted (Essex) 17.3
Boxted (Suffolk) 41.6
Boxwell with Leighterton 18.5
Boxworth 6.5

Boyatt Wood 20.9
Boyden Gate 25.5
Boylestone 11.3
Boyn Hill 3.4
Boyndie S1
Boynton 15.2
Boythorpe 11.2
Boyton (Corn) 9.1
Boyton (Suffolk) 41.5
Boyton (Wilts) 48.1
Boyton Cross 17.7
Bozeat 31.6
Brabourne 25.12
Brabourne Lees 25.12
Bracadale S17
Braceborough 28.6
Bracebridge Heath 28.4
Braceby & Sapperton 28.6
Bracewell 26.13
Brackenborough with Little Grimsby 28.2
Brackenfield 11.4
Brackenhall 47.4
Brackla S17
Bracklesham 46.2
Brackley 31.7
Brackmills 31.5
Bracknell 3.6
Braco S24
Bracon Ash 30.7
Bracora S17
Bradbourne 11.3
Bradbury 14.1
Bradden 31.7
Bradeley 40.3
Braden Heath 37.1
Bradenham (Bucks) 5.3
Bradenham, East & West (Norfolk) 30.3
Bradenstoke 48.1
Bradfield (Berks) 3.1
Bradfield (Essex) 17.4
Bradfield (Norfolk) 30.1
Bradfield (S Yorks) 39.3
Bradfield Combust with Stanningfield 41.3
Bradfield Green 7.5
Bradfield St Clare 41.3
Bradfield St George 41.3
Bradford (Devon) 12.1
Bradford (Gtr M'chester) 19.6
Bradford (W Yorks) 47.1
Bradford Abbas 13.1
Bradford Moor 47.1
Bradford Peverell 13.1
Bradford and Melksham Without 48.1
Bradford-on-Avon 48.1
Bradford-on-Tone 38.4
Brading 24.1
Bradley (Cheshire) 7.3
Bradley (Derbys) 11.3
Bradley (E Lincs) 28.9
Bradley (Hants) 20.1
Bradley (Staffs) 40.4
Bradley (W Mids) (see Bilston)

Bradley (W Yorks) 47.4
Bradley (Wrexham) W22
Bradley Fold 19.3
Bradley Green (part) 49.3, 49.6
Bradley Lakes (Longdon) 40.8
Bradley Mills 47.4
Bradley-in-the-Moors (part) 40.1, 40.5
Bradleyfield 10.5
Bradleys Both 33.5
Bradmore (Notts) 34.8
Bradmore (Wolverhampton) 45.1
Bradninch 12.4
Bradnock's Marsh 45.6
Bradnop 40.1
Bradpole 13.1
Bradshaw (Gtr M'chester) 19.2
Bradshaw (W Yorks) 47.3
Bradstone 12.3
Bradville 5.1
Bradwall 7.5
Bradwell (Bucks) 5.1
Bradwell (Derbys) 11.3
Bradwell (Essex) 17.2
Bradwell (Norfolk) 30.6
Bradwell (Staffs) 40.2
Bradwell Abbey 5.1
Bradwell Common 5.1
Bradwell-on-Sea 17.8
Bradworthy 12.1
Brae S26
Brae of Downie S2
Braehead (S Lanarks) S28
Braehead of Lunan S2
Braemar S1
Braemore S17
Brafferton (Durham) 14.8
Brafferton (N Yorks) 33.2
Brafield-on-the-Green 31.7
Bragar S32
Braggington 44.5
Braichmelyn W11
Braidwood S28
Brailes 44.5
Brailsford 11.3
Braintree & Bocking 17.2
Braiseworth 41.4
Braishfield 20.4
Braithwaite (Cumbria) 10.2
Braithwaite (S Yorks) 39.2
Braithwaite (W Yorks) 47.1
Braithwell 39.2
Bramber 46.3
Brambles Farm 33.9
Brambridge 20.5
Bramcote (Notts) 34.5
Bramcote (Warks) 44.3
Bramdean 20.5
Bramerton 30.7
Bramfield (Herts) 22.3
Bramfield (Suffolk) 41.5
Bramford 41.4
Bramhall 19.9
Bramham 47.2
Bramhope 47.2
Bramley (Hants) 20.1
Bramley (S Yorks) 39.4
Bramley (Surrey) 42.11
Bramley Green 20.1
Bramley Vale 11.5
Bramling 25.5
Brampford Speke 12.7
Brampton (Cambs) 6.3
Brampton (Cumbria) 10.1
Brampton (Derbys) (part) 11.2, 11.4
Brampton (Lincs) 28.1
Brampton (Norfolk) 30.5
Brampton (Suffolk) 41.1
Brampton Abbots 21.1
Brampton Ash 31.2
Brampton Bierlow 39.4
Brampton Bryan 21.1
Brampton Old Road 10.1
Brampton-en-le-Morthen 39.4
Bramshall 40.5
Bramshaw 20.7
Bramshill 20.2
Bramshott (part) 20.6
Bramwell 38.5
Brancaster 30.2
Brancepeth 14.1
Branderburgh (see Lossiemouth)
Brandesburton 15.2
Brandeston 41.5
Brandhall 45.4
Brandiston 30.5
Brandlesholme 19.3
Brandon (Durham) 14.1
Brandon (Lincs) 28.6
Brandon (Suffolk) 41.2
Brandon (Warks) 44.3
Brandon Hill 4.1
Brandon Parva 30.7
Brandsby-cum-Stearsby 33.2
Brandwood 37.1
Brandy Wharf 28.1
Branksome 13.6
Branksome Park 13.6
Bransby 28.1
Branscombe 12.7
Bransdale 33.3
Bransford 49.4
Bransgore 20.7
Branshaw 47.1
Branston (Leics) 27.3
Branston (Lincs) 28.4
Branston (Staffs) 40.5
Brant Broughton 28.4
Brantham 41.6
Brantingham 15.2
Branton (N'land) 32.1
Branton (S Yorks) 39.2
Brantwood 10.5
Branxton 32.1
Brasside 14.1
Brassington 11.3
Brasted 25.8
Brasted Chart 25.8
Bratoft 28.2
Brattleby 28.1
Bratton (Shrop) 37.4
Bratton (Som) 38.3
Bratton (Wilts) 48.1
Bratton Clovelly 12.3
Bratton Fleming 12.2
Bratton Seymour 38.5
Braughing 22.3
Brauncewell 28.4
Braunston (N'hants) 31.4
Braunston-in-Rutland 36.1
Braunstone (part) 27.6
Braunton 12.2
Brawby 33.3
Brawdy W16
Brawith (see Knayton)
Bray 3.4
Bray Shop (part) 9.1
Braybrooke 31.2
Braydon 48.1
Brayford 12.2
Brayton 33.8
Braywick 3.4
Braywood 3.4
Brea 9.1
Breachwood Green 22.1
Breadsall Hilltop 11.7
Breadsall Village 11.8
Breadsall* 11.7, 11.8
Breage 9.1
Bream 18.2
Breamore 20.7
Brean 38.1
Breanish S32
Brearley 47.3
Brearton 33.6
Breaston 11.8
Brechfa W6
Brechin S2
Breckenbrough (see Newsham)
Breckfield 29.2
Breckles 30.3
Brecknock W17
Brecks 39.4
Brecon W17
Bredbury 19.9
Brede 16.2
Bredenbury 21.1
Bredfield 41.5
Bredgar 25.4
Bredhurst 25.10
Bredicot 49.6
Bredon 49.6
Bredons' Norton 49.6
Bredwardine 21.1
Breedon-on-the-Hill 27.1
Breich S31
Breightmet (part) 19.3
Breighton 15.2
Breinton 21.1
Brelstone Green 21.1
Bremhill 48.1
Brenchley 25.11
Brendon 12.2
Brendon Hill 38.3
Brenkley 43.1
Brenley 25.4
Brent L4
Brent Eleigh 41.6
Brent Knoll 38.1
Brent Pelham 22.3
Brentingby 27.3
Brentor 12.3
Brentry 4.1
Brents, The 25.4
Brentwood 17.9
Brenzett 25.13
Brereton 7.5, 40.7
Brereton (part) 40.8
Bressay S26
Bressingham 30.7
Bretby 11.9
Bretford 44.3
Bretforton 49.6
Bretherton 26.9
Brettenham (Norfolk) 30.3
Brettenham (Suffolk) 41.6
Bretton (Cambs) 6.1
Bretton (Flint) W10
Brewham 38.5
Brewood 40.6
Briantspuddle 13.5
Briar Hill 31.5
Brickendon Liberty 22.3
Bricket Wood 22.5
Bricklehampton 49.6
Brickwalls (Alkington) 37.1
Bridekirk 10.2
Bridell W16
Bridestowe 12.3
Bridford 12.5
Bridge (Corn) 9.1
Bridge (Kent) 25.5
Bridge Hewick 33.6
Bridge Mill S27
Bridge Sollars 21.1
Bridge Trafford 7.3
Bridge of Allan S29
Bridge of Balgie S24
Bridge of Cally S24
Bridge of Dee S10
Bridge of Don S4
Bridge of Dun S2
Bridge of Earn S24
Bridge of Ericht S24
Bridge of Forss S17
Bridge of Gaur S24
Bridge of Orchy S3
Bridge of Tilt S24
Bridge of Weir S25
Bridgecastle S31
Bridgehampton 38.5
Bridgemary 20.11
Bridgemere 37.1
Bridgend W3
Bridgend (Argyll & Bute) S3
Bridgend (Moray) S20
Bridgend (W Lothian) S31
Bridgend of Lintrathen S2
Bridgerule 12.1
Bridgetown 38.3
Bridgeyate 18.7
Bridgham 30.3
Bridgmere 7.5

Bridgnorth 37.1
Bridgtown 40.7
Bridgwater 38.1
Bridgwater Without 38.1
Bridlington 15.2
Bridport 13.1
Bridstow 21.1
Briercliffe 26.12
Brierfield 26.13
Brierley (Gloucs) 18.2
Brierley (S Yorks) 39.1
Brierley Gap 47.5
Brierley Hill 45.3
Brierton 14.9
Briestfield 47.4
Brig O'Turk S29
Brigg 28.8
Briggate 30.1
Briggswath 33.4
Brigham (Cumbria) 10.2
Brigham (E Yorks) 15.2
Brighouse 47.3
Brighstone 24.1
Brightholmlee 39.3
Brightling 16.2
Brightlingsea 17.4
Brighton (East Sussex) 16.3
Brighton (Grampound Rd, Truro) (Corn) (part) 9.1
Brighton Hill 20.1
Brighton Hill South 20.1
Brightons S15
Brightwalton 3.1
Brightwell 41.5
Brightwell Baldwin 35.3
Brightwell-cum-Sotwell 35.3
Brigmerston 48.1
Brignall 14.1
Brigsley 28.9
Brigsteer 10.5
Brigstock 31.3
Brill 5.2
Brilley 21.1
Brimfield 21.1
Brimington 11.2
Brimington Common 11.2
Brimpsfield 18.5
Brimpton 3.1
Brimrod 19.4
Brimscombe 18.6
Brimstage 29.5
Brind 15.2
Brindle 26.9
Brindley 7.5
Brindley Ford (part) 40.1, 40.3
Brindley Heath 40.7
Brindwoodgate 11.4
Bringhurst 27.8
Brington (Cambs) 6.3
Brington, Gt & Little (N'hants) 31.4
Briningham 30.1
Brinkburn 32.1
Brinkhill 28.2
Brinkley 6.4
Brinklow (Bucks) 5.1
Brinklow (Warks) 44.3
Brinkworth 48.1
Brinscall 26.9
Brinsea 38.7
Brinsford 40.6
Brinsley (part) 34.4, 34.5
Brinsop 21.1
Brinsworth 39.4
Brinton 30.1
Brisco 10.1
Brisley 30.3
Brislington 4.1
Bristol 4.1
Briston 30.1
Britannia W4
Britford 48.1
Brithdir (Caerph) W4
Brithdir (Gwynedd) W11
Brithdir (Powys) W17
Brithembottom 12.4
Briton Ferry W14
Brittania 26.14
Britwell 3.5
Britwell Salome 35.3
Brixham (part) 12.9
Brixham South Devon (part) 12.10
Brixton (Devon) 12.9
Brixton (London) L22
Brixton Deverill 48.1
Brixworth 31.4
Brize Norton 35.1
Broad Acre 38.5
Broad Campden 18.5
Broad Chalke 48.1
Broad Haven W16
Broad Hinton 48.1
Broad Lane 9.1
Broad Oak (Carm) W6
Broad Oak (E Sussex) 16.1
Broad Oak (Here) 21.1
Broad Oak (Kent) 25.5
Broad Oak (Mersey) 29.3
Broad Oak (Som) 38.5
Broad Oak, Brede 16.2
Broad Street 48.1
Broad Town 48.1
Broadbottom 19.10
Broadbridge 46.2
Broadbridge Heath 46.3
Broadclyst 12.7
Broadfield 46.1
Broadford S17
Broadgreen 29.2
Broadhalgh 19.4
Broadheath (Gtr M'chester) 19.8
Broadheath (Worcs) 49.4
Broadhembury 12.7
Broadhempston 12.5
Broadholme (Lincs) 28.1
Broadlay W6
Broadlayings 20.1
Broadley 26.14
Broadley Common 17.6
Broadmayne 13.1
Broadmeadows 11.5
Broadmere 20.1
Broadmoor (Pemb) W16
Broadmoor (Surrey) 42.8
Broadoak (Corn) 9.1
Broadoak (Gloucs) 18.2
Broads Green 17.7
Broadstairs 25.7
Broadstone (Dorset) 13.6
Broadstone (Shrop) 37.1
Broadwas 49.4
Broadwater 46.6
Broadwath 10.1
Broadway (Carm) W6
Broadway (Som) 38.5
Broadway (Worcs) 49.6
Broadway Pound 38.5
Broadwell (Gloucs)* 18.2, 18.5
Broadwell (Oxon) 35.1
Broadwell (Warks) 44.3
Broadwindsor 13.1
Broadwoodkelly 12.3
Broadwoodwidger 12.1
Brobury 21.1
Brochel S17
Brock Hill 3.6
Brockdish 30.7
Brockencote 49.1
Brockenhurst 20.7
Brocketsbrae S28
Brockford (see Wetheringsett)
Brockhall 31.4
Brockham 42.8
Brockhampton (Gloucs) 18.5
Brockhampton (Worcs) 21.1
Brockhill 49.3
Brockholes (Shrop) (part) 37.4
Brockholes (W Yorks) 47.4
Brockhurst (Derbys) 11.4
Brockhurst (Hants) 20.11
Brocklesby 28.1
Brockley L23
Brockley (Som) 38.7
Brockley (Suffolk) 41.3
Brockmoor 45.3
Brocks Green 20.1
Brockton (part) 37.1, 37.4
Brockweir 18.2
Brockwell 11.2
Brockworth 18.1
Brocton 40.4
Brodick S21
Brodie S20
Brodsworth 39.2
Brogborough 2.2
Brogden 26.13
Brokenborough 48.1
Brokenheugh 32.1
Bromborough 29.5
Brome 41.4
Bromeswell 41.5
Bromfield (Cumbria) 10.2
Bromfield (Shrop) 37.1
Bromford 45.5
Bromham (Beds) 2.1
Bromham (Wilts) 48.1
Bromley L5
Bromley by Bow L30
Bromley Cross 19.2
Bromley Hayes 40.8
Bromlow 37.1
Brompton L20
Brompton (Kent) 25.3
Brompton (N Yorks)* 33.2, 33.4
Brompton (Shrop) 37.1
Brompton Ralph 38.3
Brompton Regis 38.3
Brompton-on-Swale 33.1
Bromsash 21.1
Bromsberrow 18.2
Bromsgrove 49.2
Bromyard & Winslow 21.1
Bronaber W11
Broncroft 37.1
Brongwyn W7
Bronington W22
Bronllys W17
Bronwydd Arms W6
Bronygarth 37.1
Brook (Hants) 20.7
Brook (I of W) 24.1
Brook (Kent) 25.12
Brook (Surrey) 42.11
Brook End (Essex) 17.7
Brook End (Longdon) (Staffs) 40.8
Brook Furlong 5.1
Brook Green 38.5
Brooke (Norfolk) 30.7
Brooke (Rutland) 36.1
Brookenby 28.1
Brookfield (Lancs) 26.6
Brookfield (Middlesbrough) 33.9
Brookfield (Renfrew) S25
Brookfoot 47.3
Brookhampton (Som) 38.5
Brookhampton (Str-u-Avon) 44.5
Brookhay 40.8
Brookhouse (Lancs) 26.1
Brookhouse (S Yorks) 39.4
Brookhouse (Staffs) 40.3
Brookland 25.13
Brooklands 5.1, 19.6
Brookmans Park 22.6
Brooks W17
Brooksbottoms 19.3
Brooksby 27.3
Brookside (Berks) (part) 3.4, 3.6
Brookside (Derbys) 11.2
Brookside (Shrop) 37.4
Brookthorpe 18.6
Brookwood 42.4
Broom (Beds) 2.2
Broom (Warks) 44.5
Broom Hill (Bristol) 4.1
Broome (Norfolk) 30.7
Broome (Shrop) 37.1
Broome (Worcs) 49.1
Broomedge 7.1
Broomfield (Essex) 17.7
Broomfield (Som) 38.1

2

Broomfield* 25.5, 25.10
Broomfleet 15.2
Broomhall 7.5
Broomhaugh 32.1
Broomhill S19
Broomhill (Dorset) 13.3
Broomhill (N'land) 32.1
Broomhill (Norfolk) (see Weeting)
Broomhill (Staffs) 40.7
Broomhill (T & W) 43.5
Broomieknowe S19
Broomley 32.1
Broompark 14.1
Brora S17
Broseley 37.1
Brothertoft 28.5
Brotherton 33.8
Brotton 33.10
Brough & Shatton 11.1
Brough (Cumbria) 10.3
Brough (E Yorks) 15.2
Brough (Highland) S17
Brough (Notts) 34.3
Brough Sowerby 10.3
Brough with St Giles 33.1
Broughall 37.1
Brougham 10.3
Broughton W10
Broughton (Bucks) 5.1
Broughton (Cambs) 6.3
Broughton (Cumbria) 10.2
Broughton (Gtr M'chester) 19.5
Broughton (Hants) 20.4
Broughton (Lancs) 26.6
Broughton (Lincs) 28.8
Broughton (N Yorks)* 33.3, 33.5
Broughton (N'hants) 31.2
Broughton (Oxon) 35.2
Broughton (Scottish Borders) S30
Broughton (Shrop) 37.1
Broughton (Vale of Glamorgan) W21
Broughton Astley 27.8
Broughton Beck 10.5
Broughton Gate 5.1
Broughton Gifford 48.1
Broughton Hackett 49.6
Broughton Mills 10.5
Broughton Moor 10.2
Broughton Poggs (see Filkins)
Broughton-in-Furness 10.5
Brown Candover 20.1
Brown Edge (Mersey) 29.3
Brown Edge (Staffs) 40.1
Brown Heath 37.1
Brown Lees 40.1
Brown Moss 37.1
Brownhills (Shrop) 37.1
Brownhills (W Mids) 45.2
Browning Hill Green 20.1
Brownlow 7.5
Browns Lane 40.9
Browns Wood 5.1
Brownsbrook 37.1
Brownshill 18.6
Brownshill Green 45.7
Brownside (Derbys) 11.1
Brownside (Lancs) 26.12
Browston 30.6
Broxa 33.4
Broxbourne 22.7
Broxburn S31
Broxholme 28.1
Broxmore Park 48.1
Broxted 17.1
Broxton 7.3
Broxtowe Estate 34.6
Bruche 7.1
Bruen Stapleford 7.3
Bruern 35.1
Bruichladdich S3
Bruisyard 41.5
Brumby 28.8
Brumstead 30.1
Brundall 30.5
Brundish 41.4
Brunshaw 26.12
Brunstock 10.1
Brunswick 43.1
Bruntcliffe 47.2
Brunthwaite 47.1
Bruntingthorpe 27.8
Brushes, The 11.2
Brushfield 11.3
Brushford (Devon) 12.4
Brushford (Som) 38.3
Bruton 38.5
Bryanston 13.2
Brydekirk S10
Bryher 50.1
Brymbo W22
Brympton 38.5
Bryn (Carm) W6
Bryn (Neath) W14
Bryn (Shrop) 37.1
Bryn Bela W11
Bryn Du W1
Bryn y Baal W10
Bryn, The (Monmth) W13
Bryn-y-maen W8
Brynamman W6
Brynbach Park (part) W2, W4
Bryncenydd W4
Bryncethin W3
Bryncir W11
Bryncoch W14
Bryncroes W11
Bryncrug W11
Bryneglwys W9
Brynford W10
Bryngwran W1
Bryngwyn (Monmth) W13
Bryngwyn (Powys) W17
Brynhyfryd W19
Brynmawr (Blaenau) W2
Brynmawr (Gwynedd) W11
Brynmenyn W3
Brynmill W19
Brynna W18
Brynore 37.1
Brynrefail W11
Brynrhydyrarian W8
Brynsadler W18
Brynsiencyn W1
Brynteg W22
Brynygwenin W13
Bualnaluib S17
Bubbenhall 44.4
Bubwith 15.2
Buchanan Smithy S29
Buchanhaven S1
Buchlyvie S29
Buckabank 10.1
Buckby Wharf 31.4
Buckden (Cambs) 6.3
Buckden (N Yorks) 33.5
Buckenham Tofts 30.3
Buckenham, Old & New 30.3
Buckerell 12.7
Buckeridge (Rock) 49.1
Buckfastleigh 12.5
Buckhaven S16
Buckholt 20.4
Buckhorn Weston 13.2
Buckhurst Hill (part) L26, 17.6
Buckie S20
Buckingham 5.2
Buckland (Bucks) 5.2
Buckland (Gloucs) 18.1
Buckland (Herts) 22.3
Buckland (Oxon) 35.4
Buckland (Surrey) 42.8
Buckland Brewer 12.1
Buckland Common 5.4
Buckland Dinham 38.2
Buckland Down 38.2
Buckland End 45.5
Buckland Filleigh 12.1
Buckland Monachorum 12.3
Buckland Newton 13.1
Buckland Ripers 13.1
Buckland St Mary 38.5
Buckland in the Moor 12.5
Buckland-tout-Saints 12.9
Bucklebury 3.1
Bucklers Hard 20.7
Bucklesham 41.5
Buckley W10
Buckminster 27.3
Bucknall (Lincs) 28.2
Bucknall (Staffs) (part) 40.1, 40.3
Bucknell (Oxon) 35.2
Bucknell (Shrop) 37.1
Buckover 18.7
Bucks Green 46.3
Bucks Horn Oak 20.6
Bucksburn S4
Buckshaw Village (part) 26.9, 40.8
Buckskin 20.1
Buckton 15.2
Buckton & Coxall 21.1
Buckworth 6.3
Budbrooke 44.4
Budby (see Perlethorpe)
Bude 9.1
Budleigh Salterton 12.7
Budock 9.1
Budock Water 9.1
Buerton 7.5
Buffler's Holt 5.2
Bugbrooke 31.7
Bugle 9.1
Bugthorpe 15.2
Buildwas 37.1
Builth Wells W17
Bulby 28.6
Bulcote 34.3
Bulford 48.1
Bulkeley 7.5
Bulkington (Warks) 44.2
Bulkington (Wilts) 48.1
Bulkworthy 12.1
Bull Bay W1
Bull Hill 20.7
Bullbridge 11.6
Bullbrook 3.6
Bullinghope 21.1
Bullington (Hants) 20.4
Bullington (Lincs) 28.1
Bullockstone (Herne Bay) 25.5
Bulls Bushes 20.1
Bulls Hill 21.1
Bully Hill Top 28.1
Bulmer (Essex) 17.2
Bulmer (N Yorks) 33.3
Bulmershe 3.3
Bulphan 17.12
Bulwell 34.6
Bulwick 31.3
Bumbles Green 17.6
Bunavoullin S17
Bunbury 7.5
Bunford 38.5
Bungay 41.1
Bunkers Hill (part) 10.1, 47.4
Bunny 34.8
Buntingford 22.3
Buntingsdale 37.1
Bunwell 30.7
Burbage (Derbys) 11.1
Burbage (Leics) 27.4
Burbage (Wilts) 48.1
Burchells Green 4.1
Burchett's Green 3.4
Burcombe 48.1
Burcot (Oxon) 35.3
Burcot (Worcs) 49.2
Burcott (Bucks) 5.2
Burcott (Som) 38.2
Burderop 48.2
Burdon 43.5
Burdon Park 43.5
Burdrop 35.2
Bures Hamlet 17.2
Bures St Mary 41.6
Burfa W17
Burford 37.1
Burford, Upton & Signet 35.1
Burgate 41.4

Burgess Green 25.6
Burgess Hill 46.4
Burgh 41.5
Burgh & Tuttington 30.5
Burgh by Sands 10.1
Burgh Castle 30.6
Burgh Heath 42.9
Burgh St Margaret 30.6
Burgh St Peter 30.7
Burgh Stubbs 30.1
Burgh le Marsh 28.2
Burgh on Bain 28.2
Burghclere 20.1
Burghead S20
Burghfield 3.1
Burghill 21.1
Burghope 21.1
Burghwallis 39.2
Burham (Kent) 25.9
Buriton 20.6
Burland 7.5
Burlawn 9.1
Burleigh 37.4
Burlescombe 12.4
Burleston 13.1
Burley (Hants) 20.7
Burley (Rutland) 36.1
Burley (Shrop) 37.1
Burley Woodhead 47.1
Burley-in-Wharfedale 47.1
Burleydam 7.5
Burlingham (see Lingwood)
Burlingjobb W17
Burlton 37.1
Burmarsh 25.13
Burmington 44.5
Burn 33.8
Burnage 19.6
Burnaston 11.9
Burnbank S28
Burnby 15.2
Burncoose 9.1
Burncross 39.3
Burndell 46.5
Burnedge 19.4
Burneside 10.5
Burneston 33.2
Burnett 38.6
Burnham 5.5
Burnham Market 30.2
Burnham Norton 30.2
Burnham Overy 30.2
Burnham Thorpe 30.2
Burnham Without 38.1
Burnham-on-Crouch 17.8
Burnham-on-Sea 38.1
Burnhill Green 40.6
Burnhope 14.1
Burnhouse S21
Burniston 33.4
Burnley 26.12
Burnmouth S30
Burnopfield 14.1
Burnrigg 10.1
Burnsall 33.5
Burnside (Fencehouse, Houghton le Spring) 43.5
Burnt Edge Todmorden 47.3
Burnt Fen 6.4
Burntisland S16
Burnton S11
Burntwood 40.8
Burpham (Surrey) 42.7
Burpham (W Sussex) 46.5
Burra Isle S26
Burradon 43.2
Burras 9.1
Burraton 9.1
Burrator 12.3
Burravoe S26
Burray S23
Burrells 10.3
Burrelton S24
Burridge 20.10
Burrill with Cowling 33.2
Burringham 28.8
Burrington (Devon) 12.2
Burrington (Here) 21.1
Burrington (Som) 38.7
Burrough Green 6.4
Burrough-on-the-Hill 27.3
Burrow with Burrow 26.1
Burrow* 38.3, 38.5
Burrowbridge 38.4
Burrs 19.3
Burry Port W6
Burscough 26.8
Burshill 15.2
Bursledon 20.9
Burslem 40.3
Burstall 41.6
Burstock 13.1
Burston 30.7
Burstow 42.10
Burstwick 15.2
Burtholme 10.1
Burthwaite 10.1
Burtle 38.1
Burton (Cheshire)* 7.3
Burton (Dorset) 13.8
Burton (Lincs) 28.1
Burton (Pemb) W16
Burton (Som) 38.5
Burton (W Sussex) 46.2
Burton (Wilts) 48.1
Burton (Wrexham) W22
Burton Agnes 15.2
Burton Bradstock 13.1
Burton Coggles 28.6
Burton Constable 15.2
Burton Dassett 44.5
Burton Fleming 15.2
Burton Green (part) 44.4, 45.6
Burton Hastings 44.3
Burton Hill 48.1
Burton Joyce 34.7
Burton Latimer 31.2
Burton Lazars 27.3
Burton Leonard 33.6
Burton Overy 27.8
Burton Pedwardine 28.4
Burton Pidsea 15.2
Burton Pynsent 38.5
Burton Salmon 33.8
Burton upon Stather 28.8
Burton upon Trent 40.5
Burton-cum-Walden 33.1
Burton-in-Kendal 10.5
Burton-in-Lonsdale 33.5
Burton-on-the-Wolds 27.2
Burton-upon-Yore 33.6
Burtonwood 7.1
Burwardsley (part) 7.3, 7.5
Burwarton 37.1
Burwash 16.2
Burwash Common 16.2
Burwash Weald 16.2
Burwell (Cambs) 6.4
Burwell (Lincs) 28.2
Bury (Cambs) 6.3
Bury (Gtr M'chester) 19.3
Bury (Som) 38.3
Bury (W Sussex) 46.2
Bury Hill (Gloucs) 18.7
Bury Hill (Here) 21.1
Bury St Edmunds 41.3
Buryas Bridge 9.1
Burythorpe 33.3
Busbridge 42.11
Busby S14
Busby Stoop (Sandhutton) 33.2
Buscot 35.4
Bushbury 45.1
Bushby 27.8
Bushey 22.10
Bushey Heath 22.10
Bushley 49.4
Bushmead (part) 2.1, 2.2
Bushmoor 37.1
Bushton 48.1
Bushwood 44.4
Buslingthorpe 28.1
Bussage 18.6
Busveal 9.1
Butcombe 38.7
Butetown (part) W4, W5
Butleigh 38.2
Butleigh Wootton 38.2
Butlers Cross 5.3
Butlers Marston 44.5
Butley 41.5
Butlocks Heath 20.9
Butsfield 14.1
Butt Lane 40.2
Buttercrambe with Bossall 33.3
Butterknowle 14.1
Butterleigh 12.4
Butterley 11.4
Buttermere (Cumbria) 10.2
Buttermere (Wilts) 48.1
Buttershaw 47.1
Butterstone S24
Butterton* 40.1, 40.2
Butterwick (Cumbria) 10.3
Butterwick (Durham) 14.1
Butterwick (Lincs) 28.5
Butterwick (N Yorks) 33.3
Butterwick with Newsham (Malton) 33.3
Butteryhaugh 32.1
Buttington W17
Button Street 25.8
Butts Batch 38.7
Butts Green (Essex) 17.7
Butts Green (Hants) 20.4
Buttsash 20.7
Buxbury 48.1
Buxhall 41.4
Buxted 16.1
Buxton (Derbys) 11.1
Buxton with Lammas 30.5
Buxworth 11.1
Bwlch (Anglesey) W1
Bwlch (Powys) W17
Bwlchderwin W11
Bwlchgwyn (part) W10, W22
Bwlchtocyn W11
Bwlchycibau W17
Bwlchyffridd W17
Byards Leap 28.4
Byermoor 43.3
Byers Green 14.1
Byfield 31.4
Byfleet 42.4
Byford 21.1
Bygrave 22.1
Byker 43.1
Byland with Wass 33.3
Bylaugh 30.3
Byley (part) 7.3, 7.5
Bynea W6
Byngs Heath* 37.1
Byram-cum-Sutton 33.8
Byrness 32.1
Bythorn 6.3
Byton 21.1
Bywell 32.1
Byworth 46.2
Cabourne 28.1
Cabrach S20
Cabus 26.2
Cadbury 12.4
Cadbury Heath 18.7
Caddington 2.2
Cadeby (Leics) 27.4
Cadeby (S Yorks) 39.2
Cadeleigh 12.4
Cadfarch W17
Cadgwith 9.1
Cadham S16
Cadishead 19.5
Cadle W19
Cadley 48.1
Cadmore End 5.3
Cadnam 20.7
Cadney 28.8
Cadole W10
Cadoxton W14
Cadwell 28.2
Cae Shon W8
Caeathro W11
Caego W22
Caeharris W12
Caehopkin W17
Caenby 28.1
Caeo W6
Caerau (part) W3, W5
Caerbragdy W4
Caerbryn W6

2

Caereinion Fechan W17
Caergeiliog W1
Caergwrle W10
Caerhun* W8, W11
Caerleon W15
Caernarfon W11
Caerphilly W4
Caersws W17
Caerwent W13
Caerwys W10
Caewern W14
Cainscross 18.6
Cairnbaan S3
Cairnbulg S1
Cairndow S3
Cairneyhill S16
Cairngorm S17
Cairnie S1
Cairnpapple S31
Cairnryan S10
Caister-on-Sea 30.6
Caistor 28.1
Caistor St Edmund 30.7
Cakebole 49.1
Calbourne 24.1
Calceby 28.2
Calcethorpe with Kelstern 28.2
Calcot (Coln St Aldwyn) 18.5
Calcot (Flint) W10
Calcot (Tetbury) 18.5
Calcutt 44.3
Caldbeck 10.2
Caldbergh with E Scrafton 33.1
Caldecote (Cambs) (part) 6.3, 6.5
Caldecote (Herts) 22.1
Caldecote (N'hants) 31.7
Caldecote (Norfolk) 30.3
Caldecote (Warks) 44.1
Caldecott (Cheshire) 7.3
Caldecott (N'hants) (see Chelveston)
Caldecott (Rutland) 36.1
Caldecotte 5.1
Calder S17
Calder Grove 47.5
Calderbank S22
Calderbrook 19.4
Caldercruix S22
Calderdale 47.3
Caldershaw 19.4
Caldey Island W16
Caldicot W13
Caldwell 33.1
Caldy 29.5
Caledfryn W4
Calendra 9.1
California (Falkirk) S15
California (Norfolk) 30.6
Calke 11.9
Callaly 32.1
Callander S29
Callands 7.1
Callanish S32
Callestick 9.1
Callington 9.1
Callow (Derbys) 11.3
Callow (Here) 21.1
Callow Hill 49.3
Callow Hill (Rock) 49.1
Calmore 20.7
Calmsden 18.5
Calne, Within & Without 48.1
Calow 11.4
Calshot 20.7
Calstock 9.1
Calstone 48.1
Calthorpe 30.1
Calthwaite 10.3
Calton (N Yorks) 33.5
Calton (Staffs) 40.1
Calveley 7.5
Calver 11.3
Calverhall 37.1
Calverleigh 12.4
Calverley 47.2
Calvert 5.2
Calverton (Bucks) 5.1
Calverton (Notts) 34.7
Calvine S24
Calvington 37.4
Calwich 40.5
Cam 18.6
Camber 16.2
Camberley 42.3
Camberwell (part) L22, L28
Camblesforth 33.8
Cambo 32.1
Cambois 32.1
Camborne 9.1
Cambourne (Cambs) 6.5
Cambridge (Cambs) 6.6
Cambridge (Gloucs) 18.6
Cambridge Batch 38.7
Cambrose 9.1
Cambus S8
Cambusbarron S29
Cambuslang S28
Camden L6
Camden Town L6
Camel Hill 38.5
Cameley 38.6
Camelford 9.1
Camelon S15
Camels 9.1
Camelsdale 46.2
Camerton (Cumbria) 10.2
Camerton (E Yorks) 15.2
Camerton (Som) 38.6
Cammeringham 28.1
Camp Hill 31.5
Camp Hill (W Mids) 45.5
Camp Hill (Warks) 44.2
Campbeltown S3
Camperdown 43.2
Campsall 39.2
Campsea Ash 41.5
Campsie Glen S12
Campton 2.2
Camrose W16
Camserney S24
Camusnagaul S17
Camusterrach S17
Camustiel S17
Canada (Hants) 20.4
Canada, Upper & Lower (Som) 38.7
Canary Wharf L30
Candlesby with Gunby 28.2
Candovers, The 20.1
Cane End 35.3
Canewdon 17.11
Canford Cliffs 13.6
Canford Heath 13.6
Canford Magna 13.6
Canisbay S17
Canley 45.7
Cann 13.2
Cann Hall L31
Canna S17
Cannards Grave 38.2
Cannich S17
Cannington 38.1
Cannock 40.7
Cannock Wood (part) 40.7, 40.8
Cannon Heath 20.1
Cannon Hill 45.5
Cannop 18.2
Canon Bridge 21.1
Canon Frome 21.1
Canon Pyon 21.1
Canonbie S10
Canonbury L19
Canons Ashby 31.4
Canons Marsh 4.1
Canonstown 9.1
Canterbury 25.5
Canterton 20.7
Cantley (Norfolk) 30.5
Cantley (S Yorks) 39.2
Canton W5
Cantref W17
Cantsfield 26.1
Canvey Island 17.13
Canwell 40.8
Canwick 28.4
Canworthy Water 9.1
Caol S17
Cape Cornwall 9.1
Cape Hill 45.4
Capel (Kent) 25.11
Capel (Surrey) 42.8
Capel Coch W1
Capel Colman W16
Capel Curig W8
Capel Dewi W6
Capel Garmon W8
Capel Graig W11
Capel Hendre W6
Capel Isaac W6
Capel Iwan W6
Capel St Andrew 41.5
Capel St Mary 41.6
Capel Seion W6
Capel-le-Ferne (part) 25.6, 25.13
Capel-y-Ffin W17
Capenhurst 7.3
Capheaton 32.1
Capitol Valley (Pontlottyn) W4
Capland 38.4
Cappercleuch S30
Capton 38.3
Caputh S24
Car Colston 34.8
Caradon Town 9.1
Carbis Bay 9.1
Carbost S17
Carbrooke 30.3
Carburton 34.1
Carclaze 9.1
Carcroft 39.2
Carden 7.3
Cardenden S16
Cardeston (see Alberbury)
Cardewless 10.1
Cardigan W7
Cardington (Beds) 2.1
Cardington (Shrop) (part) 37.1
Cardinham 9.1
Cardross S3
Careby 28.6
Careston S2
Carew W16
Carey 21.1
Carfin S22
Cargill S24
Cargo 10.1
Cargo Fleet (part) 33.9, 33.10
Cargreen 9.1
Cargurrel 9.1
Carham 32.1
Carhampton 38.3
Carharrack (part) 9.1
Carinish S32
Carisbrooke 24.1
Cark-in-Cartmel 10.5
Carkeel 9.1
Carkin (see Forcett)
Carlatton 10.1
Carlby 28.6
Carlecotes 39.1
Carleton (Cumbria)* 10.1, 10.3
Carleton (Lancs) 26.4
Carleton (N Yorks) 33.5
Carleton (Pontefract) 47.5
Carleton Forehoe 30.7
Carleton Rode 30.7
Carleton St Peter 30.7
Carley Hill 43.5
Carlin How 33.10
Carlingcott 38.6
Carlinghow 47.4
Carlisle 10.1
Carlogie S2
Carlops S30
Carloway S32
Carlton (Beds) 2.1
Carlton (Cambs) 6.5
Carlton (Leics) 27.4
Carlton (N Yorks)* 33.2, 33.8

Carlton (Notts) (part) 34.6, 34.7
Carlton (Stockton) 14.10
Carlton (W Yorks), Aireborough 47.2
Carlton (W Yorks), Rothwell 47.2
Carlton Colville 41.1
Carlton Curlieu 27.8
Carlton Highdale 33.1
Carlton Husthwaite 33.2
Carlton Miniott 33.2
Carlton Scroop 28.6
Carlton Town 33.1
Carlton-in-Lindrick 34.1
Carlton-le-Moorland 28.4
Carlton-on-Trent 34.3
Carluke S28
Carlyon Bay 9.1
Carmarthen W6
Carmel (Anglesey) W1
Carmel (Carm) W6
Carmel (Flint) W10
Carmel (Gwynedd) W11
Carmichael S28
Carmunnock S7
Carmyle S7
Carmyllie S2
Carn Brea 9.1
Carn Marth 9.1
Carnaby 15.2
Carnach S32
Carnan S32
Carnbee S16
Carnbo S24
Carneddi W11
Carnetown W18
Carnforth 26.1
Carnhell Green 9.1
Carnhot 9.1
Carnkie Redruth 9.1
Carnkie Wendron 9.1
Carnkief 9.1
Carnmenellis 9.1
Carno W17
Carnock S16
Carnon Crease 9.1
Carnon Downs 9.1
Carnoustie S2
Carnwath S28
Carnyorth 9.1
Carpenders Park 22.8
Carperby-cum-Thoresby 33.1
Carr (Gtr M'chester) 19.3
Carr (S Yorks) 39.4
Carr Bank 10.5
Carr Gate 47.5
Carr Hill 43.3
Carr Mill 29.3
Carr Vale 11.5
Carradale S3
Carrbridge S17
Carreghofa W17
Carreglefn W1
Carrick S3
Carrington S19
Carrington (Gtr M'chester) 19.8
Carrington (Lincs) 28.2
Carrington (Notts) 34.6
Carrog W9
Carron S15
Carronbridge S10
Carronshore S15
Carroway Head 40.8
Carrshield 32.1
Carrutherstown S10
Carrville 14.1
Carsethorn S10
Carsie S24
Carsington 11.3
Carskiey S3
Carsluith S10
Carsphairn S10
Carstairs S28
Carstairs Junction S28
Carswell Marsh 35.4
Carters Clay 20.4
Carters Green 45.4
Carterton 35.1
Carthew 9.1
Carthorpe 33.2
Cartington 32.1
Cartland S28
Cartmel 10.5
Cartmel Fell 10.5
Cartworth 47.4
Carway W6
Carwinley 10.1
Cary Fitzpaine 38.5
Cascade, Hengoed W4
Cascob W17
Casewick 28.6
Cashmoor 13.3
Cassington 35.1
Cassop-cum-Quarrington 14.1
Casterton 10.5
Castle Acre 30.2
Castle Ashby 31.7
Castle Bolton with East & West Bolton 33.1
Castle Bromwich 45.6
Castle Bytham 28.6
Castle Caereinion W17
Castle Camps 6.5
Castle Carlton 28.2
Castle Carrock 10.1
Castle Cary 38.5
Castle Church 40.4
Castle Combe 48.1
Castle Donington 27.1
Castle Douglas S10
Castle Eaton 48.2
Castle Eden 14.1
Castle Frome 21.1
Castle Green 37.4
Castle Gresley 11.9
Castle Hedingham 17.2
Castle Kennedy S10
Castle Levington 14.10
Castle Rising 30.2
Castle Sowerby 10.3
Castle Vale 45.5
Castlebay S32
Castlebythe W16
Castlecary S22
Castledean 13.7
Castlefields W4
Castleford 47.5
Castlelaw S19
Castlemartin W16
Castlemorton 49.4
Castlenau L27
Castlerigg (see St John's)
Castleside 14.1
Castlethorpe (Bucks) 5.1
Castlethorpe (Lincs) 28.8
Castleton (Derbys) 11.1
Castleton (Dorset) 13.1
Castleton (Gtr M'chester) 19.4
Castleton (N Yorks) 33.4
Castleton (Newport) W15
Castletown (Highland) S17
Castletown (T & W) 43.5
Castley 33.6
Caston 30.3
Castor 6.1
Caswell W19
Catbank, Coniston 10.5
Catbrain 18.7
Catbrook W13
Catchburn 32.1
Catchgate 14.1
Catcleugh 32.1
Catcliffe 39.4
Catcott 38.1
Catcune S19
Caterham 42.10
Catesby, Upper & Lower 31.4
Catfield 30.1
Catford L23
Catforth 26.6
Catfoss 15.2
Cathays W5
Cathedine W17
Cathedral Close (see St Davids)
Catherine Slack 47.1
Catherine-de-Barnes 45.6
Catherington 20.6
Catherston Leweston 13.1
Catherton 37.1
Cathiron 44.3
Catisfield 20.10
Catlodge S17
Catlowdy 10.1
Catmore 3.1
Caton with Littledale 26.1
Catrine S11
Catsfield 16.2
Catsgore 38.5
Catshill 49.2
Cattal 33.6
Catterall 26.2
Catterick 33.1
Catterlen 10.3
Catterton 33.8
Catteshall 42.11
Catthorpe 27.8
Cattistock 13.1
Catto (see Landmoth)
Catton (Derbys) 11.9
Catton (E Yorks) 15.2
Catton (N Yorks) 33.2
Catton (N'land) 32.1
Catton (Norwich) 30.4
Catwick 15.2
Catworth 6.3
Caudle Green 18.5
Caughall 7.3
Caulcott (Beds) 2.2
Caulcott (Oxon) 35.2
Cauldon 40.1
Cauldon Lowe 40.1
Cauldwell 11.9
Caundle Marsh 13.1
Caunsall 49.1
Caunton 34.3
Causeway Foot 47.3
Causeway Green 45.4
Causeway Head 47.3
Causey Park 32.1
Cautley 10.5
Cava S23
Cavendish 41.3
Cavenham 41.2
Caversfield 35.2
Caversham 3.2
Caverswall 40.1
Cawburn 32.1
Cawdor S17
Cawkwell 28.2
Cawood 33.8
Cawsand 9.1
Cawston (Norfolk) 30.5
Cawston (Warks) 44.3
Cawthorne (N Yorks) 33.3
Cawthorne (S Yorks) 39.1
Cawthorpe 28.6
Cawton 33.3
Caxton 6.5
Caynham 37.1
Caynton (part) 37.1, 37.4
Caythorpe (Lincs) 28.6
Caythorpe (Notts) 34.3
Cayton 33.4
Cayton (see South Stainley)
Cefn W8
Cefn Berain W8
Cefn Brith W8
Cefn Bryn Brain W6
Cefn Bychan W10
Cefn Coch W17
Cefn Coed W12
Cefn Cribbwr (part) W3, W14
Cefn Eurgain W10
Cefn Fforest W4
Cefn Hengoed W4
Cefn Mably W4
Cefn Mawr W17
Cefn y Bedd (part) W10, W22
Cefnblodwel 37.1
Cefnbrynbrain W6
Cefneithin W6
Cefnllys W17

Cefnmeiriadog W9
Cefnpennar W18
Cefnypant W6
Ceidio W11
Ceinws W17
Ceirog Ucha W22
Cellan W7
Cellarhead 40.1
Cemaes W1
Cemlyn W1
Cemmaes W17
Cenarth (part) W6, W7
Cennin W11
Central Milton Keynes 5.1
Ceres S16
Cerne Abbas 13.1
Cerney Wick 18.5
Cernioge W8
Cerrig-y-drudion W8
Cerrigceinwen W1
Cerrigman W1
Cesarea W11
Ceulanmaesmawr W7
Ceunant W11
Chaceley 18.1
Chacewater 9.1
Chackmore 5.2
Chackmore (see Radclive)
Chacombe 31.7
Chadderton 19.7
Chaddesden 11.7
Chaddesley Corbett 49.1
Chaddleworth 3.1
Chadlington 35.1
Chadshunt 44.5
Chadsmoor 40.7
Chadstone 31.7
Chadwell 27.3
Chadwell Heath (part) L1, L26
Chadwell St Mary 17.12
Chadwick End (part) 44.4, 45.6
Chaffcombe 38.5
Chafford Hundred, Grays 17.12
Chagford 12.3
Chaigley 26.3
Chailey 16.4
Chailey Green 16.4
Chainhurst, Marden 25.10
Chalbury 13.3
Chaldon 42.10
Chaldon Herring 13.5
Chale 24.1
Chale Green 24.1
Chalfont St Giles 5.4
Chalfont St Peter 5.4
Chalford (Gloucs) 18.6
Chalford (Oxon) 35.3
Chalgrave 2.2
Chalgrove 35.3
Chalk 25.2
Chalk End 17.7
Chalk Farm L6
Chalk Hill 2.2
Chalkhouse Green 35.3
Chalkshire 5.3
Chalkway 38.5
Chalkwell 25.4
Challaborough 12.9
Challacombe 12.2
Challock 25.12
Chalmington 13.1
Chalton (Beds) 2.2
Chalton (Hants) 20.6
Chalvey 3.5
Chalvington 16.1
Chanctonbury 46.3
Chandler's Ford (part) 20.4, 20.9
Chandler's Green (Hartley Wespall) 20.1
Chandlers Cross 22.8
Chantry 38.2
Chapel & Hill Chorlton 40.2
Chapel Allerton (Som) 38.1
Chapel Amble 9.1
Chapel Ascote 44.5
Chapel Brampton 31.4
Chapel Cleeve 38.3
Chapel End* 44.1, 44.2
Chapel Field 19.3
Chapel Haddlesey 33.8
Chapel Hill 28.4
Chapel Hill (Errol) S24
Chapel Lawn 37.1
Chapel Leigh 38.4
Chapel Milton 11.1
Chapel St Leonards 28.2
Chapel Stile 10.5
Chapel of Garioch S1
Chapel-en-le-Frith 11.1
Chapel-le-Dale 33.5
Chapelgarth Estate, Sunderland 43.5
Chapelhall S22
Chapelhill (Glenalmond) S24
Chapelknowe S10
Chapelton S28
Chapeltown (Glenlivet) S20
Chapeltown (Lancs) 26.10
Chapeltown (S Yorks) 39.3
Chapmansford 20.1
Chapmanslade (part) 38.2, 48.1
Chappel 17.3
Charcott 25.8
Chard 38.5
Chard Elm 38.5
Chard Junction 38.5
Chardleigh Green 38.5
Chardstock 12.7
Charfield 18.7
Charing 25.12
Charing Cross L33
Charingworth 18.5
Charity Banks 44.2
Charlbury 35.1
Charlcombe 38.6, 38.7
Charlcott 20.1
Charlcutt 48.1
Charlecote 44.5
Charlemont Farm 45.4
Charles 12.2
Charleston (Aberdeen) S1
Charleston (Angus) S2
Charlestown S16
Charlestown (Dorset) 13.1
Charlestown (Gtr M'chester) 19.6
Charlestown (St Austell) (Corn) 9.1
Charlestown (W Yorks)* 47.1, 47.3
Charlestown of Aberlour (see Aberlour)
Charlesworth 11.1
Charleton (East & West) 12.9
Charley 27.1
Charlinch 38.1
Charlton (Greenwich) L11
Charlton (Hants) 20.4
Charlton (Herts) 22.1
Charlton (N'hants) 31.7
Charlton (N'land) 32.1
Charlton (Shrop) 37.4
Charlton (Som) 38.2
Charlton (Surrey) 42.2
Charlton (W Sussex) 46.2
Charlton (Wilts) 48.1
Charlton (Worcs) 49.6
Charlton Adam 38.5
Charlton Horethorne 38.5
Charlton Kings 18.4
Charlton Mackrell 38.5
Charlton Marshall 13.2
Charlton Musgrove 38.5
Charlton St Peter 48.1
Charlton-All-Saints 48.1
Charlton-on-Otmoor 35.2
Charltons 33.10
Charlwood (part) 42.8, 46.1
Charminster (Bournemouth) 13.7
Charminster (W Dorset) 13.1
Charmouth 13.1
Charndon 5.2
Charney Bassett 35.4
Charnock Richard 26.9
Charsfield 41.5
Chart Sutton 25.10
Charter Alley 20.1
Charterhouse 38.2
Charterhouse (part) L19
Chartershall S29
Chartham 25.5
Chartham Hatch 25.5
Chartridge 5.4
Charvil 3.3
Charwelton 31.4
Chase Terrace 40.8
Chasetown 40.8
Chastleton 35.1
Chatburn 26.3
Chatham (Caerph) W4
Chatham (Kent) 25.3
Chatham Docks 25.3
Chatham Green 17.7
Chatham Maritime 25.3
Chatsworth 11.3
Chattenden 25.3
Chatter Alley 20.2
Chatteris 6.2
Chatterton 26.14
Chattisham 41.6
Chatton 32.1
Chavey Down 3.6
Chawleigh 12.4
Chawston 2.1
Chawton 20.6
Chazey Heath 35.3
Cheadle (Gtr M'chester) 19.9
Cheadle (Staffs) 40.1
Cheadle Hulme 19.9
Cheam (part) 42.6
Cheapside (part) 3.4, 3.6
Chearsley 5.2
Chebsey 40.4
Checkendon 35.3
Checkley (Here) 21.1
Checkley (Staffs) 40.1
Checkley-cum-Wrinehill 7.5
Chedburgh 41.3
Cheddar 38.1
Cheddington 5.2
Cheddleton 40.1
Cheddon Fitzpaine 38.4
Chedglow 48.1
Chedgrave 30.7
Chedington 13.1
Chediston 41.5
Chedworth 18.5
Chedzoy 38.1
Cheetham 19.6
Cheldon 12.2
Chelford 7.5
Chell 40.3
Chellaston 11.7
Chellington 2.1
Chellow Dene 47.1
Chelmarsh 37.1
Chelmer Village 17.7
Chelmick 37.1
Chelmondiston 41.6
Chelmorton 11.3
Chelmsford 17.7
Chelmsley Wood 45.6
Chelsea L20
Chelsfield L5
Chelsham 42.10
Chelston (Som) 38.4
Chelsworth 41.6
Cheltenham 18.4
Chelveston-cum-Caldecott 31.3
Chelvey 38.7
Chelvey Batch 38.7
Chelwood 38.6
Chelwood Gate 16.1
Chelworth 48.1
Chelynch 38.2
Cheney Longville 37.1
Chenies 5.4
Chepstow W13
Cherhill 48.1
Cherington (Gloucs) 18.5
Cherington (Warks) 44.5

Cheriton (Hants) 20.5
Cheriton (Kent) 25.13
Cheriton (Swansea) W19
Cheriton Bishop 12.4
Cheriton Fitzpaine 12.4
Cherrington 37.4
Cherry Burton 15.2
Cherry Hinton (part) 6.5, 6.6
Cherry Orchard 45.4
Cherry Willingham 28.1
Chertsey 42.1
Cheselbourne 13.1
Chesham (Bucks) 5.4
Chesham (Gtr M'chester) 19.3
Chesham Bois 5.4
Cheshunt 22.7
Cheslyn Hay 40.6
Chessington L21
Chester 7.3
Chester Moor 14.1
Chester Park 4.1
Chester-le-Street 14.1
Chesterblade 38.2
Chesterfield (Derbys) 11.2
Chesterfield (Staffs) 40.8
Chesters S30
Chesterton (Oxon) 35.2
Chesterton (Staffs) 40.2
Chesterton (Warks) 44.5
Chesterton* (Peterborough) 6.3
Chesterwood 32.1
Chestfield 25.5
Cheswardine 37.1
Cheswell 37.4
Cheswick 32.1
Cheswick Green 45.6
Chetnole 13.1
Chettisham 6.4
Chettle 13.2
Chetton 37.1
Chetwode 5.2
Chetwynd 37.4
Chetwynd Aston 37.4
Cheveley 6.4
Chevening 25.8
Cheverell, Gt & Little 48.1
Chevet 47.5
Chevington 41.3
Chevington Moor 32.1
Chevington Station 32.1
Chevithorne 12.4
Chew Magna 38.6
Chew Stoke 38.6
Chewton Keynsham 38.6
Chewton Mendip 38.2
Cheylesmore 45.7
Chibbet Post 38.3
Chibley 38.5
Chicheley 5.1
Chichester 46.2
Chickenley 47.4
Chickerell 13.1
Chickerell Road (part) 13.1, 13.4
Chicklade 48.1
Chickney 17.1
Chicksands 2.2
Chicksgrove 48.1
Chiddingfold 42.11
Chiddingly 16.1
Chiddingstone 25.8
Chiddingstone Causeway 25.8
Chiddingstone Hoath 25.8
Chideock 13.1
Chidham 46.2
Chidlow 7.3
Chidswell 47.4
Chieveley 3.1
Chignall 17.7
Chignall St James 17.7
Chignall Smealey 17.7
Chigwell (part) L26, 17.6
Chigwell Row 17.6
Chilbolton 20.4
Chilcombe (Dorset) 13.1
Chilcombe (Hants) 20.5
Chilcombe (Som) 38.3
Chilcompton 38.2
Chilcote (Leics) 27.1
Chilcote (Som) 38.2
Child Okeford 13.2
Childer Thornton 7.3
Childerley 6.5
Childrey 35.4
Childs Ercall 37.1
Childswickham 49.6
Childwall 29.2
Childwickbury 22.5
Chilfrome 13.1
Chilgrove 46.2
Chilham 25.12
Chilhampton 48.1
Chillaton 12.3
Chillenden 25.6
Chillerton 24.1
Chillesford 41.5
Chillingham 32.1
Chillington 38.5
Chilly Bridge 38.3
Chilmark 48.1
Chilson (Oxon) 35.1
Chilson (Som) 38.5
Chilson Common 38.5
Chilsworthy 9.1
Chiltern District 22.4
Chilthorne Domer 38.5
Chilton (Bucks) 5.2
Chilton (Durham) 14.1
Chilton (Oxon) 35.4
Chilton (Suffolk) 41.6
Chilton Candover 20.1
Chilton Cantelo 38.5
Chilton Foliat 48.1
Chilton Moor (part) 43.5
Chilton Polden 38.1
Chilton Trinity 38.1
Chilvers Coton 44.2
Chilwell 34.5
Chilworth (Hants) 20.4
Chilworth (Surrey) 42.7
Chilworthy (Som) 38.5
Chineham 20.1
Chineham (District Centre) 20.1
Chingford (London) (part) L31, 17.6
Chingford Hatch L31
Chinley 11.1
Chinnor 35.3
Chipnal 37.1
Chippenham (Cambs) 6.4
Chippenham, Within & Without (Wilts) 48.1
Chipperfield (part) 22.4, 22.8
Chipping 26.3
Chipping Campden 18.5
Chipping Norton 35.1
Chipping Ongar 17.6
Chipping Sodbury 18.7
Chipping Warden 31.7
Chipstable 38.4
Chipstead (Kent) 25.8
Chipstead (Surrey) 42.9
Chirbury 37.1
Chirk W22
Chirnside S30
Chirton 48.1
Chisbury 48.1
Chiselborough 38.5
Chiseldon 48.2
Chisenbury 48.1
Chislehampton 35.3
Chislehurst L5
Chislet 25.5
Chiswell Green 22.5
Chiswick (part) L9, L13, L18
Chisworth 11.1
Chithurst 46.2
Chitterne 48.1
Chittlehamholt 12.2
Chittlehampton 12.2
Chittoe & Westbrook 48.1
Chivelstone 12.9
Chivery 5.2
Chobham 42.3
Cholderton (part) 20.4, 48.1
Cholesbury-cum-St Leonards 5.4
Chollerford 32.1
Chollerton 32.1
Cholmondeley 7.5
Cholmondeston 7.5
Cholsey 35.3
Chop Gate (Bilsdale Midcable) 33.2
Choppington 32.1
Chopwell 43.3
Chorley (Cheshire) (part) 7.5
Chorley (Lancs) 26.9
Chorley (Staffs) 40.8
Chorley Hill 38.5
Chorleywood 22.8
Chorleywood Bottom 22.8
Chorlton (Cheshire) 7.5
Chorlton (Gtr M'chester) 19.6
Chorlton by Backford 7.3
Chorlton-cum-Hardy 19.6
Chorlton-on-Medlock 19.6
Choseley 30.2
Choulston 48.1
Choulton 37.1
Chowdene 43.3
Chowley 7.3
Chrishall (part) 6.5, 17.1
Christ's Hospital 46.3
Christchurch (Cambs) 6.2
Christchurch (Dorset) 13.8
Christchurch (Gloucs) 18.2
Christchurch (Newport) W15
Christchurch East 13.8
Christian Malford 48.1
Christians Cross 38.5
Christleton 7.3
Christmas Common 35.3
Christon 38.7
Christow 12.5
Chryston S22
Chudleigh 12.5
Chudleigh Knighton 12.5
Chulmleigh (part) 12.2, 12.4
Church (Lancs) 26.11
Church (Mersey) 29.2
Church Aston 37.4
Church Bay W1
Church Brampton 31.4
Church Brough 10.3
Church Broughton 11.9
Church Crookham 20.2
Church Eaton 40.4
Church End L2
Church End (Essex) 17.7
Church End (Hants) 20.1
Church End (Herts) 22.8
Church Farm 44.2
Church Fenton 33.8
Church Gresley 11.9
Church Hill (part) 49.3, 49.6
Church Knowle 13.5
Church Langley 17.5
Church Langton 27.8
Church Lawford 44.3
Church Lawton 7.5
Church Lench 49.6
Church Minshull 7.5
Church Oakley 20.1
Church Preen 37.1
Church Pulverbatch 37.1
Church Shocklach 7.3
Church Stowe 31.4
Church Stretton 37.1
Church Town 38.7
Church Village W18
Church Warsop 34.2
Church Westcote 18.5
Church Wilne 11.8
Churcham 18.2
Churchdown 18.1
Churchend (Gloucs) 18.7
Churchill (Oxon) 35.1
Churchill (Som) 38.7
Churchill (nr Kidderminster) (Worcs) 49.1
Churchill Green 38.7
Churchill Park W4
Churchmoor 37.1

2

Churchover 44.3
Churchstanton 38.4
Churchstoke W17
Churchstow 12.9
Churchtown (Lancs) 26.2
Churchtown (Mersey) 29.1
Churston Ferrers 12.10
Churt (part) 20.6, 42.11
Churton by Aldford 7.3
Churton by Farndon 7.3
Churton Heath 7.3
Churwell 47.2
Chute 48.1
Chute Forest 48.1
Chwilog W11
Chycoose 9.1
Chycowling 9.1
Cicelyford W13
Cilcain W10
Cilcennin W7
Cilfrew W14
Cilfynydd W18
Cilgerran W16
Cilgwyn W11
Ciliau Aeron W7
Cilmaengwyn W14
Cilmery W17
Cilybebyll W14
Cilycwm W6
Cilymaenllwyd W6
Cimla W14
Cinderford 18.2
Cinderhill (Notts/S Yorks) (part) 34.6, 39.4
Cinnamon Brow 7.1
Cippenham 3.5
Cirencester 18.5
City (Cowbridge) W21
City of London, The L7
Clachaig S3
Clachan (Argyll & Bute)) S3
Clachan (W Isles) S32
Clackmannan S8
Clackmarras S20
Clacton-on-Sea 17.4
Claife 10.5
Claines (part) 49.5, 49.6
Clanfield (Hants) 20.6
Clanfield (Oxon) 35.1
Clannaborough 12.4
Clanville (Hants) 20.4
Clanville (Som) 38.5
Claonaig S3
Clapham (Beds) 2.1
Clapham (Devon) 12.5
Clapham (W Sussex) 46.5
Clapham (part) L22
Clapham Common (part) L22, L32
Clapham Junction L32
Clapham-cum-Newby 33.5
Clappersgate 10.5
Clapton L12
Clapton (Gloucs) 18.5
Clapton (Som)* 38.2, 38.5
Clapton Common L12
Clapton Wick 38.7
Clapton-in-Gordano 38.7
Clara Vale 43.3
Clarbeston W16
Clarbeston Road W16
Clarborough 34.1
Clare (Oxon) 35.3
Clare (Suffolk) 41.3
Claremont 19.5
Clarencefield S10
Clarendon Park 48.1
Clareton (see Coneythorpe)
Clarks Green 42.8
Clarkston S14
Clase W19
Clashmore S17
Clashnessie S17
Clatford 48.1
Clathy S24
Clatt S1
Clatter W17
Clatterbridge 29.5
Clattercot 35.2
Clatterford End 17.7
Clatworthy 38.3
Claughton (Lancs) 26.1
Claughton (Mersey) 29.5
Claughton-on-Brock 26.2
Claverdon 44.5
Claverham 38.7
Clavering 17.1
Claverley 37.1
Claverton (Cheshire) 7.3
Claverton (Som) 38.6
Claverton (Wilts) 48.1
Clawddcoch (Cowbridge) W21
Clawddnewydd W9
Clawthorpe 10.5
Clawton 12.1
Claxby Pluckacre 28.2
Claxby St Andrew 28.2
Claxby with Moorby 28.2
Claxton (Co Durham) 14.9
Claxton (N Yorks) 33.3
Claxton (Norfolk) 30.7
Clay Bottom 4.1
Clay Coton 31.4
Clay Cross 11.4
Clay Hill 4.1
Claybrooke Magna 27.8
Claybrooke Parva 27.8
Claydon (Oxon) 35.2
Claydon (Suffolk) 41.4
Claygate 42.5
Claygate Cross 25.9
Clayhanger (Devon) 12.4
Clayhanger (Som) 38.5
Clayhanger (W Mids) 45.2
Clayhidon 12.4
Clayholes S2
Claypole 28.6
Claythorpe 28.2
Clayton (Gtr M'chester) 19.6
Clayton (Staffs) (part) 40.2, 40.4
Clayton (W Sussex) 46.4
Clayton (W Yorks) 47.1
Clayton Heights 47.1
Clayton West 47.4
Clayton with Frickley 39.2
Clayton-le-Dale 26.3
Clayton-le-Moors 26.11
Clayton-le-Woods (part) 26.9
Clayworth 34.1
Cleadale S17
Cleadon 43.4
Clearbrook 12.3
Clearwell 18.2
Cleasby 33.1
Cleatlam 14.1
Cleator Moor 10.4
Cleckheaton 47.4
Cleddon W13
Clee Hill 37.1
Clee St Margaret 37.1
Cleedownton 37.1
Cleestanton 37.1
Cleethorpes 28.9
Cleeton St Mary 37.1
Cleeve 38.7
Cleeve Hill 38.3
Cleeve Prior 49.6
Cleghorn S28
Clehonger 21.1
Cleish S24
Cleland S22
Clementhorpe 33.7
Clements End 18.2
Clench Common 48.1
Clenchwarton 30.2
Clent 49.2
Cleobury Mortimer 37.1
Cleobury North 37.1
Clephanton S17
Clerk Green 47.4
Clerkenwell L19
Clevedon 38.7
Cleverton (Wilts) 48.1
Cleverton (see Lea & Cleverton)
Clewer 3.4
Cley-next-the-Sea 30.1
Cliburn 10.3
Cliddesden 20.1
Cliff 47.4
Cliffe & South Duffield 33.8
Cliffe (Kent) 25.3
Cliffe (N Yorks) 33.1
Cliffe Woods 25.3
Clifford (Here) 21.1
Clifford (W Yorks) 47.2
Clifford Chambers 44.5
Clifford Mesne 18.2
Cliffsend (Ramsgate) 25.7
Clifton (Beds) 2.2
Clifton (Bristol) 4.1
Clifton (Cumbria) 10.3
Clifton (Derbys) 11.3
Clifton (Gtr M'chester) 19.5
Clifton (Lancs) 26.5
Clifton (N'land) 32.1
Clifton (Notts) 34.6
Clifton (Oxon) 35.2
Clifton (S Yorks) 39.2
Clifton (W Yorks) 47.3
Clifton (York) 33.7
Clifton Campville 40.8
Clifton Hampden 35.3
Clifton Maybank 13.1
Clifton Reynes 5.1
Clifton Village 34.6
Clifton Without 33.7
Clifton Wood 4.1
Clifton-on-Yore 33.2
Clifton-upon-Dunsmore 44.3
Clifton-upon-Teme 49.4
Cliftonville (Margate) 25.7
Climping 46.5
Clint 33.6
Clintmains S30
Clippesby 30.6
Clipsham 36.1
Clipston 31.4
Clipston on the Wolds 34.8
Clipstone (Beds) 2.2
Clipstone (Notts) (part) 34.2, 34.3
Clitheroe 26.3
Clive 37.1
Cliviger 26.12
Clixby 28.1
Clocaenog W9
Clock Face 29.3
Clodock 21.1
Cloford 38.2
Cloigyn W6
Clola S1
Clophill 2.2
Clopton (N'hants) 31.3
Clopton (Suffolk) 41.5
Close House 14.1
Closeburn S10
Closworth 38.5
Clothall 22.1
Clotley 37.4
Clotton Hoofield 7.3
Clough Dene 14.1
Clough Fold 26.14
Clough Foot 47.3
Cloughton 33.4
Cloutsham 38.3
Clova S2
Clovelly 12.1
Cloven Rocks 38.3
Clovenfords S30
Clowbridge 26.12
Clowne 11.5
Clows Top (part) 21.1, 49.1
Clubmoor 29.2
Cluddley 37.4
Clun 37.1
Clunas S17
Clunbury 37.1
Clungunford 37.1
Clunie S24
Clunton 37.1
Cluny (Aberdeen) S1
Cluny (Fife) S16
Clutton (Cheshire) 7.3
Clutton (Som) 38.6
Clwt Grugoer W8
Clwydyfagwr W12
Clydach (Monmth) W13
Clydach (Swansea) W19

Clydach Vale W18
Clydebank S9
Clydey W16
Clyffe Pypard 48.1
Clynderwen W16
Clyne W14
Clynnog W11
Clyro W17
Clyst Honiton 12.7
Clyst Hydon 12.7
Clyst St George 12.7
Clyst St Lawrence 12.7
Clyst St Mary 12.7
Clytha W13
Coads Green 9.1
Coal Aston 11.4
Coalbrookdale 37.4
Coalburn (N'land) 32.1
Coalburn (S Lanarks) S28
Coaley 18.6
Coalhill 17.7
Coalmoor 37.4
Coalpit Fields 44.2
Coalpit Heath 18.7
Coalport 37.4
Coalsnaughton S8
Coaltown of Balgonie S16
Coaltown of Wemyss S16
Coalville 27.1
Coalway 18.2
Coanwood 32.1
Coast S17
Coat 38.5
Coatbridge S22
Coate* 48.1, 48.2
Coates (Cambs) 6.2
Coates (Gloucs) 18.5
Coates (W Sussex) 46.2
Coates by Stow 28.1
Coatham Mundeville 14.8
Cobbinshaw S31
Cobbs 7.1
Coberley 18.5
Cobhall 21.1
Cobham (Kent) 25.2
Cobham (Surrey) 42.5
Cobley 49.2
Cobnor 46.2
Cobridge 40.3
Cock Clarks 17.8
Cockayne Hatley 2.2
Cockburnspath S30
Cockenzie S13
Cockerham 26.1
Cockermouth 10.2
Cockernhoe 22.1
Cockett W19
Cockfield (Durham) 14.1
Cockfield (Suffolk) 41.6
Cockhill 38.5
Cocking 46.2
Cockington 12.10
Cocklake 38.1
Cockle Park 32.1
Cockleford 18.5
Cockley Cley 30.3
Cockpen S19
Cockpole Green (part) 3.3, 3.4
Cocks (Perranzabuloe) 9.1
Cockshutford 37.1
Cockshutt 37.1
Cockthorpe 30.1
Cockwells 9.1
Cockwood 12.5
Coddenham 41.4
Coddington (Cheshire) 7.3
Coddington (Notts) 34.3
Coddington (Worcs) 21.1
Codford 48.1
Codicote 22.1
Codnor 11.6
Codnor Park 11.6
Codrington 18.7
Codsall 40.6
Codsend 38.3
Coed Cae W4
Coed Coch W8
Coed Eva W20
Coed Talon W10
Coed-y-cwm W18
Coed-y-parc W11
Coed-yr-allt (part) 37.1
Coedana W1
Coedcanlas, Martletwy W16
Coedely W18
Coedkernew W15
Coedpenmaen W18
Coedpoeth W22
Coedway W17
Coedybrain (Llanbradach) W4
Coelbren W17
Coffee Hall 5.1
Coffinswell 12.5
Cofton 12.5
Cofton Hackett 49.2
Cogenhoe 31.7
Coggeshall 17.2
Coignafearn S17
Coity W3
Coker Marsh 38.5
Colan 9.1
Colaton Raleigh 12.7
Colburn 33.1
Colbury 20.7
Colby (Cumbria) 10.3
Colby (Norfolk) 30.1
Colchester 17.3
Cold Ash 3.1
Cold Ashby 31.4
Cold Ashton 18.7
Cold Aston 18.5
Cold Blow W16
Cold Brayfield 5.1
Cold Hanworth 28.1
Cold Hatton 37.4
Cold Hesledon 14.1
Cold Hiendley 47.5
Cold Higham 31.7
Cold Inn W16
Cold Kirby 33.3
Cold Newton 27.8
Cold Norton 17.8
Cold Overton 27.3
Coldbackie S17
Coldbrook W13
Coldean 16.3
Colden 47.3
Colden Common 20.5
Coldham 6.2
Coldharbour (Oxon) 35.5
Coldharbour (Surrey) 42.8
Coldingham S30
Coldred 25.6
Coldridge 12.4
Coldstream S30
Coldwaltham 46.3
Coldwell (Gentleshaw) 40.8
Coldweston 37.1
Coldwind 9.1
Cole 38.5
Cole Green 22.3
Cole Henley 20.1
Colebatch 37.1
Colebrooke 12.4
Coleby* 28.4, 28.8
Coleford (Devon) 12.4
Coleford (Gloucs) 18.2
Coleford (Som) 38.2
Coleford Water 38.3
Colehill 13.3
Colehurst 37.1
Colemans Hatch 16.1
Colemere 37.1
Colemore 20.6
Coleorton 27.1
Colerne 48.1
Colesbourne 18.5
Colesden 2.1
Coleshill (Bucks) 5.4
Coleshill (Flint) W10
Coleshill (Oxon) 35.4
Coleshill (Warks) 44.1
Coley (Berks) 3.2
Coley (W Yorks) 47.3
Colgate 46.3
Colinsburgh S16
Colinton S6
Colintraive S3
Colkirk 30.3
Coll, Isle of S3
Collace S24
Collafirth S26
College Town 3.6
Collenan S27
Collessie S16
Collier Row L16
Collier St, Marden 25.10
Collier St, Yalding 25.10
Colliers Wood L24
Colliery Row 43.5
Collieston S1
Collin S10
Collingbourne Ducis 48.1
Collingbourne Kingston 48.1
Collingham (Notts) 34.3
Collingham (W Yorks) 47.2
Collington 21.1
Collingtree 31.5
Collins Green 7.1
Collycroft 44.2
Collyhurst 19.6
Collyweston 31.3
Colmonell S27
Colmworth 2.1
Coln Rogers 18.5
Coln St Aldwyn 18.5
Coln St Dennis 18.5
Colnbrook & Poyle 3.5
Colne (Cambs) 6.3
Colne (Lancs) 26.13
Colne Bridge 47.4
Colne Engaine 17.2
Colne Valley 47.4
Colney 30.7
Colney Heath 22.5
Colney Street 22.5
Colonsay, Isle of S3
Colsterdale 33.6
Colsterworth 28.6
Colston Bassett 34.8
Colthouse 10.5
Coltishall 30.5
Colton (Cumbria) 10.5
Colton (N Yorks) 33.8
Colton (Norfolk) 30.7
Colton (Staffs) 40.8
Columbia 43.5
Colva W17
Colvend S10
Colveston 30.3
Colwall 21.1
Colwell 32.1
Colwell Bay 24.1
Colwich 40.4
Colwick (part) 34.6, 34.7
Colwinston W21
Colworth 46.2
Colwyn W17
Colwyn Bay W8
Colyton 12.7
Combe (Berks) 3.1
Combe (Devon) (see Haccombe)
Combe (Here) 21.1
Combe (Huish Episcopi) 38.5
Combe (Oxon) 35.1
Combe (W Crewkerne) 38.5
Combe Common 38.5
Combe Florey 38.4
Combe Hay 38.6
Combe Martin 12.2
Combe Raleigh 12.7
Combe St Nicholas 38.5
Combe Street 38.5
Combe Sydenham 38.3
Combe Throop 38.5
Combefishacre 12.5
Combeinteignhead 12.5
Comberbach 7.3
Comberford 40.8
Combermere (Cheshire) 7.5
Combermere (Shrop) 37.1
Comberton 6.5
Combeshead 38.3
Combpyne Rousdon 12.7
Combrook 44.5
Combs (Derbys) 11.1
Combs (Suffolk) 41.4

2

Combs (W Yorks) 47.4
Combses 38.5
Combwich 38.1
Comeytrowe 38.4
Comford 9.1
Comfort* 9.1
Commins Coch W17
Common Hill 21.1
Common Moor 9.1
Common Platt (part) 48.1, 48.2
Common Wood (Shrop) 37.1
Commondale 33.4
Commonside 11.4
Commonwood 22.8
Compstall 19.9
Compton (Berks) 3.1
Compton (Surrey) 42.7
Compton (W Sussex) 46.2
Compton Abbas 13.2
Compton Abdale 18.5
Compton Bassett 48.1
Compton Beauchamp 35.4
Compton Bishop 38.1
Compton Chamberlayne 48.1
Compton Dando 38.6
Compton Dundon 38.5
Compton Durville 38.5
Compton Greenfield 18.7
Compton Martin (part) 38.2, 38.6
Compton Pauncefoot 38.5
Compton Scorpion 44.5
Compton Valence 13.1
Compton Verney 44.5
Compton Wynyates 44.5
Comrie S24
Concord 43.5
Conderton 49.6
Condicote 18.5
Condorrat S22
Condover 37.1
Coney Hill 18.3
Coney Weston 41.3
Coneypark S15
Coneysthorpe 33.3
Coneythorpe & Clareton 33.6
Conford 20.6
Congdon's Shop 9.1
Congerstone 27.4
Congham 30.2
Congleton 7.5
Congresbury 38.7
Conham (part) 4.1, 18.7
Coningsby 28.2
Conington (part) 6.3, 6.5
Conisborough 39.2
Conisborough Parks 39.2
Conisholme 28.2
Coniston (Cumbria) 10.5
Coniston (E Yorks) 15.2
Coniston Cold 33.5
Conistone with Kilnsey 33.5
Connah's Quay W10
Connel S3
Conniburrow 5.1
Connor Downs 9.1
Conon Bridge S17
Cononley 33.5
Conquermoor Heath 37.4
Consall 40.1
Consett 14.1
Constable Burton 33.1
Constantine 9.1
Constantine Bay 9.1
Contin S17
Conwil Elfed W6
Conwy W8
Cookbury 12.1
Cookham 3.4
Cookham Dean 3.4
Cookhill (Worcs) 49.6
Cookley Green 35.3
Cooksbridge 16.4
Cooksmill Green 17.7
Coole Pilate 7.5
Coolham 46.3
Cooling 25.3
Coombe (part) 9.1
Coombe Bissett 48.1
Coombe Dingle 4.1
Coombe Fields 44.3
Coombes 46.7
Cooper St 25.6
Coopersale 17.6
Cootham 46.3
Cop Street 25.6
Copdock & Washbrook 41.6
Copford with Easthorpe 17.3
Copgrove 33.6
Cople 2.1
Copley (Durham) 14.1
Copley (W Yorks) 47.3
Copley Hill 47.4
Copmanthorpe 33.7
Coppenhall (Cheshire) 7.5
Coppenhall (Staffs) 40.6
Coppett Hill 21.1
Coppingford 6.3
Coppleham Cross 38.3
Copplestone 12.4
Coppull 26.9
Copster Green 26.3
Copston Magna 44.3
Copt Hewick 33.6
Copt Oak 27.4
Copthorne 46.4
Coptiviney 37.1
Copythorne 20.7
Corbridge 32.1
Corbriggs 11.4
Corby 31.1
Corby Glen 28.6
Corby Hill 10.1
Corehouse S28
Coreley 37.1
Corfe 38.4
Corfe Castle 13.5
Corfe Mullen 13.3
Corfton 37.1
Corgarff S1
Corhampton 20.5
Corley 44.1
Corley Moor (part) 44.1
Cormiston S28
Cornbank S19
Cornborough (see Sheriff Hutton)
Cornbury & Wychwood 35.1
Cornforth 14.1
Cornforth Lane 14.1
Cornhill (Aberdeen) S1
Cornhill (Staffs) 40.3
Cornhill-on-Tweed 32.1
Cornholme 47.3
Cornish Hall End (Findingfield) 17.2
Cornsay 14.1
Cornsay Colliery 14.1
Corntown (Vale of Glamorgan) W21
Cornwell 35.1
Cornwood 12.9
Cornworthy 12.9
Coronation 14.1
Corpach S17
Corpusty 30.1
Corran, North S17
Corrie S21
Corrie Common S10
Corringham (Essex) 17.12
Corringham (Lincs) 28.1
Corris W11
Corrour Station S17
Corscombe 13.1
Corse 18.2
Corsenside 32.1
Corsham 48.1
Corsley 48.1
Corsock S10
Corston (Som) 38.6
Corston (Wilts) 48.1
Cortachy S2
Corton (Suffolk) 41.1
Corton (Wilts) 48.1
Corton Denham 38.5
Corwen W9
Coryton 12.3
Cosby 27.6
Coseley (part) 45.1, 45.3
Cosford 44.3
Cosgrove 31.7
Cosheston W16
Cossall 34.5
Cossington (Leics) 27.2
Cossington (Som) 38.1
Cost-is-Lost 9.1
Costessey, Old & New 30.7
Costhorpe 34.1
Costock 34.8
Coston (Lincs) 27.3
Coston (Norfolk) 30.7
Cotcliffe (Sowerby-under-Cotcliffe) 33.2
Cote Heath 11.1
Cotebrook 7.3
Cotehill 10.1
Cotes (Leics) 27.2
Cotes Heath 40.4
Cotes, Levens (Cumbria) 10.5
Cotesbach 27.8
Cotgrave 34.8
Cotham (Bristol) 4.1
Cotham (Notts) 34.3
Cothelstone 38.4
Cotheridge 49.4
Cotherstone 14.1
Cothill 35.4
Cotleigh 12.7
Coton (Cambs) 6.5
Coton (N'hants) 31.4
Coton (Shrop) 37.1
Coton (Staffs) 40.4
Coton (Warks) 44.2
Coton Green (part) 40.8, 40.9
Coton-in-the-Clay 40.5
Coton-in-the-Elms 11.9
Cottam (E Yorks) 15.2
Cottam (Lancs) 26.6
Cottam (Notts) 34.1
Cottenham 6.5
Cottered 22.3
Cotteridge 45.5
Cotterstock 31.3
Cottesbrooke 31.4
Cottesmore 36.1
Cottingham (E Yorks) 15.2
Cottingham (N'hants) 31.1
Cottingley 47.1
Cottingtons Hill 20.1
Cottingwith 15.2
Cottisford 35.2
Cotton (Staffs) 40.1
Cotton (Suffolk) 41.4
Cotton Abbotts 7.3
Cotton Edmunds 7.3
Cotton End 2.1
Cotwall 37.4
Couch's Mill 9.1
Coughton (Here) 21.1
Coughton (Warks) 44.5
Coulby Newham 33.9
Coulsdon (part) L8
Coulston 48.1
Coulter S28
Coultershaw 46.2
Coulton 33.3
Cound 37.1
Coundon 14.1
Coundon (W Mids) 45.7
Coundon Gate 14.1
Coundon Grange 14.1
Countesthorpe 27.6
Counthorpe 28.6
Countisbury 12.2
County 29.2
County Gate 38.3
County Oak 46.1
Coupar Angus S24
Court Hill 48.1
Court Place 38.3
Court-at-Street 25.13
Courteenhall 31.7
Cousland S19
Cousley Wood 16.1
Cove (Aberdeen) S4
Cove (Devon) 12.4

Cove (Hants) 20.3
Cove (Highland) S17
Covehithe 41.1
Coven 40.6
Coven Heath 40.6
Coveney 6.4
Covenham St Bartholomew 28.2
Covenham St Mary 28.2
Covent Garden (part) L6, L33
Coventry 45.7
Coverack 9.1
Coverham with Agglethorpe 33.1
Covington (Cambs) 6.3
Covington (S Lanarks) S28
Cowan Head, Burneside 10.5
Cowark 26.3
Cowbar 33.10
Cowbit 28.7
Cowbridge (Lincs) 28.2
Cowbridge (Vale Glam) W21
Cowden (E Yorks) 15.2
Cowden (Kent) 25.8
Cowden Pound 25.8
Cowdenbeath S16
Cowes 24.1
Cowesby 33.2
Cowesfield 48.1
Cowfold 46.3
Cowgate 43.1
Cowgill, Dent 10.5
Cowgrove 13.3
Cowhill 18.7
Cowick (see Snaith)
Cowie S29
Cowlam 15.2
Cowlands 9.1
Cowlersley 47.4
Cowley (Gloucs) 18.5
Cowley (Oxon) 35.5
Cowling 33.5
Cowlinge 41.3
Cowpe 26.14
Cowpen Bewley 14.10
Cowplain 20.13
Cowshill 14.1
Cowslip Green 38.7
Cox Green (Berks) 3.4
Cox Green (Essex) 17.7
Cox Hill 9.1
Coxbench 11.6
Coxford 20.8
Coxgreen (T & W) 43.5
Coxheath 25.10
Coxhoe 14.1
Coxley 38.2
Coxlodge 43.1
Coxwold 33.2
Coychurch W3
Coylton S27
Coylumbridge S17
Coytrahen W3
Crabbs Cross 49.3
Crackenedge 47.4
Crackenthorpe 10.3
Crackington Haven 9.1
Cracoe 33.5
Cradley (W Mids) (part) 45.3, 45.4
Cradley (Worcs) 21.1
Cradley Heath 45.4
Cradoc W17
Crafthole 9.1
Crafton 5.2
Cragg Vale 47.3
Craghead 14.1
Craichie S2
Craig Cefn Parc W19
Craig Penllyne (Cowbridge) W21
Craig Rhymney W4
Craiganour S24
Craigellachie S20
Craigend S24
Craighouse S3
Craigie S27
Craignant 37.1
Craigneuk S22
Craignure S3
Craigo S2
Craigrothie S16
Craigton S2
Crail S16
Crailing S30
Crakehall 33.2
Crakehill (see Eldmire)
Crakemarsh 40.5
Crambe 33.3
Cramlington 32.1
Cramond S6
Crampmoor 20.4
Cranage 7.5
Cranborne 13.3
Cranbourne 3.6
Cranbrook (Devon) 12.7
Cranbrook (Kent) 25.11
Crane Moor 39.1
Cranfield 2.2
Cranford L18
Cranford (Cranford St John & Cranford St Andrews) 31.2
Cranham 18.6
Cranham (London) L16
Cranhill 44.5
Crank 29.3
Cranleigh 42.11
Cranmore (I of W) 24.1
Cranmore (Som) 38.2
Cranoe 27.8
Cransford 41.5
Cranshaws S30
Cransley 31.2
Cranston S19
Cranswick 15.2
Crantock 9.1
Cranwell 28.4
Cranwich 30.3
Cranworth 30.3
Craster 32.1
Craswall 21.1
Cratfield 41.5
Crathie S1
Crathorne 33.2
Craven Arms 37.1
Crawcrook 43.3
Crawford S28
Crawfordjohn S28
Crawley (Hants) 20.5
Crawley (Oxon) 35.1
Crawley (W Sussex) 46.1
Crawley Down 46.4
Crawshawbooth 26.14
Crawtor Hill 38.3
Cray W17
Crayford L3
Crayke 33.2
Crays Hill 17.10
Crays Pond 35.3
Crazies Hill (part) 3.3, 3.4
Creacombe 12.2
Creagorry S32
Creamore 37.1
Crean 9.1
Creaton, Gt & Little 31.4
Creca S10
Credenhill 21.1
Crediton 12.4
Creech Heathfield 38.4
Creech St Michael 38.4
Creed 9.1
Creegbrawse 9.1
Creekmoor 13.6
Creeting St Mary 41.4
Creeting St Peter 41.4
Creeton 28.6
Creetown S10
Cregrina W17
Cremyll 9.1
Crendell Cripplestyle 13.3
Creslow 5.2
Cressage 37.1
Cressbrook 11.3
Cresselly W16
Cressing 17.2
Cressingham, Gt & Little 30.3
Cresswell (N'land) 32.1
Creswell (Derbys) (see Elmton)
Creswell (Staffs) (part) 40.1, 40.4
Creswell Green 40.8
Cretingham 41.5
Crew Green (Powys) W17
Crewe 7.5
Crewe by Farndon 7.3
Crewe Green (Cheshire) 7.5
Crewkerne 38.5
Crews Hole 4.1
Crianlarich S29
Cribbs Causeway 18.7
Criccieth W11
Crich 11.6
Crichton S19
Crick (Monmth) W13
Crick (N'hants) 31.4
Crickadarn W17
Cricket Hill 20.2
Cricket Malherbie 38.5
Cricket St Thomas 38.5
Crickett 37.1
Crickheath 37.1
Crickhowell W17
Cricklade 48.1
Crickleaze 38.5
Cricklewood (part) L2, L4, L6
Crickmerry 37.1
Criddlestyle 20.7
Cridling Stubbs 33.8
Crieff S24
Criftins 37.1
Criggion (see Bausley)
Crigglestone 47.5
Crimchard 38.5
Crimond S1
Crimplesham 30.2
Crimps 37.1
Crimscote 44.5
Crinan S3
Cringleford 30.7
Cringles 47.1
Crinow W16
Cripple Hill 38.5
Cripplesease 9.1
Cripps Corner 16.2
Croachy S17
Croanford 9.1
Crock Street 38.5
Crockenhill 25.8
Crocker End 35.3
Crockerhill 46.2
Crockernwell 12.3
Crockers Ash 21.1
Crockerton 48.1
Crocketford S10
Crockford Lane 20.1
Crockham Hill 25.8
Croes Bychan W13
Croeserw W14
Croesor W11
Croespenmaen W4
Croesyceiliog (Carm) W6
Croesyceiliog (Torfaen) W20
Croford 38.4
Croft (Cheshire) 7.1
Croft (Here) 21.1
Croft (Leics) 27.6
Croft (Lincs) 28.2
Croft End 4.1
Croft Pool 44.2
Croft-on-Tees 33.1
Croftamie (Stirling) S29
Crofthandy (part) 9.1
Crofton (Hants) 20.10
Crofton (W Yorks) 47.5
Crofton (Wilts) 48.1
Crofty W19
Croglin 10.3
Croick S17
Cromarty S17
Crombie S16
Cromdale S17
Cromer (Herts) 22.3
Cromer (Norfolk) 30.1
Cromford 11.3

2

Cromhall 18.7
Cromore S32
Crompton 19.7
Cromwell 34.3
Crondall 20.2
Cronton 29.4
Crook (Cumbria) 10.5
Crook (Durham) 14.1
Crookedholm S11
Crookfur S14
Crookgate 14.1
Crookhall 14.1
Crookham 32.1
Crookham Village 20.2
Crooklands 10.5
Crooksbarn 14.10
Croome D'Abitot 49.4
Cropredy 35.2
Cropthorne 49.6
Cropton 33.3
Cropwell Bishop 34.8
Cropwell Butler 34.8
Crosby (Lincs) 28.8
Crosby (Mersey) 29.1
Crosby (N Yorks) 33.2
Crosby Garett 10.3
Crosby Ravensworth 10.3
Crosby-on-Eden 10.1
Croscombe 38.2
Crosemere 37.1
Crosland Moor 47.4
Cross (Shrop) 37.1
Cross (Som) 38.1
Cross Ash 40.8, W13
Cross Bank (Rock) 49.1
Cross Hands W6
Cross Heath 40.2
Cross Houses 37.1
Cross Keys W4
Cross Roads 47.1
Cross Stones 47.3
Cross-in-Hand 16.1
Crossacres 19.6
Crossbost S32
Crossbush 46.5
Crosscanonby 10.2
Crosscoombe 9.1
Crosscrake 10.5
Crossens 29.1
Crossflatts 47.1
Crossford (Fife) S16
Crossford (S Lanarks) S28
Crossgates (Fife) S16
Crossgates (N Yorks) 33.4
Crosshill (Fife) S16
Crosshill (S Ayrs) S27
Crosshills 33.5
Crosshouse S11
Crosslee S25
Crossmichael S10
Crossway Green 49.6
Crossways 13.1
Crosthwaite 10.5
Croston 26.9
Crostwick 30.5
Crostwight 30.1
Crouch (Kent) 25.9
Crouch End (part) L14, L19
Croucheston 48.1
Croughton (Cheshire) 7.3
Croughton (N'hants) 31.7
Crow 20.7
Crow Edge 39.1
Crow Hill 21.1
Crow's Nest 9.1
Crowan 9.1
Crowborough 16.1
Crowcombe 38.3
Crowcombe Heathfield 38.3
Crowd Hill 20.9
Crowell 35.3
Crowfield (N'hants) 31.7
Crowfield (Suffolk) 41.4
Crowhill Park 44.2
Crowhurst (E Sussex) 16.2
Crowhurst (Surrey) 42.10
Crowland (part) 6.1, 28.7
Crowlas 9.1
Crowle (N Lincs) 28.8
Crowle (Worcs) 49.6
Crowmarsh Gifford 35.3
Crown Wood 3.6
Crownhill 5.1
Crownthorpe 30.7
Crowntown 9.1
Crows-an-wra 9.1
Crowsley 35.3
Crowther 43.5
Crowthorne (part) 3.3, 3.6
Crowton 7.3
Croxall 40.8
Croxby 28.1
Croxdale 14.1
Croxden 40.5
Croxley Green 22.8
Croxteth 29.2
Croxton & Kirmington (Lincs) 28.8
Croxton (Cambs) 6.5
Croxton (Norfolk) (part) 30.1, 30.3
Croxton (Staffs) 40.4
Croxton Kerrial 27.3
Croy (Highland) S17
Croy (N Lanarks) S22
Croydon L8
Croydon (Cambs) 6.5
Cruckton 37.1
Cruden Bay S1
Crudgington 37.4
Crudie S1
Crudwell 48.1
Crugsillick 9.1
Crugybar W6
Crulivig S32
Crumlin W4
Crumpsall 19.6
Crumpsbrook 37.1
Crundale 25.12
Crunwere W16
Cruwys Morchard 12.4
Crux Easton 20.1
Crwbin W6
Cryers Hill 5.3
Crymlyn Burrows W14
Crymych W16
Crynant W14
Crystal Palace (part) L5, L22
Cubbington 44.4
Cubert 9.1
Cubitt Town L30
Cubley 11.3
Cublington 5.2
Cuby 9.1
Cuckfield 46.4
Cuckfield Rural 46.4
Cucklington 38.5
Cuckney 34.1
Cuckney Hill 34.1
Cuckoo Oak 37.4
Cuddesdon 35.3
Cuddington (Bucks) 5.2
Cuddington (Cheshire)* 7.3
Cudworth (S Yorks) 39.1
Cudworth (Som) 38.5
Cudworth (Surrey) 42.8
Cuerdale (see Samlesbury)
Cuerden (part) 26.7, 26.9
Cuerdley 7.1
Cuffley 22.6
Cuikenburn S19
Culbokie S17
Culbone 38.3
Culcheth 7.1
Culdrose 9.1
Culford 41.3
Culgaith 10.3
Culham 35.3
Culkein S17
Culkerton 18.5
Cullen S20
Cullercoats 43.2
Cullicudden S17
Cullingworth 47.1
Cullingworth Gate 47.1
Cullipool S3
Culloden S17
Cullompton 12.4
Culm Davy 12.4
Culmhead 38.4
Culmington 37.1
Culmstock 12.4
Culpho 41.5
Culrain S17
Culross S16
Culsalmond S1
Culter S4
Cults S4
Culverstone 25.2
Culverthorpe 28.4
Culworth 31.7
Cumbernauld S22
Cumberworth (Lincs) 28.2
Cumberworth (W Yorks) 47.4
Cumdivock 10.1
Cuminestown S1
Cummersdale 10.1
Cummertrees S10
Cummingston S20
Cumnock S11
Cumnor 35.4
Cumrew 10.1
Cumwhinton 10.1
Cumwhitton 10.1
Cundall with Leckby 33.6
Cunningsburgh S26
Cunsey 10.5
Cupar S16
Cupernham 20.4
Curbar 11.3
Curborough 40.8
Curbridge (Hants) 20.5
Curbridge (Oxon) 35.1
Curdworth 44.1
Curin S17
Curland 38.4
Currie S6
Curriott Hill 38.5
Curry Mallet 38.5
Curry Rivel 38.5
Curtisden Green 25.11
Curtisknowle 12.9
Cury 9.1
Cury Cross Lanes 9.1
Cusgarne 9.1
Cushuish 38.4
Cusop 21.1
Cusworth 39.2
Cut Mill 46.2
Cutcombe 38.3
Cutler Heights 47.1
Cutnall Green 49.6
Cutsdean 18.5
Cutsyke 47.5
Cutteslowe 35.5
Cutthorpe 11.4
Cuttiford's Door 38.5
Cutting Hill 48.1
Cuxham 35.3
Cuxton 25.3
Cuxwold 28.1
Cwm W2, W9
Cwm Bargoed W4
Cwm Cych W6
Cwm Gwaun W16
Cwm Penanner W8
Cwm Pennant W11
Cwm-y-glo W11
Cwmaman W18
Cwmamman W6
Cwmann W6
Cwmavon (Neath) W14
Cwmavon (Torfaen) W20
Cwmbach W18
Cwmbach (Carm) W6
Cwmbran W20
Cwmbwrla W19
Cwmcarn W4
Cwmcarvon W13
Cwmdare W18
Cwmdu (Carm) W6
Cwmdu (Powys) W17
Cwmduad W6
Cwmdwyfran W6
Cwmeldeg W4
Cwmfarm (Caerph) W4
Cwmfelin (Bedlinog) W12
Cwmfelin (Maesteg) W3
Cwmfelin Boeth W6
Cwmfelin Mynach W6

Cwmfelinfach W4
Cwmffrwd W6
Cwmgors W14
Cwmgwili W6
Cwmgwrach W14
Cwmifor W6
Cwmisfael W6
Cwmllin W17
Cwmllynfell W14
Cwmmawr W6
Cwmmiles W6
Cwmnantygwynt W4
Cwmnantymeichiad W17
Cwmparc W18
Cwmpengraig W6
Cwmpennar W18
Cwmrheidol W7
Cwmrhydyceirw W19
Cwmsyfiog W4
Cwmtillery W2
Cwmtwrch (Lower & Upper) (part) W14, W17
Cwmyoy W13
Cwmystradllyn W11
Cyfarthfa W12
Cyffylliog W9
Cymau W10
Cymmer W14
Cyncoed W5
Cynghordy W6
Cynheidre W6
Cynonville W14
Cynwyd W9
Cynwyl Caeo W6
Cynwyl Elfed W6
Daccombe 12.5
Dacre (Cumbria) 10.3
Dacre (N Yorks) 33.6
Daddry Shield 14.1
Dadford 5.2
Dadlington 27.4
Dafen W6
Daglingworth 18.5
Dagnall 5.2
Dagworth (see Old Newton)
Dailly S27
Dainton 12.5
Dairsie S16
Dairy Lane 43.5
Daisy Hill (Durham) 14.1
Daisy Hill (W Yorks) 47.1
Daisy Hill Burstwick (E Yorks) 15.2
Dalbeattie S10
Dalbury Lees 11.9
Dalby 28.2
Dalby-cum-Skewsby 33.2
Dalderby 28.2
Dale W16
Dale Abbey 11.8
Dale Town 33.3
Dalehall 40.3
Dalgety Bay S16
Dalginross S24
Dalguise S24
Dalhalvaig S17
Dalham 41.2
Daliburgh S32
Dalkeith S19
Dall S24
Dallam 7.1
Dallas S20
Dalleagles S11
Dallinghoo 41.5
Dallington (E Sussex) 16.2
Dallington (N'hants) 31.5
Dalmally S3
Dalmellington S11
Dalmeny S6
Dalnaspidal S24
Dalquharran S27
Dalreavoch S17
Dalreoch S9
Dalry (Dumfries & Galloway) S10
Dalry (N Ayrs) S21
Dalrymple S11
Dalscote 31.7
Dalserf S28
Dalston L12, 10.1
Dalswinton S10
Dalton S10
Dalton (Lancs) 26.8
Dalton (N Yorks)* 33.2
Dalton (N'land) 32.1
Dalton (S Yorks) 39.4
Dalton (W Yorks) 47.4
Dalton Holme 15.2
Dalton Piercy 14.9
Dalton, Magna & Parva 39.4
Dalton-in-Furness 10.6
Dalton-le-Dale 14.1
Dalton-on-Tees 33.1
Dalwhinnie S17
Dalwood 12.7
Damerham 20.7
Damery (part) 18.7
Damhead S19
Damson Wood 45.6
Dan y Bont W14
Danbury 17.7
Danby Castleton 33.4
Danby Wiske 33.2
Dancers End 5.2
Dancing Cross 38.5
Danderhall S19
Dane End 22.3
Danebridge 40.1
Danehill 16.1
Daneshill 20.1
Danesmoor 11.4
Danestone S4
Danthorpe 15.2
Danygraig W19
Danzey Green 44.5
Darby Green 20.2
Darbys Hill 45.4
Darenth 25.1
Daresbury (part) 7.1, 7.2
Darfield 39.1
Dargate 25.4
Darite 9.1
Darland 25.3
Darlaston 45.2
Darley (see Menwith)
Darley Abbey 11.7
Darley Dale 11.3
Darley Ford 9.1
Darlingscott 44.5
Darlington 14.8
Darliston 37.1
Darlton 34.1
Darmsden 41.4
Darncombe 33.4
Darnford 40.8
Darnhall (part) 7.3, 7.5
Darowen W17
Darranlas W18
Darras Hall 32.1
Darren Valley W4
Darrington 47.5
Darsham 41.5
Dartford 25.1
Dartington 12.9
Dartmoor Forest 12.3
Dartmouth 12.9
Dartmouth Park (part) L6, L19
Darton 39.1
Darvel S11
Darvole 38.5
Darwen 26.10
Datchet 3.4
Datchworth 22.3
Dauntsey 48.1
Davenham 7.3
Daventry 31.4
Davidston S17
Davidstow 9.1
Davington Hill 25.4
Daviot (Aberdeen) S1
Daviot (Highland) S17
Davis Street 3.3
Davyhulme 19.8
Dawes Green 42.8
Dawley 37.4
Dawley Bank 37.4
Dawlish 12.5
Dawlish Warren 12.5
Dawn W8
Daybrook (part) 34.6, 34.7
Daylesford 18.5
Daymer Bay 9.1
Deadman's Cross 2.2
Deal 25.6
Dean (Cumbria) 10.2
Dean (Hants) 20.5
Dean (Som) 38.2
Dean Head 47.4
Dean Lane End 46.2
Dean Prior 12.9
Dean, Lower & Upper (Beds) 2.1
Deanburn S19
Deane 20.1
Deanend 13.3
Deanhouse 47.4
Deanland 13.3
Deanshanger 31.7
Deanston S29
Dearham 10.2
Dearnley 19.4
Debach 41.5
Debden 17.1
Debenham 41.4
Dechmont S31
Deckham 43.3
Deddington 35.2
Dedham 17.3
Dedworth 3.4
Deene 31.3
Deenethorpe 31.3
Deepcar 39.3
Deepcut 42.3
Deepdale (Beds) 2.2
Deepdale (Lancs) 26.6
Deepdale, Dent (Cumbria) 10.5
Deeping Gate 6.1
Deeping St James 28.6
Deeping St Nicholas 28.7
Deeplish 19.4
Deepthwaite 10.5
Deerhurst 18.1
Deerness S23
Deeside W10, S1
Defford 49.6
Defynnog W17
Deighton (N Yorks) 33.7
Deighton (W Yorks) 47.4
Deiniolen W11
Delabole 9.1
Delamere (part) 7.3
Delapre 31.5
Delaware 9.1
Dell Quay 46.2
Delny S17
Delph 19.7
Delves 45.2
Delves Lane 14.1
Dembleby 28.4
Denaby 39.2
Denbeath (Buckhaven) S16
Denbigh W9
Denbigh East 5.1
Denbigh Hall 5.1
Denbigh North 5.1
Denbigh West 5.1
Denbury 12.5
Denby 11.6
Denby Dale 47.4
Denchworth 35.4
Dendron 10.5
Denford 31.3
Dengie 17.8
Denhall Farm Est 7.3
Denham (Bucks) 5.5
Denham (Suffolk) 41.4
Denham-cum-Barrow 41.3
Denholm S30
Denholme 47.1
Denholme Gate 47.1
Denmark Hill (part) L28
Denmead 20.5
Dennington (Suffolk) 41.5
Denny S15
Denny Lodge 20.7
Dennyloanhead S15
Denshaw 19.7
Densole 25.13
Denston 41.3
Denstone 40.5

2

Dent 10.5
Denton (Cambs) 6.3
Denton (Durham) 14.8
Denton (E Sussex) 16.4
Denton (Gtr M'chester) 19.10
Denton (Kent) 25.6
Denton (Lincs) 28.6
Denton (N Yorks) 33.6
Denton (N'hants) 31.7
Denton (Norfolk) 30.7
Denton (Oxon) 35.3
Denton Burn 43.1
Denton, Nether & Upper 10.1
Dentons Green 29.3
Denver 30.2
Denwick 32.1
Deopham 30.7
Depden 41.3
Deppers Bridge 44.5
Deptford (Sunderland) 43.5
Deptford (part) L11, L23, L28
Derby 11.7
Dereham (East) 30.3
Deri W4
Derimysg W6
Deritend 45.5
Derringstone 25.5
Derrington 40.4
Derry Hill 48.1
Dersingham 30.2
Dervaig S3
Derwen W9
Derwen Fawr W19
Derwenlas W17
Derwent 11.1
Desborough 31.2
Desford 27.4
Deskford S20
Dethick 11.6
Detling 25.10
Deuxhill 37.1
Devauden W13
Devil's Bridge W7
Devitts Green 44.1
Devizes 48.1
Devonburn S28
Devonside S8
Devoran 9.1
Dewarton S19
Dewlish 13.1
Dewsall 21.1
Dewsbury 47.4
Dexthorpe 28.2
Dhustone 37.1
Diabaig S17
Dial Green 46.2
Dibden Purlieu 20.7
Dickens Heath 45.6
Dicker, Upper & Lower 16.1
Dickleburgh 30.7
Didcot 35.3
Diddington 6.3
Diddlebury 37.1
Didley 21.1
Didling 46.2
Didlington 30.3
Didmarton 18.5
Didsbury 19.6
Digbeth 45.5
Digby 28.4
Diggle 19.7
Digswell 22.6
Dihewyd W7
Dilham 30.1
Dilhorne 40.1
Dillarburn S28
Dillicar 10.5
Dillington 38.5
Dilston 32.1
Dilton Marsh 48.1
Dilwyn 21.1
Dimmer 38.5
Dimsdale 40.2
Dimson 9.1
Dinas (Gwynedd) W11
Dinas (Rhondda) W18
Dinas Cross W16
Dinas Dinlle W11
Dinas Mawddwy W11
Dinas Powys W21
Dinbych (Denbigh) W9
Dinckley 26.3
Dinder 38.2
Dinedor 21.1
Dingestow W13
Dinghurst 38.7
Dingle 29.2
Dingley 31.2
Dingwall S17
Dinmael W8
Dinmore 21.1
Dinmore (part) 21.1
Dinnet S1
Dinnington (Som) 38.5
Dinnington (T & W) 43.1
Dinnington St John's 39.4
Dinorwig W11
Dinton (Bucks) 5.2
Dinton (Wilts) 48.1
Dipford 38.4
Dipley 20.2
Dippenhall 20.2
Diptford 12.9
Dipton 14.1
Dipton Foot 32.1
Dirleton S13
Discoed W17
Discove 38.5
Diseworth 27.1
Dishforth 33.6
Disley 7.5
Diss 30.7
Disserth & Trecoed W17
Dissington 32.1
Distington (part) 10.2, 10.4
Ditcham (part) 20.6, 46.2
Ditcheat 38.2
Ditchford Friary 44.5
Ditchingham 30.7
Ditchling 16.4
Dittisham 12.9
Ditton (Kent) 25.9
Ditton Priors 37.1
Dobcross 19.7
Dobshill W10
Dobsons Bridge 37.1
Dobwalls 9.1
Dockenfield (part) 20.6, 42.11
Docker 10.5
Docking 30.2
Docklands L30
Docklow 21.1
Dockray 10.3
Dodbrooke (Kingsbridge) 12.9
Dodcott-cum-Wilkesley 7.5
Doddenham 49.4
Dodderhill 49.6
Doddinghurst 17.9
Doddington (Cambs) 6.2
Doddington (Cheshire) 7.5
Doddington (Kent) 25.4
Doddington (Lincs) 28.4
Doddington (N'land) 32.1
Doddington (Shrop) 37.1
Doddiscombsleigh 12.5
Dodford (N'hants) 31.4
Dodford (Worcs) 49.2
Dodford with Grafton 49.2
Dodington (Gloucs) 18.7
Dodington (Som) 38.3
Dodleston 7.3
Dodwell 44.5
Dodworth 39.1
Doe Bank 45.4
Doe Lea 11.5
Dogdyke (part) 28.2, 28.4
Dogmersfield 20.2
Dogsthorpe 6.1
Dolanog W17
Dolfor W17
Dolgarrog W8
Dolgellau W11
Dolgran W6
Dollar S8
Dolphinton S28
Dolton 12.1
Dolwen (Conwy) W8
Dolwen (Powys) W17
Dolwilym W6
Dolwyddelan W8
Dolydd W11
Dolygaer W17
Dommett 38.5
Donaldson's Lodge 32.1
Doncaster 39.2
Donhead St Andrew 48.1
Donhead St Mary 48.1
Doniford 38.3
Donington (Lincs) 28.7
Donington (Shrop) 37.1
Donington le Heath 27.1
Donington-on-Bain 28.2
Donisthorpe 27.1
Donkleywoods 32.1
Donna Nook 28.2
Donnington (Berks) (see Shaw)
Donnington (Gloucs) 18.5
Donnington (Shrop) 37.4
Donnington (W Sussex) 46.2
Donnington (Worcs) 21.1
Donnington Woods 37.4
Donwell 43.5
Donyatt 38.5
Dorcan 48.2
Dorchester (Dorset) 13.1
Dorchester-on-Thames 35.3
Dordon 44.1
Dore & Bredwardine 21.1
Dores S17
Dorking 42.8
Dormansland 42.10
Dormanstown 33.10
Dormington 21.1
Dormston 49.6
Dorn 18.5
Dorney 5.5
Dornie S17
Dornoch S17
Dornock S10
Dorridge 45.6
Dorrington (Lincs) 28.4
Dorrington (Shrop)* 37.1
Dorsington 44.5
Dorstone 21.1
Dorton 5.2
Doseley 37.4
Dosthill (part) 40.9, 44.1
Dothan W1
Dottery 13.1
Dougarie S21
Doughton 18.5
Douglas S28
Douglas Water S28
Douglas West S28
Douglastown S2
Doulting 38.2
Dounby S23
Doune S29
Dounreay S17
Dovaston 37.1
Dove Holes 11.1
Dovecot 29.2
Dovendale 28.2
Dover 25.6
Dovercourt 17.4
Doverdale 49.6
Doverhay 38.3
Doveridge 11.3
Dowally S24
Dowbiggin 10.5
Dowdeswell 18.5
Dowlais W12
Dowlais Top W12
Dowland 12.1
Dowles Green 3.3
Dowlish Ford 38.5
Dowlish Wake 38.5
Down Ampney 18.5
Down Hatherley 18.1
Down St Mary 12.4
Down Thomas (Wembury) 12.9
Downall Green 29.3
Downderry 9.1
Downe L5

Downend (part) 4.1, 18.7
Downgate 9.1
Downham (Essex) 17.7
Downham (Lancs) 26.3
Downham (Lond) (part) L5, L23
Downham (Norfolk) 30.7
Downham Market 30.2
Downham West 30.2
Downhead Park 5.1
Downhead* 38.2, 38.5
Downhill 43.5
Downholland 26.8
Downholme 33.1
Downies S1
Downley 5.3
Downs Barn 5.1
Downscombe 38.3
Downside (Som) 38.2, 38.7
Downside (Surrey) 42.5
Downswood, nr Otham 25.10
Downton (Here) 21.1
Downton (Wilts) 48.1
Dowsby 28.6
Dowsdale 28.7
Doxford Park 43.5
Doynton 18.7
Draethen W4
Dragonby 28.8
Drakeholes 34.1
Drakeley Heath 37.1
Drakelow (Derbys) 11.9
Drakelow (Worcs) 49.1
Drakes Broughton 49.6
Drakewalls 9.1
Draughton (N Yorks) 33.5
Draughton (N'hants) 31.4
Drax 33.8
Draycot Cerne 48.1
Draycote 44.3
Draycott (Derbys) 11.8
Draycott (Gloucs) 18.5
Draycott (Som)* 38.2, 38.5
Draycott Foliat 48.2
Draycott-in-the-Clay 40.5
Draycott-in-the-Moors 40.1
Draynes 9.1
Drayton (Leics) 27.8
Drayton (Norfolk) 30.5
Drayton (Oxon)* 35.2, 35.4
Drayton (Som) 38.5
Drayton (Sth Petherton) 38.5
Drayton (Warks) 44.5
Drayton (Worcs) 49.1
Drayton Bassett 40.8
Drayton Beauchamp 5.2
Drayton Parslow 5.2
Drayton St Leonard 35.3
Draytons 38.5
Drefach Felindre W6
Drefach, Llanelli W6
Dreghorn S21
Drem S13
Dresden 40.3
Drewsteignton 12.3
Driby 28.2
Driffield (E Yorks) 15.2
Driffield (Gloucs) 18.5
Drift 9.1
Drigg & Carleton 10.4
Drighlington 47.2
Drimnin S17
Dringhouses 33.7
Drinkstone 41.4
Driver 38.3
Droitwich 49.6
Dron S24
Dronfield 11.4
Drongan S11
Droxford 20.5
Droylsden 19.10
Drub 47.4
Druids Heath (part) 45.5, 49.2
Drum S24
Drumbeg S17
Drumblade S1
Drumclog S28
Drumelzier S30
Drumgask S17
Drumlithie S1
Drummore S10
Drummuir S20
Drumnadrochit S17
Drumoak S1
Drumsmittal S17
Druridge 32.1
Drury W10
Dry Crouds 38.5
Dry Doddington 28.6
Dry Drayton 6.5
Dry Sandford 35.4
Drybeck 10.3
Drybridge S21
Drybrook 18.2
Drymen S29
Drynachan S17
Dryslwyn W6
Dubmire 43.5
Duckington (Cheshire) 7.3
Ducklington (Oxon) 35.1
Duckmanton (part) 11.2, 11.4
Duddeston 45.5
Duddington 31.3
Duddlestone 38.4
Duddo 32.1
Duddon (Cheshire) 7.3
Duddon (Cumbria) 10.5
Dudleston 37.1
Dudleston Heath 37.1
Dudley (T & W) 43.2
Dudley (W Mids) 45.3
Dudley Hill 47.1
Dudley Wood 45.3
Dudswell 22.4
Duffield 11.6
Duffryn W15
Dufftown S20
Duffus S20
Dufton 10.3
Duggleby 33.3
Duhonw W17
Dukinfield 19.10
Dulas (Anglesey) W1
Dulas (Here) 21.1
Dulcote 38.2
Dull S24
Dullatur S22
Dullingham 6.4
Dulnain Bridge S17
Duloe (Beds) 2.1
Duloe (Corn) 9.1
Dulsie S17
Dulverton 38.3
Dulwich (part) L22, L28
Dulwich Village L28
Dumbarton S9
Dumbleton 18.1
Dumfries S10
Dummer 20.1
Dumpton (Ramsgate) (Broadstairs) 25.7
Dunadd S3
Dunalastair S24
Dunaskin S11
Dunball 38.1
Dunbar S13
Dunbeath S17
Dunblane S29
Dunbridge 20.4
Duncanston S17
Dunces Houses 32.1
Dunchideock 12.5
Dunchurch 44.3
Duncote 31.7
Duncow S10
Duncrievie S24
Duncton 46.2
Dundee S5
Dundon 38.5
Dundon Hayes 38.5
Dundonald (Fife) S16
Dundonald (S Ayrs) S27
Dundonnel S17
Dundraw 10.2
Dundrennan S10
Dundridge 20.5
Dundry 38.7
Dunfermline S16
Dunfield 18.5
Dunford Bridge 39.1
Dungeness 25.13
Dungworth 39.3
Dunham Massey 19.8
Dunham, Gt & Little (Norfolk) 30.3
Dunham-on-Trent 34.1
Dunham-on-the-Hill 7.3
Dunholme 28.1
Dunino S16
Dunipace S15
Dunira S24
Dunk's Green 25.9
Dunkeld S24
Dunkerton 38.6
Dunkeswell 12.7
Dunkeswick 33.6
Dunkirk 18.7
Dunley 20.1
Dunlop S11
Dunmere 9.1
Dunmore S15
Dunnerdale with Seathwaite 10.5
Dunnet S17
Dunnichen S2
Dunning S24
Dunning Glen S24
Dunnington (E Yorks) 15.2
Dunnington (Warks) 44.5
Dunnington (York) 33.7
Dunnockshaw 26.12
Dunnottar S1
Dunoon S3
Dunragit S10
Dunrobin S17
Dunrossness S26
Duns S30
Duns Tew 35.2
Dunsby 28.6
Dunscar 19.2
Dunscore S10
Dunscroft 39.2
Dunsdale 33.10
Dunsden 35.3
Dunsfold 42.11
Dunsford 12.5
Dunsforth 33.6
Dunshalt S16
Dunsley (part) 33.4, 40.6
Dunsmore (part) 5.2, 5.3
Dunsop Bridge 26.3
Dunstable (Beds) 2.2
Dunstable (Wilts) 48.1
Dunstall (Staffs) 40.5
Dunster 38.3
Dunston (Derbys) 11.2
Dunston (Lincs) 28.4
Dunston (Norfolk) 30.7
Dunston (Staffs) 40.6
Dunston (T & W) 43.3
Dunsville 39.2
Dunswell 15.2
Dunsyre S28
Dunterton 12.3
Duntisbourne Abbots 18.5
Duntisbourne Leer 18.5
Duntisbourne Rouse 18.5
Duntish 13.1
Duntocher S9
Dunton (Beds) 2.2
Dunton (Bucks) 5.2
Dunton (Norfolk) 30.1
Dunton Bassett 27.8
Dunton Green 25.8
Duntulm S17
Dunure S27
Dunvant W19
Dunvegan S17
Dunwich 41.5
Durdar Road 10.1
Durfold Wood 46.2
Durford Wood 46.2
Durham & Framwellgate 14.1
Durham City 14.1
Duriodoor S10
Durkar 47.5
Durleigh 38.1

2

Durleigh Marsh 46.2
Durlett 48.1
Durley (Hants) 20.5
Durley (Wilts) 48.1
Durnamuck S17
Durness S17
Durnford 48.1
Durns Town 20.7
Duror S17
Durrington (W Sussex) 46.6
Durrington (Wilts) 48.1
Durris S1
Dursley 18.6
Durston 38.4
Durweston 13.2
Duston 31.5
Duthill S17
Dutton (Cheshire) 7.3
Dutton (Lancs) 26.3
Duxford 6.5
Duxmoor 37.1
Dwr y Felin W14
Dwyran W1
Dwyriw W17
Dyce S4
Dyche 38.3
Dyers Common 18.7
Dyffryn W21
Dyffryn Ardudwy W11
Dyffryn Arth W7
Dyffryn Cellwen W14
Dyffryn Clydach W14
Dyffryn Rhondda W14
Dyke (Lincs) 28.6
Dyke (Moray) S20
Dykehead S2
Dylife W17
Dymchurch 25.13
Dymock 18.2
Dyrham 18.7
Dysart S16
Dyserth W9
Eachwick 32.1
Eagle 28.4
Eaglesbush Valley W14
Eaglescliffe 14.10
Eaglesfield S10
Eaglesham S14
Eaglestone 5.1
Eagley 19.2
Eakring 34.3
Ealing L9
Eamont Bridge 10.3
Earby 26.13
Eardington 37.1
Eardisland 21.1
Eardisley 21.1
Eardiston 37.1
Earis Colne 17.2
Earith 6.3
Earith Bridge 6.4
Earl Shilton 27.4
Earl Soham 41.5
Earl Sterndale 11.3
Earle 32.1
Earlestown 29.3
Earley (part) 3.2, 3.3
Earlham 30.4
Earlish S17
Earls Barton 31.6
Earls Court (part) L13, L20
Earls Croome 49.4
Earlsdon 45.7
Earlsferry S16
Earlsfield L32
Earlsheaton 47.4
Earlston S30
Earlstone Common 20.1
Earlswood (Monmth) W13
Earlswood (Surrey) 42.9
Earlswood (W Mids/Warks) (part) 44.5, 45.6
Earnley 46.2
Earnock S28
Earsdon (N'land) 32.1
Earsdon (T & W) 43.2
Earsham 30.7
Earswick 33.7
Eartham 46.2
Earthcott 18.7
Earthcott Green 18.7
Easby* 33.1, 33.2
Easebourne 46.2
Easenhall 44.3
Easington (Bucks) 5.2
Easington (Durham) 14.1
Easington (E Yorks) 15.2
Easington (Lancs) 26.3
Easington (N Yorks) 33.10
Easington (N'land) 32.1
Easington Lane 43.5
Easingwold 33.2
Eassie S2
East Acton (part) L9, L13
East Allington 12.9
East Anstey (part) 12.2
East Anton 20.4
East Ashling 46.2
East Ayton 33.4
East Barkwith 28.2
East Barnby 33.4
East Barns S13
East Bergholt 41.6
East Bierley 47.4
East Bilney 30.3
East Boldon 43.4
East Boldre 20.7
East Bolton (see Castle Bolton)
East Bowling 47.1
East Brent 38.1
East Bridgford 34.8
East Buckland 12.2
East Budleigh 12.7
East Burton 13.5
East Butterwick 28.8
East Calder S31
East Carleton 30.7
East Carlton 31.1
East Challow 35.4
East Chelborough 13.1
East Chevington 32.1
East Chiltington 16.4
East Chinnock 38.5
East Cholderton 20.4
East Clandon 42.7
East Claydon 5.2
East Clevedon 38.7
East Cliff 13.7
East Coker 38.5
East Combe 38.4
East Compton 38.2
East Cottingwith 15.2
East Cowes 24.1
East Cowick 15.2
East Cowton 33.2
East Cranmore 38.2
East Dean (E Sussex) 16.1
East Dean (Hants) 20.4
East Dean (W Sussex) 46.2
East Denton 43.1
East Donyland 17.3
East Down 12.2
East Drayton 34.1
East Dulwich L28
East Dundry 38.7
East Elrington 32.1
East End (Hants) 20.1
East End (Som) 38.5
East Farleigh 25.10
East Farndon 31.4
East Ferry 28.1
East Finchley (part) L2, L14
East Firsby 28.1
East Fortune S13
East Garston 3.1
East Garton 15.2
East Ginge 35.4
East Goscote 27.2
East Grinstead 46.4
East Guldeford 16.2
East Haddon 31.4
East Hagbourne 35.3
East Halton 28.8
East Ham L25
East Hamlet 37.1
East Hanney 35.4
East Hanningfield 17.7
East Hardwick 47.5
East Harlsey 33.2
East Harptree (part) 38.2, 38.6
East Hartford 32.1
East Hauxwell 33.1
East Heckington 28.4
East Hedleyhope 14.1
East Hendred 35.4
East Herrington 43.5
East Hewish 38.7
East Hill 25.8
East Hoathly 16.1
East Holme 13.5
East Horrington 38.2
East Horsley 42.7
East Howdon 43.2
East Howe 13.7
East Hunsbury 31.5
East Huntingtower S24
East Huntspill 38.1
East Ilsley 3.1
East Keal 28.2
East Kennett 48.1
East Keswick 47.2
East Kilbride S28
East Kirkby 28.2
East Knoyle 48.1
East Lambrook 38.5
East Langdon 25.6
East Langton 27.8
East Lavington 46.2
East Layton 33.1
East Leake 34.8
East Lilburn 32.1
East Linton S13
East Liss 20.6
East Lulworth 13.5
East Lydeard 38.4
East Lydford 38.2
East Lynch 38.3
East Malling 25.9
East Marden 46.2
East Markham 34.1
East Meon 20.6
East Mersea 17.3
East Molesden 32.1
East Molesey 42.5
East Moor 11.4
East Morton 47.1
East Newbiggin 14.8
East Newton & Leysthorpe 33.3
East Newton (E Yorks) 15.2
East Norton 27.8
East Oakley 20.1
East Orchard 13.2
East Ord 32.1
East Peckham 25.9
East Pennard 38.2
East Portlemouth 12.9
East Prawle 12.9
East Preston 46.5
East Putford 12.1
East Putney L32
East Quantoxhead 38.3
East Rainton 43.5
East Ravendale 28.9
East Rolstone 38.7
East Rounton 33.2
East Rudham 30.2
East Ruston 30.1
East Saltoun S13
East Scrafton (see Caldbergh)
East Sheen L27
East Somerton (see Somerton)
East Stanley 14.1
East Stockwith 28.1
East Stoke (Dorset) 13.5
East Stoke (Notts) 34.3
East Stoke (Som) 38.5
East Stour 13.2
East Stourmouth 25.6
East Stratton 20.5
East Studdal 25.6
East Sutton 25.10
East Tanfield 33.2
East Tilbury 17.12
East Tisted 20.6
East Torrington 28.1
East Tytherley 20.4
East Tytherton 48.1

East Village 12.4
East Walton 30.2
East Wellow 20.4
East Wemyss S16
East Whitburn S31
East Wiliamston W16
East Winch 30.2
East Wittering 46.2
East Witton Out 33.1
East Witton Town 33.1
East Woodburn 32.1
East Woodlands 38.2
East Woodyates 13.3
East Worldham 20.6
East Worlington 12.2
East Worthing 46.6
East Wykeham 28.2
Eastborough 47.4
Eastbourne 16.5
Eastburn (E Yorks) 15.2
Eastburn (W Yorks) 47.1
Eastby (see Embsay)
Eastchurch 25.4
Eastcombe 18.6
Eastcote (N'hants) 31.7
Eastcote (W Mids) 45.6
Eastcott (Som) 38.3
Eastcott (Wilts) 48.1
Eastcotts 2.1
Eastdon 12.5
Easter Balgeddie S24
Easter Compton 18.7
Eastergate 46.5
Easterlands 38.4
Eastern Green 45.7
Eastern Piercy 48.1
Easterside 33.9
Easterton 48.1
Eastfield (Bristol) 4.1
Eastfield (Cambs) 6.1
Eastfield (Midlothian) S19
Eastfield (N Yorks) 33.4
Eastfield (N'hants) 31.5
Eastgate (Cambs) 6.1
Eastgate (Durham) 14.1
Eastham (Here) 49.4
Eastham (Mersey) 29.5
Easthampnett 46.2
Easthampstead 3.6
Easthaven S2
Eastheath 3.3
Easthope 37.1
Easthorpe (Essex) (see Copford)
Easthorpe (N Yorks) 33.3
Easthouses S19
Eastington* 18.5, 18.6
Eastleach 18.5
Eastleaze 48.2
Eastleigh 20.9
Eastling 25.4
Eastnor 21.1
Eastoft 28.8
Easton (Bristol) 4.1
Easton (Cambs) 6.3
Easton (Cumbria) 10.1
Easton (Hants) 20.5
Easton (Lincs) 28.6
Easton (Norfolk) 30.7
Easton (Som) 38.2
Easton (Suffolk) 41.5
Easton Bavents (see Reydon)
Easton Grey 48.1
Easton Maudit 31.6
Easton Neston 31.7
Easton Royal 48.1
Easton-in-Gordano 38.7
Easton-on-the-Hill 31.3
Eastrea 6.2
Eastriggs S10
Eastrington 15.2
Eastrop 20.1
Eastry 25.6
Eastville (Bristol) 4.1
Eastville (Lincs) 28.2
Eastwell (Kent) 25.12
Eastwell (Leics) 27.3
Eastwick (Herts) 22.3
Eastwick (Shrop) 37.1
Eastwood (Essex) 17.14
Eastwood (Notts) 34.5
Eastwood (W Yorks) 47.3
Eastwoodhay 20.1
Eathorpe 44.4
Eaton (Cheshire)* 7.3, 7.5
Eaton (Leics) 27.3
Eaton (Norwich) 30.4
Eaton (Notts) 34.1
Eaton (Oxon) (see Appleton)
Eaton Bishop 21.1
Eaton Bray 2.2
Eaton Constantine 37.1
Eaton Ford 6.3
Eaton Hastings 35.4
Eaton Park 40.3
Eaton Socon (part) 2.1, 6.3
Eaton on Tern 37.1
Eaton-under-Heywood 37.1
Eau Withington 21.1
Eavestone 33.6
Ebberston, North & South 33.3
Ebbesbourne Wake 48.1
Ebbw Vale W2
Ebchester 14.1
Ebdon 38.7
Ebernoe 46.2
Ebony (see Stone)
Ebrington 18.5
Ebury L33
Ecchinswell 20.1
Ecclefechan S10
Ecclerigg, Windermere 10.5
Eccles S30
Eccles (Gtr M'chester) 19.5
Eccles (Kent) 25.9
Eccles (Norfolk)* 30.1, 30.3
Ecclesfield 39.3
Eccleshall 40.4
Eccleshill (Lancs) 26.10
Eccleshill (W Yorks) 47.1
Ecclesmachan S31
Eccleston (Cheshire) 7.3
Eccleston (Lancs) 26.9
Eccleston Park 29.3
Echt S1
Eckford S30
Eckington (Derbys) 11.4
Eckington (Worcs) 49.6
Ecton 31.6
Ecton Brook 31.5
Edale 11.1
Eday S23
Edbrooke 38.3
Edburton 46.3
Edderton S17
Eddleston S30
Eddlewood S28
Edenbridge 25.8
Edenfield 26.14
Edenhall 10.3
Edenham 28.6
Edensor 11.3
Edenthorpe 39.2
Edern W11
Edgbaston 45.5
Edgcote 31.7
Edgcott (Bucks) 5.2
Edgcott (Som) 38.3
Edgcumbe 9.1
Edge (Cheshire) 7.3
Edge (Gloucs) 18.6
Edge End 18.2
Edge Hill (Mersey) 29.2
Edge Hill (Warks) 44.5
Edgebolton 37.1
Edgefield 30.1
Edgehead S19
Edgeley, Whitchurch 37.1
Edgerton 47.4
Edgeside 26.14
Edgeworth 18.5
Edgmond 37.4
Edgton 37.1
Edgware (part) L4, L15
Edgworth 26.10
Edinburgh S6
Edingale 40.8
Edingley 34.3
Edingthorpe 30.1
Edington (Som) 38.1
Edington (Wilts) 48.1
Edith Weston 36.1
Edithmead 38.1
Edlaston 11.3
Edlesborough 5.2
Edleston 7.5
Edlingham 32.1
Edlington 39.2
Edlington with Wispington 28.2
Edmondestown W18
Edmondsham 13.3
Edmondsley 14.1
Edmondthorpe 27.3
Edmonton (Cornwall) 9.1
Edmundbyers 14.1
Ednam S30
Ednaston 11.3
Edney Common 17.7
Ednol W17
Edrom S30
Edstaston 37.1
Edstone (Warks) 44.5
Edstone, Gt & Little 33.3
Edvin Loach 21.1
Edwalton 34.8
Edwardstone 41.6
Edwardsville W12
Edwinstowe 34.3
Edworth 2.2
Edwyn Ralph 21.1
Edzell S2
Efail Fach W14
Efailnewydd W11
Efailwen W6
Efenechtyd W9
Effingham 42.7
Egbury 20.1
Egdean 46.2
Egerley 7.3
Egerton (Cheshire) 7.5
Egerton (Gtr M'chester) 19.2
Egerton (Kent) 25.12
Egford 38.2
Eggborough 33.8
Eggesford 12.4
Eggington (Beds) 2.2
Egginton (Derbys) 11.9
Egglescliffe 14.10
Eggleston 14.1
Egglestone Abbey 14.1
Eggleton 21.1
Egham 42.1
Egilsay S23
Egleton 36.1
Eglingham 32.1
Egloshayle 9.1
Egloskerry 9.1
Eglwys Brewis W21
Eglwys Wen W16
Eglwysbach W8
Eglwyscummin W6
Eglwyseg W9
Eglwysilan Senghenydd W4
Eglwyswrw W16
Egmanton 34.3
Egmere 30.1
Egremont (Cumbria) 10.4
Egremont (Mersey) 29.5
Egton 33.4
Egton Bridge 33.4
Egton with Newland 10.5
Egypt (Hants) 20.5
Egypt (W Yorks) 47.1
Eigg S17
Eight Ash Green 17.3
Eightlands 47.4
Eighton Banks 43.3
Eilean Iarmain S17
Elan Valley W17
Elberton 18.7
Elborough 38.7
Elbridge (Shrops) 37.1
Elbridge (W Sussex) 46.5
Elcocks Brook (part) 49.3
Elcombe 48.2
Eldene 48.2
Eldersfield 49.4
Elderslie S25
Eldindean S19

Eldmire with Crakehill 33.2
Eldon Lane 14.1
Eldroth 33.5
Eldwick 47.1
Eleighwater 38.5
Elemore Lane 43.5
Elephant & Castle L28
Elfield Park 5.1
Elford 40.8
Elgin S20
Elgol S17
Elham 25.13
Elie S16
Eling 20.7
Elkesley 34.1
Elkington 31.4
Elkstone 18.5
Elkstones 40.1
Elland 47.3
Ellastone 40.5
Ellel 26.1
Ellenhall 40.4
Ellens Green 42.11
Ellenthorpe 33.6
Ellerbeck 33.2
Ellerby (E Yorks) 15.2
Ellerby (N Yorks) 33.4
Ellerdine Heath 37.4
Ellerdine* 37.1, 37.4
Ellerker 15.2
Ellerton (E Yorks) 15.2
Ellerton (Shrop) 37.1
Ellerton Abbey 33.1
Ellerton-on-Swale 33.1
Ellesborough* 5.3
Ellesmere 37.1
Ellesmere Port 7.3
Ellicombe 38.3
Ellingham (Hants) 20.7
Ellingham (N'land) 32.1
Ellingham (Norfolk) 30.7
Ellingstring 33.6
Ellington (Cambs) 6.3
Ellington (N'land) 32.1
Ellington, High & Low (N Yorks) 33.6
Elliot S2
Elliotstown W4
Ellisfield 20.1
Ellistown 27.1
Ellon S1
Ellonby 10.3
Ellough 41.1
Elloughton 15.2
Ellwood 18.2
Elm (Cambs) 6.2
Elm (Som) 38.2
Elm Park L16
Elm Tree 14.10
Elmbridge (Gloucs) 18.3
Elmbridge (Worcs) 49.6
Elmdon (Essex) 17.1
Elmdon (W Mids) 45.6
Elmdon Heath 45.6
Elmer 46.5
Elmesthorpe 27.6
Elmham, North 30.3
Elmhurst 40.8
Elmington (Oundle) 31.3
Elmley 25.4
Elmley Castle 49.6
Elmley Lovett 49.6
Elmore 18.6
Elmsett 41.6
Elmstead (Essex) 17.4
Elmsted (Kent) 25.13
Elmstone 25.6
Elmstone Hardwicke 18.1
Elmswell (E Yorks) 15.2
Elmswell (Suffolk) 41.4
Elmton with Creswell 11.5
Elphin S17
Elphinstone S13
Elrig S10
Elsdon 32.1
Elsecar 39.1
Elsenham 17.1
Elsfield 35.3
Elsham 28.8
Elsing 30.3
Elslack 33.5
Elson (Hants) 20.11
Elson (Shrops) 37.1
Elsrickle S28
Elstead 42.11
Elsted 46.2
Elsthorpe 28.6
Elstob Farm Estate 43.5
Elston 34.3
Elstow 2.1
Elstree 22.10
Elstronwick 15.2
Elswick (Lancs) 26.5
Elswick (T & W) 43.1
Elsworth 6.5
Elterwater 10.5
Eltham (part) L3, L11
Eltisley 6.5
Elton (Cambs) 6.3
Elton (Cheshire) 7.3
Elton (Derbys) 11.3
Elton (Gloucs) 18.2
Elton (Gtr M'chester) 19.3
Elton (Here) 21.1
Elton (Notts) 34.8
Elton (Stockton) 14.10
Eltons Marsh 21.1
Elvanfoot S28
Elvaston 11.9
Elveden 41.2
Elvetham 20.2
Elvetham Heath 20.2
Elvington (Kent) 25.6
Elvington (York) 33.7
Elwick 14.9
Elworthy 38.3
Ely (Cambs) 6.4
Ely (Cardiff) W5
Emberton 5.1
Embleton (Cumbria) 10.2
Embleton (Durham) 14.1
Embleton (N'land) 32.1
Embo S17
Emborough 38.2
Embsay with Eastby 33.5
Emerson 43.5
Emerson Valley 5.1
Emery Down 20.7
Emley 47.4
Emley Moor 47.4
Emmbrook 3.3
Emmer Green 3.2
Emmotland 15.2
Emneth 30.2
Empingham 36.1
Empshott 20.6
Emsworth (part) 20.13, 46.2
Enborne 3.1
Enderby 27.6
Endmoor 10.5
Endon 40.1
Energlyn W4
Enfield L10
Enfield (Worcs) 49.3
Enford 48.1
Engedi W1
Engine Common 18.7
Englefield 3.1
Englefield Green 42.1
Englesea Brook 7.5
English Bicknor 18.2
English Frankton 37.1
Englishcombe 38.6
Engollan 9.1
Enham Alamein 20.4
Enmore 38.1
Ennerdale & Kinniside 10.4
Enniscaven 9.1
Enochdhu S24
Ensbury Park 13.7
Enslow 35.2
Enson 40.4
Enstone 35.1
Enterkinfoot S10
Enton 42.11
Enville 40.6
Eoropie S32
Epney 18.6
Epperstone 34.3
Epping 17.6
Epping Green (Essex) 17.6
Epping Green (Herts) 22.3
Epping Upland 17.6
Eppleby 33.1
Eppleton 43.5
Epsom (part) 42.6, 42.9
Epsom Downs (part) 42.6, 42.9
Epwell 35.2
Epworth 28.8
Erbistock W22
Ercall Heath 37.1
Ercall Magna 37.4
Erddig W22
Erdington 45.5
Eridge 16.1
Eriskay S32
Eriswell 41.2
Erith L3
Erleigh 38.5
Erlestoke 48.1
Ermington 12.9
Erpingham 30.1
Erringden 47.3
Errogie S17
Errol S24
Erskine S25
Ervie S10
Erwood W17
Eryholme 33.1
Escomb 14.1
Escott 38.3
Escrick 33.8
Esgair W6
Esgerdawe W6
Esh 14.1
Esh Winning (part) 14.1
Esher 42.5
Esholt 47.1
Eshott 32.1
Eshton 33.5
Eskbank S19
Eskdale 10.4
Eskdalemuir S10
Eskdaleside 33.4
Eskgrove S19
Eskham 28.2
Eskhill S19
Espley 32.1
Esprick 26.5
Essendine 36.1
Essendon 22.6
Essich S17
Essington (part) 40.6, 45.2
Eston 33.10
Etal 32.1
Etchilhampton 48.1
Etching Hill 40.7
Etchingham 16.2
Etchinghill 25.13
Etherley 14.1
Ethiehaven S2
Eton 3.4
Eton Wick 3.4
Etruria 40.3
Ettington 44.5
Etton (Cambs) 6.1
Etton (E Yorks) 15.2
Ettrickbridge S30
Etwall 11.9
Euston (London) (part) L6, L33
Euston (St Edmundsbury) 41.3
Euxton 26.9
Evanstown (part) W3, W18
Evanton S17
Eve's Corner 17.7
Evedon 28.4
Evenjobb W17
Evenley 31.7
Evenlode 18.5
Evenwood 14.1
Evercreech 38.2
Everdon, Gt & Little 31.4
Everingham 15.2
Everleigh 48.1
Everley (see Suffield)
Eversholt 2.2
Evershot 13.1
Eversley 20.2
Eversley Centre 20.2

Eversley Cross 20.2
Everthorpe 15.2
Everton (Beds) 2.2
Everton (Hants) 20.7
Everton (Mersey) 29.2
Everton (Notts) 34.1
Evertown S10
Evesbatch 21.1
Evesham 49.6
Evie S23
Ewden Village 39.3
Ewell Minnis 25.6
Ewell, East & West 42.6
Ewelme 35.3
Ewen 18.5
Ewenny (part) W3, W21
Ewerby 28.4
Ewhurst (E Sussex) 16.2
Ewhurst (Surrey) 42.11
Ewhurst House 20.1
Ewloe W10
Ewood Bridge 26.14
Ewshot 20.2
Ewyas Harold 21.1
Exbourne 12.3
Exbury 20.7
Exebridge (Devon) 12.4
Exebridge (Som) 38.3
Exelby 33.2
Exeter (City) 12.6
Exford (Som) 38.3
Exhall (Warks) (part) 44.2, 44.5
Exley Head 47.1
Exminster 12.5
Exmoor 38.3
Exmouth 12.7
Exning 41.2
Exted 25.13
Exton (Hants) 20.5
Exton (Rutland) 36.1
Exton (Som) 38.3
Eyam 11.3
Eydon 31.7
Eye (Cambs) 6.1
Eye (Suffolk) 41.4
Eye, Moreton & Ashton 21.1
Eyemouth S30
Eyeworth 2.2
Eyford 18.5
Eyke 41.5
Eynesbury 6.3
Eynesbury Hardwicke 6.3
Eynsford 25.8
Eynsham 35.1
Eype 13.1
Eythorne 25.6
Eythrope 5.2
Eyton (Here) 21.1
Eyton (Shrop) 37.1
Eyton-upon-the-Weald Moors 37.4
Faberstown 48.1
Faccombe 20.4
Faceby 33.2
Fachwen W11
Facit 26.14
Faddiley 7.5
Fadmoor 33.3
Faenor W7
Fagley 47.1
Faifley S9
Failand 38.7
Failsworth 19.7
Fair Garden 38.3
Fair Isle S26
Fair Oak (Hants) 20.9
Fair Oak (Staffs) 40.4
Fair Oak Green 20.1
Fairbourne W11
Fairburn 33.8
Faircross 20.1
Fairfield (Cheshire) 7.1
Fairfield (Derbys) 11.1
Fairfield (Gtr M'chester) 19.3
Fairfield (Kent) 25.13
Fairfield (Stockton) 14.10
Fairfield (Worcs) 49.2
Fairford 18.5
Fairhaven 26.5
Fairhill S28
Fairlie S21
Fairlight 16.2
Fairmile 13.8
Fairmoor 32.1
Fairseat 25.9
Fairstead 17.2
Fairview W4
Fairwarp 16.1
Fairwater W5
Fairwater (Torfaen) W20
Fairways W4
Fairweather Green 47.1
Fakenham 30.1
Fakenham Magna 41.3
Fala S19
Fala Dam S19
Falcutt 31.7
Faldingworth 28.1
Falfield 18.7
Falinge 19.4
Falkenham 41.5
Falkirk S15
Falkland S16
Fallin S29
Fallowfield 19.6
Falmer 16.4
Falmouth 9.1
Falstone 32.1
Fancott 2.2
Fangdale Beck (part) 33.2, 33.3
Fangfoss 15.2
Fankerton S15
Fanners Green 17.7
Far Arnside 10.5
Far Coton (Leics) 27.4
Far Cotton 31.5
Far Forest (Rock) 49.1
Far Oakridge 18.6
Far Sawrey 10.5
Farcet (part) 6.1, 6.3
Fareham 20.10
Farewell 40.8
Farforth 28.2
Faringdon 35.4
Farington 26.7
Farington Moss 26.7
Farlam 10.1
Farleigh (Som) 38.7
Farleigh Hungerford 38.2
Farleigh Wallop 20.1
Farlesthorpe 28.2
Farleton (Cumbria) 10.5
Farleton (N Yorks) (see Hornby)
Farley (Staffs) 40.1
Farley (Wilts) 48.1
Farley Chamberlayne 20.5
Farlington (N Yorks) 33.2
Farlow 37.1
Farmborough 38.6
Farmbridge End 17.7
Farmcote 18.5
Farmers W6
Farmington 18.5
Farmoor 35.4
Farnborough L5
Farnborough (Berks) 3.1
Farnborough (Hants) 20.3
Farnborough (Warks) 44.5
Farncombe 42.11
Farndale, East & West 33.3
Farndish 2.1
Farndon (Cheshire) 7.3
Farndon (Notts) 34.3
Farnell S2
Farnham (Berks) 3.5
Farnham (Dorset) 13.2
Farnham (Essex) 17.1
Farnham (N Yorks) 33.6
Farnham (Suffolk) 41.5
Farnham (Surrey) 42.11
Farnham Common 5.5
Farnham Royal (Bucks) 5.5
Farnhill 33.5
Farningham 25.8
Farnley (N Yorks) 33.6
Farnley (N'land) 32.1
Farnley Tyas 47.4
Farnsfield 34.3
Farnworth 19.2
Farr S17
Farringdon (Devon) 12.7
Farringdon (Hants) 20.6
Farringdon (T & W) 43.5
Farrington Gurney 38.6
Farsley 47.2
Farthinghoe 31.7
Farthingstone 31.4
Farthorpe 28.2
Fartown 47.4
Fartown (Pudsey) 47.2
Farway 12.7
Fassaig S17
Fatfield 43.5
Faugh 10.1
Fauld 40.5
Fauldhouse S31
Faulkbourne 17.2
Faulkland 38.2
Fauls 37.1
Fauls Green 37.1
Faversham 25.4
Faversham Without 25.4
Fawcett Forest 10.5
Fawdington 33.2
Fawdon 43.1
Fawfieldhead 40.1
Fawke Common 25.8
Fawkham 25.8
Fawkham Green 25.8
Fawler 35.1
Fawley (Berks) 3.1
Fawley (Bucks) 5.3
Fawley (Hants) 20.7
Fawley (Here) 21.1
Fawley Bottom 5.3
Fawley Green 5.3
Fawsley 31.4
Faxfleet 15.2
Faxton 31.4
Faygate 46.3
Fazakerley 29.2
Fazeley 40.8
Fazeley Road (part) 40.9
Fearby 33.6
Fearn S17
Fearnan S24
Fearnhead (see Poulton)
Featherstone (N'land) 32.1
Featherstone (Staffs) 40.6
Featherstone (W Yorks) 47.5
Feckenham (part) 49.3
Feering 17.2
Fegg Hayes 40.3
Feizor 33.5
Felbridge 42.10
Felbrigg 30.1
Felhampton 37.1
Felindre (Velindre) (Swansea) W19
Felindre, Berriew (Powys) W17
Felinfach W17
Felinfoel W6
Felingerrig W17
Felingwm W6
Felixkirk 33.2
Felixstowe 41.5
Felley 34.4
Felling 43.3
Felliscliffe 33.6
Felmersham 2.1
Felmingham 30.1
Felpham 46.5
Felsham 41.4
Felsted 17.1
Feltham (Middx) L18
Feltham (Som) 38.4
Felthorpe 30.5
Felton (N'land) 32.1
Felton (Som) 38.7
Felton (Worcs) 21.1
Feltwell 30.2
Fen Ditton 6.5
Fen Drayton 6.5
Fen End 45.6
Fenay Bridge 47.4
Fence (Lancs) 26.13

Fence (S Yorks) 39.4
Fence Houses (part) 14.1, 43.5
Fencote (see Kirby Fleetham)
Fencote, Gt & Little 33.2
Fencott 35.2
Fenemere 37.1
Fengate 6.1
Fenham 43.1
Feniscowles 26.10
Feniton 12.7
Fennifach W17
Fennington 38.4
Fenny Bentley 11.3
Fenny Castle 38.2
Fenny Compton 44.5
Fenny Drayton 27.4
Fenny Stratford 5.1
Fenrother 32.1
Fenstanton 6.3
Fenton (Cambs) 6.3
Fenton (Cumbria) 10.1
Fenton (Lincs)* 28.1, 28.6
Fenton (Staffs) 40.3
Fenton Barns S13
Fenwick S11
Fenwick (Castle Morpeth) 32.1
Fenwick (N'land) 32.1
Fenwick (S Yorks) 39.2
Feock 9.1
Ferintosh S17
Ferme Park L14
Fern S2
Fern Splatt 9.1
Ferncliffe 47.1
Ferndale W18
Ferndown 13.3
Ferness S17
Ferneydale Wood 37.1
Ferngrove 19.3
Fernham 35.4
Fernhill (part) 19.3, 46.1
Fernhill Heath 49.6
Fernhurst 46.2
Ferniegair S28
Fernilee 11.1
Fernwood 34.3
Ferrensby 33.6
Ferring 46.5
Ferry Fryston 47.5
Ferrybridge 47.5
Ferryden S2
Ferryhill 14.1
Ferryside W6
Fersfield 30.7
Festival Park 40.3
Fetcham 42.8
Fetlar S26
Fetterangus S1
Fettercairn S1
Fetteresso S1
Fewcott 35.2
Fewston 33.6
Ffairfach W6
Ffaldybrenin W6
Ffestiniog W11
Fforddygyfraith W3
Fforest W6
Fforest Coalpit W13
Fforest Goch W14
Fforestfach W19
Ffrith W10
Ffrwd (part) W10, W22
Ffynnonddrain W6
Ffynnongroyw W10
Fiddington 38.1
Fiddlers Green 21.1
Field Broughton 10.5
Field Dalling 30.1
Field Head 27.4
Fifehead Magdalen 13.2
Fifehead Neville 13.2
Fifield (Berks) 3.4
Fifield (Oxon) 35.1
Fifield Bavant 48.1
Figheldean 48.1
Figsbury 48.1
Filby 30.6
Filey 33.4
Filgrave (see Tyringham)
Filkins & Broughton Poggs 35.1
Filleigh 12.2
Fillingham 28.1
Fillongley 44.1
Filton (part) 4.1, 18.7
Filton Park 18.7
Filwood Park 4.1
Fimber 15.2
Finavon S2
Fincastle S24
Fincham 30.2
Finchampstead 3.3
Finchdean 20.6
Finchingfield 17.2
Finchley L2
Findern 11.9
Findhorn S20
Findo Gask S24
Findochty S20
Findon Valley 46.6
Findon Village 46.5
Findowrie S2
Finedon 31.6
Fineshade 31.3
Fingask S24
Fingest 5.3
Finghall 33.1
Finglesham 25.6
Fingringhoe 17.3
Finham 45.7
Finmere 35.2
Finningham 41.4
Finningley 39.2
Finsbay S32
Finsbury Park (part) L14, L19
Finstall 49.2
Finsthwaite 10.5
Finstock 35.1
Finstown S23
Fintray S1
Fintry S29
Fionnphort S3
Fir Tree 14.1
Firbank 10.5
Firbeck 39.4
Firby* 33.2, 33.3
Firgrove 19.4
Firle 16.4
Firsby 28.2
Firsdown 48.1
Firth S23
Fishbourne (W Sussex) 46.2
Fishburn 14.1
Fishcross S8
Fishergate 33.7
Fishermead 5.1
Fishers Pond 20.5
Fishersgate 46.7
Fisherstreet 46.2
Fisherton S27
Fisherton-de-la-Mere (part) 48.1
Fisherwick 40.8
Fishguard & Goodwick W16
Fishlake 39.2
Fishley (see Upton)
Fishponds (Bristol) 4.1
Fishponds (Dorset) 13.1
Fishpool 19.3
Fishtoft 28.5
Fiskerton (Lincs) 28.1
Fiskerton-cum-Morton 34.3
Fitling 15.2
Fittleton 48.1
Fittleworth 46.2
Fitz 37.1
Fitzhead 38.4
Fitzroy 38.4
Fitzwilliam 47.5
Five Acres 18.2
Five Ash Down 16.1
Five Ashes 16.1
Five Bells 38.3
Five Lane Ends 47.1
Five Lanes 9.1
Five Oak Green 25.11
Five Roads W6
Fivehead 38.5
Fiveways S27
Fixby 47.4
Flackwell Heath 5.3
Fladbury 49.6
Fladdabister S26
Flagg 11.3
Flamborough 15.2
Flamstead 22.4
Flanderwell 39.4
Flansham 46.5
Flappit Spring 47.1
Flasby with Winterburn 33.5
Flash 40.1
Flaunden 22.4
Flawborough 34.8
Flawith 33.2
Flax Bourton 38.7
Flaxby 33.6
Flaxpool 38.3
Flaxton 33.3
Fleckney 27.8
Flecknoe 44.3
Fledborough 34.1
Fleet (Dorset) 13.1
Fleet (Hants) 20.2
Fleet (Lincs) 28.7
Fleet Marston 5.2
Fleetwood 26.2
Flegg (see Blofield)
Fleggburgh 30.6
Fleming 25.6
Flemingston W21
Flempton 41.3
Fletcher's Bridge 9.1
Fletching 16.1
Fletton 6.1
Fleur-de-Lys W4
Flexbury 9.1
Flichity S17
Flimwell 16.2
Flint W10
Flint Hill 14.1
Flint Mountain W10
Flintham 34.8
Flinton 15.2
Flitcham with Appleton 30.2
Flitholme 10.3
Flitton 2.2
Flitwick 2.2
Flixborough 28.8
Flixton (East) (Lowestoft) (Suffolk) 41.1
Flixton (Gtr M'chester) 19.8
Flixton (N Yorks) 33.4
Flixton (West) (Bungay) (Suffolk) 41.1
Flockton 47.4
Flookburgh 10.5
Flordon 30.7
Flore 31.4
Florence 40.3
Florence Park 35.5
Floriston 10.1
Flotta S23
Flotterstone S19
Flowton 41.4
Flush 47.4
Flushdyke 47.5
Flushing 9.1
Flyford Flavell 49.6
Fobbing (part) 17.10, 17.12
Fochabers S20
Fochriw W4
Fockbury 49.2
Fodderty S17
Foddington 38.5
Foel W17
Foelgastell W6
Foggathorpe 15.2
Fogo S30
Folda S2
Fole (part) 40.1, 40.5
Folke 13.1
Folkestone 25.13
Folkingham 28.6
Folkington 16.1
Folksworth 6.3
Folkton 33.4
Follifoot 33.6
Folly Gate 12.3

Fonaby 28.1
Fonmon W21
Fonthill Bishop 48.1
Fonthill Gifford 48.1
Fontley (part) 20.5, 20.10
Fontmell Magna 13.2
Fontwell 46.5
Foolow 11.3
Footherley 40.8
Forbes (see Tullynessle)
Force Forge 10.5
Forcett with Carkin 33.1
Ford (Argyll & Bute) S3
Ford (Bucks) 5.2
Ford (Gloucs) 18.5
Ford (Here) 21.1
Ford (Mersey) 29.1
Ford (Midlothian) S19
Ford (N'land) 32.1
Ford (Shrop) 37.1
Ford (Som) 38.4
Ford (W Sussex) 46.5
Ford (Wilts) 48.1
Ford End 17.7
Ford Estate 43.5
Ford Green 40.3
Ford Street 38.4
Fordbridge 45.6
Fordcombe 25.8
Forde Abbey 13.1
Forden W17
Forder 9.1
Fordhall 37.1
Fordham (Cambs) 6.4
Fordham (Essex) 17.3
Fordham (Norfolk) 30.2
Fordhouses 45.1
Fordingbridge 20.7
Fordington (see Ulceby)
Fordon 15.2
Fordoun S1
Fordwich 25.5
Fordyce S1
Foremark 11.9
Foreness (Broadstairs) 25.7
Forest Gate (part) L25, L31
Forest Green 42.8
Forest Hall 43.2
Forest Head 10.1
Forest Hill 35.3
Forest Hill (part) L23, L28
Forest Park 3.6
Forest Row 16.1
Forest Town 34.2
Forest-in-Teesdale 14.1
Forestfields 34.6
Forestmill S8
Forestside 46.2
Forfar S2
Forgandenny S24
Forgewood S22
Forglen S1
Forgue S1
Formby 29.1
Forncett (St Mary & St Peter) 30.7
Forneth S24
Fornham All Saints 41.3
Fornham St Genevieve 41.3
Fornham St Martin 41.3
Forrabury & Minster 9.1
Forres S20
Forsbrook 40.1
Forshaw Heath 44.5
Forsinard S17
Forstal (part) 25.9, 25.10
Fort Augustus S17
Fort William S17
Forteviot S24
Forth S28
Forthampton 18.1
Fortingall S24
Forton (Hants)* 20.4, 20.11
Forton (Lancs) 26.2
Forton (Som) 38.5
Forton (Staffs) 40.4
Fortrose S17
Forty Green* 5.3, 5.4
Fosbury 48.1
Foscote 31.7
Foscott 5.2
Fosdyke 28.5
Fosham 15.2
Foss S24
Fosse Cross 18.5
Fossebridge 18.5
Fossoway S24
Fosterhouses 39.2
Fosters Booth 31.7
Foston (Derbys) 11.9
Foston (Lincs) 28.6
Foston (N Yorks) 33.3
Foston on the Wolds 15.2
Fotherby 28.2
Fotheringhay 31.3
Foula S26
Foulby 47.5
Foulden (Borders) S30
Foulden (Norfolk) 30.3
Foulk Stapleford 7.3
Foulness 17.11
Foulridge 26.13
Foulsham 30.5
Fountainhall S30
Fountains Earth 33.6
Four Alls 37.1
Four Ashes 40.6
Four Crosses (Powys) W17
Four Crosses (Staffs) 40.6
Four Elms 25.8
Four Lane Ends (Gtr M'chester) 19.3
Four Lane Ends (T & W) 43.5
Four Lane Ends (W Yorks) 47.1
Four Lane Ends (Warks) 44.2
Four Lanes 9.1
Four Marks 20.6
Four Mile Bridge W1
Four Oaks (W Mids) 45.5
Four Roads W6
Fourstones 32.1
Fovant 48.1
Foveran S1
Fowey 9.1
Fowlis Wester S24
Fowlmere 6.5
Fownhope 21.1
Fox Milne 5.1
Foxborough 3.5
Foxcote 38.2
Foxcotte 20.4
Foxearth 17.2
Foxfield 10.5
Foxhall 41.5
Foxham 48.1
Foxhill 48.2
Foxhole 9.1
Foxholes (N Yorks) 33.3
Foxholes (Shrop) 37.1
Foxley (N'hants) 31.7
Foxley (Norfolk) 30.3
Foxley (Wilts) 48.1
Foxmoor 38.4
Foxt 40.1
Foxton (Cambs) 6.5
Foxton (Durham) 14.1
Foxton (Leics) 27.8
Foxup 33.5
Foy 21.1
Foyers S17
Fraddam 9.1
Fraddon 9.1
Fradley 40.8
Fradley Junction 40.8
Fradswell 40.4
Fraisthorpe 15.2
Framfield 16.1
Framingham Earl 30.7
Framingham Pigot 30.7
Framlingham 41.5
Frampton (Dorset) 13.1
Frampton (Lincs) 28.5
Frampton (Llantwit Major) W21
Frampton Cotterell 18.7
Frampton Mansell 18.5
Frampton-on-Severn 18.6
Framsden 41.4
Framwellgate Moor 14.1
Frankby 29.5
Frankfort (Sloley) 30.1
Frankley (part) 45.5, 49.2
Frankton 44.3
Fransham, Gt & Little 30.3
Frant 16.1
Fraserburgh S1
Frating 17.4
Freathy 9.1
Freckenham 41.2
Freckleton 26.5
Free Town 19.3
Freeby 27.3
Freefolk 20.1
Freefolk Manor 20.1
Freefolk Priors 20.1
Freeford 40.8
Freehay 40.1
Freeland 35.1
Freemantle 20.8
Freemantle Park Farm 20.1
Freethorpe 30.5
Freiston 28.5
Fremington (Devon) 12.2
Fremington (N Yorks) 33.1
Frenchay (part) 4.1, 18.7
Frenchmoor 20.4
Frensham (part) 20.6, 42.11
Frenze 30.7
Freshbrook 48.2
Freshfield 29.1
Freshford 38.6
Freshwater 24.1
Freshwater East-West W16
Fressingfield 41.4
Freston 41.6
Freswick S17
Fretherne 18.6
Frettenham 30.5
Freuchie S16
Freystrop W16
Friar Park 45.4
Friars Cliff 13.8
Frickley (see Clayton)
Friday Hill L31
Friday Street 42.8
Fridaybridge 6.2
Fridays Hill 46.2
Fridaythorpe 15.2
Friendly 47.3
Friesthorpe 28.1
Frieston 28.6
Frieth 5.3
Frilford Heath 35.4
Frilsham 3.1
Frimley 42.3
Frimley Green 42.3
Frindsbury 25.3
Fring 30.2
Fringford 35.2
Frinsted 25.10
Frinton-on-Sea 17.4
Friockheim S2
Friog W11
Frisby 27.8
Frisby on the Wreake 27.3
Friskney 28.2
Friston (E Sussex) 16.1
Friston (Suffolk) 41.5
Fritchley 11.6
Frith (Cheshire) (see Wrenbury)
Frith (Durham) (see Forest)
Frith Bank 28.2
Fritham 20.7
Frithelstock 12.1
Frithend 20.6
Frithsden 22.4
Frithville 28.2
Frittenden 25.11
Fritton* 30.6, 30.7
Fritwell 35.2
Frizinghall 47.1
Frizington (see Arlecdon)
Frocester 18.6
Frodesley 37.1
Frodingham 28.8
Frodsham 7.3
Frog Street 38.5
Froggatt 11.3

Froghall (Beds) 2.2
Froghall (Staffs) 40.1
Frogham (Hants) 20.7
Frogham (Kent) 25.6
Frogholt 25.13
Frogmore (Devon) 12.9
Frogmore (Hants) 20.2
Frogmore (Herts) 22.5
Frognall 28.6
Frogpool 9.1
Frolesworth 27.8
Frome 38.2
Frome St Quintin 13.1
Frome Vauchurch 13.1
Frome Whitfield 13.1
Fron W17
Froncysyilte W22
Frongoch W11
Frost Hill 38.7
Frostenden 41.1
Frosterley 14.1
Frostrow 10.5
Froxfield (Hants) 20.6
Froxfield (Wilts) 48.1
Froyle 20.6
Fryerning (see Ingatestone)
Fryton 33.3
Fulbeck (Lincs) (part) 28.4, 28.6
Fulbeck (N'land) 32.1
Fulbourn 6.5
Fulbrook (Oxon) 35.1
Fulbrook (Warks) 44.5
Fulfen 40.8
Fulford (Som) 38.4
Fulford (Staffs) 40.4
Fulford (York) 33.7
Fulham (part) L13, L20
Fulking 46.4
Full Sutton 15.2
Fullers Slade 5.1
Fullerton 20.4
Fulletby 28.2
Fullready 44.5
Fulmer 5.5
Fulmodestone 30.1
Fulnetby 28.1
Fulney 28.7
Fulstone 47.4
Fulstow 28.2
Fulwell (Oxon) 35.2
Fulwell (T & W) 43.5
Fulwood (Lancs) 26.6
Fulwood (Som) 38.4
Fundenhall 30.7
Funtington 46.2
Funtley (part) 20.5, 20.10
Furnace S3
Furnace (Carm) W6
Furnace (Derbys) 11.4
Furnace Green 46.1
Furneaux Pelham 22.3
Furness Vale 11.1
Furnham 38.5
Furtho 31.7
Furze Hill 20.7
Furze Platt 3.4
Furzedown L32
Furzley 20.7
Furzton 5.1
Furzy Park & Portfield W16
Fyfield (Essex) 17.6
Fyfield (Gloucs) 18.5
Fyfield (Hants) 20.4
Fyfield (Oxon) 35.4
Fyfield (Pewsey & Marlborough) (Wilts) 48.1
Fylingdales 33.4
Fylingthorpe 33.4
Fyvie S1
Gabwell 12.5
Gadbrook 42.8
Gaddesby 27.3
Gaddesden Row 22.4
Gadlas 37.1
Gadlys W18
Gaerfawr W13
Gaerwen W1
Gailey 40.6
Gainfield 35.4
Gainford 14.1
Gainsborough 28.1
Gairloch S17
Gairlochy S17
Gairsay S23
Gaisgill 10.3
Gaitsgill 10.1
Galashiels S30
Galgate 26.1
Galhampton 38.5
Galley Common 44.2
Galley Hill (Bucks) 5.1
Galley Hill (Kent) 25.1
Galleyend 17.7
Galleywood 17.7
Gallowstree Common 35.3
Gallt-y-foel W11
Galmington 38.4
Galmpton (Kingswear) (part) 12.9
Galmpton (S Huish) 12.9
Galmpton (Torbay) (part) 12.10
Galon Uchaf W12
Galson S32
Galston S11
Gamblesby 10.3
Gamesley 11.1
Gamlingay 6.5
Gamrie S1
Gamston* 34.1, 34.8
Ganarew 21.1
Gangbridge 20.1
Ganllwyd W11
Ganstead 15.2
Ganthorpe 33.3
Ganton 33.3
Ganwick Corner 22.10
Garbhalt S3
Garboldisham 30.3
Garden City W10
Garden Village W19
Gardeners Green 3.3
Gardenstown S1
Garenin S32
Garford 35.4
Garforth 47.2
Gargrave 33.5
Gargunnock S29
Garguston S17
Garlieston S10
Garlinge (Margate) 25.7
Garlinge Green (Petham) 25.5
Garmond S1
Garmouth S20
Garnant W6
Garndiffaith W20
Garndolbenmaen W11
Garnett Bridge 10.5
Garnfadryn W11
Garnswllt W19
Garras 9.1
Garretts Green 45.5
Garrigill (see Alston)
Garriston 33.1
Garrowby 15.2
Garrowhill S7
Garsdale 10.5
Garsdon 48.1
Garsington 35.3
Garstang 26.2
Garston (Herts) (part) 22.8, 22.9, 22.10
Garston (Mersey) 29.2
Garswood 29.3
Garth (Powys) W17
Garth (Wrexham) W22
Garth Row 10.5
Garthbeibio W17
Garthbrengy W17
Gartheli W7
Garthmyl W17
Garthorpe (Leics) 27.3
Garthorpe (N Lincs) 28.8
Gartly S1
Gartmore S29
Gartness S22
Garton-on-the-Wolds 15.2
Garvald S13
Garve S17
Garvestone 30.3
Garway 21.1
Garynahine S32
Gasper (see Stourton)
Gastard 48.1
Gasthorpe 30.3
Gatcombe 24.1
Gate Burton 28.1
Gate Helmsley 33.3
Gateacre 29.2
Gatebeck 10.5
Gateforth 33.8
Gatehead S11
Gatehouse of Fleet S10
Gateley 30.3
Gatenby 33.2
Gateshead 43.3
Gateside (Angus) S2
Gateside (Fife) S16
Gateside (N Ayrs) S21
Gatley 19.9
Gatton 42.9
Gattonside S30
Gaulby 27.8
Gauldry S16
Gaunts 13.3
Gaunts Common 13.3
Gaunts Earthcott 18.7
Gautby 28.2
Gauxholme 47.3
Gavinton S30
Gawber 39.1
Gawbridge 38.5
Gawcott 5.2
Gawsworth 7.5
Gawthorpe 47.5
Gawthrop 10.5
Gawthwaite 10.5
Gay Bowers 17.7
Gaydon 44.5
Gayhurst 5.1
Gayles 33.1
Gayton (Mersey) 29.5
Gayton (N'hants) 31.7
Gayton (Norfolk) 30.2
Gayton (Staffs) 40.4
Gayton le Marsh 28.2
Gayton le Wold 28.2
Gazeley 41.2
Geanies S17
Gear (Perranporth) 9.1
Gear Sands 9.1
Geddes S17
Gedding 41.4
Geddington 31.2
Gedgrave 41.5
Gedling 34.7
Gedney 28.7
Gedney Hill 28.7
Geldeston 30.7
Gelli W18
Gellideg W12
Gellifor W9
Gelligaer W4
Gelligroes W4
Gellihaf W4
Gellilydan W11
Gellinudd W14
Gellyburn S24
Gellywen W6
Gelston (Dumfries & Galloway) S10
Gelston (Lincs) 28.6
Geltsdale 10.1
Gembling 15.2
Geneu'rglyn W7
Gentleshaw 40.8
George Green (Wexham) 5.5
George Nympton 12.2
Georgeham 12.2
Georgetown W2, W12
Gerards Bridge 29.3
Gerlan W11
Germansweek 12.3
Germoe 9.1
Gerrans 9.1
Gerrards Cross (part) 5.4, 5.5
Gestingthorpe 17.2
Ghyliheugh 32.1

Gibraltar 5.2
Gidea Park L16
Gidleigh 12.3
Giffard Park 5.1
Giffnock S14
Gifford S13
Giggleswick 33.5
Gigha, Isle of S3
Gilberdyke 15.2
Gilchriston S13
Gilcrux 10.2
Gildersome 47.2
Gildingwells 39.4
Gilesgate 14.1
Gilesgate Moor 14.1
Gileston W21
Gilfach W4
Gilfach Goch W18
Gillamoor 33.3
Gillars Green 29.3
Gilley Law 43.5
Gilling East 33.3
Gilling with Hartforth & Sedbury 33.1
Gillingham (Dorset) 13.2
Gillingham (Kent) 25.3
Gillingham (Norfolk) 30.7
Gillingstool 18.7
Gillmoss 29.2
Gillow Heath 40.1
Gillway 40.9
Gilmerton S24
Gilmonby 14.1
Gilmorton 27.8
Gilmourton S28
Gilroyd 39.1
Gilsland (part) 10.1, 32.1
Gilstead 47.1
Gilston 22.3
Gilwern W13
Gimingham 30.1
Gipping 41.4
Gipsey Bridge 28.2
Girlington 47.1
Girsby (Lincs) 28.2
Girsby (N Yorks) 33.2
Girt 38.5
Girtford 2.2
Girton (Cambs) 6.5
Girton (Notts) 34.3
Girvan S27
Gisburn 26.3
Gisburn Forest 26.3
Gisleham 41.1
Gislingham 41.4
Gissing 30.7
Gittisham 12.7
Givendale 33.6
Givons Grove 42.8
Gladestry W17
Gladsmuir S13
Glais W19
Glaisdale 33.4
Glamis S2
Glan-yr-afon W10
Glanamman W6
Glandford (see Letheringsett)
Glandy Cross W6
Glangrwyney W17
Glangwili W6
Glanrafon W11
Glanton 32.1
Glantwymyn W17
Glanvilles Wootton 13.2
Glanyant Pengam W4
Glanynant (Caerph) W4
Glanynant (Powys) W17
Glapthorn 31.3
Glapwell 11.5
Glasbury W17
Glasbury-on-Wye (Brecknock) W17
Glascoed (Conwy) W8
Glascoed (Monmth) W13
Glascote 40.9
Glascote Heath 40.9
Glascwm W17
Glasfryn W8
Glasgow S7
Glasinfryn W11
Glass S1
Glasserton S10
Glassford S28
Glasshoughton 47.5
Glassonby 10.3
Glasterlaw S2
Glaston 36.1
Glastonbury 38.2
Glatton 6.3
Glazebrook (see Rixton)
Glazebury 7.1
Glazeley 37.1
Gleaston 10.5
Glebe 43.5
Glebe, The (Norton) 14.10
Glemham, Gt & Little 41.5
Glemsford 41.6
Glen Parva (part) 27.6
Glen Village S15
Glenalmond S24
Glenbarr S3
Glenbervie S1
Glenboi W18
Glenboig S22
Glenborrodale S17
Glenbuchat S1
Glenbuck S11
Glencaple S10
Glencarse S24
Glencoe S17
Glencorse S19
Glendale S17
Glendaruel S3
Glendevon S24
Glendoick S24
Gleneagles S24
Glenelg S17
Glenfarg S24
Glenfield (part) 27.5, 27.6
Glenfields W4
Glenfinnan S17
Glenfoot S24
Glengairn (see Glenmuick)
Glengarnock S21
Glenglass S17
Glenisla S2
Glenkinchie S13
Glenlednock S24
Glenluce S10
Glenlyon S24
Glenmavis S22
Glenmuick, Tullich & Glengairn S1
Glenprosen S2
Glenridding 10.3
Glenrothes S16
Glenshee S24
Glenshiel S17
Glenskiach S17
Glentanar (see Aboyne)
Glentham 28.1
Glenthorne 38.3
Glentrool S10
Glentworth 28.1
Glespin S28
Gletness S26
Glewstone 21.1
Glinton 6.1
Glooston 27.8
Glororum 32.1
Glossop 11.1
Gloucester 18.3
Glover 43.5
Glusburn 33.5
Glympton 35.1
Glyn W17
Glyn Abbey W6
Glyn Gaer W4
Glyn Morlas 37.1
Glyn Tarell W17
Glyncoch W18
Glyncorrwg W14
Glynde 16.4
Glynfach W17
Glynneath W14
Glyntaff W18
Glyntawe W17
Glyntraian W22
Gnosall 40.4
Goadby 27.8
Goadby Marwood 27.3
Goadsbarrow 10.5
Goatacre 48.1
Goathill 13.1
Goathland 33.4
Goathurst 38.1
Goathurst Common 25.8
Gobowen 37.1
Godalming 42.11
Godden Green 25.8
Godington 35.2
Godmanchester 6.3
Godmanstone 13.1
Godmersham 25.12
Godminster 38.5
Godney 38.2
Godolphin Cross 9.1
Godre'rgraig W14
Godshill (Hants) 20.7
Godshill (I of W) 24.1
Godstone 42.10
Goetre W13
Goff's Oak 22.7
Goginan W7
Golan W11
Golant 9.1
Golberdon 9.1
Golborne 19.1
Golborne Bellow 7.3
Golborne David 7.3
Golcar 47.4
Goldcliff W15
Golden Bank 9.1
Golden Cross 16.1
Golden Green 25.9
Golden Grove W6
Golden Hill 38.5
Golden Valley 11.6
Goldenhill 40.3
Golders Green L2
Goldhanger 17.8
Goldicote 44.5
Goldings 31.5
Golds Hill 45.4
Goldsborough* 33.4, 33.6
Goldsithney 9.1
Goldstone (Shrop) 37.1
Goldsworth Park 42.4
Goldthorpe 39.1
Gollawater 9.1
Golsoncott 38.3
Golspie S17
Goltho 28.1
Gomersal 47.4
Gomshall 42.7
Gonalston 34.3
Gonfirth S26
Good Easter 17.7
Gooderstone 30.3
Goodleigh 12.2
Goodley Stock 25.8
Goodmanham 15.2
Goodnestone* 25.4, 25.6
Goodrich 21.1
Goodshaw 26.14
Goodwick (see Fishguard)
Goodwood 46.2
Goodworth Clatford 20.4
Goodyers End 44.2
Goole 15.2
Goole Fields 15.2
Goonbell 9.1
Goongumpas 9.1
Goonhavern 9.1
Goonown 9.1
Goonpiper 9.1
Goonvrea 9.1
Goose Eye 47.1
Goose Green 25.9
Goose Hill 20.1
Goosemoor 38.3
Goosenford 38.4
Goosey 35.4
Goosnargh 26.6
Goostrey 7.5
Gordon S30
Gore End 20.1
Gore Street, Monkton (Kent) 25.7
Gorebridge S19
Gorefield 6.2

Goring 35.3
Goring Heath 35.3
Goring-by-Sea 46.6
Gorleston on Sea 30.6
Gornal Wood 45.3
Gorran Churchtown 9.1
Gorran Haven 9.1
Gorse Covert 7.1
Gorsedd W10
Gorseinon W19
Gorsey Bank 37.1
Gorslas W6
Gorsley (part) 18.2, 21.1
Gorst Hill (Rock) 49.1
Gorstage 7.3
Gorstan S17
Gorsty 7.5
Gorsty Common 21.1
Gorton 19.6
Gosbeck 41.4
Gosberton 28.7
Gosfield 17.2
Gosford 35.2
Gosforth (Cumbria) 10.4
Gosforth (T & W) 43.1
Gosforth Valley 11.4
Gosling Street 38.5
Gosmore 22.1
Gospel Ash 38.5
Gospel End 40.6
Gospel Oak L6, 45.4
Gosport 20.11
Goss Moor (St Columb) 9.1
Gossops Green 46.1
Goswick 32.1
Gotham (Dorset) 13.3
Gotham (Notts) 34.8
Gotherington 18.1
Gothers 9.1
Gotton 38.4
Goudhurst 25.11
Goulceby 28.2
Gourock S18
Govilon W13
Gowan Bank S2
Gowanbank (Colliston) S2
Gowdall 15.2
Gower W19
Gowerton W19
Gowkshill S19
Gowthorpe 15.2
Goxhill (E Yorks) 15.2
Goxhill (Lincs) 28.8
Goytre W14
Graby 28.6
Gracedieu 27.1
Graces Cross 17.7
Gradbach 40.1
Graddfa W4
Grade Ruan 9.1
Graemsay S23
Graffham 46.2
Grafham 6.3
Grafton & Radcot 35.1
Grafton (Cheshire) 7.3
Grafton (Here) 21.1
Grafton (N Yorks) (see Marton)
Grafton (Wilts) 48.1
Grafton (Worcs) 49.6
Grafton Flyford 49.6
Grafton Manor 49.2
Grafton Regis 31.7
Grafton Underwood 31.2
Grafty Green, nr Lenham 25.10
Grahamston Cottages S2
Graig (Rhondda) W18
Graig Rhymney W4
Graig-y-Rhacca W4
Grain 25.3
Grain (Isle of) (see Isle of Grain)
Grainsby 28.2
Grainthorpe 28.2
Grampound 9.1
Grampound Rd 9.1
Granborough 5.2
Granby (Bucks) 5.1
Granby (Dorset) 13.1
Granby (Mersey) 29.2
Granby (Notts) 34.8
Grandborough 44.3
Grandpont 35.5
Grandtully S24
Grane 26.14
Grange S20
Grange (Dorset) 13.3
Grange (Kent) 25.3
Grange (Mersey) 29.5
Grange Court 18.2
Grange Farm 5.1
Grange Moor 47.4
Grange Park (Mersey) 29.3
Grange Park (N'hants) 31.7
Grange Park (Wilts) 48.2
Grange Villa 14.1
Grange de Lings 28.1
Grange of Lindores S16
Grange-over-Sands 10.5
Grangefield 14.10
Grangemouth S15
Grangetown W5
Grangetown (N Yorks) 33.10
Grangetown (T & W) 43.5
Grangewood 11.2
Gransmoor 15.2
Granston W16
Grantchester 6.5
Grantham 28.6
Grantley 33.6
Grantown-on-Spey S17
Grantshouse S30
Grappenhall 7.1
Grasby 28.1
Grasmere 10.5
Grasscroft 19.7
Grassendale 29.2
Grassington 33.5
Grassmoor 11.4
Grassthorpe 34.3
Grasswell 43.5
Grateley 20.4
Gratton (Derbys) 11.3
Gratton (Staffs) 40.1
Gratwich 40.5
Graveley (Cambs) 6.5
Graveley (Herts) 22.1
Gravelly Hill 45.5
Gravels 37.1
Graveney 25.4
Gravenhunger 37.1
Gravenhurst 2.2
Gravesend 25.2
Gravir S32
Grayingham 28.1
Grayrigg 10.5
Grays 17.12
Grayshott 20.6
Grayswood 42.11
Graythwaite 10.5
Grea Harwood 26.11
Greasbrough 39.4
Greasby 29.5
Greasley 34.5
Gt Abington 6.5
Gt Addington 31.3
Gt Alne 44.5
Gt Altcar 26.8
Gt Amwell 22.3
Gt Asby 10.3
Gt Ashby (part) 21.1, 22.1, 22.2
Gt Ashfield 41.4
Gt Aycliffe 14.1
Gt Ayton 33.2
Gt Baddow 17.7
Gt Badminton 18.7
Gt Bardfield 17.2
Gt Barford 2.1
Gt Barr (part) 45.2, 45.4, 45.5
Gt Barrington (see Barrington) (Gloucs)
Gt Barton 41.3
Gt Bavington 32.1
Gt Bedwyn 48.1
Gt Bentley 17.4
Gt Billing 31.5
Gt Blakenham 41.4
Gt Blencowe 10.3
Gt Bolas 37.4
Gt Bookham 42.8
Gt Boughton 7.3
Gt Bourton 35.2
Gt Bowden 27.8
Gt Bradley 41.3
Gt Braxted 17.8
Gt Bricett 41.4
Gt Brickhill 5.2
Gt Bridge 45.4
Gt Bromley 17.4
Gt Broughton 33.2
Gt Budworth 7.3
Gt Burdon 14.8
Gt Burstead 17.10
Gt Busby 33.2
Gt Canfield 17.1
Gt Carlton 28.2
Gt Casterton 36.1
Gt Chart 25.12
Gt Chatwell 40.6
Great Chesterford 17.1
Gt Chishill 6.5
Gt Clacton 17.4
Gt Clifton 10.2
Gt Coates 28.9
Gt Comberton 49.6
Gt Corby 10.1
Gt Cornard 41.6
Gt Coxwell 35.4
Gt Cressingham 30.3
Gt Crosby 29.1
Gt Dalby 27.3
Great Doddington 31.6
Gt Doward 21.1
Gt Dunham 30.3
Great Dunmow 17.1
Great Easton (Essex) 17.1
Gt Easton (Leics) 27.8
Gt Eccleston 26.2
Gt Ellingham 30.3
Gt Elm 38.2
Gt Eversden 6.5
Gt Faringdon 35.4
Gt Fenton 40.3
Gt Finborough 41.4
Gt Gaddesden 22.4
Gt Gidding 6.3
Gt Givendale 15.2
Gt Glen 27.8
Gt Gonerby 28.6
Gt Gransden 6.3
Great Hale 28.4
Great Hallingbury 17.1
Great Hampden 5.3
Great Hanwood 37.1
Great Harrowden 31.6
Great Haseley 35.3
Great Haywood 40.4
Gt Henny 17.2
Gt Hinton 48.1
Gt Holland 17.4
Gt Hollands 3.6
Gt Holm 5.1
Gt Horkesley 17.3
Gt Horton 47.1
Gt Horwood 5.2
Gt Houghton (N'hants) 31.5
Gt Houghton (S Yorks) 39.1
Gt Hucklow 11.3
Gt Humby 28.6
Gt Kelk 15.2
Great Kimble 5.3
Gt Kingshill (part) 5.4
Gt Langdale 10.5
Gt Langton 33.2
Gt Lea 3.3
Gt Leighs 17.7
Gt Limber 28.1
Gt Linford 5.1
Gt Livermere 41.3
Gt Longstone 11.3
Gt Lumley 14.1
Gt Maplestead 17.2
Gt Massingham 30.2
Gt Melton 30.7
Great Milton 35.3
Gt Missenden 5.4
Gt Mitton 26.3
Gt Mongeham 25.6

Gt Moulton 30.7
Gt Munden 22.3
Gt Musgrave 10.3
Great Ness 37.1
Gt Notley 17.2
Gt Oakley (Essex) 17.4
Gt Oakley (N'hants) 31.1
Gt Ormside 10.3
Gt Orton 10.1
Gt Ouseburn 33.6
Gt Oxenden 31.4
Gt Packington 44.1
Gt Parndon 17.5
Gt Paxton 6.3
Gt Plumpton (see Westby with Plumpton)
Gt Ponton 28.6
Gt Preston 47.2
Gt Purston 31.7
Gt Ribston with Walshford 33.6
Gt Rissington 18.5
Gt Ryburgh 30.1
Gt Saling (see Salings, The)
Gt Salkeld 10.3
Great Sampford 17.1
Gt Sankey 7.1
Gt Saxham 41.3
Gt Shefford 3.1
Gt Shelford 6.5
Gt Smeaton 33.2
Gt Snoring 30.1
Gt Somerford 48.1
Great Soudley 37.1
Gt Stainton 14.8
Gt Stanney 7.3
Gt Staughton 6.3
Gt Steeping 28.2
Gt Stoke 18.7
Gt Stretton 27.8
Gt Strickland 10.3
Gt Stukeley 6.3
Gt Sturton 28.2
Gt Sutton 7.3
Gt Tew 35.1
Gt Tey 17.3
Gt Thurlow 41.3
Gt Timble 33.6
Gt Torrington 12.1
Gt Totham 17.8
Gt Urswick 10.5
Gt Wakering 17.11
Gt Waldingfield 41.6
Gt Walsingham 30.1
Gt Waltham 17.7
Gt Warford 7.5
Gt Whelnetham 41.3
Gt Whittington 32.1
Gt Wigborough 17.3
Gt Wilbraham 6.5
Gt Wilne 11.9
Gt Wishford 48.1
Gt Witchingham 30.5
Gt Witcombe 18.1
Gt Witley 49.4
Gt Wolford 44.5
Gt Wratting 41.3
Gt Wymondley 22.1
Gt Wyrley 40.6
Gt Yarmouth 30.6
Gt Yeldham 17.2
Greatfield 48.1
Greatford 28.6
Greatham (Co Durham) 14.9
Greatham (Hants) 20.6
Greatham (W Sussex) 46.3
Greatstone 25.13
Greatt Kingshill (part) 5.3
Greatt Marlow 5.3
Greatwood (Mylor) 9.1
Greatworth 31.7
Greaves Ground 10.5
Green Fairfield 11.1
Green Hailey 5.3
Green Hammerton 33.6
Green Haume 10.6
Green Haworth 26.11
Green Ore 38.2
Green Street Green (Darenth) 25.1
Greenaleigh 38.3
Greenbottom (Corn) 9.1
Greenbottom (Gloucs) 18.2
Greencroft 14.1
Greenfield (Beds) 2.2
Greenfield (Flint) W10
Greenfield (Gtr M'chester) 19.7
Greenfield (Lincs) (see Aby)
Greenfoot S22
Greenford L9
Greengairs S22
Greengates 47.1
Greenhalgh 26.5
Greenham (Berks) 3.1
Greenham (Dorset) 13.1
Greenham (Som)* 38.4, 38.5
Greenhaugh 32.1
Greenhead 32.1
Greenhill S15
Greenhill (Herne Bay) 25.5
Greenhill (Wilts) 48.1
Greenhill Bank 37.1
Greenhithe 25.1
Greenholm (see Newmilns)
Greenland 38.4, 38.5
Greenlands 49.3
Greenlaw S30
Greenlaw Mains S19
Greenleys 5.1
Greenloaning S24
Greenmeadow (Caerph) W4
Greenmeadow (Torfaen) W20
Greenmeadow (Wilts) 48.2
Greenmoor 39.1
Greenmount 19.3
Greenock S18
Greenodd 10.5
Greenrigg S31
Greens Norton 31.7
Greenscoe 10.6
Greenside (T & W) 43.3
Greenstead Green 17.2
Greensted 17.6
Greenway 38.4
Greenwich L11
Greenwich (Wilts) 48.1
Greenwith Common 9.1
Greet 45.5
Greete 37.1
Greetham 36.1
Greetham with Somersby 28.2
Greetland 47.3
Greetwell 28.1
Greinton 38.1
Grendon (N'hants) 31.6
Grendon (Warks) 44.1
Grendon Bishop 21.1
Grendon Underwood 5.2
Grenoside 39.3
Gresford W22
Gresham 30.1
Gressenhall 30.3
Gressingham 26.1
Gresty (see Shavington)
Greta Bridge 14.1
Gretna S10
Gretna Green S10
Gretton 18.1
Grewelthorpe 33.6
Greylees 28.4
Greys Green 35.3
Greysouthen 10.2
Greystead 32.1
Greystoke 10.3
Greystone S2
Greywell 20.2
Gribthorpe (E Yorks) 15.2
Griff 44.2
Griffiths Crossing W11
Griffithstown W20
Griffydam 27.1
Grimblethorpe 28.2
Grimethorpe 39.1
Grimley 49.4
Grimoldby 28.2
Grimpo 37.1
Grimsargh 26.6
Grimsby 28.9
Grimscote 31.7
Grimscott 9.1
Grimsdyke 48.1
Grimstead 48.1
Grimsthorpe 28.6
Grimston (E Yorks) 15.2
Grimston (Leics) 27.3
Grimston (N Yorks) 33.8
Grimston (Norfolk) 30.2
Grimstone 33.3
Grindale 15.2
Grindleford 11.3
Grindleton 26.3
Grindley (see Tushingham)
Grindley Brook 37.1
Grindlow 11.3
Grindon (Staffs) 40.1
Grindon (Stockton) 14.10
Grindon (T & W) 43.6
Gringley-on-the-Hill 34.1
Grinkle 33.10
Grinsdale 10.1
Grinshill 37.1
Grinton 33.1
Gristhorpe 33.4
Griston 30.3
Grittenham 48.1
Grittleton 48.1
Grizebeck 10.5
Grizedale, Garsdale 10.5
Grizedale, Satterthwaite 10.5
Groby 27.4
Groes W8
Groesfaen (part) W4, W18
Groesffordd W17
Groesffordd Marli W8
Groeslon W11
Groeslon Marc W11
Groespluan W17
Groeswen W4
Grogley 9.1
Gronant W10
Grondre W14
Groombridge (part) 16.1, 25.11
Grosmont (Monmth) W13
Grosmont (N Yorks) 33.4
Groton 41.6
Grotton 19.7
Grove (Bucks) 5.2
Grove (Kent) 25.5
Grove (Notts) 34.1
Grove (Oxon) 35.4
Grove Ferry 25.5
Grove Green, Boxley 25.10
Grove Hill 33.9
Grove, The (Durham) 14.1
Grovesend (Gloucs) 18.7
Grovesend (Swansea) W19
Grumbla 9.1
Grundisburgh 41.5
Gruting S26
Gt & Little Plumstead 30.5
Guard House 47.1
Guardbridge S16
Guarlford 49.4
Gubbions Green 17.7
Gubeon 32.1
Guestling 16.2
Guestwick 30.5
Guide Post 32.1
Guilden Morden 6.5
Guilden Sutton 7.3
Guildford 42.7
Guildhall 33.7
Guildtown S24
Guilsborough 31.4
Guilsfield Rural W17
Guilsfield Village W17
Guilton 25.6
Guisborough 33.10
Guiseley 47.2
Guist 30.3
Guiting Power 18.5
Gullane S13
Gullom 10.3
Gulval 9.1
Gulworthy 12.3

Gumfreston W16
Gumley 27.8
Gunby (part) 28.2, 28.6
Gundleton 20.5
Gunnerside 33.1
Gunnerton 32.1
Gunness 28.8
Gunnislake 9.1
Gunnista S26
Guns Village 45.4
Gunthorpe (Cambs) 6.1
Gunthorpe (Norfolk) 30.1
Gunthorpe (Notts) 34.3
Gunthorpe (Rutland) 36.1
Gunton Park 30.1
Gunville 24.1
Gunwalloe 9.1
Gupworthy 38.3
Gurnard 24.1
Gurney Slade 38.2
Gurnos W12, W17
Gussage All Saints 13.3
Gussage St Michael 13.3
Gustard Wood (part) 22.5
Guston 25.6
Gutcher S26
Guthrie S2
Guy's Cliffe (see Leek Wootton)
Guycroft (Otley) 47.2
Guyhirn 6.2
Gwaelodybrithdir W4
Gwaenysgor W10
Gwaithla W17
Gwalchmai W1
Gwarafog W17
Gwaun-Cae-Gurwen W14
Gweek 9.1
Gwehelog W13
Gwenddwr W17
Gwennap 9.1
Gwernaffield W10
Gwernesney W13
Gwernffrwd (see Wernffrud)
Gwernogle W6
Gwernyfed W17
Gwernymynydd W10
Gwersyllt W22
Gwespyr W10
Gwinear-Gwithian 9.1
Gwyddelwern W9
Gwyddgrug W6
Gwynfe W6
Gwynfryn W22
Gwytherin W8
Gyrn Goch W11
Habberley 37.1
Habblesthorpe 34.1
Habergham Eaves 26.12
Habertoft 28.2
Habrough 28.9
Habton, Gt & Little 33.3
Haccombe with Combe 12.5
Haceby 28.4
Hacheston 41.5
Hack Green 7.5
Hackford 30.7
Hackforth 33.2
Hackington 25.5
Hackleton 31.7
Hackmans Gate (Broome) 49.1
Hackness 33.4
Hackney (part) L7, L12
Hackney Wick L12
Hackthorn 28.1
Hackthorne 48.1
Hackthorpe 10.3
Hackwood Park 20.1
Haconby 28.6
Haddenham (Bucks) 5.2
Haddenham (Cambs) 6.4
Haddington (E Lothian) S13
Haddington (Lincs) 28.4
Haddiscoe 30.7
Haddon (part) 6.1, 6.3
Hade Edge 47.4
Haden Cross 45.4
Haden Hill 45.4
Hadfield 11.1
Hadleigh (Essex) 17.13
Hadleigh (Suffolk) 41.6
Hadley 37.4
Hadley End 40.5
Hadley Gate 40.8
Hadlow (Cheshire) 7.3
Hadlow (Kent) 25.9
Hadlow Down 16.1
Hadnall 37.1
Hadspen 38.5
Hadstock 17.1
Hadston 32.1
Hady 11.2
Hadzor 49.6
Hafod W19
Hafodyrynys W4
Haggate 26.12
Haggerston L12
Haggs S15
Hagley 49.2
Hagley (South Hereford) 21.1
Hagnaby 28.2
Hague Bar 11.1
Hagworthingham 28.2
Haigh (Gtr M'chester) 19.1
Haigh (W Yorks) 47.5
Haighton 26.6
Hail Weston 6.3
Haile & Wilton 10.4
Hailey 35.1
Hailsham 16.1
Hainford 30.5
Hainton 28.2
Hainworth 47.1
Haisthorpe 15.2
Halam 34.3
Halbeath S16
Halberton 12.4
Haldon 12.5
Hale (Cumbria) 10.5
Hale (Gtr M'chester) 19.8
Hale (Hants) 20.7
Hale (Som) 38.5
Hale (Surrey) 42.11
Hale Barns 19.8
Hale Coombe 38.7
Hale End L31
Hale Street 25.9
Hale Village (Liverpool) 7.2
Hales (Norfolk) 30.7
Hales (Staffs) 40.2
Halesfield 37.4
Halesowen 45.3
Halesworth 41.1
Halewood 29.4
Half Acre 19.3
Halford (Shrop) 37.1
Halford (Warks) 44.5
Halfpenny 10.5
Halfpenny Furze W6
Halfway W6
Halfway Bridge (Gwynedd) W11
Halfway Bridge (W Sussex) 46.2
Halfway House 37.1
Halfway Houses 25.4
Halghton W22
Halifax 47.3
Halkirk S17
Halkyn W10
Hall Bower 47.4
Hall End 18.7
Hall Farm 43.5
Hall Green (W Mids) 45.5
Hall Green (W Yorks) 47.5
Halland 16.1
Hallas Bridge 47.1
Hallaton 27.8
Hallatrow 38.6
Hallbankgate 10.1
Hallen 18.7
Hallfieldgate 11.4
Hallglen S15
Halliford 42.2
Halling 25.3
Hallington (Lincs) 28.2
Hallington (Tynedale) 32.1
Halloughton 34.3
Hallow 49.4
Halls Green 22.1
Hallside S7
Hallworthy 9.1
Halmer End 40.2
Halnaker 46.2
Halsall 26.8
Halse (N'hants) 31.7
Halse (Som) 38.4
Halsetown 9.1
Halsham 15.2
Halstead (Essex) 17.2
Halstead (Kent) 25.8
Halstead (Leics) 27.8
Halstead (Lincs) 28.2
Halstead Rural 17.2
Halstock 13.1
Halsway 38.3
Haltcliffe 10.3
Haltham 28.2
Halton (Bucks) 5.2
Halton (N Yorks) East & West 33.5
Halton (Wrexham) W22
Halton Gill 33.5
Halton Holegate 28.2
Halton Lea Gate 32.1
Halton Shields 32.1
Halton with Aughton 26.1
Haltwhistle 32.1
Halvergate 30.5
Halwell 12.9
Halwill 12.1
Halwill Junction (Torridge) 12.1
Ham (Gloucs) 18.6
Ham (Kent) 25.6
Ham (London) L27
Ham (Som)* 38.4, 38.5
Ham (Wilts) 48.1
Ham Green (Kent) 25.4
Ham Green (Som) 38.7
Ham Green (Worcs) (part) 49.3
Ham Hill 25.9
Hamble 20.9
Hambleden (Bucks) 5.3
Hambledon (Hants) 20.5
Hambledon (Surrey) 42.11
Hambleton (Lancs) 26.2
Hambleton (N Yorks) 33.8
Hambleton (Rutland) 36.1
Hambridge 38.5
Hambrook (Gloucs) 18.7
Hambrook (W Sussex) 46.2
Hameringham 28.2
Hamerton 6.3
Hamfallow 18.6
Hamilton S28
Hamlet 13.1
Hamley (Colton) 40.8
Hammer 46.2
Hammer Vale 20.6
Hammerpot 46.5
Hammersmith L13
Hammersmith & Fulham L13
Hammerwich 40.8
Hammerwood 16.1
Hammill 25.6
Hammoon 13.2
Hamnavoe S26
Hampden Park 16.5
Hampden* 5.3
Hampen 18.5
Hampnett 18.5
Hampole 39.2
Hampreston 13.3
Hampstead (part) L2, L6
Hampstead Norreys 3.1
Hampsthwaite 33.6
Hampton (Cheshire) 7.3
Hampton (Herne Bay) 25.5
Hampton (Richmond) L27
Hampton Bank 37.1
Hampton Bishop 21.1
Hampton Charles 21.1
Hampton Gay 35.2
Hampton Hargate 6.1
Hampton Hill L27
Hampton Lovett 49.6
Hampton Lucy 44.5

Hampton Poyle 35.2
Hampton Vale 6.1
Hampton Wafer 21.1
Hampton Wainhill 35.3
Hampton Wick L27
Hampton-in-Arden 45.6
Hamptworth 48.1
Hamsey 16.4
Hamstall Ridware 40.8
Hamstead (W Mids) 45.4
Hamstead Marshall 3.1
Hamsterley (Durham) 14.1
Hamsterley Colliery 14.1
Hamstreet 25.12
Hamwood 38.7
Hamworthy 13.6
Hanborough Long & Church 35.1
Hanbury (Staffs) 40.5
Hanbury (Worcs) 49.6
Hanby 28.6
Hanch 40.8
Hanchurch 40.4
Handcross 46.4
Handforth 7.5
Handley (Cheshire) 7.3
Handley (Derbys) 11.4
Handley Green 17.7
Handsacre (see Armitage)
Handsworth 45.5
Handsworth Wood 45.5
Hanford (Dorset) 13.2
Hanford (Staffs) 40.3
Hangersley Hill 20.7
Hanging Heaton 47.4
Hanging Houghton 31.4
Hanging Langford 48.1
Hangleton 16.3
Hanham 18.7
Hanham Abbots 18.7
Hankelow 7.5
Hankerton 48.1
Hankham 16.1
Hanley (Here) 49.4
Hanley (Staffs) 40.3
Hanley Castle 49.4
Hanlith 33.5
Hanmer W22
Hannah-cum-Hagnaby 28.2
Hanney, East & West 35.4
Hannington (Hants) 20.1
Hannington (N'hants) 31.4
Hannington (Wilts) 48.2
Hannington Wick 48.2
Hanslope 5.1
Hanthorpe 28.6
Hanwell (Ealing) L9
Hanwell (Oxon) 35.2
Hanworth (Norfolk) 30.1
Happisburgh 30.1
Hapsford (Cheshire) 7.3
Hapsford (Som) 38.2
Hapton (Lancs) 26.12
Hapton (Norfolk) 30.7
Harberton 12.9
Harbertonford 12.9
Harbledown 25.5
Harborne 45.5
Harborough Magna 44.3
Harborough Parva 44.3
Harbottle 32.1
Harbridge 20.7
Harburn S31
Harbury 44.5
Harby (Leics) 27.3
Harby (Notts) 34.3
Harcles Hill 19.3
Harcourt 9.1
Harcourt (Shrop) 37.1
Harden (W Mids) 45.2
Harden (W Yorks) 47.1
Hardendale 10.3
Hardgate S9
Hardingham 30.3
Hardingstone 31.5
Hardington 38.2
Hardington Mandeville 38.5
Hardington Marsh 38.5
Hardington Moor 38.5
Hardley (Hants) 20.7
Hardley (Norfolk) (see Langley)
Hardmead 5.1
Hardstoft 11.5
Hardstoft Common 11.5
Hardway (Hants) 20.11
Hardway (Som) 38.5
Hardwick (Bucks) 5.2
Hardwick (Cambs) 6.5
Hardwick (Lincs) 28.1
Hardwick (N'hants) 31.6
Hardwick (Norfolk) 30.7
Hardwick (Oxon) 35.2
Hardwick (Shrop) 37.1
Hardwick (Stockton) 14.10
Hardwick Wood 11.4
Hardwick with Yelford 35.1
Hardwicke 18.6
Hare 38.5
Hare Hatch 3.3
Hare Law 14.1
Hare Warren 20.1
Hareby 28.2
Harecroft 47.1
Harefield (Hants) 20.8
Harelaw 32.1
Hareleeshill S28
Harescombe 18.6
Haresfield 18.6
Haresfinch 29.3
Harestock 20.5
Harewood (Here) 21.1
Harewood (W Yorks) 47.2
Harford (Carm) W6
Harford (Devon) 12.9
Hargham 30.3
Hargrave (N'hants) 31.3
Hargrave (Suffolk) 41.3
Haringey L14
Harker 10.1
Harkstead 41.6
Harlaston 40.8
Harlaxton 28.6
Harle Syke 26.12
Harlech W11
Harlesden (part) L4, L13
Harleston (Norfolk) (see Redenhall)
Harleston (Suffolk) 41.4
Harlestone, Upper & Lower 31.4
Harley (S Yorks) 39.4
Harley (Shrop) 37.1
Harling, East & West 30.3
Harlington (Beds) 2.2
Harlington (S Yorks) 39.2
Harlow 17.5
Harlow Hill 32.1
Harlthorpe 15.2
Harlton 6.5
Harlyn Bay 9.1
Harmanswater 3.6
Harmby 33.1
Harmer Hill 37.1
Harmston 28.4
Harnham 32.1
Harnhill 18.5
Harold Wood L16
Haroldston West W16
Haroldswick S26
Harome 33.3
Harpenden Rural 22.5
Harpenden Town 22.5
Harperrig S31
Harpfields 40.3
Harpford (see Newton Poppleford)
Harpham 15.2
Harpley 30.2
Harpole 31.7
Harprigg 10.5
Harpsden 35.3
Harpswell 28.1
Harpton W17
Harpur Hill 11.1
Harpurhey 19.6
Harraton 43.5
Harray S23
Harrietfield S24
Harrietsham 25.10
Harringay (part) L12, L14
Harrington (Lincs) 28.2
Harrington (N'hants) 31.2
Harringworth 31.3
Harriseahead 40.2
Harrogate 33.6
Harrold 2.1
Harrow L15
Harrow Hill (Gloucs) 18.2
Harrow Way, The (Basingstoke) 20.1
Harrow Weald L15
Harrowbarrow 9.1
Harrowby Without 28.6
Harry Stoke 18.7
Harston (Cambs) 6.5
Harston (Leics) 27.3
Harswell 15.2
Hart (Co Durham) 14.9
Hart District Council (Hants) 20.2
Hartburn (part) 14.10, 32.1
Hartcliffe 4.1
Hartest 41.6
Hartfield 16.1
Hartford (Cambs) 6.3
Hartford (Cheshire) 7.3
Hartford (Som) 38.3
Hartfordbridge 20.2
Hartforth (see Gilling)
Hartham 48.1
Harthill S22
Harthill (Cheshire) 7.3
Harthill (Derbys) 11.3
Harthill with Woodhall 39.4
Harting 46.2
Hartington Middle Quarter 11.3
Hartington Nether Quarter 11.3
Hartington Town Quarter 11.3
Hartland 12.1
Hartlebury 49.6
Hartlepool 14.9
Hartley (Cumbria) 10.3
Hartley Mauditt 20.6
Hartley Wespall 20.1
Hartley Wintney 20.2
Hartley* 25.8
Hartleyburn 32.1
Hartlington 33.5
Hartlip 25.4
Hartoft 33.3
Harton 33.3
Hartpury 18.2
Harts Grounds 28.5
Hartshay 11.6
Hartshead 47.4
Hartshead Moor (part) 47.3, 47.4
Hartshill (Staffs) 40.3
Hartshill (Warks) 44.1
Hartshorne 11.9
Hartsop 10.3
Hartwell (Bucks) 5.2
Hartwell (N'hants) 31.7
Hartwith-cum-Winsley 33.6
Harvel 25.2
Harvington (Worcs) 49.6
Harvington (nr Kidderminster) 49.1
Harwell (Notts) 34.1
Harwell (Oxon) 35.4
Harwich 17.4
Harwood (Gtr M'chester) 19.2
Harwood Dale 33.4
Harwood, East & West (Som) 38.3
Harwood-in-Teesdale 14.1
Harworth Bircotes 34.1
Hasbury 45.3
Hascombe 42.11
Haselbech 31.4
Haselbury Plucknett 38.5
Haseley 44.4
Haselor 44.5
Haselour 40.8
Hasfield 18.1
Hasguard W16
Hasketon 41.5

Hasland (part) 11.2, 11.4
Haslemere (part) 42.11, 46.2
Haslingbourne 46.2
Haslingden 26.14
Haslingfield 6.5
Haslington 7.5
Hassage 38.2
Hassall 7.5
Hassocks 46.4
Hassop 11.3
Haster S17
Hasthorpe 28.2
Hastingleigh (part) 25.12, 25.13
Hastings (E Sussex) 16.6
Hastings (Som) 38.5
Hastings Hill 43.5
Haston 37.1
Haswell 14.1
Haswell Plough 14.1
Hatch (Beds) 2.2
Hatch (Hants) 20.1
Hatch (Wilts) 48.1
Hatch Beauchamp 38.4
Hatch End L15
Hatch Green 38.4
Hatch Warren 20.1
Hatchett Green 20.7
Hatcliffe 28.9
Hateley Heath 45.4
Hatfield (E Yorks) 15.2
Hatfield (Here) 21.1
Hatfield (Herts) 22.6
Hatfield (S Yorks) 39.2
Hatfield Broad Oak 17.1
Hatfield Heath (part) 17.1, 17.6
Hatfield Peverel 17.2
Hatfield Woodhouse 39.2
Hatford 35.4
Hatherden 20.4
Hatherleigh 12.3
Hathern 27.2
Hatherop 18.5
Hathersage 11.3
Hatherton (Cheshire) 7.5
Hatherton (Staffs) 40.6
Hatley 6.5
Hatt 9.1
Hatt Common 20.1
Hattingley 20.6
Hatton S1
Hatton (Cheshire)* 7.1, 7.3
Hatton (Derbys) 11.9
Hatton (Lincs) 28.2
Hatton (Shrop) 37.1
Hatton (Warks) 44.4
Hatton of Fintray S1
Haugh 28.2
Haugh of Urr S10
Haugham 28.2
Haughhead S12
Haughley 41.4
Haughs of Kinnaird S2
Haughton (Cheshire) 7.5
Haughton (N'land) 32.1
Haughton (Notts) 34.1
Haughton (Staffs) 40.4
Haughurst Hill 20.1
Haultwick 22.3
Haunton 40.8
Hauxley 32.1
Hauxton 6.5
Havant 20.13
Haven, The 15.2
Havenhouses 28.2
Havens, The W16
Havenstreet 24.1
Haverah Park 33.6
Havercroft 47.5
Haverfordwest W16
Haverhill 41.3
Havering-atte-Bower L16
Haveringland 30.5
Haversham 5.1
Haverthwaite 10.5
Haverton Hill 14.10
Havyatt 38.2
Havyatt Green 38.7
Hawarden W10
Hawcoat Village 10.6
Hawerby-cum-Beesby 28.9
Hawes 33.1
Hawick S30
Hawk Street 48.1
Hawkchurch 12.7
Hawkcombe 38.3
Hawkedon 41.3
Hawkenbury (nr Headcorn) 25.10
Hawkesbury (Gloucs) 18.7
Hawkesbury (Warks) (part) 44.2, 45.7
Hawkesbury Upton 18.7
Hawkesley 45.5
Hawkhouse Green 39.2
Hawkhurst 25.11
Hawkinge (part) 25.6, 25.13
Hawkington 38.3
Hawkley 20.6
Hawkridge 38.3
Hawks Green 40.7
Hawkshaw 19.3
Hawkshead 10.5
Hawksland S28
Hawkstone 37.1
Hawkswick 33.5
Hawksworth (Notts) 34.8
Hawksworth (W Yorks) 47.1
Hawkwell (Essex) 17.11
Hawkwell (N'land) 32.1
Hawley (Hants) (part) 20.2, 20.3
Hawley (Kent) 25.1
Hawling 18.1
Hawnby 33.3
Haworth 47.1
Hawridge 5.4
Hawsbank, Coniston 10.5
Hawsker 33.4
Hawstead 41.3
Hawthorn W18
Hawthorn (Durham) 14.1
Hawthorn (Wilts) 48.1
Hawthorn Hill (part) 3.4, 3.6
Hawthornden S19
Hawthorpe 28.6
Hawthwaite 10.5
Hawtin Park W4
Hawton 34.3
Haxby 33.7
Haxey 28.8
Haxton 48.1
Hay W17
Hay Mills 45.5
Hay Rural W17
Haybridge (Shrop) 37.4
Haybridge (Som) 38.2
Haydock 29.3
Haydon (Dorset) 13.1
Haydon (N'land) 32.1
Haydon (Som)* 38.2, 38.4
Haydon Bridge 32.1
Haydon Wick 48.2
Hayes L5
Hayfield 11.1
Haylands 24.1
Hayle 9.1
Hayley Green (Berks) 3.6
Hayley Green (W Mids) 45.3
Hayling Island 20.13
Haymill 3.5
Haynes 2.2
Haynes West End 2.2
Hayscastle W16
Haysden 25.9
Haythorne 13.3
Hayton & Mealo 10.2
Hayton (Cumbria) 10.1
Hayton (E Yorks) 15.2
Hayton (Notts) 34.1
Hayton (Shrop) 37.1
Haytor 12.5
Haywards Heath 46.4
Haywood (Here) 21.1
Haywood (S Yorks) 39.2
Hazel Grove 19.9
Hazel Slade 40.7
Hazelbadge 11.3
Hazelbury Bryan 13.2
Hazeleigh 17.8
Hazeley 5.1
Hazeley Bottom 20.2
Hazeley Heath 20.2
Hazeley Lea 20.2
Hazelhurst 19.3
Hazelslack 10.5
Hazelwood 11.6
Hazelwood (see Stutton)
Hazelwood with Storiths 33.5
Hazlemere 5.3
Hazlerigg 43.1
Hazleton 18.5
Heacham 30.2
Head of Muir S15
Headbourne Worthy 20.5
Headcorn 25.10
Headington (part) 35.3, 35.5
Headington Quarry 35.5
Headlam 14.1
Headless Cross 49.3
Headley (Hants) 20.6
Headley (Hants)* 20.1
Headley (Surrey) 42.8
Headley Heath 49.2
Headon Cross 38.3
Headon-cum-Upton 34.1
Heads Nook 10.1
Heage 11.6
Healaugh* 33.1, 33.8
Heald Green 19.9
Heale* 38.4, 38.5
Healey (Gtr M'chester/Lancs) (part) 19.4, 26.14
Healey (N Yorks) 33.6
Healey (N'land) 32.1
Healeyfield 14.1
Healing 28.9
Heamoor 9.1
Heanor 11.6
Heanton Punchardon 12.2
Heap Bridge (part) 19.3, 19.4
Heapey 26.9
Heapham 28.1
Hearts Delight 25.6
Heartsease (Norwich) 30.4
Heasandford 26.12
Heaste S17
Heath W5
Heath & Reach 2.2
Heath (Beds) 2.2
Heath (Derbys) 11.4
Heath (Shrop) 37.1
Heath (W Yorks) 47.5
Heath Charnock 26.9
Heath Common 46.3
Heath End (Gloucs) 18.7
Heath End (Hants) 20.1
Heath End (Surrey) 42.11
Heath End (Warks) 44.2
Heath Hayes 40.7
Heathcote 37.1
Heathencote 31.7
Heather 27.1
Heather Row 20.1
Heatherton 11.7
Heathfield (Devon) 12.5
Heathfield (E Sussex) 16.1
Heathfield (Oxon) 35.2
Heathfield (Som) 38.4
Heathylee 40.1
Heatley 7.1
Heaton (Staffs) 40.1
Heaton (T & W) 43.1
Heaton (W Yorks) 47.1
Heaton Park (part) 19.3, 19.6
Heaton with Oxcliffe 26.1
Heaval S32
Heaverham 25.8
Heaves 10.5
Hebburn 43.4
Hebden 33.5
Hebden Bridge 47.3
Hebron (Carm) W6
Hebron (N'land) 32.1
Heck 33.8
Heckfield 20.2

Heckingham 30.7
Heckington 28.4
Hecklegirth S10
Heckmondwike 47.4
Heddington 48.1
Heddon Oak 38.3
Heddon-on-the-Wall 32.1
Hedenham 30.7
Hedge End 20.9
Hedgeley 32.1
Hedgerley 5.5
Hedley 32.1
Hedley Hope 14.1
Hednesford 40.7
Hedon 15.2
Hedsor 5.3
Heelands 5.1
Heighington (Durham) 14.8
Heighington (Lincs) 28.4
Heighley 32.1
Heightington 49.1
Heiton S30
Helbeck 10.3
Hele (part) 12.4, 38.4
Helensburgh S3
Helford 9.1
Helhoughton 30.1
Heligan 9.1
Helions Bumpstead 17.2
Hellaby 39.4
Helland (Corn) 9.1
Helland (Som) 38.4
Hellesdon 30.5
Hellesveor 9.1
Hellidon 31.4
Hellifield 33.5
Hellingly 16.1
Hellington 30.7
Helmdon 31.7
Helme 47.4
Helmingham 41.4
Helmington Row 14.1
Helmsdale S17
Helmshore 26.14
Helmsley 33.3
Helperby 33.2
Helperthorpe (Luttons) 33.3
Helpringham 28.4
Helpston 6.1
Helsby 7.3
Helsington 10.5
Helston 9.1
Helston Water 9.1
Helstone 9.1
Helton 10.3
Helwith Bridge 33.5
Hem Heath 40.3
Hemblington 30.5
Hemel Hempstead 22.4
Hemford 37.1
Hemingbrough 33.8
Hemingby 28.2
Hemingfield 39.1
Hemingford Abbots 6.3
Hemingford Grey 6.3
Hemingstone 41.4
Hemington (Leics) 27.1
Hemington (N'hants) 31.3
Hemington (Som) 38.2
Hemley 41.5
Hemlington 33.9
Hempholme 15.2
Hempnall 30.7
Hempstead (Essex) 17.1
Hempstead (Kent) 25.3
Hempstead (Norfolk) 30.1
Hempsted (Cambs) 6.1
Hempsted (Glouc) 18.3
Hempton (Norfolk) 30.1
Hempton (Oxon) 35.2
Hemsby 30.6
Hemscott Hill 32.1
Hemswell 28.1
Hemswell Cliff 28.1
Hemsworth 47.5
Hemyock 12.4
Henbury (Bristol) 4.1
Henbury (Cheshire) 7.5
Henbury (Kent) 25.13
Henderskelfe 33.3
Hendon (London) L2
Hendon (T & W) 43.5
Hendra* 9.1
Hendre (Caerph) W4
Hendre (Flint) W10
Hendred, East & West 35.4
Hendredenny W4
Hendy W6
Heneglwys W1
Henfield (Gloucs) 18.7
Henfield (W Sussex) 46.3
Henfynyw W7
Hengoed W4
Hengoed, Upper & Lower (Shrop) 37.1
Hengrave 41.3
Hengrove 4.1
Henham (Essex) 17.1
Henham (Suffolk) 41.1
Henhull 7.5
Henlade 38.4
Henleaze 4.1
Henley (High Ham) 38.5
Henley (Shrop) 37.1
Henley (Suffolk) 41.4
Henley (W Crewkerne) 38.5
Henley (W Sussex) 46.2
Henley-in-Arden 44.5
Henley-on-Thames 35.3
Henllan W9
Henllanfallteg W6
Henllys W20
Henlow 2.2
Hennock 12.5
Henry's Moat W16
Henryd W8
Hensall 33.8
Henshaw 32.1
Henstead (Norfolk) (see Forehoe & Henstead)
Henstead with Hulver Street 41.1
Hensting 20.5
Henstridge 38.5
Henstridge Ash 38.5
Henstridge Bowden 38.5
Henstridge Marsh 38.5
Hentland 21.1
Henton (Oxon) 35.3
Henton (Som) 38.2
Henwood 9.1
Heol y Glo W14
Heolgerrig W12
Heolycyw W3
Hepple 32.1
Hepscott 32.1
Hepthorne Lane 11.4
Heptonstall 47.3
Hepworth (Suffolk) 41.3
Hepworth (W Yorks) 47.4
Herbrandston W16
Hereford City 21.1
Hereson (Ramsgate) 25.7
Heriot S30
Hermitage (Berks) 3.1
Hermitage (Dorset) 13.1
Hermitage (W Sussex) 46.2
Hermon W6
Herne 25.5
Herne Bay 25.5
Herne Hill (part) L22, L28
Hernhill 25.4
Herodsfoot 9.1
Heron Cross 40.3
Heronden 25.6
Herongate 17.9
Herons Ghyll 16.1
Heronsgate 22.8
Herriard 20.1
Herringby (see Stokesby)
Herringfleet 41.1
Herringswell 41.2
Herrington Burn 43.5
Hersden 25.5
Hersham 42.5
Herstmonceux 16.1
Hertburn 43.5
Hertford 22.3
Hertford Heath 22.3
Hertingfordbury 22.3
Hesket 10.3
Hesketh Bank 26.8
Hesketh Park 29.1
Hesketh with Becconsall 26.8
Heskin 26.9
Hesleden 14.1
Heslerton East & West 33.3
Hesleyhurst 32.1
Hesleyside 32.1
Heslington 33.7
Hessay 33.7
Hessenford 9.1
Hessett 41.4
Hessle (E Yorks) 15.2
Hessle (W Yorks) 47.5
Hest (see Slyne)
Hest Bank 26.1
Heston L18
Heswall 29.5
Hethe 35.2
Hethel 30.7
Hethersett 30.7
Hethersgill 10.1
Hett 14.1
Hetton (N Yorks) 33.5
Hetton (T & W) 43.5
Hetton Downs 43.5
Hetton Lyons 43.5
Hetton-le-Hole 43.5
Heugh 32.1
Heveningham 41.5
Hever 25.8
Heversham 10.5
Hevingham 30.5
Hewaswater 9.1
Hewelsfield 18.2
Hewenden 47.1
Hewish* 38.5, 38.7
Hewood 13.1
Heworth (T & W) 43.3
Heworth (York) 33.7
Heworth Without 33.7
Hexham 32.1
Hexhamshire 32.1
Hextable 25.8
Hexthorpe 39.2
Hexton 22.1
Heybridge 17.8
Heybridge Basin 17.8
Heybrook Bay (Wembury) 12.9
Heydon (Cambs) 6.5
Heydon (Norfolk) 30.5
Heydour 28.6
Heylor S26
Heyope W17
Heysham 26.1
Heyshott 46.2
Heytesbury 48.1
Heythrop 35.1
Heywood (Gtr M'chester) 19.4
Heywood (Wilts) 48.1
Hibaldstow 28.8
Hickleton 39.2
Hickling (Norfolk) 30.1
Hickling (Notts) 34.8
Hicks Forstal (Sturry) 25.5
Hicks Mill 9.1
Hickstead 46.4
Hidcote Bartrim 18.5
Hidcote Boyce 18.5
High Abbotside 33.1
High Ackworth 47.5
High Angerton 32.1
High Barnes 43.5
High Beach 17.6
High Bentham 33.5
High Bickington 12.1, 12.2
High Biggins 10.5
High Blantyre S28
High Bonnybridge S15
High Bray 12.2
High Brooms 25.11
High Brunthwaite 47.1
High Callerton 32.1
High Casterton 10.5
High Catton 15.2
High Clarence 14.10
High Coniscliffe 14.8
High Cross (Hants) 20.6

High Cross (Herts) 22.3
High Cunsey 10.5
High Easter 17.1
High Ellington 33.6
High Ercall 37.4
High Flatts 47.4
High Grange 14.1
High Green (N'land) 32.1
High Green, Troutbeck 10.5
High Halden 25.12
High Halstow 25.3
High Ham 38.5
High Handenhold 14.1
High Hatton 37.1
High Hawsker 33.4
High Heath (Pelsall) 45.2
High Heaton 43.1
High Hesket 10.3
High Holborn L6
High Hoyland 39.1
High Hurstwood 16.1
High Kelling 30.1
High Lands 14.1
High Lane 19.9
High Laver 17.6
High Legh 7.5
High Leven 14.10
High Littleton 38.6
High Melton 39.2
High Mickley 32.1
High Midgeholme 10.1
High Moorsley 43.5
High Newton 10.5
High Nibthwaite 10.5
High Offley 40.4
High Ongar 17.6
High Park 29.1
High Roothing 17.1
High Salvington 46.6
High Shincliffe 14.1
High Spen 43.3
High Stott Park 10.5
High Street 9.1
High Toynton 28.2
High Urpeth 14.1
High Valleyfield S16
High Warden 32.1
High Westwood 14.1
High Worsall 33.2
High Wray 10.5
High Wych 22.3
High Wycombe 5.3
Higham (Derbys) 11.4
Higham (Kent) 25.2
Higham (Lancs) 26.13
Higham (S Yorks) 39.1
Higham (Suffolk)* 41.2, 41.6
Higham Ferrers 31.3
Higham Gobion 2.2
Higham-on-the-Hill 27.4
Highampton 12.3
Highams Park L31
Highbridge 38.1
Highburton 47.4
Highbury L19
Highbury (Som) 38.2
Highbury Vale 34.6
Highclere 20.1
Highcliffe 13.8
Higher Bal 9.1
Higher Chillington 38.5
Higher Halstock Leigh 13.1
Higher Heath 37.1
Higher Horton 38.5
Higher Hurdsfield 7.5
Higher Kinnerton W10
Higher Marsh 38.5
Higher Melcombe 13.1
Higher Ogden 19.4
Higher Pertwood 48.1
Higher Ridge 37.1
Higher Rowe 13.3
Higher Town 38.3
Higher Trevella 9.1
Higher Trevethan 9.1
Higher Walton 26.7
Higher Waterston 13.1
Higher Woodhill 19.3
Higher Woodsford 13.1
Higher Wraxall 13.1
Highertown 9.1
Highfield (Hants) 20.8
Highfield (T & W) 43.3
Highfields (Caerph) W4
Highfields (Shrop) 37.1
Highgate (part) L6, L14
Highgreen (S Yorks) 39.3
Highleadon (see Rudford)
Highleigh 46.2
Highley 37.1
Highlow 11.3
Highmoor 35.3
Highmoor Cross 35.3
Highnam 18.1
Highridge (Bristol) 4.1
Highstead (Chislet) 25.5
Hightae S10
Highters Heath 45.5
Hightown (Hants) 20.7
Hightown (Mersey) 29.1
Hightown (Staffs) 40.7
Hightown (W Yorks) 47.4
Highway 38.5
Highwood 17.7
Highworth 48.2
Hilborough 30.3
Hilcot 48.1
Hilcote 11.5
Hildenborough 25.9
Hildenley 33.3
Hildersham 6.5
Hilderstone 40.4
Hilgay 30.2
Hill & Moor 49.6
Hill (Gloucs) 18.7
Hill (Warks) 44.3
Hill Brow (part) 20.6, 46.2
Hill Cliffe 7.1
Hill Croome 49.4
Hill Deverill 48.1
Hill End 38.5
Hill Gate 21.1
Hill Head 20.10
Hill Pool 49.1
Hill Ridware 40.8
Hill Terrace (Balrownie) S2
Hill Top (W Mids) 45.4
Hill Top (W Yorks) 47.5
Hill View 43.5
Hill-of-Beath S16
Hillam 33.8
Hillbeck 10.3
Hillborough (Herne Bay) (Kent) 25.5
Hillborough (Warks) 44.5
Hillbutts 13.3
Hillcommon 38.4
Hilldale 26.8
Hillend S19
Hillersland 18.2
Hillesden 5.2
Hillesley 18.6
Hillfarrance 38.4
Hillfield 13.1
Hillfields 4.1
Hillhampton 49.4
Hillhouse S28
Hilliards Cross 40.8
Hillingdon L17
Hillington 30.2
Hillside (Angus) S2
Hillside (Mersey) 29.1
Hillstown 11.5
Hillstreet 20.7
Hillswick S26
Hilmarton 48.1
Hilperton 48.1
Hilston 15.2
Hiltingbury 20.9
Hilton S17
Hilton (Cambs) 6.3
Hilton (Cumbria) 10.3
Hilton (Derbys) 11.9
Hilton (Dorset) 13.2
Hilton (Durham) 14.1
Hilton (Staffs)* 40.6, 40.8
Hilton (Stockton) 14.10
Hilton Park 19.3
Himbleton 49.6
Himley 40.6
Hincaster 10.5
Hinchley Wood 42.5
Hinchliffe Mill 47.4
Hinckley 27.4
Hincks, The 37.4
Hinderclay 41.4
Hinderton 7.3
Hinderwell 33.4
Hindford* 37.1
Hindhead 42.11
Hindley (Gtr M'chester) 19.1
Hindley (N'land) 32.1
Hindlip 49.6
Hindolveston 30.1
Hindon (Som) 38.3
Hindon (Wilts) 48.1
Hindringham 30.1
Hingham 30.7
Hinkshay 37.4
Hinstock 37.1
Hintlesham 41.6
Hinton (Hants) 20.7
Hinton (Som) 38.5
Hinton Ampner 20.5
Hinton Blewitt 38.6
Hinton Charterhouse 38.6
Hinton Marsh 20.5
Hinton Martell 13.3
Hinton Parva (Dorset) 13.3
Hinton Parva (Wilts) 48.2
Hinton St George 38.5
Hinton St Mary 13.2
Hinton Waldrist 35.4
Hinton* (Gloucs) 18.6, 18.7
Hinton-in-the-Hedges 31.7
Hinton-on-the-Green 49.6
Hints 40.8
Hinwick 2.1
Hinxhill 25.12
Hinxton 6.5
Hinxworth 22.1
Hipley 20.5
Hipperholme 47.3
Hipswell 33.1
Hiraeth W6
Hiraethog W8
Hirnant W17
Hirst Courtney 33.8
Hirwaun W18
Histon 6.5
Hitcham 41.6
Hitchin 22.1
Hittisleigh 12.4
Hixon 40.4
Hoaden 25.6
Hoar Cross 40.5
Hoarwithy 21.1
Hoath 25.5
Hobson 14.1
Hoby 27.3
Hockenhull 7.3
Hockering 30.3
Hockerton 34.3
Hockham, Gt & Little 30.3
Hockley (Essex) 17.11
Hockley (Staffs) 40.9
Hockley (W Mids) 45.5
Hockley Heath (part) 44.4, 44.5, 45.6
Hockliffe 2.2
Hockwold-cum-Wilton 30.2
Hockworthy 12.4
Hoddesdon 22.7
Hoddington 20.1
Hoddom S10
Hodge Hill 45.5
Hodge Lea 5.1
Hodgeston W16
Hodley W17
Hodnell 44.5
Hodnet 37.1
Hodsock 34.1
Hodsoll Street 25.8
Hodson 48.2
Hodthorpe 11.5
Hoe 30.3
Hoff 10.3
Hogdigging 20.1
Hoggeston 5.2
Hoghton (part) 26.7, 26.9
Hognaston 11.3
Hogshaw 5.2

Hogsthorpe 28.2
Holbeach 28.7
Holbeach Hurn 28.7
Holbeach St. Johns 28.7
Holbeach St. Marks 28.7
Holbeach St. Mathews 28.7
Holbeck (Cumbria) 10.6
Holbeck (Lincs) 28.2
Holbeck (Notts) 34.1
Holbeton 12.9
Holborn L6
Holbrook (Derbys) 11.6
Holbrook (Shrop) 37.1
Holbrook (Suffolk) 41.6
Holbrooks 45.7
Holbury 20.7
Holcombe (Devon) 12.5
Holcombe (Gtr M'chester) 19.3
Holcombe (Som) 38.2
Holcombe Brook 19.3
Holcombe Burnell 12.5
Holcombe Rogus 12.4
Holcot 31.4
Holden Vale 26.14
Holdenby 31.4
Holdenhurst 13.7
Holdfast 49.4
Holdgate 37.1
Holdingham 28.4
Holditch (Dorset) 13.1
Holditch (Staffs) 40.2
Holebiggerah 10.5
Holeslack 10.5
Holford 38.3
Holgate 33.7
Holker 10.5
Holkham 30.1
Hollacombe 12.1
Hollam 38.3
Holland Fen 28.5
Holland Park L20
Holland-on-Sea 17.4
Hollesley 41.5
Hollicondane (Ramsgate) 25.7
Hollinfare 7.1
Hollingbourne 25.10
Hollingbury 16.3
Hollingdean 16.3
Hollingdon 5.2
Hollinghill 32.1
Hollington (Derbys) 11.3
Hollington (Hants) 20.1
Hollington (Staffs) 40.1
Hollingwood 11.2
Hollingworth 19.10
Hollins 19.7
Hollins (part) 19.3, 19.4
Hollins Green 7.1
Hollinsclough 40.1
Hollinswood* 37.1, 37.4
Hollow Meadows 39.3
Holloway (Derbys) 11.6
Holloway (London) L19
Hollowcombe 38.3
Hollowell 31.4
Hollowells 38.5
Holly Green 5.3
Hollyberry End 45.6
Hollybush (Caerph) W4
Hollybush (E Ayrs) S11
Hollycarrside 43.5
Hollycombe 46.2
Hollym 15.2
Hollywood 49.2
Holm S23
Holman Clavel 38.4
Holmbridge 47.4
Holmbury St Mary (part) 42.7, 42.8, 42.11
Holmbush 9.1
Holme (Cambs) 6.3
Holme (Cumbria) 10.5
Holme (Lincs) 28.8
Holme (N Yorks) 33.2
Holme (Notts) 34.3
Holme (W Yorks) 47.4
Holme Abbey 10.2
Holme East Waver 10.2
Holme Green 3.3
Holme Hale 30.3
Holme Hall 11.2
Holme Lacy 21.1
Holme Low 10.2
Holme Pierrepont 34.8
Holme St Cuthbert 10.2
Holme Wood (W Yorks) 47.1
Holme-next-the-Sea 30.2
Holme-on-Spalding-Moor 15.2
Holmer 21.1
Holmer Green 5.4
Holmer Lake 37.4
Holmes Chapel 7.5
Holmesfield 11.4
Holmewood (Derbys) 11.4
Holmfield 47.3
Holmfirth 47.4
Holmgate 11.4
Holmhead S11
Holmpton 15.2
Holmside 14.1
Holmwood 42.8
Holne 12.9
Holnest 13.1
Holnicote 38.3
Holsworthy 12.1
Holsworthy Hamlets 12.1
Holt (Dorset) 13.3
Holt (Norfolk) 30.1
Holt (Wilts) 48.1
Holt (Worcs) 49.4
Holt (Wrexham) W22
Holt Ball 38.3
Holt End 49.2
Holt Fleet 49.6
Holt Pound (part) 20.6
Holtby 33.7
Holtby (see Ainderby Miers)
Holton (Oxon) 35.3
Holton (Som) 38.5
Holton (Suffolk) 41.1
Holton Heath 13.5
Holton St Mary 41.6
Holton le Clay 28.2
Holton le Moor 28.1
Holton-cum-Beckering 28.1
Holtwood 13.3
Holtye 16.1
Holverston 30.7
Holway (Flint) W10
Holway (part) 38.4
Holwell (Dorset) 13.1
Holwell (Herts) 22.1
Holwell (Leics) 27.3
Holwell (Oxon) 35.1
Holwell (Som) 38.2
Holwick 14.1
Holy Cross 49.2
Holy Island 32.1
Holybourne 20.6
Holyhead W1
Holyhead Mountain W1
Holyport 3.4
Holystone 43.2
Holytown S22
Holywell (Cambs) 6.3
Holywell (Corn) 9.1
Holywell (Dorset) 13.1
Holywell (Flint) W10
Holywell (Lincs) 28.6
Holywell (N'land) 32.1
Holywell (Som) 38.5
Holywell Bay 9.1
Holywell Green 47.3
Holywell Lake 38.4
Holywell Row 41.2
Holywellmoor 37.1
Holywood S10
Hom Green 21.1
Homanton 48.1
Homersfield (South Elmham St Mary) 41.1
Homerton L12
Homington 48.1
Honddu Isaf W17
Honey Hall 38.7
Honey Hill (Blean) 25.5
Honeybourne 49.6
Honeycombe Leaze 18.5
Honeydon 2.1
Honeystreet 48.1
Honiley 44.4
Honing 30.1
Honingham 30.5
Honington (Lincs) 28.6
Honington (Suffolk) 41.3
Honington (Warks) 44.5
Honiton 12.7
Honley 47.4
Honnington 37.4
Honor Oak Park (part) L28
Hoo 41.5
Hoo St Werburgh 25.3
Hoober 39.4
Hood Grange 33.2
Hood Green 39.1
Hood Hill 39.4
Hood Manor 7.1
Hooe 16.1
Hook (E Riding) 15.2
Hook (Hants)* 20.2, 20.10
Hook (Pemb) (see Llangwm)
Hook (Surrey) L21
Hook (Wilts) 48.1
Hook Common 20.2
Hook End 17.9
Hook Gate 40.2
Hook Green 25.2
Hook Heath 42.4
Hook Norton 35.2
Hook-a-Gate (see Bayston Hill)
Hooke 13.1
Hookway 12.4
Hookwood 42.8
Hoole Village 7.3
Hooley 42.9
Hoon 11.9
Hooton (part) 7.3
Hooton Green 7.3
Hooton Levitt 39.4
Hooton Pagnell 39.2
Hooton Roberts 39.4
Hopcott 38.3
Hope (Derbys) 11.1
Hope (Durham) 14.1
Hope (Flint) W10
Hope (Shrop) 37.1
Hope (Staffs) 40.1
Hope Bagot 37.1
Hope Bowdler 37.1
Hope Cove 12.9
Hope Mansell 21.1
Hope Woodlands 11.1
Hope-under-Dinmore 21.1
Hopefield S19
Hopeman S20
Hopesay 37.1
Hopetoun S31
Hopkinstown W18
Hopperton (see Allerton Mauleverer)
Hopsford 44.3
Hopshort 37.1
Hopton (Derbys) 11.3
Hopton (Shrop) 37.1
Hopton (Staffs) 40.4
Hopton (Suffolk) 41.3
Hopton Bank 37.1
Hopton Cangeford 37.1
Hopton Castle 37.1
Hopton Heath 37.1
Hopton Wafers 37.1
Hopton on Sea 30.6
Hopwas 40.8
Hopwell 11.8
Hopwood (Gtr M'chester) 19.4
Hopwood (Worcs) 49.2
Horam 16.1
Horbling 28.6
Horbury 47.5
Horbury Junction 47.5
Horcott 18.5
Horden 14.1
Horderley 37.1
Hordle 20.7
Hordley 37.1
Horeb W6

2

Horeston Grange 44.2
Horfield 4.1
Horham 41.4
Horkstow 28.8
Horley (Oxon) 35.2
Horley (Surrey) (part) 42.8 42.9
Hormead 22.3
Horn (Rutland) 36.1
Horn (Som) 38.5
Horn Ash 13.1
Horn Hill 22.8
Horn Moor 38.5
Hornblotton 38.2
Hornby 33.2
Hornby with Farleton 26.1
Horncastle 28.2
Hornchurch L16
Horncliffe 32.1
Horndean 20.6
Horndon on the Hill 17.12
Horne 42.10
Horne Row 17.7
Horner 38.3
Horning 30.1
Horninghold 27.8
Horninglow 40.5
Horningsea 6.5
Horningsham 48.1
Horningtoft 30.3
Horningtops 9.1
Horns Cross 25.1
Hornsbury 38.5
Hornsea 15.2
Hornsey (part) L14, L19
Hornsey Rise L14, L19
Hornton 35.2
Horrabridge 12.3
Horringer 41.3
Horris Hill 20.1
Horsebridge 20.4
Horsecastle 38.7
Horsehay 37.4
Horseheath 6.5
Horseley Heath 45.4
Horsell 42.4
Horsenden 5.3
Horseshoe Green 25.8
Horsey 30.1
Horsford 30.5
Horsforth 47.2
Horsham 46.3
Horsham St Faith & Newton St Faith 30.5
Horsington (Lincs) 28.2
Horsington (Som) 38.5
Horsington Marsh 38.5
Horsley (Derbys) 11.6
Horsley (Gloucs) 18.6
Horsley (N'land) 32.1
Horsley Woodhouse 11.6
Horsleys Green 5.3
Horsmonden 25.11
Horspath 35.3
Horstead with Stanninghall 30.5
Horsted Keynes 46.4
Hortham 18.7
Horton (Berks) 3.4
Horton (Bucks) 5.2
Horton (Dorset) 13.3
Horton (Gloucs) 18.7
Horton (N'hants) 31.7
Horton (Shrop)* 37.1, 37.4
Horton (Som) 38.5
Horton (Staffs) 40.1
Horton (Swansea) W19
Horton (Wilts) 48.1
Horton Bank Top 47.1
Horton Cross 38.5
Horton Grange 43.1
Horton Heath 20.9
Horton Kirby 25.8
Horton Wood 37.4
Horton in Craven 26.3
Horton-by-Malpas 7.3
Horton-cum-Peel 7.3
Horton-cum-Studley 35.2
Horton-in-Ribblesdale 33.5
Horwich 19.2
Horwood 12.2
Hose 27.3
Hoswick S26
Hotham 15.2
Hothersall 26.3
Hothfield 25.12
Hothorpe 31.4
Hoton 27.2
Hotwells 4.1
Hough 7.5
Hough-on-the-Hill 28.6
Hougham (Kent) 25.6
Hougham (Lincs) 28.6
Houghton (Cambs) 6.3
Houghton (Cumbria) 10.1
Houghton (E Yorks) 15.2
Houghton (Hants) 20.4
Houghton (N'land) 32.1
Houghton (Norfolk) 30.2
Houghton (T & W) (see Houghton le Spring)
Houghton (W Sussex) 46.5
Houghton Conquest 2.2
Houghton Green 7.1
Houghton Regis 2.2
Houghton St Giles 30.1
Houghton le Side 14.8
Houghton le Spring (part) 43.5
Houghton-on-the-Hill (Leics) 27.8
Houghton-on-the-Hill (Norfolk) 30.3
Houlsyke 33.4
Hound 20.9
Hound Green 20.2
Houndmills 20.1
Houndsmoor 38.4
Houndstone 38.5
Hounsdown 20.7
Hounsley Batch 38.7
Hounslow L18
Houses Hill 47.4
Houston S25
Houstry S17
Hove 16.3
Hove Edge 47.3
Hoveringham 34.3
Hoveton 30.1
Hovingham 33.3
How Caple 21.1
How End 2.2
How Green 44.1
How Mill 10.1
How Wood 22.5
Howbrook 39.1
Howden 15.2
Howden Clough 47.4
Howden-le-Wear 14.1
Howdendyke 15.2
Howdon 43.2
Howe (N Yorks) 33.2
Howe (Norfolk) 30.7
Howe Green 17.7
Howe Street 17.7
Howell 28.4
Howey W17
Howgate S19
Howgill 10.5
Howgrave 33.2
Howle Hill 21.1
Howle* 37.1, 37.4
Howleigh 38.4
Howley (Cheshire) 7.1
Howley (Som) 38.5
Hownam S30
Howsham (Lincs) 28.8
Howsham (N Yorks) 33.3
Howtown 10.3
Howwood S25
Hoxne 41.4
Hoy S23
Hoylake 29.5
Hoyland 39.1
Hoylandswaine 39.1
Hubberston W16
Hubberton Green 47.3
Hubberts Bridge 28.5
Huby (N Yorks)* 33.2
Hucclecote (part) 18.1, 18.3
Huckerby 28.1
Hucking 25.10
Hucknall 34.4
Huddersfield 47.4
Huddington 49.6
Huddlesford 40.8
Huddleston with Newthorpe 33.8
Hudswell 33.1
Huggate 15.2
Hugglescote 27.1
Hughenden Valley 5.3
Hughley 37.1
Hugill 10.5
Huish (Devon) 12.1
Huish (Wilts) 48.1
Huish Champflower 38.3
Huish Episcopi 38.5
Hulam 14.1
Hulberry 25.8
Hulcote (Beds) 2.2
Hulcote (N'hants) 31.7
Hulcott 5.2
Hulland 11.3
Hulland Ward 11.3
Hullavington 48.1
Hullbridge 17.11
Hulme (Cheshire) 7.1
Hulme (Gtr M'chester) 19.6
Hulme (Staffs) (part) 40.1, 40.3
Hulme End 40.1
Hulme Walfield 7.5
Hulverstone 24.1
Humber 21.1
Humbers, The 37.4
Humberston 28.9
Humberton 33.6
Humbie S13
Humbledon 43.5
Humbleton 15.2
Humbley Grove 20.1
Hume S30
Hummer 13.1
Hummerbeck 14.1
Humshaugh 32.1
Huncoat 26.11
Huncote 27.6
Hundall 11.4
Hunderthwaite 14.1
Hundleby 28.2
Hundleton W16
Hundon 41.3
Hundred Acres 20.5
Hundred House W17
Hundredstone 38.5
Hungarton 27.8
Hungary Hatton 37.1
Hungerford (Berks) 3.1
Hungerford (Hants) 20.7
Hungerford (Shrop) 37.1
Hungerford (Som) 38.3
Hungerton (see Wyville)
Hungry Bentley 11.3
Hunmanby 33.4
Hunningham 44.4
Hunnington 49.2
Hunscote 44.5
Hunsdon 22.3
Hunsingore 33.6
Hunsonby 10.3
Hunstanton 30.2
Hunstanworth 14.1
Hunsterson 7.5
Hunston (Suffolk) 41.4
Hunston (W Sussex) 46.2
Hunstrete 38.6
Hunsworth 47.4
Hunt End 49.3
Hunterfield S19
Hunters Forstal 25.5
Huntham 38.4
Huntingdon 6.3
Huntingfield 41.5
Huntingford (part) 18.7
Huntington (Cheshire) 7.3
Huntington (Here) 21.1
Huntington (Shrop) 37.4
Huntington (Staffs) 40.6
Huntington (York) 33.7
Huntingtower S24
Huntley 18.2

Huntley Fold 19.3
Huntly S1
Hunton (Kent) 25.10
Hunton (N Yorks) 33.1
Hunton Bridge 22.8
Hunts Cross 29.2
Huntscott 38.3
Huntsham 12.4
Huntshaw 12.1
Huntspill, East & West 38.1
Huntwick 47.5
Hunwick 14.1
Hunworth 30.1
Hurbuck 14.1
Hurcot 38.5
Hurleston 7.5
Hurley (Berks) 3.4
Hurley (Warks) 44.1
Hurlford S11
Hurlingham L13
Hurn 13.8
Hursley 20.5
Hurst (Berks) 3.3
Hurst (Som) 38.5
Hurst Green (E Sussex) 16.2
Hurst Green (Lancs) 26.3
Hurst Green (Surrey) 42.10
Hurst Green (W Mids) 45.3
Hurst Hill (part) 45.1, 45.3
Hurstbourne Priors 20.1
Hurstbourne Tarrant 20.4
Hurstpierpoint 46.4
Hurstwood (see Worsthorne)
Hurworth 14.8
Hurworth Place 14.8
Husbands Bosworth 27.8
Husborne Crawley 2.2
Hushinish S32
Husthwaite 33.2
Huthwaite 34.4
Huttoft 28.2
Hutton S30
Hutton (Cumbria) 10.3
Hutton (E Yorks) 15.2
Hutton (Essex) 17.9
Hutton (Lancs) 26.7
Hutton (Som) 38.7
Hutton Bonville 33.2
Hutton Buscel 33.4
Hutton Conyers 33.6
Hutton Cranswick 15.2
Hutton End 10.3
Hutton Hang 33.1
Hutton Henry 14.1
Hutton John 10.3
Hutton Magna 14.1
Hutton Mulgrave 33.4
Hutton Roof 10.5
Hutton Rudby 33.2
Hutton Sessay 33.2
Hutton-in-the-Forest 10.3
Hutton-le-Hole 33.3
Huttons Ambo 33.3
Huxham 12.7
Huxley 7.3
Huyton 29.4
Huyton with Roby (part) 29.2, 29.4
Hyde (Beds) 2.2
Hyde (Gtr M'chester) 19.10
Hyde (Hants) 20.7
Hyde End 3.3
Hyde Heath 5.4
Hyde Park L33, 39.2
Hyde, The (part) L2, L4
Hylton Castle 43.5
Hylton Red House 43.5
Hyndford Bridge S28
Hyson Green 34.6
Hyssington W17
Hythe (Hants) 20.7
Hythe (Kent) 25.13
Hythe (Surrey) 42.1
Hythe End 3.4
Ibberton 13.2
Ible 11.3
Ibsley 20.7
Ibstock 27.1
Ibstone 5.3
Ibthorpe 20.4
Ibworth 20.1
Icelton 38.7
Ickburgh 30.3
Ickford 5.2
Ickham 25.5
Ickham & Well 25.5
Ickleford 22.1
Icklesham 16.2
Ickleton 6.5
Icklingham 41.2
Ickwell Green 2.2
Ickworth 41.3
Icomb 18.5
Idbury 35.1
Iddesleigh 12.3
Iddinshall 7.3
Ide 12.5
Ide Hill 25.8
Ideford 12.5
Iden 16.2
Iden Green, Benenden 25.11
Idle 47.1
Idless 9.1
Idlicote 44.5
Idmiston 48.1
Idole W6
Idridgehay 11.6
Idrigill S17
Idstone 35.4
Idsworth 20.6
Iffley 35.5
Iffley Lock 35.4
Ifield (Kent) 25.2
Ifield (W Sussex) 46.1
Ifold 46.2
Iford (Dorset) 13.7
Iford (E Sussex) 16.4
Ifton Heath 37.1
Ightenhill 26.12
Ightfield 37.1
Ightfield Heath 37.1
Ightham 25.9
Iken 41.5
Ilam 40.1
Ilchester 38.5
Ilderton 32.1
Ilford (Essex) L26
Ilford (Som) 38.5
Ilfracombe 12.2
Ilkeston 11.8
Ilketshall St Andrew 41.1
Ilketshall St John 41.1
Ilketshall St Lawrence 41.1
Ilketshall St Margaret 41.1
Ilkley 47.1
Illington 30.3
Illingworth 47.3
Illmer 5.3
Illogan 9.1
Illogan Highway 9.1
Illshaw Heath 45.6
Illston on the Hill 27.8
Ilmington 44.5
Ilminster 38.5
Ilsington 12.5
Ilston W19
Ilton 38.5
Ilton-cum-Pott 33.6
Imber 48.1
Immingham 28.9
Impington 6.5
Ince 7.3
Ince Blundell 29.1
Ince-in-Makerfield 19.1
Inchbare S2
Incheril S17
Inchinnan S25
Inchture S24
Inchyra S24
Incline Top W12
Indian Queens 9.1
Ingarsby 27.8
Ingatestone & Fryerning 17.9
Ingbirchworth 39.1
Ingestre 40.4
Ingham (Lincs) 28.1
Ingham (Norfolk) 30.1
Ingham (Suffolk) 41.3
Ingleby (Derbys) 11.9
Ingleby (Lincs) 28.1
Ingleby Arncliffe 33.2
Ingleby Barwick 14.10
Ingleby Cross (Ingleby Arncliffe) 33.2
Ingleby Greenhow 33.2
Inglesbatch 38.6
Inglesham 48.2
Inglestone Common 18.7
Ingleton (Durham) 14.1
Ingleton (N Yorks) 33.5
Inglewhite 26.6
Ingoe 32.1
Ingol 26.6
Ingoldisthorpe 30.2
Ingoldmells 28.2
Ingoldsby 28.6
Ingram 32.1
Ingrams Green 46.2
Ingrave 17.9
Ingrow 47.1
Ings 10.5
Ingst 18.7
Ingworth 30.1
Inkberrow 49.6
Inkersall 11.2
Inkersall Green 11.2
Inkpen 3.1
Inmarsh 48.1
Innellan S3
Innerleithen S30
Innerwick (E Lothian) S13
Innerwick (Perth) S24
Inns Court 4.1
Innsworth 18.1
Insch S1
Inskip with Sowerby 26.2
Instow 12.2
Insworke 9.1
Intake 39.2
Intwood 30.7
Invemettie S1
Inver (Highland) S17
Inver (Perth) S24
Inverallochy S1
Inveralmond S24
Inveraray S3
Inverarity S2
Inverasdale S17
Inverbervie S1
Inverdruie S17
Inveresk Village S13
Invergarry S17
Invergordon S17
Invergowrie S24
Inverie S17
Inverinate S17
Inverkeilor S2
Inverkeithing S16
Inverkeithny S1
Inverkip S18
Inverlochy S17
Invermoriston S17
Inverness S17
Inverpolly S17
Inversnaid S29
Inverugie S1
Inverurie S1
Invervar S24
Inwardleigh 12.3
Inworth (see Messing)
Iona, Isle of S3
Iping 46.2
Ipplepen 12.5
Ipsden 35.3
Ipsley 49.3
Ipstones 40.1
Ipswich 41.7
Irby (Mersey) 29.5
Irby in the Marsh 28.2
Irby upon Humber 28.9
Irchester 31.6
Ireby 10.2
Ireby with Leck 26.1
Ireland 2.2
Irelands Cross 37.1
Ireleth 10.6
Ireshopeburn 14.1
Irlam 19.5

2

Irnham 28.6
Iron Acton 18.7
Iron Cross 44.5
Ironbridge 37.4
Ironmasters 33.9
Ironville 11.6
Irstead 30.1
Irthington 10.1
Irthlingborough 31.3
Irton 33.4
Irton with Santon 10.4
Irvine S21
Irwell Vale 26.14
Iscoyd W22
Isfield 16.1
Isham 31.6
Isington 20.6
Islands Brow 29.3
Islay, Isle of S3
Isle Abbots 38.5
Isle Brewers 38.5
Isle of Arran S21
Isle of Cumbrae (see Millport)
Isle of Dogs L30
Isle of Grain 25.3
Isle of Sheppey 25.4
Isle of Skye S17
Isle of Whithorn S10
Isleham 6.4
Isleworth L18
Isley Walton 27.1
Isley-cum-Langley 27.1
Islington L19
Islington (Shrop) 37.4
Islip (N'hants) 31.3
Islip (Oxon) 35.2
Islivig S32
Isombridge 37.4
Istead Rise 25.2
Isycoed W22
Isygarreg W17
Itchen Abbas 20.5
Itchen Stoke 20.5
Itchen Valley 20.5
Itchenor 46.2
Itchingfield 46.3
Itchington 18.7
Itlay 18.5
Itteringham 30.1
Itton W13
Ivegill 10.3
Iver & Iver Heath 5.5
Iver Richings Park 5.5
Iverley 40.6
Iveston 14.1
Ivinghoe 5.2
Ivinghoe Aston 5.2
Ivonbrook Grange 11.3
Ivy Hatch 25.9
Ivybridge 12.9
Ivychurch 25.13
Iwade 25.4
Iwerne Courtney (or Shroton) 13.2
Iwerne Minster 13.2
Iwerne Stepleton 13.2
Iwood 38.7
Ixworth 41.3
Ixworth Thorpe 41.3
Jackfield 37.4
Jacksdale 34.4
Jackson Bridge 47.4
Jackton S28
Jacobstow 9.1
Jacobstowe 12.3
Jagger Green 47.3
Jameston W16
Jamestown (Highland) S17
Jamestown (W Dunbarton) S9
Janetstown S17
Jarrow 43.4
Jarvis Brook 16.1
Jaywick 17.4
Jealotts Hill 3.6
Jedburgh S30
Jeffreyston W16
Jemimaville S17
Jericho S2
Jericho (Gtr M'chester) 19.3
Jericho (Oxon) 35.5
Jersey Marine W14
Jerviston S22
Jesmond 43.1
Jevington 16.1
Jockey Green 48.1
John O'Groats S17
Johnby 10.3
Johnshaven S1
Johnston W16
Johnstone S25
Johnstone Bridge S10
Johnstown (Carm) W6
Johnstown (Wrexham) W22
Joiners Square 40.3
Jollys Bottom 9.1
Joppa (S Ayrs) S27
Jordans 5.4
Jordanston* W16
Joydens Wood 25.1
Joys Green 18.2
Jubilee 34.4
Jump 39.1
Jumpers 13.8
Juniper Green S6
Juniper Hill 35.2
Jura S3
Justicetown 10.1
Kaber 10.3
Kames S3
Kathernes 17.5
Kea 9.1
Keadby with Althorpe 28.8
Keal Coates 28.2
Kearby with Netherby 33.6
Kearn (see Auchendoir)
Kearsley 19.2
Kearsney 25.6
Keasden 33.5
Kebroyd 47.3
Keddington 28.2
Kederminster 3.5
Kedington 41.3
Kedleston 11.6
Keelby 28.1
Keele 40.2
Keelham 47.1
Keevil 48.1
Kegworth 27.1
Kehelland 9.1
Keig S1
Keighley 47.1
Keillour S24
Keinton Mandeville 38.5
Keisby 28.6
Keiss S17
Keith S20
Keithhall & Kinkell S1
Kelbrook 26.13
Kelby 28.4
Keld 10.3
Kelfield 33.8
Kelham 34.3
Kelhead S10
Kelk 15.2
Kellah 32.1
Kellaton 12.9
Kelleythorpe 15.2
Kelling 30.1
Kellington 33.8
Kelloe 14.1
Kelloholm S10
Kelly 12.3
Kelly Bray 9.1
Kelmarsh 31.4
Kelmscott 35.1
Kelsale 41.5
Kelsall 7.3
Kelshall 22.1
Kelso S30
Kelstedge 11.4
Kelstern 28.2
Kelston 38.6
Keltneyburn S24
Kelty S16
Kelvedon 17.2
Kelvedon Hatch 17.9
Kelvinhead S22
Kelynack 9.1
Kemback S16
Kemberton 37.1
Kemble (Gloucs) 18.5
Kemble (Wilts) 48.1
Kemble Wick 18.5
Kemerton 49.6
Kemeys Inferior W15
Kemnay S1
Kemp Town 16.3
Kempley 18.2
Kemprow 22.10
Kempsey 49.4
Kempsford 18.5
Kempshott 20.1
Kempshott Park 20.1
Kempston 2.1
Kempston Hardwick 2.1
Kempston Rural 2.1
Kempstone 30.3
Kempton 37.1
Kemsing 25.8
Kemsley Down 25.4
Kenardington 25.12
Kenchester 21.1
Kencot 35.1
Kendal 10.5
Kenderchurch 21.1
Kendleshire 18.7
Kenfig W3
Kenfig Hill W3
Kenfig Industrial Estate, nr Margam W14
Kenilworth 44.4
Kenley (Shrop) 37.1
Kenley (Surrey) (part) L8
Kenmore S24
Kenn (Devon) 12.5
Kenn (Som) 38.7
Kennerleigh 12.4
Kennethmont S1
Kennett (Cambs) 6.4
Kennett (Suffolk) 41.2
Kennford 12.5
Kenninghall 30.3
Kennington (Kent) 25.12
Kennington (Oxon) 35.4
Kennington (part) L22, L28
Kennoway S16
Kenny 38.5
Kenny Hill 41.2
Kensal Green (part) L13
Kensalyre S17
Kensington & Chelsea L20
Kensington (London) L20
Kensington (Mersey) 29.2
Kensington Park 4.1
Kenstone 37.1
Kenswick 49.4
Kensworth 2.2
Kent Street 16.2
Kentallen S17
Kentchurch 21.1
Kentford 41.2
Kentisbeare 12.4
Kentisbury 12.2
Kentish Town L6
Kentmere 10.5
Kenton (Devon) 12.5
Kenton (Suffolk) 41.4
Kenton (T & W) 43.1
Kenton (part) L4, L15
Kenton Bank Foot 43.1
Kenton Bar 43.1
Kentra S17
Kents Bank, Grange 10.5
Kents Hill 5.1
Kents Hill Park 5.1
Kents Oak 20.4
Kentwood Hill 3.2
Kenwick 37.1
Kenwyn 9.1
Kepwick 33.2
Keresley (part) 44.2, 45.7
Kerley Downs 9.1
Kermincham 7.5
Kernborough 12.9
Kerrera S3
Kerry W17
Kersal 19.5
Kersall 34.3
Kersey 41.6
Kershader S32

Kersham 38.3
Kershopefoot (part) 10.1, S30
Kesgrave 41.5
Kessingland 41.1
Kestle Mill (part) 9.1
Keston L5
Keswick (Cumbria) 10.2
Keswick (Norfolk) 30.7
Ketley 37.4
Ketley Bank 37.4
Ketsby (see South Ormsby)
Kettering 31.2
Ketteringham 30.7
Kettins S24
Kettlebaston 41.6
Kettlebrook 40.9
Kettleburgh 41.5
Kettleby 28.1
Kettleness 33.4
Kettleshulme 7.5
Kettlestone 30.1
Kettlethorpe (Lincs) 28.1
Kettlethorpe (W Yorks) 47.5
Kettlewell with Starbotton 33.5
Ketton 36.1
Keverstone (see Raby)
Kew L27
Kewstoke 38.7
Kexborough 39.1
Kexby (Lincs) 28.1
Kexby (N Yorks) 33.7
Keyham (Leics) 27.8
Keyhaven 20.7
Keyingham 15.2
Keymer 46.4
Keynsham 38.6
Keysoe 2.1
Keyston 6.3
Keythorpe 27.8
Keyworth 34.8
Kibblesworth 43.3
Kibworth Beauchamp 27.8
Kibworth Harcourt 27.8
Kidbrooke L11
Kidderminster 49.1
Kiddington with Asterleigh 35.1
Kidlington 35.2
Kidmore End 35.3
Kidsgrove 40.2
Kidwelly W6
Kielder 32.1
Kigetty W16
Kilbarchan S25
Kilberry S3
Kilbirnie S21
Kilbride (Argyll & Bute) S3
Kilbride (W Isles) S32
Kilburn (Derbys) 11.6
Kilburn (N Yorks) 33.2
Kilburn (part) L6, L33
Kilburn Park (part) L6, L33
Kilby 27.6
Kilby Bridge 27.7
Kilchattan Bay S3
Kilchoan S17
Kilchoman S3
Kilchrenan S3
Kilconquhar S16
Kilcot 18.2
Kildale 33.2
Kildalton S3
Kildary S17
Kildonan (Highland) S17
Kildonan (N Ayrs)* S21, S27
Kildrummy S1
Kildwick 33.5
Kilfinan S3
Kilgwrrwg W13
Kilham (E Yorks) 15.2
Kilham (N'land) 32.1
Kilkenzie S3
Kilkhampton 9.1
Killamarsh 11.4
Killay W19
Killean S3
Killearn S29
Killearnan S17
Killen S17
Killerby (Durham) 14.8
Killerby (N Yorks) 33.2
Killiechonan S24
Killiecrankie S24
Killiganoon 9.1
Killigarth 9.1
Killilan S17
Killin S29
Killinghall 33.6
Killington 10.5
Killingworth New Town 43.2
Killingworth Village 43.2
Killiow 9.1
Kilmacolm S18
Kilmaluag S17
Kilmany S16
Kilmarnock S11
Kilmartin S3
Kilmaurs S11
Kilmelford S3
Kilmersdon 38.2
Kilmeston 20.5
Kilmichael of Inverlussa S3
Kilmington (Devon) 12.7
Kilmington (Wilts) 48.1
Kilmore S3
Kilmory S17
Kilmuir S17
Kilmun S3
Kiln Farm 5.1
Kiln Green 3.3
Kilncadzow S28
Kilndown 25.11
Kilnhurst 39.4
Kilninver S3
Kilnsea 15.2
Kilnsey (see Conistone)
Kilnwick 15.2
Kilnwick Percy 15.2
Kiloran S3
Kilpeck 21.1
Kilpin 15.2
Kilrenny S16
Kilry S2
Kilsby 31.4
Kilspindie Errol S24
Kilsyth S22
Kiltarlity S17
Kilton 33.10
Kilvaxter S17
Kilve 38.3
Kilverstone 30.3
Kilvey W19
Kilvington 34.3
Kilwinning S21
Kimberley (Norfolk) 30.7
Kimberley (Notts) 34.5
Kimblesworth 14.1
Kimblewick 5.3
Kimbolton (Cambs) 6.3
Kimbolton (Here) 21.1
Kimcote 27.8
Kimmeridge 13.5
Kimpton (Hants) 20.4
Kimpton (Herts) 22.1
Kinbrace S17
Kinbuck S29
Kincardine (Fife) S16
Kincardine (Highland) S17
Kincardine O'Neil S1
Kinclaven S24
Kincraig S17
Kincraigie S24
Kindallachan S24
Kinellar S1
Kineton (Gloucs) 18.5
Kineton (Warks) 44.5
Kinfauns S24
King Edward S1
King Sterndale 11.1
King's Lynn 30.2
King's Norton (Leics) 27.8
King's Pyon 21.1
King's Somborne 20.4
King's Sutton 31.7
King's Walden 22.1
King's Worthy 20.5
Kingairloch S17
Kingcoed W13
Kingdown 38.7
Kingerby 28.1
Kingfield 42.4
Kingham 35.1
Kingholm Quay S10
Kinghorn S16
Kinglassie S16
Kinglochhourn S17
Kingmoor 10.1
Kingoldrum S2
Kings Bromley 40.8
Kings Caple 21.1
Kings Coughton 44.5
Kings Cross (part) L6, L19
Kings Furlong 20.1
Kings Heath (N'hants) 31.5
Kings Heath (W Mids) 45.5
Kings Hill (Kent) 25.9
Kings Hill (W Mids) (part) 45.4
Kings Langley (part) 22.4, 22.8
Kings Marsh 7.3
Kings Meaburn 10.3
Kings Newnham 44.3
Kings Newton 11.9
Kings Norton (Birmingham) 45.5
Kings Nympton 12.2
Kings Park 13.7
Kings Ripton 6.3
Kings Stanley 18.6
Kings' Cliffe 31.3
Kingsand 9.1
Kingsbarns S16
Kingsbridge (Devon) 12.9
Kingsbridge (Som) 38.3
Kingsbridge (Swansea) W19
Kingsbury 44.1
Kingsbury Episcopi 38.5
Kingsbury Regis 38.5
Kingsclere 20.1
Kingscote 18.5
Kingsdon 38.5
Kingsdown (Bristol) 4.1
Kingsdown (Kent)* 25.4, 25.6
Kingsdown (Wilts) 48.1
Kingseat S16
Kingsey 5.2
Kingsfold 46.3
Kingsford (Staffs) 40.6
Kingsford (Worcs) 49.1
Kingsgate (Broadstairs) 25.7
Kingsholm 18.3
Kingshurst 45.6
Kingskerswell 12.5
Kingskettle S16
Kingsland L12
Kingsland (Here) 21.1
Kingsland (Surrey) 42.8
Kingsley (Cheshire) 7.3
Kingsley (Hants) 20.6
Kingsley (N'hants) 31.5
Kingsley (Staffs) 40.1
Kingsley Green 46.2
Kingsley Holt 40.1
Kingsley Moor 40.1
Kingsmead 5.1
Kingsmuir S2
Kingsnorth 25.12
Kingstanding 45.5
Kingsteignton 12.5
Kingsthorne 21.1
Kingsthorpe (part) 31.5
Kingston (Bucks) 5.1
Kingston (Cambs) 6.5
Kingston (Devon) 12.9
Kingston (Dorset) 13.5
Kingston (E Lothian) S13
Kingston (E Sussex) 16.4
Kingston (Kent) 25.5
Kingston (Moray) S20
Kingston (W Sussex) 46.5
Kingston (Warks) 44.5
Kingston Bagpuize with Southmoor 35.4
Kingston Blount 35.3
Kingston Deverill 48.1
Kingston Lacy 13.3
Kingston Lisle 35.4
Kingston Maurward 13.1

2

Kingston Russell 13.1
Kingston St Mary 38.4
Kingston Seymour 38.7
Kingston Stert 35.3
Kingston Winslow 35.4
Kingston upon Hull 15.1
Kingston upon Thames (part) L21, L27
Kingston-on-Soar 34.8
Kingstone (Here) 21.1
Kingstone (Som) 38.5
Kingstone (Staffs) 40.5
Kingstown 10.1
Kingsway (part) L6, L33
Kingswear 12.9
Kingswells S4
Kingswinford 45.3
Kingswood (Bristol) (part) 4.1, 18.7
Kingswood (Bucks) 5.2
Kingswood (Gloucs) (part) 18.6
Kingswood (Kent) 25.10
Kingswood (Som) 38.3
Kingswood (Surrey) 42.9
Kingthorpe (Lincs) 28.1
Kingthorpe (N Yorks) 33.3
Kington (Gloucs) 18.7
Kington (Here) 21.1
Kington (Worcs) 49.6
Kington Langley 48.1
Kington Magna 13.2
Kington Rural 21.1
Kington St Michael 48.1
Kingussie S17
Kingwater 10.1
Kingweston 38.5
Kingwood 35.3
Kingwood Common 35.3
Kinkell Bridge S24
Kinlet 37.1
Kinloch (Perth & Kinross) S24
Kinloch Rannoch S24
Kinlochard S29
Kinlochbervie S17
Kinlocheil S17
Kinlochewe S17
Kinlochleven S17
Kinloss S20
Kinmel Bay W8
Kinnaber S2
Kinnaird S24
Kinneff S1
Kinnell S2
Kinnerley 37.1
Kinnersley 21.1
Kinnerton W17
Kinnesswood S24
Kinnettles S2
Kinniside (see Ennerdale)
Kinoulton 34.8
Kinross S24
Kinrossie S24
Kinsbourne Green (part) 2.2, 22.5
Kinsham (part) 21.1, 49.6
Kinsley 47.5
Kinson 13.7
Kintbury 3.1
Kintillo S24
Kintore S1
Kinver 40.6
Kinwarton 44.5
Kiplin 33.2
Kippax 47.2
Kippen S29
Kippford S10
Kippielaw S19
Kirby Bedon 30.7
Kirby Bellars 27.3
Kirby Cane 30.7
Kirby Cross 17.4
Kirby Fleetham with Fencote 33.2
Kirby Grindalythe 33.3
Kirby Hall 33.6
Kirby Hill (part) 33.1, 33.6
Kirby Knowle 33.2
Kirby Misperton 33.3
Kirby Muxloe 27.6
Kirby Sigston 33.2
Kirby Underdale 15.2
Kirby Wiske 33.2
Kirby-le-Soken 17.4
Kirdford 46.2
Kirk Bramwith 39.2
Kirk Deighton 33.6
Kirk Hallam 11.8
Kirk Hammerton 33.6
Kirk Ireton 11.3
Kirk Langley 11.6
Kirk Lea 43.5
Kirk Merrington 14.1
Kirk O'Shotts S22
Kirk Sandall (see Barnby Dun)
Kirk Smeaton 33.8
Kirk Yetholm S30
Kirkabister S26
Kirkandrews 10.1
Kirkbampton 10.2
Kirkbean S10
Kirkbride 10.2
Kirkburn 15.2
Kirkburton 47.4
Kirkby (Mersey) 29.4
Kirkby (N Yorks) 33.2
Kirkby Green 28.4
Kirkby Lonsdale 10.5
Kirkby Malham 33.5
Kirkby Mallory 27.4
Kirkby Malzeard 33.6
Kirkby Overblow 33.6
Kirkby Stephen 10.3
Kirkby Thore 10.3
Kirkby Underwood 28.6
Kirkby Wharfe with North Milford 33.8
Kirkby Woodhouse 34.4
Kirkby in Ashfield 34.4
Kirkby in Furness 10.5
Kirkby la Thorpe 28.4
Kirkby on Bain 28.2
Kirkby-cum-Osgodby 28.1
Kirkbymoorside 33.3
Kirkcaldy S16
Kirkcambeck 10.1
Kirkcolm S10
Kirkconnel S10
Kirkcowan S10
Kirkcudbright S10
Kirkdale 29.2
Kirkella 15.2
Kirkfieldbank S28
Kirkgunzeon S10
Kirkham 26.5
Kirkhamgate 47.5
Kirkharle 32.1
Kirkhaugh (see Knarsdale)
Kirkheaton (N'land) 32.1
Kirkheaton (W Yorks) 47.4
Kirkhill (Highland) S17
Kirkhill (Midlothian) S19
Kirkholt 19.4
Kirkhouse 10.1
Kirkhouse Green 39.2
Kirkinner S10
Kirkintilloch S12
Kirkland (Cumbria) 10.3
Kirkland (Lancs) 26.2
Kirkleatham 33.10
Kirklees, Tottington 19.3
Kirklevington 14.10
Kirkley 32.1
Kirklington 34.3
Kirklington-cum-Upsland 33.2
Kirklinton 10.1
Kirkliston S6
Kirkmabreck S10
Kirkmaiden S10
Kirkmichael (Perth & Kinross) S24
Kirkmichael (S Ayrs) S27
Kirkmuirhill S28
Kirknewton (N'land) 32.1
Kirknewton (W Lothian) S31
Kirkoswald (Cumbria) 10.3
Kirkoswald (S Ayrs) S27
Kirkpatrick Durham S10
Kirkpatrick Fleming S10
Kirkstead 28.2
Kirkstead Bridge 28.4
Kirkthorpe 47.5
Kirkton S10
Kirkwall S23
Kirkwhelpington 32.1
Kirland 9.1
Kirmington (Lincs) (see Croxton)
Kirmond le Mire 28.1
Kirriemuir S2
Kirstead 30.7
Kirtlebridge S10
Kirtling 6.4
Kirtlington 35.2
Kirtomy S17
Kirton (Lincs) 28.5
Kirton (Notts) 34.3
Kirton (Suffolk) 41.5
Kirton-in-Lindsey 28.8
Kishorn S17
Kislingbury 31.7
Kite Green 44.5
Kites Hardwick 44.3
Kittisford 38.4
Kittle W19
Kitts End 22.10
Kitts Green 45.5
Kittwhistle 13.1
Kiveton Park 39.4
Kiveton Park Station 39.4
Knaith 28.1
Knaith Park 28.1
Knaphill 42.4
Knapp 38.4
Knaptoft 27.8
Knapton (Norfolk) 30.1
Knapton (Scampston) 33.3
Knapwell 6.5
Knaresborough 33.6
Knaresborough Outer 33.6
Knarsdale with Kirkhaugh 32.1
Knatts Valley 25.8
Knavesmire 33.7
Knayton with Brawith 33.2
Knebworth 22.1
Knedlington 15.2
Kneesall 34.3
Kneeton 34.8
Knelston W19
Knettishall 41.3
Knightcote 44.5
Knightcott 38.7
Knighton (I of W) (see Newchurch)
Knighton (Oxon) 35.4
Knighton (Powys) W17
Knighton (Som) 38.5
Knighton (Staffs)* 40.2, 40.4
Knighton-on-Teme 49.4
Knights Enham 20.4
Knightsbridge (part) L20, L33
Knightsbridge House & Farm 20.1
Knightwick 49.4
Knill 21.1
Knipton 27.3
Kniveton 11.3
Knock 10.3
Knock (Argyll & Bute) S3
Knock (W Isles) S32
Knockando S20
Knockentiber S11
Knockfarrel S17
Knockholt 25.8
Knockholt Pound 25.8
Knockin 37.1
Knockin Heath 37.1
Knodishall 41.5
Knole 38.5
Knook 48.1
Knorren Fell 10.1
Knossington 27.3
Knotbury 40.1
Knott End-on-Sea 26.2
Knotting 2.1
Knottingley 47.5
Knotty Ash 29.2

Knotty Green 5.4
Knowbury 37.1
Knowe S10
Knowl Hill (part) 3.3, 3.4
Knowle (Bristol) 4.1
Knowle (Devon) 12.4
Knowle (Hants) 20.5
Knowle (Som) 38.3
Knowle (W Mids) 45.6
Knowle Green 26.3
Knowle Park 47.1
Knowle St Giles 38.5
Knowle West 4.1
Knowlhill 5.1
Knowlton (Dorset) 13.3
Knowlton (Kent) 25.6
Knowsley 29.4
Knowstone 12.2
Knoydart S17
Knutsford 7.5
Knutton 40.2
Knuzden (part) 26.10, 26.11
Knypersley 40.1
Krumlin 47.3
Kyle of Lochalsh S17
Kyleakin S17
Kylerhea S17
Kyloe 32.1
Kynaston 21.1
Kyneton 18.7
Kynnersley 37.4
Kyre 49.4
La Feock 9.1
Laceby 28.9
Lacey Green 5.3
Lach Dennis 7.3
Lache (see Marlston)
Lackenby 33.10
Lackford 41.3
Lacock 48.1
Lacon 37.1
Ladbroke 44.5
Ladbroke Grove (part) L20, L33
Ladderedge 40.1
Laddingford, Yalding 25.10
Ladock 9.1
Ladybank S16
Ladycross 9.1
Ladygrove 11.6
Ladykirk S30
Ladyridge 21.1
Ladywell S2
Ladywood S19
Ladywood (W Mids) 45.5
Ladywood (Worcs) 49.6
Laffak 29.3
Lagavullin S3
Laggan S17
Lagness 46.5
Laide S17
Laindon 17.10
Lairg S17
Laisterdyke 47.1
Laithes 10.3
Lake (I of W) 24.1
Lake (Som) 38.5
Lake (Wilts) (see Wilsford)
Lakenham (Norwich) 30.4
Lakenheath 41.2
Lakesend 30.2
Lakeside (Cumbria) 10.5
Lakeside (Worcs) 49.3
Lakeview 31.5
Laleham 42.2
Laleston W3
Lamarsh 17.2
Lamberhurst 25.11
Lamberton S30
Lambeth L22
Lambley (N'land) 32.1
Lambley (Notts) 34.7
Lambourn 3.1
Lambourne End 17.6
Lambrigg 10.5
Lambrook 38.5
Lambs Green 46.3
Lambston W16
Lambton 14.1, 43.5
Lambwood Hill 3.3
Lamerton 12.3
Lamesley 43.3
Lamington S28
Lamlash S21
Lammas (see Buxton)
Lamonby 10.3
Lamorna 9.1
Lamorran 9.1
Lampeter W7
Lampeter Velfrey W16
Lamphey W16
Lamplugh 10.4
Lamport 31.4
Lamyatt 38.2
Lanark S28
Lancaster 26.1
Lanchester 14.1
Lancing 46.7
Land's End 9.1
Landare W18
Landbeach 6.5
Landcross 12.1
Landewednack 9.1
Landford 48.1
Landford Wood 48.1
Landimore W19
Landkey 12.2
Landmoth-cum-Catto 33.2
Landore W19
Landulph 9.1
Lane Bottom 26.12
Lane End (Bucks) 5.3
Lane End (Here) 21.1
Lane End (Kent) 25.1
Lane Head (W Yorks) 47.3
Lane Head, Willenhall 45.2
Laneast 9.1
Laneham 34.1
Lanehead 14.1
Lanercost 10.1
Laneshawbridge 26.13
Laneside (Queensbury) 47.1
Laneside (Wilsden) 47.1
Langaller 38.4
Langar-cum-Barnstone 34.8
Langbank S25
Langbar (see Nesfield)
Langcliffe 33.5
Langdale 10.5
Langdale End 33.4
Langdon 25.6
Langdon Hills (part) 17.10, 17.12
Langdown 20.7
Langenhoe 17.3
Langeview W13
Langford (Beds) 2.2
Langford (Essex) 17.8
Langford (Norfolk) 30.3
Langford (Notts) 34.3
Langford (Oxon) 35.1
Langford (Som) 38.7
Langford Budville 38.4
Langford Green 38.7
Langham (Essex) 17.3
Langham (Lincs) 28.2
Langham (Norfolk) 30.1
Langham (Rutland) 36.1
Langham (Som) 38.5
Langham (Suffolk) 41.4
Langho 26.3
Langholm S10
Langland W19
Langlees S15
Langley (Berks) 3.5
Langley (Cheshire) 7.5
Langley (Essex) 17.1
Langley (Hants) 20.7
Langley (Herts) 22.1
Langley (Kent) 25.10
Langley (Leics) (see Isley)
Langley (N'land) 32.1
Langley (Shrop) 37.1
Langley (Som) 38.4
Langley (W Mids) 45.4
Langley (W Sussex) 46.2
Langley (Warks) 44.5
Langley Burrell Without 48.1
Langley Green 46.1
Langley Marsh 38.4
Langley Mill 11.6
Langley Moor 14.1
Langley Park 14.1
Langley Vale 42.6
Langley with Hardley 30.7
Langleybury 22.8
Langleydale 14.1
Langmere 30.7
Langney 16.5
Langold 34.1
Langore 9.1
Langport 38.5
Langrick 28.2
Langridge 38.6
Langrish 20.6
Langriville 28.2
Langsett 39.1
Langshaw S30
Langstone W15
Langthorne 33.2
Langthorpe 33.6
Langtoft (E Yorks) 15.2
Langtoft (Lincs) 28.6
Langton (Durham) 14.1
Langton (N Yorks) 33.3
Langton by Horncastle 28.2
Langton by Spilsby 28.2
Langton by Wragby 28.2
Langton Green 25.11
Langton Herring 13.1
Langton Long Blandford 13.2
Langton Matravers 13.5
Langtree (Devon) 12.1
Langtree (Gtr M'chester) (see Standish)
Langwathby 10.3
Langwith 11.5
Langwith Basset 11.5
Langwith Junction 11.5
Langworth 28.1
Langworthy 19.5
Lanhydrock 9.1
Lanivet 9.1
Lanjeth 9.1
Lanlivery 9.1
Lanner 9.1
Lanreath 9.1
Lansallos 9.1
Lansbury L30
Lansbury Park W4
Lansdown 38.6
Lanteglos 9.1
Lanton S30
Lapford 12.4
Lapley 40.6
Lapworth (part) 44.4, 44.5
Larbert S15
Larbreck (see Little Eccleston)
Largoward S16
Largs S21
Larkbarrow 38.3
Larkfield 25.9
Larkhall S28
Larkhill 48.1
Larkton 7.3
Larling 30.3
Lartington 14.1
Lasborough (see Westonbirt)
Lascelles Hall 47.4
Lasham (part) 20.1, 20.6
Lask Edge 40.1
Laskill Pasture 33.3
Lasswade S19
Lastingham 33.3
Latchbrook 9.1
Latchford (Cheshire) 7.1
Latchford (Herts) 22.3
Latchingdon 17.8
Latchley 9.1
Latchmere Green 20.1
Latebrook 40.3
Lathbury 5.1
Latheron S17
Latheronwheel S17
Lathom 26.8
Latimer 5.4
Latteridge 18.7
Lattiford 38.5
Latton (Essex) 17.5
Latton (Wilts) 48.1

2

Lauder S30
Laugharne Township W6
Laughterton 28.1
Laughton (E Sussex) 16.1
Laughton (Leics) 27.8
Laughton (Lincs) (part) 28.1, 28.6
Laughton (S Yorks) 39.4
Laughton Common 39.4
Launcells 9.1
Launceston 9.1
Launcherley 38.2
Launde 27.8
Launditch (see Mitford & Launditch)
Launton 35.2
Laurencekirk S1
Laurieston (Dumfries & Galloway) S10
Laurieston (Falkirk) S15
Lavant 46.2
Lavendon 5.1
Lavenham 41.6
Lavernock W21
Laversdale 10.1
Laverstock 48.1
Laverstoke 20.1
Laverton (N Yorks) 33.6
Laverton (Som) 38.2
Law S28
Lawers S24
Lawford (Essex) 17.4
Lawford (Som) 38.3
Lawhitton 9.1
Lawkholme 47.1
Lawkland 33.5
Lawley 37.4
Lawrence Weston 4.1
Lawrenny W16
Lawshall 41.6
Lawton Heath End 7.5
Laxay S32
Laxfield 41.4
Laxo S26
Laxton (E Riding) 15.2
Laxton (N'hants) 31.3
Laxton (Notts) 34.3
Laycock 47.1
Layer Breton 17.3
Layer Marney 17.3
Layer-de-la-Haye 17.3
Layham 41.6
Laymore 13.1
Laytham 15.2
Lazenby* 33.2, 33.10
Lazonby 10.3
Lea & Cleverton 48.1
Lea (Cheshire) 7.5
Lea (Derbys) 11.6
Lea (Here) 21.1
Lea (Lancs) 26.6
Lea (Lincs) 28.1
Lea Bailey (part) 18.2, 21.1
Lea Bridge (part) L12, L31
Lea Green 29.3
Lea Hall (Birm) 45.5
Lea Hall (Derbys) 11.3
Lea Marston 44.1
Lea Newbold 7.3
Lea-by-Backford 7.3
Leabridge 11.6
Leabrooks 11.6
Leacroft (part) 40.6, 40.7
Lead 33.8
Leadburn S19
Leaden Roding 17.1
Leadenhall 5.1
Leadenham 28.4
Leadgate (Cumbria) 10.3
Leadgate (Durham) 14.1
Leadhills S28
Leafield 35.1
Leagram (see Bowland)
Leake 33.2
Lealholm 33.4
Leam Lane 43.3
Leamington Hastings 44.3
Leamington Spa, Royal 44.4
Leamore 45.2
Leamside 14.1
Leasgill 10.5
Leasingham 28.4
Leasingthorne 14.1
Leasowe 29.5
Leatherhead 42.8
Leathley 33.6
Leaton 37.1
Leaveland 25.4
Leavenheath 41.6
Leavening 33.3
Leavesden (part) 22.8, 22.9
Lebberston 33.4
Lechlade 18.5
Leck (see Ireby)
Leckby (see Cundall)
Leckford 20.4
Leckhampstead (Berks) 3.1
Leckhampstead (Bucks) 5.2
Leckmelm S17
Leckwith W21
Leconfield 15.2
Ledaig S3
Ledburn 5.2
Ledbury 21.1
Ledsham (Cheshire) 7.3
Ledsham (W Yorks) 47.2
Ledston 47.2
Lee (Shrop) 37.1
Lee (part) L11, L23
Lee Brockhurst 37.1
Lee Mill 12.9
Lee Moor 47.5
Lee Mount 47.3
Lee, The 5.4
Lee-on-the-Solent 20.11
Leebotwood 37.1
Leece 10.5
Leechmere 43.5
Leeds (Kent) 25.10
Leeds (W Yorks) 47.2
Leedstown (part) 9.1
Leegomery 37.4
Leeholme 14.1
Leek 40.1
Leek Wootton & Guy's Cliffe 44.4
Leekfrith 40.1
Leeming (N Yorks) 33.2
Leeming (W Yorks) 47.1
Leeming Bar (Aiskew) 33.2
Lees (Gtr M'chester) 19.7
Lees (W Yorks) 47.1
Leeshill 10.1
Leesthorpe 27.3
Leeswood W10
Leetown S24
Legbourne 28.2
Legerwood S30
Legsby 28.1
Leicester 27.5
Leicester Forest East 27.6
Leicester Forest West 27.6
Leigh (Dorset) 13.1
Leigh (Gloucs) 18.1
Leigh (Gtr M'chester) 19.1
Leigh (Kent) 25.8
Leigh (Staffs) 40.5
Leigh (Surrey) 42.8
Leigh (Wilts) 48.1
Leigh (Worcs) 49.4
Leigh Common 38.5
Leigh Delamere 48.1
Leigh Park 20.13
Leigh Woods 38.7
Leigh-on-Mendip 38.2
Leigh-on-Sea (part) 17.13, 17.14
Leighfield 36.1
Leighland Chapel 38.3
Leighterton (see Boxwell)
Leighton (Cheshire) 7.5
Leighton (Powys) W17
Leighton (Shrop) 37.1
Leighton Bromswold 6.3
Leighton Buzzard 2.2
Leighton Linslade 2.2
Leinthall Starkes 21.1
Leintwardine 21.1
Leire 27.8
Leiston 41.5
Leith S6
Leith Hill 42.8
Leitholm S30
Lelant 9.1
Lelant Downs 9.1
Lelley 15.2
Lemington (Gloucs) 18.5
Lemington (T & W) 43.1
Lemreway S32
Lemsford 22.6
Lenborough 5.2
Lenchwick 49.6
Lenham 25.10
Lenham Heath 25.10
Lennoxtown S12
Lenton (Lincs) 28.6
Lenton (Notts) 34.6
Lenzie S12
Leochel Cushnie S1
Leominster 21.1
Leonard Stanley 18.6
Lepe 20.7
Lepton 47.4
Lerryn 9.1
Lerwick S26
Lesbury 32.1
Leslie (Aberdeen) S1
Leslie (Fife) S16
Lesmahagow S28
Lesnewth 9.1
Lessingham 30.1
Leswalt S10
Letchmore Heath 22.10
Letchworth 22.1
Letcombe Bassett 35.4
Letcombe Regis 35.4
Letham (Angus) S2
Letham (Falkirk) S15
Letham (Fife) S16
Lethen S17
Letheringham 41.5
Letheringsett with Glandford 30.1
Lethnot S2
Letters S17
Letterston W16
Letton (Here) 21.1
Letton (Norfolk) 30.3
Letty Green 22.3
Letwell 39.4
Leurbost S32
Leusdon 12.5
Leven (E Yorks) 15.2
Leven (Fife) S16
Levens 10.5
Levenshulme 19.6
Levenwick S26
Leverburgh S32
Leverington 6.2
Leverton 28.5
Levington 41.5
Levisham 33.3
Lew 35.1
Lewannick 9.1
Lewcombe 13.1
Lewes 16.4
Leweston 13.1
Lewisham (part) L11, L23
Lewiston S17
Lewistown W3
Lewknor 35.3
Lewtrenchard 12.3
Lexham (East & West) 30.3
Ley (Som) 38.3
Ley Green 22.1
Ley Hill (Bucks) 5.4
Leybourne 25.9
Leyburn 33.1
Leycett 40.2
Leyfields 40.3, 40.9
Leyhill (Gloucs) 18.7
Leyland 26.7
Leymoor 47.4
Leys Hill 21.1
Leys, The 40.9
Leysdown on Sea 25.4
Leysmill S2
Leysters 21.1
Leysthorpe (see East Newton)
Leyton L31
Leyton Marshes L31

Leytonstone L31
Lezant 9.1
Leziate 30.2
Lhanbryde S20
Libanus W17
Libberton S28
Lichfield 40.8
Lickey 49.2
Lickey End 49.2
Lickfold 46.2
Liddington 48.2
Liden 48.2
Lidgate 41.3
Lidget 47.1
Lidget Green 47.1
Lidlington 2.2
Lidsey 46.5
Lidsing, nr Boxley 25.10
Lifton 12.3
Light Oaks 40.3
Lightbowne 19.6
Lightcliffe 47.3
Lighthorne 44.5
Lighthorne Heath 44.5
Lightmoor 37.4
Lightwater 42.3
Lightwood (Derbys) 11.4
Lightwood (Staffs) 40.3
Lilbourne 31.4
Lilbourne Furze 31.4
Lilford-cum-Wigsthorpe 31.3
Lillesdon 38.4
Lilleshall (part) 37.4
Lilley 22.1
Lilliesleaf S30
Lillings Ambo 33.3
Lillingstone Dayrell 5.2
Lillingstone Lovell 5.2
Lillington (Dorset) 13.1
Lilliput 13.6
Lillycombe 38.3
Limefield 19.3
Limehouse L30
Limekilns S16
Limerigg S15
Limeslade W19
Limington 38.5
Limpley Stoke 48.1
Limpsfield 42.10
Limpsfield Chart 42.10
Linacre Woods (part) 11.2, 11.4
Linbrook 20.7
Linby 34.7
Linch 46.2
Linchmere 46.2
Lincoln 28.3
Lindal-in-Furness (part) 10.5, 10.6
Lindale 10.5
Linden 32.1
Lindfield 46.4
Lindfield Rural 46.4
Lindford 20.6
Lindley (N Yorks) 33.6
Lindley (W Yorks) 47.4
Lindrick Common 39.4
Lindrick Dale 39.4
Lindrick with Studley Roger 33.6
Lindridge 49.4
Lindsell 17.1
Lindsey 41.6
Linford (Essex) 17.12
Linford (Hants) 20.7
Linford Wood 5.1
Lingbob 47.1
Lingdale 33.10
Lingen 21.1
Lingfield 42.10
Lings 31.5
Lingwell Gate 47.5
Lingwood & Burlingham 30.5
Linkenholt 20.4
Linkinhorne 9.1
Links View 31.5
Links, The 37.1
Linley 37.1
Linlithgow S31
Linlithgow Bridge S31
Linslade 2.2
Linstead, Magna & Parva 41.5
Linstock 10.1
Linthorpe 33.9
Linthwaite 47.4
Linton S30
Linton (Cambs) 6.5
Linton (Derbys) 11.9
Linton (Here)* 21.1
Linton (Kent) 25.10
Linton (N Yorks) 33.5
Linton (N'land) 32.1
Linton (W Yorks) 47.2
Linton (Worcs) 21.1
Linton-on-Ouse 33.2
Lintrathem, Bridgend of (see Bridgend of Lintrathem)
Lintz 14.1
Linwood S25
Linwood (Hants) 20.7
Linwood (Lincs) 28.1
Lionaclate S32
Lionthorn S15
Liphook (part) 20.6, 46.2
Lipyeate 38.2
Liscard 29.5
Liskeard 9.1
Lismore, Isle of S3
Liss 20.6
Lissett 15.2
Lissington 28.1
Lisson Grove L33
Listerhills 47.1
Listock 38.4
Listoft 28.2
Liston 17.2
Lisvane (Caerph) W4
Lisvane (Cardiff) W5
Litcham 30.3
Litchard W3
Litchborough 31.7
Litchfield (Hants) 20.1
Litherland 29.1
Litlington (E Sussex) 16.1
Litlington (S Cambs) 6.5
Litmarsh 21.1
Little Abington 6.5
Little Addington 31.3
Little Alne 44.5
Little Ann 20.4
Little Arrow 10.5
Little Asby 10.3
Little Aston 40.8
Little Ayton 33.2
Little Baddow 17.7
Little Badminton 18.7
Little Ballinluig S24
Little Bardfield 17.1
Little Barford 2.1
Little Barningham 30.1
Little Barrington (see Barrington) (Gloucs)
Little Basing 20.1
Little Bedworth Heath 44.2
Little Bedwyn 48.1
Little Bentley 17.4
Little Berkhamsted 22.3
Little Billing 31.5
Little Birch 21.1
Little Blakenham 41.4
Little Blencowe 10.3
Little Bloxwich 45.2
Little Bognor 46.2
Little Bolas 37.1
Little Bollington 7.5
Little Bookham 42.8
Little Bourton 35.2
Little Bowden 27.8
Little Bradley 41.3
Little Brampton (Here) (see Rodd, Nash & Little Brampton)
Little Brampton (Shrop) 37.1
Little Braxted 17.8
Little Brechin S2
Little Brickhill 5.1
Little Bristol 18.7
Little Bromley 17.4
Little Broughton 33.2
Little Budworth 7.3
Little Burstead 17.10
Little Busby 33.2
Little Bytham 28.6
Little Canfield 17.1
Little Carharrack 9.1
Little Carlton (Lincs) 28.2
Little Carlton (Notts) 34.3
Little Casterton 36.1
Little Cawthorpe 28.2
Little Chalfont 5.4
Little Chart 25.12
Little Chell 40.3
Little Chesterford 17.1
Little Chesterton 35.2
Little Chishill 6.5
Little Clacton 17.4
Little Clifton 10.2
Little Comberton 49.6
Little Compton 44.5
Little Corby 10.1
Little Cornard 41.6
Little Cowarne 21.1
Little Coxwell 35.4
Little Cransley 31.2
Little Crawley 5.1
Little Cressingham 30.3
Little Crosby 29.1
Little Dalby 27.3
Little Dassett 44.5
Little Dawley 37.4
Little Dewchurch 21.1
Little Doward 21.1
Little Downham 6.4
Little Driffield 15.2
Little Dronfield 38.5
Little Dunham 30.3
Little Dunmow 17.1
Little Earnock S28
Little Easton 17.1
Little Eaton 11.8
Little Eccleston with Larbreck 26.5
Little Ellingham 30.3
Little Eversden 6.5
Little Faringdon 35.1
Little Fenton 33.8
Little Fields 38.5
Little Finborough 41.4
Little Gaddesden 22.4
Little Gidding 6.3
Little Gransden 6.5
Little Grimsby 28.2
Little Hadham 22.3
Little Hale 28.4
Little Hales 37.4
Little Hallingbury 17.1
Little Hampden 5.3
Little Harrowden 31.6
Little Haseley 35.3
Little Haven W16
Little Hay 40.8
Little Haywood 40.4
Little Heath 22.6
Little Henny 17.2
Little Hereford 21.1
Little Hinton 48.2
Little Holland (see Holland-on-Sea)
Little Hoole 26.7
Little Horkesley 17.3
Little Horsted 16.1
Little Horton 47.1
Little Horwood 5.2
Little Houghton (N'hants) 31.7
Little Houghton (S Yorks) 39.1
Little Hucklow 11.3
Little Hulton 19.5
Little Humby 28.6
Little Ickford 5.2
Little Irchester 31.6
Little Kelk 15.2
Little Kimble 5.3
Little Kineton 44.5
Little Kingshill 5.4
Little Langdale 10.5
Little Langford 48.1
Little Langton 33.2
Little Laver 17.6

2

Little Lawford 44.3
Little Leigh 7.3
Little Leighs 17.7
Little Lever 19.2
Little Limber 28.1
Little Linford 5.1
Little Livermere 41.3
Little Load 38.5
Little London (W Yorks) 47.1
Little London, Pamber 20.1
Little London, St Mary Bourne 20.1
Little Longstone 11.3
Little Lumley 14.1
Little Lyde 38.5
Little Malvern 49.4
Little Maplestead 17.2
Little Marcle 21.1
Little Marlow 5.3
Little Massingham 30.2
Little Melton 30.7
Little Mill (Kent) 25.9
Little Mill (Monmth) W13
Little Milton 35.3
Little Missenden 5.4
Little Mitton 26.3
Little Mongeham 25.6
Little Munden 22.3
Little Musgrave 10.3
Little Ness 37.1
Little Neston 7.3
Little Newcastle W16
Little Normans 18.3
Little Norton 38.5
Little Oakley (Essex) 17.4
Little Oakley (N'hants) 31.2
Little Ormside 10.3
Little Orton (Cumbria) 10.1
Little Orton (Leics) 27.4
Little Ouse 6.4
Little Ouseburn 33.6
Little Packington 44.1
Little Parndon 17.5
Little Paxton 6.3
Little Petherick 9.1
Little Petherton 38.5
Little Ponton 28.6
Little Preston (N'hants) 31.4
Little Preston (W Yorks) 47.2
Little Purston 31.7
Little Reedness 15.2
Little Ribston 33.6
Little Rissington 18.5
Little Ryburgh 30.1
Little Salkeld 10.3
Little Sampford 17.1
Little Sandhurst 3.6
Little Saxham 41.3
Little Shelford 6.5
Little Singleton 26.5
Little Smeaton* 33.2, 33.8
Little Snoring 30.1
Little Sodbury 18.7
Little Somborne 20.4
Little Somerford 48.1
Little Stainton 14.8
Little Stanney* 7.3
Little Staughton 2.1
Little Steeping 28.2
Little Stoke (Gloucs) 18.7
Little Stoke (Oxon) 35.3
Little Stonham 41.4
Little Stretton (Leics) 27.8
Little Stretton (Shrop) 37.1
Little Strickland 10.3
Little Stukeley 6.3
Little Sutton (Cheshire) 7.3
Little Sutton (Lincs) 28.7
Little Tew 35.1
Little Thetford 6.4
Little Thornage 30.1
Little Thurlow 41.3
Little Thurrock 17.12
Little Timble 33.6
Little Tingewick 5.2
Little Torrington 12.1
Little Totham 17.8
Little Urswick 10.5
Little Venice L33
Little Wakering 17.11
Little Waldingfield 41.6
Little Walsingham 30.1
Little Waltham 17.7
Little Walton 44.3
Little Warford 7.5
Little Weighton 15.2
Little Wenlock 37.4
Little Weston 38.5
Little Whelnetham 41.3
Little Wigborough 17.3
Little Wilbraham 6.5
Little Willicote 44.5
Little Witchingham 30.5
Little Witley 49.4
Little Wittenham 35.3
Little Wolford 44.5
Little Wratting 41.3
Little Wymondley 22.1
Little Wyrley 40.6
Little Wytheford 37.1
Little Yeldham 17.2
Littlebeck 33.4
Littleborough 19.4
Littlebourne 25.5
Littlebredy 13.1
Littlebury 17.1
Littledale (see Caton)
Littledean 18.2
Littledown 13.7
Littleferry S17
Littlefield Green 3.4
Littleham 12.1
Littlehampton 46.5
Littlehempston 12.9
Littlemill S17
Littlemore 35.5
Littleover 11.7
Littleport 6.4
Littlesea 13.1
Littlestone 25.13
Littlethorpe (Leics) 27.6
Littlethorpe (N Yorks) 33.6
Littleton (Cheshire) 7.3
Littleton (Hants) 20.5
Littleton (Som) 38.5
Littleton (Surrey) 42.2
Littleton (Worcs), Middle, North & South 49.6
Littleton Drew 48.1
Littleton Panell 48.1
Littleton-upon-Severn 18.7
Littletown (Durham) 14.1
Littletown (W Yorks) 47.4
Littlewick Green 3.4
Littleworth (Oxon)* 35.3, 35.4
Littleworth (Staffs) 40.7
Littleworth (Wilts) 48.1
Littleworth (Worcs) 49.6
Littley Green 17.7
Litton (Derbys) 11.3
Litton (N Yorks) 33.5
Litton (Som) 38.2
Litton Cheney 13.1
Litton Mill 11.3
Liverpool 29.2
Liversedge 47.4
Liverton (Devon) 12.5
Liverton (Redcar) 33.10
Livesey 26.10
Livingston S31
Lixwm W10
Lizard, The 9.1
Llaingoch W1
Llanaber W11
Llanaelhaearn W11
Llanafan W7
Llanafanfawr W17
Llanafanfechan W17
Llanallgo W1
Llananno W17
Llanarmon W11
Llanarmon Dyffryn Ceiriog W22
Llanarmon-yn-Ial W9
Llanarth (Card) W7
Llanarth (Monmth) W13
Llanarthney W6
Llanasa W10
Llanbabo W1
Llanbadarn Fawr (Card) W7
Llanbadarn Fynydd W17
Llanbadarn-y-garreg W17
Llanbadarnfawr (Powys) W17
Llanbadoc W13
Llanbadrig W1
Llanbedr W11
Llanbedr Painscastle W17
Llanbedr Ystradwy W17
Llanbedr-Dyffryn-Clwyd W9
Llanbedr-y-cennin W8
Llanbedrgoch W1
Llanbedrog W11
Llanberis W11
Llanbethery W21
Llanbeulan W1
Llanbister W17
Llanblethian W21
Llanboidy W6
Llanbradach W4
Llanbrynmair W17
Llancadle W21
Llancaiach W4
Llancarfan W21
Llancayo W13
Llancillo 21.1
Llancynfelin W7
Llandaff W5
Llandaff North W5
Llandanwg W11
Llandarcy W14
Llanddanielfab W1
Llanddarog W6
Llanddeiniol W7
Llanddeiniolen W11
Llandderfel W11
Llanddetty W17
Llanddeusant (Anglesey) W1
Llanddeusant (Carm) W6
Llanddew W17
Llanddewi W19
Llanddewi Abergwesyn W17
Llanddewi Brefi W7
Llanddewi Rhydderch W13
Llanddewi Sgyrrid W13
Llanddewi Velfrey W16
Llanddewi Ystradenni W17
Llanddewi'r Cwm W17
Llanddewifach W17
Llanddinorwic W11
Llanddoged W8
Llanddona W1
Llanddowror W6
Llanddulas W8
Llanddyfnan W1
Llandecwyn W11
Llandefaelog Fach W17
Llandefalle W17
Llandegfan W1
Llandegfedd W13
Llandegla W9
Llandegwning W11
Llandeilo W6
Llandeilo Abercywyn W6
Llandeilo Llwydarth W16
Llandeilo'r Fan W17
Llandeloy W16
Llandenny W13
Llandevaud W15
Llandevenny (part) W13, W15
Llandilo Graban W17
Llandinabo 21.1
Llandinam W17
Llandissilio East W6, W16
Llandissilio West W16
Llandogo W13
Llandough (Cowbridge) W21
Llandough (Penarth) W21
Llandovery W6
Llandow W21
Llandrillo W9
Llandrindod Wells W17
Llandrinio W17
Llandrygarn W1
Llandudno W8
Llandudwen W11
Llandulas W17

Llandwrog W11
Llandybie W6
Llandyfaelog W6
Llandyfan W6
Llandyfodwg W3
Llandyfriog W7
Llandyfrydog W1
Llandygai W11
Llandygwydd W7
Llandyrnog W9
Llandysilio W17
Llandysiliogogo W7
Llandyssil W17
Llandysul W7
Llanedeyrn W5
Llanedwen W1
Llanedy W6
Llaneglwys W17
Llanegryn W11
Llanegwad W6
Llaneilian W1
Llanelian-yn-Rhos W8
Llanelidan W9
Llanelieu W17
Llanellen W13
Llanelli W6
Llanelltyd W11
Llanelly W13
Llanelwedd W17
Llanenddwyn W11
Llanengan W11
Llanerchymedd W1
Llanerchymor W10
Llanerfyl W17
Llaneugrad W1
Llanfabon (Nelson) W4
Llanfach W4
Llanfachraeth W1
Llanfachreth W11
Llanfaelog W1
Llanfaelrhys W11
Llanfaes W1
Llanfaethlu W1
Llanfaglan W11
Llanfair (Gwynedd) W11
Llanfair (Vale Glam) W21
Llanfair Caereinion W17
Llanfair Clydogau W7
Llanfair Discoed W13
Llanfair Dyffryn Clwyd W9
Llanfair Green W13
Llanfair Kilgeddin W13
Llanfair Talhaiarn W8
Llanfair Waterdine 37.1
Llanfair-Mathafarneithaf W1
Llanfair-ar-y-Bryn W6
Llanfairfechan W8
Llanfairpwllgwyngyll W1
Llanfairyneubwll W1
Llanfairynghornwy W1
Llanfallteg W6
Llanfapley W13
Llanfaredd W17
Llanfarian W7
Llanfechain W17
Llanfechan W17
Llanfechell W1
Llanfedw W4
Llanferres W9
Llanfflewyn W1
Llanfigael W1
Llanfigan W17
Llanfihangel W17
Llanfihangel Aberbythych W6
Llanfihangel Abergwesyn W17
Llanfihangel Brynpabuan W17
Llanfihangel Crucorney W13
Llanfihangel Fechan W17
Llanfihangel Glyn Myfyr W8
Llanfihangel Helygen W17
Llanfihangel Nant Bran W17
Llanfihangel Penbedw W16
Llanfihangel Rhos-y-Corn W6
Llanfihangel Rhydithon W17
Llanfihangel Rogiet W13
Llanfihangel Tal-y-llyn W17
Llanfihangel Ystrad W7
Llanfihangel-Trerbeirdd W1
Llanfihangel-ar-Arth W6
Llanfihangel-nant-melan W17
Llanfihangel-uwch-Gwili W6
Llanfihangel-y-Creuddyn W7
Llanfihangel-y-pennant W11
Llanfihangel-ystern-Llewern W13
Llanfihangelysceifiog W1
Llanfilo W17
Llanfoist W13
Llanfor W11
Llanfrechfa Lower W20
Llanfrothen W11
Llanfrynach W17
Llanfwrog (Anglesey) W1
Llanfyllin W17
Llanfynydd (Carm) W6
Llanfynydd (Flint) W10
Llanfyrnach W16
Llanfythin W21
Llangadfan W17
Llangadog W6
Llangadwaladr (Anglesey) W1
Llangaffo W1
Llangain W6
Llangammarch Wells W17
Llangan W21
Llanganten W17
Llangarron 21.1
Llangasty-Talyllyn W17
Llangathen W6
Llangattock W17
Llangattock Lingoed W13
Llangattock-Vibon-Avel W13
Llangattock-nigh-Usk W13
Llangedwyn W17
Llangefni W1
Llangeinor W3
Llangeinwen W1
Llangoitho W7
Llangeler W6
Llangelynin W11
Llangennech W6
Llangennith W19
Llangenny W17
Llangernyw W8
Llangian W11
Llanglydwen W6
Llangoed W1
Llangoedmor W7
Llangollen W9
Llangolman W16
Llangorse W17
Llangorwen W7
Llangoven W13
Llangrannog W7
Llangristiolus W1
Llangrove 21.1
Llangua W13
Llanguicke W14
Llangunllo (Powys) W17
Llangunnor W6
Llangurig W17
Llangwm & Hook (Pemb) W16
Llangwm (Conwy) W8
Llangwnnadl W11
Llangwyfan W1
Llangwyllog W1
Llangwyryfon W7
Llangybi (Card) W7
Llangybi (Gwynedd) W11
Llangybi Fawr W13
Llangyfelach W19
Llangyndeyrn W6
Llangynhafal W9
Llangynidr W17
Llangyniew W17
Llangynin W6
Llangynog (Carm) W6
Llangynog (Powys)* W17
Llangynwyd W3
Llangywer W11
Llanhamlach W17
Llanharan W18
Llanharry W18
Llanhennock W13
Llanhilleth W2
Llanidan W1
Llanidloes W17
Llanidloes Without W17
Llaniestyn (Anglesey) W1
Llaniestyn (Gwynedd) W11
Llanigon W17
Llanilar W7
Llanilid W18
Llanina W7
Llanishen W5
Llanllawddog W6
Llanllechid W11
Llanlleonfel W17
Llanllugan W17
Llanllwch W6
Llanllwchaiarn Newtown W17
Llanllwni W6
Llanllyfni W11
Llanmadoc W19
Llanmaes W21
Llanmartin W15
Llanmerewig W17
Llanmihangel W21
Llanmiloe W6
Llanmorlais W19
Llannefydd W8
Llannon W6
Llannor W11
Llanover W13
Llanpumsaint W6
Llanreithan W16
Llanrhaeadr-ym-Mochnant W17
Llanrhaeadr-yng-Nghinmeirch W9
Llanrhian W16
Llanrhidian, Higher & Lower W19
Llanrhychwyn W8
Llanrhyddlad W1
Llanrhystud W7
Llanrothal 21.1
Llanrug W11
Llanrwst W8
Llansadurnen W6
Llansadwrn (Anglesey) W1
Llansadwrn (Carm) W6
Llansaint W6
Llansamlet W19
Llansanffraid Glan Conwy W8
Llansannan W8
Llansannor W21
Llansantffraed (Powys) W17
Llansantffraed Cwmdeuddwr W17
Llansantffraed-in-Elvel W17
Llansantffraid W7
Llansantffraid Deytheur W17
Llansantffraid Glyn Ceiriog W22
Llansantffraid Pool W17
Llansawel W6
Llansilin W17
Llansoy W13
Llanspyddid W17
Llanstadwell W16
Llanstephan (Carm) W6
Llanstephan (Powys) W17
Llantarnam (part) W15, W20
Llanthony W13
Llantilio Crossenny W13
Llantilio Pertholey W13
Llantood W16
Llantrisant (Anglesey) W1
Llantrisant (Monmth) W13
Llantrisant (Rhondda) W18
Llantrithyd W21
Llantwit Fardre W18
Llantwit Major W21
Llanuwchllyn W11
Llanvaches (part) W13, W15
Llanvetherine W13
Llanveynoe 21.1
Llanwarne 21.1
Llanwddyn W17
Llanwenarth W13
Llanwenog W7
Llanwern (Newport) W15

Llanwern (Powys) W17
Llanwinio W6
Llanwnda (Gwynedd) W11
Llanwnda (Pemb) W16
Llanwnnen W7
Llanwnog W17
Llanwonno W18
Llanwrda W6
Llanwrin W17
Llanwrthwl W17
Llanwrtyd Wells W17
Llanwrtyd Without W17
Llanwyddelan W17
Llanyblodwel 37.1
Llanybri W6
Llanybydder (part) W6, W7
Llanycefn W16
Llanychaer W16
Llanychaiarn W7
Llanychllwydog W16
Llanycil W11
Llanycrwys W6
Llanymawddwy W11
Llanymynech (part) 37.1, W17
Llanynghenedl W1
Llanynys W9
Llanyravon W20
Llanyre W17
Llanystumdwy W11
Llawhaden W16
Llawnt 37.1
Llawryglyn W17
Llay W22
Llechcynfarwy W1
Llechfaen W17
Llechryd W4, W7
Llechylched W1
Lledrod W7
Llewitha W19
Llidiad Nennog W6
Llidiartywaen W17
Llithfaen W11
Lloc W10
Lloiney W17
Llong W10
Llowes W17
Llwchwr W19
Llwydcoed W18
Llwydiarth W17
Llwyncelyn W4
Llwyndyrys W11
Llwyngwril W11
Llwynhendy W6
Llwynhudol W11
Llwynypia W18
Llyn-Helyg W10
Llyn-y-Pandy W10
Llynclys 37.1
Llys-y-fran W16
Llysdinam W17
Llysfaen W8
Llyswen W17
Llysworney W21
Llywel W17
Load Brook 39.3
Loanhead S19
Loanstone S19
Lobley Hill 43.3
Lobthorpe 28.6
Loch Lomond (part) S3, S9
Lochailort S17
Lochaline S17
Lochans S10
Lochavich S3
Lochboisdale S32
Lochbroom S17
Lochcarron S17
Lochearnhead S29
Lochfoot S10
Lochgair S3
Lochgelly S16
Lochgilphead S3
Lochgoilhead S3
Lochinver S17
Lochluichart S17
Lochmaben S10
Lochmaddy S32
Lochore S16
Lochranza S21
Lochs S32
Lochussie S17
Lochwinnoch S25
Lockengate 9.1
Lockerbie S10
Lockeridge 48.1
Lockerley 20.4
Locking 38.7
Locking Stumps 7.1
Lockinge 35.4
Lockington (E Yorks) 15.2
Lockington (Leics) 27.1
Lockleaze 4.1
Lockley Wood 37.1
Locks Heath 20.10
Lockton 33.3
Lockwood 47.4
Loddington (Leics) 27.8
Loddington (N'hants) 31.2
Loddiswell 12.9
Loddon 30.7
Loddon Bridge 3.3
Lode 6.4
Loders 13.1
Lodge W22
Lodge Farm 31.5
Lodge Park 49.3
Lodsworth 46.2
Lodway 38.7
Lofthouse 47.2
Lofthouse Gate (part) 47.2, 47.5
Loftus 33.10
Logan S11
Loganlea S31
Loggans 9.1
Loggerheads (Denbigh) W9
Loggerheads (Staffs) 40.2
Logie (Angus) S2
Logie (Lochbroom) (Highland) S17
Logie Buchan S1
Logie Coldstone S1
Logie Durno S1
Logie Easter S17
Logie Pert S2
Logiealmond S24
Logierait S24
Login W6
Lolworth 6.5
Lon-y-llyn W4
Londesborough 15.2
London Apprentice 9.1
London Colney (part) 22.5, 22.10
London E1 (part) L7, L30
London E2 (part) L12, L30
London E3 L30
London E4 L31
London E5 L12
London E6 L25
London E7 (part) L25, L31
London E8 L12
London E9 (part) L12, L30
London E10 L31
London E11 (part) L26, L31
London E12 (part) L25, L26
London E13 L25
London E14 L30
London E15 (part) L12, L25, L31
London E16 L25
London E17 L31
London E18 L26
London EC1 (part) L6, L7, L19
London EC2 (part) L6, L7, L19
London EC3 (part) L7, L30
London EC4 (part) L7
London Fields L12
London N1 (part) L6, L12, L19
London N2 (part) L2, L14
London N3 L2
London N4 (part) L14, L19
London N5 L19
London N6 (part) L6, L14
London N7 (part) L6, L19
London N8 (part) L14, L19
London N9 L10
London N10 (part) L2, L14
London N11 (part) L2, L10, L14
London N12 L2
London N13 (part) L10
London N14 (part) L2, L10
London N15 (part) L12, L14
London N16 (part) L12, L14
London N17 L14
London N18 L10
London N19 (part) L6, L19
London N20 L2
London N21 L10
London N22 (part) L10, L14
London NW1 (part) L6, L33
London NW2 (part) L2, L4, L6
London NW3 (part) L2, L6
London NW4 L2
London NW5 L6
London NW6 (part) L6, L33
London NW7 L2
London NW8 (part) L6, L33
London NW9 (part) L2, L4
London NW10 (part) L4, L9, L13
London NW11 L2
London SE1 (part) L22, L28
London SE2 (part) L3, L11
London SE3 (part) L11, L23
London SE4 L23
London SE5 (part) L22, L28
London SE6 L23
London SE7 L11
London SE8 (part) L11, L23, L28
London SE9 (part) L5, L11, L23
London SE10 (part) L11, L23
London SE11 (part) L22, L28
London SE12 (part) L11, L23
London SE13 (part) L11, L23
London SE14 (part) L23, L28
London SE15 (part) L23, L28
London SE16 (part) L23, L28
London SE17 L28
London SE18 (part) L11
London SE19 (part) L5, L8, L22, L28
London SE20 L5
London SE21 (part) L22, L28
London SE22 L28
London SE23 (part) L23, L28
London SE24 (part) L22, L28
London SE25 L8
London SE26 (part) L5, L23, L28
London SE27 (part) L22
London SE28 (part) L3, L11
London SW1 (part) L20, L33
London SW2 L22
London SW3 L20
London SW4 (part) L22, L32
London SW5 L20
London SW6 L13
London SW7 (part) L20, L33
London SW8 (part) L22, L32
London SW9 L22
London SW10 (part) L13, L20
London SW11 L32
London SW12 (part) L22, L32
London SW13 L27
London SW14 L27
London SW15 (part) L21, L27, L32
London SW16 (part) L8, L22, L32
London SW17 (part) L24, L32

London SW18 (part) L24, L32
London SW19 L32
London SW19 (part) L24
London SW20 L24
London W1 (part) L6, L33
London W2 L33
London W3 (part) L9, L13, L18
London W4 (part) L9, L13, L18
London W5 L9
London W6 L13
London W7 L9
London W8 L20
London W9 (part) L6, L33
London W10 (part) L13, L20, L33
London W11 (part) L13, L20, L33
London W12 (part) L9, L13
London W13 L9
London W14 (part) L13, L20
London WC1 (part) L6, L7, L19
London WC2 (part) L6, L7, L33
Londonderry (N Yorks) 33.2
Londonderry (W Mids) 45.4
Londonthorpe 28.6
Lonemore S17
Long Ashton 38.7
Long Bennington 28.6
Long Bredy 13.1
Long Buckby 31.4
Long Clawson 27.3
Long Compton 44.5
Long Crendon 5.2
Long Crichel 13.3
Long Ditton 42.5
Long Drax 33.8
Long Eaton 11.8
Long Itchington 44.5
Long Lane 37.4
Long Lawford 44.3
Long Lee 47.1
Long Load 38.5
Long Marston (Herts) 22.4
Long Marston (N Yorks) 33.6
Long Marston (Warks) 44.5
Long Marton 10.3
Long Meadowend 37.1
Long Melford 41.6
Long Newnton (Gloucs) 18.5
Long Newton (Stockton) 14.10
Long Preston 33.5
Long Rock 9.1
Long Stratton 30.7
Long Sutton (Hants) 20.2
Long Sutton (Lincs) 28.7
Long Sutton (Som) 38.5
Long Waste 37.4
Long Whatton 27.1
Long Wittenham 35.3
Longbarn 7.1
Longbenton 43.2
Longborough 18.5
Longbridge 45.5
Longbridge Deverill 48.1
Longbridge Hayes 40.2
Longburgh 10.1
Longburton 13.1
Longcot 35.4
Longcroft (Falkirk) S15
Longcroft (Som) 38.5
Longcross 42.1
Longden 37.1
Longdon (Staffs) 40.8
Longdon (Worcs) 49.4
Longdon Green 40.8
Longdon-upon-Tern 37.4
Longdown 12.5
Longdowns 9.1
Longfield 25.1
Longfield Hill 25.1
Longford (Cheshire) 7.1
Longford (Derbys) 11.3
Longford (Gloucs) (part) 18.1, 18.3
Longford (Neath) W14
Longford (Shrop)* 37.1, 37.4
Longford (W Mids/Warks) (part) 44.2, 45.7
Longford Turning 37.1
Longforgan S24
Longformacus S30
Longframlington 32.1
Longham (Dorset) 13.3
Longham (Norfolk) 30.3
Longhirst 32.1
Longhope 18.2
Longhorsley 32.1
Longhoughton 32.1
Longlevens 18.3
Longley 47.4
Longmanhill S1
Longmoor 20.6
Longmorn S20
Longney 18.6
Longniddry S13
Longnor (Shrop) 37.1
Longnor (Staffs) 40.1
Longparish 20.4
Longport 40.3
Longridge (Lancs) (part) 26.3, 26.6
Longridge (W Lothian) S31
Longriggend S22
Longsdon 40.1
Longside S1
Longsight 19.6
Longsleddale 10.5
Longslow 37.1
Longstanton 6.5
Longstock 20.4
Longstone 9.1
Longstowe 6.5
Longswood 37.4
Longthorpe 6.1
Longton (Lancs) 26.7
Longton (Staffs) 40.3
Longtown (Cumbria) 10.1
Longtown (Here) 21.1
Longville in the Dale 37.1
Longwell Green 18.7
Longwick 5.3
Longwitton 32.1
Longwood 47.4
Longworth 35.4
Lonlas W14
Lonmay S1
Looe 9.1
Loose 25.10
Loosley Row 5.3
Lopcombe Corner (part) 20.4, 48.1
Lopen 38.5
Lopham, North & South 30.3
Loppergarth 10.5
Loppington 37.1
Lordington 46.2
Lordshill 20.8
Lordswood (part) 25.3, 25.10
Lorton 10.2
Loscoe 11.6
Lossiemouth & Branderburgh S20
Lostford 37.1
Lostock 19.2
Lostock Gralam 7.3
Lostock Green 7.3
Lostock Hall 26.7
Lostwithiel 9.1
Lothersdale 33.5
Lotherton-cum-Aberford 47.2
Lothianburn S19
Lottisham 38.2
Loudwater (Bucks) 5.3
Loudwater (Herts) 22.8
Loughborough 27.2
Loughor W19
Loughrigg 10.5
Loughton (Bucks) 5.1
Loughton (Essex) 17.6
Loughton (Shrop) 37.1
Loughton Lodge 5.1
Lound (Lincs) (see Toft)
Lound (Notts) 34.1
Lound (Suffolk) 41.1
Loundsley Green 11.2
Lount 27.1
Louth 28.2
Loveclough 26.14
Lovedean (part) 20.6, 20.13
Lovel Hill 3.6
Lover 48.1
Loversall 39.2
Loves Green 17.7
Lovesome Hill 33.2
Loveston W16
Lovington 38.5
Low Abbotside 33.1
Low Ackworth 47.5
Low Angerton 32.1
Low Bentham 33.5
Low Biggins 10.5
Low Bradfield 39.3
Low Burthwaite 10.1
Low Catton 15.2
Low Caythorpe 15.2
Low Coniscliffe 14.8
Low Cunsey 10.5
Low Dinsdale 14.8
Low Ellington 33.6
Low Etherley 14.1
Low Fell 43.3
Low Ford 43.5
Low Fulney 28.7
Low Ham 38.5
Low Hameringham 28.2
Low Hawsker 33.4
Low Hesket 10.3
Low Hill 45.1
Low Juniper 32.1
Low Lands 14.1
Low Moor 47.1
Low Moorsley 43.5
Low Park 10.5
Low Row 10.1
Low Skirlington 15.2
Low Southwick 43.5
Low Stott Park 10.5
Low Toynton 28.2
Low Valley 39.1
Low Valleyfield S16
Low Waters S28
Low Westwood 14.1
Low Worsall 33.2
Low Wray 10.5
Lowca 10.4
Lowdham 34.3
Lowe 37.1
Lower Almondsbury 18.7
Lower Assendon 35.3
Lower Beeding 46.3
Lower Benefield 31.3
Lower Bockhampton 13.1
Lower Boddington 31.7
Lower Brynamman (part) W6, W14
Lower Bullingham 21.1
Lower Cadsden 5.3
Lower Caldecote 2.2
Lower Chapel W17
Lower Clapton L12
Lower Clent 49.2
Lower College 37.1
Lower Common (Gloucs) 18.7
Lower Common (Hants) 20.2
Lower Cumberworth 47.4
Lower Cwmtwrch (part) W14, W17
Lower Dean 18.5
Lower Denby 47.4
Lower Down 37.1
Lower Earley 3.3
Lower Edmonton L10
Lower Failand 38.7
Lower Frankton 37.1
Lower Froyle 20.6
Lower Godney 38.2
Lower Gornal 45.3
Lower Green 17.7
Lower Halstock Leigh 13.1
Lower Halstow 25.4

Lower Hamswell 18.7
Lower Hardres 25.5
Lower Harford 18.5
Lower Harpton 21.1
Lower Hartshay 11.6
Lower Hazel 18.7
Lower Heath 37.1
Lower Heyford 35.2
Lower Holker 10.5
Lower Holloway L19
Lower Hopton 47.4
Lower Kilcot 18.6
Lower Kingswood 42.9
Lower Kinnerton 7.3
Lower Langford 38.7
Lower Largo S16
Lower Machen (part) W4, W15
Lower Maescoed 21.1
Lower Moor 49.6
Lower Morton 18.7
Lower Oddington (see Oddington) (Gloucs)
Lower Ogden 19.4
Lower Penn 40.6
Lower Penponds 9.1
Lower Peover 7.3
Lower Pilsley 11.4
Lower Pollicott 5.2
Lower Popeley 47.4
Lower Radbourne 44.5
Lower Rainham 25.3
Lower Ridge 37.1
Lower Rowe 13.3
Lower Sapey 49.4
Lower Severalls 38.5
Lower Shiplake 35.3
Lower Shirlowe 37.4
Lower Shuckburgh 44.5
Lower Slaughter 18.5
Lower Stoford 38.4
Lower Stoke 25.3
Lower Stondon 2.2
Lower Stonnall 40.8
Lower Stratton 38.5
Lower Swanwick 20.10
Lower Tadmarton 35.2
Lower Temple 48.1
Lower Town (Frogpool) 9.1
Lower Upham 20.5
Lower Vexford 38.3
Lower Wanborough 48.2
Lower Waterston 13.1
Lower Withington 7.5
Lower Woolston 38.5
Lower Wyke (Hants) 20.1
Lower Wyke (W Yorks) 47.4
Lowercroft 19.3
Lowerhouse 26.12
Lowerhouses 47.4
Lowerplace 19.4
Lowesby 27.8
Lowestoft 41.1
Loweswater 10.2
Lowfield Heath 46.1
Lowford 20.9
Lowgates 11.2
Lowgill 10.5
Lowick (N'hants) 31.3
Lowick (N'land) 32.1
Lowick Bridge 10.5
Lowick Green 10.5
Lownie Moor S2
Lowside Quarter 10.4
Lowsonford 44.4
Lowther 10.3
Lowthorpe 15.2
Lowton (Gtr M'chester) 19.1
Lowton (Som) 38.4
Lowtown (Pudsey) 47.2
Loxbeare 12.4
Loxhole Bridge 38.3
Loxhore 12.2
Loxley (S Yorks) 39.3
Loxley (Staffs) 40.5
Loxley (Warks) 44.5
Loxton 38.7
Loxwood 46.2
Lozells 45.5
Lubbesthorpe 27.6
Lubenham 27.8
Luccombe 38.3
Lucker (see Adderstone)
Luckett 9.1
Luckington 48.1
Luckwell Bridge 38.3
Lucott 38.3
Lucton 21.1
Ludag S32
Ludborough 28.2
Ludchurch W16
Luddenden 47.3
Luddendenfoot 47.3
Luddenham 25.4
Luddesdown 25.2
Luddington 31.3
Luddington (N Lincs) 28.8
Luddington (Warks) 44.5
Luddington-in-the-Brook (N'hants) 31.3
Ludford (Lincs) 28.2
Ludford (Shrop) 37.1
Ludgershall (Bucks) 5.2
Ludgershall (Wilts) 48.1
Ludgvan 9.1
Ludham 30.1
Ludlow 37.1
Ludney (Lincs) 28.2
Ludney (Som) 38.5
Ludwell 48.1
Ludworth 14.1
Luffenhall 22.1
Luffield Abbey 5.2
Luffincott 12.1
Lufton 38.5
Lugar S11
Luggiebank S22
Lugshorn 38.5
Lugton (E Ayrs) (part) S11
Lugton (Midlothian) S19
Lugton (N Ayrs) (part) S21
Lugwardine 21.1
Luib S17
Luing, Isle of S3
Lullingstone 25.8
Lullington (Derbys) 11.9
Lullington (E Sussex) 16.1
Lullington (Som) 38.2
Lulsgate Bottom 38.7
Lulsley 49.4
Lumb (Irwell Vale) 26.14
Lumb (Lancs) 26.14
Lumb (W Yorks) 47.3
Lumbertubs 31.5
Lumbutts 47.3
Lumley 46.2
Lumphanan S1
Lumphinnans S16
Lumsden S1
Lunan S2
Lunanbank S2
Lunanhead S2
Luncarty S24
Lund 15.2
Lundin Links S16
Lunds, Sedbergh 10.5
Lundy Bay 9.1
Lundy Island 12.1
Lunedale 14.1
Lunna S26
Lunning S26
Lunnon W19
Lunt 29.1
Luppitt 12.7
Lupton 10.5
Lurgashall 46.2
Lusby with Winceby 28.2
Luss S3
Lustleigh 12.5
Luston 21.1
Lusty 38.5
Luthrie S16
Luton (Beds) 2.4
Luton (Devon) 12.5
Lutterworth 27.8
Lutton (Lincs) 28.7
Lutton (N'hants) 31.3
Luttons (East & West) 33.3
Luxborough 38.3
Luxulyan 9.1
Lyatts 38.5
Lybster S17
Lychpit 20.1
Lydart W13
Lydbrook 18.2
Lydbury North 37.1
Lydd 25.13
Lydd-on-Sea 25.13
Lydden* 25.6, 25.7
Lyddington 36.1
Lyde (see Pipe)
Lydeard St Lawrence 38.4
Lydford 12.3
Lydford on Fosse 38.2
Lydgate (Gtr M'chester) 19.7
Lydgate (W Yorks) 47.3
Lydham 37.1
Lydiard Millicent 48.1
Lydiard Tregoze (part) 48.1, 48.2
Lydiate 29.1
Lydiate Ash 49.2
Lydlinch 13.2
Lydmarsh 38.5
Lydney 18.2
Lydstep W16
Lye 45.3
Lye Cross 38.7
Lye Head (Rock) 49.1
Lye Hole 38.7
Lyford 35.4
Lyme Handley 7.5
Lyme Regis 13.1
Lyminge 25.13
Lymington 20.7
Lyminster 46.5
Lymm 7.1
Lympne 25.13
Lympsham 38.1
Lympstone 12.7
Lynch 38.3
Lynch Hill 20.1
Lyncroft 40.8
Lyndhurst (Hants) 20.7
Lyndhurst (Notts) 34.3
Lyndon 36.1
Lyne 42.1
Lyneal 37.1
Lyneham (Oxon) 35.1
Lyneham (Wilts) 48.1
Lynemouth 32.1
Lynesack 14.1
Lynford 30.3
Lyng (Norfolk) 30.3
Lyng (Som) 38.1
Lyngate 30.1
Lynmouth 12.2
Lynn (Shrop) 37.4
Lynn (Staffs) 40.8
Lynsted 25.4
Lynstone 9.1
Lynton 12.2
Lyons 43.5
Lyons Gate 13.1
Lyonshall 21.1
Lyonswood 37.1
Lypiatt (see Bisley)
Lytchett Matravers 13.5
Lytchett Minster 13.5
Lytes Cary 38.5
Lyth (Cumbria) 10.5
Lyth (Shrop) 37.1
Lytham 26.5
Lythe 33.4
Mabe Burnthouse 9.1
Mablethorpe 28.2
Macclesfield 7.5
Macclesfield Forest 7.5
Macduff S1
Macefen 7.3
Machen W4
Machrihanish S3
Machynlleth W17
Machynys W6
Mackworth (part) 11.6, 11.7
Macmerry S13
Madderty S24
Maddiston S15
Madehurst 46.5
Madeley (Shrop) 37.4
Madeley (Staffs) 40.2

Madeley Heath (Staffs) 40.2
Madeley Heath (Worcs) 49.2
Madeley Wood 37.4
Maders 9.1
Madingley 6.5
Madley 21.1
Madresfield 49.4
Madron 9.1
Maenaddwyn W1
Maenan W8
Maenclochog W16
Maendy W21
Maenporth (part) 9.1
Maentwrog W11
Maer 40.2
Maerdy (Conwy) W8
Maerdy (Rhondda) W18
Maes-y-Groes W11
Maesbrook 37.1
Maesbury 37.1
Maescar W17
Maesgeirchen W11
Maeshafn W9
Maesmynis W17
Maesteg W3
Maesybont W6
Maesycmmer W4
Maesycoed W18
Maesycrugiau (part) W6, W7
Magdalen Laver 17.6
Magham Down 16.1
Maghull 29.1
Magna Park 5.1
Magor W13
Magpie Bottom 25.8
Maida Hill L33
Maida Vale (part) L6, L33
Maiden Bradley 48.1
Maiden Erleigh 3.3
Maiden Law 14.1
Maiden Newton 13.1
Maiden's Green 3.6
Maidenbower 46.1
Maidencombe (part) 12.10
Maidendown 12.4
Maidenhead 3.4
Maidens S27
Maidensgrove 35.3
Maidenwell 28.2
Maidford 31.7
Maids Moreton 5.2
Maidstone 25.10
Maidwell 31.4
Maincombe 38.5
Mainholm S27
Mainsforth 14.1
Mainstone 37.1
Maisemore 18.1
Maiseyhampton (see Meysey Hampton)
Majors Green 49.2
Maker 9.1
Makerstoun S30
Malborough 12.9
Malden Rushett L21
Maldon 17.8
Malham 33.5
Malham Moor 33.5
Malinslee 37.4
Malkin's Bank 7.5
Mallaig S17
Mallerstang 10.3
Mallsburn 10.1
Malltraeth W1
Mallwyd W11
Malmesbury, Within & Without 48.1
Malpas (Cheshire) 7.3
Malpas (Corn) 9.1
Malshanger 20.1
Malswick 18.2
Maltby (Lincs) (see Raithby)
Maltby (S Yorks) 39.4
Maltby (Stockton) 14.10
Maltby le Marsh 28.2
Malton 33.3
Malvern 49.4
Malvern Wells 49.4
Mamble 49.4
Mamhead 12.5
Mamhilad W13
Manaccan 9.1
Manafon W17
Manaton 12.5
Manby 28.2
Mancetter 44.1
Mancot W10
Mancroft 38.5
Manea 6.2
Maney 45.5
Manfield 33.1
Mangerton 13.1
Mangotsfield 18.7
Mangreen 30.7
Mankinholes 47.3
Manley 7.3
Manmoel W4
Manningford-Bruce, Bohune Abbots 48.1
Manningham 47.1
Mannings Heath 46.3
Mannington (Dorset) 13.3
Mannington (Norfolk) 30.1
Mannington (Wilts) 48.2
Manningtree 17.4
Manod W11
Manor Park (W Yorks) 47.1
Manor Park (part) L25, L26
Manorbier W16
Manordeifi W16
Manordeilo W6
Manorowen W16
Mansel Lacy 21.1
Mansell Gamage 21.1
Manselton W19
Mansergh 10.5
Mansfield 34.2
Mansfield Woodhouse 34.2
Mansriggs 10.5
Manston (Dorset) 13.2
Manston (Kent) 25.7
Manswood 13.3
Manthorpe (Bourne) (Grantham) 28.6
Manton (Lincs) 28.8
Manton (Notts) 34.1
Manton (Rutland) 36.1
Manton Downs 48.1
Manuden 17.1
Maperton 38.5
Maple Cross 22.8
Maple Hayes 40.8
Maplebeck 34.3
Mapledurham 35.3
Mapledurwell 20.1
Mapperley (Derbys) 11.6
Mapperley (Notts) (part) 34.6, 34.7
Mapperley Park 34.6
Mapperton 13.3
Mappleborough Green 44.5
Mappleton (Derbys) 11.3
Mappleton (E Yorks) 15.2
Mapplewell 39.1
Mappowder 13.2
Marazanvose 9.1
Marazion 9.1
Marbury 7.3
Marbury-cum-Quoisley 7.5
March 6.2
Marcham 35.4
Marchamley 37.1
Marchington 40.5
Marchwiel W22
Marchwood 20.7
Marcross Monknash W21
Mardale 10.3
Marden (Here) 21.1
Marden (Kent) 25.10
Marden (T & W) 43.2
Marden (Wilts) 48.1
Marden Ash 17.6
Mardu 37.1
Mardy W13
Mare Green 38.4
Marefield 27.8
Mareham le Fen 28.2
Mareham on the Hill 28.2
Marehay 11.6
Maresfield 16.1
Marford W22
Margam W14
Margaret Marsh 13.2
Margaret Roding 17.1
Margaretting 17.7
Margaretting Tye 17.7
Margate 25.7
Margrove Park 33.10
Marham 30.2
Marhamchurch 9.1
Marholm 6.1
Marian W10
Marianglas W1
Mariansleigh 12.2
Marishes 33.3
Maritime Quarter W19
Mark 38.1
Mark Beech 25.8
Mark Cross 16.1
Mark Hall 17.5
Markby 28.2
Markenfield Hall 33.6
Market Bosworth 27.4
Market Deeping 28.6
Market Drayton 37.1
Market End 44.2
Market Harborough 27.8
Market Lavington 48.1
Market Overton 36.1
Market Rasen 28.1
Market Stainton 28.2
Market Weighton 15.2
Market Weston 41.3
Markfield 27.4
Markham W4
Markham Moor 34.1
Markinch S16
Markington with Wallerthwaite 33.6
Marks Tey 17.3
Marksbury 38.6
Marksdanes 38.5
Markshall 30.7
Markyate 22.4
Marlborough 48.1
Marlbrook 49.2
Marlcliff 44.5
Marldon 12.9
Marlesford 41.5
Marley (W Sussex) 46.2
Marley (W Yorks) 47.1
Marley Hill 43.3
Marley Mount 20.7
Marley Potts 43.5
Marlingford 30.7
Marloes & St Brides W16
Marlow 5.3
Marlow Bottom 5.3
Marlpit Hill 25.8
Marlpool 11.6
Marlston-cum-Lache 7.3
Marnham 34.1
Marnhull 13.2
Marnoch S1
Marple 19.9
Marr 39.2
Marriage Hill 48.1
Marrick 33.1
Marros W6
Marsden 47.4
Marsh (Bucks) 5.3
Marsh (Cleckheaton) (W Yorks)* 47.4
Marsh (Huddersfield) (W Yorks)* 47.4
Marsh (W Yorks)* 47.1
Marsh Baldon 35.3
Marsh Chapel 28.2
Marsh Common 18.7
Marsh Gibbon 5.2
Marsh Green (Kent) 25.8
Marsh Green (Shrops) 37.4
Marsh Lane 11.4
Marshalls Cross 29.3
Marshalswick 22.5
Marsham 30.5
Marshborough 25.6
Marshbrook 37.1
Marshfield (Gloucs) 18.7
Marshfield (Newport) W15

Marshgate 9.1
Marshland St James 30.2
Marshside 29.1
Marshside (Chislet) 25.5
Marshwood 13.1
Marske 33.1
Marske-by-the-Sea 33.10
Marston (Cheshire) 7.3
Marston (Lincs) 28.6
Marston (Oxon) 35.5
Marston (Staffs) 40.4
Marston (Warks) 44.1
Marston (Wilts) 48.1
Marston Bigot 38.2
Marston Green 45.6
Marston Jabbett 44.2
Marston Magna 38.5
Marston Meysey 48.1
Marston Montgomery 11.3
Marston Moretaine 2.2
Marston St Lawrence 31.7
Marston Trussell 31.4
Marston-on-Dove 11.9
Marstow 21.1
Marsworth 5.2
Marten 48.1
Marthall 7.5
Martham 30.6
Marthwaite 10.5
Martin (Hants) 20.7
Martin (Kent) 25.6
Martin (Lincs) 28.4
Martin Hussingtree 49.6
Martin Mill 25.6
Martindale 10.3
Martinhoe 12.2
Martins Heron 3.6
Martinscroft 7.1
Martinsthorpe 36.1
Martlesham 41.5
Martletwy W16
Martley 49.4
Martock 38.5
Marton (Cheshire)* 7.3, 7.5
Marton (E Yorks) 15.2
Marton (Lincs) 28.1
Marton (Middlesbrough) 33.9
Marton (N Yorks) 33.3
Marton (Shrop) (part) 37.1
Marton (Warks) 44.3
Marton Grove 33.9
Marton-cum-Grafton 33.6
Marton-cum-Moxby 33.2
Marton-le-Moor 33.6
Martons Both 33.5
Martyr Worthy 20.5
Marwood (Devon) 12.2
Marwood (Durham) 14.1
Mary Tavy 12.3
Marybank S17
Maryburgh S17
Maryculter S1
Marykirk S1
Marylebone L33
Maryport 10.2
Marystow 12.3
Maryton S2
Marywell S2
Masbury 38.2
Mascalles 10.5
Masham 33.6
Mashbury 17.7
Mastin Moor (part) 11.2, 11.5
Matchborough, East and West 49.3
Matching 17.6
Matching Green 17.6
Matching Tye 17.6
Matfen 32.1
Matfield 25.11
Mathern W13
Mathon 21.1
Mathry W16
Matlaske 30.1
Matlock 11.3
Matlock Bath 11.3
Matson 18.3
Matterdale 10.3
Mattersey 34.1
Matthews Green 3.3
Mattingley 20.2
Mattishall 30.3
Mattishall Burgh 30.3
Mauchline S11
Maud S1
Maugersbury 18.5
Maulden 2.2
Maulds Meaburn 10.3
Maunby 33.2
Maundown 38.4
Mauricewood S19
Mautby 30.6
Mavesyn Ridware 40.8
Mavis Enderby 28.2
Mavisbank S19
Mawdesley 26.9
Mawgan Porth 9.1
Mawgan-in-Meneage 9.1
Mawla (part) 9.1
Mawnan 9.1
Mawnan Smith 9.1
Mawsley 31.2
Mawthorpe 28.2
Maxey 6.1
Maxstoke 44.1
Maxton S30
May Bank 40.2
May Hill 18.2
May's Green 38.7
Mayals W19
Maybole S27
Mayburn S19
Maybury 42.4
Maybush 20.8
Mayes Green 42.8
Mayfair L33
Mayfield S19
Mayfield (E Sussex) 16.1
Mayfield (Staffs) 40.5
Mayfield Park 4.1
Mayford 42.4
Mayhill W19
Mayland 17.8
Maypole (Kent) 25.5
Maypole (W Mids) (part) 45.5, 49.2
McDuff (E Wemys) S16
Meadle 5.3
Meadowfield 14.1
Meadows 34.6
Meadowtown 37.1
Meads 16.5
Meadvale 42.9
Mealbank 10.5
Meare 38.2
Meare Green 38.4
Mearley 26.3
Mears Ashby 31.6
Measham 27.1
Meathop 10.5
Meavy 12.3
Medbourne (Bucks) 5.1
Medbourne (Leics) 27.8
Medburn 32.1
Meden Vale 34.2
Medmenham 5.3
Medomsley 14.1
Medstead 20.6
Meer End 45.6
Meerbrook 40.1
Meesden 22.3
Meeson 37.4
Meeth 12.3
Meeting Hill 30.1
Meidrim W6
Meifod W17
Meigle S24
Meikle Earnock S28
Meikle Wartle S1
Meiklour S24
Meinciau W6
Meir 40.3
Meir Hay 40.3
Meir Heath 40.4
Meir Park 40.3
Melbecks 33.1
Melbost S32
Melbourn 6.5
Melbourne (Derbys) 11.9
Melbourne (E Yorks) 15.2
Melbury Abbas 13.2
Melbury Bubb 13.1
Melbury Osmond 13.1
Melbury Sampford 13.1
Melchbourne 2.1
Melchet Park 20.4
Melcombe Horsey 13.1
Meldon 32.1
Meldon Park 32.1
Meldreth 6.5
Meldrum S1
Meliden W9
Melin Cryddan W14
Melin Crythan W14
Melin y Wig W9
Melincourt W14
Melindwr W7
Meline W16
Melinycoed W8
Melkinthorpe 10.3
Melkridge 32.1
Melksham 48.1
Melksham Without 48.1
Melling 29.1
Melling with Wrayton 26.1
Mellis 41.4
Mellon Charles S17
Mellon Udrigle S17
Mellor (Lancs) 26.3
Mellor Brook (part) 26.7, 26.10
Mells (Som) 38.2
Mells (Suffolk) (see Wenhaston)
Melmerby* 33.1, 33.6
Melplash 13.1
Melrose (Borders) S30
Melrose (Mersey) 29.2
Melsonby 33.1
Meltham 47.4
Meltham Mills 47.4
Melton (E Yorks) 15.2
Melton (Suffolk) 41.5
Melton Constable 30.1
Melton Mowbray 27.3
Melton Ross 28.8
Meltonby 15.2
Melvaig S17
Melverley 37.1
Melvich S17
Melyn W14
Melyn Court W14
Membury 12.7
Memsie S1
Memus S2
Menagissy 9.1
Menai Bridge W1
Mendham 41.4
Mendlesham 41.4
Meneage (see Mawgan)
Meneage (see St Anthony)
Meneage (see St Martin)
Menethorpe 33.3
Menheniot 9.1
Mennock S10
Menston (part) 47.1, 47.2
Menstrie S8
Mentmore 5.2
Menwith with Darley 33.6
Meols 29.5
Meols Cop (part) 29.1
Meonstoke 20.5
Meopham 25.2
Mepal 6.4
Meppershall 2.2
Mercaston 11.3
Mere (Cheshire) 7.5
Mere (Lincs) 28.4
Mere (Wilts) 48.1
Mere Green 45.5
Mereclough 26.12
Meretown 37.4
Merevale 44.1
Mereworth 25.9
Meriden 45.6
Merley 13.6
Merlins Bridge W16
Merriott 38.5
Merriottsford 38.5
Merrow 42.7

Merry Hill Green 3.3
Merrybent 14.8
Merrymeet 9.1
Mersham 25.12
Merstham 42.9
Merston 46.2
Merstone 24.1
Merthyr W6
Merthyr Cynog W17
Merthyr Tydfil W12
Merthyr Vale W12
Merthyrmawr W3
Merton L24
Merton (Devon) 12.1
Merton (Norfolk) 30.3
Merton (Oxon) 35.2
Merton Park L24
Mertoun S30
Meshaw 12.2
Messing-cum-Inworth 17.3
Messingham 28.8
Metfield 41.4
Metherell 9.1
Metheringham 28.4
Methil S16
Methilhill S16
Methley 47.2
Methlick S1
Methven S24
Methwold 30.2
Mettingham 41.1
Metton 30.1
Mevagissey 9.1
Mewith 33.5
Mexborough 39.2
Mey S17
Meysey Hampton 18.5
Miavig S32
Michaelchurch Escley 21.1
Michaelchurch-on-Arrow W17
Michaelston-le-Pit W21
Michaelston-super-Ely W5
Michaelston-y-Fedw W4
Michaelstone-y-Fedw W15
Michaelstow 9.1
Micheldever 20.5
Michelmersh 20.4
Mickfield 41.4
Mickle Trafford 7.3
Micklebring 39.2
Mickleby 33.4
Micklefield (Sarratt) (Herts) 22.8
Micklefield (W Yorks) 47.2
Micklegate 33.7
Mickleham 42.8
Micklehead Green 29.3
Mickleover (part) 11.7, 11.9
Micklethwaite 47.1
Mickleton (Durham) 14.1
Mickleton (Gloucs) 18.5
Mickletown (Methley) 47.2
Mickley (Derbys) 11.4
Mickley (N'land) 32.1
Mickley (Shrop) 37.1
Mid Calder S31
Mid Holmwood 42.8
Mid Yell S26
Midanbury 20.8
Middle Assendon 35.3
Middle Aston 35.2
Middle Barton 35.1
Middle Chinnock 38.5
Middle Claydon 5.2
Middle Duntisbourne 18.5
Middle Handley 11.4
Middle Herrington 43.5
Middle Lambrook 38.5
Middle Moor 38.5
Middle Morrey 37.1
Middle Park L11
Middle Rasen 28.1
Middle Stoke 25.3
Middle Taphouse 9.1
Middle Wallop 20.4
Middlebie S10
Middlecliff 39.1
Middlecroft 11.2
Middleham 33.1
Middlemarsh 13.1
Middleport 40.3
Middlesbrough 33.9
Middleshaw 10.5
Middlestown 47.5
Middleton (Bucks) 5.1
Middleton (Cumbria) 10.5
Middleton (Essex) 17.2
Middleton (Gtr M'chester) 19.4
Middleton (Hants) 20.4
Middleton (Lancs) 26.1
Middleton (N Yorks) 33.6
Middleton (N'hants) 31.1
Middleton (N'land) (part) 32.1
Middleton (Norfolk) 30.2
Middleton (Pickering) (N Yorks) 33.3
Middleton (Shrop) 37.1
Middleton (Suffolk) 41.5
Middleton (W Sussex) 46.5
Middleton (Warks) 44.1
Middleton by Wirksworth 11.3
Middleton by Youlgreave 11.3
Middleton Cheney 31.7
Middleton Green 40.5
Middleton Junction 19.4
Middleton Quernhow 33.6
Middleton St George 14.8
Middleton Scriven 37.1
Middleton Stoney 35.2
Middleton Tyas 33.1
Middleton-in-Teesdale 14.1
Middleton-on-Leven 33.2
Middleton-on-the-Hill 21.1
Middleton-on-the-Wolds (E Yorks) 15.2
Middletown (Powys) W17
Middletown (Som) 38.7
Middlewich 7.5
Middlewood (Devon) 12.5
Middlewood (Here) 21.1
Middlezoy 38.1
Middop 26.3
Midelney 38.5
Midford 38.6
Midgeholme 10.1
Midgham 3.1
Midgley (part) 47.4, 47.5
Midhopestones 39.3
Midhurst 46.2
Midlem S30
Midloe (see Southoe)
Midmar S1
Midney 38.5
Midsomer Norton 38.6
Midsomer Norton Edge 38.2
Midthorpe 28.2
Midville 28.2
Midway 11.9
Migvie S1
Milborne Down 38.5
Milborne Port 38.5
Milborne Port Stn 38.5
Milborne St Andrew 13.2
Milborne Wick 38.5
Milbourne (N'land) 32.1
Milbourne (Wilts) 48.1
Milburn 10.3
Milbury Heath 18.7
Milby 33.6
Milcombe 35.2
Milcote 44.5
Milden 41.6
Mildenhall (Suffolk) 41.2
Mildenhall (Wilts) 48.1
Mile Cross 30.4
Mile End L30, 18.2
Mile End Green 25.1
Mile Oak (E Sussex) 16.3
Mile Oak (Staffs) 40.8
Mileham 30.3
Milehouse 40.2
Miles Green 40.2
Miles Platting 19.6
Milfield 32.1
Milford (Derbys) 11.6
Milford (Pemb) W16
Milford (Surrey) 42.11
Milford on Sea 20.7
Milkhouse Water 48.1
Milkwall 18.2
Mill Bank 47.3
Mill Bridge (see Bridge Mill)
Mill End 22.8
Mill Green 37.1
Mill Hill (London) L2
Mill Hill (T & W) 43.5
Mill Holme 10.5
Milland 46.2
Millbank (Hoath) 25.5
Millbridge 47.4
Millbrook (Beds) 2.2
Millbrook (Corn) 9.1
Millbrook (Hants) 20.8
Milldale 40.1
Millendreath 9.1
Millerhill S19
Millersdale 11.3
Millfield (Cambs) 6.1
Millfield (T & W) 43.5
Millhead 26.1
Millhouse 10.3
Millhouse Green 39.1
Millhousebridge S10
Millington (Cheshire) 7.5
Millington (E Yorks) 15.2
Millknowe S13
Millness 10.5
Millom 10.4
Millom Without 10.4
Millpool 9.1
Millport (Isle of Cumbrae) S21
Millside 10.5
Millthorpe 28.6
Millthrop 10.5
Milltimber S4
Milltown (Derbys) 11.4
Milltown (Lostwithiel) (Corn) 9.1
Milltown (Som) 38.3
Milnathort S24
Milngavie S12
Milnrow 19.4
Milnsbridge 47.4
Milnthorpe 10.5
Milovaig S17
Milson 37.1
Milstead 25.4
Milston 48.1
Milton (Caithness) S17
Milton (Cambs) 6.5
Milton (Cumbria) 10.1
Milton (Derbys) 11.9
Milton (Highland) S17
Milton (Oxon)* 35.2, 35.4
Milton (Som)* 38.5, 38.7
Milton (Staffs) 40.3
Milton (W Dunbarton) S9
Milton Abbas 13.2
Milton Abbot 12.3
Milton Bridge S19
Milton Bryan 2.2
Milton Clevedon 38.2
Milton Combe 12.3
Milton Common 35.3
Milton Damerel 12.1
Milton Ernest 2.1
Milton Keynes 5.1
Milton Keynes Village 5.1
Milton Lilbourne 48.1
Milton Malsor 31.7
Milton Regis 25.4
Milton of Balgonie S16
Milton of Buchanan S29
Milton of Campsie S12
Milton of Ogilvie S2
Milton-under-Wychwood 35.1
Miltonduff S20
Miltons 38.3
Milverton 38.4
Milwall L30
Milwich 40.4
Milwr W10
Minard S3
Minchington 13.3
Minchinhampton 18.6

Minehead 38.3
Minehead Without 38.3
Minera W22
Minety 48.1
Minffordd, Bangor W11
Mingarry S17
Minginish S17
Mingoose 9.1
Miningsby 28.2
Minions 9.1
Minishant S27
Minnigaff S10
Minnow End 17.7
Minshull Vernon 7.5
Minstead 20.7
Minsted 46.2
Minster (Corn) (see Forrabury & Minster)
Minster (Kent) 25.7
Minster (Sheppey) 25.4
Minster Lovell 35.1
Minsterley (part) 37.1
Minsterworth 18.1
Minterne Magna 13.1
Minting 28.2
Mintlaw S1
Minto S30
Minton 37.1
Minwere W16
Minworth 45.5
Mirfield 47.4
Misbrooks Green 42.8
Miserden 18.6
Miskin (Mountain Ash) W18
Miskin Pontyclun W18
Mislingford 20.5
Misson 34.1
Misterton (Leics) 27.8
Misterton (Notts) 34.1
Misterton (Som) 38.5
Mistley 17.4
Mitcham (part) L8, L24
Mitchel Troy W13
Mitcheldean 18.2
Mitchell 9.1
Mitford 32.1
Mithian 9.1
Mixbury 35.2
Mixenden 47.3
Mixtow 9.1
Moat 10.1
Mobberley (Cheshire) 7.5
Mobberley (Staffs) 40.1
Moccas 21.1
Mochdre (Conwy) W8
Mochdre (Powys) W17
Mochrum S10
Mockbeggar 20.7
Modbury 12.9
Moddershall 40.4
Modrydd W17
Moel-y-Crio W10
Moelfre (Anglesey) W1
Moelfre (Conwy) W8
Moffat S10
Moffat Mills S22
Mogador 42.9
Moggerhanger 2.2
Mohope 32.1
Mohuns Park 38.5
Moidart S17
Moira 27.1
Molash 25.12
Mold W10
Moldgreen 47.4
Molescroft 15.2
Molesdon 32.1
Molesworth 6.3
Molland 12.2
Mollington (Cheshire) 7.3
Mollington (Oxon) 35.2
Mona W1
Monach Islands S32
Monar S17
Monewden 41.5
Moneydie S24
Mongewell 35.3
Mongleath 9.1
Moniaive S10
Monifieth S2
Monikie S2
Monimail S16
Monington W16
Monk 33.7
Monk Bretton 39.1
Monk Fryston 33.8
Monk Sherbourne 20.1
Monk Soham 41.4
Monkhill 10.1
Monkhopton 37.1
Monkland 21.1
Monkleigh 12.1
Monknash W21
Monkokehampton 12.3
Monks Eleigh 41.6
Monks Gate 46.3
Monks Green 42.8
Monks Horton 25.13
Monks Kirby 44.3
Monks Risborough 5.3
Monkseaton 43.2
Monksilver 38.3
Monkston 5.1
Monkston Park 5.1
Monkswood W13
Monkton S27
Monkton (Devon) 12.7
Monkton (Kent) 25.7
Monkton Combe 38.6
Monkton Deverill 48.1
Monkton Farleigh 48.1
Monkton Heathfield 38.4
Monkton Wyld 13.1
Monkwearmouth 43.5
Monmarsh 21.1
Monmouth W13
Monnington-on-Wye 21.1
Monquhitter S1
Monreith S10
Monsall 19.6
Montacute 38.5
Montford 37.1
Montgomery W17
Montpelier 4.1
Montrose S2
Monxton 20.4
Monyash 11.3
Monymusk S1
Monzie S24
Moodiesburn S22
Moolham 38.5
Moons Moat, South and North 49.3
Moor 38.5
Moor Hall 11.4
Moor Monkton 33.6
Moor Park 22.8
Moorby 28.2
Moordown 13.7
Moore 7.2
Moorends 39.2
Moorfields 4.1
Moorgate 19.3
Moorgreen (Hants) 20.9
Moorhead 47.1
Moorhouse 34.3
Moorhouse (Cumbria) 10.1
Moorhouse (S Yorks) 39.2
Moorland 38.1
Moorlinch 38.1
Moors Bank 37.1
Moorsholm 33.10
Moorside (Durham) 14.1
Moorside (Gtr M'chester) 19.7
Moorside (T & W) 43.5
Moorsley 43.5
Moorthorpe 47.5
Moortown (Lincs) 28.1
Moorwood Moor 11.6
Morar S17
Morborne 6.3
Morchard Bishop 12.4
Morcombelake 13.1
Morcott 36.1
Morda 37.1
Morden (Dorset) 13.5
Morden (London) (part) L24, L29
Mordiford 21.1
Mordington S30
Mordon 14.1
More 37.1
More Crichel 13.3
Morebath 12.4
Morebattle S30
Morecambe 26.1
Morehall 25.13
Moreleigh 12.9
Moresby 10.4
Morestead 20.5
Moreton (Cheshire) (see Newbold Astbury)
Moreton (Dorset) 13.5
Moreton (Essex) 17.6
Moreton (Here) (see Eye, Moreton & Ashton)
Moreton (Mersey) 29.5
Moreton (Oxon) 35.3
Moreton (Staffs) 40.4
Moreton Corbet 37.1
Moreton Jeffries 21.1
Moreton Mill 37.1
Moreton Morrell 44.5
Moreton Paddox 44.5
Moreton Pinkney 31.7
Moreton Say 37.1
Moreton Valence 18.6
Moreton Wood 37.1
Moreton-cum-Alcumlow 7.5
Moreton-in-Marsh 18.5
Moreton-on-Lugg 21.1
Moretonhampstead 12.5
Morfa W8
Morfa Bychan W11
Morfa Nefyn W11
Morfabach W6
Morgan Town W12
Morgans Vale 48.1
Morganstown W5
Morham S13
Morland 10.3
Morley (Derbys) (part) 11.6, 11.8
Morley (Durham) 14.1
Morley St Botolph 30.7
Morley St Peter 30.7
Morningthorpe 30.7
Mornington Meadows W4
Morpeth 32.1
Morrilow Heath 40.5
Morriston W19
Morston 30.1
Mortehoe 12.2
Mortimer West End 20.1
Mortlake L27
Mortomley 39.3
Morton (Derbys) 11.4
Morton (Gloucs) 18.7
Morton (Lincs)* 28.1, 28.6
Morton (Notts) (see Fiskerton)
Morton (Shrop) 37.1
Morton (W Yorks) 47.1
Morton Bagot 44.5
Morton Palms 14.8
Morton Tinmouth 14.1
Morton on Swale 33.2
Morton-on-the-Hill 30.5
Morvah 9.1
Morval 9.1
Morven S17
Morvil W16
Morville 37.1
Morwenstow 9.1
Mosborough (S Yorks) 39.3
Moscow (E Ayrs) S11
Moscow (W Yorks) 47.1
Mosedale 10.3
Moseley 45.5
Moses Gate 19.2
Moss (S Yorks) 39.2
Moss (Wrexham) W22
Moss Bank 29.3
Moss Side (Gtr M'chester) 19.6
Moss Side (Lancs) 26.5
Mossbank S26
Mossblown S27
Mossborough 29.3
Mossend (Midlothian) S19
Mossend (N Lanarks) S22

Mossey Green 37.4
Mossley (Gtr M'chester) 19.10
Mossley (W Mids) 45.2
Mossley Hill 29.2
Mosstodloch S20
Mosterton 13.1
Moston (Ches)* 7.3, 7.5
Moston (Gtr M'chester) 19.6
Moston (Shrop) 37.1
Mostyn W10
Motcombe 13.2
Motherby 10.3
Motherwell S22
Mottingham (part) L5, L23
Mottisfont 20.4
Mottram St Andrew 7.5
Mottram in Longdendale 19.10
Mouldsworth 7.3
Moulin S24
Moulsecoomb 16.3
Moulsford 35.3
Moulsoe 5.1
Moulton (Cheshire) 7.3
Moulton (Lincs) 28.7
Moulton (N Yorks) 33.1
Moulton (N'hants) (part) 31.4, 31.5
Moulton (Suffolk) 41.2
Moulton (Vale Glam) W21
Moulton Chapel 28.7
Moulton Leys 31.5
Moulton Park 31.5
Moulton Seas End 28.7
Mount (Corn) (part)* 9.1
Mount (W Yorks) 47.4
Mount Ambrose 9.1
Mount Bures 17.3
Mount Farm 5.1
Mount Hawke 9.1
Mount Pleasant (Cheshire) 7.5
Mount Pleasant (Gtr M'chester) 19.3
Mount Pleasant (Merthyr Vale) W12
Mount Pleasant (Swansea) W19
Mount Pleasant (T & W) 43.3
Mount Pleasant (W Yorks) 47.4
Mount Tabor 47.3
Mount Vernon S7
Mount, The (Hants) 20.1
Mountain 47.1
Mountain Ash W18
Mountain Bower 48.1
Mountain Hare W12
Mountainhall S10
Mountfield 16.2
Mountjoy (Colan, Newquay) 9.1
Mountnessing 17.9
Mountsorrel 27.2
Mousehole 9.1
Mouswald S10
Mow Cop (part) 7.5, 40.1, 40.2
Mowsley 27.8
Moxby (see Marton)
Moxhull (see Wishaw)
Moxley (part) 45.2, 45.4
Moy S17
Moylegrove W16
Moze (see Beaumont)
Muasdale S3
Much Birch 21.1
Much Cowarne 21.1
Much Dewchurch 21.1
Much Hadham 22.3
Much Hoole 26.7
Much Marcle 21.1
Much Wenlock 37.1
Muchalls S1
Muchelney 38.5
Muchelney Ham 38.5
Muck S17
Muckhart (see Pool O'Muckhart)
Mucking 17.12
Muckle Roe S26
Muckleford 13.1
Mucklestone 40.2
Muckleton 37.1
Muckleton Moss 37.1
Muckley Corner 40.8
Muckton 28.2
Mudeford 13.8
Mudford 38.5
Mudford Sock 38.5
Mugdock S29
Mugginton 11.6
Muggleswick 14.1
Mugswell 42.9
Muie S17
Muir of Ord S17
Muirdrum S2
Muiredge (Buckhaven) S16
Muirend (part) S7, S14
Muirhead (N Lanarks) S22
Muirhouse S22
Muirhouses S15
Muirkirk S11
Muker 33.1
Mulbarton 30.7
Mulben S20
Mulbuie S17
Mull, Isle of S3
Mullion 9.1
Mulwith (see Newby)
Mumbles W19
Mumbleys 18.7
Mumby 28.2
Muncaster 10.4
Munden 22.10
Mundesley 30.1
Mundford 30.3
Mundham 30.7
Mundon 17.8
Mungrisdale 10.3
Munlochy S17
Munsley 21.1
Munslow 37.1
Munstone 21.1
Muntham 46.5
Murcott 35.2
Murrell Green 20.2
Murrow 6.2
Mursley 5.2
Murston 25.4
Murthly S24
Murton (Cumbria) 10.3
Murton (D'ham) 14.1
Murton (Helmsley) 33.3
Murton (Swansea) W19
Murton (York) 33.7
Murton Village 43.2
Murtry 38.2
Musbury (Devon) 12.7
Musbury (Lancs) 26.14
Muscliff 13.7
Muscoates 33.3
Musgrave 10.3
Musselburgh S13
Muston (Leics) 27.3
Muston (N Yorks) 33.4
Muswell Hill (part) L2, L14
Mutford 41.1
Muthill S24
Mutterton 12.4
Muxton 37.4
Mybster S17
Myddfai W6
Myddle 37.1
Myddlewood 37.1
Myerscough 26.2
Mylor 9.1
Mynachlogddu W16
Myndtown 37.1
Mynydd Bach W13
Mynydd Isa W10
Mynydd Llandygai W11
Mynydd Mechell W1
Mynydd Nefyn W11
Mynyddcerrig W6
Mynyddislwyn W4
Mynyddygarreg W6
Mynytho W11
Mytchett 42.3
Mytholmroyd 47.3
Myton-on-Swale 33.2
Naast S17
Nab Wood 47.1
Nabb, The 37.4
Naburn 33.7
Nackington 25.5
Nacton 41.5
Nadderwater 12.5
Nafferton 15.2
Nailbridge 18.2
Nailsea (Som) 38.7
Nailstone 27.4
Nailsworth 18.6
Nairn S17
Nancegollan 9.1
Nancekuke 9.1
Nancledra 9.1
Nanhoron W11
Nankilly 9.1
Nannerch W10
Nanpean 9.1
Nansladron 9.1
Nansough 9.1
Nanstallon 9.1
Nant Ffrancon W11
Nant Peris W11
Nant-y-Patrick W8
Nantcwnlle W7
Nantgaredig W6
Nantgarw (part) W4, W18
Nantgwynant W11
Nantlle W11
Nantmawr 37.1
Nantmel W17
Nantmor W11
Nantwich 7.5
Nanty Cafn W14
Nantycaws (Carm) W6
Nantycaws (Shrop) 37.1
Nantyderry W13
Nantyffin W6
Nantyffyllon W3
Nantyglo W2
Nantymoel W3
Naphill 5.3
Nappa 33.5
Napsbury 22.5
Napton-on-the-Hill 44.5
Narberth, North & South W16
Narborough (Leics) 27.6
Narborough (Norfolk) 30.3
Narford 30.3
Narkurs 9.1
Narth, The W13
Narthwaite (part) 10.3, 10.5
Naseby 31.4
Nash (Bucks) 5.2
Nash (H & W) (see Rodd, Nash & Little Brampton)
Nash (Kent) 25.6
Nash (Newport) W15
Nash (Pemb) W16
Nash (Shrop) 37.1
Nash (Som) 38.5
Nash (Vale Glam) W21
Nash Lee 5.3
Nash Mills 22.8
Nashes Green 20.1
Nassington 31.3
Nateby (Cumbria) 10.3
Nateby (Lancs) 26.2
Nately Scures 20.1
Natland 10.5
Naughton (see Nedging)
Naunton 18.5
Naunton Beauchamp 49.6
Navenby 28.4
Navestock 17.9
Nawton 33.3
Nayland with Wissington 41.6
Nazareth W11
Nazeing 17.6
Neacroft 20.7
Neal's Green 44.2
Nealhouse 10.1
Neap S26
Near Sawrey 10.5
Neasden L4

2

Neasham 14.8
Neath W14
Neath Abbey W14
Neath Hill 5.1
Neatham 20.6
Neatishead 30.1
Nebo (Anglesey) W1
Nebo (Carm) W6
Nebo (Conwy) W8
Nebo (Gwynedd) W11
Nechells 45.5
Necton 30.3
Nedderton 32.1
Nedging with Naughton 41.6
Needham 30.7
Needham Market 41.4
Needingworth 6.3
Needwood 40.5
Neen Savage 37.1
Neen Sollars 37.1
Neenton 37.1
Nefyn W11
Neighbourne 38.2
Neilston S14
Nelson (Caerph) W4
Nelson (Lancs) 26.13
Nelson Village 32.1
Nemphlar S28
Nempnett Thrubwell 38.6
Nenthall 10.3
Nenthead 10.3
Nenthorn S30
Nentsbury 10.3
Neopardy 12.4
Nercwys W10
Neroche 38.4
Nerston S28
Nesbitt 14.1
Nesfield with Langbar 33.6
Ness (Cheshire) 7.3
Ness (N Yorks) 33.3
Ness Holt 7.3
Nesscliffe 37.1
Nesting, North S26
Nesting, South S26
Neston (Cheshire) 7.3
Neston (Wilts) 48.1
Neswick 15.2
Netham 4.1
Nether Alderley 7.5
Nether Broughton 27.3
Nether Cerne 13.1
Nether Compton 13.1
Nether Dallachy S20
Nether Denton 10.1
Nether Haddon 11.3
Nether Haugh 39.4
Nether Heage 11.6
Nether Heyford 31.7
Nether Kellet 26.1
Nether Langwith (part) 11.5, 34.1
Nether Levens 10.5
Nether Padley 11.3
Nether Peover 7.3
Nether Poppleton 33.7
Nether Silton 33.2
Nether Stowey 38.1
Nether Street 48.1
Nether Wallop 20.4
Nether Warden 32.1
Nether Wasdale 10.4
Nether Westcote 18.5
Nether Whitacre 44.1
Nether Winchendon 5.2
Nether Wyresdale 26.2
Netheravon 48.1
Netherburn S28
Netherbury 13.1
Netherby (see Kearby)
Nethercote (Oxon) 35.2
Nethercote (Warks) 44.3
Nethercourt 25.7
Netherend 18.2
Netherexe 12.7
Netherfield (Bucks) 5.1
Netherfield (E Sussex) 16.2
Netherfield (Notts) 34.7
Netherfields 33.9
Netherhampton 48.1
Netherlee S14
Netherley 29.2
Netherne on the Hill 42.9
Netheroyd Hill 47.4
Netherseal 11.9
Netherstowe 40.8
Netherthong 47.4
Netherthorpe (Derbys) 11.2
Netherthorpe (S Yorks) 39.4
Netherton S22
Netherton (Cambs) 6.1
Netherton (Devon) 12.5
Netherton (Mersey) 29.1
Netherton (N'land)* 32.1
Netherton (Oxon) 35.4
Netherton (Som) 38.5
Netherton (W Mids) 45.3
Netherton (W Yorks) 47.5
Netherton (Worcs) 49.6
Nethertown 40.8
Netherwitton 32.1
Nethybridge S17
Netley 20.9
Netley Abbey 20.9
Netley Marsh 20.7
Netterswell 17.5
Nettlebed 35.3
Nettlebridge 38.2
Nettlecombe (Dorset) 13.1
Nettlecombe (Som) 38.3
Nettleden with Potten End 22.4
Nettleham 28.1
Nettlestead (Kent) 25.10
Nettlestead (Suffolk) 41.4
Nettlestone 24.1
Nettlesworth 14.1
Nettleton (Lincs) 28.1
Nettleton (Wilts) 48.1
Nettleton Hill 47.4
Netton 48.1
Nevendon 17.10
Nevern W16
Nevill Holt 27.8
Neville's Cross 14.1
New Abbey S10
New Aberdour S1
New Alresford 20.5
New Alston 32.1
New Alyth S24
New Ash Green 25.8
New Barn 25.1
New Bolingbroke 28.2
New Bolsover 11.5
New Bradwell 5.1
New Brancepeth 14.1
New Brighton (Flint) W10
New Brighton (Mersey) 29.5
New Brotton 33.10
New Broughton W22
New Buckenham 30.3
New Byth S1
New Covent Garden L32
New Coylton S27
New Cricket 37.1
New Cross (London) L23
New Cross (Som) 38.5
New Cumnock S11
New Deer S1
New Earswick 33.7
New Eltham L11
New England (Cambs) 6.1
New England (Som) 38.5
New Ferry 29.5
New Forest (Hants) 20.7
New Forest (N Yorks) 33.1
New Galloway S10
New Gilston S16
New Hartley 32.1
New Haw 42.1
New Hedges W16
New Herrington 43.5
New Hinksey 35.5
New Holland 28.8
New Houghton 11.5
New Hutton 10.5
New Hythe 25.9
New Inn (Carm) W6
New Inn (Leics) 27.8
New Inn (Torfaen) W20
New Invention (Shrop) 37.1
New Invention (Som) 38.3
New Invention, Willenhall 45.2
New Kyo 14.1
New Lanark S28
New Leake 28.2
New Leeds S1
New Longton 26.7
New Luce S10
New Malden (part) L21, L24
New Marske 33.10
New Marton 37.1
New Mill (Carm) W6
New Mill (W Yorks) 47.4
New Mill (Wilts) 48.1
New Mills (Derbys) 11.1
New Mills (Powys) W17
New Milton 20.7
New Moat W16
New Oscott 45.5
New Packington 27.1
New Pitsligo S1
New Place 38.3
New Polzeath 9.1
New Quay (Card) W7
New Radnor W17
New Ridley 32.1
New Romney 25.13
New Sharlston 47.5
New Silksworth 43.5
New Southgate (part) L2, L10
New Stevenston S22
New Street 25.6
New Swanington 27.1
New Toft 28.1
New Town (Som)* 38.5
New Tredegar W4
New Waltham 28.9
New Whittington 11.2
New Winton S13
New Woodhouses 37.1
New Works 37.4
New York (Lincs) 28.2
New York (T & W) 43.2
New Zealand 48.1
Newall 47.2
Newall with Clifton 33.6
Newark (Cambs) 6.1
Newark (Notts) 34.3
Newarthill S22
Newbald 15.2
Newball 28.1
Newbarns Village 10.6
Newbattle S19
Newbie S10
Newbiggin (Croglin) 10.3
Newbiggin (N Yorks) 33.1
Newbiggin (S'th Lakeland) 10.5
Newbiggin (Stainton) 10.3
Newbiggin (Temple Sowerby) 10.3
Newbiggin-by-the-Sea 32.1
Newbiggin-in-Teesdale 14.1
Newbiggin-on-Lune 10.3
Newbigging (Angus) S2
Newbigging (Strath) S28
Newbold (Derbys) 11.2
Newbold (Gtr M'chester) 19.4
Newbold (Leics) 27.1
Newbold Astbury-cum-Moreton 7.5
Newbold Moor 11.2
Newbold Pacey 44.5
Newbold Verdon 27.4
Newbold on Stour 44.5
Newborough (Anglesey) W1
Newborough (Cambs) 6.1
Newborough (Staffs) 40.5
Newbottle (N'hants) 31.7
Newbottle (T & W) 43.5
Newbourn 41.5
Newbridge (Caerph) W4
Newbridge (Corn)* 9.1
Newbridge (Edin) S6
Newbridge (Hants) 20.7
Newbridge (I of W) 24.1
Newbrough 32.1
Newburgh (Aberdeen) S1

Newburgh (Fife) S16
Newburgh (Lancs) 26.8
Newburgh (N Yorks) 33.2
Newburn 43.1
Newbury (Berks) 3.1
Newbury (Som) 38.2
Newby (Cumbria)* 10.1, 10.3
Newby (N Yorks)* 33.2, 33.4, 33.6
Newby Bridge 10.5
Newby Wiske 33.2
Newby with Mulwith 33.6
Newcarron Village S15
Newcastle (Monmth) W13
Newcastle (Powys) W17
Newcastle (Shrop) 37.1
Newcastle Emlyn W6
Newcastle upon Tyne 43.1
Newcastle-under-Lyme 40.2
Newcastleton (Borders) S30
Newcastleton (Cumbria) 10.1
Newchapel (Staffs) 40.2
Newchapel (Surrey) 42.10
Newchurch (Carm) W6
Newchurch (I of W) 24.1
Newchurch (Kent) 25.13
Newchurch (Lancs) 26.14
Newchurch (Powys) W17
Newchurch (Staffs) 40.5
Newchurch West W13
Newchurch in Pendle 26.13
Newdale 37.4
Newdigate 42.8
Newenden 25.12
Newent 18.2
Newfield* 14.1
Newfound 20.1
Newgale W16
Newhall S17
Newhall (Cheshire) 7.5
Newhall (Derbys) 11.9
Newham L25
Newhampton 21.1
Newhaven 16.4
Newhey 19.4
Newholm 33.4
Newhouse S22
Newick 16.4
Newingreen 25.13
Newington (Kent)* 25.7, 25.13
Newington (Notts) 34.1
Newington (Oxon) 35.3
Newington (part) L28
Newland (Berks) 3.3
Newland (E Yorks) 15.2
Newland (Gloucs) 18.2
Newland (N Yorks) 33.8
Newland (Worcs) 49.4
Newland Bottom 10.5
Newland-cum-Woodhouse 47.5
Newlandrig S19
Newlands (Bucks) 5.1
Newlands (Cumbria) 10.3
Newlyn 9.1
Newlyn East 9.1
Newmachar S1
Newmains S22
Newmarket S32
Newmarket (Cambs) (part) 6.4
Newmarket (Suffolk) 41.2
Newmill (Corn) 9.1
Newmill (Moray) S20
Newmillerdam 47.5
Newmills (Corn) 9.1
Newmilns & Greenholm S11
Newnes 37.1
Newney Green 17.7
Newnham (Gloucs) 18.2
Newnham (Hants) 20.1
Newnham (Herts) 22.1
Newnham (Kent) 25.4
Newnham (N'hants) 31.4
Newnham (Warks) 44.5
Newnham Hill 31.4
Newport (E Riding) 15.2
Newport (Essex) 17.1
Newport (I of W) 24.1
Newport (Middlesbrough) 33.9
Newport (Norfolk) 30.6
Newport (Pemb) W16
Newport (S Yorks) 43.5
Newport (Shrop) 37.4
Newport (Som) 38.4
Newport Pagnell 5.1
Newport-on-Tay S16
Newquay (Corn) 9.1
Newsham (N Yorks) 33.1
Newsham (N'land) 32.1
Newsham (Stockton) 14.10
Newsham with Breckenbrough 33.2
Newsholme (E Yorks) 15.2
Newsholme (Lancs) 26.3
Newsholme (W Yorks) 47.1
Newsome 47.4
Newstead S30
Newstead (Notts) 34.7
Newstead (Staffs) 40.3
Newthorpe (N Yorks) (see Huddlestone)
Newtimber 46.4
Newton 37.1
Newton (Argyll & Bute) S3
Newton (Beds) 2.2
Newton (Cambs) (part) 6.2, 6.5
Newton (Cowbridge) (Vale Glam) W21
Newton (Derbys) 11.5
Newton (Dumfries) S10
Newton (Here) 21.1
Newton (Lincs) 28.4
Newton (Mersey) 29.5
Newton (N Yorks) 33.3
Newton (N'hants) 31.2
Newton (N'land) 32.1
Newton (Norfolk) (see Trowse)
Newton (Notts) 34.8
Newton (Porthcawl) W3
Newton (Staffs) 40.5
Newton (Suffolk) 41.6
Newton (Swansea) W19
Newton (W & Midlothian)* S19, S31
Newton (Warks) 44.3
Newton (Wilts) 48.1
Newton Abbot 12.5
Newton Aycliffe 14.1
Newton Bewley 14.9
Newton Blossomville 5.1
Newton Bromswold 31.3
Newton Burgoland 27.1
Newton by Castle Acre 30.3
Newton by Toft 28.1
Newton Ferrers 12.9
Newton Flotman 30.7
Newton Grange 11.3
Newton Hall 14.1
Newton Harcourt 27.8
Newton Heath 19.6
Newton Kyme-cum-Toulson 33.8
Newton Leys (part) 5.1
Newton Longville 5.2
Newton Mearns S14
Newton Morrell (N Yorks) 33.1
Newton Morrell (Oxon) 35.2
Newton Mulgrave 33.4
Newton Poppleford 12.7
Newton Purcell 35.2
Newton Regis 44.1
Newton Reigny 10.3
Newton St Cyres 12.4
Newton St Loe 38.6
Newton St Petrock 12.1
Newton Solney 11.9
Newton Stewart S10
Newton Tony 48.1
Newton Tracey 12.2
Newton Valence 20.6
Newton on Derwent 15.2
Newton on Rawcliffe 33.3
Newton on Trent 28.1
Newton under Roseberry 33.10
Newton with Clifton 26.5
Newton with Scales 26.5
Newton-by-Malpas 7.3
Newton-by-Tattenhall 7.3
Newton-by-the-Sea 32.1
Newton-in-Bowland 26.3
Newton-in-Cartmel 10.5
Newton-in-Furness 10.6
Newton-le-Willows (part) 29.3, 33.1
Newton-on-Ouse 33.2
Newton-on-the-Hill 37.1
Newton-on-the-Moor 32.1
Newtongrange S19
Newtonhill S1
Newtonmore S17
Newtown (Bristol) 4.1
Newtown (Dorset) 13.6
Newtown (Hants) (part) 20.1, 20.4, 20.5, 20.7, 20.8
Newtown (I of W) 24.1
Newtown (Powys) W17
Newtown (Rhondda) W18
Newtown (Shrop) 37.1
Newtown (Staffs) 40.1
Newtown (W Mids) 45.4
Newtown (Wilts) (part) 48.1
Newtown Linford 27.2
Newtown St Boswells S30
Newtown Unthank 27.4
Newtyle S2
Next Ness 10.5
Neyland W16
Nibley 18.7
Nibthwaite 10.5
Nicholashayne 12.4
Nicholaston W19
Nicholforest 10.1
Nichols Town 20.8
Nidd 33.6
Nigg S17
Nimmer 38.5
Nine Ashes 17.6
Nine Elms L32, 48.2
Nine Mile Burn S19
Ninebanks 32.1
Ninfield 16.1
Niton 24.1
Nixonville W12
No Mans Heath (part) 40.8, 44.1
No Place 14.1
Nobottle 31.4
Nocton 28.4
Noctorum 29.5
Noke 35.2
Nolton & Roch W16
Nomansland (Corn) 9.1
Nomansland (Devon) 12.4
Nomansland (Wilts) (part) 20.7, 48.1
Noneley 37.1
Nonington 25.6
Nook 10.5
Nookside 43.5
Norbriggs 11.2
Norbury L8
Norbury (Cheshire) 7.5
Norbury (Derbys) 11.3
Norbury (Shrop) 37.1
Norbury (Staffs) 40.4
Norby (N Yorks) 33.2
Nordelph 30.2
Norden 19.4
Nordrach-on-Mendip 38.2
Norham 32.1
Norham Manor 35.5
Nork 42.9
Norland Town 47.3
Norley 7.3
Norleywood 20.7
Normacot 40.3
Norman Cross 6.3
Normanby (Lincs) 28.8
Normanby (N Yorks)* 33.3, 33.10
Normanby by Spital 28.1
Normanby by Stow 28.1

2

Normanby le Wold 28.1
Normandy 42.7
Normans Bay 16.2
Normanton (Derby) 11.7
Normanton (Leics) 27.3
Normanton (Lincs) 28.6
Normanton (Notts)* 34.3, 34.9
Normanton (Rutland) 36.1
Normanton (W Yorks) 47.5
Normanton (Wilts) 48.1
Normanton-le-Heath 27.1
Normanton-on-Soar 34.8
Normanton-on-Trent 34.1
Normanton-on-the-Wolds 34.8
Norrington 48.1
Norris Green (Corn) 9.1
Norris Green (Mersey) 29.2
Norristhorpe 47.4
North Acton L9
North Anston 39.4
North Ashton 29.3
North Aston 35.2
North Baddesley 20.4
North Barningham 30.1
North Barrow 38.5
North Benfleet 17.10
North Berwick S13
North Bitchburn 14.1
North Blyth 32.1
North Boarhunt 20.5
North Bovey 12.5
North Bowood 13.1
North Bradley 48.1
North Bradon 38.5
North Brewham 38.5
North Broomhill 32.1
North Cadbury 38.5
North Camp 20.3
North Carlton 28.1
North Cave 15.2
North Cerney 18.5
North Chailey 16.4
North Charford 20.7
North Cheriton 38.5
North Chideock 13.1
North Claines 49.6
North Cliffe 15.2
North Clifton 34.3
North Coates 28.2
North Cockerington 28.2
North Coker 38.5
North Combe 38.3
North Cornelly W3
North Country 9.1
North Cove 41.1
North Cowton 33.1
North Crawley 5.1
North Creake 30.2
North Curry 38.4
North Dalton 15.2
North Deighton 33.6
North Duffield 33.8
North Elkington 28.2
North Elmsall 47.5
North End (East Woodhay) 20.1
North End (Essex) 17.7
North End (Som) 38.7
North Erradale S17
North Fambridge 17.8
North Ferriby 15.2
North Finchley L2
North Foreland (Broadstairs) 25.7
North Frodingham 15.2
North Gorley 20.7
North Gosforth 43.1
North Grimston 33.3
North Hawkwell 38.3
North Heath 46.3
North Hill (Corn) 9.1
North Hill (Som) 38.3
North Hinksey 35.4
North Holme 33.3
North Holmwood 42.8
North Huish 12.9
North Hykeham 28.4
North Hylton 43.5
North Kelsey 28.1
North Kensington (part) L13, L20
North Kenton 43.1
North Kessock S17
North Killingholme 28.8
North Kilvington 33.2
North Kilworth 27.8
North Kyme 28.4
North Lee 5.3
North Leigh (Oxon) 35.1
North Leverton 34.1
North Lodge 14.1
North Luffenham 36.1
North Marden 46.2
North Marston 5.2
North Meads 46.5
North Meols 26.8
North Middleton S19
North Milford (see Kirby Wharfe)
North Molton 12.2
North Moreton 35.3
North Motherwell S22
North Mundham 46.2
North Muskham 34.3
North Mymms 22.6
North Newbald 15.2
North Newington 35.2
North Newnton 48.1
North Newton 38.1
North Nibley 18.6
North Oakley 20.1
North Ockendon L16
North Ormesby 33.9
North Ormsby 28.2
North Otterington 33.2
North Owersby 28.1
North Perrott 38.5
North Petherton 38.1
North Petherwin 9.1
North Piddle 49.6
North Quarme 38.3
North Queensferry S16
North Rauceby 28.4
North Reston 28.2
North Rigton 33.6
North Rode 7.5
North Roe S26
North Ronaldsay S23
North Runcton 30.2
North Scale 10.6
North Scarle 28.4
North Seaton 32.1
North Sheen L27
North Shields 43.2
North Somercotes 28.2
North Stainley with Slenningford 33.6
North Stainmore 10.3
North Stifford 17.12
North Stoke (Oxon) 35.3
North Stoke (Som) 38.6
North Stoneham (part) 20.4, 20.9
North Sunderland 32.1
North Tamerton 9.1
North Tawton 12.3
North Thoresby 28.2
North Tolsta S32
North Town (Hants) 20.3
North Town (Som) 38.5
North Uist S32
North Walbottle 43.1
North Walsham 30.1
North Waltham 20.1
North Warnborough 20.2
North Weald 17.6
North Weirs 20.7
North Weston (Oxon) 35.3
North Weston (Som) 38.7
North Wheatley 34.1
North Willingham 28.1
North Wingfield 11.4
North Witham 28.6
North Woolwich L25
North Wootton (Dorset) 13.1
North Wootton (Norfolk) 30.2
North Wootton (Som) 38.2
North Wraxall 48.1
North Wylam 32.1
Northall 5.2
Northallerton 33.2
Northam (Devon) 12.1
Northam (Hants) 20.8
Northampton 31.5
Northaw 22.6
Northay 38.5
Northborough 6.1
Northbourne (Bournemouth) 13.7
Northbourne (Dover) 25.6
Northbrook 35.2
Northbrook (Hants) 20.5
Northchapel 46.2
Northchurch 22.4
Northcott Hamlet 12.1
Northdown (Margate) 25.7
Northedge 11.4
Northend (Bucks) 5.3
Northend (Oxon) 35.3
Northend (Warks) 44.5
Northenden 19.6
Northfield (Bucks) 5.1
Northfield (W Mids) 45.5
Northfleet 25.2
Northgate 46.1
Northiam 16.2
Northill 2.2
Northington* 20.1, 20.5
Northlands 28.2
Northleach with Eastington 18.5
Northleaze 38.5
Northleigh 12.7
Northlew 12.3
Northmoor (Oxon) 35.1
Northmoor (Som) 38.3
Northmoor Green 38.1
Northolt (part) L9
Northop W10
Northop Hall W10
Northorpe 28.6
Northorpe (part) 28.1, 28.6
Northover 38.5
Northowram 47.3
Northpunds S26
Northrepps 30.1
Northton S32
Northville (Gloucs) 18.7
Northville (Torfaen) W20
Northway 18.1
Northwich 7.3
Northwick 18.7
Northwold 30.2
Northwood (3) (Shrop) 37.1
Northwood (Derbys) 11.3
Northwood (Herts) 22.8
Northwood (I of W) 24.1
Northwood (Kirkby) 29.4
Northwood (Ramsgate) (Kent) 25.7
Northwood (Staffs) 40.3
Northwood Green 18.2
Norton & Lenchwick 49.6
Norton (Gloucs) 18.1
Norton (I of W) 24.1
Norton (Kent) 25.4
Norton (Malton) (N Yorks) 33.3
Norton (N'hants) 31.4
Norton (Notts) 34.1
Norton (Powys) W17
Norton (S Yorks) 39.2
Norton (Selsey) 46.2
Norton (Som) 38.7
Norton (Staffs) 40.3
Norton (Stockton) 14.10
Norton (Suffolk) 41.4
Norton (W Sussex) 46.5
Norton (Wilts) 48.1
Norton (Worcs) 21.1
Norton Bavant 48.1
Norton Bridge 40.4
Norton Canes 40.7
Norton Canon 21.1
Norton Conyers 33.6
Norton Disney 28.4
Norton Fitzwarren 38.4
Norton Green 40.3
Norton Heath 17.6

Norton Lindsey 44.4
Norton Malreward 38.6
Norton Mandeville 17.6
Norton Radstock 38.6
Norton St Philip 38.2
Norton Subcourse 30.7
Norton Tower 47.3
Norton-in-Hales 37.1
Norton-in-the-Moors (part) 40.1, 40.3
Norton-juxta-Kempsey 49.6
Norton-juxta-Twycross 27.4
Norton-le-Clay 33.6
Norton-sub-Hamdon 38.5
Norwell 34.3
Norwell Woodhouse 34.3
Norwich 30.4
Norwood 33.6
Norwood (part) L22, L28
Norwood Green 47.3
Norwood Hill 42.8
Noseley 27.8
Noss Mayo 12.9
Nostell 47.5
Nosterfield (West Tanfield) 33.2
Notgrove 18.5
Nottage W3
Notter Bridge 9.1
Notting Hill L20
Nottingham 34.6
Notton (W Yorks) 47.5
Notton (Wilts) 48.1
Nowton 41.3
Nuffield 35.3
Nun Monkton 33.6
Nunburnholme 15.2
Nuncargate 34.4
Nuneaton 44.2
Nuneham Courtenay 35.3
Nunhead L28
Nunkeeling 15.2
Nunney 38.2
Nunnington (Here) 21.1
Nunnington (N Yorks) 33.3
Nunnykirk 32.1
Nunriding 32.1
Nunroyd 47.4
Nunthorpe (part) 33.9, 33.10
Nunton 48.1
Nunwick (N'land) 32.1
Nupdown 18.7
Nursling 20.4
Nursteed 48.1
Nurston W21
Nutbourne (part) 46.2, 46.3
Nutfield 42.10
Nutgrove 29.3
Nuthall 34.5
Nuthampstead 22.1
Nuthurst 46.3
Nutley (E Sussex) 16.1
Nutley (Hants) 20.1
Nuttall 19.3
Nuttall Lane 19.3
Nye 38.7
Nyetimber 46.5
Nyewood 46.2
Nymet Rowland 12.4
Nympsfield 18.6
Nynehead 38.4
Nyton 46.5
Oadby 27.7
Oak Gate 19.3
Oakamoor 40.1
Oakbank 10.5
Oakdale (Caerph) W4
Oakdale (Dorset) 13.6
Oake 38.4
Oakengates 37.4
Oakenholt W10
Oakenshaw (Durham) 14.1
Oakenshaw (W Yorks) (part) 47.1, 47.4
Oakenshaw (Worcs) 49.3
Oakerthorpe 11.6
Oakes 47.4
Oakfield W20
Oakford 12.4
Oakgrove 5.1
Oakham (Rutland) 36.1
Oakham (W Mids) 45.4
Oakhanger (Cheshire) 7.5
Oakhanger (Hants) 20.6
Oakhill (Bucks) 5.1
Oakhill (Som) 38.2
Oakhill (Staffs) 40.3
Oakington & Westwick 6.5
Oakley (Beds) 2.1
Oakley (Bucks) 5.2
Oakley (Fife) S16
Oakley (Hants) 20.1
Oakley (Suffolk) 41.4
Oakmere 7.3
Oakridge (Gloucs) 18.6
Oakridge (Hants) 20.1
Oakridge (Som) 38.7
Oakridge Lynch 18.6
Oakridge Park 5.1
Oaks in Charnwood 27.1
Oaksey 48.1
Oakthorpe 27.1
Oakwell 47.4
Oakwood (Cheshire) 7.1
Oakwood (Derby) 11.7
Oakwood (N'land) 32.1
Oakwood Hill 42.8
Oakworth 47.1
Oare (Kent) 25.4
Oare (Som) 38.3
Oare (Wilts) 48.1
Oareford 38.3
Oasby 28.6
Oath 38.5
Oathill 38.5
Oathlaw S2
Oatlands 42.5
Oban S3
Obley 37.1
Oborne 13.1
Obthorpe 28.6
Oby 30.6
Occaney (see Walkingham Hill)
Occold 41.4
Ochiltree S11
Ockbrook 11.8
Ocker Hill 45.4
Ockham 42.7
Ockley 42.8
Ocle Pychard 21.1
Octon 15.2
Odcombe 38.5
Odd Rode 7.5
Odder 28.1
Oddingley 49.6
Oddington (Gloucs) 18.5
Oddington (Oxon) 35.2
Odell 2.1
Odiham 20.2
Odsal 47.1
Odstock 48.1
Odstone 27.4
Offchurch 44.4
Offcote & Underwood 11.3
Offenham 49.6
Offerton (Derbys) 11.3
Offerton (T & W) 43.5
Offham (E Sussex) 16.4
Offham (Kent) 25.9
Offham (W Sussex) 46.5
Offington 46.6
Offley 22.1
Offord Cluny 6.3
Offord D'arcy 6.3
Offton 41.4
Offwell 12.7
Ogbourne Maizey 48.1
Ogbourne St Andrew 48.1
Ogbourne St George 48.1
Ogden 47.3
Ogle 32.1
Ogmore by Sea W21
Ogmore Vale W3
Ogwell 12.5
Okeford Fitzpaine 13.2
Okehampton 12.3
Okehampton Hamlets 12.3
Okeover 40.5
Oker & Snitterton 11.3
Okewood Hill 42.8
Old 31.4
Old Alresford 20.5
Old Basing 20.1
Old Bolingbroke 28.2
Old Bursledon 20.9
Old Byland 33.3
Old Castle (Monmth) W13
Old Catton 30.5
Old Cleeve 38.3
Old Colwyn W8
Old Crickett 37.1
Old Dalby 27.3
Old Deer S1
Old Down 18.7
Old Farm Park 5.1
Old Fletton 6.1
Old Ford L30
Old Forge 21.1
Old Furnace W20
Old Hall (Cheshire) 7.1
Old Hall (Gtr M'chester) 19.3
Old Harlow 17.5
Old Hill 45.4
Old Hunstanton 30.2
Old Hutton 10.5
Old Kilpatrick S9
Old Knebworth 22.1
Old Leake 28.5
Old Lindley 47.3
Old Linslade 2.2
Old Marton 37.1
Old Milverton 44.4
Old Netley 20.9
Old Newton with Dagworth 41.4
Old Park 37.4
Old Penshaw 43.5
Old Pentland S19
Old Radnor W17
Old Romney 25.13
Old Royston 47.5
Old Scone S24
Old Sodbury 18.7
Old Somerby 28.6
Old St. Mellons W15
Old Stratford (N'hants) 31.7
Old Stratford (Warks) 44.5
Old Swan 29.2
Old Teversal Village 34.4
Old Toll S27
Old Town (Cumbria) 10.5
Old Town (W Yorks) 47.3
Old Trafford 19.8
Old Warden 2.2
Old Weston 6.3
Old Whittington 11.2
Old Windsor 3.4
Old Wives Lees 25.12
Old Woking 42.4
Old Wolverton 5.1
Old Woodhouses 37.1
Oldberrow 44.5
Oldbrook 5.1
Oldbury (W Mids) 45.4
Oldbury (Warks) 44.1
Oldbury Naite 18.7
Oldbury-on-Severn 18.7
Oldbury-on-the-Hill 18.5
Oldcastle (Cheshire) 7.3
Oldcotes (see Styrrup)
Oldcroft 18.2
Oldfield* 47.1, 47.4
Oldford 38.2
Oldham 19.7
Oldhamstocks S13
Oldhurst 6.3
Oldland 18.7
Oldmeldrum S1
Oldmixon 38.7
Oldstead 33.3
Oldswinford 45.3
Oldway 38.5
Oldways End 38.3
Oliffe (see Shipton Oliffe)
Olivers Battery 20.5
Ollaberry S26
Ollerton (Cheshire) 7.5
Ollerton (Notts) 34.3
Ollerton (Shrop) 37.1
Olney 5.1

2

Olney Park 5.1
Olton 45.6
Olveston 18.7
Ombersley 49.6
Ompton 34.3
Onecote 40.1
Onehouse 41.4
Onen, The W13
Onesacre 39.3
Onibury 37.1
Onich S17
Onllwyn W14
Onneley (Shrop) 37.1
Onneley (Staffs) 40.2
Onston 7.3
Openwoodgate 11.6
Opinan S17
Orby 28.2
Orchard Portman 38.4
Orchard Wyndham 38.3
Orcheston 48.1
Orcop 21.1
Ord 32.1
Ordiquhill S1
Ordsall 19.5
Orford (Cheshire) 7.1
Orford (Suffolk) 41.5
Organford 13.5
Orgreave (S Yorks) 39.4
Orgreave (Staffs) 40.8
Orlestone 25.12
Orleton (Here) (see Stanford)
Orleton (Shrop) 37.4
Orlingbury 31.6
Ormesby (part) 33.9, 33.10
Ormesby St Margaret 30.6
Ormesby St Michael 30.6
Ormiston S13
Ormsary S3
Ormside 10.3
Ormskirk 26.8
Orphir S23
Orpington L5
Orrell (Gtr M'chester) 19.1
Orrell (Mersey) (part) 29.1, 29.2
Orrell Park 29.2
Orsett 17.12
Orsett Heath 17.12
Orslow 40.6
Orston 34.8
Orton (Cumbria)* 10.1, 10.3
Orton (N'hants) 31.2
Orton Brimbles 6.1
Orton Goldhay 6.1
Orton Grange 10.1
Orton Longueville 6.1
Orton Malborne 6.1
Orton Southgate 6.1
Orton Waterville 6.1
Orton Wistow 6.1
Orton-on-the-Hill 27.4
Orwell 6.5
Osbaldeston 26.3
Osbaldwick 33.7
Osbaston (Leics) 27.4
Osbaston (Shrop) 37.4
Osborne 24.1
Osbournby 28.4
Osgathorpe 27.1
Osgodby (Lincs)* 28.1, 28.6
Osgodby (N Yorks)* 33.2, 33.4
Oskamull S3
Osleston 11.9
Osmaston 11.3
Osmere 37.1
Osmington 13.1
Osmotherley (Cumbria) 10.5
Osmotherley (N Yorks) 33.2
Osney 35.5
Ospringe 25.4
Ossendyke (see Ryther)
Ossett 47.5
Ossington 34.3
Oswaldkirk 33.3
Oswaldtwistle 26.11
Oswestry 37.1
Oteley 37.1
Otford 25.8
Otham 25.10
Othery 38.1
Otley (Suffolk) 41.5
Otley (W Yorks) 47.2
Otterbourne 20.5
Otterburn (N Yorks) 33.5
Otterburn (N'land) 32.1
Otterden 25.10
Otterford 38.4
Otterham 9.1
Otterhampton 38.1
Ottershaw 42.1
Otterton 12.7
Ottery St Mary 12.7
Ottinge 25.13
Ottringham 15.2
Oughtershaw 33.5
Oughterside 10.2
Oughtibridge 39.3
Oughtrington 7.1
Oulston 33.2
Oulton (Norfolk) 30.5
Oulton (Stone) (Staffs) 40.4
Oulton (Suffolk) 41.1
Oulton (W Yorks) 47.2
Oundle 31.3
Ousby 10.3
Ousden 41.3
Ousefleet 15.2
Ousethorpe 15.2
Ouston (Durham) 14.1
Out Elmstead (Barham) 25.5
Out Hill 44.5
Out Newton 15.2
Out Rawcliffe 26.2
Out Skerries S26
Outgate 10.5
Outlane (part) 47.3, 47.4
Outseats 11.3
Outwell 30.2
Outwood (Gtr M'chester) 19.3
Outwood (Surrey) 42.10
Outwood (W Yorks) 47.5
Outwood Gate 19.3
Outwoods 40.5
Ouzelwell Green (Rothwell) 47.2
Ovenden 47.3
Over (Cambs) 6.5
Over (Gloucs) 18.7
Over Alderley 7.5
Over Compton 13.1
Over Dinsdale 33.2
Over Haddon 11.3
Over Hulton 19.2
Over Kellet 26.1
Over Norton 35.1
Over Silton 33.2
Over Stowey 38.1
Over Stratton 38.5
Over Wallop 20.4
Over Whitacre 44.1
Over Wyresdale 26.1
Overbury 49.6
Overdale 37.4
Overley 37.4
Overpool 7.3
Overseal (part) 11.9, 27.1
Oversley Green 44.5
Overstone 31.4
Overstone Lodge 31.5
Overstrand 30.1
Overthorpe (N'hants) 31.7
Overthorpe (W Yorks) 47.4
Overton (Cheshire) 7.3
Overton (Derbys) 11.4
Overton (Hants) 20.1
Overton (Lancs) 26.1
Overton (N Yorks) 33.2
Overton (Swansea) W19
Overton (W Yorks) 47.5
Overton (Wrexham) W22
Overtown S22
Oving (Bucks) 5.2
Oving (W Sussex) 46.2
Ovingdean (part) 16.3
Ovingham 32.1
Ovington (Durham) 14.1
Ovington (Essex) 17.2
Ovington (Hants) 20.5
Ovington (N'land) 32.1
Ovington (Norfolk) 30.3
Ower (Cadnam) 20.7
Ower (Calshot) 20.7
Owermoigne 13.1
Owersby 28.1
Owlpen 18.6
Owlsmoor 3.6
Owlswick 5.3
Owmby (see Searby)
Owmby by Spital 28.1
Owselbury 20.5
Owston & Newbold (Leics) 27.8
Owston (S Yorks) 39.2
Owston Ferry 28.8
Owstwick 15.2
Owthorne 15.2
Owthorpe 34.8
Oxborough 30.3
Oxbridge 13.1
Oxcliffe (see Heaton)
Oxclose 43.5
Oxcombe 28.2
Oxen Fell 10.5
Oxen Park 10.5
Oxendon, Gt & Little 31.4
Oxenford 38.5
Oxenhall 18.2
Oxenholme 10.5
Oxenhope 47.1
Oxenpill 38.2
Oxenton 18.1
Oxenwood 48.1
Oxford (Oxon) 35.5
Oxford (Staffs) 40.3
Oxhey (part) 22.8, 22.9
Oxhill (Durham) 14.1
Oxhill (Warks) 44.5
Oxley Park 5.1
Oxlode 6.4
Oxnam S30
Oxney Green, Gt & Little 17.7
Oxshott 42.5
Oxspring 39.1
Oxted 42.10
Oxton (Mersey) 29.5
Oxton (N Yorks) 33.8
Oxton (Notts) 34.3
Oxton (Scottish Borders) S30
Oxton Rakes 11.4
Oxwich W19
Oxwick 30.3
Oyne S1
Oystermouth W19
Ozleworth 18.5
Pachesham 42.8
Packington (Leics) 27.1
Packington (Staffs) 40.8
Packmoor 40.3
Packwood 45.6
Padanaram S2
Padbury 5.2
Paddington (Cheshire) 7.1
Paddington (London) L33
Paddlesworth 25.13
Paddock 47.4
Paddock Lane 43.5
Paddock Stile 43.5
Paddock Wood 25.11
Paddol Green 37.1
Padgate 7.1
Padiham 26.12
Padside (see Thornthwaite)
Padstow 9.1
Padworth 3.1
Page Bank 14.1
Pagham 46.5
Paglesham Church End 17.11
Paglesham North End 17.11
Paignton 12.10
Pailton 44.3
Painscastle W17
Painsthorpe 15.2
Painswick 18.6
Painthorpe 47.5

Paisley S25
Pakenham 41.3
Palestine 20.4
Palewell L27
Paley Street 3.4
Palgrave (Norfolk) (see Sporle)
Palgrave (Suffolk) 41.4
Pallion 43.5
Pallister Park 33.9
Palmarsh 25.13
Palmer's Green L10
Palmers Flat 18.2
Palmersville 43.2
Palms Hill 37.1
Palnackie S10
Palnure S10
Palterton 11.5
Pamber 20.1
Pamber End 20.1
Pamber Green 20.1
Pamber Heath 20.1
Pamphill 13.3
Pampisford 6.5
Panbride S2
Pancrasweek 12.1
Pandy (Carm) W6
Pandy (Monmth) W13
Pandy (Powys) W17
Pandy (Wrexham) W22
Pandy Tudur W8
Panfield 17.2
Pangbourne 3.1
Pankeymoor 37.1
Pannal 33.6
Pant (Merthyr) W12
Pant (Shrop) 37.1
Pant Glas (Shrop) 37.1
Pant-glas (Gwynedd) W11
Pantasaph W10
Panteg W20
Panton 28.2
Pantperthog W11
Pantside W4
Pantybuarth W10
Pantyffynon W6
Pantygasseg W20
Pantygelli W13
Pantygog W3
Pantygraigwen W18
Pantymwyn W10
Pantyscallog W12
Pantywaun W4
Papa Stour S26
Papa Westray S23
Papcastle 10.2
Papplewick 34.7
Papworth Everard 6.5
Papworth St Agnes 6.5
Par 9.1
Paradise (Cumbria) 10.6
Paradise (Som) 38.5
Paradise Green 47.1
Paradwys W1
Parbold 26.8
Parbrook 38.2
Parc W11
Parc Seymour W15
Pardown 20.1
Parham (Suffolk) 41.5
Parham (W Sussex) 46.3
Park Barn 38.5
Park Bottom 9.1
Park End (Middlesbrough) 33.9
Park End (N'land) 32.1
Park Farm 49.3
Park Gate (Cumbria) 10.5
Park Gate (Hants) 20.10
Park Hall (Shrop) 37.1
Park Hall (W Mids) 45.2
Park Lane 19.3
Park Mill 47.4
Park Prewett 20.1
Park Royal (part) L4, L9
Park Street 22.5
Park Town 35.5
Park Village 32.1
Park Wood 25.10
Parkend 18.2
Parkeston 17.4
Parkfield (see Coseley)
Parkgate S10
Parkgate (Cheshire) 7.3
Parkgate (S Yorks) 39.4
Parkgate (Surrey) 42.8
Parkham 12.1
Parkhead 47.4
Parkhouse W13
Parkhurst 24.1
Parklands 31.5
Parkmill W19
Parksite 40.2
Parkstone (Upper & Lower) 13.6
Parkway 38.5
Parkwood* 25.3
Parlington 47.2
Parnwell 6.1
Parr 29.3
Parr Stocks 29.3
Parracombe 12.2
Parsley 9.1
Parson Drove 6.2
Parsonage Green 17.7
Parsons 43.5
Parsons Green L13
Partington 19.8
Partney 28.2
Parton (Cumbria) 10.4
Parton (Dumfries) S10
Partridge Green (Essex) 17.7
Partridge Green (W Sussex) 46.3
Partridge Hill 48.1
Partrishow W17
Parwich 11.3
Paslow Common 17.6
Passenham 31.7
Passfield 20.6
Passmonds 19.4
Paston (Cambs) 6.1
Paston (Norfolk) 30.1
Patcham 16.3
Patchetts Green 22.10
Patching 46.5
Patchway 18.7
Pately Bridge 33.6
Path of Condie S24
Pathhead S19
Pathlow 44.5
Patna S11
Patney 48.1
Patrick Brompton 33.1
Patricroft 19.5
Patrington 15.2
Patrixbourne 25.5
Patshull (part) 37.1, 40.6
Patterdale 10.3
Pattesley 30.3
Pattiesmuir S16
Pattingham 40.6
Pattishall 31.7
Pattison 43.5
Pattiswick 17.2
Patton 10.5
Paul 9.1
Paulerspury 31.7
Paull 15.2
Paulton 38.6
Pauntley 18.2
Pave Lane 37.4
Pavenham 2.1
Pavenhill 48.1
Pawlett 38.1
Paxford 18.5
Paxton S30
Payhembury 12.7
Paynes Green 42.8
Paynters Lane End 9.1
Paythorne 26.3
Paytoe & Grange 21.1
Payton 38.4
Peacehaven 16.4
Peak Dale 11.1
Peak Forest 11.1
Peakirk 6.1
Pear Ash 38.5
Peartree (Durham) 14.1
Peartree (Hants) 20.8
Peartree Bridge 5.1
Pease Pottage 46.4
Peasedown St John 38.6
Peasemore 3.1
Peasenhall 41.5
Peaslake 42.7
Peasley Cross 29.3
Peasmarsh (E Sussex) 16.2
Peasmarsh (Som) 38.5
Peasmarsh (Surrey) 42.7
Peat Inn S16
Peatling, Magna & Parva 27.8
Peatmoor 48.2
Peaton 37.1
Peblig Hill W11
Pebmarsh 17.2
Pebworth 49.6
Pecket Well 47.3
Peckforton 7.5
Peckham L28
Peckham Bush (Kent) 25.9
Peckleton 27.4
Pedairffordd W17
Pedlinge 25.13
Pedmore 45.3
Pednor 5.4
Pedwell 38.1
Peebles S30
Peel 26.5
Peel (see Horton)
Peel Common (part) 20.10, 20.11
Peel Green 19.5
Peene 25.13
Peggs Green 27.1
Pegsdon 2.2
Pegswood 32.1
Pegwell (Ramsgate) 25.7
Pelaw 43.3
Peldon 17.3
Pelenna W14
Pelhams Lands 28.5
Pell Wall 37.1
Pellon 47.3
Pelsall 45.2
Pelton 14.1
Pelton Fell 14.1
Pelton Lane Ends 14.1
Pelynt 9.1
Pemberton W6
Pembrey W6
Pembridge 21.1
Pembroke W16
Pembroke Dock W16
Pembury 25.11
Pen Alt 21.1
Pen Mill 38.5
Pen Pant W19
Pen-y-banc W6
Pen-y-bont (Carm) W6
Pen-y-bont (Powys/Shrop) (part) 37.1, W17
Pen-y-bryn W4
Pen-y-cae W22
Pen-y-cae-mawr W13
Pen-y-cefn W10
Pen-y-clawdd W13
Pen-y-coedcae W18
Pen-y-felin W10
Pen-y-garn W20
Pen-y-garnedd W17
Pen-yr-heol (Torfaen) W20
Penair 9.1
Penallt W13
Penally W16
Penarth W21
Penberth 9.1
Penboyr W6
Penbryn W7
Penbuallt W17
Pencader W6
Pencaenewydd W11
Pencaer W16
Pencaerau W11
Pencaerav W14
Pencaitland S13
Pencarnisiog W1
Pencarrog W6
Pencelli W17
Penclawdd W19

2

Pencoed W3
Pencombe 21.1
Pencoyd 21.1
Pencoys 9.1
Pencraig 21.1
Pendeen 9.1
Pendeford (part) 40.6, 45.1
Penderleath 9.1
Penderyn W18
Pendine W6
Pendlebury 19.5
Pendleton (Gtr M'chester) 19.5
Pendleton (Lancs) 26.3
Pendock 49.4
Pendoggett 9.1
Pendomer 38.5
Pendoylan W21
Penegoes W17
Penelewey 9.1
Pengam W4
Penge L5
Pengegon 9.1
Pengover Green 9.1
Pengraigwen W1
Pengroeslon W11
Penhale (Fraddon, St Columb) 9.1
Penhalvean 9.1
Penhow W15
Penicuik S19
Peniel (Carm) W6
Peniel (Denbigh) W9
Penisarwaen W11
Penistone 39.1
Penketh 7.1
Penkhull 40.3
Penkridge 40.6
Penlan W19
Penley (Wrexham) W22
Penllergaer W19
Penllyn W21
Penmachno W8
Penmaen (Caerph) W4
Penmaen (Swansea) W19
Penmaenhead W8
Penmaenmawr W8
Penmaenpool W11
Penmaenrhos W8
Penmark W21
Penmon W1
Penmorfa W11
Penmount 9.1
Penmynydd W1
Penn (Bucks) 5.4
Penn Common 40.6
Penn Hill (Som) 38.5
Penn Street 5.4
Pennal W11
Pennan S1
Pennant W17
Pennard W19
Pennerley 37.1
Pennington (Cumbria) 10.5
Pennington (Hants) 20.7
Pennorth W17
Pennsylvania 18.7
Penny Bridge 10.5
Penny Hill 38.3
Pennyghael S3
Pennyland 5.1
Pennymoor 12.4
Pennywell 43.5
Penpedairheol W4
Penpergwm W13
Penperlleni W13
Penpol 9.1
Penponds 9.1
Penpont (Dumfries) S10
Penpont (Powys) W17
Penrherber W6
Penrhiwceiber W18
Penrhiwfer W18
Penrhos (Gwynedd) W11
Penrhos (Monmth) W13
Penrhos (Powys) W17
Penrhosgarnedd W11
Penrhoslligwy W1
Penrhyndeudraeth W11
Penrhys W18
Penrice W19
Penrith 10.3
Penrose (North Petherwin) 9.1
Penrose (St Ervan) 9.1
Penruddock 10.3
Penryn 9.1
Pensarn (Carm) W6
Pensarn (Conwy) W8
Pensax (part) 49.1, 49.4
Pensby 29.5
Penselwood 38.5
Pensford 38.6
Penshaw 43.5
Penshurst 25.8
Pensilva 9.1
Pensnett 45.3
Pensthorpe 30.1
Penstraze 9.1
Penstrowed W17
Pentewan 9.1
Pentir W11
Pentire 9.1
Pentland S19
Pentlepoir W16
Pentlow 17.2
Pentney 30.2
Penton 10.1
Penton Grafton 20.4
Penton Mewsey 20.4
Pentonville (part) L6, L19
Pentraeth W1
Pentre (Denbigh) W9
Pentre (Flint) W10
Pentre (Rhondda) W18
Pentre (Shrop) 37.1
Pentre Berw W1
Pentre Broughton W22
Pentre Halkyn W10
Pentre Morgan W6
Pentre-Coed 37.1
Pentre-Morgan (part) 37.1, W22
Pentrebach W12
Pentrebeirdd W17
Pentrebychan W22
Pentrecagal W6
Pentrecelyn W9
Pentrecwrt W6
Pentredwr W9
Pentrefelin W17
Pentrefoelas W8
Pentregwenlais W6
Pentrellyncymer W8
Pentremeyrick W21
Pentrepiod W20
Pentretygwyn W6
Pentreuchaf W11
Pentrich 11.6
Pentridge 13.3
Pentrobin W10
Pentwyn (Caerph) W4
Pentwyn (Cardiff) W5
Pentwyn (Merthyr) W12
Pentwyn (Torfaen) W20
Pentwynmawr W4
Pentyrch W5
Penwartha Coombe 9.1
Penweathers 9.1
Penwithick 9.1
Penwood 20.1
Penwortha 9.1
Penwortham 26.7
Penyard (Here) 21.1
Penyard (Merthyr) W12
Penybontfawr W17
Penycae W17
Penycwm W16
Penydarren W12
Penyfai W3
Penyfan W13
Penyffordd* (Buckley/Holywell) W10
Penygraig W18
Penygroes (Carm) W6
Penygroes (Gwynedd) W11
Penymynydd W10
Penyrenglyn W18
Penyrheol W4
Penyrheolferthyr W12
Penyrheolgerrig W12
Penysarn W1
Penywaun W18
Penzance 9.1
Peopleton 49.6
Peover, Inferior (part) 7.3, 7.5
Peover, Superior 7.5
Peper Harow 42.11
Peplow 37.1
Peppard Common 35.3
Pepper Arden (South Cowton) 33.2
Percy Main 43.2
Periton 38.3
Perivale L9
Perkinsville 14.1
Perlethorpe-cum-Budby 34.3
Perranarworthal 9.1
Perrancombe 9.1
Perranporth 9.1
Perranuthnoe 9.1
Perranwell 9.1
Perranzabuloe 9.1
Perrotts Brook 18.5
Perry (Cambs) 6.3
Perry (Kent) 25.6
Perry Barr 45.5
Perry Common 45.5
Perry Green 22.3
Perry Street (Kent) 25.2
Perry Street (Som) 38.5
Perrycrofts 40.9
Pershall 40.4
Pershore 49.6
Pertenhall 2.1
Perth S24
Perthcelyn W18
Perthy 37.1
Perton 40.6
Pertwood 48.1
Peter Tavy 12.3
Peterborough 6.1
Peterburn S17
Peterchurch 21.1
Peterhead S1
Peterlee 14.1
Peters Green 22.1
Peters Marland 12.1
Petersfield 20.6
Petersfinger 48.1
Petersham L27
Peterston-super-Ely W21
Peterstone Wentlooge W15
Peterstow 21.1
Peterville 9.1
Petham 25.5
Petrockstowe 12.1
Petsoe Manor 5.1
Pett 16.2
Pett Bottom 25.5
Pettaugh 41.4
Pettinain S28
Pettistree 41.5
Petton 37.1
Petts Wood L5
Petworth 46.2
Pevensey (E Sussex) 16.1
Pevensey Bay 16.1
Peveril 11.2
Pewsey 48.1
Pewsham 48.1
Pheasey 45.2
Philadelphia 43.5
Philips Park 19.3
Phillack 9.1
Philleigh 9.1
Phillipstown W4
Philpstoun S31
Phocle Green 21.1
Phoenix Green 20.2
Pibsbury 38.5
Picadilly L33
Pickburn 39.2
Pickenham, North & South 30.3
Pickering 33.3
Pickering Nook 14.1
Picket Piece 20.4
Picket Twenty 20.4
Picketston W21

Pickhill with Roxby 33.2
Picklescott 37.1
Pickmere 7.5
Pickney 38.4
Pickstock 37.4
Picktree 14.1
Pickup Bank 26.10
Pickwell 27.3
Pickworth (Lincs) 28.6
Pickworth (Rutland) 36.1
Picton (Cheshire) 7.3
Picton (Flint) W10
Picton (Mersey) 29.2
Picton (N Yorks) 33.2
Picts Cross 21.1
Picts Hill 38.5
Piddinghoe 16.4
Piddington (Bucks) 5.3
Piddington (N'hants) 31.7
Piddington (Oxon) 35.2
Piddlehinton 13.1
Piddletrenthide 13.1
Pidley 6.3
Piercebridge (part) 14.8
Pigdon 32.1
Pikes Hill 20.7
Pilcot 20.2
Pile Marsh 4.1
Pilgrims Hatch 17.9
Pilham 28.1
Pill 38.7
Pill Point 9.1
Pillaton 9.1
Pillerton Hersey 44.5
Pillerton Priors 44.5
Pilleth W17
Pilley 20.7
Pilley (S Yorks) 39.1
Pilley Bailey 20.7
Pilling 26.2
Pillowell 18.2
Pilning 18.7
Pilsdon 13.1
Pilsgate 6.1
Pilsley (Derbyshire Dales) 11.3
Pilsworth 19.3
Piltdown 16.1
Pilton (N'hants) 31.3
Pilton (Rutland) 36.1
Pilton (Som) 38.2
Pilton West 12.2
Pimhole 19.3
Pimlico L33
Pimlico (Herts) (part) 22.5, 22.8
Pimperne 13.2
Pinchbeck 28.7
Pinchinthorpe 33.10
Pineham 25.6
Pineham (Bucks) 5.1
Pinewood 41.6
Pinged W6
Pinkney 48.1
Pinley 45.7
Pinmore S27
Pinner (part) L15
Pinnocks Moor 13.3
Pinvin 49.6
Pinwall 27.4
Pinwherry S27
Pinxton 11.5
Pipe & Lyde 21.1
Pipe Aston 21.1
Pipe Gate (Shrop) 37.1
Pipe Gate (Staffs) 40.2
Pipe Hill 40.8
Pipe Ridware 40.8
Piperhill S17
Pipers Pool 9.1
Pipewell 31.2
Pipton W17
Pirbright 42.7
Pirnmill S21
Pirrie 29.2
Pirton (Herts) 22.1
Pirton (Worcs) 49.6
Pishill 35.3
Pistyll W11
Pitagowan S24
Pitcairngreen S24
Pitcalnie S17
Pitcaple S1
Pitcarity S2
Pitch Green 5.3
Pitchcombe 18.6
Pitchcott 5.2
Pitchcroft 37.4
Pitchford 37.1
Pitcombe 38.5
Pitfour S24
Pitkennedy S2
Pitlessie S16
Pitlochry S24
Pitmedden S1
Pitminster 38.4
Pitney 38.5
Pitroddie S24
Pitsea 17.10
Pitsford 31.4
Pitsford Hill 38.3
Pitstone 5.2
Pitsworthy 38.3
Pitt (Hants) 20.5
Pitt (Som) 38.3
Pittenweem S16
Pittington 14.1
Pitton 48.1
Pittshill 40.3
Pitway 38.5
Pityme 14.1
Pityoulish S17
Pixley 21.1
Pizien Well 25.9
Plaidy 9.1
Plains S22
Plains Farm 43.5
Plaistow L25
Plaistow (W Sussex) 46.2
Plaistow Green 11.6
Plaitford 20.4
Plantation Bridge 10.5
Plas Gwyn W11
Plas Madoc W22
Plas-y-coed W20
Plashetts 32.1
Plasmarl W19
Plaster's Green 38.6
Plasterdown 12.3
Plasterfield S32
Plastow Green 20.1
Platt 25.9
Platt Bridge 19.1
Platts Common 39.1
Platts Heath, Lenham 25.10
Plawsworth 14.1
Plaxtol 25.9
Playden 16.2
Playford 41.5
Playhatch 35.3
Playing Place 9.1
Plealey 37.1
Pleamore Cross 38.4
Plean S29
Pleasington 26.10
Pleasley (part) 11.5, 34.2
Plenmeller with Whitfield 32.1
Pleshey 17.7
Plockton S17
Plompton 33.6
Plot Gate 38.5
Plowden 37.1
Pluckley 25.12
Plucks Gutter 25.6
Pludds 18.2
Plumbland 10.2
Plumgarths 10.5
Plumley 7.5
Plumpton (Cumbria) 10.3
Plumpton (E Sussex) 16.4
Plumpton (Lancs) (see Westby)
Plumpton (N'hants) 31.7
Plumpton Green 16.4
Plumpton Park 47.1
Plumstead L11
Plumstead (Norfolk) 30.1
Plumtree 34.8
Plungar 27.3
Pluscarden S20
Plush 13.1
Plushabridge 9.1
Plymouth 12.8
Plympton 12.8
Plymstock 12.8
Plymtree 12.7
Pockley 33.3
Pocklington 15.2
Pockthorpe 15.2
Podimore 38.5
Podington 2.1
Podsmead 18.3
Point (Corn) 9.1
Point (W Isles) S32
Point Clear 17.4
Pointon 28.6
Pokesdown 13.7
Polbain S17
Polbathic 9.1
Polbeth S31
Pole Moor 47.4
Polebrook 31.3
Polegate 16.1
Polesden Lacey 42.8
Polesworth 44.1
Polgigga 9.1
Polglass S17
Polgooth 9.1
Polhampton 20.1
Poling 46.5
Polkerris (Par) 9.1
Pollard Park 47.1
Pollington 15.2
Polmanter 9.1
Polmont S15
Polmorla 9.1
Polperro 9.1
Polruan 9.1
Polsham 38.2
Polstead 41.6
Poltimore 12.7
Polton S19
Poltonhall S19
Polwarth S30
Polwhele 9.1
Polzeath 9.1
Ponciau W22
Ponden 47.1
Pondersbridge 6.2
Ponsanooth 9.1
Ponsmain 9.1
Ponsonby 10.4
Ponsticill W12
Ponsworthy 12.5
Pontantwm W6
Pontardawe W14
Pontarddulais W19
Pontarfynach W7
Pontarsais W6
Pontblyddyn W10
Pontcanna W5
Pontcynon W18
Pontcysyllte W22
Pontdolgoch W17
Pontefract 47.5
Ponteland 32.1
Pontesbury 37.1
Pontfadog W22
Pontfaen W17
Ponthenry W6
Ponthir (part) W15, W20
Pontlasse W19
Pontllanfraith W4
Pontlliw W19
Pontllogel W17
Pontllyfni W11
Pontlottyn W4
Pontmorlais W12
Pontneathvaughan W14
Pontnewydd W20
Pontprennau W5
Pontrhyddallt W11
Pontrhydycyff W3
Pontrhydyfen W14
Pontrhydyrun W20
Pontrilas 21.1
Pontrobert W17
Pontrug W11
Pontsarn W12
Pontshill 21.1
Pontsticill (Powys) W17

Pontwalby W14
Pontweli W6
Pontyates W6
Pontyberem W6
Pontybodkin W10
Pontyclun W18
Pontycymmer W3
Pontygwaith W18
Pontymister W4
Pontymoile W20
Pontypandy W4
Pontypool W20
Pontypridd W18
Pontyrhyl W3
Pontywaun W4
Pool O'Muckhart S8
Pool Quay W17
Pool-in-Wharfedale 47.2
Pooldole 40.3
Poole (Cheshire) 7.5
Poole (Dorset) 13.6
Poole (Som) 38.4
Poole Keynes 18.5
Poolewe S17
Pooley Bridge 10.3
Poolfields 40.2
Poolham 28.2
Poolhead 37.1
Poolhill 37.4
Poolmill 21.1
Poolsbrook 11.2
Poorton, North & South 13.1
Popham 20.1
Poplar L30
Poplar Farm 44.2
Popley 20.1
Popples 47.3
Porchester (Notts) (part) 34.6, 34.7
Porchfield 24.1
Poringland 30.7
Porkellis 9.1
Porlock 38.3
Porlock Weir 38.3
Porlockford 38.3
Porset (Rudry) W4
Port Askaig S3
Port Charlotte S3
Port Clarence 14.10
Port Dinoric (see Y Felinheli)
Port Ellen S3
Port Eynon W19
Port Gaverne 9.1
Port Glasgow S18
Port Henderson S17
Port Isaac 9.1
Port Logan S10
Port Mulgrave 33.4
Port Quin 9.1
Port Seton S13
Port Sunlight 29.5
Port Talbot W14
Port Tennant W19
Port William S10
Port of Menteith S29
Port of Ness S32
Portbury 38.7
Portchester (part) 20.10, 20.12
Portesham 13.1
Portfield (Pemb) (see Furzy Park)
Portfield (Som) 38.5
Portgordon S20
Porth (Corn) 9.1
Porth (Rhondda) W18
Porth Dinllaen W11
Porth Navas 9.1
Porth-y-waen 37.1
Porthallow 9.1
Porthcawl W3
Porthcurno 9.1
Porthdafen W6
Porthgwarra 9.1
Porthill 40.2
Porthkerry W21
Porthleven 9.1
Porthmadog W11
Porthoustock 9.1
Porthpean 9.1
Porthtowan (part) 9.1
Porthyrhyd (Carmarthen) W6
Porthyrhyd (Llandovery) W6
Portico 29.3
Portington 15.2
Portishead 38.7
Portknockie S20
Portland 13.4
Portlethen S1
Portloe 9.1
Portmahomack S17
Portmellon 9.1
Portmore 20.7
Portnahaven S3
Portnalong S17
Portobello (Edin) S6
Portobello (T & W) 43.3
Porton 48.1
Portpatrick S10
Portreath 9.1
Portree S17
Portscatho 9.1
Portskerra S17
Portskewett W13
Portslade-by-Sea 16.3
Portsmouth (Hants) 20.12
Portsmouth (W Yorks) 47.3
Portsoy S1
Portswood 20.8
Portway (Here) (part) 21.1
Portway (Som) 38.5
Portway (W Mids) 45.4
Portway (Warks) 44.5
Portway (Worcs) (part) 49.2
Portwrinkle 9.1
Posbury 12.4
Poslingford 41.3
Postbridge 12.3
Postcombe 35.3
Postern 11.6
Postling 25.13
Postwick 30.5
Potsgrove 2.2
Pott (see Ilton)
Pott Shrigley 7.5
Potten End (see Nettleden)
Potter Heigham 30.1
Potterhanworth 28.4
Potterne 48.1
Potters Bar 22.10
Potters Cross 40.6
Potters Crouch 22.5
Potters Marston 27.6
Pottershill 38.7
Potterspury 31.7
Potto 33.2
Potton 2.2
Potton Island 17.11
Poughill (Corn) 9.1
Poughill (Devon) 12.4
Poulner 20.7
Poulshot 48.1
Poulton (Cheshire) 7.3
Poulton (Gloucs) 18.5
Poulton with Fearnhead 7.1
Poulton-le-Fylde 26.2
Pound 38.5
Pound Bank (Rock) 49.1
Pound Corner 38.5
Pound Green 3.3
Pound Hill 46.1
Poundon 5.2
Poundsbridge 25.8
Poundsgate 12.5
Poundstock 9.1
Povey Cross (part) 42.8, 46.1
Powderham 12.5
Powerstock 13.1
Powfoot S10
Powick 49.4
Powmill S24
Powntley Copse 20.1
Poxwell 13.1
Poynings 46.4
Poyntington 13.1
Poynton (Shrop) 37.4
Poynton Green 37.4
Poynton with Worth 7.5
Poyntzfield S17
Praa Sands 9.1
Pratts Bottom (part) L5, 25.8
Praze 9.1
Praze-an-Beeble 9.1
Prees 37.1
Prees Green 37.1
Prees Heath 37.1
Prees Wood 37.1
Preesall 26.2
Preese (see Weeton)
Preesgweene 37.1
Premnay S1
Prendergast W16
Prenteg W11
Prenton 29.5
Prescot 29.4
Prescote 35.2
Prescott (Gloucs) 18.1
Prescott (Shrop) 37.1
Preshute 48.1
Press 11.4
Prestatyn W9
Prestbury (Cheshire) 7.5
Presteigne W17
Prestleigh 38.2
Prestolee 19.2
Preston S30
Preston (E Sussex) 16.3
Preston (E Yorks) 15.2
Preston (Gloucs) 18.5
Preston (Herts) 22.1
Preston (Lancs) 26.6
Preston (Rutland) 36.1
Preston (Shrop) 37.4
Preston (Wilts) 48.1
Preston Bagot 44.5
Preston Bissett 5.2
Preston Bowyer 38.4
Preston Brockhurst 37.1
Preston Brook 7.2
Preston Candover 20.1
Preston Capes 31.4
Preston Crowmarsh 35.3
Preston Deanery 31.7
Preston Grange 43.2
Preston Gubbals 37.1
Preston Patrick 10.5
Preston Plucknett 38.5
Preston Richard 10.5
Preston St Mary 41.6
Preston Village 43.2
Preston Wynne 21.1
Preston-le-Skerne 14.1
Preston-on-Stour 44.5
Preston-on-Tees 14.10
Preston-on-Wye 21.1
Preston-on-the-Hill 7.2
Preston-under-Scar 33.1
Preston-upon-the-Weald 37.4
Prestonkirk S13
Prestonpans S13
Prestwich (Gtr M'chester) 19.3
Prestwick S27
Prestwick (N'land) 32.1
Prestwold 27.2
Prestwood 5.4
Prey Heath 42.4
Prickwillow 6.4
Priddy 38.2
Priest Hutton 26.1
Priestfields 33.9
Priestthorpe 47.1
Priestweston (part) 37.1, W17
Primrose Hill L6, 47.4
Primrose Valley 33.4
Princes End 45.4
Princes Gate W16
Princes Risborough 5.3
Princethorpe 44.3
Princetown (Devon) 12.3
Princetown (Rhymney) W4
Prinsted 46.2
Prion W9
Prior's Heys 7.3
Priors Dean 20.6
Priors Frome 21.1
Priors Hardwick 44.5

Priors Marston 44.5
Priorslee 37.4
Priory Wood 21.1
Prisk W21
Priston 38.6
Prittlewell 17.14
Privett 20.6
Prizet 10.5
Probus 9.1
Prospect Village 40.7
Prudhoe 32.1
Publow 38.6
Puckeridge 22.3
Puckington 38.5
Pucklechurch 18.7
Pudding Norton 30.1
Puddington (Cheshire) 7.3
Puddington (Devon) 12.4
Puddle Town (Som) 38.5
Puddlebridge 38.5
Puddletown (Dorset) 13.1
Pudleston 21.1
Pudsey 47.2
Pugeston S2
Pulborough 46.3
Puleston 37.4
Pulford 7.3
Pulham 13.2
Pulham Market 30.7
Pulham St Mary 30.7
Pull Woods 10.5
Pulloxhill 2.2
Pumpherston S31
Pumpsaint W6
Puncheston W16
Puncknowle 13.1
Punnetts Town 16.1
Purbrook 20.13
Purdis Farm 41.5
Purewell 13.8
Purfleet 17.12
Puriton 38.1
Purleigh 17.8
Purley L8
Purley-on-Thames 3.1
Purlogue 37.1
Purse Caundle 13.1
Purslow 37.1
Purston 47.5
Purtington 38.5
Purton 48.1
Purton Stoke 48.1
Pury End 31.7
Pusey 35.4
Puthill 38.5
Putley 21.1
Putney (part) L27, L32
Putney Heath L32
Putney Vale L32
Puttenham (Herts) 22.4
Puttenham (Surrey) 42.7
Puxley 31.7
Puxton 38.7
Pwll W6
Pwllcrochan W16
Pwlldu W13
Pwllglas W9
Pwllheli W11
Pwllmeyric W13
Pwlltrap W6
Pwlly Glaw W14
Pwllypant W4
Pye Bridge (part) 11.6, 34.4
Pye Green 40.7
Pyecombe 46.4
Pyle W3
Pyleigh 38.4
Pylle 38.2
Pymoor 6.4
Pymore (Dorset) 13.1
Pype Hayes 45.5
Pyrford 42.4
Pyrland 38.4
Pyrton 35.3
Pytchley 31.2
Pyworthy 12.1
Quadring 28.7
Quadring Eaudyke 28.7
Quainton 5.2
Quaker's Yard W12
Quaking Houses 14.1
Quanea 6.4
Quar, The W12
Quarff S26
Quarles 30.1
Quarley 20.4
Quarmby 47.4
Quarndon 11.6
Quarnford 40.1
Quarr 24.1
Quarrendon 5.2
Quarrington (Durham) (see Cassop)
Quarrington (Lincs) 28.4
Quarrington Hill 14.1
Quarry Bank 45.3
Quarter S28
Quarter Bach W6
Quatt Malvern 37.1
Quebec 14.1
Quedgeley (part) 18.3, 18.6
Queen Adelaide 6.4
Queen Camel 38.5
Queen Charlton 38.6
Queen's Park 13.7
Queenborough-in-Sheppey 25.4
Queenhill 49.4
Queens Gate L20
Queens Gate (part) L33
Queens Head 37.1
Queensbury 47.1
Queensferry (Flint) W10
Queensnympton 12.2
Queenzieburn S22
Quenby 27.8
Quenchwell 9.1
Quendale S26
Quendon & Rickling 17.1
Queniborough 27.2
Quenington 18.5
Quernmore 26.1
Quethiock 9.1
Quidenham 30.3
Quidhampton (Hants) 20.1
Quidhampton (Wilts) 48.1
Quina Brook 37.1
Quinta 37.1
Quinton (N'hants) 31.7
Quinton (Warks) 44.5
Quintrell Downs 9.1
Quiraing S17
Quoisley (see Marbury)
Quorn 27.2
Quothquan S28
Quy (see Stow)
Raasay S17
Rabley 22.10
Rabley Heath 22.1
Raby 29.5
Raby Mere 29.5
Raby Park 7.3
Raby with Keverstone 14.1
Racecourse 37.1
Rachan S30
Rachub W11
Rackenford 12.2
Rackham 46.3
Rackheath 30.5
Racks S10
Racton 46.2
Radbourne 11.9
Radcliffe (part) 19.2, 19.3
Radcliffe-on-Trent 34.8
Radclive-cum-Chackmore 5.2
Radcot (see Grafton)
Raddington 38.4
Radfall (Whitstable) 25.5
Radford (Notts) 34.6
Radford (W Mids) 45.7
Radford Semele 44.4
Radlett 22.10
Radley 35.4
Radley Green 17.7
Radnage 5.3
Radnor 9.1
Radstock 38.6
Radstone 31.7
Radway 44.5
Radway Green (part) 7.5
Radwell (Beds) 2.1
Radwell (Herts) 22.1
Radwinter 17.1
Radyr W5
Rafford S20
Ragdale 27.3
Ragged Appleshaw 20.4
Raglan W13
Ragnall 34.1
Rainford 29.3
Rainham (Kent) 25.3
Rainham (London) L16
Rainhill 29.3
Rainow 7.5
Rainsbury 38.3
Rainsough 19.3
Rainton Bridge 43.5
Rainton with Newby 33.6
Rainworth (part) 34.2, 34.3
Raisbeck 10.3
Rait S24
Raithby 28.2
Raithby-cum-Maltby 28.2
Rake 46.2
Rakewood 19.4
Raleigh's Cross 38.3
Ram W6
Ram Alley 48.1
Ram Hill 18.7
Rame (see Maker)
Rame Cross 9.1
Rampisham 13.1
Rampside 10.6
Rampton (Cambs) 6.5
Rampton (Notts) 34.1
Ramsaycleuch S30
Ramsbottom 19.3
Ramsbury 48.1
Ramscombe 38.3
Ramsdean 20.6
Ramsdell 20.1
Ramsden 35.1
Ramsden Bellhouse 17.10
Ramsden Heath 17.7
Ramsey (Cambs) 6.3
Ramsey (Essex) 17.4
Ramsey Forty Foot 6.3
Ramsey Heights 6.3
Ramsey Mereside 6.3
Ramsey St Mary's 6.3
Ramsgate 25.7
Ramsgreave 26.3
Ramshaw 14.1
Ramsholt 41.5
Ramshorn 40.5
Ranby (Lincs) 28.2
Ranby (Notts) 34.1
Rand 28.1
Rand Grange 33.2
Randlay 37.4
Randlay Fields 37.4
Randwick 18.6
Rangemore 40.5
Rangeworthy 18.7
Rankinston S11
Ranmore 42.8
Rannoch Station S24
Ranskill 34.1
Ranton 40.4
Rapps 38.5
Raskelf 33.2
Rassau W2
Rastrick 47.3
Ratby 27.4
Ratcliffe Culey 27.4
Ratcliffe-on-Soar 34.8
Ratcliffe-on-the-Wreake 27.2
Ratford 48.1
Rathen S1
Rathillet S16
Rathmell 33.5
Ratho S6
Ratho Station S6
Rathven (Buckie) S20
Ratley 44.5
Ratlinghope 37.1
Rattery 12.9
Rattlesden 41.4
Rattray S24

Raughton Head (part) 10.1, 10.3
Raunds 31.3
Raveleys, The, Gt & Little 6.3
Ravenfield 39.4
Ravenhill W19
Raveningham 30.7
Ravenscar 33.4
Ravenscliffe 47.1
Ravensdale Park 11.6
Ravensden 2.1
Ravensfleet 28.1
Ravenshead 34.7
Ravensmoor 7.5
Ravensthorpe (Cambs) 6.1
Ravensthorpe (N'hants) 31.4
Ravensthorpe (W Yorks) 47.4
Ravenstone (Bucks) 5.1
Ravenstone (Leics) 27.1
Ravenstonedale 10.3
Ravenstown 10.5
Ravenstruther S28
Ravensworth 33.1
Rawcliffe (E Yorks) 15.2
Rawcliffe (York) 33.7
Rawdon 47.2
Rawmarsh 39.4
Rawnsley 40.7
Rawreth 17.11
Rawtenstall 26.14
Rawthorpe 47.4
Raydon 41.6
Rayleigh 17.11
Rayne (Aberdeen) S1
Rayne (Essex) 17.2
Raynes Park L24
Raynes Park (part) L21
Raynham 30.1
Reach (Beds) 2.2
Reach (Cambs) 6.4
Read 26.3
Reading 3.2
Reading Street (Tenterden) 25.12
Ready Token 18.5
Reagill 10.3
Rearsby 27.2
Reaseheath 7.5
Reawick S26
Reay S17
Rectory Farm 31.5
Reculver 25.5
Red Hill (Shrop) 37.1
Red Hill (Som) 38.5
Red House 43.5
Red Lake 37.4
Red Lodge 41.2
Red Post Cross 38.5
Red Roses W6
Red Row 32.1
Red Scar 26.6
Red Street 40.2
Red Wharf Bay W1
Redberth W16
Redbourn 22.5
Redbourne 28.8
Redbridge L26
Redbridge (Hants) 20.8
Redbrook (Gloucs/Monmth) (part) 18.2, W13
Redburn 32.1
Redburn Row 43.5
Redcar 33.10
Redcastle S17
Redcliff 4.1
Redcliff Bay 38.7
Redding S15
Reddingmuirhead S15
Redditch 49.3
Rede 41.3
Redenhall with Harleston 30.7
Redenham 20.4
Redesmouth 32.1
Redfield 4.1
Redfields Industrial Park 20.2
Redford (Angus) S2
Redford (W Sussex) 46.2
Redgorton S24
Redgrave 41.4
Redhill (Herts) 22.1
Redhill (Notts) 34.7
Redhill (Som) 38.7
Redhill (Surrey) 42.9
Redhill Park 13.7
Redhouse Park 5.1
Redisham 41.1
Redland 4.1
Redlands 38.5
Redlingfield 41.4
Redlynch (Som) 38.5
Redlynch (Wilts) 48.1
Redmarley D'Abitot 18.2
Redmarshall 14.10
Redmile 27.3
Redmire 33.1
Redmoor 9.1
Redmoor (Bucks) 5.1
Rednal (Shrop) 37.1
Rednal (W Mids) 45.5
Redpoint S17
Redruth 9.1
Redvales 19.3
Redwick (Gloucs) 18.7
Redwick (Newport) W15
Reed 22.1
Reedham 30.5
Reedley Hallows 26.13
Reedness 15.2
Reedsholme 26.14
Reepham (Lincs) 28.1
Reepham (Norfolk) 30.5
Reeth 33.1
Reiff S17
Reigate 42.9
Reighton 33.4
Reiss S17
Releath 9.1
Relubbus 9.1
Remenham 3.3
Rempstone 34.8
Rendall S23
Rendcomb 18.5
Rendham 41.5
Rendlesham 41.5
Renfrew S25
Renhold 2.1
Renishaw (part) 11.4, 11.5
Rennington 32.1
Renton S9
Renwick 10.3
Repps with Bastwick 30.6
Repton 11.9
Rescorla (Penwithick, St Austell) 9.1
Reskadinnick 9.1
Reskivers 9.1
Resolis S17
Resolven W14
Reston (Borders) S30
Reston (Cumbria) 10.5
Restronguet 9.1
Restronguet Point 9.1
Retford 34.1
Rettendon 17.7
Revesby 28.2
Rewe 12.7
Reybridge 48.1
Reydon with Easton Bavents 41.1
Reymerston 30.3
Reynalton W16
Reynoldston W19
Rhandirmwyn W6
Rhayader W17
Rhesycae W10
Rhewl W9
Rhewl Mostyn W10
Rhiews 37.1
Rhigos W18
Rhinefield 20.7
Rhiroy S17
Rhiw (Conwy) W8
Rhiw (Gwynedd) W11
Rhiwbina W5
Rhiwceiliog W3
Rhiwfawr W14
Rhiwlas (Gwynedd) W11
Rhiwlas (Monmth) W13
Rhodes (part) 19.3, 19.4
Rhodes Minnis 25.13
Rhodesia 34.1
Rhodogeidio W1
Rhodyate 38.7
Rhondda W18
Rhonehouse S10
Rhoose W21
Rhos (Carm) W6
Rhos (Neath) W14
Rhos Isaf W11
Rhos on Sea W8
Rhosbodrual W11
Rhoscefnhir W1
Rhoscolyn W1
Rhoscrowther W16
Rhosddu (Wrexham) W22
Rhosesmor W10
Rhosfawr W11
Rhosferig W17
Rhosgadfan W11
Rhosgoch W1
Rhoshirwaun W11
Rhoslan W11
Rhoslefain W11
Rhosllanerchrugog W22
Rhosmaen W6
Rhosmeirch W1
Rhosneigr W1
Rhosrobin W22
Rhossili W19
Rhostrehwfa W1
Rhostryfan W11
Rhostyllen W22
Rhoswiel 37.1
Rhosybol W1
Rhosygwaliau W11
Rhu (Highland) S17
Rhuallt W9
Rhuddlan W9
Rhulen W17
Rhum S17
Rhuthun W9
Rhyd W11
Rhyd-Ddu W11
Rhyd-y-clafdy W11
Rhyd-y-foel W8
Rhydargaeau W6
Rhydcymerau W6
Rhyddings W14
Rhydlios W11
Rhydlydan W8
Rhydowen W6
Rhydtalog W10
Rhyduchaf W11
Rhydwyn W1
Rhydycar W12
Rhydycroesau 37.1
Rhydyfelin W18
Rhydyfro W14
Rhydygwern Machen W4
Rhydymain W11
Rhydymwyn W10
Rhydypandy W19
Rhyl W9
Rhymney (Caerphilly) W4
Rhymney Bridge W4
Rhynd S24
Rhyndwyclydach W19
Rhynie S1
Ribbesford 49.1
Ribblehead Part 33.5
Ribchester 26.3
Riber 11.3
Ribston, Gt with Walshford 33.6
Ribston, Little 33.6
Riby 28.1
Riccall 33.8
Rich's Holford 38.4
Richards Castle (part) 21.1, 37.1
Richborough 25.6
Richdore (Waltham) 25.5
Richmond (N Yorks) 33.1
Richmond upon Thames (part) L21, L27
Rickerby 10.1
Rickford 38.7

Rickinghall, Inferior & Superior 41.4
Rickleton (part) 14.1, 43.5
Rickling (see Quendon)
Rickmansworth 22.8
Riddings 11.6
Riddlesden 47.1
Riddlesworth 30.3
Ridge (Dorset) 13.5
Ridge (Herts) 22.10
Ridge Hill 21.1
Ridge Lane 44.1
Ridgehill (Som) 38.7
Ridgeway (Bristol/Som) 38.2
Ridgeway (S Yorks/Derbys) (part) 11.4, 39.3
Ridgewell 17.2
Ridgewood 16.1
Ridgmont 2.2
Ridgwardine 37.1
Riding Gate 38.5
Riding Mill 32.1
Ridley (Cheshire) 7.5
Ridley (Kent) 25.8
Ridley (N'land) 32.1
Ridlington (Norfolk) 30.1
Ridlington (Rutland) 36.1
Rievaulx 33.3
Rigg S10
Righoul S17
Rigsby with Ailby 28.2
Rigside S28
Rigton (see Bardsey)
Rigton North 33.6
Riley Hill 40.8
Rilla Mill 9.1
Rillington 33.3
Rimington 26.3
Rimpton 38.5
Rimswell 15.2
Ring's End 6.2
Ringford S10
Ringinglow 39.3
Ringland 30.5
Ringley (part) 19.2, 19.3
Ringmer 16.4
Ringmore 12.9
Ringsfield 41.1
Ringshall (Suffolk) 41.4
Ringshall (part) 5.2, 22.4
Ringstead (N'hants) 31.3
Ringstead (Norfolk) 30.2
Ringstead Bay 13.1
Ringtail Green 17.7
Ringway 19.6
Ringwood (Dorest/Hants) (part) 20.7
Ringwood (Dorset/Hants) (part) 13.3
Ringwould 25.6
Ripe 16.1
Ripley (Derbys) 11.6
Ripley (Hants) 20.7
Ripley (N Yorks) 33.6
Ripley (Surrey) 42.7
Ripon 33.6
Rippingale 28.6
Ripple (Kent) 25.6
Ripple (Worcs) 49.4
Ripponden 47.3
Risby (Lincs) (see Roxby cum Risby)
Risby (Suffolk) 41.3
Risca W4
Riscombe 38.3
Rise 15.2
Rise Park 34.6
Rise, The (Llanbradach) W4
Riseholme 28.1
Riseley 2.1
Rishangles 41.4
Rishton 26.11
Rishworth 47.3
Rising Bridge 26.14
Rising Sun 9.1
Risinghurst & Sandhills 35.5
Risley (Cheshire) 7.1
Risley (Derbys) 11.8
Riston 15.2
Rivacre 7.3
Rivenhall 17.2
River (Kent) 25.6
River (W Sussex) 46.2
Riverhead 25.8
Rivermead 48.2
Riversdale 11.6
Riverside (Cardiff) W5
Riverside (Mersey) 29.2
Riverside (Worcs) 49.3
Riversway 26.6
Rivington 26.9
Rivock 47.1
Rixton with Glazebrook 7.1
Roa Island 10.6
Roade 31.7
Roadhead 10.1
Roadside W8
Roadside of Kinneff S1
Roadwater 38.3
Roanhead 10.6
Roath W5
Roberton (Borders) S30
Roberton (S Lanarks) S28
Robertsbridge 16.2
Robertstown W18
Roberttown 47.4
Robeston Wathen W16
Robeston West W16
Robin Hood (W Yorks) 47.2
Robin Hood's Bay 33.4
Robinson's End 44.2
Roborough* 12.1
Robsheugh 32.1
Roby (see Huyton)
Rocester 40.5
Roch (see Nolton)
Rochdale 19.4
Roche 9.1
Rochester (Kent) 25.3
Rochester (N'land) 32.1
Rochford 49.4
Rochford (Essex) 17.11
Rochford (Here) 21.1
Rock (Corn) 9.1
Rock (Worcs) 49.1
Rock Cross (Rock) 49.1
Rock Ferry 29.5
Rock, The 37.4
Rockall S32
Rockbeare 12.7
Rockbourne 20.7
Rockcliffe (Cumbria) 10.1
Rockcliffe (Dumfries) S10
Rockfield W13
Rockford 20.7
Rockhampton 18.7
Rockingham 31.1
Rockland All Saints 30.3
Rockland St Mary 30.7
Rockland St Peter 30.3
Rocklands 30.3
Rockley (Notts) 34.1
Rockley (Wilts) 48.1
Rockwell End 5.3
Rockwell Green 38.4
Rocombe 12.5
Rodborough 18.6
Rodbourne 48.1
Rodd, Nash & Little Brampton 21.1
Roddam 32.1
Rodden 13.1
Roddymoor 14.1
Rode 38.2
Rode Heath 7.5
Rodel S32
Roden 37.4
Rodgrove 38.5
Rodhuish 38.3
Rodington 37.4
Rodley 47.2
Rodmarton 18.5
Rodmell 16.4
Rodmersham 25.4
Rodney Stoke 38.2
Rodsley 11.3
Roeburndale 26.1
Roecliffe 33.6
Roedean 16.3
Roehampton L32
Roffey 46.3
Rogart S17
Rogate 46.2
Roger Ground 10.5
Rogerstone (part) W4, W15
Rogiet W13
Roke 35.3
Rokeby 14.1
Rokemarsh 35.3
Roker 43.5
Rollesby 30.6
Rolleston (Leics) 27.8
Rolleston (Notts) 34.3
Rolleston-on-Dove (Staffs) 40.5
Rollright 35.1
Rolphy Green 17.7
Rolston 15.2
Rolstone 38.7
Rolvenden 25.12
Romaldkirk 14.1
Romanby 33.2
Romansleigh 12.2
Romford L16
Romiley 19.9
Romney Marsh 25.13
Romney Street 25.8
Romsey 20.4
Romsey Extra 20.4
Romsley (Shrop) 37.1
Romsley (Worcs) 49.2
Rona (Highland) S17
Rona (W Isles) S32
Rood End 45.4
Rook's Nest 38.3
Rookham 38.2
Rookhope 14.1
Rookley 24.1
Rooksbridge 38.1
Rooksley 5.1
Rookwith 33.2
Roos 15.2
Roose 10.6
Rope 7.5
Ropehaugh 32.1
Ropley 20.6
Ropsley 28.6
Rora S1
Rorrington 37.1
Roscroggan 9.1
Rose 9.1
Rose Ash 12.2
Rose Green (Bristol) 4.1
Rose Green (W Sussex) 46.5
Rose Hill (Corn) 9.1
Rose Hill (Oxon) 35.5
Roseacre 26.5
Rosebank S28
Rosedale, East & West 33.3
Rosegrove 26.12
Rosehall S17
Rosehearty S1
Rosehill (Lancs) 26.12
Rosehill (Shrop) 37.1
Roseisle S20
Rosemarket W16
Rosemarkie S17
Rosemount S24
Rosemundy 9.1
Rosenannon 9.1
Roseville 45.3
Rosevine 9.1
Rosewell S19
Roseworth 14.10
Roseworthy* 9.1
Rosgill 10.3
Roslin S19
Rosliston 11.9
Ross 45.4
Ross Rural 21.1
Ross-on-Wye 21.1
Rossendale 26.14
Rossett W22
Rosside 10.5
Rossie Braes S2
Rossington 39.2
Rossmoor 15.2
Rostherne 7.5
Roston 11.3
Rosudgeon 9.1
Rosyth S16

Rothbury 32.1
Rotherby 27.3
Rotherfield 16.1
Rotherfield Greys 35.3
Rotherfield Peppard 35.3
Rotherham 39.4
Rotherhithe L28
Rothersthorpe 31.7
Rotherwas 21.1
Rotherwick 20.2
Rothes S20
Rothesay S3
Rothiemay S20
Rothienorman S1
Rothley (Leics) 27.2
Rothley (N'land) 32.1
Rothwell (Lincs) 28.1
Rothwell (N'hants) 31.2
Rothwell (W Yorks) 47.2
Rottingdean 16.3
Rotton Park 45.5
Roudham 30.3
Rough Close 40.4
Rough Common (Harbledown) 25.5
Rough Park 37.4
Rougham (Norfolk) 30.3
Rougham (Suffolk) (see Rushbrooke)
Roughlee Booth 26.13
Roughmoor 48.2
Roughton (Lincs) 28.2
Roughton (Norfolk) 30.1
Roughway 25.9
Round Spinney 31.5
Roundbush 22.10
Roundham 38.5
Roundhurst 46.2
Rounds Green 45.4
Roundthwaite 10.3
Roundway 48.1
Roundwood 47.5
Roundyhill S2
Rous Lench 49.6
Rousay S23
Rousham 35.1
Routh 15.2
Rowanburn S10
Rowarth 11.1
Rowberrow 38.1
Rowde 48.1
Rowell 10.5
Roweltown 10.1
Rowfoot 32.1
Rowhedge 17.3
Rowington 44.4
Rowland 11.3
Rowlands Castle 20.6
Rowlands Gill 43.3
Rowledge (part) 20.6, 42.11
Rowlestone 21.1
Rowley (E Yorks) 15.2
Rowley (Shrop) 37.1
Rowley Regis (part) 45.3, 45.4
Rowley's Green (part) 44.2, 45.7
Rowling 25.6
Rownall 40.1
Rowner 20.11
Rowney Green 49.2
Rownhams 20.4
Rowsham 5.2
Rowsley 11.3
Rowstock 35.4
Rowston 28.4
Rowthorne 11.5
Rowton (Cheshire) 7.3
Rowton (Shrop) 37.4
Rowtown 42.1
Roxburgh S30
Roxby 33.4
Roxby (see Pickhill with Roxby)
Roxby-cum-Risby 28.8
Roxholm 28.4
Roxton 2.1
Roxwell 17.7
Roy Bridge S17
Roydon (Essex) 17.6
Roydon (Norfolk)* 30.2, 30.7
Royston (Herts) 22.1
Royston (S Yorks) 39.1
Royston Water 38.4
Royton 19.7
Ruabon W22
Ruan Minor 9.1
Ruanhighlanes 9.1
Ruanlanihorne 9.1
Ruardean 18.2
Ruardean Hill 18.2
Ruardean Woodside 18.2
Rubery (part) 45.5, 49.2
Ruckcroft 10.3
Ruckhall Common 21.1
Ruckinge 25.12
Ruckland 28.2
Ruckley 37.1
Rudbaxton W16
Rudby 33.2
Rudchester 32.1
Ruddington 34.8
Ruddlemoor 9.1
Rudford & Highleadon 18.2
Rudge (Shrop) 37.1
Rudge (Som) 38.2
Rudgeway 18.7
Rudgwick 46.3
Rudheath 7.3
Rudloe 48.1
Rudry W4
Rudston 15.2
Rudyard 40.1
Rueval S32
Ruewood 37.1
Rufford (Lancs) 26.8
Rufford (Notts) 34.3
Rufforth 33.7
Rugby 44.3
Rugeley 40.7
Ruggin 38.4
Ruishton 38.4
Ruleholme 10.1
Rumbling Bridge S24
Rumburgh 41.1
Rumford (Corn) 9.1
Rumford (Falkirk) S15
Rumwell 38.4
Runcorn 7.2
Runcton 46.2
Runcton Holme 30.2
Runfold 42.11
Runhall 30.7
Runham 30.6
Runham Vauxhall 30.6
Runnington 38.4
Runsell Green 17.7
Runswick Bay 33.4
Runton, East & West 30.1
Runwell 17.7
Ruscombe (Berks) 3.3
Ruscombe (Gloucs) 18.6
Rush Green (part) L16
Rushall (Norfolk) 30.7
Rushall (W Mids) 45.2
Rushall (Wilts) 48.1
Rushbrooke with Rougham 41.3
Rushbury 37.1
Rushden (Herts) 22.1
Rushden (N'hants) 31.3
Rushenden 25.4
Rushey Platt 48.2
Rushford 30.3
Rushlake Green 16.1
Rushmere (N'hants) 31.5
Rushmere (Suffolk) 41.1
Rushmere St Andrew 41.5
Rushmoor (Tilford) 42.11
Rushock 49.1
Rusholme 19.6
Rushton (Cheshire) 7.3
Rushton (N'hants) 31.2
Rushton (Staffs) 40.1
Rushwick 49.4
Ruskington 28.4
Rusland 10.5
Rusper 46.3
Ruspidge 18.2
Russell Green 17.7
Russell Town 4.1
Russells Water 35.3
Rusthall 25.11
Rustington 46.5
Ruston 33.4
Ruston Parva 15.2
Ruswarp 33.4
Rutherglen S28
Ruthernbridge 9.1
Ruthin W9
Ruthven S2
Ruthvenfield S24
Ruthvoes (St Columb) 9.1
Ruthwell S10
Ruyton-XI-Towns (part) 37.1
Ryal 32.1
Ryall 13.1
Ryarsh 25.9
Rycote 35.3
Rydal 10.5
Ryde 24.1
Rye 16.2
Rye Bank 37.1
Rye Foreign 16.2
Rye Harbour 16.2
Ryecroft 47.1
Ryecroft Gate 40.1
Ryeford 21.1
Ryhall 36.1
Ryhill (E Yorks) 15.2
Ryhill (W Yorks) 47.5
Ryhope 43.5
Rylstone 33.5
Ryme Intrinseca 13.1
Ryston 30.2
Ryther-cum-Ossendyke 33.8
Ryton (N Yorks) 33.3
Ryton (Shrop) 37.1
Ryton (T & W) 43.3
Ryton-on-Dunsmore 44.3
Sabden 26.3
Sacombe 22.3
Sacriston 14.1
Sadberge 14.8
Saddington 27.8
Saddleworth 19.7
Saffron Walden 17.1
Saham Toney 30.3
Saighton 7.3
St Abbs S30
St Agnes (Cornwall) 9.1
St Agnes (Scilly) 50.1
St Albans 22.5
St Allen 9.1
St Andrews S16
St Andrews (Orkney) S23
St Andrews Major W21
St Ann Without 16.4
St Annes 26.5
St Annes (Bristol) 4.1
St Annes Park 4.1
St Anns S10
St Anns (Gwynedd) W11
St Anns (Kent) 25.4
St Anns (Notts) 34.6
St Anns Chapel 9.1
St Anthony's 43.1
St Anthony-in-Meneage 9.1
St Arvans W13
St Asaph W9
St Athan W21
St Audries 38.3
St Augustines 11.2
St Austell 9.1
St Bees 10.4
St Blazey 9.1
St Boltophs 46.3
St Boswells S30
St Breock 9.1
St Breward 9.1
St Briavels 18.2
St Brides (see Marloes)
St Brides Major (Vale Glam) W21
St Brides Netherwent W13
St Brides Wentlooge W15
St Brides-super-Ely W21
St Bridget Beckermet 10.4
St Buryan 9.1
St Catherine 38.6
St Catherine's S3

St Clears W6
St Cleer 9.1
St Clement 9.1
St Clement's 35.5
St Clether 9.1
St Columb Major 9.1
St Columb Minor 9.1
St Combs S1
St Cosmus & St Damian in the Blean 25.5
St Cuthbert Out 38.2
St Cuthbert Without 10.1
St Cyrus S1
St Damian (see St Cosmus)
St Davids S24
St Davids & Cathedral Close W16
St Day (part) 9.1
St Decumans 38.3
St Dennis 9.1
St Denys 20.8
St Devereux 21.1
St Dials W20
St Dogmaels W16
St Dogwells W16
St Dominick 9.1
St Donats W21
St Edrins (see Hayscastle)
St Endellion 9.1
St Enoder 9.1
St Erme 9.1
St Erth 9.1
St Erth Praze 9.1
St Ervan 9.1
St Eval 9.1
St Ewe 9.1
St Fagans W5
St Fergus S1
St Fillans S24
St Florence W16
St Gabriel's 43.5
St Gennys 9.1
St George (Bristol) 4.1
St George (Conwy) W8
St Georges (Shrop) 37.4
St Georges (Som) 38.7
St Georges (Worcs) 49.3
St Georges Hill 42.5
St Georges-super-Ely W21
St Germans 9.1
St Giles (see Brough)
St Giles-in-the-Wood 12.1
St Giles-on-the-Heath 12.1
St Gluvias 9.1
St Goran 9.1
St Harmon W17
St Helen Without 35.4
St Helens (I of W) 24.1
St Helens (Mersey) 29.3
St Helens Auckland 14.1
St Hilary (Corn) 9.1
St Hilary (Vale Glam) W21
St Hilda's 33.9
St Ipollitts 22.1
St Ishmael W6
St Ishmaels W16
St Issells W16
St Issey 9.1
St Ive 9.1
St Ives (Cambs) 6.3
St Ives (Corn) 9.1
St James L33
St James (N'hants) 31.5
St John 9.1
St John Beckermet 10.4
St John Without 16.4
St John's 42.4
St John's & Castlerigg 10.2
St John's Chapel 14.1
St Johns Wood (part) L6, L33
St Just 9.1
St Just-in-Roseland 9.1
St Keverne 9.1
St Kew 9.1
St Kew Highway 9.1
St Keyne 9.1
St Kilda S32
St Lawrence (Essex) 17.8
St Lawrence (I of W) 24.1
St Lawrence (Pemb) (see Hayscastle)
St Lawrence (Ramsgate) (Kent) 25.7
St Leonard Shoreditch L12
St Leonards & St Ives (Dorset) 13.3
St Leonards (Bucks) (see Cholesbury)
St Leonards-on-Sea 16.6
St Levan 9.1
St Lythans W21
St Mabyn 9.1
St Madoes S24
St Margaret's Hope S23
St Margaret's Island W16
St Margarets (Here) 21.1
St Margarets Bay 25.6
St Margarets-at-Cliffe 25.6
St Martha 42.7
St Martin (Corn) 9.1
St Martin Without 6.1
St Martin's (Scilly) 50.1
St Martin-in-Meneage 9.1
St Martins (N Yorks) 33.1
St Martins (Perth) S24
St Martins (Shrop) (part) 37.1
St Mary Bourne 20.1
St Mary Cray L5
St Mary Hill W21
St Mary Hoo 25.3
St Mary in the Marsh 25.13
St Mary's (Mersey) 29.2
St Mary's (Scilly) 50.1
St Mary's Bay 25.13
St Mary's Island 25.3
St Mary-out-Liberty W16
St Marychurch W21
St Maughans W13
St Mawes 9.1
St Mawgan-in-Pydar 9.1
St Mellion 9.1
St Mellons (part) W5, W15
St Merryn 9.1
St Mewan 9.1
St Michael (Herts) 22.5
St Michael Caerhays 9.1
St Michael Penkevil 9.1
St Michael's Mount 9.1
St Michaels-on-Wyre 26.2
St Minver, Highlands & Lowlands 9.1
St Monans S16
St Neot 9.1
St Neots 6.3
St Newlyn East 9.1
St Nicholas (Pemb) W16
St Nicholas (Vale Glam) W21
St Nicholas Hurst 3.3
St Nicholas-at-Wade 25.7
St Nicolas Park 44.2
St Ola S23
St Olaves 30.6
St Osyth 17.4
St Owens Cross 21.1
St Pancras L6
St Paul's (Bristol) 4.1
St Paul's Cray L5
St Paul's Walden 22.1
St Peter-the-Great (part) 49.5
St Peters 25.7
St Petrox (see Stackpole Elidor)
St Philips 4.1
St Phillips Marsh 4.1
St Pinnock 9.1
St Quivox S27
St Sampson 9.1
St Stephen (Herts) 22.5
St Stephen-in-Brannel 9.1
St Stephens-by-Launceston 9.1
St Teath 9.1
St Thomas (Corn) 9.1
St Thomas (Swansea) W19
St Tudwal's Island (East & West) W11
St Tudy 9.1
St Twynnells W16
St Veep 9.1
St Vigeans S2
St Wenn 9.1
St Weonards 21.1
St Winnow 9.1
Saintbridge 18.3
Saintbury 18.5
Salcombe 12.9
Salcot & Virley 17.3
Sale 19.8
Saleby with Thoresthorpe 28.2
Salehurst 16.2
Salem (Carm) W6
Salem (Swansea) W19
Salen (Argyll & Bute) S3
Salen (Highland) S17
Salendine Nook 47.4
Salesbury 26.3
Salford (Beds) 2.2
Salford (Gtr M'chester) 19.5
Salford (Oxon) 35.1
Salford (Powys) W17
Salford Priors 44.5
Salfords 42.9
Salhouse 30.5
Saline S16
Salings, The (Bardfield Saling & Great Saling) 17.2
Salisbury 48.1
Salle 30.5
Salmonby 28.2
Salperton 18.5
Salsburgh S22
Salt 40.4
Saltaire 47.1
Saltash 9.1
Saltburn 33.10
Saltburn (Highland) S17
Saltby 27.3
Saltcoats S21
Saltdean, East 16.4
Saltdean, West 16.3
Saltend 15.2
Salterforth 26.13
Salters Heath 20.1
Saltersgill 33.9
Salterton 48.1
Saltfleet Haven (see Skidbrooke)
Saltfleetby All Saints 28.2
Saltfleetby St Clement 28.2
Saltfleetby St Peter 28.2
Saltford 38.6
Salthouse 30.1
Saltley 45.5
Saltmarsh (E Yorks) 15.2
Saltney (part) 7.3, W10
Saltney Ferry W10
Salton 33.3
Saltoun S13
Saltwick 32.1
Saltwood 25.13
Salvington 46.6
Salwarpe 49.6
Salway Ash 13.1
Salwick 26.5
Sambourne 44.5
Sambrook (part) 37.1, 37.4
Samlesbury & Cuerdale 26.7
Sampford Arundel 38.4
Sampford Brett 38.3
Sampford Courtenay 12.3
Sampford Peverell 12.4
Sampford Spiney 12.3
Sancreed 9.1
Sancton 15.2
Sand S17
Sand Bay 38.7
Sand Hutton* 33.3
Sandal 47.5
Sanday S23
Sandbach 7.5
Sandbank S3
Sandbanks 13.6
Sandbeds 47.3
Sandbeds (Cullingworth) 47.1

Sandbeds (Keighley) 47.1
Sandbeds (Queensbury) 47.1
Sandend S1
Sandfields W14
Sandford S28
Sandford (Cumbria) 10.3
Sandford (Devon) 12.4
Sandford (Dorset) 13.5
Sandford (Hants) 20.7
Sandford (Shrop) 37.1
Sandford (Som) 38.7
Sandford Batch 38.7
Sandford Hill 40.3
Sandford Orcas 13.1
Sandford St Martin 35.1
Sandford-on-Thames 35.3
Sandgate 25.13
Sandhall 15.2
Sandhaven S1
Sandhead S10
Sandhill Park 38.4
Sandhills (Oxon) (see Risinghurst)
Sandhills (Surrey) 42.11
Sandhills (W Mids) 45.2
Sandhoe 32.1
Sandholme (see Scalby)
Sandhurst (Berks) 3.6
Sandhurst (Gloucs) 18.1
Sandhurst (Kent) 25.11
Sandhutton* 33.2
Sandiacre 11.8
Sandilands S28
Sandiway 7.3
Sandleheath 20.7
Sandling* 25.10, 25.13
Sandness S26
Sandon (Essex) 17.7
Sandon (Herts) 22.1
Sandon (Staffs) 40.4
Sandown 24.1
Sandplace 9.1
Sandridge 22.5
Sandringham 30.2
Sandscale 10.6
Sandsend 33.4
Sandside (Beetham) 10.5
Sandside (Kirkby) 10.5
Sandway 25.10
Sandwell 45.4
Sandwich 25.6
Sandwich Bay 25.6
Sandwick S26
Sandwick (Orkney) S23
Sandy 2.2
Sandy Bank 28.2
Sandy Cove W8
Sandy Lane (W Yorks) 47.1
Sandy Lane (Wilts) 48.1
Sandycroft W10
Sandyford (Staffs) 40.3
Sandyford (T & W) 43.1
Sandyway 38.3
Sanquhar S10
Sansaw 37.1
Santon (Cumbria) (see Irton)
Santon (Lincs) 28.8
Santon Downham (part) 30.3, 41.2
Sapcote 27.6
Sapiston 41.3
Sapley 6.3
Sapperton (Gloucs) 18.5
Sapperton (Lincs) 28.6
Saracens Head 28.7
Sardis* W6, W16
Saredon 40.6
Sarisbury 20.10
Sarn (Bridgend) W3
Sarn (Flint) W10
Sarn (Powys) W17
Sarn Bach W11
Sarn Mellteyrn W11
Sarnau (Gwynedd) W11
Sarnau (Powys) W17
Sarnay W17
Sarnesfield 21.1
Saron (Carm) W6
Saron (Denbigh) W9
Saron, Llanwda W11
Sarratt 22.8
Sarre 25.7
Sarsden 35.1
Satley 14.1
Satterleigh 12.2
Satterthwaite 10.5
Satwell 35.3
Saucher S24
Sauchie S8
Saughall 7.3
Saughall Massie 29.5
Saughtree S30
Saul 18.6
Saundby 34.1
Saundersfoot W16
Saunderton 5.3
Sausthorpe 28.2
Saverley Green 40.4
Savernake 48.1
Savile Town 47.4
Sawbridge 44.3
Sawbridgeworth (part) 17.6, 22.3
Sawdon 33.4
Sawley (Derbys) 11.8
Sawley (Lancs) 26.3
Sawley (Leics) 27.1
Sawley (N Yorks) 33.6
Sawmills 11.6
Sawston 6.5
Sawtry 6.3
Saxby (Leics) 27.3
Saxby (Lincs) 28.1
Saxby All Saints 28.8
Saxelby 27.3
Saxilby with Ingleby 28.1
Saxlingham 30.1
Saxlingham Green 30.7
Saxlingham Nethergate 30.7
Saxlingham Thorpe 30.7
Saxmundham 41.5
Saxon Street 6.4
Saxondale 34.8
Saxonfields 40.3
Saxtead 41.5
Saxthorpe 30.1
Saxton-cum-Scarthingwell 33.8
Scackleton 33.3
Scaftworth 34.1
Scagglethorpe 33.3
Scalby 33.4
Scalby & Sandholme 15.2
Scaldwell 31.4
Scaleby 10.1
Scaleby Hill 10.1
Scales 10.5
Scalford 27.3
Scaling (part) 33.4, 33.10
Scalloway S26
Scalpay (Highland) S17
Scalpay (W Isles) S32
Scalthwaiterigg 10.5
Scamblesby 28.2
Scammonden (part) 47.3, 47.4
Scampston 33.3
Scampton 28.1
Scapegoat Hill 47.4
Scar Top 47.1
Scarborough 33.4
Scarcliffe 11.5
Scarcroft 47.2
Scardroy S17
Scarfskerry S17
Scargill 14.1
Scarinish S3
Scarisbrick 26.8
Scarlet Heights 47.1
Scarletts 3.3
Scarning 30.3
Scarrington 34.8
Scarthingwell (see Saxton)
Scartho 28.9
Scatwell S17
Scawby 28.8
Scawby Brooke 28.8
Scawsby 39.2
Scawthorpe 39.2
Scawton 33.3
Scaynes Hill 46.4
Scethrog W17
Scholar Green 7.5
Scholemoor 47.1
Scholes 47.2
Scholes (Cleckheaton) 47.4
Scholes (Holmfirth) 47.4
Scholes (Rotherham) 39.4
School Green 47.1
Scissett 47.4
Scleddau W16
Sco Ruston 30.1
Scole 30.7
Sconce 47.1
Scone S24
Sconser S17
Scopwick 28.4
Scoraig S17
Scorrier (part) 9.1
Scorton 26.2, 33.1
Scosthrop 33.5
Scot Hay 40.2
Scotby 10.1
Scotforth 26.1
Scotgate 47.4
Scothern 28.1
Scotland Gate 32.1
Scotlandwell S24
Scots Gap 32.1
Scotsburn S17
Scotsgrove 5.2
Scotstown S17
Scotswood 43.1
Scott Willoughby 28.4
Scotter 28.1
Scotter Common 28.1
Scotterthorpe 28.1
Scottlethorpe 28.6
Scotton (Lincs) 28.1
Scotton (N Yorks)* 33.1, 33.6
Scottow 30.1
Scoulton 30.3
Scourie S17
Scousburgh S26
Scouthead 19.7
Scrabster S17
Scrafield 28.2
Scraptoft 27.8
Scrapton 38.5
Scratby 30.6
Scrayingham 33.3
Scredington 28.4
Scremby (see Ashby)
Scremerston 32.1
Screveton 34.8
Scrivelsby 28.2
Scriven 33.6
Scrogwood 32.1
Scrooby 34.1
Scropton 11.9
Scruton 33.2
Sculthorpe 30.1
Scunthorpe 28.8
Scupholme 28.2
Scurlage W19
Sea 38.5
Sea Mills 4.1
Sea Palling 30.1
Seaborough 13.1
Seabridge 40.2
Seaburn 43.5
Seaburn Dene 43.5
Seacombe 29.5
Seafield S31
Seaford 16.4
Seaforth 29.1
Seagrave 27.2
Seagry 48.1
Seaham 14.1
Seahouses 32.1
Seal 25.8
Seal Chart 25.8
Seal Sands 14.10
Sealand W10
Seale 42.7
Seamans Green 42.8
Seamer* 33.2, 33.4
Searby-cum-Owmby 28.1
Seasalter 25.5
Seascale 10.4

Seathwaite (see Dunnerdale)
Seaton (Corn) 9.1
Seaton (Cumbria) 10.2
Seaton (Devon) 12.7
Seaton (E Yorks) 15.2
Seaton (Rutland) 36.1
Seaton Burn 43.2
Seaton Croft 43.2
Seaton Delaval 32.1
Seaton Ross 15.2
Seaton Sluice 32.1
Seaton with Slingley 14.1
Seatown 13.1
Seaview 24.1
Seavington St Mary 38.5
Seavington St Michael 38.5
Sebastopol W20
Sebergham 10.2
Seckington 44.1
Sedbergh 10.5
Sedbury (Gloucs) 18.2
Sedbury (N Yorks) (see Gilling)
Seddington 2.2
Sedgeberrow 49.6
Sedgebrook 28.6
Sedgefield 14.1
Sedgeford (Norfolk) 30.2
Sedgeford (Shrop) 37.1
Sedgehill 48.1
Sedgley (part) 45.1, 45.3
Sedgley Park 19.3
Sedgwick 10.5
Sedlescombe 16.2
Sedrup 5.2
Seedfield 19.3
Seedley 19.5
Seend 48.1
Seend Cleeve 48.1
Seend Head 48.1
Seend Row 48.1
Seer Green 5.4
Seething 30.7
Sefton 29.1
Sefton Park 29.2
Seghill 32.1
Seifton 37.1
Seighford 40.4
Seion W11
Seisdon 40.6
Selattyn 37.1
Selborne 20.6
Selby 33.8
Selham 46.2
Selkirk S30
Sellack 21.1
Sellicks Green 38.4
Sellindge 25.13
Selling 25.4
Sells Green 48.1
Selly Oak 45.5
Selly Park 45.5
Selmeston 16.1
Selsey 46.2
Selside (Cumbria) 10.5
Selside (N Yorks) 33.5
Selsley 18.6
Selson 25.6
Selsted 25.13
Selston 34.4
Selwood 38.2
Selworthy 38.3
Semer 41.6
Semilong 31.5
Semington 48.1
Semley 48.1
Sempringham 28.6
Send 42.7
Seneley Green 29.3
Senghenydd W4
Sennen 9.1
Sennen Cove 9.1
Senni W17
Sennybridge W17
Serlby 34.1
Serrington 48.1
Sessay 33.2
Sesswick W22
Setley 20.7
Setmurthy 10.2
Settle 33.5
Settlingstones 32.1
Settrington 33.3
Seven Ash 38.4
Seven Sisters W14
Seven Wells Down 38.5
Sevenhampton (Gloucs) 18.5
Sevenhampton (Wilts) 48.2
Sevenoaks 25.8
Sevenoaks Weald 25.8
Severn Beach 18.7
Severn Stoke 49.4
Sevington (Kent) 25.12
Sevington (Wilts) 48.1
Sewardstonebury 17.6
Sewell 2.2
Seworgan 9.1
Sewston 27.3
Sexhow 33.2
Sezincote 18.5
Shabbington 5.2
Shackerstone 27.4
Shackleford 42.7
Shacklewell L12
Shader S32
Shadfen 32.1
Shadforth 14.1
Shadingfield 41.1
Shadoxhurst 25.12
Shadwell L30, 47.2
Shaftesbury 13.2
Shafton 39.1
Shakeford 37.1
Shalbourne 48.1
Shalden 20.6
Shaldon 12.5
Shalfleet 24.1
Shalford (Essex) 17.2
Shalford (Som) 38.5
Shalford (Surrey) 42.7
Shalmsford Street (Chartham) 25.5
Shalstone 5.2
Shamley Green 42.11
Shandwick S17
Shangton 27.8
Shanklin 24.1
Shap 10.3
Shapinsay S23
Shapwick (Dorset) 13.3
Shapwick (Som) 38.1
Sharcott (Som) 38.3
Sharcott (Wilts) 48.1
Shard End 45.5
Shardlow (part) 11.9, 27.1
Shareshill 40.6
Sharlston 47.5
Sharlston Common 47.5
Sharnbrook 2.1
Sharneyford 26.14
Sharnford 27.6
Sharow 33.6
Sharpenhoe 2.2
Sharpham 38.2
Sharpness 18.6
Sharpthorne (part) 16.1, 46.4
Sharptor 9.1
Sharrington 30.1
Sharston 19.6
Shatterling 25.6
Shatton 11.1
Shaugh Prior 12.9
Shave Cross 13.1
Shavington 37.1
Shavington-cum-Gresty 7.5
Shaw (Gtr M'chester) 19.7
Shaw (Wilts) 48.1
Shaw Cross 47.4
Shaw-cum-Donnington 3.1
Shawbirch 37.4
Shawbury 37.1
Shawclough 19.4
Shawell 27.8
Shawford 20.5
Shawforth 26.14
Shawhead S10
Shawsburn S28
Shearsby 27.8
Shebbear 12.1
Shebdon 40.4
Shedfield 20.5
Sheen 40.1
Sheep Green 42.8
Sheepbridge 11.2
Sheepridge 47.4
Sheepscombe 18.6
Sheepstor 12.3
Sheepwash 12.1
Sheepway 38.7
Sheepy, Magna & Parva 27.4
Sheering 17.6
Sheerness 25.4
Sheerwater 42.4
Sheet (Hants) 20.6
Sheet (Shrop) 37.1
Sheffield (Corn) 9.1
Sheffield (S Yorks) 39.3
Shefford 2.2
Sheinton 37.1
Shelderton 37.1
Sheldon (Derbys) 11.3
Sheldon (Devon) 12.7
Sheldon (W Mids) 45.5
Sheldwich 25.4
Shelf 47.3
Shelfanger 30.7
Shelfield (W Mids) 45.2
Shelfield (Warks) 44.5
Shelford 34.8
Shell Ness 25.4
Shelland 41.4
Shellbrook 27.1
Shelley (Essex) 17.6
Shelley (Suffolk) 41.6
Shelley (W Yorks) 47.4
Shellingford 35.4
Shellow Bowells 17.6
Shelsley Beauchamp 49.4
Shelsley Kings 49.4
Shelsley Walsh 49.4
Shelswell 35.2
Shelton (Beds) 2.1
Shelton (Norfolk) 30.7
Shelton (Notts) 34.8
Shelton (Staffs) 40.3
Shelton Lock 11.7
Shelve 37.1
Shelwick 21.1
Shenfield 17.9
Shenington 35.2
Shenley 22.10
Shenley Brook End 5.1
Shenley Church End 5.1
Shenley Lodge 5.1
Shenley Wood 5.1
Shenleybury 22.10
Shenstone (Staffs) 40.8
Shenstone (Worcs) 49.1
Shenstone Wood End 40.8
Shenton 27.4
Shepeau Stow 28.7
Shepherd's Bush (part) L9, L13
Shepherds Green 35.3
Shepherdswell 25.6
Shepley 47.4
Shepperdine 18.7
Shepperton 42.2
Sheppey (Isle of) 25.4
Shepreth 6.5
Shepshed 27.2
Shepton Beauchamp 38.5
Shepton Mallet 38.2
Shepton Montague 38.5
Shepway* 25.10
Sheraton 14.1
Sherborne (Dorset) 13.1
Sherborne (Gloucs) 18.5
Sherborne St John 20.1
Sherbourne 44.4
Sherburn (Durham) 14.1
Sherburn (N Yorks) 33.3
Sherburn Hill 14.1
Sherburn House 14.1
Sherburn-in-Elmet 33.8
Shere 42.7
Shereford 30.1
Sherfield English 20.4
Sherfield Green 20.1

Sherfield Park 20.1
Sherfield-on-Loddon 20.1
Sherford (Devon) 12.9
Sherford (Som) 38.4
Sheriff Hutton with Cornborough 33.3
Sheriffhales 37.1
Sheriffs Lench 49.6
Sheringham 30.1
Sherington 5.1
Shermanbury 46.3
Shermel Gate 48.1
Shernborne 30.2
Sherrington 48.1
Sherston 48.1
Sherwood (Midlothian) S19
Sherwood (Notts) 34.6
Sherwood Rise 34.6
Shevington 19.1
Sheviock 9.1
Shiant Islands S32
Shibden 47.3
Shield Row 14.1
Shieldaig S17
Shieldfield 43.1
Shieldhill S15
Shifford (see Aston Bampton)
Shifnal 37.1
Shilbottle 32.1
Shilburn 32.1
Shildon 14.1
Shillettwood 38.3
Shillingford (Devon) 12.4
Shillingford (Oxon) 35.3
Shillingford Abbot 12.5
Shillingford Hill 35.3
Shillingford St George 12.5
Shillinglee 46.2
Shillingstone 13.2
Shillington 2.2
Shilton (Oxon) 35.1
Shilton (Warks) 44.3
Shilvinghampton 13.1
Shilvington 32.1
Shimpling (Norfolk) 30.7
Shimpling (Suffolk) 41.6
Shincliffe 14.1
Shinfield 3.3
Shingay-cum-Wendy 6.5
Shingham 30.3
Shipbourne 25.9
Shipdham 30.3
Shipham 38.1
Shiplake 35.3
Shiplake Cross 35.3
Shiplate 38.7
Shipley (Derbys) 11.6
Shipley (W Sussex) 46.3
Shipley (W Yorks) 47.1
Shipley Bridge (part) 42.10, 46.1
Shipmeadow 41.1
Shippea Hill (part) 6.4
Shippon 35.4
Shipston-on-Stour 44.5
Shipton (Bucks) 5.2
Shipton (Gloucs) 18.5
Shipton (N Yorks) 33.2
Shipton (Shrop) 37.1
Shipton Bellinger 20.4
Shipton Gorge 13.1
Shipton Green 46.2
Shipton Moyne 18.5
Shipton Oliffe 18.5
Shipton-on-Cherwell 35.2
Shipton-under-Wychwood 35.1
Shiptonthorpe 15.2
Shirburn 35.3
Shire Oak 45.2
Shirebrook 11.5
Shirehampton 4.1
Shiremoor 43.2
Shirenewton W13
Shireoaks 34.1
Shirland 11.4
Shirley (Derbys) 11.3
Shirley (W Mids) 45.6
Shirley Holmes 20.7
Shirley Warren 20.8
Shirlowe 37.4
Shirrell Heath 20.5
Shirwell 12.2
Shobdon 21.1
Shobley 20.7
Shobrooke 12.4
Shoby 27.3
Shockerwick 38.6
Shocklach Oviatt 7.3
Shoe, The 48.1
Shoeburyness 17.14
Sholden 25.6
Sholing 20.8
Shootash 20.4
Shooters Hill (Shrop) 37.1
Shopland 17.11
Shopnoller 38.4
Shore (Gtr M'chester) 19.4
Shore (W Yorks) 47.3
Shoreditch (London) (part) L12, L30
Shoreditch (Som) 38.4
Shoreham (Kent) 25.8
Shoreham-by-Sea 46.7
Shoresdean 32.1
Shoreswood 32.1
Shorncliffe 25.13
Shorne 25.2
Short Heath 45.5
Shortheath 20.6
Shortheath, Willenhall 45.2
Shortlands L5
Shortlanesend 9.1
Shortstanding 18.2
Shortstown 2.1
Shortwood 18.7
Shorwell 24.1
Shoscombe 38.6
Shotatton 37.1
Shotesham 30.7
Shothanger 20.1
Shotley (N'hants) 31.3
Shotley (Suffolk) 41.6
Shotley Bridge (part) 14.1, 32.1
Shotley Low Quarter 32.1
Shotover (see Forest Hill)
Shottenden 25.12
Shottermill (part) 42.11, 46.2
Shottery 44.5
Shottesbrooke 3.4
Shotteswell 44.5
Shottisham 41.5
Shottle 11.6
Shotton (Durham) 14.1
Shotton (Flint) W10
Shotton (Shrop) 37.1
Shotts S22
Shotwick 7.3
Shotwick Park 7.3
Shouldham 30.2
Shouldham Thorpe 30.2
Shrawardine 37.1
Shrawley 49.4
Shray Hill 37.4
Shrewley 44.4
Shrewsbury 37.1
Shrewton 48.1
Shripney 46.5
Shrivenham 35.4
Shropham 30.3
Shroton (or Iwerne Courtney) 13.2
Shucknall 21.1
Shudy Camps 6.5
Shurdington 18.1
Shustoke 44.1
Shute 12.7
Shute End 48.1
Shutford 35.2
Shutlanger 31.7
Shuttington 44.1
Shuttlewood 11.5
Shuttleworth 19.3
Sibbaldbie S10
Sibbertoft 31.4
Sibdon Carwood 37.1
Sibford Ferris 35.2
Sibford Gower 35.2
Sible Hedingham 17.2
Sibsey 28.2
Sibson (Cambs) 6.3
Sibson (Leics) 27.4
Sibthorpe 34.8
Sibton 41.5
Sicklinghall 33.6
Sidbrook 38.4
Sidbury 37.1
Sidcot 38.7
Sidcup L3
Siddal 47.3
Siddington (Cheshire) 7.5
Siddington (Gloucs) 18.5
Siddown Hill 20.1
Sidemoor 49.2
Sidestrand 30.1
Sideway 40.3
Sidlesham 46.2
Sidlow 42.9
Sidmouth 12.7
Sigginstone W21
Sigglesthorne 15.2
Sigwells 38.5
Silchester 20.1
Sileby 27.2
Silfield 30.7
Silian W7
Silk Willoughby 28.4
Silkstone 39.1
Silkstone Common 39.1
Silksworth 43.5
Silloth 10.2
Siloh W6
Silpho 33.4
Silsden 47.1
Silsoe 2.2
Silton 13.2
Silver End 17.2
Silver Knapp 38.5
Silver Street 20.7
Silverburn S19
Silverdale (Lancs) 26.1
Silverdale (Notts) 34.6
Silverdale (Staffs) 40.2
Silverly (see Ashley)
Silverstone 31.7
Silverton 12.4
Silvertonhill S28
Silvington 37.1
Simister 19.3
Simmondley 11.1
Simonburn 32.1
Simonsbath 38.3
Simonstone 26.3
Simonswood 26.8
Simpson 5.1
Simpson Green 47.1
Sinderby 33.2
Sinderhope 32.1
Sinfin (part) 11.7, 11.9
Singleborough 5.2
Singleton (Kent) 25.12
Singleton (Lancs) 26.5
Singleton (W Sussex) 46.2
Singlewell 25.2
Sinnington 33.3
Sinope 27.1
Sirhowy W2
Sisland 30.7
Sissinghurst 25.11
Siston 18.7
Sithney 9.1
Sittingbourne 25.4
Six Ashes 40.6
Six Bells W2
Six Mile Bottom (part) 6.4, 6.5
Sixhills 28.1
Sixpenny Handley 13.3
Sizergh 10.5
Skeabost S17
Skeeby 33.1
Skeet Hill 25.8
Skeffington 27.8
Skeffling 15.2
Skegby 34.4
Skegness 28.2
Skelbrooke 39.2
Skelding 33.6
Skeldon S27
Skellingthorpe 28.4

Skellister S26
Skellow 39.2
Skelmanthorpe 47.4
Skelmersdale 26.8
Skelmorlie S21
Skelpick S17
Skelsmergh 10.5
Skelton (Cumbria) 10.3
Skelton (York) 33.7
Skelwith Bridge 10.5
Skelwith Fold 10.5
Skendleby 28.2
Skene S1
Skenfrith W13
Sker W3
Skerne 15.2
Skerray S17
Sketty W19
Skewen W14
Skewsby (see Dalby)
Skeyton 30.1
Skidbrooke with Saltfleet Haven 28.2
Skidby 15.2
Skigersta S32
Skilgate 38.3
Skillington 28.6
Skinflats S15
Skinnand 28.4
Skinners Bottom 9.1
Skinningrove 33.10
Skiplam 33.3
Skipness S3
Skipsea 15.2
Skipton 33.5
Skipton-on-Swale 33.2
Skipwith 33.8
Skircoat Green 47.3
Skirlaugh 15.2
Skirling S30
Skirmett 5.3
Skirpenbeck 15.2
Skirwith 10.3
Skittle Green 5.3
Skutterskelfe 33.2
Skyborry Green 37.1
Skye S17
Slack 47.3
Slackhead 10.5
Slad 18.6
Slade Heath 40.6
Slade Hooton 39.4
Sladesbridge 9.1
Slaggyford 32.1
Slaidburn 26.3
Slains S1
Slaithwaite 47.4
Slaley 32.1
Slamannan S15
Slapewath 33.10
Slapton (Bucks) 5.2
Slapton (Devon) 12.9
Slapton (N'hants) 31.7
Slatepitdale 11.4
Slattocks 19.4
Slaugham 46.4
Slaughterford 48.1
Slawston 27.8
Sleaford (Hants) 20.6
Sleaford (Lincs) 28.4
Sleagill 10.3
Sleap 37.1
Sleap (part) 37.4
Sleapford 37.4
Sleapshyde 22.5
Slebech W16
Sledmere 15.2
Sleekburn, East & West 32.1
Sleight 48.1
Sleights 33.4
Slenningford (see North Stainley)
Slett S26
Sligachan S17
Slimbridge 18.6
Slindon (Staffs) 40.4
Slindon (W Sussex) 46.5
Slinfold 46.3
Sling (Gloucs) 18.2
Sling (Gwynedd) W11
Slingley (see Seaton)
Slingsby 33.3
Slip End 2.2
Slipton 31.3
Slitting Mill 40.7
Sloley 30.1
Sloothby (see Willoughby)
Slough 3.5
Slough Green 38.4
Slyne with Hest 26.1
Sma Glen S24
Smailholm S30
Small Heath 45.5
Small Hythe (Tenterden) 25.12
Smallbridge 19.4
Smallburgh 30.1
Smallburn 32.1
Smalldole 46.3
Smalley 11.6
Smallfield 42.10
Smallford 22.5
Smallthorne 40.3
Smallway 38.5
Smallwood (Cheshire) 7.5
Smallwood (Worcs) 49.3
Smannell 20.4
Smardale 10.3
Smarden 25.12
Smeeth 25.12
Smeeton Westerby 27.8
Smethcott 37.1
Smethwick 45.4
Smisby 11.9
Smithdown 29.2
Smithfield 10.1
Smithincott 12.4
Smithton S17
Smithy Bridge 19.4
Smythemoor 37.1
Snailbeach 37.1
Snailwell 6.4
Snainton, North & South 33.4
Snaith 15.2
Snap Ant 38.5
Snape (Suffolk) 41.5
Snape with Thorpe 33.2
Snarehill, Gt & Little 30.3
Snarestone 27.1
Snarford 28.1
Snargate 25.13
Snatchwood W20
Snave 25.13
Sneaton 33.4
Snedshill 37.4
Sneinton 34.6
Snelland 28.1
Snellsgate 9.1
Snelshall 5.1
Snelson 7.5
Snelston 11.3
Snetterton 30.3
Snettisham 30.2
Sneyd Green 40.3
Sneyd Park 4.1
Snibston 27.1
Snilesworth 33.3
Snitter 32.1
Snitterby 28.1
Snitterfield 44.5
Snitterton (see Oker)
Snitton 37.1
Snodland 25.9
Snowden Hill 38.5
Snowdown 25.6
Snowshill 18.1
Snydale 47.5
Soar W17
Soay, Isle of S17
Soberton 20.5
Sock Dennis 38.5
Sockbridge 10.3
Sockburn 14.8
Sodbury 18.7
Sodyllt 37.1
Sofrydd W2
Softley (see Lynesack)
Soham 6.4
Soho L33
Soho (part) 45.4, 45.5
Soke 20.1
Soldridge 20.6
Sole Street 25.2
Solihull 45.6
Solihull Lodge 45.6
Sollas S32
Sollers Hope 21.1
Solport 10.1
Solva W16
Somerby (Leics) 27.8
Somerby (Lincs) 28.1
Somercotes 11.6
Somerford (Cheshire) 7.5
Somerford (Dorset) 13.8
Somerford Booths 7.5
Somerford Keynes 18.5
Somerley 46.2
Somerleyton 41.1
Somersal Herbert 11.3
Somersall 11.2
Somersby 28.2
Somersham (Cambs) 6.3
Somersham (Suffolk) 41.4
Somerton (Oxon) 35.2
Somerton (Som) 38.5
Somerton (Suffolk) 41.6
Somerton, East & West (Norfolk) 30.6
Somerwood (part) 37.1, 37.4
Sompting 46.7
Sonning 3.3
Sonning Common 35.3
Sonning Eye 35.3
Sookholme 34.2
Soothill 47.4
Sopley 20.7
Sopworth 48.1
Sorbie S10
Sorn S11
Sotby 28.2
Sotherton 41.1
Sots Hole 28.4
Sotterley 41.1
Sotwell (see Brightwell)
Soudley (Gloucs) 18.2
Soudley (Shrop) 37.1
Soudley, Gt & Little 37.1
Sough 26.13
Soulbury 5.2
Soulby 10.3
Souldern 35.2
Souldrop 2.1
Soulton 37.1
Sound 7.5
Soundwell 18.7
Sourton 12.3
Soutergate 10.5
South Acre 30.3
South Acton L9
South Allington 12.9
South Alloa S15
South Ambersham 46.2
South Anston 39.4
South Baddesley 20.7
South Bank 33.10
South Barrow 38.5
South Bedburn 14.1
South Bents 43.5
South Bowood 13.1
South Bradon 38.5
South Bramwith 39.2
South Brent 12.9
South Brewham 38.5
South Bromley L30
South Broomhill 32.1
South Cadbury 38.5
South Carlton 28.1
South Cary 38.5
South Cave 15.2
South Cerney 18.5
South Chailey 16.4
South Chard 38.5
South Cheriton 38.5
South Church 14.1
South Cleatham 14.1
South Cliffe 15.2
South Clifton 34.3
South Cockerington 28.2
South Cornelly W3

South Cove 41.1
South Cowton 33.2
South Creake 30.2
South Crosland 47.4
South Croxton 27.2
South Croydon L8
South Damerham 20.7
South Darenth (part) 25.1, 25.8
South Darley 11.3
South Duffield (see Cliffe)
South Ealing L9
South Elkington 28.2
South Ella 15.2
South Elmham All Saints 41.1
South Elmham St Cross 41.1
South Elmham St James 41.1
South Elmham St Margaret 41.1
South Elmham St Mary (Homersfield) 41.1
South Elmham St Michael 41.1
South Elmham St Nicholas 41.1
South Elmham St Peter 41.1
South Elmsall 47.5
South Erradale S17
South Fambridge 17.11
South Ferriby 28.8
South Frodingham 15.2
South Godstone 42.10
South Gorley 20.7
South Gosforth 43.1
South Gulham 28.1
South Hackney L12
South Ham (Hants) 20.1
South Hanningfield 17.7
South Harp 38.5
South Harrow L15
South Heath 5.4
South Heighton 16.4
South Hetton 14.1
South Hiendley 47.5
South Hill (Corn) 9.1
South Hill (Som) 38.5
South Hinksey 35.4
South Holme 33.3
South Holmwood 42.8
South Horrington 38.2
South Huish 12.9
South Hykeham 28.4
South Hylton 43.5
South Kelsey 28.1
South Kensington (part) L20, L33
South Killingholme 28.8
South Kilvington 33.2
South Kilworth 27.8
South Kirkby 47.5
South Kyme 28.4
South Lambeth (part) L22
South Leigh (Oxon) 35.1
South Leverton 34.1
South Luffenham 36.1
South Marsh 38.5
South Marston (Wilts) 48.2
South Milford 33.8
South Milton 12.9
South Mimms 22.10
South Molton 12.2
South Moor (Durham) 14.1
South Moreton 35.3
South Mundham 46.2
South Muskham 34.3
South Newbald 15.2
South Newington 35.2
South Newton 48.1
South Normanton 11.5
South Norwood L8
South Nutfield 42.10
South Ockenden 17.12
South Ormsby-cum-Ketsby 28.2
South Otterington 33.2
South Owersby 28.1
South Oxhey 22.8
South Pelaw 14.1
South Perrot 13.1
South Petherton 38.5
South Petherwin 9.1
South Pool 12.9
South Queensferry S6
South Rauceby 28.4
South Reston 28.2
South Ronaldsay S23
South Scarle 34.3
South Shields 43.4
South Somercotes 28.2
South Stainley with Cayton 33.6
South Stainmore 10.3
South Stifford 17.12
South Stoke (Oxon) 35.3
South Stoke (Som) 38.6
South Stoke (W Sussex) 46.5
South Tawton 12.3
South Thoresby 28.2
South Tottenham (part) L12, L14
South Uist S32
South Walsham 30.5
South Warnborough (part) 20.1, 20.2
South Weald 17.9
South Wellfield 43.2
South Weston 35.3
South Wheatley 34.1
South Wigston 27.7
South Willesborough 25.12
South Willingham 28.2
South Wimbledon L24
South Wingfield 11.6
South Witham 28.6
South Wonston 20.5
South Woodford L26
South Woodham Ferrers 17.7
South Wootton 30.2
South Wraxall 48.1
South Zeal 12.3
Southall (Shrop) 37.4
Southall (part) L9, L18
Southam (Gloucs) 18.1
Southam (Warks) 44.5
Southampton 20.8
Southay 38.5
Southborough 25.11
Southbourne (Dorset) 13.7
Southbourne (W Sussex) 46.2
Southburgh 30.3
Southburn 15.2
Southchurch 17.14
Southcrest 49.3
Southdene (Kirkby) 29.4
Southdown 9.1
Southease 16.4
Southend S3
Southend (Bucks) 5.3
Southend-on-Sea 17.14
Southern Green 22.1
Southernby 10.3
Southerndown W21
Southerness S10
Southery 30.2
Southfields L32
Southfields (N'hants) 31.5
Southfleet 25.1
Southgate (Swansea) W19
Southgate (W Sussex) 46.1
Southgate (part) L2, L10
Southill 2.2
Southington 20.1
Southlea 20.1
Southleigh (Devon) 12.7
Southley 20.1
Southmead 4.1
Southminster 17.8
Southmoor (Oxon) (see Kingston Bagpuize)
Southoe & Midloe 6.3
Southolt 41.4
Southorpe (Cambs) 6.1
Southorpe (Lincs) 28.1
Southowram 47.3
Southport 29.1
Southrepps 30.1
Southrey 28.1
Southrop 18.5
Southrope 20.1
Southsea (Hants) 20.12
Southsea (Wrexham) W22
Southtown 38.5
Southville (Bristol) 4.1
Southville (Torfaen) W20
Southwaite 10.3
Southwark L28
Southwater 46.3
Southwell 34.3
Southwick (Hants) 20.5
Southwick (N'hants) 31.3
Southwick (T & W) 43.5
Southwick (W Sussex) 46.7
Southwick (Wilts) 48.1
Southwold 41.1
Southwood S27
Southwood (Hants) 20.3
Southwood (Ramsgate) (Kent) 25.7
Soutra S19
Sowerby (Lancs) (see Inskip)
Sowerby (Thirsk) 33.2
Sowerby (W Yorks) 47.3
Sowerby Bridge 47.3
Sowerby Row 10.3
Sowerby-under-Cotcliffe 33.2
Sowood 47.3
Sowton (part) 12.6, 12.7
Soyland 47.3
Spa Common 30.1
Spalding 28.7
Spaldington 15.2
Spaldwick 6.3
Spalford 34.3
Spanby 28.4
Spanish Green 20.1
Sparcells 48.2
Sparham 30.3
Spark Bridge 10.5
Sparkbrook 45.5
Sparket 10.3
Sparkford 38.5
Sparkhill 45.5
Sparkwell 12.9
Sparnon Gate 9.1
Sparrowpit 11.1
Sparsholt (Hants) 20.5
Sparsholt (Oxon) 35.4
Sparty Lee 32.1
Spaunton 33.3
Spaxton 38.1
Spean Bridge S17
Speckington 38.5
Speedwell 4.1
Speen (Bucks) 5.3
Speeton 33.4
Speke 29.2
Speldhurst 25.11
Spelsbury 35.1
Spenborough 47.4
Spencer 31.5
Spencer's Wood 3.3
Spennithorne 33.1
Spennymoor 14.1
Spernall 44.5
Spetchley 49.6
Spetisbury 13.2
Spexhall 41.1
Spey Bay S20
Spilsby 28.2
Spinkhill (part) 11.4, 11.5
Spinney Hill 31.5
Spinningdale S17
Spion Kop 34.2
Spital (Derbys) 11.2
Spital (Mersey) 29.5
Spital Hill (N'land) 32.1
Spital Tongues 43.1
Spital in the Street 28.1
Spitewinter 11.4
Spithurst 16.4
Spittal (E Yorks) 15.2
Spittal (N'land) 32.1
Spittal (Pemb) W16

Spittal of Glenshee S24
Spittalfield S24
Spixworth 30.5
Splott W5
Spofforth with Stokeld 33.6
Spon End 45.7
Spondon 11.7
Spooner Row 30.7
Spoonley 37.1
Sporle with Palgrave 30.3
Spotland 19.4
Spott S13
Spratton 31.4
Spreyton 12.3
Spridlington 28.1
Spring Cottage 27.1
Spring Grove 38.4
Springboig S7
Springbourne 13.7
Springfield L12
Springfield (Bucks) 5.1
Springfield (Dumfries) S10
Springfield (Essex) 17.7
Springfield (Fife) S16
Springfield (Som) 38.4
Springfield (W Mids)* 45.4, 45.5
Springfield Estate L32
Springhead 19.7
Springholm S10
Springside S21
Springthorpe 28.1
Springwell 43.5
Springwell Estate (not Village) 43.3
Springwell Village 43.5
Sproatley 15.2
Sproston 7.3
Sprotbrough 39.2
Sproughton 41.6
Sprouston S30
Sprowston 30.5
Sproxton (Leics) 27.3
Sproxton (N Yorks) 33.3
Spun Hill 37.1
Spurstow 7.5
Stable Green 32.1
Stacey Bushes 5.1
Stackhouses 33.5
Stackpole Elidor & St Petrox W16
Stacksteads 26.14
Staddlethorpe 15.2
Stadhampton 35.3
Staffield 10.3
Staffin S17
Stafford 40.4
Stafford Park 37.4
Stagsden 2.1
Stain (see Withern)
Stainborough 39.1
Stainburn 33.6
Stainby 28.6
Staincliffe 47.4
Staincross 39.1
Staindrop 14.1
Staines (part) 19.12, 42.1, 42.2
Stainfield* 28.1, 28.6
Stainforth (N Yorks) 33.5
Stainforth (S Yorks) 39.2
Staining (part) 26.4, 26.5
Stainland 47.3
Stainmore 10.3
Stainsacre 33.4
Stainsby (Derbys) 11.5
Stainsby (Lincs) 28.2
Stainsby Common 11.5
Stainton (Carlisle)* 10.1
Stainton (Durham) (see Streatlam)
Stainton (Kendal)* 10.5
Stainton (Middlesbrough) 33.9
Stainton (N Yorks) 33.1
Stainton (S Yorks) 39.2
Stainton by Langworth 28.1
Stainton Grove 14.1
Stainton le Vale 28.1
Stainton with Adgarley 10.5
Staintondale 33.4
Stair S11
Staithes 33.10
Stakeford 32.1
Stakenbridge 49.1
Stalbridge 13.2
Stalham 30.1
Stalisfield 25.4
Stallingborough 28.9
Stalmine with Staynall 26.2
Stalybridge 19.10
Stamborough 38.3
Stambourne 17.2
Stambridge 17.11
Stamford 28.6
Stamford Bridge 15.2
Stamford Hill (part) L12, L14
Stamfordham 32.1
Stamingfield (see Bradfield Combust)
Stamperland S14
Stanage W17
Stanbridge (Beds) 2.2
Stanbridge (Dorset) 13.3
Stanbridgeford 2.2
Stanbury 47.1
Stancil 39.2
Stand 19.3
Standburn S15
Standens Barn 31.5
Standerwick 38.2
Standford 20.6
Standing Stone 32.1
Standish 18.6
Standish with Langtree 19.1
Standlake 35.1
Standon (Herts) 22.3
Standon (Staffs) 40.4
Stanfield* 30.3, 30.7
Stanfields 40.3
Stanford (Beds) 2.2
Stanford (Kent) 25.13
Stanford (Norfolk) 30.3
Stanford Bishop 21.1
Stanford Bridge 37.4
Stanford Dingley 3.1
Stanford Rivers 17.6
Stanford in the Vale 35.4
Stanford with Orleton 49.4
Stanford-le-Hope 17.12
Stanford-on-Avon (N'hants) 31.4
Stanford-on-Soar 34.8
Stanfree 11.5
Stanghow 33.10
Stanground 6.1
Stanhill 26.11
Stanhoe 30.2
Stanhope 14.1
Stanion 31.1
Stank 10.6
Stanley (Derbys) 11.8
Stanley (Durham) 14.1
Stanley (E Renfrews) S24
Stanley (Notts) 34.4
Stanley (Staffs) 40.1
Stanley (W Yorks) 47.5
Stanley (Wilts) 48.1
Stanley Common 11.8
Stanley Crook 14.1
Stanley Green 37.1
Stanleytown W18
Stanlow (part) 7.3
Stanmer 16.3
Stannersburn 32.1
Stanney 7.3
Stanningfield 41.3
Stanninghall (see Horstead)
Stanningley 47.2
Stannington (N'land) 32.1
Stannington (S Yorks) 39.3
Stannycliffe 19.4
Stanpit 13.8
Stansfield 41.3
Stanshawes 18.7
Stanshope 40.1
Stanstead (Suffolk) 41.6
Stanstead Abbots 22.3
Stanstead St Margarets 22.3
Stansted (Kent) 25.9
Stansted Mountfitchet 17.1
Stanthorne 7.3
Stanton (Derbys/Staffs) 40.5
Stanton (Gloucs) 18.1
Stanton (N'land) 32.1
Stanton (Suffolk) 41.3
Stanton Drew 38.6
Stanton Fitzwarren 48.2
Stanton Harcourt 35.1
Stanton Hill 34.4
Stanton Lacy 37.1
Stanton Lees 11.3
Stanton Long 37.1
Stanton Prior 38.6
Stanton St Bernard 48.1
Stanton St Gabriel 13.1
Stanton St John 35.3
Stanton St Quintin 48.1
Stanton-by-Bridge 11.9
Stanton-by-Dale 11.8
Stanton by Nowhall 11.9
Stanton-in-Peak 11.3
Stanton-on-the-Wolds 34.8
Stanton-under-Bardon 27.4
Stanton-upon-Hine-Heath 37.1
Stantonbury 5.1
Stantonbury Fields 5.1
Stanwardine 37.1
Stanwardine in the Fields 37.1
Stanway (Essex) 17.3
Stanway (Gloucs) 18.1
Stanway (Here) 21.1
Stanwell 42.2
Stanwell Moor 42.2
Stanwick 31.3
Stanwick St John 33.1
Stanwix 10.1
Stape (Pickering) 33.3
Stapehill 13.3
Stapeley 7.5
Stapenhill 40.5
Staple (Kent) 25.6
Staple (Som) 38.3
Staple Fitzpaine 38.4
Staple Hill 18.7
Staplecross 16.2
Staplefield 46.4
Stapleford (Cambs) 6.5
Stapleford (Herts) 22.3
Stapleford (Leics) 27.3
Stapleford (Lincs) 28.4
Stapleford (Notts) 34.5
Stapleford (Wilts) 48.1
Stapleford Abbotts 17.6
Stapleford Tawney 17.6
Staplegrove 38.4
Staplehay 38.4
Staplehurst 25.10
Stapleton (Bristol) 4.1
Stapleton (Cumbria) 10.1
Stapleton (Here) 21.1
Stapleton (Leics) 27.4
Stapleton (N Yorks)* 33.1, 33.8
Stapleton (Shrop) 37.1
Stapleton (Som) 38.5
Stapley 38.4
Staploe 2.1
Star (Anglesey) W1
Star (Fife) S16
Starbotton (see Kettlewell)
Starcross 12.5
Starling 19.3
Starmore (see Westrill)
Starston 30.7
Startforth 14.1
Startley 48.1
Statfold 40.8
Statham 7.1
Stathe (part) 38.4, 38.5
Stathern 27.3
Station Town 14.1
Staunton (Gloucs) 18.2
Staunton (Notts) 34.3
Staunton Coleford 18.2
Staunton Harold 27.1
Staunton-on-Arrow 21.1
Staunton-on-Wye 21.1
Staveley (Cumbria) 10.5

2

Staveley (Derbys) 11.2
Staveley (N Yorks) 33.6
Staveley in Cartmel 10.5
Staverton (Devon) 12.9
Staverton (Gloucs) 18.1
Staverton (N'hants) 31.4
Staverton (Wilts) 48.1
Stawell 38.1
Stawley 38.4
Staxigoe S17
Staxton (Scarborough) 33.3
Staylittle W17
Staynall (see Stalmine)
Staythorpe 34.3
Stead 47.1
Steam Mills 18.2
Steanbow 38.2
Steane 31.7
Stearsby (see Brandsby)
Steart* 38.3, 38.5
Stebbing 17.1
Stechford 45.5
Stedham 46.2
Steel 32.1
Steele Heath 37.1
Steep 20.6
Steeple (Dorset) 13.5
Steeple (Essex) 17.8
Steeple Ashton 48.1
Steeple Aston 35.2
Steeple Barton 35.1
Steeple Bumpstead 17.2
Steeple Claydon 5.2
Steeple Gidding 6.3
Steeple Langford 48.1
Steeple Morden 6.5
Steeraway 37.4
Steetley 11.5
Steeton (N Yorks) 33.8
Steeton (W Yorks) 47.1
Stein S17
Stelling 25.13
Stelling Minnis 25.13
Stembridge (Som) 38.5
Stembridge (Vale Glam) W21
Stenalees 9.1
Stenhousemuir S15
Stenigot 28.2
Stenness S23
Stenson 11.9
Stenson Fields (part) 11.7, 11.9
Stenton S13
Stepaside W16
Stephenson 43.5
Stepney L30
Steppingley 2.2
Stepps S22
Sterndale Moor 11.1
Sternfield 41.5
Stert 48.1
Stetchworth 6.4
Stevenage 22.2
Stevenston S21
Steventon (Hants) 20.1
Steventon (Oxon) 35.4
Stevington 2.1
Stewards 17.5
Stewartby 2.1
Stewarton S11
Stewkley 5.2
Stewley 38.5
Stewton 28.2
Steyning 46.3
Steynton W16
Stibbard 30.1
Stibbington 6.3
Stichill S30
Sticker 9.1
Stickford 28.2
Sticklepath (Okehampton, Devon)* 12.3
Sticklepath (Som) 38.5
Sticklynch 38.2
Stickney 28.2
Stidcot 18.7
Stiffkey 30.1
Stifford Clays 17.12
Stile 38.3
Stillingfleet 33.8
Stillington (N Yorks) 33.2
Stillington (Stockton) 14.10
Stilton 6.3
Stinchcombe 18.6
Stinsford 13.1
Stiperstones 37.1
Stirchley (Shrop) 37.4
Stirchley (W Mids) 45.5
Stirling S29
Stirton with Thorlby 33.5
Stisted 17.2
Stithians 9.1
Stittenham 33.3
Stivichall 45.7
Stixwould with Woodhall 28.2
Stoak 7.3
Stoborough 13.5
Stobswood 32.1
Stock & Bradley 49.6
Stock (Essex) 17.7
Stock (Som) 38.7
Stockbridge (Hants) 20.4
Stockbridge (W Yorks) 47.1
Stockbridge Village (part) 29.2, 29.4
Stockbury 25.10
Stockdalewath 10.1
Stockerston 27.8
Stockgrove 5.2
Stockham 38.4
Stocking Pelham 22.3
Stockingford 44.2
Stockland 12.7
Stockland Bristol 38.1
Stockland Green 45.5
Stockleigh English 12.4
Stockleigh Pomeroy 12.4
Stockley 48.1
Stockley Hill 21.1
Stocklinch 38.5
Stockport (Gtr M'chester) 19.9
Stockport (Wilts) 48.1
Stocks Green 25.9
Stocksbridge 39.3
Stocksfield 32.1
Stocksmoor (part) 47.4, 47.5
Stockton (Cheshire) 7.3
Stockton (Norfolk) 30.7
Stockton (Shrop)* 37.1, 37.4
Stockton (Warks) 44.5
Stockton (Wilts) 48.1
Stockton Brook (part) 40.1, 40.3
Stockton Heath 7.1
Stockton-on-Forest 33.7
Stockton-on-Tees 14.10
Stockton-on-Teme 49.4
Stockwell L22
Stockwell Heath 40.8
Stockwitch Cross 38.5
Stockwood (Bristol) 4.1
Stockwood (Dorset) 13.1
Stodday (see Ashton)
Stodmarsh 25.5
Stody 30.1
Stoer S17
Stoford (Som)* 38.4, 38.5
Stoford (Wilts) 48.1
Stogumber 38.3
Stogursey 38.3
Stoke (Berks) 3.5
Stoke (Cheshire) 7.5
Stoke (Hants) 20.1
Stoke (Kent) 25.3
Stoke (W Mids) 45.7
Stoke Abbot 13.1
Stoke Albany 31.2
Stoke Ash 41.4
Stoke Bardolph 34.7
Stoke Bishop 4.1
Stoke Bliss 49.4
Stoke Bruerne 31.7
Stoke Canon 12.7
Stoke Charity 20.5
Stoke Climsland 9.1
Stoke D'Abernon 42.5
Stoke Doyle 31.3
Stoke Dry 36.1
Stoke Edith 21.1
Stoke Ferry 30.2
Stoke Fleming 12.9
Stoke Gabriel 12.9
Stoke Gifford 18.7
Stoke Golding 27.4
Stoke Goldington 5.1
Stoke Hammond 5.2
Stoke Heath (Shrop) 37.1
Stoke Heath (W Mids) 45.7
Stoke Heath (Worcs) 49.2
Stoke Holy Cross 30.7
Stoke Lacy 21.1
Stoke Lyne 35.2
Stoke Mandeville 5.2
Stoke Newington L12
Stoke Orchard 18.1
Stoke Pero 38.3
Stoke Poges 5.5
Stoke Prior (Hereford) 21.1
Stoke Prior (Worcs) 49.2
Stoke Rivers 12.2
Stoke Rochford 28.6
Stoke Row 35.3
Stoke St Gregory 38.4
Stoke St Mary 38.4
Stoke St Michael 38.2
Stoke St Milborough 37.1
Stoke Talmage 35.3
Stoke Trister 38.5
Stoke Wake 13.2
Stoke-by-Clare 41.3
Stoke-by-Nayland 41.6
Stoke-on-Tern 37.1
Stoke-sub-Hamdon 38.5
Stoke-upon-Trent 40.3
Stokeham 34.1
Stokeinteignhead 12.5
Stokeld (see Spofforth)
Stokenchurch 5.3
Stokenham 12.9
Stokesay 37.1
Stokesby with Herringby 30.6
Stokesley 33.2
Stoketon 9.1
Ston Easton 38.2
Stondon Massey (part) 17.6, 17.9
Stone (Bucks) 5.2
Stone (Gloucs) 18.6
Stone (Kent)* 25.1, 25.4
Stone (S Yorks) 39.4
Stone (Som) 38.2
Stone (Staffs) 40.4
Stone (Worcs) 49.1
Stone Cross (E Sussex) 16.1
Stone Cross (W Mids) 45.4
Stone Edge Batch 38.7
Stone Street 25.8
Stone-cum-Ebony 25.12
Stonea 6.2
Stonebeck, Down & Up 33.6
Stonebridge 38.7
Stonebridge (Bucks) 5.1
Stonebroom 11.4
Stoneclough 19.2
Stonedge 11.4
Stonefold 26.14
Stonegate 16.2
Stonegrave 33.3
Stonegravels 11.2
Stonehaugh 32.1
Stonehaven S1
Stonehill 42.1
Stonehouse (Gloucs) 18.6
Stonehouse (Strath) S28
Stoneleigh (Surrey) 42.6
Stoneleigh (Warks) 44.4
Stonesby 27.3
Stonesfield 35.1
Stoneton 44.5
Stoney Cross 20.7
Stoney Down 13.3
Stoney Heath 20.1
Stoney Hill (Shrop) 37.4
Stoney Hill (Worcs) 49.2
Stoney Middleton 11.3
Stoney Ridge 47.1
Stoney Stanton 27.6

Stoney Stoke 38.5
Stoney Stratton 38.2
Stoneybridge (W Isles) S32
Stoneybridge (Worcs) 49.2
Stoneyburn S31
Stoneycroft 29.2
Stoneygate-Houghton-le-Spring 43.5
Stoneyholme 26.12
Stoneykirk S10
Stoneywood (Aberdeen) S4
Stoneywood (Denny) S15
Stonham Aspal 41.4
Stonham Earl 41.4
Stonham Parva 41.4
Stonnall (part) 40.8, 45.2
Stonor 35.3
Stonton Wyville 27.8
Stony Houghton 11.5
Stony Stratford 5.1
Stonydelph 40.9
Stonyhurst 26.3
Stoodleigh 12.4
Stopham 46.2
Storeton 29.5
Storiths (see Hazelwood)
Stormontfield S24
Stormy Down W3
Stornoway S32
Storr, The S17
Storrington 46.3
Storrs 10.5
Storth 10.5
Storwood 15.2
Stotfold 2.2
Stottesdon 37.1
Stoughton (Leics) 27.8
Stoughton (W Sussex) 46.2
Stoulton 49.6
Stour Provost 13.2
Stourbridge 45.3
Stourmouth (part) 25.5, 25.6, 25.7
Stourpaine 13.2
Stourport-on-Severn 49.1
Stourton (Staffs) 40.6
Stourton (W Yorks) 47.2
Stourton (Warks) 44.5
Stourton Caundle 13.2
Stourton with Gasper 48.1
Stourvale 13.7
Stout 38.5
Stoven 41.1
Stover 18.7
Stow S30
Stow Bardolph 30.2
Stow Bedon 30.3
Stow Longa 6.3
Stow Maries 17.8
Stow* 28.1, 28.4
Stow-cum-Quy 6.5
Stow-on-the-Wold 18.5
Stowe (Bucks) 5.2
Stowe (Lincs) 28.6
Stowe (Shrop) 37.1
Stowe-Nine-Churches 31.4
Stowe-by-Chartley (Staffs) 40.4
Stowell 38.5
Stowey 38.6
Stowey Sutton 38.6
Stowford 12.3
Stowlangtoft 41.4
Stowmarket 41.4
Stowting 25.13
Stowupland 41.4
Stracathro S2
Strachan S1
Strachur S3
Stradbroke 41.4
Stradishall 41.3
Stradsett 30.2
Stragglethorpe (Lincs) 28.4
Stragglethorpe (Notts) 34.8
Straiton S19
Straloch S24
Stranraer S10
Strata Florida W7
Stratfield Mortimer 3.1
Stratfield Saye 20.1
Stratfield Turgis 20.1
Stratford (part) L12, L25, L31
Stratford St Andrew 41.5
Stratford St Mary 41.6
Stratford Tony 48.1
Stratford-on-Avon 44.5
Stratford-sub-Castle 48.1
Strath, Gairloch S17
Strathallan S24
Strathaven S28
Strathblane S29
Strathconon S17
Strathdon S1
Strathgarve S17
Strathkinness S16
Strathmiglo S16
Strathpeffer S17
Strathtay S24
Strathtummel S24
Strathy S17
Strathyre S29
Stratton (Corn) 9.1
Stratton (Dorset) 13.1
Stratton (Gloucs) 18.5
Stratton Audley 35.2
Stratton Hall 41.5
Stratton St Margaret 48.2
Stratton Strawless 30.5
Stratton-on-the-Fosse 38.2
Stream 38.3
Streat 16.4
Streatham (part) L8, L22
Streatlam & Stainton 14.1
Streatley (Beds) 2.2
Streatley (Berks) 3.1
Street 38.2
Street Ashton 44.3
Street End 38.7
Street End (Lower Hardres) (Kent) 25.5
Streethay 40.8
Streethouse 47.5
Streetlam (Danby Wiske) 33.2
Streetly 45.5
Streetly (part) 40.8, 45.2
Strefford 37.1
Strelley Village 34.5
Strensall 33.7
Strensham 49.6
Strete 12.9
Stretford (Gtr M'chester) 19.8
Stretford (Here) 21.1
Strethall 17.1
Stretham 6.4
Strettington 46.2
Stretton (Cheshire)* 7.1, 7.3
Stretton (Derbys) 11.4
Stretton (Rutland) 36.1
Stretton (Staffs)* 40.5, 40.6
Stretton Baskerville 44.3
Stretton Grandison 21.1
Stretton Sugwas 21.1
Stretton-en-le-Field 27.1
Stretton-on-Dunsmore 44.3
Stretton-on-Fosse 44.5
Stretton-under-Fosse 44.3
Strichen S1
Stringston 38.3
Strixton 31.6
Strode 38.7
Stromness S23
Stronachlachar S29
Strone of Cally S24
Strongstry 26.14
Stronsay S23
Strontian S17
Strood 25.3
Strood Green (Surrey) 42.8
Strood Green (W Sussex) 46.2
Stroud (Gloucs) 18.6
Stroud (Hants) 20.6
Strouden Park 13.7
Stroxton 28.6
Strubby with Woodthorpe 28.2
Strumpshaw 30.5
Stuartfield S1
Stubbington 20.10
Stubbins 26.14
Stubley 19.4
Stubton 28.6
Stubwood 40.5
Stuckton 20.7
Studd Hill (Herne Bay) 25.5
Studdal 25.6
Studfold 33.5
Studham 2.2
Studland 13.5
Studley (Oxon) (see Horton)
Studley (Warks) 44.5
Studley (Wilts) 48.1
Studley Roger (see Lindrick)
Stuntney 6.4
Sturgate 28.1
Sturmer 17.2
Sturminster Marshall 13.3
Sturminster Newton 13.2
Sturry 25.5
Sturston 30.3
Sturton (Lincs) 28.8
Sturton by Stow 28.1
Sturton-le-Steeple 34.1
Stuston 41.4
Stutchbury 31.7
Stutton 41.6
Stutton-cum-Hazelwood 33.8
Styal 7.5
Stychbrook 40.8
Styche 37.1
Styrrup with Oldcotes 34.1
Subberthwaite 10.5
Success 43.5
Suckley 49.4
Sudborough 31.3
Sudbourne 41.5
Sudbrook (Lincs) 28.6
Sudbrook (Monmth) W13
Sudbrooke 28.1
Sudbury (Derbys) 11.3
Sudbury (Suffolk) 41.6
Sudden 19.4
Sudeley 18.1
Suffield 30.1
Suffield-cum-Everley 33.4
Sugdon 37.4
Sula Sgeir S32
Sulby 31.4
Sulgrave (N'hants) 31.7
Sulgrave (T & W) 43.5
Sulham (see Tidmarsh)
Sulhamstead 3.1
Sullington 46.3
Sullom Voe S26
Sully (Som) 38.3
Sully (Vale Glam) W21
Sumburgh S26
Summercourt 9.1
Summerfield 25.6
Summerhill 40.8
Summerhouse 14.8
Summerlands (Cumbria) 10.5
Summerlands (Som) 38.5
Summerley 11.4
Summerseat 19.3
Summertown 35.5
Summit 19.4
Sumners 17.5
Sunart S17
Sunbiggin 10.3
Sunbury-on-Thames 42.2
Sundays Hill 18.7
Sunderland 43.5
Sunderland Bridge 14.1
Sundon 2.2
Sundridge 25.8
Sunk Island 15.2
Sunningdale (Berks) 3.4
Sunningdale (Caerph) W4
Sunninghill 3.4
Sunningwell 35.4
Sunniside (Durham) 14.1
Sunniside (T & W) 43.3
Sunny Corner 9.1
Sunnybank 10.3
Sunnybrow 14.1
Sunnyhill 11.7

2

Sunnymead 35.5
Sunnyside 39.4
Sunnywood 19.3
Surbiton (part) L21
Surfeit Hill 45.4
Surfleet 28.7
Surlingham 30.7
Surrey Quays L28
Sustead 30.1
Susworth 28.1
Sutcombe 12.1
Suton 30.7
Sutterby 28.2
Sutterton 28.5
Suttieslea S19
Sutton L29
Sutton (Beds) 2.2
Sutton (Cambs) 6.1, 6.4
Sutton (Cheshire)* 7.3, 7.5
Sutton (Dorset) 13.3
Sutton (Kent) 25.6
Sutton (Mersey) 29.3
Sutton (N Yorks) (see Byram)
Sutton (Norfolk) 30.1
Sutton (Notts) 34.1
Sutton (Peterborough) 6.1
Sutton (S Yorks) 39.2
Sutton (Suffolk) 41.5
Sutton (W Sussex) 46.2
Sutton Bassett 31.2
Sutton Benger 48.1
Sutton Bingham 38.5
Sutton Bonington 34.8
Sutton Bridge 28.7
Sutton Cheney 27.4
Sutton Courtenay 35.4
Sutton Green (Cheshire) 7.3
Sutton Green (Surrey) 42.4
Sutton Heath 29.3, 41.5
Sutton Heights 37.4
Sutton Hill 37.4
Sutton Howgrave 33.2
Sutton Leach 29.3
Sutton Maddock 37.1
Sutton Mallet 38.1
Sutton Mandeville 48.1
Sutton Manor 29.3
Sutton Montis 38.5
Sutton St Edmund 28.7
Sutton St James 28.7
Sutton St Nicholas 21.1
Sutton Scarsdale 11.4
Sutton Scotney 20.5
Sutton Spring Wood 11.4
Sutton Stop 44.2
Sutton Valence 25.10
Sutton Veny 48.1
Sutton Waldron 13.2
Sutton Weaver (part) 7.2, 7.3
Sutton-at-Hone 25.1
Sutton-cum-Duckmanton 11.4
Sutton-cum-Granby 34.8
Sutton-in-Ashfield 34.4
Sutton-in-Craven 33.5
Sutton-on-Derwent 15.2
Sutton-on-Forest 33.2
Sutton-on-Hull 15.1
Sutton-on-Sea 28.2
Sutton-on-Trent 34.3
Sutton-on-the-Hill 11.9
Sutton-under-Brailes 44.5
Sutton-under-Whitestonecliffe 33.2
Sutton-upon-Tern 37.1
Swaby 28.2
Swadlincote 11.9
Swaffham 30.3
Swaffham Bulbeck 6.4
Swaffham Prior 6.4
Swafield 30.1
Swainby (Whorlton) 33.2
Swainby with Allerthorpe 33.2
Swainsford (part) 48.1
Swainshill 21.1
Swainsthorpe 30.7
Swainswick 38.6
Swalcliffe 35.2
Swalecliffe 25.5
Swallow 28.1
Swallowcliffe 48.1
Swallowfield 3.3
Swallownest 39.4
Swalwell 43.3
Swampton 20.1
Swan 43.5
Swan Village 45.4
Swanage 13.5
Swanbourne 5.2
Swanbridge (Penarth) W21
Swanland 15.2
Swanley (Cheshire) 7.5
Swanley (Kent) 25.8
Swanley Village (Kent) 25.8
Swanmore 20.5
Swannington (Leics) 27.1
Swannington (Norfolk) 30.5
Swanscombe 25.1
Swansea W19
Swanton Abbott 30.1
Swanton Morley 30.3
Swanton Novers 30.1
Swanvale 9.1
Swanwick (Derbys) 11.6
Swanwick (Hants) 20.10
Swarby 28.4
Swardeston 30.7
Swarkestone 11.9
Swarland 32.1
Swarraton 20.5
Swartha 47.1
Swarthmoor 10.5
Swaton 28.4
Swavesey 6.5
Sway 20.7
Swayfield 28.6
Swaythling 20.8
Sweatmere 37.1
Sweeney 37.1
Sweeney Mountain 37.1
Sweethay 38.4
Sweetshouse 9.1
Sweetworthy 38.3
Sweffling 41.5
Swell (Gloucs) 18.5
Swell (Som) 38.5
Swepstone 27.1
Swerford 35.1
Swettenham 7.5
Swilland 41.5
Swillington 47.2
Swimbridge 12.2
Swinbrook & Widford 35.1
Swinburn 32.1
Swincliffe 47.4
Swinden 33.5
Swinderby 28.4
Swindon (Staffs) 40.6
Swindon (Wilts) 48.2
Swine 15.2
Swinefleet 15.2
Swineford 18.7
Swineshead (Beds) 2.1
Swineshead (Lincs) 28.5
Swinethorpe 28.4
Swinfen 40.8
Swinford (Leics) 27.8
Swinford (Oxon) 35.4
Swingfield 25.13
Swinhoe 32.1
Swinhope 28.1
Swinscoe (see Blore)
Swinstead 28.6
Swinton (Borders) S30
Swinton (Gtr M'chester) 19.5
Swinton (Malton) (N Yorks) 33.3
Swinton (S Yorks) 39.4
Swinton with Warthermarske 33.6
Swiss Cottage L6
Swiss Valley W6
Swithland 27.2
Swyncombe 35.3
Swynnerton 40.4
Swyre 13.1
Sychdyn W10
Sychtyn 37.1
Syde 18.5
Sydenham (Oxon) 35.3
Sydenham (part) L5, L23, L28
Sydenham Damerel 12.3
Syderstone 30.2
Sydling St Nicholas 13.1
Sydmonton 20.1
Syerston 34.3
Sykehouse 39.2
Syleham 41.4
Sylen W6
Symington* S27, S28
Symonds Yat 21.1
Symondsbury 13.1
Syndercombe 38.3
Syreford 18.5
Syresham 31.7
Syston (Leics) 27.2
Syston (Lincs) 28.6
Sytchampton 49.6
Sywell 31.6
Tabley (Inferior & Superior) 7.5
Tackley 35.1
Tacolneston 30.7
Tadcaster, East & West 33.8
Taddington 11.3
Tadley 20.1
Tadlow 6.5
Tadworth 42.9
Tafarnaubach W2
Taffs Well W18
Tai'n Lôn W11
Tai'rgwaith W14
Taibach W14
Tain S17
Tairheol W4
Takeley 17.1
Tal-y-Bont (Gwynedd) W11
Tal-y-Wern W17
Tal-y-bont (Card) W7
Tal-y-llyn W17
Talachddu W17
Talacre W10
Talaton 12.7
Talbenny W16
Talbot Green W18
Talbot Woods 13.7
Talerddig W17
Talgarth W17
Taliesin W7
Talisker S17
Talke 40.2
Talke Pits 40.2
Talkin 10.1
Talland 9.1
Talley W6
Tallington 28.6
Talmine S17
Talog W6
Talrych W8
Talsarnau W11
Talskiddy 9.1
Talwrn W1
Talybont-on-Usk W17
Talysarn W11
Talywain W20
Tame Bridge (Stokesley) 33.2
Tamfourhill S15
Tamworth 40.9
Tan-y-fron W8
Tan-y-lan W8
Tandridge 42.10
Tanfield 14.1
Tanfield Lea 14.1
Tanfield Tye 17.7
Tang Hall 33.7
Tangley 20.4
Tangmere 46.2
Tankersley 39.1
Tankerton (Kent) 25.5
Tanlan W10
Tannadice S2
Tannington 41.4
Tannochside S22
Tansley 11.3
Tansor 31.3

Tansterne 15.2
Tanterton 26.6
Tantobie 14.1
Tanvats 28.4
Tanworth-in-Arden 44.5
Tanygrisiau W11
Taphouse 9.1
Taplow 5.5
Tapton 11.2
Tarbat S17
Tarbert (Argyll & Bute) S3
Tarbert (W Isles) S32
Tarbock 29.4
Tarbolton S27
Tarbrax S28
Tardebigge 49.2
Tarfside S2
Tarland S1
Tarleton 26.8
Tarlton 18.5
Tarnacre (see Upper Rawcliffe)
Tarporley 7.3
Tarr Steps 38.3
Tarraby 10.1
Tarrant Crawford 13.2
Tarrant Gunville 13.2
Tarrant Hinton 13.2
Tarrant Keynston 13.2
Tarrant Launceston 13.2
Tarrant Monkton 13.2
Tarrant Rawston 13.2
Tarrant Rushton 13.2
Tarring 46.6
Tarring Neville 16.4
Tarrington 21.1
Tarset 32.1
Tarskavaig S17
Tarves S1
Tarvin 7.3
Tasburgh 30.7
Tasley 37.1
Tat Bank 45.4
Tatenhill 40.5
Tatham 26.1
Tathwell 28.2
Tatsfield 42.10
Tattenhall 7.3
Tattenhams 42.9
Tattenhoe 5.1
Tattenhoe Park 5.1
Tatterford 30.1
Tattersett 30.1
Tattershall 28.2
Tattershall Bridge 28.4
Tattershall Thorpe 28.2
Tattingstone 41.6
Tatton 7.5
Tatworth 38.5
Taunton 38.4
Taverham 30.5
Tavernspite (part) W6, W16
Tavistock 12.3
Tawe Uchaf W17
Tawstock 12.2
Taxal 11.1
Tayinloan S3
Taylor Hill 47.4
Taynton (Gloucs) 18.2
Taynton (Oxon) 35.1
Taynuilt S3
Tayock S2
Tayport S16
Tayvallich S3
Tea Green 22.1
Tealby 28.1
Team Valley 43.3
Teams 43.3
Teangue S17
Tebay 10.3
Tebworth 2.2
Tedburn St Mary 12.5
Teddesley Hay 40.6
Teddington (Gloucs) 18.1
Teddington (Middx) L27
Tedston Delamere 21.1
Tedstone Wafre 21.1
Teesdale 14.10
Teesville 33.10
Teeton 31.4
Teffont 48.1
Tehidy 9.1
Teigh 36.1
Teigngrace 12.5
Teignmouth 12.5
Telford 37.4
Telham 16.2
Tellisford 38.2
Telscombe Cliffs 16.4
Telscombe Village 16.4
Templand S10
Temple 9.1
Temple (Midlothian) S19
Temple Balsall 45.6
Temple Bruer 28.4
Temple Cloud 38.6
Temple Cowley 35.5
Temple Ewell 25.6
Temple Grafton 44.5
Temple Guiting 18.5
Temple Herdewyke 44.5
Temple High Grange 28.4
Temple Hirst 33.8
Temple Mills L31
Temple Normanton 11.4
Temple Sowerby 10.3
Temple Thornton 32.1
Templecombe 38.5
Templeton (Devon) 12.4
Templeton (Pemb) W16
Tempsford 2.2
Tenbury Wells 49.4
Tenby W16
Tendring 17.4
Tenterden 25.12
Terling 17.2
Tern Hill 37.1
Terregles S10
Terrick 5.3
Terrington St Clement 30.2
Terrington St John 30.2
Terrington with Wiganthorpe 33.3
Testerton 30.1
Teston 25.10
Testwood 20.7
Tetbury 18.5
Tetbury Upton 18.5
Tetchill 37.1
Tetcott 12.1
Tetford 28.2
Tetney 28.2
Tetsworth 35.3
Tettenhall 45.1
Tetworth 6.3
Teversal 34.4
Teversham 6.5
Teviothead S30
Tewin 22.3
Tewkesbury 18.1
Teynham 25.4
Thackley 47.1
Thackthwaite 10.3
Thakeham 46.3
Thame 35.3
Thames Ditton 42.5
Thamesmead (part) L3, L11
Thanet 25.7
Thanington 25.5
Thanington Without 25.5
Thankerton S28
Tharston 30.7
Thatcham 3.1
Thatto Heath 29.3
Thaxted 17.1
The Beacon 9.1
The Blythe 40.5
The Dings 4.1
The Flatts 47.4
The Middles 14.1
The Spinney 43.2
Theakston 33.2
Thealby 28.8
Theale (Berks) 3.1
Theale (Som) 38.1
Theberton 41.5
Theddingworth 27.8
Theddlethorpe All Saints 28.2
Theddlethorpe St Helen 28.2
Thelbridge 12.4
Thelnetham 41.3
Thelveton 30.7
Thelwall 7.1
Themelthorpe 30.5
Thenford 31.7
Theobalds Green 48.1
Therfield 22.1
Thetford 30.3
Theydon Bois 17.6
Theydon Garnon 17.6
Theydon Mount 17.6
Thickhorn 38.5
Thimbleby (Lincs) 28.2
Thimbleby (N Yorks) 33.2
Thingley 48.1
Thingwall 29.5
Thirkleby, High & Low 33.2
Thirlby 33.2
Thirlwall 32.1
Thirn 33.2
Thirsk 33.2
Thirston, East & West 32.1
Thirtleby 15.2
Thistleberry 40.2
Thistleton 26.5
Thistleton (Lancs) (see Greenhalgh)
Thistleton (Rutland) 36.1
Thixendale 33.3
Thockrington 32.1
Tholthorpe 33.2
Thomas Chapel W16
Thomas Town W12
Thomastown W18
Thomley 35.3
Thompson 30.3
Thong 25.2
Thongsbridge 47.4
Thonock 28.1
Thoralby 33.1
Thoresby (see Carperby)
Thoresthorpe (see Saleby)
Thoresway 28.1
Thorganby (Lincs) 28.1
Thorganby (N Yorks) 33.8
Thorington 41.5
Thorlby (see Stirton)
Thorley 22.3
Thormanby 33.2
Thorn 2.2
Thornaby 14.10
Thornage 30.1
Thornborough (Bucks) 5.2
Thornborough (N Yorks) 33.2
Thornbury (Devon)* 12.1
Thornbury (Gloucs) 18.7
Thornbury (Plymouth) 12.8
Thornbury (W Yorks) (part) 47.1, 47.2
Thornbury (Worcs) 21.1
Thornby 31.4
Thorncliffe 40.1
Thorncombe 13.1
Thorncote Green 2.2
Thorndon 41.4
Thorne (S Yorks) 39.2
Thorne St Margaret 38.4
Thorne/Thorne Coffin (Som) 38.5
Thorner 47.2
Thorney (Cambs) 6.1
Thorney (Notts) 34.3
Thorney (Som) 38.5
Thorney Close 43.5
Thorney Gate 32.1
Thorney Hill (Hants) 20.7
Thorney Hill (T & W) 43.1
Thorney Island 46.2
Thorney Toll 6.2
Thornfalcon 38.4
Thornford 13.1
Thorngrafton 32.1
Thorngumbald 15.2
Thornham (Gtr M'chester) 19.4
Thornham (Norfolk) 30.2
Thornham, Magna & Parva (Suffolk) 41.4
Thornhaugh 6.1

2

Thornhill (Cardiff) W5
Thornhill (Derbys) 11.1
Thornhill (Dumfries) S10
Thornhill (Hants) (part) 20.8, 20.9
Thornhill (Middlesbrough) 33.9
Thornhill (Stirling) S29
Thornhill (T & W) 43.5
Thornhill (Torfaen) W20
Thornhill (W Yorks) 47.4
Thornhill Edge 47.4
Thornhill Farm 44.2
Thornhill Lees 47.4
Thornholme 15.2
Thornley 14.1
Thornley with Wheatley 26.3
Thornliebank (part) S14
Thornthwaite with Padside 33.6
Thornton S16
Thornton (Bucks) 5.2
Thornton (E Yorks) 15.2
Thornton (Leics) 27.4
Thornton (Lincs) 28.2
Thornton (Mersey) 29.1
Thornton (Middlesbrough) 33.9
Thornton (W Yorks) 47.1
Thornton (Warks) 44.5
Thornton Bridge 33.6
Thornton Cleveleys (part) 26.2, 26.4
Thornton Curtis 28.8
Thornton Dale 33.3
Thornton Heath L8
Thornton Hough 29.5
Thornton Lodge 47.4
Thornton Riseborough 33.3
Thornton Rust 33.1
Thornton Steward 33.1
Thornton Watlass 33.2
Thornton le Fen 28.2
Thornton-in-Craven 33.5
Thornton-in-Lonsdale 33.5
Thornton-le-Beans 33.2
Thornton-le-Clay 33.3
Thornton-le-Moor (Lincs) 28.1
Thornton-le-Moor (N Yorks) 33.2
Thornton-le-Moors 7.3
Thornton-le-Street 33.2
Thornton-on-the-Hill 33.2
Thorntonhall S28
Thorntree 33.9
Thornville 33.6
Thornwood 17.6
Thornybank S19
Thoroton 34.8
Thorp Arch 47.2
Thorpe (Derbys) 11.3
Thorpe (Durham) (see Wycliffe)
Thorpe (N Yorks) 33.5
Thorpe (N Yorks) (see Snape)
Thorpe (Notts) 34.3
Thorpe (Suffolk) (see Ashfield)
Thorpe (Surrey) 42.1
Thorpe (W Yorks) 47.2
Thorpe Abbotts 30.7
Thorpe Achurch 31.3
Thorpe Arnold 27.3
Thorpe Audlin 47.5
Thorpe Bassett 33.3
Thorpe Bay 17.14
Thorpe Common 39.4
Thorpe Constantine 40.8
Thorpe Dales 28.2
Thorpe Edge 47.1
Thorpe Hamlet (Norwich) 30.4
Thorpe Hesley 39.4
Thorpe Langton 27.8
Thorpe Larches 14.10
Thorpe Latimer 28.4
Thorpe Lubenham 31.4
Thorpe Malsor 31.2
Thorpe Mandeville 31.7
Thorpe Market 30.1
Thorpe Morieux 41.6
Thorpe Parva 30.7
Thorpe St Andrew 30.5
Thorpe St Peter 28.2
Thorpe Salvin 39.4
Thorpe Satchville 27.3
Thorpe Thewles 14.10
Thorpe Tilney 28.4
Thorpe Underwood 31.2
Thorpe Underwoods 33.6
Thorpe Waterville (Thorpe Achurch) 31.3
Thorpe Willoughby 33.8
Thorpe in the Glebe 34.8
Thorpe le Vale 28.2
Thorpe next Haddiscoe 30.7
Thorpe on the Hill (Lincs) 28.4
Thorpe on the Hill (W Yorks) 47.2
Thorpe-by-Water 36.1
Thorpe-in-Balne 39.2
Thorpe-in-the-Fallows 28.1
Thorpe-le-Soken 17.4
Thorpe-le-Willows 33.3
Thorpeness (see Aldringham)
Thorplands 31.5
Thorrington 17.4
Thorverton 12.4
Thrandeston 41.4
Thrapston 31.3
Threapland 10.2
Threapwood (Cheshire) 7.3
Threapwood (Staffs) 40.1
Three Ashes (Hants) 20.1
Three Ashes (Som) 38.5
Three Bridges 46.1
Three Burrows 9.1
Three Cocks W17
Three Crosses W19
Three Gates 27.8
Three Holes 30.2
Three Legged Cross 13.3
Three Oaks, Guestling 16.2
Threekingham 28.4
Threemilestone 9.1
Threemiletown S31
Threlkeld (part) 10.2, 10.3
Threshfield 33.5
Threxton 30.3
Thrigby 30.6
Thrimby 10.3
Thringstone 27.1
Thrintoft 33.2
Thriplow 6.5
Throapham 39.4
Throckenholt (Cambs) 6.2
Throckenholt (Lincs) 28.7
Throckley 43.1
Throckmorton 49.6
Throop* 13.5, 13.7
Throphill 32.1
Thropton 32.1
Throsk S29
Throwleigh 12.3
Throwley 25.4
Thrumpton 34.8
Thrumster S17
Thrupp (Gloucs) 18.6
Thrupp (Oxon) 35.2
Thruscross 33.6
Thrushelton 12.3
Thrussington 27.2
Thruxton (Hants) 20.4
Thruxton (Here) 21.1
Thrybergh 39.4
Thulston 11.9
Thunderbridge 47.4
Thundersley 17.13
Thundridge 22.3
Thurcaston 27.2
Thurcroft 39.4
Thurgarton (Norfolk) 30.1
Thurgarton (Notts) 34.3
Thurgoland 39.1
Thurlaston (Leics) 27.6
Thurlaston (Warks) 44.3
Thurlbear 38.4
Thurlby* 28.2, 28.4, 28.6
Thurleigh 2.1
Thurlestone 12.9
Thurloxton 38.1
Thurlstone 39.1
Thurlton 30.7
Thurmaston (part) 27.2, 27.5
Thurnby 27.8
Thurne 30.6
Thurnham (Kent) 25.10
Thurnham (Lancs) 26.1
Thurning (N'hants) 31.3
Thurning (Norfolk) 30.1
Thurnscoe 39.1
Thurrock 17.12
Thursby 10.2
Thursford 30.1
Thursley 42.11
Thurso S17
Thurstaston 29.5
Thurston 41.4
Thurstonfield 10.1
Thurstonland 47.4
Thurton 30.7
Thurvaston 11.9
Thuxton 30.3
Thwaite (Norfolk) 30.7
Thwaite (Norfolk) (see Alby)
Thwaite (Suffolk) 41.4
Thwaite Flat 10.6
Thwaites 47.1
Thwaites Brow 47.1
Thwing 15.2
Tibbermore S24
Tibberton (Gloucs) 18.2
Tibberton (Shrop)* 37.1, 37.4
Tibberton (Worcs) 49.6
Tibenham 30.7
Tibshelf 11.5
Tibthorpe 15.2
Ticehurst 16.2
Tichborne 20.5
Tickencote 36.1
Tickenham 38.7
Tickhill 39.2
Ticklerton 37.1
Ticknall 11.9
Tickton 15.2
Tidbury Green 45.6
Tidcombe 48.1
Tiddington (Oxon) 35.3
Tiddington (Warks) 44.5
Tiddycross 37.4
Tideford 9.1
Tidenham 18.2
Tidenham Chase 18.2
Tideswell 11.3
Tidgrove 20.1
Tidmarsh with Sulham 3.1
Tidmington 44.5
Tidworth 48.1
Tiers Cross W16
Tiffield 31.7
Tigerton S2
Tighnabruaich S3
Tilbrook (Bucks) 5.1
Tilbrook (Cambs) 6.3
Tilbury 17.12
Tilbury-juxta-Clare 17.2
Tile Cross 45.5
Tilehurst (part) 3.1, 3.2
Tilford 42.11
Tilgate 46.1
Tiliside 32.1
Tilland 9.1
Tilley 37.1
Tilley Green 37.1
Tillicoultry S8
Tillietudlem S28
Tillingham 17.8
Tillington (Here) 21.1
Tillington (W Sussex) 46.2
Tilmanstone 25.6
Tilney All Saints 30.2
Tilney St Lawrence 30.2
Tilshead 48.1
Tilstock 37.1
Tilston 7.3
Tilstone Fearnall 7.3

Tilsworth 2.2
Tilton on the Hill 27.8
Tilty 17.1
Timberhonger 49.2
Timberland 28.4
Timberscombe 38.3
Timperley 19.8
Timsbury (Hants) 20.4
Timsbury (Som) 38.6
Timworth 41.3
Tincleton 13.1
Tindale Crescent 14.1
Tindale Fell 10.1
Tingewick 5.2
Tingley 47.2
Tingrith 2.2
Tingwall S26
Tinkers Bridge 5.1
Tinkers Cross 20.7
Tintagel 9.1
Tintern W13
Tintinhull 38.5
Tintwistle 11.1
Tinwald S10
Tinwell 36.1
Tippity Green 45.4
Tiptoe 20.7
Tipton (part) 45.3, 45.4
Tipton Green 45.4
Tiptree 17.3
Tirabad W17
Tircoed W19
Tirdeunaw W19
Tiree, Isle of S3
Tirley 18.1
Tiroran S3
Tirphil W4
Tirril 10.3
Tiryberth W4
Tirydail W6
Tirymynach W7
Tisbury 48.1
Tismans Common 46.3
Tissington 11.3
Titchfield 20.10
Titchmarsh 31.3
Titchwell 30.2
Tithby 34.8
Tithill 38.4
Titley 21.1
Titsey 42.10
Tittenley 37.1
Tittensor 40.4
Tittesworth 40.1
Tittleshall 30.3
Tiumpan S32
Tiverton (Cheshire) 7.3
Tiverton (Devon) 12.4
Tivetshall St Margaret 30.7
Tivetshall St Mary 30.7
Tividale 45.4
Tivington 38.3
Tivington Knowle 38.3
Tixall 40.4
Tixover 36.1
Toab S26
Toadhole 11.4
Tobermory S3
Toberonochy S3
Tockenham 48.1
Tocketts 33.10
Tockholes 26.10
Tockington 18.7
Tockwith 33.6
Todber 13.2
Toddington 2.2
Toddington (Gloucs) 18.1
Toddington (W Sussex) 46.5
Todds Green (part) 22.1, 22.2
Todenham 18.5
Todhills 10.1
Todmorden 47.3
Todpool 9.1
Todwick 39.4
Toft (Cambs) 6.5
Toft (Cheshire) 7.5
Toft (Warks) 44.3
Toft Hill 14.1
Toft Monks 30.7
Toft Newton 28.1
Toft with Lound 28.6
Toftrees 30.1
Tofts, West 30.3
Toghill 18.7
Togston 32.1
Tokers Green 35.3
Toll End 45.4
Tolland 38.4
Tollard Royal 48.1
Tolldown 18.7
Toller Fratrum 13.1
Toller Porcorum 13.1
Toller Whelme 13.1
Tollerton (N Yorks) 33.2
Tollerton (Notts) 34.8
Tollesbury 17.8
Tollesby 33.9
Tolleshunt D'Arcy 17.8
Tolleshunt Knights 17.8
Tolleshunt Major 17.8
Tolob S26
Tolpuddle 13.1
Tolworth (Surbiton) L21
Tomatin S17
Tomdoun S17
Tomich S17
Tomintoul S20
Tomlow 44.5
Tomnavoulin S20
Ton Pentre W18
Tonbridge 25.9
Tondu W3
Tone Vale 38.4
Tonedale 38.4
Tong (Shrop) 37.1
Tong (W Yorks) 47.1
Tong Park 47.1
Tonge (Kent) 25.4
Tonge (Leics) 27.1
Tongham 42.7
Tongue S17
Tongue End 28.7
Tongwell 5.1
Tongwynlais W5
Tonmawr W14
Tonna W14
Tonteg W18
Tonyfelin W4
Tonypandy W18
Tonyrefail W18
Toot Baldon 35.3
Toot Hill (Essex) 17.6
Toothill (Wilts) 48.2
Tooting L32
Tooting Graveney (part) L24, L32
Top Valley (part) 34.6
Topcliffe 33.2
Topcroft 30.7
Toppesfield 17.2
Torbay 12.10
Torbryan 12.5
Tore S17
Torksey 28.1
Tormarton 18.7
Toronto 14.1
Torpantau W17
Torpenhow 10.2
Torphichen S31
Torphins S1
Torpoint 9.1
Torquay 12.10
Torrance S12
Torre 38.3
Torridon S17
Torrin S17
Torrington (see Gt Torrington)
Torryburn S16
Torthorwald S10
Tortington 46.5
Tortworth 18.7
Torver 10.5
Torweston 38.3
Torwood S15
Torworth 34.1
Toscaig S17
Toseland 6.3
Tosside (part) 26.3, 33.5
Tosson 32.1
Tostock 41.4
Tothby 28.2
Tothill (Hants) 20.1
Tothill (Lincs) 28.2
Totland 24.1
Totnell 13.1
Totnes 12.9
Toton 34.5
Tottenham L14
Tottenham Vale L14
Tottenhill 30.2
Totterdown 4.1
Totternhoe 2.2
Totterton 37.1
Totties 47.4
Tottington (Gtr M'chester) 19.3
Tottington (Norfolk) 30.3
Totton 20.7
Touchen End 3.4
Tough S1
Toulson (see Newton Kyme)
Tovil 25.10
Tow Law 14.1
Towan Cross 9.1
Toward S3
Towcester 31.7
Towednack 9.1
Tower Gate 5.1
Tower Hamlets L30
Tower Hill (Kirkby) 29.4
Tower Hill (London) L30
Tower, The 38.5
Towerhead 38.7
Towersey 35.3
Towie S1
Town End (Cumbria) 10.5
Town End (W Yorks) 47.1
Town End Farm 43.5
Town Littleworth 16.4
Town Yetholm S30
Townhill W19
Townhill Farm 20.9
Towns End (Som) 38.5
Townsend (Corn) (part) 9.1
Townsend (Dorset) 13.7
Townsend (Gloucs) 18.7
Townsend (Hants) 20.1
Townsend (Staffs) 40.3
Townville 47.5
Townwell 18.7
Towthorpe (E Yorks) 15.2
Towthorpe (York) 33.7
Towton 33.8
Towyn W8
Toxteth 29.2
Toynton All Saints 28.2
Toynton St Peter 28.2
Toys Hill 25.8
Tracebridge 38.4
Trafford Park 19.8
Traianglas W17
Traianmawr W17
Trajan Gate 22.3
Trallong W17
Trallwn W18
Trallwn (Swansea) W19
Tranch W20
Tranent S13
Tranmere (Mersey) 29.5
Tranmere Park (W Yorks) 47.2
Trannack 9.1
Tranwell 32.1
Trapwell (Rudry) W4
Traquair S30
Trawden 26.13
Trawscoed W7
Trawsfynydd W11
Trawsmawr W6
Treadam W13
Trealaw W18
Treales 26.5
Trearddur Bay W1
Treaubrey W21
Trebanog W18
Trebanos W14
Trebetherick 9.1
Trebles Holford 38.4
Treboeth W19
Treborough 38.3

Treborth W11
Trebudannon (Newquay) 9.1
Trebullett 9.1
Treburley 9.1
Treburrick 9.1
Trecastle W17
Trecenydd W4
Trecoed (see Disserth)
Trecwn W16
Trecynon W18
Tredarvah 9.1
Tredavoe 9.1
Tredegar W2
Tredington 44.5
Tredinnick 9.1
Tredinnickpits 9.1
Tredodridge W21
Tredogan W21
Tredomen W4
Tredrizzick 9.1
Tredunnock W13
Tredworth 18.3
Treen 9.1
Treeton 39.4
Trefdraeth W1
Trefechan W12
Trefeglwys W17
Trefeurig W7
Treffgarne W16
Trefil W2
Trefilan W7
Treflach 37.1
Treflys W17
Trefnanney W17
Trefnant W9
Trefonen 37.1
Trefor W11
Trefor (Anglesey) W1
Treforest W18
Trefriw W8
Tregadillett 9.1
Tregagle W13
Tregaian W1
Tregare W13
Tregaron W7
Tregarth W11
Tregavethan 9.1
Tregele W1
Tregellist 9.1
Tregeseal 9.1
Tregonetha 9.1
Tregongon 9.1
Tregoniggie 9.1
Tregony 9.1
Tregorrick 9.1
Tregoss 9.1
Tregoyd W17
Tregrehan 9.1
Tregurrian 9.1
Tregynon W17
Trehafod W18
Trehan 9.1
Treharris W12
Treherbert (Carm) W6
Treherbert (Rhondda) W18
Trehunist 9.1
Trelawnyd W10
Trelech W6
Trelech-a'r-Bettws W6
Treleigh 9.1
Trelewis W12
Treligga 9.1
Trelights 9.1
Trelill 9.1
Treliske 9.1
Trellech W13
Trelogan W10
Trelonk 9.1
Trelowth (St Mewan) 9.1
Trelystan W17
Tremadog W11
Tremaine 9.1
Tremar 9.1
Trematon 9.1
Tremeirchion W9
Tremoilet W6
Tremostyn W10
Trenance (Mawgan Porth) 9.1
Trenance (St Austell) 9.1
Trench (part) 37.1, 37.4
Trendeal 9.1
Trenear 9.1
Treneglos 9.1
Trenona 9.1
Trent 13.1
Trent Vale 40.3
Trentham 40.3
Trentishoe 12.2
Treoes W21
Treorchy W18
Treovis 9.1
Treowen W4
Trequite 9.1
Trerhyngyll W21
Trerice (St Dennis) 9.1
Trerulefoot 9.1
Tresawsen 9.1
Tresco 50.1
Trescott 40.6
Trescowe 9.1
Tresean 9.1
Tresham 18.6
Tresillian 9.1
Treskerby 9.1
Treslothan 9.1
Tresmeer 9.1
Tressait S24
Tresta S26
Treswell 34.1
Treswithian 9.1
Trethem 9.1
Trethewell 9.1
Trethomas W4
Trethowel 9.1
Trethurgy 9.1
Tretire 21.1
Tretower W17
Treuddyn W10
Trevalga 9.1
Trevanson 9.1
Trevarren 9.1
Trevarrian 9.1
Trevaughan (Carmarthen) W6
Trevaughan (Whitland) W6
Treveal 9.1
Treveighan 9.1
Trevellas 9.1
Treveor (St Stephen, St Austell) 9.1
Trevethin W20
Trevigro 9.1
Treville 21.1
Treviscoe 9.1
Treviskey 9.1
Trevone 9.1
Trevor W22
Trewalder 9.1
Trewellard 9.1
Trewen 9.1
Trewern (Powys) W17
Trewethern 9.1
Trewidland 9.1
Trewince 9.1
Trewint 9.1
Trewithen 9.1
Trewoon 9.1
Treworga 9.1
Treyford 46.2
Triangle 47.3
Triangle (Chasetown) (Staffs) 40.8
Tricketts Cross 13.3
Trimdon Station (Deaf Hill) 14.1
Trimdon, Colliery, Grange & Village 14.1
Trimingham 30.1
Trimley St Martin 41.5
Trimley St Mary 41.5
Trimpley 49.1
Trimsaran W6
Trinafour S24
Trinant W4
Tring 22.4
Tring Hill 5.2
Trinity S2
Trispen 9.1
Tritlington 32.1
Trochry S24
Troedrhiwfuwch W4
Troedyraur W7
Troedyrhiw W12
Trofarth W8
Troon (Corn) 9.1
Troon (S Ayrs) S27
Troston 41.3
Trostre W13
Trotternish S17
Trottiscliffe 25.9
Trotton 46.2
Troutbeck Bridge 10.5
Troutbeck, Windermere 10.5
Troutsdale 33.4
Troway 11.4
Trowbridge 48.1
Trowbridge Estate L12
Trowell 34.5
Trowse with Newton 30.7
Troytes 38.3
Trub 19.4
Trudoxhill 38.2
Trull 38.4
Trumfleet 39.2
Trumpington 6.6
Trunch 30.1
Truro City 9.1
Trusham 12.5
Trusley 11.9
Trusthorpe 28.2
Trysull 40.6
Tubney 35.4
Tuckingmill (Corn) 9.1
Tuckingmill (Wilts) 48.1
Tuckton 13.7
Tucoyse 9.1
Tuddenham St Martin 41.5
Tuddenham* (Suffolk) 41.2
Tuddenham, East & North (Norfolk) 30.3
Tudeley 25.11
Tudhoe 14.1
Tudweiliog W11
Tuebrook 29.2
Tuffley 18.3
Tufnel Park L19
Tufton 20.1
Tugby 27.8
Tugford 37.1
Tullibardine S24
Tullibody S8
Tullich (see Glenmuick)
Tulliemet S24
Tullynessle & Forbes S1
Tumble W6
Tumby 28.2
Tummel Bridge S24
Tunbridge Wells, Royal 25.11
Tunley 38.6
Tunstall (E Yorks) 15.2
Tunstall (Kent) 25.4
Tunstall (Lancs) 26.1
Tunstall (N Yorks) 33.1
Tunstall (Shrop) 37.1
Tunstall (Staffs) 40.3
Tunstall (Suffolk) 41.5
Tunstall (T & W) 43.5
Tunstall Village 43.5
Tunstead 30.1
Tunworth 20.1
Tupholme 28.2
Tupton 11.4
Tur Langton 27.8
Turgis Green 20.1
Turkdean 18.5
Turn 26.14
Turnastone 21.1
Turnberry S27
Turnbridge 47.4
Turnditch 11.6
Turners Hill 46.4
Turners Puddle 13.5
Turnerwood 39.4
Turnford 22.7
Turnham Green (part) L9
Turnhurst 40.3
Turnworth 13.2
Turriff S1
Tursdale 14.1

Turton, North 26.10
Turton, South 19.2
Turves 6.2
Turvey 2.1
Turville (Bucks) 5.3
Turweston 5.2
Tushingham-cum-Grindley 7.3
Tusmore 35.2
Tutbury 40.5
Tutnall 49.2
Tutshill (Gloucs) 18.2
Tuxford 34.1
Twechar S12
Tweedale 37.4
Tweedmouth 32.1
Tweedsmuir S30
Twemlow 7.5
Twenty 28.6
Twickenham L27
Twigmoor 28.8
Twigworth 18.1
Twin Rivers 15.2
Twineham 46.4
Twinstead 17.2
Twiston 26.3
Twitchen (Devon) 12.2
Twitchen (Shrop) 37.1
Twitham 25.6
Twitton 25.8
Two Burrows 9.1
Two Gates 40.9
Two Locks W20
Two Mile Ash 5.1
Two Mile Hill 4.1
Twowatersfoot 9.1
Twycross 27.4
Twydall 25.3
Twyford (Berks) 3.3
Twyford (Bucks) 5.2
Twyford (Derbys) 11.9
Twyford (Hants) 20.5
Twyford (Here) 21.1
Twyford (Leics) 27.3
Twyford (Norfolk) 30.3
Twyn Shon Evan W4
Twyn, The (Caerph) W4
Twyn-yr-odyn (Vale Glam) W21
Twynholm S10
Twyning 18.1
Twynyrodyn (Merthyr) W12
Twywell 31.3
Ty Croes (Anglesey) W1
Ty Nant W8
Ty'n-y-Maes W11
Ty-Isaf W4
Ty-Sign (Risca) W4
Ty-broughton W22
Tyberton 21.1
Tyburn 45.5
Tycoch W19
Tycroes (Carm) W6
Tydd Gote (part) 6.2, 28.7
Tydd St Giles 6.2
Tydd St Mary 28.7
Tye Green 17.5
Tye Green (part) 17.7
Tyersal (part) 47.1, 47.2
Tyldesley 19.1
Tyler Hill 25.5
Tylers Green 5.3
Tylorstown W18
Tyn Lon W1
Tyn-y-morfa W10
Tynant W18
Tyndalls Park 4.1
Tyndrum S29
Tyneham 13.5
Tynehead S19
Tynemouth 43.2
Tynewydd W18
Tyninghame S13
Tynron S10
Tyntesfield 38.7
Tynygongl W1
Tyrie S1
Tyringham-cum-Filgrave 5.1
Tyrley (Shrop) 37.1
Tyrley (Staffs) 40.2
Tyrrells Wood 42.8
Tyseley 45.5
Tysoe 44.5
Tythegston (part) W3, W14
Tytherington (Gloucs) 18.7
Tytherington (Som) 38.2
Tytherington (Wilts) 48.1
Tytherton Lucas 48.1
Tyttenhanger (part) 22.5, 22.10
Tywardreath 9.1
Tywyn (Gwynedd) W11
Ubbeston 41.5
Ubley (part) 38.2, 38.6
Uckerby 33.1
Uckfield 16.1
Uckington 18.1
Uddingston (part) S22, S28
Udimore 16.2
Udny S1
Udston S28
Uffculme 12.4
Uffington (Lincs) 28.6
Uffington (Oxon) 35.4
Uffington (Shrop) (part) 37.1, 37.4
Ufford (Cambs) 6.1
Ufford (Suffolk) 41.5
Ufton 44.5
Ufton Nervet 3.1
Ugborough 12.9
Uggeshall 41.1
Ugglebarnby 33.4
Ughill 39.3
Ugley 17.1
Ugthorpe 33.4
Uig (Highland) S17
Uig (W Isles) S32
Ulceby (Lincs) (part) 28.1, 28.8
Ulceby with Fordington 28.2
Ulcombe 25.10
Uldale 10.2
Uley 18.6
Ulgham 32.1
Ulgham Grange 32.1
Ullapool S17
Ullenhall 44.5
Ulleskelf 33.8
Ullesthorpe 27.8
Ulley 39.4
Ullingswick 21.1
Ulnes Walton 26.9
Ulpha (part) 10.4, 10.5
Ulrome 15.2
Ulting 17.8
Ulva Ferry S3
Ulverscroft 27.2
Ulverston 10.5
Umberleigh (part) 12.2, 12.4
Umberslade 44.5
Uncleby 15.2
Underbarrow 10.5
Underbridge W14
Undercliffe 47.1
Underdown (Chartham) 25.5
Underriver 25.8
Underskiddaw 10.2
Underwood (Derbys) (see Offcote)
Underwood (Notts) 34.4
Undley 41.2
Undy W13
Unst S26
Unstone 11.4
Unsworth 19.3
Unthank (part) 10.1, 10.3
Up Cerne 13.1
Up Holland 26.8
Up Marden 46.2
Up Mudford 38.5
Up Nateley 20.1
Up Somborne 20.4
Upavon 48.1
Upchurch 25.4
Uphall S31
Uphall Station S31
Upham (Hants) 20.5
Upham, Upper & Lower (Wilts) 48.1
Uphampton 49.6
Uphill 38.7
Upland Arms W6
Uplands W19
Uplawmoor S14
Upleadon 18.2
Upleatham 33.10
Uploders 13.1
Uplowman 12.4
Uplyme 12.7
Upminster L16
Upnor 25.3
Upottery 12.7
Upper Arley 49.1
Upper Batley 47.4
Upper Beeding 46.3
Upper Benefield (Benefield) 31.3
Upper Boddington 31.7
Upper Broughton 34.8
Upper Bruntingthorpe 27.8
Upper Brynamman W6
Upper Caldecote 2.2
Upper Chapel W17
Upper Cheddon 38.4
Upper Chirk Bank 37.1
Upper Chute 48.1
Upper Clapton L12
Upper Clatford 20.4
Upper College 37.1
Upper Colwyn Bay W8
Upper Cumberworth 47.4
Upper Cwmtwrch (part) W14, W17
Upper Denby 47.4
Upper Denton 10.1
Upper Edmonton L10
Upper Fivehead 38.5
Upper Gatton 42.9
Upper Gornal 45.3
Upper Halling 25.3
Upper Harbledown 25.5
Upper Hardres 25.5
Upper Hartshay 11.6
Upper Haugh 39.4
Upper Haysden 25.11
Upper Heaton 47.4
Upper Helmsley 33.3
Upper Heyford (N'hants) 31.7
Upper Heyford (Oxon) 35.2
Upper Hill (Gloucs) 18.7
Upper Hill (Here) 21.1
Upper Holloway L19
Upper Hopton 47.4
Upper Kilcot 18.7
Upper Killay W19
Upper Langford 38.7
Upper Langwith 11.5
Upper Largo S16
Upper Littleton 38.7
Upper Llandwrog W11
Upper Longdon 40.8
Upper Morton 18.7
Upper Newbold (part) 11.2
Upper Norwood (Bromley) (part) L5, L22
Upper Norwood (Graffham) (W Sussex) 46.2
Upper Oldfield 47.4
Upper Pollicott 5.2
Upper Poppleton 33.7
Upper Race W20
Upper Radbourne 44.5
Upper Rawcliffe with Tarnacre 26.2
Upper Rissington 18.5
Upper Sapey 21.1
Upper Shelton 2.2
Upper Sheringham 30.1
Upper Shuckburgh 44.5
Upper Slaughter 18.5
Upper Stoke 25.3
Upper Stondon 2.2
Upper Stowe 31.4
Upper Tadmarton 35.2
Upper Tooting (part) L24, L32
Upper Town (Som) 38.7
Upper Trench (part) 37.1
Upper Walthamstow L31
Upper Wanborough 48.2

Upper Winchedon 5.2
Upper Wootton 20.1
Upper Wyke 20.1
Upperhulme 40.1
Upperkeith S13
Uppermidhope 39.3
Uppermill 19.7
Upperthong 47.4
Upperton 46.2
Uppertown (Derbys) 11.4
Uppingham 36.1
Uppington (Dorset) 13.3
Uppington (Shrop) (part) 37.1, 37.4
Uppington (Wilts) 48.1
Uppleby (Easingwold) 33.2
Upsall (part) 33.2, 33.10
Upshire 17.6
Upsland (see Kirklington)
Upstreet 25.5
Upton (Berks) 3.5
Upton (Bucks) 5.2
Upton (Cambs) 6.1
Upton (Dorset) (part) 13.5, 13.6
Upton (Hants) 20.4
Upton (Leics) 27.4
Upton (Lincs) 28.1
Upton (Mersey) 29.5
Upton (N'hants) 31.5
Upton (Notts) 34.3
Upton (Oxon) 35.4
Upton (Som)* 38.3, 38.5
Upton (W Yorks) 47.5
Upton (Warks) 44.5
Upton (Wilts) 48.1
Upton Bishop 21.1
Upton Cheyney 18.7
Upton Cressett 37.1
Upton Crews 21.1
Upton Cross 9.1
Upton Grey 20.1
Upton Hellions 12.4
Upton Lovell 48.1
Upton Magna (part) 37.1, 37.4
Upton Noble 38.2
Upton Pyne 12.7
Upton St Leonards 18.6
Upton Scudamore 48.1
Upton Snodsbury 49.6
Upton Warren 49.6
Upton with Fishley 30.5
Upton-by-Chester 7.3
Upton-upon-Severn 49.4
Upwaltham 46.2
Upware 6.4
Upwell 30.2
Upwood (Cambs) 6.3
Upwood (Dorset) 13.3
Urchany S17
Urchfont 48.1
Urgashay 38.5
Urmston 19.8
Urpeth 14.1
Urpeth Grange 14.1
Urquhart S20
Urray S17
Usan S2
Ushaw Moor 14.1
Usk W13
Usselby 28.1
Usworth 43.5
Utkinton 7.3
Utley 47.1
Utterby 28.2
Uttoxeter 40.5
Uwchmynydd W11
Uwchygarreg W17
Uzmaston & Boulston W16
Vagg 38.5
Vale 47.3
Vale of Grwyney, Velindre W17
Valley (Anglesey) W1
Valley (Mersey) 29.2
Valley Park 20.4
Valtos S32
Van (Carm) W6
Van (Powys) W17
Vange (part) 17.10, 17.12
Varteg W20
Vatersay S32
Vauxhall 37.4
Vauxhaull (Mersey) 29.2
Vaynol Park W11
Vaynor W12
Velindre W14
Venn 38.5
Venn Cross 38.4
Ventnor 24.1
Vernham Dean 20.4
Vernolds Common 37.1
Verrington 38.5
Verwood 13.3
Veryan 9.1
Viables 20.1
Victoria L33
Victoria (part) 9.1
Victoria Dock L25
Victoria Garesfield 43.3
Victoria Park 4.1
Viewpark S22
Vigo 25.2
Village on the Green 44.2
Vines Cross 16.1
Viney Bridge 38.5
Viney Hill 18.2
Virginia Water 42.1
Virginstow 12.1
Virley (see Salcot)
Vobster 38.2
Voe S26
Vogue 9.1
Voguebeloth 9.1
Vowchurch 21.1
Vyne 20.1
Waberthwaite 10.4
Wackerfield 14.1
Wacton (Norfolk) 30.7
Wacton (Worcs) 21.1
Wadborough 49.6
Waddesdon 5.2
Waddingham 28.1
Waddington (Lancs) 26.3
Waddington (Lincs) 28.4
Waddingworth 28.2
Waddon 13.1
Wadebridge 9.1
Wadeford 38.5
Wadenhoe 31.3
Wadesmill 22.3
Wadhurst 16.1
Wadingburn S19
Wadshelf 11.4
Wadsworth 47.3
Wadwick 20.1
Wadworth 39.2
Waen (Denbigh) W9
Waen (Gwynedd) W11
Wagg 38.5
Wainfelin W20
Wainfleet All Saints 28.2
Wainfleet St Mary 28.2
Waingroves 11.6
Wainscott 25.3
Wainstalls 47.3
Waitby 10.3
Waithe 28.2
Wakebridge 11.6
Wakefield 47.5
Wakerley 31.3
Wakes Colne 17.3
Walberswick 41.5
Walberton 46.5
Walbottle 43.1
Walburn 33.1
Walcombe 38.2
Walcot (Lincs) 28.4
Walcot (Norfolk) 30.1
Walcot (Shrop) 37.4
Walcote (Leics) 27.8
Walcote (Warks) 44.5
Walcott 28.4
Walden Stubbs 33.8
Waldershare 25.6
Walderslade (part) 25.3, 25.9, 25.10
Walderton 46.2
Waldridge 14.1
Waldringfield 41.5
Waldron 16.1
Wales (S Yorks) 39.4
Wales (Som) 38.5
Wales Bar 39.4
Walesby (Lincs) 28.1
Walesby (Notts) 34.3
Walford (Dorset) 13.3
Walford (Here) 21.1
Walford (Shrop) 37.1
Walford (Som) 38.4
Walford Heath 37.1
Walford, Letton & Newton 21.1
Walgherton 7.5
Walgrave 31.4
Walham Green L13
Walhampton 20.7
Walk Mill 26.12
Walkden 19.5
Walker 43.1
Walkerburn S30
Walkerdene 43.1
Walkergate 43.1
Walkeringham 34.1
Walkerith 28.1
Walkern 22.3
Walkers Heath (part) 45.5, 49.2
Walkerville 43.1
Walkford 13.8
Walkhampton 12.3
Walkingham Hill with Occaney 33.6
Walkington 15.2
Walkwood 49.3
Wall (N'land) 32.1
Wall (Staffs) 40.8
Wall End 10.5
Wall Heath 45.3
Wall Village 40.8
Wall-under-Haywood 37.1
Wallacestone S15
Wallasea Island 17.11
Wallasey 29.5
Wallerthwaite (see Markington)
Wallingford 35.3
Wallington (Hants) 20.10
Wallington (Herts) 22.1
Wallington Demesne 32.1
Wallingwells 34.1
Wallisdown (part) 13.6, 13.7
Walliswood 42.8
Wallridge 32.1
Walls S26
Wallsend 43.2
Wallyford S13
Walmer 25.6
Walmer Bridge 26.7
Walmersley 19.3
Walmgate 33.7
Walmley 45.5
Walmsgate 28.2
Walney Island 10.6
Walnut Tree 5.1
Walpole (Norfolk) 30.2
Walpole (Suffolk) 41.5
Walpole Cross Keys 30.2
Walpole Highway 30.2
Walronds Park 38.5
Walsall 45.2
Walsall Wood 45.2
Walsden 47.3
Walsgrave-on-Sowe 45.7
Walsham-le-Willows 41.4
Walshaw (Gtr M'chester) 19.3
Walshaw (W Yorks) 47.3
Walshford (see Gt Ribston)
Walsoken 30.2
Walston S28
Walters Ash 5.3
Walterston W21
Walterstone 21.1
Waltham 28.9
Waltham (Kent) 25.5
Waltham Abbey (part) 17.6, 22.7
Waltham Chase 20.5
Waltham Cross (part) L10, 22.7

Waltham Forest L31
Waltham St Lawrence 3.4
Waltham on the Wolds 27.3
Walthamstow L31
Walton (Bucks) 5.1
Walton (Cambs) 6.1
Walton (Cheshire) 7.1
Walton (Cumbria) 10.1
Walton (Derbys) (part) 11.2, 11.4
Walton (Leics) 27.8
Walton (Mersey) 29.2
Walton (Powys) W17
Walton (Shrop) 37.4
Walton (Som) 38.2
Walton (W Yorks)* 47.2, 47.5
Walton (Warks) 44.5
Walton Bay 38.7
Walton Cardiff 18.1
Walton East W16
Walton Hall 5.1
Walton Manor 35.5
Walton Park 5.1, 38.7
Walton Pool 49.2
Walton St Mary 38.7
Walton West W16
Walton on the Wolds 27.2
Walton-in-Gordano 38.7
Walton-le-Dale 26.7
Walton-on-Thames 42.5
Walton-on-the-Hill 42.9
Walton-on-the-Naze 17.4
Walton-upon-Trent 11.9
Walwick 32.1
Walworth (Durham) 14.8
Walworth (London) L28
Walwyns Castle W16
Wambrook 38.5
Wamphray S10
Wanborough (Surrey) 42.7
Wanborough (Wilts) 48.2
Wandsworth L32
Wangford* 41.1, 41.2
Wanlip 27.2
Wanlockhead S10
Wansford (Cambs) (part) 6.1, 6.3
Wansford (E Yorks) 15.2
Wanstrow 38.2
Wantage 35.4
Wantisden 41.5
Wapley 18.7
Waplington 15.2
Wappenbury 44.4
Wappenham 31.7
Wappenshall 37.4
Wapping L30
Warbleton 16.1
Warborough 35.3
Warboys 6.3
Warbreck 29.2
Warbstow 9.1
Warburton 19.8
Warcop 10.3
Ward End 45.5
Ward Green 39.1
Warden (Kent) 25.4
Warden (N'land) 32.1
Warden Law 43.5
Wardhedges 2.2
Wardington (Upper & Lower) 35.2
Wardle (Cheshire) 7.5
Wardle (Gtr M'chester) 19.4
Wardleworth 19.4
Wardley (Rutland) 36.1
Wardley (T & W) 43.3
Wardley (W Sussex) 46.2
Wardley Green 46.2
Wardlow 11.3
Wardour 48.1
Wardy Hill 6.4
Ware (Herts) 22.3
Ware (Kent) 25.6
Wareham 13.5
Warehorne 25.12
Warenford 32.1
Waresley 6.3
Warfield 3.6
Wargrave (Berks) 3.3
Wargrave (Mersey) 29.3
Warham 30.1
Wark* 32.1
Warkleigh 12.2
Warkton 31.2
Warkworth (N'hants) 31.7
Warkworth (N'land) 32.1
Warlaby 33.2
Warland 47.3
Warleggan 9.1
Warleigh 38.6
Warley (Essex) 17.9
Warley (W Mids) 45.4
Warley (W Yorks) 47.3
Warlingham (part) L8, 42.10
Warmfield 47.5
Warmingham 7.5
Warmington (N'hants) 31.3
Warmington (Warks) 44.5
Warminster 48.1
Warmley 18.7
Warmsworth 39.2
Warmwell 13.1
Warndon 49.5
Warnford 20.5
Warnham 46.3
Warningcamp 46.5
Warninglid 46.4
Warrant, The 37.1
Warren W16
Warren Hill 34.7
Warren Wood 34.7
Warren, The 3.6
Warrenby 33.10
Warrenrow 3.4
Warrington (Bucks) 5.1
Warrington (Cheshire) 7.1
Warsash 20.10
Warsill 33.6
Warslow 40.1
Warsop 34.2
Warsop Vale 34.2
Warstock 45.5
Warter 15.2
Warthermarske (see Swinton)
Warthill 33.3
Wartling 16.1
Wartnaby 27.3
Warton (Lancs) 26.1, 26.5
Warton (Warks) 44.1
Warton Carnforth 26.1
Warwick 44.4
Warwick Bridge 10.1
Warwick-on-Eden 10.1
Wash Water (Highclere) 20.1
Washaway 9.1
Washbattle Bridge 38.3
Washbrook (see Copdock)
Washfield 12.4
Washford (Som) 38.3
Washford (Worcs) 49.3
Washford Pyne 12.4
Washingborough 28.4
Washingley 6.3
Washington (T & W) 43.5
Washington (W Sussex) 46.3
Washington Station 43.5
Washington Village 43.5
Washwood Heath 45.5
Wasing 3.1
Waskerley 14.1
Wasperton 44.4
Wass (see Byland)
Wassand 15.2
Watchet 38.3
Watchfield 35.4
Watchgate 10.5
Water 26.14
Water Eaton 35.2
Water End 5.3
Water Fryston 47.5
Water Orton 44.1
Water Stratford 5.2
Water Yeat 10.5
Waterbeach (Cambs) 6.5
Waterbeach (W Sussex) 46.2
Waterbeck S10
Watercombe 13.1
Waterditch 20.7
Waterend 20.1
Waterfall 40.1
Waterfoot S14
Waterfoot (Haslingden) 26.14
Waterfoot (Rawtenstall) 26.14
Waterford 22.3
Watergall 44.5
Watergore 38.5
Waterhead (Cumbria) 10.1
Waterhead (Gtr M'chester) 19.7
Waterhead, Ambleside 10.5
Waterhouses (Durham) 14.1
Waterhouses (Staffs) 40.1
Wateringbury (part) 25.9, 25.10
Waterlip 38.2
Waterloo S24
Waterloo (Mersey) 29.1
Waterloo (Shrop) 37.1
Waterloo (W Yorks) 47.4
Waterloo (part) L28
Waterloo Crescent 38.5
Waterlooville 20.13
Watermillock 10.3
Waternewton 6.3
Waternish S17
Waterperry 35.3
Waterrow 38.4
Waters Upton 37.4
Watersfield 46.3
Waterside* S11
Waterstock 35.3
Watford (Herts) 22.9
Watford (N'hants) 31.4
Wath 33.3
Wath-upon-Dearne 39.4
Watleys End 18.7
Watlington (Norfolk) 30.2
Watlington (Oxon) 35.3
Watten S17
Wattisfield 41.4
Wattisham 41.6
Wattlefield 30.7
Watton (E Yorks) 15.2
Watton (Norfolk) 30.3
Watton Woodhall 22.3
Watton-at-Stone 22.3
Wattstown W18
Wattsville W4
Waulkmill S2
Waun Wen W19
Waunarlwydd W19
Waunceirch W14
Waunfawr W11
Waungilwen W6
Wavendon 5.1
Wavendon Gate 5.1
Waverton (Cheshire) 7.3
Waverton (Cumbria) 10.2
Wavertree 29.2
Wawne 15.2
Waxham 30.1
Waxholme 15.2
Way Wick 38.7
Wayford (Som) 38.5
Wayford Bridge 30.1
Waytown 13.1
Weacombe 38.3
Wealdstone L15
Wear 43.5
Wearde 9.1
Weare 38.1
Weare Giffard 12.1
Wearhead 14.1
Wearne 38.5
Weasenham All Saints 30.3
Weasenham St Peter 30.3
Weaste 19.5
Weaverham 7.3
Weavering Street, Boxley 25.10
Weaverthorpe 33.3
Webbers Post 38.3
Webheath 49.3

Weddicar 10.4
Weddington (Kent) 25.6
Weddington (Warks) 44.2
Wedmore 38.1
Wednesbury (part) 45.2, 45.4
Wednesfield 45.1
Weedon (Bucks) 5.2
Weedon Bec 31.4
Weedon Lois 31.7
Weedon, Upper & Lower (N'hants) 31.4
Weeford 40.8
Week St Mary 9.1
Weekley 31.2
Weeley 17.4
Weeley Heath 17.4
Weem S24
Weethley 44.5
Weeting Broomhill 30.3
Weeton (E Yorks) 15.2
Weeton (N/W Yorks) 33.6
Weeton with Preese 26.5
Weir 26.14
Weirbrook 37.1
Weirend 21.1
Weisdale S26
Welbeck 34.1
Welborne 30.7
Welbourn 28.4
Welburn (Kirkbymoorside) 33.3
Welburn (York) 33.3
Welbury 33.2
Welby (Leics) 27.3
Welby (Lincs) 28.6
Welcombe 12.1
Weldon 31.1
Welford (Berks) 3.1
Welford (N'hants) 31.4
Welford-on-Avon 44.5
Welham (Leics) 27.8
Welham (Som) 38.5
Welham Green 22.6
Well (Hants) 20.2
Well (Lincs) 28.2
Well (N Yorks) 33.2
Well End 5.3
Well Heads 47.1
Well Hill 25.8
Welland 49.4
Wellers Town 25.8
Wellesbourne 44.5
Wellham 38.5
Wellhead 2.2
Welling L3
Wellingborough 31.6
Wellingham 30.3
Wellingore 28.4
Wellington (Here) 21.1
Wellington (Shrop) 37.4
Wellington (Som) 38.4
Wellington Heath 21.1
Wellow (Hants) 20.4
Wellow (I of W) 24.1
Wellow (Notts) 34.3
Wellow (Som) 38.6
Wells 38.2
Wells of Ythan S1
Wells-next-the-Sea 30.1
Wellsborough 27.4
Wellshead 38.3
Welney 30.2
Welsh Bicknor 21.1
Welsh End 37.1
Welsh Frankton 37.1
Welsh Newton 21.1
Welsh St Donats W21
Welshampton 37.1
Welshpool W17
Welton (E Yorks) 15.2
Welton (Lincs) 28.1
Welton (N'hants) 31.4
Welton le Marsh 28.2
Welton le Wold 28.2
Welwick 15.2
Welwyn 22.6
Welwyn Garden City 22.6
Wem 37.1
Wem Moss 37.1
Wembdon 38.1
Wemberham 38.7
Wembley L4
Wembury 12.9
Wembworthy 12.4
Wemyss Bay S18
Wenden Lofts 17.1
Wendens Ambo 17.1
Wendlebury 35.2
Wendling 30.3
Wendover 5.2
Wendover Dean 5.2
Wendron 9.1
Wendy (see Shingay)
Wenford Bridge 9.1
Wenham Magna 41.6
Wenham Parva 41.6
Wenhaston with Mells 41.5
Wennington (Cambs) 6.3
Wennington (Lancs) 26.1
Wensley (Derbys) 11.3
Wensley (N Yorks) 33.1
Wentbridge 47.5
Wentnor 37.1
Wentworth (Cambs) 6.4
Wentworth (S Yorks) 39.4
Wentworth (Surrey) 42.1
Wenvoe W21
Weobley 21.1
Weoley Castle 45.5
Wepham 46.5
Wereham 30.2
Wern 37.1
Wern Tarw W3
Wern-y-gaer W10
Wernddu W4
Werneth 19.7
Wernffrwd W19
Werrington (Cambs) 6.1
Werrington (Corn) 9.1
Werrington (Staffs) 40.1
Wervin 7.3
Wesham 26.5
Wessington 11.4
West Acre 30.2
West Acton L9
West Allen 32.1
West Allotment 43.2
West Alvington 12.9
West Anstey 12.2
West Ardnamurchan S17
West Ashby 28.2
West Ashling 46.2
West Ashton 48.1
West Auckland (part) 14.1
West Ayton 33.4
West Bagborough 38.4
West Balmirmer S2
West Barkwith 28.2
West Barnby 33.4
West Barns S13
West Bay 13.1
West Benridge 32.1
West Bergholt 17.3
West Bexington 13.1
West Blatchington 16.3
West Boldon 43.4
West Bolton (see Castle Bolton)
West Bowling 47.1
West Bradford 26.3
West Bradley 38.2
West Bretton 47.5
West Bridgford 34.8
West Brompton L13
West Bromwich 45.4
West Buckfastleigh 12.9
West Buckland (Devon) 12.2
West Buckland (Som) 38.4
West Burton (Notts) 34.1
West Burton (W Sussex) 46.2
West Butterwick 28.8
West Byfleet 42.4
West Caister 30.6
West Calder S31
West Camel 38.5
West Challow 35.4
West Chelborough 13.1
West Chevin (Otley) 47.2
West Chevington 32.1
West Chiltington 46.3
West Chinnock 38.5
West Cilrhedyn W16
West Clandon 42.7
West Cliff (Dorset) 13.7
West Close Booth (see Higham)
West Coker 38.5
West Common 20.7
West Compton (Dorset) 13.1
West Compton (Som) 38.2
West Cowick 15.2
West Cranmore 38.2
West Crewkerne 38.5
West Cross W19
West Dean (Hants) 20.4
West Dean (W Sussex) 46.2
West Dean (Wilts) 48.1
West Deeping 28.6
West Denton 43.1
West Derby 29.2
West Dereham 30.2
West Down 12.2
West Drayton (Middx) L17
West Drayton (Notts) 34.1
West Dulwich (part) L28
West Dumpton (Ramsgate) 25.7
West Ealing L9
West Ella 15.2
West Elrington 32.1
West End (Gloucs) 18.7
West End (Hants) 20.9
West End (Som)* 38.5
West End (Surrey) 42.3
West End (Wilts) 48.1
West End (part) L6, L33
West End Green 20.1
West Ewell (part) L21
West Farleigh 25.10
West Farndon 31.4
West Felton 37.1
West Fen 28.2
West Firsby 28.1
West Ginge 35.4
West Green (Hants) 20.2
West Green (W Sussex) 46.1
West Grinstead 46.3
West Haddlesey 33.8
West Haddon 31.4
West Hagbourne 35.3
West Hagley 49.2
West Hall (Cumbria) 10.1
West Hallam 11.8
West Halton 28.8
West Hampstead L6
West Handley 11.4
West Hanney 35.4
West Hanningfield 17.7
West Hardwick 47.5
West Harptree (part) 38.2, 38.6
West Harsley 33.2
West Hatch 38.4
West Hauxwell 33.1
West Hay (Som) 38.7
West Heath (Birm'ham) 45.5
West Heath (Hants) 20.1
West Hendred 35.4
West Herrington 43.5
West Hewish 38.7
West Hill L32
West Hoathly 46.4
West Holme 13.5
West Horndon (part) 17.9, 17.12
West Horrington 38.2
West Horsley 42.7
West Hougham 25.6
West Howe 13.7
West Howeton 38.3
West Hunsbury 31.5
West Huntspill 38.1
West Hyde 22.8
West Hythe 25.13
West Ilsley 3.1
West Itchenor 46.2
West Jesmond 43.1

West Keal 28.2
West Kennett 48.1
West Kensington (part) L13, L20
West Kilbride S21
West Kingsdown 25.8
West Kington 48.1
West Kirby 29.5
West Knighton (Dorset) 13.1
West Knoyle 48.1
West Lambrook 38.5
West Langdon 25.6
West Langton 27.8
West Lavington (W Sussex) 46.2
West Lavington (Wilts) 48.1
West Layton 33.1
West Leake 34.8
West Linton S30
West Liss 20.6
West Littleton 18.7
West Luccombe 38.3
West Lulworth 13.5
West Lydford 38.2
West Malling 25.9
West Malvern 49.4
West Marden 46.2
West Markham 34.1
West Meads 46.5
West Melton 39.4
West Meon 20.5
West Mersea 17.3
West Mickley 32.1
West Milton 13.1
West Minster (Kent) 25.4
West Molesey 42.5
West Monkseaton 43.2
West Monkton 38.4
West Moor 43.2
West Moors 13.3
West Morton 47.1
West Mudford 38.5
West Newbiggin 14.8
West Newton 15.2
West Norwood (part) L22
West Orchard 13.2
West Overton 48.1
West Park 29.3
West Parley 13.3
West Peckham 25.9
West Pelton 14.1
West Pennard 38.2
West Pinchbeck 28.7
West Pontnewydd W20
West Putford 12.1
West Quantoxhead 38.3
West Rainton 14.1
West Rasen 28.1
West Ravendale 28.9
West Rounton 33.2
West Row 41.2
West Rudham 30.2
West Saltoun S13
West Sandwick S26
West Scholes 47.1
West Scrafton 33.1
West Smethwick 45.4
West Southbourne 13.7
West Stafford 13.1
West Stockwith 34.1
West Stoke (Som) 38.5
West Stoke (W Sussex) 46.2
West Stour 13.2
West Stourmouth 25.6
West Stow 41.3
West Stratton 20.5
West Studdal 25.6
West Tanfield 33.2
West Thorney 46.2
West Thurrock 17.12
West Tilbury 17.12
West Tisbury 48.1
West Tisted 20.6
West Tolgus 9.1
West Torrington 28.2
West Town (Som) 38.7
West Tytherley 20.4
West Vale (W Yorks) 47.3
West Walton 30.2
West Wellow 20.4
West Wemyss S16
West Wick (Som) 38.7
West Wickham (Cambs) 6.5
West Wickham (London) L5
West Williamson W16
West Willoughby 28.6
West Wimbledon L24
West Winch 30.2
West Wittering 46.2
West Witton 33.1
West Wood (Som) 38.5
West Woodburn 32.1
West Woodhay 3.1
West Woodlands 38.2
West Worthing 46.6
West Wratting 6.5
West Wycombe 5.3
West Wylam 32.1
Westbere 25.5
Westborough (Lincs) 28.6
Westborough (W Yorks) 47.4
Westbourne (Dorset) 13.7
Westbourne (W Sussex) 46.2
Westbrook (Cheshire) 7.1
Westbrook (Margate) (Kent) 25.7
Westbury (Bucks) 5.2
Westbury (Shrop) 37.1
Westbury (Wilts) 48.1
Westbury Park (Bristol) 4.1
Westbury Park (Staffs) 40.2
Westbury-on-Severn 18.2
Westbury-on-Trym 4.1
Westbury-sub-Mendip 38.2
Westby 28.6
Westby with Plumpton (inc Gt Plumpton) 26.5
Westcliff-on-Sea 17.14
Westcombe 38.5
Westcot 35.4
Westcot Barton 35.1
Westcote 18.5
Westcott (Bucks) 5.2
Westcott (Surrey) 42.8
Westcott Brake 38.3
Westcraigs S31
Westcroft 5.1
Westdean (E Sussex) 16.1
Westdene (E Sussex) 16.3
Westenhanger 25.13
Wester Balgedie S24
Wester Essendy S24
Wester Lochewe S17
Westerdale 33.4
Westerfield 41.5
Westergate 46.5
Westerham 25.8
Westerhope 43.1
Westerleigh 18.7
Westerton (Durham) 14.1
Westerton (W Sussex) 46.2
Westfield S31
Westfield (E Sussex) 16.2
Westfield (Norfolk) 30.3
Westfield (Surrey) 42.4
Westfield (York) 33.7
Westford 38.4
Westgate (Co Durham) 14.1
Westgate (W Yorks) 47.4
Westgate Hill (part) 47.1, 47.4
Westgate on Sea 25.7
Westhall (Suffolk) 41.1
Westham 16.1
Westhampnett 46.2
Westhay (Som) 38.2
Westhide 21.1
Westhill S1
Westhope 37.1
Westhorpe (Suffolk) 41.4
Westhoughton 19.2
Westhouses 11.5
Westhumble 42.8
Westlands 40.2
Westlea 48.2
Westleigh (Devon)* 12.2, 12.4
Westleton 41.5
Westley 41.3
Westley Waterless 6.4
Westlington 5.2
Westlinton 10.1
Westmancote 49.6
Westmarsh 25.6
Westmead 48.2
Westmeston 16.4
Westmill 22.3
Westminster L33
Westmuir S2
Westnewton 10.2
Weston (Cheshire) 7.5
Weston (Hants)* 20.6, 20.8
Weston (Here) 21.1
Weston (Herts) 22.1
Weston (Lincs) 28.7
Weston (N Yorks) 33.6
Weston (N'hants) 31.7
Weston (Notts) 34.3
Weston (Staffs) 40.4
Weston (Suffolk) 41.1
Weston Bampfylde 38.5
Weston Beggard 21.1
Weston Colville 6.5
Weston Common (Hants) 20.1
Weston Common (Shrop) 37.1
Weston Corbett 20.1
Weston Coyney 40.3
Weston Favell 31.5
Weston Green 42.5
Weston Hills 28.7
Weston Longville 30.5
Weston Lullingfields 37.1
Weston Park 40.3
Weston Patrick 20.1
Weston Rhyn 37.1
Weston Sprink 40.3
Weston Subedge 18.5
Weston Turville 5.2
Weston Underwood (Bucks) 5.1
Weston Underwood (Derbys) 11.6
Weston-by-Welland 31.2
Weston-in-Arden 44.2
Weston-in-Gordano 38.7
Weston-on-Avon 44.5
Weston-on-the-Green 35.2
Weston-super-Mare 38.7
Weston-under-Lizard 40.6
Weston-under-Penyard 21.1
Weston-under-Redcastle 37.1
Weston-under-Wetherley 44.4
Weston-upon-Trent 11.9
Westonbirt (Wilts) 48.1
Westonbirt with Lasborough 18.5
Westone 31.5
Westoning 2.2
Westonzoyland 38.1
Westow 33.3
Westowe 38.4
Westport 38.5
Westquarter S15
Westray S23
Westridge 20.1
Westrill & Starmore 27.8
Westruther S30
Westtown (W Yorks) 47.4
Westvale (Kirkby) 29.4
Westville 28.2
Westward 10.2
Westward Ho! 12.1
Westwell (Kent) 25.12
Westwell (Oxon) 35.1
Westwick (Cambs) (see Oakington)
Westwick (Durham) 14.1
Westwick (N Yorks) 33.6
Westwick (Norfolk) 30.1
Westwood (Broadstairs) (Kent) 25.7
Westwood (Cambs) 6.1
Westwood (Devon) 12.5
Westwood (Notts) 34.4
Westwood (Wilts) 48.1

2

Westwood (Worcs) 49.6
Westwood Heath 45.7
Westy 7.1
Wetheral 10.1
Wetherby 47.2
Wetherden 41.4
Wetheringsett-cum-Brockford 41.4
Wethersfield 17.2
Wetley Rocks 40.1
Wettenhall 7.5
Wetton 40.1
Wetwang 15.2
Wetwood 40.4
Wexham (Berks) 3.5
Wexham (Bucks) 5.5
Weybourne (Norfolk) 30.1
Weybourne (Surrey) 42.11
Weybread 41.4
Weybridge 42.5
Weyhill 20.4
Weymouth 13.4
Whaddon (Bucks) 5.2
Whaddon (Cambs) 6.5
Whaddon (Gloucs) 18.6
Whaddon (Wilts) 48.1
Whale 10.3
Whaley 11.5
Whaley Bridge 11.1
Whaley Common 11.5
Whaley Thorns 11.5
Whalley 26.3
Whalley Range 19.6
Whalsay S26
Whalton 32.1
Whaplode 28.7
Whaplode Drove 28.7
Wharfe 33.5
Wharles 26.5
Wharley End 2.2
Wharncliffe Side 39.3
Wharram 33.3
Wharton 10.3
Whashton 33.1
Whasset 10.5
Whatcote 44.5
Whatcroft 7.3
Whatfield 41.6
Whatley* 38.2, 38.5
Whatlington 16.2
Whatstandwell 11.6
Whatton 34.8
Whauphill S10
Wheal Kitty 9.1
Wheatacre 30.7
Wheatcroft 11.6
Wheatfield 35.3
Wheathampstead 22.5
Wheathill (Shrop) 37.1
Wheathill (Som) 38.5
Wheathold Green 20.1
Wheatley (Oxon) 35.3
Wheatley (S Yorks) 39.2
Wheatley (Som) (see Thornley)
Wheatley (W Yorks) 47.3
Wheatley Hill 14.1
Wheaton Aston 40.6
Wheatsheaf Enclosure 46.2
Wheddon Cross 38.3
Wheelbarrow Town 25.13
Wheeler End 5.3
Wheelock Heath (part) 7.5
Wheelton 26.9
Wheldrake 33.7
Whelford 18.5
Whelpley 48.1
Whelpley Hill 5.4
Whenby 33.2
Whepstead 41.3
Whereley Rough 37.1
Wherstead 41.6
Wherwell 20.4
Whessoe 14.8
Wheston 11.3
Whetstone (Leics) 27.6
Whetstone (London) L2
Whicham 10.4
Whichford 44.5
Whickham 43.3
Whiddon Down 12.3
Whig Street S2
Whilborough 12.5
Whilton 31.4
Whilton Locks 31.4
Whimple 12.7
Whinburgh 30.3
Whinfell 10.5
Whinney Banks 33.9
Whinney Hill 14.10
Whinnyfold S1
Whippingham 24.1
Whipsnade 2.2
Whisby 28.4
Whissendine 36.1
Whissonsett 30.3
Whistley 48.1
Whiston (Mersey) 29.4
Whiston (Newport) W15
Whiston (N'hants) 31.7
Whiston (S Yorks) 39.4
Whiston (Staffs) 40.1
Whitbourne 21.1
Whitburn 43.4
Whitburn (W Lothian) S31
Whitburn Bents 43.5
Whitby (Cheshire) 7.3
Whitby (N Yorks) 33.4
Whitchurch (Bristol) (part) 4.1
Whitchurch (Bucks) 5.2
Whitchurch (Cardiff) W5
Whitchurch (Devon) 12.3
Whitchurch (Hants) 20.1
Whitchurch (Here) 21.1
Whitchurch (Pemb) W16
Whitchurch (Shrop) 37.1
Whitchurch (Som) 38.6
Whitchurch (Warks) 44.5
Whitchurch Hill 35.3
Whitchurch-on-Thames 35.3
Whitcliffe Mount 47.4
Whitcombe (Dorset) 13.1
Whitcombe (Som) 38.5
Whitcott 37.1
White Ball 38.4
White City L13, 20.1
White Colne 17.2
White Coppice 26.9
White Cross (W Yorks) 47.2
White Gate (Som) 38.5
White Gritt W17
White Hill (Overton) 20.1
White Horse Common 30.1
White Ladies Aston 49.6
White Lee 47.4
White Moss 10.5
White Notley 17.2
White Roding 17.1
White Waltham 3.4
White-le-Head 14.1
Whitebridge S17
Whitebrook W13
Whitecastle W13
Whitechapel 26.6
Whitechurch 38.5
Whitechurch Canonicorum 13.1
Whitechurch Eglwyswrw W16
Whiteclosegate 10.1
Whitecraig S13
Whitecraigs S14
Whitecroft 18.2
Whitecross (Cheshire) 7.1
Whitecross (Corn)* 9.1
Whitecross (Linlithgow) S15
Whitecross (Oxon) 35.4
Whitecross (Som) 38.5
Whitedale 15.2
Whitefield (Gtr M'chester) 19.3
Whitegate (Cheshire) 7.3
Whitehall 4.1
Whitehaven 10.4
Whitehawk 16.3
Whiteheath 45.4
Whitehill S28
Whitehill (Hants) 20.6
Whitehill (Staffs) 40.2
Whitehill by Dalkeith S19
Whitehills (Aberdeen) S1
Whitehills (N'hants) 31.5
Whitehills, North (Angus) S2
Whitehough 11.1
Whitehouse S3
Whitekirk S13
Whitelackington 38.5
Whiteleaf 5.3
Whiteley (part) 20.5, 20.10
Whiteley Bank 24.1
Whitely 20.5
Whitelye W13
Whitemere 37.1
Whitemill W6
Whitemoor 13.3
Whitemoor (Corn) 9.1
Whitemore (Cheshire/Staffs) 40.1
Whiteness S26
Whiteparish 48.1
Whitesheet 13.3
Whiteshill (Bristol/Gloucs) (part) 18.6, 18.7
Whitestake 26.7
Whitestaunton 38.5
Whitestone (Devon) 12.5
Whitestone (Here) 21.1
Whitestone (Warks) 44.2
Whitestreet 9.1
Whiteway (Bristol) 4.1
Whiteway (Gloucs) 18.6
Whitewell 26.3
Whitfield (Derbys) 11.1
Whitfield (Gloucs) 18.7
Whitfield (Kent) 25.6
Whitfield (N'hants) 31.7
Whitfield (N'land) (see Plenmeller)
Whitford W10
Whitford Bridge 49.2
Whitgift 15.2
Whitgreave 40.4
Whithorn S10
Whitland W6
Whitley (Berks) 3.2
Whitley (Cheshire) 7.3
Whitley (N Yorks) 33.8
Whitley (W Mids) 45.7
Whitley (W Yorks) 47.4
Whitley Bay 43.2
Whitley Bridge 33.8
Whitley Chapel 32.1
Whitley, Lower 47.4
Whitlingham 30.7
Whitminster 18.6
Whitmore 40.2
Whitnash 44.4
Whitney-on-Wye 21.1
Whitsbury 20.7
Whitsome S30
Whitson (see Goldcliffe)
Whitstable 25.5
Whitstone 9.1
Whitstones 38.3
Whittingehame S13
Whittingham (Lancs) 26.6
Whittingham (N'land) 32.1
Whittingslow 37.1
Whittington 37.1
Whittington (Gloucs) 18.5
Whittington (Lancs) 26.1
Whittington (Shrop) (part) 37.1
Whittington (Staffs) 40.8
Whittington (Worcs) 49.6
Whittington Barracks 40.8
Whittington Heath 40.8
Whittington Hurst 40.8
Whittington Moor 11.2
Whittle-le-Woods 26.9
Whittlebury 31.7
Whittlefield 26.12
Whittleford 44.2
Whittlesey 6.2
Whittlesford 6.5
Whitton (Lincs) 28.8
Whitton (Powys) W17
Whitton (Richmond) L27
Whitton (Shrop) 37.1
Whitton (Stockton) 14.10

Whitton (Suffolk) (part) 41.4, 41.7
Whittonstall 32.1
Whitway 20.1
Whitwell (Derbys) 11.5
Whitwell (Herts) 22.1
Whitwell (I of W) 24.1
Whitwell (N Yorks) 33.2
Whitwell (Rutland) 36.1
Whitwell Bottom 26.14
Whitwell House 14.1
Whitwell-on-the-Hill 33.3
Whitwick 27.1
Whitwood 47.5
Whitworth 26.14
Whixall 37.1
Whixley 33.6
Whorlton (Durham) 14.1
Whorlton (N Yorks) 33.2
Whorlton Grange 43.1
Whyteleafe (part) L8, 42.10
Wibsey 47.1
Wibtoft (part) 27.8, 44.3
Wichenford 49.4
Wick S17
Wick (Dorset) 13.7
Wick (Gloucs) 18.7
Wick (Som) 38.5
Wick (Vale Glam) W21
Wick (W Sussex) 46.5
Wick (Wilts) 48.1
Wick (Worcs) 49.6
Wick St Lawrence 38.7
Wicken (Cambs) 6.4
Wicken (N'hants) 31.7
Wicken Bonhunt 17.1
Wicken Green Village 30.1
Wickenby 28.1
Wickersley 39.4
Wickets Beer 38.5
Wickford (part) 17.7, 17.10
Wickham 20.5
Wickham Bishops 17.8
Wickham Market 41.5
Wickham St Paul 17.2
Wickham Skeith 41.4
Wickhambreaux 25.5
Wickhambrook 41.3
Wickhamford 49.6
Wicklewood 30.7
Wickmere 30.1
Wickwar 18.7
Widdington 17.1
Widdop 47.3
Widdrington 32.1
Widecombe in the Moor 12.5
Widemouth Bay 9.1
Wideopen 43.2
Widford (Essex) 17.7
Widford (Herts) 22.3
Widford (Oxon) (see Swinbrook)
Widley (part) 20.5, 20.12, 20.13
Widmer End 5.3
Widmerpool 34.8
Widnes 7.2
Widworthy 12.7
Wield 20.6
Wigan 19.1
Wiganthorpe (see Terrington)
Wigbeth 13.3
Wigborough (Som) 38.5
Wigfach W3
Wigfair W8
Wiggenhall St Germans 30.2
Wiggenhall St Mary Magdalen 30.2
Wigginton (Herts) 22.4
Wigginton (Oxon) 35.2
Wigginton (Staffs) 40.8
Wigginton (York) 33.7
Wigglesworth 33.5
Wighill 33.6
Wighton 30.1
Wigland 7.3
Wigley 20.7
Wigmore (Here) 21.1
Wigmore (Kent) 25.3
Wigsley 34.3
Wigsthorpe (N'hants) 31.3
Wigsthorpe (see Lilford)
Wigston 27.7
Wigston Parva 27.6
Wigtoft 28.5
Wigton 10.2
Wigtown S10
Wike 47.2
Wilbarston 31.2
Wilberfoss 15.2
Wilberlee 47.4
Wilburton 6.4
Wilby (N'hants) 31.6
Wilby (Norfolk) 30.3
Wilby (Suffolk) 41.4
Wilcot (Shrop) 37.1
Wilcot (Wilts) 48.1
Wilcove 9.1
Wilcrick W13
Wilday Green 11.4
Wildboarclough 7.5
Wilden 2.1
Wildhern 20.4
Wildmill W3
Wildmoor (Hants) 20.1
Wildmoor (Worcs) 49.2
Wildmore 28.2
Wildon Grange 33.2
Wildsworth 28.1
Wilford 34.6
Wilkesley (see Dodcott)
Wilkhaven S17
Wilkieston S31
Wilkin Throop 38.5
Wilkins Green (part) 22.5, 22.6
Wilksby 28.2
Willand (Devon) 12.4
Willaston (Cheshire)* 7.3, 7.5
Willaston (Shrop) 37.1
Willen 5.1
Willen Lake 5.1
Willen Park 5.1
Willenhall (W Mids) (part) 45.1, 45.2, 45.7
Willerby (Staxton, Scarborough) 33.3
Willersey 18.5
Willersley 21.1
Willesborough 25.12
Willesden L4, L9
Willesley (Leics) 27.1
Willesley (Wilts) 48.1
Willett 38.3
Willey (Here) 21.1
Willey (Warks) 44.3
Willhayne 38.5
Williamscote 35.2
Williamstown* W12, W18
Williamwood S14
Willian 22.1
Willicote 44.5
Willimoteswick 32.1
Willingale 17.6
Willingdon (part) 16.1, 16.5
Willingham (Cambs) 6.5
Willingham (Lincs) 28.1
Willingham St Mary 41.1
Willington (Beds) 2.1
Willington (Cheshire) 7.3
Willington (Derbys) 11.9
Willington (Durham) 14.1
Willington (Warks) 44.5
Willington (Wrexham) W22
Willington Quay 43.2
Willington St, Bearsted 25.10
Willisham 41.4
Willitoft 15.2
Williton 38.3
Willoughbridge 40.2
Willoughby 44.3
Willoughby Waterleys 27.8
Willoughby with Sloothby 28.2
Willoughby-on-the-Wolds 34.8
Willoughton 28.1
Wills Pastures 44.5
Willsbridge 18.7
Willtown 38.5
Wilmcote 44.5
Wilmington (E Sussex) 16.1
Wilmington (Kent) 25.1
Wilmorton 11.7
Wilmslow 7.5
Wilnecote 40.9
Wilpshire 26.3
Wilsden 47.1
Wilsden (Brent) L4
Wilsden Hill 47.1
Wilsford (Lincs) 28.4
Wilsford (Wilts) 48.1
Wilsford-cum-Lake 48.1
Wilshaw 47.4
Wilson 27.1
Wilsontown S28
Wilstead 2.1
Wilsthorpe (E Yorks) 15.2
Wilsthorpe (Lincs) 28.6
Wilstone 22.4
Wilstrop 33.6
Wilton (Norfolk) (see Hockwold)
Wilton (Som) 38.4
Wilton* 33.3, 33.10
Wilton* (Wilts) 48.1
Wimbish 17.1
Wimblebury 40.7
Wimbledon (part) L24
Wimblington 6.2
Wimbolds Trafford 7.3
Wimboldsley 7.3
Wimborne 13.3
Wimborne Minster 13.3
Wimborne St Giles 13.3
Wimbotsham 30.2
Wimpole 6.5
Wimpstone 44.5
Wincanton 38.5
Winceby 28.2
Winch Fawr W12
Winch Wen W19
Wincham 7.3
Winchburgh S31
Winchcombe 18.1
Winchelsea 16.2
Winchelsea Beach 16.2
Winchester 20.5
Winchfield 20.2
Winchmore Hill (Bucks) 5.4
Winchmore Hill (London) L10
Wincle 7.5
Wincombe 48.1
Windermere 10.5
Winderton 44.5
Windhill 47.1
Windle 29.3
Windle Hill 7.3
Windlehurst 29.3
Windlesham 42.3
Windlestone 14.1
Windley 11.6
Windmill Hill 4.1
Windmill Hill (N'land) 32.1
Windmill Hill (Som) 38.5
Windrush 18.5
Windsor 3.4
Windwhistle 38.5
Windy Nook 43.3
Windygates S16
Wineham 46.3
Winestead 15.2
Winfarthing 30.7
Winford (I of W) 24.1
Winford (Som) 38.7
Winforton 21.1
Winfrith Newburgh 13.5
Wing (Bucks) 5.2
Wing (Rutland) 36.1
Wingate 14.1
Wingerworth 11.4
Wingfield (Beds) 2.2
Wingfield (Suffolk) 41.4
Wingfield (Wilts) 48.1
Wingham 25.6
Wingham Green 25.6

2

Wingham Well 25.6
Wingland 28.7
Wingmore 25.13
Wingrave 5.2
Winkburn 34.3
Winkfield 3.6
Winkhill 40.1
Winkhurst Green 25.8
Winklebury 20.1
Winkleigh 12.1
Winksley 33.6
Winkton 13.8
Winlaton 43.3
Winlaton Mill 43.3
Winmarleigh 26.2
Winnall (Hants) 20.5
Winnall (Here) 21.1
Winnards Perch 9.1
Winnersh 3.3
Winnothdale 40.1
Winscales 10.2
Winscombe 38.7
Winscombe Hill (part) 38.1, 38.7
Winsford (Cheshire) 7.3
Winsford (Som) 38.3
Winsham 38.5
Winshill 40.5
Winsick 11.4
Winskill 10.3
Winslade 20.1
Winsley (N Yorks) (see Hartwith)
Winsley (Wilts) 48.1
Winslow (Bucks) 5.2
Winson 18.5
Winson Green 45.5
Winsor 20.7
Winster (Cumbria) 10.5
Winster (Derbys) 11.3
Winston (Durham) 14.1
Winston (Suffolk) 41.4
Winstone 18.5
Winter Hill 5.1
Winterborne Came 13.1
Winterborne Clenston 13.2
Winterborne Herringston 13.1
Winterborne Houghton 13.2
Winterborne Kingston 13.2
Winterborne Monkton 13.1
Winterborne St Martin 13.1
Winterborne Stickland 13.2
Winterborne Whitechurch 13.2
Winterborne Zelston 13.2
Winterbourne (Berks) 3.1
Winterbourne (Gloucs) 18.7
Winterbourne Abbas 13.1
Winterbourne Bassett 48.1
Winterbourne Dauntsey 48.1
Winterbourne Down 18.7
Winterbourne Earls 48.1
Winterbourne Gunner 48.1
Winterbourne Monkton 48.1
Winterbourne Steepleton 13.1
Winterbourne Stoke 48.1
Winterburn (see Flashby)
Winterhead (part) 38.1, 38.7
Winteringham 28.8
Winterley 7.5
Wintersett 47.5
Winterslow 48.1
Winterton 28.8
Winterton-on-Sea 30.6
Winthorpe (Lincs) 28.2
Winthorpe (Notts) 34.3
Winton 19.5
Winton (Cumbria) 10.3
Winton (Dorset) 13.7
Winton Stank & Hallikeld 33.2
Wintringham 33.3
Winwick (Cambs) 6.3
Winwick (Cheshire) 7.1
Winwick (N'hants) 31.4
Winyates Green 49.3
Winyates, East and West 49.3
Wirehill 49.3
Wirksworth 11.3
Wirral 29.5
Wirswall 7.5
Wisbech 6.2
Wisbech St Mary 6.2
Wisborough Green 46.2
Wiseton 34.1
Wishaw S22
Wishaw & Moxhull 44.1
Wisley 42.7
Wispington 28.2
Wissett 41.1
Wissington (see Nayland)
Wistanstow 37.1
Wistanswick 37.1
Wistaston 7.5
Wiston S28
Wiston (Pemb) W16
Wiston (W Sussex) 46.3
Wistow (Cambs) 6.3
Wistow (Leics) 27.8
Wistow (N Yorks) 33.8
Wiswell 26.3
Witcham 6.4
Witchampton 13.3
Witchford 6.4
Witcombe 38.5
Witcombe Bottom 38.5
Witham 17.2
Witham Friary 38.2
Witham St Hughs 28.4
Witham on the Hill 28.6
Withcall 28.2
Withcote (part) 27.3, 27.8
Withdean 16.3
Withergate 30.1
Witheridge (part) 12.2
Witheridge Hill 35.3
Witherley 27.4
Withern with Stain 28.2
Withernsea 15.2
Withernwick 15.2
Withersfield 41.3
Witherslack 10.5
Witherwack 43.5
Withiel 9.1
Withiel Florey 38.3
Withington (Gloucs) 18.5
Withington (Gtr M'chester) 19.6
Withington (Here) 21.1
Withington (Shrop) 37.1
Withleigh 12.4
Withnell 26.9
Withybrook 44.3
Withycombe 38.3
Withyham 16.1
Withypool 38.3
Withywood 4.1
Witley 42.11
Witnesham 41.5
Witney 35.1
Witney Bottom 38.5
Wittering 6.1
Wittersham 25.12
Witton (Norfolk) 30.1
Witton (W Mids) 45.5
Witton Gilbert 14.1
Witton Park (part) 14.1
Witton-le-Wear 14.1
Wiveliscombe 38.4
Wivelsfield 16.4
Wivelsfield Green 16.4
Wivenhoe 17.3
Wiverton 34.8
Wiveton 30.1
Wix 17.4
Wixford 44.5
Wixoe 41.3
Wiyam 2.1
Woburn 2.2
Woburn Sands (part) 2.2, 5.1
Wokefield 3.1
Woking 42.4
Wokingham 3.3
Wokingham Without 3.3
Wold Newton* 15.2, 28.9
Woldingham 42.10
Wolferlow 21.1
Wolfhampcote 44.3
Wolfhill S24
Wolfpits W17
Wolfscastle W16
Wollaston (N'hants) 31.6
Wollaston (Shrop) 37.1
Wollaston (W Mids) 45.3
Wollaton (part) 34.6
Wollerton 37.1
Wollescote 45.3
Wolsingham 14.1
Wolstanton 40.2
Wolston 44.3
Wolterton 30.1
Wolvercote 35.5
Wolverham 7.3
Wolverhampton 45.1
Wolverley (Shrop) 37.1
Wolverley (Worcs) 49.1
Wolvershill 38.7
Wolverton (Bucks) 5.1
Wolverton (Hants) 20.1
Wolverton (Kent) 25.6
Wolverton (Warks) 44.5
Wolverton Mill 5.1
Wolvesnewton W13
Wolvey 44.3
Wolviston 14.10
Womaston W17
Wombleton 33.3
Wombourne 40.6
Wombridge 37.4
Wombwell 39.1
Womenswold 25.5
Womersley 33.8
Wonderstone 38.7
Wonersh 42.11
Wonston 20.5
Wooburn 5.3
Wooburn Green 5.3
Wood 38.5
Wood Broughton 10.5
Wood Burcote 31.7
Wood Dalling 30.5
Wood End (W Yorks) 47.2
Wood End (Warks) 44.1
Wood Enderby 28.2
Wood Farm 35.5
Wood Green (W Mids) 45.4
Wood Green (part) L10, L14
Wood Lane 40.2
Wood Norton 30.1
Wood Rising 30.3
Wood Road 19.3
Woodbank 7.3
Woodbastwick 30.5
Woodbatch 37.1
Woodbeck 34.1
Woodbine 10.6
Woodborough (Notts) 34.7
Woodborough (Som) 38.7
Woodborough (Wilts) 48.1
Woodbridge (Suffolk) 41.5
Woodbridge (Wilts) 48.1
Woodburn S19
Woodbury (Devon) 12.7
Woodchester 18.6
Woodchurch (Kent) 25.12
Woodchurch (Mersey) 29.5
Woodcock Heath 40.5
Woodcocks 38.3
Woodcombe 38.3
Woodcote (Oxon) 35.3
Woodcote (Shrop) 37.4
Woodcote (Worcs) 49.2
Woodcott (Cheshire) 7.5
Woodcott (Hants) 20.1
Woodcroft 18.2
Woodcross 45.1
Woodcutts 13.3
Woodditton 6.4
Woodeaton 35.3
Wooden W16
Woodend S27
Woodend (N'hants) 31.7
Woodfalls 48.1
Woodfield 18.6
Woodfieldside W4
Woodford (N'hants) 31.3
Woodford (Wilts) 48.1

Woodford (part) L26
Woodford Bridge (part) L26, 17.6
Woodford Green (part) L31
Woodford Halse 31.4
Woodford and South Woodford (part) L26
Woodgarston Farm 20.1
Woodgate (Cumbria) 10.5
Woodgate (W Mids) 45.5
Woodgate (W Sussex) 46.5
Woodgate (Worcs) 49.2
Woodgate Hill 19.3
Woodgreen (Hants) 20.7
Woodhall (Herts) 22.3
Woodhall (Lincs) 28.2
Woodhall (S Yorks) (see Harthill)
Woodhall Park 48.2
Woodhall Spa 28.2
Woodham (Bucks) 5.2
Woodham (Durham) 14.1
Woodham (Surrey) (part) 42.1, 42.4
Woodham Ferrers 17.7
Woodham Mortimer 17.8
Woodham Walter 17.8
Woodhatch 42.9
Woodhead S1
Woodhey 19.3
Woodhill (Bucks) 5.1
Woodhill (Essex) 17.7
Woodhill (Gtr M'chester) 19.3
Woodhill (Som) 38.4, 38.7
Woodhorn 32.1
Woodhouse (Leics) 27.2
Woodhouse (S Yorks) 39.3
Woodhouse (Som) 38.5
Woodhouse (W Yorks) (see Newland)
Woodhouse Down 18.7
Woodhouse Eaves 27.2
Woodhouse Hill 47.4
Woodhouse Mill (part) 39.3, 39.4
Woodhouse Park 19.6
Woodhouse, Haversham 10.5
Woodhouselea S19
Woodhouses 40.8
Woodhouses (Gtr M'chester) 19.7
Woodhouses (Shrop) 37.1
Woodhurst 6.3
Woodingdean 16.3
Woodkirk (part) 47.2, 47.4
Woodland (Cumbria) 10.5
Woodland (Devon) 12.5
Woodland (Durham) 14.1
Woodlands (Dorset) 13.3
Woodlands (Hants) 20.7
Woodlands (Kent) 25.8
Woodlands (S Yorks) 39.2
Woodlands (Som) 38.5
Woodlands Park 44.2
Woodleigh 12.9
Woodlesford 47.2
Woodley (Berks) 3.3
Woodmancote (Gloucs)* 18.1, 18.5
Woodmancote (W Sussex) (part) 46.2, 46.3
Woodmancott 20.5
Woodmans Green 46.2
Woodmansey 15.2
Woodmansterne 42.9
Woodnesborough 25.6
Woodnewton 31.3
Woodnook 28.6
Woodperry 35.3
Woodplumpton 26.6
Woodrow 49.3
Woods Estate 45.4
Woods Lane 20.1
Woodsbirds Hill 38.5
Woodseaves (Shrop) 37.1
Woodseaves (Staffs) 40.4
Woodsetton 45.3
Woodsetts 39.4
Woodsford 13.1
Woodside S24
Woodside (Beds) 2.2
Woodside (Cumbria) 10.2
Woodside (Shrop) 37.4
Woodside (W Yorks) 47.1
Woodstock (Oxon) 35.1
Woodston 6.1
Woodthorpe (Derbys) (part) 11.2, 11.4
Woodthorpe (Lincs) (see Strubby)
Woodthorpe (Notts) 34.7
Woodton 30.7
Woodvale (part) 29.1
Woodville (Angus) S2
Woodville (Cumbria) 11.9
Woodwalton 6.3
Woodyates 13.3
Woofferton 37.1
Wookey 38.2
Wookey Hole 38.2
Wool 13.5
Woolacombe 12.2
Woolage Green 25.5
Woolaston 18.2
Woolavington 38.1
Woolbeding 46.2
Woolcofts 38.3
Wooldale 47.4
Wooler 32.1
Woolfardisworthy* 12.1, 12.4
Woolfold 19.3
Woolfords S28
Woolhampton 3.1
Woolhope 21.1
Woolland 13.2
Woollard 38.6
Woolley (Cambs) 6.3
Woolley (Som) 38.6
Woolley (W Yorks) 47.5
Woolley Moor 11.4
Woolmer Green 22.6
Woolminstone 38.5
Woolpit 41.4
Woolscott 44.3
Woolsery 12.1
Woolsington 43.1
Woolstanwood 7.5
Woolstaston 37.1
Woolsthorpe by Belvoir 28.6
Woolsthorpe by Colsterworth 28.6
Woolston (Cheshire) 7.1
Woolston (Hants) 20.8
Woolston (Shrop) 37.1
Woolston (Som)* 38.3, 38.5
Woolstone 35.4
Woolstone (Bucks) 5.1
Woolton 29.2
Woolton Hill 20.1
Woolverstone 41.6
Woolverton 38.2
Woolwich L11
Woore 37.1
Woosehill 3.3
Wootton (Beds) 2.1
Wootton (Hants) 20.7
Wootton (Kent) 25.6
Wootton (Lincs) 28.8
Wootton (N'hants) 31.5
Wootton (Oxon)* 35.1, 35.4
Wootton (Shrop) 37.1
Wootton (Staffs) 40.5
Wootton Bassett 48.1
Wootton Bridge 24.1
Wootton Courtenay 38.3
Wootton Fields (part) 31.5
Wootton Fitzpaine 13.1
Wootton Knowle 38.3
Wootton Rivers 48.1
Wootton St Lawrence 20.1
Wootton Wawen 44.5
Worcester 49.5
Worcester Park (Kingston) (part) L21
Worcester Park (Surrey) (part) 42.6
Worcester Park (Sutton) (part) L29
Wordsley 45.3
Wordwell 41.3
Worfield 37.1
Workington 10.2
Worksop 34.1
Worlaby* (Lincs) 28.2, 28.8
Worldham 20.6
Worlds End 20.5
Worle 38.7
Worlebury 38.7
Worleston 7.5
Worlingham 41.1
Worlington 41.2
Worlingworth 41.4
Wormbridge 21.1
Wormegay 30.2
Wormelow 21.1
Wormhill 11.1
Wormingford 17.3
Worminghall 5.2
Worminster 38.2
Wormit S16
Wormleighton 44.5
Wormley (Herts) 22.7
Wormley West End 22.3
Worms Ash 49.2
Wormshill 25.10
Wormsley 21.1
Worplesdon 42.7
Worrall 39.3
Worrall Hill 18.2
Worsbrough 39.1
Worsley (part) 19.1
Worstead 30.1
Worsthorne with Hurstwood 26.12
Worston 26.3
Worth (Cheshire) (see Poynton)
Worth (Kent) 25.6
Worth (Som) 38.2
Worth (W Sussex) (part) 46.1, 46.4
Worth Matravers 13.5
Worth Village 47.1
Wortham 41.4
Wortheal 38.5
Worthen 37.1
Worthenbury W22
Worthing (Norfolk) 30.3
Worthing (W Sussex) 46.6
Worthington (Gtr M'chester) 19.1
Worthington (Leics) 27.1
Worthy 38.3
Worting 20.1
Wortley (S Yorks) (part) 39.1, 39.3
Wortley Hill 18.6
Worton (Oxon) 35.1
Worton (Wilts) 48.1
Wortwell 30.7
Wothersome 47.2
Wotherton 37.1
Wothorpe 6.1
Wotton (Surrey) 42.8
Wotton Underwood 5.2
Wotton-under-Edge 18.6
Woughton Park 5.1
Woughton-on-the-Green 5.1
Wouldham 25.9
Wrabness 17.4
Wragby (Lincs) 28.2
Wragby (W Yorks) 47.5
Wragholme 28.2
Wramplingham 30.7
Wrangbrook 47.5
Wrangle 28.5
Wrangway 38.4
Wrantage 38.4
Wrawby 28.8
Wraxall (Dorset) 13.1
Wraxall (Som) 38.2, 38.7
Wray with Botton 26.1
Wraysbury 3.4
Wrayton (see Melling)
Wrea Green 26.5
Wreath 38.5
Wreay (part) 10.1, 10.3
Wrecclesham 42.11
Wrekenton 43.3

2

Wrelton (Pickering) 33.3
Wrenbury 7.5
Wrenbury-cum-Frith 7.5
Wreningham 30.7
Wrentham 41.1
Wrenthorpe 47.5
Wressle 15.2
Wrestlingworth 2.2
Wretham, East & West 30.3
Wretton 30.2
Wrexham W22
Wrightington 26.8
Wrinehill (Cheshire) (see Checkley)
Wrinehill (Staffs) 40.2
Wrington 38.7
Wringworthy 9.1
Writhlington 38.2
Writtle 17.7
Wrockwardine 37.4
Wrockwardine Wood 37.4
Wroot 28.8
Wrose 47.1
Wrotham 25.9
Wroughton 48.2
Wroxall (I of W) 24.1
Wroxall (Warks) 44.4
Wroxeter 37.1
Wroxham 30.5
Wroxton 35.2
Wyaston 11.3
Wyatts Green 17.9
Wyberton 28.5
Wyboston 2.1
Wybunbury 7.5
Wychbold 49.6
Wychling 25.10
Wychnor 40.5
Wychough 7.3
Wychwood (see Cornbury)
Wyck Rissington 18.5
Wycliffe 14.1
Wycomb 27.3
Wyddial 22.3
Wydon 38.3
Wye 25.12
Wyfordby 27.3
Wyham-cum-Cadeby 28.2
Wyke (Hants) 20.1
Wyke (W Yorks) 47.1
Wyke Champflower 38.5
Wyke Common (part) 47.1, 47.4
Wykeham 33.4
Wykey* 37.1
Wylam 32.1
Wylde Green 45.5
Wyllie W4
Wylye 48.1
Wymbush 5.1
Wymeswold 27.2
Wymington 2.1
Wymondham (Leics) 27.3
Wymondham (Norfolk) 30.7
Wyndham W3
Wynford Eagle 13.1
Wynyard 14.10
Wyre S23
Wyre Piddle 49.6
Wysall 34.8
Wythall 49.2
Wytham 35.4
Wytheford 37.1
Wythenshawe 19.6
Wythop 10.2
Wyton (Cambs) 6.3
Wyton (E Yorks) 15.2
Wyverstone 41.4
Wyville-cum-Hungerton 28.6
Y Felinheli W11
Y Ferwig W7
Y Ffôr W11
Y Waun W22
Yaddlethorpe 28.8
Yafforth 33.2
Yalding 25.10
Yanley 38.7
Yanwath 10.3
Yanworth 18.5
Yapham 15.2
Yapton 46.5
Yarberry 38.7
Yarburgh 28.2
Yarcombe 12.7
Yarde 38.3
Yardley 45.5
Yardley Gobion 31.7
Yardley Hastings 31.7
Yardley Wood 45.5
Yarford 38.4
Yarkhill 21.1
Yarley 38.2
Yarlington 38.5
Yarm 14.10
Yarmouth 24.1
Yarnbrook 48.1
Yarnfield (Staffs) 40.4
Yarnfield (Wilts) 48.1
Yarningale 44.5
Yarnscombe 12.1
Yarnton 35.2
Yarpole 21.1
Yarrow (Borders) S30
Yarrow (N'land) 32.1
Yarwell 31.3
Yate (Gloucs) 18.7
Yate (Lancs) 26.10
Yate Rocks 18.7
Yateley 20.2
Yatesbury 48.1
Yattendon 3.1
Yatton (Here) 21.1
Yatton (Som) 38.7
Yatton Keynell 48.1
Yatts (Pickering) 33.3
Yaverland 24.1
Yawthorpe 28.1
Yaxham 30.3
Yaxley (Cambs) part 6.1, 6.3
Yaxley (Suffolk) 41.4
Yazor 21.1
Yeabridge 38.5
Yeadon (part) 47.1, 47.2
Yealand Conyers 26.1
Yealand Redmayne 26.1
Yealmpton 12.9
Yearby 33.10
Yearnor 38.3
Yearsley 33.2
Yeaton 37.1
Yeaveley 11.3
Yedingham 33.3
Yeldersley 11.3
Yell S26
Yelland 12.2
Yelling 6.3
Yelsted 25.10
Yelvertoft 31.4
Yelverton (Devon) 12.3
Yelverton (Norfolk) 30.7
Yelves, The 37.1
Yenston 38.5
Yenworthy 38.3
Yeoford 12.4
Yeolmbridge 9.1
Yeovil 38.5
Yeovil Marsh 38.5
Yeovilton 38.5
Yerbeston W16
Yester S13
Yetminster 13.1
Yetts of Muckhart (part) S8, S24
Yews Green 47.1
Yielden 2.1
Yieldingtree 49.1
Ynys Enlli (Bardsey Island) W11
Ynysarwed W14
Ynysawdre W3
Ynysboeth W18
Ynysddu W4
Ynysfach W12
Ynysforgan W19
Ynyshir W18
Ynysmaerdy W18
Ynysmeudwy W14
Ynystawe W19
Ynyswen W17
Ynysybwl W18
Yockenthwaite 33.5
Yockleton 37.1
Yokefleet 15.2
York 33.7
Yorkletts (Whitstable) 25.5
Yorkley 18.2
Yorktown 3.6
Yorton 37.1
Yorton Heath 37.1
Youlgreave 11.3
Youlthorpe 15.2
Youlton 33.2
Yoxall 40.5
Yoxford 41.5
Ysbyty Ifan W8
Ysbyty Ystwyth W7
Ysceifiog W10
Yscir W17
Ysclydach W17
Ysgubor-y-coed W7
Yspitty W6
Ystalyfera W14
Ystrad W18
Ystrad Fflur W7
Ystrad Mynach W4
Ystradfellte W17
Ystradgynlais, Higher & Lower W17
Ystradmeurig W7
Ystradowen (C'marthenshire) W6
Ystradowen (Vale Glam) W21
Ythanbank S1
Zeal Monachorum 12.4
Zeals 48.1
Zelah 9.1
Zennor 9.1
Zouch 34.8

Part 3

Principal Mortgage Lenders

Applications for redemption figures and deeds and documents should be made to the head office (the address given) unless otherwise indicated, ie by a subsequent alternative address.

The Building Societies Association

The Building Societies Association
Website: www.bsa.org.uk
Head Office: 6th Fl, York Ho, 23 Kingsway, London WC2B 6UJ
Tel: 020 7520 5900 Fax: 020 7240 5290
e-mail: simon.rex@bsa.org.uk

Council of Mortgage Lenders

Council of Mortgage Lenders
Website: www.cml.org.uk
Head Office: Bush Ho, North West Wing, Aldwych, London WC2B 4PJ
Tel: 0845 373 6771 Fax: 0845 373 6778
Note: Note: The Council of Mortgage Lenders is a member-only trade association.

Principal Mortgage Lenders

AIB Group (UK) plc
Website: www.aibgb.co.uk
Head Office: Allied Irish Bank (GB), St Helen's, 1 Undershaft, London EC3A 8AB
Tel: 020 7647 3300
e-mail: mortgages.gb@aib.ie

Abbey National *(see Santander)*

Accrington *(see Cheshire)*

Aid to Thrift *(see Bank of Ireland)*

Alfreton *(see Co-operative Bank)*

Alliance & Leicester plc *(see Santander)*

Alliance *(see Santander)*

Anglia *(see Nationwide)*

Argyle *(see Norwich & Peterborough)*

Banffshire *(see Scottish)*

Bank of Ireland
Website: www.bankofirelandmortgages.co.uk
Head Office: Mortgage Customer Services Dept, PO Box 27, 1 Temple Quay, Bristol BS99 7AX
Tel: 0117 979 2222 Fax: 0117 929 3787
DX: 98850 Bristol 2

Bank of Scotland *(see Halifax)*

Barclays Bank plc
Website: www.barclays.co.uk
Head Office: 1 Churchill Place, Canary Wharf, London E14 5HP
Tel: 020 7116 1000
Mortgage Head Office: Barclays Mortgages, Mortgage Loan Services, PO Box 8575, Leicester LE18 9AW
Tel: 0800 022 4022

Barnsley Building Society
Website: www.barnsley-bs.co.uk
Head Office: Yorkshire Ho, Yorkshire Dr, Bradford BD5 8LJ
Tel: 0845 1200 898 Fax: 01226 287374

Bedford *(see Cheltenham & Gloucester)*

Bedford Crown *(see Cheltenham & Gloucester)*

Beverley Building Society
Website: www.beverleybs.co.uk
Head Office: 57 Market Pl, Beverley HU17 8AA
Tel: 01482 881510 Fax: 01482 872680
e-mail: website@beverleybs.co.uk

Bideford *(see Nationwide)*

Birmingham & Bridgwater *(see Birmingham Midshires)*

Birmingham Midshires
Website: www.bmmortgages.co.uk
Corporate Centre: PO Box 81, Pendeford Business Park, Wobaston Rd, Wolverhampton WV9 5HZ
Tel: 0845 300 2627
DX: 718030 Wolverhampton 17
e-mail: info@birminghammidshires.co.uk

Blackheath *(see Co-operative Bank)*

Blyth & Morpeth *(see Virgin Money)*

Bolton *(see Cheltenham & Gloucester)*

Bradford & Bingley
Website: www.bradford-bingley.co.uk
Crossflatts Service Centre: PO Box 629, Durham DH1 9JQ
Tel: 0844 892 2590

Bristol & Economic *(see Coventry)*

Bristol & West plc *(see Bank of Ireland)*

Britannia Building Society *(see Co-operative Bank)*

Buckinghamshire Building Society
Website: www.bucksbs.co.uk
Head Office: High St, Chalfont St Giles, Bucks HP8 4QB
Tel: 01494 879517/500 Fax: 01494 876256
e-mail: info@bucksbs.co.uk

Burnley *(see Santander)*

Bury St Edmunds *(see Cheltenham & Gloucester)*

Cambridge Building Society
Website: www.cambridgebs.co.uk
Head Office: Membership Services Dept, PO Box 232, 51 Newmarket Rd, Cambridge CB5 8FF
Tel: 01223 727727 Fax: 01223 727700
DX: 133158 Cambridge 8
e-mail: enquiries@cambridgebs.co.uk

Cardiff *(see Cheltenham & Gloucester)*

Catholic Building Society *(see Chelsea)*

Century Building Society *(see Scottish Building Society)*

Chatham *(see Principality)*

Chelsea Building Society
Website: www.thechelsea.co.uk
Head Office: Timbercombe Ho, Charlton Kings Business Pk, Cirencester Rd, Cheltenham, Glos GL53 8DZ
Tel: 0845 1200 842 Fax: 01242 226605
DX: 32850 Cheltenham 2
Note: DX: 32853 Cheltenham 2 (for Deeds)

Cheltenham & Gloucester plc
Website: www.cheltglos.co.uk
Head Office: Chief Office, Barnett Way, Gloucester GL4 3RL
Tel: 0800 028 0639 Fax: 01452 373955
DX: 55251 Gloucester 2; deeds only DX 55250

Chesham Building Society *(see Skipton)*

Cheshire Building Society *(see Nationwide)*

Cheshunt *(see Bank of Ireland)*

Chester & North Wales *(see Cheshire)*

Chilterns *(see Bradford & Bingley)*

Chorley & District Building Society
Website: www.chorleybs.co.uk
Head Office: Key House, Foxhole Rd, Chorley, Lancs PR7 1NZ
Tel: 01257 235000 / 01257 419110 Fax: 01257 241371
DX: 18419 Chorley
e-mail: mortgages@chorleybs.co.uk

Citizens Regency *(see Nationwide)*

City & Metropolitan *(see Coventry)*

City of Derry Building Society
Website: www.cityofderrybs.co.uk
Head Office: Progressive Ho, 33–37 Wellington Pl, Belfast BT1 6HH
Tel: 028 7137 0037 Fax: 028 7137 1508
e-mail: info@cityofderrybs.co.uk

Civil Service *(see Birmingham Midshires)*

Clapham *(see Bradford & Bingley)*

Co-operative Bank plc
Website: www.co-operativebank.co.uk
Head Office: PO Box 101, 1 Balloon St, Manchester M60 4EP
Tel: 0161 832 3456 Fax: 0161 829 4475
DX: 700003 Manchester 6

Colchester *(see Cheltenham & Gloucester)*

Cotswold *(see Cheltenham & Gloucester)*

Country *(see Nationwide)*

Coventry Building Society
Website: www.coventrybuildingsociety.co.uk
Head Office: 'Economic House', PO Box 9, High St, Coventry CV1 5QN
Tel: 0845 766 5522 Fax: 024 7684 1209
DX: 18855 Coventry 2
e-mail: support@coventrybuildingsociety.co.uk

Coventry Economic *(see Coventry)*

Coventry Provident *(see Coventry)*

Cumberland Building Society
Website: www.cumberland.co.uk
Head Office: Cumberland Hse, Cooper Way, Carlisle CA3 0JF
Tel: 0845 601 8396 / 01228 403141 Fax: 01228 525309
DX: 63025 Carlisle
e-mail: mortgages@cumberland.co.uk

Darlington Building Society
Website: www.darlington.co.uk
Head Office: Sentinel Ho, Lingfield Way, Darlington DL1 4PR
Tel: 01325 366366 Fax: 01325 741000
DX: 712851 Darlington 6
e-mail: sales@darlington.co.uk

Denton *(see Co-operative Bank)*

Derbyshire Building Society *(see Nationwide)*

Dillwyn *(see Swansea)*

Dover & Folkestone *(see Bradford & Bingley)*

Driffield *(see Co-operative Bank)*

Dudley Building Society
Website: www.dudleybuildingsociety.co.uk
Head Office: 7 Harbour Bldgs, The Waterfront, Brierley Hill DY5 1LN
Tel: 0845 850 2369 Fax: 01384 233250
e-mail: enquiries@dudleybuildingsociety.co.uk

Dunfermline Building Society *(see Nationwide)*

Ealing & Acton *(see Birmingham Midshires)*

Earl Shilton Building Society
Website: www.esbs.co.uk
Head Office: 22 The Hollow, Earl Shilton, Leicester LE9 7NB
Tel: 01455 844422 Fax: 01455 845857
e-mail: enquire@esbs.co.uk / mortgages@esbs.co.uk

Ecology Building Society
Website: www.ecology.co.uk
Head Office: 7 Belton Rd, Silsden, Keighley, W.Yorkshire BD20 0EE
Tel: 0845 674 5566 / 01535 650770 Fax: 01535 650780
e-mail: info@ecology.co.uk / mortgages@ecology.co.uk

Essex Equitable *(see Cheltenham & Gloucester)*

Furness Building Society
Website: www.furnessbs.co.uk
Head Office: Mortgage Dept, 51–55 Duke St, Barrow-in-Furness, Cumbria LA14 1RT
Tel: 0800 220 568 Fax: 01229 837043
DX: 63922 Barrow
e-mail: furness.direct@furness-bs.co.uk

Gateway *(see Barclays)*

Glamorgan *(see Bradford & Bingley)*

Greenwich *(see Nationwide)*

Hadrian *(see Virgin Money)*

Halifax plc
Website: www.halifax.co.uk
Head Office: PO Box 548, Leeds LS1 1WU
Tel: 08458 503705
DX: 11896 Halifax
Redemption figs: apply to local branch of Halifax

Hampshire *(see Bradford & Bingley)*

Hanley Economic Building Society
Website: www.thehanley.co.uk
Head Office: Granville Ho, Festival Park, Hanley, Stoke-on-Trent ST1 5TB
Tel: 01782 255000 Fax: 01782 873167
e-mail: hebs@thehanley.co.uk

Harpenden Building Society
Website: www.harpendenbs.co.uk
Head Office: Mardall Ho, 9–11 Vaughan Rd, Harpenden AL5 4HU
Tel: 01582 463133 Fax: 01582 766967
DX: 80470 Harpenden
e-mail: enquiries@harpendenbs.co.uk

Harrow *(see Birmingham Midshires)*

Hartlepool & District *(see Virgin Money)*

Haslemere *(see Santander)*

Haywards Heath *(see Yorkshire)*

Hearts of Oak & Enfield *(see Bradford & Bingley)*

Hemel Hempstead *(see Birmingham Midshires)*

Herne Bay *(see Kent Reliance)*

Hibernian *(see Bradford & Bingley)*

Hinckley and Rugby Building Society
Website: www.hrbs.co.uk
Head Office: Principal Office, 81 Upper Bond St, Hinckley LE10 1DG
Tel: 0800 434 6343 Fax: 01455 618506
DX: 716435 Hinckley
e-mail: enquiry@hrbs.co.uk

Holmesdale Building Society
Website: www.holmesdale.co.uk
Head Office: 43 Church St, Reigate RH2 0AE
Tel: 01737 245716 Fax: 01737 246962
DX: 54107 Reigate 2
e-mail: mail@holmesdale.org.uk

Horsham *(see Bradford & Bingley)*

Housing & General *(see Bradford & Bingley)*

Huntly *(see Scottish)*

Ilkeston Permanent *(see Derbyshire)*

Ipswich Building Society
Website: www.ibs.co.uk
Head Office: Lending Services, PO Box 547, Ipswich IP3 9WZ
Tel: 0845 230 8686 Fax: 01473 278625
e-mail: enquiries@ibs.co.uk

Kent & Canterbury Permanent Benefit *(see Kent Reliance)*

Kent Reliance Building Society
Website: www.krbs.co.uk
Head Office: Legal Services, Reliance Hse, PO Box 600, Chatham ME4 9DW
Tel: 0845 122 0033 Fax: 01634 830912
DX: 6710 Chatham
e-mail: mail@krbs.com

Kilmarnock *(see Virgin Money)*

King Edward *(see Birmingham Midshires)*

Leeds Building Society
Website: www.leedsbuildingsociety.co.uk
Head Office: 105 Albion St, Leeds LS1 5AS
Tel: 0113 225 7777 Fax: 0113 225 7659
DX: 12299 Leeds 1
e-mail: info@leedsbuildingsociety.co.uk

Leeds Permanent *(see Halifax)*

Leek United Building Society
Website: www.leekunited.co.uk
Head Office: Mortgage Applications, 50 St Edward St, Leek ST13 5DL
Tel: 01538 384151 Fax: 01538 399179
DX: 16354 Leek
e-mail: ruth.taylor@leekunited.co.uk

Leicester *(see Santander)*

Leigh Permanent *(see Cheshire)*

London & South of England *(see Nationwide)*

London Commercial *(see Nottingham)*

London Grosvenor *(see Barclays)*

London Permanent *(see Cheltenham & Gloucester)*

Loughborough Building Society
Website: www.theloughborough.co.uk
Head Office: 6 High St, Loughborough LE11 2QB
Tel: 01509 610707 Fax: 01509 231058
DX: 19611 Loughborough
e-mail: enquiries@theloughborough.co.uk

Manchester Building Society
Website: www.themanchester.co.uk
Head Office: 125 Portland St, Manchester M1 4QD
Tel: 0161 923 8000 Fax: 0161 923 8950
e-mail: info@themanchester.co.uk
Lending: PO Box 4256, Manchester M60 3AX
Tel: 0161 923 8050 Fax: 0161 923 8951
e-mail: mps@themanchester.co.uk

Manchester Unity *(see Virgin Money)*

Mansfield Building Society
Website: www.mansfieldbs.co.uk
Head Office: Mortgage Dept, Regent Ho, Regent St, Mansfield NG18 1SS
Tel: 01623 676300 Fax: 01623 676356
DX: 10400 Mansfield
e-mail: enquiries@mansfieldbs.co.uk

Market Harborough Building Society
Website: www.mhbs.co.uk
Head Office: Mortgage Administration, Welland Ho, The Square, Market Harborough LE16 7PD
Tel: 01858 412250 Fax: 01858 412254
DX: 27312 Market Harborough
e-mail: customersfirst@mhbs.co.uk

Marsden Building Society
Website: www.themarsden.co.uk
Head Office: 6–20 Russell St, Nelson BB9 7NJ
Tel: 01282 440500 Fax: 01282 440550
e-mail: info@themarsden.co.uk

Melton Mowbray Building Society
Website: www.themelton.co.uk
Head Office: Mutual Ho, Leicester Rd, Melton Mowbray LE13 0DB
Tel: 01664 414141 Fax: 01664 414103
e-mail: melton@mmbs.co.uk

Merseyside *(see Bradford & Bingley)*

Metrogas *(see Birmingham Midshires)*

Midshires *(see Birmingham Midshires)*

Monmouthshire Building Society
Website: www.monbs.com
Head Office: Monmouthshire Ho, John Frost Sq, Newport NP20 1PX
Tel: 01633 844351 Fax: 01633 844445
DX: 33240 Newport (Gwent)
e-mail: enquiries@monbs.com

Mornington *(see Co-operative Bank)*

Mortgage Express *(see Bradford & Bingley)*

Mortgage Trust
Website: www.mortgagetrust.co.uk
Head Office: 51 Homer Rd, Solihull, W Mids B91 3QJ
Tel: 0845 849 4040 (current customers); 4000 (new customer s) Fax: 0845 849 4041 (current customers); 4002 (new)
DX: 30718 Epsom
e-mail: mtlenquiries@mortgagetrust.co.uk (current customers), mtenquiries@paragon-group.co.uk (new customers)

Mortgage Works (UK) plc, The
Website: www.themortgageworks.co.uk
Head Office: Portman Ho, Richmond Hill, Bournemouth BH2 6EP
Tel: 0845 4545 800 Fax: 01202 562460
e-mail: tmwdirect@themortgageworks.co.uk

Musselburgh *(see Virgin Money)*

National & Provincial Building Society *(see Santander)*

National Counties Building Society
Website: www.ncbs.co.uk
Head Office: Ebbisham Ho, 30 Church St, Epsom KT17 4NL
Tel: 01372 742211 Fax: 01372 745607
DX: 30729 Epsom
e-mail: info@ncbs.co.uk
Branch: Ashley Sq, Epsom KT18 5DD
Tel: 01372 747771

National Westminster Bank plc
Website: www.natwest.com
Head Office: 135 Bishopsgate, London EC2M 3UR
Tel: 0800 200 400
Customer Relations: NatWest Customer Relations, Freepost NAT 12685, Borehamwood WD6 1BR
Tel: 0800 015 4212

Nationwide Building Society
Website: www.nationwide.co.uk
Administration centre: King's Park Rd, Moulton Pk, Northampton NN3 6NW
Tel: 01793 513513
DX: 12500 Northampton
Head Office: Nationwide Ho, Pipers Way, Swindon SN38 1NW
Tel: 01793 513513
DX: 43553 Swindon

Newbury Building Society
Website: www.newbury.co.uk
Head Office: Customer Services, 17 Bartholomew St, Newbury RG14 5LY
Tel: 01635 555700 Fax: 01635 555799
DX: 30822 Newbury
e-mail: enquiries@newbury.co.uk

Newcastle Building Society
Website: www.newcastle.co.uk
Principal Office: Legal Services, Portland Ho, New Bridge St, Newcastle upon Tyne NE1 8AL
Tel: 0845 600 4367 Fax: 0191 244 2001
e-mail: sales@newcastle.co.uk

North Kent *(see Barclays)*

North Wilts Equitable *(see Nationwide)*

North Wilts Ridgeway *(see Nationwide)*

North of England *(see Virgin Money)*

Norwich & Peterborough Building Society
Website: www.nandp.co.uk
Chief Office: Peterborough Business Park, Lynch Wood, Peterborough PE2 6WZ
Tel: 01733 372372 Fax: 01733 372373
DX: 29181 Lynch Wood

Norwich *(see Norwich & Peterborough)*

Nottingham Building Society
Website: www.thenottingham.com
Head Office: Nottingham Ho, 3 Fulforth St, Nottingham NG1 3DL
Tel: 0115 956 4704 Fax: 0115 956 4777
DX: 10000 Nottingham
e-mail: customer-services@thenottingham.com

Nottingham Imperial *(see Newcastle)*

Otley *(see Skipton)*

Over Darwen *(see Co-operative Bank)*

Paddington *(see Nationwide)*

Padiham *(see Bradford & Bingley)*

Paragon Mortgages Ltd
Website: www.paragon-mortgages.co.uk
Head Office: 51 Homer Rd, Solihull, W Mids B91 3QJ
Tel: 0845 849 4040 / 0845 849 4000 (switchboard)
Fax: 0845 849 4041 / 0845 849 4002 (switchboard)
e-mail: pmlcs@paragon-group.co.uk

Penrith Building Society
Website: www.penrithbuildingsociety.co.uk
Head Office: 7 King St, Penrith, Cumbria CA11 7AR
Tel: 01768 863675 Fax: 01768 891275

Peterborough *(see Norwich & Peterborough)*

Pioneer *(see Virgin Money)*

Portman *(see Nationwide)*

Portsmouth *(see Cheltenham & Gloucester)*

Principality Building Society
Website: www.principality.co.uk
Head Office: Mortgage Service Centre, Principality Bldgs, PO Box 89, Queen St, Cardiff CF10 1UA
Tel: 0330 333 4000 Fax: 0845 371 5310
DX: 144240 Cardiff 29
e-mail: enquiries@principality.co.uk

Progressive Building Society
Website: www.theprogressive.com
Head Office: Progressive Ho, 33–37 Wellington Pl, Belfast BT1 6HH
Tel: 028 90244926 Fax: 028 90330431
DX: 4230 NR Belfast 26
e-mail: info@theprogressive.com

Property Owners *(see Barclays)*

Ramsbury *(see Nationwide)*

Regency & West of England *(see Nationwide)*

Ridgeway *(see Nationwide)*

Rowley Regis *(see Cheltenham & Gloucester)*

Royal Bank of Scotland plc, The
Website: www.rbs.co.uk
Head Office: 1st Fl, House F, Gogarburn, Edinburgh EH12 1HQ
Tel: 0131 556 8555 Fax: 0131 557 6565
DX: 551727 Edinburgh 65

Rugby Provident *(see Hinckley & Rugby)*

Saddleworth *(see Bradford & Bingley)*

Saffron Walden Building Society
Website: www.saffronbs.co.uk
Head Office: Saffron Ho, 1A Market St, Saffron Walden CB10 1HX
Tel: 01799 522211 / 0800 072 1100
Fax: 01799 581901/513622
e-mail: saffrondirect@saffronbs.co.uk

Saint Pancras *(see Nationwide)*

Sandbach *(see Cheshire)*

Santander UK plc
Website: www.santander.co.uk
Registered Office: Abbey National Ho, 2 Triton Sq, Regents Pl, London NW1 3AN
Tel: 0870 607 6000
DX: 130181 London
Deeds Services: Deeds Dept, 101 Midsummer Boulevard, Milton Keynes MK9 1AA
Tel: 0870 607 1862
DX: 137000 Milton Keynes 2

Scottish Building Society
Website: www.scottishbs.co.uk
Head Office: SBS Ho, 193 Dalry Rd, Edinburgh EH11 2EF
Tel: 0131 313 7700 Fax: 0131 313 7711
DX: LP–158 Edinburgh–2
e-mail: mail@scottishbs.co.uk

Sheffield *(see Bradford & Bingley)*

Shepshed Building Society *(see Nottingham)*

Shields & Washington *(see Virgin Money)*

Shields Commercial *(see Virgin Money)*

Skipton Building Society
Website: www.skipton.co.uk
Head Office: Deeds Data Control, The Bailey, Skipton, N Yorks BD23 1DN
Tel: 01756 705000 Fax: 01756 705700
DX: 21757 Skipton

South Durham *(see Virgin Money)*

South Shields Sun Permanent *(see Virgin Money)*

Staffordshire Building Society *(see Nationwide)*

Standard Life Bank
Website: www.standardlife.co.uk
Head Office: 1 Baileyfield Cres, Edinburgh EH15 1ET
Tel: 0845 845 8450 Fax: 0131 246 1471
e-mail: slb.mortgages@slb.barclays.com

Stanley *(see Bradford & Bingley)*

Stockport & County Permanent *(see Virgin Money)*

Stockport Mersey *(see Bradford & Bingley)*

Strathclyde *(see Scottish)*

Stroud & Swindon *(see Coventry)*

Stroud *(see Coventry)*

Sunderland & Shields *(see Virgin Money)*

Surrey *(see Virgin Money)*

Sussex Mutual *(see Nationwide)*

Swansea Building Society
Website: www.swansea-bs.co.uk
Head Office: 11/12 Cradock St, Swansea SA1 3EW
Tel: 01792 483700 Fax: 01792 483718
DX: 39595 Swansea
e-mail: info@swansea-bs.co.uk

Swansea Park *(see Bradford & Bingley)*

Swindon Permanent *(see Coventry)*

Target *(see Bradford & Bingley)*

Teachers' Building Society
Website: www.teachersbs.co.uk
Head Office: Allenview Hse, Hanham Rd, Wimborne, Dorset BH21 1AG
Tel: 01202 843500 Fax: 01202 841694
DX: 45315 Wimborne
e-mail: karen.flaherty@teachersbs.co.uk

The Woolwich *(see Barclays)*

Thrift *(see Bank of Ireland)*

Tipton & Coseley Building Society
Website: www.thetipton.co.uk
Head Office: 70 Owen St, Tipton, W Midlands DY4 8HG
Tel: 0121 557 2551 (Switchboard), 0121 521 4000 (Mortgage s) Fax: 0121 557 8570
e-mail: info@thetipton.co.uk

Town & Country *(see Barclays)*

United Kingdom *(see Virgin Money)*

United Provinces *(see Bradford & Bingley)*

Vernon Building Society
Website: www.thevernon.co.uk
Head Office: The Secretary, 19 St Petersgate, Stockport SK1 1HF
Tel: 0161 429 6262 Fax: 0161 429 6996
e-mail: info@vernonbs.co.uk

Virgin Money
Website: www.virginmoney.com
Head Office: Jubilee Ho, Gosforth, Newcastle upon Tyne NE3 4PL
Tel: 01268 443956

Waltham Abbey *(see Cheltenham & Gloucester)*

Walthamstow *(see Cheltenham & Gloucester)*

Wellington (Somerset) & District *(see Co-operative Bank)*

Welsh Economic *(see Co-operative Bank)*

Wessex *(see Nationwide)*

West Bromwich Building Society
Website: www.westbrom.co.uk
Head Office: 374 High St, West Bromwich, W Midlands B70 8LR
Tel: 0845 330 0656 Fax: 0121 500 5961
DX: 14611 WB7

West Cumbria *(see Cumberland)*
Western Counties *(see Nationwide)*
Wigan *(see Cheshire)*
Wishaw Investment *(see Virgin Money)*

Yorkshire Building Society
Website: www.ybs.co.uk
Head Office: Yorkshire Ho, Yorkshire Drive, Bradford BD5 8LJ
Tel: 0845 1200 100 Fax: 01274 652134
DX: 11798 Bradford

Part 4

Courts

The Court Service

HM Courts Service
Website: www.hmcourts-service.gov.uk
Headquarters: Complaint Handling & Enquiries Team, Zone C, 1st Fl, 102 Petty France, London SW1H 9AJ
Tel: 0845 456 8770 Fax: 020 3334 4087
DX: 152380 Westminster 8
e-mail: customerservicecshq@hmcourts-service.gsi.gov.uk
Note: More information about County Courts can be found on the Court Service website.

Crown Courts

Aylesbury Crown Court
Court Office: Crown Court, County Hall, Market Square, Aylesbury HP20 1XD
Tel: 01296 434401 Fax: 01296 435665
DX: 157430 Aylesbury 11

Barnstaple Crown Court
Court Office: Exeter Crown & County Court, Southernhay Gardens, Exeter EX1 1UH
Tel: 01392 415300 Fax: 01392 415642
DX: 98440 Exeter 2

Basildon Crown Court
Court Office: Basildon Combined Court, The Gore, Basildon SS14 2BU
Tel: 01268 458000 Fax: 01268 458100
DX: 97633 Basildon 5

Birmingham Crown Court
Court Office: Queen Elizabeth II Law Courts, 1 Newton St, Birmingham B4 7NA
Tel: 0121 681 3300 Fax: 0121 681 3370
DX: 702033 Birmingham 8

Blackfriars Crown Court
Court Office: Crown Court, 1–15 Pocock St, London SE1 0BJ
Tel: 020 7922 5800 Fax: 0870 324 0146
DX: 400800 Lambeth 3

Bolton Crown Court
Court Office: Bolton Combined Court Centre, The Law Courts, Blackhorse St, Bolton BL1 1SU
Tel: 01204 392881 Fax: 01204 363204
DX: 702610 Bolton 3

Bournemouth Crown Court
Court Office: Bournemouth Crown and County Court, Courts of Justice, Deansleigh Rd, Bournemouth BH7 7DS
Tel: 01202 502800 Fax: 01202 502801
DX: 98420 Bournemouth 4

Bradford Crown Court
Court Office: Bradford Combined Court Centre, The Law Courts, Exchange Square, Drake St, Bradford BD1 1JA
Tel: 01274 840274 Fax: 01274 843510
DX: 702083 Bradford 2

Bristol Crown Court
Court Office: The Law Courts, Small St, Bristol BS1 1DA
Tel: 0117 976 3030 Fax: 0117 976 3074
DX: 78128 Bristol

Burnley Crown Court
Court Office: Burnley Combined Court Centre, The Law Courts, Hammerton St, Burnley BB11 1XD
Tel: 01282 855300 Fax: 01282 414911
DX: 724940 Burnley 4

Bury St Edmonds Crown Court
Court Office: Shire Hall, Bury St Edmonds IP33 1HF
Tel: 01473 228585 Fax: 01473 228560

Caernarfon Crown Court
Court Office: Caernarfon Criminal Justice Centre, Llanberis Rd, Caernarfon LL55 2DF
Tel: 01352 707340 Fax: 01352 753874

Cambridge Crown Court
Court Office: Crown Court, 83 East Rd, Cambridge CB1 1BT
Tel: 01223 488321 Fax: 01223 488333
DX: 97365 Cambridge 2

Canterbury Crown Court
Court Office: Canterbury Combined Court Centre, The Law Courts, Chaucer Rd, Canterbury CT1 1ZA
Tel: 01227 819200 Fax: 01227 819329
DX: 99710 Canterbury 3

Cardiff Crown Court
Court Office: The Law Courts, Cathays Park, Cardiff CF10 3PG
Tel: 029 2067 8830 Fax: 0870 324 0261
DX: 99450 Cardiff 5

Carlisle Crown Court
Court Office: Carlisle Combined Court Centre, Courts of Justice, Earl St, Carlisle CA1 1DJ
Tel: 01228 882120 Fax: 01228 590588
DX: 65331 Carlisle 2

Carmarthen Crown Court
Court Office: The Law Courts, St Helen's Rd, Swansea SA1 4PF
Tel: 01792 637000 Fax: 01792 637049
DX: 99540 Swansea 4

Central Criminal Court Crown Court
Court Office: Old Bailey, London EC4M 7HS
Tel: 020 7248 3277 Fax: 020 7192 2671
DX: 46700 Old Bailey

Chelmsford Crown Court
Court Office: Crown Court, PO Box 9, New St, Chelmsford CM1 1EL
Tel: 01245 603000 Fax: 01245 603011
DX: 97375 Chelmsford 3

Chester Crown Court
Court Office: Crown Court, The Castle, Chester CH1 2AN
Tel: 01244 317606 Fax: 01244 350773
DX: 702527 Chester 5

Chichester Crown Court
Court Office: Chichester Combined Court Centre, Southgate, Chichester PO19 1SX
Tel: 01243 520700

Coventry Crown Court
Court Office: Coventry Combined Court Centre, 140 Much Park St, Coventry CV1 2SN
Tel: 0300 123 557 Fax: 024 7625 1083
DX: 701580 Coventry 5

Croydon Crown Court
Court Office: The Law Courts, Altyre Rd, Croydon CR9 5AB
Tel: 020 8410 4700 Fax: 020 8781 1001
DX: 97473 Croydon 6

Derby Crown Court
Court Office: Derby Combined Court Centre, Morledge, Derby DE1 2XE
Tel: 01332 622600 Fax: 01332 622540
DX: 724060 Derby 21

Dolgellau Crown Court
Court Office: The Law Courts, County Civic Centre, Mold CH7 1AE
Tel: 01352 707340 Fax: 01352 753874
DX: 702521 Mold 2

Doncaster Crown Court
Court Office: Sheffield Crown Court, The Law Courts, West Bar, Sheffield S3 8PH
Tel: 01302 322211 Fax: 01302 329471

Dorchester Crown Court
Court Office: Crown Court, Colliton Park, Dorchester DT1 1XJ
Tel: 01305 265867 Fax: 01305 251867
DX: 8720 Dorchester

Durham Crown Court
Court Office: The Law Courts, Old Elvet, Durham DH1 3HW
Tel: 0191 386 6714 Fax: 0191 383 0605
DX: 65112 Durham 4

Exeter Crown Court
Court Office: Crown Court, Southernhay Gardens, Exeter EX1 1UH
Tel: 01392 415300 Fax: 01392 415644
DX: 98440 Exeter 2

Gloucester Crown Court
Court Office: Courthouse, Longsmith St, Gloucester GL1 2TS
Tel: 01452 420100 Fax: 01452 833557

Great Grimsby Crown Court
Court Office: Crown Court, Town Hall Square, Great Grimsby DN31 1HX
Tel: 01472 265250 Fax: 01472 265251
DX: 702007 Grimsby 3

Guildford Crown Court
Court Office: Crown Court, Bedford Rd, Guildford GU1 4ST
Tel: 01483 468500 Fax: 01483 579545
DX: 97862 Guildford 5

Harrow Crown Court
Court Office: Crown Court, Hailsham Drive, off Headstone Drive, Harrow HA1 4TU
Tel: 020 8424 2294 Fax: 0870 324 0149
DX: 97335 Harrow 5

Hereford Crown Court
Court Office: Crown Court, The Shirehall, St Peter's Sq, Hereford HR1 2HY
Tel: 01905 730823 Fax: 01905 730810

Inner London Sessions Ho Crown Court
Court Office: Sessions Ho, Newington Causeway, London SE1 6AZ
Tel: 020 7234 3100 Fax: 020 7234 3287
DX: 97345 Southwark 3

Ipswich Crown Court
Court Office: The Court House, 1 Russell Rd, Ipswich IP1 2AG
Tel: 01473 228585 Fax: 01473 228560
DX: 729480 Ipswich 19

Isleworth Crown Court
Court Office: Crown Court, 36 Ridgeway Rd, Isleworth TW7 5LP
Tel: 020 8388 4500 Fax: 0870 324 0150
DX: 97420 Isleworth 1

King's Lynn Crown Court
Court Office: The Court House, College La, King's Lynn PE30 1PQ
Tel: 01603 728200 Fax: 01603 760863

Kingston-Upon-Hull Crown Court
Court Office: Crown Court, Lowgate, Hull HU1 2EZ
Tel: 01482 586161 Fax: 01482 588527
DX: 703010 Hull 5

Kingston-Upon-Thames Crown Court
Court Office: Crown Court, 6–8 Penrhyn Rd, Kingston-Upon-Thames KT1 2BB
Tel: 020 8240 2500 Fax: 020 8240 2675
DX: 97430 Kington Upon Thames 2

Lancaster Crown Court
Court Office: The Law Courts, Openshaw Place, Ring Way, Preston PR1 2LL
Tel: 01772 844700 Fax: 01772 844759
DX: 702660 Preston 5

Leeds Crown Court
Court Office: The Court House, 1 Oxford Row, Leeds LS1 3BG
Tel: 0113 306 2800 Fax: 0113 306 2654
DX: 703016 Leeds 6

Leicester Crown Court
Court Office: Crown Court, 90 Wellington St, Leicester LE1 6HG
Tel: 0116 222 5800 Fax: 0116 222 5888
DX: 10880 Leicester 3

Lewes Crown Court
Court Office: The Law Courts, High St, Lewes BN7 1YB
Tel: 01273 480400 Fax: 01273 485269
DX: 97395 Lewes 4

Lincoln Crown Court
Court Office: Crown Court, The Castle, Castle Hill, Lincoln LN1 3GA
Tel: 01522 525222 Fax: 01522 543962
DX: 722500 Lincoln 11

Liverpool Crown Court
Court Office: The Queen Elizabeth II Law Courts, Derby Square, Liverpool L2 1XA
Tel: 0151 473 7373 Fax: 0151 471 1000
DX: 740880 liverpool 22

Luton Crown Court
Court Office: Crown Court, 7 George St, Luton LU1 2AA
Tel: 01582 522000 Fax: 01582 522001
DX: 120500 Luton 6

Maidstone Crown Court
Court Office: The Law Courts, Barker Rd, Maidstone ME16 8EQ
Tel: 01622 202000 Fax: 01622 202001
DX: 130065 Maidstone 7

Manchester Crown Court
Court Office: Crown Court, Crown Square, Manchester M3 3FL
Tel: 0161 954 1800 Fax: 0161 954 1705
DX: 702539 Manchester 11
Court Office: Crown Court, Minshull St, Manchester M1 3FS
Tel: 0161 954 7500 Fax: 0161 954 7600
DX: 724860 Manchester 43

Merthyr Tydfil Crown Court
Court Office: The Law Courts, Glebeland Place, Merthyr Tydfil CF47 8BH
Tel: 01685 727600 Fax: 01685 722702
DX: 99582 Merthyr Tydfil 2

Mold Crown Court
Court Office: The Law Courts, County Civic Centre, Mold CH7 1AE
Tel: 01352 707340 Fax: 01352 753874
DX: 702621 Mold 2

Newcastle-Upon-Tyne Crown Court
Court Office: The Law Courts, Quayside, Newcastle-Upon-Tyne NE1 3LA
Tel: 0191 201 2000 Fax: 0191 201 2001
DX: 65127 Newcastle-Upon-Tyne 2

Newport (IOW) Crown Court
Court Office: The Law Courts, Quay St, Newport PO30 5YT
Tel: 01983 535100 Fax: 01983 554977
DX: 98460 Newport (IOW) 2

Newport (Wales) Crown Court
Court Office: The Law Courts, Cathays Park, Cardiff CF10 3PG
Tel: 029 2067 8830 Fax: 0870 324 0261
DX: 99450 Cardiff 5

Northampton Crown Court
Court Office: Northampton Combined Court Centre, 85/87 Lady's Ln, Northampton NN1 3HQ
Tel: 01604 470400 Fax: 01604 632728
DX: 725380 Northampton 21

Norwich Crown Court
Court Office: The Law Courts, Bishopgate, Norwich NR3 1UR
Tel: 01603 728200 Fax: 01603 760863
DX: 97385 Norwich 5

Nottingham Crown Court
Court Office: The Law Courts, 60 Canal St, Nottingham NG1 7EL
Tel: 0115 910 3551 Fax: 0115 910 3599
DX: 702383 Nottingham 7

Oxford Crown Court
Court Office: Oxford Combined Court Centre, St Aldates, Oxford OX1 1TL
Tel: 01865 264200 Fax: 01865 790773
DX: 96450 Oxford 4

Peterborough Crown Court
Court Office: Peterborough Combined Court Centre, Crown Buildings, Rivergate, Peterborough PE1 1EJ
Tel: 01733 349161 Fax: 01733 557348
DX: 702302 Peterborough 8

Plymouth Crown Court
Court Office: The Law Courts, Armada Way, Plymouth PL1 2ER
Tel: 01752 677400 Fax: 01752 208292
DX: 98470 Plymouth 7

Portsmouth Crown Court
Court Office: The Court of Justice, Winston Churchill Avenue, Portsmouth PO1 2EB
Tel: 023 9289 3000 Fax: 023 9201 6859
DX: 98490 Portsmouth 5

Preston Crown Court
Court Office: The Law Courts, Openshaw Place, Ring Way, Preston PR1 2LL
Tel: 01772 844700 Fax: 01772 844759
DX: 702660 Preston 5

Reading Crown Court
Court Office: The Old Shire Hall, The Forbury, Reading RG1 3EH
Tel: 0118 967 4400 Fax: 0118 967 4444
DX: 97440 Reading 5

Salisbury Crown Court
Court Office: The Law Courts, Wilton Rd, Salisbury SP2 7EP
Tel: 01722 345200 Fax: 01722 345201
DX: 98500 Salisbury 2

Sheffield Crown Court
Court Office: The Law Courts, 50 West Bar, Sheffield S3 8PH
Tel: 0114 281 2400 Fax: 0114 281 2425
DX: 703028 Sheffield 6

Shrewsbury Crown Court
Court Office: The Shirehall, Abbey Foregate, Shrewsbury SY2 6LU
Tel: 01743 260820 Fax: 01743 244236
DX: 702022 Shrewsbury 2

Snaresbrook Crown Court
Court Office: Crown Court, 75 Hollybush Hill, London E11 1QW
Tel: 020 8530 0000 Fax: 0870 324 0165
DX: 98240 Wanstead 2

Southampton Crown Court
Court Office: The Courts of Justice, London Rd, Southampton SO15 2XQ
Tel: 023 8021 3200 Fax: 0870 761 7655
DX: 111000 Southampton 11

Southend Crown Court
Court Office: The Court Ho, Victoria Ave, Southend-on-Sea SS2 6EG
Tel: 01268 458000 Fax: 01268 458100

Southwark Crown Court
Court Office: Crown Court, 1 English Grounds (off Battlebridge Ln), London SE1 2HU
Tel: 020 7522 7200 Fax: 020 7522 7300
DX: 39913 London Bridge South

St Albans Crown Court
Court Office: The Court Building, Bricket Rd, St Albans AL1 3JW
Tel: 01727 753220 Fax: 01727 753221
DX: 99700 St Albans 3

Stafford Crown Court
Court Office: Stafford Combined Court Centre, Victoria Square, Stafford ST16 2QQ
Tel: 01785 610730 Fax: 01785 246786
DX: 703190 Stafford 4

Stoke-on-Trent Crown Court
Court Office: Bethesda St, Hanley, Stoke-on-Trent ST1 3BP
Tel: 01782 854000 Fax: 01782 854021
DX: 703360 Hanley 3

Swansea Crown Court
Court Office: The Law Courts, St Helen's Rd, Swansea SA1 4PF
Tel: 01792 637000 Fax: 01792 637049
DX: 99540 Swansea 4

Swindon Crown Court
Court Office: The Law Courts, Islington St, Swindon SN1 2HG
Tel: 01793 690500 Fax: 01793 690535
DX: 98430 Swindon 5

Taunton Crown Court
Court Office: Crown Court, Shire Hall, Taunton TA1 4EU
Tel: 01823 281100 Fax: 01823 322116
DX: 98411 Taunton 2

Teeside Crown Court
Court Office: Teesside Combined Court Centre, Russell St, Teeside TS1 2AE
Tel: 01642 340000 Fax: 01642 340002
DX: 65152 Middlesbrough 2

Truro Crown Court
Court Office: Courts of Justice, Edward St, Truro TR1 2PB
Tel: 01872 267420
DX: 135396 Truro 2

Warrington Crown Court
Court Office: The Castle, Chester CH1 2AN
Tel: 01244 317606 Fax: 01244 350773
DX: 702501 Warrington 3

Warwick Crown Court
Court Office: Warwickshire Justice Centre, Newbold Terrace, Leamington, Warwick CV32 4EL
Tel: 01926 682100 Fax: 01926 682519
DX: 701964 Leamington 7

Winchester Crown Court
Court Office: The Law Courts, Winchester SO23 9EL
Tel: 01962 814100 Fax: 0870 324 0125
DX: 98520 Winchester 3

Wolverhampton Crown Court
Court Office: Wolverhampton Combined Court Centre, Pipers Row, Wolverhampton WV1 3LQ
Tel: 01902 481000 Fax: 01902 481001
DX: 702019 Wolverhampton 4

Wood Green Crown Court
Court Office: Crown Court, Woodhall Ho, Lordship Ln, Wood Green N22 5LF
Tel: 020 8826 4100 Fax: 0870 324 0160
DX: 130346 Wood Green 3

Woolwich Crown Court
Court Office: Crown Court, 2 Belmarsh Rd, London SE28 0EY
Tel: 020 8312 7000 Fax: 020 8312 7078
DX: 117650 Woolwich 7

Worcester Crown Court
Court Office: Worcester Combined Court Centre, The Shirehall, Foregate St, Worcester WR1 1EQ
Tel: 01905 730823 Fax: 01905 730810
DX: 721120 Worcester 11

York Crown Court
Court Office: The Castle, York YO1 9WZ
Tel: 01904 645121 Fax: 01904 611689
DX: 65162 York 3

County Courts

Aberystwyth County Court
Court Office: Aberystwyth Justice Centre, Y Lanfa, Trefechan, Aberystwyth SY23 1AS
Tel: 01970 636370 Fax: 01970 625985
e-mail: enquiries@aberystwyth.countycourt.gsi.gov.uk

Accrington County Court
Court Office: Burnley County Court, The Law Courts, Hammerton St, Burnley BB11 1XD
Tel: 01254 237490 Fax: 01254 393869

Aldershot & Farnham County Court
Court Office: 84–86 Victoria Rd, Aldershot GU11 1SS
Tel: 01252 796800 Fax: 01252 345705
DX: 98530 Aldershot 2

Altrincham County Court
Court Office: Altrincham County Court, Trafford Court Ho, Ashton La, Sale, Cheshire M33 7WX
Tel: 0161 975 4760 Fax: 0161 975 4761
DX: 708292 Sale 6
e-mail: enquiries@altrincham.countycourt.gsi.gov.uk
Note: filing@altrincham.countycourt.gsi.gov.uk

Aylesbury County Court
Court Office: Aylesbury County Court, Walton St, Aylesbury, Bucks HP21 7QZ
Tel: 01296 554326/7 Fax: 01296 554320
DX: 97820 Aylesbury 10
e-mail: enquiries@aylesbury.countycourt.gsi.gov.uk

Banbury County Court
Court Office: The Court House, Warwick Rd, Banbury OX16 2AW
Tel: 01295 452090 Fax: 01295 452051
DX: 701967 Banbury 2
e-mail: enquiries@banbury.countycourt.gsi.gov.uk

Barnet Civil and Family Courts Centre
Court Office: St Mary's Court, Regents' Park Rd, Finchley, London N3 1BQ
Tel: 020 8343 4272 Fax: 020 8343 1324
DX: 122570 Finchley (Church End)
e-mail: enquiries@barnet.countycourt.gsi.gov.uk

Barnsley County Court
Court Office: The Court House, PO Box 17, Westgate, Barnsley S70 2DW
Tel: 01226 320000 Fax: 01226 320044
DX: 702080 Barnsley 3
e-mail: enquiries@barnsley.countycourt.gsi.gov.uk

Barnstaple County Court
Court Office: North Devon Courts, 8th Fl, Civic Centre, North Walk, Barnstaple EX31 1DX
Tel: 01271 340410 Fax: 01271 340415
DX: 98560 Barnstaple 2
e-mail: hearings@barnstaple.countycourt.gsi.gov.uk

Barrow-in-Furness County Court
Court Office: Court Service, Barrow County Court, Abbey Rd, Barrow-in-Furness LA14 5QX
Tel: 01229 840370 Fax: 01229 840371
DX: 65210 Barrow in Furness 2

Basildon Crown and County Courts
Court Office: Basildon Combined Court, The Gore, Basildon SS14 2BU
Tel: 01268 458000 (Crown) / 0844 892 4000 (County)
Fax: 01268 458100
DX: 97633 Basildon 5
e-mail: enquiries@basildon.crowncourt.gsi.gov.uk
Note: County Court emails to enquiries@basildon.countycourt.gsi.gov.uk

Basingstoke County Court
Court Office: The Court House, London Rd, Basingstoke RG21 4AB
Tel: 01256 318200 Fax: 01256 318217
DX: 98570 Basingstoke 3

Bath County Court
Court Office: The Law Courts, North Parade Rd, Bath BA1 5AF
Tel: 01225 476730 Fax: 01225 476724
DX: 98580 Bath 2
e-mail: av-bathcounty@hmcts.gsi.gov.uk

Bedford County Court
Court Office: PO Box 1405, Bedford MK40 9DN
Tel: 0844 892 0550 Fax: 01234 319026
DX: 97590 BEDFORD 11
e-mail: enquiries@bedford.countycourt.gsi.gov.uk

Birkenhead County Court
Court Office: The Court Manager, 76 Hamilton St, Birkenhead CH41 5EN
Tel: 0151 666 5800 Fax: 0151 666 5873
DX: 725000 Birkenhead 10
e-mail: enquiries@birkenhead.countycourt.gsi.gov.uk

Birmingham Civil Justice Centre and Family Courts
Court Office: The Court Manager, The Priory Courts, 33 Bull St, Birmingham B4 6DS
Tel: 0121 681 4441
DX: 701987 Birmingham 7
e-mail: enquiries@birmingham.countycourt.gsi.gov.uk; family@birmingham.countycourt.gsi.gov.uk

Blackburn County Court
Court Office: 64 Victoria St, Blackburn, Lancs BB1 6DJ
Tel: 01254 299852 (Civil) / 01254 299848 (Listing)
Fax: 01254 692712
DX: 702650 Blackburn 4
e-mail: blackburn.cty.cm@hmcts.gsi.gov.uk

Blackpool County Court
Court Office: The Court Service, The Law Courts, Chapel St, Blackpool FY1 5RJ
Tel: 01253 754020 Fax: 01253 295255
DX: 724900 Blackpool 10
e-mail: enquiries@blackpool.countycourt.gsi.gov.uk

Blackwood Civil & Family Court
Court Office: 8 Hall St, Blackwood, S Wales NP12 1NY
Tel: 01495 238200 Fax: 01495 238203
DX: 99470 Blackwood 2
e-mail: blackwood.enquiries@hmcts.gsi.gov.uk

Bodmin County Court
Court Office: The Law Courts, Launceston Rd, Bodmin, Cornwall PL31 2AL
Tel: 01208 261580 Fax: 01208 77255
DX: 136846 Bodmin 2
e-mail: enquiriesbodmincc@hmcts.gsi.gov.uk

Bolton Combined Court Centre
Court Office: The Law Courts, Blackhorse St, Bolton BL1 1SU
Tel: 01204 392881
Fax: 01204 373706 (County) / 01204 363204 (Crown)
DX: 702610 Bolton 3
e-mail: enquiries@bolton.countycourt.gsi.gov.uk

Boston County Court
Court Office: The Court Service, 55 Norfolk St, Boston, Lincolnshire PE21 6PE
Tel: 01205 366080 Fax: 01205 311692
DX: 701922 Boston 2
e-mail: bostonenquiries@hmcts.gsi.gov.uk

Bournemouth County Court
Court Office: Courts of Justice, Deansleigh Rd, Bournemouth BH7 7DS
Tel: 01202 502800 Fax: 01202 502801
DX: 98420 Bmth 4
e-mail: enquiries@bournemouth.countycourt.gsi.gov.uk

Bow County Court
Court Office: Court Service, 96 Romford Rd, London E15 4EG
Tel: 020 8536 5200 Fax: 020 8503 1152
DX: 97490 Stratford (London) 2
e-mail: enquiries@bow.countycourt.gsi.gov.uk

4

Bradford Combined Court Centre
Court Office: Bradford Combined Court Service, Bradford Law Courts, Exchange Sq, Drake St, Bradford BD1 1JA
Tel: 01274 840274 Fax: 01274 840275
DX: 702083 Bradford 2

Brecon Law Courts
Court Office: Merthyr Tydfil Combined Courts, The Law Courts, Glebeland Place, Merthyr Tydfil CF47 8BH
Tel: 01874 622993 Fax: 01874 622441
e-mail: breconmagscrt@hmcts.gsi.gov.uk

Brentford County Court
Court Office: Court Service, Alexandra Rd, Brentford High St, Brentford, Mddx TW8 0JJ
Tel: 020 8231 8940 Fax: 020 8568 2401
DX: 97840 Brentford 2
e-mail: enquiries@brentford.countycourt.gsi.gov.uk

Bridgend County Court
Court Office: The Law Courts, Sunnyside, Bridgend CF31 4AJ
Tel: 01656 673833 Fax: 01656 647124
DX: 99750 Bridgend 2

Brighton County Court
Court Office: William St, Brighton BN2 0RF
Tel: 01273 674421 Fax: 01273 602138
DX: 98070 Brighton 3
e-mail: enquiries@brighton.countycourt.gsi.gov.uk
Note: family@brighton.countycourt.gsi.gov.uk; bailiffs@brighton.countycourt.gsi.gov.uk; hearings@brighton.countycourt.gsi.gov.uk; e-filing@brighton.countycourt.gsi.gov.uk

Bristol County Court
Court Office: Bristol Civil Justice Centre, 2 Redcliff St, Bristol BS1 6GR
Tel: 0117 366 4800
Fax: 0117 366 4801 (Civil) / 0117 366 4802 (Family)
DX: 95903 Bristol 3
e-mail: enquiries@bristol.countycourt.gsi.gov.uk
Note: family@bristol.countycourt.gsi.gov.uk; e-filing@bristol.countycourt.gsi.gov.uk; bailiffs@bristol.countycourt.gsi.gov.uk; hearings@bristol.countycourt.gsi.gov.uk

Bromley County Court
Court Office: Court Ho, College Rd, Bromley, Kent BR1 3PX
Tel: 020 8290 9620 Fax: 020 8313 9624
DX: 98080 Bromley 2
e-mail: enquiries@bromley.countycourt.gsi.gov.uk

Burnley Combined Court Centre
Court Office: HMCTS, The Law Courts, Hammerton St, Burnley BB11 1XD
Tel: 01282 855300 Fax: 01282 414911
DX: 724940 Burnley 4
e-mail: enquiries@burnley.countycourt.gsi.gov.uk

Bury County Court
Court Office: Tenters St, Bury BL9 0HX
Tel: 0161 447 8699 Fax: 0161 763 4995
DX: 702615 Bury 2
e-mail: enquiries@bury.countycourt.gsi.gov.uk

Bury St Edmunds County Court
Court Office: Bury St Edmunds Employment Tribunal, 100 Southgate St, Bury St Edmunds IP33 2AQ
Tel: 0844 892 4000 Fax: 01284 702687
e-mail: enquiries@burystedmunds.countycourt.gsi.gov.uk

Caernarfon County Court
Court Office: The Courthouse, Llanberis Rd, Caernarfon LL55 2DF
Tel: 01286 684600 Fax: 01286 678965
DX: 702483 Caernarfon 2

Cambridge County Court
Court Office: Court Service, 197 East Rd, Cambridge CB1 1BA
Tel: 0844 892 4000 Fax: 01223 224590
DX: 97650 Cambridge 3
e-mail: cambridgecountyenquiries@hmcts.gsi.gov.uk

Canterbury Combined Court Centre
Court Office: The Law Courts, Chaucer Rd, Canterbury CT1 1ZA
Tel: 01227 819200
Fax: 01227 819283 (County) / 819329 (Crown)
DX: 99710 Canterbury 3
e-mail: enquiries@canterbury.countycourt.gsi.gov.uk

Cardiff County Court
Court Office: Civil Justice Centre, 2 Park St, Cardiff CF10 1ET
Tel: 029 2037 6400 Fax: 029 2037 6475
DX: 99500 Cardiff 6
e-mail: enquiries@cardiff.countycourt.gsi.gov.uk

Carlisle County Court
Court Office: Carlisle Combined Court Centre, Courts of Justice, Earl St, Carlisle CA1 1DJ
Tel: 01228 882140 Fax: 01228 590588
DX: 65331 Carlisle 2
e-mail: enquiries@carlisle.countycourt.gsi.gov.uk

Carmarthen County Court
Court Office: Carmarthen County Court, The Hearing Centre, Hill Ho, Picton Terrace, Carmarthen SA31 3BS
Tel: 01267 245060 Fax: 01267 245047
DX: 99570 Carmarthen 2
e-mail: enquiries@carmarthen.countycourt.gsi.gov.uk

Central London County Court
Court Office: Royal Courts of Justice, Thomas More Bldg, Strand, London WC2A 2LL
Tel: 020 7917 5000 Fax: 020 7917 5014
DX: 97325 Regents Pk 2
e-mail: enquiries@centrallondon.countycourt.gsi.gov.uk
Bankruptcy Court: Royal Courts of Justice, Room WB10 West Block, Strand, London WC2A 2LL

Chelmsford County Court
Court Office: Priory Pl, New London Rd, Chelmsford CM2 0PP
Tel: 0844 8924000 Fax: 01245 295395
DX: 97660 Chelmsford 4
e-mail: enquiries@chelmsford.countycourt.gsi.gov.uk

Chester County Court
Court Office: Chester Civil Justice Centre, Trident Ho, Little St John St, Chester, Cheshire CH1 1SN
Tel: 01244 404200 Fax: 01244 404300
DX: 702460 Chester 4
e-mail: enquiries@chester.countycourt.gsi.gov.uk

Chesterfield County Court
Court Office: Tapton La, Chesterfield S41 7TW
Tel: 01246 501200 Fax: 01246 501205

Chichester County Court
Court Office: Chichester Combined Court, Southgate, Chichester PO19 1SX
Tel: 01243 520700 Fax: 01243 533756
DX: 97460 Chichester 2

Chippenham and Trowbridge County Court
Court Office: Chippenham Law Courts, Pewsham Way, Chippenham SN15 3BF
Tel: 01249 463473 Fax: 01249 466246
DX: 744850 Chippenham 5
e-mail: enquiries@trowbridge.countycourt.gsi.gov.uk

Clerkenwell and Shoreditch County Court
Court Office: The Gee Street Courthouse, 29–41 Gee St, London EC1V 3RE
Tel: 020 7250 7200 Fax: 020 7250 7250
DX: 121000 Shoreditch 2
e-mail: enquiries@clerkenwellandshoreditch.countycourt.gsi.gov.uk

Colchester County Court
Court Office: Falkland Ho, 25 Southway, Colchester CO3 3EG
Tel: 0844 892 4000 Fax: 01206 717250
DX: 97670 Colchester 3
e-mail: enquiries@colchester.countycourt.gsi.gov.uk

Coventry Combined Court
Court Office: 140 Much Park St, Coventry CV1 2SN
Tel: 0300 123 5577 Fax: 024 7652 0443
DX: 701580 Coventry 5
e-mail: enquiries@coventry.countycourt.gsi.gov.uk

Crewe County Court
Court Office: The Court Service, The Law Courts, Civic Centre, Crewe CW1 2DP
Tel: 01270 539300 Fax: 01270 216344
DX: 702504 Crewe 2

Croydon County Court
Court Office: The Law Courts, Altyre Rd, Croydon CR9 5AB
Tel: 020 8410 4797 Fax: 020 8760 0432
DX: 97470 Croydon 6
e-mail: enquires@croydon.countycourt.gsi.gov.uk; e-filing@croydon.countycourt.gsi.gov.uk; hearings@croydon.countycourt.gsi.gov.uk; bailiffs@croydon.countycourt.gsi.gov.uk; family@croydon.countycourt.gsi.gov.uk

Darlington County Court
Court Office: 4 Coniscliffe Rd, Darlington, Co Durham DL3 7RL
Tel: 01325 463224 Fax: 01325 362829
DX: 65109 Darlington 2
e-mail: darlingtoncountycourt@hmcts.gsi.gov.uk

Dartford County Court
Court Office: Court Ho, Home Gardens, Dartford DA1 1DX
Tel: 01322 627600 Fax: 01322 270902
DX: 98090 Dartford 2

Derby Combined Court Centre
Court Office: Derby Combined Court Centre, Morledge, Derby DE1 2XE
Tel: 01332 622600 Fax: 01332 622543
DX: 724060 Derby 21
e-mail: enquiries@derbycountycourt.gsi.gov.uk
Note: e-filing@derbycountycourt.gsi.gov.uk; hearings@derbycountycourt.gsi.gov.uk; bailiffs@derbycountycourt.gsi.gov.uk; family@derbycountycourt.gsi.gov.uk

Doncaster County Court
Court Office: 74 Waterdale, Doncaster, S Yorks DN1 3BT
Tel: 01302 381730 Fax: 01302 768090
DX: 702089 Doncaster 4
e-mail: enquiries@doncaster.countycourt.gsi.gov.uk

Dudley County Court
Court Office: 7 Hagley Rd, Stourbridge DY8 1QL
Tel: 01384 394232 Fax: 01384 441736
DX: 701889 Stourbridge 2
e-mail: enquiries@dudley.countycourt.gsi.gov.uk

Durham County Court
Court Office: Civil and Family Justice Centre, Green La, Old Elvet, Durham DH1 3RG
Tel: 0191 375 1840 Fax: 0191 375 1844
DX: 65115 Durham 5

Eastbourne County Court
Court Office: The Law Courts, Old Orchard Rd, Eastbourne BN21 4UN
Tel: 01323 727518 Fax: 01323 649372
DX: 98110 Eastbourne 2

Edmonton County Court
Court Office: Court House, 59 Fore St, Edmonton, London N18 2TN
Tel: 020 8884 6500 Fax: 020 8803 0564
DX: 136686 Edmonton 3
e-mail: enquiries@edmonton.countycourt.gsi.gov.uk

Exeter Combined Court Centre
Court Office: Exeter Crown and County Court, Southernhay Gardens, Exeter EX1 1UH
Tel: 01392 415300
Fax: 01392 415642 (Civil) / 415644 (Crown)
DX: 98440 Exeter 2
e-mail: enquiries@exeter.countycourt.gsi.gov.uk

Gateshead County Court
Court Office: Gateshead Law Courts, Warwick St, Gateshead NE8 1DT
Tel: 0191 477 5821 Fax: 0191 440 7209
DX: 742120 Gateshead 2

Gloucester and Cheltenham County Court
Court Office: Gloucester & Cheltenham Civil and Family Court, Kimbrose Way, Gloucester GL1 2DE
Tel: 01452 834900 Fax: 01452 834923
DX: 98660 Gloucester 5
e-mail: enquiries@gloucester.countycourt.gsi.gov.uk

Great Grimsby Combined Court Centre
Court Office: Great Grimsby Combined Court, Town Hall Sq, Grimsby DN31 1HX
Tel: 01472 265200 (County Court) / 265250 (Crown Court)
Fax: 01472 265201 (County Court) / 265251 (Crown Court)
DX: 702007 Grimsby 3
e-mail: enquiries@grimsby.countycourt.gsi.gov.uk

Guildford County Court
Court Office: County Court and Family Court Hearing Centre, The Law Courts, Mary Rd, Guildford GU1 4PS
Tel: 01483 405300 Fax: 01483 300031
DX: 97860 Guildford 5

Halifax County Court
Court Office: Prescott St, Halifax HX1 2JJ
Tel: 01422 344700 Fax: 01422 360132
DX: 702095 Halifax 2
e-mail: halifax.cty.cm@hmcts.gsi.gov.uk

Harrogate County Court
Court Office: HMCTS, 2 Victoria Ave, Harrogate, North Yorkshire HG1 1EL
Tel: 01423 503921 Fax: 01423 528679
DX: 702098 Harrogate 3
e-mail: enquiries@harrogate.countycourt.gsi.gov.uk

Hartlepool County Court
Court Office: The Law Courts, Victoria Rd, Hartlepool, Cleveland TS24 8BS
Tel: 01429 268198 Fax: 01429 862550
DX: 65121 Hartlepool 2
e-mail: hartlepool.cty.cm@hmcts.gsi.gov.uk

Hastings County Court
Court Office: The Law Courts, Horntye Pk, Bohemia Rd, Hastings TN34 1QX
Tel: 01424 710280; 01424 710290 (Listings)
Fax: 01424 421585
DX: 98150 Hastings 2

Haverfordwest County Court
Court Office: Penffynnon, Hawthorn Rise, Haverfordwest SA61 2AX
Tel: 01437 772060 Fax: 01437 769222
DX: 99610 Haverfordwest 2
e-mail: enquiries@haverfordwest.countycourt.gsi.gov.uk

Hereford County Court
Court Office: 1st Fl, Barclays Bank Chambers, 1–3 Broad St, Hereford HR4 9BA
Tel: 01432 357233 Fax: 01432 352593
DX: 701904 Hereford 2

Hertford County Court
Court Office: PO Box 373, Hertford SG13 9HT
Tel: 0844 892 0550 Fax: 01992 501274
DX: 97710 Hertford 2
e-mail: enquiries@hertford.countycourt.gsi.gov.uk

Horsham County Court
Court Office: The Law Courts, Hurst Rd, Horsham, West Sussex RH12 2EU
Tel: 01403 252474 Fax: 01403 258844
DX: 98170 Horsham 2
e-mail: ss.cchorsham@hmcts.gsi.gov.uk

Huddersfield County Court
Court Office: Queensgate Ho, Queensgate, Huddersfield, West Yorkshire HD1 2RR
Tel: 01484 421043 Fax: 01484 426366
DX: 703013 Huddersfield 2
e-mail: enquiries@huddersfield.countycourt.gsi.gov.uk

Ipswich County Court
Court Office: 8 Arcade St, Ipswich IP1 1EJ
Tel: 0844 892 4000 Fax: 01473 251797
DX: 97731 Ipswich 3
e-mail: enquiries@ipswich.countycourt.gsi.gov.uk

Kendal County Court
Court Office: Carlisle Combined Court Centre, Courts of Justice, Earl St, Carlisle CA1 1DJ
Tel: 01228 882140 Fax: 01228 590588
DX: 65331 Carlisle 2
e-mail: kendal.cty.cm@hmcts.gsi.gov.uk

Kettering County Court
Court Office: HMCTS, Dryland St, Kettering NN16 0BE
Tel: 01536 512471 Fax: 01536 416857
DX: 701886 Kettering 2
e-mail: enquiries@kettering.countycourt.gsi.gov.uk

King's Lynn County Court
Court Office: Chequer Ho, 12 King St, King's Lynn PE30 1ES
Tel: 0844 892 4000 Fax: 01553 769824
DX: 97740 King's Lynn 2
e-mail: helpdesk@norwich.countycourt.gsi.gov.uk

Kingston-upon-Hull Combined Court
Court Office: Lowgate, Humberside HU1 2EZ
Tel: 01482 586161 Fax: 01482 588527
DX: 703010 Hull 5
e-mail: enquiries@kingstonuponhull.countycourt.gsi.gov.uk

Kingston-upon-Thames County Court
Court Office: St James's Rd, Kingston-upon-Thames KT1 2AD
Tel: 020 8972 8700 Fax: 020 8547 1426
DX: 97890 Kingston upon Thames 3
e-mail: enquiries@kingston.countycourt.gsi.gov.uk

Lambeth County Court
Court Office: Court Ho, Cleaver St, Kennington Rd, London SE11 4DZ
Tel: 020 7091 4410 Fax: 020 7587 1951
DX: 145020 Kennington 2
e-mail: enquiries@lambeth.countycourt.gsi.gov.uk

Lancaster County Court
Court Office: HMCS, Second Fl, Mitre Ho, Church St, Lancaster LA1 1UZ
Tel: 01524 68112 Fax: 01524 846478
DX: 145880 Lancaster 2
e-mail: enquiries@lancaster.countycourt.gsi.gov.uk

Leeds Combined Court
Court Office: HMCTS, Leeds County Court, The Courthouse, 1 Oxford Row, Leeds LS1 3BG
Tel: 0113 306 2800 Fax: 0113 306 2628
DX: 703016 Leeds 6
e-mail: enquiries@leeds.countycourt.gsi.gov.uk

Leicester County Court
Court Office: 90 Wellington St, Leicester LE1 6HG
Tel: 0116 222 5700 Fax: 0116 222 5763
DX: 17401 Leicester 3
e-mail: enquiries@leicester.countycourt.gsi.gov.uk

Lewes Combined Court Centre
Court Office: The Law Courts, High St, Lewes, East Sussex BN7 1YB
Tel: 01273 480400 Fax: 01273 485269
DX: 97395 Lewes 4
e-mail: enquiries@lewes.countycourt.gsi.gov.uk

Lincoln County Court
Court Office: 360 High St, Lincoln LN5 7PS
Tel: 01522 551500 Fax: 01522 551551
DX: 703231 Lincoln 6
e-mail: hearings@lincoln.countycourt.gsi.gov.uk;
enquiries@lincoln.countycourt.gsi.gov.uk;
bailiffs@lincoln.countycourt.gsi.gov.uk;
family@lincoln.countycourt.gsi.gov.uk;
e-filing@lincoln.countycourt.gsi.gov.uk

Liverpool Civil Justice Centre
Court Office: 35 Vernon St, Liverpool L2 2BX
Tel: 0151 296 2200 Fax: 0151 296 2201
DX: 702600 Liverpool 5
e-mail: enquiries@liverpool.countycourt.gsi.gov.uk

Llanelli County Court
Court Office: Second Fl, Court Bldgs, Town Hall Sq, Llanelli SA15 3AL
Tel: 01554 757171 Fax: 01554 758079
DX: 99510 Llanelli 2
e-mail: enquiries@llanelli.countycourt.gsi.gov.uk

Llangefni County Court
Court Office: Glanhwfa Rd, Llangefni, Isle of Anglesey LL77 7EN
Tel: 01248 750225 Fax: 01248 750778
DX: 702480 Llangefni 2
e-mail: enquiries@llangefni.countycourt.gsi.gov.uk

Luton County Court
Court Office: HMCS, 2nd Fl, Cresta Ho, Alma St, Luton LU1 2PU
Tel: 0844 892 0550 Fax: 01582 506 701
DX: 97760 Luton 4
e-mail: enquiries@luton.countycourt.gsi.gov.uk

Macclesfield County Court
Court Office: 2nd Fl, Silk Ho, Park Green, Macclesfield SK11 7NA
Tel: 01625 412800 Fax: 01625 501262
DX: 702498 Macclesfield 3
e-mail: enquiries@macclesfield.countycourt.gsi.gov.uk

Maidstone Combined Court
Court Office: Ministry of Justice, HMCS, The Law Courts, Barker Rd, Maidstone, Kent ME16 8EQ
Tel: 01622 202000
Fax: 01622 202001 (Crown); 01622 202002 (County)
DX: 130065 Maidstone 7
e-mail: enquiries@maidstone.countycourt.gsi.gov.uk
Note: enquiries@maidstone.crowncourt.gsi.gov.uk

Manchester County Court
Court Office: Manchester Civil Justice Centre, 1 Bridge St West, Manchester M60 9DJ
Tel: 0161 240 5000 Fax: 0161 240 5050
DX: 724783 Manchester 44
e-mail: enquiries@manchester.countycourt.gsi.gov.uk

Mansfield County Court
Court Office: Rosemary St, Mansfield NG19 6EE
Tel: 01623 451500 Fax: 01623 451502
DX: 179560 Mansfield 9

Mayor's & City of London Court
Court Office: Guildhall Buildings, Basinghall St, London EC2V 5AR
Tel: 020 7796 5400 Fax: 020 7796 5424
DX: 97520 Moorgate EC2
e-mail: enquiries@mayorsandcityoflondon.countycourt.gsi.gov.uk

Medway County Court
Court Office: Anchorage Ho, 47–67 High St, Chatham, Kent ME4 4DW
Tel: 01634 887900 Fax: 01634 811332
DX: 98180 Chatham 4

Merthyr Tydfil Combined Court Centre
Court Office: HMCS, The Law Courts, Glebeland Pl, Merthyr Tydfil CF47 8BH
Tel: 01685 727600 Fax: 01685 727703
DX: 99582 Merthyr Tydfil 2
e-mail: enquiries@merthyrtydfil.countycourt.gsi.gov.uk

Middlesbrough County Court
Court Office: Teesside Combined Court Centre, Russell St, Middlesbrough TS1 2AE
Tel: 01642 340000 Fax: 01642 340002
DX: 65152 Middlesbrough 2

Milton Keynes County Court
Court Office: 351 Silbury Boulevard, Witan Gate East, Central Milton Keynes MK9 2DT
Tel: 01908 302800 (Civil); 01908 302801 (Family)
Fax: 01908 230063
DX: 136266 Milton Keynes 6
e-mail: enquiries@miltonkeynes.countycourt.gsi.gov.uk
Note: family@miltonkeynes.countycourt.gsi.gov.uk; hearings@miltonkeynes.countycourt.gsi.gov.uk; bailiffs@miltonkeynes.countycourt.gsi.gov.uk

Morpeth and Berwick County Court
Court Office: Court Service, Fountain Ho, Newmarket, Morpeth, Northumberland NE61 1LA
Tel: 01670 512221 Fax: 01670 504188
DX: 65124 Morpeth 2
e-mail: no-morpethcc@hmcts.gsi.gov.uk
Note: Principal office of Berwick-upon-Tweed County Court

Neath & Port Talbot County Court
Court Office: HMCS, Forster Rd, Neath SA11 3BN
Tel: 01639 642267 Fax: 01639 633505
DX: 99550 Neath 2

Newcastle upon Tyne Combined County Court
Court Office: The Law Courts, Quayside, Newcastle upon Tyne NE1 3LA
Tel: 0191 201 2000 Fax: 0191 201 2001
DX: 65127 Newcastle 2
e-mail: enquiries@newcastle.countycourt.gsi.gov.uk

Newport (Gwent) Civil and Family Court
Court Office: Her Majesty's Court Service, 5th Fl Clarence Ho, Clarence Place, Newport NP19 7AA
Tel: 01633 245040 Fax: 01633 245041
DX: 99480 Newport (South Wales) 4
e-mail: enquiries@newportgwent.countycourt.gsi.gov.uk

North Shields County Court
Court Office: HMCS, 2nd Fl, Kings Court, Earl Grey Way, Royal Quays, North Shields, Tyne & Wear NE29 6AR
Tel: 0191 298 2339 Fax: 0191 298 2337
DX: 65137 North Shields 2

Northampton Combined Court
Court Office: Combined Court Centre, 85–87 Lady's La, Northampton NN1 3HQ
Tel: 01604 470400
Fax: 01604 232398; 01604 470445 (Family)
DX: 725380 Northampton 21
e-mail: enquiries@northampton.countycourt.gsi.gov.uk

Norwich Combined Court
Court Office: The Law Courts, Bishopgate, Norwich, Norfolk NR3 1UR
Tel: 0844 892 4000 Fax: 01603 760863
DX: 97385 Norwich 5
e-mail: enquiries@norwich.countycourt.gsi.gov.uk
Note: family@norwich.countycourt.gsi.gov.uk

Nottingham County Court
Court Office: 60 Canal St, Nottingham NG1 7EJ
Tel: 0115 910 3500 Fax: 0115 910 3510
DX: 702380 Nottingham 7
e-mail: enquiries@nottingham.countycourt.gsi.gov.uk

Nuneaton County Court
Court Office: Warwickshire Justice Centre, PO Box 3878, Vicarage St, Nuneaton CV11 4JU
Tel: 0300 123 5577 Fax: 02476 352835
DX: 701940 Nuneaton 2
e-mail: enquiries@nuneaton.countycourt.gsi.gov.uk

Oldham County Court
Court Office: County Court, New Radcliffe St, Oldham OL1 1NL
Tel: 0161 290 4200 Fax: 0161 290 4222
DX: 702595 Oldham 2
e-mail: enquiries@oldham.countycourt.gsi.gov.uk

Oxford Combined Court Centre
Court Office: St Aldates, Oxford OX1 1TL
Tel: 01865 264200
Fax: 01865 790773 (Civil) / 264253 (Crown)
DX: 96450 Oxford 4
e-mail: enquiries@oxford.countycourt.gsi.gov.uk

Peterborough Combined Court
Court Office: HMCS, Crown Bldgs, Rivergate, Peterborough PE1 1EJ
Tel: 0844 8924000 (County Helpdesk); 01733 426955 (Crown) Fax: 01733 557348
DX: 702302 Peterborough 8
e-mail: helpdesk@norwich.countycourt.gsi.gov.uk

Plymouth Combined Court
Court Office: The Law Courts, 10 Armada Way, Plymouth PL1 2ER
Tel: 01752 677400
Fax: 01752 208286 (Fam); 208292 (Crown); 677455 (Civil)
DX: 98470 Plymouth 7
e-mail: enquiries@plymouth.countycourt.gsi.gov.uk

Pontypridd County Court
Court Office: The Courthouse, Courthouse St, Pontypridd CF37 1JR
Tel: 01443 490800 Fax: 01443 480305
DX: 99620 Pontypridd 2
e-mail: enquiries@pontypridd.countycourt.gsi.gov.uk

Portsmouth Combined Court Centre
Court Office: The Courts of Justice, Winston Churchill Ave, Portsmouth, Hampshire PO1 2EB
Tel: 023 9289 3000 Fax: 023 9282 6385
DX: 98490 Portsmouth 5
e-mail: enquiries@portsmouth.countycourt.gsi.gov.uk

Preston Combined Court Centre
Court Office: The Law Courts, Openshaw Pl, Ring Way, Preston PR1 2LL
Tel: 01772 844700
Fax: 01772 844759 (Crown); 01772 844710 (County)
DX: 702660 Preston 5
e-mail: enquiries@preston.countycourt.gsi.gov.uk

Reading County Court
Court Office: 160–163 Friar St, Reading RG1 1HE
Tel: 0118 987 0500 Fax: 0118 987 0555
DX: 98010 Reading 6
e-mail: enquiries@reading.countycourt.gsi.gov.uk

Reigate County Court
Court Office: The Law Courts, Mary Rd, Guildford GU1 4PS
Tel: 01737 763637 Fax: 01737 766917

Rhyl County Court
Court Office: HMCTS, The Courthouse, Clwyd St, Rhyl LL18 3LA
Tel: 01745 352940 Fax: 01745 336726
DX: 702489 Rhyl 2

Romford County Court
Court Office: 2A Oaklands Ave, Romford, Essex RM1 4DP
Tel: 01708 775 353 Fax: 01708 756 653
DX: 97530 Romford 2
e-mail: enquiries@romford.countycourt.gsi.gov.uk

Rotherham Law Courts
Court Office: Rotherham Law Courts, The Statutes, PO Box 15, Rotherham S60 1YW
Tel: 01709 839339 Fax: 01709 370082
DX: 703025 Rotherham 4

Salisbury Law Courts
Court Office: Wilton Rd, Salisbury SP2 7EP
Tel: 01722 345200 Fax: 01722 345201
DX: 98500 Salisbury 2

Scarborough County Court
Court Office: The Law Courts, Northway, Scarborough YO11 7AE
Tel: 01723 505000 Fax: 01723 501992
e-mail: enquiries@scarborough.countycourt.gsi.gov.uk

Scunthorpe County Court
Court Office: Scunthorpe Court Centre, Corporation Rd, Scunthorpe DN15 6QB
Tel: 01724 281100 Fax: 01724 281890
DX: 742212 Scunthorpe 10

Sheffield Combined Court
Court Office: The Law Courts, 50 West Bar, Sheffield, S Yorks S3 8PH
Tel: 0114 281 2400 Fax: 0114 281 2425
DX: 703028 Sheffield 6

Skipton County Court
Court Office: The Court House, Otley St, Skipton, N Yorks BD23 1RH
Tel: 01756 692650 Fax: 01756 692655
DX: 703031 Skipton 2

Slough County Court
Court Office: The Law Courts, Windsor Rd, Slough SL1 2HE
Tel: 01753 690300 Fax: 01753 575990
DX: 98030 Slough 3
e-mail: enquiries@slough.countycourt.gsi.gov.uk

South Shields County Court
Court Office: South Tyneside Law Courts, Millbank, Secretan Way, South Shields NE33 1RG
Tel: 0191 456 3343 Fax: 0191 427 4499
DX: 65143 South Shields 3
e-mail: southshields.cty.cm@hmcts.gsi.gov.uk

Southampton Combined Court Centre
Court Office: The Courts of Justice, London Rd, Southampton SO15 2XQ
Tel: 023 8021 3200
Fax: 023 8021 3222 (County) / 023 8021 3234 (Crown)
DX: 111000 Southampton 11
e-mail: enquiries@southhampton.countycourt.gsi.gov.uk

Southend County Court
Court Office: Tylers Ho, Tylers Ave, Southend-on-Sea SS1 2AW
Tel: 0844 892 4000 Fax: 01702 603090
DX: 97780 Southend 2
e-mail: enquiries@southend.countycourt.gsi.gov.uk

St Albans County Court
Court Office: The Court Building, Bricket Rd, St Albans, Herts AL1 3JW
Tel: 0844 892 0550 Fax: 01727 753234
DX: 97770 St Albans 2
e-mail: Behcchelpdesk@hmcts.gsi.gov.uk

St Helens County Court
Court Office: St Helens Courthouse, Corporation St, St Helens, Merseyside WA10 1SZ
Tel: 01744 620244 Fax: 01744 20484
DX: 725020 St Helens 4

Stafford Combined Court Centre
Court Office: Stafford Combined Court Centre, Victoria Sq, Stafford ST16 2QQ
Tel: 01785 610730 Fax: 01785 213250
DX: 703190 Stafford 4
e-mail: enquiries@stafford.countycourt.gsi.gov.uk

Staines County Court
Court Office: The Law Courts, Mary Rd, Guildford GU1 4PS
Tel: 01784 895900 Fax: 01784 895530

Stockport County Court
Court Office: The Courthouse, Edward St, Stockport SK1 3NF
Tel: 0161 477 2020 Fax: 0161 968 9733
DX: 702620 Stockport 4
e-mail: enquiries@stockport.countycourt.gsi.gov.uk

Stoke-on-Trent Combined Court
Court Office: Bethesda St, Hanley, Stoke-on-Trent ST1 3BP
Tel: 01782 854000 Fax: 01782 854046
DX: 703360 Hanley 3

Sunderland County Court
Court Office: The Court Ho, 44 John St, Sunderland SR1 1RB
Tel: 0191 568 0750 Fax: 0191 514 3028
DX: 65149 Sunderland 2
e-mail: enquiries@sunderland.countycourt.gsi.gov.uk

Swansea Civil and Family Justice Centre
Court Office: Caravella Ho, Quay West, Quay Parade, Swansea SA1 1SP
Tel: 01792 485800 Fax: 01792 485810
DX: 99740 Swansea 5

Swindon Combined Court
Court Office: The Law Courts, Islington St, Swindon, Wilts SN1 2HG
Tel: 01793 690500 Fax: 01793 690555
DX: 98430 Swindon 5
e-mail: swindon.cty.enq@hmcts.gsi.gov.uk

Tameside County Court
Court Office: PO Box 166, Henry Sq, Ashton-under-Lyne, Lancashire OL6 7TP
Tel: 0161 331 5614 Fax: 0161 331 5649
DX: 702625 Ashton-under-Lyne 2
e-mail: tameside.cty@hmcts.gsi.gov.uk

Taunton County Court
Court Office: The Shire Hall, Taunton TA1 4EU
Tel: 01823 281110
DX: 98410 Taunton 2
e-mail: enquiries@taunton.countycourt.gsi.gov.uk

Teesside Combined Court *(see Middlesbrough)*

Telford County Court
Court Office: Telford Sq, Malinsgate, Town Centre, Telford TF3 4JP
Tel: 01952 238280 Fax: 01952 291601
DX: 701976 Telford 3

Thanet County Court
Court Office: The Court Ho, 2nd Fl, Cecil Sq, Margate, Kent CT9 1RL
Tel: 01843 221722 Fax: 01843 222730
DX: 98210 Cliftonville 2
e-mail: enquiries@thanet.countycourt.gsi.gov.uk

Torquay and Newton Abbot County Court
Court Office: The Willows, Nicholson Rd, Torquay TQ2 7AZ
Tel: 01803 616791 Fax: 01803 616795
DX: 98740 Torquay 4

Trowbridge County Court *(see Chippenham and Trowbridge)*

Truro County Court
Court Office: HMCS, The Courts of Justice, Edward St, Truro TR1 2PB
Tel: 01872 267460
DX: 135396 Truro 2
Note: email:
civilsection.trurocountycourt@hmcourts-service.gsi.gov.uk;
familysection@trurocountycourt@hmcourts-service.gsi.gov.uk

Uxbridge County Court
Court Office: 501 Uxbridge Rd, Hayes UB4 8HL
Tel: 020 8756 3520 Fax: 020 8561 2020
DX: 44658 Hayes (Mddx)
e-mail: enquiries@uxbridge.countycourt.gsi.gov.uk

Wakefield County Court
Court Office: Wakefield Civil and Family Justice Centre, 1 Mulberry Way, Wakefield, W Yorks WF1 2QN
Tel: 01924 207903 Fax: 01924 207959
e-mail: wakefield.cty.cm@hmcts.gsi.gov.uk

Walsall County Court
Court Office: Bridge Ho, Bridge St, Walsall WS1 1JQ
Tel: 01922 728855 Fax: 01922 728891
DX: 701943 Walsall 2
e-mail: enquiries@walsall.countycourt.gsi.gov.uk

Wandsworth County Court
Court Office: 76–78 Upper Richmond Rd, Putney, London SW15 2SU
Tel: 020 8333 4351 Fax: 020 8877 9854
DX: 97540 Putney 2
e-mail: enquiries@wandsworth.countycourt.gsi.gov.uk

Warrington and Runcorn County Courts
Court Office: Law Courts, Legh St, Warrington WA1 1UR
Tel: 01925 256700 Fax: 01925 413335
DX: 702501 Warrington 3

Warwick Combined Court
Court Office: Warwickshire Justice Centre, Newbold Terr, Leamington Spa CV32 4EL
Tel: 01926 682100 / 0300 123 5577
Fax: 01926 682519 (Crown) / 682517 (County)
DX: 701964 Leamington 7
e-mail: enquiries@warwick.countycourt.gsi.gov.uk
Note: crowncourtenquiries@warwick.crowncourt.gsi.gov.uk

Watford County Court
Court Office: 3rd Fl, Cassiobury Ho, 11–19 Station Rd, Watford, Herts WD17 1EZ
Tel: 0844 892 0550 Fax: 01923 699479
DX: 122740 Watford 5
e-mail: enquiries@watford.countycourt.gsi.gov.uk

Welshpool and Newtown County Court *(see Wrexham)*

West Cumbria County Court
Court Office: Hall Park, Ramsey Brow, Workington CA14 4AS
Tel: 01900 609609 Fax: 01900 609636
DX: 743420 Workington 5
e-mail: enquiries@westcumbria.countycourt.gsi.gov.uk

West London County Court
Court Office: West London Family Court, Gloucester Ho, 4 Dukes Green Ave, Feltham TW14 0LR
Tel: 020 8600 6868 Fax: 020 8600 6860
DX: 97550 Hammersmith 8
e-mail: enquiries@westlondon.countycourt.gsi.gov.uk

Weston-super-Mare County Court
Court Office: North Somerset Courthouse, The Hedges, St Georges, Weston-super-Mare BS22 7BB
Tel: 01934 528686 Fax: 01934 528594
DX: 152361 Weston-Super-Mare 5
e-mail: weston-s-marecountycourt@hmcts.gsi.gov.uk

Weymouth and Dorchester Combined Court Centre
Court Office: Westwey Ho, Westwey Rd, Weymouth DT4 8TE
Tel: 01305 752510 Fax: 01305 788293
DX: 98820 Weymouth 3
e-mail: enquiries@weymouth.countycourt.gsi.gov.uk

Wigan County Court
Court Office: Wigan and Leigh Courthouse, Darlington St, Wigan WN1 1DW
Tel: 01942 405405 Fax: 01942 405499
DX: 724820 Wigan 9
e-mail: enquiries@wigan.countycourt.gsi.gov.uk

Willesden County Court
Court Office: 9 Acton La, Harlesden, London NW10 8SB
Tel: 020 8963 8200 Fax: 020 8453 0946
DX: 97560 Harlesden 2
e-mail: enquiries@willesden.countycourt.gsi.gov.uk

Winchester Combined Court
Court Office: The Law Courts, Winchester, Hampshire SO23 9EL
Tel: 01962 814100 Fax: 01962 853821
DX: 98520 Winchester 3
e-mail: carolyn.ormsby@hmcts.gsi.gov.uk

Wolverhampton Combined Court Centre
Court Office: Pipers Row, Wolverhampton WV1 3LQ
Tel: 01902 481000 Fax: 01902 481001
DX: 702019 Wolverhampton 4
e-mail: enquiries@wolverhampton.countycourt.gsi.gov.uk

Woolwich County Court
Court Office: 165 Powis St, Woolwich, London SE18 6JW
Tel: 020 8301 8700 Fax: 020 8316 4842
DX: 123450 Woolwich 8
e-mail: enquiries@woolwich.countycourt.gsi.gov.uk

Worcester Combined Court
Court Office: The Shirehall, Foregate St, Worcester WR1 1EQ
Tel: 01905 730800 Fax: 01905 730801
DX: 721120 Worcester 11

Worthing County Court
Court Office: The Law Courts, Christchurch Rd, Worthing BN11 1JD
Tel: 01903 221920 Fax: 01903 235559
DX: 98230 Worthing 4

Wrexham County Court
Court Office: Wrexham Law Courts, Bodhyfryd, Wrexham LL12 7BP
Tel: 01978 317400 Fax: 01978 358213
DX: 745320 Wrexham 9
e-mail: enquiries@wrexham.countycourt.gsi.gov.uk

Yeovil County Court
Court Office: 22 Hendford, Yeovil BA20 2QD
Tel: 01935 382150 (Gen.Enqs); 01935 382164 (Family)
Fax: 01935 410004
DX: 98830 Yeovil 2
e-mail: info@yeovil.countycourt.gsi.gov.uk

York County Court
Court Office: Piccadilly Ho, 55 Piccadilly, York YO1 9WL
Tel: 01904 688550 Fax: 01904 679963
DX: 65165 York 4
e-mail: enquiries@york.countycourt.gsi.gov.uk

Coroners

Chief Coroner of England
Coroner: His Honour Judge Peter Thornton QC

Coroner for the Royal Household
Coroner: Senior Coroner M J C Burgess

Avon Coroner
Coroner's Office: The Court House, Old Western Rd, Flax Bourton, Bristol BS48 1UL
Tel: 01275 461920 Fax: 01275 462749

Bedfordshire and Luton Coroner
Coroner's Office: The Court House, Woburn Rd, Ampthill MK45 2HZ
Tel: 0300 300 6557/8 Fax: 01234 273014

Berkshire Coroner
Coroner's Office: Yeomanry Ho, 131 Castle Hill, Reading RG1 7TA
Tel: 0118 937 3528 Fax: 0118 937 5448

Birmingham and Solihull Coroner
Coroner's Office: 50 Newton St, Birmingham B4 6NE
Tel: 0121 303 3228 Fax: 0121 233 4841

Blackburn, Hyndburn and Ribble Valley Coroner
Coroner's Office: King George's Hall, Northgate, Blackburn BB2 1AA
Tel: 01254 588680 Fax: 01254 588681

Blackpool and Fylde Coroner
Coroner's Office: 283 Church St, Blackpool FY1 3PG
Tel: 01282 438446

Bournemouth, Poole and Eastern Dorset Coroner
Coroner's Office: Stafford Rd, Bournemouth BH1 1PA
Tel: 01202 310049 Fax: 01202 780423

Bridgend and Glamorgan Valleys Coroner
Coroner's Office: Rock Grounds, Aberdare CF44 7AE
Tel: 01685 885202 Fax: 01685 885250

Brighton and Hove Coroner
Coroner's Office: Woodvale, Lewes Rd, Brighton BN2 3QB
Tel: 01273 292046 Fax: 01273 292047

Buckinghamshire Coroner
Coroner's Office: 29 Windsor End, Beaconsfield HP9 2JJ
Tel: 01494 475505 Fax: 01494 673760

Cambridgeshire Coroner
Coroner's Office: Lawrence Court, Princes St, Huntingdon PE29 3PA
Tel: 0345 045 1364 Fax: 01480 372777

Cardiff and the Vale of Glamorgan Coroner
Coroner's Office: Central Police Station, Cathays Park, Cardiff CF10 3NN
Tel: 029 2022 2111 Fax: 029 2023 3886

Carmarthenshire and Pembrokeshire Coroner
Coroner's Office: The Town Hall, Hamilton Terrace, Milford Haven SA73 3JW
Tel: 01646 698129 Fax: 01646 690607

Ceredigionshire Coroner
Coroner's Office: 6 Upper Portland St, Aberystwyth SY23 2DU
Tel: 01970 612567 Fax: 01970 615572

Cheshire Coroner
Coroner's Office: The West Annexe, Town Hall, Sankey St, Warrington WA1 1UH
Tel: 01925 444216 Fax: 01925 444219

Cornwall Coroner
Coroner's Office: 15 Barrack Ln, Truro TR1 2DW
Tel: 01872 261612 Fax: 01872 262738

County Durham and Darlington Coroner
Coroner's Office: PO Box 282, Bishop Auckland DL14 4FY
Tel: 01388 761564 Fax: 01388 765430

Coventry Coroner
Coroner's Office: Little Park St, Coventry CV1 2JX
Tel: 02476 539017 Fax: 02476 539804

Cumbria North and West Coroner
Coroner's Office: Fairfield Station Rd, Cockermouth CA13 9PT
Tel: 01900 706902 Fax: 01900 706915

Cumbria South and East Coroner
Coroner's Office: Central Police Station, Market St, Barrow-in-Furness LA14 2LE
Tel: 01229 848966 Fax: 01229 848953

Derby and South Derbyshire Coroner
Coroner's Office: St Katherine's Ho, St Mary's Wharf, Mansfield Rd, Derby DE1 3TQ
Tel: 01332 343225 Fax: 01332 294942

Dorset West Coroner
Coroner's Office: Stafford Rd, Bournemouth BH1 1PA
Tel: 01202 310049

East Riding and Kingston-upon-Hull Coroner
Coroner's Office: The Guildhall, Kingston-Upon-Hull HU1 2AA
Tel: 01482 613009 Fax: 01482 613020

East Sussex Coroner
Coroner's Office: 28/29 Grand Parade, St Leonard's-on-Sea TN37 6DR
Tel: 01424 200144 Fax: 01424 200145

Essex Coroner
Coroner's Office: New Bridge Ho, 60–68 New London Rd, Chelmsford CM2 0PD
Tel: 01245 506837 Fax: 01245 506839

Exeter and Greater Devon Coroner
Coroner's Office: Room 226, Devon County Hall, Topsham Rd, Exeter EX2 4QD
Tel: 01392 383636 Fax: 01392 383635

Gateshead and South Tyneside Coroner
Coroner's Office: 35 Station Rd, Hevvum NE31 1LA
Tel: 0191 483 8771 Fax: 0191 428 6699

Gloucestershire Coroner
Coroner's Office: Corinium Avenue, Barnwood, Gloucester GL4 3DJ
Tel: 01452 305661 Fax: 01452 412618

Greater Manchester Central Coroner
Coroner's Office: Crown Square, Deansgate, Greater Manchester M60 1PR
Tel: 0161 830 4222 Fax: 0161 274 7329

Greater Manchester North Coroner
Coroner's Office: The Phoenix Centre, Church St, Heywood OL10 1LR
Tel: 01706 924815 Fax: 0844 963 2383

Greater Manchester South Coroner
Coroner's Office: Mottram St, Stockport SK1 3PA
Tel: 0161 474 3993 Fax: 0161 474 3994

Greater Manchester West Coroner
Coroner's Office: Paderborn Ho, Civic Centre, Howell Croft North, Bolton BL1 1JW
Tel: 01204 338799 Fax: 01204 338798

Gwent Coroner
Coroner's Office: Victoria Chambers, 11 Clytha Park Rd, Newport NP20 4PB
Tel: 01633 264194 Fax: 01633 841146

Hampshire Central Coroner
Coroner's Office: Castle Hill, The Castle, Winchester SO23 8UL
Tel: 01962 667884 Fax: 01962 667893

Hampshire North East Coroner
Coroner's Office: Goldings, London Rd, Basingstoke RG21 4AN
Tel: 01256 478119 Fax: 01256 814292

Hartlepool Coroner
Coroner's Office: Donnelly McArdle Adamson Solicitors, 155 York St, Hartlepool Coroner TS26 9EQ
Tel: 01429 861563 Fax: 01429 260199

Herefordshire Coroner
Coroner's Office: The Civic, Martins Way, Stourport-on-Severn DY13 8UJ
Tel: 01905 766066

Hertfordshire Coroner
Coroner's Office: The Old Court House, St Albans Rd East, Hatfield AL10 0ES
Tel: 01707 292707 Fax: 01707 897399

Isle of Wight Coroner
Coroner's Office: 3–9 Quay St, Isle of Wight PO30 5BB
Tel: 01983 520697 Fax: 01983 527678

Isles of Scilly Coroner
Coroner's Office: 1 Palk St, Torquay TQ2 5EL
Tel: 01803 380705 Fax: 01803 380704

Kent Central and South East Coroner
Coroner's Office: West St, Hunton, Maidstone ME15 0SB
Tel: 01622 820412 Fax: 01622 820800

Kent North East Coroner
Coroner's Office: St Peter's Ho, Dane Valley Rd, St Peters CT10 3JJ
Tel: 01843 863260 Fax: 01843 603927

Kent North West Coroner
Coroner's Office: The Old Town Hall, High St, Gravesend DA11 0AZ
Tel: 01474 815747 Fax: 01474 815356

Lancashire East Coroner
Coroner's Office: 6a Hargreaves St, Burnley BB11 1ES
Tel: 01282 438446 Fax: 01282 446525

Leicester City and South Leicestershire Coroner
Coroner's Office: The Town Hall, Leicester LE1 9BG
Tel: 0116 225 2534 Fax: 0116 225 2537

Lincolnshire Central Coroner
Coroner's Office: Lindium Ho, 10 Queen St, Spilsbury PE23 5JE
Tel: 01522 552500 Fax: 01522 516055

Lincolnshire North and Grimsby Coroner
Coroner's Office: The Town Hall, Knoll St, Cleethorpes DN35 8LN
Tel: 01472 324005 Fax: 01472 324007

Lincolnshire South Coroner
Coroner's Office: Unit 1, Gilbert Drive, Endeavour Park, Boston PE21 7QT
Tel: 01522 552064

Liverpool Coroner
Coroner's Office: Liverpool and Wirral Coroner Areas Courthouse, Boundary St, Liverpool L5 2QD
Tel: 0151 225 5770 Fax: 0151 703 6838

London City Coroner
Coroner's Office: Walbrook Wharf, 78–83 Upper Thames St, London EC4R 3TD
Tel: 020 7332 1598 Fax: 020 7332 1800

London East Coroner
Coroner's Office: Queens Rd, Walthamstow E17 8QP
Tel: 020 8496 5000 Fax: 020 8496 3378/9

London Inner North Coroner
St Pancras Coroner's Office: Camley St, London N1C 4PP
Tel: 020 7387 4882 Fax: 020 7383 2485
Poplar Coroner's Office: 127 Poplar High St, London E14 0AE
Tel: 020 7538 1201 Fax: 020 7538 0565

London Inner South Coroner
Coroner's Office: 1 Tennis St, London SE1 1YD
Tel: 020 7525 4200 Fax: 020 7525 6356

London Inner West Coroner
Westminster Coroner's Office: 65 Horseferry Rd, London SW1P 2ED
Tel: 020 7802 4750 Fax: 020 7828 2837
Battersea Coroner's Office: City Hall, 5th Fl, Victoria St, London SW1E 6QP
Tel: 020 7641 5305 Fax: 020 7641 5351

London North Coroner
Coroner's Office: 29 Wood St, Barnet, London EN6 4BE
Tel: 020 8447 7680 Fax: 020 8447 7689

London South Coroner
Coroner's Office: Barclay Rd, Croydon CR9 3NE
Tel: 020 8681 3275 Fax: 020 8680 0999

London West Coroner
Coroner's Office: 25 Bagleys Ln, Fulham, London SW6 2QA
Tel: 020 8753 6800 Fax: 020 8753 6803

Mid Kent and Medway Coroner
Coroner's Office: The Archbishop's Palace, Mill St, Maidstone ME15 6YE
Tel: 01622 701927 Fax: 01622 663690

Milton Keynes Coroner
Coroner's Office: Civic Offices, 1 Saxon Gate, Milton Keynes MK9 3EJ
Tel: 01908 254327 Fax: 01908 253636

Newcastle-Upon-Tyne Coroner
Coroner's Office: Civic Centre, Barras Bridge, Newcastle-upon-Tyne NE1 8PS
Tel: 0191 277 7280 Fax: 0191 261 2952

Norfolk Coroner
Coroner's Office: 69–75 Thorpe Rd, Norwich NR1 1UA
Tel: 01603 663302 Fax: 01603 665511

North East and Central Wales Coroner
Coroner's Office: County Hall, Wynnstay Rd, Ruthin LL15 1YN
Tel: 01824 708047 Fax: 01824 708048

North Tyneside Coroner
Coroner's Office: 3 Stanley St, Blyth NE24 2BS
Tel: 01670 354777 Fax: 01670 797891

North West Wales Coroner
Coroner's Office: 37 Castle Square, Caernarfon LL55 2NN
Tel: 01286 672804 Fax: 01286 675217

North Yorkshire Eastern Coroner
Coroner's Office: Sentinel Ho, Peasholme Green, York YO1 7PP
Tel: 01904 716000 Fax: 01904 716100
Coroner's Office: Rose Cottage, Oswaldkirk, York YO62 5XT
Tel: 01439 788339

North Yorkshire Western Coroner
Coroner's Office: 21 Grammar School Ln, Northallerton DL7 8ES
Tel: 01609 533805 Fax: 01609 780793

Northamptonshire Coroner
Coroner's Office: 110 Whitworth Rd, Northampton NN1 4HJ
Tel: 01604 624732 Fax: 01604 623681

Northumberland North Coroner
Coroner's Office: 17 Church St, Berwick-Upon-Tweed TD15 1EE
Tel: 01289 304318 Fax: 01289 303591

Northumberland South Coroner
Coroner's Office: 3 Stanley St, Blyth NE24 2BS
Tel: 01670 354777 Fax: 01670 797891

Nottinghamshire Coroner
Coroner's Office: The Council Ho, Old Market Square, Nottingham NG1 2DT
Tel: 0115 841 5553 Fax: 0115 876 5689

Oxfordshire Coroner
Coroner's Office: 1 Tidmarsh La, Oxford OX1 1NS
Tel: 01865 815020 Fax: 01865 783391

Peterborough Coroner
Coroner's Office: 10 Briggate Quay, Whittlesey, Peterborough PE7 1DH
Tel: 01733 452275 Fax: 0870 238 4085

Plymouth, Torbay and South Devon
Coroner's Office: 3 The Crescent, Plymouth PL1 3AB
Tel: 01752 204636 Fax: 01752 313297

Portsmouth and South East Hampshire Coroner
Coroner's Office: The Guildhall, Guildhall Square, Portsmouth PO1 2AB
Tel: 023 9268 8326 Fax: 023 9268 8331

Powys, Bridgend and Glamorgan Valleys Coroner
Coroner's Office: 1st Fl, Rock Ground, Aberdare CF44 7AE
Tel: 01685 885202 Fax: 01865 885250

Preston and West Lancashire Coroner
Coroner's Office: 2 Faraday Drive, Fulwood, Preston PR2 9NB
Tel: 01772 703700 Fax: 01772 704422

Rutland and North Leicestershire Coroner
Coroner's Office: Southfield Rd, Loughborough LE11 2TR
Tel: 0116 305 7732 Fax: 01509 550473

Scarsdale and High Peak Coroner
Coroner's Office: Ground Fl, 5–6 Royal Court, Basil Close, Chesterfield S41 7SL
Tel: 01246 201391 Fax: 01246 273058

Sefton, Knowsley and St Helens Coroner
Coroner's Office: Southport Town Hall, Lord St, Southport PR8 1DA
Tel: 0151 934 2746 Fax: 01704 534321
Coroner's Office: Southport Police Station, Law Courts, Southport PR9 0LL
Tel: 0151 777 3480 Fax: 01704 512784
Coroner's Office: Whiston Hospital, Whiston L35 5DR
Tel: 0151 430 1238 Fax: 0151 426 6694

Shropshire, Telford and Wrekin Coroner
Coroner's Office: Third Fl, Guildhall, Frankwell Quay, Shrewsbury SY2 5RW
Tel: 01743 281297 Fax: 01743 281289

Somerset Eastern Coroner
Coroner's Office: Argyll Ho, Bath St, Frome BA11 1DP
Tel: 0117 973 4259 Fax: 0117 973 6430

Somerset Western Coroner
Coroner's Office: Blackbrook Gate, Blackbrook Park Avenue, Taunton TA1 2PG
Tel: 0845 209 1796 Fax: 01845 209 2572

South Yorkshire East Coroner
Coroner's Office: 5 Union St, off St Sepulchre Gate West, Doncaster DN1 3AE
Tel: 01302 320844 Fax: 01302 364833

South Yorkshire West Coroner
Coroner's Office: Medico-Legal Centre, Watery St, Sheffield S3 7ET
Tel: 0114 273 8721 Fax: 0114 272 6247

Southampton and New Forest Coroner
Coroner's Office: 12–18 Hulse Rd, Southampton SO15 2JX
Tel: 023 8071 0452 Fax: 023 8067 4479

Staffordshire South Coroner
Coroner's Office: 1 Staffordshire Place, Stafford ST16 2LP
Tel: 01785 276127 Fax: 01785 276128

Stoke-on-Trent and North Staffordshire Coroner
Coroner's Office: 547 Hartshill Rd, Hartshill, Stoke-on-Trent ST4 6HF
Tel: 01782 234777 Fax: 01782 232074

Suffolk Coroner
Coroner's Office: 1st Fl, Landmark Ho, 4 Egerton Rd, Ipswich IP1 5PF
Tel: 01473 613888 Fax: 01473 613619

Sunderland Coroner
Coroner's Office: Civic Centre, Burdon Rd, Sunderland SR2 7DN
Tel: 0191 561 7843 Fax: 0191 553 7803

Surrey Coroner
Coroner's Office: Station Approach, Woking GU22 7AP
Tel: 01483 776138 Fax: 01483 765460

Swansea, Neath and Port Talbot Coroner
Coroner's Office: The Civic Centre, Oystermouth, Swansea SA1 3SN
Tel: 01792 636237 Fax: 01792 636603

Teesside Coroner
Coroner's Office: Corporation Rd, Middlesbrough TS1 2DA
Tel: 01642 729350 Fax: 01642 729948

The Black Country Coroner
Coroner's Office: Smethwick Council Ho, High St, Smethwick B66 3NT
Tel: 0845 352 7483 Fax: 0121 569 5384

Warwickshire Coroner
Coroner's Office: Warwickshire Justice Centre, Newbold Terrace, Leamington Spa CV32 4EL
Tel: 01926 684065 Fax: 01926 682513

West Sussex Coroner
Coroner's Office: Centenary Ho, Durrington Ln, Worthing BN13 2QB
Tel: 01243 404012 Fax: 01243 404020

West Yorkshire Eastern Coroner
Coroner's Office: 71 Northgate, Wakefield WF1 3BS
Tel: 01924 302180 Fax: 01924 302184

West Yorkshire Western Coroner
Coroner's Office: City Courts, The Tyrls, Bradford BD1 1LA
Tel: 01274 391362 Fax: 01274 721794

Wiltshire and Swindon Coroner
Coroner's Office: 26 Endless St, Salisbury SP1 1DP
Tel: 01722 438900 Fax: 01722 332223

Wirral Coroner
Coroner's Office: South Annexe, Town Hall, Brighton St, Wallasey, Wirral CH44 8ED
Tel: 0151 691 8648 Fax: 0151 691 8474

Part 5

Government Departments

Charity Commission

Charity Commission
Website: www.charitycommission.gov.uk
London: Please refer to website,
Tel: 0845 300 0218
e-mail: contact via website

Communities and Local Government

Department for Communities and Local Government
Website: www.gov.uk/government/organisations/department-for-communities-and-local-government
London: 2 Marsham St, London SW1P 4DF
Tel: 0303 444 0000
e-mail: contact via website

Crown Prosecution Service

The Crown Prosecution Service
Website: www.cps.gov.uk
Head Office: Rose Ct, 2 Southwark Bridge, London SE1 9HS
Tel: 020 3357 0000
e-mail: enquiries@cps.gsi.gov.uk

Education and Skills

Department for Business, Innovation and Skills
Website: www.gov.uk/government/organisations/department-for-business-innovation-skills
Head Office: 1 Victoria St, London SW1H 0ET
Tel: 020 7215 5000
e-mail: enquiries@bis.gsi.gov.uk
Note: minicom: 020 7215 6740

Department for Education
Website: www.gov.uk/government/organisations/department-for-education
Head Office: Piccadilly Gate, Store St, Manchester M1 2WD
Tel: 0370 000 2288 Fax: 01928 794248
e-mail: contact via website

Environment, Food & Rural Affairs

Department for Environment, Food & Rural Affairs (Defra)
Website: www.gov.uk/government/organisations/department-for-environment-food-rural-affairs
Head Office: Nobel Ho, 17 Smith Sq, London SW1P 3JR
Tel: 0845 933 5577
e-mail: defra.helpline@defra.gsi.gov.uk
Note: minicom: 0845 300 1998

Foreign & Commonwealth Office

Foreign & Commonwealth Office
Website: www.gov.uk/government/organisations/foreign-commonwealth-office
Head Office: King Charles St, London SW1A 2AH
Tel: 020 7008 1500
e-mail: fcocorrespondence@fco.gov.uk

HM Revenue & Customs

HM Revenue & Customs
Website: www.hmrc.gov.uk
Head Office: Written Enquiries Section, Alexander Ho, Victoria Ave, Southend SS99 1BD
Tel: National Advice Service 0845 010 9000
e-mail: contact via website
VAT Enquiries: Contact local VAT offices

HM Treasury

HM Treasury
Website: www.gov.uk/government/organisations/hm-treasury
Head Office: The Correspondence and Enquiries Unit, 1 Horse Guards Rd, Whitehall, London SW1A 2HQ
Tel: 020 7270 5000
e-mail: public.enquiries@hmtreasury.gsi.gov.uk

Health

Department of Health
Website: www.gov.uk/government/organisations/department-of-health
Head Office: Ministerial Correspondence and Public Enquiries Unit, Richmond Ho, 79 Whitehall, London SW1A 2NS
Tel: 020 7210 4850 Fax: 020 7210 5952
e-mail: contact via website

Home Office

Home Office
Website: www.homeoffice.gov.uk
Head Office: Direct Communications Unit, 2 Marsham St, London SW1P 4DF
Tel: 020 7035 4848 Fax: 020 7035 4745
e-mail: public.enquiries@homeoffice.gsi.gov.uk
Note: Minicom: 020 7035 4742

Ministry of Justice

Ministry of Justice
Website: www.justice.gov.uk
Head Office: 102 Petty France, London SW1H 9AJ
Tel: 020 3334 3555 Fax: 020 3334 4455
DX: 152380 Westminster 8
e-mail: general.queries@justice.gsi.gov.uk

Scotland

Scottish Government
Website: www.gov.scot
Head Office: St Andrew's Ho, Regent Rd, Edinburgh EH1 3DG
Tel: 0300 244 4000 Fax: 01397 795 001
e-mail: ceu@scotland.gsi.gov.uk

The Scotland Office
Website: www.gov.uk/government/organisations/scotland-office
Head Office: Dover Ho, Whitehall, London SW1A 2AU
Tel: 020 7270 6754 Fax: 020 7270 6812
e-mail: contact via website
Other offices: 1 Melville Crescent, Edinburgh EH3 7HW
Tel: 0131 244 9010 Fax: 0131 244 9028
e-mail: contact via website

Transport

Department for Transport
Website: www.gov.uk/government/organisations/department-for-transport
Head Office: Great Minster Ho, 33 Horseferry Rd, London SW1P 4DR
Tel: 0300 330 3000
e-mail: contact via website
Information Rights Unit: Ashdown Ho, Sedlescombe Rd North, St Leonards-on-Sea TN37 7GA
Tel: 0300 330 3000
e-mail: foi-advice-team-dft@dft.gsi.gov.uk
Marine Accident Investigation Branch: Mountbatten Ho, Grosvenor Sq, Southampton SO15 2JU
Tel: 023 8039 5500 Fax: 023 8023 2459
e-mail: maib@dft.gsi.gov.uk
Rail Accident Investigation Branch: The Wharf, Stores Rd, Derby DE21 4BA
Tel: 01332 253 300 Fax: 01332 253 301
e-mail: enquiries@raib.gov.uk

Wales

Wales Office
Website: www.gov.uk/government/organisations/wales-office
Head Office: 1 Caspian Point, Caspian Way, Cardiff CF10 4PJ
Tel: 029 2092 4220
e-mail: correspondence@walesoffice.gsi.gov.uk

Welsh Government
Website: www.wales.gov.uk
Head Office: Cathays Park, Cardiff CF10 3NQ
Tel: 0300 0603 300
e-mail: customerhelp@wales.gsi.gov.uk

Work and Pensions

Department for Work and Pensions
Website: www.gov.uk/government/organisations/department-for-work-pensions
Head Office: Caxton Ho, Tothill St, London SW1H 9NA
e-mail: ministers@dwp.gsi.gov.uk

Part 6

Police Forces

UK Police Forces: London

City of London Police
Website: www.cityoflondon.police.uk
Headquarters: 37 Wood St, London EC2P 2NQ
Tel: 020 7601 2222
e-mail: firstname.lastname@cityoflondon.pnn.police.uk
Commissioner: Adrian Leppard QPM MBA, Assistant Commissioner, Ian Dyson
Strategic Planning: Head of Strategic Development: Stuart Phoenix
Professional Standards: Director: Det Supt Martin Kapp
Media and Communications: Director: Teresa La Thangue

Metropolitan Police
Website: www.met.police.uk
Headquarters: New Scotland Yard, Broadway, London SW1H 0BG
Tel: 020 7230 1212
e-mail: mso@met.police.uk
Commissioner: Sir Bernard Hogan-Howe, Deputy Commissioner, Craig Mackay
Strategic Planning: Director: Denise Milani
Professional Standards: Director: Fiona Taylor
Legal Services: Director: H Giles
Media and Communications: Director: Martin Fewell
Specialist Operations: Assistant Commissioner: Cressida Dick
Counter Terrorism: Deputy Assistant Commissioner: Helen Ball
Royalty Protection: Royalty Protection: OCU Commander: Chief Supt Bert Moore
Diplomatic Protection: Diplomatic Protection: Chief Supt Elaine Van-Orden

Metropolitan Police Marine Police Unit
Headquarters: 98 Wapping High St, London E1W 2NE
Tel: 020 7275 4452

Metropolitan Police Mayor's Office for Policing and Crime
Website: www.london.gov.uk/policing
Headquarters: City Hall, The Queen's Walk, London SE1 2AA
Tel: 020 7983 6532
e-mail: firstname.lastname@mopac.london.gov.uk

Metropolitan Police Training
Headquarters: Aerodrome Rd, London NW9 5JE

UK Police Forces: England and Wales

Avon and Somerset Police
Website: www.avonandsomerset.police.uk
Headquarters: PO Box 37, Portishead, Bristol BS20 8QL
e-mail: firstname.lastname@avonandsomerset.pnn.police.uk
Commissioner: Ms Sue Mountstevens
Strategic Planning: Head of Strategic Service Improvement: Mrs M Hardwell
Professional Standards: Head of Professional Standards Unit: Supt P Richards
Legal Services: Head of Legal Services: Ms S Dauncey
Media and Communications: Head of Communications: Mrs A Hirst
Specialist Operations: Head of Operations: Chief Supt M Carter

Bedfordshire Police
Website: www.bedfordshire.police.uk
Headquarters: Woburn Rd, Kempston, Bedford MK43 9AX
Tel: 01234 841212
e-mail: firstname.lastname@bedfordshire.pnn.police.uk
Police and Crime Commissioner: Mr Olly Martins
Legal Services: Head of Legal Services: Mr Afzal Chowdhury
Media and Communications: Media Relations Manager: Ms Jo Hobbs

Cambridge Police Constabulary
Website: www.cambs.police.uk
Headquarters: Hinchingbrooke Park, Huntingdon PE29 6NP
e-mail: firstname.lastname@cambs.pnn.police.uk
Police and Crime Commissioner: Sir Graham Bright
Professional Standards: Head of Operational HR & Policy: Sarah Knight
Media and Communications: Head of Corporate Communications: Sarah Cooper

Cheshire Police Constabulary
Website: www.cheshire.police.uk
Headquarters: Clemonds Hey, Oakmere Rd, Winsford CW7 2UA
e-mail: firstname.lastname@cheshire.pnn.police.uk
Police and Crime Commissioner: Mr J Dwyer
Strategic Planning: Head of Planning & Performance: Mr P Woods
Professional Standards: Head of Professional Standards: Det Supt J Armstrong
Legal Services: Force Solicitor: Mr David Bryan
Counter Terrorism: Head: Det Insp M Byrne

Cleveland Police
Website: www.cleveland.police.uk
Headquarters (postal): Ash Ho, III Acres, Princeton Drive, Thornaby, Stockton on Tees TS17 6AJ
e-mail: firstname.lastname@cleveland.pnn.police.uk
Police and Crime Commissioner: Barry Coppinger

Cumbria Police Constabulary
Website: www.cumbria.police.uk
Headquarters: Carleton Hall, Penrith CA10 2AU
e-mail: comms@cumbria.pnn.police.uk
Police and Crime Commissioner: Richard Rhodes

Derbyshire Police Constabulary
Website: www.derbyshire.police.uk
Headquarters: Butterley Hall, Ripley DE5 3RS
e-mail: foi@derbyshire.pnn.police.uk
Police and Crime Commissioner: Mr A Charles
Professional Standards: Head of Professional Standards Department: Supt R Walker
Legal Services: Head of Legal Services: Mr C W Sutherland
Media and Communications: Miss J Walden

Devon and Cornwall Police Constabulary
Website: www.devon-cornwall.police.uk
Headquarters: Middlemoor, Exeter EX2 7HQ
e-mail: firstname.lastname@devonandcornwall.pnn.police.uk
Police and Crime Commissioner: Mr Tony Hogg

Professional Standards: Head of Professional Standards: Det Supt Sam De Reya
Legal Services: Senior Legal Advisors: Mrs Jill Gratwick and Miss Lucy Seymour
Media and Communications: Head of Corporate Communications: Ms Tanya Croft
Specialist Operations: Commander: Chief Supt Jim Nye

Dorset Police
Website: www.dorset.police.uk
Headquarters: Winforth, Dorchester DT2 8DZ
e-mail: firstname.lastname@dorset.pnn.police.uk
Police and Crime Commissioner: Martyn Underhill
Strategic Planning: Head of Department: Ms J Yates
Professional Standards: Head of Department: Supt P Windle
Media and Communications: Head of Communications and Engagement: Mr N Cloak
Specialist Operations: Head of Operational Planning: Supt N Searle

Durham Police Constabulary
Website: www.durham.police.uk
Headquarters: Aykley Heads, Durham DH1 5TT
e-mail: durham@pnn.police.uk
Police and Crime Commissioner: Mr R Hogg
Professional Standards: Head of Department: Supt D Ellis
Media and Communications: Media & Corporate Communications Manager: Mr N Preston
Specialist Operations: Head of Operational Planning & Change: Supt W Dutton

Dyfed-Powys Police
Website: www.dyfed-powys.police.uk
Headquarters: PO Box 99, Llangunnor, Carmarthen SA31 2PF
e-mail: firstname.lastname@dyfed-powys.pnn.police.uk
Police and Crime Commissioner: Mr Christopher Salmon
Strategic Planning: Head of Corporate Development: Mrs L Davies
Legal Services: Head of Legal Services: Ms S Waters
Media and Communications: Senior Manager Corporate Communications: Rhian Moore
Specialist Operations: Head of Operational Support: Chief Supt H Rees

Essex Police
Website: www.essex.police.uk
Headquarters: PO Box 2, Springfield, Chelmsford CM2 6DA
e-mail: firstname.lastname@essex.pnn.police.uk
Police and Crime Commissioner: Nicholas Alston
Strategic Planning: Head of Business Services: Dave Marshall
Professional Standards: Director of Joint Support Services: Mark Gilmartin
Legal Services: Force Solicitor: Mr Adam Hunt

Gloucester Police Constabulary
Website: www.gloucestershire.police.uk
Headquarters: No.1 Waterwells, Waterwells Drive, Quedgeley, Glouscester GL2 2AN
e-mail: firstname.lastname@gloucestershire.pnn.police.uk
Police and Crime Commissioner: Martin Surl
Professional Standards: Head of Department: Supt Bridget Woodhall
Specialist Operations: Det Chief Supt Bernie Kinsella

Greater Manchester Police
Website: www.gmp.police.uk
Headquarters: Central Park, Northampton Rd, Manchester M40 5BP
e-mail: GMPOperational.Enquiries@gmp.pnn.police.uk
Police and Crime Commissioner: Tony Lloyd
Strategic Planning: Planning & Policy Manager: George Burns
Legal Services: Director of Legal Services: Sandra Pope
Media and Communications: Head of Corporate Communications: Amanda Coleman
Specialist Operations: Supt Martin Greenhalgh
Counter Terrorism: Branch Head: Det Chief Supt T Mole
Force Museum: Force Museum, Newton St, Manchester M1 1ES
Note: Museum Curator: Duncan Broady

Gwent Police
Website: www.gwent.police.uk
Headquarters: Croesyceiliog, Cwmbran NP44 2XJ
e-mail: firstname.lastname@gwent.pnn.police.uk
Police and Crime Commissioner: Mr Ian Johnston
Professional Standards: Head: Det Supt Ruth Price
Media and Communications: Head: Stuart John

Hampshire Police Constabulary
Website: www.hampshire.police.uk
Headquarters: West Hill, Winchester SO22 5DB
Tel: 0845 045 4545
e-mail: firstname.lastname@hampshire.pnn.police.uk
Police and Crime Commissioner: Mr Simon Hayes
Strategic Planning: Head of Force Change Programme: Mrs Mairead Whiting
Professional Standards: Head of Professional Standards Department: Chief Supt Mark Chatterton
Legal Services: Force Solicitor: Mr Roger Trencher
Media and Communications: Head of Corporate Communications: Ben Pratt
Specialist Operations: Assistant Chief Constable Chris Shead

Hertfordshire Police Constabulary
Website: www.herts.police.uk
Headquarters: Stanborough Rd, Welwyn Garden City AL8 6XF
e-mail: firstname.lastname@herts.pnn.police.uk
Police and Crime Commissioner: David Lloyd
Strategic Planning: Head of Strategy & Programmes: Diana Wyers
Professional Standards: Head of Professional Standards: Det Supt Mark Hodgson
Legal Services: Head of Legal Services: Mr Afzal Chowdhury
Media and Communications: Head of Corporate Communication: Colin Connolly
Specialist Operations: Head of Crime & Operational Support: Det Chief Supt Mick Campbell

Humberside Police
Website: www.humberside.police.uk
Headquarters: Priory Rd, Hull HU5 5SF
e-mail: firstname.lastname@humberside.pnn.police.uk
Police and Crime Commissioner: Matthew Grove
Professional Standards: Branch Head: Det Supt Judi Heaton
Legal Services: Legal Services Manager: Mr Stephen Hodgson
Media and Communications: Marketing & Communications: Mr James Newall
Specialist Operations: Branch Head: T/Chief Supt Steven Graham

Kent Police
Website: www.kent.police.uk
Headquarters: Sutton Rd, Maidstone ME15 9BZ
e-mail: firstname.lastname@kent.pnn.police.uk
Police and Crime Commissioner: Mrs Ann Barnes
Professional Standards: Head of Professional Services Department: Det Supt Rachel Ireland
Legal Services: Head of Legal Services: Bev Newman

Media and Communications: Head of Corporate Communications: Gavin McKinnon
Specialist Operations: Head of Strategic Operations: Supt Stuart Kehily
Kent Police Museum: Kent Police Museum, The Historic Dockyard, Chatham ME4 4TZ

Lancashire Police Constabulary
Website: www.lancashire.police.uk
Headquarters: PO Box 77, Hutton, Nr Preston PR4 5SB
Tel: 01772 614444
e-mail: firstname.lastname@lancashire.pnn.police.uk
Police and Crime Commissioner: Clive Grunshaw
Strategic Planning: Strategic Business Development Manager: Sharon Cunningham
Professional Standards: Head of Professional Standards: Supt Jenny Gomery
Media and Communications: Head of Corporate Communications: Elizabeth Riding
Specialist Operations: Operations Manager: T/Supt Nicola Evans
Counter Terrorism: Head of Counter Terrorism Branch: Det Supt Stephen Pemberton

Leicestershire Police
Website: www.leics.police.uk
Headquarters: St John's, Enderby, Leicester LE19 2BX
e-mail: firstname.lastname@leicestershire.pnn.police.uk
Police and Crime Commissioner: Sir Clive Loader
Professional Standards: Head of Department & Civil Claims: Supt Jim Holyoak
Specialist Operations: Det Insp Joe Elliott

Lincolnshire Police
Website: www.lincs.police.uk
Headquarters: PO Box 999, Lincoln LN5 7PH
e-mail: forcehq@lincs.pnn.police.uk
Police and Crime Commissioner: Alan Hardwick
Strategic Planning: Head of Strategic Development: Mrs Julie Hogan
Professional Standards: D/Supt S Morrison
Media and Communications: Head of Corporate Communications: Mr Tony Diggins
Specialist Operations: Operations Manager: Miss A Driver

Merseyside Police
Website: www.merseyside.police.uk
Headquarters: PO Box 59, Liverpool L69 1JD
e-mail: firstname.lastname@merseyside.pnn.police.uk
Police and Crime Commissioner: Jane Kennedy
Strategic Planning: Head: Chief Supt S Richards
Professional Standards: Head: D/Chief Supt Karen Cummings
Legal Services: Legal Services: Miss C Ashcroft

Norfolk Police Constabulary
Website: www.norfolk.police.uk
Headquarters: Operations and Communications Centre, Jubilee Ho, Falconers Chase, Wymondham NR18 0WW
e-mail: lastnameinitial@norfolk.pnn.police.uk
Police and Crime Commissioner: Mr Stephen Bett
Professional Standards: Head of Professional Standards: Det Supt K Elliott
Legal Services: Head of Legal Services: Mrs A Ings
Media and Communications: Head of Corporate Communications: Mrs B Durham
Royalty and VIP Protection: Supt K Clarke

North Wales Police
Website: www.north-wales.police.uk
Headquarters: Glan-y-Don, Colwyn Bay LL29 8AW
Tel: 0300 330 0101
e-mail: northwalespolice@north-wales.police.uk
Police and Crime Commissioner: Winston Roddick
Professional Standards: Head of Information Standards & Compliance: Judith Roberts
Legal Services: Force Solicitors: Ann Warman
Media and Communications: Head of Corporate Communications: Sue Appleton

North Yorkshire
Website: www.northyorkshire.police.uk
Headquarters: Newby Wiske Hall, Northallerton DL7 9HA
e-mail: firstname.lastname@northyorkshire.pnn.police.uk
Police and Crime Commissioner: Julia Mulligan
Professional Standards: Head of Professional Standards: Mr Steven Read
Legal Services: Head of Legal and Compliance Services: Jane Wintermeyer
Media and Communications: Head of Communications: Louise Wood
Specialist Operations: Head of Operations: Supt Dave Hannan

Northamptonshire Police
Website: www.northants.police.uk
Headquarters: Wootton Hall, Northampton NN4 0JQ
e-mail: firstname.lastname@northants.pnn.police.uk
Police and Crime Commissioner: Mr Adam Simmonds
Professional Standards: Head of Professional Standards: Supt Jan Meagher
Specialist Operations: Head of EMSOU-SOC: T/Det Chief Supt Jason Caunt

Northumbria Police
Website: www.northumbria.police.uk
Headquarters: Ponteland, Newcastle-upon-Tyne NE20 0BL
Tel: 01660 872555
e-mail: chief.constable@northumbria.pnn.police.uk
Police and Crime Commissioner: Vera Baird
Strategic Planning: Head of Strategy and Performance Unit: Inspector Karl Wilson
Professional Standards: Supt D Bryne
Legal Services: Head of Department: Mr R Heron
Media and Communications: Head of Corporate Communications: Mrs M Berne

Nottinghamshire Police
Headquarters: Sherwood Lodge, Arnold, Nottingham NG5 8PP
e-mail: firstname.lastname@nottinghamshire.pnn.police.uk
Police and Crime Commissioner: Paddy Tipping
Strategic Planning: Performance & Insight Manager: Chief Insp Andy Burton
Professional Standards: Head of Professional Standards: Det Supt Jackie Alexander
Media and Communications: Head of Corporate Communications: Paul Coffey
Specialist Operations: Head of Operational Support: Supt Chris Haward

South Wales Police
Website: www.south-wales.police.uk
Headquarters: Cowbridge Rd, Bridgend CF31 3SU
Tel: 01656 655555
e-mail: firstname.lastname@south-wales.pnn.police.uk
Police and Crime Commissioner: Rt Hon Alun Michael
Strategic Planning: Head of Performance & Inspection: Supt Stephen Jones
Professional Standards: Head of Professional Standards: Det Chief Supt Tim Jones
Legal Services: Head of Joint Legal Services: Mrs Nia Brennan

Media and Communications: Communications Manager: Mr Paul Dierden
Specialist Operations: Chief Supt Josh Jones

South Yorkshire Police
Website: www.southyorks.police.uk
Headquarters: Snig Hill, Sheffield S3 8LY
Tel: 0114 220 2020
e-mail: firstname.lastname@southyorks.pnn.police.uk
Police and Crime Commissioner: Shaun Wright
Professional Standards: Head of Department: Det Supt Terry Mann
Specialist Operations: Chief Supt Rachel Barber

Staffordshire Police
Website: www.staffordshire.police.uk
Headquarters: Weston Rd, Stafford ST18 0YY
e-mail: firstname.lastname@staffordshire.pnn.police.uk
Police and Crime Commissioner: Matthew Ellis
Professional Standards: People Performance Assessment Manager: Chief Insp Paul Barker
Legal Services: Miss Lisa-Marie Smith
Media and Communications: Head of Corporate Communications: Mr David Bailey

Suffolk Police Constabulary
Website: www.suffolk.police.uk
Headquarters: Martlesham Heath, Ipswich IP5 3QS
Tel: 01473 613500
e-mail: headquarters@suffolk.pnn.police.uk
Police and Crime Commissioner: Mr T Passmore
Strategic Planning: Head of Strategic Change & Planning: Supt L Pepper
Professional Standards: Head of Professional Standards: Det Supt K Elliott
Media and Communications: Head of Corporate Communications: Mrs B Durham

Surrey Police
Website: www.surrey.police.uk
Headquarters: PO Box 101, Guildford GU1 9PE
e-mail: customerservice@surrey.pnn.police.uk
Police and Crime Commissioner: Kevin Hurley
Strategic Planning: Chief Insp (Strategic Planning): Dave Kelley
Professional Standards: Head of Professional Standards: Det Supt Ray Marley
Media and Communications: Head of Corporate Communications: Ruth Shulver

Sussex Police
Website: www.sussex.police.uk
Headquarters: Church Ln, Lewes BN7 2DZ
Tel: 01273 470101
e-mail: chief.constable@sussex.pnn.police.uk
Police and Crime Commissioner: Katy Bourne
Professional Standards: Supt Lisa Bell
Media and Communications: Chief Supt Wayne Jones
Specialist Operations: Chief Supt Paul Morrison

Thames Valley Police
Website: www.thamesvalley.police.uk
Headquarters: Oxford Rd, Kidlington OX5 2NX
e-mail: firstname.lastname@thamesvalley.pnn.police.uk
Police and Crime Commissioner: Anthony Stansfeld
Professional Standards: Head of Professional Standards: Chief Supt Tim de Meyer
Legal Services: Head of Legal Services: Guy Lemon
Media and Communications: Head of Corporate Communications: Michelle Nichols
Specialist Operations: Assistant Chief Constable (Operations): Chris Shead

Warwickshire Police
Website: www.warwickshire.police.uk
Headquarters: PO Box 4, Leek Wootton, Warwick CV35 7QB
Tel: 01926 415000
e-mail: firstname.lastname@warwickshire.pnn.police.uk
Police and Crime Commissioner: Mr Ron Ball
Media and Communications: Head of Corporate Communications: Mr Carl Baldacchino
Specialist Operations: Head of Specialist Operations: Det Supt Daryn Elton

West Mercia Police
Website: www.westmercia.police.uk
Headquarters: Hindlip Hall, PO Box 55, Hindlip, Worcester WR3 8SP
Tel: 0300 333 3000
e-mail: firstname.lastname@westmercia.pnn.police.uk
Police and Crime Commissioner: Mr Bill Longmore
Media and Communications: Head of Corporate Communications: Ms Kate Quilley
Specialist Operations: T/Head of Specialist Operations: T/Det/Supt Jason Wells

West Midlands Police
Headquarters: PO Box 52, Lloyd Ho, Colmore Circus Queensway, Birmingham B4 6NQ
Tel: 0345 113 5000
e-mail: initial.lastname@west-midlands.pnn.police.uk
Police and Crime Commissioner: Mr David Jamieson
Strategic Planning: Strategic Planning Manager: Mr D Leyland
Professional Standards: Head of Professional Standards: Chief Supt A Nicholson
Legal Services: Acting Director Legal Services: Ms Lisa-Marie Smith
Media and Communications: Head of Corporate Communications: D Barton
Specialist Operations: Commander: Chief Supt S Johnson

West Yorkshire Police
Website: www.westyorkshire.police.uk
Headquarters: PO Box 9, Wakefield WF1 3QP
e-mail: firstname.lastname@westyorkshire.pnn.police.uk
Police and Crime Commissioner: Mark Burns-Williamson
Professional Standards: Head of Department: Det Chief Supt Clive Wain
Legal Services: Head of Legal Services: Mr Mike Percival
Media and Communications: Head of Corporate Communications: Mr Nigel Swift
Specialist Operations: Head of Operations: Chief Supt Dickie Whitehead

Wiltshire Police
Website: www.wiltshire.police.uk
Headquarters: London Rd, Devizes SN10 2DN
e-mail: firstname.lastname@wiltshire.pnn.police.uk
Police and Crime Commissioner: Mr Angus MacPherson
Professional Standards: Head of People Standards & Support: T/DCI Sarah Robbins
Media and Communications: Head of Communications: Clare Mills

UK Police Forces: Scotland

Aberdeen City Divisional Police
Headquarters: Queen St, Aberdeen AB10 1ZA
Divisional Commander: Chief Supt Adrian Watson

Aberdeenshire and Moray Divisional Police
Headquarters: Blackhall Rd, Inverurie AB51 3QD
Divisional Commander: Chief Supt Mark McLaren

Argyll and West Dunbartonshire Divisional Police
Headquarters: Stirling Rd, Dumbarton G82 3PT
Divisional Commander: Chief Supt Helen Swann

Ayrshire Divisional Police
Headquarters: 10 St Marnock St, Kilmarnock KA1 1TJ
Divisional Commander: Chief Supt Gillian MacDonald

Dumfries and Galloway Divisional Police
Headquarters: Cornwall Mount, Dumfries DG1 1PZ
Divisional Commander: T/Chief Supt Robert Moore

Edinburgh Divisional Police
Headquarters: Fettes Avenue, Edinburgh EH4 1RB
Divisional Commander: Chief Supt Mark Williams

Fife Divisional Police
Headquarters: Detroit Rd, Glenrothes KY6 2RJ
Divisional Commander: Chief Supt Garry McEwan

Forth Valley Divisional Police
Headquarters: West Bridge St, Falkirk FK1 5AP
Divisional Commander: Chief Supt David Flynn

Greater Glasgow Divisional Police
Headquarters: 923 Helen St, Glasgow G52 1EE
Divisional Commander: Chief Supt Andy Bates

Highland and Islands Divisional Police
Headquarters: Old Perth Rd, Inverness IV2 3SY
Divisional Commander: Chief Supt Julian Innes

Lanarkshire Divisional Police
Headquarters: 217 Windnillhill St, Motherwell ML1 1RZ
Divisional Commander: Chief Supt Nelson Telfer

Renfrewshire and Inverclyde Divisional Police
Headquarters: Mill St, Paisley PA1 1JU
Divisional Commander: Chief Supt Alan Speirs

Scottish Police Authority
Website: www.spa.police.uk.
Headquarters: 1 Pacific Quay, Glasgow G51 1DZ
Tel: 0141 585 8300
e-mail: enquiries@spa.pnn.police.uk
Chair: Vic Emery
Media and Communications: Director of Communications & Relationships: John McCroskie

Tayside Divisional Police
Headquarters: West Bell St, Dundee DD1 9JU
Divisional Commander: Chief Supt Eddie Smith

The Lothian and Scottish Borders Divisional Police
Headquarters: Newbattle Rd, Dalkeith EH22 3AX
Divisional Commander: Chief Supt Gill Imery

UK Police Forces: Dependencies

Guernsey Police
Website: www.guernsey.police.uk
Headquarters: Hospital Ln, St. Peter Port, Guernsey GY1 2QN
Tel: 01481 725111
e-mail: hq@guernsey.pnn.police.uk
Lieutenant-Governor and Commander-in-Chief: Air Marshal Peter Walker
Professional Standards: Det Insp A Whitton
Specialist Operations: Head of Operations: Supt R Hardy

Isle of Man Constabulary
Website: www.gov.im/categories/home-and-neighbourhood/emergency-services/police/
Headquarters: Dukes Avenue, Douglas IM2 4RG
Tel: 01624 631212
e-mail: firstname.lastname@gov.im
Lieutenant-Governor: His Excellency the Lieutenant Governor Mr Adam Wood
Strategic Planning: Supt Kevin Willson
Media and Communications: Mr Dave Caley

States of Jersey Police
Website: www.jersey.police.uk
Headquarters: PO Box 789, St. Helier, Jersey JE4 8ZD
Tel: 01534 612612
e-mail: sojp@jersey.pnn.police.uk
Lieutenant-Governor: General Sir John McColl
Legal Services: Mr Laurence O'Donnell
Media and Communications: Media and Public Information Officer: Ms Hannah Collier

Airports Police

Airports Police
Aberdeen: Aberdeen Airport, Viscount Ho, Brent Rd, Dyce AB21 0NU
Tel: 0845 600 5700
Belfast (George Best): Belfast (George Best) City Airport, 1–5 Dundela Avenue, Belfast BT4 3BQ
Tel: 028 9090 1758
Belfast International: Belfast International Airport, Belfast BT29 4AB
Tel: 028 9448 4400
Birmingham: Birmingham Airport, Diamond Ho, Birmingham B26 3QJ
Bournemouth: Bournemouth Airport, Barrack Rd, Christchurch BH23 1PN
Tel: 01202 222908
Bristol: Bristol Airport, Lulsgate, Bristol BS48 3DY
Tel: 01275 473764
Cardiff: Cardiff Airport, Cowbridge Rd, Bridgend CF31 3SU
Carlisle: Cumbria Police Constabulary
Durham: Durham Police Constabulary
East Midlands: Leicestershire Police Constabulary
Edinburgh: Edinburgh Airport, Almond Ho, Almond Rd, Edinburgh EH12 9DN
Tel: 0131 335 5000
Farnborough: (see Southampton Airport)
Glasgow International: Glasgow International Airport, St Andrew's Drive, Abbotsinch PA3 2ST
Isle of Man: Isle of Man Airport, Ballasalla, Isle of Man IM9 2AS
Tel: 01624 821712
Leeds/Bradford: West Yorkshire Police
Liverpool (John Lennon): Merseyside Police
London City: London City Airport, SO18 Aviation Security,
Tel: 020 3276 1460
London Gatwick: London Gatwick Airport, Perimeter Rd North, Gatwick Airport RH6 0JE
Tel: 0845 607 0999
London Heathrow: London Heathrow Airport, SO18 Aviation Security,
Tel: 020 3276 1460
London Stansted: London Stansted Airport, Enterprise Ho, Bassingbourn Rd, Stansted Airport CM24 1PS
Tel: 01279 680298

Luton: Bedfordshire Police
Manchester: Manchester Airport, Airport Section, Wythenshawe, Manchester M90 1NN
Tel: 0161 856 0250
Newcastle: Newcastle Airport, Main Terminal Building, Woolsington, Newcastle-upon-Tyne NE13 8BZ
Tel: 0191 214 3603
Prestwick International: Prestwick International Airport, Police Scotland, Tactical Command Building, RVP South, McIntyre Rd, Prestwick KA9 0BU
Southampton: Inkerman Building, Inkerman Building, Hamble, Southampton SO31 4TS
Tel: 02380 744605

Armed Forces Police

Royal Air Force Police
Headquarters: Service Police Crime Bureau, Southwick Park, Fareham PO17 6EJ

Royal Marines Police Troop
Headquarters: RM Barracks, StoneHo, Plymouth PL1 3QS

Royal Military Police
Army Headquarters (Provost Marshal): 2nd Fl, Zone 5, Ramillies Building (1DL 431), Marlborough Lines, Monxton Rd, Andover SP11 8HJ

Royal Navy Police
Headquarters (Eastern): HMS Nelson, Queen St, Portsmouth PO1 3HH
Headquarters (Northern): 9–12 Churchill Square, Helensburgh, Argyll and Bute G84 9HL
Headquarters (Western): HMS Drake, Plymouth PL2 2BG

British Transport Police

British Transport Police
England Headquarters: 25 Camden Rd , London NW1 9LN
Scotland Headquarters: 90 Cowcaddens Rd, Glasgow G4 0LU
Sub Division – Pennines: 1st Fl, West Gate Ho, Grace St, Leeds LS1 2RP
C Division: Suite 2b, 1 Portland St, Manchester M1 3BE
Sub Division – Midlands: 1st Fl, The Axis, 10 Holliday St, Birmingham B1 1UP
Sub Division – East: 423–425 Caledonian Rd, London N7 9BQ
Sub Division – South: Ivason Ho, 8a London Bridge St, London SE1 9SG
Sub Division – London, South & East England, London Underground & DLR: Central London Police Station, 16–24 Whitfield St, London W1T 2RA
Sub Division – Wales: 3 Callaghan Sq, Cardiff CF10 5BT
Sub Division – Western: Reading Police Station, Station Hill, Reading RG1 1LT

Civil Nuclear Police Constabulary

Civil Nuclear Police Constabulary
Website: www.cnc.police.uk
Headquarters: Building F6, Culham Science Centre, Abingdon OX14 3DB
Tel: 01235 466466
e-mail: ccc@cnc.pnn.police.uk

Ministry of Defence Police

Ministry of Defence Police
Headquarters: Wethersfield, Braintree CM7 4AZ
Tel: 01371 854000

Parks Police

Epping Forest: Forest Keepers
Headquarters: The Warren, Loughton IG10 4RW
e-mail: epping.forest@cityoflondon.gov.uk

Hampstead Heath Police Constabulary
Headquarters: Kenwood Staff Yard, Hampstead Ln, London N6 4NU
e-mail: hh-constabulary@cityoflondon.gov.uk

Parks Police Service
Headquarters: Stable Yard, Holland Park, London W8 6LU
e-mail: parkspolice@rbkc.gov.uk
Note: Covers the Royal Borough of Kensington & Chelsea and Hammersmith & Fulham

Royal Botanic Gardens Kew Constabulary
Headquarters: The Royal Botanic Gardens, Kew, Richmond TW9 3AB
e-mail: j.deer@kew.org

Wandsworth Events Police Service
Headquarters: Battersea Park, London SW11 4NJ
e-mail: sbiggs@wandsworth.gov.uk

Port, Waterways and Tunnels Police

Belfast Harbour Police
Headquarters: Port Operations Centre, Barnett Dock Rd, Belfast Harbour Estate, Belfast BT3 9AF

Broads Authority Police
Headquarters: Yare Ho, 62–64 Thorpe Rd, Norwich NR1 1RY

Canal and River Trust Enforcement
Headquarters: 1st Fl North, Station Ho, 500 Elder Gate, Milton Keynes MK9 1BB

Falmouth Police
Headquarters: The Falmouth Docks and Engineering Co Ltd, The Docks, Falmouth TR11 4NR

Kent Ports Police
Headquarters: Ports Co-ordination Centre, Longport Police Station, Ashford Rd, Newington, Folkstone CT18 8AP
Note: Including Eurotunnel Terminal in Coquelles, France

Larne Police
Headquarters: Larne Harbour Ltd, 9 Olderfleet Rd, Larne BT40 1AS

Mersey Tunnels Police
Headquarters: Merseyside Integrated Transport Authority, Merseytravel, PO Box 1976, Liverpool L69 3HN

Port Dover Police
Headquarters: Fl 4, Terminal Control Building, Eastern Docks, Dover CT16 1JA

Port of Bristol Police
Headquarters: Royal Portbury Dock, Bristol BS20 7XQ

Port of Felixstowe Police
Headquarters: Port of Felixtowe Security & Port Police Unit, The Dock, Felixstowe IP11 3SY

Port of Isle of Man Police
Headquarters: Sea Terminal Building, Douglas IM1 2RF

Port of Liverpool Police
Headquarters: Liverpool Freeport, Liverpool L21 1JD

Port of London Police
Headquarters: Tilbury Freeport, Tilbury RM18 7DU

Portland Police
Headquarters: Castledown, Portland DT5 1PP

Tees and Hartlepool Harbour Police
Headquarters: Harbour Master's Office, Tees Dock, Grangetown, Middlesbrough TS6 6UD

Wildlife Police

UK National Wildlife Crime Unit
Headquarters: Old Livingston Police Station, Almondvale South, Livingston EH54 6PX
e-mail: ukwildlifecrime@nwcu.pnn.police.uk

Part 7

Health Authorities

England

NHS England
Website: www.england.nhs.uk
Head Office name: Head Office, Customer Services, PO Box 16738, Redditch B97 9PT
Tel: 0300 311 2233
e-mail: england.contactus@nhs.net

Scotland

Ayrshire and Arran NHS
Website: www.nhsaaa.net
Head Office: John Burns, Chief Executive, Eglinton Ho, Ailsa Hospital, Dalmellington Rd, Ayr KA6 6AB
Tel: 01292 513628
e-mail: contact via website

Borders NHS
Website: www.nhsborders.org.uk
Head Office: Jane Davidson (Interim), Newstead, Melrose, Roxburghshire TD6 9DA
Tel: 01896 826 000 Fax: 01896 825 580
e-mail: bordershb@borders.scot.nhs.uk

Dumfries & Galloway NHS
Website: www.nhsdg.scot.nhs.uk
Head Office: Jeff Ace, Chief Executive, Crichton Hall, Bankend Rd, Dumfries DG1 4TG
Tel: 01387 272705
e-mail: dg.feedback@nhs.net

Fife NHS
Website: www.nhsfife.org
Head Office: Brian Montgomery, Interim Chief Executive, Hayfield Ho, Hayfield Rd, Kirkcaldy KY2 5AH
Tel: 01592 643 355 Fax: 01592 648 142

Forth Valley NHS
Website: www.nhsforthvalley.com
Head Office: Jane Grant, Chief Executive, Carseview Ho, Castle Business Pk, Stirling FK9 4SW
Tel: 01786 463 031
e-mail: fv-uhb.yourhealthservice@nhs.net

Grampian NHS
Website: www.nhsgrampian.org
Head Office: Malcolm Wright, (Interim) Chief Executive, Summerfield Ho, 2 Eday Rd, Aberdeen AB15 6RE
Tel: 01224 558552

Greater Glasgow and Clyde NHS
Website: www.nhsggc.org.uk
Head Office: Robert Calderwood, Chief Executive, J B Russell Ho, Gartnavel Royal Hospital Campus, 1055 Gt Western Rd, Glasgow G12 0XH
Tel: 0141 201 4444 Fax: 0141 201 4403
Note: textphone: 0141 201 4400

Highland NHS
Website: www.nhshighland.scot.nhs.uk
Head Office: Elaine Mead, Chief Executive, Assynt Ho, Beechwood Pk, Inverness IV2 3BW
Tel: 01463 717 123
e-mail: nhs.highland@nhs.net

Lanarkshire NHS
Website: www.nhslanarkshire.org.uk
Head Office: Calum Campbell, Chief Executive, Kirklands, Fallside Rd, Bothwell G71 8BB
Tel: 01698 858 184
e-mail: calum.campbell@lanarkshire.scot.nhs.uk

Lothian NHS
Website: www.nhslothian.scot.nhs.uk
Head Office: Tim Davison, Chief Executive, Waverley Gate, 2–4 Waterloo Pl, Edinburgh EH1 3EG
Tel: 0131 536 9000

NHS National Services Scotland
Website: www.nhsnss.org
Head Office: Gyle Sq, 1 South Gyle Cres, Edinburgh EH12 9EB
Tel: 0131 275 6000
e-mail: nss.communications@nhs.net
Central Legal Office: Anderson Ho, Breadalbane St, Bonnington Rd, Edinburgh EH6 5JR
Tel: 0131 275 7800 Fax: 0131 275 7990
DX: ED 154
e-mail: nss.clo@nhs.net

Orkney NHS
Website: www.ohb.scot.nhs.uk
Head Office: Board HQ, Garden Ho, New Scapa Rd, Kirkwall KW15 1BH
Tel: 01856 888 000
e-mail: ork-hb.feedback@nhs.net

Shetland NHS
Website: www.shb.scot.nhs.uk
Head Office: Ralph Roberts, Chief Executive, Upper Floor Montfield, Burgh Rd, Lerwick ZE1 0LA
Tel: 01595 743 060 Fax: 01595 696 727
e-mail: shet-hb.information@nhs.net

State Hospitals' Board for Scotland
Website: www.tsh.scot.nhs.uk
Head Office: James Crichton, Chief Executive, Carstairs, Lampits Rd, Lanark ML11 8RP
Tel: 01555 840 293 Fax: 01555 840 024
e-mail: tsh.info@nhs.net

Tayside NHS
Website: www.nhstayside.scot.nhs.uk
Head Office: Lesley McLay, Chief Executive, Level 10, Ninewells Hospital, Dundee DD1 9SY
Tel: 01382 660 111
e-mail: generalcomments.tayside@nhs.net

Western Isles NHS
Website: www.wihb.scot.nhs.uk
Head Office: Gordon Jamieson, Chief Executive, 37 South Beach St, Stornoway, Isle of Lewis HS1 2BB
Tel: 01851 702 997 Fax: 01851 704 405
e-mail: gordon.jamieson@nhs.net

Wales

Abertawe Bro Morgannwg University Local Health Board
Website: www.abm.wales.nhs.uk
Head Office: Paul Roberts, Chief Executive, One Talbot Gateway, Baglan Energy Pk, Baglan, Port Talbot SA12 7BR
Tel: 01656 752 752 Fax: 01639 687 675
Bridgend Office: Innovations Centre, Ewenny Science Pk, Ewenny, Bridgend CF31 3NA
Tel: 01656 642 760
Neath/Port Talbot Office: Suite A, Britannic Ho, D'Arcy Business Pk, Llandarcy, Neath SA10 6JQ
Tel: 01792 326500
Swansea Office: 12th Fl, The Oldway Centre, 36 Orchard St, Swansea SA1 5AN
Tel: 01792 601 800

Betsi Cadwaladr University Local Health Board
Website: www.bcu.wales.nhs.uk
Head Office: Prof Trevor Purt, Chief Executive, Ysbyty Gwynedd, Penrhosgarnedd, Bangor LL57 2PW
Tel: 01248 384 384
e-mail: info.bcu@wales.nhs.uk
Anglesey/Gwynedd Office: Eryldon, Campbell Rd, Caernarfon, Gwynedd LL55 1HU
Tel: 01286 672 451
Flintshire Office: Preswylfa, Hendy Rd, Mold, Flintshire CH7 1PZ
Tel: 01352 803 434

Cardiff and Vale University Health Board
Website: www.cardiffandvaleuhb.wales.nhs.uk
Head Office: Adam Cairns, Chief Executive, Heath Park, Cardiff CF14
Tel: 029 2074 7747 Fax: 029 2074 6406
e-mail: intranews@wales.nhs.uk

Cwm Taf Local Health Board
Website: www.cwmtaf.wales.nhs.uk
Head Office: Alison Williams, Chief Executive, Ynysmeurig Ho, Navigation Pk, Abercynon CF45 4SN
Tel: 01443 744 800 Fax: 01443 744 888

Hywel Dda Local Health Board
Website: www.hywelddahb.wales.nhs.uk
Head Office: Steve Moore, Chief Executive, Merlin's Ct, Winch La, Haverfordwest SA61 1SB
Tel: 01437 771 220
e-mail: contact via website

Powys Teaching Health Board
Website: www.powysthb.wales.nhs.uk
Head Office: Carol Shillabeer, Chief Executive, Mansion Ho, Bronllys, Brecon LD3 0LS
Tel: 01874 711 661 Fax: 01874 712554
e-mail: andrew.cottom@wales.nhs.uk

Public Health Wales
Website: www.publichealthwales.wales.nhs.uk
Head Office: Dr Tracey Cooper, Chief Executive, 14 Cathedral Rd, Cardiff CF11 9LJ
Tel: 02920 227 744 Fax: 02920 226 749
e-mail: general.enquiries@wales.nhs.uk

Part 8

Land Registry

Registration of title to land is compulsory on sale throughout the whole of England and Wales. The table following indicates the land registry office serving each authority and also the dates on which compulsory registration was applied to each district. Owing to numerous boundary changes and reorganisations of local government, it is not always practicable to rely upon the names of the districts given as having always applied to the area in question. If it is important to ascertain the precise date when compulsory registration first applied to a particular property, enquiry may be made of the appropriate district land registry office or Land Registry Practice Guide 51 accessible in the publications section of their primary website (see below).{HLB}

Land Registry

Land Registry
Website: www.gov.uk/government/organisations/land-registry
Head Office: Trafalgar Ho, 1 Bedford Pk, Croydon CR0 2AQ
Tel: 0844 892 1111 / 0300 006 0001 (switchboard)
DX: 2699 Croydon 3
e-mail: foi@landregistry.gsi.gov.uk

Land Registry Offices

Land Registry Birkenhead Office
Website: www.gov.uk/government/organisations/land-registry
All titles: Rosebrae Court, Woodside Ferry Approach, Birkenhead CH41 6DU
Tel: 0844 892 1111 Fax: 03000 065789
DX: 24270 Birkenhead 4

Land Registry Coventry Office
Website: www.gov.uk/government/organisations/land-registry
All titles: Leigh Ct, Torrington Ave, Tile Hill, Coventry CV4 9XZ
Tel: 0844 892 1111 Fax: 03000 060025
DX: 18900 Coventry 3

Land Registry Croydon Office
Website: www.gov.uk/government/organisations/land-registry
All titles: Trafalgar Ho, 1 Bedford Pk, Croydon CR0 2AQ
Tel: 0844 892 1111 Fax: 03000 060024
DX: 2699 Croydon 3

Land Registry Durham Office
Website: www.gov.uk/government/organisations/land-registry
All titles: Southfield Ho, Southfield Way, Durham DH1 5TR
Tel: 0844 892 1111 Fax: 03000 060030
DX: 60200 Durham 3

Land Registry Fylde Office
Website: www.gov.uk/government/organisations/land-registry
All titles: Wrea Brook Court, Lytham Rd, Warton, Preston PR4 1TE
Tel: 0844 892 1111 Fax: 03000 060035
DX: 721560 Lytham St Annes 6

Land Registry Gloucester Office
Website: www.gov.uk/government/organisations/land-registry
All titles: Twyver Ho, Bruton Way, Gloucester GL1 1DQ
Tel: 0844 892 1111 Fax: 03000 060050
DX: 7599 Gloucester 3

Land Registry Kingston upon Hull Office
Website: www.gov.uk/government/organisations/land-registry
All titles: Earle Ho, Colonial St, Kingston upon Hull HU2 8JN
Tel: 0844 892 1111 Fax: 03000 060031
DX: 26700 Hull 4

Land Registry Leicester Office
Website: www.gov.uk/government/organisations/land-registry
All titles: Westbridge Pl, Leicester LE3 5DR
Tel: 0844 892 1111 Fax: 03000 060023
DX: 11900 Leicester 5

Land Registry Nottingham Office
Website: www.gov.uk/government/organisations/land-registry
All titles: Castle Wharf Ho, 2 Canal St, Nottingham NG1 7AU
Tel: 0844 892 1111 Fax: 03000 060028
DX: 10298 Nottingham 3

Land Registry Peterborough Office
Website: www.gov.uk/government/organisations/land-registry
All titles: Stuart Ho, West Wing, Peterborough PE1 1QF
Tel: 0844 892 1111 Fax: 03000 060027
DX: 12598 Peterborough 4

Land Registry Plymouth Office
Website: www.gov.uk/government/organisations/land-registry
All titles: Seaton Ct, 2 William Prance Rd, Plymouth PL6 5WS
Tel: 0844 892 1111 Fax: 03000 066123
DX: 8299 Plymouth 4

Land Registry Telford Office
Website: www.gov.uk/government/organisations/land-registry
All titles: Parkside Ct, Hall Park Way, Telford, Shropshire TF3 4LR
Tel: 0844 892 1111 Fax: 03000 060026
DX: 28100 Telford 2

Land Registry Wales (Cofrestrfa Tir Ddosbarthol Cymru) Office
Website: www.gov.uk/government/organisations/land-registry
All titles: Ty Cwm Tawe, Phoenix Way, Llansamlet, Swansea SA7 9FQ
Tel: 0844 892 1111 Fax: 03000 060029
DX: 82800 Swansea 2
Note: Serves some titles in England and all titles in Wales

Land Registry Weymouth Office
Website: www.gov.uk/government/organisations/land-registry
All titles: Melcombe Ct, 1 Cumberland Dr, Weymouth DT4 9TT
Tel: 0844 892 1111 Fax: 03000 060034
DX: 8799 Weymouth 2

Land Charges/Agricultural Credits

Land Charges Department
Website: www.gov.uk/government/organisations/land-registry
Head Office: Seaton Ct, 2 William Prance Rd, Plymouth PL6 5WS
Tel: 03000 066616 Fax: 03000 066665
DX: 8249 Plymouth 3

Scottish Land Registry

Registers of Scotland Executive Agency
Website: www.ros.gov.uk
Head Office: Edinburgh Customer Service Centre, Meadowbank Ho, 153 London Rd, Edinburgh EH8 7AU
Tel: 0800 169 9391
DX: 550906 Edinburgh 9
e-mail: customer.services@ros.gov.uk
Glasgow Customer Service Centre: Hanover Ho, 24 Douglas St, Glasgow G2 7NQ
Tel: 0800 169 9391 Fax: 0141 306 1721
DX: 501752 Glasgow 9
e-mail: customer.services@ros.gov.uk

	Local Authority	No. of stages	From	To	Land Registry Office
Greater London	Barking & Dagenham	1	1 September 1966		Telford
	Barnet	1	1 April 1965		Wales
	Bexley	1	1 January 1961		Croydon
	Brent	1	1 January 1937		Wales
	Bromley	1	1 January 1961		Croydon
	Camden	1	1899		Croydon
	City of London	1	1 July 1902		Wales
	Croydon	2	1 January 1939	15 March 1952	Croydon
	Ealing	1	1 January 1937		Wales
	Enfield	1	1 January 1937		Wales
	Greenwich	1	1900		Telford
	Hackney	1	1899		Wales
	Hammersmith & Fulham	1	1899		Birkenhead
	Haringey	1	1 January 1937		Wales
	Harrow	1	1 January 1937		Wales
	Havering	1	1 February 1967		Birkenhead
	Hillingdon	1	1 January 1937		Wales
	Hounslow	1	1 January 1937		Wales
	Islington	1	1899		Wales
	Kensington & Chelsea	1	1899		Birkenhead
	Kingston upon Thames	1	15 March 1952		Croydon
	Lambeth	1	1900		Telford
	Lewisham	1	1900		Telford
	Merton	1	15 March 1952		Croydon
	Newham	2	1 September 1900	1 April 1965	Telford
	Redbridge	1	1 September 1966		Birkenhead
	Richmond upon Thames	1	1 January 1937		Telford
	Southwark	1	1900		Telford
	Sutton	1	15 March 1952		Croydon
	Tower Hamlets	1	1899		Wales
	Waltham Forest	1	1 February 1967		Wales
	Wandsworth	1	1900		Telford
	Westminster	1	1899		Croydon
Bedfordshire	Bedford	2	1 October 1969	1 September 1974	Peterborough
	Luton	1	1 October 1969		Peterborough
	Mid Bedfordshire (former council)	1	1 November 1985		Peterborough
	South Bedfordshire (former council)	2	1 October 1969	1 September 1974	Peterborough
Berkshire	Bracknell Forest	1	1 April 1963		Gloucester
	Reading	1	1 October 1962		Gloucester
	Slough	1	1 June 1975		Gloucester
	West Berkshire	1	1 April 1963		Gloucester
	Windsor & Maidenhead	2	1 April 1963	1 January 1974	Gloucester
	Wokingham	1	1 April 1963		Gloucester
Bristol	Bristol	1	1 December 1967		Gloucester
Buckinghamshire	Aylesbury Vale	1	1 November 1986		Leicester
	Chiltern	1	1 November 1986		Leicester
	Milton Keynes	1	1 November 1986		Leicester
	South Bucks	1	1 December 1975		Leicester
	Wycombe	1	1 November 1986		Leicester

	Local Authority	No. of stages	From	To	Land Registry Office
Cambridgeshire	Cambridge	1	1 May 1974		Peterborough
	East Cambridgeshire	1	1 December 1988		Peterborough
	Fenland	1	1 December 1988		Peterborough
	Huntingdon	1	1 November 1986		Peterborough
	Peterborough	1	1 March 1977		Peterborough
	South Cambridgeshire	1	1 November 1986		Peterborough
Cheshire	Chester (former council)	2	1 March 1966	1 May 1974	Birkenhead
	Congleton (former council)	1	1 February 1978		Birkenhead
	Crewe & Nantwich (former council)	2	1 July 1967	1 May 1974	Birkenhead
	Ellesmere Port & Neston (former council)	1	1 October 1977		Birkenhead
	Halton	1	1 October 1977		Birkenhead
	Macclesfield (former council)	1	1 February 1978		Birkenhead
	Vale Royal (former council)	1	1 October 1977		Birkenhead
	Warrington	2	1 March 1966	1 September 1974	Birkenhead
Cornwall	Caradon (former council)	1	1 April 1985		Plymouth
	Carrick (former council)	1	1 December 1988		Plymouth
	Kerrier (former council)	1	1 December 1988		Plymouth
	North Cornwall (former council)	1	1 December 1988		Plymouth
	Penwith (former council)	1	1 December 1988		Plymouth
	Restormel (former council)	1	1 April 1985		Plymouth
Cumbria	Allerdale	1	1 November 1986		Durham
	Barrow-in-Furness	1	1 March 1977		Durham
	Carlisle	1	1 November 1986		Durham
	Copeland	1	1 December 1987		Durham
	Eden	1	1 December 1987		Durham
	South Lakeland	1	1 December 1987		Durham
Derbyshire	Amber Valley	1	1 April 1985		Nottingham
	Bolsover	1	1 March 1977		Nottingham
	Chesterfield	1	1 March 1977		Nottingham
	Derby City	1	1 April 1968		Nottingham
	Derbyshire Dales	1	1 December 1987		Nottingham
	Erewash	2	1 December 1969	1 September 1974	Nottingham
	High Peak	1	1 December 1987		Nottingham
	North East Derbyshire	1	1 April 1985		Nottingham
	South Derbyshire	1	1 February 1978		Nottingham
Devon	East Devon	1	1 February 1978		Plymouth
	Exeter	1	1 May 1974		Plymouth
	Mid Devon	1	1 April 1986		Plymouth
	North Devon	1	1 April 1986		Plymouth
	Plymouth	2	1 October 1969	1 January 1974	Plymouth
	South Hams	1	1 February 1978		Plymouth
	Teignbridge	1	1 February 1978		Plymouth
	Torbay	1	1 May 1974		Plymouth
	Torridge	1	1 December 1988		Plymouth
	West Devon	1	1 December 1988		Plymouth

	Local Authority	No. of stages	From	To	Land Registry Office
Dorset	Bournemouth	1	1 March 1977		Weymouth
	Christchurch	1	1 March 1977		Weymouth
	East Dorset	1	1 October 1977		Weymouth
	North Dorset	1	1 April 1990		Weymouth
	Poole	1	1 June 1975		Weymouth
	Purbeck	1	1 April 1990		Weymouth
	West Dorset	1	1 April 1990		Weymouth
	Weymouth & Portland	1	1 October 1977		Weymouth
Durham, Co	Chester-le-Street (former council)	1	1 December 1975		Durham
	City of Durham (former council)	2	1 March 1967	1 May 1974	Durham
	Darlington	2	1 February 1968	1 May 1974	Durham
	Derwentside (former council)	1	1 December 1987		Durham
	Easington (former council)	2	1 February 1968	1 May 1974	Durham
	Hartlepool	2	1 February 1968	1 May 1974	Durham
	Sedgefield (former council)	1	1 December 1975		Durham
	Stockton-on-Tees	2	1 September 1970	1 May 1974	Durham
	Teesdale (former council)	1	1 December 1987		Durham
	Wear Valley (former council)	1	1 December 1987		Durham
East Riding of Yorkshire	East Riding of Yorkshire	3	1 December 1975	1 November 1985	Kingston upon Hull
	Kingston upon Hull	1	1 December 1975		Kingston upon Hull
East Sussex	Brighton & Hove	1	1 October 1965		Durham
	Eastbourne	1	1 January 1926		Durham
	Hastings	1	1 January 1929		Durham
	Lewes	2	1 October 1966	1 June 1975	Durham
	Rother	2	1 October 1966	1 June 1975	Durham
	Wealden	1	1 February 1978		Durham
Essex	Basildon	1	1 March 1977		Peterborough
	Braintree	1	1 November 1986		Peterborough
	Brentwood	1	1 June 1975		Peterborough
	Castle Point	1	1 December 1990		Peterborough
	Chelmsford	1	1 November 1985		Peterborough
	Colchester	1	1 November 1986		Peterborough
	Epping Forest	1	1 March 1977		Peterborough
	Harlow	1	1 March 1977		Peterborough
	Maldon	1	1 December 1990		Peterborough
	Rochford	1	1 December 1990		Peterborough
	Southend-on-Sea	1	1 April 1968		Peterborough
	Tendring	1	1 December 1990		Peterborough
	Thurrock	1	1 June 1975		Peterborough
	Uttlesford	1	1 November 1986		Peterborough
Gloucestershire	Cheltenham	1	1 November 1985		Gloucester
	Cotswold	1	1 November 1986		Gloucester
	Forest of Dean	1	1 November 1986		Gloucester
	Gloucester	1	1 April 1967		Gloucester
	South Gloucestershire	3	1 December 1967	1 April 1985	Gloucester
	Stroud	1	1 November 1986		Gloucester
	Tewkesbury	1	1 November 1986		Gloucester

	Local Authority	No. of stages	From	To	Land Registry Office
Greater Manchester	Bolton	2	1 December 1965	1 January 1974	Fylde
	Bury	2	1 December 1965	1 January 1974	Fylde
	Manchester	2	2 October 1961	1 January 1974	Fylde
	Oldham	4	15 October 1956	1 January 1974	Fylde
	Rochdale	3	1 January 1963	1 January 1974	Fylde
	Salford	4	2 October 1961	1 January 1974	Fylde
	Stockport	2	1 June 1965	1 January 1974	Fylde
	Tameside	2	1 September 1967	1 January 1974	Fylde
	Trafford	2	1 July 1967	1 January 1974	Fylde
	Wigan	1	1 December 1975		Fylde
Hampshire	Basingstoke & Deane	1	1 April 1986		Weymouth
	East Hampshire	1	1 March 1988		Weymouth
	Eastleigh	1	1 October 1977		Weymouth
	Fareham	1	1 October 1977		Weymouth
	Gosport	1	1 October 1977		Weymouth
	Hart	1	1 March 1988		Weymouth
	Havant	1	1 February 1978		Weymouth
	New Forest	1	1 February 1978		Weymouth
	Portsmouth	1	1 December 1975		Weymouth
	Rushmoor	1	1 March 1988		Weymouth
	Southampton	1	1 December 1975		Weymouth
	Test Valley	1	1 March 1988		Weymouth
	Winchester	1	1 March 1988		Weymouth
Herefordshire	Herefordshire	1	1 March 1977		Telford
Hertfordshire	Broxbourne	1	1 March 1977		Leicester
	Dacorum	1	1 November 1985		Leicester
	East Hertfordshire	1	1 February 1978		Leicester
	Hertsmere	3	1 January 1937	1 May 1974	Leicester
	North Hertfordshire	1	1 November 1985		Leicester
	St Albans	1	1 October 1977		Leicester
	Stevenage	1	1 May 1974		Leicester
	Three Rivers	2	1 April 1968	1 May 1974	Leicester
	Watford	1	1 April 1968		Leicester
	Welwyn Hatfield	1	1 March 1977		Leicester
Isle of Wight	Isle of Wight	1	1 April 1986		Weymouth
Isles of Scilly	Isles of Scilly				Plymouth
Kent	Ashford	1	1 October 1958		Nottingham
	Canterbury	2	1 January 1958	1 October 1958	Nottingham
	Dartford	2	1 March 1957	1 January 1961	Nottingham
	Dover	1	1 January 1958		Nottingham
	Gravesham	1	1 March 1957		Nottingham
	Maidstone	1	1 October 1958		Nottingham
	Medway	1	1 March 1957		Nottingham
	Sevenoaks	1	1 January 1961		Nottingham
	Shepway	1	1 October 1958		Nottingham
	Swale	1	1 October 1958		Nottingham
	Thanet	1	1 January 1958		Nottingham
	Tonbridge & Malling	2	1 October 1958	1 January 1961	Nottingham
	Tunbridge Wells	2	1 October 1958	1 January 1961	Nottingham

	Local Authority	No. of stages	From	To	Land Registry Office
Lancashire	Blackburn with Darwen	2	1 June 1962	1 May 1974	Fylde
	Blackpool	1	1 March 1977		Fylde
	Burnley	2	1 October 1965	1 September 1974	Fylde
	Chorley	1	1 April 1986		Fylde
	Fylde	1	1 March 1977		Fylde
	Hyndburn	1	1 April 1985		Fylde
	Lancaster	1	1 March 1988		Fylde
	Pendle	1	1 April 1985		Fylde
	Preston	2	1 October 1965	1 May 1974	Fylde
	Ribble Valley	2	1 September 1974	1 March 1988	Fylde
	Rossendale	1	1 October 1977		Fylde
	South Ribble	1	1 April 1986		Fylde
	West Lancashire	1	1 April 1986		Fylde
	Wyre	1	1 March 1988		Fylde
Leicestershire	Blaby	1	1 March 1977		Leicester
	Charnwood	1	1 October 1977		Leicester
	Harborough	1	1 November 1985		Leicester
	Hinckley & Bosworth	1	1 October 1977		Leicester
	Leicester	1	1 October 1957		Leicester
	Melton	1	1 November 1985		Leicester
	North West Leicestershire	1	1 October 1977		Leicester
	Oadby & Wigston	1	1 March 1977		Leicester
Lincolnshire	Boston	1	1 December 1989		Kingston upon Hull
	East Lindsey	1	1 February 1989		Kingston upon Hull
	Lincoln	1	1 December 1975		Kingston upon Hull
	North East Lincolnshire	2	1 December 1975	1 March 1977	Kingston upon Hull
	North Kesteven	1	1 December 1989		Kingston upon Hull
	North Lincolnshire	2	1 December 1975	1 November 1985	Kingston upon Hull
	South Holland	1	1 December 1989		Kingston upon Hull
	South Kesteven	1	1 December 1989		Kingston upon Hull
	West Lindsey	1	1 February 1989		Kingston upon Hull
Merseyside	Knowsley	1	1 June 1975		Birkenhead
	Liverpool	1	1 December 1969		Birkenhead
	Sefton	1	1 June 1975		Birkenhead
	St Helens	2	1 July 1967	1 March 1974	Birkenhead
	Wirral	2	1 June 1965	1 March 1974	Birkenhead
Norfolk	Breckland	1	1 December 1989		Kingston upon Hull
	Broadland	1	1 December 1989		Kingston upon Hull
	Great Yarmouth	1	1 November 1985		Kingston upon Hull
	King's Lynn & West Norfolk	1	1 December 1989		Kingston upon Hull
	North Norfolk	1	1 December 1989		Kingston upon Hull
	Norwich	2	1 April 1968	1 January 1974	Kingston upon Hull
	South Norfolk	1	1 December 1989		Kingston upon Hull
Northamptonshire	Corby	1	1 November 1985		Leicester
	Daventry	1	1 November 1986		Leicester
	East Northamptonshire	1	1 November 1986		Leicester
	Kettering	1	1 February 1978		Leicester
	Northampton	2	1 April 1968	1 January 1974	Leicester
	South Northamptonshire	1	1 November 1986		Leicester
	Wellingborough	1	1 November 1985		Leicester

	Local Authority	No. of stages	From	To	Land Registry Office
Northumberland	Alnwick (former council)	1	1 December 1989		Durham
	Berwick-upon-Tweed (former council)	1	1 December 1989		Durham
	Blyth Valley (former council)	1	1 June 1975		Durham
	Castle Morpeth (former council)	1	1 November 1986		Durham
	Tynedale (former council)	1	1 December 1989		Durham
	Wansbeck (former council)	1	1 October 1977		Durham
North Yorkshire	City of York	1	1 March 1977		Durham
	Craven	2	1 September 1974	1 November 1985	Durham
	Hambleton	1	1 December 1988		Durham
	Harrogate	1	1 November 1986		Durham
	Middlesbrough	2	1 September 1970	1 January 1974	Durham
	Redcar & Cleveland	2	1 September 1970	1 May 1974	Durham
	Richmondshire	1	1 December 1988		Durham
	Ryedale	1	1 December 1988		Durham
	Scarborough	1	1 December 1988		Durham
	Selby	1	1 November 1986		Durham
4Nottinghamshire	Ashfield	1	1 December 1975		Nottingham
	Bassetlaw	1	1 April 1986		Nottingham
	Broxtowe	2	1 December 1969	1 September 1974	Nottingham
	Gedling	2	1 December 1969	1 September 1974	Nottingham
	Mansfield	1	1 December 1975		Nottingham
	Newark & Sherwood	1	1 April 1986		Nottingham
	Nottingham	2	1 December 1969	1 January 1974	Nottingham
	Rushcliffe	2	1 December 1969	1 September 1974	Nottingham
Oxfordshire	Cherwell	1	1 November 1986		Gloucester
	Oxford	1	1 March 1954		Gloucester
	South Oxfordshire	2	1 April 1963	1 September 1974	Gloucester
	Vale of White Horse	1	1 April 1963		Gloucester
	West Oxfordshire	1	1 November 1986		Gloucester
Rutland	Rutland	1	1 November 1985		Leicester
Shropshire	Bridgnorth (former council)	1	1 April 1988		Telford
	North Shropshire (former council)	1	1 January 1990		Telford
	Oswestry (former council)	1	1 January 1990		Telford
	Shrewsbury & Atcham (former council)	1	1 January 1990		Telford
	South Shropshire (former council)	1	1 January 1990		Telford
	Telford & Wrekin	1	1 April 1986		Telford
Somerset	Bath & North East Somerset	2	1 May 1974	1 April 1985	Plymouth
	Mendip	1	1 December 1989		Weymouth
	North Somerset	1	1 April 1985		Plymouth
	Sedgemoor	1	1 December 1989		Plymouth
	South Somerset	1	1 December 1989		Weymouth
	Taunton Deane	1	1 April 1985		Plymouth
	West Somerset	1	1 April 1986		Plymouth
South Yorkshire	Barnsley	1	1 September 1974		Nottingham
	Doncaster	1	1 September 1974		Nottingham
	Rotherham	1	1 November 1974		Nottingham
	Sheffield	2	1 October 1970	1 March 1974	Nottingham

	Local Authority	No. of stages	From	To	Land Registry Office
Staffordshire	Cannock Chase	1	1 February 1978		Birkenhead
	East Staffordshire	1	1 December 1988		Birkenhead
	Lichfield	1	1 October 1977		Birkenhead
	Newcastle-under-Lyme	1	1 March 1977		Birkenhead
	South Staffordshire	1			Birkenhead
	Stafford	1	1 December 1988		Birkenhead
	Staffordshire Moorlands	1	1 December 1988		Birkenhead
	Stoke-on-Trent	1	1 April 1968		Birkenhead
	Tamworth	1	1 October 1977		Birkenhead
Suffolk	Babergh	1	1 December 1990		Kingston upon Hull
	Forest Heath	1	1 December 1990		Kingston upon Hull
	Ipswich	1	1 May 1974		Kingston upon Hull
	Mid Suffolk	1	1 December 1990		Kingston upon Hull
	St Edmundsbury	1	1 December 1990		Kingston upon Hull
	Suffolk Coastal	1	1 December 1990		Kingston upon Hull
	Waveney	1	1 November 1985		Kingston upon Hull
Surrey	Elmbridge	1	15 March 1952		Durham
	Epsom & Ewell	1	15 March 1952		Durham
	Guildford	1	15 March 1952		Durham
	Mole Valley	1	15 March 1952		Durham
	Reigate & Banstead	1	15 March 1952		Durham
	Runnymede	1	15 March 1952		Durham
	Spelthorne	1	1 January 1937		Durham
	Surrey Heath	1	15 March 1952		Durham
	Tandridge	1	15 March 1952		Durham
	Waverley	1	15 March 1952		Durham
	Woking	1	15 March 1952		Durham
Tyne & Wear	Gateshead	1	1 June 1975		Durham
	Newcastle upon Tyne	2	1 December 1969	1 January 1974	Durham
	North Tyneside	1	1 May 1974		Durham
	South Tyneside	2	1 February 1968	1 January 1974	Durham
	Sunderland	2	1 February 1968	1 January 1974	Durham
Warwickshire	North Warwickshire	1	1 February 1978		Gloucester
	Nuneaton & Bedworth	1	1 February 1965		Gloucester
	Rugby	2	1 February 1965	1 September 1974	Gloucester
	Stratford-upon-Avon	1	1 November 1985		Gloucester
	Warwick	2	1 October 1965	1 September 1974	Gloucester
West Midlands	Birmingham	2	1 February 1965	2 May 1966	Birkenhead
	Coventry	2	1 December 1964	1 March 1974	Birkenhead
	Dudley	2	1 April 1967	1 March 1974	Birkenhead
	Sandwell	1	1 April 1967		Birkenhead
	Solihull	2	1 April 1968	1 March 1974	Birkenhead
	Walsall	2	1 April 1967	1 January 1974	Birkenhead
	Wolverhampton	1	1 April 1967		Birkenhead
West Sussex	Adur	1	1 March 1977		Durham
	Arun	1	1 February 1978		Durham
	Chichester	1	1 April 1986		Durham
	Crawley	2	15 March 1952	1 September 1974	Durham
	Horsham	1	1 April 1986		Durham
	Mid Sussex	2	1 December 1966	1 September 1974	Durham
	Worthing	1	1 March 1977		Durham

	Local Authority	No. of stages	From	To	Land Registry Office
West Yorkshire	Calderdale	1	1 June 1975		Nottingham
	City of Bradford	1	1 September 1974		Nottingham
	Kirklees	2	2 April 1962	1 March 1974	Nottingham
	Leeds	2	1 October 1970	1 March 1974	Nottingham
	Wakefield	1	1 September 1974		Nottingham
Wiltshire	Kennet (former council)	1	1 April 1990		Weymouth
	North Wiltshire (former council)	1	1 April 1990		Weymouth
	Salisbury (former council)	1	1 April 1990		Weymouth
	Swindon	1	1 April 1985		Weymouth
	West Wiltshire (former council)	1	1 April 1986		Weymouth
Worcestershire	Bromsgrove	1	1 March 1977		Gloucester
	Malvern Hills	1	1 December 1990		Gloucester
	Redditch	1	1 April 1986		Gloucester
	Worcester	1	1 March 1977		Gloucester
	Wychavon	1	1 December 1990		Gloucester
	Wyre Forest	1	1 December 1990		Gloucester
Wales	Anglesey	1	1 March 1988		Wales
	Blaenau Gwent	1	1 November 1985		Wales
	Bridgend	1	1 June 1975		Wales
	Caerphilly	2	1 March 1977	1 November 1985	Wales
	Cardiff	2	1 May 1974	1 October 1977	Wales
	Carmarthenshire	2	1 March 1977	1 December 1988	Wales
	Ceredigion (formerly Cardiganshire)	1	1 December 1988		Wales
	Conwy	2	1 March 1988	1 December 1988	Wales
	Denbighshire	2	1 April 1986	1 March 1988	Wales
	Flintshire	1	1 April 1986		Wales
	Gwynedd	1	1 December 1988		Wales
	Merthyr Tydfil	1	1 November 1985		Wales
	Monmouthshire	1	1 November 1985		Wales
	Neath Port Talbot	2	1 June 1975	1 December 1975	Wales
	Newport	2	1 May 1974		Wales
	Pembrokeshire	1	1 December 1988		Wales
	Powys	1	1 March 1988		Wales
	Rhondda Cynon Taff	2	1 October 1977	1 November 1985	Wales
	Swansea	1	1 December 1975		Wales
	Torfaen	1	1 November 1985		Wales
	Vale of Glamorgan	2	1 June 1975	1 December 1975	Wales
	Wrexham	1	1 March 1988		Wales

Part 9

HM Revenue & Customs

HM Revenue & Customs

HM Revenue & Customs
Website: www.gov.uk/government/organisations/hm-revenue-customs
Head Office: 100 Parliament St, London SW1A 2BQ
Tel: 020 7438 6622 (Switchboard) / 0845 3000 627 (Helpline)

Inheritance Tax

Inheritance Tax
Website: www.gov.uk/inheritance-tax
England: Ferrers Ho, PO Box 38, Castle Meadow Rd, Nottingham NG2 1BB
Tel: 0845 302 0900 Fax: 0115 974 2432
DX: 701201 Nottingham 4
Belfast: Dorchester Ho, Level 3, 52–58 Great Victoria St, Belfast BT2 7QL
Tel: 0845 302 0900 Fax: 028 9050 5305
DX: 2001 N R Belfast 2
Scotland: St Mungo's Rd, Cumbernauld, Glasgow G70 5WY
Tel: 0845 302 0900

Stamp Offices

Birmingham Stamp Office
Website: www.gov.uk/business-tax/stamp-taxes
Head Office: 9th Fl, City Centre Ho, 30 Union St, Birmingham B2 4AR
Tel: 0845 603 0135 (Helpline) Fax: 0121 643 7538
DX: 15001 Birmingham 1
Note: Note: All regional correspondence goes to the Birmingham Stamp Office

Valuation Office Agency

Valuation Office Agency
Website: www.gov.uk/government/organisations/valuation-office-agency
Chief Executive's Office: Head Office, Wingate Ho, 93–107 Shaftesbury Ave, London W1D 5BU
Tel: 03000 561700 Fax: 03000 500690
e-mail: dsohelp@voa.gsi.gov.uk

Valuation Offices: England

Valuation Office Agency – Barking
Head Office: 10th Fl, Crown Ho, Linton Rd, Barking IG11 8HJ
Tel: 03000 501501 Fax: 03000 505090
e-mail: ctsouth@voa.gsi.gov.uk

Valuation Office Agency – Barnstaple
Head Office: 2nd Fl, Princess Ho, Queen St, Barnstaple, Devon EX32 8HJ
Tel: 03000 501501 Fax: 03000 504399
e-mail: ctwest@voa.gsi.gov.uk

Valuation Office Agency – Birmingham
Head Office: 14–17 George Rd, Edgbaston, Birmingham B15 1NU
e-mail: ctwest@voa.gsi.gov.uk

Valuation Office Agency – Bournemouth
Head Office: 20 Oxford Rd, Bournemouth BH8 8EF
Tel: 03000 501501 Fax: 03000 501540
e-mail: ctwest@voa.gsi.gov.uk

Valuation Office Agency – Bristol
Head Office: 4th Fl, Citypoint, Temple Gate, Bristol BS1 6PL
Tel: 03000 501501 Fax: 03000 505246
e-mail: ctwest@voa.gsi.gov.uk

Valuation Office Agency – Bromley
Head Office: Unicorn Ho, 28 Elmfield Rd, Bromley, Kent BR1 1LR
Tel: 03000 501501 Fax: 03000 506631
e-mail: ctsouth@voa.gsi.gov.uk

Valuation Office Agency – Cambridge
Head Office: 1st Fl, Eastbrook, Shaftesbury Rd, Cambridge CB2 2DU
Tel: 03000 501501 Fax: 03000 507189
e-mail: cteast@voa.gsi.gov.uk

Valuation Office Agency – Carlisle
Head Office: Rufus Ho, Castle St, Carlisle CA3 8TJ
Tel: 03000 501501 Fax: 03000 505850
e-mail: ctnorth@voa.gsi.gov.uk

Valuation Office Agency – Chatham
Head Office: Anchorage Ho, High St, Chatham, Kent ME4 4WD
Tel: 03000 501501 Fax: 03000 506012
e-mail: ctsouth@voa.gsi.gov.uk

Valuation Office Agency – Coventry
Head Office: 5th Fl, Sherbourne Ho, 1 Manor House Dr, Coventry CV1 2TG
Tel: 03000 501501 Fax: 03000 508901
e-mail: ctwest@voa.gsi.gov.uk

Valuation Office Agency – Crewe
Head Office: 2nd Fl, Wellington Ho, Delamere St, Crewe CW1 2LQ
Tel: 03000 501501 Fax: 03000 507395
e-mail: ctnorth@voa.gsi.gov.uk

Valuation Office Agency – Dorchester
Head Office: 2nd Fl, Vespasian Ho, Bridport Rd, Dorchester, Dorset DT1 1TN
Tel: 01305 327101 Fax: 01305 327199
e-mail: ctwest@voa.gsi.gov.uk

Valuation Office Agency – Durham
Head Office: Wycliffe Ho, Green Lane, Durham DH1 3UW
Tel: 03000 501501 Fax: 03000 501511
e-mail: ctnorth@voa.gsi.gov.uk

Valuation Office Agency – Eastbourne
Head Office: 4th & 5th Fl, St Anne's Ho, 2 St Anne's Rd, Eastbourne, E Sussex BN21 3LG
Tel: 03000 501501 Fax: 03000 500099
e-mail: ctsouth@voa.gsi.gov.uk

Valuation Office Agency – Enfield
Head Office: Chase Ho, 305 Chase Rd, Southgate, London N14 6LZ
Tel: 03000 501501 Fax: 03000 508780
e-mail: ctsouth@voa.gsi.gov.uk

Valuation Office Agency – Exeter
Head Office: 4th Fl, Broadwalk Ho, Southernhay West, Exeter EX1 1TS
Tel: 03000 501501 Fax: 03000 500161
e-mail: ctwest@voa.gsi.gov.uk

Valuation Office Agency – Folkestone
Head Office: 2nd Fl, Palting Ho, Trinity Rd, Folkestone, Kent CT20 2TP
Tel: 03000 501501 Fax: 03000 503755
e-mail: ctsouth@voa.gsi.gov.uk

Valuation Office Agency – Gloucester
Head Office: Ley Court, Barnett Way, Gloucester GL4 7RT
Tel: 03000 501501 Fax: 03000 507799
e-mail: ctwest@voa.gsi.gov.uk

Valuation Office Agency – Guildford
Head Office: 3rd Fl, Bridge Ho, 1 Walnut Tree Cl, Guildford GU1 4GA
Tel: 03000 501501 Fax: 03000 506961
e-mail: ctsouth@voa.gsi.gov.uk

Valuation Office Agency – Halifax
Head Office: 1st, 2nd, 3rd, 4th Floors, 60 Crown St, Halifax HX1 1HY
Tel: 03000 501501 Fax: 03000 502881
e-mail: ctnorth@voa.gsi.gov.uk

Valuation Office Agency – Harrow
Head Office: 3rd Fl, Aspect Gate, 166 College Rd, Harrow HA1 1BH
Tel: 03000 501501 Fax: 020 8427 3609
e-mail: ctsouth@voa.gsi.gov.uk

Valuation Office Agency – Huddersfield (London Support Unit)
Head Office: Ramsden Ho, New St, Huddersfield HD1 2UU
Tel: 03000 501501 Fax: 03000 508151
e-mail: ctsouth@voa.gsi.gov.uk

Valuation Office Agency – Hull
Head Office: Market Place, Hull HU1 1RT
Tel: 03000 501501 Fax: 03000 503497
e-mail: ctnorth@voa.gsi.gov.uk

Valuation Office Agency – Ipswich
Head Office: St Clare House, Greyfriars, Ipswich IP1 1LR
Tel: 03000 501501 Fax: 03000 506022
e-mail: cteast@voa.gsi.gov.uk

Valuation Office Agency – Isle of Wight
Head Office: Broadlands Ho, Staplers Rd, Newport, Isle of Wight PO30 2HX
Tel: 03000 501501 Fax: 01983 558377
e-mail: ctwest@voa.gsi.gov.uk

Valuation Office Agency – Lancaster
Head Office: 1st & 2nd Fl, Mitre Ho, Church St, Lancaster LA1 1HG
Tel: 03000 501501 Fax: 03000 508099
e-mail: ctnorth@voa.gsi.gov.uk

Valuation Office Agency – Leeds
Head Office: Castle Ho, 31 Lisborn St, Leeds LS1 4SA
Tel: 03000 501501 Fax: 03000 508911
e-mail: ctnorth@voa.gsi.gov.uk

Valuation Office Agency – Leicester
Head Office: Grd & 1st Fl, Enkalon Ho, 92 Regent Rd, Leicester LE1 7DD
Tel: 03000 501501 Fax: 03000 505145
e-mail: cteast@voa.gsi.gov.uk

Valuation Office Agency – Lincoln
Head Office: 2nd, 3rd & 4th Fl, Queensgate Ho, 12 Silver St, Lincoln LN2 1EW
Tel: 03000 501501 Fax: 03000 505310
e-mail: cteast@voa.gsi.gov.uk

Valuation Office Agency – Liverpool
Head Office: 2nd & 3rd Fl, 72 Church St, Liverpool L1 3AY
Tel: 03000 501501 Fax: 03000 504140
e-mail: ctnorth@voa.gsi.gov.uk

Valuation Office Agency – Manchester
Head Office: 17th Fl, 53 Portland Tower, Portland St, Manchester M1 3LD
Tel: 03000 501501 Fax: 03000 503683
e-mail: ctnorth@voa.gsi.gov.uk

Valuation Office Agency – Newcastle
Head Office: Eagle Star Ho, Regent Centre, Newcastle-upon-Tyne NE3 3TW
Tel: 03000 501501 Fax: 03000 507303
e-mail: ctnorth@voa.gsi.gov.uk

Valuation Office Agency – Northampton
Head Office: 3rd Fl, Northgate Ho, Sheep St, Northampton NN1 2LL
Tel: 03000 501501 Fax: 03000 506599
e-mail: cteast@voa.gsi.gov.uk

Valuation Office Agency – Norwich
Head Office: 1st Fl, Rosebery Ct, Central Ave, St Andrew's Business Park, Norwich NR7 0HS
Tel: 03000 501501 Fax: 03000 505454
e-mail: cteast@voa.gsi.gov.uk

Valuation Office Agency – Nottingham
Head Office: Ferrers Ho, Castle Meadow Rd, Nottingham NG2 1AB
Tel: 03000 501501 Fax: 03000 500975
e-mail: cteast@voa.gsi.gov.uk

Valuation Office Agency – Oxford
Head Office: 4400 Nash Ct, Oxford Business Centre, Garsington Rd, Oxford OX4 2RU
Tel: 03000 501501 Fax: 03000 506365
e-mail: cteast@voa.gsi.gov.uk

Valuation Office Agency – Peterborough
Head Office: 3rd Fl, Churchgate, New Road, Peterborough PE1 1TT
Tel: 03000 501501 Fax: 03000 507104
e-mail: cteast@voa.gsi.gov.uk

Valuation Office Agency – Plymouth
Head Office: 3rd & 4th Fl, 190 Armada Way, Plymouth, Devon PL1 1EG
Tel: 03000 501501 Fax: 03000 503798
e-mail: ctwest@voa.gsi.gov.uk

Valuation Office Agency – Preston
Head Office: 5th–7th Fl, 104 Lancaster Rd, Preston PR1 1LX
Tel: 03000 501501 Fax: 03000 501041
e-mail: ctnorth@voa.gsi.gov.uk

Valuation Office Agency – Reading
Head Office: 3rd & 4th Fl, Kings Wharf, 20–30 Kings Rd, Reading, Berks RG1 3ER
Tel: 03000 501501 Fax: 03000 501255
e-mail: cteast@voa.gsi.gov.uk

Valuation Office Agency – Reigate
Head Office: Betchworth Ho, 57–65 Station Rd, Redhill RH1 1QB
Tel: 03000 501501 Fax: 03000 503950
e-mail: ctsouth@voa.gsi.gov.uk

Valuation Office Agency – Sheffield
Head Office: Greenfield Ho, 32 Scotland St, Sheffield S3 7DQ
Tel: 03000 501501
e-mail: ctnorth@voa.gsi.gov.uk

Valuation Office Agency – Shrewsbury
Head Office: Darwin Ho, 2 The Mount, Shrewsbury, Shropshire SY3 8PU
Tel: 03000 501501 Fax: 03000 507440
e-mail: ctwest@voa.gsi.gov.uk

Valuation Office Agency – Southampton
Head Office: 2nd Fl, Overline Ho, Central Station, Blechynden Terr, Southampton SO15 1GW
Tel: 03000 501501 Fax: 03000 504370
e-mail: ctwest@voa.gsi.gov.uk

Valuation Office Agency – St Albans
Head Office: St Peters Ho, 45 Victoria St, St Albans AL1 3WZ
Tel: 03000 501501 Fax: 03000 501323
e-mail: cteast@voa.gsi.gov.uk

Valuation Office Agency – St Austell
Head Office: 2nd Fl, Penhaligon Ho, Trinity St, St Austell, Cornwall PL25 5BG
Tel: 03000 501501 Fax: 03000 502799
e-mail: ctwest@voa.gsi.gov.uk

Valuation Office Agency – Stoke-on-Trent
Head Office: 2nd & 3rd Fl, Blackburn Ho, Old Hall St, Hanley, Stoke-on-Trent ST1 3BS
Tel: 03000 501501 Fax: 03000 505771
e-mail: ctwest@voa.gsi.gov.uk

Valuation Office Agency – Taunton
Head Office: Quantock Ho, Paul St, Taunton TA1 3PB
Tel: 03000 501501 Fax: 03000 507025
e-mail: ctwest@voa.gsi.gov.uk

Valuation Office Agency – Teesside
Head Office: 1st Fl, St Marks Ho, St Marks Ct, Thornaby, Stockton-on-Tees TS17 6QS
Tel: 03000 501501 Fax: 03000 504232
e-mail: ctnorth@voa.gsi.gov.uk

Valuation Office Agency – Tower Hamlets
Head Office: 2nd Fl, Cityside, 40 Adler St, London E1 1EE
Tel: 03000 501501 Fax: 03000 504729
e-mail: ctsouth@voa.gsi.gov.uk

Valuation Office Agency – Ulverston
Head Office: 1st & 2nd Fl, Glynis Ho, 25–27 Brogden St, Ulverston LA12 7AT
Tel: 03000 501501 Fax: 03000 505991
e-mail: ctnorth@voa.gsi.gov.uk

Valuation Office Agency – Westminster
Head Office: 2nd Fl, Wingate Ho, 93–107 Shaftesbury Ave, London W1D 5BU
Tel: 03000 501501 Fax: 03000 500692
e-mail: ctsouth@voa.gsi.gov.uk

Valuation Office Agency – Wimbledon
Head Office: 2nd Fl, 1 Francis Grove, Wimbledon, London SW19 4DT
Tel: 03000 501501 Fax: 03000 501182
e-mail: ctsouth@voa.gsi.gov.uk

Valuation Office Agency – Wolverhampton
Head Office: 5th Fl, Crown Ho, Birch St, Wolverhampton WV1 4DS
Tel: 03000 501501 Fax: 03000 507250
e-mail: ctwest@voa.gsi.gov.uk

Valuation Office Agency – Worcester
Head Office: Grd Fl, Block A, Government Bldgs, Whittington Rd, Worcester WR5 2LB
Tel: 03000 501501 Fax: 03000 507707
e-mail: ctwest@voa.gsi.gov.uk

Valuation Office Agency – Worthing
Head Office: 5th & 6th Fl, Westmoreland Ho, Strand Parade, Goring by Sea, Worthing, W.Sussex BN12 6EA
Tel: 03000 501501 Fax: 03000 505672
e-mail: ctsouth@voa.gsi.gov.uk

Valuation Office Agency – York
Head Office: Leeman Ho, Station Business Park, York YO26 4GB
Tel: 03000 501501 Fax: 03000 506435
e-mail: ctnorth@voa.gsi.gov.uk

Valuation Offices: Scotland

Valuation Office Agency – Dumfries
Head Office: Room 001, 3rd Fl, 52–60 Queensberry St, Dumfries DG1 1BF
Tel: 01387 269755 Fax: 01387 250612
e-mail: dumfries.vo@voa.gsi.gov.uk

Valuation Office Agency – North East District Valuer
Head Office: Aberdeen Valuation Office Agency, Greyfriars Ho, Gallowgate, Aberdeen AB10 1JW
Tel: 03000 506240 Fax: 03000 506244
e-mail: scotlandne.vo@voa.gsi.gov.uk

Valuation Office Agency – North West District Valuer
Head Office: Inverness Valuation Office Agency, Baron Taylor's St, Inverness IV1 1QL
Tel: 03000 506300 Fax: 03000 506305
e-mail: scotlandnw.vo@voa.gsi.gov.uk

Valuation Office Agency – South East District Valuer
Head Office: Edinburgh Valuation Agency Office, 50 Frederick St, Edinburgh EH2 1NG
Tel: 03000 506272 Fax: 03000 506277
e-mail: scotlandse.vo@voa.gsi.gov.uk

Valuation Office Agency – South West District Valuer
Glasgow Office: Glasgow Valuation Agency Office, 6th Fl, Portcullis Ho, 21 India St, Glasgow G2 4JJ
Tel: 03000 502750 Fax: 03000 502758
e-mail: scotlandsw.vo@voa.gsi.gov.uk

Valuation Offices: Wales

Valuation Office Agency – Bangor
Head Office: 1st & 2nd Fl, Ty Glyder, 339 High St, Bangor, North Wales LL57 1YA
Tel: 03000 505505 Fax: 03000 504269
e-mail: ctwales@voa.gsi.gov.uk

Valuation Office Agency – Cardiff
Head Office: Ty Rhodfa, Ty Glas Rd, Llanishen, Cardiff CF14 5GR
Tel: 03000 505505 Fax: 03000 507581
e-mail: ctwales@voa.gsi.gov.uk

Valuation Office Agency – Carmarthen
Head Office: 2nd & 3rd Fl, Government Bldgs, Picton Terr, Carmarthen, Dyfed SA31 3BT
Tel: 03000 505505 Fax: 03000 500040
e-mail: ctwales@voa.gsi.gov.uk

Valuation Office Agency – Merthyr Tydfil
Head Office: 1st Fl, Government Bldgs, Castle St, Merthyr Tydfil CF47 8TX
Tel: 03000 505505 Fax: 03000 508026
e-mail: ctwales@voa.gsi.gov.uk

Valuation Office Agency – Newport
Head Office: 2nd Fl, Crown Bldgs, 11 Chepstow Rd, Newport, South Wales NP19 8WA
Tel: 03000 505505 Fax: 03000 507655
e-mail: southwalesgroup.vo@gsi.gov.uk

Valuation Office Agency – Rhyl
Network Support Office: Llys Anwyl, Churton Rd, Rhyl LL18 3NB
Tel: 03000 508387

Valuation Office Agency – Swansea
Head Office: Grd & 1st Fl, Ty Nant, 180 High St, Swansea SA1 1JR
Tel: 03000 505505 Fax: 03000 504194
e-mail: ctwales@voa.gsi.gov.uk

Valuation Office Agency – Wrexham
Head Office: 2nd & 3rd Fl, Regent Ho, Regent St, Wrexham LL11 1PR
Tel: 03000 505505 Fax: 03000 505446
e-mail: ctwales@voa.gsi.gov.uk

Part 10

Probate Registries

Principal Registry

Principal Registry of the Family Division
Website: courttribunalfinder.service.gov.uk/courts/london-probate-department
Court Office: Probate Dept, Principal Registry of the Family Division, First Avenue Ho, 42–49 High Holborn, London WC1V 6NP
Tel: 020 7947 6939 Fax: 020 7947 6946
DX: 941 Lon/Chancery Ln
General Enquiries: Probate Dept – General Enquiries, Principal Registry of the Family Division, as before,
Tel: 0845 302 0900; applications 020 7947 7462/7414
Fax: 020 7947 6946
DX: 941 Lon/Chancery Ln
Office Manager: Probate Dept – Office Manager, G39, Principal Registry of the Family Division, as before,
Tel: 020 7947 6945 Fax: 020 7947 6946
DX: 941 Lon/Chancery Ln
e-mail: ade.ojo@hmcourts-service.gsi.gov.uk

District Probate Registries

Birmingham District Probate Registry
Website: courttribunalfinder.service.gov.uk/courts/birmingham-district-probate-registry
District Registry: Birmingham District Probate Registry, 3rd Fl, Priory Courts, 33 Bull St, Birmingham B4 6DU
Tel: 0121 681 3401
DX: 701990 Birmingham 7
e-mail: birminghamdprsolicitorsenquiries@hmcts.gsi.gov.uk
Subregistry: Nottingham Probate Sub Registry, 60 Canal St, Nottingham NG1 7EJ
Tel: 0121 681 3400
Subregistry: Stoke on Trent Probate Sub Registry, Combined Court Centre, Bethesda St, Hanley, Stoke-on-Trent ST1 3BP
Tel: 01782 854065 Fax: 01782 274916
DX: 703363 Hanley 3

Brighton District Probate Registry
Website: courttribunalfinder.service.gov.uk/courts/brighton-district-probate-registry
District Registry: William St, Brighton BN2 0RF
Tel: 01273 573510 Fax: 01273 625845
DX: 98073 Brighton 3
e-mail: brightondprsolicitorsenquiries@hmcourts-service.gsi.gov.uk
Subregistry: Subregistry, Law Courts, Barker Rd, Maidstone ME18 8EQ
Tel: 01622 202047/8
DX: 130066 Maidstone 7
e-mail: maidstonepsrsolicitorsenquiries@hmcourts-service.gsi.gov.uk

Bristol District Probate Registry
Website: courttribunalfinder.service.gov.uk/courts/bristol-district-probate-registry
District Registry: The Civil Justice Centre, 2 Redcliff St, Bristol BS1 6GR
Tel: 0117 366 4961 Fax: 0117 376 3656
DX: 94400 Bristol 5
e-mail: bristoldprsolicitorsenquiries@hmcourts-service.gsi.gov.uk
Subregistry: Exeter Probate Sub-Registry, Exeter Crown & County Courts, Southernhay Gdns, Exeter EX1 1UH
Tel: 01392 415370 Fax: 01392 415608
DX: 98442 Exeter 2
e-mail: exeterpsrsolicitorsenquiries@hmcourts-service.gsi.gov.uk
Subregistry: Subregistry, Bodmin Probate Sub-Registry, The Law Courts, Launceston Rd, Bodmin PL31 2AL
Tel: 01208 261581 Fax: 01208 775 42
DX: 136847 Bodmin 2
e-mail: bodminpsrsolicitorsenquiries@hmcourts-service.gsi.gov.uk

Ipswich District Probate Registry
Website: courttribunalfinder.service.gov.uk/courts/ipswich-district-probate-registry
District Registry: Ground Fl, 8 Arcade St, Ipswich IP1 1EJ
Tel: 01473 284260
DX: 97733 Ipswich 3
e-mail: ipswichdprsolicitorsenquiries@hmcts.gsi.gov.uk
Subregistry: The Law Courts, Bishopsgate, Norwich NR3 1UR
Tel: 01603 728267
DX: 97390 Norwich 5
Subregistry: 1st Fl, Crown Bldg, Rivergate, Peterborough PE1 1EJ
Tel: 01473 284260
DX: 97733 Ipswich 3

Leeds District Probate Registry
Website: courttribunalfinder.service.gov.uk/courts/leeds-district-probate-registry
District Registry: 2nd Fl, York Ho, 31 York Pl, Leeds LS1 2BA
Tel: 0113 386 3540 Fax: 0113 247 1893
DX: 26451 Park Sq Leeds
e-mail: leedsdprsolicitorsenquiries@hmcts.gsi.gov.uk
Subregistry: 360 High St, Lincoln LN5 7PS
Tel: 01522 523648 Fax: 01522 539903
DX: 703233 Lincoln 6
e-mail: lincolnpsrsolicitorsenquiries@hmcourts-service.gsi.gov.uk
Subregistry: The Law Courts, PO Box 832, 50 West Bar, Sheffield S3 8YR
Tel: 0114 281 2596 Fax: 0114 273 0848
DX: 742916 Sheffield 6
e-mail: sheffieldpsrsolicitorsenquiries@hmcourts-service.gsi.gov.uk

Liverpool District Probate Registry
Website: courttribunalfinder.service.gov.uk/courts/liverpool-district-probate-registry
District Registry: Main Registry, Queen Elizabeth II Law Courts, 2nd Fl East Wing, Derby Sq, Liverpool L2 1XA
Tel: 0151 236 8264 Fax: 0151 227 4634
DX: 14246 Liverpool 1
e-mail: liverpooldprsolicitorsenquiries@hmcts.gsi.gov.uk
Subregistry: Trident Ho, Little John St, Chester CH1 1SN
DX: 702470 Chester 18
Subregistry: 111 Mitre Ho, Church St, Lancaster LA1 1HE
DX: 145883 Lancaster 2

Manchester District Probate Registry
Website: courttribunalfinder.service.gov.uk/courts/manchester-district-probate-registry
District Registry: Civil Justice Centre, Ground Fl, 1 Bridge St West, PO Box 4240, Manchester M60 1WJ
Tel: 0161 240 5702 / 240 5701
DX: 724784 Manchester 44
e-mail: manchesterdprsolicitorsenquiries@hmcts.gsi.gov.uk

Newcastle upon Tyne District Probate Registry
Website: courttribunalfinder.service.gov.uk/courts/newcastle-district-probate-registry
District Registry: 1 Waterloo Sq, Newcastle upon Tyne NE1 4DR
Tel: 0191 211 2170 Fax: 0191 211 2184
DX: 61081 Newcastle 14
e-mail: newcastledprsolicitorsenquiries@hmcts.gsi.gov.uk
Subregistry: Teesside Combined Court Centre, Russell St, Middlesbrough TS1 2AE
Tel: 0191 211 2170
e-mail: newcastledprsolicitorsenquiries@hmcts.gsi.gov.uk
Subregistry: Piccadilly Ho, 55 Piccadilly, York YO1 9WL
Tel: 0113 389 6133
DX: 26451 Leeds Park Sq
e-mail: newcastledprsolicitorsenquiries@hmcts.gsi.gov.uk

Oxford District Probate Registry
Website: courttribunalfinder.service.gov.uk/courts/oxford-district-probate-registry
District Registry: Oxford District Probate Registry, St Aldates, Oxford OX1 1LY
Tel: 01865 793050
DX: 96454 Oxford 4
e-mail: oxforddprenquiries@hmcts.gsi.gov.uk
Subregistry: 2nd Fl, Combined Court Buildings, Kimbrose Way, Gloucester GL1 2DG
Tel: 01452 834966
DX: 98663 Gloucester
e-mail: gloucesterpsrenquiries@hmcts.gsi.gov.uk
Subregistry: 90 Wellington St, Leicester LE1 6HG
Tel: 0116 285 3380
DX: 17403 Leicester 3
e-mail: leicesterpsrenquiries@hmcts.gsi.gov.uk

Winchester District Probate Registry
Website: courttribunalfinder.service.gov.uk/courts/winchester-district-probate-registry
District Registry: 4th Fl, Cromwell Ho, Andover Rd, Winchester SO23 7EW
Tel: 01962 897024
DX: 96900 Winchester 2
e-mail: winchesterdprsolicitorsenquiries@hmcts.gsi.gov.uk

Probate Registry of Wales
Website: courttribunalfinder.service.gov.uk/courts/cardiff-probate-registry-of-wales
District Registry: 3rd Fl, Cardiff Magistrates Court, Fitzalan Pl, Cardiff CF24 0RZ
Tel: 02920 474373
DX: 743940 Cardiff 38
e-mail: cardiffdprenquiries@hmcourts-service.gsi.gov.uk
Subregistry: Carmarthen Hearing Centre, Hill Ho, Picton Terrace, Carmarthen SA31 3BT
Tel: 01267 245035 Fax: 01267 229067
DX: 99574 Carmarthen 2
e-mail: carmarthenpsr@hmcts.gsi.gov.uk
Subregistry: Caernarfon Criminal Justice Centre, Llanberis Rd, Caernarfon LL55 2DF
Tel: 01286 669755 Fax: 01286 671509
DX: 744381 Caernarfon 6
e-mail: caernarfonpsrenquiries@hmcourts-service.gsi.gov.uk

Commissary Registry of Scotland
Website: www.scotcourts.gov.uk
District Registry: Sheriff's Clerk, HM Commissary Office, 27 Chambers St, Edinburgh EH1 1LB
Tel: 0131 225 2525 Fax: 0131 247 2850
DX: 550313 Edinburgh 37
e-mail: cru@scotcourts.gov.uk

Part 11

Rent Assessment Panels and the Rent Service

The Rent Service (TRS) was established on 1 October 1999 as an Executive Agency of the Department for Transport, Local Government and the Regions (DTLR, formerly known as the DETR). It took over the responsibilities of the former Rent Officer Service (established in 1965) which operated through 77 separate units based in local authorities. TRS provides local authorities, tenants, and landlords with expertise in rental evaluations. The Scottish Rent Registration Service fulfils a function similar to the England and Wales Rent Service.

The Residential Property Tribunal Service (RPTS) is an independent body that provides an alternative to the court service in England and Wales. It aims to assist with landlord, tenant and leaseholder disputes over rent and leasehold property. The RPTS comprises one Welsh and five English Rent Assessment Panels. The Scottish Rent Assessment Panel is a non-departmental public body of the Scottish Executive which fulfils the same function.

The Rent Service: England

The Rent Service (within the VOA Office)
Website: www.gov.uk/government/organisations/valuation-office-agency
Head Office: VOA Housing Allowances, Wycliffe Ho, Green Lane, Durham DH1 3UW
Tel: 03000 501501 Fax: 03000 501506
e-mail: nsohelpdesk@voa.gsi.gov.uk
Note: Note: All correspondence for England goes via the Network Support Office

The Rent Officer Service: Wales

North Wales Rent Officer Service
Website: gov.wales/topics/housing-and-regeneration/welfare-reform/rentofficers/
Head Office: Welsh Govt, Sarn Mynach, Llandudno Junction LL31 9RZ
Tel: 0300 062 5106 Fax: 0300 062 5014
e-mail: rentofficerhelpdesk@wales.gsi.gov.uk

South East Wales Rent Officer Service
Website: gov.wales/topics/housing-and-regeneration/welfare-reform/rentofficers/
Head Office: Grnd Fl (North Wing), Welsh Assembly Govt, Merthyr Tydfil Office, Rhydycar, Merthyr Tydfil CF48 1UZ
Tel: 01685 729017 Fax: 01685 729006
e-mail: rentofficerhelpdesk@wales.gsi.gov.uk

South West Wales Rent Officer Service
Website: gov.wales/topics/housing-and-regeneration/welfare-reform/rentofficers/
Head Office: Rent Officers Wales, Government Bldgs, Picton Terrace, Carmarthen SA31 3BT
Tel: 01267 245113 Fax: 01267 245114
e-mail: rentofficerhelpdesk@wales.gsi.gov.uk

Rent Registration Service: Scotland

Rent Service Scotland
Website: www.scotland.gov.uk/rrs
Head Office: 2nd Fl, Endeavor Ho, 1 Greenmarket, Dundee DD1 4QB
Tel: 01382 427555 Fax: 01382 427527
e-mail: rrs.dundee@scotland.gsi.gov.uk

Rent Assessment Panels

Eastern Rent Assessment Panel
Head Office: Residential Property Tribunal Service, Unit C4, Quern Ho, Mill Court, Great Shelford, Cambridge CB22 5LD
Tel: 0845 100 2616 / 01223 841524 Fax: 01223 785129
e-mail: rpeastern@hmcts.gsi.gov.uk

London Rent Assessment Panel
Head Office: Residential Property Tribunal Service, 10 Alfred Pl, London WC1E 7LR
Tel: 020 7446 7700 Fax: 01264 785060
DX: 134205 Tottenham Court Road 2
e-mail: rplondon@hmcts.gsi.gov.uk

Midland Rent Assessment Panel
Head Office: Residential Property Tribunal Service, 3rd Fl, Temple Ct, 35 Bull St, Birmingham B4 6AF
Tel: 0121 681 3084 Fax: 01264 785122
e-mail: rpmidland@hmcts.gsi.gov.uk

Northern Rent Assessment Panel
Head Office: Residential Property Tribunal Service, 1st Fl, Piccadilly Exchange, Piccadilly Plaza, Manchester M1 4AH
Tel: 0845 100 2614/0161 237 9491 Fax: 01264 785128
e-mail: rpnorthern@hmcts.gsi.gov.uk

Scotland Rent Assessment Panel
Website: www.prhpscotland.gov.uk
Head Office: Europa Bldg, 450 Argyle St, Glasgow G2 4LH
Tel: 0141 242 0142 Fax: 0141 242 0141
e-mail: prhpadmin@scotland.gsi.gov.uk

Southern Rent Assessment Panel
Head Office: Residential Property Tribunal Service, round Floor, Magistrates Court and Tribunals Centre, 6 Market Avenue, Chichester PO19 1YE
Tel: 01243 779394 Fax: 0870 7395 900
e-mail: southern.rap@hmcts.gsi.gov.uk

Wales Residential Property Tribunal
Website: rpt.wales.gov.uk
Head Office: Residential Property Tribunal, 1st Fl, West Wing, Southgate Ho, Wood St, Cardiff CF10 1EW
Tel: 029 2092 2777 Fax: 029 2023 6146
e-mail: rpt@wales.gsi.gov.uk

Part 12

High Court Enforcement Officers

As from April 1, 2004, a new regime for High Court enforcement came into effect in England and Wales.

Previous to this date, enforcement of High Court writs of fieri facias and Writs of possession (collectively known as 'writs of execution') was carried out in the name of the High Sheriff for each bailiwick. (A 'bailiwick' being the area under the jurisdiction of the High Sheriff, these areas being roughly equivalent to the pre–1974 county boundaries).

From April 1, 2004, all this changed. Incoming High Sheriffs who take office from that date are being removed from their obligation from enforcing these High Court writs.

Instead, High Court writs of execution are now being enforced by "enforcement officers" appointed and assigned to districts by the Lord Chancellor or his nominated delegate. This directory contains a list of all those appointed as enforcement officers, and the postal districts to which they have been assigned. It also contains their contact details.

An enforcement officer is obliged to accept any writ forwarded to him or her for the postal districts to which they have been assigned. They also have the discretion to accept writs for anywhere in England and Wales, but may decline to accept the writ if it is for an area to which they have not sought assignment.

Many regular court users may already have regular dealings with High Court enforcement officers, and may know who they wish to approach to enforce their writs. However, many creditors may be unfamiliar with the system of High Court enforcement, and not know who they wish to enforce their writs on their behalf. This directory contains details of all those appointed and to which areas they have been assigned. It also contains the address of the National Information Centre for Enforcement, where you may send your writ for automatic allocation to a High Court enforcement officer for the relevant postal district, using the "cab rank" principle.

Their contact details are below:

National Information Office

National Information Centre for Enforcement
Head Office: c/o Registry Trust Ltd, 153–157 Cleveland St, London W1T 6QW
Tel: 020 7391 7299
DX: 134211 Tottenham Ct Rd 2

Enforcement Officers by District

Bath BA
ANDERSON, Michael
ARNOLD, John
ASKER, David
BADGER, Chris
BARNETT, Simon
DEAN, Derek
DEAN, Gordon
DUNCAN, Andrew
EGMORE, Angela
EVANS, Philip
FARRINGTON, Patrick
GATER, Jonathan
HARRISON, Karl
HORNER, Nigel
JAMES, John (AW)
KIMBER, Michael
LEYSHON, Martin
MARSTON, John
METCALFE, James William
MORGAN, Ian
PEPPER, Nigel
SANDBROOK, Claire
SMITH, Alan (S)
SOUTHERN, Norman
THOMSON, Patricia
VANN, Edward
WILSON, Andrew

Birmingham B
ANDERSON, Michael
ARNOLD, John
ASKER, David
BADGER, Chris
BUTLER, Malcolm
CADDY, Paul
DEAN, Derek
DEAN, Gordon
DUNCAN, Andrew
EDDOWES, Mark
EVANS, Philip
FARRINGTON, Patrick
GATER, Jonathan
HARRISON, Karl
HUGHES, Gareth
HORNER, Nigel
JAMES, John (A)
JACKSON, Michael
JAMES, John (AW)
KIMBER, Michael
LEYSHON, Martin
MARSTON, John
METCALFE, James William
MORGAN, Ian
PEPPER, Nigel
SANDBROOK, Claire
SMITH, Alan (JM)
SMITH, Alan (S)
SOUTHERN, Norman

THOMSON, Patricia
VANN, Edward
WILLIAMSON, Simon
WILSON, Andrew

Blackburn BB
ARNOLD, John
ASKER, David
BADGER, Chris
BOVAN, Gary
DEAN, Derek
DEAN, Gordon
HARRISON, Karl
MARSTON, John
METCALFE, James William
MORGAN, Ian
SANDBROOK, Claire
SMITH, Alan (S)
SOUTHERN, Norman
THOMSON, Patricia
VANN, Edward
WILSON, Andrew

Bolton BL
ARNOLD, John
ASKER, David
BADGER, Chris
DEAN, Derek
DEAN, Gordon
HARRISON, Karl
MARSTON, John
METCALFE, James William
MORGAN, Ian
SANDBROOK, Claire
SMITH, Alan (S)
SOUTHERN, Norman
THOMSON, Patricia
VANN, Edward
WILSON, Andrew

Bournemouth BH
ARNOLD, John
ASKER, David
BADGER, Chris
BARNETT, Simon
DEAN, Derek
DEAN, Gordon
EGMORE, Angela
GATER, Jonathan
HARRISON, Karl
MARSTON, John
METCALFE, James William
MORGAN, Ian
SANDBROOK, Claire
SMITH, Alan (S)
SOUTHERN, Norman
THOMSON, Patricia
VANN, Edward
WATT, Peter
WILSON, Andrew

Bradford BD
ARNOLD, John
ASKER, David
BADGER, Chris
BOVAN, Gary
DEAN, Derek
DEAN, Gordon
HARRISON, Karl
MARSTON, John
METCALFE, James William
MORGAN, Ian
SANDBROOK, Claire
SMITH, Alan (S)
SOUTHERN, Norman
THOMSON, Patricia
VANN, Edward
WHITWORTH, Frank
WILSON, Andrew

Brighton BN
ARNOLD, John
ASKER, David
BADGER, Chris
DEAN, Derek
DEAN, Gordon
GATER, Jonathan
HARRISON, Karl
MARSTON, John
METCALFE, James William
MORGAN, Ian
SANDBROOK, Claire
SMITH, Alan (S)
SOUTHERN, Norman
THOMSON, Patricia
VANN, Edward
WATT, Peter
WILSON, Andrew

Bristol BS
ALEXANDER, Nicholas
ANDERSON, Michael
ARNOLD, John
ASKER, David
BADGER, Chris
DEAN, Derek
DEAN, Gordon
DUNCAN, Andrew
EVANS, Philip
EWART-JAMES, Andrew
FARRINGTON, Patrick
GATER, Jonathan
HARRISON, Karl
HORNER, Nigel
JAMES, John (AW)
KIMBER, Michael
LEYSHON, Martin
MARSTON, John
METCALFE, James William
MORGAN, Ian
PEPPER, Nigel
SANDBROOK, Claire
SMITH, Alan (S)
SOUTHERN, Norman
THOMSON, Patricia
VANN, Edward
WATT, Peter
WILSON, Andrew

Bromley BR
ARNOLD, John
ASKER, David
BADGER, Chris
BUTLER, Malcolm
CADDY, Paul
DEAN, Derek
DEAN, Gordon
EDDOWES, Mark
GATER, Jonathan
HARRISON, Karl
HUGHES, Gareth

JACKSON, Michael
JAMES, John (A)
MARSTON, John
METCALFE, James William
MORGAN, Ian
SANDBROOK, Claire
SMITH, Alan (JM)
SMITH, Alan (S)
SOUTHERN, Norman
THOMSON, Patricia
VANN, Edward
WATT, Peter
WILLIAMSON, Simon
WILSON, Andrew

Cambridge CB
ARNOLD, John
ASKER, David
BADGER, Chris
DEAN, Derek
DEAN, Gordon
HALL, Brian
HARRISON, Karl
MARSTON, John
METCALFE, James William
MORGAN, Ian
SANDBROOK, Claire
SMITH, Alan (S)
SOUTHERN, Norman
THOMSON, Patricia
VANN, Edward
WATT, Peter
WILSON, Andrew

Canterbury CT
ARNOLD, John
ASKER, David
BADGER, Chris
DEAN, Derek
DEAN, Gordon
GATER, Jonathan
HARRISON, Karl
MARSTON, John
METCALFE, James William
MORGAN, Ian
SANDBROOK, Claire
SMITH, Alan (S)
SOUTHERN, Norman
THOMSON, Patricia
VANN, Edward
WILSON, Andrew

Cardiff CF
ANDERSON, Michael
ARNOLD, John
ASKER, David
BADGER, Chris
DEAN, Derek
DEAN, Gordon
DUNCAN, Andrew
EVANS, Philip
FARRINGTON, Patrick
GATER, Jonathan
HARRISON, Karl
HORNER, Nigel
JAMES, John (AW)
KIMBER, Michael
LEYSHON, Martin
MARSTON, John
METCALFE, James William
MORGAN, Ian
PEPPER, Nigel
SANDBROOK, Claire
SMITH, Alan (S)
SOUTHERN, Norman
THOMSON, Patricia
VANN, Edward
WATT, Peter
WILSON, Andrew

Carlisle CA
ARNOLD, John
ASKER, David
BADGER, Chris
DEAN, Derek
DEAN, Gordon
HARRISON, Karl
MARSTON, John
METCALFE, James William
MORGAN, Ian
SANDBROOK, Claire
SMITH, Alan (S)
SOUTHERN, Norman
THOMSON, Patricia
VANN, Edward
WILSON, Andrew

Chelmsford CM
ARNOLD, John
ASKER, David
BADGER, Chris
BUTLER, Malcolm
CADDY, Paul
DEAN, Derek
DEAN, Gordon
EDDOWES, Mark
HARRISON, Karl
HUGHES, Gareth
JACKSON, Michael
JAMES, John (A)
MARSTON, John
METCALFE, James William
MORGAN, Ian
SANDBROOK, Claire
SMITH, Alan (JM)
SMITH, Alan (S)
SOUTHERN, Norman
THOMSON, Patricia
TUNSTILL, Peter
VANN, Edward
WATT, Peter
WILLIAMSON, Simon
WILSON, Andrew

Chester CH
ANDERSON, Michael
ARNOLD, John
ASKER, David
BADGER, Chris
BOVAN, Gary
DEAN, Derek
DEAN, Gordon
DUNCAN, Andrew
EVANS, Philip
FARRINGTON, Patrick
GATER, Jonathan
HARRISON, Karl
HORNER, Nigel
JAMES, John (AW)
KIMBER, Michael

LEYSHON, Martin
MARSTON, John
MASON, David
METCALFE, James William
MORGAN, Ian
PEPPER, Nigel
SANDBROOK, Claire
SMITH, Alan (S)
SOUTHERN, Norman
THOMSON, Patricia
VANN, Edward
WILSON, Andrew

Cleveland (Teesside) TS
ARNOLD, John
ASKER, David
BADGER, Chris
DAVIES, Malcolm
DEAN, Derek
DEAN, Gordon
FELLOWS, Kathleen
HARRISON, Karl
MARSTON, John
METCALFE, James William
MORGAN, Ian
SANDBROOK, Claire
SMITH, Alan (S)
SOUTHERN, Norman
THOMSON, Patricia
VANN, Edward
WILSON, Andrew

Colchester CO
ARNOLD, John
ASKER, David
BADGER, Chris
DEAN, Derek
DEAN, Gordon
HARRISON, Karl
MARSTON, John
METCALFE, James William
MORGAN, Ian
SANDBROOK, Claire
SMITH, Alan (S)
SOUTHERN, Norman
THOMSON, Patricia
VANN, Edward
WATT, Peter
WILSON, Andrew

Coventry CV
ANDERSON, Michael
ARNOLD, John
ASKER, David
BADGER, Chris
BUTLER, Malcolm
CADDY, Paul
DEAN, Derek
DEAN, Gordon
DUNCAN, Andrew
EDDOWES, Mark
EVANS, Philip
FARRINGTON, Patrick
GATER, Jonathan
HARRISON, Karl
HUGHES, Gareth
HORNER, Nigel
JACKSON, Michael
JAMES, John (A)
JAMES, John (AW)
KIMBER, Michael
LEYSHON, Martin
MARSTON, John
METCALFE, James William
MORGAN, Ian
PEPPER, Nigel
SANDBROOK, Claire
SMITH, Alan (JM)
SMITH, Alan (S)
SOUTHERN, Norman
THOMSON, Patricia
VANN, Edward
WILLIAMSON, Simon
WILSON, Andrew

Crewe CW
ANDERSON, Michael
ARNOLD, John
ASKER, David
BADGER, Chris
BOVAN, Gary
DEAN, Derek
DEAN, Gordon
DUNCAN, Andrew
EVANS, Philip
FARRINGTON, Patrick
GATER, Jonathan
HARRISON, Karl
HORNER, Nigel
JAMES, John (AW)
KIMBER, Michael
LEYSHON, Martin
MARSTON, John
MASON, David
METCALFE, James William
MORGAN, Ian
PEPPER, Nigel
SANDBROOK, Claire
SMITH, Alan (S)
SOUTHERN, Norman
THOMSON, Patricia
VANN, Edward
WILSON, Andrew

Croydon CR
ARNOLD, John
ASKER, David
BADGER, Chris
BUTLER, Malcolm
CADDY, Paul
DEAN, Derek
DEAN, Gordon
EDDOWES, Mark
GATER, Jonathan
HARRISON, Karl
HUGHES, Gareth
JACKSON, Michael
JAMES, John (A)
MARSTON, John
METCALFE, James William
MORGAN, Ian
SANDBROOK, Claire
SMITH, Alan (JM)
SMITH, Alan (S)
SOUTHERN, Norman
THOMSON, Patricia
VANN, Edward
WATT, Peter
WILLIAMSON, Simon

WILSON, Andrew

Darlington DL
ARNOLD, John
ASKER, David
BADGER, Chris
DAVIES, Malcolm
DEAN, Derek
DEAN, Gordon
FELLOWS, Kathleen
HARRISON, Karl
MARSTON, John
METCALFE, James William
MORGAN, Ian
SANDBROOK, Claire
SMITH, Alan (S)
SOUTHERN, Norman
THOMSON, Patricia
VANN, Edward
WILSON, Andrew

Dartford DA
ARNOLD, John
ASKER, David
BADGER, Chris
BUTLER, Malcolm
CADDY, Paul
DEAN, Derek
DEAN, Gordon
EDDOWES, Mark
GATER, Jonathan
HARRISON, Karl
HUGHES, Gareth
JACKSON, Michael
JAMES, John (A)
MARSTON, John
METCALFE, James William
MORGAN, Ian
SANDBROOK, Claire
SMITH, Alan (JM)
SMITH, Alan (S)
SOUTHERN, Norman
THOMSON, Patricia
VANN, Edward
WATT, Peter
WILLIAMSON, Simon
WILSON, Andrew

Derby DE
ANDERSON, Michael
ARNOLD, John
ASKER, David
BADGER, Chris
BUTLER, Malcolm
CADDY, Paul
DEAN, Derek
DEAN, Gordon
DUNCAN, Andrew
EDDOWES, Mark
EVANS, Philip
FARRINGTON, Patrick
GATER, Jonathan
HARRISON, Karl
HUGHES, Gareth
HORNER, Nigel
JACKSON, Michael
JAMES, John (A)
JAMES, John (AW)
KIMBER, Michael
LEYSHON, Martin
MARSTON, John
METCALFE, James William
MORGAN, Ian
PEPPER, Nigel
SANDBROOK, Claire
SMITH, Alan (JM)
SMITH, Alan (S)
SOUTHERN, Norman
THOMSON, Patricia
VANN, Edward
WILLIAMSON, Simon
WILSON, Andrew

Doncaster DN
ARNOLD, John
ASKER, David
BADGER, Chris
BAITSON, Michael
BUTLER, Malcolm
CADDY, Paul
DEAN, Derek
DEAN, Gordon
EDDOWES, Mark
HARRISON, Karl
HUGHES, Gareth
JACKSON, Michael
JAMES, John (A)
MARSTON, John
METCALFE, James William
MORGAN, Ian
SANDBROOK, Claire
SMITH, Alan (JM)
SMITH, Alan (S)
SOUTHERN, Norman
THOMSON, Patricia
VANN, Edward
WILLIAMSON, Simon
WILSON, Andrew

Dorchester DT
ARNOLD, John
ASKER, David
BADGER, Chris
BARNETT, Simon
DEAN, Derek
DEAN, Gordon
EGMORE, Angela
HARRISON, Karl
MARSTON, John
METCALFE, James William
MORGAN, Ian
SANDBROOK, Claire
SMITH, Alan (S)
SOUTHERN, Norman
THOMSON, Patricia
VANN, Edward
WILSON, Andrew

Dudley DY
ANDERSON, Michael
ARNOLD, John
ASKER, David
BADGER, Chris
BUTLER, Malcolm
CADDY, Paul
DEAN, Derek
DEAN, Gordon
DUNCAN, Andrew
EDDOWES, Mark
EVANS, Philip

FARRINGTON, Patrick
GATER, Jonathan
HARRISON, Karl
HUGHES, Gareth
HORNER, Nigel
JACKSON, Michael
JAMES, John (A)
JAMES, John (AW)
KIMBER, Michael
LEYSHON, Martin
MARSTON, John
METCALFE, James William
MORGAN, Ian
PEPPER, Nigel
SANDBROOK, Claire
SMITH, Alan (JM)
SMITH, Alan (S)
SOUTHERN, Norman
THOMSON, Patricia
VANN, Edward
WILLIAMSON, Simon
WILSON, Andrew

Durham DH
ARNOLD, John
ASKER, David
BADGER, Chris
DAVIES, Malcolm
DEAN, Derek
DEAN, Gordon
FELLOWS, Kathleen
HARRISON, Karl
MARSTON, John
METCALFE, James William
MORGAN, Ian
SANDBROOK, Claire
SMITH, Alan (S)
SOUTHERN, Norman
THOMSON, Patricia
VANN, Edward
WILSON, Andrew

Enfield EN
ARNOLD, John
ASKER, David
BADGER, Chris
BUTLER, Malcolm
CADDY, Paul
DEAN, Derek
DEAN, Gordon
EDDOWES, Mark
HARRISON, Karl
HUGHES, Gareth
JACKSON, Michael
JAMES, John (A)
MARSTON, John
METCALFE, James William
MORGAN, Ian
SANDBROOK, Claire
SMITH, Alan (JM)
SMITH, Alan (S)
SOUTHERN, Norman
THOMSON, Patricia
TUNSTILL, Peter
VANN, Edward
WATT, Peter
WILLIAMSON, Simon
WILSON, Andrew

Exeter EX
ARNOLD, John
ASKER, David
BADGER, Chris
BARNETT, Simon
DEAN, Derek
DEAN, Gordon
EGMORE, Angela
HARRISON, Karl
MARSTON, John
METCALFE, James William
MORGAN, Ian
SANDBROOK, Claire
SMITH, Alan (S)
SOUTHERN, Norman
THOMSON, Patricia
VANN, Edward
WILSON, Andrew

Fylde (Blackpool) FY
ARNOLD, John
ASKER, David
BADGER, Chris
DEAN, Derek
DEAN, Gordon
HARRISON, Karl
MARSTON, John
METCALFE, James William
MORGAN, Ian
SANDBROOK, Claire
SMITH, Alan (S)
SOUTHERN, Norman
THOMSON, Patricia
VANN, Edward
WILSON, Andrew

Gloucester GL
ALEXANDER, Nicholas
ANDERSON, Michael
ARNOLD, John
ASKER, David
BADGER, Chris
DEAN, Derek
DEAN, Gordon
DUNCAN, Andrew
EVANS, Philip
EWART-JAMES, Andrew
FARRINGTON, Patrick
GATER, Jonathan
HARRISON, Karl
HORNER, Nigel
JAMES, John (AW)
KIMBER, Michael
LEYSHON, Martin
MARSTON, John
METCALFE, James William
MORGAN, Ian
PEPPER, Nigel
SANDBROOK, Claire
SMITH, Alan (S)
SOUTHERN, Norman
THOMSON, Patricia
VANN, Edward
WATT, Peter
WILSON, Andrew

Guildford GU
ANDERSON, Michael
ARNOLD, John
ASKER, David

BADGER, Chris
BUTLER, Malcolm
CADDY, Paul
DEAN, Derek
DEAN, Gordon
DUNCAN, Andrew
EDDOWES, Mark
EVANS, Philip
FARRINGTON, Patrick
GATER, Jonathan
HARRISON, Karl
HUGHES, Gareth
HORNER, Nigel
JACKSON, Michael
JAMES, John (A)
JAMES, John (AW)
KIMBER, Michael
LEYSHON, Martin
MARSTON, John
METCALFE, James William
MORGAN, Ian
PEPPER, Nigel
SANDBROOK, Claire
SMITH, Alan (JM)
SMITH, Alan (S)
SOUTHERN, Norman
THOMSON, Patricia
VANN, Edward
WATT, Peter
WILLIAMSON, Simon
WILSON, Andrew

Halifax HX
ARNOLD, John
ASKER, David
BADGER, Chris
BOVAN, Gary
DEAN, Derek
DEAN, Gordon
HARRISON, Karl
MARSTON, John
METCALFE, James William
MORGAN, Ian
SANDBROOK, Claire
SMITH, Alan (S)
SOUTHERN, Norman
THOMSON, Patricia
VANN, Edward
WHITWORTH, Frank
WILSON, Andrew

Harrogate HG
ARNOLD, John
ASKER, David
BADGER, Chris
BOVAN, Gary
DEAN, Derek
DEAN, Gordon
HARRISON, Karl
MARSTON, John
METCALFE, James William
MORGAN, Ian
SANDBROOK, Claire
SMITH, Alan (S)
SOUTHERN, Norman
THOMSON, Patricia
VANN, Edward
WHITWORTH, Frank
WILSON, Andrew

Harrow HA
ARNOLD, John
ASKER, David
BADGER, Chris
BUTLER, Malcolm
CADDY, Paul
DEAN, Derek
DEAN, Gordon
EDDOWES, Mark
GATER, Jonathan
HARRISON, Karl
HUGHES, Gareth
JACKSON, Michael
JAMES, John (A)
KIMBER, Michael
MARSTON, John
METCALFE, James William
MORGAN, Ian
SANDBROOK, Claire
SMITH, Alan (JM)
SMITH, Alan (S)
SOUTHERN, Norman
THOMSON, Patricia
VANN, Edward
WATT, Peter
WILLIAMSON, Simon
WILSON, Andrew

Hemel Hempstead HP
ANDERSON, Michael
ARNOLD, John
ASKER, David
BADGER, Chris
BUTLER, Malcolm
CADDY, Paul
DEAN, Derek
DEAN, Gordon
DUNCAN, Andrew
EDDOWES, Mark
EVANS, Philip
FARRINGTON, Patrick
GATER, Jonathan
HARRISON, Karl
HUGHES, Gareth
HORNER, Nigel
JACKSON, Michael
JAMES, John (A)
JAMES, John (AW)
KIMBER, Michael
LEYSHON, Martin
MARSTON, John
METCALFE, James William
MORGAN, Ian
PEPPER, Nigel
SANDBROOK, Claire
SMITH, Alan (JM)
SMITH, Alan (S)
SOUTHERN, Norman
THOMSON, Patricia
TUNSTILL, Peter
VANN, Edward
WATT, Peter
WILLIAMSON, Simon
WILSON, Andrew

Hereford HR
ALEXANDER, Nicholas
ANDERSON, Michael
ARNOLD, John

ASKER, David
BADGER, Chris
BUTLER, Malcolm
CADDY, Paul
DEAN, Derek
DEAN, Gordon
DUNCAN, Andrew
EDDOWES, Mark
EVANS, Philip
EWART-JAMES, Andrew
FARRINGTON, Patrick
GATER, Jonathan
HARRISON, Karl
HUGHES, Gareth
HORNER, Nigel
JACKSON, Michael
JAMES, John (A)
JAMES, John (AW)
KIMBER, Michael
LEYSHON, Martin
MARSTON, John
METCALFE, James William
MORGAN, Ian
PEPPER, Nigel
SANDBROOK, Claire
SMITH, Alan (JM)
SMITH, Alan (S)
SOUTHERN, Norman
THOMSON, Patricia
VANN, Edward
WATT, Peter
WILLIAMSON, Simon
WILSON, Andrew

Huddersfield HD
ARNOLD, John
ASKER, David
BADGER, Chris
BOVAN, Gary
DEAN, Derek
DEAN, Gordon
HARRISON, Karl
MARSTON, John
METCALFE, James William
MORGAN, Ian
SANDBROOK, Claire
SMITH, Alan (S)
SOUTHERN, Norman
THOMSON, Patricia
VANN, Edward
WHITWORTH, Frank
WILSON, Andrew

Hull HU
ARNOLD, John
ASKER, David
BADGER, Chris
BAITSON, Michael
DEAN, Derek
DEAN, Gordon
HARRISON, Karl
MARSTON, John
METCALFE, James William
MORGAN, Ian
SANDBROOK, Claire
SMITH, Alan (S)
SOUTHERN, Norman
THOMSON, Patricia
VANN, Edward
WILSON, Andrew

Ilford IG
ARNOLD, John
ASKER, David
BADGER, Chris
BUTLER, Malcolm
CADDY, Paul
DEAN, Derek
DEAN, Gordon
EDDOWES, Mark
GATER, Jonathan
HARRISON, Karl
HUGHES, Gareth
JACKSON, Michael
JAMES, John (A)
MARSTON, John
METCALFE, James William
MORGAN, Ian
SANDBROOK, Claire
SMITH, Alan (JM)
SMITH, Alan (S)
SOUTHERN, Norman
THOMSON, Patricia
VANN, Edward
WATT, Peter
WILLIAMSON, Simon
WILSON, Andrew

Ipswich IP
ARNOLD, John
ASKER, David
BADGER, Chris
DEAN, Derek
DEAN, Gordon
HALL, Brian
HARRISON, Karl
MARSTON, John
METCALFE, James William
MORGAN, Ian
SANDBROOK, Claire
SMITH, Alan (S)
SOUTHERN, Norman
THOMSON, Patricia
VANN, Edward
WATT, Peter
WILSON, Andrew

Kingston upon Thames KT
ARNOLD, John
ASKER, David
BADGER, Chris
BUTLER, Malcolm
CADDY, Paul
DEAN, Derek
DEAN, Gordon
EDDOWES, Mark
GATER, Jonathan
HARRISON, Karl
HUGHES, Gareth
JACKSON, Michael
JAMES, John (A)
KIMBER, Michael
MARSTON, John
METCALFE, James William
MORGAN, Ian
SANDBROOK, Claire
SMITH, Alan (JM)
SMITH, Alan (S)
SOUTHERN, Norman

THOMSON, Patricia
VANN, Edward
WATT, Peter
WILLIAMSON, Simon
WILSON, Andrew

Lancaster LA
ARNOLD, John
ASKER, David
BADGER, Chris
DEAN, Derek
DEAN, Gordon
HARRISON, Karl
MARSTON, John
METCALFE, James William
MORGAN, Ian
SANDBROOK, Claire
SMITH, Alan (S)
SOUTHERN, Norman
THOMSON, Patricia
VANN, Edward
WILSON, Andrew

Leeds LS
ARNOLD, John
ASKER, David
BADGER, Chris
BOVAN, Gary
DEAN, Derek
DEAN, Gordon
HARRISON, Karl
MARSTON, John
METCALFE, James William
MORGAN, Ian
SANDBROOK, Claire
SMITH, Alan (S)
SOUTHERN, Norman
THOMSON, Patricia
VANN, Edward
WHITWORTH, Frank
WILSON, Andrew

Leicester LE
ANDERSON, Michael
ARNOLD, John
ASKER, David
BADGER, Chris
BUTLER, Malcolm
CADDY, Paul
DEAN, Derek
DEAN, Gordon
DUNCAN, Andrew
EDDOWES, Mark
EVANS, Philip
FARRINGTON, Patrick
GATER, Jonathan
HARRISON, Karl
HUGHES, Gareth
HORNER, Nigel
JACKSON, Michael
JAMES, John (A)
JAMES, John (AW)
KIMBER, Michael
LEYSHON, Martin
MARSTON, John
METCALFE, James William
MORGAN, Ian
PEPPER, Nigel
SANDBROOK, Claire
SMITH, Alan (JM)
SMITH, Alan (S)
SOUTHERN, Norman
THOMSON, Patricia
VANN, Edward
WATT, Peter
WILLIAMSON, Simon
WILSON, Andrew

Lincoln LN
ARNOLD, John
ASKER, David
BADGER, Chris
BAITSON, Michael
BUTLER, Malcolm
CADDY, Paul
DEAN, Derek
DEAN, Gordon
EDDOWES, Mark
HARRISON, Karl
HUGHES, Gareth
JACKSON, Michael
JAMES, John (A)
MARSTON, John
METCALFE, James William
MORGAN, Ian
SANDBROOK, Claire
SMITH, Alan (JM)
SMITH, Alan (S)
SOUTHERN, Norman
THOMSON, Patricia
VANN, Edward
WILLIAMSON, Simon
WILSON, Andrew

Liverpool L
ARNOLD, John
ASKER, David
BADGER, Chris
BOVAN, Gary
DEAN, Derek
DEAN, Gordon
HARRISON, Karl
MARSTON, John
MASON, David
METCALFE, James William
MORGAN, Ian
SANDBROOK, Claire
SMITH, Alan (S)
SOUTHERN, Norman
THOMSON, Patricia
VANN, Edward
WILSON, Andrew

Llandrindod Wells LD
ANDERSON, Michael
ARNOLD, John
ASKER, David
BADGER, Chris
DEAN, Derek
DEAN, Gordon
DUNCAN, Andrew
EVANS, Philip
FARRINGTON, Patrick
GATER, Jonathan
HARRISON, Karl
HORNER, Nigel
JAMES, John (AW)
KIMBER, Michael
LEYSHON, Martin
MARSTON, John

METCALFE, James William
MORGAN, Ian
PEPPER, Nigel
SANDBROOK, Claire
SMITH, Alan (S)
SOUTHERN, Norman
THOMSON, Patricia
VANN, Edward
WATT, Peter
WILSON, Andrew

Llandudno LL
ANDERSON, Michael
ARNOLD, John
ASKER, David
BADGER, Chris
DEAN, Derek
DEAN, Gordon
DUNCAN, Andrew
EVANS, Philip
FARRINGTON, Patrick
GATER, Jonathan
HARRISON, Karl
HORNER, Nigel
JAMES, John (AW)
KIMBER, Michael
LEYSHON, Martin
MARSTON, John
METCALFE, James William
MORGAN, Ian
PEPPER, Nigel
SANDBROOK, Claire
SMITH, Alan (S)
SOUTHERN, Norman
THOMSON, Patricia
VANN, Edward LL
WILSON, Andrew

London East E
ARNOLD, John
ASKER, David
BADGER, Chris
BUTLER, Malcolm
CADDY, Paul
DEAN, Derek
DEAN, Gordon
EDDOWES, Mark
GATER, Jonathan
HARRISON, Karl
HUGHES, Gareth
JACKSON, Michael
JAMES, John (A)
MARSTON, John
METCALFE, James William
MORGAN, Ian
SANDBROOK, Claire
SMITH, Alan (JM)
SMITH, Alan (S)
SOUTHERN, Norman
THOMSON, Patricia
VANN, Edward
WATT, Peter
WILLIAMSON, Simon
WILSON, Andrew

London East Central EC
ARNOLD, John
ASKER, David
BADGER, Chris
BUTLER, Malcolm
CADDY, Paul
DEAN, Derek
DEAN, Gordon
EDDOWES, Mark
GATER, Jonathan
HARRISON, Karl
HENTY, Charles
HUGHES, Gareth
JACKSON, Michael
JAMES, John (A)
MARSTON, John
METCALFE, James William
MORGAN, Ian
SANDBROOK, Claire
SMITH, Alan (JM)
SMITH, Alan (S)
SOUTHERN, Norman
THOMSON, Patricia
VANN, Edward
WATT, Peter
WILLIAMSON, Simon
WILSON, Andrew

London North N
ARNOLD, John
ASKER, David
BADGER, Chris
BUTLER, Malcolm
CADDY, Paul
DEAN, Derek
DEAN, Gordon
EDDOWES, Mark
GATER, Jonathan
HARRISON, Karl
HUGHES, Gareth
JACKSON, Michael
JAMES, John (A)
MARSTON, John
METCALFE, James William
MORGAN, Ian
SANDBROOK, Claire
SMITH, Alan (JM)
SMITH, Alan (S)
SOUTHERN, Norman
THOMSON, Patricia
VANN, Edward
WATT, Peter
WILLIAMSON, Simon
WILSON, Andrew

London North West NW
ARNOLD, John
ASKER, David
BADGER, Chris
BUTLER, Malcolm
CADDY, Paul
DEAN, Derek
DEAN, Gordon
EDDOWES, Mark
GATER, Jonathan
HARRISON, Karl
HUGHES, Gareth
JACKSON, Michael
JAMES, John (A)
KIMBER, Michael
MARSTON, John
METCALFE, James William
MORGAN, Ian
SANDBROOK, Claire

SMITH, Alan (JM)
SMITH, Alan (S)
SOUTHERN, Norman
THOMSON, Patricia
VANN, Edward
WATT, Peter
WILLIAMSON, Simon
WILSON, Andrew

London South East SE
ARNOLD, John
ASKER, David
BADGER, Chris
BUTLER, Malcolm
CADDY, Paul
DEAN, Derek
DEAN, Gordon
EDDOWES, Mark
GATER, Jonathan
HARRISON, Karl
HUGHES, Gareth
JACKSON, Michael
JAMES, John (A)
MARSTON, John
METCALFE, James William
MORGAN, Ian
SANDBROOK, Claire
SMITH, Alan (JM)
SMITH, Alan (S)
SOUTHERN, Norman
THOMSON, Patricia
VANN, Edward
WATT, Peter
WILLIAMSON, Simon
WILSON, Andrew

London South West SW
ARNOLD, John
ASKER, David
BADGER, Chris
BUTLER, Malcolm
CADDY, Paul
DEAN, Derek
DEAN, Gordon
EDDOWES, Mark
GATER, Jonathan
HARRISON, Karl
HUGHES, Gareth
JACKSON, Michael
JAMES, John (A)
MARSTON, John
METCALFE, James William
MORGAN, Ian
SANDBROOK, Claire
SMITH, Alan (JM)
SMITH, Alan (S)
SOUTHERN, Norman
THOMSON, Patricia
VANN, Edward
WATT, Peter
WILLIAMSON, Simon
WILSON, Andrew

London West W
ARNOLD, John
ASKER, David
BADGER, Chris
BUTLER, Malcolm
CADDY, Paul
DEAN, Derek
DEAN, Gordon
EDDOWES, Mark
GATER, Jonathan
HARRISON, Karl
HUGHES, Gareth
JACKSON, Michael
JAMES, John (A)
KIMBER, Michael
MARSTON, John
METCALFE, James William
MORGAN, Ian
SANDBROOK, Claire
SMITH, Alan (JM)
SMITH, Alan (S)
SOUTHERN, Norman
THOMSON, Patricia
VANN, Edward
WATT, Peter
WILLIAMSON, Simon
WILSON, Andrew

London West Central WC
ARNOLD, John
ASKER, David
BADGER, Chris
BUTLER, Malcolm
CADDY, Paul
DEAN, Derek
DEAN, Gordon
EDDOWES, Mark
GATER, Jonathan
HARRISON, Karl
HUGHES, Gareth
JACKSON, Michael
JAMES, John (A)
KIMBER, Michael
MARSTON, John
METCALFE, James William
MORGAN, Ian
SANDBROOK, Claire
SMITH, Alan (JM)
SMITH, Alan (S)
SOUTHERN, Norman
THOMSON, Patricia
VANN, Edward
WATT, Peter
WILLIAMSON, Simon
WILSON, Andrew

Luton LU
ARNOLD, John
ASKER, David
BADGER, Chris
DEAN, Derek
DEAN, Gordon
HALL, Brian
HARRISON, Karl
MARSTON, John
METCALFE, James William
MORGAN, Ian
SANDBROOK, Claire
SMITH, Alan (S)
SOUTHERN, Norman
THOMSON, Patricia
VANN, Edward
WATT, Peter
WILSON, Andrew

Manchester M
ARNOLD, John

ASKER, David
BADGER, Chris
DEAN, Derek
DEAN, Gordon
HARRISON, Karl
MARSTON, John
MASON, David
METCALFE, James William
MORGAN, Ian
SANDBROOK, Claire
SMITH, Alan (S)
SOUTHERN, Norman
THOMSON, Patricia
VANN, Edward
WILSON, Andrew

Medway ME
ARNOLD, John
ASKER, David
BADGER, Chris
BUTLER, Malcolm
CADDY, Paul
DEAN, Derek
DEAN, Gordon
EDDOWES, Mark
GATER, Jonathan
HARRISON, Karl
HUGHES, Gareth
JACKSON, Michael
JAMES, John (A)
MARSTON, John
METCALFE, James William
MORGAN, Ian
SANDBROOK, Claire
SMITH, Alan (JM)
SMITH, Alan (S)
SOUTHERN, Norman
THOMSON, Patricia
VANN, Edward
WATT, Peter
WILLIAMSON, Simon
WILSON, Andrew

Milton Keynes MK
ARNOLD, John
ASKER, David
BADGER, Chris
DEAN, Derek
DEAN, Gordon
HALL, Brian
HARRISON, Karl
MARSTON, John
METCALFE, James William
MORGAN, Ian
SANDBROOK, Claire
SMITH, Alan (S)
SOUTHERN, Norman
THOMSON, Patricia
VANN, Edward
WATT, Peter
WILSON, Andrew

Newcastle NE
ARNOLD, John
ASKER, David
BADGER, Chris
DAVIES, Malcolm
DEAN, Derek
DEAN, Gordon
FELLOWS, Kathleen
HARRISON, Karl
MARSTON, John
METCALFE, James William
MORGAN, Ian
SANDBROOK, Claire
SMITH, Alan (S)
SOUTHERN, Norman
THOMSON, Patricia
VANN, Edward
WILSON, Andrew

Newport NP
ALEXANDER, Nicholas
ANDERSON, Michael
ARNOLD, John
ASKER, David
BADGER, Chris
DEAN, Derek
DEAN, Gordon
DUNCAN, Andrew
EVANS, Philip
EWART-JAMES, Andrew
FARRINGTON, Patrick
GATER, Jonathan
HARRISON, Karl
HORNER, Nigel
JAMES, John (AW)
KIMBER, Michael
LEYSHON, Martin
MARSTON, John
METCALFE, James William
MORGAN, Ian
PEPPER, Nigel
SANDBROOK, Claire
SMITH, Alan (S)
SOUTHERN, Norman
THOMSON, Patricia
VANN, Edward
WILSON, Andrew

Northampton NN
ARNOLD, John
ASKER, David
BADGER, Chris
DEAN, Derek
DEAN, Gordon
HALL, Brian
HARRISON, Karl
MARSTON, John
METCALFE, James William
MORGAN, Ian
SANDBROOK, Claire
SMITH, Alan (S)
SOUTHERN, Norman
THOMSON, Patricia
VANN, Edward
WATT, Peter
WILSON, Andrew

Norwich NR
ARNOLD, John
ASKER, David
BADGER, Chris
DEAN, Derek
DEAN, Gordon
HALL, Brian
HARRISON, Karl
MARSTON, John
METCALFE, James William
MORGAN, Ian

SANDBROOK, Claire
SMITH, Alan (S)
SOUTHERN, Norman
THOMSON, Patricia
VANN, Edward
WATT, Peter
WILSON, Andrew

Nottingham NG
ANDERSON, Michael
ARNOLD, John
ASKER, David
BADGER, Chris
BUTLER, Malcolm
CADDY, Paul
DEAN, Derek
DEAN, Gordon
DUNCAN, Andrew
EDDOWES, Mark
EVANS, Philip
FARRINGTON, Patrick
GATER, Jonathan
HARRISON, Karl
HUGHES, Gareth
HORNER, Nigel
JACKSON, Michael
JAMES, John (A)
JAMES, John (AW)
KIMBER, Michael
LEYSHON, Martin
MARSTON, John
METCALFE, James William
MORGAN, Ian
PEPPER, Nigel
SANDBROOK, Claire
SMITH, Alan (JM)
SMITH, Alan (S)
SOUTHERN, Norman
THOMSON, Patricia
VANN, Edward
WILLIAMSON, Simon
WILSON, Andrew

Oldham OL
ARNOLD, John
ASKER, David
BADGER, Chris
BOVAN, Gary
DEAN, Derek
DEAN, Gordon
HARRISON, Karl
MARSTON, John
METCALFE, James William
MORGAN, Ian
SANDBROOK, Claire
SMITH, Alan (S)
SOUTHERN, Norman
THOMSON, Patricia
VANN, Edward
WHITWORTH, Frank
WILSON, Andrew

Oxford OX
ALEXANDER, Nicholas
ANDERSON, Michael
ARNOLD, John
ASKER, David
BADGER, Chris
DEAN, Derek
DEAN, Gordon
DUNCAN, Andrew
EVANS, Philip
EWART-JAMES, Andrew
FARRINGTON, Patrick
GATER, Jonathan
HARRISON, Karl
HORNER, Nigel
JAMES, John (AW)
KIMBER, Michael
LEYSHON, Martin
MARSTON, John
METCALFE, James William
MORGAN, Ian
PEPPER, Nigel
SANDBROOK, Claire
SMITH, Alan (S)
SOUTHERN, Norman
THOMSON, Patricia
VANN, Edward
WATT, Peter
WILSON, Andrew

Peterborough PE
ARNOLD, John
ASKER, David
BADGER, Chris
DEAN, Derek
DEAN, Gordon
HALL, Brian
HARRISON, Karl
MARSTON, John
METCALFE, James William
MORGAN, Ian
SANDBROOK, Claire
SMITH, Alan (S)
SOUTHERN, Norman
THOMSON, Patricia
VANN, Edward
WATT, Peter
WILSON, Andrew

Plymouth PL
ARNOLD, John
ASKER, David
BADGER, Chris
BARNETT, Simon
DEAN, Derek
DEAN, Gordon
EGMORE, Angela
HARRISON, Karl
MARSTON, John
METCALFE, James William
MORGAN, Ian
REED, Philip
SANDBROOK, Claire
SMITH, Alan (S)
SOUTHERN, Norman
THOMSON, Patricia
VANN, Edward
WILSON, Andrew

Portsmouth PO
ANDERSON, Michael
ARNOLD, John
ASKER, David
BADGER, Chris
DEAN, Derek
DEAN, Gordon
DUNCAN, Andrew
EVANS, Philip

FARRINGTON, Patrick
GATER, Jonathan
HARRISON, Karl
HORNER, Nigel
JAMES, John (AW)
KIMBER, Michael
LEYSHON, Martin
MARSTON, John
METCALFE, James William
MORGAN, Ian
PEPPER, Nigel
SANDBROOK, Claire
SMITH, Alan (S)
SOUTHERN, Norman
THOMSON, Patricia
VANN, Edward
WATT, Peter
WILSON, Andrew

Preston PR
ARNOLD, John
ASKER, David
BADGER, Chris
BOVAN, Gary
DEAN, Derek
DEAN, Gordon
HARRISON, Karl
MARSTON, John
METCALFE, James William
MORGAN, Ian
SANDBROOK, Claire
SMITH, Alan (S)
SOUTHERN, Norman
THOMSON, Patricia
VANN, Edward
WILSON, Andrew

Reading RG
ANDERSON, Michael
ARNOLD, John
ASKER, David
BADGER, Chris
DEAN, Derek
DEAN, Gordon
DUNCAN, Andrew
EVANS, Philip
FARRINGTON, Patrick
GATER, Jonathan
HARRISON, Karl
HORNER, Nigel
JAMES, John (AW)
KIMBER, Michael
LEYSHON, Martin
MARSTON, John
METCALFE, James William
MORGAN, Ian
PEPPER, Nigel
SANDBROOK, Claire
SMITH, Alan (S)
SOUTHERN, Norman
THOMSON, Patricia
VANN, Edward
WATT, Peter
WILSON, Andrew

Redhill RH
ARNOLD, John
ASKER, David
BADGER, Chris
BUTLER, Malcolm
CADDY, Paul
DEAN, Derek
DEAN, Gordon
EDDOWES, Mark
GATER, Jonathan
HARRISON, Karl
HUGHES, Gareth
JACKSON, Michael
JAMES, John (A)
MARSTON, John
METCALFE, James William
MORGAN, Ian
SANDBROOK, Claire
SMITH, Alan (JM)
SMITH, Alan (S)
SOUTHERN, Norman
THOMSON, Patricia
VANN, Edward
WATT, Peter
WILLIAMSON, Simon
WILSON, Andrew

Romford RM
ARNOLD, John
ASKER, David
BADGER, Chris
BUTLER, Malcolm
CADDY, Paul
DEAN, Derek
DEAN, Gordon
EDDOWES, Mark
GATER, Jonathan
HARRISON, Karl
HUGHES, Gareth
JACKSON, Michael
JAMES, John (A)
MARSTON, John
METCALFE, James William
MORGAN, Ian
SANDBROOK, Claire
SMITH, Alan (JM)
SMITH, Alan (S)
SOUTHERN, Norman
THOMSON, Patricia
VANN, Edward
WATT, Peter
WILLIAMSON, Simon
WILSON, Andrew

Salisbury SP
ARNOLD, John
ASKER, David
BADGER, Chris
BARNETT, Simon
DEAN, Derek
DEAN, Gordon
EGMORE, Angela
GATER, Jonathan
HARRISON, Karl
MARSTON, John
METCALFE, James William
MORGAN, Ian
SANDBROOK, Claire
SMITH, Alan (S)
SOUTHERN, Norman
THOMSON, Patricia
VANN, Edward
WILSON, Andrew

Sheffield S
ARNOLD, John
ASKER, David
BADGER, Chris
BOVAN, Gary
BUTLER, Malcolm
CADDY, Paul
DEAN, Derek
DEAN, Gordon
EDDOWES, Mark
HARRISON, Karl
HUGHES, Gareth
JACKSON, Michael
JAMES, John (A)
MARSTON, John
METCALFE, James William
MORGAN, Ian
SANDBROOK, Claire
SMITH, Alan (JM)
SMITH, Alan (S)
SOUTHERN, Norman
THOMSON, Patricia
TODD, Nicholas
VANN, Edward
WILLIAMSON, Simon
WILSON, Andrew

Shrewsbury SY
ANDERSON, Michael
ARNOLD, John
ASKER, David
BADGER, Chris
DEAN, Derek
DEAN, Gordon
DUNCAN, Andrew
EVANS, Philip
FARRINGTON, Patrick
GATER, Jonathan
HARRISON, Karl
HORNER, Nigel
JAMES, John (AW)
KIMBER, Michael
LEYSHON, Martin
MARSTON, John
MASON, David
METCALFE, James William
MORGAN, Ian
PEPPER, Nigel
SANDBROOK, Claire
SMITH, Alan (S)
SOUTHERN, Norman
THOMSON, Patricia
VANN, Edward
WILSON, Andrew

Slough SL
ANDERSON, Michael
ARNOLD, John
ASKER, David
BADGER, Chris
DEAN, Derek
DEAN, Gordon
DUNCAN, Andrew
EVANS, Philip
FARRINGTON, Patrick
GATER, Jonathan
HARRISON, Karl
HORNER, Nigel
JAMES, John (AW)
KIMBER, Michael
LEYSHON, Martin
MARSTON, John
METCALFE, James William
MORGAN, Ian
PEPPER, Nigel
SANDBROOK, Claire
SMITH, Alan (S)
SOUTHERN, Norman
THOMSON, Patricia
VANN, Edward
WATT, Peter
WILSON, Andrew

Southall (Uxbridge) UB
ARNOLD, John
ASKER, David
BADGER, Chris
BUTLER, Malcolm
CADDY, Paul
DEAN, Derek
DEAN, Gordon
EDDOWES, Mark
GATER, Jonathan
HARRISON, Karl
HUGHES, Gareth
JACKSON, Michael
JAMES, John (A)
KIMBER, Michael
MARSTON, John
METCALFE, James William
MORGAN, Ian
SANDBROOK, Claire
SMITH, Alan (JM)
SMITH, Alan (S)
SOUTHERN, Norman
THOMSON, Patricia
VANN, Edward
WATT, Peter
WILLIAMSON, Simon
WILSON, Andrew

Southampton SO
ANDERSON, Michael
ARNOLD, John
ASKER, David
BADGER, Chris
DEAN, Derek
DEAN, Gordon
DUNCAN, Andrew
EVANS, Philip
FARRINGTON, Patrick
GATER, Jonathan
HARRISON, Karl
HORNER, Nigel
JAMES, John (AW)
KIMBER, Michael
LEYSHON, Martin
MARSTON, John
METCALFE, James William
MORGAN, Ian
PEPPER, Nigel
SANDBROOK, Claire
SMITH, Alan (S)
SOUTHERN, Norman
THOMSON, Patricia
VANN, Edward
WATT, Peter
WILSON, Andrew

Southend on Sea SS
ARNOLD, John
ASKER, David
BADGER, Chris
BUTLER, Malcolm
CADDY, Paul
DEAN, Derek
DEAN, Gordon
EDDOWES, Mark
HARRISON, Karl
HUGHES, Gareth
JACKSON, Michael
JAMES, John (A)
MARSTON, John
METCALFE, James William
MORGAN, Ian
SANDBROOK, Claire
SMITH, Alan (JM)
SMITH, Alan (S)
SOUTHERN, Norman
THOMSON, Patricia
VANN, Edward
WATT, Peter
WILLIAMSON, Simon
WILSON, Andrew

St. Albans AL
ARNOLD, John
ASKER, David
BADGER, Chris
BUTLER, Malcolm
CADDY, Paul
DEAN, Derek
DEAN, Gordon
EDDOWES, Mark
HARRISON, Karl
HUGHES, Gareth
JACKSON, Michael
JAMES, John (A)
MARSTON, John
METCALFE, James William
MORGAN, Ian
SANDBROOK, Claire
SMITH, Alan (JM)
SMITH, Alan (S)
SOUTHERN, Norman
THOMSON, Patricia
TUNSTILL, Peter
VANN, Edward
WATT, Peter
WILLIAMSON, Simon
WILSON, Andrew

Stevenage SG
ARNOLD, John
ASKER, David
BADGER, Chris
BUTLER, Malcolm
CADDY, Paul
DEAN, Derek
DEAN, Gordon
EDDOWES, Mark
HALL, Brian
HARRISON, Karl
HUGHES, Gareth
JACKSON, Michael
JAMES, John (A)
MARSTON, John
METCALFE, James William
MORGAN, Ian
SANDBROOK, Claire
SMITH, Alan (JM)
SMITH, Alan (S)
SOUTHERN, Norman
THOMSON, Patricia
TUNSTILL, Peter
VANN, Edward
WATT, Peter
WILLIAMSON, Simon
WILSON, Andrew

Stockport SK
ARNOLD, John
ASKER, David
BADGER, Chris
BUTLER, Malcolm
CADDY, Paul
DEAN, Derek
DEAN, Gordon
EDDOWES, Mark
HARRISON, Karl
HUGHES, Gareth
JACKSON, Michael
JAMES, John (A)
MARSTON, John
MASON, David
METCALFE, James William
MORGAN, Ian
SANDBROOK, Claire
SMITH, Alan (JM)
SMITH, Alan (S)
SOUTHERN, Norman
THOMSON, Patricia
VANN, Edward
WILLIAMSON, Simon
WILSON, Andrew

Stoke on Trent ST
ANDERSON, Michael
ARNOLD, John
ASKER, David
BADGER, Chris
BUTLER, Malcolm
CADDY, Paul
DEAN, Derek
DEAN, Gordon
DUNCAN, Andrew
EDDOWES, Mark
EVANS, Philip
FARRINGTON, Patrick
GATER, Jonathan
HARRISON, Karl
HUGHES, Gareth
HORNER, Nigel
JACKSON, Michael
JAMES, John (A)
JAMES, John (AW)
KIMBER, Michael
LEYSHON, Martin
MARSTON, John
METCALFE, James William
MORGAN, Ian
PEPPER, Nigel
SANDBROOK, Claire
SMITH, Alan (JM)
SMITH, Alan (S)
SOUTHERN, Norman
THOMSON, Patricia

VANN, Edward
WILLIAMSON, Simon
WILSON, Andrew

Sunderland SR
ARNOLD, John
ASKER, David
BADGER, Chris
DAVIES, Malcolm
DEAN, Derek
DEAN, Gordon
FELLOWS, Kathleen
HARRISON, Karl
MARSTON, John
METCALFE, James William
MORGAN, Ian
SANDBROOK, Claire
SMITH, Alan (S)
SOUTHERN, Norman
THOMSON, Patricia
VANN, Edward
WILSON, Andrew

Sutton SM
ARNOLD, John
ASKER, David
BADGER, Chris
BUTLER, Malcolm
CADDY, Paul
DEAN, Derek
DEAN, Gordon
EDDOWES, Mark
GATER, Jonathan
HARRISON, Karl
HUGHES, Gareth
JACKSON, Michael
JAMES, John (A)
MARSTON, John
METCALFE, James William
MORGAN, Ian
SANDBROOK, Claire
SMITH, Alan (JM)
SMITH, Alan (S)
SOUTHERN, Norman
THOMSON, Patricia
VANN, Edward
WATT, Peter
WILLIAMSON, Simon
WILSON, Andrew

Swansea SA
ANDERSON, Michael
ARNOLD, John
ASKER, David
BADGER, Chris
DEAN, Derek
DEAN, Gordon
DUNCAN, Andrew
EVANS, Philip
FARRINGTON, Patrick
GATER, Jonathan
HARRISON, Karl
HORNER, Nigel
JAMES, John (AW)
KIMBER, Michael
LEYSHON, Martin
MARSTON, John
METCALFE, James William
MORGAN, Ian
PEPPER, Nigel
SANDBROOK, Claire
SMITH, Alan (S)
SOUTHERN, Norman
THOMSON, Patricia
VANN, Edward
WATT, Peter
WILSON, Andrew

Swindon SN
ALEXANDER, Nicholas
ANDERSON, Michael
ARNOLD, John
ASKER, David
BADGER, Chris
DEAN, Derek
DEAN, Gordon
DUNCAN, Andrew
EVANS, Philip
EWART-JAMES, Andrew
FARRINGTON, Patrick
GATER, Jonathan
HARRISON, Karl
HORNER, Nigel
JAMES, John (AW)
KIMBER, Michael
LEYSHON, Martin
MARSTON, John
METCALFE, James William
MORGAN, Ian
PEPPER, Nigel
SANDBROOK, Claire
SMITH, Alan (S)
SOUTHERN, Norman
THOMSON, Patricia
VANN, Edward
WATT, Peter
WILSON, Andrew

Taunton TA
ARNOLD, John
ASKER, David
BADGER, Chris
BARNETT, Simon
DEAN, Derek
DEAN, Gordon
EGMORE, Angela
HARRISON, Karl
MARSTON, John
METCALFE, James William
MORGAN, Ian
SANDBROOK, Claire
SMITH, Alan (S)
SOUTHERN, Norman
THOMSON, Patricia
VANN, Edward
WILSON, Andrew

Telford TF
ANDERSON, Michael
ARNOLD, John
ASKER, David
BADGER, Chris
DEAN, Derek
DEAN, Gordon
DUNCAN, Andrew
EVANS, Philip
FARRINGTON, Patrick
GATER, Jonathan
HARRISON, Karl
HORNER, Nigel

JAMES, John (AW)
KIMBER, Michael
LEYSHON, Martin
MARSTON, John
METCALFE, James William
MORGAN, Ian
PEPPER, Nigel
SANDBROOK, Claire
SMITH, Alan (S)
SOUTHERN, Norman
THOMSON, Patricia
VANN, Edward
WILSON, Andrew

Tonbridge TN
ARNOLD, John
ASKER, David
BADGER, Chris
BUTLER, Malcolm
CADDY, Paul
DEAN, Derek
DEAN, Gordon
EDDOWES, Mark
GATER, Jonathan
HARRISON, Karl
HUGHES, Gareth
JACKSON, Michael
JAMES, John (A)
MARSTON, John
METCALFE, James William
MORGAN, Ian
SANDBROOK, Claire
SMITH, Alan (JM)
SMITH, Alan (S)
SOUTHERN, Norman
THOMSON, Patricia
VANN, Edward
WATT, Peter
WILLIAMSON, Simon
WILSON, Andrew

Torquay TQ
ARNOLD, John
ASKER, David
BADGER, Chris
BARNETT, Simon
DEAN, Derek
DEAN, Gordon
EGMORE, Angela
HARRISON, Karl
MARSTON, John
METCALFE, James William
MORGAN, Ian
SANDBROOK, Claire
SMITH, Alan (S)
SOUTHERN, Norman
THOMSON, Patricia
VANN, Edward
WILSON, Andrew

Truro TR
ARNOLD, John
ASKER, David
BADGER, Chris
BARNETT, Simon
DEAN, Derek
DEAN, Gordon
EGMORE, Angela
HARRISON, Karl
MARSTON, John
METCALFE, James William
MORGAN, Ian
REED, Philip
SANDBROOK, Claire
SMITH, Alan (S)
SOUTHERN, Norman
THOMSON, Patricia
VANN, Edward
WILSON, Andrew

Tweeddale (Berwick upon Tweed) TD
ARNOLD, John
ASKER, David
BADGER, Chris
DAVIES, Malcolm
DEAN, Derek
DEAN, Gordon
HARRISON, Karl
MARSTON, John
METCALFE, James William
MORGAN, Ian
SANDBROOK, Claire
SMITH, Alan (S)
SOUTHERN, Norman
THOMSON, Patricia
VANN, Edward
WILSON, Andrew

Twickenham TW
ARNOLD, John
ASKER, David
BADGER, Chris
BUTLER, Malcolm
CADDY, Paul
DEAN, Derek
DEAN, Gordon
EDDOWES, Mark
GATER, Jonathan
HARRISON, Karl
HUGHES, Gareth
JACKSON, Michael
JAMES, John (A)
KIMBER, Michael
MARSTON, John
METCALFE, James William
MORGAN, Ian
SANDBROOK, Claire
SMITH, Alan (JM)
SMITH, Alan (S)
SOUTHERN, Norman
THOMSON, Patricia
VANN, Edward
WATT, Peter
WILLIAMSON, Simon
WILSON, Andrew

Wakefield WF
ARNOLD, John
ASKER, David
BADGER, Chris
BOVAN, Gary
BRADLEY, Andrew
DEAN, Derek
DEAN, Gordon
HARRISON, Dion
HARRISON, Karl
LAMBERT, Stephen
MARSTON, John
METCALFE, James William
MORGAN, Ian

SANDBROOK, Claire
SMITH, Alan (S)
SOUTHERN, Norman
THOMSON, Patricia
VANN, Edward
WHITWORTH, Frank
WILSON, Andrew

Walsall WS
ANDERSON, Michael
ARNOLD, John
ASKER, David
BACHE, Penny
BADGER, Chris
BUTLER, Malcolm
CADDY, Paul
DEAN, Derek
DEAN, Gordon
DUNCAN, Andrew WS
EVANS, Philip
EDDOWES, Mark
FARRINGTON, Patrick
GATER, Jonathan
HARRISON, Karl
HUGHES, Gareth
HORNER, Nigel
JACKSON, Michael
JAMES, John (A)
JAMES, John (AW)
KIMBER, Michael
LEYSHON, Martin
MARSTON, John
METCALFE, James William
MORGAN, Ian
PEPPER, Nigel
SANDBROOK, Claire
SMITH, Alan (JM)
SMITH, Alan (S)
SOUTHERN, Norman
THOMSON, Patricia
VANN, Edward
WILLIAMSON, Simon
WILSON, Andrew

Warrington WA
ARNOLD, John
ASKER, David
BADGER, Chris
DEAN, Derek
DEAN, Gordon
HARRISON, Karl
MARSTON, John
MASON, David
METCALFE, James William
MORGAN, Ian
SANDBROOK, Claire
SMITH, Alan (S)
SOUTHERN, Norman
THOMSON, Patricia
VANN, Edward
WILSON, Andrew

Watford WD
ARNOLD, John
ASKER, David
BADGER, Chris
BUTLER, Malcolm
CADDY, Paul
DEAN, Derek
DEAN, Gordon
EDDOWES, Mark
HARRISON, Karl
HUGHES, Gareth
JACKSON, Michael
JAMES, John (A)
MARSTON, John
METCALFE, James William
MORGAN, Ian
SANDBROOK, Claire
SMITH, Alan (JM)
SMITH, Alan (S)
SOUTHERN, Norman
THOMSON, Patricia
TUNSTILL, Peter
VANN, Edward
WATT, Peter
WILLIAMSON, Simon
WILSON, Andrew

Wigan WN
ARNOLD, John
ASKER, David
BADGER, Chris
DEAN, Derek
DEAN, Gordon
HARRISON, Karl
MARSTON, John
MASON, David
METCALFE, James William
MORGAN, Ian
SANDBROOK, Claire
SMITH, Alan (S)
SOUTHERN, Norman
THOMSON, Patricia
VANN, Edward
WILSON, Andrew

Wolverhampton WV
ANDERSON, Michael
ARNOLD, John
ASKER, David
BADGER, Chris
BUTLER, Malcolm
CADDY, Paul
DEAN, Derek
DEAN, Gordon
DUNCAN, Andrew
EDDOWES, Mark
EVANS, Philip
FARRINGTON, Patrick
GATER, Jonathan
HARRISON, Karl
HUGHES, Gareth
HORNER, Nigel
JACKSON, Michael
JAMES, John (A)
JAMES, John (AW)
KIMBER, Michael
LEYSHON, Martin
MARSTON, John
METCALFE, James William
MORGAN, Ian
PEPPER, Nigel
SANDBROOK, Claire
SMITH, Alan (JM)
SMITH, Alan (S)
SOUTHERN, Norman
THOMSON, Patricia
VANN, Edward

WILLIAMSON, Simon
WILSON, Andrew

Worcester WR
ALEXANDER, Nicholas
ANDERSON, Michael
ARNOLD, John
ASKER, David
BACHE, Penny
BADGER, Chris
BUTLER, Malcolm
CADDY, Paul
DEAN, Derek
DEAN, Gordon
DUNCAN, Andrew
EDDOWES, Mark
EVANS, Philip
EWART-JAMES, Andrew
FARRINGTON, Patrick
GATER, Jonathan
HARRISON, Karl
HUGHES, Gareth
HORNER, Nigel
JACKSON, Michael
JAMES, John (A)
JAMES, John (AW)
KIMBER, Michael
LEYSHON, Martin
MARSTON, John
METCALFE, James William
MORGAN, Ian
PEPPER, Nigel
SANDBROOK, Claire
SMITH, Alan (JM)
SMITH, Alan (S)
SOUTHERN, Norman
THOMSON, Patricia
VANN, Edward
WILLIAMSON, Simon
WILSON, Andrew

York YO
ARNOLD, John
ASKER, David
BADGER, Chris
BAITSON, Michael
BOVAN, Gary
DEAN, Derek
DEAN, Gordon
FELLOWS, Kathleen
HARRISON, Karl
MARSTON, John
METCALFE, James William
MORGAN, Ian
SANDBROOK, Claire
SMITH, Alan (S)
SOUTHERN, Norman
THOMSON, Patricia
VANN, Edward
WILSON, Andrew

Enforcement Officers

ALEXANDER, Nicholas
Office: Adept Enforcement, 2nd Fl, 65 London Rd, Gloucester GL1 3HF
Tel: 01452 429883/01531 636108 Fax: 01452 300922
DX: 7514 Gloucester
e-mail: nicholasalexander@wspsolicitors.com
Note: Bristol BS, Gloucester GL, Hereford HR, Newport NP, Oxford OX, Swindon SN, Worcester WR

ANDERSON, Michael
Website: www.hcegroup.co.uk
Office: High Court Enforcement Group Ltd, 141 Walter Rd, Swansea SA1 5RW
Tel: 01792 466771 Fax: 01792 455755
DX: 52966 Swansea
e-mail: manderson@hcegroup.co.uk
Note: Bath BA, Birmingham B, Bristol BS, Cardiff CF, Chester CH, Coventry CV, Crewe CW, Derby DE, Dudley DY, Gloucester GL, Guildford GU, Hemel Hempstead HP, Hereford HR, Leicester LE, Llandridnod Wells LD, Llandudno LL, Newport NP, Nottingham NG, Oxford OX, Portsmouth PO, Reading RG, Shrewsbury SY, Slough SL, Southampton SO, Stoke on Trent ST, Swansea SA, Swindon SN, Telford TF, Walsall WS, Wolverhampton WV, Worcester WR

ARNOLD, John
Office: Marston Group Limited, Cullimore Dutton, Solicitors, 20 White Friars, Chester CH1 1XS
Tel: 01244 321066 Fax: 01244 312582
DX: 19985 Chester
e-mail: john.arnold@cullimoredutton.co.uk
Note: Bath BA, Birmingham B, Blackburn BB, Bolton BL, Bournemouth BH, Bradford BD, Brighton BN, Bristol BS, Bromley BR, Cambridge CB, Canterbury CT, Cardiff CF, Carlisle CA, Chelmsford CM, Chester CH, Cleveland (Teesside) TS, Colchester CO, Coventry CV, Crewe CW, Croydon CR, Darlington DL, Dartford DA, Derby DE, Doncaster DN, Dorchester DT, Dudley DY, Durham DH, Enfield EN, Exeter EX, Fylde (Blackpool) FY, Gloucester GL, Guildford GU, Halifax HX, Harrogate HG, Harrow HA, Hemel Hempstead HP, Hereford HR, Huddersfield HD, Hull HU, Ilford IG, Ipswich IP, Kingston upon Thames KT, Lancaster LA, Leeds LS, Leicester LE, Lincoln LN, Liverpool L, Llandrindod Wells LD, Llandudno LL, London East E, London East Central EC, London North N, London North West NW, London South East SE, London South West SW, London West W, London West Central WC, Luton LU, Manchester M, Medway ME, Milton Keynes MK, Newcastle NE, Newport NP, Northampton NN, Norwich NR, Nottingham NG, Oldham OL, Oxford OX, Peterborough PE, Plymouth PL, Portsmouth PO, Preston PR, Reading RG, Redhill RH, Romford RM, Salisbury SP, Sheffield S, Shrewsbury SY Slough SL, Southall (Uxbridge) UB, Southampton SO, Southend on Sea SS, St Albans AL, Stevenage SG, Stockport SK, Stoke on Trent ST, Sunderland SR, Sutton SM, Swansea SA, Swindon SN, Taunton TA, Telford TF, Tonbridge TN, Torquay TQ, Truro TR, Tweeddale (Berwick on Tweed) TD, Twickenham TW, Wakefield WF, Walsall WS, Warrington WA, Watford WD, Wigan WN, Wolverhampton WV, Worcester WR, York YO

ASKER, David
Website: www.sherforce.net
Office: Sherforce, 1 Fetter Lane, London EC4 1BR
Tel: 0845 890 9200 Fax: 0845 890 9201
e-mail: d.asker@shergroup.net
Note: Bath BA, Birmingham B, Blackburn BB, Bolton BL, Bournemouth BH, Bradford BD, Brighton BN, Bristol BS, Bromley BR, Cambridge CB, Canterbury CT, Cardiff CF,

Carlisle CA, Chelmsford CM, Chester CH, Cleveland (Teesside) TS, Colchester CO, Coventry CV, Crewe CW, Croydon CR, Darlington DL, Dartford DA, Derby DE, Doncaster DN, Dorchester DT, Dudley DY, Durham DH, Enfield EN, Exeter EX, Fylde (Blackpool) FY, Gloucester GL, Guildford GU, Halifax HX, Harrogate HG, Harrow HA, Hemel Hempstead HP, Hereford HR, Huddersfield HD, Hull HU, Ilford IG, Ipswich IP, Kingston upon Thames KT, Lancaster LA, Leeds LS, Leicester LE, Lincoln LN, Liverpool L, Llandrindod Wells LD, Llandudno LL, London East E, London East Central EC, London North N, London North West NW, London South East SE, London South West SW, London West W, London West Central WC, Luton LU, Manchester M, Medway ME, Milton Keynes MK, Newcastle NE, Newport NP, Northampton NN, Norwich NR, Nottingham NG, Oldham OL, Oxford OX, Peterborough PE, Plymouth PL, Portsmouth PO, Preston PR, Reading RG, Redhill RH, Romford RM, Salisbury SP, Sheffield S, Shrewsbury SY Slough SL, Southall (Uxbridge) UB, Southampton SO, Southend on Sea SS, St Albans AL, Stevenage SG, Stockport SK, Stoke on Trent ST, Sunderland SR, Sutton SM, Swansea SA, Swindon SN, Taunton TA, Telford TF, Tonbridge TN, Torquay TQ, Truro TR, Tweeddale (Berwick on Tweed) TD, Twickenham TW, Wakefield WF, Walsall WS, Warrington WA, Watford WD, Wigan WN, Wolverhampton WV, Worcester WR, York YO

BACHE, Penny
Website: www.marstongroup.co.uk
Office: Marston Group Enforcement Centre, Embassy Ho, 60 Church St, Birmingham B3 2DJ
Tel: 0845 340 7250 Fax: 0121 200 7401
DX: 13014 Birmingham
e-mail: hccs@marstongroup.co.uk
Note: Walsall WS, Worcester WR

BADGER, Chris
Website: www.thesheriffsoffice.com
Office: The Sheriff's Office, Airport Ho, Purley Way, Croydon CR0 0XZ
Tel: 0845 688 9750 Fax: 0845 688 9760
DX: 156870 Croydon 41
e-mail: cb@thesheriffsoffice.com
Note: Bath BA, Birmingham B, Blackburn BB, Bolton BL, Bournemouth BH, Bradford BD, Brighton BN, Bristol BS, Bromley BR, Cambridge CB, Canterbury CT, Cardiff CF, Carlisle CA, Chelmsford CM, Chester CH, Cleveland (Teesside) TS, Colchester CO, Coventry CV, Crewe CW, Croydon CR, Darlington DL, Dartford DA, Derby DE, Doncaster DN, Dorchester DT, Dudley DY, Durham DH, Enfield EN, Exeter EX, Fylde (Blackpool) FY, Gloucester GL, Guildford GU, Halifax HX, Harrogate HG, Harrow HA, Hemel Hempstead HP, Hereford HR, Huddersfield HD, Hull HU, Ilford IG, Ipswich IP, Kingston upon Thames KT, Lancaster LA, Leeds LS, Leicester LE, Lincoln LN, Liverpool L, Llandrindod Wells LD, Llandudno LL, London East E, London East Central EC, London North N, London North West NW, London South East SE, London South West SW, London West W, London West Central WC, Luton LU, Manchester M, Medway ME, Milton Keynes MK, Newcastle NE, Newport NP, Northampton NN, Norwich NR, Nottingham NG, Oldham OL, Oxford OX, Peterborough PE, Plymouth PL, Portsmouth PO, Preston PR, Reading RG, Redhill RH, Romford RM, Salisbury SP, Sheffield S, Shrewsbury SY Slough SL, Southall (Uxbridge) UB, Southampton SO, Southend on Sea SS, St Albans AL, Stevenage SG, Stockport SK, Stoke on Trent ST, Sunderland SR, Sutton SM, Swansea SA, Swindon SN, Taunton TA, Telford TF, Tonbridge TN, Torquay TQ, Truro TR, Tweeddale (Berwick on Tweed) TD, Twickenham TW, Wakefield WF, Walsall WS, Warrington WA, Watford WD, Wigan WN, Wolverhampton WV, Worcester WR, York YO

BAITSON, Michael
Website: www.gilbert-baitson.co.uk
Office: High Court Enforcement Office, 389–395 Anlaby Rd, Hull, East Yorks HU3 6AB
Tel: 01482 500500 Fax: 01482 500501
e-mail: hceo@gilbert-baitson.co.uk
Note: Doncaster DN, Hull HU, Lincoln LN, York YO

BARNETT, Simon
Website: www.hcegroup.co.uk
Office: High Court Enforcement Group Ltd, 141 Walter Rd, Swansea SA1 5RW
Tel: 01792 466771 Fax: 01792 455755
DX: 52966 Swansea
e-mail: simon.barnett@michelmores.com
Note: Bath BA, Bournemouth BH, Dorchester DT, Exeter EX, Plymouth PL, Salisbury SP, Taunton TA, Torquay TQ, Truro TR

BOVAN, Gary
Website: www.hcegroup.co.uk
Office: High Court Enforcement Group Ltd, City Hub, 9–11 Peckover St, Bradford, W Yorks BD1 5BE
Tel: 01274 391929 Fax: 01274 734773
DX: 11701 Bradford
e-mail: gary.bovan@hcegroup.co.uk
Note: Blackburn BB, Bradford BD, Chester CH, Crewe CW, Halifax HX, Harrogate HG, Huddersfield HD, Leeds LS, Liverpool L, Oldham OL, Preston PR, Sheffield S, Wakefield WF, York YO

BRADLEY, Andrew
Website: www.harrisonhce.co.uk
Office: Harrison High Court Enforcement, Milner Way, Ossett WF5 9JQ
Tel: 01924 279005 Fax: 01924 280114
DX: 707162 Ossett 2
e-mail: post@harrisonhce.co.uk
Note: Wakefield WF

BUTLER, Malcolm
Website: www.marstongroup.co.uk
Office: Marston Group Enforcement, Embassy Ho, 60 Church St, Birmingham B3 2DJ
Tel: 0845 340 7250 Fax: 0121 200 7401
DX: 13014 Birmingham
e-mail: hccs@marstongroup.co.uk
Note: Birmingham B, Bromley BR, Chelmsford CM, Coventry CV, Croydon CR, Dartford DA, Derby DE, Doncaster DN, Dudley DY, Enfield EN, Guildford GU, Harrow HA, Hemel Hempstead HP, Hereford HR, Ilford IG, Kingston upon Thames KT, Leicester LE, Lincoln LN, London East E, London East Central EC, London North N, London North West NW, London South East SE, London South West SW, London West W, London West Central WC, Medway ME, Nottingham NG, Redhill RH, Romford RM, Sheffield S, Southall (Uxbridge) UB, Southend on Sea SS, St. Albans AL, Stevenage SG, Stockport SK, Stoke on Trent ST, Sutton SM, Tonbridge TN, Twickenham TW, Walsall WS, Watford WD, Wolverhampton WV, Worcester WR

CADDY, Paul
Website: www.marstongroup.co.uk
Office: Marston Group Enforcement Centre, Embassy Ho, 60 Church St, Birmingham B3 2DJ
Tel: 0845 340 7250 Fax: 0121 200 7401
DX: 13014 Birmingham
e-mail: hccs@marstongroup.co.uk
Note: Birmingham B, Bromley BR, Chelmsford CM, Coventry CV, Croydon CR, Dartford DA, Derby DE, Doncaster DN, Dudley DY, Enfield EN, Guildford GU, Harrow HA, Hemel Hempstead HP, Hereford HR, Ilford IG, Kingston upon Thames KT, Leicester LE, Lincoln LN, London East E, London East Central EC, London North N, London North West NW, London South East SE, London South West SW, London West W, London West Central WC, Medway ME, Nottingham NG, Redhill RH, Romford RM, Sheffield S, Southall (Uxbridge) UB, Southend on Sea SS, St. Albans AL, Stevenage SG, Stockport SK, Stoke on Trent ST, Sutton SM, Tonbridge TN, Twickenham TW, Walsall WS, Watford WD, Wolverhampton WV, Worcester WR

DAVIES, Malcolm
Website: www.elliottdavies.com
Office: Wellbar Central, 36 Gallowgate, Newcastle Upon Tyne NE1 4TD
Tel: 0191 488 8800 Fax: 0191 488 8811
e-mail: info@elliottdavies.com
Note: Cleveland (Teeside) TS, Darlington DL, Durham DH, Newcastle NE, Sunderland SR, Tweeddale (Berwick upon Tweed) TD

DEAN, Derek
Website: www.hcegroup.co.uk
Office: High Court Enforcement Group Ltd, 27 Lord St, Liverpool L2 9SA
Tel: 0151 236 4751 Fax: 0151 236 8071
DX: 14104 Liverpool
e-mail: derek.dean@hcegroup.co.uk
Note: Bath BA, Birmingham B, Blackburn BB, Bolton BL, Bournemouth BH, Bradford BD, Brighton BN, Bristol BS, Bromley BR, Cambridge CB, Canterbury CT, Cardiff CF, Carlisle CA, Chelmsford CM, Chester CH, Cleveland (Teesside) TS, Colchester CO, Coventry CV, Crewe CW, Croydon CR, Darlington DL, Dartford DA, Derby DE, Doncaster DN, Dorchester DT, Dudley DY, Durham DH, Enfield EN, Exeter EX, Fylde (Blackpool) FY, Gloucester GL, Guildford GU, Halifax HX, Harrogate HG, Harrow HA, Hemel Hempstead HP, Hereford HR, Huddersfield HD, Hull HU, Ilford IG, Ipswich IP, Kingston upon Thames KT, Lancaster LA, Leeds LS, Leicester LE, Lincoln LN, Liverpool L, Llandrindod Wells LD, Llandudno LL, London East E, London East Central EC, London North N, London North West NW, London South East SE, London South West SW, London West W, London West Central WC, Luton LU, Manchester M, Medway ME, Milton Keynes MK, Newcastle NE, Newport NP, Northampton NN, Norwich NR, Nottingham NG, Oldham OL, Oxford OX, Peterborough PE, Plymouth PL, Portsmouth PO, Preston PR, Reading RG, Redhill RH, Romford RM, Salisbury SP, Sheffield S, Shrewsbury SY Slough SL, Southall (Uxbridge) UB, Southampton SO, Southend on Sea SS, St Albans AL, Stevenage SG, Stockport SK, Stoke on Trent ST, Sunderland SR, Sutton SM, Swansea SA, Swindon SN, Taunton TA, Telford TF, Tonbridge TN, Torquay TQ, Truro TR, Sweeddale (Berwick on Tweed) TD, Twickenham TW, Wakefield WF, Walsall WS, Warrington WA, Watford WD, Wigan WN, Wolverhampton WV, Worcester WR, York YO

DEAN, Gordon
Website: www.hcegroup.co.uk
Office: High Court Enforcement Group Ltd, 27 Lord St, Liverpool L2 9SA
Tel: 0151 236 4751 Fax: 0151 236 8071
DX: 14104 Liverpool
e-mail: gordon.dean@hcegroup.co.uk
Note: Bath BA, Birmingham B, Blackburn BB, Bolton BL, Bournemouth BH, Bradford BD, Brighton BN, Bristol BS, Bromley BR, Cambridge CB, Canterbury CT, Cardiff CF, Carlisle CA, Chelmsford CM, Chester CH, Cleveland (Teesside) TS, Colchester CO, Coventry CV, Crewe CW, Croydon CR, Darlington DL, Dartford DA, Derby DE, Doncaster DN, Dorchester DT, Dudley DY, Durham DH, Enfield EN, Exeter EX, Fylde (Blackpool) FY, Gloucester GL, Guildford GU, Halifax HX, Harrogate HG, Harrow HA, Hemel Hempstead HP, Hereford HR, Huddersfield HD, Hull HU, Ilford IG, Ipswich IP, Kingston upon Thames KT, Lancaster LA, Leeds LS, Leicester LE, Lincoln LN, Liverpool L, Llandrindod Wells LD, Llandudno LL, London East E, London East Central EC, London North N, London North West NW, London South East SE, London South West SW, London West W, London West Central WC, Luton LU, Manchester M, Medway ME, Milton Keynes MK, Newcastle NE, Newport NP, Northampton NN, Norwich NR, Nottingham NG, Oldham OL, Oxford OX, Peterborough PE, Plymouth PL, Portsmouth PO, Preston PR, Reading RG, Redhill RH, Romford RM, Salisbury SP, Sheffield S, Shrewsbury SY Slough SL, Southall (Uxbridge) UB, Southampton SO, Southend on Sea SS, St Albans AL, Stevenage SG, Stockport SK, Stoke on Trent ST, Sunderland SR, Sutton SM, Swansea SA, Swindon SN, Taunton TA, Telford TF, Tonbridge TN, Torquay TQ, Truro TR, Sweeddale (Berwick on Tweed) TD, Twickenham TW, Wakefield WF, Walsall WS, Warrington WA, Watford WD, Wigan WN, Wolverhampton WV, Worcester WR, York YO

DUNCAN, Andrew
Website: www.hcegroup.co.uk
Office: High Court Enforcement Group Ltd, 141 Walter Rd, Swansea SA1 5RW
Tel: 01792 466771 Fax: 01792 455755
DX: 52966 Swansea
e-mail: a.duncan@wwf.co.uk
Note: Bath BA, Birmingham B, Bristol BS, Cardiff CF, Chester CH, Coventry CV, Crewe CW, Derby DE, Dudley DY, Gloucester GL, Guildford GU, Hemel Hempstead HP, Hereford HR, Leicester LE, Llandridnod Wells LD, Llandudno LL, Newport NP, Nottingham NG, Oxford OX, Portsmouth PO, Reading RG, Shrewsbury SY, Slough SL, Southampton SO, Stoke on Trent ST, Swansea SA, Swindon SN, Telford TF, Walsall WS, Wolverhampton WV, Worcester WR

EDDOWES, Mark
Website: www.marstongroup.co.uk
Office: Marston Group Enforcement Centre, Embassy Ho, 60 Church St, Birmingham B3 2DJ
Tel: 0845 340 7250 Fax: 0121 200 7401
DX: 13014 Birmingham
e-mail: hccs@marstongroup.co.uk
Note: Birmingham B, Bromley BR, Chelmsford CM, Coventry CV, Croydon CR, Dartford DA, Derby DE, Doncaster DN, Dudley DY, Enfield EN, Guildford GU, Harrow HA, Hemel Hempstead HP, Hereford HR, Ilford IG, Kingston upon Thames KT, Leicester LE, Lincoln LN, London East E, London East Central EC, London North N, London North West NW, London South East SE, London South West SW, London West W, London West Central WC, Medway ME, Nottingham NG, Redhill RH, Romford RM, Sheffield S, Southall (Uxbridge) UB, Southend on Sea SS, St. Albans AL,

Stevenage SG, Stockport SK, Stoke on Trent ST, Sutton SM, Tonbridge TN, Twickenham TW, Walsall WS, Watford WD, Wolverhampton WV, Worcester WR

EGMORE, Angela
Website: www.hcegroup.co.uk
Office: High Court Enforcement Group Ltd, 141 Walter Rd, Swansea SA1 5RW
Tel: 01792 466771 Fax: 01792 455755
DX: 52966 Swansea
e-mail: devon@hcegroup.co.uk
Note: Bath BA, Bournemouth BH, Dorchester DT, Exeter EX, Plymouth PL, Salisbury SP, Taunton TA, Torquay TQ, Truro TR

EVANS, Philip
Website: www.hcegroup.co.uk
Office: High Court Enforcement Group Ltd, 141 Walter Rd, Swansea SA1 5RW
Tel: 01792 466771 Fax: 01792 455755
DX: 52966 Swansea
e-mail: pevans@cardiff-law.co.uk
Note: Bath BA, Birmingham B, Bristol BS, Cardiff CF, Chester CH, Coventry CV, Crewe CW, Derby DE, Dudley DY, Gloucester GL, Guildford GU, Hemel Hempstead HP, Hereford HR, Leicester LE, Llandridnod Wells LD, Llandudno LL, Newport NP, Nottingham NG, Oxford OX, Portsmouth PO, Reading RG, Shrewsbury SY, Slough SL, Southampton SO, Stoke on Trent ST, Swansea SA, Swindon SN, Telford TF, Walsall WS, Wolverhampton WV, Worcester WR

EWART-JAMES, Andrew
Office: Adept Enforcement Group Ltd, 2nd Fl, 65 London Rd, Gloucester, Gloucestershire GL1 3HF
Tel: 01452 429883 Fax: 01452 300922
DX: 7514 Gloucester
e-mail: andrew.ewart-james@adept-enforcement.co.uk
Note: Bristol BS, Gloucester GL, Hereford HR, Newport NP, Oxford OX, Swindon SN, Worcester WR

FARRINGTON, Patrick
Website: www.hcegroup.co.uk
Office: High Court Enforcement Group Ltd, 141 Walter Rd, Swansea SA1 5RW
Tel: 01792 466771 Fax: 01792 455755
DX: 52966 Swansea
e-mail: pfarrington@hmo.co.uk
Note: Bath BA, Birmingham B, Bristol BS, Cardiff CF, Chester CH, Coventry CV, Crewe CW, Derby DE, Dudley DY, Gloucester GL, Guildford GU, Hemel Hempstead HP, Hereford HR, Leicester LE, Llandridnod Wells LD, Llandudno LL, Newport NP, Nottingham NG, Oxford OX, Portsmouth PO, Reading RG, Shrewsbury SY, Slough SL, Southampton SO, Stoke on Trent ST, Swansea SA, Swindon SN, Telford TF, Walsall WS, Wolverhampton WV, Worcester WR

FELLOWS, Kathleen
Website: www.albertchambers.co.uk
Office: Storey & Fellows, Albert Chambers, 50 Albert Rd, Middlesbrough TS1 1QD
Tel: 01642 218819 Fax: 01642 246546
DX: 60534 Middlesbrough
e-mail: hceo@albertchambers.co.uk
Note: Cleveland (Teeside) TS, Darlington DL, Durham DH, Newcastle NE, Sunderland SR, York YO

GATER, Jonathan
Website: www.hcegroup.co.uk
Office: High Court Enforcement Group Ltd, 141 Walter Rd, Swansea SA1 5RW
Tel: 01792 466771 Fax: 01792 455755
DX: 52966 Swansea
e-mail: hceo@blandy.co.uk
Note: Bath BA, Birmingham B, Bournemouth BH, Brighton BN, Bristol BS, Bromley BR, Canterbury CT, Cardiff CF, Chester CH, Coventry CV, Crewe CW, Croydon CR, Dartford DA, Derby DE, Dudley DY, Gloucester GL, Guildford GU, Harrow HA, Hemel Hempstead HP, Hereford HR, Ilford IG, Kingston upon Thames KT, Leicester LE, Llandridnod Wells LD, Llandudno LL, London East E, London East Central EC, London North N, London North West NW, London South East SE, London South West SW, London West W, London West Central WC, Medway ME, Newport NP, Nottingham NG, Oxford OX, Portsmouth PO, Reading RG, Redhill RH, Romford RM, Salisbury SP, Shrewsbury SY, Slough SL, Southall (Uxbridge) UB, Southampton SO, Stoke on Trent ST, Sutton SM, Swansea SA, Swindon SN, Telford TF, Tonbridge TN, Twickenham TW, Walsall WS, Wolverhampton WV, Worcester WR

HALL, Brian
Website: www.woodfines.co.uk
Office: MEA Enforcement, 6 Bedford Rd, Sandy, Bedfordshire SG19 1EN
Tel: 01767 680251 Fax: 01767 691775
DX: 47801 Sandy
e-mail: bhall@woodfines.co.uk
Note: Cambridge CB, Ipswich IP, Luton LU, Milton Keynes MK, Northampton NN, Norwich NR, Peterborough PE, Stevenage SG

HARRISON, Dion
Website: www.harrisonhce.co.uk
Office: Harrison High Court Enforcement, Milner Way, Ossett WF5 9JQ
Tel: 01924 279000 Fax: 01924 280114
DX: 707162 OSSETT 2
e-mail: post@harrisonhce.co.uk
Note: Wakefield WF

HARRISON, Karl
Website: www.andrewwilsonandco.com
Office: The Sheriffs Office, 26 Missouri Ave, Salford, Manchester M50 2NP
Tel: 0161 925 1800 Fax: 0161 925 1801
DX: 710252 Manchester 3
e-mail: karl.harrison@andrewwilsonandco.com
Note: Bath BA, Birmingham B, Blackburn BB, Bolton BL, Bournemouth BH, Bradford BD, Brighton BN, Bristol BS, Bromley BR, Cambridge CB, Canterbury CT, Cardiff CF, Carlisle CA, Chelmsford CM, Chester CH, Cleveland (Teesside) TS, Colchester CO, Coventry CV, Crewe CW, Croydon CR, Darlington DL, Dartford DA, Derby DE, Doncaster DN, Dorchester DT, Dudley DY, Durham DH, Enfield EN, Exeter EX, Fylde (Blackpool) FY, Gloucester GL, Guildford GU, Halifax HX, Harrogate HG, Harrow HA, Hemel Hempstead HP, Hereford HR, Huddersfield HD, Hull HU, Ilford IG, Ipswich IP, Kingston upon Thames KT, Lancaster LA, Leeds LS, Leicester LE, Lincoln LN, Liverpool L, Llandrindod Wells LD, Llandudno LL, London East E, London East Central EC, London North N, London North West NW, London South East SE, London South West SW, London West W, London West Central WC, Luton LU, Manchester M, Medway ME, Milton Keynes MK, Newcastle NE, Newport NP, Northampton NN, Norwich NR, Nottingham NG, Oldham OL, Oxford OX, Peterborough PE, Plymouth PL, Portsmouth PO,

Preston PR, Reading RG, Redhill RH, Romford RM, Salisbury SP, Sheffield S, Shrewsbury SY Slough SL, Southall (Uxbridge) UB, Southampton SO, Southend on Sea SS, St Albans AL, Stevenage SG, Stockport SK, Stoke on Trent ST, Sunderland SR, Sutton SM, Swansea SA, Swindon SN, Taunton TA, Telford TF, Tonbridge TN, Torquay TQ, Truro TR, Tweeddale (Berwick on Tweed) TD, Twickenham TW, Wakefield WF, Walsall WS, Warrington WA, Watford WD, Wigan WN, Wolverhampton WV, Worcester WR, York YO

HENTY, Charles
Office: Office of the Secondary Central Criminal Court, Old Bailey, London EC4M 7EH
Tel: 020 7248 3277 ext 2326/2323/2338 Fax: 020 7192 2444
e-mail: charles.henty@corpoflondon.gov.uk
Note: London East Central EC

HORNER, Nigel
Website: www.hcegroup.co.uk
Office: High Court Enforcement Group Ltd, 141 Walter Rd, Swansea SA1 5RW
Tel: 01792 466771 Fax: 01792 455755
DX: 52966 Swansea
e-mail: n.horner@wwf.co.uk
Note: Bath BA, Birmingham B, Bristol BS, Cardiff CF, Chester CH, Coventry CV, Crewe CW, Derby DE, Dudley DY, Gloucester GL, Guildford GU, Hemel Hempstead HP, Hereford HR, Leicester LE, Llandridnod Wells LD, Llandudno LL, Newport NP, Nottingham NG, Oxford OX, Portsmouth PO, Reading RG, Shrewsbury SY, Slough SL, Southampton SO, Stoke on Trent ST, Swansea SA, Swindon SN, Telford TF, Walsall WS, Wolverhampton WV, Worcester WR

HUGHES, Gareth
Website: www.marstongroup.co.uk
Office: Marston Group Enforcement Centre, Embassy Ho , 60 Church St, Birmingham B3 2DJ
Tel: 0845 340 7250 Fax: 0121 200 7401
DX: 13014 Birmingham
e-mail: hccs@marstongroup.co.uk
Note: Birmingham B, Bromley BR, Chelmsford CM, Coventry CV, Croydon CR, Dartford DA, Derby DE, Doncaster DN, Dudley DY, Enfield EN, Guildford GU, Harrow HA, Hemel Hempstead HP, Hereford HR, Ilford IG, Kingston upon Thames KT, Leicester LE, Lincoln LN, London East E, London East Central EC, London North N, London North West NW, London South East SE, London South West SW, London West W, London West Central WC, Medway ME, Nottingham NG, Redhill RH, Romford RM, Sheffield S, Southall (Uxbridge) UB, Southend on Sea SS, St. Albans AL, Stevenage SG, Stockport SK, Stoke on Trent ST, Sutton SM, Tonbridge TN, Twickenham TW, Walsall WS, Watford WD, Wolverhampton WV, Worcester WR

JACKSON, Michael
Website: www.marstongroup.co.uk
Office: Marston Group Enforcement Centre, Embassy Ho, 60 Church St, Birmingham B3 2DJ
Tel: 0845 340 7250 Fax: 0121 200 7401
DX: 13014 Birmingham
e-mail: hccs@marstongroup.co.uk
Note: Birmingham B, Bromley BR, Chelmsford CM, Coventry CV, Croydon CR, Dartford DA, Derby DE, Doncaster DN, Dudley DY, Enfield EN, Guildford GU, Harrow HA, Hemel Hempstead HP, Hereford HR, Ilford IG, Kingston upon Thames KT, Leicester LE, Lincoln LN, London East E, London East Central EC, London North N, London North West NW, London South East SE, London South West SW, London West W, London West Central WC, Medway ME, Nottingham NG, Redhill RH, Romford RM, Sheffield S, Southall (Uxbridge) UB, Southend on Sea SS, St Albans AL, Stevenage SG, Stockport SK, Stoke on Trent ST, Sutton SM, Tonbridge TN, Twickenham TW, Walsall WS, Watford WD, Wolverhampton WV, Worcester WR

JAMES, John A
Website: www.marstongroup.co.uk
Office: Embassy House, 60 Church St, Birmingham B3 2DJ
Tel: 0845 340 7250 Fax: 0121 200 7401
DX: 13014 Birmingham
e-mail: hccs@marstongroup.co.uk
Note: Birmingham B, Bromley BR, Chelmsford CM, Coventry CV, Croydon CR, Dartford DA, Derby DE, Doncaster DN, Dudley DY, Enfield EN, Guildford GU, Harrow HA, Hemel Hempstead HP, Hereford HR, Ilford IG, Kingston upon Thames KT, Leicester LE, Lincoln LN, London East E, London East Central EC, London North N, London North West NW, London South East SE, London South West SW, London West W, London West Central WC, Medway ME, Nottingham NG, Redhill RH, Romford RM, Sheffield S, Southall (Uxbridge) UB, Southend on Sea SS, St Albans AL, Stevenage SG, Stockport SK, Stoke on Trent ST, Sutton SM, Tonbridge TN, Twickenham TW, Walsall WS, Watford WD, Wolverhampton WV, Worcester WR

JAMES, John A W
Website: www.hcegroup.co.uk
Office: High Court Enforcement Group Ltd, 141 Walter Rd, Swansea SA1 5RW
Tel: 01792 466771 Fax: 01792 455755
DX: 52966 Swansea
e-mail: jjames@hmo.co.uk
Note: Bath BA, Birmingham B, Bristol BS, Cardiff CF, Chester CH, Coventry CV, Crewe CW, Derby DE, Dudley DY, Gloucester GL, Guildford GU, Hemel Hempstead HP, Hereford HR, Leicester LE, Llandridnod Wells LD, Llandudno LL, Newport NP, Nottingham NG, Oxford OX, Portsmouth PO, Reading RG, Shrewsbury SY, Slough SL, Southampton SO, Stoke on Trent ST, Swansea SA, Swindon SN, Telford TF, Walsall WS, Wolverhampton WV, Worcester WR

KIMBER, Michael
Website: www.hcegroup.co.uk
Office: High Court Enforcement Group Ltd, 141 Walter Rd, Swansea SA1 5RW
Tel: 01792 466771 Fax: 01792 455755
DX: 52966 Swansea
e-mail: michael@tsauction.co.uk
Note: Bath BA, Birmingham B, Bristol BS, Cardiff CF, Chester CH, Coventry CV, Crewe CW, Derby DE, Dudley DY, Gloucester GL, Guildford GU, Harrow HA, Hemel Hempstead HP, Hereford HR, Kingston upon Thames KT, Leicester LE, Llandridnod Wells LD, Llandudno LL, London North West NW, London West W, London West Central WC, Newport NP, Nottingham NG, Oxford OX, Portsmouth PO, Reading RG, Shrewsbury SY, Slough SL, Southall (Uxbridge) UB, Southampton SO, Stoke on Trent ST, Swansea SA, Swindon SN, Telford TF, Twickenham TW, Walsall WS, Wolverhampton WV, Worcester WR

LAMBERT, Stephen
Website: www.harrisonhce.co.uk
Office: Harrison High Court Enforcement, Milner Way, Ossett WF5 9JQ
Tel: 01924 279005 Fax: 01924 280114
DX: 707162 Ossett 2
e-mail: post@harrisonhce.co.uk
Note: Wakefield WF

LEYSHON, Martin
Website: www.hcegroup.co.uk
Office: High Court Enforcement Group Limited, 141 Walter Rd, Swansea SA1 5RW
Tel: 01792 466771 Fax: 01792 455755
DX: 52966 Swansea
e-mail: m.leyshon@hcegroup.co.uk
Note: Bath BA, Birmingham B, Bristol BS, Cardiff CF, Chester CH, Coventry CV, Crewe CW, Derby DE, Dudley DY, Gloucester GL, Guildford GU, Hemel Hempstead HP, Hereford HR, Leicester LE, Llandridnod Wells LD, Llandudno LL, Newport NP, Nottingham NG, Oxford OX, Portsmouth PO, Reading RG, Shrewsbury SY, Slough SL, Southampton SO, Stoke on Trent ST, Swansea SA, Swindon SN, Telford TF, Walsall WS, Wolverhampton WV, Worcester WR

MARSTON, John
Website: www.marstongroup.co.uk
Office: Marston Group Enforcement, Embassy Ho, 60 Church St, Birmingham B3 2DJ
Tel: 0845 340 7250 Fax: 0121 200 7401
DX: 13014 Birmingham
e-mail: hccs@marstongroup.co.uk
Note: Bath BA, Birmingham B, Blackburn BB, Bolton BL, Bournemouth BH, Bradford BD, Brighton BN, Bristol BS, Bromley BR, Cambridge CB, Canterbury CT, Cardiff CF, Carlisle CA, Chelmsford CM, Chester CH, Cleveland (Teesside) TS, Colchester CO, Coventry CV, Crewe CW, Croydon CR, Darlington DL, Dartford DA, Derby DE, Doncaster DN, Dorchester DT, Dudley DY, Durham DH, Enfield EN, Exeter EX, Fylde (Blackpool) FY, Gloucester GL, Guildford GU, Halifax HX, Harrogate HG, Harrow HA, Hemel Hempstead HP, Hereford HR, Huddersfield HD, Hull HU, Ilford IG, Ipswich IP, Kingston upon Thames KT, Lancaster LA, Leeds LS, Leicester LE, Lincoln LN, Liverpool L, Llandrindod Wells LD, Llandudno LL, London East E, London East Central EC, London North N, London North West NW, London South East SE, London South West SW, London West W, London West Central WC, Luton LU, Manchester M, Medway ME, Milton Keynes MK, Newcastle NE, Newport NP, Northampton NN, Norwich NR, Nottingham NG, Oldham OL, Oxford OX, Peterborough PE, Plymouth PL, Portsmouth PO, Preston PR, Reading RG, Redhill RH, Romford RM, Salisbury SP, Sheffield S, Shrewsbury SY Slough SL, Southall (Uxbridge) UB, Southampton SO, Southend on Sea SS, St Albans AL, Stevenage SG, Stockport SK, Stoke on Trent ST, Sunderland SR, Sutton SM, Swansea SA, Swindon SN, Taunton TA, Telford TF, Tonbridge TN, Torquay TQ, Truro TR, Tweeddale (Berwick on Tweed) TD, Twickenham TW, Wakefield WF, Walsall WS, Warrington WA, Watford WD, Wigan WN, Wolverhampton WV, Worcester WR, York YO

MASON, David
Website: www.cullimoredutton.co.uk
Office: Cullimore Dutton, Solicitors, 20 White Friars, Chester CH1 1XS
Tel: 01244 356789 Fax: 01244 312582
DX: 19985 Chester
e-mail: david.mason@cullimoredutton.co.uk
Note: Chester CH, Crewe CW, Liverpool L, Manchester M, Shrewsbury SY, Stockport SK, Warrington WA, Wigan WN

METCALFE, James
Website: www.hcegroup.co.uk
Office: High Court Enforcement Group Ltd, City Hub, 9–11 Peckover St, Bradford, West Yorks BD1 5BE
Tel: 01274 391929 Fax: 01274 734773
DX: 11701 Bradford
e-mail: jim.metcalfe@hcegroup.co.uk
Note: Bath BA, Birmingham B, Blackburn BB, Bolton BL, Bournemouth BH, Bradford BD, Brighton BN, Bristol BS, Bromley BR, Cambridge CB, Canterbury CT, Cardiff CF, Carlisle CA, Chelmsford CM, Chester CH, Cleveland (Teesside) TS, Colchester CO, Coventry CV, Crewe CW, Croydon CR, Darlington DL, Dartford DA, Derby DE, Doncaster DN, Dorchester DT, Dudley DY, Durham DH, Enfield EN, Exeter EX, Fylde (Blackpool) FY, Gloucester GL, Guildford GU, Halifax HX, Harrogate HG, Harrow HA, Hemel Hempstead HP, Hereford HR, Huddersfield HD, Hull HU, Ilford IG, Ipswich IP, Kingston upon Thames KT, Lancaster LA, Leeds LS, Leicester LE, Lincoln LN, Liverpool L, Llandrindod Wells LD, Llandudno LL, London East E, London East Central EC, London North N, London North West NW, London South East SE, London South West SW, London West W, London West Central WC, Luton LU, Manchester M, Medway ME, Milton Keynes MK, Newcastle NE, Newport NP, Northampton NN, Norwich NR, Nottingham NG, Oldham OL, Oxford OX, Peterborough PE, Plymouth PL, Portsmouth PO, Preston PR, Reading RG, Redhill RH, Romford RM, Salisbury SP, Sheffield S, Shrewsbury SY Slough SL, Southall (Uxbridge) UB, Southampton SO, Southend on Sea SS, St Albans AL, Stevenage SG, Stockport SK, Stoke on Trent ST, Sunderland SR, Sutton SM, Swansea SA, Swindon SN, Taunton TA, Telford TF, Tonbridge TN, Torquay TQ, Truro TR, Tweeddale (Berwick on Tweed) TD, Twickenham TW, Wakefield WF, Walsall WS, Warrington WA, Watford WD, Wigan WN, Wolverhampton WV, Worcester WR, York YO

MORGAN, Ian
Website: www.marstongroup.co.uk
Office: Marston Group Enforcement, Embassy Ho, 60 Church St, Birmingham B3 2DJ
Tel: 0845 340 7250 Fax: 0121 200 7401
DX: 13014 Birmingham
e-mail: hccs@marstongroup.co.uk
Note: Bath BA, Birmingham B, Blackburn BB, Bolton BL, Bournemouth BH, Bradford BD, Brighton BN, Bristol BS, Bromley BR, Cambridge CB, Canterbury CT, Cardiff CF, Carlisle CA, Chelmsford CM, Chester CH, Cleveland (Teesside) TS, Colchester CO, Coventry CV, Crewe CW, Croydon CR, Darlington DL, Dartford DA, Derby DE, Doncaster DN, Dorchester DT, Dudley DY, Durham DH,

Enfield EN, Exeter EX, Fylde (Blackpool) FY, Gloucester GL, Guildford GU, Halifax HX, Harrogate HG, Harrow HA, Hemel Hempstead HP, Hereford HR, Huddersfield HD, Hull HU, Ilford IG, Ipswich IP, Kingston upon Thames KT, Lancaster LA, Leeds LS, Leicester LE, Lincoln LN, Liverpool L, Llandrindod Wells LD, Llandudno LL, London East E, London East Central EC, London North N, London North West NW, London South East SE, London South West SW, London West W, London West Central WC, Luton LU, Manchester M, Medway ME, Milton Keynes MK, Newcastle NE, Newport NP, Northampton NN, Norwich NR, Nottingham NG, Oldham OL, Oxford OX, Peterborough PE, Plymouth PL, Portsmouth PO, Preston PR, Reading RG, Redhill RH, Romford RM, Salisbury SP, Sheffield S, Shrewsbury SY Slough SL, Southall (Uxbridge) UB, Southampton SO, Southend on Sea SS, St Albans AL, Stevenage SG, Stockport SK, Stoke on Trent ST, Sunderland SR, Sutton SM, Swansea SA, Swindon SN, Taunton TA, Telford TF, Tonbridge TN, Torquay TQ, Truro TR, Tweeddale (Berwick on Tweed) TD, Twickenham TW, Wakefield WF, Walsall WS, Warrington WA, Watford WD, Wigan WN, Wolverhampton WV, Worcester WR, York YO

PEPPER, Nigel
Website: www.hcegroup.co.uk
Office: High Court Enforcement Group Ltd, 141 Walter Rd, Swansea SA3 5RW
Tel: 01792 466771 Fax: 01792 455755
DX: 52966 Swansea
e-mail: npepper@hmo.co.uk
Note: Bath BA, Birmingham B, Bristol BS, Cardiff CF, Chester CH, Coventry CV, Crewe CW, Derby DE, Dudley DY, Gloucester GL, Guildford GU, Hemel Hempstead HP, Hereford HR, Leicester LE, Llandridnod Wells LD, Llandudno LL, Newport NP, Nottingham NG, Oxford OX, Portsmouth PO, Reading RG, Shrewsbury SY, Slough SL, Southampton SO, Stoke on Trent ST, Swansea SA, Swindon SN, Telford TF, Walsall WS, Wolverhampton WV, Worcester WR

REED, Philip
Office: Cornwall High Court Recovery, Stephens & Scown, Osprey Ho, Malpas Rd, Truro TR1 1UT
Tel: 01872 265100 Fax: 01872 279137
e-mail: debtlink@stephens-scown.co.uk
Note: Plymouth PL, Truro TR

SANDBROOK, Claire
Website: www.sherforce.net
Office: Sherforce, 1 Fetter La, London EC4 1BR
Tel: 0845 890 9207 Fax: 0845 890 9208
e-mail: c-sandbrook@sherforce.net
Note: Bath BA, Birmingham B, Blackburn BB, Bolton BL, Bournemouth BH, Bradford BD, Brighton BN, Bristol BS, Bromley BR, Cambridge CB, Canterbury CT, Cardiff CF, Carlisle CA, Chelmsford CM, Chester CH, Cleveland (Teeside) TS, Colchester CO, Coventry CV, Crewe CW, Croydon CR, Darlington DL, Dartford DA, Derby DE, Doncaster DN, Dorchester DT, Dudley DY, Durham DH, Enfield EN, Exeter EX, Fylde (Blackpool) FY, Gloucester GL, Guildford GU, Halifax HX, Harrogate HG, Harrow HA, Hemel Hempstead HP, Hereford HR, Huddersfield HD, Hull HU, Ilford IG, Ipswich IP, Kingston upon Thames KT, Lancaster LA, Leeds LS, Leicester LE, Lincoln LN, Liverpool L, Llandridnod Wells LD, Llandudno LL, London East E, London East Central EC, London North N, London North West NW, London South East SE, London South West SW, London West W, London West Central WC, Luton LU, Manchester M, Medway ME, Milton Keynes MK, Newcastle NE, Newport NP, Northampton NN, Norwich NR, Nottingham NG, Oldham OL, Oxford OX, Peterborough PE, Plymouth PL, Portsmouth PO, Preston PR, Reading RG, Redhill RH, Romford RM, Salisbury SP, Sheffield S, Shrewsbury SY, Slough SL, Southall (Uxbridge) UB, Southampton SO, Southend on Sea SS, St. Albans AL, Stevenage SG, Stockport SK, Stoke on Trent ST, Sunderland SR, Sutton SM, Swansea SA, Swindon SN, Taunton TA, Telford TF, Tonbridge TN, Torquay TQ, Truro TR, Tweeddale (Berwick upon Tweed) TD, Twickenham TW, Wakefield WF, Walsall WS, Warrington WA, Watford WD, Wigan WN, Wolverhampton WV, Worcester WR, York YO

SMITH, Alan J M
Website: www.hcegroup.co.uk
Office: Enforcement Centre, 3rd Fl, 27 Lord St, Liverpool L2 9SA
Tel: 0151 236 4751 Fax: 0151 236 8071
DX: 14104 Liverpool
e-mail: alan.smith@hcegroup.co.uk
Note: Bath BA, Birmingham B, Blackburn BB, Bolton BL, Bournemouth BH, Bradford BD, Brighton BN, Bristol BS, Bromley BR, Cambridge CB, Canterbury CT, Cardiff CF, Carlisle CA, Chelmsford CM, Chester CH, Cleveland (Teesside) TS, Colchester CO, Coventry CV, Crewe CW, Croydon CR, Darlington DL, Dartford DA, Derby DE, Doncaster DN, Dorchester DT, Dudley DY, Durham DH, Enfield EN, Exeter EX, Fylde (Blackpool) FY, Gloucester GL, Guildford GU, Halifax HX, Harrogate HG, Harrow HA, Hemel Hempstead HP, Hereford HR, Huddersfield HD, Hull HU, Ilford IG, Ipswich IP, Kingston upon Thames KT, Lancaster LA, Leeds LS, Leicester LE, Lincoln LN, Liverpool L, Llandrindod Wells LD, Llandudno LL, London East E, London East Central EC, London North N, London North West NW, London South East SE, London South West SW, London West W, London West Central WC, Luton LU, Manchester M, Medway ME, Milton Keynes MK, Newcastle NE, Newport NP, Northampton NN, Norwich NR, Nottingham NG, Oldham OL, Oxford OX, Peterborough PE, Plymouth PL, Portsmouth PO, Preston PR, Reading RG, Redhill RH, Romford RM, Salisbury SP, Sheffield S, Shrewsbury SY Slough SL, Southall (Uxbridge) UB, Southampton SO, Southend on Sea SS, St Albans AL, Stevenage SG, Stockport SK, Stoke on Trent ST, Sunderland SR, Sutton SM, Swansea SA, Swindon SN, Taunton TA, Telford TF, Tonbridge TN, Torquay TQ, Truro TR, Tweeddale (Berwick on Tweed) TD, Twickenham TW, Wakefield WF, Walsall WS, Warrington WA, Watford WD, Wigan WN, Wolverhampton WV, Worcester WR, York YO

SMITH, Alan S
Website: www.equita.co.uk
Office: Equita Ltd, 42–44 Henry St, Northampton NN1 4BS
Tel: 01604 250116 Fax: 01604 633489
DX: 724180 Leamington Spa 6
e-mail: alan.smith2@capita.co.uk
Note: Bath BA, Birmingham B, Blackburn BB, Bolton BL, Bournemouth BH, Bradford BD, Brighton BN, Bristol BS, Bromley BR, Cambridge CB, Canterbury CT, Cardiff CF, Carlisle CA, Chelmsford CM, Chester CH, Cleveland (Teesside) TS, Colchester CO, Coventry CV, Crewe CW, Croydon CR, Darlington DL, Dartford DA, Derby DE, Doncaster DN, Dorchester DT, Dudley DY, Durham DH, Enfield EN, Exeter EX, Fylde (Blackpool) FY, Gloucester GL, Guildford GU, Halifax HX, Harrogate HG, Harrow HA, Hemel Hempstead HP, Hereford HR, Huddersfield HD, Hull HU, Ilford IG, Ipswich IP, Kingston upon Thames KT, Lancaster LA, Leeds LS, Leicester LE, Lincoln LN, Liverpool L, Llandrindod Wells LD, Llandudno LL, London East E, London East Central EC, London North N, London North West NW, London South East SE, London South West SW, London West W, London West Central WC, Luton LU, Manchester M, Medway ME, Milton Keynes MK, Newcastle NE, Newport NP, Northampton NN, Norwich NR, Nottingham NG, Oldham OL,

Oxford OX, Peterborough PE, Plymouth PL, Portsmouth PO, Preston PR, Reading RG, Redhill RH, Romford RM, Salisbury SP, Sheffield S, Shrewsbury SY Slough SL, Southall (Uxbridge) UB, Southampton SO, Southend on Sea SS, St Albans AL, Stevenage SG, Stockport SK, Stoke on Trent ST, Sunderland SR, Sutton SM, Swansea SA, Swindon SN, Taunton TA, Telford TF, Tonbridge TN, Torquay TQ, Truro TR, Tweeddale (Berwick on Tweed) TD, Twickenham TW, Wakefield WF, Walsall WS, Warrington WA, Watford WD, Wigan WN, Wolverhampton WV, Worcester WR, York YO

SOUTHERN, Norman
Website: www.hcegroup.co.uk
Office: 3rd Fl, 27 Lord St, Liverpool L2 9SA
Tel: 0151 236 4751 Fax: 0151 236 8071
DX: 14104 Liverpool
e-mail: liverpool@hcegroup.co.uk
Note: Bath BA, Birmingham B, Blackburn BB, Bolton BL, Bournemouth BH, Bradford BD, Brighton BN, Bristol BS, Bromley BR, Cambridge CB, Canterbury CT, Cardiff CF, Carlisle CA, Chelmsford CM, Chester CH, Cleveland (Teesside) TS, Colchester CO, Coventry CV, Crewe CW, Croydon CR, Darlington DL, Dartford DA, Derby DE, Doncaster DN, Dorchester DT, Dudley DY, Durham DH, Enfield EN, Exeter EX, Fylde (Blackpool) FY, Gloucester GL, Guildford GU, Halifax HX, Harrogate HG, Harrow HA, Hemel Hempstead HP, Hereford HR, Huddersfield HD, Hull HU, Ilford IG, Ipswich IP, Kingston upon Thames KT, Lancaster LA, Leeds LS, Leicester LE, Lincoln LN, Liverpool L, Llandrindod Wells LD, Llandudno LL, London East E, London East Central EC, London North N, London North West NW, London South East SE, London South West SW, London West W, London West Central WC, Luton LU, Manchester M, Medway ME, Milton Keynes MK, Newcastle NE, Newport NP, Northampton NN, Norwich NR, Nottingham NG, Oldham OL, Oxford OX, Peterborough PE, Plymouth PL, Portsmouth PO, Preston PR, Reading RG, Redhill RH, Romford RM, Salisbury SP, Sheffield S, Shrewsbury SY Slough SL, Southall (Uxbridge) UB, Southampton SO, Southend on Sea SS, St Albans AL, Stevenage SG, Stockport SK, Stoke on Trent ST, Sunderland SR, Sutton SM, Swansea SA, Swindon SN, Taunton TA, Telford TF, Tonbridge TN, Torquay TQ, Truro TR, Tweeddale (Berwick on Tweed) TD, Twickenham TW, Wakefield WF, Walsall WS, Warrington WA, Watford WD, Wigan WN, Wolverhampton WV, Worcester WR, York YO

THOMSON, Patricia
Website: www.andrewwilsonandco.com
Office: The Sheriffs Office, 26 Missouri Ave, Salford, Manchester M50 2NP
Tel: 0161 925 1800 Fax: 0161 925 1801
DX: 710252 Manchester 3
e-mail: tricia.thomson@andrewwilsonandco.com
Note: Bath BA, Birmingham B, Blackburn BB, Bolton BL, Bournemouth BH, Bradford BD, Brighton BN, Bristol BS, Bromley BR, Cambridge CB, Canterbury CT, Cardiff CF, Carlisle CA, Chelmsford CM, Chester CH, Cleveland (Teesside) TS, Colchester CO, Coventry CV, Crewe CW, Croydon CR, Darlington DL, Dartford DA, Derby DE, Doncaster DN, Dorchester DT, Dudley DY, Durham DH, Enfield EN, Exeter EX, Fylde (Blackpool) FY, Gloucester GL, Guildford GU, Halifax HX, Harrogate HG, Harrow HA, Hemel Hempstead HP, Hereford HR, Huddersfield HD, Hull HU, Ilford IG, Ipswich IP, Kingston upon Thames KT, Lancaster LA, Leeds LS, Leicester LE, Lincoln LN, Liverpool L, Llandrindod Wells LD, Llandudno LL, London East E, London East Central EC, London North N, London North West NW, London South East SE, London South West SW, London West W, London West Central WC, Luton LU, Manchester M, Medway ME, Milton Keynes MK, Newcastle NE, Newport NP, Northampton NN, Norwich NR, Nottingham NG, Oldham OL, Oxford OX, Peterborough PE, Plymouth PL, Portsmouth PO, Preston PR, Reading RG, Redhill RH, Romford RM, Salisbury SP, Sheffield S, Shrewsbury SY Slough SL, Southall (Uxbridge) UB, Southampton SO, Southend on Sea SS, St Albans AL, Stevenage SG, Stockport SK, Stoke on Trent ST, Sunderland SR, Sutton SM, Swansea SA, Swindon SN, Taunton TA, Telford TF, Tonbridge TN, Torquay TQ, Truro TR, Tweeddale (Berwick on Tweed) TD, Twickenham TW, Wakefield WF, Walsall WS, Warrington WA, Watford WD, Wigan WN, Wolverhampton WV, Worcester WR, York YO

TODD, Nicholas
Website: www.burlingtongroup.co.uk
Office: Burlington Group, 227–228 Strand, London WC2R 1BE
Tel: 0330 900 8000 Fax: 0330 900 7000
DX: 86 London Chancery Lane
e-mail: nicholas.todd@burlingtongroup.net
Note: Sheffield S

TUNSTILL, Peter
Website: www.breezeandwyles.co.uk
Office: Breeze & Wyles, 2nd Fl, Old London Rd, Hertford, Hertfordshire SG13 7LA
Tel: 01992 558411 Fax: 01992 503889
DX: 57901 Hertford
e-mail: peter.tunstill@breezeandwyles.co.uk
Note: Chelmsford CM, Enfield EN, Hemel Hempstead HP, St. Albans AL, Stevenage SG, Watford WD

VANN, Edward
Website: www.hcegroup.co.uk
Office: Enforcement Centre, 3rd Fl, 27 Lord St, Liverpool L2 9SA
Tel: 0151 236 4751 Fax: 0151 236 8071
DX: 14104 Liverpool
e-mail: liverpool@hcegroup.co.uk
Note: Bath BA, Birmingham B, Blackburn BB, Bolton BL, Bournemouth BH, Bradford BD, Brighton BN, Bristol BS, Bromley BR, Cambridge CB, Canterbury CT, Cardiff CF, Carlisle CA, Chelmsford CM, Chester CH, Cleveland (Teesside) TS, Colchester CO, Coventry CV, Crewe CW, Croydon CR, Darlington DL, Dartford DA, Derby DE, Doncaster DN, Dorchester DT, Dudley DY, Durham DH, Enfield EN, Exeter EX, Fylde (Blackpool) FY, Gloucester GL, Guildford GU, Halifax HX, Harrogate HG, Harrow HA, Hemel Hempstead HP, Hereford HR, Huddersfield HD, Hull HU, Ilford IG, Ipswich IP, Kingston upon Thames KT, Lancaster LA, Leeds LS, Leicester LE, Lincoln LN, Liverpool L, Llandrindod Wells LD, Llandudno LL, London East E, London East Central EC, London North N, London North West NW, London South East SE, London South West SW, London West W, London West Central WC, Luton LU, Manchester M, Medway ME, Milton Keynes MK, Newcastle NE, Newport NP, Northampton NN, Norwich NR, Nottingham NG, Oldham OL, Oxford OX, Peterborough PE, Plymouth PL, Portsmouth PO, Preston PR, Reading RG, Redhill RH, Romford RM, Salisbury SP, Sheffield S, Shrewsbury SY Slough SL, Southall (Uxbridge) UB, Southampton SO, Southend on Sea SS, St Albans AL, Stevenage SG, Stockport SK, Stoke on Trent ST, Sunderland SR, Sutton SM, Swansea SA, Swindon SN, Taunton TA, Telford TF, Tonbridge TN, Torquay TQ, Truro TR, Tweeddale (Berwick on Tweed) TD, Twickenham TW, Wakefield WF, Walsall WS, Warrington WA, Watford WD, Wigan WN, Wolverhampton WV, Worcester WR, York YO

WATT, Peter
Website: www.thesherrifsoffice.com
Office: Sheriffs High Court Enforcement Ltd, The Sheriff's Office, Airport Ho, Purley Way, Croydon CR0 0XZ
Tel: 0845 688 9750 Fax: 0845 688 9760
DX: 156870 Croydon 41
e-mail: peter.watt@thesheriffsoffice.com
Note: Bournemouth BH, Brighton BN, Bristol BS, Bromley BR, Cambridge CB, Cardiff CF, Chelmsford CM, Colchester CO, Croydon CR, Dartford DA, Enfield EN, Gloucester GL, Guildford GU, Harrow HA, Hemel Hempstead HP, Hereford HR, Ipswich IP, Kingston upon Thames KT, Leicester LE, Llandrindod Wells LD, London East E, London East Central EC, London North N, London North West NW, London South East SE, London South West SW, London West W, London West Central WC, Luton LU, Medway ME, Milton Keynes MK, Northampton NN, Norwich NR, Oxford OX, Peterborough PE, Portsmouth PO, Reading EG, Redhill RH, Romford RM, Slough SL, Southall (Uxbridge) UB, Southampton SO, St Albans AL, Stevenage SG, Sutton SM, Swansea SA, Swindon SN, Tonbridge TN, Twickenham TW, Watford WD

WHITWORTH, Frank
Website: www.frankgwhitworth-hce.co.uk
Office: 17 Cloth Hall St, Huddersfield HD1 2DX
Tel: 01484 427467 Fax: 01484 484313
DX: 713001 Huddersfield
e-mail: frank.whitworth@btconnect.com
Note: Bradford BD, Halifax HX, Harrogate HG, Huddersfield HD, Leeds LS, Oldham OL, Wakefield WF

WILLIAMSON, Simon
Website: www.millbankgroup.com
Office: Millbank Group, Millbank Business Centre, 72–94 Millbank St, Southampton SO14 5QN
Tel: 02380 236329 Fax: 02380 332159
e-mail: simon@millbankgroup.com
Note: Birmingham B, Bromley BR, Chelmsford CM, Coventry CV, Croydon CR, Dartford DA, Derby DE, Doncaster DN, Dudley DY, Enfield EN, Guildford GU, Harrow HA, Hemel Hempstead HP, Hereford HR, Ilford IG, Kingston upon Thames KT, Leicester LE, Lincoln LN, London East E, London East Central EC, London North N, London North West NW, London South East SE, London South West SW, London West W, London West Central WC, Medway ME, Nottingham NG, Redhill RH, Romford RM, Sheffield S, Southall (Uxbridge) UB, Southend on Sea SS, St Albans AL, Stevenage SG, Stockport SK, Stoke on Trent ST, Sutton SM, Tonbridge TN, Twickenham TW, Walsall WS, Watford WD, Wolverhampton WV, Worcester WR

WILSON, Andrew
Website: www.andrewwilsonandco.com
Office: The Sheriffs Office, 26 Missouri Ave, Salford, Manchester M50 2NP
Tel: 0161 925 1800 Fax: 0161 925 1801
DX: 710252 Manchester 3
e-mail: andrew@andrewwilsonandco.com
Note: Bath BA, Birmingham B, Blackburn BB, Bolton BL, Bournemouth BH, Bradford BD, Brighton BN, Bristol BS, Bromley BR, Cambridge CB, Canterbury CT, Cardiff CF, Carlisle CA, Chelmsford CM, Chester CH, Cleveland (Teesside) TS, Colchester CO, Coventry CV, Crewe CW, Croydon CR, Darlington DL, Dartford DA, Derby DE, Doncaster DN, Dorchester DT, Dudley DY, Durham DH, Enfield EN, Exeter EX, Fylde (Blackpool) FY, Gloucester GL, Guildford GU, Halifax HX, Harrogate HG, Harrow HA, Hemel Hempstead HP, Hereford HR, Huddersfield HD, Hull HU, Ilford IG, Ipswich IP, Kingston upon Thames KT, Lancaster LA, Leeds LS, Leicester LE, Lincoln LN, Liverpool L, Llandrindod Wells LD, Llandudno LL, London East E, London East Central EC, London North N, London North West NW, London South East SE, London South West SW, London West W, London West Central WC, Luton LU, Manchester M, Medway ME, Milton Keynes MK, Newcastle NE, Newport NP, Northampton NN, Norwich NR, Nottingham NG, Oldham OL, Oxford OX, Peterborough PE, Plymouth PL, Portsmouth PO, Preston PR, Reading RG, Redhill RH, Romford RM, Salisbury SP, Sheffield S, Shrewsbury SY Slough SL, Southall (Uxbridge) UB, Southampton SO, Southend on Sea SS, St Albans AL, Stevenage SG, Stockport SK, Stoke on Trent ST, Sunderland SR, Sutton SM, Swansea SA, Swindon SN, Taunton TA, Telford TF, Tonbridge TN, Torquay TQ, Truro TR, Tweeddale (Berwick on Tweed) TD, Twickenham TW, Wakefield WF, Walsall WS, Warrington WA, Watford WD, Wigan WN, Wolverhampton WV, Worcester WR, York YO

Part 13

Utilities

Electricity and Gas Companies

AES Ballylumford
Website: www.aes.com
Head Office: Ballylumford, Islandmagee, Larne BT40 3RS
Tel: 028 9338 1100 Fax: 028 9338 1240
e-mail: information@aes.com

AES Kilroot Power
Website: www.aes.com
Head Office: Kilroot Power Stn, Larne Rd, Carrickfergus BT38 7LX
Tel: 028 9335 1644 Fax: 028 9335 6265
e-mail: information@aes.com

British Gas Trading Limited
Website: www.britishgas.co.uk
Head Office: Lakeside, 30 The Causeway, Staines, Middx TW18 3BY
Tel: 01784 874000 Fax: 01784 878719
e-mail: customerservice@britishgas.co.uk

Centrica plc
Website: www.centrica.com
Head Office: Millstream, Maidenhead Rd, Windsor SL4 5GD
Tel: 01753 494000 Fax: 01753 494001

E.ON UK (formerly Powergen plc)
Website: www.eon-uk.com
Head Office: Westwood Way, Westwood Business Pk, Coventry CV4 8LG
Tel: 02476 424 000 Fax: 02476 425 432

EDF Energy
Website: www.edfenergy.com
Head Office: 3rd Fl, Cardinal Pl, 80 Victoria St, London SW1E 5JL
Tel: 020 7061 4000 Fax: 020 7061 5000
e-mail: info@edfenergy.com
Note: Customer Enqs: 0800 096 2270; Customer Relations: 0800 028 4587

Guernsey Electricity
Website: www.electricity.gg
Head Office: PO Box 4, Electricity Ho, Northside, Vale, Guernsey GY1 3AD
Tel: 01481 200700 Fax: 01481 246942
e-mail: admin@electricity.gg

Jersey Electricity
Website: www.jec.co.uk
Head Office: The Powerhouse, PO Box 45, Queens Rd, St Helier JE4 8NY
Tel: 01534 505460 Fax: 01534 505565
e-mail: jec@jec.co.uk

Manweb Scottish Power
Website: www.scottishpower.co.uk
Head Office: 1 Atlantic Quay, Glasgow G2 8SP
Tel: 0141 568 2000 Fax: 0141 248 8300

Manx Electricity Authority
Website: www.manxelectricity.com
Head Office: PO Box 177, Douglas, Isle of Man IM99 1PS
Tel: 01624 687687 Fax: 01624 687612
e-mail: mea@gov.im

National Grid
Website: www.nationalgrid.com
Office for National Transmission: National Grid-UKT, National Grid Ho, Warwick Technology Pk, Gallows Hill, Warwick CV34 6DA
Tel: 01926 653000 Fax: 01926 654378
General Enquiries: National Grid-UKD, Brick Kiln St, Hinckley LE10 0NA
Tel: 0845 835 1111
e-mail: customersupport@nationalgrid.com

Northern Ireland Electricity
Website: www.nie.co.uk
Head Office: 120 Malone Rd, Belfast BT9 5HT
Tel: 08457 643643
Note: Contact via website

Northern Powergrid
Website: www.northernpowergrid.com
Head Office: Lloyds Ct, 78 Grey St, Newcastle upon Tyne NE1 6AF
Tel: 0845 070 7172 (general) / 0870 160 0910 (records)
Note: Contact via website

RWE Npower plc
Website: www.rwe.com
Headquarters: Windmill Hill Business Pk, Whitehill Way, Swindon SN5 6PB
Tel: 01793 877777 Fax: 01793 892525

SSE plc
Website: www.sse.co.uk
Head Office: Legal Services, Inveralmond Ho, 200 Dunkeld Rd, Perth PH1 3AQ
Tel: 01738 456000
e-mail: info@sse.co.uk

Scottish Power
Website: www.scottishpower.com
Head Office: Corporate Office, 1 Atlantic Quay, Glasgow G2 8SP
Tel: 0141 248 8200 Fax: 0141 248 8300

Southern Electric (SSE plc)
Website: www.southern-electric.co.uk
Head Office: Inveralmond Ho, 200 Dunkeld Rd, Perth PH1 3AQ
Tel: 01738 456000
e-mail: customerservice@southern-electric.co.uk
Customer Service Centre: Customer Service Centre, PO Box 6009, Basingstoke RG21 8ZD
Tel: 0845 7444555
e-mail: customerservice@southern-electric.co.uk
Mapping Services: Mapping Services, PO Box 6206, Basingstoke RG24 8BW
Tel: 01256 337292
e-mail: mapping.services@sse.com
Scottish Hydro Electric: PO Box 7506, Perth PH1 3QR
Tel: 0845 300 2141
e-mail: customerservice@hydro.co.uk

United Utilities
Website: www.unitedutilities.com
Head Office: Haweswater Ho, Lingley Mere Business Pk, Great Sankey, Warrington WA5 3LP
Tel: 01925 237000 Fax: 01925 237073
e-mail: info@uuplc.co.uk
Business Enquiries: Legal, Grasmere Ho, Lingley Mere Business Pk, Great Sankey, Warrington WA5 3LP
Tel: 01925 237000
Water and Drainage Services: Property Searches, Stephen's Way, Goose Green, Wigan WN3 6PJ
Tel: 0870 7510101 Fax: 0870 7510102
DX: 719690 Wigan 8
e-mail: property.searches@uuplc.co.uk

Western Power Distribution
Website: www.westernpower.co.uk
Head Office: Avonbank, Feeder Rd, Bristol BS2 0TB
Tel: 0117 933 2000 Fax: 0117 933 2001
e-mail: info@westernpower.co.uk

Environment Agencies

Anglian Region Environment Agency
Website: www.gov.uk/government/organisations/environment-agency
Head Office: Kingfisher Ho, Goldhay Way, Orton Goldhay, Peterborough PE2 5ZR
Tel: 03708 506506 Fax: 01733 464487
DX: 701640 Orton Goldhay
e-mail: enquiries@environment-agency.gov.uk
Central Area Office: Bromholme La, Brampton, Huntingdon, Cambs PE28 4NE
Tel: 03708 506506
e-mail: enquiries@environment-agency.gov.uk
Eastern Area Office: Cobham Rd, Ipswich, Suffolk IP3 9JD
Tel: 03708 506506
e-mail: enquiries@environment-agency.gov.uk
Northern Area Office: Waterside Ho, Waterside North, Lincoln, Lincs LN2 5HA
Tel: 03708 506506
e-mail: enquiries@environment-agency.gov.uk

Environment Agency
Website: www.environment-agency.gov.uk
Head Office: Ergon Ho, Horseferry Rd, London SW1P 2AL
Tel: 0370 8506 506
e-mail: enquiries@environment-agency.gov.uk
Flood & Coastal Risk, Finance & Resource: Horizon Ho, Deanery Rd, Bristol BS1 5AH
Tel: 0370 850 6506 Fax: 0117 934 5115
DX: 121225 Bristol 43
e-mail: enquiries@environment-agency.gov.uk
Note: minicom: 08702 422 549

Midlands Region Environment Agency
Website: www.environment-agency.gov.uk
Head Office: Midlands Regional Office, Sapphire East, 550 Streetsbrook Rd, Solihull B91 1QT
Tel: 03708 506506 Fax: 0121 711 5859
DX: 702280 Solihull 3
e-mail: enquiries@environment-agency.gov.uk
Central Area Office: Sentinel Ho, 9 Wellington Cres, Fradley Pk, Lichfield, Staffs WS13 8RR
Tel: 03708 506506
e-mail: enquiries@environment-agency.gov.uk
East Area Office: Trentside Offices, Scarrington Rd, West Bridgford, Nottingham, Notts NG2 5FA
Tel: 03708 506506
e-mail: enquiries@environment-agency.gov.uk
West Area Office: Riversmeet Ho, Northway La, Tewkesbury, Glos GL20 8JG
Tel: 03708 506506
e-mail: enquiries@environment-agency.gov.uk

Natural Resources Wales
Website: www.cyfoethnaturiolcymru.gov.uk / www.naturalresourceswales.gov.uk
Head Office (Regional): Cambria Ho, 29 Newport Rd, Cardiff CF24 0TP
Tel: 0300 065 3000 Fax: 029 2046 6417
DX: 121376 Cardiff
e-mail: enquiries@naturalresourceswales.gov.uk
Northern Area Office: Ffordd Penlan, Parc Menai, Bangor, Gwynedd LL57 4DE
Tel: 0300 065 3000
e-mail: enquiries@naturalresourceswales.gov.uk
South East Area Office: Rivers Ho, St Mellons Business Pk, St Mellons, Cardiff CF3 0EY
Tel: 0300 065 3000
e-mail: enquiries@naturalresourceswales.gov.uk
South West Area Office: Maes Newydd, Llandarcy, Neath, Glamorgan SA10 6JQ
Tel: 0300 065 3000
e-mail: enquiries@naturalresourceswales.gov.uk

North West Region Environment Agency
Website: www.environment-agency.gov.uk
Regional & South Area Office: North West Regional Office, Richard Fairclough Ho, Knutsford Rd, Latchford, Warrington WA4 1HT
Tel: 03708 506506 Fax: 01925 574736
DX: 709290 Warrington 5
e-mail: enquiries@environment-agency.gov.uk
Central Area Office: Lutra Ho, Dodd Way, Walton Summit, Bamber Bridge, Preston, Lancs PR5 8BX
Tel: 03708 506506
e-mail: enquiries@environment-agency.gov.uk
North Area Office: Ghyll Mount, Gilian Way, Penrith 40 Business Pk, Penrith, Cumbria CA11 9BP
Tel: 03708 506506
e-mail: enquiries@environment-agency.gov.uk

South East Region Environment Agency
Website: www.environment-agency.gov.uk
Head Office: Regional Office, Kings Meadow Ho, Kings Meadow Rd, Reading RG1 8DQ
Tel: 03708 506506 Fax: 0118 950 9440
DX: 121325 Reading 10
e-mail: enquiries@environment-agency.gov.uk
Kent/South London Office: Orchard Ho, Endeavour Pk, London Rd, Addington, West Malling ME19 5SH
Tel: 03708 506506
e-mail: enquiries@environment-agency.gov.uk
North East Thames Area Office: Apollo Ct, 2 St Bishops Sq Business Pk, St Albans Rd West, Hatfield AL10 9EX
Tel: 03708 506506
e-mail: enquiries@environment-agency.gov.uk
Solent and South Downs Area Office: Regional Office, Guildborne Ho, Chatsworth Rd, Worthing BN11 1LD
Tel: 03708 506506 Fax: 01903 832058
DX: 3713 Worthing
e-mail: enquiries@environment-agency.gov.uk
West Thames Area Office: West Area Office, Howbery Pk, Crowmarsh Gifford, Wallingford OX10 8BD
Tel: 0370 8506 506
e-mail: enquiries@environment-agency.gov.uk

South West Region Environment Agency
Website: www.environment-agency.gov.uk
Head Office: Regional Office, Manley Ho, Kestrel Way, Exeter EX2 7LQ
Tel: 03708 506506 Fax: 01392 442112
DX: 121350 Exeter 12
e-mail: enquiries@environment-agency.gov.uk
Cornwall Area Office: Sir John Moore Ho, Victoria Sq, Bodmin, Cornwall PL31 1EB
Tel: 03708 506506
e-mail: enquiries@environment-agency.gov.uk
North Wessex Area Office: Rivers Ho, East Quay, Bridgewater, Somerset TA6 4YS
Tel: 03708 506506
e-mail: enquiries@environment-agency.gov.uk
South Wessex Area Office: Rivers Ho, Sunrise Business Pk, Higher Shaftesbury Rd, Blandford, Dorset DT11 8ST
Tel: 03708 506506
e-mail: enquiries@environment-agency.gov.uk

Yorkshire and North East Region Environment Agency
Website: www.environment-agency.gov.uk
Yorkshire Area Office: Regional Office, Lateral, 8 City Walk, Leeds LS11 9AT
Tel: 03708 506506 Fax: 0113 819 6400
DX: 14095 Leeds Park Square
e-mail: enquiries@environment-agency.gov.uk
North East Area Office: Regional Office, Tyneside Ho, Skinnerburn Rd, Newcastle Business Pk, Newcastle upon Tyne NE4 7AR
Tel: 03708 506506
e-mail: enquiries@environment-agency.gov.uk

National Water Companies

Anglian Water plc
Website: www.anglianwater.co.uk
Head Office: Anglian Water Services, Lancaster Ho, Lancaster Way, Ermine Business Park , Huntingdon PE29 6YJ
Tel: 01480 323000 Fax: 01480 323115
Note: minicom: 0800 917 5901
Drainage Enquiries: Geodesys, Osprey Ho, 1 Percy Rd, Huntingdon, Cambs PE29 6SZ
Tel: 0845 070 9109 Fax: 01480 323890
DX: 123730 Huntingdon 6
e-mail: customer.services@geodesys.com

Dwr Cymru Welsh Water
Website: www.dwrcymru.com
Head Office: Pentwyn Rd, Nelson, Treharris, Mid Glamorgan CF46 6LY
Tel: 01443 452300 / 0800 052 0145 (General Enquiries)
Fax: 01443 452323
e-mail: contact via website

Northumbrian Water Ltd
Website: www.nwpropertysolutions.co.uk
Head Office: Northumbria Ho, Abbey Rd, Pity Me, Durham DH1 5FJ
Tel: 0845 607 7468
DX: 717042 Durham 15
e-mail: propertysolutions@nwl.co.uk

Severn Trent Water Ltd
Website: www.stwater.co.uk
Head Office: 2 St Johns St, Coventry CV1 2LZ
Tel: 0247 771 5000 Fax: 0247 771 5871
e-mail: customercare@severntrent.co.uk

South West Water Ltd
Website: www.sourceforsearches.co.uk
Head Office: Source for Searches, Peninsula Ho, Rydon La, Exeter EX2 7HR
Tel: 08453 303401 Fax: 01392 443912
DX: 119851 Exeter 10
e-mail: contactus@sourceforsearches.co.uk

Southern Water Services Ltd
Website: www.southernwater.co.uk
Registered Head Office: Southern Ho, Yeoman Rd, Worthing BN13 3NX
Tel: 01903 264444; Enquiries 0845 2780845
Fax: 01903 272609
DX: 400500 Goring-by-Sea 3
e-mail: customerservices@southernwater.co.uk
Accounts Office: PO Box 41, Worthing BN13 3NZ
Tel: 0845 272 0845
Land Searches: Southern Water Land Searches, Southern Ho, Capstone Rd, Chatham ME5 7QA
Tel: 0845 270 0212 Fax: 01634 844514
DX: 400450 Chatham 5
e-mail: searches@southernwater.co.uk

Thames Water Utilities Ltd
Website: www.thameswater.co.uk
Head Office: Clearwater Ct, Vastern Rd, Reading RG1 8DB
Tel: 0118 373 8000
Operational/Emergency & General Enquiry: Customer Services, PO Box 286, Swindon SN38 2RA
Tel: 0845 920 0800 (Water enqs) / 0845 920 0888 (accounts)
e-mail: customer.feedback@thameswater.co.uk
Solicitor Searches/Drainage Enquiries: Thames Water Property Searches, PO Box 3189, Slough SL1 4WW
Tel: 0118 925 1504
DX: 151280 Slough 13
e-mail: onlinecustomers@thameswater.co.uk

United Utilities (formerly North West Water Ltd)
Website: www.unitedutilities.co.uk
Head Office: Haweswater Ho, Lingley Mere Business Pk, Lingley Mere Ave, Great Sankey, Warrington WA5 3LP
Tel: 01925 237000 Fax: 01925 237073
e-mail: info@uuplc.co.uk
Legal Dept: Legal Services, Grasmere Ho, Lingley Mere Business Pk, Great Sankey, Warrington WA5 3LP
Tel: 01925 731345 Fax: 01925 678957
DX: 715567 Warrington 7
e-mail: legalservices@uuplc.co.uk
Water and Drainage Searches: Property Searches, Grasmere Ho, Linley Mere Business Pk, Great Sankey, Warrington WA5 3LP
Tel: 0870 7510101 Fax: 0870 7510102
DX: 715568 Warrington 7
e-mail: property.searches@uuplc.co.uk

Wessex Water Enterprises
Website: www.wessexsearches.co.uk
Head Office: Operations Centre, Claverton Down, Bath BA2 7WW
Tel: 01225 526000 Fax: 01225 528994
e-mail: contactus@wessexsearches.co.uk
Accounts Office: Operations Centre, Claverton Down, Bath BA2 7WW
Tel: 01225 526000 Fax: 01225 528994
e-mail: contactus@wessexsearches.co.uk
Note: Area split. Contact either Planning Services, Council Offices, as above or Exmoor National Park, Exmoor Ho, Dulverton

Emergencies & Operational Problems: Operations Centre, Claverton Down, Bath BA2 7WW
Tel: 0845 600 4600
e-mail: contactus@wessexsearches.co.uk

Regional Water Companies

Affinity Water
Website: www.affinitywater.co.uk
Central Office: Tamblin Way, Hatfield, Herts AL10 9EZ
Tel: 01707 268111 Fax: 01707 277333
Note: minicom: 01206 399277@office = *South East Office:* Cherry Garden Lane, Folkestone, Kent CT19 4QB
Tel: 01303 298800 Fax: 01303 276712
e-mail: enquiries.southeast@veoliawater.co.uk
East Office: Mill Hill, Mannington, Essex CO11 2AZ
Tel: 0845 1489 288 (general) / 0845 1489 299 (emergency)
Fax: 01206 399210

Bristol Water plc
Website: www.bristolwater.co.uk
Head Office: PO Box No 218, Bridgwater Rd, Bristol BS99 7AU
Tel: 0117 966 5881
e-mail: customer.services@bristolwater.co.uk

Cambridge Water plc
Website: www.cambridge-water.co.uk
Head Office: Operations Office, 90 Fulbourn Rd, Cambridge CB1 9JN
Tel: 01223 706050 Fax: 01223 214052
e-mail: info@cambridge-water.co.uk
Note: Areas of responsibility: Water supply

Cholderton & District Water Co
Website: www.choldertonwater.co.uk
Head Office: The Estate Office, Cholderton, Salisbury, Wiltshire SP4 0DR
Tel: 01980 629 203
e-mail: admin@cholderton-estate.co.uk

Dee Valley Group plc
Website: www.deevalleygroup.com
Head Office: Packsaddle, Wrexham Rd, Rhostyllen, Wrexham LL14 4EH
Tel: 01978 846946 / Accounts 01978 833200
Fax: 01978 846888
e-mail: contact@deevalleygroup.com
Note: Water supply. Group incorporates Dee Valley Water plc

Hartlepool Water
Website: www.hartlepoolwater.co.uk
Head Office: Operations Support, 3 Lancaster Rd, Hartlepool TS24 8LW
Tel: 01429 858050 Fax: 01429 858000
e-mail: enquiries@hartlepoolwater.co.uk
Note: Areas of responsibility: Water supply only, Hartlepool area

Independent Water Networks
Head Office: Driscoll 2, Ellen St, Cardiff CF10 4BP
Tel: 02920 028711 Fax: 0871 429 0589
e-mail: enquiries@iwnl.co.uk

Portsmouth Water Ltd
Website: www.portsmouthwater.co.uk
Head Office: PO Box 8, West St, Havant PO9 1LG
Tel: 023 92499888 Fax: 023 92453632
e-mail: head.office@portsmouthwater.co.uk

Sembcorp Bournemouth Water Ltd
Website: www.sembcorpbw.co.uk
Head Office: George Jessel Ho, Francis Ave, Bournemouth BH11 8NX
Tel: 01202 591111 Fax: 01202 597022
e-mail: customerservice@sembcorpbw.co.uk

South East Water Ltd
Website: www.southeastwater.co.uk
Head Office: Rocfort Rd, Snodland, Kent ME6 5AH
Tel: 0333 000 0001 Fax: 01634 242764
Note: Contact via website

South Staffordshire Water plc
Website: www.south-staffs-water.co.uk
Head Office: Green Lane, Walsall WS2 7PD
Tel: 01922 638282 Fax: 01922 723621
Note: Contact via website; minicom: 01922 618025

Sutton and East Surrey Water plc
Website: www.waterplc.com
Head Office: London Rd, Redhill RH1 1LJ
Tel: 01737 772000 Fax: 01737 766807
e-mail: sesw@waterplc.com

Yorkshire Water, Safe-move
Website: www.safe-move.co.uk
Head Office: PO Box 99, Bradford BD3 7YB
Tel: 0800 1385 385 Fax: 01274 253502
DX: 723020 Bradford 20
e-mail: safemove@yorkshirewater.com
Note: For Searches see www.safe-move.co.uk

Scottish Water Authorities

Scottish Water
Website: www.scottishwater.co.uk
Head Office: Castle Ho, 6 Castle Dr, Carnegie Campus, Dunfermline KY11 8GG
Tel: 0845 601 8855
e-mail: customer.services@scottishwater.co.uk
Customer Enquiries: PO Box 8855, Edinburgh EH10 6YQ
Tel: 0845 601 8855
e-mail: customer.services@scottishwater.co.uk

Part 14

General Addresses

Architects Registration Board

Architects Registration Board
Website: www.arb.org.uk
Head Office: 8 Weymouth St, London W1W 5BU
Tel: 020 7580 5861 Fax: 020 7436 5269
e-mail: info@arb.org.uk

Architectural Association

Architectural Association (AA) School of Architecture
Website: www.aaschool.ac.uk
Head Office: 36 Bedford Sq, London WC1B 3ES
Tel: 020 7887 4000 Fax: 020 7414 0782
e-mail: webmaster@aaschool.ac.uk

Associated British Ports

Associated British Ports
Website: www.abports.co.uk
Head Office: Aldwych Ho, 71–91 Aldwych, London WC2B 4HN
Tel: 020 7430 1177 Fax: 020 7406 7896
e-mail: abpsales@abports.co.uk

Association of British Insurers

The Association of British Insurers
Website: www.abi.org.uk
Head Office: 51 Gresham St, London EC2V 7HQ
Tel: 020 7600 3333 Fax: 020 7696 8999
e-mail: info@abi.org.uk

Association of Building Engineers

Association of Building Engineers
Website: www.cbuilde.com
Head Office: Chief Executive, Lutyens Ho, Billing Brook Rd, Weston Favell, Northampton NN3 8NW
Tel: 01604 404121 Fax: 01604 784220
e-mail: building.engineers@cbuilde.com

BAA Ltd

BAA Ltd
Website: www.heathrowairport.com/about-us
Head Office: The Compass Centre, Nelson Rd, London Heathrow Airport, Hounslow TW6 2GW
Tel: 0844 335 1801
e-mail: web.queries@computershare.co.uk

Births, Marriages and Deaths (certificates)

General Register Office
Website: www.gro.gov.uk
Post: Identity & Passport Service, General Register Office for England and Wales, PO Box 2, Southport, Merseyside PR8 2JD
Tel: 0300 123 1837
DX: 709741 Birkdale 2
e-mail: certificate.services@ips.gsi.gov.uk

British Insurance Brokers Association

British Insurance Brokers Association
Website: www.biba.org.uk
Head Office: 8th Fl, John Stow Ho, 18 Bevis Marks, London EC3A 7JB
Tel: 0870 950 1790 Fax: 020 7626 9676
e-mail: enquiries@biba.org.uk

British Telecommunications plc

British Telecommunications plc
Website: www.bt.com
Head Office: BT Centre, 81 Newgate St, London EC1A 7AJ
Tel: 020 7356 5000 Fax: 020 7356 5520
Customer Services (nationwide):
Tel: x150 (residential); x152 (business) Ext: 152 (business)

British Waterways

Canal and River Trust
Website: www.canalrivertrust.org.uk
Head Office: 1st Fl Nth, Station Ho, 500 Elder Gate, Milton Keynes MK9 1BB
Tel: 0303 040 4040
e-mail: customer.services@canalrivertrust.org.uk
Central Shires & West Midlands Waterways: Peel's Wharf, Lichfield St, Fazeley, Tamworth, Staffs B78 3QZ
Tel: 01827 252000 Fax: 01827 288071
e-mail: enquiries.westmidlands@canalrivertrust.org.uk
East Midlands Waterways: The Kiln, Mather Rd, Newark, Notts NG24 1FB
Tel: 01636 704481 Fax: 01636 705584
e-mail: enquiries.eastmidlands@canalrivertrust.org.uk
Kennet and Avon Waterways: The Locks, Bath Rd, Devizes SN10 1QR
Tel: 01380 722859
e-mail: enquiries.kennetavon@canalrivertrust.org.uk
London Waterways: Docklands Office, 420 Manchester Rd, London E14 9ST
Tel: 020 7985 7200 Fax: 020 7985 7201
e-mail: enquiries.london@canalrivertrust.org.uk
Manchester and Pennine Waterways: Red Bull Wharf, Congleton Rd Sth, Church Lawton, Stoke-on-Trent ST7 3AP
Tel: 01782 785703
e-mail: enquiries.manchesterpennine@canalrivertrust.org.uk

North East Waterways: Fearns Wharf, Neptune St, Leeds LS9 8PB
Tel: 0113 281 6800 Fax: 0113 281 6886
e-mail: enquiries.northeast@canalrivertrust.org.uk
North Wales & Border Counties Waterways: Navigation Rd, Northwich, Cheshire CW8 1BH
Tel: 01606 723800 Fax: 01606 871471
e-mail: enquiries.northwalesborders@canalrivertrust.org.uk
North West Waterways: Waterside Ho, Waterside Dr, Wigan WN3 5AZ
Tel: 01942 405700 Fax: 01942 405710
e-mail: enquiries.northwest@canalrivertrust.org.uk
South East Waterways: 1st Fl Nth, Station Ho, 500 Elder Gate, Milton Keynes MK9 1BB
Tel: 01908 302500 Fax: 01908 302510
e-mail: enquiries.southeast@canalrivertrust.org.uk
South Wales and Severn Waterways: The Dock Office, Commercial Rd, Gloucester GL1 2EB
Tel: 01452 318000 Fax: 01452 318076
e-mail: enquiries.southwalessevern@canalrivertrust.org.uk

Scottish Canals
Website: www.scottishcanals.co.uk
Lowlands Canal Office (Head Office): Canal Ho, Applecross St, Glasgow G4 9SP
Tel: 0141 332 6936 Fax: 0141 331 1688
e-mail: enquiries@scottishcanals.co.uk
Caledonian Canal Office: Seaport Marina, Muirtown Wharf, Inverness IY3 5LS
Tel: 01463 725500 Fax: 0141 331 1688
e-mail: enquiries@scottishcanals.co.uk
Crinan Canal Office: Pier Sq, Ardrishaig, Argyll PA30 8DZ
Tel: 01546 603210
e-mail: enquiries@scottishcanals.co.uk

Building Research Establishment Ltd

Building Research Establishment Ltd
Website: www.bre.co.uk
Head Office: Building Research Establishment Ltd, Bucknalls La, Garston, Watford WD25 9XX
Tel: 01923 664000 Fax: 01923 664010
e-mail: enquiries@bre.co.uk
Irish Office: BRE Ireland, Bucknalls La, Garston, Watford WD25 9XX
Tel: 0333 321 8811
e-mail: enquiries@bre.co.uk
Scottish Office: BRE Scotland, Scottish Enterprise Technology Pk, East Kilbride, Glasgow G75 0RD
Tel: 01355 576200 Fax: 01355 576210
e-mail: eastkilbride@bre.co.uk
South West & Welsh Office: Ethos, Kings Rd, Swansea Waterfront SA1 8AS
Tel: 01792 630100
e-mail: walesenq@bre.co.uk; southwest@bre.co.uk

Building and Engineering Services Association

Building and Engineering Services Association
Website: www.b-es.org
Head Office: ESCA Ho, 34 Palace Ct, Bayswater, London W2 4JG
Tel: 020 7313 4900 Fax: 020 7727 9268
e-mail: contact@b-es.org

Campaign for the Protection of Rural Wales

Campaign for the Protection of Rural Wales
Website: www.cprw.org.uk
Head Office: Ty Gwyn, 31 High St, Welshpool SY21 7YD
Tel: 01938 552525/556212 Fax: 01938 871552
e-mail: info@cprwmail.org.uk

Central Office Queen's Bench Division

Central Office Queen's Bench Division
Website: www.justice.gov.uk/courts/rcj-rolls-building/queens-bench
Head Office: Queen's Bench Action Dept, Royal Courts of Justice, Strand, London WC2A 2LL
Tel: 020 7947 7228 / 6437
DX: 44450 Strand
e-mail: qbcaseman@hmcts.gsi.gov.uk

Chartered Accountants in England and Wales

The Institute of Chartered Accountants in England and Wales
Website: www.icaew.com
Head Office: Chartered Accountants' Hall, Moorgate Pl, London EC2P 6EA
Tel: 020 7920 8100 Fax: 020 7920 0547
DX: 877 Lon/City
e-mail: generalenquiries@icaew.com
Brussels: European Union Office, The Institute of Chartered Accountants in England & Wales, 227 rue de la Loi, B–1040 Brussels, Belgium
Tel: +322 230 3272 Fax: +322 230 2851
e-mail: europe@icaew.com
Milton Keynes: Level 1, Metropolitan Ho, 321 Avebury Boulevard, Milton Keynes MK9 2FZ
Tel: 01908 248100 Fax: 01908 248088
e-mail: generalenquiries@icaew.com

Chartered Institute of Arbitrators

The Chartered Institute of Arbitrators
Website: www.ciarb.org
Head Office: International Arbitration & Mediation Centre, 12 Bloomsbury Sq, London WC1A 2LP
Tel: 020 7421 7444 Fax: 020 7404 4023
e-mail: info@ciarb.org

Chartered Institute of Building

The Chartered Institute of Building
Website: www.ciob.org.uk
Head Office: 1 Arlington Sq, Downshire Way, Bracknell RG12 1WA
Tel: 01344 630700 Fax: 01344 630777
e-mail: reception@ciob.org.uk
London Office: 50 Broadway, London SW1H 0RG

Chartered Insurance Institute

Chartered Insurance Institute
Website: www.cii.co.uk
Head Office: Customer Service Centre, 42–48 High Rd, South Woodford, London E18 2JP
Tel: 020 8989 8464 Fax: 020 8530 3052
e-mail: customer.serv@cii.co.uk

Cheshire Brine Subsidence Compensation Board

Cheshire Brine Subsidence Compensation Board
Website: www.cheshirebrine.com
Head Office: Sir Henry Doulton Ho, Forge La, Etruria, Stoke-on-Trent ST1 5BD
Tel: 0845 002 0562 Fax: 0845 111 8888
e-mail: info@cheshirebrine.com

Church Commissioners for England

Church Commissioners for England
Website: www.churchofengland.org
Head Office: Legal Office, Church Ho, Great Smith St, London SW1P 3AZ
Tel: 020 7898 1000 Fax: 020 7898 1718/1721
DX: 148403 Westminster 5
e-mail: webmaster@churchofengland.org

College of Arms

College of Arms
Website: www.college-of-arms.gov.uk
Head Office: 130 Queen Victoria St, London EC4V 4BT
Tel: 020 7248 2762 Fax: 020 7248 6448
e-mail: enquiries@college-of-arms.gov.uk

Commission for Racial Equality

Equality and Human Rights Commission
Website: www.equalityhumanrights.com
Head Office: Fleetbank Ho, 2–6 Salisbury Sq, London EC4Y 8JX
Tel: 020 7832 7800 Fax: 020 7832 7801
e-mail: info@equalityhumanrights.com
Scotland: Equality and Human Rights Commission (Scotland), 151 West George St, Glasgow G2 2JJ
Tel: 0141 228 5910 Fax: 0141 228 5912
e-mail: scotland@equalityhumanrights.com
Wales: Equality and Human Rights Commission, 1 Caspian Point, Caspian Way, Cardiff Bay CF10 4DQ
Tel: 029 20 447710 Fax: 029 20 447713
e-mail: wales@equalityhumanrights.com

Community Matters

Community Matters (The National Federation of Community Organisations)
Website: www.communitymatters.org.uk
Head Office: 12–20 Baron St, Islington, London N1 9LL
Tel: 020 7837 7887 Fax: 020 7278 9253
e-mail: info@communitymatters.org.uk

Companies House

The Chief Executive and Registrar of Companies for England and Wales
Website: www.gov.uk/government/organisations/companies-house
Head Office: Companies Ho, Crown Way, Maindy, Cardiff CF14 3UZ
Tel: 0303 1234500
DX: 33050 Cardiff
e-mail: enquiries@companieshouse.gov.uk
Belfast: 2nd Fl, The Linenhall, 32–38 Linenhall St, Belfast BT2 8BG
DX: 481 N.R.Belfast 1
Edinburgh: 4th Fl Edinburgh Quay 2, 139 Fountainbridge, Edinburgh EH3 9FF
Tel: 0303 1234500
DX: ED 235 Edinburgh
e-mail: enquiries@companieshouse.gov.uk
London: London Information Centre, Companies Ho, 4 Abbey Orchard St, London SW1P 2HT
Tel: 0303 1234 500 Fax: 020 7637 6210
e-mail: enquiries@companieshouse.gov.uk

Competition and Markets

Competition and Markets Authority
Website: www.gov.uk/government/organisations/competition-and-markets-authority
Head Office: Victoria Ho, 37 Southampton Row, London WC1B 4AD
Tel: 020 3738 6000
e-mail: general.enquiries@cma.gsi.gov.uk

Cornwall Consultants (Mining Searches)

Cornwall Consultants Ltd
Website: www.cornwallconsultants.co.uk
Head Office: Mining Searches, Park Vean Ho, Coach La, Redruth TR15 2TT
Tel: 01209 313511 Fax: 01209 313512
e-mail: enquiries@cornwallconsultants.co.uk

Council for Licensed Conveyancers

Council for Licensed Conveyancers (CLC)
Website: www.clc-uk.org
Head Office: 16 Glebe Rd, Chelmsford CM1 1QG
Tel: 01245 349599 Fax: 01245 341300
DX: 121925 Chelmsford 6
e-mail: clc@clc-uk.org

Country Land & Business Association

Country Land & Business Association Limited
Website: www.cla.org.uk
Head Office: Legal Dept, 16 Belgrave Sq, London SW1X 8PQ
Tel: 020 7235 0511 Fax: 020 7235 4696
e-mail: mail@cla.org.uk

Criminal Injuries Compensation Authority

Criminal Injuries Compensation Authority
Website: www.gov.uk/government/organisations/criminal-injuries-compensation-authority
Head Office: Alexander Bain Ho, Atlantic Quay, 15 York St, Glasgow G2 8JQ
Tel: 0300 003 3601 Fax: 0141 331 2287
DX: 1GW 379 Glasgow
e-mail: general.enquiries@circa.gsi.gov.uk

Crown Estate

The Crown Estate
Website: www.thecrownestate.co.uk
Head Office: Legal Dept, 16 New Burlington Pl, London W1S 2HX
Tel: 020 7851 5000 Fax: 020 7851 5125
e-mail: legal@thecrownestate.co.uk

Deeds Registries

Bedford Level Deeds Registry
Website: www.cambridgeshire.gov.uk/leisure/archives/
County Record Office: Cambridgeshire Archives, Box SH 1009, Shire Hall, Castle Hill, Cambridge CB3 0AP
Tel: 01223 699399 Fax: 01223 703895
DX: 137870 Cambridge 9
e-mail: cals@cambridgeshire.gov.uk
Note: Conveyances, leases, etc of 'Adventurers' Lands' within the Bedford Level were registered with the Bedford Level Corp between 1649 and 1920.

Middlesex Deeds Registry
Website: www.cityoflondon.gov.uk/lma
London Metropolitan Archives: 40 Northampton Rd, London EC1R 0HB
Tel: 020 7332 3820 Fax: 020 7833 9136
e-mail: ask.lma@cityoflondon.gov.uk

Yorkshire Deeds Registries
Website: www.northyorks.gov.uk/archives
North Riding: North Yorkshire County Record Office, County Hall, Northallerton DL7 8AD
Tel: 01609 777585 Fax: 01609 777078
e-mail: archives@northyorks.gov.uk
Note: 1736 to 1970. No deeds made after 31 August 1970 registered.

Document Exchanges

DX
Website: www.thedx.co.uk
Head Office: DX Ho, Ridgeway, Iver SL0 9JQ
Tel: 01753 657350 Fax: 01753 631631
DX: 1 Iver
e-mail: info@thedx.co.uk

Economic and Social Research Council

Economic and Social Research Council
Website: www.esrcsocietytoday.ac.uk
Head Office: Communications Division, Polaris Ho, North Star Ave, Swindon SN2 1UJ
Tel: 01793 413000 Fax: 01793 413001
e-mail: comms@esrc.ac.uk

Electrical Contractors' Association

Electrical Contractors' Association
Website: www.eca.co.uk
Head Office: ESCA Ho, 34 Palace Ct, London W2 4HY
Tel: 020 7313 4800 Fax: 020 7221 7344
e-mail: info@eca.co.uk

Employment Tribunals (England, Wales & Scotland)

Employment Tribunals Service
Website: www.gov.uk/employment-tribunals
Head Office: Employment Judicial Support, Head Office, Victory Ho, 5th Fl, 30–34 Kingsway, London WC2B 6EX
Tel: 0845 795 9775 (enqs); minicom: 0845 757 3722
e-mail: ets.secretariat@hmcts.gsi.gov.uk
Note: The service also has temporary sites around the country for the purpose of hearing cases only.@office =
Aberdeen: Employment Tribunals Regional Office, Mezzanine Fl, Atholl Ho, 84–88 Guild St, Aberdeen AB11 6LT
Tel: 01224 593137 Fax: 01224 593138
DX: Ab77 Aberdeen
e-mail: aberdeenet@hmcts.gsi.gov.uk
Ashford: Employment Tribunals Regional Office, 1st Fl, Ashford Ho, County Square Shopping Centre, Ashford TN23 1YB
Tel: 01233 621 346 Fax: 01233 624 423
DX: 157160 Ashford (Kent) 8
e-mail: ashfordet@hmcts.gsi.gov.uk
Bedford, Bury St Edmunds & Huntingdon: Employment Tribunals Regional Office, Walden Rd, Huntingdon PE29 3DW
Tel: 01480 415600
e-mail: huntingdonet@hmcts.gsi.gov.uk
Birmingham: Employment Tribunals Regional Office, Centre City Tower, 7 Hill St, Birmingham B5 4UU
Tel: 0121 600 7780 Fax: 01264 347999
e-mail: birminghamet@hmcts.gsi.gov.uk
Bristol: Employment Tribunals Regional Office, Ground Fl, The Crescent Centre, Temple Back, Bristol BS1 6EZ
Tel: 0117 929 8261 Fax: 0870 739 4009
e-mail: bristolet@hmcts.gsi.gov.uk
Cardiff: Employment Tribunals Regional Office, Caradog Ho, 1–6 St Andrew's Pl, Cardiff CF10 3BE
Tel: 029 2067 8100 Fax: 029 2022 5906
DX: 33027 Cardiff
e-mail: cardiffet@hmcts.gsi.gov.uk
Dundee: Employment Tribunals Regional Office, Grnd Fl, Block C, Caledonian Ho, Greenmarket, Dundee DD1 4QB
Tel: 01382 221578 Fax: 01382 227136
DX: DD51 Dundee
e-mail: dundeeet@hmcts.gsi.gov.uk
Edinburgh: Employment Tribunals Regional Office, 54–56 Melville St, Edinburgh EH3 7HF
Tel: 0131 226 5584 Fax: 0131 220 6847
DX: ED147 Edinburgh
e-mail: edinburghet@hmcts.gsi.gov.uk
Exeter: Employment Tribunals Regional Office, 2nd Fl, Keble Ho, Southernhay Gdns, Exeter EX1 1NT
Tel: 01392 279 665 Fax: 01392 430 063
e-mail: exeteret@hmcts.gsi.gov.uk
Glasgow: Employment Tribunals Central Office, The Eagle Bldg, 215 Bothwell St, Glasgow G2 7TS
Tel: 0141 204 0730 Fax: 0141 204 0732
DX: 580003 Glasgow 17
e-mail: glasgowet@hmcts.gsi.gov.uk

Leeds: Employment Tribunals Regional Office, 4th Fl, City Exchange, Albion Towers, 11 Albion St, Leeds LS1 5ES
Tel: 0113 245 9741 Fax: 0113 242 8843
DX: 742940 Leeds 75
e-mail: leedset@hmcts.gsi.gov.uk
London Central: Employment Tribunals Regional Office, Victory Ho, 30–34 Kingsway, London WC2B 6EX
Tel: 020 7273 8603 Fax: 020 7273 8686
DX: 141420 Bloomsbury 7
e-mail: londoncentralet@hmcts.gsi.gov.uk
London East: Employment Tribunals Regional Office, 2nd Fl, Anchorage Ho, 2 Clove Ct, London E14 2BE
Tel: 020 7538 6161 Fax: 020 7538 6210
e-mail: eastlondon@hmcts.gsi.gov.uk
London South: Employment Tribunals Regional Office, Montague Ct, 101 London Rd, West Croydon CR0 2RF
Tel: 020 8667 9131 Fax: 020 8649 9470
DX: 155062 Croydon 39
e-mail: londonsouthet@hmcts.gsi.gov.uk
Manchester: Employment Tribunals Regional Office, Alexandra Ho, 14–22 The Parsonage, Manchester M3 2JA
Tel: 0161 833 6100 Fax: 0870 739 4433
DX: 743570 Manchester 66
e-mail: manchesteret@hmcts.gsi.gov.uk
Newcastle: Employment Tribunals Regional Office, Quayside Ho, 110 Quayside, Newcastle upon Tyne NE1 3DX
Tel: 0191 260 6900 Fax: 0870 739 4206
DX: 742283
e-mail: newcastleet@hmcts.gsi.gov.uk
Nottingham: Employment Tribunals Regional Office, Carrington St, Nottingham NG2 1EE
Tel: 0115 947 5701 Fax: 0115 950 7612
e-mail: nottinghamet@hmcts.gsi.gov.uk
Reading: Employment Tribunals Regional Office, 5th Fl, 30–31 Friar St, Reading RG1 1DX
Tel: 0118 959 4917 Fax: 0118 956 8066
DX: 155830 Reading 31
e-mail: readinget@hmcts.gsi.gov.uk
Sheffield: Employment Tribunals Regional Office, 14 East Parade, Sheffield S1 2ET
Tel: 0114 276 0348 Fax: 0114 276 2551
DX: 10531 Sheffield
e-mail: sheffieldet@hmcts.gsi.gov.uk
Shrewsbury: Employment Tribunals Regional Office, Shrewsbury Magistrates' Court, The Court House, Preston St, Shrewsbury SY2 5NX
Tel: 01743 358 341 Fax: 01743 244 186
e-mail: shrewsburyet@hmcts.gsi.gov.uk
Southampton: Employment Tribunals Regional Office, 100 The Avenue, Southampton SO17 1EY
Tel: 023 8038 4200 Fax: 0870 739 4190
e-mail: southamptonet@hmcts.gsi.gov.uk
Watford: Employment Tribunals Regional Office, 3rd Fl, Radius Ho, 51 Clarendon Rd, Watford, Herts WD17 1HP
Tel: 01923 281750 Fax: 01923 281781
DX: 155650 Watford 3
e-mail: watfordet@hmcts.gsi.gov.uk

Energy Institute

Energy Institute
Website: www.energyinst.org.uk
Head Office: 61 New Cavendish St, London W1G 7AR
Tel: 020 7467 7100 Fax: 020 7255 1472
e-mail: info@energyinst.org

Federation of Master Builders

Federation of Master Builders
Website: www.fmb.org.uk
Head Office: David Croft Ho, 25 Ely Pl, London EC1N 6TD
Tel: 020 7025 2900 Fax: 020 7025 2929
e-mail: fmblondon@fmb.org.uk
Eastern and Midlands: John Watson, Mercer Ho, 780a Hagley Rd West, Oldbury B68 0PJ
Tel: 0121 421 2241 Fax: 0121 423 2017
e-mail: fmbcentral@fmb.org.uk
Northern Ireland: Maire Nawaz, Unit 10, Kilbegs Business Centre, Plasketts Cl, Antrim BT41 4LY
Tel: 028 9446 0416 Fax: 028 9446 0408
e-mail: mairenawaz@fmb.org.uk
Northern, North West, Yorkshire & Trent: Phil Parkinson, Viscount Ct, 245 Leeds Rd, Rothwell, Leeds LS26 0GR
Tel: 0113 393 4040 Fax: 0113 393 4141
e-mail: fmbnorth@fmb.org.uk
Scotland: Grahame Barn, 5 New Mart Place, Edinburgh EH14 1RW
Tel: 0131 442 8830 Fax: 0131 442 8833
e-mail: grahamebarn@fmb.org.uk
Southern and South West: Ron Willers, 83 Alma Rd, Clifton, Bristol BS8 2DP
Tel: 0117 973 6891 Fax: 0117 946 7906
e-mail: fmbsouth@fmb.org.uk
Wales: Richard Jenkins, Unit 5, Bridgend Business Centre, Bridgend CF31 3SH
Tel: 01656 750955
e-mail: richardjenkins@fmb.org.uk

Fields in Trust

Fields in Trust (operating name of National Playing Fields Association)
Website: www.fieldsintrust.org
Head Office: 15 Crinan St, London N1 9SQ
Tel: 020 7427 2110 Fax: 020 8264 2410
e-mail: info@fieldsintrust.org
Cymru: Welsh Institute of Sport, Sophia Gdns, Cardiff CF11 9SW
Tel: 029 2033 4935 Fax: 029 2023 0643
e-mail: cymru@fieldsintrust.org
Scotland: Dewar Ho, Claverhouse, Staffa Pl, Dundee DD2 3SX
Tel: 01382 817427 Fax: 01382 828444
e-mail: scotland@fieldsintrust.org

Financial Conduct

Financial Conduct Authority
Website: www.fca.org.uk
Head Office: 25 The North Colonnade, Canary Wharf, London E14 5HS
Tel: 0300 500 0597 (companies), 0800 111 6768 (consumers)
e-mail: firm.queries@fca.org.uk (companies),consumer.queries@fca.org.uk (consumers)

Fire and Emergency Planning Authorities

London Fire and Emergency Planning Authority
Website: www.london-fire.gov.uk
Brigade Headquarters: Commissioner for Fire & Emergency Planning, 169 Union St, Southwark, London SE1 0LL
Tel: 020 8555 1200 x 30000 Fax: 020 7960 3600
e-mail: ron.dobson@london-fire.gov.uk

London Office: Head of Legal & Democratic Services, 169 Union St, Southwark, London SE1 0LL
Tel: 020 8555 1200 x 30117 Fax: 020 7960 3617
e-mail: david.atkinson@london-fire.gov.uk

Merseyside Fire and Rescue Authority
Website: www.merseyfire.gov.uk
Head Office: Director of Law, Fire Service HQ, Bridle Rd, Bootle, Liverpool L30 4YD
Tel: 0151 296 4000 Fax: 0151 296 4333
e-mail: janethenshaw@merseyfire.gov.uk

South Yorkshire Fire and Civil Rescue Authority
Website: www.southyorks.org.uk/fire
Head Office: Clerk & Treasurer, 18 Regent St, Barnsley S70 2HG
Tel: 01226 772800 Fax: 01226 772899
e-mail: bwilkinson@syjs.gov.uk

Tyne & Wear Fire and Rescue Authority
Website: www.twfire.gov.uk
Head Office: The Chief Fire Officer, Service Headquarters, Nissan Way, Sunderland SR5 3QY
Tel: 0191 444 1500 Fax: 0191 444 1512
DX: 60729 Sunderland
e-mail: kate.cuthbert@sunderland.gov.uk

West Midlands Fire and Civil Defence Authority
Website: www.wmfs.net
Headquarters: 99 Vauxhall Rd, Nechells, Birmingham B7 4HW
Tel: 0121 380 7404 Fax: 0121 380 7007
e-mail: contact@wmfs.net

West Yorkshire Fire and Rescue Authority
Website: www.westyorksfire.gov.uk
Head Office: Clerk & Solicitor, Oakroyd Hall, Bradford Rd, Birkenshaw BD11 2DY
Tel: 01274 682311 Fax: 01274 652231

Gambling Commission

Gambling Commission
Website: www.gamblingcommission.gov.uk
Head Office: Victoria Sq Ho, Victoria Sq, Birmingham B2 4BP
Tel: 0121 230 6666 Fax: 0121 230 6720
e-mail: info@gamblingcommission.gov.uk

General Council of the Bar

The General Council of the Bar
Website: www.barcouncil.org.uk
Main Office: 289–293 High Holborn, London WC1V 7HZ
Tel: 020 7242 0082 Fax: 020 7831 9217
DX: 240 LDE

Geological Society of London

Geological Society of London
Website: www.geolsoc.org.uk
Head Office: Burlington Ho, Piccadilly, London W1J 0BG
Tel: 020 7434 9944 Fax: 020 7439 8975
e-mail: enquiries@geolsoc.org.uk

Historic Buildings and Monuments

CADW
Website: cadw.wales.gov.uk
Head Office: Cadw, Plas Carew, Unit 5/7 Cefn Coed, Parc Nantgarw, Cardiff CF15 7QQ
Tel: 01443 336000 Fax: 01443 336001
e-mail: cadw@wales.gsi.gov.uk

Historic Buildings and Monuments Commission for England
Website: www.english-heritage.org.uk
Head Office: 1 Waterhouse Sq, 138–142 Holborn, London EC1N 2ST
Tel: 020 7973 3000 Fax: 020 7973 3001
e-mail: london@english-heritage.org.uk

Historic Scotland
Website: www.historic-scotland.gov.uk
Head Office: Historic Scotland's Heritage Management Directorate, Longmore Ho, Salisbury Place, Edinburgh EH9 1SH
Tel: 0131 668 8600 Fax: 0131 668 8722

Immigration Appeals

Immigration and Asylum Chamber
Website: www.tribunals.gov.uk/immigrationasylum
Head Office: First-Tier Tribunal, Immigration and Asylum Chamber, PO Box 6987, Leicester LE1 6ZX
Tel: 0845 6000 877 Fax: 0116 249 4192
Note: minicom: 0845 606 0766

Incorporated Council of Law Reporting for England and Wales

Incorporated Council of Law Reporting for England and Wales
Website: www.iclr.co.uk
Head Office: The Law Reports and the Weekly Law Reports, Megarry Ho, 119 Chancery La, London WC2A 1PP
Tel: 020 7242 6471 Fax: 020 7831 5247
e-mail: enquiries@iclr.co.uk

Industrial Injuries Advisory Council

Industrial Injuries Advisory Council
Website: www.gov.uk/government/organisations/industrial-injuries-advisory-council
Head Office: Department for Work and Pensions, Health and Wellbeing Directorate, 2nd Fl, Caxton Ho, Tothill St, London SW1H 9NA
Tel: 020 7449 5618
e-mail: iiac@dwp.gsi.gov.uk

Institute of Chartered Secretaries and Administrators

Institute of Chartered Secretaries and Administrators
Website: www.icsa.org.uk
Head Office: Saffron Ho, 6–10 Kirby St, London EC1N 8TS
Tel: 020 7580 4741 Fax: 020 7232 1132
e-mail: info@icsaglobal.com

Institute of Legal Executives

Institute of Legal Executives
Website: www.cilex.org.uk
Head Office: Kempston Manor, Kempston, Bedford MK42 7AB
Tel: 01234 841000 Fax: 01234 840373
DX: 124780 Kempston 2
e-mail: info@cilex.org.uk

Institute of Trade Mark Attorneys

Institute of Trade Mark Attorneys
Website: www.itma.org.uk
Head Office: ITMA, 5th Fl, Outer Temple, 222–225 Strand, London WC2R 1BA
Tel: 020 7101 6090 Fax: 020 7101 6099
e-mail: tm@itma.org.uk

Institution of Civil Engineers

Institution of Civil Engineers
Website: www.ice.org.uk
Head Office: One Gt George St, Westminster, London SW1P 3AA
Tel: 020 7222 7722 Fax: 020 7222 7500
e-mail: communications@ice.org.uk

Integrated Transport Authorities

Merseyside Integrated Transport Authority
Website: www.merseytravel.gov.uk
Head Office: PO Box 1976, Liverpool L69 3HN
Tel: 0151 330 1234 Fax: 0151 236 2457
Note: Contact via website; minicom: 0151 300 1087

North East Combined Authority
Website: www.northeastca.gov.uk
Head Office: Quadrant, Cobalt Business Park, The Silverlink North, Newcastle upon Tyne NE27 0BY
Tel: 0191 232 8520
Note: Contact via website

South Yorkshire Integrated Transport Authority
Website: www.southyorks.gov.uk
Head Office: South Yorkshire Joint Secretariat, 18 Regent St, Barnsley S70 2HG
Tel: 01226 772 800 Fax: 01226 772 899

Transport for Greater Manchester Committee
Website: www.transportforgreatermanchestercommittee.gov.uk
Head Office: PO Box 532, Town Hall, Manchester M60 2LA
Tel: 0161 234 4619
e-mail: tfgmc@manchester.gov.uk

West Midlands Integrated Transport Authority
Website: www.centro.org.uk
Head Office: Centro Ho, 16 Summer La, Birmingham B19 3SD
Tel: 0121 214 7214
Note: Contact via website
WMPTA: WMPTA Committee Team, Room 120, 16 Summer La, Birmingham B19 3SD
Tel: 0121 214 7505 Fax: 0121 233 1841
DX: 712531 Birmingham 30

Intellectual Property Office

Intellectual Property Office
Website: www.gov.uk/government/organisations/intellectual-property-office
Head Office: Concept Ho, Cardiff Rd, Newport NP10 8QQ
Tel: 0300 300 2000 Fax: 01633 817 777
e-mail: information@ipo.gov.uk
Note: minicom: 0300 0200 015

Kaolin and Ball Clay Association

Kaolin and Ball Clay Association (UK)
Website: www.kabca.org
Head Office: Par Moor Centre, Par Moor Rd, Par PL24 2SQ
Tel: 01726 811311 Fax: 01726 811200
e-mail: adrian.mutton@imerys.com

Land Charges Department

Land Charges Department
Website: www.gov.uk/government/organisations/land-registry
Head Office: Land Registry, Land Charges Dept, Seaton Ct, 2 William Prance Rd, Plymouth PL6 5WS
Tel: 0300 006 6000 Fax: 0300 006 6123
DX: 8299 Plymouth (4)
Note: Tel No above is for general enquiries. Telephone Searches, please dial 08709 088063 for registrations in England; 08709 088069 for registrations in Wales

Landscape Institute

Landscape Institute
Website: www.landscapeinstitute.org
Head Office: Charles Darwin Ho, 12 Roger St, London WC1N 2JU
Tel: 020 7685 2640 Fax: 020 7685 2641
e-mail: mail@landscapeinstitute.org

Law Commission

Law Commission
Website: lawcommission.justice.gov.uk
Head Office: 1st Fl, Tower, 52 Queen Anne's Gate, London SW1H 9AG
Tel: 020 3334 0200 Fax: 020 3334 0201
e-mail: chief.executive@lawcommission.gsi.gov.uk

Law Society

The Law Society
Website: www.lawsociety.org.uk
Head Office: Law Society's Hall, 113 Chancery La, London WC2A 1PL
Tel: 020 7242 1222 Fax: 020 7831 0344
DX: 56 London/Chancery Lane
e-mail: contact@lawsociety.org.uk

Legal Aid Agency

Legal Aid Agency
Website: www.gov.uk/government/organisations/legal-aid-agency
Head Office: Head Office, Unit B8, Berkley Way, Viking Business Park, Jarrow NE31 1SF
Tel: 0345 345 4 345
Note: Contact via website

Lloyd's Register

Lloyd's Register
Website: www.lr.org
Head Office: 71 Fenchurch St, London EC3M 4BS
Tel: 020 7709 9166 Fax: 020 7488 4796
e-mail: emea@lr.org

Lloyd's of London

Lloyd's of London
Website: www.lloyds.com
Head Office: One Lime St, London EC3M 7HA
Tel: 020 7327 1000 Fax: 020 7626 2389
e-mail: enquiries@lloyds.com

Local Government Association

Local Government Association
Website: www.local.gov.uk
Head Office: Smith Sq, London SW1P 3HZ
Tel: 020 7664 3000 Fax: 020 7664 3030
DX: 119450 Westminster 2
e-mail: info@local.gov.uk
Note: Information Line: 020 7664 3131

London Councils

London Councils
Website: www.londoncouncils.gov.uk
Head Office: 59½ Southwark St, London SE1 0AL
Tel: 020 7934 9999

London Gazette

The London Gazette
Website: www.thegazette.co.uk
Head Office: PO Box 3584, Norwich NR7 7WD
Tel: 0870 600 3322
e-mail: london.gazette@tso.co.uk

Medical Research Council

Medical Research Council
Website: www.mrc.ac.uk
Head Office: 14th Fl, One Kemble St, London WC2B 4AN
Tel: 01793 416 200
e-mail: corporate@headoffice.mrc.ac.uk

Mersey Docks and Harbour Co

Mersey Docks and Harbour Co
Website: www.merseydocks.co.uk
Head Office: Company Secretary, Maritime Centre, Port of Liverpool, Liverpool L21 1LA
Tel: 0151 949 6000 Fax: 0151 949 6300

Mutual Societies Registration

Mutual Societies Registration
Website: www.fsa.gov.uk/doing/small_firms/msr
Head Office: Mutual Team, 25 The North Colonnade, Canary Wharf, London E14 5HS
Tel: 0845 606 9966
e-mail: mutual.societies@fsa.gov.uk

NICEIC Group Ltd

NICEIC Group Ltd
Website: www.niceic.com
Head Office: NICEIC, Warwick Ho, Houghton Hall Pk, Houghton Regis, Dunstable LU5 5ZX
Tel: 0870 013 0382 Fax: 01582 539 090
e-mail: enquiries@niceic.com

National Archives

The National Archives
Website: www.nationalarchives.gov.uk
Head Office: Advice and Records Knowledge, National Archives, Kew, Richmond TW9 4DU
Tel: 020 8876 3444
Note: Contact via website. Minicom: 020 8392 91900

National Association of Estate Agents

National Association of Estate Agents
Website: www.naea.co.uk
Head Office: Arbon Ho, 6 Tournament Ct, Edgehill Dr, Warwick, Warwickshire CV34 6LG
Tel: 0845 250 6001 Fax: 0845 250 6061

National Association of Local Councils

National Association of Local Councils
Website: www.nalc.gov.uk
Head Office: 109 Gt Russell St, London WC1B 3LD
Tel: 020 7637 1865 Fax: 020 7436 7451
e-mail: nalc@nalc.gov.uk

National Federation of Builders

National Federation of Builders
Website: www.builders.org.uk
Head Office: National Office, Spectrum Ho, Suite AF29, Beehive Ring Rd, Gatwick RH6 0LG
Tel: 08450 578160 Fax: 08450 578161
e-mail: national@builders.org.uk

National House-Building Council

The National House-Building Council
Website: www.nhbc.co.uk
Head Office: NHBC Ho, Davy Ave, Knowlhill, Milton Keynes MK5 8FB
Tel: 0844 633 1000 Fax: 01908 747 255
DX: 84759 Milton Keynes 3
e-mail: cssupport@nhbc.co.uk

National Housing Federation

National Housing Federation
Website: www.housing.org.uk
Head Office: Lion Ct, 25 Procter St, London WC1V 6NY
Tel: 020 7067 1010 Fax: 020 7067 1011
e-mail: info@housing.org.uk

National Library of Wales

National Library of Wales
Website: www.llgc.org.uk
Head Office: Aberystwyth, Ceredigion SY23 3BU
Tel: 01970 632800 Fax: 01970 615709
e-mail: holi@llgc.org.uk

National Park Authorities

Brecon Beacons National Park Authority
Website: www.breconbeacons.org
Head Office: Plas-y-Ffynnon, Cambrian Way, Brecon LD3 7HP
Tel: 01874 624437 Fax: 01874 622574
e-mail: enquiries@breconbeacons.org

Broads Authority
Website: www.broads-authority.gov.uk
Head Office: Yare Ho, 62–64 Thorpe Rd, Norwich NR3 1RY
Tel: 01603 610 734
Note: Contact via website

Cairngorms National Park Authority
Website: www.cairngorms.co.uk
Head Office: 14 The Square, Grantown on Spey PH26 3HG
Tel: 01479 873535 Fax: 01479 873527
e-mail: enquiries@cairngorms.co.uk

Dartmoor National Park Authority
Website: www.dartmoor.gov.uk
Head Office: Parke, Bovey Tracey, Newton Abbot TQ13 9JQ
Tel: 01626 832 093 Fax: 01626 834 684
e-mail: hq@dartmoor.gov.uk

Exmoor National Park Authority
Website: www.exmoor-nationalpark.gov.uk
Head Office: Exmoor Ho, Dulverton TA22 9HL
Tel: 01398 323 665
e-mail: info@exmoor-nationalpark.gov.uk

Lake District National Park Authority
Website: www.lakedistrict.gov.uk
Head Office: Legal Services, National Park Office, Murley Moss, Oxenholme Rd, Kendal, Cumbria LA9 7RL
Tel: 01539 724 555 Fax: 01539 740 822
e-mail: julie.wood@lakedistrict.gov.uk
Note: Contact via website

Loch Lomond and the Trossachs National Park Authority
Website: www.lochlomond-trossachs.org
Head Office: Carrochan, Carrochan Rd, Balloch G83 8EG
Tel: 01389 722600 Fax: 01389 722633
e-mail: info@lochlomond-trossachs.org

New Forest National Park Authority
Website: www.newforestnpa.gov.uk
Head Office: Lymington Town Hall, Avenue Rd, Lymington SO41 9ZG
Tel: 01590 646 600
e-mail: enquiries@newforestnpa.gov.uk

North York Moors National Park Authority
Website: www.northyorkmoors.org.uk
Head Office: The Old Vicarage, Bondgate, Helmsley YO62 5BP
Tel: 01439 772700 Fax: 01439 770691
e-mail: info@northyorkmoors.org.uk

Northumberland National Park Authority
Website: www.northumberlandnationalpark.org.uk
Head Office: Eastburn, South Park, Hexham NE46 1BS
Tel: 01434 605 555
Note: Contact via website

Peak District National Park Authority
Website: www.peakdistrict.gov.uk
Head Office: Aldern Ho, Baslow Rd, Bakewell DE45 1AE
Tel: 01629 816 200
e-mail: customer.service@peakdistrict.gov.uk

Pembrokeshire Coast National Park Authority
Website: www.pcnpa.org.uk
Head Office: Llanion Pk, Pembroke Dock, Pembrokeshire SA72 6DY
Tel: 0845 345 7275 Fax: 01646 689 076
e-mail: info@pembrokeshirecoast.org.uk

Snowdonia National Park Authority
Website: www.eryri-npa.co.uk
Head Office: National Park Office, Penrhyndeudraeth LL48 6LF
Tel: 01766 770 274 Fax: 01766 771 211
e-mail: parc@snowdonia-npa.gov.uk

South Downs National Park
Website: www.southdowns.gov.uk
Head Office: North St, Midhurst GU29 9DH
Tel: 0300 303 1053
Note: Contact via website

Yorkshire Dales National Park
Website: www.yorkshiredales.org.uk
Yorkshire Dales National Park North: Yoredale, Bainbridge, Leyburn DL8 3EL
Tel: 01969 652300 Fax: 01969 652399
e-mail: info@yorkshiredales.org.uk
Yorkshire Dales National Park South: Colvend, Grassington, Skipton BD23 5LB
Tel: 01756 751600 Fax: 01756 751699
e-mail: info@yorkshiredales.org.uk

National Trust

The National Trust
Website: www.nationaltrust.org.uk
Head Office: Heelis, Kemble Dr, Swindon SN2 2NA
Tel: 0844 800 1895 Fax: 0844 800 4642
e-mail: enquiries@nationaltrust.org.uk

Office for National Statistics

Office for National Statistics
Website: www.ons.gov.uk
Head Office: Customer Contact Centre, Room 1.101, Government Bldgs, Cardiff Rd, Newport, South Wales NP10 8XG
Tel: 0845 601 3034 Fax: 01633 652 747
e-mail: info@statistics.gov.uk
Note: minicom: 01633 815 044

Office of Fair Trading

Office of Fair Trading *(see Competition and Markets Authority or Financial Conduct Authority)*

Office of the Public Guardian

Office of the Public Guardian
Website: www.gov.uk/government/organisations/office-of-the-public-guardian
Head Office: PO Box 16185, Birmingham B2 2WH
Tel: 0300 456 0300 Fax: 0870 739 5780
DX: 744240 Birmingham 79
e-mail: customerservices@publicguardian.gsi.gov.uk

Offices of the Police and Crime Commissioner

Police and Crime Commissioners *(see Part 6 Police Forces)*

Official Solicitor to the Supreme Court

Official Solicitor and Public Trustee
Website: www.gov.uk/government/organisations/official-solicitor-and-public-trustee
Head Office: Victory Ho, 30–34 Kingsway, London WC2B 6EX
Tel: 020 3681 2752 Fax: 020 3681 2762
DX: 141423 Bloomsbury 7
e-mail: enquiries@offsol.gsi.gov.uk

Open Spaces Society

The Open Spaces Society
Website: www.oss.org.uk
Head Office: 25a Bell St, Henley-on-Thames RG9 2BA
Tel: 01491 573535 Fax: 01491 573051
e-mail: hq@oss.org.uk

Ordnance Survey

Ordnance Survey
Website: www.ordnancesurvey.co.uk
Head Office: Customer Service Centre, Adanac Dr, Nursling, Southampton SO16 0AS
Tel: 0845 605 0505 Fax: 0845 099 0494
e-mail: customerservices@ordnancesurvey.co.uk
Note: textphone: 023 8005 6146

Passenger Transport Executives

Merseytravel
Website: www.merseytravel.gov.uk
Head Office: PO Box 1976, Liverpool L69 3HN
Tel: 0151 330 1234 Fax: 0151 236 2457
Note: Contact via website

South Yorkshire Passenger Transport Executive
Website: www.sypte.co.uk
Head Office: Legal, 11 Broad St West, Sheffield S1 2BQ
Tel: 0114 276 7575 Fax: 0114 275 9908

Transport for Greater Manchester
Website: www.tfgm.com
Head Office: GMPTE Legal Department, 2 Piccadilly Pl, Manchester M1 3BG
Tel: 0161 244 1000 Fax: 0161 244 1011
e-mail: publicity@gmpte.gov.uk

Transport for London
Website: www.tfl.gov.uk
Office of the Secretary & Legal Director: 4th Fl, Zone Y4, 14 Pier Walk, North Greenwich, London SE10 0ES
Fax: 020 3054 5306
e-mail: enquire@tfl.gov.uk

Tyne & Wear Passenger Transport Executive (Nexus)
Website: www.nexus.org.uk
Head Office: Nexus Ho, St James Blvd, Newcastle upon Tyne NE1 4AX
Tel: 0191 2020 747
e-mail: customerservices@nexus.org.uk

West Midlands Passenger Transport Executive
Website: www.centro.org.uk
Centro (WMPTE): Centro Ho, 16 Summer Lane, Birmingham B19 3SD
Tel: 0121 200 2787 Fax: 0121 214 7010
Note: Contact via website

West Yorkshire Passenger Transport Executive (Metro)
Website: www.wymetro.com
Head Office: Wellington Ho, 40–50 Wellington St, Leeds LS1 2DE
Tel: 0113 245 7676
e-mail: metroline@wypte.gov.uk

Privy Council Office

Privy Council Office
Website: http://privycouncil.independent.gov.uk
Head Office: Privy Council Office, 2 Carlton Gdns, London SW1Y 5AA
Tel: 020 7747 5310
e-mail: pcosecretariat@pco.x.gsi.gov.uk

Regeneration & Development

Homes and Communities Agency
Website: www.homesandcommunities.co.uk
Head Office: Palestra, 197 Blackfriars Rd, Southwark, London SE1 8AA
Tel: 0300 123 4500 Fax: 020 7633 3500
e-mail: mail@englishpartnerships.co.uk
Corporate Centre (London): Maple Ho, 149 Tottenham Ct Rd, London W1T 7BN
Tel: 0300 1234 300
Corporate Centre (Milton Keynes):
Tel: 0300 1234 500
e-mail: mail@homesandcommunities.co.uk

Corporate Centre (Warrington): Arpley Ho, 110 Birchwood Blvd, Birchwood, Warrington WA3 7QH
Note: Registered address for legal documents@office =
Birmingham Office: 5 St Phillips Place, Colmore Row, Birmingham B3 2PW
Bristol Office: 2 Rivergate, Temple Quay, Bristol BS1 6EH
Tel: 0300 1234 500
Cambridge Office: Eastbrook, Shaftesbury Rd, Cambridge CB2 8BF
Tel: 01223 374 003
Chatham Office: 2nd Fl, The Observatory, Brunel, Chatham Maritime ME4 4NT
Gateshead Office: St George's Ho, Kingsway, Team Valley, Gateshead NE11 0NA
Tel: 0300 1234 500
Guildford Office: Bridge Ho, 1 Walnut Tree Cl, Guildford GU1 4GA
Leeds Office: 1st Fl, 8 City Walk, Leeds LS11 9AT
Manchester Office: 4th Fl, One Picadilly Gardens, Manchester M1 1RG
Tel: 0300 1234 500
Nottingham Office: 3rd Fl, Block C, Cumberland Pl, Park Row, Nottingham NG1 6HJ

Room: The National Council for Housing and Planning

Royal Town Planning Institute
Website: www.rtpi.org.uk
Head Office: 41 Botolph La, London EC3R 8DL
Tel: 020 7929 9494 Fax: 020 7929 9490
Note: Contact via website

Royal Commission on the Ancient and Historical Monuments of Wales

Royal Commission on the Ancient and Historical Monuments of Wales
Website: www.rcahmw.gov.uk
Head Office: Library and Enquiries Service, Plas Crug, Aberystwyth SY23 1NJ
Tel: 01970 621 200 Fax: 01970 627 701
e-mail: nmr.wales@rcahmw.gov.uk
Note: Note: Enquiries regarding specific monuments and buildings should be addressed to the National Monuments Record of Wales (telephone number, e-mail, fax as above).

Royal Forestry Society

Royal Forestry Society
Website: www.rfs.org.uk
Head Office: The Hay Barns, Home Farm Drive, Upton Estate, Banbury OX15 6HU
Tel: 01295 678588 Fax: 01295 670798
e-mail: rfshq@rfs.org.uk

Royal Institute of British Architects

Royal Institute of British Architects
Website: www.architecture.com
Head Office: 66 Portland Pl, London W1B 1AD
Tel: 020 7580 5533 Fax: 020 7255 1541
e-mail: info@inst.riba.org

Royal Institution of Chartered Surveyors

Royal Institution of Chartered Surveyors (RICS)
Website: www.rics.org
Head Office: 12 Great George St, Parliament Sq, London SW1P 3AD
Tel: 0870 333 1600 Fax: 020 7334 3811
e-mail: contactrics@rics.org

Scottish Government

Scottish Court Service
Website: www.scotcourts.gov.uk
Head Office: Saughton Ho, Broomhouse Dr, Edinburgh EH11 3XD
Tel: 0131 441 3300 Fax: 0131 443 2610
DX: 557007 Edinburgh 20
e-mail: enquiries@scotcourts.gov.uk

Scottish Government
Website: www.gov.scot
Head Office: St Andrew's Ho, Regent Rd, Edinburgh EH1 3DG
Tel: 0131 556 8400 Fax: 01397 795001
DX: 557007 Edinburgh 20
Note: minicom: 0131 244 1829

Search Agents

Jordans
Website: www.jordansproperty.co.uk
Head Office: 21 St Thomas St, Bristol BS1 6JS
Tel: 0117 923 0600 Fax: 0117 923 0063
DX: 78161 Bristol
e-mail: propertyservices@jordans.co.uk

TM Property Group (UK) Ltd
Website: www.tmgroup.co.uk
Head Office: 1200 Delta Business Pk, Swindon SN5 7XD
Tel: 0844 249 9200
DX: 743360 Swindon 31
e-mail: helpdesk@tmgroup.co.uk

Society for the Protection of Ancient Buildings

Society for the Protection of Ancient Buildings
Website: www.spab.org.uk
Head Office: 37 Spital Sq, London E1 6DY
Tel: 020 7377 1644 Fax: 020 7247 5296
e-mail: info@spab.org.uk

Society of Local Authority Chief Executives and Senior Managers

Society of Local Authority Chief Executives and Senior Managers
Website: www.solace.org.uk
Head Office: PO Box 199, Pontefract WF8 1WT
London Office: Hope Ho, 1st Fl, 45 Great Peter St, London SW1P 3LT
Tel: 0845 652 4010 Fax: 0845 652 4011
e-mail: hope.house@solace.org.uk

Stationery Office

The Stationery Office Ltd
Website: www.tso.co.uk
Head Office: St Crispins, Duke St, Norwich NR3 1PD
Tel: 01603 622 211
e-mail: customer.services@tso.co.uk
London: Parliament Press, Mandela Way, London SE1 5SS
Tel: 020 7394 4200
TSO Ireland: Weavers Ct, Belfast BT12 5GH
Tel: 02890 238 451
e-mail: enquiries@tsoireland.com
TSO Scotland: 26 Rutland Sq, Edinburgh EH1 2BW
Tel: 0131 659 7020 Fax: 0131 659 7040
e-mail: enquiries@tsoscotland.com

The Upper Tribunal (Lands Chamber)

The Upper Tribunal (Lands Chamber)
Website: www.gov.uk/appeal-upper-tribunal-lands
Head Office: Ministry of Justice, Tribunal Service, 5th Fl, Rolls Bldg, 7 Rolls Buildings, Fetter La, London EC4A 1N
Tel: 020 7612 9710 Fax: 020 7612 9723
e-mail: lands@hmcts.gsi.gov.uk

Town and Country Planning Association

Town and Country Planning Association
Website: www.tcpa.org.uk
Head Office: 17 Carlton House Terr, London SW1Y 5AS
Tel: 020 7930 8903 Fax: 020 7930 3280
e-mail: tcpa@tcpa.org.uk

Treasury Solicitor

The Treasury Solicitor's Department
Website: www.gov.uk/government/organisations/treasury-solicitor-s-department
Head Office: Treasury Solicitor, One Kemble St, London WC2B 4TS
Tel: 020 7210 3000
DX: 123240 Kingsway 6
e-mail: thetreasurysolicitor@tsol.gsi.gov.uk

Valuation Tribunal

Valuation Tribunal
Website: www.valuationtribunal.gov.uk
Head Office: 2nd Fl, 120 Leman St, London E1 8EU
Tel: 020 7426 3900 Fax: 020 7247 6598
e-mail: ceo.office@vts.gsi.gov.uk
Doncaster: Hepworth Ho, 2 Trafford Ct, Doncaster DN1 1PN
Tel: 0300 123 2035 Fax: 01302 321 447
e-mail: vtdoncaster@vts.gsi.gov.uk

WRc-NSF

WRc-NSF
Website: www.wrcnsf.com
Oakdale: WRc-NSF Ltd, Unit 30, Fern Cl, Pen-y-fan Industrial Estate, Oakdale, Gwent NP11 3EH
Tel: 01495 236260 Fax: 01495 242499
e-mail: info@wrcnsf.com
Reading: WRc-NSF Ltd, Unit 25, Robert Cort Estate, Britten Rd, Reading RG2 0AU

Part 15

Conveyancing Fees and Charges

This part covers Land Registry fees, Land Charges Registry fees and local authority search fees. It does not include stamp duties.

Land Registry fees

Land Registry fees are presently governed by the Land Registration Fee Order 2013, which came into effect on 17 March 2014.

The principal fees are contained in Schedules 1 and 2 to the Order (Scales 1 and 2).

First registration of and dealings with freehold or leasehold land

Schedule 1 (Scale 1) applies to

(a) an application for first registration,

(b) a transfer for monetary consideration of a registered estate,

(c) a transfer giving effect to a disposition of a share in a registered estate for monetary consideration, and

(d) the surrender of a registered leasehold estate for monetary consideration (subject to exemption (3) see "Exemptions" below), But Scale 1 does not apply to "large scale applications" (as to which, see below). The Scale 1 fees are as follows.

Value (£)	Reduced Fee (£)	Fee (£)
0–80,000	30	40
80,001–100,000	60	80
100,001–200,000	140	190
200,001–500,000	200	270
500,001–1,000,000	400	540
1,000,001 and over	680	910

Notes

1 The reduced fee in the table above is payable on voluntary first registration applications, other than those for first registration of rentcharges, franchises or profit à prendre in gross. A 25 per cent reduction, reduced to the nearest £10, applies to large scale applications (see below) as well.

2 On an application by the original lessee or his personal representative for the registration of a title to a lease, or to register the grant of a lease, (whether or not it is granted out of a registered title), the "value" for the purposes of this table is an amount equal to the sum of the premium and the rent.

However, if there is no rent, or the rent cannot be quantified in money at the time the application is made, then—

(a) If there is a premium, the "value" for the purpose of the table is the amount of the premium

(b) If there is no premium, the value for the purposes of the table is the maximum amount for which the lease could be sold on the open market at the date of the application free from any charge, subject to a minimum fee of £40.

"Premium" means the amount or value of any monetary consideration given by the lessee by way of fine, premium or otherwise. However, where that consideration includes the surrender of a registered leasehold estate of substantially the same land as is comprised in the lease being granted, then the value of the surrendered lease is not treated as part of the premium. "Rent" means the amount or value of the annual rent, or the amount or value of the rent for the term if the lease is for a term of less than one year. Where the rent varies or can be varied, it is the largest amount of annual rent that the lease may reserve in the first five years of its term, or in any year where the term is less than five years. A peppercorn rent or other rent having no money value is treated as if it were an annual rent of one penny.

3 On an application for first registration of a freehold or any other leasehold estate in land, or a franchise or profit à prendre in gross, the "value" for the purposes of this table is the maximum amount for which it could be sold on the open market at the date of the application free from any charge.

4 The fee for an application for first registration of a rentcharge is £40.

5 On an application to register a transfer of a registered estate, or a share in a registered estate, for monetary consideration, the "value" for the purposes of this table is the amount or value of the consideration.

6 See the Scale 2 table (Transfers other than for monetary consideration/charges) for the fees for certain other transactions.

7 Where the amount of the value is a figure that includes odd pence, the value must be rounded down to the nearest £1.

8 The Scale 1 fee payable on the transfer or surrender of the whole of a registered title is reduced by 50% if the application for the registration of that transfer or surrender is delivered by electronic means.

Transfers other than for monetary consideration etc/charges

Schedule 2 (Scale 2) applies – subject to exemption 9 (see "Exemptions", below) – in the case of an application to register:

(a) a transfer of a registered estate otherwise than for monetary consideration;

(b) a surrender of a registered leasehold estate otherwise than for monetary consideration (whether effected by deed or otherwise);

(c) a transfer by operation of law on death or bankruptcy of an individual proprietor;

(d) an assent (including a vesting assent) – but see Scale 1 for assents inducing first registration;

(e) an appropriation of a registered estate;

(f) a vesting order or declaration to which section 27(5) of the Land Registration Act 2002 applies;

(g) a transfer of a matrimonial or civil partnership home made pursuant to an order of the court;

(h) a transfer otherwise than for monetary consideration for the purpose of giving effect to the disposition of a share in a registered estate;

(i) a charge;

(j) the transfer of a registered charge.

(k) the transfer of for the purpose of giving effect to a transfer of a share in a registered charge.

Value (£)	Fee (£)
0–100,000	40
100,001–200,000	60
200,001–500,000	80
500,001–1,000,000	120
1,000,001 and over	250

Notes

1 The expression "monetary consideration" is defined as a consideration in money or money's worth (other than a nominal consideration or a consideration consisting solely of a covenant to pay money owing under a mortgage), and "share" as an interest in land under a trust of land.

2 Where the amount of the value includes odd pence, the figure must be rounded down to the nearest £1.

3 No fee is payable to register a charge that either accompanies, or is lodged before the completion of a 'scale fee application' which will result in the applicant being registered as proprietor of the estate charged, except that:

(a) if the application to register a charge does not accompany, but is lodged before the completion of, a voluntary first registration application attracting the reduced fee (see note 1 to the scale 1 table above) the charge is not exempt and will attract a Scale 2 fee;

(b) 4if the charge also includes a registered estate which is not the subject of the application, a fee is payable under Scale 2 on the proportion of the charge which the additional estate not so subject bears to the value of the whole security.

"Scale fee application" means an application that attracts a scale fee, or would do so if it were not a "large scale application".

4 The Scale 2 fee payable on the disposition or charge or transfer of charge is reduced by 50% if the disposition or charge is of the whole of a registered title and the application for the registration of that disposition, charge or transfer of charge is delivered by electronic means.

Large scale applications

A "large scale application" is one that relates to 20 or more "land units", which in turn are defined as:

(a) the land registered under a single title number, or

(b) on a first registration application, a separate area of land not adjoining any other unregistered land affected by the same application.

Where a large scale application would otherwise attract a fee under Scale 1 or Scale 2, the fee payable is the greater of:

(a) the scale fee, and

(b) a fee calculated on the following basis:

(i) where the application relates to not more than 500 land units, £10 per land unit; or

(ii) where the application relates to more than 500 land units, £5,000 plus £5 per land unit over 500, up to a maximum fee of £40,000.

Notes

1 Except on first registration, an application where the value of the land or amount of the charge to which it relates does not exceed £30,000 is not treated as a large scale application. Instead, the minimum Scale 1 or Scale 2 fee of £40 is payable.

2 If a large scale application is a voluntary application for first registration, the fee is reduced by 25 per cent, and the maximum fee is £30,000.

3 In the case of an application to register a charge, any registered title affected, in respect of which no fee is payable because the charge is lodged with or before the completion of a transfer, should be excluded when assessing the number of land units in the application.

4 Where a freehold estate in commonhold land is registered in the name of the developer under more than one title number, a disposition by the developer affecting all or some of those titles is not treated as a large scale application.

Applications and services fixed fees

These are prescribed by, respectively, Parts 1 and 2 to 4 of Schedule 3 to the 2012 Order. The fees are as follows. References to "the rules" are to the Land Registration Rules 2003 and references to "the Act" are to the Land Registration Act 2002. "Electronic means" means electronically in accordance with a notice given under Schedule 2 to the rules but not by fax.

Application or Service	**Fee (£)**
Applications	
(1) To register:	
(a) a standard form of restriction contained in Schedule 4 to the rules,	
(b) a notice,	
(c) a new or additional beneficiary of a unilateral notice,	
(d) an obligation to make further advances under rule 108,	
(e) an agreement of a maximum amount of security under rule 109, or	
(f) an alteration of priority of registered charges under rule 102	
fee for up to three registered titles affected where delivered by electronic means	£20
where delivered by any other permitted means	£40
Additional fee for each subsequent registered title affected where delivered by electronic means	£10
where delivered by any other permitted means	£20
3total fee for up to three registered titles affected	£40
additional fee for each subsequent registered title affected	£20

Provided that no such fee is payable if, in relation to each registered title affected, the application is accompanied by a scale fee application or another application which attracts a fee under this paragraph.

No fee is payable to register a restriction in Form A in Schedule 4 to the rules (see exemption 13 below).

(2) To register a restriction in a form not contained in Schedule 4 to the rules for each registered title

where delivered by electronic means £45

where delivered by any other permitted means £90

(3) To register a caution against first registration £40

(4) To alter the cautions register for each individual cautions register £40

(5) To close or partly close a registered leasehold or a registered rentcharge title other than on surrender for each registered title closed or partly closed

where delivered by electronic means £20

where delivered by any other permitted means £40

Provided that no such fee is payable if the application is accompanied by a scale fee application.

(6) To upgrade from one class of registered title to another

where delivered by electronic means £20

where delivered by any other permitted means £40

Provided that no such fee is payable if the application for upgrading is accompanied by a scale fee application.

(7) To cancel an entry in the register of notice of an unregistered lease or an unregistered rentcharge which has determined for each registered title affected

where delivered by electronic means £20

where delivered by any other permitted means £40

Provided that no such fee is payable if the application is accompanied by a scale fee application.

(8) To enter or remove a record of a defect in title pursuant to section 64(1) of the Act

where delivered by electronic means £20

where delivered by any other permitted means £40

Provided that no such fee is payable if the application is accompanied by a scale fee application.

(9) An outline application made under rule 54:

(a) where delivered by electronic means £2

(b) where delivered by any other permitted means £5

Such fee is payable in addition to any other fee which is payable in respect of the application.

(10) For an order in respect of a restriction under section 41(2) of the Act for each registered title affected

where delivered by electronic means £20

where delivered by any other permitted means £40

(11) To register a person in adverse possession of a registered estate for each registered title affected. £130

(12) For registration as a person entitled to be notified of an application for adverse possession for each registered title affected

where delivered by electronic means £20

where delivered by any other permitted means £40

(13) For the determination of the exact line of a boundary under rule 118 for each application £90

(14) To alter the register – for each application

where delivered by electronic means £20

where delivered by any other permitted means £40

(15) To register a freehold estate in land as a freehold estate in commonhold land which is not accompanied by a statement under section 9(1)(b) of the Commonhold and Leasehold Reform Act 2002:

(a) up to 20 commonhold units £40

(b) for every 20 commonhold units, or up to 20 commonhold units, thereafter £10

(16) To add land to a commonhold:

(a) adding land to the common parts title £40

(b) adding land to a commonhold unit £40

(c) adding commonhold units

up to 20 commonhold units £40

for every 20 commonhold units, or up to 20 commonhold units, thereafter £10

(17) To apply for a freehold estate in land to cease to be registered as a freehold estate in commonhold land during the transitional period, as defined in the Commonhold and Leasehold Reform Act 2002 £40

(18) To register a freehold estate in land as a freehold estate in commonhold land, which is accompanied by a statement under section 9(1)(b) of the Commonhold and Leasehold Reform Act 2002

for each commonhold unit converted £40

(19) To register an amended commonhold community statement which changes the extent of the common parts or any commonhold unit:

(a) for the common parts £40

(b) for up to three commonhold units £40

(c) for each subsequent commonhold unit £20

Provided that no such fee shall be payable if, in relation to each registered title affected, the application is accompanied by a scale fee application or another application that attracts a fee under this Part

(20) To register an amended commonhold community statement, which does not change the extent of a registered title within the commonhold £40

Provided that no such fee shall be payable if, in relation to each registered title affected, the application is accompanied by a scale fee application or another application that attracts a fee under this Part

(21) To register an alteration to the Memorandum or Articles of Association of a commonhold association £40

(22) 2 To make a termination application (as defined in the Commonhold and Leasehold Reform Act 2002)
for each registered title affected £40

(23) To note the surrender of a development right under section 58 of the Commonhold and Leasehold Reform Act 2002 £40

Notes

1 Where an application of a kind specified in paragraphs (1), (2) or (10) above affects the whole or part of a freehold estate in commonhold land which is registered in the name of the developer under more than one title number, the fee is to be assessed as if the application affects only one title.

2 3Where an application of the kind specified in paragraph (18) is accompanied by an application to register a charge, the provisions explained in note 3 to the Scale 2 table above apply.

Services inspection and copying

(1) Inspection, by electronic means:
- (a) for each individual register £3
- (b) for each title plan £3
- (c) for each document referred to in an individual register or kept by the registrar which relates to an application to the registrar £3
- (d) for the individual register and title plan of a commonhold common parts title for each registered title £3
- (e) for each individual caution register £3
- (f) for each caution plan £3

(2) Inspection by other permitted means:
- (a) for each individual register £7
- (b) for each title plan £7
- (c) for each document referred to in an individual register or kept by the registrar which relates to an application to the registrar £7
- (d) for the individual register and title plan of a commonhold common parts title for each registered title £7
- (fe for each individual caution register £7
- (f) for each caution plan £7

(3) Official copy in respect of a registered title:
- (a) for each individual register
  - (i) where an official copy is requested by electronic means £3
  - (ii) where an official copy in paper form is requested by any other permitted means £7
- (b) for each title plan
  - (i) where an official copy is requested by electronic means £3
  - (ii) where an official copy in paper form is requested by any other permitted means £7
- (c) for each commonhold common parts individual register and title plan
  - (i) where an official copy is requested by electronic means £3
  - (ii) where an official copy in paper form is requested by any other permitted means £7

(4) Official copy in respect of the cautions register
- (a) for each individual caution register
  - (i) where an official copy is requested by electronic means £3
  - (ii) where an official copy in paper form is requested by any other permitted means £7
- (b) for each caution plan
  - (i) where an official copy is requested by electronic means £3
  - (ii) where an official copy in paper form is requested by any other permitted means £7

(5) Official copy of documents referred to in an individual register or kept by the registrar which relates to an application to the registrar for each document
- (a) where an official copy is requested by electronic means £3
- (b) where an official copy in paper form is requested by any other permitted means £7

(6) Copy of an historical edition
- (a) of an individual register of a registered title, where a copy is requested by electronic means – for each title £3
- (b) of a registered title or part of the edition of a registered title, where a copy is requested by any other permitted means for each title £7

Services searches

(1) An official search of an individual register or of a pending first registration application made to the registrar by electronic means for each title £3

(2) An official search of an individual register by a mortgagee for the purpose of section 56(3) of the Family Law Act 1996 made to the registrar by electronic means £3

(3) An official search of an individual register or of a pending first registration application other than as described in paragraphs (1) and (2) for each title £7

(4) The issue of a certificate of inspection of a title plan £7

(5) An official search of the index map
- (a) where no or not more than fice registered titles are disclosed £4
- (b) where more than five registered titles are disclosed–
  - (i) for the first five titles £4
  - (ii) for every ten titles, or up to ten titles, thereafter £2

(6) Search of the index of proprietors' names for each name £11

(7) An official search of the index of relating franchises and manors for each administrative area:
- (a) where the application is delivered by electronic means £3
- (b) where the application is delivered by any other permitted means £7

Services other information

(1)	Application for return of a document under rule 204	£9
(2)	Application that the registrar designate a document an exempt information document	
	where delivered by electronic means	£12
	where delivered by any other permitted means	£25
(3)	The fee for an application under rule 140 is the aggregate of the fees for the services provided.	

Exemptions

By Schedule 4 to the 2012 Order, no fee is payable for:

(1) reflecting a change in the name, address or description of a registered proprietor or other person referred to in the register, or in the cautions register, or changing the description of a property,

(2) giving effect in the register to a change of proprietor where the registered estate or the registered charge, as the case may be, has become vested without further assurance (other than on the death or bankruptcy of a proprietor) in some person by the operation of any statute (other than the Land Registration Act 2002), statutory instrument or scheme taking effect under any statute or statutory instrument,

(3) registering the surrender of a registered leasehold estate where the surrender is consideration or part consideration for the grant of a new lease to the registered proprietor of substantially the same premises as were comprised in the surrendered lease and where a scale fee is paid for the registration of the new lease,

(4) registering a discharge of a registered charge,

(5) registering a home rights notice, or renewal of such a notice, or renewal of a home rights caution under the Family Law Act 1996,

(6) entering in the register the death of a joint proprietor,

(7) cancelling the registration of a notice, (other than a notice in respect of an unregistered lease or unregistered rentcharge), caution against first registration, caution against dealings, including a withdrawal of a deposit or intended deposit, inhibition, restriction, or note,

(8) the removal of the designation of a document as an exempt information document,

(9) approving an estate layout plan or any draft document with or without a plan,

(10) an order by the registrar (other than an order under section 41(2) of the Land Registration Act 2002),

(11) deregistering a manor,

(12) an entry in the register of a note of the dissolution of a corporation,

(13) registering a restriction in form A in Schedule 4 to the Land Registration Rules 2003,

(14) an application for day list information on any one occasion delivered by electronic means.

Land Charges Registry fees

The current fees are those prescribed by the Land Charges (Fees) Rules 1990, as amended. The most recent amendment was by the Land Charges Fees (Amendment) Rules 2012, which came into force on 17 December 2012. The fees are as follows.

	Type of Application	Fee (£)
1	Registration, renewal, rectification or cancellation of an entry in the register per name	1.00
2	Certificate of cancellation per name	1.00
3	Entry of priority notice per name	1.00
4	Inspection of an entry in the register per entry	1.00
5	Office copy of an entry in the register (including any plan) per copy	1.00
6	Official search in the index (including issue of certificate of result):	
	(a) application by post, document exchange or delivery by hand) per name	1.00
	(b) application by other permitted means of communication (see below) per name	2.00

Land Charges applications can be made by post or DX, or by personal attendance at the Land Charges Department. Searches can also be made and office copies applied for by other means:

– By fax, in form K15, K16 or K19, to 0300 006 6699. Only users who maintain a Land Registry credit account or who have entered into a variable direct debit agreement with the registrar can use this service. Lines are open between 08:00 hours Monday and 15:00 hours Friday (except on public holidays, after 15:00 on the day before a public holiday, and before 08:00 on the day after a public holiday). Results are issued by post or DX.

– Land charge searches can also be made and office copies applied for by remote terminal using the Land Registry portal or Business Gateway, by organisations who have registered as a Land Registry Business e-services user and have set up a Variable Direct Debit. This service is available between 06:30 and 22:00 hours Monday to Friday excluding public holidays and between 07:00 and 17:00 hours Saturdays excluding Christmas Day. See www.landregistry.gov.uk for full details.

– The telephone service has been withdrawn.

– Land Registry Practice Guide 63, available at www.landregistry.gov.uk, contains further information about land charge applications.

Local land charges registries

In England each registering authority must prescribe its own fees in relation to local land charges as required by section 13A of the Local Land Charges Act 1975, inserted by the Constitutional Reform Act 2005, s.15(1) and Schedule 4 Part 1 paragraphs 82 and 83. Guidance on doing so was published by the then Department for Constitutional Affairs in January 2007 (Cm 7026).

The fee for making a personal search of a local land charges register has been abolished in both England and Wales (Local Land Charges (Amendment) Rules 2010 and Local Land Charges (Amendment) (Wales) Rules 2010).

In Wales, the power to make rules prescribing fees is exercised by the Welsh Ministers. At the time of going to press, no such rules had been made, and fees prescribed by Schedule 3 to the Local Land Charges Rules 1977, as substituted by the Local Land Charges (Amendment) Rules 2003, remain in force. They are as follows:

Type of Application	Fee (£)
1 Registration of a charge in Part 11 of the register (light obstruction notice)	67.00
2 Filing a definitive certificate of the Upper Tribunal under rule 10(3) of the Local Land Charges Rules 1977.	2.50
3 Filing a judgment, order or application for the variation or cancellation of an entry in Part 11 of the register.	7.00
4 Inspection of documents filed under rule 10 in respect of each parcel of land.	2.50
5 3Personal search in the whole or in part of the register	11.00
and in addition, in respect of each parcel of land above one, where under rule 11(3) the search extends to more than one parcel, subject to a maximum of £16.	1.00
6 Official search (including issue of official certificate of search):	
(a) in any one part of the register	2.00
(b) in the whole of the register	
(i) 1where the requisition is made by electronic means in accordance with rule 16	4.00
(ii) in any other case	6.00
and in addition, in respect of each parcel of land above one, where under rule 11(3) more than one parcel is included in the same requisition (whether the requisition is for a search in the whole or in any part of the register), subject to a maximum of £16.	1.00
7 Office copy of any entry in the register (not including a copy or extract of any plan or document filed pursuant to the Rules).	1.50
8 3Office copy of any plan or other document filed pursuant to the Rules—such fee as may be reasonable according to the time and work involved.	

The list below includes in each case the combined fees for an offical search and Part 1 enquiries.

Enquiries of local authorities

Local authorities must set their own fees for answering enquiries, in accordance with the Local Authorities (England) (Charges for Property Searches) Regulations 2008 or the Local Authorities (Charges for Property Searches) (Wales) Regulations 2009, as appropriate. These regulations came into force on 23 December 2008 and 3 March 2009 respectively. They do not apply to searches in the local land charges register, as to which see above. Guidance ("Local Authority Property Search Services – Costing and Charging Guidance") was issued by the Department for Communities and Local Government on 22 January 2009. The list that follows gives the fees charged by every authority. In the list:

Part I plus search gives the combined fee for an official search and replies to Part I enquiries for one residential plot of land. (Some authorities make a higher charge for business premises.) It is therefore the "basic search fee".

Part II enquiries gives the fee for each printed Part II enquiry.

Part II additional gives the fee for each additional Part II enquiry.

A blank space indicates that the authority states that it will not reply to such enquiries; except where indicated that a discretionary fee will be charged having regard to the work involved. In some cases additional enquiries are referred to the department responsible for the subject matter of the enquiry and that department will fix the fee.

Plans

Most authorities especially where the property in question is outside a town or city require a plan or plans of the property to be submitted with the search.

Drainage and water searches

The list below shows the basic fees, inclusive of VAT at 20 per cent, charged at the time of going to press by each water company (or its associated search company) for residential searches (Form CON 29 DW) and commercial drainage and water searches, and, where applicable, any higher fee for an expedited search. However, several of the companies offer discounted fees for online searches, and have different fees for multi-site searches or where other types of search are purchased at the same time. See the company websites listed below for details of these, and for the terms of commercial property searches and any expedited service.

Anglian Water (www.geodesys.com)	residential £46.20, £64.20 expedited; commercial (below 5 hectares) £120.00, £180.00 expedited; (above 5 hectares) £240, £360 expedited
Northumbrian Water (www.nwpropertysolutions.co.uk)	residential £43.40, commercial £108.00
Severn-Trent Water (www.severntrentsearches.com)	residential £52.80, £45.60 if delivered electronically, £72.00 expedited; commercial—three different packages at £90.00, £108.00 and £258.00
Southern Water (www.southernwater.co.uk)	residential £54.36, £75.00 expedited; commercial £123.60, £162.00 expedited; commercial (premium) £204.00, £242.40 expedited
South West Water (www.sourceforsearches.co.uk)	residential £54.36, £75.00 expedited; commercial 1£123.60, £162.00 expedited; commercial (premium) £204.00, £242.40 expedited
Thames Water (www.thameswater-propertysearches.co.uk)	residential £54.90, £102.90 expedited; commercial—three different packages at £126.60, £158.40 and £207.60 (£252.00, £284.40 and £333.60 expedited)
United Utilities (formerly North West Water) (www.unitedutilities.com)	residential £43.63, £67.21 expedited; commercial £103.10, £128.73 expedited; commercial mixed/small £77.46, £96.69 expedited

Welsh Water/Dwr Cymru (www.dwrcymru.com)	Residential and commercial £32.00 (Dwr Cymru answers CON29DW regardless of the type of property)
Wessex Water (www.wessexsearches.co.uk)	residential £45.60; commercial—three different packages at £72.00, £115.20 and £244.80
Yorkshire Water (www.safe-move.co.uk)	residential £45.36; commercial "standard" £113.40, commercial "plus" £204.00

Addresses for the water companies are given in Part 12.

NLIS

The National Land Information Service has two channels offering online conveyancing searches via the internet. These are SearchFlow and Thames Water Property Searches. Search fees set by these providers are listed online when a search is conducted so these fees are not listed in the Conveyancing Fees and Charges table. For more information, visit the NLIS website at www.nlis.org.uk.

County	Authority	Part I plus search (LLCI/ Con29(R))	Part II enquiries (Con29(O) enquiries)	Part II additional (own questions)	Notes
Residential property					
Greater London	Barking & Dagenham	150.00	16.00		Drainage etc: Thames; 2 plans required; additional parcel £25
	Barnet	210.00	23.50	46.50	Drainage etc: Thames; additional parcel £46.40
	Bexley	110.00	33.00	55.00	Drainage etc: Thames; additional parcel £42
	Brent	200.00	10.00	20.00	Drainage etc: Thames; additional parcel £21
	Bromley	64.00	13.00	40.00	Drainage etc: Thames; additional parcel £22
	Camden	118.00	16.00	26.00	Drainage etc: Thames; additional parcel £17
	City of London	146.00	6.00	30.00	Drainage etc: Thames; additional parcel £30
	Croydon	260.00	30.00	48.00	Drainage etc: Thames; additional parcel £48
	Ealing	115.00	12.00		Additional enquiries discretionary; Drainage etc: Thames; additional parcel £15
	Enfield	100.00	10.00	10.00	Drainage etc: Thames; 2 plans required; Q22: £14; additional parcel £7
	Greenwich	108.00	10.00	10.00	Drainage etc: Thames; Q4: £28; additional parcel £31
	Hackney	130.00	8.00		Additional enquiries discretionary; Drainage etc: Thames; Q22: £15; additional parcel £41
	Hammersmith & Fulham	264.00	14.00	24.00	Drainage etc: Thames; 2 plans required; additional parcel £24
	Haringey	135.00	5.00	6.00	Drainage etc: Thames; Q22: £14; 2 plans required; additional parcel £27
	Harrow	200.00	22.00	25.00	Drainage etc: Thames; Q22: £22; additional parcel £3
	Havering	85.00	17.00	28.50	Drainage etc: Thames; additional parcel £29.50; Q4: £26.50; 2 plans required
	Hillingdon	60.00		15.00	Additional enquiries discretionary; Drainage etc: Thames; additional parcel £1
	Hounslow	207.00	15.00		Drainage etc: Thames; Q22: £14; additional parcel £30
	Islington	110.00	10.00	20.00	Additional enquiries discretionary; additional parcel £21; Drainage etc: Thames
	Kensington & Chelsea	257.50	12.00	55.00	Drainage etc: Thames; 2 plans required; additional parcel £44
	Kingston upon Thames	83.00	1.00	40.00	Additional enquiries discretionary; Drainage etc: Thames; Q6 & Q9: £5; 2 plans required; additional parcel £15
	Lambeth	249.00	30.00		Additional enquiries discretionary; Q22: £14; 1 plan sufficient; Drainage etc: Thames; additional parcel £45
	Lewisham	132.00	10.00	25.00	Drainage etc: Thames; Do not answer Q9 & Q10; additional parcel £25; 2 plans required
	Merton	87.00	10.00		Additional enquiries discretionary; Q22: £23; Drainage etc: Thames; 2 plans required; additional parcel £37
	Newham	140.00	20.00	50.00	Drainage etc: Thames; 2 plans required; additional parcel £30
	Redbridge	140.00	30.00	50.00	Drainage etc: Thames; 2 plans required; additional parcel £40
	Richmond upon Thames	85.00	13.00	35.00	Drainage etc: Thames; 2 plans required, outlining area in red; additional parcel £15
	Southwark	177.00	12.00	30.00	Drainage etc: Thames; Q22: £14; additional parcel £30
	Sutton	100.00	30.00	45.00	Do not answer Q9-refer to Transco; Q22: £14; Drainage etc: Thames; additional parcel £30
	Tower Hamlets	200.00	35.00	32.00	Additional enquiries discretionary; Drainage etc: Thames; additional parcel £35
	Waltham Forest	230.00		36.00	Drainage etc: Thames; Q22: £15; additional parcel £15 (LLC1 only)
	Wandsworth	67.00			Additional enquiries discretionary; Drainage etc: Thames; additional parcel £42
	Westminster	160.00	25.00	35.00	Drainage etc: Thames; 2 plans required; additional parcel £42

County	Authority	Part I plus search (LLCI/ Con29(R))	Part II enquiries (Con29(O) enquiries)	Part II additional (own questions)	Notes
Residential property					
Bedfordshire	Bedford	169.00	24.00	24.00	Drainage etc: Anglian; additional parcel £23
	Central Bedfordshire	133.00	15.00	25.00	Drainage etc: Anglian; Q22: £16; additional parcel £13.50
	Luton	97.00	11.00	11.00	Drainage etc: Thames and Anglian; Q22: £14; 2 plans required; additional parcel £25
Berkshire	Bracknell Forest	104.15	10.50	21.00	Drainage etc: Thames; additional parcel (garage): £13; additional parcel (non-garage): £25
	Reading	98.00	12.00	25.00	Drainage etc: Thames; Q22: £14; 2 plans required; additional parcel £20
	Slough	118.00	12.00	20.00	Drainage etc: Thames; additional parcel £15
	West Berkshire	100.00	20.00	38.00	Drainage etc: Thames; additional parcel £70
	Windsor & Maidenhead	108.00	36.00	36.00	Drainage etc: Thames; additional parcel £56
	Wokingham	107.00	17.00	27.20	Drainage etc: Thames; 2 plans required; additional parcel £15.20
Bristol	Bristol	110.00	7.00	16.00	Drainage etc: Wessex; Q22: £14; additional parcel £14
Buckinghamshire	Aylesbury Vale	99.00	12.00	12.00	Will not answer Q4; Drainage etc: Anglian and Thames; Q22: £16; additional parcel £16
	Chiltern	92.50	15.00	30.00	Drainage etc: Thames; additional parcel £15; 2 plans required
	Milton Keynes	113.50	14.00	20.50	Drainage etc: Geodesys; 2 plans required; additional parcel £28
	South Bucks	95.00	15.00	25.00	Drainage etc: Thames; additional parcel £20; 2 plans required
	Wycombe	90.00	10.00	15.00	Drainage etc: Thames; Q4: £50 (apply directly to Planning Dept); additional parcel £20
Cambridgeshire	Cambridge	122.00	8.00	12.00	Drainage etc: Anglian; Q5: £9; Q9: refer to Transco; Q17: £10; Q22: £7; additional parcel £12
	East Cambridgeshire	80.10	55.10	6.00	Part II enquiries individually priced; Drainage etc: Anglian; 2 plans required; additional parcel £12
	Fenland	134.20	12.00	15.00	Drainage etc: Anglian; additional parcel £15
	Huntingdon	76.00	6.00	11.00	Drainage etc: Anglian; Q5: £12; Q9; £8; Q17: £13; Q22: £12; additional parcel £29.50; 2 plans required if searching extra piece of land
	Peterborough	150.00	30.00	35.00	Drainage etc: Anglian; additional parcel £25
	South Cambridgeshire	86.00	8.00	15.00	Discretionary charges for Part II enquiries; Drainage etc: Anglian; additional parcel £20
Cheshire	Cheshire East	90.00	13.00	40.00	Drainage etc: United; 2 plans required; Q22: £20.50; additional parcel £20
	Cheshire West and Chester	90.00	13.00	15.00	Drainage etc: United; Q22: £18; additional parcel £15
	Halton	110.00	12.00	26.00	Drainage etc: United; Q22: £14; additional parcel £26
	Warrington	133.00	15.00		Additional enquiries discretionary; Drainage etc: United; additional parcel £10
Cornwall	Cornwall	125.00	12.00	20.00	Drainage etc: South West; Q4: £20; additional parcel £12; send all correspondence to appropriate area office

15

County	Authority	Part I plus search (LLCI/ Con29(R))	Part II enquiries (Con29(O) enquiries)	Part II additional (own questions)	Notes
Residential property					
Cumbria	Allerdale	90.00	11.00	15.00	Drainage etc: United; Q22 £18; additional parcel £15
	Barrow-in-Furness	99.00	11.00	11.00	Drainage etc: United; Q22: £15; additional parcel £22.50
	Carlisle	131.00	10.00	10.50	Drainage etc: United; Q22: £13.50; additional parcel £16.50
	Copeland	105.00	10.00	20.00	Drainage etc: United; Q5: £10; Q22: £17; additional parcel £15; optional additional enquiries £9 or £11
	Eden	90.00	12.90		Additional enquiries discretionary; Drainage etc: Northumbrian and United; Q5: £17.10; Q22: £18; additional parcel £15.50
	South Lakeland	89.00	11.00		Will not answer solicitor's own queries; north pointed grid reference must accompany each search; Q22: £25; additional parcel £12
Derbyshire	Amber Valley	98.50	11.00	15.00	Drainage etc: Severn Trent; additional parcel £12
	Bolsover	60.00	10.00	10.00	Drainage etc: Severn Trent, Yorkshire; Q4: £30; additional parcel £37
	Chesterfield	109.00	7.80	7.80	Drainage etc: Yorkshire; additional parcel £10
	Derby City	82.50	15.00	30.00	Drainage etc: Severn Trent; additional parcel £25
	Derbyshire Dales	100.00	10.00	12.00	Drainage etc: Severn Trent; additional parcel £11; 2 plans required; Peak Park and not Peak Park same level of fees since 1 April 2007
	Erewash	120.00	15.50	27.00	Drainage etc: Severn Trent; additional parcel £17
	High Peak	80.00	8.00	16.00	Drainage etc: United and Severn Trent; additional parcel £20
	North East Derbyshire	85.00	10.00	10.00	Drainage etc: Severn Trent and Yorkshire; will not answer landfill or neighbouring land; Q22: £14; additional parcel £15; if property also in Peak Park: extra £17
	South Derbyshire	75.00	15.00	20.00	Drainage etc: Severn Trent; 2 plans required; additional parcel £30
Devon	East Devon	70.00	5.00	20.00	Pt II enquiries individually priced; Qs 12–15: will not answer; Drainage etc: South West; additional parcel £12
	Exeter	85.00	4.00	10.00	Drainage etc: South West; Qs 5, 22: £4.50; additional parcel £2
	Mid Devon	70.60		12.50	Part II enquiries individually priced; Drainage etc: South West; Q22: £14; additional parcel £14
	North Devon	71.00	6.00	12.00	Drainage etc: South West; will not answer landfill enquiries; 3 plans required; additional parcel £11
	Plymouth	88.00	10.00	20.00	Drainage etc: South West; additional parcel £15; 3 plans required outlined in red
	South Hams	83.00		15.00	Pt II enquiries individually priced; Q4 not applicable; Drainage etc: South West; additional parcel £15.50; 3 plans required
	Teignbridge	85.00	8.00	10.00	Drainage etc: South West; additional parcel £11
	Torbay	89.00	10.00	15.00	Drainage etc: South West; additional parcel £17; 2 plans required
	Torridge	82.50		8.60	Pt II enquiries individually priced; Q15: not applicable; Drainage etc: South West; additional parcel £15; 2 plans required
	West Devon	64.50		20.00	Part II enquiries individually priced; Drainage etc: South West; additional parcel £13.75; 3 plans required

County	Authority	Part I plus search (LLCI/ Con29(R))	Part II enquiries (Con29(O) enquiries)	Part II additional (own questions)	Notes
Residential property					
Dorset	Bournemouth	53.00	13.00	16.00	Drainage etc: Wessex; additional parcel £16
	Christchurch	90.00	12.00	12.00	Drainage etc: Wessex; additional parcel £12; 2 plans required
	East Dorset	118.00	15.00	20.00	Drainage etc: Wessex; additional parcel £16; will not answer Q4, Q9, Q17
	North Dorset	95.00	14.00	20.00	Drainage etc: Wessex; additional parcel £16; 3 plans required edged in red
	Poole	123.00	12.00	25.00	Drainage etc: Wessex; 2 plans required; additional parcel £20
	Purbeck	124.00	10.00	12.00	Drainage etc: Wessex; 2 plans required; additional parcel £13
	West Dorset	125.00	10.00	20.00	Drainage etc: Wessex and South West; will not answer Q4; additional parcel £10
	Weymouth & Portland	112.00	12.00	20.00	Drainage etc: Wessex; additional parcel £15; 2 plans required
Durham, Co	Darlington	79.00	5.00	5.00	Drainage etc: Northumbrian; additional parcel £20; 2 plans required
	Durham	121.00	10.00	10.00	Drainage etc: Northumbrian; additional parcel £15; 2 plans required
	Hartlepool	95.00	7.00	54.38	Drainage etc: Northumbrian; additional parcel £8.10
	Stockton-on-Tees	61.50	10.00	25.00	Drainage etc: Northumbrian; additional parcel £14
East Riding of Yorkshire	East Riding of Yorkshire	130.00	20.00	30.00	Drainage etc: Yorkshire; Q22: £14; additional parcel £9.30; 2 plans required
	Kingston upon Hull	115.00	10.00	11.50	Will not answer Q4; Drainage etc: Yorkshire; additional parcel £1; 2 plans required
East Sussex	Brighton & Hove	115.00	15.00	30.00	Drainage etc: Southern; additional parcel £20; 2 plans required
	Eastbourne	140.00	10.00	20.00	Drainage etc: Southern; Q22: £24; additional parcel £10
	Hastings	202.00	12.50	26.00	Drainage etc: Southern; Q4, 5, 22: £15; additional parcel £13.50
	Lewes	83.00	5.00	20.00	Drainage etc: Southern; Q4, 5, 22: £15; additional parcel £10
	Rother	110.00	12.00	18.00	Drainage etc: Southern; additional parcel £12; 2 plans required
	Wealden	90.00	15.00	22.00	Drainage etc: Southern; additional parcel £10; 2 plans required

County	Authority	Part I plus search (LLCI/ Con29(R))	Part II enquiries (Con29(O) enquiries)	Part II additional (own questions)	Notes
Residential property					
Essex	Basildon	145.00	10.00	20.00	Drainage etc: Anglian; Q22: £24; additional parcel £6.30; 2 plans required
	Braintree	90.00	15.00		Additional enquiries discretionary; Drainage etc: Anglian; additional parcel £15; 4 copies of plan required
	Brentwood	101.65	11.75	28.75	Drainage etc: Anglian and Thames; Q22: £14; additional parcel £35.80
	Castle Point	106.00	20.00	30.00	Drainage etc: Anglian; Q22: £14; additional parcel £10
	Chelmsford	87.65	16.00	40.00	Drainage etc: Anglian; 2 plans required; additional parcel £16; will not answer Q9
	Colchester	90.00	10.00	17.00	Drainage etc: Anglian; Q22: £14; additional parcel £14
	Epping Forest	85.00	10.00	20.00	Drainage etc: Thames; Q22: £14; additional parcel £15
	Harlow	110.65	12.00	18.00	Drainage etc: Thames; Q22: £14; additional parcel £20; 2 plans required
	Maldon	140.00	15.00	31.00	Drainage etc: Anglian; Q22: £21; additional parcel £15; 2 plans required
	Rochford	172.00	20.00	36.00	Drainage etc: Anglian; 2 plans required; additional parcel £31
	Southend-on-Sea	115.00	15.00		Additional enquiries discretionary; Drainage etc: Anglian; additional parcel £15; 2 plans required
	Tendring	64.00	10.00	10.00	Drainage etc: Anglian; Q22: £20; 4 plans required; additional parcel £13.50
	Thurrock	110.00	22.00		Additional enquiries discretionary; Drainage etc: Anglian; 2 plans required; additional parcel £28
	Uttlesford	98.00	15.00	20.00	Drainage etc: Anglian and Thames; additional parcel £15; 5 plans required
Gloucestershire	Cheltenham	99.00	10.00	25.00	Drainage etc: Severn Trent; 3 plans required; Q22: £25; additional parcel £3.50
	Cotswold	147.50	20.00	20.00	Drainage etc: Thames, Severn Trent and Wessex; additional parcel £20; 3 plans required
	Forest of Dean	117.00	16.00	16.00	Drainage etc: Severn Trent and Welsh Water; Q22: £24; additional parcel £10.50; 2 plans required
	Gloucester	110.00		20.00	Pt II enquiries individually priced; Drainage etc: Severn Trent; additional parcel £15.05; 2 plans required
	South Gloucestershire	100.00	15.00	20.00	Drainage etc: Wessex; additional parcel £20; 2 plans required
	Stroud	98.00	11.00	10.00	Drainage etc: Severn Trent and Wessex; Q22: £22; additional parcel £26; 5 plans required
	Tewkesbury	120.00	20.00	20.00	Drainage etc: Severn Trent; additional parcel £20; 2 plans required
Greater Manchester	Bolton	135.00	20.00	25.00	Drainage etc: United; additional parcel £10
	Bury	131.00	12.00	17.00	Drainage etc: United; Q22: £14; additional parcel £22; 2 plans required
	Manchester	75.60	5.00	19.00	Drainage etc: United; additional parcel percentage of total cost
	Oldham	90.00	13.00	21.00	Drainage etc: United; Q22: £14; additional parcel £24
	Rochdale	135.00	23.00	26.00	Drainage etc: United; Q22: £14; additional parcel £20
	Salford	135.00	10.00	12.50	Drainage etc: United; additional parcel £16
	Stockport	121.00	14.00	30.00	Drainage etc: United; Q4, Q5, Q6, Q11: £30; additional parcel £32
	Tameside	60.00	12.00	25.00	Drainage etc: United; additional parcel £12
	Trafford	62.00	12.00	15.00	Drainage etc: United; Q6, Q22: £15; additional parcel £20
	Wigan	135.00	10.00	15.00	Drainage etc: United; additional parcel £10

County	Authority	Part I plus search (LLCI/ Con29(R))	Part II enquiries (Con29(O) enquiries)	Part II additional (own questions)	Notes
Residential property					
Hampshire	Basingstoke & Deane	130.00	22.00	20.45	Drainage etc: Southern and Thames; additional parcel £22
	East Hampshire	138.30	10.00	15.00	Drainage etc: Southern and Thames; Q22: £21; additional parcel £15; 2 plans required
	Eastleigh	149.00	15.00	17.60	Drainage etc: Southern; additional parcel £20; 3 plans required
	Fareham	164.00	23.00	41.00	Drainage etc: Southern; additional parcel £41; 2 plans required
	Gosport	118.00	7.00	7.00	Drainage etc: Southern; additional parcel £12
	Hart	160.00	15.00	40.00	Drainage etc: Thames; Q4, 5 & 22: £18; additional parcel £25
	Havant	160.00	15.00	20.00	Drainage etc: Southern; Qs 18, 19, 22: £30; additional parcel £20
	New Forest	120.00	20.00	40.00	Drainage etc: Southern and Wessex; additional parcel £20
	Portsmouth	50.00	12.00	15.00	Drainage etc: Southern; additional parcel £12; 2 plans required
	Rushmoor	120.00	10.00	20.00	Drainage etc: Thames; 2 plans required; Q4, 5 & 22: £18; additional parcel £15
	Southampton	80.00	3.00	16.00	Drainage etc: Southern; 4 plans required; additional parcel £31
	Test Valley	97.00	14.00	20.00	Drainage etc: Southern; additional parcel £15; electronic search available
	Winchester	160.00	16.00	20.00	Drainage etc: Southern; 2 plans required; Q22: £14; additional parcel £100
Herefordshire	Herefordshire	119.00	5.00		Additional enquiries discretionary; Q5: £10; Qs 10, 19, 20: £7.50; Q22: £25; Drainage etc: Severn Trent and Welsh Water; additional parcel £35; 2 plans required
Hertfordshire	Broxbourne	75.00	15.00	15.00	Drainage etc: Thames; Q22: £14; additional parcel £30; 2 plans required
	Dacorum	99.00	12.00		Additional enquiries discretionary; Q22: £20; 3 plans required; Drainage etc: Thames; additional parcel £20
	East Hertfordshire	87.00	12.00	25.00	Drainage etc: Thames; Q22: £20; 2 plans required; additional parcel £20
	Hertsmere	68.00	10.00	20.00	Enquiries on specific or authorised use discretionary; Q22: £20; Drainage etc: Thames; additional parcel £15; 2 plans required
	North Hertfordshire	90.00	9.00	15.00	Drainage etc: Anglian and Thames; Q22: £20; additional parcel £13; 4 plans required
	St Albans	100.00	9.00	10.00	Drainage etc: Thames; Q22: £14; additional parcel £12.50; 2 plans required
	Stevenage	66.00		9.00	Pt II enquiries priced individually. Drainage etc: Anglian and Thames; additional parcel £9
	Three Rivers	65.00	10.00	10.00	Drainage etc: Thames; Q22: £20; additional parcel £15
	Watford	64.00	7.50	10.00	Drainage etc: Thames; Q22: £16.59; additional parcel £13.50; 3 plans required
	Welwyn Hatfield	75.00	15.00	20.00	Drainage etc: Thames; additional parcel £15
Isle of Wight	Isle of Wight	145.00	11.00	16.00	Drainage etc: Southern; additional parcel £16; 2 plans required
Isles of Scilly	Isles of Scilly	115.50	13.25	20.00	Contact directly for drainage enquiries £49.50; Q22: £14; additional parcel £16.50; 2 plans required

County	Authority	Part I plus search (LLCI/ Con29(R))	Part II enquiries (Con29(O) enquiries)	Part II additional (own questions)	Notes
Residential property					
Kent	Ashford	85.00	10.00	30.00	Drainage etc: Southern; Q22: £15; 2 plans required; additional parcel £10
	Canterbury	109.00	10.00	10.00	Drainage etc: Southern; additional parcel £10; 2 plans required
	Dartford	95.00	10.00	10.00	Drainage etc: Southern and Thames; additional parcel £10; 2 plans required
	Dover	115.50	14.50	15.00	Drainage etc: Southern; additional parcel £13; 5 plans required
	Gravesham	120.00	10.00	20.00	Drainage etc: Southern; Q22: £14; additional parcel £10.80; 2 plans required
	Maidstone	95.00	15.00	20.00	Drainage etc: Southern; Q22: contact Kent County Council; 2 plans required; additional parcel £10
	Medway	75.00	10.00	10.00	Drainage etc: Southern; Qs 5 & 22: £15; additional parcel £35; 2 plans required
	Sevenoaks	105.00	15.00	25.00	Drainage etc: Southern and Thames; additional parcel £15; 2 plans required
	Shepway	115.00	10.00	15.00	Drainage etc: Southern; 2 plans required; additional parcel £13
	Swale	115.50	16.00	21.00	Drainage etc: Southern; additional parcel £12; 3 plans required
	Thanet	143.00	10.00	10.00	Drainage etc: Southern; Q22: £14; additional parcel £19; 2 plans required
	Tonbridge & Malling	148.00	15.00	18.00	Drainage etc: Southern; additional parcel £10; 2 plans required
	Tunbridge Wells	125.00	10.00	16.00	Drainage etc: Southern; Q22: £14; additional parcel £10; 2 plans required
Lancashire	Blackburn with Darwen	117.42	14.70	14.70	Drainage etc: United; Q22: £14; additional parcel £12; 2 plans required
	Blackpool	111.00	9.00		Drainage etc: United; Q22: £20; additional parcel £16; additional enquiries discretionary
	Burnley	136.60	29.45	25.55	Drainage etc: United; Q4, Q5 & Q22: £29.45; additional parcel £10; 2 plans required
	Chorley	130.71	12.77	21.42	Will not answer Q4; Q22: £27; 2 plans required; additional parcel £12.40
	Fylde	79.00	15.00	20.00	Drainage etc: United; additional parcel £15; 2 plans required
	Hyndburn	90.50	7.50	9.25	Drainage etc: United; Q22: £15; additional parcel £10.50
	Lancaster	99.00	7.00		Additional enquiries discretionary; Q22: £22; 2 plans required; additional parcel £2
	Pendle	65.00	25.00	30.00	Drainage etc: United; additional parcel £20
	Preston	135.00	10.00	15.00	Drainage etc: United; Q22: £14; additional parcel £16; 2 plans required
	Ribble Valley	119.35	13.50	10.00	Drainage etc: United; Q22: £15.50; additional parcel £8.90
	Rossendale	80.00	10.00	17.50	Drainage etc: United; Q22: £20; additional parcel £15
	South Ribble	125.00	15.00	25.00	Drainage etc: United; Q22: £15; additional parcel £30
	West Lancashire	75.00	10.00	12.00	Drainage etc: United; Q22: £15; additional parcel £12; 2 plans required
	Wyre	97.00	15.00		Additional enquiries discretionary; Drainage etc: United; additional parcel £25; 2 plans required

County	Authority	Part I plus search (LLCI/ Con29(R))	Part II enquiries (Con29(O) enquiries)	Part II additional (own questions)	Notes
Residential property					
Leicestershire	Blaby	75.00	10.00	20.00	Drainage etc: Severn Trent; Q22: £14; additional parcel £11.80
	Charnwood	104.00	10.00	15.00	Drainage etc: Severn Trent; Q22: £15; additional parcel £11; 2 plans required
	Harborough	70.00	7.00	10.00	Part II questions individually priced; Drainage etc: Severn Trent and Anglian; Q22: £14; additional parcel £11
	Hinckley & Bosworth	75.00	10.00	20.00	Drainage etc: Severn Trent; Q22: £14; additional parcel £11.80; 2 plans required
	Leicester	80.00	12.00	15.00	Drainage etc: Severn Trent; Q22: £14; additional parcel £11; 2 plans required
	Melton	107.00	11.00	16.00	Drainage etc: Severn Trent; Q22: £14; additional parcel £9; 2 plans required
	North West Leicestershire	104.00	15.00	20.00	Drainage etc: Severn Trent; Q4: £30; Q22: £14; additional parcel £20; 2 plans required
	Oadby & Wigston	92.00	12.00	15.00	Drainage etc: Severn Trent; Q22: £14; additional parcel £19; 2 plans required
Lincolnshire	Boston	93.00	11.50	18.00	Drainage etc: Anglian; Qs 4 & 22: £22.50; additional parcel £18
	East Lindsey	90.00	12.00	13.00	Drainage etc: Anglian; Q22: £14; additional parcel £13
	Lincoln	87.50	15.50	15.50	Drainage etc: Anglian; additional parcel £15.50
	North East Lincolnshire	100.00	10.00	20.00	Drainage etc: Anglian; Q22: £14; additional parcel £15; 2 plans required
	North Kesteven	90.00	11.25	14.30	Drainage etc: Anglian; Q5: £14; Q22: £14; additional parcel £13
	North Lincolnshire	85.00	5.00	6.50	Pt II enquiries individually priced; additional enquiries discretionary. Drainage etc: Anglian and Severn Trent; additional parcel £12; 2 plans required
	South Holland	115.00	10.00	20.00	Drainage etc: Anglian; Q22: £15; additional parcel £12.80; 4 plans required
	South Kesteven	100.40	14.90	12.80	Drainage etc: Anglian and Severn Trent; additional parcel £13.50; Q5 & Q22: £15.90
	West Lindsey	100.00	15.00	26.00	Drainage etc: Anglian and Severn Trent; additional parcel £14.50; 2 plans required
Merseyside	Knowsley	58.00	7.00		Additional enquiries discretionary. Drainage etc: United; additional parcel £5
	Liverpool	75.00	5.00		Additional enquiries discretionary; Drainage etc: United; additional parcel £10; 2 plans required
	Sefton	50.00	5.00	30.00	Drainage etc: United; additional parcel £10
	St Helens	121.00	17.50	17.50	Drainage etc: United; additional parcel £12
	Wirral	91.58	10.00	10.00	Drainage etc: United and Welsh Water; Q22: £14; additional parcel £15; 2 plans required
Norfolk	Breckland	114.20	8.50	12.50	Drainage etc: Anglian; Q22: £17; additional parcel £13.70
	Broadland	105.00	17.00	17.00	Drainage etc: Anglian; additional parcel £17; 4 plans required
	Great Yarmouth	135.00	8.00	8.50	Drainage etc: Anglian; Q22: refer to Norfolk County Council; additional parcel £12.50
	King's Lynn & West Norfolk	52.00	12.00	14.00	Drainage etc: Geodesys; Q22: refer to Norfolk County Council; additional parcel £11.30; 3 plans required
	North Norfolk	105.00	15.00	11.50	Drainage etc: Anglian; Q22: £26; additional parcel £16.50
	Norwich	120.00	15.00	21.00	Drainage etc: Anglian; Qs 5 & 22: refer to Norfolk County Council; additional parcel £17; 2 plans required
	South Norfolk	147.00	12.50	16.00	Drainage etc: Anglian; Q22: £16; additional parcel £16; 3 plans required

County	Authority	Part I plus search (LLCI/ Con29(R))	Part II enquiries (Con29(O) enquiries)	Part II additional (own questions)	Notes
Residential property					
Northamptonshire	Corby	126.50	15.00	6.00	Drainage etc: Anglian; Q4–5: £8.50, Q6–21: £3, Q22: £12; 2 plans required; additional parcel £11
	Daventry	120.00	20.00	20.00	Drainage etc: Anglian, Severn Trent and Thames; additional parcel £15.50
	East Northamptonshire	132.00	14.00	24.00	Drainage etc: Anglian; 4 plans required; additional parcel £18.50
	Kettering	79.00	10.00	25.00	Additional enquiries discretionary; Q22: £13.50; Drainage etc: Anglian; additional parcel £11; 2 plans required
	Northampton	98.00	15.00	20.00	Drainage etc: Anglian; additional parcel £11.50; 2 plans required
	South Northamptonshire	63.00	10.00		Drainage etc: Anglian and Thames; additional enquiries £30-£75; Q4–5: £8.50; Q22: £12; additional parcel £15
	Wellingborough	70.50	10.00	20.00	Drainage etc: Anglian; 2 plans required; Q22: £12; additional parcel £11
Northumberland	Northumberland	95.00	15.00	20.00	Drainage etc: Northumbrian; additional parcel £26
North Yorkshire	City of York	90.00	21.00	42.00	Drainage etc: Yorkshire; Q22: £14; additional parcel £9.50; 2 plans required
	Craven	127.00	21.00	17.00	Drainage etc: United, Safe-Move; additional parcel £14; 2 plans required
	Hambleton	60.00	6.00	20.00	Drainage etc: Northumbrian and Yorkshire; Q4–5: £10; Q22: £15; additional parcel £1
	Harrogate	112.50	23.50	23.50	Drainage etc: Yorkshire; additional parcel £23.50; 2 plans required
	Middlesbrough	83.50	17.50	17.50	Drainage etc: Northumbrian; additional parcel £7.75
	Redcar & Cleveland	104.00	6.50		Drainage etc: Northumbrian; additional enquiries variable; Q22: £14; additional parcel £14
	Richmondshire	75.00	15.00	6.00	Outside National Park. Drainage etc: Northumbrian and Yorkshire; Qs 4,5 & 9: £10; Q22: £15; additional parcel £1
		90.00	17.00	6.00	Inside National Park. Drainage etc: Northumbrian and Yorkshire; Qs 4,5 & 9: £10; Q22: £15; additional parcel £1
	Ryedale	82.70	17.00	17.00	Outside National Park. Drainage etc: Yorkshire; additional parcel £15; 2 plans required
		98.00	17.00	17.00	Inside National Park. Drainage etc: Yorkshire; additional parcel £15; 2 plans required
	Scarborough	69.00		10.00	Drainage etc: Safe-Move; additional parcel £12; advised to check before raising additional enquiries; National Park £80
	Selby	118.00	20.00		Additional enquiries discretionary; Drainage etc: Safe-Move; additional parcel £15
Nottinghamshire	Ashfield	91.00	14.00	14.00	Drainage etc: Severn Trent; additional parcel £14
	Bassetlaw	90.00	14.00	21.00	Drainage etc: Severn Trent; Q5: £6; Q22: £14; additional parcel £18
	Broxtowe	93.00	10.00	15.00	Drainage etc: Severn Trent; Q5: £16; Q22: £24; additional parcel £12
	Gedling	118.70	10.00	13.00	Drainage etc: Severn Trent; Q22: £14; additional parcel £15.50
	Mansfield	92.00	29.00	15.00	Drainage etc: Severn Trent; Q22: £14; additional parcel £15
	Newark & Sherwood	85.00	10.00	17.00	Drainage etc: Severn Trent; Q5: £17; Q22: £14; additional parcel £15; 2 plans required
	Nottingham	92.00	15.30	15.30	Drainage etc: Severn Trent; Q5: £10; Q22: £14; additional parcel £8.85
	Rushcliffe	98.00	5.00	10.00	Drainage etc: Severn Trent; Q22: £14; additional parcel £10; 2 plans required

County	Authority	Part I plus search (LLCI/ Con29(R))	Part II enquiries (Con29(O) enquiries)	Part II additional (own questions)	Notes
Residential property					
Oxfordshire	Cherwell	128.00	10.00	20.00	Drainage etc: Severn Trent and Thames; Q22: £20; additional parcel £20; 2 plans required
	Oxford	120.00	17.00	22.00	Drainage etc: Thames; Q22: £22; additional parcel £16
	South Oxfordshire	163.00	13.00	25.00	Will not answer Q4; Q22: £22; Drainage etc: Thames; additional parcel £27; 2 plans required
	Vale of White Horse	162.00	14.00	25.00	Will not answer Q4; Q22: £22. Drainage etc: Thames; additional parcel £40
	West Oxfordshire	130.39	15.38	18.45	Drainage etc: Thames; Q4: £20; Q5: £18; Q22: £22.55; additional parcel £19.30
Rutland	Rutland	100.00	13.50	35.00	Drainage etc: Anglian and Severn Trent; additional parcel £38
Shropshire	Shropshire	80.00	15.00	25.00	Drainage etc: Severn Trent and Welsh; additional parcel £30
	Telford & Wrekin	56.00	27.00	4.00	Drainage etc: Severn Trent; 2 plans required; additional parcel £7.50
Somerset	Bath & North East Somerset	98.00		15.00	Drainage etc: Wessex; Part II enquiries individually priced; additional parcel £15; 2 plans required
	Mendip	98.00	11.00	16.00	Drainage etc: Wessex; additional parcel £16
	North Somerset	105.00	20.00	29.00	Drainage etc: Wessex; 2 plans required; additional parcel £24
	Sedgemoor	140.00	7.50	10.00	Drainage etc: Wessex; Q22: £25.55; additional parcel £10.50; 4 plans required
	South Somerset	157.00	9.50	13.50	Drainage etc: South West and Wessex; Q22: £27.90; additional parcel £13.70; 2 plans required
	Taunton Deane	140.55	8.00	12.00	Drainage etc: South West and Wessex; additional parcel £12; cheques only from solicitor and firm; no drainage or sewage enquiries; no DX; 3 plans required
	West Somerset	99.00	7.50	10.00	Drainage etc: Wessex; optional printed enquiries £7.50 + £20 admin fee; additional parcel £10
South Yorkshire	Barnsley	80.00	8.00		Will not answer Q4; Drainage etc: Safe-Move; additional parcel £5; 2 plans required
	Doncaster	77.70	10.00	2.70	Drainage etc: Anglian, Severn Trent and Yorkshire; Q22: £7; will not answer Q4; additional parcel £10; 2 plans required
	Rotherham	66.00	10.00		Additional enquiries discretionary; Drainage etc: Severn Trent and Yorkshire; Q4: Free; Q22: £20; 2 plans required; additional parcel £2
	Sheffield	78.00	7.50	15.00	Drainage etc: Yorkshire; additional parcel £10.80; 2 plans required

County	Authority	Part I plus search (LLCI/ Con29(R))	Part II enquiries (Con29(O) enquiries)	Part II additional (own questions)	Notes
Residential property					
Staffordshire	Cannock Chase	87.00	5.00	5.00	Drainage etc: Severn Trent; 2 plans required; no DX; additional parcel £29.35
	East Staffordshire	75.00	14.00	40.00	Drainage etc: Severn Trent; additional parcel £42; 2 plans required
	Lichfield	99.00	30.00	30.00	Drainage etc: Severn Trent; Q22: £30; additional parcel £50; 2 plans required
	Newcastle-under-Lyme	92.00	18.00		Additonal enquiries discretionary; Drainage etc: United and Severn Trent; additional parcel £35
	South Staffordshire	115.00	15.00	20.00	Drainage etc: Severn Trent; will not answer landfill enquiries; Q22: £15; additional parcel £15; 2 plans required
	Stafford	98.00	26.00	26.00	Will not answer landfill enquiries; Drainage etc: Severn Trent; Q22: £25; additional parcel £10; 2 plans required
	Staffordshire Moorlands	80.00	8.00	16.00	Outside Peak Park; Drainage etc: United and Severn Trent; Qs 5, 9 & 22: £3.25; Q8: £6.50; additional parcel £25
		80.00	8.00	8.00	In Peak Park; Drainage etc: United and Severn Trent; Qs 5, 9 & 22: £3.25; Q8: £6.50; additional parcel £25
	Stoke-on-Trent	48.60		15.00	Part II enquiries: variable; Drainage etc: Severn Trent; Q22: £0.95; additional parcel £15; 2 plans required
	Tamworth	118.00	15.00	20.50	Will not answer landfill enquiries; Drainage etc: Severn Trent; additional parcel £11; 2 plans required
Suffolk	Babergh	148.00	12.00	40.00	Drainage etc: Geodesys (Anglian); additional parcel £16; 2 plans required
	Forest Heath	127.570	13.00	34.10	Drainage etc: Geodesys (Anglian); 2 plans required; additional parcel £15.70
	Ipswich	95.00	10.00	20.00	Drainage etc: Geodesys (Anglian); additional parcel £14; 2 plans required
	Mid Suffolk	149.00	12.00	15.00	Drainage etc: Geodesys (Anglian); Q5, Q22: £12; additional parcel £13; 2 plans required
	St Edmundsbury	100.00	10.50	16.50	Drainage etc: Geodesys (Anglian); Q5, Q22: £15; additional parcel £13
	Suffolk Coastal	100.00	12.50	15.00	Drainage etc: Geodesys (Anglian); additional parcel £12; 2 plans required
	Waveney	100.00	12.50	15.00	Drainage etc: Geodesys (Anglian); Q9: £5; Qs 5 & 22: £12.50; additional parcel £13
Surrey	Elmbridge	98.00	14.00	20.00	Drainage etc: Thames; additional parcel £18.20; 2 plans required
	Epsom & Ewell	140.00	11.00	25.00	Drainage etc: Thames; additional parcel £25
	Guildford	90.00	12.00	20.00	Drainage etc: Thames; additional parcel £10
	Mole Valley	205.00	16.00	31.00	Drainage etc: Thames and Southern; additional parcel £34
	Reigate & Banstead	191.00	15.00	15.00	Drainage etc: Thames; Q22: refer to Surrey County Council; additional parcel £15
	Runnymede	215.00	20.00	40.00	Drainage etc: Thames; Additional enquiries regarding highways should be directed to Surrey CC; additional parcel £14.12; 2 plans required
	Spelthorne	204.00	15.00	20.00	Will not answer highways enquiries; Drainage etc: Thames; additional parcel £15.40
	Surrey Heath	171.50	15.60	20.80	Drainage etc: Thames; Q22: £15; additional parcel £16.65
	Tandridge	224.00	15.00	45.00	Drainage etc: Thames and Southern; additional parcel £20; 2 plans required
	Waverley	195.00	15.00	20.00	Drainage etc: Thames and Southern; Q4, Q5, Q22: £12; additional parcel £20; 2 plans required
	Woking	162.37	13.00	20.00	Drainage etc: Thames; additional parcel £57.02

County	Authority	Part I plus search (LLCI/ Con29(R))	Part II enquiries (Con29(O) enquiries)	Part II additional (own questions)	Notes
Residential property					
Tyne & Wear	Gateshead	135.30		27.30	Part II enquiries individually priced; Drainage etc: Northumbrian; additional parcel £12; 2 plans required
	Newcastle upon Tyne	139.50	12.50	22.00	Drainage etc: Northumbrian; Q22: £14; additional parcel £21
	North Tyneside	80.73	6.00	12.00	Drainage etc: Northumbrian; Q9: Transco; Q22: £14; additional parcel £11
	South Tyneside	140.55		25.65	Part II enquiries individually priced; Drainage etc: Northumbrian; additional parcel £23
	Sunderland	98.00	14.00	30.00	Additional enquiries discretionary; Q22: £14; Drainage etc: Northumbrian; additional parcel £20; 4 plans required
Warwickshire	North Warwickshire	115.00	1.00	1.00	Drainage etc: Severn Trent; Q22: £10; additional parcel £10.80; 2 plans required
	Nuneaton & Bedworth	113.50	15.50	25.00	Drainage etc: Severn Trent; additional parcel £17; 2 plans required
	Rugby	85.00	10.00	30.00	Cannot answer Q4, Q17; Drainage etc: Severn Trent; additional parcel £20; 2 plans required
	Stratford-upon-Avon	98.00	5.00	10.00	Landfill enquiries: £38 (write separately addressed to the Environmental Health Team); cannot answer Q4; Q22: £15; Drainage etc: Thames and Severn Trent; additional parcel £10
	Warwick	145.00	10.00	20.00	Landfill enquiries or those about planning within 200m should be directed to Planning; Drainage etc: Severn Trent; additional parcel £10; 2 plans required
West Midlands	Birmingham	100.00	10.00		Additional enquiries discretionary; Drainage etc: Severn Trent; additional parcel £20
	Coventry	110.00	10.00		Additional enquiries discretionary; Drainage etc: Severn Trent; additional parcel £21; 2 plans required
	Dudley	92.45	14.35		Additional enquiries discretionary; Drainage etc: Severn Trent; additional parcel £16.30; 2 plans required
	Sandwell	99.00	10.00		Additional enquiries discretionary; Drainage etc: Severn Trent; Q4: do not answer; Qs5–22: £10; additional parcel £18
	Solihull	145.60	16.00	20.00	Drainage etc: Severn Trent; Q4: £25.25; Q22: £14.50; additional parcel £10
	Walsall	131.50	10.75		Additional enquiries discretionary; limestone, landfill: £10.15; Severn Trent search £52.80; Coal Authority search £32.40; additional parcel £11.05
	Wolverhampton	61.00	10.00	10.00	Drainage etc: Severn Trent; additional parcel £11; 2 plans required
West Sussex	Adur & Worthing	133.00	7.00		Drainage etc: Southern; additional parcel £6
	Arun	75.00	7.75	13.50	Drainage etc: Southern; additional parcel £11
	Chichester	85.00	15.00	18.00	Drainage etc: Southern and Thames; additional parcel £20; 2 plans required
	Crawley	83.00	10.00	20.00	Drainage etc: Thames; no highway questions; additional parcel £20
	Horsham	110.00		35.00	Part II enquiries individually priced; Drainage etc: Thames (the Rusper area) and Southern; additional parcel £15; 3 plans required
	Mid Sussex	73.00	2.30	25.00	Drainage etc: Southern and Thames; Qs 4, 5, & 22: £15; additional parcel £30; 2 plans required

County	Authority	Part I plus search (LLCI/ Con29(R))	Part II enquiries (Con29(O) enquiries)	Part II additional (own questions)	Notes
Residential property					
West Yorkshire	Calderdale	144.00	10.60	27.00	Drainage etc: Yorkshire; additional parcel £29
	City of Bradford	134.00	11.50		Additional enquiries discretionary; no drainage questions; additional parcel £25; 2 plans required
	Kirklees	75.00	7.00		Additional enquiries discretionary; Drainage etc: Yorkshire; Q4: Free; Q22: £14; additional parcel £21
	Leeds	49.00	5.50	7.00	Q22: £4.50; Drainage etc: Yorkshire; additional parcel £2
	Wakefield	40.00	5.00		Additional enquiries discretionary; Q22: £14; Drainage etc: Yorkshire; additional parcel £5
Wiltshire	Swindon	57.00			Pt II enquiries individually priced; additional enquiries discretionary. Drainage etc: Thames; 2 plans required; additional parcel £28
	Wiltshire	125.00	15.50	21.00	Drainage etc: Thames, Southern and Wessex; additional parcel £12; 2 plans required
Worcestershire	Bromsgrove	108.00		45.50	Pt II enquiries individually priced; Q22: £21.50; Drainage etc: Severn Trent; additional parcel £18; £40 for landfill enquiries
	Malvern Hills	100.00	20.00	30.00	Drainage etc: Severn Trent; additional parcel £16.50
	Redditch	94.50	6.00	6.00	Drainage etc: Severn Trent; Q4, Q5, Q9: £12.50; Q22: £20; additional parcel £12.50
	Worcester	110.50	22.00	22.00	Pt II enquiries individually priced; Q22: £17; Drainage etc: Severn Trent; additional parcel £18
	Wychavon	113.00	2.50	21.00	Drainage etc: Severn Trent; Q4, Q5: £8.50; Q22: £17; 2 plans required; additional parcel £14.40
	Wyre Forest	108.00	17.00		Additional enquiries discretionary; Drainage etc: Severn Trent; additional parcel £39
Isles of Scilly	Isles of Scilly	115.50	13.25	20.00	Contact directly for drainage enquiries £49.50; Q22: £14; additional parcel £16.50; 2 plans required

County	Authority	Part I plus search (LLCI/ Con29(R))	Part II enquiries (Con29(O) enquiries)	Part II additional (own questions)	Notes
Residential property					
Wales	Anglesey	102.00	7.00		Additional enquiries discretionary; Drainage etc: Welsh Water; 7 plans required; Q22: £14; additional parcel £10
	Blaenau Gwent	90.00	8.00	10.00	Drainage etc: Welsh Water; Q22: £5; additional parcel £10; 2 plans required
	Bridgend	109.00	18.00	28.00	Drainage etc: Welsh Water; additional parcel £17
	Caerphilly	78.00	12.00	15.00	Drainage etc: Welsh Water; 2 plans required; additional parcel £13
	Cardiff	85.80	8.00	15.00	Drainage etc: Welsh Water; Q22: £14; 2 plans required; additional parcel £11
	Carmarthenshire	110.00	10.00	15.00	Drainage: Welsh Water; 2 plans required; additional parcel £11
	Ceredigion (formerly Cardiganshire)	99.00	10.00	15.00	Drainage etc: Welsh Water; 2 plans required; additional parcel £12.50
	Conwy	101.00	10.00	15.00	Drainage etc: Welsh Water; additional parcel £10.40; Q22: £14
	Denbighshire	65.00	6.00	10.00	Additional enquiries discretionary; Drainage etc: Welsh Water; additional parcel £15; Q22: £25
	Flintshire	123.00	11.00	25.00	Drainage etc: Welsh Water; 2 plans required; additional parcel £11
	Gwynedd	96.00	7.00	21.00	Drainage etc: Welsh Water; Q22: £14; 2 plans required; additional parcel £16
	Merthyr Tydfil	111.00	10.00	15.00	Drainage etc: Welsh Water; 2 plans required; additional parcel £15
	Monmouthshire	97.00	12.00		Additional enquiries discretionary; Drainage etc: Welsh Water; Q5, Q22: £15; 3 plans required; additional parcel £45
	Neath Port Talbot	70.00	6.00		Additional enquiries £35 if accepted; Drainage etc: Hyder; Q22: £21.90; 2 plans required; additional parcel £12.20
	Newport	110.00	12.00	25.00	Drainage etc: Welsh Water; Contaminated land and landfill enquiries should be directed to Environmental Health; additional parcel £25
	Pembrokeshire	90.00	7.00		Additional enquiries £15 if accepted; Drainage etc: Welsh Water; additional parcel £11.70
	Powys	102.00	12.00	22.00	Drainage etc: Welsh Water, Hyder and Severn Trent; Q5, Q22: £20; 1 plan sufficient; additional parcel £11
	Rhondda Cynon Taf	127.00	16.00	20.00	Drainage etc: Welsh Water; 2 plans required; additional parcel £17
	Swansea	90.50	10.50	10.50	Drainage etc: Welsh Water; Q22: £23; additional parcel £10.50; 2 plans required
	Torfaen	86.00	12.00	20.00	Additional enquiries discretionary; Drainage etc: Welsh Water; Q22: £14; additional parcel £15; 1 plan sufficient
	Vale of Glamorgan	125.00	13.51	11.00	Drainage etc: Welsh Water; Q22: £14; additional parcels £15
	Wrexham	105.00	11.00	20.00	Drainage etc: Welsh Water; additional parcel £12

County	Authority	Part I plus search (LLCI/ Con29(R))	Part II enquiries (Con29(O))	Part II additional (own questions)	Notes
Commercial property					
Greater London	Barking & Dagenham	150.00	16.00		Drainage etc: Thames; 2 plans required; additional parcel £25
	Barnet	210.00	23.50	46.50	Drainage etc: Thames; additional parcel £46.50
	Bexley	110.00	33.00	55.00	Drainage etc: Thames; additional parcel £42
	Brent	200.00	10.00	20.00	Drainage etc: Thames; additional parcel £21
	Bromley	120.00	13.00	40.00	Drainage etc: Thames; additional parcel £22
	Camden	118.00	16.00	26.00	Drainage etc: Thames; additional parcel £17
	City of London	146.00	6.00	30.00	Drainage etc: Thames; additional parcel £30
	Croydon	260.00	30.00	48.00	Drainage etc: Thames; additional parcel £48
	Ealing	115.00	12.00		Additional enquiries discretionary; Drainage etc: Thames; additional parcel £15
	Enfield	165.00	10.00	10.00	Drainage etc: Thames; 2 plans required; Q22: £14; additional parcel £7
	Greenwich	108.00	10.00	10.00	Drainage etc: Thames; Q4: £28; additional parcel £31
	Hackney	130.00	8.00		Additional enquiries discretionary; Drainage etc: Thames; additional parcel £41; Q22: £15
	Hammersmith & Fulham	264.00	14.00	24.00	Drainage etc: Thames; 2 plans required; additional parcel £24
	Haringey	135.00	5.00	6.00	Drainage etc: Thames; Q22: £14; 2 plans required; additional parcel £27
	Harrow	200.00	22.00	25.00	Drainage etc: Thames; Q2: £22; additional parcel £23
	Havering	85.00	17.00	28.50	Drainage etc: Thames; additional parcel £29.50; Q4: £26.50; 2 plans required
	Hillingdon	70.00		15.00	Additional enquiries discretionary; Drainage etc: Thames; additional parcel £1
	Hounslow	252.00	15.00		Drainage etc: Thames; Q22: £14; additional parcel £30
	Islington	110.00	10.00	20.00	Additional enquiries discretionary; additional parcel £21; Drainage etc: Thames
	Kensington & Chelsea	257.50	12.00	55.00	Drainage etc: Thames; 2 plans required; additional parcel £44
	Kingston upon Thames	83.00	1.00	40.00	Additional enquiries discretionary; Drainage etc: Thames; Q6 & Q9: £5; 2 plans required; additional parcel £15
	Lambeth	249.00	30.00		Additional enquiries discretionary; Q22: £14; 1 plan sufficient; Drainage etc: Thames; additional parcel £45
	Lewisham	132.00	10.00	25.00	Drainage etc: Thames; Do not answer Q9 or Q10; 2 plans required; additional parcel £25
	Merton	87.00	10.00		Additional enquiries discretionary; Q22: £23; Drainage etc: Thames; 2 plans required; additional parcel £37
	Newham	140.00	20.00	50.00	Drainage etc: Thames; 2 plans required; additional parcel £30
	Redbridge	140.00	30.00	50.00	Drainage etc: Thames; 2 plans required; additional parcel £40
	Richmond upon Thames	85.00	13.00	35.00	Drainage etc: Thames; 2 plans required, outlining area in red; additional parcel £15
	Southwark	177.00	12.00	30.00	Drainage etc: Thames; Q22: £14; additional parcel £30
	Sutton	100.00	30.00	45.00	Do not answer Q9-refer to Transco; Q22: £14; Drainage etc: Thames; additional parcel £30
	Tower Hamlets	200.00	35.00	32.00	Additional enquiries discretionary; Drainage etc: Thames; additional parcel £35
	Waltham Forest	230.00		36.00	Drainage etc: Thames; Q22: £15; additional parcel £15 (LLC1 only)
	Wandsworth	67.00			Additional enquiries discretionary; Drainage etc: Thames; additional parcel £42
	Westminster	160.00	25.00	35.00	Drainage etc: Thames; 2 plans required; additional parcel £40

County	Authority	Part I plus search (LLCI/ Con29(R))	Part II enquiries (Con29(O))	Part II additional (own questions)	Notes
Commercial property					
Bedfordshire	Bedford	163.00	23.00	23.00	Drainage etc: Anglian; additional parcel £23
	Central Bedfordshire	201.00	15.00	25.00	Drainage etc: Anglian; Q22: £16; additional parcel £13.50
	Luton	225.00	11.00	11.00	Drainage etc: Thames and Anglian; Q22: £14; 2 plans required; additional parcel £50
Berkshire	Bracknell Forest	109.15	10.50	21.00	Drainage etc: Thames; additional parcel (garage): £13; additional parcel (non-garage): £25
	Reading	98.00	12.00	25.00	Drainage etc: Thames; Q22: £14; 2 plans required; additional parcel £20
	Slough	118.00	12.00	20.00	Drainage etc: Thames; additional parcel £15
	West Berkshire	100.00	20.00	38.00	Drainage etc: Thames; additional parcel £70
	Windsor & Maidenhead	108.00	36.00	36.00	Drainage etc: Thames; additional parcel £56
	Wokingham	107.00	17.00	27.20	Drainage etc: Thames; 2 plans required; additional parcel £15.20
Bristol	Bristol	150.00	7.00	16.00	Drainage etc: Wessex; Q22: £14; additional parcel £14
Buckinghamshire	Aylesbury Vale	99.00	12.00	12.00	Will not answer Q4; Drainage etc: Anglian and Thames; Q22: £16; additional parcel £16
	Chiltern	92.50	15.00	30.00	Drainage etc: Thames; additional parcel £15; 2 plans required
	Milton Keynes	113.50	13.00	19.50	Drainage etc: Geodesys; 2 plans required; additional parcel £28
	South Bucks	111.00	14.00	20.50	Drainage etc: Thames; additional parcel £20; 2 plans required
	Wycombe	90.00	10.00	15.00	Drainage etc: Thames; Q4: £50 (apply directly to Planning Dept); additional parcel £20
Cambridgeshire	Cambridge	122.00	8.00	12.00	Drainage etc: Anglian; Q5: £9; Q9: refer to Transco; Q17: £10; Q22: £7; additional parcel £12
	East Cambridgeshire	80.10	55.10	6.00	Part II enquiries individually priced; Drainage etc: Anglian; 2 plans required; additional parcel £12
	Fenland	222.20	12.00	15.00	Drainage etc: Anglian; additional parcel £15
	Huntingdon	110.50	6.00	11.00	Drainage etc: Anglian; Q5: £12; Q17: £13; Q22: £11; additional parcel £29.50; 2 plans required if searching extra piece of land
	Peterborough	150.00	30.00	35.00	Drainage etc: Anglian; additional parcel £25
	South Cambridgeshire	182.00	8.00	15.00	Discretionary charges for Part II enquiries; Drainage etc: Anglian; additional parcel £20
Cheshire	Cheshire East	146.00	13.00	40.00	Drainage etc: United; 2 plans required; Q22: £20.50; additional parcel £20
	Cheshire West and Chester	115.00	13.00	15.00	Drainage etc: United; Q22: £18; additional parcel £15
	Halton	110.00	12.00	26.00	Drainage etc: United; Q22: £14; additional parcel £26
	Warrington	133.00	15.00		Additional enquiries discretionary; Drainage etc: United; additional parcel £10
Cornwall	Cornwall	125.00	12.00	20.00	Drainage etc: South West; Q4: £20; additional parcel £12; send all correspondence to appropriate area office

15

County	Authority	Part I plus search (LLC1/ Con29(R))	Part II enquiries (Con29(O))	Part II additional (own questions)	Notes
Commercial property					
Cumbria	Allerdale	90.00	11.00	15.00	Drainage etc: United; Q22 £5; additional parcel £15
	Barrow-in-Furness	99.00	11.00	11.00	Drainage etc: United; Q22: £15; additional parcel £22.50
	Carlisle	131.00	10.00	10.50	Drainage etc: United; Q22: £13.50; additional parcel £16.50
	Copeland	105.00	10.00	20.00	Drainage etc: United; Q5: £10; Q22: £17; additional parcel £15; optional additional enquiries £9 or £11
	Eden	90.00	12.90		Additional enquiries discretionary; Drainage etc: Northumbrian and United; Q5: £17.10; Q22: £18; additional parcel £15.50
	South Lakeland	89.00	11.00		Will not answer solicitor's own queries; north pointed grid reference must accompany each search; Q22: £25; additional parcel £12
Derbyshire	Amber Valley	98.50	11.00	15.00	Drainage etc: Severn Trent; additional parcel £12
	Bolsover	105.00	10.00	10.00	Drainage etc: Severn Trent, Yorkshire; Q4: £30; additional parcel £37
	Chesterfield	109.00	7.80	7.80	Drainage etc: Yorkshire; additional parcel £10
	Derby City	82.50	15.00	30.00	Drainage etc: Severn Trent; additional parcel £25
	Derbyshire Dales	100.00	10.00	12.00	Drainage etc: Severn Trent; additional parcel £11; 2 plans required; Peak Park and not Peak Park same level of fees since 1 April 2007
	Erewash	140.00	15.50	27.00	Drainage etc: Severn Trent; additional parcel £17
	High Peak	125.00	80.00	16.00	Drainage etc: United and Severn Trent; additional parcel £20
	North East Derbyshire	85.00	10.00	10.00	Drainage etc: Severn Trent and Yorkshire; will not answer landfill or neighbouring land; Q22: £14; additional parcel £15; if property also in Peak Park: extra £17
	South Derbyshire	150.00	15.00	20.00	Drainage etc: Severn Trent; 2 plans required; additional parcel £30
Devon	East Devon	70.00	5.00	20.00	Pt II enquiries individually priced; Qs 12–15: will not answer; Drainage etc: South West; additional parcel £12
	Exeter	85.00	4.00	10.00	Drainage etc: South West; Qs5,22: £4.50; additional parcel £2
	Mid Devon	70.60		12.50	Part II enquiries individually priced; Drainage etc: South West; Q22: £14; additional parcel £14
	North Devon	71.00	6.00	12.00	Drainage etc: South West; will not answer landfill enquiries; 3 plans required; additional parcel £11
	Plymouth	88.00	10.00	20.00	Drainage etc: South West; additional parcel £15; 3 plans required outlined in red
	South Hams	83.00		15.00	Pt II enquiries individually priced; Q4 not applicable; Drainage etc: South West; additional parcel £15.50; 3 plans required
	Teignbridge	85.00	8.00	10.00	Drainage etc: South West; additional parcel £11
	Torbay	89.00	10.00	15.00	Drainage etc: South West; additional parcel £17; 2 plans required
	Torridge	82.50		8.60	Pt II enquiries individually priced; Q15: not applicable; Drainage etc: South West; additional parcel £15; 2 plans required
	West Devon	64.50		20.00	Part II enquiries individually priced; Drainage etc: South West; additional parcel £13.75; 3 plans required

County	Authority	Part I plus search (LLCI/ Con29(R))	Part II enquiries (Con29(O))	Part II additional (own questions)	Notes
Commercial property					
Dorset	Bournemouth	53.00	15.00	20.00	Drainage etc: Wessex; additional parcel £25
	Christchurch	90.00	12.00	12.00	Drainage etc: Wessex; additional parcel £12; 2 plans required
	East Dorset	118.00	15.00	20.00	Drainage etc: Wessex; additional parcel £16; will not answer Q4, Q9, Q17
	North Dorset	95.00	14.00	20.00	Drainage etc: Wessex; additional parcel £16; 3 plans required edged in red
	Poole	210.00	12.00	25.00	Drainage etc: Wessex; 2 plans required; additional parcel £20
	Purbeck	124.00	10.00	12.00	Drainage etc: Wessex; 2 plans required; additional parcel £13
	West Dorset	125.00	10.00	20.00	Drainage etc: Wessex and South West; will not answer Q4; additional parcel £10
	Weymouth & Portland	112.00	12.00	20.00	Drainage etc: Wessex; additional parcel £15; 2 plans required
Durham, Co	Darlington	119.00	5.00	5.00	Drainage etc: Northumbrian; additional parcel £20; 2 plans required
	Durham	182.00	30.00	30.00	Drainage etc: Northumbrian; additional parcel £30; 2 plans required
	Hartlepool	95.00	7.00	54.38	Drainage etc: Northumbrian; additional parcel £8.10
	Stockton-on-Tees	81.50	10.00	25.00	Drainage etc: Northumbrian; additional parcel £14
East Riding of Yorkshire	East Riding of Yorkshire	160.00	20.00	30.00	Drainage etc: Yorkshire; Q22: £14; additional parcel £9.30; 2 plans required
	Kingston upon Hull	140.00	10.00	11.50	Will not answer Q4; Drainage etc: Yorkshire; additional parcel £1; 2 plans required
East Sussex	Brighton & Hove	115.00	15.00	30.00	Drainage etc: Southern; additional parcel £20; 2 plans required
	Eastbourne	140.00	10.00	20.00	Drainage etc: Southern; Q22: £24; additional parcel £10
	Hastings	202.00	12.50	26.00	Drainage etc: Southern; Q4, 5, 22: £15; additional parcel £13.50
	Lewes	83.00	5.00	20.00	Drainage etc: Southern; Q4, 5, 22: £15; additional parcel £10
	Rother	110.00	12.00	18.00	Drainage etc: Southern; additional parcel £12; 2 plans required
	Wealden	90.00	15.00	22.00	Drainage etc: Southern; additional parcel £10; 2 plans required

County	Authority	Part I plus search (LLCI/ Con29(R))	Part II enquiries (Con29(O))	Part II additional (own questions)	Notes
Commercial property					
Essex	Basildon	145.00	10.00	20.00	Drainage etc: Anglian; Q22: £24; additional parcel £6.30; 2 plans required
	Braintree	90.00	15.00		Additional enquiries discretionary; Drainage etc: Anglian; additional parcel £15; 4 copies of plan required
	Brentwood	101.65	11.75	28.75	Drainage etc: Anglian and Thames; Q22: £14; additional parcel £35.80
	Castle Point	106.00	20.00	30.00	Drainage etc: Anglian; Q22: £14; additional parcel £10
	Chelmsford	87.65	16.00	40.00	Drainage etc: Anglian; 2 plans required; additional parcel £16; will not answer Q9
	Colchester	128.00	10.00	17.00	Drainage etc: Anglian; Q22: £14; additional parcel £14
	Epping Forest	85.00	10.00	20.00	Drainage etc: Thames; Q22: £14; additional parcel £15
	Harlow	110.65	12.00	18.00	Drainage etc: Thames; Q22: £14; additional parcel £20; 2 plans required
	Maldon	161.00	15.00	31.00	Drainage etc: Anglian; Q22: £21; additional parcel £15; 2 plans required
	Rochford	172.00	20.00	36.00	Drainage etc: Anglian; 2 plans required; additional parcel £31
	Southend-on-Sea	115.00	15.00		Additional enquiries discretionary; Drainage etc: Anglian; additional parcel £15; 2 plans required
	Tendring	64.00	10.00	10.00	Drainage etc: Anglian; Q22: £20; 4 plans required; additional parcel £13.50
	Thurrock	160.00	22.00		Additional enquiries discretionary; Drainage etc: Anglian; 2 plans required; additional parcel £35
	Uttlesford	118.00	15.00	20.00	Drainage etc: Anglian and Thames; additional parcel £15; 5 plans required
Gloucestershire	Cheltenham	99.00	10.00	25.00	Drainage etc: Severn Trent; Q22: £25; 3 plans required; additional parcel £3.50
	Cotswold	147.50	20.00	20.00	Drainage etc: Thames, Severn Trent and Wessex; additional parcel £20; 3 plans required
	Forest of Dean	117.00	16.00	16.00	Drainage etc: Severn Trent and Welsh Water; Q22: £24; additional parcel £10.50; 2 plans required
	Gloucester	110.00		20.00	Pt II enquiries individually priced; Drainage etc: Severn Trent; additional parcel £15.05; 2 plans required
	South Gloucestershire	150.00	15.00	20.00	Drainage etc: Wessex; additional parcel £20; 2 plans required
	Stroud	98.00	11.00	10.00	Drainage etc: Severn Trent and Wessex; Q22: £22; additional parcel £26; 5 plans required
	Tewkesbury	120.00	20.00	20.00	Drainage etc: Severn Trent; additional parcel £20; 2 plans required
Greater Manchester	Bolton	135.00	20.00	25.00	Drainage etc: United; additional parcel £10
	Bury	131.00	12.00	17.00	Drainage etc: United; Q22: £14; additional parcel £22; 2 plans required
	Manchester	75.60	5.00	19.00	Drainage etc: United; additional parcel percentage of total cost
	Oldham	100.00	13.00	21.00	Drainage etc: United; Q22: £14; additional parcel £24
	Rochdale	135.00	23.00	26.00	Drainage etc: United; Q22: £14; additional parcel £20
	Salford	135.00	10.00	12.50	Drainage etc: United; additional parcel £16
	Stockport	121.00	14.00	30.00	Drainage etc: United; Q4, Q5, Q6, Q11: £30; additional parcel £32
	Tameside	60.00	12.00	25.00	Drainage etc: United; additional parcel £12
	Trafford	62.00	12.00	15.00	Drainage etc: United; Q6, Q22: £15; additional parcel £20
	Wigan	135.00	10.00	15.00	Drainage etc: United; additional parcel £10

County	Authority	Part I plus search (LLCI/ Con29(R))	Part II enquiries (Con29(O))	Part II additional (own questions)	Notes
Commercial property					
Hampshire	Basingstoke & Deane	130.00	22.00	20.45	Drainage etc: Southern and Thames; additional parcel £22
	East Hampshire	138.30	10.00	15.00	Drainage etc: Southern and Thames; Q22: £21; additional parcel £15; 2 plans required
	Eastleigh	149.00	15.00	17.60	Drainage etc: Southern; additional parcel £20; 3 plans required
	Fareham	164.00	23.00	41.00	Drainage etc: Southern; additional parcel £41; 2 plans required
	Gosport	118.00	7.00	7.00	Drainage etc: Southern; additional parcel £12
	Hart	160.00	15.00	40.00	Drainage etc: Thames; Q4, 5 & 22: £18; additional parcel £25
	Havant	160.00	15.00	20.00	Drainage etc: Southern; Qs 18, 19, 22: £30; additional parcel £20
	New Forest	160.00	20.00	40.00	Drainage etc: Southern and Wessex; additional parcel £20
	Portsmouth	50.00	12.00	15.00	Drainage etc: Southern; additional parcel £12; 2 plans required
	Rushmoor	120.00	10.00	20.00	Drainage etc: Thames; Q4, 5 & 22: £18; 2 plans required; additional parcel £15
	Southampton	80.00	3.00	16.00	Drainage etc: Southern; 4 plans required; additional parcel £31
	Test Valley	97.00	14.00	20.00	Drainage etc: Southern; additional parcel £15; electronic search available
	Winchester	160.00	16.00	20.00	Drainage etc: Southern; 2 plans required; Q22: £14; additional parcel £100
Herefordshire	Herefordshire	119.00	5.00		Additional enquiries discretionary; Q5: £10; Qs 10, 19 & 20: £7.50; Q22: £25; Drainage etc: Severn Trent and Welsh Water; additional parcel £35; 2 plans required
Hertfordshire	Broxbourne	75.00	15.00	15.00	Drainage etc: Thames; Q22: £14; additional parcel £30; 2 plans required
	Dacorum	190.00	12.00		Additional enquiries discretionary; Q22: £14; 3 plans required; Drainage etc: Thames; additional parcel £20
	East Hertfordshire	87.00	12.00	25.00	Drainage etc: Thames; Q22: £20; 2 plans required; additional parcel £20
	Hertsmere	68.00	10.00	20.00	Enquiries on specific or authorised use discretionary; Q22: £20; Drainage etc: Thames; additional parcel £15; 2 plans required
	North Hertfordshire	100.00	9.00	15.00	Drainage etc: Anglian and Thames; Q22: £20; additional parcel £13; 4 plans required
	St Albans	100.00	9.00	10.00	Drainage etc: Thames; Q22: £14; additional parcel £25; 2 plans required
	Stevenage	88.00		9.00	Pt II enquiries priced individually. Drainage etc: Anglian and Thames; additional parcel £9
	Three Rivers	90.00	10.00	10.00	Drainage etc: Thames; Q22: £20; additional parcel £15
	Watford	120.00	7.50	10.00	Drainage etc: Thames; Q22: £16.59; additional parcel £13.50; 3 plans required
	Welwyn Hatfield	75.00	15.00	20.00	Drainage etc: Thames; additional parcel £15
Isle of Wight	Isle of Wight	145.00	11.00	16.00	Drainage etc: Southern; additional parcel £16; 2 plans required
Isles of Scilly	Isles of Scilly	115.50	13.25	20.00	Contact directly for drainage enquiries £49.50; Q22: £14; additional parcel £16.50; 2 plans required

County	Authority	Part I plus search (LLCI/ Con29(R))	Part II enquiries (Con29(O))	Part II additional (own questions)	Notes
Commercial property					
Kent	Ashford	190.00	10.00	30.00	Drainage etc: Southern; Q22: £15; 2 plans required; additional parcel £10
	Canterbury	109.00	10.00	10.00	Drainage etc: Southern; additional parcel £10; 2 plans required
	Dartford	130.00	10.00	10.00	Drainage etc: Southern and Thames; additional parcel £10; 2 plans required
	Dover	115.50	14.50	15.00	Drainage etc: Southern; additional parcel £13; 5 plans required
	Gravesham	240.00	10.00	20.00	Drainage etc: Southern; Q22: £14; additional parcel £10.80; 2 plans required
	Maidstone	95.00	15.00	20.00	Drainage etc: Southern; Q22: contact Kent County Council; 2 plans required; additional parcel £10
	Medway	75.00	10.00	10.00	Drainage etc: Southern; Qs 5 & 22: £15; additional parcel £35; 2 plans required
	Sevenoaks	105.00	15.00	25.00	Drainage etc: Southern and Thames; additional parcel £15; 2 plans required
	Shepway	150.00	10.00	15.00	Drainage etc: Southern; 2 plans required; additional parcel £13
	Swale	131.00	16.00	21.00	Drainage etc: Southern; additional parcel £12; 3 plans required
	Thanet	143.00	10.00	10.00	Drainage etc: Southern; Q22: £14; additional parcel £19; 2 plans required
	Tonbridge & Malling	299.00	15.00	18.00	Drainage etc: Southern; additional parcel £10; 2 plans required
	Tunbridge Wells	125.00	10.00	16.00	Drainage etc: Southern; Q22: £14; additional parcel £10; 2 plans required
Lancashire	Blackburn with Darwen	179.20	14.70	14.70	Drainage etc: United; Q22: £14; additional parcel £12; 2 plans required
	Blackpool	120.00	9.00		Drainage etc: United; Q22: £20; additional parcel £16; additional enquiries discretionary
	Burnley	136.60	29.45	25.55	Drainage etc: United; Q4, Q5 & Q22: £29.45; additional parcel £10; 2 plans required
	Chorley	130.71	12.77	21.42	Will not answer Q4; Q22: £27; 2 plans required; additional parcel £12.40
	Fylde	79.00	15.00	20.00	Drainage etc: United; additional parcel £15; 2 plans required
	Hyndburn	90.50	7.50	9.25	Drainage etc: United; Q22: £15; additional parcel £10.50
	Lancaster	99.00	7.00		Additional enquiries discretionary; Q22: £22; 2 plans required; additional parcel £2
	Pendle	125.00	25.00	30.00	Drainage etc: United; additional parcel £20
	Preston	135.00	10.00	15.00	Drainage etc: United; Q22: £14; additional parcel £16; 2 plans required
	Ribble Valley	119.35	13.50	10.00	Drainage etc: United; Q22: £21; additional parcel £8.90
	Rossendale	80.00	10.00	17.50	Drainage etc: United; Q22: £20; additional parcel £15
	South Ribble	125.00	15.00	25.00	Drainage etc: United; Q22: £15.50; additional parcel £30
	West Lancashire	75.00	10.00	12.00	Drainage etc: United; Q22: £15; additional parcel £12; 2 plans required
	Wyre	97.00	15.00		Additional enquiries discretionary; Drainage etc: United; additional parcel £25; 2 plans required

County	Authority	Part I plus search (LLCI/ Con29(R))	Part II enquiries (Con29(O))	Part II additional (own questions)	Notes
Commercial property					
Leicestershire	Blaby	75.00	10.00	20.00	Drainage etc: Severn Trent; Q22: £14; additional parcel £11.80
	Charnwood	104.00	10.00	15.00	Drainage etc: Severn Trent; Q22: £15; additional parcel £11; 2 plans required
	Harborough	70.00	7.00	10.00	Part II questions individually priced; Drainage etc: Severn Trent and Anglian; Q22: £14; additional parcel £11
	Hinckley & Bosworth	75.00	10.00	20.00	Drainage etc: Severn Trent; Q22: £14; additional parcel £11.80; 2 plans required
	Leicester	80.00	12.00	15.00	Drainage etc: Severn Trent; Q22: £14; additional parcel £11; 2 plans required
	Melton	145.00	11.00	16.00	Drainage etc: Severn Trent; Q22: £14; additional parcel £9; 2 plans required
	North West Leicestershire	134.00	15.00	20.00	Drainage etc: Severn Trent; Q4: £30; Q22: £14; additional parcel £20; 2 plans required
	Oadby & Wigston	92.00	12.00	15.00	Drainage etc: Severn Trent; Q22: £14; additional parcel £19; 2 plans required
Lincolnshire	Boston	93.00	11.50	18.00	Drainage etc: Anglian; Qs 4 & 22: £22.50; additional parcel £18
	East Lindsey	90.00	12.00	13.00	Drainage etc: Anglian; Q22: £14; additional parcel £13
	Lincoln	87.50	15.50	15.50	Drainage etc: Anglian; additional parcel £15.50
	North East Lincolnshire	100.00	10.00	20.00	Drainage etc: Anglian; Q22: £14; additional parcel £15; 2 plans required
	North Kesteven	90.00	11.25	14.30	Drainage etc: Anglian; Q5: £14; Q22: £14; additional parcel £13
	North Lincolnshire	85.00	5.00	6.50	Pt II enquiries individually priced; additional enquiries discretionary. Drainage etc: Anglian and Severn Trent; additional parcel £12; 2 plans required
	South Holland	115.00	10.00	20.00	Drainage etc: Anglian; Q22: £15; additional parcel £12.80; 4 plans required
	South Kesteven	129.00	14.90	12.80	Drainage etc: Anglian and Severn Trent; additional parcel £13.50; Q5 & Q22: £15.90
	West Lindsey	100.00	15.00	26.00	Drainage etc: Anglian and Severn Trent; additional parcel £14.50; 2 plans required
Merseyside	Knowsley	58.00	7.00		Additional enquiries discretionary. Drainage etc: United; additional parcel £5
	Liverpool	75.00	5.00		Additional enquiries discretionary; Drainage etc: United; additional parcel £10; 2 plans required
	Sefton	50.00	5.00	30.00	Drainage etc: United; additional parcel £10
	St Helens	121.00	17.50	17.50	Drainage etc: United; additional parcel £12
	Wirral	91.58	10.00	10.00	Drainage etc: United and Welsh Water; Q22: £14; additional parcel £15; 2 plans required
Norfolk	Breckland	114.20	8.50	12.50	Drainage etc: Anglian; Q22: £17; additional parcel £13.70
	Broadland	115.00	17.00	17.00	Drainage etc: Anglian; additional parcel £17; 4 plans required
	Great Yarmouth	135.00	8.00	8.50	Drainage etc: Anglian; Q22: refer to Norfolk CC; additional parcel £12.50
	King's Lynn & West Norfolk	52.00	12.00	14.00	Drainage etc: Geodesys; Q22: refer to Norfolk CC; additional parcel £11.30; 3 plans required
	North Norfolk	105.00	15.00	11.50	Drainage etc: Anglian; Q22: £26; additional parcel £16.50
	Norwich	170.00	15.00	21.00	Drainage etc: Anglian; Qs 5 & 22: refer to Norfolk CC; additional parcel £23.50; 2 plans required
	South Norfolk	147.00	12.50	16.00	Drainage etc: Anglian; Q22: £16; additional parcel £16; 3 plans required

County	Authority	Part I plus search (LLCI/ Con29(R))	Part II enquiries (Con29(O))	Part II additional (own questions)	Notes
Commercial property					
Northamptonshire	Corby	126.50	15.00	6.00	Drainage etc: Anglian; Q4–5: £8.50, Q6–21: £3, Q22: £12; 2 plans required; additional parcel £11
	Daventry	177.00	20.00	20.00	Drainage etc: Anglian, Severn Trent and Thames; additional parcel £15.50
	East Northamptonshire	132.00	14.00	24.00	Drainage etc: Anglian; 4 plans required; additional parcel £18.50
	Kettering	99.00	10.00	25.00	Additional enquiries discretionary; Q22: £13.50; Drainage etc: Anglian; additional parcel £11; 2 plans required
	Northampton	98.00	15.00	20.00	Drainage etc: Anglian; additional parcel £11.50; 2 plans required
	South Northamptonshire	63.00	10.00		Drainage etc: Anglian and Thames; additional enquiries £30-£75; Q4–5: £8.50; Q22: £12; additional parcel £15
	Wellingborough	70.50	10.00	20.00	Drainage etc: Anglian; 2 plans required; Q22: £12; additional parcel £11
Northumberland	Northumberland	95.00	15.00	20.00	Drainage etc: Northumbrian; additional parcel £26
North Yorkshire	City of York	165.00	21.00	42.00	Drainage etc: Yorkshire; Q22: £14; additional parcel £9.50; 2 plans required
	Craven	127.00	21.00	17.00	Drainage etc: United, Safe-Move; additional parcel £14; 2 plans required
	Hambleton	60.00	6.00	20.00	Drainage etc: Northumbrian and Yorkshire; Q4–5: £10; Q22: £15; additional parcel £1
	Harrogate	217.00	23.50	23.50	Drainage etc: Yorkshire; additional parcel £23.50; 2 plans required
	Middlesbrough	83.50	17.50	17.50	Drainage etc: Northumbrian; additional parcel £7.75
	Redcar & Cleveland	104.00	6.50		Additional enquiries variable; Drainage etc: Northumbrian; Q22: £14; additional parcel £14
	Richmondshire	75.00	15.00	6.00	Outside National Park. Drainage etc: Northumbrian and Yorkshire; Qs 4,5 & 9: £10; Q22: £15; additional parcel £1
		90.00	17.00	6.00	Inside National Park. ??
	Ryedale	132.70	17.00	17.00	Outside National Park. Drainage etc: Yorkshire; additional parcel £15; 2 plans required
		148.00	17.00	17.00	Inside National Park. Drainage etc: Yorkshire; additional parcel £15; 2 plans required
	Scarborough	69.00		10.00	Drainage etc: Safe-Move; additional parcel £12; advised to check before raising additional enquiries; National Park: £80
	Selby	118.00	20.00		Additional enquiries discretionary; Drainage etc: Safe-Move; additional parcel £15
Nottinghamshire	Ashfield	91.00	16.00	14.00	Drainage etc: Severn Trent; additional parcel £14
	Bassetlaw	90.00	14.00	21.00	Drainage etc: Severn Trent; Q5: £6; Q22: £14; additional parcel £18
	Broxtowe	93.00	10.00	15.00	Drainage etc: Severn Trent; Q5: £16; Q22: £24; additional parcel £12
	Gedling	118.70	10.00	13.00	Drainage etc: Severn Trent; Q22: £14; additional parcel £15.50
	Mansfield	116.30	29.00	15.00	Drainage etc: Severn Trent; Q22: £14; additional parcel £15
	Newark & Sherwood	110.00	10.00	17.00	Drainage etc: Severn Trent; Q5: £17; Q22: £14; additional parcel £15; 2 plans required
	Nottingham	116.30	15.30	15.30	Drainage etc: Severn Trent; Q5: £10; Q22: £14; additional parcel £8.85
	Rushcliffe	98.00	5.00	10.00	Drainage etc: Severn Trent; Q22: £14; additional parcel £10; 2 plans required

County	Authority	Part I plus search (LLCI/ Con29(R))	Part II enquiries (Con29(O))	Part II additional (own questions)	Notes
Commercial property					
Oxfordshire	Cherwell	128.00	10.00	20.00	Drainage etc: Severn Trent and Thames; Q22: £20; additional parcel £20; 2 plans required
	Oxford	120.00	17.00	22.00	Drainage etc: Thames; Q22: £22; additional parcel £16
	South Oxfordshire	213.00	13.00	25.00	Will not answer Q4; Q22: £22; Drainage etc: Thames; additional parcel £27; 2 plans required
	Vale of White Horse	212.00	14.00	25.00	Will not answer Q4; Q22: £22. Drainage etc: Thames; additional parcel £40
	West Oxfordshire	130.39	15.38	18.45	Drainage etc: Thames; Q4: £20; Q5: £18; Q22: £22.55; additional parcel £19.30
Rutland	Rutland	100.00	13.50	35.00	Drainage etc: Anglian and Severn Trent; additional parcel £38
Shropshire	Shropshire	100.00	15.00	25.00	Drainage etc: Severn Trent and Welsh; additional parcel £30
	Telford & Wrekin	56.00	27.00	4.00	Drainage etc: Severn Trent; 2 plans required; additional parcel £7.50
Somerset	Bath & North East Somerset	98.00		15.00	Drainage etc: Wessex; Part II enquiries individually priced; additional parcel £15; 2 plans required
	Mendip	98.00	11.00	16.00	Drainage etc: Wessex; additional parcel £16
	North Somerset	150.00	20.00	29.00	Drainage etc: Wessex; 2 plans required; additional parcel £24
	Sedgemoor	140.00	7.50	10.00	Drainage etc: Wessex; Q22: £25.55; additional parcel £10.50; 4 plans required
	South Somerset	157.00	9.50	13.50	Drainage etc: South West and Wessex; Q22: £27.90; additional parcel £13.70; 2 plans required
	Taunton Deane	140.55	8.00	12.00	Drainage etc: South West and Wessex; additional parcel £12; cheques only from solicitor and firm; no drainage or sewage enquiries; no DX; 3 plans required
	West Somerset	99.00	7.50	10.00	Drainage etc: Wessex; optional printed enquiries £7.50 + £20 admin fee; additional parcel £10
South Yorkshire	Barnsley	80.00	8.00		Will not answer Q4; Drainage etc: Safe-Move; additional parcel £5.10; 2 plans required
	Doncaster	77.70	10.00	2.70	Drainage etc: Anglian, Severn Trent and Yorkshire; Q22: £7; will not answer Q4; additional parcel £10; 2 plans required
	Rotherham	66.00	10.00		Additional enquiries discretionary; Drainage etc: Severn Trent and Yorkshire; Q4: Free; Q22: £20; 2 plans required; additional parcel £2
	Sheffield	78.00	7.50	15.00	Drainage etc: Yorkshire; additional parcel £10.80; 2 plans required

15

County	Authority	Part I plus search (LLCI/ Con29(R))	Part II enquiries (Con29(O))	Part II additional (own questions)	Notes
Commercial property					
Staffordshire	Cannock Chase	161.84	5.00	5.00	Drainage etc: Severn Trent; 2 plans required; no DX; additional parcel £29.35
	East Staffordshire	140.00	14.00	40.00	Drainage etc: Severn Trent; additional parcel £42; 2 plans required
	Lichfield	200.00	30.00	30.00	Drainage etc: Severn Trent; Q22: £30; additional parcel £50; 2 plans required
	Newcastle-under-Lyme	260.00	18.00		Additonal enquiries discretionary; Drainage etc: United and Severn Trent; additional parcel £35
	South Staffordshire	115.00	15.00	20.00	Drainage etc: Severn Trent; will not answer landfill enquiries; Q22: £15; additional parcel £15; 2 plans required
	Stafford	175.00	32.00	32.00	Will not answer landfill enquiries; Drainage etc: Severn Trent; Q22: £25; additional parcel £10; 2 plans required
	Staffordshire Moorlands	125.00	8.00	16.00	Outside Peak Park; Drainage etc: United and Severn Trent; Qs 5, 9 & 22: £3.25; Q8: £6.50; additional parcel £25
		115.70	8.00	8.00	In Peak Park; Drainage etc: United and Severn Trent; Qs 5, 9 & 22: £3.25; Q8: £6.50; additional parcel £25
	Stoke-on-Trent	54.60		15.00	Part II enquiries variable; Drainage etc: Severn Trent; Q22: £0.95; additional parcel £15; 2 plans required
	Tamworth	155.00	15.00	20.50	Will not answer landfill enquiries; Drainage etc: Severn Trent; additional parcel £11; 2 plans required
Suffolk	Babergh	148.00	12.00	40.00	Drainage etc: Geodesys (Anglian); additional parcel £16; 2 plans required
	Forest Heath	127.50	13.00	34.10	Drainage etc: Geodesys (Anglian); 2 plans required; additional parcel £15.70
	Ipswich	95.00	10.00	20.00	Drainage etc: Geodesys (Anglian); additional parcel £14; 2 plans required
	Mid Suffolk	148.00	12.00	15.00	Drainage etc: Geodesys (Anglian); Q5, Q22: £12; additional parcel £13; 2 plans required
	St Edmundsbury	100.00	10.50	16.50	Drainage etc: Geodesys (Anglian); Q5, Q22: £15; additional parcel £13; 1 plan required
	Suffolk Coastal	100.00	12.50	15.00	Drainage etc: Geodesys (Anglian); additional parcel £12; 2 plans required
	Waveney	100.00	12.50	15.00	Drainage etc: Geodesys (Anglian); Q9: £5; Qs 5 & 22: £12.50; additional parcel £13
Surrey	Elmbridge	98.00	14.00	20.00	Drainage etc: Thames; additional parcel £18.20; 2 plans required
	Epsom & Ewell	160.00	11.00	25.00	Drainage etc: Thames; additional parcel £25
	Guildford	90.00	12.00	20.00	Drainage etc: Thames; additional parcel £10
	Mole Valley	205.00	16.00	31.00	Drainage etc: Thames and Southern; additional parcel £34
	Reigate & Banstead	191.00	15.00	15.00	Drainage etc: Thames; additional parcel £15
	Runnymede	250.00	15.00	30.00	Drainage etc: Thames; Additional enquiries regarding highways should be directed to Surrey CC; additional parcel £14.12; 2 plans required
	Spelthorne	201.00	15.00	20.00	Will not answer highways enquiries; Drainage etc: Thames; additional parcel £15.40
	Surrey Heath	208.00	15.60	20.80	Drainage etc: Thames; Q22: £15; additional parcel £16.65
	Tandridge	224.00	15.00	45.00	Drainage etc: Thames and Southern; additional parcel £20; 2 plans required
	Waverley	195.00	15.00	20.00	Drainage etc: Thames and Southern; Q4, Q5, Q22: £12; additional parcel £20; 2 plans required
	Woking	162.37	13.00	20.00	Drainage etc: Thames; additional parcel £57.02

County	Authority	Part I plus search (LLCI/ Con29(R))	Part II enquiries (Con29(O))	Part II additional (own questions)	Notes
Commercial property					
Tyne & Wear	Gateshead	188.80		27.30	Part II enquiries individually priced; Drainage etc: Northumbrian; additional parcel £12.10; 2 plans required
	Newcastle upon Tyne	139.50	12.50	22.00	Drainage etc: Northumbrian; Q22: £14; additional parcel £21
	North Tyneside	148.61	6.00	12.00	Drainage etc: Northumbrian; Q9: Transco; Q22: £14; additional parcel £11
	South Tyneside	140.55		25.65	Part II enquiries individually priced; Drainage etc: Northumbrian; additional parcel £23
	Sunderland	220.00	14.00	30.00	Additional enquiries discretionary; Q22: £14; Drainage etc: Northumbrian; additional parcel £20; 4 plans required
Warwickshire	North Warwickshire	115.00	1.00	1.00	Drainage etc: Severn Trent; Q22: £10.25; additional parcel £10.80; 2 plans required
	Nuneaton & Bedworth	113.50	15.50	25.00	Drainage etc: Severn Trent; additional parcel £17; 2 plans required
	Rugby	85.00	10.00	30.00	Cannot answer Q4, Q17; Drainage etc: Severn Trent; additional parcel £20; 2 plans required
	Stratford-upon-Avon	98.00	5.00	10.00	Landfill enquiries: £38 (write separately addressed to the Environmental Health Team); cannot answer Q4; Q22: £15; Drainage etc: Thames and Severn Trent; additional parcel £10
	Warwick	145.00	10.00	20.00	Landfill enquiries or those about planning within 200m should be directed to Planning; Drainage etc: Severn Trent; additional parcel £10; 2 plans required
West Midlands	Birmingham	100.00	10.00		Additional enquiries discretionary; Drainage etc: Severn Trent; additional parcel £20
	Coventry	150.00	10.00		Additional enquiries discretionary; Drainage etc: Severn Trent; additional parcel £21; 2 plans required
	Dudley	92.45	14.35		Additional enquiries discretionary; Drainage etc: Severn Trent; additional parcel £16.30; 2 plans required
	Sandwell	176.00	10.00		Additional enquiries discretionary; Drainage etc: Severn Trent; Q4: do not answer; Qs5–22: £10; additional parcel £18
	Solihull	156.00	16.00	20.00	Drainage etc: Severn Trent; Q4: £25.25; Q22: £14.50; additional parcel £10
	Walsall	174.50	10.75		Additional enquiries discretionary; additional parcel £11.05
	Wolverhampton	61.00	10.00	10.00	Drainage etc: Severn Trent; additional parcel £11
West Sussex	Adur & Worthing	133.00	7.00		Drainage etc: Southern; additional parcel £6
	Arun	75.00	7.75	13.50	Drainage etc: Southern; additional parcel £11
	Chichester	85.00	15.00	18.00	Drainage etc: Southern and Thames; additional parcel £20; 2 plans required
	Crawley	83.00	10.00	20.00	Drainage etc: Thames; no highway questions; additional parcel £20
	Horsham	110.00		35.00	Part II enquiries individually priced; Drainage etc: Thames (the Rusper area) and Southern; additional parcel £15; 3 plans required
	Mid Sussex	73.00	2.30	25.00	Drainage etc: Southern and Thames; Qs 4 & 5: £15; Q22: £14; additional parcel £30; 2 plans required

15

County	Authority	Part I plus search (LLCI/ Con29(R))	Part II enquiries (Con29(O))	Part II additional (own questions)	Notes
Commercial property					
West Yorkshire	Calderdale	144.00	10.60	27.00	Drainage etc: Yorkshire; additional parcel £29
	City of Bradford	134.00	11.50		Additional enquiries discretionary; no drainage questions; additional parcel £25; 2 plans required
	Kirklees	85.00	7.00		Additional enquiries discretionary; Drainage etc: Yorkshire; Q4: Free; Q22: £14; additional parcel £20
	Leeds	49.00	5.50	7.00	Q22: £4.50; Drainage etc: Yorkshire; additional parcel £2
	Wakefield	40.00	5.00		Additional enquiries discretionary; Drainage etc: Yorkshire; Q22: £14; additional parcel £5
Wiltshire	Swindon	179.00			Pt II enquiries individually priced; additional enquiries discretionary. Drainage etc: Thames; 2 plans required; additional parcel £28
	Wiltshire	125.00	15.50	21.00	Drainage etc: Thames, Southern and Wessex; additional parcel £12; 2 plans required
Worcestershire	Bromsgrove	147.00		45.50	Pt II enquiries individually priced; Q22: £21.50; Drainage etc: Severn Trent; additional parcel £19.40; £43 for landfill enquiries
	Malvern Hills	100.00	20.00	30.00	Drainage etc: Severn Trent; additional parcel £16.50
	Redditch	94.50	6.00	6.00	Drainage etc: Severn Trent; Q4, Q5, Q9: £12.50; Q22: £20; additional parcel £12.50
	Worcester	110.50	22.00	22.00	Pt II enquiries individually priced; Q22: £17; Drainage etc: Severn Trent; additional parcel £18
	Wychavon	113.00	2.50	21.00	Drainage etc: Severn Trent; Q4, Q5: £8.50; Q22: £17; 2 plans required; additional parcel £14.40
	Wyre Forest	135.00	17.00		Additional enquiries discretionary; Drainage etc: Severn Trent; additional parcel £45
Isles of Scilly	Isles of Scilly	115.50	13.25	20.00	Contact directly for drainage enquiries £49.50; Q22: £14; additional parcel £16.50; 2 plans required

County	Authority	Part I plus search (LLCI/ Con29(R))	Part II enquiries (Con29(O))	Part II additional (own questions)	Notes
Commercial property					
Wales	Anglesey	102.00	7.00		Additional enquiries discretionary; Drainage etc: Welsh Water; 7 plans required; Q22: £14; additional parcel £10
	Blaenau Gwent	90.00	8.00	10.00	Drainage etc: Welsh Water; Q22: £14; additional parcel £10; 2 plans required
	Bridgend	150.00	18.00	28.00	Drainage etc: Welsh Water; additional parcel £17
	Caerphilly	101.50	12.00	15.00	Drainage etc: Welsh Water; 2 plans required; additional parcel £13
	Cardiff	85.80	8.00	15.00	Drainage etc: Welsh Water; Q22: £14; 2 plans required; additional parcel £11
	Carmarthenshire	110.00	10.00	15.00	Drainage: Welsh Water; 2 plans required; additional parcel £11
	Ceredigion (formerly Cardiganshire)	99.00	10.00	15.00	Drainage etc: Welsh Water; 2 plans required; additional parcel £12.50
	Conwy	101.00	10.00	15.00	Drainage etc: Welsh Water; Q22: £14; additional parcel £10.40
	Denbighshire	105.00	6.00	10.00	Additional enquiries discretionary; Drainage etc: Welsh Water; additional parcel £15; Q22: £25
	Flintshire	123.00	11.00	25.00	Drainage etc: Welsh Water; additional parcel £11; 2 plans required
	Gwynedd	96.00	7.00	21.00	Drainage etc: Welsh Water; Q22: £14; 2 plans required; additional parcel £16
	Merthyr Tydfil	121.00	10.00	15.00	Drainage etc: Welsh Water; 2 plans required; additional parcel £15
	Monmouthshire	97.00	12.00		Additional enquiries discretionary; Drainage etc: Welsh Water; Q5, Q22: £15; 3 plans required; additional parcel £45
	Neath Port Talbot	176.00	6.00		Additional enquiries £35 if accepted; Drainage etc: Hyder; Q22: £21.90; 2 plans required; additional parcel £12.20
	Newport	110.00	12.00	25.00	Drainage etc: Welsh Water; Contaminated land and landfill enquiries should be directed to Environmental Health; additional parcel £25
	Pembrokeshire	90.00	7.00		Additional enquiries £15 if accepted; Drainage etc: Welsh Water; additional parcel £11.70
	Powys	102.00	12.00	22.00	Drainage etc: Welsh Water, Hyder and Severn Trent; Q5, Q22: £20; additional parcel £11; 1 plan sufficient
	Rhondda Cynon Taf	127.00	16.00	20.00	Drainage etc: Welsh Water; 2 plans required; additional parcel £17
	Swansea	120.00	10.50	10.50	Drainage etc: Welsh Water; Q22: £23; additional parcel £10.50; 2 plans required
	Torfaen	86.00	12.00	20.00	Additional enquiries discretionary; Drainage etc: Welsh Water; Q22: £14; additional parcel £15; 1 plan sufficient
	Vale of Glamorgan	125.00	13.51	11.00	Drainage etc: Welsh Water; Q22: £14; additional parcels £15
	Wrexham	130.00	11.00	20.00	Drainage etc: Welsh Water; additional parcel £12